SAGE
Premium
Video

BOOST COMPREHENSION. BOLSTER ANALYSIS.

- SAGE Premium Video **EXCLUSIVELY CURATED FOR THIS TEXT**
- **BRIDGES BOOK CONTENT** with application & critical thinking
- Includes short, auto-graded quizzes that **DIRECTLY FEED TO YOUR LMS GRADEBOOK**
- Premium content is **ADA COMPLIANT WITH TRANSCRIPTS**
- Comprehensive media guide to help you **QUICKLY SELECT MEANINGFUL VIDEO** tied to your course objectives

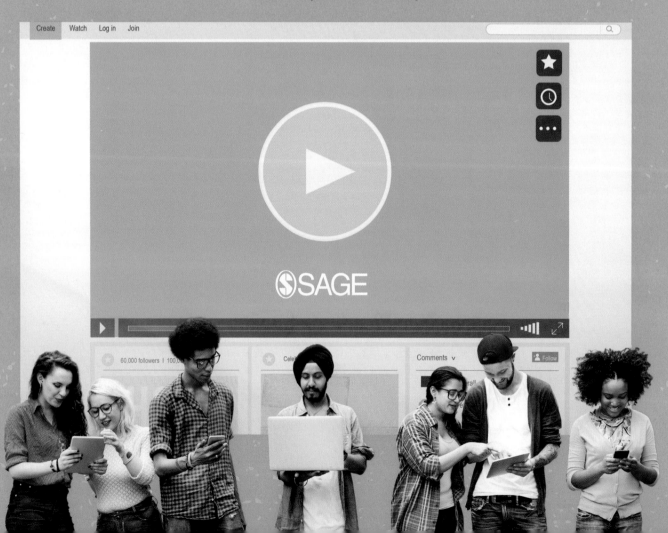

The
Hallmark
Features

Human Resource Management: People, Data, and Analytics introduces students to the fundamentals of talent management with integrated coverage of data analytics.

- Includes a unique **DATA MANAGEMENT AND HRIS CHAPTER** that explores the pivotal role of data along with the challenges and opportunities of managing data.

- **DATA AND ANALYTICS EXERCISES** and **EXCEL EXTENSIONS** offer hands-on opportunities for students to practice using data in Microsoft Excel® to make decisions.

- **INSIDE HR ORIGINAL VIDEOS INTERVIEW REAL-WORLD PROFESSIONALS** demonstrating how they use HR concepts in their day-to-day work. Each video is tied to assessment questions.

Data Management and Human Resource Information Systems

Opening Case

Shifting to a Data-Driven Organization with HRIS: The Case of Nissan

As former Nissan CEO Carlos Ghosn tells it, in 1999 the Japanese carmaker Nissan was in trouble. The company had not been profitable for 8 years, its margins were low, and it was estimated that the car company gave away $1,000 for every car it sold in the United States. In addition, plant capacity was much larger than demand, leading to high overhead costs. In the hopes of turning things around, French carmaker Renault invested $5.4 billion in Nissan for an equity stake in the company. After their strategic alliance governed by cross-sharing agreements was struck, Renault-Nissan became the fourth-largest car company in the world. But the alliance made sense only if Nissan could turn things around. Ghosn was asked to do just that.

One of the major ways that Ghosn set out to turn things around was to transform HR to a "shared services model." This entailed a multitier HR service delivery system in which employees first had access to technology that allowed them to answer their own questions and to make most of their HR-related decisions on their own. If employees still needed help, then their question could be escalated to the next level of service, which included sending a ticket to a shared service desk. Finally, if the HR concern was not resolved at that level, it was escalated to HR experts. This change was transformational in allowing HR staff to shift from spending

LEARNING OBJ

After reading and st chapter, you should able to:

3.1 Describe key as management.

3.2 Apply opportuniti management and

3.3 Identify and addre for data managem

3.4 Describe basic tec of developing an H

3.5 Address key points of HRIS implementa

3.6 Apply core informatic concepts in HR mana

Carlos Ghosn at the Toyota Motor Show in 2015.

DATA AND ANALYTICS EXERCISE: DATA CLEANING

One of the overarching goals of any HRIS is to provide users with accurate data. Further, the integrity of the data directly influences the integrity of the insights gleaned from the data, or in other words: garbage in, garbage out. Unfortunately, the data that reside within an HRIS are not always what we would hope or expect. There are a number of reasons for this, but one of the most common reasons is human error.

Imagine that your HRIS is built around a relational database consisting of a number of different tables. In one of the tables, you store basic employee information, such as employee ID, employee name, job level, location, and department. Here is an excerpt of the table:

EMPLOYEE ID	EMPLOYEE NAME	JOB LEVEL	LOCATION	DEPARTMENT
EA44312	Kim, Yeongjin	1	beaverton	Customer Service
EB58521	Dowsett, Jane	3	Hillsboro	
EA84533	Henderson, Lynn	4	Hillsboro	Customer Service
EA89575	Mitchell, Terrance	1	Hillsboro	Customer Service
ET58748	Smith, John	1	Beaverton	Marketing
ET96461	Martinez, David	4	Beavertn	Customer Service
EB11248	Liu, Patricia	11	Beaverton	

First, take a close look at the Location field. Do you notice anything? Note how the Beaverton location is spelled with a "B" for three of the cases and how it is spelled without the "o" for one case. Most likely, this difference in spelling was the r an error during data entry. Errors like this might not seem like such a big deal, but down the road, they can lead to issues comes to merging and analyzing the data. Namely, many software programs such as Microsoft Access Excel will treat the ferent versions of the word "Beaverton" (i.e., Beaverton, Beavertn) location as two distinct categories. That is, instead of trea

SAGE Publishing:
Our Story

Founded in 1965 by 24-year-old entrepreneur Sara Miller McCune, SAGE continues its legacy of making research accessible and fostering **CREATIVITY** and **INNOVATION**. We believe in creating fresh, cutting-edge content to help you prepare your students to thrive in the modern business world and be **TOMORROW'S LEADING ENTREPRENEURS**.

- By partnering with **TOP BUSINESS AUTHORS** with just the right balance of research, teaching, and industry experience, we bring you the most current and applied content.

- As a **STUDENT-FRIENDLY PUBLISHER**, we keep our prices affordable and provide multiple formats of our textbooks so your students can choose the option that works best for them.

- Being permanently **INDEPENDENT** means we are fiercely committed to publishing the highest-quality resources for you and your students.

Human Resource Management

People, Data, and Analytics

Talya Bauer
Portland State University

Berrin Erdogan
Portland State University

David Caughlin
Portland State University

Donald Truxillo
University of Limerick, Ireland

Los Angeles | London | New Delhi
Singapore | Washington DC | Melbourne

FOR INFORMATION:

SAGE Publications, Inc.
2455 Teller Road
Thousand Oaks, California 91320
E-mail: order@sagepub.com

SAGE Publications Ltd.
1 Oliver's Yard
55 City Road
London EC1Y 1SP
United Kingdom

SAGE Publications India Pvt. Ltd.
B 1/I 1 Mohan Cooperative Industrial Area
Mathura Road, New Delhi 110 044
India

SAGE Publications Asia-Pacific Pte. Ltd.
18 Cross Street #10-10/11/12
China Square Central
Singapore 048423

Library of Congress Cataloging-in-Publication Data

Names: Bauer, Talya, author. | Erdogan, Berrin, author. | Caughlin, David Ellis, author.

Title: Human resource management : people, data, and analytics / Talya Bauer, Portland State University, USA, Berrin Erdogan, Portland State University, USA, David Caughlin, Portland State University, USA, Donald Truxillo, University of Limerick, Ireland.

Description: Thousand Oaks : SAGE Publications, [2019] | Includes bibliographical references and index.

Identifiers: LCCN 2018032223 | ISBN 9781506363127 (pbk. : alk. paper)

Subjects: LCSH: Personnel management.

Classification: LCC HF5549 .B3148 2019 | DDC 658.3—dc23
LC record available at https://lccn.loc.gov/2018032223

This book is printed on acid-free paper.

SUSTAINABLE FORESTRY INITIATIVE
Certified Sourcing
www.sfiprogram.org
SFI-01268

SFI label applies to text stock

Acquisitions Editor: Maggie Stanley
Content Development Editor: Lauren Holmes
Editorial Assistants: Alissa Nance,
                       Janeane Calderon
Production Editor: Tracy Buyan
Copy Editor: Kim Husband
Typesetter: C&M Digitals (P) Ltd.
Proofreader: Talia Greenberg
Indexer: Maria Sosnowski
Cover Designer: Scott Van Atta
Marketing Manager: Sarah Panella

19 20 21 22 23 10 9 8 7 6 5 4 3 2 1

Brief Contents

Part IV. Special Topics in HR

Detailed Contents

Chapter 2 • Strategic HRM, Data-Driven Decision Making, and HR Analytics   32

Chapter 3 • Data Management and Human Resource Information Systems 66

Chapter 7 • Selection Processes and Procedures   212

Chapter 10 • Managing Employee Separations and Retention 330

Part III. Reward System

Chapter 11 • Developing a Pay Structure 364

Chapter 12 • Rewarding Performance

Preface

Welcome to *Human Resource Management: People, Data, and Analytics*. We set out to write this book because we believe that human resource management (HRM) has the potential to be an essential business partner in making data-informed decisions within organizations. The potential for HRM has never been greater than it is today. However, that potential will only be realized if business students are well versed in how people, data, and analytics work together as legs of a three-legged stool. If we only focus on one or two legs, the stool tips over. But when each part is understood and functioning, the results are stable and powerful. As you will read throughout this book, fluency in people, data, and analytics involves asking the right questions, gathering the right data to address questions, choosing appropriate analyses, and interpreting and communicating findings in a meaningful way. Moreover, recognizing and addressing ethical and legal challenges are critical for success. Today, organizations that are able to manage people, data, and analytics effectively are positioned to leverage HRM to inform and support organizational strategy.

Thus, a unique feature of this book is a focus on how HRM is rapidly evolving into a vibrant and data-rich field while also making sure that students are well versed in the basics of HRM. While the demand for data and analytic skills is growing (as evidenced by the 2018 glassdoor.com *Best Jobs in America* list with data scientist as #1, HR manager as #5, and analytics manager as #18), business students will be well served if they understand HRM regardless of their intended major or work setting. As a result, this book is designed to help students leverage the principles of *people, data*, <u>and</u> *analytics* to focus on *leveraging data to inform decisions in business in general and HRM specifically*. With recent changes in HRM, we have observed that many of today's leading organizations use a people, data, and analytics approach to design and implement HRM systems and procedures aimed at recruiting, selecting, training, managing, developing, rewarding, and retaining talented people. We incorporate this approach through the use of several features throughout the book as well as data-informed, hands-on student experiences in every chapter. At the same time, all the time-honored HRM concepts are covered in depth for students studying all business functions including HRM.

Our Approach

This book grew from our passion for helping students succeed both in the classroom and in the workplace as well as helping businesses be effective and fair. Each of us is passionate about bridging science and practice, and we bring that into our classrooms every day. The motto of Portland State University is "*Let Knowledge Serve the City*," and we believe that an important way to bring this to life is through the use of hands-on practice and learning. The virtuous cycle of "learn–do–reflect" is one that allows students to see immediate relevance

to what they are learning, become excited about it, and want to learn more. Employers report the power of students who engage with material in such meaningful ways.

When it came to developing a textbook with a people, data, and analytics focus geared to helping students of HRM master concepts and skills, we knew that designing experiences such as exercises that would support faculty and engage students in applying HRM concepts regardless of their major was essential. Therefore, we developed end-of-the chapter HR Reasoning and Decision-Making Exercises that put the student in the decision-maker role and present them with opportunities to practice making HR-related decisions while considering relevant HR concepts. In addition, we created Data and Analytics Exercises. These appear at the end of each chapter with Excel Extensions. These activities show students how to analyze data in order to make high-quality decisions. Finally, there are Special Features including opening Chapter Cases, Spotlights on Data and Analytics, Legal Issues, Ethics, Small and Medium-Sized Businesses, and HR in Action features.

Our goal was to write about critical concepts in an accessible, compelling, and informative manner. We did this through three key approaches to the content of this book.

1. **An approachable writing style.** We carefully consider student perspectives, and we believe it is important that we make material accessible and engaging. We understand that some students have little or no work experience, others have work experience not related to HR, while others do have HR-related experience. Our goal is to appeal to all of these perspectives. We also recognize that some of those reading this book are doing so as part of their coursework for a career in HR, while others are not. What matters to us is that we communicate the importance of HR-related decisions for everyone within organizations by equipping students with the tools to make high-quality decisions.

2. **Examples, examples, and more examples.** Throughout the book, you will find examples of different types of organizations, individuals in different positions and levels within organizations, and examples of effective and ineffective HR decisions. All of these examples help attune readers to considerations, approaches to decision making, and best practices and help them avoid the mistakes made by some organizations. The examples bring material to life, make the material relevant, and help students learn from the experiences of other organizations.

3. **Evidence-based practices.** Like many areas of business, people who work in HR have traditionally made decisions based on a "gut feeling." While intuition can be an effective and efficient way to make low-stakes, moment-to-moment decisions, critical, high-stakes decisions informed by evidence and systematic problem solving help avoid failure. Evidence comes in different forms and from different sources, and our book reflects this. First and foremost, we review scholarly research to inform recommended practices and to understand and explain human behavior at work. Second, we showcase ways in which organizations have systematically analyzed and evaluated their own data to inform high-stakes HR decision making. Third, we provide opportunities for students to practice applying different approaches to collect, analyze, and interpret data.

What Makes Our Book Unique

When we set out to write this book, it was important that we didn't write just "another" HRM textbook. Rather, we wanted to write a book that is modern, approachable, and effective at communicating the importance of HRM. In doing so, we believed it should describe the effective and evidence-based approaches to HRM. At the same time, we wanted to create a textbook that helps students understand the importance of people, data, and analytics for supporting the HRM functions within organizations. We are proud of the result. For example, this textbook is the first to include an entire chapter on data management and HR information systems (Chapter 3). This is an important feature given the pivotal space that data occupy in today's business landscape. We believe that upon reading this textbook, you will appreciate the importance of this innovation. We also highlight key trends in the people, data, and analytics space, such as the importance of online privacy for individuals and organizations. While we see great potential in the merging of people, data, and analytics, we also feel that it is imperative for students to understand that just because something is possible using the most sophisticated analytic techniques does not mean it is ethical or even legal. Thus, one of our major goals is to highlight areas where the promise and the reality of people, data, and analytics have also produced challenges and ethical dilemmas for individuals and organizations alike.

We take a contemporary approach to HRM and its role in business regardless of one's formal position, title, or functional area. As HRM evolves, we are observing emerging pathways that are moving HRM beyond being simply transactional, toward becoming more transformational and strategic in nature. People are the life force of most organizations, and thus attracting, motivating, and retaining the best people is crucial for organizational success. HRM is uniquely positioned to inform the systems, policies, and practices organizations use to manage their people.

As we lay out in the next section, we accomplish this throughout the book via several approaches, including hands-on data and analytics exercises, spotlight features on data and analytics, as well as content, exercises, case studies, and spotlights features on legal and ethical issues throughout the book.

Textbook Features

In-Chapter Features

Source: Reprinted from *SHRM Competency Model* with permission of the Society for Human Resource Management (SHRM). © SHRM. All rights reserved.

Each chapter includes features that stand alone and that also align with the Society for Human Resource Management's (SHRM's) nine competencies (depicted in italics below):

- A vivid **opening case** focusing on key business and HR practices as well as the implications of data-informed decisions appears in every chapter to help students engage in *critical evaluation* and *business acumen* within a variety of organizations. Our opening cases include Chobani, Chevron, Nissan, Pinterest, SHRM, PwC, Google, Igloo, Deloitte, the trucking industry, the U.S. Women's National Soccer Team, Geisinger Health Systems, Care.com, New Seasons Market, railroads, and Mercy Corps. Our goal was to highlight small, medium, and large organizations, Fortune 500 organizations, family-owned businesses, not-for-profit organizations, and nongovernmental organizations (NGOs) in a variety of industries and settings.

- The **Manager's Toolbox** (*various SHRM HR competencies*) helps students gather tools and knowledge that will help readers become more effective now and in the future. Examples include tools to help individuals develop skills for making more effective decisions, developing effective organizational strategy, engaging in strong cybersecurity, avoiding illegal questions, choosing key performance indicators, structuring interviews, delivering feedback effectively, and retaining top talent.

- The **Spotlight on HR for Small and Medium-Sized Businesses** (*HR expertise and knowledge*) is an important highlight within our book. Of the 5.83 million employing firms in the United States, 99.7% of them consist of 500 or fewer employees. Further, organizations with fewer than 20 workers make up 89.4% of those firms. It is easy to lose sight of this given how prevalent information on the HR practices of Fortune 500 organizations is. These large organizations frequently make news, and we often read about them in the pages of *Forbes* or *The Wall Street Journal*. However, major companies were often once a small business, so it makes sense to think about HR as a powerful tool for new companies. This is especially important to keep in mind given that more than 50% of the working population is engaged in a small business. Thus, while we highlight examples of small, medium, and large-sized businesses throughout this book, we also specifically focus on HR for small and medium-sized businesses in this section of each chapter.

- The **Spotlight on Data and Analytics** (*critical evaluation*) is a major feature of our book. HRM has become more focused on data. These features offer real-world examples of how companies have collected and analyzed HR data to inform decision making, as well as explanations of key data and analytics terms, concepts, and tools. Example topics include distinguishing between descriptive, predictive, and prescriptive analytics; aligning analytics with strategy; using analytics to improve retention; using performance metrics in screening job applicants; using sentiment analysis to assess engagement; using data and analytics to evaluate pay-for-performance programs; and measuring the antecedents of workplace accidents.

- The **Spotlight on Ethics** (*ethical practice*) provides a focus on ethical issues central to HR and organizational decisions. The number and complexity of these issues has led to more sophisticated analytics. These include issues around data privacy of employees and job applicants; the implementation of "ban-the-box" laws; the management of employee layoffs; and ethical issues in multinational corporations. By taking the time to dive more deeply into these topics, you will see examples of both ethical and unethical situations and approaches to dealing with the large variety of challenges within the organizational landscape.

- The **Spotlight on Legal Issues** (*ethical practice and business acumen*) recognizes that HRM is influenced and shaped by laws. Specifically, legal issues around civil rights legislation have shaped today's approach to diversity management and elevated job analysis from a "nice to have" activity to a foundational legal underpinning of HRM, recruitment, and selection. These legal issues will continue to shape the HRM landscape. Such legislation also has implications for how individuals are trained, developed, managed, and rewarded; the benefits they receive; and how their labor rights are managed and protected; as well as their occupational safety and health. And it is impossible to do work globally without understanding the laws of the countries within which one does business, an issue that is addressed in our chapter on global HRM. Examples of topics covered in these spotlight features include the legal issues associated with obtaining and maintaining data in organizations, the use of "data scraping" by organizations, and pay discrimination. In each chapter, we highlight important legal issues such as these.

- The **Spotlight on Global Issues** (*global and cultural effectiveness*) features provide glimpses into HRM from an international perspective. In each chapter, we highlight the way the topic discussed in that chapter may need to be modified, changed, and adapted to business in a global context. This may include how a specific practice would work when doing business overseas and how a specific HR decision may need to be adapted to a context in which there is cultural diversity. When designing selection, rewards, benefits, and performance management systems, companies need to make modifications for the different locales in which the systems would be utilized. We are aware that our readers may end up working in organizations that do significant international business, have cultural diversity, or enjoy a global career spanning across national boundaries. Therefore, we include discussions of cross-cultural research as it relates to HR, as well as the implications of globalization on the way that work is done. Our author team brings significant international research and practice experience and is involved in international efforts professionally, which results in our culturally sensitive focus to HRM.

- **HR in Action** (*HR expertise and knowledge*) is a key feature that allows us to highlight approaches, individuals, and organizations engaged in HRM in a variety of situations. These examples focus on specific approaches, programs, and decisions made in real time. Examples of HR in Action include Accenture, ADP, Costco, L'Oréal, Mars Inc., Procter & Gamble, Salesforce.com, and Valve.

- **Decision-Making Exercises** for each chapter put the student in the role of a decision maker. Each exercise describes a scenario and asks the student to make a decision that is fair and ethical, fosters healthy employer–employee relationships, and is evidence based. These exercises require students to read and understand the material discussed in each chapter but then also weigh the pros and cons of different alternatives to arrive at a decision that meets the needs of all stakeholders. We find this approach useful in our own teaching, and therefore we included both a mini case study and a decision-making exercise at the end of each chapter.

- **Data and Analytics Exercises** for each chapter are also included for instructors to assign as they choose. These end-of-chapter activities provide illustrations and applications of how data can be used to answer a question relevant to the chapter content. The feature in the textbook can also be paired with lifelike data available to instructors in the Excel Extensions should they be interested in having students analyze the data to answer the question. Done individually or in teams, this allows students to engage in *relationship management*, *leadership and navigation*, and *consultation* for organizational decision makers identified in the exercises. Example exercises cover techniques like describing data using descriptive statistics and data visualizations, using regression to understand performance, determining the amount of turnover using metrics, and evaluating a merit pay program using data visualizations.

- **Excel Extensions** for each chapter are included for instructors to assign as they choose. They offer hands-on opportunities for students to practice using data analytics in Microsoft Excel to inform decision making. These activities extend the Data and Analytics Exercises.

- **Summaries** and **Key Terms** serve to help students master the critical terminology with ease. Learning the vocabulary of HR is important to be able to communicate with other HR professionals more efficiently and to access most up-to-date materials on a particular topic more easily.

- **Supplements** at the end of each chapter highlight extra HR information, forms, and tools. These are useful resources for those who want to engage in effective HR practices whether they are managers or HR professionals. Examples of these supplements include the history and evolution of HRM, steps for strategy formulation, HR metrics, sample job descriptions, Equal Employment Opportunity forms, O*NET information, the Uniform Guidelines, Occupational Safety and Health Administration training requirements, sample performance appraisal forms and policies for employee separations, and management–union communication guidelines.

Content and Organization

Part I: HRM in Context opens by covering an introduction of HRM and its relevance for all business segments (not just for those interested in HRM as a profession), how data and analytics allow for strategic decisions within HRM, an overview of the legal context and ethical issues around HRM and analytics, a discussion of HRM in the context of diversity, followed by coverage of job analysis and design as important tools for the remainder of HR practices.

Chapter 1, "Introduction to Human Resource Management," describes what HRM is; why it is foundational to business success; how it is changing due to larger changes and trends such as changing demographics; the emergence of the gig economy, globalization, technology, and the availability of data; as well as ethical codes for HRM.

Chapter 2, "Strategic HRM, Data-Driven Decision Making, and HR Analytics," defines strategy, describes how strategic HRM has evolved, and explains how HR analytics can be used to inform and support both HRM strategy and organizational strategy. It also examines the importance of the scientific process in HR analytics and explains how organizations can successfully leverage HR analytics.

Chapter 3, "Data Management and Human Resource Information Systems," describes key aspects of data management, opportunities and challenges for human resource information systems (HRIS), and keys to successful HRIS implementation. It also introduces the basics of information systems and technical aspects of developing an HRIS. All of this is critical in understanding how to address integrated questions utilizing a people, data, and analytics approach.

Chapter 4, "Diversity, Inclusion, and Equal Employment Laws," describes the challenges and benefits of managing diversity effectively, presents an overview of equal employment opportunity laws, and identifies ways in which organizations may comply with the law and help create an inclusive workplace.

Chapter 5, "The Analysis and Design of Work," explains the importance of analyzing work for effective HR practice and introduces different types of job analysis and competency modeling practices. It also explains how to effectively design jobs to increase workers' motivation, performance, and well-being.

Part II: Managing Across the Talent Life Cycle covers the core employee life cycle functions of HRM (employee recruitment and selection, training, career development, performance management, and management of employee exit).

Chapter 6, "Workforce Planning and Recruitment," highlights the importance of workforce planning to maintain appropriate employment levels and understand and engage in effective recruitment practices. It also explains the role of internal and external recruitment sources, recruiting for diversity, maintaining applicant interest, and influencing ultimate job choice.

Chapter 7, "Selection Processes and Procedures," explains the key role of employee selection to organizational effectiveness, including the concepts of reliability and validity and how to enhance the financial value of hiring procedures. It also covers how to choose the most effective hiring procedures; the role of HR analytics; legal, ethical, and global issues in selection; and how to enhance the job applicant's experience.

Chapter 8, "Training, Development, and Career," describes current best practices in the delivery of training in organizations. This includes conducting an effective training needs assessment, enhancing training effectiveness, key training methods and media available to employers, and how to evaluate training effectiveness. It also describes processes for effective career development and management.

Chapter 9, "Performance Management," differentiates between performance management and appraisal, introduces different ways of measuring performance, and explains how to give feedback to employees as well as create a feedback culture.

Chapter 10, "Managing Employee Separations and Retention," discusses the costs of voluntary and involuntary turnover in organizations, describes ways in which organizations can manage different types of turnover, and highlights best practices for managing employee separations in a way that is ethical, fair, and supportive of organizational objectives.

Part III: Reward Systems covers key areas of HRM policy including pay structures, pay-for-performance programs, and benefits.

Chapter 11, "Developing a Pay Structure," describes pay as a type of reward, discusses the importance of the fairness of rewards, and explains how to develop an equitable pay structure. It also describes person-based pay structures and challenges associated with compensating executives and examines the challenges and opportunities associated with pay administration.

Chapter 12, "Rewarding Performance," describes how pay can be used to motivate employees, discusses the importance of aligning organizational strategy with pay-for-performance programs, describes common pay-for-performance programs, and describes the challenges and opportunities organizations face when rewarding performance using pay.

Chapter 13, "Managing Benefits," examines employee benefits as a type of reward, reviewing legally required benefits associated with Social Security, workers' compensation, unemployment insurance, family and medical leave, and other required health care benefits. It discusses voluntary benefits associated with health care insurance, disability insurance, retirement insurance, life insurance, wellness and work–life programs, and perks. It also describes the ways in which benefits programs are administered and communicated.

Part IV: Special Topics in HR covers the topics of managing HRM in a unionized context, managing health and safety of workers, and managing global HRM.

Chapter 14, "Employee and Labor Relations," explains what employee relations are and the factors that influence them, including culture, fair treatment, and working conditions. This chapter also outlines organizational policies and procedures, the labor movement, the collective bargaining process, and what happens if disputes are not resolved.

Chapter 15, "Employee Safety, Well-Being, and Wellness," describes the importance of employee well-being in organizations and the role of regulatory agencies. The chapter also describes the main safety outcomes measured by organizations, the concept of safety promotion, the variety of wellness programs and well-being interventions available to employers, and the role of an integrated Total Worker Health™ approach to employee well-being.

Chapter 16, "Opportunities and Challenges in International HRM," explains the benefits and downsides of standardizing HR practices in a firm operating in multiple countries and discusses best practices in expatriate management and international mobility.

Online Resources

SAGE edge for Instructors

A password-protected instructor resource site at **edge.sagepub.com/bauer** supports teaching with high-quality content to help in creating a rich learning environment for students. The SAGE edge site for this book includes the following instructor resources:

- **Test banks** built on AACSB and SHRM standards, the book's learning objectives, and Bloom's Taxonomy provide a diverse range of test items with **ExamView test generation**. Each chapter includes 100 test questions to give instructors options for assessing students.

- Editable, chapter-specific **PowerPoint® slides** offer complete flexibility for creating a multimedia presentation for the course.

- **Lecture notes** for each chapter align with PowerPoint slides to serve as an essential reference, summarizing key concepts to ease preparation for lectures and class discussion.

- **Instructor's Manual** includes answers to in-text questions, discussion questions, exercises, case notes, and answers to case questions.

- Carefully selected **video and multimedia content** aligned with the book's learning objectives enhances exploration of key topics to reinforce concepts and provide further insights.

- Author-created **supplemental exercises and activities** help students apply the concepts they learn to see how they work in various contexts, providing new perspectives. Each chapter will include an exercise with a link to relevant journal articles and thoughtful review questions.

- **Spotlight on HR Research** boxes highlight articles on new and exciting research in the field of HR such as the influence of technology on HRM and how data combination methods affect hiring decisions.

- EXCLUSIVE, influential **SAGE journal and reference content**, built into course materials and assessment tools, ties important research and scholarship to chapter concepts to strengthen learning.

- **Tables and figures** from the book are available for download.

- **SAGE coursepacks** provide easy LMS integration.

SAGE edge for Students

The open-access companion website helps students accomplish their coursework goals in an easy-to-use learning environment, featuring:

- **Learning objectives** with summaries reinforce the most important material.

- Mobile-friendly practice **quizzes** encourage self-guided assessment and practice.

- Mobile-friendly **flashcards** strengthen understanding of key concepts.

- EXCLUSIVE, influential **SAGE journal and reference content**, built into course materials and assessment tools, ties important research and scholarship to chapter concepts to strengthen learning.

- Carefully selected **video and multimedia content** enhances exploration of key topics to reinforce concepts and provide further insights.

SAGE coursepacks

SAGE coursepacks makes it easy to import our quality instructor and student resource content into your school's learning management system (LMS) with minimal effort. Intuitive and simple to use, **SAGE coursepacks** gives you the control to focus on what really matters: customizing course content to meet your students' needs. The SAGE coursepacks, created specifically for this book, are customized and curated for use in Blackboard, Canvas, Desire2Learn (D2L), and Moodle.

In addition to the content available on the SAGE edge site, the coursepacks include:

- **Pedagogically robust assessment tools** that foster review, practice, and critical thinking and offer a better, more complete way to measure student engagement, including:

  - ○ **Diagnostic chapter pretests and posttests** that identify opportunities for student improvement, track student progress, and ensure mastery of key learning objectives.
  - ○ **Instructions** on how to use and integrate the comprehensive assessments and resources provided.
  - ○ **Assignable video tied to learning objectives, with corresponding multimedia assessment tools** bring concepts to life that increase student engagement and appeal to different learning styles. The **video assessment questions** feed to your gradebook.
  - ○ **Integrated links to the eBook version** that make it easy to access the mobile-friendly version of the text, which can be read anywhere, anytime.

Interactive eBook

Human Resource Management is also available as an **Interactive eBook** that can be packaged with the text for just $5 or purchased separately. The Interactive eBook offers hyperlinks to original videos, including **Inside HR** video interviews of HR professionals and general managers at Blount International and Procore Technologies, Inc., explaining how concepts in the text are applied in a real-world organization. The Interactive eBook also includes additional case studies from the SAGE Business Case Collection, TED Talks, as well as carefully chosen articles from the web. Users will also have immediate access to study tools such as highlighting, bookmarking, note-taking/sharing, and more!

Acknowledgments

The authors would like to thank the following people who supported this book both personally and professionally. Special thanks to Dean Cliff Allen and Associate Deans Melissa Appleyard and Erica Wagner for their ongoing support of human resource management as a key part of business success as well as the manner in which they embrace the importance of celebrating HRM with a people, data, and analytics focus. Their ability to lead into the future is inspirational. They have created an entrepreneurial and positive environment for us to all learn, experiment, and grow in our teaching and scholarship. We thank them for all that they do for students, faculty, organizations, and the larger community. We feel fortunate to get to work with them every day to help make the world, and the world of work, a better place.

We also offer our heartfelt thanks to Maggie Stanley, our acquisitions editor at SAGE, who supported our vision every step of the way. It has been a great working relationship from the first time we met. Thanks are also due to Lauren Holmes, our development editor, who has great editorial instincts and who worked tirelessly to keep us all on track and moving in the right direction. It was a pleasure to work with you both. Elsa Peterson was invaluable at aligning our outlines, learning objectives, and chapter content as we worked toward production. We would also like to thank our editorial assistant, Alissa Nance, who kept us on track; our copy editors, Jared Leighton and Kim Husband; and our cover designer, Scott Van Atta. Tracy Buyan, our production editor, did a fantastic job bringing our book to life and keeping us on schedule throughout the process. We also send sincere thanks to Amy Lammers, our marketing manager; associate marketing manager Victoria Velasquez; and marketing communications manager Andrew Lee. They helped champion this textbook and communicate our people, data, and analytics HRM approach. This talented SAGE team worked with us to develop compelling content and experiential exercises to help faculty teach the material, and more importantly, to help students learn to engage in HRM from a strategic and analytic perspective regardless of their position within the organization.

We give special thanks to Alex Alonso and Nancy Woolever at SHRM for the invaluable resources they provide to individuals and organizations to engage in effective HR practices. As the world's largest and leading organization for human resources, SHRM provides thought leadership, certification, community, and advocacy for the effectiveness and practice of organizations and HR individuals and functions. Throughout this book, we drew upon SHRM's guidance and competencies to outline the key HR practices and approaches to cover across the 16 chapters of this book.

No textbook acknowledgment is complete without recognizing the significant role that instructor feedback and reviews play in developing a vibrant, responsive, and useful book that helps faculty teach and students learn key concepts and to develop their skills in applying what they learn. With this in mind, we offer special thanks to the following reviewers for their expertise, insights, questions, and suggestions throughout the development of each chapter of this book as well as the themes.

The authors and SAGE would like to thank the following instructors who participated in reviews and market development for this book:

Susan Flannery Adams, Sonoma State University

Joann Adeogun, Point University

Devi Akella, Albany State University

Ron Alexandrowich, York University

Lisa M. Amoroso, Dominican University

Stephanie Bae, East Carolina University

Stacy Ball, Southwest Minnesota State University

Rimjhim Banerjee, Santa Fe College

Linda Barrenchea, University of Nevada, Reno

Robyn Berkley, Southern Illinois University, Edwardsville

Mike Bojanski, Methodist College

Emmanuele Bowles, Florida International University

Yvonne Brinson, Union University

Ronald Brownie, Northern State University

Otha Carlton Hawkins, Alamance Community College

Brian Cawley, Calvin College

Hyeran Choi, Columbus State University

Gwendolyn M. Combs, University of Nebraska Lincoln

Joseph Cooper, University of Toledo

Cody Cox, St. Mary's University

Stan Dale, University of LaVerne

Diana L. Deadrick, Old Dominion University

Caitlin A. Demsky, Oakland University

Karen Ehrhart, San Diego State University

Allison Ellis, California Polytechnic University, San Luis Obispo

John Fazio, Marieta College

Diane D. Galbraith, Slippery Rock University

Bruce Gillies, California Lutheran University

Deborah Good, University of Pittsburgh

Patricia Greer, University of Denver

Sheri Grotrian, Peru State College

Bruce L. Haller, Molloy College

Robert W. Halliman, Austin Peay State University

Robert Hanks, Portland State University

Jeffrey Hefel, Saint Mary's University of Minnesota

Heidi Helgren, Delta College

Terrill C. Herring, Lindenwood University

Michael W. Hill, University of Georgia

Kevin J. Hurt, Columbus State University

Patricia A. Ippoliti, Rutgers University

Sayeedul Islam, Farmingdale State College

Kathleen Jones, University of North Dakota

Jie Ke, Jackson State University

Chris Krull, Indiana University–Purdue University Indianapolis

Jeffrey D. Kudisch, University of Maryland College Park

Ann Langlois, Palm Beach Atlantic University

Julia Levashina, Kent State University

Waheeda Lillevik, The College of New Jersey

Kurt Loess, East Tennessee State University

Erin E. Makarius, University of Akron

Elizabeth Malatestinic, Indiana University

Gery Markova, Wichita State University

Lowell Matthews, Southern New Hampshire University

Randy McCamey, Tarleton State University

Jalane Meloun, Barry University

Ian Mercer, Auburn University

Mark S. Miller, Carthage College

Edwin Mourino, Rollins College

Steven Nichols, Metropolitan Community College

Lisa Nieman, Indiana Wesleyan University

Victor Oladapo, Webster University

Candice A. Osterfeld Ottobre, University of Akron

Deborah Powell, University of Guelph

Norma Raiff, Chatham University

Anushri Rawat, Eastern Michigan University

Kendra Reed, Loyola University of New Orleans

Kate Rowbotham, Queen's University

Lou L. Sabina, Stetson University

Terry J. Schindler, University of Indianapolis

Lewis Schlossinger, Fordham University

Tom See, California State University, Bakersfield

Joseph Simon, Casper College

Lauren Simon, University of Arkansas

Shamira Soren Malekar, City University of New York–Borough of Manhattan Community College

Alicia Stachowski, University of Wisconsin, Stout

Heather Staples, Texas A&M University

Steven Stovall, Southeast Missouri State University

Gary Stroud, Franklin University

Kyra Leigh Sutton, Rutgers University

Charmaine Tener, Thompson Rivers University

Neal F. Thomason, Columbus State University

Justice Tillman, Baruch College

Lee J. Tyner, University of Central Oklahoma

Stephen H. Wagner, Governor's State University

Carlotta S. Walker, Lansing Community College

Stacy Wassell, Frostburg State University

Brian D. Webster, Ball State University

Joseph R. Weintraub, Babson College

Don Wlodarski, Roosevelt University

Benjamin B. Yumol, Claflin University

SAGE would also like to thank Susan Schanne of Eastern Michigan University, Bruce Gillies of California Lutheran University, and Jessica McCulley at Graphic World, Inc. for contributing to the digital resources for this book.

Finally, we would like to offer special thanks to the thousands of students we have taught over the years. Each one of you has made us better teachers and scholars.

Thank you!

About the Authors

Talya Bauer, PhD
Gerry & Marilyn Cameron Professor of Management

Talya Bauer earned her PhD in business with an emphasis in organizational behavior and human resources from Purdue University. She is an award-winning teacher and was awarded the Innovation in Teaching Award from the HR Division of the Academy of Management. She teaches HR analytics, introduction to HRM, training and development, organizational behavior, and negotiations courses and has been recognized by the Society for Industrial and Organizational Psychology (SIOP) with the Distinguished Teaching Award. She conducts research about HR and relationships at work. More specifically, she works in research areas across the employee life cycle including recruitment and selection, new employee onboarding, and coworker and leader relationships. This work has resulted in dozens of journal publications, book chapters, and research grants including from NSF and NIH. She has acted as a consultant for government, Fortune 1,000, and start-up organizations. She has been quoted and her work covered in the *New York Times, Harvard Business Review, Wall Street Journal, Fortune*, the *Washington Post, Business Week, Talent Management, USA Today*, as well as appearing on NPR's *All Things Considered*. Previously, she worked as a computer consultant and as a trainer in California, Idaho, Oregon, and Hong Kong. She has been a visiting professor in France, Spain, and at Google, Inc. Talya is involved in professional organizations and conferences at the national level such as serving on the Human Resource Management Executive Committee of the Academy of Management and as SIOP president. She has received several Society for Human Resource Management (SHRM) research grants and authored SHRM's "Onboarding New Employees: Maximizing Success" and coauthored SHRM's "Applicant Reactions to Selection: HR's Best Practices" white papers. She is an associate editor for the *Journal of Applied Psychology*, the former editor of *Journal of Management*, and on the editorial boards for *Personnel Psychology, Journal of Management*, and *Industrial and Organizational Psychology: Perspectives on Science and Practices*. She has coauthored multiple textbooks including *Organizational Behavior, Principles of Management*, and *Psychology and Work: Introduction to Industrial and Organizational Psychology*. She is a fellow of SIOP, APA, APS, and IAAP.

Berrin Erdogan, PhD
Express Employment Professionals Professor of Management

Berrin Erdogan completed her PhD in human resource management at the University of Illinois, Chicago, and her B.S. degree in business administration at Bogazici University, Istanbul, Turkey. Prior to her graduate studies, she worked as a corporate trainer at a private bank. She teaches human resource management, performance management and compensation, and global human resource management at undergraduate and graduate levels. Her research focuses on the flow of people into and out of organizations, with a focus on applicant reactions to employee selection systems, newcomer onboarding, manager–employee relationships and skill utilization, and employee retention. Her studies have been conducted in a variety of industries including manufacturing, clothing and food retail, banking, health care, education, and information technology in the United States, UK, Turkey, Spain, India, China, France, Germany, and Vietnam. She authored over 60 articles and book chapters that appeared in journals including *Academy of Management Journal, Journal of Applied Psychology, Journal of Management, Personnel Psychology*, and *Human Resource Management,* and have been discussed in media outlets including the *New York Times, Harvard Business Review, Wall Street Journal, BBC Capital*, and *The Oregonian*. In addition, she coauthored the textbooks *Organizational Behavior, Psychology and Work: Introduction to Industrial and Organizational Psychology*, and *Principles of Management*. Berrin served as an associate editor for *Personnel Psychology* and *European Journal of Work and Organizational Psychology* and has served on numerous editorial boards. She is a fellow of SIOP. She was a visiting scholar and gave invited talks at universities in Australia, Canada, Greece, Singapore, Spain, Turkey, the United Kingdom, and the United States.

David Caughlin, PhD
Cameron Professor of HR Analytics, Instructor of Management

David Caughlin earned his master's in industrial and organizational psychology from Indiana University Purdue University–Indianapolis and his PhD in industrial/organizational psychology with concentrations in quantitative methodology and occupational health psychology from Portland State University. He has taught a number of courses related to human resource management (HRM) and data analytics, such as introduction to HRM, reward systems and performance management, HR information systems, HR analytics, organizational behavior, organizational psychology, practical statistical skills in psychology, and research methods in psychology. In his HR analytics courses, David teaches students how to use the statistical programming language R to manage, analyze, and visualize HR data to improve high-stakes decision making; in the process, students build their data literacy and develop valuable critical thinking and reasoning skills. He was recognized by the School of Business at Portland State University with the Teaching Innovation Award. David conducts research on topics related to supervisor support, employee motivation, and occupational safety and health. As a faculty member, he is affiliated with Portland State University's Advancement of Interdisciplinary Methodology for Social Science. He has worked with a variety of organizations on projects related to employee selection, performance management, compensation, organizational culture, mistreatment prevention, and employee survey development. His work has been published in academic journals such as *Journal of Occupational Health Psychology*; *Stress & Health*; and *Psychology, Public Policy, and Law*.

Donald Truxillo, PhD
Professor of Work and Employment Studies

Donald Truxillo earned his PhD from Louisiana State University. He is a professor at the Kemmy Business School, University of Limerick, Ireland. Previously, he worked in the areas of selection, employee development, and promotions in the public sector as an industrial psychologist and as a professor in the industrial/organizational psychology program at Portland State University. He studies the methods employers use to hire workers and the experiences of job applicants during recruitment and hiring. In addition, Donald examines issues related to workplace safety and health as well as age differences at work. He served as associate editor for the *Journal of Management* and is currently an associate editor at *Work, Aging and Retirement*. He is a member of nine editorial boards including *Journal of Applied Psychology*, *Personnel Psychology*, and *Human Resource Management Review*. He is the author of more than 100 peer-reviewed journal articles and book chapters. Donald is the recipient of SIOP's 2017 Distinguished Teaching Contributions Award and a coauthor of the textbook *Psychology and Work: Introduction to Industrial and Organizational Psychology*. His research has been supported by the SHRM Foundation, the National Institute of Occupational Safety and Health (NIOSH), and the National Science Foundation (NSF), most recently to study privacy and security issues associated with online hiring. He has taught courses in human resource management, training and development, research methods, and industrial psychology. He has received three Fulbright grants to study abroad and has visited at universities in Italy, Portugal, Spain, Switzerland, Ireland, and Germany. Since 2010, he has been a member of the Doctoral Training Committee, Department of Psychological Science and Education, University of Trento, Italy. He is a fellow of SIOP, APA, APS, and IAAP.

Human Resource Management

Introduction to Human Resource Management

1

1 ←

Opening Case

HRM in Context: The Case of Chobani's Evolving HR Culture[1]

Hamdi Ulukaya, founder and CEO of Chobani, LLC, left his family dairy business in Turkey to learn English in the United States. Soon after he arrived, he noticed that the strained yogurt popular in Greece and Turkey, known for its rich flavor and high levels of protein, was not widely available in U.S. grocery stores. In 2005, that realization and Ulukaya's dairy background led him to take the opportunity to purchase a 100-year-old dairy plant in central New York state. He started out small. As he recalls, "I hired five people from the 55 [applicants], and those five are still with me." It took 2 years of work to perfect the yogurt recipe; the company's first order didn't ship until 2007. However, Chobani caught on quickly, with annual sales of $1 billion in 2012. That same year, Chobani opened its second plant. Today, Chobani is the best-selling Greek yogurt in the United States, employs over 2,000 people, and boasts the world's largest yogurt plant at its state-of-the art, million-square-foot location in Twin Falls, Idaho.

However, the company has experienced its share of highs and lows. In 2013, Ulukaya was named the Ernst & Young World Entrepreneur of the Year, but Chobani was plagued with a recall of some of the yogurt produced in its new plant. Chobani recovered and in 2015 had sales of $1.6 billion. Again, in 2016, Chobani and its founder were making headlines when Ulukaya surprised 2,000 full-time Chobani employees with shares worth 10% of the company, redeemable when Chobani is sold or goes public. Ulukaya tied the number of shares to the length of time an employee had been with Chobani so that the five original employees received the greatest number of shares. These shares come directly from Ulukaya, as he was the sole owner of the 100% independent company—a status that enabled him to create what he calls a "people-centered company." He said in a memo to employees that the shares were not just a gift. They were "a mutual promise to work together with a shared purpose and responsibility." In 2017, Chobani implemented a new paid parental leave policy offering 100% paid parental leave for 6 weeks for all full-time employees.

Along the way, Chobani's HRM system needed to evolve in response to the company's astronomical growth. How did Chobani's 30 full-time HR professionals help manage the 3,000 full- and part-time employees in Australia and the United States who make over 2.2 million cases of

LEARNING OBJECTIVES

After reading and studying this chapter, you should be able to do the following:

1.1 Define human resource management (HRM).

1.2 Articulate why HRM matters, giving concrete examples.

1.3 Explain the changing context of HRM and the developing role of analytics and technology.

1.4 Summarize the HRM profession.

Hamdi Ulukaya

yogurt each week? Craig Gomez, Chobani's former chief people officer, describes how his experience in HR at PepsiCo, GE, and Cisco helped him strike a balance between where Chobani's HR had grown organically and where it needed to go. Gomez's strategy was to find solutions to existing organizational "pain points." He and his HR colleagues realized that they couldn't do everything all at once. "We have picked items that add tremendous value and do not unduly burden the client with administrative headaches," Gomez says. He further notes, "I think, with all due respect to all of my peers in HR, a lot of times HR comes at an organization with a set playbook and they just lead with a set list of things they think that every organization should have instead of really listening to the client and really matching up what they deliver with what the specific client's points of pain are."

When it comes to insights, Chobani's HR team has had a few. For example, they developed orientation programs that new employees can view on a laptop. They also realized that even though they couldn't hire every person who applied to work at Chobani, it is important to treat applicants with respect. Gomez explained, "We want to bring the same level of sensitivity to job applicants as we do to consumers." As you will see in this textbook, these are HR insights that are backed up by research studies on the topics. As for Chobani, it is clear that HR is a partner in helping the business grow and generate solutions.

An important point in this case is the fact that organizations evolve. You will see examples throughout this book of small start-up companies, governmental agencies, and not-for-profit organizations as well as small, medium, and large organizations, including Fortune 500 companies. If you examine the histories of organizations, you can begin to see a pattern where today's large corporations often began as small start-ups employing just a handful of individuals. The HRM needs of start-up organizations certainly differ from those of large Fortune 500 companies, but the principles of HRM remain the same. Beginning with solid, tested HRM practices and ethical guidelines makes it much easier for organizations to stay effective as they grow.

Case Discussion Questions

1. Chobani has grown a great deal since its founding in 2005. How do you think growth has influenced its HR practices beyond what is mentioned in this case? Please share specific insights.

2. Craig Gomez, Chobani's former chief people officer, makes a strong case for HR being in the business of solving problems for the organization. Do you agree with this position? Why or why not?

3. Why do you think that Chobani's founder, Hamdi Ulukaya, gave away 10% of his company to his current full-time employees? Do you think this is a wise idea or a foolish one? Why?

4. Do you consider Chobani's policy of offering 6 weeks of paid parental leave to all full-time employees a waste of money or a wise investment? Why? Be prepared to defend your response.

▶ Click to learn more...

View Hamdi Ulukaya's story at https://youtu.be/578FODRPRa0

Human resource management (HRM) is defined as the constellation of decisions and actions associated with managing individuals throughout the employee lifecycle to maximize employee and organizational effectiveness. HRM relates to all aspects of organizational life. The first chapter of this book gives you an overview of what HRM is and why it is important.

Human resource management (HRM) The decisions and actions associated with managing individuals throughout the employee life cycle to maximize employee and organization effectiveness

What Is Human Resource Management?

LO 1.1 Define human resource management (HRM).

This textbook provides an introduction to the field of human resource management (HRM). This includes what HRM is, the evolving context and landscape of HRM, best practices, and some of the issues and controversies associated with HRM today. We suspect that, unlike some other areas of study in business, HRM is a subject you already know a great deal about even before reading this book or taking this class. For example, if you have ever filled out a job application or been interviewed for a job, you have been exposed to a major function within HRM called *selection*. Even if you have never applied for a job, you have still interacted with thousands of people who have. Every teacher you have had in the classroom and every customer service interaction you have encountered was the result of HRM in some way or another: Teachers and customer service specialists are hired, trained, paid, and managed via their organization's HRM system. Interactions such as these may have given you some preconceived notions of what HRM is all about. This is a great thing because it means you can jump right in and start participating and discussing the material. But we suspect, as you progress through this book, you will also find yourself seeing the strategic value of HRM practices and why HRM is a key factor in organizational success regardless of the area of business that you intend to focus on in your own career. That is why we set out to write this book.

The world of HRM is changing in new and innovative ways. Much like the *Industrial Revolution* of the mid-1800s, where machines changed the way that manufacturing work was done, we are currently in the midst of a *knowledge revolution*. Never before in history has it been easier to access information, connect globally, and manage employees remotely. We discuss the implications of this recent shift in this chapter, and it is integrated throughout the book. Chapter 2 specifically addresses how this knowledge revolution has created exciting opportunities for HRM to become invaluable within organizations in a variety of ways, including informing managers with best practices and data to aid decision making throughout the organization. As valued business partners, HRM specialists and generalists can span the range of activities from following procedures to creating and testing hypotheses regarding the most effective ways to manage employees. It is clear that there is a lot to learn, so let us get started with addressing the basic question of what HRM is exactly, who is involved, and where HR is located within organizations.

Human resource management refers to the constellation of decisions and actions associated with managing individuals throughout the employee life cycle to maximize employee and organizational effectiveness in attaining goals. This includes functions that range from analyzing and designing jobs; managing diversity and complying with local, national, and global employee laws; recruiting individuals to apply for jobs; selecting individuals to join organizations; training and developing people while they are employed; helping to manage their performance; rewarding and compensating employee performance while maintaining healthy labor relations and helping to keep them safe; as well as managing their exit, or departure, from the organization.

If you have ever applied for a job and had an interview, you have experienced HRM in action.

©iStock.com/sturti

Ultimately, HRM is about making decisions about people. This decision-making process involves many questions that those within an organization must ask and answer. Over time, the answers may change as the firm experiences growth or decline, external factors change, or the organizational culture evolves. For example, those involved in HRM need to address questions such as these:

- What type of employees do we need to hire?
- Where will we find the best and most diverse employees?
- How do we manage diversity to maximize its benefits and minimize group conflicts?

- How should we select the people who will join our company?
- How can we help them be safe and experience well-being at work?
- How should we motivate and reward employees to be effective, innovative, and loyal?
- What benefits would our employees find the most attractive?
- What training do our employees need, and how can we further develop them?
- How can we help to ensure that employment relations between employees and managers remain healthy and include healthy feedback and voice from both sides?
- What can we do to ensure that employees engage in ethical decision making and behaviors?
- What do we need to do to remain competitive locally and globally?
- Why are employees leaving, and what can we learn from their exits?

All of these questions and more are part of managing the HRM system of decisions and actions associated with managing individuals throughout the employee life cycle (see Figure 1.1) from the hiring stage through the exit of an employee through voluntary or involuntary turnover.

Viewing HRM from a decision-making perspective has important implications for the success of employees and organizations. First, HRM systems can help overcome *biases*—types of favoritism or prejudice—that can be inherent in organizational decisions. A preponderance of evidence indicates that individuals have biases, often unconscious, when engaging in decision making. Each of these biases represents a shortcut to making decisions. Based on years of experience, each of us has developed the ability to sort through copious amounts of information to arrive at decisions. Some are small, and we hardly ever give them a thought, but those can be dangerous decisions because biases such as availability, anchoring, or confirmation can influence the outcome unconsciously. Other choices, such as whether to hire one of three candidates, also have consequences.

For example, consider the *availability bias*, which is the tendency to rely more on information that is readily available to us, and thus we discount alternative information. To the degree that the information relating to the job candidates is subjective, such as when interviews are used, our past experiences will influence us to a greater degree, and bias can creep into the process. The bias might be subtle, such as your recollection that

Biases A tendency, feeling, or opinion, especially one that is preconceived, unreasoned, and unsupported by evidence

Availability bias The tendency to rely more on information that is more readily available than alternative information

■ **FIGURE 1.1** The Employee Life Cycle

A critical aspect of HRM is managing key aspects of work throughout the entire employee life cycle.

the last employee you hired from State University has done a great job. This might lead you to lean toward the one candidate on your short list from this same school. But is this a reasonable thing, given that State University graduates 8,000 students per year and the other two candidates graduated from schools from which your company has employed dozens of successful candidates? It probably is not. To avoid this as well as the other types of biases, take concrete steps, including recognizing that such biases exist; taking the other side of your argument, including others in the decision making; assigning a devil's advocate; and considering the consequences of a suboptimal hire. In other words, one of the functions of HRM is to be aware of and design systems that prevent systemic biases from exerting undue influence over decision making, resulting in better decisions. ***Anchoring bias***, the tendency to rely too much on the first piece of information given, can

Anchoring bias The tendency when making a judgment to rely on the first piece of information that one receives

MANAGER'S TOOLBOX

Am I Making a Good Decision?

Making decisions is not easy. Research shows that only about 50% of all decisions made within organizations are successful.[2] However, to help you understand whether a particular decision has the hallmarks of success, it makes sense to consider the following key characteristics. Doing so won't guarantee success, but it can help you develop more robust decision-making criteria that help to meet the needs of the entire organization rather than just solving a problem today that may create a larger problem tomorrow.

Ask yourself these questions:

- *Is this course of action legal? Is it ethical? Is it fair?* Just being legal is a good first step, but it is not enough. How would you feel if your course of action were shared on the Internet or on the front page of your local newspaper? If the answer is "not so great," that's an indication that the course of action you are considering may be legal but may not be ethical or fair.

- *Is this decision based on evidence and data?* While decisions should not be made solely based on prior evidence and relevant data, they should consider both and try to leverage what is possible to know to rule out alternative courses of action.

- *Will pursuing this course of action help to make the organization healthier?* It is easy to make decisions and pursue courses of action in isolation from the larger organization. However, doing so can create problems. Stopping to consider whether you are doing something that is likely to help or hinder positive employee–employer relations is helpful in avoiding problems down the line.

- *Is this course of action time and resource efficient?* If the course of action you are considering is not time or resource efficient, it is not likely to be sustainable over time. This can lead to resource constraints, including employee energy and burnout as well as financial constraints.

- *Does this course of action take a systematic perspective and consider various stakeholders?* You might have all the information necessary to make a good decision. But you might not. And even if you do have the relevant information, including stakeholders in the decision-making process is a helpful way of securing acceptance of a decision. Thus, skipping this step will most likely lead to less effective decisions in the long run.

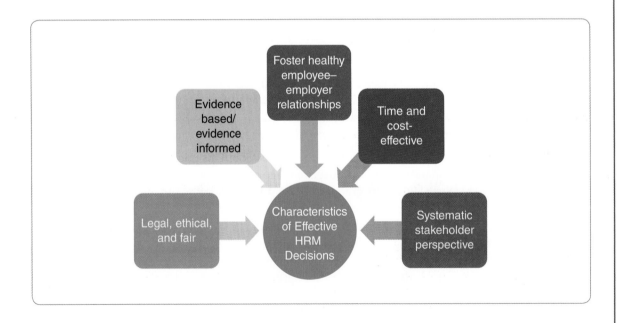

be just as dangerous, as your decision can be influenced simply by the way others present information. Finally, **overconfidence bias**, the tendency to seek confirmation of one's own beliefs or expectations, can shortcut the exploration of a full range of options. All of these biases can hurt the quality of decisions made.

Another important implication for approaching HRM as a set of decision-making activities is to address the core issue of what makes a good decision. Manager's Toolbox details the hallmarks of a good decision.

Overconfidence bias The tendency for an individual to be more confident in their own beliefs than reality would suggest

Why HRM Matters

You might be taking this class because it is required at your school even if you are not an HRM major. Regardless of your major, HR is valuable for you and your career. For example, knowing about HR policies and practices is important because as a manager or future manager, you will be required to make employee-related decisions. You might be involved in recruiting and hiring employees, and in fact, you will be on the front line of the hiring process. You may play an important role in managing the performance of employees and allocating rewards. You may need to discipline employees or manage their exit. Your decisions, actions, and inactions will be used to assess compliance with the law. Therefore, much of the information included in this book is relevant as you build your managerial skills. For any HR practice to be implemented effectively, HR and line managers will need to be partners. This involves each party understanding the rationale behind each practice, line managers remaining true to the spirit of the system in place and giving feedback to HR, and HR departments designing systems that meet the needs of line managers. Moreover, if you end up working in an area outside of HR, such as accounting or marketing, you will still be a consumer of the HR systems and services available at your organization. For example, your department may require a new training program, and thus, it will be essential to partner with the HR department to design and implement the new training program. As such, it is important to understand how HR systems and services work. In short, even if you have no interest in working in HR, learning about HRM will be a good investment of your time.

LO 1.2   Articulate why HRM matters, giving concrete examples.

People Matter

It is well documented that the individuals who work within an organization matter when it comes to what an organization is like as a place to work and what it is able to do. Individuals influence its culture, informal rules, how hard individuals work, how they should treat one another, how much risk employees should take, as well as what is considered acceptable in terms of performance and ethics. Influence happens through who is attracted to join the organization, who is selected to join the organization, and who decides to remain or leave the organization. Benjamin Schneider called this the **A-S-A framework**, standing for attraction-selection-attrition in organizations. In other words, organizations vary in terms of the human capital they have access to based on whom they attract, hire, and retain. *Human capital* refers to the knowledge, skills, and abilities, as well as other characteristics (KSAOs) embodied in people.[3] As you saw in the opening case on Chobani, human capital might refer to the KSAOs of a handful of people when a company is starting out to thousands of employees if the organization grows. Clearly, the human capital needs change over time as well. Chobani did not have a formal HRM department when it started out, and it continued to be quite successful. However, as it grew, the decision to shift toward less outsourcing of HRM and more in-house HRM functions was made.

A-S-A framework The process of attraction, selection, and attrition that defines an organization's culture

HR IN ACTION
Costco

Barry Sweet/Bloomberg via Getty Images

Former Costco president and CEO James Sinegal is pictured in one of the company's stores near its headquarters in Issaquah, Washington.

Costco is known as a desirable employer, in part, because it pays an average of $21 per hour to employees in retail environments where $10.50 is closer to the average hourly pay. Costco also covers 90% of health insurance expenses for both full-time and part-time employees, which is rare. James Sinegal, former CEO of Costco, is quoted as saying, "When employees are happy, they are your very best ambassadors." Although HR at Costco is not directly run by its CEO, you can imagine how such a strong set of values at the executive level influences all HR practices at Costco. These values, together with the facts that Costco promotes from within, encourages and listens to employee suggestions, and gives managers autonomy to experiment with their departments and stores with an eye toward increasing sales and/or reducing costs (as long as products are never marked up more than 15%), and the fact that he made a modest salary as CEO, are among the reasons why Sinegal was named one of the 100 Most Influential People in Business Ethics in 2008. As a founder and CEO, he made a big profit for the company while putting people first, so it is hard to argue with his success. Although Costco pays considerably more than the industry average, including bonuses and other incentives, its revenues and stock price continue to grow. In fact, the value of Costco stock from 1985 until Sinegal's retirement in 2012 increased by 5,000%. The next CEO, W. Craig Jelinek, continued this trend. In 2015, Costco's stock rose more than 15% under his leadership, and he was named CEO of the Year by CNN. Costco's stock price has continued to be strong in subsequent years.[4]

Richard Branson, founder of the Virgin Group, famously said, "Take care of your employees, and they'll take care of your business."[5] He argues that creating a great place to work involves a work climate where people are appreciated, engaged in their work, productive, and thriving rather than simply surviving. Research supports this idea, showing that large percentages of disengaged employees (68% to 70% of survey respondents) cost U.S. businesses up to $550 billion per year in lost productivity.[6] Disengaged employees also have 49% more accidents on the job and 60% more errors in their work, and their companies have a 65% lower share price over time than those with more engaged employees.[7] Organizations increasingly understand that treating individuals isn't just about "being nice" to them; it is a win-win, as those employees who feel valued also tend to be more engaged and productive. And we know that organizations that value their employees are more profitable than those that do not.[8]

If employing people who are valued, highly supported, and engaged at work promotes company success, why don't all organizations create such cultures? That is a great question. The answer is complex, but reasons include not understanding or believing the connection between organizational culture and success and not knowing how to create this connection.

Organizational Culture Matters

Organizational culture refers to shared, "taken-for-granted" assumptions that members of an organization have that affect the way they act, think, and perceive their environment.[9] Because of this, organizational culture influences how decisions are made within organizations, and it is also influenced by those decisions. For example, if being polite is highly valued within an organization,

Organizational culture
Assumptions shared by organization members, which affect their actions, thoughts, and perceptions

the approach taken when giving performance feedback would be much different than in an organization that values directness. During the initial pilot of a managerial training program, which involved a simulation and role play conducted with employees at Hewlett Packard in the 1990s, the entire role play had to be rewritten when the participants insisted that the role of an employee who argues with their manager vigorously just would never happen. As participants explained, they didn't know how to react to this because it was so far out of the norm of their business. Since that time, HP's culture has evolved to be more in line with other cultures, which are more direct and aggressive. However, this is a useful reminder of how powerful cultures can be. Thus, it makes sense to take some time to understand the different types of organizational cultures that exist within organizations.

Types of Organizational Culture

One popular typology of organizational cultures, called the Competing Values Framework, characterizes them by their emphasis on collaboration, creating, controlling, or competing (see Figure 1.2).[10] In the Competing Values Framework, **clan cultures** are collaboration oriented and are characterized by valuing being cohesive, people oriented, team players, and empowering employees. Based on our understanding of Chobani from the opening case, it appears to be consistent with a clan culture. Other examples of organizations that can be seen

Clan culture Organizations with clan cultures are collaboration and people oriented and value cohesion, employee empowerment, and team players

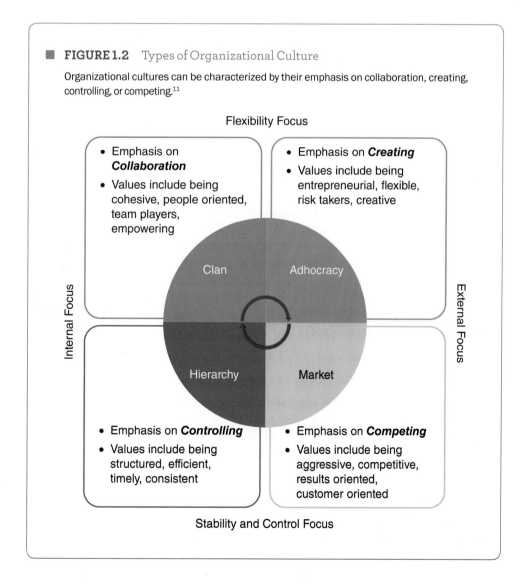

■ FIGURE 1.2   Types of Organizational Culture

Organizational cultures can be characterized by their emphasis on collaboration, creating, controlling, or competing.[11]

Flexibility Focus

- Emphasis on **Collaboration**
- Values include being cohesive, people oriented, team players, empowering

- Emphasis on **Creating**
- Values include being entrepreneurial, flexible, risk takers, creative

Internal Focus

External Focus

Clan   Adhocracy

Hierarchy   Market

- Emphasis on **Controlling**
- Values include being structured, efficient, timely, consistent

- Emphasis on **Competing**
- Values include being aggressive, competitive, results oriented, customer oriented

Stability and Control Focus

as having clan cultures are Costco, Southwest Airlines Company, and SAS Institute. ***Adhocracy cultures*** focus on creating and emphasize being entrepreneurial, flexible, taking risks, and being creative. Examples of adhocracy cultures are 3M, Google, and Facebook. ***Market cultures*** are characterized by competition and value being aggressive, competitive, and customer oriented. Examples of companies showing signs of a market culture are Amazon, Intel, and Netflix. ***Hierarchy cultures*** focus on controlling and value being efficient, timely, and consistent. Organizations such as Walmart and Boeing are examples of this type of culture.

How HRM Affects Organizational Culture

There is no one type of culture that leads to success and happy employees. The examples given for different cultures are all successful businesses in their industries. However, it is important to remember that there is a close connection between company culture and HR practices adopted, and in turn, the HR practices adopted will influence and shape the culture into the future. Company HR practices are often a reflection of company culture. For example, Marriott developed an online recruiting platform called "My Marriott Hotel" where candidates manage different areas of the hotel's operations, where they lose or gain points for customer satisfaction and profitability. Such a recruitment tool reflects the company's values, such as being results and customer oriented.[12] You would not expect to see such a system in place in a company that emphasizes efficient and cost-effective hiring to fill specific positions.

Similarly, the HR practices in use will shape a company's culture. For example, imagine a company that adopts a performance review system that involves ranking employees on a bell curve and distributing rewards accordingly, such as Yahoo's adoption of such a system in 2013. Requiring managers to compare employees with each other will shape the culture of the company toward a market culture, as survival in such a system will require competition among employees. Therefore, effective HR decisions will need to consider the implications of every decision for the culture the company has and the culture the company would like to have.

LO 1.3   Explain the changing context of HRM and the developing role of analytics and technology.

The Changing Context of HRM

Human resource management does not exist in a vacuum. Companies have gone from personnel departments exclusively using paper forms and tracking benefits to HR becoming a strategic partner in organizational decisions. Because of this, as the world and the fundamental characteristics of work continue to evolve, so must human resource management. This section outlines a number of these important changes in the contextual landscape that have major implications for HRM. These include changing demographics, the emerging gig economy, increased globalization, technology, the availability of data, and the ongoing and rising importance of ethics and corporate social responsibility (see Figure 1.3).

Changing Demographics

One of the largest impacts on HRM is that of the increasingly changing demographics of individuals in the United States and around the world (see Figure 1.4). Changes include the aging population and increasing demographic diversity. Given how prevalent this topic is, you are probably aware that the American workforce is aging. By 2030, 20% or more of those in the United States are projected to be aged 65 or older, which is more than double the percentage in 1970.[13] This represents a major shift in the working population, as nearly 75 million baby boomers (those born between 1946 and 1964) are expected to retire in the next 25 years, with only 46 million new workers from later generations joining the organizational ranks. More recently, however, we are also seeing greater numbers of non-U.S.-born entrants into the American workforce, which is helping to fill the labor gap.

■ **FIGURE 1.3**   The Changing Context of HRM

Forces shaping human resource management continue to evolve.

Source: Photos via Shutterstock.

Whereas the aging workforce is a key demographic shift, increasing diversity in the workplace is also an aspect of the changing demographic landscape, which has implications for HRM. For example, race is an area where we still see challenges with equal pay for equal work. Research finds that ethnic subgroups experience both an earnings gap and a glass ceiling. In 2015, for every dollar a Caucasian male employee made, Asian males made $1.20, whereas African American males made around 76 cents, and Hispanic employees made 69 cents.[14] In 2018, only three Fortune 500 companies (Merck & Co, Inc., JCPenney's, and TIAA) are run by African American chairpersons and CEOs. It is interesting that although, as a group, ethnic subgroups face challenges in terms of pay and promotion, the demographic trends are such that by 2055, Caucasians are estimated to constitute less than one half of the population in the United States.[15] This demographic shift has already taken place in some parts of the United States, such as the Los Angeles area, where only 29% of the population is Caucasian, non-Hispanic.[16]

Such core changes in who is available to work has major implications for how to recruit, select, train, reward, and manage the workforce. Given that HRM is responsible for these functions, being aware of the changes as well as their associated challenges and opportunities is essential for organizations to remain competitive.

Emergence of the Gig Economy

A ***gig economy*** is characterized by the prevalence of temporary employment positions, and individuals are employed as independent workers rather than actual employees of an organization. And a ***gig*** is defined as a single project or task that a worker is hired to do on demand. Think of

Gig economy The prevalence of temporary employment positions, where individuals are employed as independent workers instead of actual employees of an organization

Gig A single project or task that a worker is hired to do on demand

■ **FIGURE 1.4**   Percent Aged 65 and Over by Race and Hispanic Origin for the United States: 2012 and 2050 (percent of each group's total population)

The distribution of U.S. population continues to change, which has implications for HR.

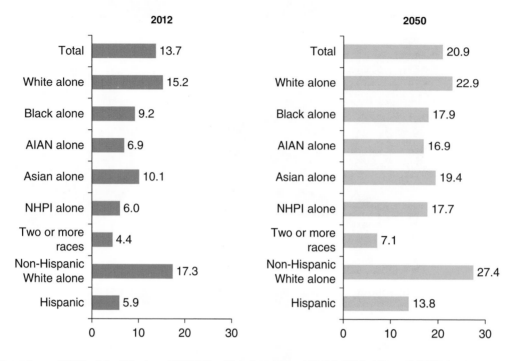

Sources: U.S. Census Bureau, 2012 Population Estimates and 2012 National Projections; Ortman, J. M., Velkoff, V. A., & Hogan, H. (2014). An aging nation: The older population in the United States. U.S. Department of Commerce. Retrieved August 2, 2018, from https://www.census.gov/prod/2014pubs/p25-1140.pdf

Notes: AIAN = American Indian and Alaska Native. NHPI = Native Hawaiian and Other Pacific Islander.

Uber drivers or substitute teachers. In 2018, of the 161 million employed in the United States, nearly 21 million (or 13%) reported working part-time jobs for noneconomic reasons.[17] A survey found that 75% of full-time and 68% of part-time freelance employees noted scheduling flexibility as a key reason for their attraction to freelance work.[18] Other positives reported are variety and the ability to pursue one's interests. Reported downsides include inconsistency in pay and scheduling and the lack of benefits associated with this type of employment contract. As the U.S. Department of Labor noted about the gig economy, "These workers often get individual gigs using a website or mobile app that helps to match them with customers. Some gigs may be brief. . . . Others are much longer but still of limited duration, such as an 18-month database management project. When one gig is over, workers who earn a steady income this way must find another. And sometimes, that means juggling multiple jobs at once."[19] Some occupations are more likely than others to employ contract workers. Arts and design, computer and information technology, construction and extraction, media and communications, as well as transportation and material moving are industry sectors at the top of the list for contract work. The implications of the emerging gig economy are vast. Because this class of employment is so relatively new, the legal environment has not yet kept up, and it remains an area that is unclear.

Globalization

U.S.-based businesses recognize the importance of international business and international presence. India and China are the fastest growing economies, each of them being home to around 18% of the world's population. Major U.S. businesses are realizing that a big portion of their revenues

SPOTLIGHT ON GLOBAL ISSUES
Labor Laws Diverge Globally

A key aspect to global HRM success is to recognize that beyond cultural differences, different countries have fundamentally different approaches to work that may be instituted into labor laws. For example, France is a country known for having strong protections for workers. Within France, the workweek is limited to 35 hours, and employees have the "right to disconnect," or have the right to hours during which they are not required to check or answer e-mail. Another example is the General Data Protection Regulation (GDPR), which took effect in 2018 and mandates that the European Union's (EU) 500 million citizens have specific data privacy rights and that companies with a presence in the EU must adhere to the rules or face stiff fines. In Sweden, while legislation requires boards of directors to have at least 40% of board seats filled by women, it is strongly encouraged that they strive for gender balance. These are just a few examples of how fundamental HRM policies may differ in terms of defining the workweek, contact outside of working hours, how data may be collected and reported, and the composition of governing entities. Thus, it is clear that organizations interested in working on a global scale need to pay close attention to HRM and develop their own strategic plan for addressing both organizational and national rules, guidelines, and policies.[20]

come from overseas. For example, Intel receives 82% of its revenue from overseas. For Qualcomm, this ratio is over 98%. Half the revenue of Dow Chemical, Exxon Mobil, Apple, and Johnson & Johnson comes from overseas.[21] If you are not convinced that international business is here to stay, consider these iconic, everyday brands: Budweiser, 7-Eleven, Holiday Inn, Shell, and T-Mobile. All of these are foreign-owned. Globalization of business introduces a number of HRM challenges. Businesses recruit and hire employees from a more diverse pool of applicants given the realities of global mobility of potential employees. Businesses will need to consider the local laws and regulations in the different operations they run. It is also important to consider the role of cultural differences in the use of different HRM practices around the world. It is tempting to transport best practices developed in corporate headquarters, but such efforts, without sensitivity to the local culture, are often doomed to fail. As a result, in companies operating worldwide, effective HRM takes into account local differences in local laws and norms to create an effective global organization.

Technology

Technology has been evolving at a rapid pace. A key reason behind this can be explained via Moore's Law, put forth in 1965, which states the capacity of computer chips would double roughly every 2 years at around the same cost. George E. Moore was the cofounder of Intel Corporation. As part of its 50-year celebration of Moore's Law, Intel calculated that if fuel efficiency were to improve at the same rate as the law over 50 years, a person could drive their car for a lifetime on a single tank of gas.[22] Moore's Law is important to HRM because it illustrates how rapidly technology will continue to evolve as the cost and availability of processing power becomes increasingly accessible. This aligns with the increasing rate of technology's impact on HRM processes and procedures. As you will see throughout this book—and especially in Chapter 3—technology matters a great deal when it comes to HRM.

Availability of Data

It may seem like everyone is talking about big data. We discuss this in greater detail in the next two chapters, but for now, it is helpful to know that *big data* refers to data that are large in volume, variety, and velocity. Technology has allowed for greater and greater computing power, and the Internet has generated so much data that recent estimates are that Amazon, Facebook, Google, and Microsoft stored at least 1,200 petabytes among them in 2013 alone. A petabyte is 1 million

SPOTLIGHT ON DATA AND ANALYTICS

Descriptive, Predictive, and Prescriptive Analytics

A survey of business leaders conducted by Deloitte found that concerns exist regarding the gap between the perceived need for data-driven approaches to HR and the existing skill base. Of the companies surveyed, 75% reported a belief that HR analytics is important, but just 8% reported a belief that their own organization is strong in this area.[23] A SHRM Foundation report on analytics found that two key skills are lacking: analytics skills and the ability to present findings in a convincing way to senior executives.[24] However, as more organizations such as Pfizer, AOL, and Facebook continue to focus on analytics, we suspect that other organizations will continue to follow suit.

As you consider how analytics in general and HR analytics in particular may play a role in your future, keep in mind these different levels of analytics: *descriptive*, *predictive*, and *prescriptive*.

Descriptive analytics is focused on understanding what has happened. By definition, it is focused on understanding the past. Descriptive analytics might include understanding what percentage of an employee sample has a college education versus a high school education. *Predictive analytics* focuses on what is likely to happen given what is known. By definition it is forward looking. For example, predictive analytics might focus on understanding how going to high school versus continuing to college relates to job performance based on probabilities. *Prescriptive analytics* focuses on what should be done in the future based on what is known. By definition it is also forward looking. Prescriptive analytics might focus on what the best mix of high school– versus college-educated employees the firm *should* have for optimal firm performance.

Descriptive Analytics	• **What has happened?** • Most of HRM employs descriptive analytics • Includes sums, averages, percentages that describe the situation • For example, for HRM, how many employees went through training last year?
Predictive Analytics	• **What could happen?** • Includes forecasts, developing models to predict and explain employee and organizational outcomes • For example, for HRM, understanding which types of employees will benefit the most from different training programs
Prescriptive Analytics	• **What should be done?** • Consider different possible outcomes of actions and optimal solutions; rarely used • Advice on which course of action the organization *should* take • For example, for HRM, what should the organization do so employees will benefit most from training?

gigabytes. Every second, there are over 8,000 tweets, nearly 1,000 Instagram photos uploaded, over 1,500 Tumblr posts, 3,000 Skype calls, over 65,000 Google search queries, and 2.7 million e-mails sent. These numbers continue to grow over time.[25] That's a lot of data. In addition, companies often gather annual opinion surveys, as well as other employment data from millions of workers each year. As more and more transactions, communications, and shopping move online, more information is available each day. Thus, over 70% of business executives are investing, or plan to invest, in analytics related to big data, but only 2% say they have yet achieved what they called "broad, positive impact."[26]

This book explicitly focuses on the importance of data in making effective HRM decisions. We offer examples and insights throughout the book as well as special features to help bring data analytics to help you become more familiar and more effective at thinking about and leveraging the availability of data. Chapters 2 and 3 include much more depth on data. But for now, knowing that technology and big data are major trends that affect HRM throughout the world are the key points we want you to take way from this section.

Ethical Challenges and Corporate Social Responsibility

Business ethics is a system of principles that govern how businesses operate, how decisions are made, and how people are treated. It includes the conduct of individual employees as well as the entire organization. These concepts should look familiar from our earlier discussion of the characteristics of effective HRM decision making. The concept of business ethics arose in the 1960s and 1970s in the United States as values shifted from strict loyalty to the organization to a stronger loyalty toward one's own guiding principles and ideals.[27] This manifested itself through environmental issues, increasing employee-versus-employer tension, human rights issues surrounding unfair and unsafe labor practices, and civil rights issues. Over time, additional issues surfaced, such as bribes and illegal contracting practices, deception in advertising, and lack of transparency in business transactions.

By the early 2000s, concerns regarding business scandals such as financial mismanagement, increased corporate liability for personal damage, and fraud had come to the forefront. Such scandals led to several changes on the global stage, such as the UN Convention Against Corruption and the 2004 Global Compact adopting the 10th principle against corruption, and the Association of Advanced Collegiate Schools of Business (AACSB) included ethics as part of an accredited business education including a key provision on the importance of ethical decision making.[28] Given that HRM is defined as the constellation of decisions and actions associated with managing individuals throughout the employee life cycle, addressing ethical challenges and corporate social responsibility are key aspects of HRM. Thus, you will find a feature called *Spotlight on Ethics* in each chapter of this book. We encourage you to take the time to consider the ethical challenges you have and may encounter at work.

Business ethics A system of principles that govern how business operates, how decisions are made, and how people are treated

HRM as a Profession

Not every person reading this book plans to go into HRM as a profession. Nevertheless, understanding who is involved in HRM, the types of HR careers available, and what the core HRM competencies are should be helpful to all interested in business. We start with an overview of who is involved in HRM.

LO 1.4 Summarize the HRM profession.

Who Is Involved in HRM?

The short answer to this question is everyone within an organization. This is because everyone is responsible for helping the organization be successful. However, some individuals, groups, and departments are more involved in HRM decision making and actions on a

SPOTLIGHT ON ETHICS

SHRM Code of Ethics

Ethics is critically important to the effective practice of HRM. Ethical decisions and actions lead to greater trust and engagement within organizations and allow for all types of information to emerge, which is important for effective decision making. Given the importance of ethics to HRM, the Society for Human Resource Management (SHRM), which is the world's largest professional society for human resource management, developed a code of ethics. We encourage you to read this code of ethics whether you are an aspiring manager or HRM professional or one who is seasoned. The core principles noted are easily transferable to different organizational roles, and following them can help you avoid serious problems as you are faced with ethical dilemmas and decisions throughout your career. The six core principles described in the code provisions include the idea that professionals should engage in their work with a focus on professional responsibility, professional development, ethical leadership, fairness and justice, conflicts of interest, and use of information.

Questions

1. Describe a hypothetical scenario in which you would benefit from applying certain principles from the SHRM Code of Ethics.

2. Choose a business situation from the news or the HR literature where principles from the SHRM Code of Ethics could have made a difference. Specifically, what did the decision makers do right, or what could they have done better?

| Professional Responsibility | As HR professionals, we are responsible for adding value to the organizations we serve and contributing to the ethical success of those organizations. We accept professional responsibility for our individual decisions and actions. We are also advocates for the profession by engaging in activities that enhance its credibility and value. |

| Professional Development | As professionals, we must strive to meet the highest standards of competence and commit to strengthen our competencies on a continuous basis. |

| Ethical Leadership | HR professionals are expected to exhibit individual leadership as role models for maintaining the highest standards of ethical conduct. |

| Fairness and Justice | As human resource professionals, we are ethically responsible for promoting and fostering fairness and justice for all employees and their organizations. |

| Conflicts of Interest | As HR professionals, we must maintain a high level of trust with our stakeholders. We must protect the interests of our stakeholders as well as our professional integrity and should not engage in activities that create actual, apparent, or potential conflicts of interest. |

| Use of Information | HR professionals consider and protect the rights of individuals, especially in the acquisition and dissemination of information while ensuring truthful communications and facilitating informed decision making. |

SPOTLIGHT ON HR FOR SMALL AND MEDIUM-SIZED BUSINESSES

By the Numbers

Of the 5.83 million employing firms in the United States, 99.7% consist of 500 or fewer employees. Further, organizations with fewer than 20 workers make up 89.4% of those firms. But those numbers are only for organizations with employees. There are over 24 million small businesses in the United States classified as self-employment, with no additional payroll or employees. Smaller businesses are also big money. In 2011 alone, revenue from nonemployer businesses (those with no employees) was $989.6 billion. The number of self-employed individuals soared by 19% from 2005 to 2015. This is, in part, due to the rise of the gig economy, as noted earlier in this chapter. Thus, it is accurate to say that when it comes to business in the United States, it is overwhelmingly smaller businesses that make up a majority of the firms.

It is easy to lose sight of this, given how prevalent information is on the HR practices of Fortune 500 organizations. They frequently make news, and we often read about them in the pages of *Forbes* or the *Wall Street Journal*. However, every major company was once a small business, so it makes sense to think about HR as a powerful tool for new companies. This is especially important to keep in mind knowing that over 50% of the working population works in a small business. Although we highlight examples of small, medium-, and large-sized businesses throughout this book, we also specifically spotlight HR for small and medium-sized businesses in each chapter to make sure no one forgets how critical they are to the economy.[29]

day-to-day basis than others. These include CEOs and the associated leadership team, HR managers, line managers, as well as HR specialists and generalists. In addition, other areas of the organization, such as information systems technology, play an important role in making sure the right people have the right information in place in order to make the most effective decisions possible. The marketing of products influences whether potential applicants know about and are attracted to the organization. The accounting and finance functions are critical to the fiscal health of an organization, and therefore, they also play an important role in keeping the organization's finances supporting human capital. They may be involved in compensation and benefits-related decisions as well.

Enrique Washington is an executive talent acquisition leader. In the past, he has recruited executives at sports organizations such as the Portland Trail Blazers, video game maker Electronic Arts, and Nike. A key part of his job is advising hiring leaders on establishing role requirements to identify, assess, select, and integrate new executive leaders in alignment with their business goals.

And every one of these departments also has managers who oversee them. Thus, it would be a missed opportunity to *only* focus on what happens within the Department of Human Resource Management within a firm.

Because this book is written with a special focus on best practices and functions of HRM, we focus primarily on the ways in which four important groups affect the culture and functioning of HRM within an organization. These include the top management leadership team, line managers, HRM practitioners, and finally, HR departments.

Top Management Teams and HRM

The top members of the organizational team, such as the CEO, top management team, and/or owner of the organization, set the tone for HR and how much or how little human capital is valued. They also set the tone for how much HRM is valued as a strategic function to enhance the organization's effectiveness. The organization's chief human resource officer (CHRO) is also critical in this regard. Organizations often use executive recruiting functions within their organizations or hire external search firms to help them find the right talent at this level.

HR Managers and HRM

An HR manager is someone who oversees the personnel department or HR functions within a group. The degree to which they are passive versus proactive in terms of asking questions, gathering data, and helping to address the major challenges and opportunities of the organization can influence how effective HRM and relatedly the organization ultimately becomes. One of the other major functions of these individuals is to partner with other managers across the organization. This is a critical coordination function. These individuals might hold a variety of job titles such as HR manager/director, which is the most frequently advertised job position in HR.

Line Managers and HRM

Managers also play a critical role in making people decisions. For example, a hiring manager's opinion can be the difference between a person being hired, promoted, or fired. Managers also play a critical day-to-day role in managing work flows, helping support new employee development, and developing talent for greater responsibilities over time. Managers help to set the tone of a work group or department. Research shows that the climate managers set can influence the level of innovation, safe behaviors, and ethical behaviors within the group.[30] Most position announcements for HR manager require 3 to 5 years of HR-related experience to be considered for the job.

HR Careers

HR practitioners work on HR-related activities and regularly engage in HR-related strategic and process-related people or personnel decisions within the organization. They might be called HR manager, HR partner, or HR specialist (see Figure 1.5). Each of these titles connotes different

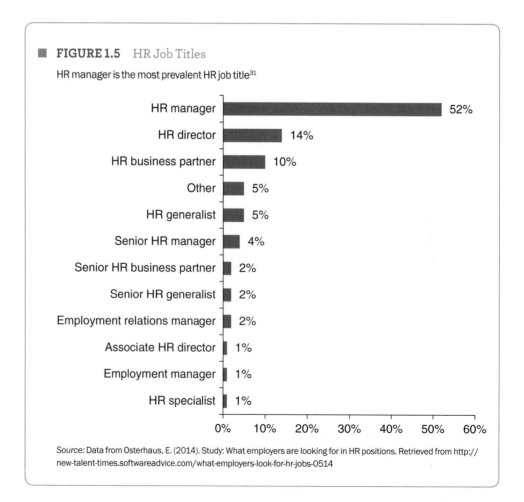

■ **FIGURE 1.5**   HR Job Titles

HR manager is the most prevalent HR job title[31]

Job Title	Percentage
HR manager	52%
HR director	14%
HR business partner	10%
Other	5%
HR generalist	5%
Senior HR manager	4%
Senior HR business partner	2%
Senior HR generalist	2%
Employment relations manager	2%
Associate HR director	1%
Employment manager	1%
HR specialist	1%

Source: Data from Osterhaus, E. (2014). Study: What employers are looking for in HR positions. Retrieved from http://new-talent-times.softwareadvice.com/what-employers-look-for-hr-jobs-0514

aspects of the HR practitioner's core job functions. And each might perform an ***HR specialist*** function where they attend to all aspects of one specific HRM function, such as recruitment, compensation, or training. Or they might be an ***HR generalist*** function where they span the multiple HR functions. As you might imagine, the needs for specialists versus generalists is related to the size and scope of the HR function, as well as the industry the organization is in. The larger the organization is, the more likely it is to employ specialists. Thus, you might see job titles such as recruiter, compensation analyst, or HR analysts.

HR Business Partners and HRM

HR business partner (HRBP) is the second most frequently advertised job position in HR. An ***HR business partner*** is a more recent term and refers to someone who serves as a consultant to management on HR-related issues. As the Society for Human Resource Management notes, the "HRBP is responsible for aligning business objectives with employees and management in designated business units. . . . The successful HRBP will act as an employee champion and agent of change." The key aspect of HRBP is that their role is to anticipate HR-related needs, as well as being available to share advice and proactively address small problems before they become big ones.

What Employers Look for in HR Applicants

The answer to this question depends on the level of the HR position in the organization, as well as the degree to which HR plays a strategic role within the organization. For example, an HR assistant position typically only requires a high school diploma. However, to move up in the organization, a college degree can make a big difference. An analysis of HR position announcements for jobs found that the top requested areas of college study included human resource management, business administration, psychology, and organizational development. Getting the first job and some HRM experience is only the first step. Those in HR need to stay up to date on the latest developments—especially as they relate to the ever-shifting legal environment.

There are organizations that exist in order to help HR practitioners stay informed of best practices and up to date on the latest trends that might affect HR. One such organization is the Society for Human Resource Management (SHRM). SHRM is the world's largest HR professional society, representing 285,000 members in more than 165 countries. Its headquarters are located in Alexandria, Virginia, and it has 575 affiliated local chapters throughout the United States, China, India, and the United Arab Emirates.[32] One of the key benefits of such professional organizations is that they have a wide view of what it takes to be effective in HRM. In fact, SHRM has spent a great deal of time and energy studying just that, as seen in the section on competencies.

Salary and Job Outlook

The Bureau of Labor Statistics (see Table 1.1) reports that the median pay for an HR manager in 2017 was $110,120 per year, which equals $52.94 per hour. Moving up to become an HR manager happens, on average, about 5 years after starting out. In addition, job growth is projected to be 9% in the next 10 years, which is above the average for all jobs that year.[33] Overall, HRM is considered to have solid career prospects and to be an attractive job. For example, a 2018 survey by Glassdoor .com found that human resource manager was the fifth-best job based on job projections, median base salary, and career opportunity ratings.[34] Shari Ballard, former chief HR officer and president of U.S. retail (and now senior executive VP) at Best Buy Co. Inc., was the highest-paid HR executive in 2015 at $6.6 million, based on Securities and Exchange Commission findings. In 2015, 7 of the 10 highest-paid HR executives at publicly traded companies were women. In 2016, she became president of Best Buy's Multi-Channel Retail and Operations.

HRM certifications. HRCI began offering certification in HR in 1976 and originally partnered with SHRM. However, starting in 2015, SHRM began offering its own certification based on its HR competency model. Thus, the two major certifications in HRM are administered by SHRM (SHRM-CP and SHRM-SCP) and the HR Certification Institute (HRCI) (SPHR and PHR). (We discuss what a competency model is later in this chapter and in greater depth in Chapter 5.)

HR specialist A person who fulfills an HR specialist function attends to all aspects of one specific HRM function

HR generalist A person who fulfills an HR generalist function attends to multiple HR functions

HR business partner Someone who serves as a consultant to management on HR-related issues

Tona Brewer, Director of Global Talent Management at Blount International, Inc, focuses on developing a range of approaches designed to improve individual and organizational performance. She leads teams and organizations focused on identifying metrics that matter.

TABLE 1.1   HRM Careers by the Numbers

HR Specialists

Human resources specialists recruit, screen, interview, and place workers. They often handle other human resources work, such as those related to employee relations, compensation and benefits, and training.

2017 Median Pay	$60,350 per year ($29.01 per hour)
Typical Entry-Level Education	Bachelor's degree
Work Experience in a Related Occupation	None
Number of Jobs, 2016	547,800
Job Outlook, 2016–2026	7% (average)
Employment Change, 2016–2026	38,900 new jobs

HR Managers

Human resources managers plan, direct, and coordinate the administrative functions of an organization. They oversee the recruiting, interviewing, and hiring of new staff; consult with top executives on strategic planning; and serve as a link between an organization's management and its employees.

2017 Median Pay	$110,120 per year ($52.94 per hour)
Typical Entry-Level Education	Bachelor's degree
Work Experience in a Related Occupation	5+ years
Number of Jobs, 2016	136,100
Job Outlook, 2016–2026	9% (faster than average)
Employment Change, 2016–2026	12,300 new jobs

Source: Bureau of Labor Statistics.[35]

One question that those interested in business and HRM practitioners alike ask is the value of HRM certifications. In an analysis of job postings for HRM, 42% noted a preference or requirement for certification. Further, some positions, such as HR business partner, were more likely than not to require certification, which indicates that certification may be beneficial in securing a job.[36] In addition, having a deeper knowledge of HRM should help the individual to master the HRM knowledge domain more fully and signals a deeper interest in HRM than noncertified individuals.[37]

HR Competencies

Competency A cluster of knowledge, skills, abilities, and other characteristics (KSAOs) necessary to be effective at one's job

You probably know what it means to be competent. A person who is competent is perceived to be able to perform specific functions reasonably well. A ***competency*** is a cluster of knowledge, skills, abilities, and other characteristics (KSAOs) necessary to be effective at one's job. Competencies are much like this but at a broader level, as they refer to a set of technical or behavioral KSAOs that, together, help to define what it takes to be successful within a specific job, organization, or profession.[38]

SHRM developed its competency model based on 111 focus groups consisting of 1,200 participants and completed surveys from over 32,000 HR professionals (see Figure 1.6). Its goal was to create a model that is applicable to all HR professionals regardless of characteristics such as job function or career level, organization size, industry, or location. What emerged was a set of core technical competencies called *HR expertise/knowledge*. In addition, it identified eight behavioral

■ **FIGURE 1.6**   SHRM Competency Model

SHRM developed the SHRM Competency Model. Technical competencies are encompassed within HR expertise/knowledge. Interpersonal competencies include relationship management, communication, and global and cultural effectiveness. Business competencies include business acumen, critical evaluation, and consultation. Leadership competencies include leadership and navigation and ethical practice.

competencies that form three additional clusters of competencies with *interpersonal competencies* including relationship management, communication, and global and cultural effectiveness; *business competencies* including business acumen, critical evaluation, and consultation; and *leadership competencies* including leadership and navigation and ethical practice.

Staying Up to Date: Evidence-Based Management

We have seen how important learning the functions of HRM is. It is also important to stay abreast of changes in the field as they evolve by taking workshops and education courses (and continuing education) separately or as part of being certified. Another important way that managers, HRM practitioners, consultants, and researchers stay up to date on the latest findings and changes in the field is by learning about research findings conducted by others. In this way, practitioners can learn best practices to give their organization a competitive advantage by saving time by learning from others' mistakes and considering their successes.

Information regarding HRM comes from three main places. First, organizations often engage in benchmarking. **Benchmarking** refers to a measurement of the quality of an organization's practices in comparison with peer organizations using similar metrics. The best benchmarking follows the standards of good decision making and includes identifying the goal and

Benchmarking The measurement of the quality of an organization's practices in comparison with those of a peer organization

parameters of the benchmarking, gathering data, analyzing data, and communicating the results. Benchmarking might occur within a specific industry sector or across functions such as HRM benchmarking. Benchmarking is often done at different levels as well, with Fortune 500 organizations often benchmarking against one another. For example, asking what the top 10 best companies in your industry do in terms of surveys with departing employees could be useful information if you are planning to make changes to your own exit process. One thing to keep in mind is that simply meeting benchmarks is not an advantage, but understanding them and moving beyond them can be.

Second, reports are written based on surveys and trends by HR organizations such as SHRM, The Conference Board, or the Association for Talent Development, and HR consulting firms such as PwC, SAP/SuccessFactors, and Aberdeen Group. These findings might be shared at industry conferences or in practitioner outlets such as *HR Focus, HR Magazine, Harvard Business Review, People Management, Workforce,* and *T+D* as well as via blogs or newsletters. These outlets may be reviewed but do not go under the same scrutiny as peer-reviewed research articles.

Third, researchers within universities and in industry in the fields of HRM and I-O psychology[39] generate new knowledge about best practices through their research streams. The findings are published in academic journals, which are *peer reviewed* by experts in that research area who evaluate the rigor of the studies and their contribution to the research and practice of HRM. Research findings are also presented at annual conferences such as the Academy of Management and Society for Industrial and Organizational Psychology.[40] Papers presented at these particular conferences are also peer reviewed but with less detailed peer review than for a journal, and attending sessions at conferences allows HRM practitioners and researchers to learn what some of the most current research is on a given topic. And of course, books on HRM topics are also important ways to stay up to date.

Given how important we feel evidence-based practice is, we include research findings throughout the book. When we can, we focus on key findings from meta-analyses in each chapter. Although we base much of this textbook on findings across many individual studies, a meta-analysis is unique in that it summarizes and synthesizes everything that researchers have found on a given topic up to that point using a statistical process. Another way to think about staying up to date is to follow the scientific process in gathering information within your own organization. We cover what this scientific process includes and how helpful it can be to HRM best practices in Chapter 2.

SPOTLIGHT ON LEGAL ISSUES

U.S. Equal Employment Opportunity Commission

The U.S. EEOC is the primary federal agency responsible for handling workplace discrimination claims. In 2017, the agency received over 84,000 individual filings. In the U.S., federal law prohibits discrimination in employment decisions based on protected characteristics. These laws are referred to as equal employment opportunity (EEO) laws. Most EEO laws pertaining to private, government, and state institutions are monitored and enforced by the EEOC, which is an independent federal agency. The EEOC ensures compliance with the law, in addition to providing outreach activities and preventing discrimination from occurring in the first place. EEO laws typically apply to organizations with 15 or more employees and cover business, private employers, government agencies, employment agencies, and labor unions and aim to prevent discrimination against employees, job applicants, and participants in training and apprenticeship programs. You will learn more about the laws that the EEOC covers in Chapter 4, but for now, the key point is to understand that this agency exists.[41]

CHAPTER SUMMARY

The case of Chobani yogurt illustrates how HRM influences a company's success from start-up through years of expansion, including successes and setbacks. At this point, you know a great deal about what HRM is, why it matters, and different types of organizational cultures. We also covered an overview of six key aspects of the changing context of HRM, including changing demographics, the emergence of a gig economy, globalization, technology, availability of data, and ethical challenges and corporate social responsibility. The overview of HRM as a profession included understanding who is involved in HRM, different aspects of HRM careers, and HRM competencies. Finally, Spotlights on global issues, HR analytics, ethics, HR for small and medium-sized businesses, and legal issues, as well as HR in Action, highlighted key points and examples.

KEY TERMS

human resource management (HRM) 5
biases 6
availability bias 6
anchoring bias 7
overconfidence bias 9
A-S-A framework 9
organizational culture 10

clan cultures 11
adhocracy cultures 12
market cultures 12
hierarchy cultures 12
gig economy 13
gig 13
business ethics 17
HR specialist 21

HR generalist 21
HR business partner 21
competency 22
benchmarking 23
sign 28
magnitude 28
spurious correlation 28
Hawthorne Effect 29

Visit **edge.sagepub.com/bauer** to help you accomplish your coursework goals in an easy-to-use learning environment.

- Master the learning objectives using key study tools
- Watch, listen, and connect with online multimedia resources

- Access mobile-friendly quizzes and flashcards to check your understanding

HR REASONING AND DECISION-MAKING EXERCISES

MINI-CASE ANALYSIS EXERCISE: INFORMATION SEEKING AS A NEW EMPLOYEE

You have started work at a small company, Johnson Natural Shoes, which designs and produces children's shoes. The company has an innovative approach and uses all-natural materials. Its product has been increasing in demand in the few short years since it began. The company was founded by Shannon McKenzie. You found out about the position because you are friends with Shannon's daughter, who is an old friend of yours from high school. You were hired after you met with the founder, who remembered you from soccer games and birthday parties.

You do not have a job description or formal job title. But you are the only person in the organization with a degree in business, and Shannon mentioned to you that you were hired in the hopes you could help the company manage its rapid growth. At this point, the company is on track to double in size this year compared with last year, when it only had 28 employees.

You notice from the first days on the job that employees enjoy collaborating and making decisions together, and you feel welcomed right away. You see great things in the company's future and want to help make Johnson Natural Shoes an international brand. You can't wait to start making a contribution.

Now it is your turn to decide how to help:

1. Given that you are still new to the company, how would you approach learning more about the company and its employees?

2. What are specific key questions you might want to ask employees about the company?

3. Based on your knowledge of business, what would you advise Shannon to consider as HR priorities as the organization experiences high growth?

HR DECISION ANALYSIS EXERCISE: UNLIMITED VACATION?

In this chapter, we presented a lot of information regarding HRM and approaches to business in general. Given how many different things you have considered, we would like you to take some time to focus on some key aspects of making effective HRM decisions. Read on about some different HRM decisions that have been made.

Your company is considering giving everyone in the organization unlimited vacation time regardless of how long they have been with the company or how much they currently make. This is following the popularity of this approach at several major organizations such as Netflix, General Electric, and the Virgin Group. Your boss has asked you to take the perspective of wanting to ensure that HRM decisions are effective, and using the figure below as a guide, determine what questions should be asked to address how wise this policy change might be from a variety of angles.

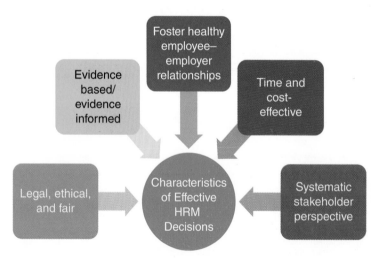

Please generate questions and provide the rationale for them around each of the following characteristics. In other words, what questions do you need to have answered to determine if this is an effective HRM decision?

Legal, ethical, and fair

_____
_____
_____
_____

Evidence based/evidence informed

_____
_____
_____
_____

Fosters healthy employee–employer relationships

_____
_____
_____
_____

Timely and cost effective

_____
_____
_____
_____

Takes a systematic stakeholder perspective

_____
_____
_____
_____
_____
_____

Considering your analysis, overall, is this an effective decision? Why or why not?

_____
_____
_____
_____
_____
_____

What, if anything, do you think should be taken into consideration to help make this decision most effective?

_____
_____
_____
_____

HR DECISION-MAKING EXERCISE: THE CHANGING CONTEXT OF HRM

Making HRM decisions is often a group activity, as seldom does one person have all the required information, context, and expertise to tackle every HR issue. Working in a group, review the six trends we identified as impacting HRM today and into the future (changing demographics, the emerging gig economy, increasing globalization, technology, availability of data, and ethical and corporate social responsibility challenges).

1. Form your group.

2. Decide if there are additional trends your group believes might be as important or more important than these six.

3. As a group, decide which trend your group collectively feels is the *most* important factor that will influence HRM. It is as important to justify your answer in terms of your selection of the most important factor as it is to defend why the others are not seen as equally important.

DATA AND ANALYTICS EXERCISE: CORRELATION DOES NOT EQUAL CAUSATION

Sign The positive or negative direction of a relationship between variables

Magnitude The size of a relationship

Correlation is an important statistical tool, and it is utilized in different ways in the context of HRM. A correlation coefficient is a number that conveys two important pieces of information: sign and magnitude. The ***sign*** (positive or negative) refers to the direction of a relationship, and the size of that relationship is its ***magnitude***.

A correlation coefficient can range from -1.00 to $+1.00$ (i.e., its greatest possible magnitude is 1.00, and its sign can be either positive or negative). A correlation coefficient of -1.00 indicates that two variables are "perfectly" correlated and share a negative (inverse) relationship such that as scores on one variable get larger, scores on the other variable get smaller. Conversely, a correlation of $+1.00$ indicates that two variables are perfectly correlated and share a positive relationship such that as scores on one variable get larger, scores on the other variable also get larger. Specifically, the absolute value of a correlation coefficient indicates how strong the relationship is, where an absolute value of 1.00 indicates a perfect relationship, and a value of 0.00 indicates no relationship. In HRM, we often describe the size of a correlation using qualitative descriptors. For instance, we might describe a correlation coefficient of 0.10 as *small*, 0.30 as *medium*, and 0.50 as *large*. Thus, a correlation coefficient provides a very efficient description of how much two variables are related in terms of the sign and magnitude of their relationship.

Spurious correlation A correlation observed between two variables that are not actually related

With all that said, we must still remember that *correlation does not mean causation*. That is, two variables may covary with one another without being directly related. When a correlation is found between two variables that are not directly related, we refer to this as a ***spurious correlation***, which may be the result of two variables that are not directly related but that share a common cause. For example, imagine that you find a large positive correlation (e.g., $r = .52$) between construction workers' self-reported annual consumption of ice cream and their level of self-reported job satisfaction. That is, as the amount of ice cream consumed by construction workers increases, their level of job satisfaction tends to increase as well. At first glance, we might look at this finding and conclude that ice cream consumption causes job satisfaction. Taking a closer look, we might think, "Well, this relationship doesn't make much sense given what we know about job satisfaction."

What, then, is a possible explanation for this potentially spurious correlation? The finding could be due to a third variable that causes both increases in ice cream consumption and increases in job satisfaction. Perhaps construction workers in this sample work in multiple locations around the United States. Accordingly, those who work in warmer climates consume more ice cream per year to cool off. In addition, those who work in warmer climates feel more satisfied with their job because they work outdoors in more pleasant temperatures. In this scenario, ice cream consumption does not cause job satisfaction, and job satisfaction does not cause ice cream consumption; rather, warmer climate is the common cause that leads to more ice cream consumption and higher job satisfaction, thereby resulting in the spurious correlation.

In sum, we should remain cautious when interpreting correlations and remind ourselves that *correlation does not equal causation*. To avoid making this mistake, we should evaluate each correlation coefficient through the lens of existing theory to make better decisions and draw more appropriate conclusions.

✔ EXCEL EXTENSION: NOW YOU TRY!

- On **edge.sagepub.com/bauer**, you will find an Excel tutorial that shows how to compute a correlation coefficient.

- Using Excel, answer the following questions:

  ○ What is the correlation between employee engagement and sales revenue?

  ○ Consider the sign and the magnitude of the correlation. How would you describe the nature of the relation between engagement and sales revenue to a manager who does not know what a correlation coefficient means?

  ○ What is the correlation between job satisfaction and customer satisfaction?

CHAPTER 1 SUPPLEMENT: THE EVOLUTION OF HRM

To understand modern HRM, we find it helpful to take a quick look back through history to understand how HRM developed and transformed over the years. The following section will review HRM from the early years through the modern changes and trends within HRM of today.

EARLY YEARS

With the Industrial Revolution in the 19th century, organizations became increasingly large and hierarchical. This increased number of employees required that organizations think more carefully about how to manage their employees. This included

new techniques for helping employees to get the work done, as well as the need for entire departments that would help support the management of a large number of workers. In the early part of the 20th century, as a precursor to modern HRM, the mechanical engineer Frederick W. Taylor developed a method he termed *scientific management*, which emphasized the study of actions in order to establish the most efficient possible way to do a task. These *time and motion studies* were a mechanical approach for improving productivity and efficiency. In one classic example, Taylor devised the "science of shoveling" and determined that 21 pounds was the optimal amount to be shoveled at one time, balancing how much weight a worker could lift and sustainability so that the worker was not too tired. In those days, every worker brought their own shovel to work, and not all shovels were able to handle a 21-pound load. So Taylor provided workers with the optimal shovel for each density of materials: coal, dirt, snow, and so on. With the right tools, workers became 3 or 4 times more productive, and they were rewarded with pay increases.[42]

Henry Ford adopted Taylor's scientific management approach. Although it made workers efficient, it also made the work less fulfilling, resulting in high turnover rates and training costs. Here, workers are constructing a Model T engine on an assembly line in a Ford Motor Company factory circa 1914.

Although methods like Taylor's did lead to greater output by employees, the changing nature of work made these methods less important. Furthermore, society began demanding—and employees began expecting—that workers be treated more humanely and less like interchangeable cogs in a wheel. A major shift occurred as workers organized and began to demand better treatment. For example, National Cash Register Company was originally established to manufacture and sell the first mechanical cash register, which had been invented in 1879. Following a bitter strike, in 1901, the company set up what is believed to be the first HR department (then called personnel department).[43]

HUMAN RELATIONS ERA

These events exemplify what was happening during the early years of HR's origin. As working conditions got worse and societal pressure became greater, businesses were forced to respond by setting up procedures to treat employees in more humane and predictable ways, such as set wages and hours.

Up until the 1920s, workers were thought of as interchangeable parts of the organizational machine, with little attention paid to how their own thoughts or desires might influence how much or how well the work was done. However, that all changed with the beginning of the Hawthorne studies conducted by Harvard Business School professor Elton Mayo at the Western Electric Hawthorne Works near Chicago, Illinois. His team began by examining differences in the physical aspects of the plant, such as the lighting, temperature, and humidity conditions, on the assembly of electronic components. But no consistent effects were found. They made the factory brighter, and the employees went faster. They dimmed the lights, and employees responded by assembling the components more quickly. In other words, employees continued to work harder, even under conditions (low lighting) where they should not. This was a frustrating outcome, but it led to a new concept called the ***Hawthorne Effect***, which refers to the alteration of one's behavior to fit what you think is wanted of you, due to the knowledge of being studied or observed. The idea that psychological and social factors mattered as much as the physical environment was big news at this point in the history of understanding productivity.

Hawthorne Effect The alteration of one's behavior to fit what you think is wanted of you, as a result of the knowledge of being studied or observed

WORLD WAR II AND POSTWAR ERA

During World War I, selection was a major emphasis as exams were developed to help select and place soldiers with the right skills into the right positions. This work continued throughout World War II and into today, where the military branches in the United States place a great deal of time and attention into the HRM practices of recruiting, selecting, training, and maintaining a huge workforce. From the 1930s to the 1950s, the United States also saw increases in union membership, which have dwindled over time. During this time, other important milestones in HRM included Cornell University establishing the School of Industrial and Labor Relations as the first university program to focus on HRM issues and SHRM originally forming in 1948.

TABLE 1.2   Human Resource Management Evolution and Timeline

1870–1920s	1927–1940	1941–1963	1964–PRESENT	1995–PRESENT	2005–PRESENT
Early Years and World War I Era	**Human Relations Era Begins**	**World War II and Postwar Era**	**Civil Rights Era**	**Strategic and Technology HR Era**	**Competencies and Analytics Era**
Personnel Administration	*Human Resource Management*	*Personnel Management*	*Human Resource Management*	*Strategic Human Resource Management*	*Human Resource Business Partners*
Factories set up procedures to attend to employee wages and welfare and labor concerns. **1901:** National Cash Register Company establishes the first HR department. **1905–1920:** Scientific Management **1910:** Ford and Tata Steel institute 8-hour day. **1913:** The oldest known HR organization, known as the Chartered Institute of Personnel and Development (CIPD) since 2000, formed in the UK. It was then called the Welfare Workers' Association. **1917:** Army Alpha and Army Beta Exams are developed to help select soldiers (Walter Scott & Walter Bingham).	**1927–1932:** Elton Mayo conducts Hawthorne Studies and stumbled upon the Hawthorne Effect.	**1935–1950:** Surge in union membership. **1945:** Cornell University established the School of Industrial and Labor Relations as the first institution of higher education in the U.S. to focus on HR issues. **Post-WWII** **1948:** SHRM originally formed as the American Society for Personnel Administration this year. It became SHRM in 1998.	**1963:** Equal Pay Act **1964:** U.S. Civil Rights Act **1976:** HR Certification Institute begins to offer certifications. **1978:** Uniform Guidelines on Employee Selection Procedures (see Chapter 6) **1990:** Americans with Disabilities Act **2009:** Lilly Ledbetter Fair Pay Act amends the Civil Rights Act.	**1997:** David Ulrich publishes *Human Resource Champions.* **2001:** Brian Becker, Mark Huselid, David Ulrich publish *The HR Scorecard.* Beginning of online and high-tech delivery of HR functions.	**2004:** Todd Carlisle, later VP of HR at Twitter, becomes the first member of People Analytics team at Google. **2015:** SHRM develops its competency model and offers its own certifications, breaking away from the HR Certification Institute. **2018:** Continued development of online HR functionality. Availability of cloud computing, big data, and analytics proliferate. Beginning of robotics and cognitive automation.

Sources: The historical background of human resource management. (n.d.). http://www.whatishumanresource.com/the-historical-background-of-human-resource-man agement; Truxillo, D., Bauer, T., & Erdogan, B. (2016). *Psychology and work: Perspectives in industrial and organizational psychology.* London and New York: Routledge Press.

CIVIL RIGHTS ERA

In 1964, the U.S. Civil Rights Act was a major change in the way HRM was done. The act outlawed discrimination on the basis of race, color, religion, sex, or national origin in regards to voter registration, racial segregation in schools, and toward applicants or employees at the workplace. Employment practices such as hiring decisions, promotion decisions, and decisions regarding who gets training and development opportunities suddenly came into the spotlight. We cover this act, as well as other key legal decisions, in much greater depth in Chapter 4. In the United States, acts of Congress can be altered over time. For example, the Equal Pay Act of 1963, which "prohibits sex-based wage discrimination between men and women in the same establishment who perform jobs that require substantially equal skill, effort, and responsibility under similar working conditions," and the Civil Rights Act of 1964 were modified by the Lilly Ledbetter Fair Pay Act of 2009. A key aspect of this act redefines the statute of limitation for pay discrimination to be reset every time a person receives a paycheck that does not represent fair pay.

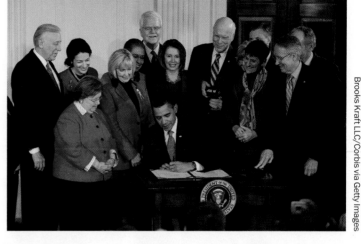

Brooks Kraft LLC/Corbis via Getty Images

President Barack Obama signing the Lilly Ledbetter Act into law on January 29, 2009, while Ledbetter, to his left, watches.

MODERN HRM

Both the Strategic and Technology HR and Competencies and Analytics Eras marked major shifts in the evolution of HRM. Rather than simply considering HRM to be about processing and controlling employees and being considered part of the cost of doing business for organizations, it became clear that employing strategy and technology to help employees and organizations be more effective and efficient was possible. Today, the idea that specific competencies can be identified for effectiveness and that data and analytics can help individuals within organizations be more effective is becoming more commonplace. For example, it was not until 2004 that Todd Carlisle became the first member of the People Analytics team at Google.

Strategic HRM, Data-Driven Decision Making, and HR Analytics

2

Opening Case

Strategic HRM in Context: The Case of Strategy and HR Analytics at Chevron

Chevron is a large energy company based in San Ramon, California. In 2014, the company launched a centralized human resource analytics team, which it refers to as a talent analytics team. **Human resource (HR) analytics** goes by different terms, such as people analytics, workforce analytics, human capital analytics, and talent analytics; it refers to the process of collecting, analyzing, and reporting people-related data for the purpose of improving decision making, achieving strategic objectives, and sustaining a competitive advantage.

From the beginning, Chevron's analytics team made it clear that its mission is to "support Chevron's business strategies with better, faster workforce decisions informed by data." To that end, R. J. Milnor, the former head of talent analytics for Chevron, stated that "[HR] analytics is really about informing and supporting business strategy, and we do that through people data." In other words, the analytics team at Chevron understands the important role that people data can play in strategy realization. After all, people are valuable resources for companies, and making data-driven and evidence-based decisions provides companies such as Chevron with an opportunity to attract, motivate, and retain talented people with the right knowledge, skills, and abilities.

Over time, Chevron's HR analytics team has moved from running simple descriptive analytics, which represent a snapshot of the past, to more advanced predictive and prescriptive analytics, which provide a glimpse into the future. As such, managing human resources at Chevron is now more forward thinking and proactive, which allows for more strategic thinking and informed action.

As an overarching strategic objective, Chevron's HR analytics team has been tasked with improving revenue per employee. The team also consults with other units and departments, including company leadership, when it comes to major decisions such as reorganization and restructuring. With respect to workforce planning, the team built models to forecast future talent demand and supply 10 years in the future. These models identified key drivers of talent demand and supply for different geographic locations and provided estimates of future attrition (e.g., turnover) with 85% accuracy. Knowing the key drivers—or predictors—of attrition is very important when it comes to making decisions about how

LEARNING OBJECTIVES

After reading and studying this chapter, you should be able to do the following:

2.1 Identify the steps for formulating and implementing a strategy.

2.2 Define strategic HRM.

2.3 Explain the importance of strategic HRM for realizing employee, operational, stakeholder, and financial outcomes and for sustaining a competitive advantage.

2.4 Demonstrate the use of data-driven decisions in realizing organizational strategy and contrasting different HR analytics competencies and levels of HR analytics.

2.5 Summarize the arguments for a scientific, ethical, and legally compliant approach to HR decision making.

2.6 Manage the components of a successful HR analytics function.

Human resource (HR) analytics The process of collecting, analyzing, interpreting, and reporting people-related data for the purpose of improving decision making, achieving strategic objectives, and sustaining a competitive advantage

to retain talented people who can help the organization achieve its strategic objectives.

In just a few short years, Chevron's HR analytics team has transformed the way the organization leverages data. By centralizing the HR analytics function, the team created an HR hub that collects data, performs data analytics, and reports findings to HR specialty areas spread across the company. Of note, centralizing the analytics function increased the productivity of analysts by approximately 30% and substantially reduced redundant HR reporting within at least one business unit.

Chevron also established a community of practice with hundreds of members, which include HR specialists, business partners, and analysts. The community of practice encourages members to discuss topics related to data analytics and data-driven decision making during virtual meetings. In doing so, HR and non-HR workers have an opportunity to learn from one another and to share different data-modeling approaches, techniques, and programs. Ultimately, this has led to an increase in the number of projects pursued by HR analysts and a decrease in the amount of time it takes to complete such projects.

In just a handful of years, the HR analytics team at Chevron has transformed the company's approach to human resource management. Merely introducing an HR analytics function, however, is by no means a panacea. In fact, failing to align HR analytics with HR and business strategy can hinder the likelihood of success. As such, an organization will be best served by using HR analytics to inform and support strategy, as Chevron has done. In other words, HR analytics should be embedded into the fabric of the organization.[1]

Case Discussion Questions

1. How has Chevron used HR analytics to inform and support organizational strategy?

2. Chevron's HR analytics team used statistical models to predict employee turnover with a high degree of accuracy. Based on your own knowledge and experiences, what are some key drivers (i.e., predictors) of employee turnover?

3. What are some different ways in which an organization might leverage HR analytics to attract, motivate, and retain talented people?

4. Chevron has established an HR-specific analytics team. From the perspective of organizational effectiveness, what are some potential advantages of having data analytics integrated directly into the HR function as opposed to a company-wide analytics team that supports HR and other functional areas?

 Click to learn more . . .

To learn more about HR analytics at Chevron, check out the following video: https://youtu.be/LbxGL2TXzao

imply put, people matter. Jim Goodnight, CEO of SAS Institute Inc., is quoted as saying, "Ninety-five percent of my assets drive out the gate every evening. It's my job to maintain a work environment that keeps those people coming back every morning."[2] This chapter focuses on the role HR plays in managing people to achieve organizational success. *Strategic human resource management* is the process of aligning HR policies and practices with the objectives of the organization, including employee, operational, stakeholder, and financial outcomes. This chapter explains how strategy is combined with HRM to achieve organizational success and how organizations can make data-driven decisions that are accurate, fair, ethical, and legal—considerations that are becoming increasingly important as our society pushes forward into an era of big data.

What Is a Strategy?

Central to strategic human resource management—and to strategic management in general—is the concept of a strategy. What is a strategy? Think of a *strategy* as a well-devised and thoughtful plan for achieving an objective.[3] A strategy is inherently future oriented and is intended to provide a road map toward completion of an objective. More specifically, a strategy reflects the manner in which a unit, department, or organization coordinates activities to achieve planned objectives in both the short and long term.[4] In the opening case on Chevron, we learned how the HR analytics team leverages data analytics to inform and support business strategies. As such, strategy can be paired with data analytics to make data-driven decisions, which improve the likelihood of achieving strategic objectives and sustaining a competitive advantage. As you will learn later in the chapter, the *scientific process* offers a rigorous and useful framework for guiding the way in which HR departments collect, analyze, and interpret data in service of HR and organizational strategies.

Some firms keep their strategies relatively private, but others, like Tesla Motors Inc., announce their strategy to the world. With a mission to "accelerate the world's transition to sustainable energy," Tesla's strategy is multiphased and is referred to as the *Tesla Motors Master Plan* by provocative and often controversial company cofounder and CEO Elon Musk.[5] Musk unveiled Tesla's strategy in 2006, describing the overall purpose of the company as expediting a shift from a hydrocarbon (fossil fuel) economy to a solar-electric (clean energy) economy. For the first phase, Musk outlined the company's plan of initially producing a high-end electric car called the Tesla Roadster, which reached the market in 2006 and was rated the second-best invention by *Time* magazine in 2008. (The retail DNA test developed by 23andMe took top honors that year.)[6]

Using revenue and interest generated from the Tesla Roadster, the original plan was to develop increasingly more affordable cars and, ultimately, affordable family cars. So far, Tesla has followed through on the first-phase strategy. In 2012, a higher-end, yet more accessible, model called the Model S rolled out of production plants, and in 2017, the even more affordable Model 3 went into production, albeit with some newsworthy delays.[7] Based on these achievements, Tesla not only formulated a viable strategy but, to date, has largely followed through on the implementation of most aspects of its strategic plan. In 2016, Musk set the second phase of Tesla's strategy into motion by announcing plans for Tesla to acquire SolarCity, a company that produces solar panels.[8] By combining Tesla and SolarCity, Musk intends to stay true to the overall purpose of his company: shifting the world to clean energy. That is, when Tesla electric cars are charged with solar electric energy, they become truly clean-energy vehicles, and in the process, Tesla leaves its mark as an industry disrupter with its innovative approaches to car design and energy.[9]

Strategy Formulation: Developing and Refining a Strategy

In adhering to its mission, Tesla illustrates two important aspects of strategy: formulation and implementation. *Strategy formulation* involves planning what to do to achieve organizational

In 2016, Tesla announced its most affordable car to date—the Model 3—and, within 2 months of the announcement, had already taken deposits on over 350,000 reservations.[10] Pictured here is Elon Musk, Tesla CEO.

Yuriko Nakao/Bloomberg via Getty Images

Strategic human resource management The process of aligning HR policies and practices with the objectives of the organization, including employee, operational, stakeholder, and financial outcomes

LO 2.1 Identify the steps for formulating and implementing a strategy.

Strategy A well-devised and thoughtful plan for achieving an objective

Scientific process A method used for systematic and rigorous problem solving that is predicated on the assumption that knowledge requires evidence

Strategy formulation The process of planning what to do to achieve organizational objectives

■ **FIGURE 2.1**   Steps for Strategy Formulation

Formulating an organization strategy requires decision making regarding the mission, vision, values, strategy type, as well as analyzing the internal and external environments, and defining objectives designed to satisfy stakeholders.

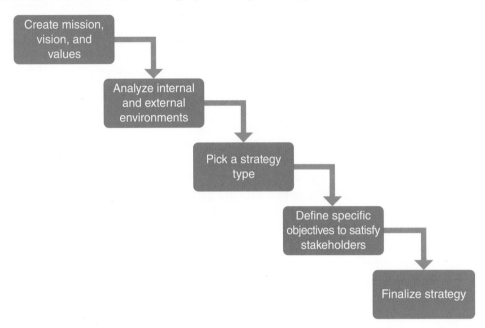

objectives—or in other words, the development and/or refinement of a strategy. To achieve its over-arching goal of shifting consumers toward clean-energy transportation and living solutions, Tesla formulated a rational and methodical strategy with multiple preplanned phases. In addition, Tesla demonstrated a top-down approach to strategy formulation in that the strategy originated with its CEO. With that said, strategy formulation can also occur in a bottom-up fashion, such that the strategy emerges from the pattern of many decisions that are made over time within an organization. And in many cases, strategy formulation occurs as the result of both top-down and bottom-up processes. Regardless of how a strategy originates, an organization's strategy is not set in stone; nor is an organization's approach to fulfilling the strategy. Rather, an organization should demonstrate strategic flexibility by remaining abreast of dynamic changes in the internal and external environment and by re-envisioning and reformulating a strategy as needed. Strategy formulation often follows the steps depicted in Figure 2.1, which ultimately set the stage for strategy implementation.

Create a Mission, Vision, and Set of Values

A ***mission*** describes a core need that an organization strives to fulfill and thus represents the organization's overarching purpose—or in other words, a *raison d'être*, or reason for existence. Recall that Tesla's espoused mission is to "accelerate the world's transition to sustainable energy," and as you have probably observed, many organizations feature their mission statements prominently on their webpages. Tesla is no exception. In addition to a mission, strategy formulation also involves stating a vision and values. An organization's ***vision*** is an extension of the mission and describes what the organization will look like or be at some point in the future. Creating a set of core ***values*** provides the organization with parameters and guidelines for decision making and bringing its vision to fruition.

Analyze Internal and External Environments

To achieve a competitive advantage, an organization must look both internally and externally to understand how to bring its mission, vision, and values to life. That is, an organization

Mission A core need that an organization strives to fulfill and thus represents the organization's overarching purpose

Vision An extension of an organization's mission that describes what the organization will look like or be at some point in the future

Values Parameters and guidelines for decision making that help an organization realize its vision

SPOTLIGHT ON ETHICS

Mission, Vision, and Values at The Body Shop

The Asahi Shimbun via Getty Images

The Body Shop is a global manufacturer and retailer of ethically made beauty and cosmetic products. When she founded The Body Shop in 1979, Anita Roddick believed that companies have the potential to do good and just things for the world, as evidenced by the company's *mission* statement: "To dedicate our business to the pursuit of social and environmental change." In other words, Roddick was an early supporter of *corporate social responsibility*. Roddick passed away in 2007 at 64 years of age, but her legacy lives on in the form of The Body Shop's following core *values*:

- Against animal testing
- Support community trade
- Activate self-esteem
- Defend human rights
- Protect our planet

When the company was acquired by L'Oréal in 2006, the CEO of L'Oréal, Lindsay Owen-Jones, expressed his admiration for The Body Shop's mission, vision, and core values. He described how his company's expertise and knowledge of international markets could bring The Body Shop and its ethically made products to new customers.[11]

Questions

1. How might The Body Shop's ethical values influence its HRM policies?

2. If you were a manager for a competitor of The Body Shop, how would you go about investigating the implications of corporate social responsibility for a company's success?

must analyze the internal *strengths* and *weaknesses* that are under its control and the external *threats* and *opportunities* that are beyond its direct control—a process commonly referred to as a **SWOT analysis**.[12] By analyzing the internal environment, an organization comes up with a plan for how to leverage its strengths and improve on its weaknesses. By analyzing the external environment, an organization identifies opportunities and threats with respect to the state of its industry and competitors, as well as other external factors like the labor market, unemployment rate, and the general state of the local, national, and/or global economies. Taken together, a SWOT analysis is a systematic and methodical decision-making tool used to formulate a *viable* strategy.

SWOT analysis An analysis of the internal strengths and weaknesses of an organization and the external opportunities and threats to that organization

Pick a Strategy Type

After analyzing internal and external environments, an organization is ready to select a strategy type. A **strategy type** provides a general approach for how an organization will bring its mission, vision, and values to life, while at the same time leveraging its strengths and improving its weaknesses. Examples include the following:[13]

Strategy type A general approach for how an organization will bring its mission, vision, and values to life

- **Differentiation:** The organization creates a product or service that is different from competitors' products or services and thus warrants a higher price or more attention from consumers.

- **Cost leadership:** The organization identifies ways to produce a product or provide a service at a lower cost compared with competitors. This can help the organization increase its margin or sell the product or service at a cheaper price than competitors.

- **Focus or niche:** The organization uses differentiation or cost leadership but identifies a narrow consumer base to appeal to a specific product or service type that might not be produced or sold by competitors.

Resource-based view
Proposes that a resource holds value to the extent that it is rare and inimitable, where example resources include physical, financial, organizational, and human resources

Define Specific Objectives to Satisfy Stakeholders

The process of operationalizing a mission and general strategy type into specific objectives hinges on the needs of key stakeholders and the organization's need for a

Resource-Based View of Apple Inc.

By adopting a **resource-based view** when conducting a SWOT analysis, an organization can identify the strengths and weaknesses of an organization in terms of its physical, financial, organizational, and human resources, and identify how the organization can use these resources to maximize opportunities and minimize threats in the external environment. Proponents of the resource-based view propose that a resource holds value to the extent that it is rare and inimitable. *Rare* refers to the extent to which a particular resource is scarce and relatively few (if any) competitors possess the resource, while *inimitable* refers to the extent to which it is difficult (if not impossible) for competitors to reproduce, attain, or deploy the same resource. The process of identifying rare and inimitable internal resources provides a way of anticipating whether the organization, upon applying the strategy, will be able to achieve its objectives and sustain a competitive advantage.

As a visionary leader, many believed that Steve Jobs (former CEO of Apple Inc.) was himself a rare and inimitable resource. For example, Walter Isaacson wrote in an authorized biography of Jobs that people were often amazed with Jobs's seemingly innate ability to envision what customers would want even before they knew they wanted it. In other words, Jobs embodied Apple's strategy and associated slogan "Think different."—even though Jobs personally despised some versions of the advertisement campaign, fearing that he might come off as an egomaniac. Leveraging Jobs as a rare and inimitable *human* resource, Apple developed the Macintosh, iMac, iPod, iTunes, and iPad under his leadership—all of which have become hallmarks of innovation. After Jobs passed away in 2011, many feared that Apple would fail to innovate moving forward. As an illustration of that fear and concern, shares in Apple dipped following the news of his death. Soon after, Tim Cook succeeded Jobs as CEO, and many have noted how Cook possesses a different management style and different capabilities. Nonetheless, under Cook's leadership, Apple's stock has more than doubled, and some attribute this success to various supply chain innovations orchestrated under Cook's leadership. Thus, while Jobs's leadership style was arguably a rare and inimitable resource for Apple that helped the company realize strategic objectives related to product innovation, Cook's leadership style—albeit different from Jobs's style—pushed Apple to achieve other critical strategic objectives. Together, the former and current CEOs of Apple illustrate just how important human resources are for the realization of strategy.[14]

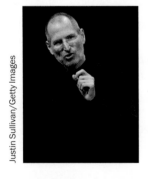 

Justin Sullivan/Getty Images

Justin Sullivan/Getty Images

Steve Jobs (left) and Tim Cook (right): former and current CEOs at Apple. Jobs and Cook showed two distinct approaches to leading and managing human resources.

sustainable competitive advantage. Ultimately, an organization formulates a strategy to meet the needs of stakeholders and—above all—to be competitive. As such, strategic objectives stemming from a mission, vision, and values and SWOT analysis should be designed to satisfy different stakeholders. **Stakeholders** include a number of different groups that an organization must appeal to, such as

- customers,
- investors and shareholders,
- employees, and
- communities.

Finalize Strategy

Once an organization defines its mission, vision, and values; analyzes the internal and external environments; chooses a general strategy type; and defines its strategic objectives, it is ready to finalize the strategy. That is, the organization must create a clear plan for the future before progressing to strategy implementation.

Strategy Implementation: Bringing a Strategy to Life

During **strategy implementation**, an organization follows through on its plan. It is during this stage that an organization builds and leverages the capabilities of its human resources (which are often referred to as **human capital** at the organizational level of analysis), as human resources will ultimately play an important role in supporting the enactment of an organization's strategy. The following section discusses how to align an organization's HR policies and practices with its strategy and how a well-designed system of HR policies and practices can improve human capital capabilities within an organization and, ultimately, performance.

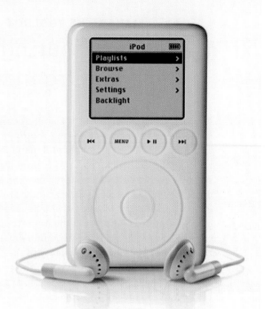

Apple Computer/Getty Images

Apple Inc. has consistently illustrated a differentiation strategy, and this approach is reflected in its "Think different" slogan. The iPod and iTunes revolutionized how people purchased, stored, and listened to music. At the time of their introduction, storing digital music files on a device (as opposed to inserting a CD into a disc drive) was a relatively novel concept, and Apple differentiated the iPod and iTunes from other products and services with clever advertising campaigns.

Stakeholders A number of different groups that an organization must appeal to, including customers and investors

Strategy implementation The enactment of a strategic plan

Human capital The knowledge, skills, and abilities that people embody across an organization

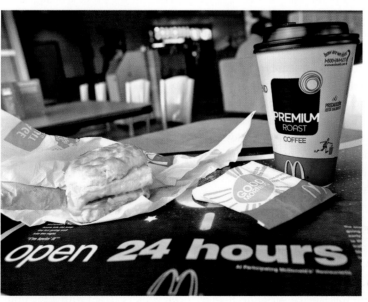

Jeff Zelevansky/Bloomberg via Getty Images

McDonald's long recognized the popularity of its breakfast menu. To boost sales by satisfying its customers, the company offered breakfast as part of its all-day menu, resulting in increased revenue.[15]

Contributing to Your Organization's Strategy

After the formulation stage, the strategy must be implemented, which requires the coordination and cooperation of employees and managers at all levels of the organization. As you might imagine, sometimes there are disconnects between an organization's espoused strategy and how it actually enacts the strategy. Managers who behave in their own self-interest—and not in the interest of the organization—can derail strategy implementation by delaying or reducing the quality of the implementation or even sabotaging the strategy! Here are some actions you can take as a manager to bring your organization's strategy to life.[16]

1. *Know what your organization's strategy is.* In a survey of employees from 20 major Australian corporations, only 29% of respondents were able to identify their company's strategy from a list of six choices. Take the following steps to understand your organization's strategy:

   - Review the organization's mission statement, vision, and values.
   - Ask your manager to explain how you can contribute to strategic objectives.
   - Pay attention to formal communications from the C-suite and upper management.
   - Stay on top of changes to your firm's strategy.

2. *Align your own goals with your organization's strategic objectives.* As a manager, it is important to align your self-interests with the interests of the organization, assuming the strategy aligns with your own personal ethics. Specifically, set goals that describe how you and your team can contribute to organizational objectives, such as decreasing turnover or increasing productivity.

3. *Communicate the strategy to your employees.* Explain the strategy to your employees, and engage them in activities that help them understand how they can contribute to the organization's strategic objectives. Remember, as a manager, you play an essential role in communicating company strategy to employees.

LO 2.2 Define Strategic HRM.

Strategic HRM: Linking Strategy With HRM

The beginning of this chapter defines *strategic HRM* as the process of aligning HR policies and practices with the strategic objectives of the organization, including achieving employee, operational, stakeholder, and financial outcomes to achieve and sustain a competitive advantage. Further, a central tenet of strategic HRM is that HR practices and employees are company assets that add value and not merely costs.[17] If implemented in a systematic and data-driven manner, strategic HRM can help an organization realize its strategy and objectives through the deployment of its human resource capabilities. As described in the opening case about Chevron, HR analytics represents an important tool for bringing an organization's strategy to life, as it can reveal how best to deploy HR systems, policies, and practices. When couched in the scientific-process framework, HR analytics offers a rigorous approach to attracting, motivating, and retaining talented people that are crucial for realizing strategic objectives and achieving a competitive advantage.

LO 2.3 Explain the importance of strategic HRM for realizing employee, operational, stakeholder, and financial outcomes and for sustaining a competitive advantage.

From Then to Now: The Origins of Strategic HRM

With a growing number of organizations focused on *strategic* HRM and using data to make better HR decisions, the activities associated with HRM have changed over the years. Historically, the function was labeled *personnel management*, which carried with it the implication that employees were an organizational expense.[18] Today, we use the term *human resource management*, as the function has evolved from a predominant focus on transactional and administrative

HR IN ACTION

Importance of HRM for Procter & Gamble Merger

Shutterstock.com

In 2005, Procter & Gamble (P&G) agreed to purchase the Gillette Company for approximately $57 billion in stock, thereby strengthening P&G's reputation as a consumer products giant. The move provided P&G with more pricing leverage with large retailers like Walmart.

To ensure the merger's success, P&G took several steps to assuage fears and to integrate Gillette employees. For instance, P&G gradually introduced Gillette employees to the P&G performance management and reward systems so that they had time to learn P&G's business strategy and objectives. In addition, although P&G had a reputation for promoting from within, management decided to replace many lower performing P&G employees with higher performing Gillette employees. This, in turn, signaled to employees that P&G valued the human capital coming from Gillette. Finally, as evidence of P&G's merger success, P&G met financial targets in the year following the merger.[19]

activities (e.g., recordkeeping) and employee relations activities to a more pronounced focus on transformational activities intended to help the organization leverage its human capital to achieve strategic organizational objectives (see Figure 2.2). This change has expanded our view of managing people from that of a cost to that of an asset and corresponds with advances in information systems and HR analytics.[20]

With the introduction of the term *strategic HRM*, the responsibilities of the HR function expanded even further. As shown in Figure 2.3, Ulrich's model of HRM indicates that strategic HRM plays the role of administrative expert, employee advocate, change agent, and

■ **FIGURE 2.2**   Evolution of HRM Activities

The amount of time spent on transactional activities has decreased over the past century as more HR functions become automated. This leaves more time for activities designed to transform the organization by strategically deploying human resources.

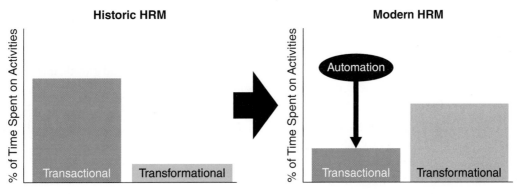

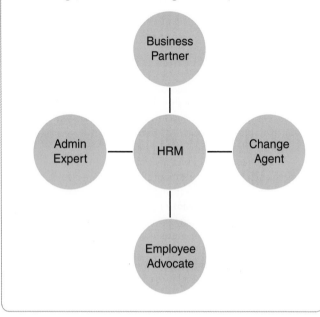

■ **FIGURE 2.3**   Ulrich's Model of Strategic HRM

Ulrich's model indicates that HRM should provide administrative expertise, serve as an employee advocate, be an agent of change, and serve as a strategic business partner.

business partner. Specifically, HRM has retained foundational activities related to administrative and employee relations activities while introducing additional activities related to orchestrating change and serving as a business partner. Strategic HRM has expanded the influence of the HR function, such that the deployment of HR practices and human resource capabilities can be used to realize strategic change initiatives, such as mergers, acquisitions, reorganizations, and restructurings, as well as gain a "seat at the table" during key business decisions and strategy formulation and implementation.

With the additional responsibilities of being a change agent and strategic business partner, the modern HR function now faces greater pressure to make sound and impactful decisions. As a result, data-driven decisions have become an integral part of effective strategic HRM. To achieve strategic objectives and a competitive advantage, a growing number of organizations collect, analyze, and interpret data via HR information systems and HR analytics. More specifically, technological advances have made it easier to capture and store HR data in HR information systems, and using HR analytics, these data can be used to improve HR systems, policies, and practices and, as a result, the performance and viability of the organization. With the scientific process as a road map, HR analysts test hypotheses to determine the best ways to manage people within the organization—or in other words, to arrive at ***data-driven decisions*** that bring the organization one step closer to meeting strategic objectives. In support of this stance, a panel of experts convened by the Society for Human Resource Management in 2012 predicted that HRM will continue moving toward a decision-based science from that of a procedures-based practice.[21]

Data-driven decisions
Decisions that are made based on the analysis and interpretation of relevant, accurate, and timely data

Conceptualizing Organizational Performance: The Balanced Scorecard

Historically, organizational performance was defined in terms of financial indicators, such as return on assets, return on equity, and market return. While achieving financial outcomes is indeed a worthwhile and necessary objective, other indicators of firm performance must also be considered. The introduction of the ***balanced scorecard*** was a game-changer in that regard, as it made the case for considering nonfinancial indicators when defining organizational success.[22] The balanced scorecard is used to evaluate organizational performance based on the extent to which the organization satisfies different stakeholder needs, such as the needs of customers, investors and shareholders, employees, and the broader community. Accordingly, consistent with the balanced scorecard approach, we conceptualize ***organizational performance*** as the extent to which employee learning and growth, internal business process efficiency, customer attitudes and behavior, and financial performance contribute to the organization's mission and strategy. Additionally, the balanced scorecard approach illustrates the value of an organization differentiating its human resources relative to competitors to gain a competitive advantage.

Balanced scorecard The evaluation of organizational performance based on the extent to which the organization satisfies different stakeholder needs, such as the needs of customers, investors, shareholders, employees, and the broader community

Organizational performance The extent to which employee learning and growth, internal business process efficiency, customer attitudes and behavior, and financial performance contribute to the organization's mission and strategy

Identifying Best Practices

Strategic HRM has roots in multiple disciplines, as it reflects the intersection of HRM and strategic management, and incorporates principles from other areas, such as industrial relations, economics, and organizational theory.[23] Together, these disciplines provide a basis for understanding how human resources can be strategically deployed in the service of organizational objectives and strategy. Understandably, they also offer different perspectives regarding how HR practices influence organizational outcomes. For instance, those working in the industrial relations and economics disciplines tend to identify HR practices that are thought to universally predict organizational outcomes regardless of context (e.g., industry, organization type, strategy type), whereas those in strategic management often focus on the context and conditions under which a *specific* bundle of HR practices predicts a given outcome or, rather, the degree to which the relation is contingent on a specific context.[24] Regarding the former, some HR practices can be thought of as *universal best practices* in that their implementation across different contexts will likely lead to favorable organizational outcomes. In HRM, evidenced-based universal best practices include enhancing perceptions of job security among employees, promoting from within the organization, providing financial incentives linked to performance, offering training, and providing flexible work arrangements.[25]

■ **FIGURE 2.4** Pfeffer's Seven Practices of Successful Organizations

Pfeffer's practices are examples of high-performance work practices that are instrumental for developing human capital capabilities across different contexts.[26]

1. *Create employment security* policies to encourage employee involvement and commitment.
2. *Selectively hire new employees* to create a highly qualified workforce that are a good fit.
3. *Organize employees into self-managed teams* to achieve higher-performing teams.
4. *Compensate employees based on performance* to attract, motivate, and retain talented employees.
5. *Train employees* to enhance the knowledge and skills necessary for high performance.
6. *Reduce status differences between employees* to leverage ideas, skills, and effort at all levels.
7. *Share information on strategy and performance* to motivate employees to contribute to the organization.

And such practices are often referred to as ***high-performance work practices***.[27] Recent meta-analytic evidence indicates that certain well-designed individual HR practices generally have positive effects on organizational outcomes.[28] For examples of evidence-based high-performance work practices, refer to Figure 2.4.

High-performance work practices Bundles of HR universal best practices, such as promoting within the organization and offering training

Considering the System and Context

In addition to identifying universal best practices, such as high-performance work practices, it is important to consider how these practices and others fit into the broader HR system. In other words, the effectiveness of some HR practices may be contingent on the context (e.g., industry,

Systems perspective The view
of how all pieces of a system and
its subsystems fit together

culture) and the configuration of other HR practices that are part of a larger system.[29] Thus, in addition to identifying universal best practices, it is advisable to adopt a contextual and configural approach to strategic HRM, which is consistent with a systems perspective on HRM. Taking a **systems perspective** means considering how all of the pieces of the HR puzzle fit together and how any misalignment can be addressed to optimize the overall system of HR practices. When a system of HR practices is well designed and well integrated, certain synergies can emerge, such that the potential of the whole system may be greater than the sum of the system's parts.

Synergy between bundled HR practices, however, is not guaranteed. Without consideration of the organization's strategy and without taking a systems perspective, it is unlikely that a system of HR practices will reach its full potential. For instance, imagine a company in which teamwork is integral for achieving a strategic objective. Accordingly, this company devised a selection tool to identify job applicants who are likely to be team players and an onboarding program to train new employees to work effectively in teams. Now imagine that the same company introduces a new compensation program that rewards only individual performance and not the performance of teams. Rather than interacting synergistically with the selection and training subsystems to improve team effectiveness, the reward subsystem may thwart team effectiveness by focusing individuals' efforts toward their own individual achievement, as opposed to the achievement of their team. In this hypothetical case, the whole might even be *less* than the sum of the parts when it comes to achieving the team-oriented strategic objective. Thus, to achieve desired organizational outcomes, it is important to develop HR practices with a strategic mindset and to focus on the entire system of HR practices as a whole and their potential configurations, as well as their interaction with the organization's culture and technology capabilities.

In recent decades, accumulated research findings have shown that a well-configured system of high-performance work practices that aligns with contextual factors does, in fact, improve organizational outcomes. Based on data from 968 organizations of various sizes and from a variety of industries, one study found that investing in an HR system can lead to valued organizational outcomes, such as lower turnover, higher productivity, and higher financial performance.[30] Offering additional support, a meta-analytic investigation of 92 studies showed that systems of high-performance work practices outperform well-designed individual HR practices with respect to organizational performance, which suggests that integrating different HR practices matters. Further, the meta-analytic investigation showed that the relationship between HR practices and organizational performance was stronger among manufacturing firms compared with service firms, which lends support to the argument that the context matters from an industry standpoint too. Table 2.1 provides examples of other factors that have been found to influence the effectiveness of HR practices.

SPOTLIGHT ON GLOBAL ISSUES

Strategic International HRM

Today, many organizations, such as Walmart, Marriott, and Microsoft, span international boundaries. Consequently, these multinational companies operate across national and cultural contexts and conditions, with different laws, customs, and values. Strategic international HRM requires a nuanced and intentional approach to deploying human resources to achieve strategic objectives. To be successful in the international arena, scholars have argued

that organizations must show flexibility in their HR practices to adapt to and fit with the different national environments. The flexible application of HR practices, however, is not without its challenges, as multinational corporations struggle with whether to integrate HR practices in a consistent manner via a global strategy or to tailor HR practices to fit the needs of each national context via an adaptive strategy.[31]

TABLE 2.1 Factors Influencing the Effectiveness of HR Practices[32]

FACTORS	DESCRIPTION
Internal Environment	
Business Strategy	Although research findings have been mixed, some evidence indicates differentiation strategies enhance the effectiveness of HR systems in relation to certain organizational outcomes, such as reducing turnover.
Culture	Most evidence to date indicates that a positive and supportive organizational culture enhances the effectiveness of HR systems in relation to organizational outcomes.
Manager Characteristics	Research has shown that having more senior managers and managers with stronger HR backgrounds enhances the effectiveness of HR systems.
External Environment	
Industry Characteristics	The type of industry an organization operates within can influence the effectiveness of HR systems. For example, the positive effects of HR systems on organizational outcomes tends to be stronger in manufacturing industries (as opposed to service industries).

Strategic HRM, Data-Driven Decision Making, and HR Analytics

LO 2.4 Demonstrate the use of data-driven decisions in realizing organizational strategy, contrasting different HR analytics competencies and levels of HR analytics.

We live in a world with ever-increasing amounts of data and big decisions to make. Data are collected and analyzed for a variety of purposes but often with the goal of making better decisions—that is, decisions informed by evidence. For example, medicine has advanced at a rapid pace due to ongoing research using randomized clinical trials and other rigorous research designs, which are predicated upon the notion that knowledge is based on data. Further, technological advances in the form of wearable devices have made it easier for us to collect data about our own behavior, enabling us to optimize our health and recognize the extent to which we are attaining our health goals. As a society, we have grown more comfortable with the idea of using data to inform decision making. This comfort has made its way into HR departments, and in recent years, the boundaries of strategic HRM have expanded to place a greater emphasis on data-driven decision making, thereby paving the way for HR analytics. At this point, you may be thinking, "Do I have to become an expert in data analysis?" The answer is no, but we do recommend that you gain some basic familiarity with mathematical and statistical concepts and data analysis tools. To that end, the remainder of the chapter discusses the different sources of HR data, as well as how to collect, analyze, and interpret data to inform and support the pursuit of strategic objectives and, above all, how to use the scientific process as a decision-making framework.

Today, data-driven decision making is an important component of strategic HRM, and increasingly, companies like Google and Microsoft have been leading the charge regarding integrating advanced and strategically aligned data analytics into their HR function. Earlier in the chapter, we described Tesla's mission and strategy; Tesla has also embraced data to make better people decisions and to inform and support strategy. With respect to electric cars, Tesla places a big emphasis on technological innovation, such as improved vehicle performance and increased battery capacity; however, at the same time, the company strives to make models that are affordable and competitive in price with nonelectric cars. As such, Tesla requires a workforce replete with talented people

How Does a System of HR Practices Influence Organizational Outcomes?

Performance = Ability x Motivation x Opportunity

The **ability-motivation-opportunity model** proposes that a system of HR practices influences employee outcomes and, ultimately, operational and financial outcomes to the extent that the practices target three different elements: ability to perform, motivation to perform, and opportunity to perform. The first element—*ability* to perform—encapsulates employees' knowledge, skills, and abilities. In a sense, ability to perform can be thought as what an employee *can do* on the job. The second element—*motivation* to perform—refers to the work-related effort that employees exert toward goal completion and captures what employees *will do* on the job. That is, just because employees have the ability to do the work does not necessarily mean they have the motivation to do the work, and vice versa. The third element—*opportunities* to perform—entails whether employees have the chance to perform on the job. Taken together, we can conceptualize employee performance as a function of their ability, motivation, and opportunity to perform. Thus, according to this model, if ability, motivation, or opportunity falls to zero, performance will be zero. We recommend using this conceptual formula to help you wrap your mind around how employees achieve high levels of performance in the workplace, as well as how different HR practices can be designed to target each of these three elements.[33]

Ability-motivation-opportunity model A model that proposes a system of HR practices that influences employee outcomes and, ultimately, operational and functional outcomes to the extent that the practices target three different elements: ability to perform, motivation to perform, and opportunity to perform

D. J. Patil, who has worked for eBay and LinkedIn, helped coin the term *data scientist*. He became the first chief data scientist in the U.S. Office of Science and Technology Policy.

who are motivated to leverage their human resource capabilities to attain those lofty objectives, and like other large companies, Tesla's HR department uses data to inform HR decision making and manage talent. For example, Tesla HR analysts mined the company's employee referral program data and found that higher-performing employees referred higher-potential job candidates, midrange employees referred lower-performing job candidates, and lower-performing employees referred all levels of job candidates. Using these data-analytic findings, the team devised ways to improve its recruitment and selection practices to attract and attain high-potential people.[34] Thus, basing decisions on evidence helps HR departments to attract, motivate, and retain talented people, which can ultimately drive organizational outcomes, such as productivity and innovation, and reduce costs associated with turnover and counter productive behaviors.

Despite the growing popularity of data analytics as decision-support tools, many organizational leaders report that they still use their gut, or intuition, to make major decisions, instead of relying on empirical evidence to inform such decisions.[35] Therefore, using data to inform people decisions requires making a business case to organizational leaders by linking data to strategic organizational objectives. One way to garner support for HR analytics and data-driven decision making in general is to convince organizational leaders and HR professionals of the value of the scientific process. That is, organizational leaders and HR professionals must think like scientists when it comes to collecting, analyzing, and interpreting people data, but at the same time, they need business acumen to make a strong case for using science-based HR practices to improve the organization.[36] Finally, when leveraging HR analytics in this way, an overarching goal should be to provide managers with actionable evidence-based practices that improve the management of people.

SPOTLIGHT ON DATA AND ANALYTICS

Aligning Analytics With Strategy

Business analytics, in general, has received a great deal of media attention, as evidenced by *New York Times* and *Wall Street Journal* headlines such as "Data-crunching is coming to help your boss manage your time"; "Big data, trying to build better workers"; and "The algorithm that tells the boss who might quit." Despite the media and organizational attention paid to analytics and big data, some argue that analytics is overhyped, misunderstood, or misused. In a recent article by Ransbotham, Kiron, and Prentice (in collaboration with SAS Institute Inc.) for the *MIT Sloan Management Review*, the authors concluded that the *idea* of analytics is now mainstream, but analytics is still not widely practiced. Further, based on the results of a survey of over 2,000 managers, the authors found that organizations with innovative analytics programs were much more likely to have an official strategy for analytics. Although awareness of analytics has increased substantially in recent years, translating analytics into practice has remained an elusive goal in many organizations. As you will learn later in the chapter, most companies rely on a basic level of analytics called descriptive analytics. Essentially, this means that these companies have the capability to report what *has* happened in the past based on data but not to predict what *will* happen in the future. Although it is important to build analytics capabilities, particularly in the area of HR analytics, companies also need to develop strategies for using analytics. That is, using analytics to achieve a competitive advantage depends on the development of a clear plan for integrating analytics into organizational decision making and for aligning analytics strategy with organizational strategy. In fact, some have even argued that a lack of alignment between HR analytics and strategy could have damaging effects on the organization and its employees.[37]

Defining HR Analytics

Given its large focus on data and scientific decision making, HR analytics has been referred to jokingly as "HR's nerdy best friend."[38] And many would argue that HR analytics has the potential to be HR's nerdy *and valuable* best friend. As described previously, collecting, analyzing, and interpreting people data can lead to valuable insights, and the emergence of HR as a strategic business partner has paved the way for HR analytics. In general, HR analytics can provide evidence supporting the links among HR systems, policies, and practices and employee, operational, stakeholder, and financial outcomes. Advanced HR analytics can even provide prescriptive recommendations for the future.

The growth in HR analytics interest signals that more and more organizations are beginning to understand the importance of making data-driven decisions to achieve a competitive advantage. To that end, after reviewing survey responses and panel discussions, the Society for Human Resource Management (SHRM) Foundation concluded in a report that leveraging HR analytics to achieve a competitive advantage is an important area of growth for HRM.[39] The report concluded that talent shortages are on the rise and that HR must provide HR analytics to aid in strategic business decision making.

What exactly is HR analytics? We define HR analytics as the process of collecting, analyzing, interpreting, and reporting people-related data for the purpose of improving decision making, achieving strategic objectives, and sustaining a competitive advantage. In other words, HR analytics is the systematic process of applying quantitative or qualitative methods to derive insights that shape and inform people-related business decisions and strategy. Thus, HR analytics, which is also referred to as people analytics, human capital analytics, talent analytics, and workforce analytics, is intended to provide data-driven decisions that improve decision making at all levels of an organization, including among frontline managers. HR analytics can be used to understand the company-wide impact of a well-designed system of integrated HR practices on employee, operational, stakeholder, and financial outcomes.

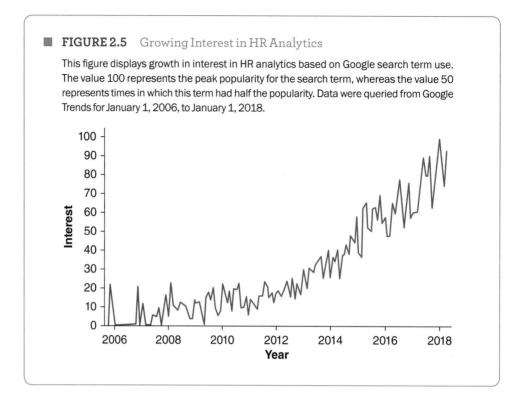

■ **FIGURE 2.5**   Growing Interest in HR Analytics

This figure displays growth in interest in HR analytics based on Google search term use. The value 100 represents the peak popularity for the search term, whereas the value 50 represents times in which this term had half the popularity. Data were queried from Google Trends for January 1, 2006, to January 1, 2018.

A number of organizations, including Chevron, T-Mobile, and Facebook, have expanded their internal HRM function by adding an HR analytics team. Further, companies like ADP Inc. and SAP SuccessFactors now provide products and services for analyzing people data in addition to those related to data collection and storage. These changes reflect the findings of a 2015 Deloitte survey, which showed that, on average, executives rated HR analytics as important for their business but, at the same time, reported feeling only somewhat ready to respond to the need.[40] Further, only 4% of executives reported that their company was excellent at leveraging people data to predict performance and improvement. Thus, many organizations and HR departments are in need of individuals who possess knowledge and skills related to HR analytics. Figure 2.5 shows the growing interest in HR analytics.

Identifying HR Analytics Competencies

Integrating HR analytics into the HRM function requires certain competencies that do not necessarily need to be held by a single individual. Ideally, HR analytics should be a team endeavor. Working as a team with diverse backgrounds and perspectives can facilitate sound judgments and good decision making, particularly when it comes to ethically or legally gray areas. While some HR analysts may have degrees in business or HRM, others may have backgrounds in industrial and organizational psychology, law, statistics, mathematics, data science, computer science, or information systems. Aside from educational differences among HR analysts, what matters most is that an HR analytics *team*, as a whole, is competent in the following seven areas: theory, business, data management, measurement, data analysis, employment law, and ethics (see Table 2.2).

Even if you have no desire to become an HR analyst but still wish to work in HR, developing data analysis skills, in particular, is wise. A common complaint from data analysts is that managers do not understand or recognize the value of data analysis and data-driven findings, leading to frustration. Conversely, a common complaint among managers is that data analysts fail to provide *understandable* answers to the questions that managers *actually* need answered, also leading to frustration. Thus, it is not uncommon for a rift to emerge between data analysts and managers.

TABLE 2.2   The Seven Competencies of Effective HR Analytics Teams

COMPETENCY	DESCRIPTION
Theory	Knowledge of psychological and social scientific theory is critical because findings from people data should be interpreted through the lens of human behavior, cognition, and emotion.
Business	Business knowledge and skills ensure that the activities of an HR analytics team are in the service of HR and organizational strategies and thus help the organization gain a competitive advantage.
Data Management	Data management knowledge and skills ensure that data are acquired, cleaned, manipulated, and stored in a way that facilitates subsequent analysis while maintaining data privacy and security.
Measurement	Measurement knowledge and skills provide a basis for developing sound HR metrics and measures that demonstrate sufficient reliability and validity.
Data Analysis	Knowledge and skills related to mathematics, statistics, and data analysis are critical, especially when it comes to identifying an appropriate analysis technique to address a given hypothesis or question.
Employment Law	Knowledge of employment law and HR legal issues separate an HR analytics team from a general business analytics team; teams lacking such knowledge might inadvertently violate laws when collecting data, analyze data that should not be analyzed, or use data in ways that may result in adverse consequences for protected groups.
Ethics	Knowledge of ethics helps the team navigate legally gray areas while also answering the question: "Just because we can, should we?"

In recognition of this communication issue, Tom Davenport, who is an independent senior advisor to Deloitte Analytics, wrote a blog post praising what he refers to as *light quants*.[41] Whereas a *heavy quant* would include the likes of a statistician, mathematician, or data scientist, a light quant is someone who knows enough about mathematics, statistics, and data analysis to communicate with a heavy quant and who knows enough about the business to communicate with a manager. Davenport contends that many organizations with an analytics function would benefit from hiring or training individuals who qualify as light quants, as such individuals can help managers pose better questions for heavy quants to answer and, in turn, translate the findings of heavy quants into words and ideas that are understood by managers. As such, Davenport refers to these individuals as *analytical translators*. We agree with Davenport and argue that all HR students and professionals should develop their competence in mathematics, statistics, and data analysis, at least to the point where they are able to bridge the communication divide between so-called heavy quants and managers.

Understanding the Levels of HR Analytics

There are three levels of HR analytics: descriptive, predictive, and prescriptive. **Descriptive analytics** focuses on understanding what has happened, which implies a focus on the past. Typically, descriptive analytics include summary statistics, such as sums, means, and percentages. Commonly reported HR metrics, such as absence rate, turnover rate, cost per hire, and training return-on-investment, are types of descriptive analytics. HR dashboards provide managers with summaries of key HR metrics and other descriptive analytics to help them understand their workforce. The Supplement discusses common descriptive HR metrics and how to calculate them. Descriptive analytics do not have to be complicated, and most involve simple arithmetic.

A more advanced form of analytics is **predictive analytics**, which focuses on what is likely to happen in the future based on available data and therefore is more forward looking. Examples of predictive analytics include statistical and computational models. What is a *model*? Broadly speaking, a model is an approximation of reality or the way that we think things work. By extension, statistical

Descriptive analytics Focuses on understanding what has already happened, which implies a focus on the past

Predictive analytics Focuses on what is likely to happen in the future based on available data

©iStock.com/Yok46233042

HR dashboards are often interactive, such that managers can manipulate the data display and drill down into different teams and units, as well as conduct "what if" analyses.

Prescriptive analytics Focuses on what actions should be taken based on what is likely to happen in the future

LO 2.5   Summarize the arguments for a scientific, ethical, and legally compliant approach to HR decision making.

models are mathematical approximations of reality based on data sampled from an underlying population. A common type of statistical model is a regression model. Using regression, we can evaluate the extent to which scores on one or more predictor variables are associated with scores on a particular outcome variable. For instance, in the context of selection, we might test whether applicants' level of extraversion predicts their future level of sales performance. Note that we do not expect 100% accuracy in our predictive models, as human behavior is influenced by many factors that may not be captured in the regression model. However, we strive to forecast future events and outcomes with as much accuracy as we can. As described by a SHRM Foundation report, very few companies have reached the level of predictive analytics, as the vast majority relies on descriptive analytics and basic reporting for HRM.[42]

Finally, the most advanced form of analytics is prescriptive analytics, and at this point, relatively few companies effectively apply prescriptive analytics to HR-related decision making. ***Prescriptive analytics*** focuses on what actions should be taken based on what is likely to happen in the future. By definition prescriptive analytics is forward-looking, just like predictive analytics, but prescriptive analytics build upon predictive analytics by taking data-informed predictions and translating them into different decision alternatives and courses of action. An overarching goal of prescriptive analytics is to optimize decision making to ultimately achieve the best outcome that is aligned with organizational strategy.

HR Analytics and the Scientific Process

Regardless of whether a company uses descriptive, predictive, or prescriptive analytics, we recommend that you envision HR analytics—and data-driven decision making, in general—as a scientific endeavor. The scientific process rests firmly in empiricism, which refers to knowledge based on evidence. In essence, the scientific process can be thought of as a rigorous and rational approach to problem solving and decision making. As described in Chapter 1, the scientific process consists of the six steps shown in Figure 2.6.

Step One: Identifying the Problem

Like any problem-solving approach, the first step of the scientific process is to identify and define the problem. That is, what specifically will you try to describe, predict, explain, or understand using analytics? For example, imagine your organization has been facing a retention issue, in which employees are voluntarily leaving the organization at a concerning rate. In general, turnover is a major cost for organizations,[43] with some estimates suggesting that selecting and training a replacement employee can cost organizations between 50% and 200% of the first-year salary for each person who leaves the organization.[44] Given the cost of voluntary turnover and your organization's latest turnover rates (which represent a type of a descriptive analytics), you might define voluntary turnover as a problem for which you wish to find a solution, as failure to do so might impair the organization's ability to achieve strategic objectives.

Step Two: Doing Background Research

It is unlikely that the problem you identified is completely novel. For example, others who came before you have investigated the problem of voluntary turnover. Universities and other academic institutions employ organizational scholars and researchers who, collectively, have investigated

■ **FIGURE 2.6**   Steps in the Scientific Process

The scientific process can be thought of as a rigorous approach to problem solving and decision making.

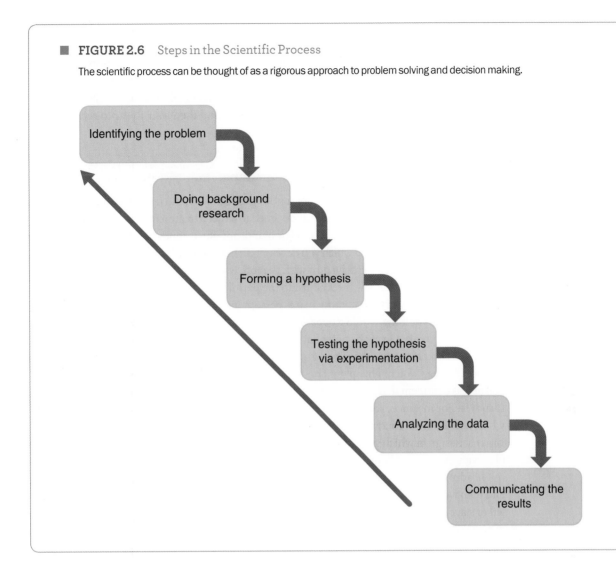

countless organizational problems. As such, before starting from scratch, look to prior theory and research to help you understand the phenomenon you wish to investigate using the scientific process. If you were to look through scholarly journal articles on the topic of voluntary turnover, for example, you would find thousands of empirical studies and theoretical explorations of the phenomenon. In doing so, you might find meta-analyses that indicate job dissatisfaction and poor person–job or person–organization fit predict voluntary turnover.[45] Never underestimate the value of a good theory to help you solve a particular problem. From a practical standpoint, doing background research can save your HR department money, as you will spend less time and energy on trying to solve a problem for which others have already found a viable solution.

Step Three: Forming a Hypothesis

A hypothesis is simply a statement of what you believe or predict to be true. In other words, it is an educated guess based on the background research you performed. We recommend stating the hypothesis as an if/then statement. For example, based on your identification of the problem and background research, you might hypothesize: "If employees perceive a low degree of fit with their job, then they will be more likely to turn over." As a suggestion, try to make your hypothesis as specific as possible by including conditional statements or qualifiers, such as "in this situation" or "for whom." For instance, you might revise your hypothesis to state: "If *new sales* employees perceive a low degree of fit with their job, then they will be more likely to turn over *within 1 year of hire.*" Remember, your hypothesis serves as a compass for enacting the remaining steps of the scientific process. First, a hypothesis informs what data you need to collect. In the turnover example, we would need to measure new sales employees' perceptions of person–job fit, as well as pull organizational turnover records for employees at 1-year post hire. Second, a hypothesis informs the type of research design you will use. In this case, we might want to measure new sales employees' perceived person–job fit within a week of being hired and then wait 1 year to record which employees left and which stayed.

Step Four: Testing the Hypothesis via Experimentation

A true experiment is one of the most rigorous designs you can use to test a hypothesis. For a true experiment, employees must be randomly assigned to either a treatment or control group. Under some circumstances it may be impractical or inappropriate to conduct a true experiment. For instance, imagine a scenario in which you developed a new onboarding module aimed at increasing new sales employees' perceived fit with the job, where *onboarding* refers to an organized process aimed at helping new hires adjust to the performance and social demands of the job.[46] Assuming the onboarding module increases person–job fit and ultimately reduces the probability of voluntarily quitting, would it be ethical to withhold the new onboarding module from those in the control group? Given the potential consequences of not participating in the new onboarding module, you may argue that a true experimental design would not be ethical in this particular scenario. Instead, you might opt for another way of testing your hypothesis, even if it means you will be less confident that participating in the onboarding module is the reason behind reduced turnover. For instance, you might conduct what are referred to as pre- or quasi-experiments, which lack a control condition or random assignment. Alternatively, you might opt for an observational design in which you survey employees or record their behavior directly through direct observation or archival organizational records. For example, to test our turnover hypothesis, we might administer a survey in which employees respond to a perceived person–job fit measure and then we gather organizational turnover records 1 year later to assess whether an employee left or stayed. Finally, regardless of how a hypothesis is tested, it is important to consider the types of data that will be collected, as the type of data informs the type of analysis.

Qualitative vs. Quantitative Data

In general, there are two types of data: qualitative and quantitative (see Table 2.3). On the one hand, **qualitative data** are non-numeric and include text or narrative data, such as interview transcripts or responses to open-ended survey questions. Additional examples of qualitative data include videos and photos. Qualitative data can be quite rich, providing important information about context and processes. Qualitative data, however, are analyzed differently than quantitative data. For instance, qualitative interview data could be content or thematically analyzed such that

Qualitative data Non-numeric information that includes text or narrative data, such as interview transcripts

---

TABLE 2.3 Example of Qualitative vs. Quantitative Data

This data table provides an example of a qualitative variable and quantitative variable. The performance description variable is qualitative because the associated data are non-numeric and text. The performance rating variable is quantitative because the data are numeric.

EMPLOYEE ID	PERFORMANCE RATING	PERFORMANCE DESCRIPTION
9082625	2.65	Peter performed satisfactorily. He still struggles with his TPS reports and arrives late to work at least once a week. Nonetheless, he showed glimpses of potential from time to time.
9077854	4.99	Lisa's performance was exceptional this quarter. She went above and beyond on her grant proposals and showed great teamwork when she helped get a team member back up to speed who had been on maternity leave.

the transcripts are coded for recurring themes. There are even software programs to facilitate this process, such as NVivo and ATLAS.ti. Sometimes HR analysts take qualitative data and transform them to quantitative data. As a simple example, an analyst might use a text analysis program to count the proportion of positive words relative to negative words an individual used in a 500-word block of text as part of a response to an open-ended survey question. This process would, in effect, translate non-numeric qualitative data to numeric quantitative data.

On the other hand, *quantitative data* are numeric and can be counted or measured in some way. Employee age is an example of a continuous quantitative variable, whereas employee voluntary turnover—when coded in binary as 0 = stayed and 1 = quit—is an example of a categorical variable. Statistical models are created using quantitative data.

Quantitative data Numeric data that can be counted or measured in some way

Big Data vs. Little Data

In addition to the qualitative vs. quantitative distinction, we can distinguish between big data and little data. The term *big data* has received a lot of attention in the popular press in recent years, and companies like Amazon, Facebook, and Google have built enormous reputations and revenues from leveraging data to optimize business decision making. Amazon, for example, tracks huge volumes of consumer data and, using sophisticated algorithms, can predict what consumers will buy.

In the realm of HRM, HR analysts have begun to use big data to make better people decisions. Signaling the growth in big data in HRM, the Equal Employment Opportunity Commission met in 2016 to discuss big data and analytics from a legal perspective.[47] But exactly what are big data? It turns out that the term *big data* means different things to different people. For some, big data simply mean a lot of data. For others, big data have to do with the structure of the data. For our purposes, *big data* refer to large (or massive) amounts of unstructured, messy, and sometimes quickly streaming data—often from sources that we did not originally intend to leverage for analytical purposes (e.g., scraping or coding résumé data). As shown in Figure 2.7, big data are also described in terms of four Vs: volume (i.e., amount of data), variety (i.e., different sources and forms of data), velocity (i.e., speed with which new data arrive), and veracity (i.e., trustworthiness of the data, data integrity, and certainty).[48] Together, these Vs provide an indication of the "bigness" and quality of big data.

Big data Large amounts of unstructured, messy, and sometimes quickly streaming data, which can be described in terms of volume, variety, velocity, and veracity

In contrast, *little data* are structured data that are gathered in smaller volumes, usually for a previously planned purpose. Consider an analogy involving a water fountain and a fire hydrant to illustrate the distinction between little data and big data. Working with little data is like drinking from a water fountain; the water flow is steady, clean, slow, predictable, and easy to manage. Alternatively, working with big data is like drinking from a fire hydrant spraying out untreated and unfiltered water; the water flow is voluminous, dirty, fast, largely unpredictable, and difficult to manage. Thus, working with big data requires a lot of up-front data management and restructuring, so much so that prepping big data for subsequent data analysis may require the expertise of a data scientist.

Little data Structured data that are gathered in small volumes, usually for a previously planned purpose

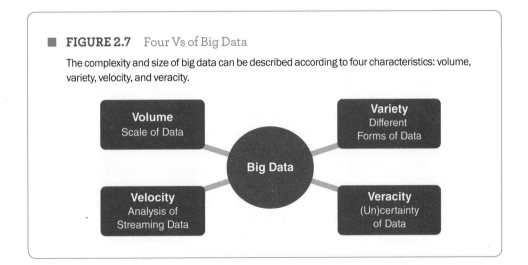

■ **FIGURE 2.7** Four Vs of Big Data

The complexity and size of big data can be described according to four characteristics: volume, variety, velocity, and veracity.

Data Collection and Measurement

Regardless of how or where data are collected, sound measurement is key. Think carefully about what is being measured and how it is being measured, and distinguish between two terms: concept and measure. A **concept** is a theoretical phenomenon or construct. Job performance is a prime example. Performance on a given job entails a number of different behaviors. For instance, a sales position requires the enactment of customer service behaviors. Different **measures** can be used to assess the concept of job performance for a sales position. For instance, an HR analyst might survey customers for feedback on their experiences working with specific sales people. Or the analyst might observe and rate sales people interacting with customers. Thus, different measurement types and sources can be used to measure the same concept.

Step Five: Analyzing the Data

After testing your hypothesis through experimentation (or alternative research designs), which implies data collection and measurement, you are ready to analyze the data to formally test your hypothesis—that is, accept (confirm) or reject (disconfirm) the hypothesis. For hypothesis testing involving quantitative data, null hypothesis significance testing has long been the standard approach. Although not a new approach, in recent years a Bayesian approach to hypothesis testing has gained more traction. A discussion of the relative merits of these two approaches is beyond the scope of this textbook, but for curious readers, we encourage an independent investigation of the two approaches.

Qualitative Data Analysis

As mentioned previously, qualitative data can be analyzed using a variety of analytical tools; however, the notion of hypothesis testing is a bit different for qualitative data analysis. True qualitative data analysis does not produce a numeric or probability-based significance test that can be used to support whether to accept or reject a hypothesis. Instead, qualitative data analysis might rely on agreement between independent coders/analysts to determine whether a phenomenon exists and the processes underlying that phenomenon. Many people approach qualitative data analysis from a different epistemological perspective (i.e., way of knowing the world), as compared with quantitative data analysis. A full discussion of qualitative data analysis is beyond the scope of this textbook, but nonetheless, we highly recommend that you learn more about qualitative data analysis tools and techniques, as qualitative data can be a rich source of data and can answer unique questions. In fact, if you are interested in seeing a rigorous example of qualitative data analysis applied to understanding a workplace phenomenon, we recommend reading a study on interviewer impression management as found in this endnote.[49]

Quantitative Data Analysis

Regarding quantitative data analysis, a number of tools exist, and determining which one to use rests on a number of assumptions, including the type(s) of data you collected and your research design. For categorical data analysis, for example, statistical techniques, such as the chi-square test of independence, are often appropriate. For designs in which the means of two or more continuous variables are compared, such as in a true or quasi-experiment, t-tests and analysis of variance (ANOVA) are often used. When testing the relation between two or more continuous variables, such as job satisfaction scores in relation to job performance scores, you might use analyses such as correlation or regression. Further, when modeling change over time, growth-modeling techniques can be applied, and when modeling the structure of social network interactions, social network analysis is appropriate. With the rise of big data, some data analysts have begun to use machine learning algorithms, which refer to models that self-update and self-adjust and identify patterns in large amounts of data. This list of examples is not meant to be a comprehensive inventory of data analysis techniques; rather, it is intended to illustrate the decisions that must be made when determining how to analyze data.

Interpreting results is the final stage of the data-analysis process. Remember, data do not "speak"; they are interpreted or evaluated. That is, the act of interpretation, like other aspects of the scientific process, requires sound judgment and decision making. This also means that interpretation is susceptible to bias and error, which is addressed next.

Concept A theoretical phenomenon or construct

Measure A tool used to assess the levels of a theoretical concept, such as a survey used to assess employee engagement

SPOTLIGHT ON LEGAL ISSUES
Legal Implications of Big Data

Organizations can benefit from big data and analytics when it comes to key HRM functions, such as recruitment and selection. For example, algorithmic systems and analytic tools, such as those based on machine learning, can provide more accurate predictions of future performance given a number of candidate attributes (e.g., personality, experiences).

Using an algorithm or an analytic tool, however, will not necessarily result in recruitment processes and selection decisions that meet legal scrutiny. To that end, a White House report from May 2016 addressed the legal implications of big data and analytics in a variety of areas, including access to credit, higher education, criminal justice, and employment. With regard to employment, the report recognized that modern algorithmic and automated recruitment and selection systems do, in fact, have the potential to reduce bias, but the report cautions that algorithms are designed by humans. As a result, bias can inevitably find its way into algorithms and models. In fact, algorithms and models can even magnify biases in the data. Nonetheless, the report contends that the use of data-driven approaches in hiring can reduce bias if designed properly.

Thus, the major challenge to using data-driven approaches is improving decision making while also adhering to legal guidelines. When building algorithms and models to predict employee behavior and outcomes, analysts must carefully consider whether it is appropriate to include variables that are directly or indirectly linked to the protected group status of individuals. This means that analysts should proceed with caution when including variables like age or race—or variables that are likely to be strongly correlated with such variables—in their algorithms and models, unless they have a clear and defensible rationale for doing so, such as identifying sources of bias or uncovering evidence of disparate impact. Further, it is important that analysts communicate data-analytic findings to managers in a manner that ensures appropriate and legally compliant actions are taken based on the findings.

As HRM continues to evolve, big data and analytics can provide a strategic advantage. However, without careful consideration, analytics can be susceptible to bias, potentially leading to poor decisions and legal issues.[50]

Biases in Model Building, Testing, and Interpretation

We have hinted throughout this chapter that HR analytics involves many judgment calls and decisions. For instance, when building a regression model, the assumption is that you have included all necessary predictor variables to explain your outcome and no irrelevant predictor variables. This is a difficult assumption to meet, and it relies on the judgment and expertise of HR analysts to determine which variables to include and which to exclude in the model. Psychological and social-scientific theory can play a helpful role when determining which variables to measure and include in a model. At this point, we also reiterate a previous point that models are, by nature, an approximation of reality—reality as perceived by humans. That is, models are inherently subjective. To that end, prominent data scientist and mathematician Cathy O'Neil reminds us of the subjective nature of models by stating, "Models are opinions embedded in mathematics."[51]

Step Six: Communicating the Results

The manner in which you communicate the results of the scientific process depends largely on where you work and the company culture. In academia, this refers to presenting a formal research paper at a conference or publishing the results in a peer-reviewed journal. In other types of organizations, it is common to communicate findings in internal presentations, technical reports, or even white papers. Amazon, for example, is known for communicating findings in technical reports that are read silently during the first part of meetings. Many other companies rely on PowerPoint presentations in which written and oral descriptions of results are provided. In recent years, more value has been placed on creating easy-to-understand data visualizations. ***Data visualizations*** refer to pictorial and graphic representations of quantitative or qualitative data. Regardless of how you communicate the results, it is important to focus on the story you are telling. When storytelling with data, try to keep the story simple, be clear and concise, use repetition, and do not overburden

Data visualization Pictorial and graphic representations of quantitative or qualitative data

■ **FIGURE 2.8**   Examples of Different Types of Data Visualizations

Data visualizations can take different forms, from simple text to bar graphs to geographic plots. Pick the visual that best represents the data and tells the most accurate story.

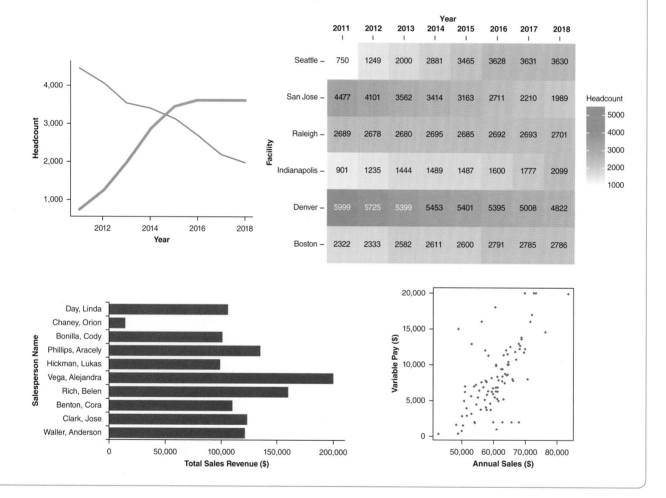

the reader or viewer with too much information.[52] Finally, when deciding upon the specific results you wish to communicate, recognize the limitations of the data you collected and the study design you employed to test your hypothesis. In other words, take care not to overstate or exaggerate your findings. At the same time, do not understate your findings, either. See Figure 2.8 for examples of different data visualizations.

LO 2.6   Manage the components of a successful HR analytics function.

Ensuring HR Analytics Success

A sustainable HR analytics function requires the consideration of a number of important issues. First, HR analytics should be integrated and embedded into HR and organizational strategies, and this requires taking a systems perspective of the organization and its various subsystems. In the

SPOTLIGHT ON HR FOR SMALL AND MEDIUM-SIZED BUSINESSES

HR Analytics

Many of the companies featured in this chapter are quite large. But even though large companies have been early adopters of HR analytics, small and medium-sized companies can also use HR analytics to their advantage.

First, HR information systems and technologies have become more affordable, making it possible for smaller companies to purchase the platforms that are similar to those that larger companies are using. For example, ADP Inc. and SAP SuccessFactors offer different platforms designed to meet the needs of small, medium, and large companies. Not only can these platforms help smaller companies store and manage their people data, but they also provide many automated descriptive analytics, such as common HR metrics.

Second, adopting the scientific process for HR decision making and problem solving is not exclusive to large companies. Rather, small and medium-sized companies can integrate the scientific process into their HR function to help the company find, motivate, and keep the right people. Recall from earlier in the chapter that the scientific process is akin to rigorous and rational problem solving.

Finally, there is a wealth of peer-reviewed, scientific research on a variety of HR systems, policies, and practices, as well as a growing literature on strategic HRM. Subscribing to academic- and practitioner-oriented journals can provide HR professionals with a treasure trove of rigorous empirical findings from other organizations that can be used to inform and support their decision making.

opening case, we described how Chevron integrated its HR analytics team into the organization and created a community of practice to bring those interested in analytics together. HR analytics can become an integral part of the HR strategic business partnership by leveraging people data to inform and support people decisions and strategy. In other words, the HR analytics function can provide data-driven recommendations regarding the design and implementation of HR practices in order to facilitate the organization's achievement of strategic objectives. Second, HR analytics should be integrated into the culture of HR and the organization. As we previously noted, many executives continue to make major decisions based on their gut instincts, or intuition. As such, developing an HR analytics function in some organizations may be difficult, especially if the culture does not ostensibly value data and data-driven decisions. By gaining manager support and creating a culture that supports evidence-based practices, the HR analytics function will have a better chance of implementing changes. Third, and related to the second point, HR analytics must be paired with good change management, where change management refers to the "systematic process of applying knowledge, tools, and resources to transform organization from one state of affairs to another."[53] People have a natural tendency to resist change, and thus, in addition to creating a culture supportive of data-driven decision making, a culture of continuous change should be cultivated as well. Fourth, an HR analytics team must comprise the right people with the right mix of competencies. We recommended the following seven competencies earlier in the chapter: theory, business, data management, measurement, data analysis, employment law, and ethics. Deficiencies in any one of these competencies within a team may result in failure to make a contribution or, worse, may use HR analytics in ways that are illegal or unethical. Finally, we cannot overstate the importance of ethics. Today, new information technologies make it easier than ever to collect, manage, and analyse potentially sensitive people and organizational data, and with these new technologies come new ethical responsibilities. For example, some platforms allow us to systematically scrape data about our employees from social media sites. Before doing so, however, we must pause and ask this question: "Just because we can, should we?" For example, just because we can scrape employees' social media data with ease and just because that data might be predictive of employee outcomes, should we do it? The same rigor that is applied to the scientific process should also be applied to decision making surrounding what data to use, how to use data, and whether to run certain analyses. Referring back to the systems perspective once more is important because it reminds us of the interconnectedness between ourselves and other organizational entities. In other words, a systems perspective reminds us that one decision—ethical or not—can result in a large ripple effect through the organization system and beyond.

CHAPTER SUMMARY

HRM has evolved immensely over the past century, with the development of strategic HRM, data-driven decision making, and HR analytics. Leading organizations leverage their HR function to inform and support organizational strategy; to realize employee, operational, stakeholder, and financial outcomes; and to achieve a competitive advantage. Data-driven decision making in the form of HR analytics plays an important role in strategy realization. An effective HR analytics function can be leveraged to improve the quality of decisions we make by informing the way an organization collects, manages, analyzes, and interprets its people data.

KEY TERMS

strategic human resource
   management   35
human resource analytics (HR
   analytics)   33
strategy   35
scientific process   35
strategy formulation   35
mission   36
vision   36
values   36
SWOT analysis   37
resource-based view   38
strategy type   37

stakeholders   39
strategy implementation   39
human capital   39
balanced scorecard   42
organizational performance   42
data-driven decisions   42
high-performance work practices   43
systems perspective   44
ability-motivation-opportunity
   model   46
descriptive analytics   49
predictive analytics   49
prescriptive analytics   50

qualitative data   52
quantitative data   53
big data   53
little data   53
concept   54
measures   54
data visualization   55
categorical variable   61
continuous variable   61
mean   61
standard deviation   61

$SAGE edge™

Visit **edge.sagepub.com/bauer** to help you accomplish your coursework goals in an easy-to-use learning environment.

- Master the learning objectives using key study tools
- Watch, listen, and connect with online multimedia resources
- Access mobile-friendly quizzes and flashcards to check your understanding

HR REASONING AND DECISION-MAKING EXERCISES

MINI-CASE ANALYSIS EXERCISE:
ORGANIZATIONAL CULTURE AND THE SUCCESS OF HR ANALYTICS

Chapter 1 discussed the importance of organizational culture in relation to HRM. Specifically, the chapter reviewed a popular organizational culture typology called the Competing Values Framework, which characterizes different culture types by their emphasis on either collaboration, creating, controlling, or competing. The culture types are as follows: clan, adhocracy, market, and hierarchy. Given what you learned in this chapter about HR analytics and data-driven people decisions, consider how the different culture types might influence an organization's acceptance of HR analytics.

Now, you decide:

1. For which organization culture type do you think HR analytics will best integrate? Is there an ideal culture type to support HR analytics? Why?

2. Which organization culture type will be least likely to accept HR analytics as a viable part of the organization's strategy? Why?

HR DECISION ANALYSIS EXERCISE: THE CASE OF GRAVITY PAYMENTS

The CEO of Gravity Payments, Dan Price, made national headlines in 2015 when he announced that he would be increasing all employees' annual pay to $70,000 over the course of several years. Price had read a study that showed that emotional well-being improved as income increased, up until about $75,000 a year, and he was inspired to raise his employees' pay with the hope that it would lift their emotional well-being. Reportedly, he moved very quickly when making this major decision. In the months that followed his compensation announcement, Price was both cheered and jeered. His supporters touted his inspirational message, while his critics argued that it was all a publicity stunt and questioned his motives. In addition, not everyone within the company was happy with this decision. Within 3 months, two of his most-valued employees had quit, citing the fact that newer and less experienced employees would make the same amount of money. Some of his company's clients commended him, while other clients said he made their job harder because they feared they would have to justify the costs of services that might come with the pay increases.[54] Now, answer the following questions regarding what you think about Price's HRM decision making in terms of the five characteristics of effective HRM decisions depicted below.

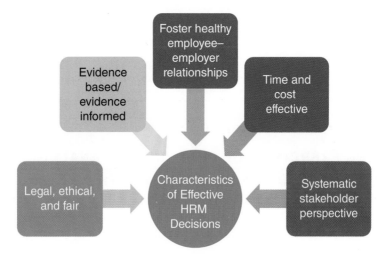

Be sure to include specific examples from the case or your own research to support your answers.

Was Dan Price's HRM decision legal, ethical, and fair?

_____
_____
_____
_____

Was it evidence based/evidence informed?

_____
_____
_____
_____

Did it foster healthy employee–employer relationships?

_____
_____
_____
_____

Was it time and cost effective?

_____
_____
_____
_____

Did it take a systematic stakeholder perspective?

_____
_____
_____
_____

Considering your analysis above, overall, do you think this was an effective decision? Why or why not?

_____
_____
_____

What, if anything, do you think should be done differently or considered to help make this decision more effective?

_____
_____

HR DECISION-MAKING EXERCISE: BUILDING YOUR HR ANALYTICS TEAM

HR analytics is an interdisciplinary field, and as a result, HR analytics teams are often composed of individuals from different disciplines, specializations, and degree programs. Critical areas of expertise in any HR analytics team include the following: theory, business, data management, measurement, data analysis, employment law, and ethics. For this exercise, work in a group to determine how you would recruit, select, and train members of an effective HR analytics team.

1. As a group, create a series of jobs for which you will ultimately recruit and select new employees. A given job may cover more than one area of expertise, and multiple jobs may overlap in terms of some areas of expertise.

2. For each job created in Step 1, identify the competencies and educational/professional experiences that are necessary for success on each job.

3. Develop a brief recruitment and selection strategy for each job. In other words, where will you recruit individuals for these positions? Why? How and why will you select and hire individuals for these positions?

DATA AND ANALYTICS EXERCISE: DESCRIBING YOUR DATA

Summarizing people data using descriptive analytics can provide valuable insights into the state of your company. Although there are a number of common HR metrics such as turnover rate and yield ratio (see Supplement for more examples and details), often it is valuable to summarize basic demographic data, survey data, and performance data using descriptive statistics like frequency, percentage, mean, median, mode, and standard deviation. Part of the challenge is determining which descriptive statistic to use to describe a particular variable. Regarding quantitative variables, one can distinguish between categorical variables and continuous variables. Although variables can be described in even more specific terms, the categorical and continuous distinction is an important one.

A *categorical variable* consists of multiple levels, but these levels do not have a particular order or inherent numeric values. For example, race is typically operationalized as a categorical variable, where the levels of the race variable correspond to the different categories of race (e.g., Asian, Black, White), in no particular order. As another example, for reporting purposes to the Equal Employment Opportunity Commission, employee sex is often reported as a dichotomous categorical variable with the following levels: male and female. When we report categorical variables, we often use frequency or percentage to describe the data. For example, imagine that a company employs 230 female and 199 male employees. We could describe sex using two frequencies: frequency of females (230) and frequency of males (199). Alternatively, we could describe each level of the gender variable as a percentage. For example, 53.6% of employees identify as female (53.6% = 230/(230 + 199) × 100), and 46.4% identify as male (46.4% = 199/(230 + 199) × 100). Data visualizations like the bar charts shown in Figures 2.9 and 2.10 facilitate the communication of such descriptive analytics findings.

> **Categorical variable** A variable that has multiple levels, without any particular order to the levels or inherent numeric values

A *continuous variable* consists of a continuum of numerically ordered values. A classic example is employee age when measured in years. Years can be ordered such that we can say someone who is 39 years is older than someone who is 38 years, and thus, one value is larger or higher than another value. Although many survey response scales technically represent what are referred to as ordinal variables, which are distinguishable from continuous variables, we often treat them like continuous variables for the purposes of data analysis. For instance, in an employee engagement survey, you might ask employees to respond to different survey items using a 5-point response scale ranging from *strongly disagree* (1) to *neither agree nor disagree* (3) to *strongly agree* (5).

> **Continuous variable** A variable that consists of a continuum of numerically ordered values
>
> **Mean** The average of a group of numeric values
>
> **Standard deviation** The amount of variation of a group of numeric values around their mean

To summarize employees' ages or their responses to the item "I am satisfied with my job," you could compute descriptive statistics of central tendency and/or dispersion. For example, you might find that the *mean* (average) employee age is 38.2 years with a *standard deviation*

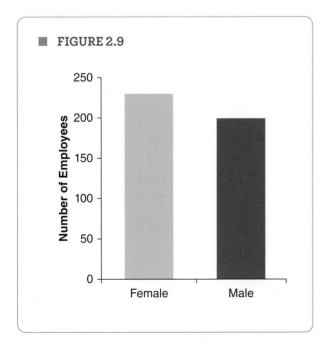

■ FIGURE 2.9

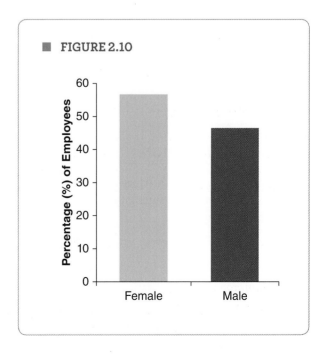

■ FIGURE 2.10

■ FIGURE 2.11

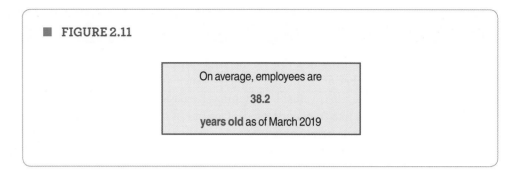

On average, employees are

38.2

years old as of March 2019

■ FIGURE 2.12

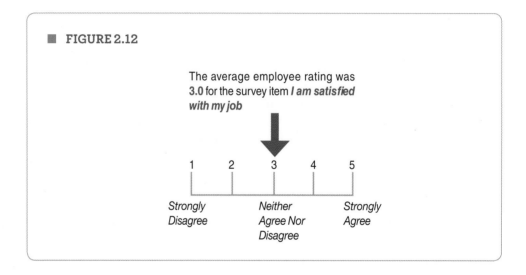

The average employee rating was **3.0** for the survey item *I am satisfied with my job*

| 1 | 2 | 3 | 4 | 5 |

Strongly Disagree   *Neither Agree Nor Disagree*   *Strongly Agree*

of 5.4 years. This means that the center of the distribution of employee ages is 38.2 years and that about two thirds of employees' ages fall within 5.4 years of 38.2 or, in other words, 32.8 to 43.6 years. Similarly, you might find that the mean response to the job satisfaction item is 3.0, which indicates that, on average, employees neither agree nor disagree with the statement: "I am satisfied with my job." A standard deviation of 1.2 for responses on that item, however, indicates that approximately two thirds of employees' responses fall within 1.2 points above and below the mean or, in other words, 1.8 to 4.2. Thus, in that example, a large proportion of employees' responses varied anywhere from slightly dissatisfied to slightly satisfied with their job. When creating a data visualization for a mean, there are many options; Figures 2.11 and 2.12 provide examples.

In summary, descriptive analytics includes basic summary statistics and the data visualizations used to communicate those summary statistics. Identifying the difference between categorical and continuous variables is the first step toward picking the right statistic to summarize your data.

✔ EXCEL EXTENSION: NOW YOU TRY!

- On **edge.sagepub.com/bauer**, you will find an Excel exercise on descriptive analytics. Specifically, you will compute basic descriptive and summary statistics for the following variables from a sample dataset: age, gender, race, engagement, and pay.

- First, you will classify each variable as either a categorical or continuous variable.

- Second, you will select and compute appropriate descriptive and summary statistics to describe the variables.

- Third, you will create a data visualization in Excel to help communicate your findings.

CHAPTER 2 SUPPLEMENT: STEPS FOR STRATEGY FORMULATION

COMMON HR METRICS[55]

HR METRICS		
Absence rate	[(No. of days absent in mo.)/ (Ave. no. of employees during mo.) × (No. of workdays)] × 100	Measures absenteeism. Determines if your company has an absenteeism problem. Analyzes why and how to address the issue. Analyzes further for effectiveness of attendance policy and effectiveness of management in applying policy. See Hollmann (2002).
Cost per hire	(Advertising + Agency fees + Employee referrals + Travel cost of applicants and staff + Relocation costs + Recruiter pay and benefits)/No. of hires	Costs involved with a new hire. Use *EMA/Cost per Hire Staffing Metrics Survey* as a benchmark for your organization (Kluttz, 2003). Can be used as a measurement to show any substantial improvements to savings in recruitment/retention costs. Determines what your recruiting function can do to increase savings/reduce costs, etc.
Health care costs per employee	Total cost of health care/Total employees	Per capita cost of employee benefits. Indicates cost of health care per employee. For benefit data from the Bureau of Labor Statistics (BLS). See BLS's publications titled *Employer Costs for Employee Compensation and Measuring Trends in the Structure and Levels of Employer Costs for Employee Compensation* (BLS, 2008) for additional information on this topic.
HR expense factor	HR expense/Total operating expense	HR expenses in relation to the total operating expenses of the organization. In addition, determines if expenditures exceeded, met, or fell below budget. Analyzes HR practices that contributed to savings, if any.
Human capital ROI	(Revenue − (Operating expense − [Compensation cost + Benefit cost])/ (Compensation cost + Benefit cost)	ROI ratio for employees. Did organization get a return on its investment? Analyzes causes of positive/negative ROI metric. Uses analysis as an opportunity to optimize investment with HR practices, such as recruitment, motivation, training, and development. Evaluates if HR practices have a causal relationship in positive changes to improving metric.
Human capital value added	(Revenue − (Operating expense − [Compensation cost + Benefit cost])/Total no. of FTE	Value of workforce's knowledge, skill, and performance. This measurement illustrates how employees add value to an organization.
Prorating merit increases	(No. of mos. actually worked/ No. of mos. under the current increase policy) × Increase in percentage the person would otherwise be entitled to	The basic steps to calculate an employee's pay increase appropriate to the period of time worked.
Revenue factor	Revenue/Total no. of FTE	Benchmark to indicate effectiveness of company and to show employees as capital rather than as an expense. Human capital can be viewed as an investment.
Time to fill	Total days elapsed to fill requisitions/No. hired	Number of days from which job requisition was approved to new hire start date. How efficient/productive is recruiting function? This is also a process measurement. See *EMA/Cost per Hire Staffing Metrics Survey* for more information.

(Continued)

(Continued)

HR METRICS		
Training investment factor	Total training cost/Headcount	Training cost per employee. Analyzes training function further for effectiveness of training (e.g., Has productivity increased as a result of acquiring new skills and knowledge? Have accidents decreased?). If not, evaluate the causes.
Training (ROI)	(Total benefit − Total costs) × 100	The total financial gain/benefit an organization realizes from a particular training program less the total direct and indirect costs incurred to develop, produce, and deliver the training program (see white paper titled *Four Steps to Computing Training ROI* [Lilly, 2001] for more information on this topic).
Turnover costs	Total of the costs of separation + vacancy + replacement + training	The separation, vacancy, replacement, and training costs resulting from employee turnover. This formula can be used to calculate the turnover cost for one position, a class code, a division, or the entire organization. *Exit interviews* (Drake & Robb, 2002) are a useful tool in determining why employees are leaving your organization (see white paper titled *Employee Turnover Hurts Small and Large Company Profitability* [Galbreath, 2002] for more information on this topic). Implements retention efforts. Evaluates if HR practices are having a causal relationship in positive changes to improving cost of turnover.
Turnover rate (monthly)	(No. of separations during mo. / Avg. no. of employees during mo.) × 100	Calculates and compares metric with national average, using business and legal reports at www.bls.gov/jlt/home.htm. This measures the rate at which employees leave a company. Is there a trend? Has metric increased/decreased? Analyzes what has caused increase/decrease to metric. Determines what an organization can do to improve retention efforts. Evaluates if HR practices have a causal relationship in positive changes to improving metric. (See white paper titled *Employee Turnover: Analyzing Employee Movement Out of the Organization* [Ofsanko & Napier, 1990].)
Turnover rate (annual)	(No. of employees exiting the job/Avg. actual no. of employees during the period) × 12)/No. of mos. in period	Calculates and compares metric with national average, using business and legal reports at www.bls.gov/jlt/home.htm. This measures the rate at which employees leave a company. Is there a trend? Has metric increased/decreased? Analyze what has caused increase/decrease to metric. Determines what organization can do to improve retention efforts. Evaluates if HR practices have a causal relationship in positive changes to improving metric. (See white paper titled *Employee Turnover: Analyzing Employee Movement Out of the Organization* [Ofsanko & Napier, 1990].)
Vacancy costs	Total of the costs of temporary workers + independent contractors + other outsourcing + overtime − Wages and benefits not paid for vacant position(s)	The cost of having work completed that would have been performed by the former employee or employees less the wages and benefits that would have been paid to the vacant position(s). This formula may be used to calculate the vacancy cost for one position, a group, a division, or the entire organization.
Vacancy rate	(Total no. of vacant positions as of today/Total no. of positions as of today) × 100	Measures the organization's vacancy rates resulting from employee turnover. This formula can be used to calculate the vacancy rate for one position, a class code, a division, or the entire organization.
Workers' compensation cost per employee	Total WC cost for year/Average no. of employees	Analyzes and compares (e.g., Year 1 to Year 2, etc.) on a regular basis. You can also analyze workers' compensation further to determine trends in types of injuries, injuries by department, jobs, and so forth. HR practices such as safety training, *disability management*, and incentives can reduce costs. Use metric as benchmark to show causal relationship between HR practices and reduced workers' compensation costs.
Workers' compensation incident rate	(No. of injuries and/or illnesses per 100 FTE/Total hours worked by all employees during the calendar year) × 200,000	The "incident rate" is the *number of injuries and/or illnesses* per 100 full-time workers. 200,000 is the base for 100 FTE workers (working 40 hours/week, 50 weeks/year). The calculated rate can be modified depending on the *nature* of the injuries and/or illnesses. For example, if you wished to determine the lost workday case rate, you would include only the cases that involved *days away from work*.

HR METRICS		
Workers' compensation severity rate	(No. of days away from work per 100 FTE/Total hours worked by all employees during the calendar year) × 200,000	The "severity rate" is the number of days away from work per 100 FTE. To calculate the severity rate, replace the number of injuries and/or illnesses per 100 FTE from the incident rate calculation with the number of days away from work per 100 FTE. More information is available regarding the types of injuries, incident rates, and comparison with other SIC codes at www.bls.gov/iif/oshdef.htm#incidence.
Yield ratio	Percentage of applicants from a recruitment source that make it to the next stage of the selection process (e.g., 100 résumés received, 50 found acceptable = 50% yield)	A comparison of the number of applicants at one stage of the recruiting process with the number at the next stage. (*Note: Success ratio* is the proportion of selected applicants who are later judged as being successful on the job.)

Data Management and Human Resource Information Systems

3

Opening Case

Shifting to a Data-Driven Organization With HRIS: The Case of Nissan[1]

In 1999 the Japanese carmaker Nissan was in trouble. The company had not been profitable for 8 years, its margins were low, and it was estimated that the car company gave away $1,000 for every car it sold in the United States. In addition, plant capacity was much larger than demand, leading to high overhead costs. In the hopes of turning things around, French carmaker Renault invested $5.4 billion in Nissan for an equity stake in the company. After their strategic alliance governed by cross-sharing agreements was struck, Renault-Nissan became the fourth-largest car company in the world. But the alliance made sense only if Nissan could turn things around. It was asked to do just that.

One of the major ways that Nissan set out to turn things around was to transform HR to a "shared services model." This entailed a multitier HR service delivery system in which employees first had access to technology that allowed them to answer their own questions and to make most of their HR-related decisions on their own. If employees still needed

LEARNING OBJECTIVES

After reading and studying this chapter, you should be able to do the following:

3.1 Describe key aspects of data management.

3.2 Apply opportunities for data management and HRIS.

3.3 Identify and address challenges for data management and HRIS.

3.4 Describe basic technical aspects of developing an HRIS.

3.5 Address key points of the process of HRIS implementation.

3.6 Apply core information system concepts in HR management.

©iStock.com/Tramino

help, then their question could be escalated to the next level of service, which included sending a ticket to a shared service desk. Finally, if the HR concern was not resolved at that level, it was escalated to HR experts. This change was transformational in allowing HR staff to shift from spending much of their time on administrative and transactional activities to spending more time on activities associated with being a strategic business partner.

Today, Renault, Nissan, and Mitsubishi are all part of a unique strategic alliance partnership. However, in 2012, Nissan was running multiple non–cloud-based HR systems across its multiple regions without a way to link them. For example, Nissan ran SuccessFactors and Oracle's PeopleSoft in North America, but SAP HR packages in Europe and outdated software in Japan. Through pressure from Nissan's board to streamline the HR systems, Alfonso Díez David, Alliance General Manager of Global Digital Human Resources at Renault-Nissan-Mitsubishi, was tasked with integrating and unifying all of Nissan's HR systems to achieve global consistency. The transition was not without its challenges, but after successfully piloting the Workday, Inc., platform in Hong Kong and South Africa, Nissan rolled it out to North America and Japan in 2016. By 2017, both the French carmaker Renault (with nearly 125,000 employees in 128 countries) and Nissan (with nearly 140,000 employees in more than 160 countries) had a global cloud-based HR software system.

Díez David explains that the rationale behind the major investment in time and money to move to a single global HR system was to allow Nissan to compare "apples to apples" when it came to employees and HR. Another major driver was the desire to leverage HR analytics to manage their talent globally. The hope was to save time for HR staff by offloading common administrative HR tasks and allowing them time to focus on high-value data analytics to help Nissan become more efficient and profitable.

Díez David recommends several things when rolling out a major HRIS project such as this one including:

- Being user centric,
- Recruiting system champions to answer questions and help with trainings locally,
- Focusing on data quality up front to avoid problems later on, and
- Investing in the management of data privacy concerns.

Of course, the changes made with Nissan's HR system and their global HRIS rollout are not the only factors influencing Nissan's successful turnaround. However, this case remains a valuable reminder of how important data management and HRIS are as a foundation to strong organizations.

Case Discussion Questions

1. Nissan underwent a great deal of change in a short period of time. How do you think the employees who were asked to make these changes reacted along the way?

2. Díez David shared four recommendations for those considering a major HRIS project. Can you think of other recommendations that might make sense to help the process go smoothly?

3. What role do you think HRIS played in Nissan's turnaround story?

4. Do you think there are any downsides to having a global HRIS in place? If so, what could be done to help mitigate those problems in the design and implementation phases?

▶ Click to learn more...

Read more about how Nissan was transformed by reading *Shift: Inside Nissan's Revival* (2004) by former Renault and Nissan CEO Carlos Ghosn.

After reading Chapters 1 and 2 of this book, you can see that our approach to covering HRM is based on the concepts and developments you will need to understand now and in the future of HR, organizations, business, and your own career. Among those concepts are the skills needed to make use of data to make sound HRM decisions. In today's business world, effective HRM requires that organizational members be knowledgeable about how data are managed, stored, retrieved, merged, analyzed, and reported to help with data-driven decision making. Even if they are not data analysts or experts in *human resource information systems (HRIS)*, all employees should be familiar with issues around data management and HRIS. Understanding these concepts will make you an effective consumer of data and its possibilities within your organization regardless of your position, functional area, or title.

Human Resource Information Systems (HRIS) Systems used to collect, store, manage, analyze, retrieve, and report HR data and allow for the automation of some HR management functions

Managing Data

Recall from Chapter 1 that the availability of people data has increased dramatically with advances in technology and data-gathering tools. *People data* refers to data associated with various groups of individuals, such as employees and other stakeholders, who might be integral for an organization's success. As described in Chapter 2, HR analytics has emerged as an approach to leveraging people data to make data-driven decisions to improve the flow of human capital into and through an organization. Because of this, strategic data management has become especially salient to HR professionals and HR analysts. As seen in the Nissan case, HR has long since outgrown the days of employee records and data stored on paper and housed in filing cabinets. Before computer-based information systems became the norm, relatively small amounts of data were accessed with regularity, and merging data from different files was a cumbersome and time-consuming process. Today, with ever-accumulating amounts of people data and sometimes easier access to such data, we must think critically, ethically, and legally about how large volumes of data about individuals are stored and managed and how advances in information systems are used to facilitate this process. HR information systems and electronic HRM (e-HRM) represent two closely related HRM data management topics that play an important role in that regard. In many organizations, HR information systems and e-HRM are integrated into a larger cross-functional data management system called an enterprise resource planning system—all of which can be broadly classified as information systems.

LO 3.1 Describe key aspects of data management.

People data Data associated with various groups of humans that are associated with an organization, such as employees and other stakeholders

Enterprise Resource Planning Systems

An *enterprise resource planning (ERP)* system refers to integrated business-management software intended to coordinate and integrate processes and data across different functional areas of a company, such as accounting, sales, finance, operations, customer service, and HRM. For instance, an ERP might capture, track, and integrate data pertaining to payroll, inventory, production capacity, applicant tracking, and purchase orders, to name a few things. By integrating

Enterprise resource planning (ERP) Integrated business-management software intended to coordinate and integrate processes and data across different functional areas of a company, such as accounting, sales, human resource management, and finance

data cross-functionally, an ERP creates a robust data ecosystem, which enables organizational stakeholders to take a systems perspective when making important decisions. For example, imagine that customer service data residing within an ERP indicates that customer service representatives have been fielding increasingly more customer complaints having to do with faulty products. Using those data, a decision maker on the manufacturing floor might investigate where mistakes are being made in the production process. Ultimately, that decision maker might reach out to someone from the HR department with expertise in employee training to help design a new training program for manufacturing employees. Thus, a well-designed and well-integrated ERP has the potential to improve decision making across different functional areas, as the entire business can be viewed as an integrated system with separate yet related subsystems.

Like most technology, an ERP was originally a luxury of large companies. As computer processing speeds and data storage capabilities improved and came down in cost, introducing a robust ERP system became a reality for smaller and smaller companies. This has been great news for small and medium-sized businesses, as ERPs were historically extremely expensive, and now many HR needs can be met for smaller businesses using ERPs at prices that are affordable.

Human Resource Information Systems

Many organizations incorporate an HR information system within their broader ERP systems, such that HR processes and data are linked to and integrated with data from other business functions. An HR information system (HRIS) refers to a "system used to acquire, store, manipulate, analyze, retrieve, and distribute pertinent information about an organization's human resources,"[2] and the concept of HRIS can be nested within the broader concept of e-HRM. At its most basic, an HRIS is simply a system of the following: input → data management → output. Broadly speaking, *e-HRM* refers to Internet-based information systems and technology that span across organizational levels.[3] HRIS represents the confluence of HRM and information technology, and when coupled with strategic HRM, HRIS offers a way to realize synergies between and across different HR practices. It can provide a wealth of readily available data to provide organizational decision makers with accurate and timely information.

e-HRM Internet-based information systems and technology that span across organizational levels

Just like the broader ERP system, an organization can use its HRIS to integrate people data across different HR functions, such as recruitment, selection, training, performance management, compensation, and benefits. Moreover, an HRIS can be designed to automate transactional HR activities, such as benefits enrollment or applicant tracking. After World War II, the payroll function was one of the first to be automated using early computers and information systems. As computer technology advanced in the following decades, organizations began to integrate web- and cloud-based services into their HRISs. An HRIS is a cost-saving tool, as it can reduce errors and increase efficiencies related to storing, accessing, and using data. For example, DHL, the largest international logistics company in the world, had employees apply for leave using physical forms that were then sent overseas to be processed, which was time consuming and frustrating to employees who wanted to know the status of their leave requests in a timely manner. In 2008, DHL transitioned from a paper-based system to something much more efficient. As Jitin Patel of DHL says, "Our employees applied for leave by filling in forms that were then sent to Malaysia payroll office for approval, such vague and lengthy process totally frustrated HR and payroll staff. It also incurred lots of leave liabilities. Leave records could not be traced without an online leave application." Following their transition, DHL now has "a simple and user-friendly system which enables DHL Supply Chain to start even with minimal training."[4] Thus, an HRIS can help HR become more efficient. Beyond efficiency, an HRIS, by definition, involves the complex collection, storage, and analysis of people data, providing an opportunity to analyze these data to make better people decisions.

As seen in the opening case of Nissan, the hallmarks of an advanced HRIS are consistency, accuracy, timely access to data, and integration. Rather than using a separate and insular information subsystem for each core HR function—such as selection, training, performance management, and retention—an advanced HRIS integrates people data across HR functions. And when integrated into a company's ERP, the comprehensiveness of the data becomes even more robust. Further, allowing subsystems to "speak" with one another means that analysts can retrieve and merge data from multiple subsystem functions for subsequent analysis and reporting. A number of vendors (e.g., Oracle, SAP) offer HRIS and ERP solutions, thereby facilitating data management and integration processes. In fact, many vendors now integrate data analytics solutions into their data management platforms. Integrated analytics solutions reflect tremendous advances in computing power such as those described in Chapter 1 regarding Moore's Law. At the click of a button, the software can run and generate off-the-shelf analyses and reports.

Some vendors, like ADP, offer proprietary data analysis algorithms to predict important outcomes, such as employee retention. Because such algorithms are proprietary and thus considered intellectual property, the specific criteria used in the algorithmic models often remain locked in a "black box" where the contents are unknown. As such, HR professionals, and all organizational members, should do their due diligence to understand, to the best of their ability, what data are being used in such models and how to properly interpret output or results from such models.

Opportunities for Data Management and HRIS

LO 3.2 Apply opportunities for data management and HRIS.

When it comes to data management and HRIS, there exist a number of opportunities, as well as challenges. Figure 3.1 illustrates several of these when it comes to developing, implementing, and maintaining an HRIS. Opportunities exist in the form of being able to track the employee

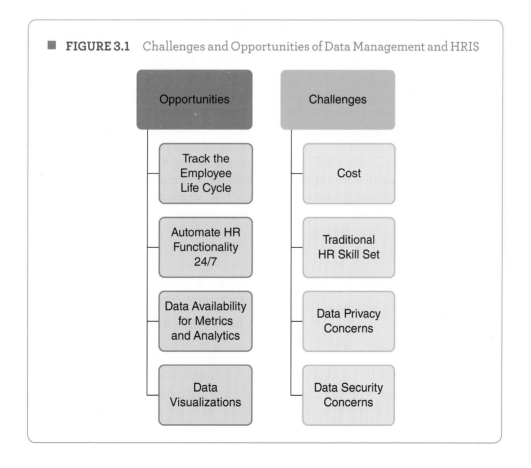

■ **FIGURE 3.1** Challenges and Opportunities of Data Management and HRIS

Opportunities
- Track the Employee Life Cycle
- Automate HR Functionality 24/7
- Data Availability for Metrics and Analytics
- Data Visualizations

Challenges
- Cost
- Traditional HR Skill Set
- Data Privacy Concerns
- Data Security Concerns

■ **FIGURE 3.2** HRM as a Linking Pin for Critical People Decisions

Critical people decisions such as what skills are needed, who to hire, what training employees need, how they are performing, and how to develop leaders and make succession plans are all facilitated by having real-time data to help inform those decisions.

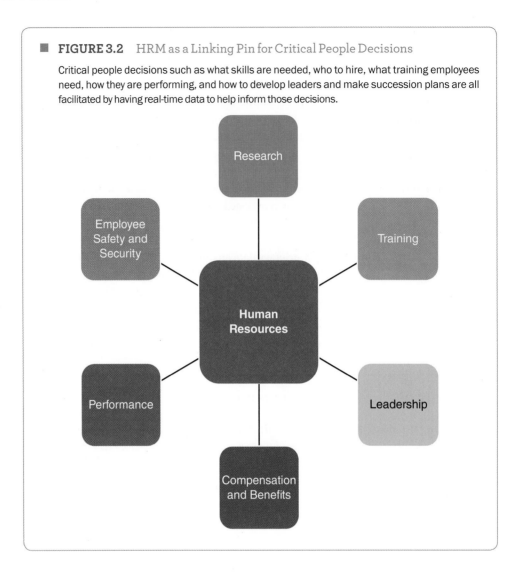

throughout their employment life cycles, automating HR functionality for employees, allowing data to be available for HR analytics, and storing and merging employee attitude surveys and other sources of people data over time. An example of HRIS in practice is Virginia Beach, Virginia (a town with more than 6,000 city employees and 45 city HRM professionals). In 2003, it embarked on what was considered an innovative approach to merging data from the city's HRIS, the Virginia Retirement System, and other data sources to enhance its workforce planning efforts. Managers can now use the system to understand projected retirement statistics, changing workforce demographics, and pending job vacancies, making the city more proactive and less reactive in terms of workforce planning.[5]

Track the Employee Life Cycle

Recall that HRM is *the constellation of decisions and actions associated with managing individuals through the employee life cycle to maximize employee and organizational effectiveness in attaining goals.* This includes a range of functions such as analyzing and designing jobs; managing diversity and complying with local, national, and global employee laws; recruiting individuals to apply for jobs; selecting individuals to join organizations; training and developing people while they are employed; helping to manage their performance; rewarding and compensating employee performance while maintaining healthy labor relations and helping to keep them safe; and managing their exit from the organization (see Figure 3.2).

Thus, a major opportunity for an organization is to manage the valuable resources that are data in a manner that helps the organization not only describe its employees and predict their future movements throughout the organization but also prescribe what the ideal state of HR will be in the future. Effective data management and HRIS are critical to realizing this potential. One study of HR executives and managers working in diverse countries, including Argentina, Brazil, China, India, Latvia, and Slovakia, found that the presence of a global HRIS was related to higher staff retention of global IT service providers in emerging markets. This was especially helpful in decreasing turnover for employees assigned to other countries, as the support of a global HRIS for scheduling and training were cited as helpful for new employees and their managers alike.[6] It is clear that "the effective management of human resources in a firm to gain a competitive advantage requires *timely and accurate information* on current employees and potential employees in the labor market."[7]

SPOTLIGHT ON DATA AND ANALYTICS
Talent Analytics for Retention

©iStock.com/RiverNorthPhotography

HR analytics has many uses, and companies have started leveraging data collected during and after hiring employees to predict and manage retention. Companies can link a wide variety of information at their disposal to employee turnover and determine the strongest drivers of turnover. Identifying employees at risk of turnover may then be used to develop targeted interventions for those employees. For example, the telecommunications company Sprint found that employees who have not signed up for the company's retirement program are at risk of leaving shortly after being hired.

In addition to identifying predictors of turnover, many companies examine low work engagement and job satisfaction as early and lagged indicators of turnover. This means that conducting regular surveys and tracking results and metrics over time will be helpful. For example, JetBlue Airways created a "crewmember net promoter score," which asks employees their willingness to recommend the company as a place to work. Net promoter scores are usually used to measure customer satisfaction, but JetBlue asks this question to all new hires on their hire dates, which means the company can regularly track these data.

Simply tracking satisfaction and engagement data may not achieve the goal of reducing employee turnover: The company will need to intervene using these data. The food service company Sysco tracks satisfaction ratings of its delivery associates and intervenes when satisfaction drops below a certain point. Using this methodology, the company was able to increase its retention rate from 65% to 85%.

It is also possible to identify the specific employees who are at risk for turnover for intervention purposes. At Credit Suisse, once employees with high turnover risk were identified, internal recruiters called employees to notify them about internal openings. This method allowed the firm to retain employees who might have left the company otherwise. Preemptive intervention is often a better strategy than providing a counteroffer to an employee who gets a job offer.

At the same time, companies will need to be careful in what type of data they use and how they intervene. It is technically possible for businesses to monitor how much time employees spend in networking sites such as LinkedIn or to use data from employee badges to see which employees may be interviewing at other locations within the company. Then the manager of the employee may have a conversation with at-risk employees about whether they are happy about their jobs. Although there is value in having career-related conversations with employees, this situation may quickly evolve into a "Big Brother is watching" scenario, violating employee feelings of trust, privacy, and fairness, depending on how the manager broaches the subject. Any intervention with individuals or groups of employees should reflect a genuine concern for employee well-being and career goals in order to be useful for turnover reduction.[8]

The Value of Automated, Employee-Centered HR Functionality

Chapters 1 and 2 point out the trend in HRM is moving away from processing paperwork and more transactional interactions toward more strategic work. We have discussed the benefits of this approach in terms of time and cost savings as HR becomes more efficient. However, it also means better customer service for employees. Rather than waiting for HR to process paperwork, answer questions, or implement changes, employees now have access to their HR systems 24 hours a day, 7 days a week. Some questions are escalated to HR professionals, but many of their more routine questions can be answered anytime and anywhere. Research shows that the perceived ease of use and perceived usefulness of an HRIS are related to higher job satisfaction and lower turnover intentions.[9] Thus, moving toward automated, employee-centered HR functionality meets two goals. First, it enables employees to access information more quickly and to verify the accuracy of the data, as they can view and detect inaccuracies more readily, which helps them feel more satisfied with their jobs.[10] Second, because HR data are increasingly accessible via the web or the cloud, data from across the organization can be retrieved and merged with greater ease, enabling timely and efficient analysis of the data for HR decision making.

Data Availability for Metrics and Analytics

The theme of technology has played a revolutionary role in the evolution of HRM. In order to make data-informed people decisions, data must be accessible. As experts state, "Data are the lifeblood of an organization."[11] As the Society for Human Resource Management (SHRM) notes, trends such as the growth of social networking and the rise in data analytics and dashboards have fundamentally changed what HR needs.[12] Another HR expert, John Sullivan, shares his thoughts about the importance of HR metrics: "I have found the largest single difference between a great HR department and an average one is the use of metrics . . . bar none, there is nothing you can do to improve yours and your department's performance that succeeds the impact of using metrics."

Having a clear data management plan and having an effective HRIS in place are critical aspects to HR analytics success, and an HRIS update, upgrade, or reenvisioning is a great opportunity to fix problems and set up the organization for success for becoming more deeply data informed when making people decisions. These are important considerations in avoiding huge problems and generating solutions while there is time to plan.

Data Quality

An important point to remember when thinking about metrics and analytics is the importance of gathering high-quality data, which starts with sound measurement. Recall from Chapter 2 that a *measure* is a tool or method used to gather data about a concept. Without sound measurement, we cannot state with any confidence whether we consistently or accurately measured a concept. With poor measurement techniques, we become susceptible to low-quality (e.g., unreliable) data—also known as "garbage data." When garbage data are collected, it does not matter how we analyze the data, as the findings and interpretations will be of low quality (e.g., invalid)—also known as "garbage findings." This phenomenon is referred to as "garbage in, garbage out," or GIGO (see Figure 3.3).

Data Structure and Storage

Databases are designed to store structured data, and a common approach to adding structure to data is to use tables, whereby the rows represent distinct entities (e.g., individual employees) and the columns represent unique fields or variables that characterize the entities (e.g., employee start date, address, job title). Databases and data warehouses were designed to deal with such data. However, with the rise of semistructured and unstructured data, new forms of storage are needed. Thus, data lakes are a solution that many organizations are turning to, because unlike

■ **FIGURE 3.3** Garbage In, Garbage Out (GIGO) Phenomenon

Below is an illustration of the "garbage in, garbage out" (GIGO) phenomenon. Analysts must collect high-quality data through sound measurement to ensure that subsequent analysis yields meaningful findings and interpretations. If poor data are used, useful conclusions cannot be drawn, regardless of how big the sample or how sophisticated the analytics.

Data

Analysis

Findings and Interpretation

Photos via Shutterstock

a data warehouse, a **data lake** stores a vast amount of raw data in its native format. Technology companies are meeting demand for data lakes such as with Microsoft's Azure and offerings by Amazon Web Services and IBM Analytics. Typically, these platforms allow users to use the open-source software framework called Apache Hadoop, which helps users process vast amounts of data across clustered computers. There are pros and cons to each storage approach, but at this point, consider what types of data you might have access to now and in the future, and plan data storage options accordingly and with the future in mind.

Data lake Stores a vast amount of raw data in its native (and often unstructured) format

Data Visualizations

Although HRIS, HR metrics, and HR analytics are critical for making data-informed people decisions, effective data visualizations and **storytelling with data** can help facilitate the interpretation and communication of the findings. Today, HR professionals and managers use data visualizations to understand, predict, explain, and communicate their human capital challenges and opportunities based on available data. And data visualizations are useful tools for telling a compelling story about HR data.

Part of telling an effective story with data is knowing how to drill down to and communicate the most important findings. In other words, analyzing data can be quite complex, and thus, a good storyteller understands how to craft a straightforward, simple, and comprehensible narrative. Doing so requires striking a careful balance between engaging the audience and remaining faithful to the analytical findings derived from the data. As the saying goes, "A picture is worth a thousand words." Effective data visualizations play an important role when interpreting and communicating data and data-analytic findings in a succinct way. In fact, research even shows that the way in which data are presented visually has an effect on how data are interpreted and which decisions are ultimately

Storytelling with data Communicating data in a manner that brings it to life for the audience with a focus on simplicity and ease of interpretation and comprehension

HR IN ACTION
Valero Energy Gets Analytical

©iStock.com/USA-TARO

When Dan Hilbert arrived as manager of Employment Services at Valero Energy, he wasn't quite sure what he wanted or needed to do. Coming from a background in operations, he was used to having information about the effectiveness of all current operations; yet, as he quickly learned, these data were not available for HR operations and programs, nor were there systems in place to generate them. He recognized the potential value of having even simple descriptive statistics about the organization's people, and its operations to highlight potential opportunities and how changes in these values could signal potential problems. However, since these data were not currently available or easily developed, he created a small team, consisting of one HR staff member who could help get access to data from the organization's current systems and a graduate student with a statistical background, who was hired as a part-time employee. The team's assignment was to collect data about the human capital in the organization in an effort to learn more about the organization and its people, which Dan was now charged with supporting.

The team's analysis highlighted a unique characteristic of the Valero workforce: all of its refinery managers were at least 55 years old. This meant that these managers, each with long tenure in one of the most critical positions for assuring operating success, would be eligible to retire in fewer than 10 years. Further, given that these managers had all joined the company at roughly the same time and had held these refinery manager positions for many years, the promotion pipeline for succession to the position was limited. In other words, promising managers who had joined the organization at lower managerial positions decided to leave the company when it was clear the upward opportunities were limited.

When Hilbert presented the results of this analysis and his conclusions to senior managers, they were shocked. No one had considered this issue of the aging of refinery managers and, likely, management would not have become aware of the situation until the refinery managers began to retire. By then, it would have been too late to act to get immediate replacements. Interestingly, as Valero's success increased and the stock price increased, the retirement age lowered, compounding the problem. The pipeline of trained managers capable of filling these positions internally would not have been sufficient to meet the demand created by the mass retirements, and the time to train them as refinery managers was lengthy. As a result, the computation of relatively simple metrics and analytics provided new insights on the current retirement status of employees. These data allowed management to engage in the training and development needed to build internal bench strength for this critical position prior to these managers retiring, likely saving the refinery millions in salary expense and reduced refinery performance.[13]

made. For example, adjusting the axis scaling of a scatterplot, as shown in Figure 3.4, can give the impression that two variables are more strongly correlated than they actually are, as the figure on the right seems to show a stronger pattern than the one on the left.[14] As such, it is important to be cognizant of the ways in which data visualization displays can be unintentionally or intentionally manipulated to affect the interpretations of different audiences. This means that choosing how to display data should be coupled with careful consideration of the ethical implications.

How does one begin to think through how to create the most effective data visualizations? Following work by experts on storytelling and data visualizations,[15] keep the following six points in mind when creating data visualizations:

1. *Understand the context*. When crafting a story, there are many ways to approach it; however, there are three key questions to ask at the highest level when thinking about storytelling. First, *what* do you want your audience to know after you are done? Second, *how* do you want them to feel? Finally, *what*, exactly, do you want them to do based on exposure to

■ **FIGURE 3.4**   Data Visualization With Scatterplots

The way in which data are presented using data visualizations can affect how the users interpret the data. Both scatterplots depict the same data; however, the x- and y-axis scaling for the scatterplot on the right is much larger, resulting in what appears to be a stronger relationship between Annual Sales and Variable Pay.

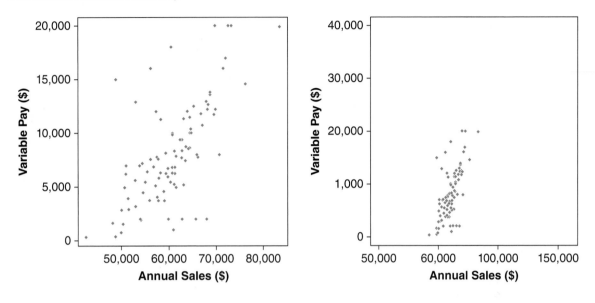

your presentation or report? In addition, it is important to determine the context, understand who your audience is, and determine the tone you want to take with them. For example, are you presenting in an informative, exploratory, or urgent way? It can be helpful to "boil down" your goal into a concise 2-minute story. If that is compelling, the presentation or written document stands a better chance of being clear and concise.

2. ***Choose an appropriate visual display***. Regarding data visualizations, there are many kinds of elements for displaying data to choose from, including simple text, tables, bar graphs, line graphs, scatterplots, heat maps, and geographic charts. Certain display types are appropriate for communicating certain types of data or for communicating different messages. For example, if there are a few key numbers that make a powerful statement, simple text might have the most impact. Alternatively, if you are interested in sharing a table full of numbers but want to emphasize patterns in the numbers, a heat map, as presented in Table 3.1, can be effective. Consider using one color for positive numbers and another for negative numbers. The key is to match your goals to an appropriate display.

    In addition, there are several tools that can help you generate data visualization, ranging from simple Microsoft Excel visuals or using SmartArt within the Microsoft Word program to more sophisticated tools such as Tableau Software and visuals generated using open-source R software. The tools available for creating data visualizations will continue to evolve, but understanding the basic principles behind effective data visualizations continues to be an important skill for managers and HR professionals alike.

3. ***Keep things simple***. By removing clutter and focusing on your main points in the most efficient and succinct manner, you make it easier for your audience to focus because you are minimizing the energy they need to process the new information. In other words, you are decreasing their cognitive load. If anything in your visual is unnecessary, *eliminate it*! An example of this is to avoid gridlines, borders, and unnecessary shading on graphs. As you see in Figure 3.5, the graph on the left looks fine, but the one on the right is simpler and clearer and communicates the trend more clearly.

TABLE 3.1   Heat Map Table

Heat map table displaying headcount by year and facility, such that darker green values represent larger head counts.

	YEAR 2011	2012	2013	2014	2015	2016	2017	2018
Seattle	750	1249	2000	2881	3465	3628	3631	3630
San Jose	4477	4101	3562	3414	3163	2711	2210	1989
Raleigh	2689	2678	2680	2695	2685	2692	2693	2701
Indianapolis	901	1235	1444	1489	1487	1600	1777	2099
Denver	5999	5725	5399	5453	5401	5395	5008	4822
Boston	2322	2333	2582	2611	2600	2791	2785	2786

FACILITY

Headcount
- 5000
- 4000
- 3000
- 2000
- 1000

FIGURE 3.5   Headcount Data Over Time

Two line graphs displaying the same headcount data over time. The graph on the right has less clutter in terms of gridlines and shading, which makes it easier to see the trend.

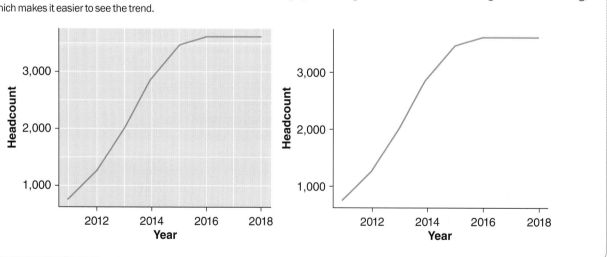

4. ***Focus attention where you want it.*** You can do this by using color and shading strategically. The use of color and bolding of lines and figures can help people see trends more quickly and accurately. Thus, as you can see in Figure 3.6, effective emphasis using color

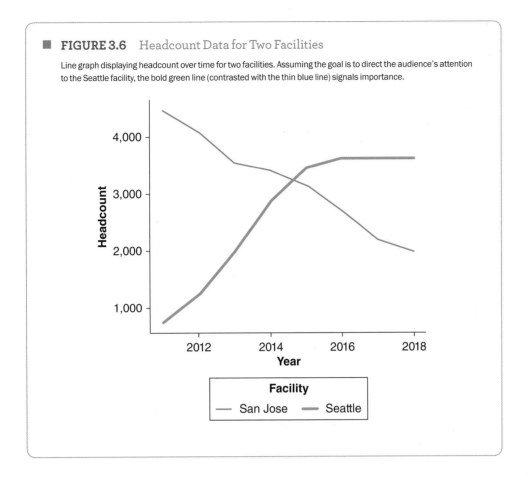

■ **FIGURE 3.6**   Headcount Data for Two Facilities

Line graph displaying headcount over time for two facilities. Assuming the goal is to direct the audience's attention to the Seattle facility, the bold green line (contrasted with the thin blue line) signals importance.

Facility

—— San Jose   —— Seattle

and shading is a factor to consider when it comes to data visualizations. However, please keep in mind that when it comes to color, less is more. Use it sparingly.

5. ***Think like a designer.*** You may have heard the phrase form follows function. It is an important phrase for designers, as it helps them focus their work. In our case, the function is what we want the audience to do with the data, and the form is the visualization created to communicate this. Designers also focus on making things visually appealing, or attractive, which is a goal of design thinking.

6. ***Tell a persuasive story.*** Research tells us that one of the most effective ways to persuade individuals is through storytelling. As Cole Nussbaumer Knaflic writes, "At a fundamental level, a story expresses how and why life changes. Stories start with balance. Then something happens—an event that throws things out of balance."[16] This dramatic tension can feature data as the event that throws things off. Now you know something new, or a key point that you had not noticed has become salient. Stories have a beginning, a middle, and an end. Stories start by introducing the plot and building the context for the reader or audience. With the audience in mind, the introduction should address the "So what?" question and explain why they should care about the topic at hand. The middle describes what could be possible, given more context and detail, and allows you to discuss potential solutions for the issues raised. The end should focus on a specific call to action so that the audience truly understands what it is expected to do after hearing your story.

These six points can help guide the generation of data visualizations. However, the availability of data in the first place rests on the quality of the HRIS of your organization and your ability to gather and merge the data necessary to tell your story.

LO 3.3   Identify and address challenges for data management and HRIS.

Challenges for Data Management and HRIS

Although there are a great number of potential opportunities for data management and HRIS, challenges also exist. Being aware of them can help organizations proactively assess needs and manage potential threats to successful implementation. The challenges include cost, the lack of analytics skills in traditional HR skill sets, and privacy concerns.

Cost

Typical HRIS costs include time, money, and/or opportunity costs. With respect to budgeting time, it is important to think about the skill sets available within your organization versus hiring a consultant to help implement a project. The cost of an HRIS varies by organization, their needs, and the sales force of the software vendor. Note that a request for proposal (RFP) is a key part of the HRIS vendor selection process. Of course, another way to think about costs is to more fully consider the potentially large cost savings due to system automation. Such cost reductions might include time entry and attendance tracking, benefits administration, recruiting, training, payroll, and performance management, to name a few. For large organizations, conducting a formal return-on-investment (ROI) analysis is a good idea when dealing with projects this large. For smaller organizations, it may simply be a matter of finding a package or platform that meets their needs into the foreseeable future.

Traditional HR Skill Sets

In 2004, 80% of organizations had an HRIS, but fewer than 40% reported using it to generate data used in strategic decision making. By 2007, the use of HRIS in strategic decision making had increased, with some organizations creating a competitive advantage through their use of data-driven decision making.[17] That means that many HRIS projects stop short of their potential to enjoy greater efficiency and reduced costs. As organizations hire and train more and more individuals with critical thinking skills, data management skills, and data analytics skills, we anticipate that the HR departments will begin to collect and store more higher-quality data in their HRIS and will apply not only descriptive analytics but more sophisticated predictive and prescriptive analytics to inform and support decisions that impact the strategic objectives. In general, we expect HR to become more scientific.

Josh Bersin of Deloitte has found that it generally takes an organization between 5 and 8 years to put all the necessary pieces together in order to become a data-driven culture using data to inform decisions about people. This includes having the right people, processes, and infrastructure (such as hardware and software) in place. This is an important challenge, and as noted by *Forbes* columnist Vorhauser-Smith, "You can have access to the right data but without the right people to analyze it and—more importantly—act on it, what good is it?"[18] Indeed, researchers report that 80% of surveyed HR directors who were relatively early adopters of HRIS reported that HRIS improved their levels of information usefulness and information sharing. Fully 90% felt that HRIS added value.[19] Aligning the skill sets of those in HRM with the new realities of data and analytics is necessary to realize the full potential for HRM via HRIS. This is especially important because we know that HRIS expertise is one of the major factors related to HRIS success across 110 companies in 10 industry sectors.[20]

Data Privacy Concerns

With great amounts of data comes great responsibility. Because HRIS is a repository for personal data, safeguarding data and maintaining data privacy and security are foundational. To begin, ***data privacy*** refers to individuals' control over the collection, storage, access, and reporting of their personal data.[21] Research shows that individuals who are able to choose

Data privacy Individual's control over the collection, storage, access, and reporting of their personal data

the types of HR systems they use report lower privacy concerns and higher satisfaction with the system. They are especially sensitive to medical data, which may be used for insurance purposes, for example, to be available to those within the organization who make decisions regarding their careers, such as managers.[22] In accordance with the Fair Labor Standards Act of 1938 and other legislation, U.S. companies are required to maintain basic employee data, such as name, Social Security number, address, pay, and hours worked. Understandably, many employees would prefer that their personal data remain private, especially their pay or Social Security numbers. Employees grow concerned about their company's HRIS and data privacy when[23]

- supervisors are able to access employee data;
- employee data are used in employment and administrative decisions, as opposed to just HR planning purposes; and
- employees are unable to verify the accuracy of their own data.

Thus, an effective HRIS must guard against unauthorized access and disclosure of employees' personal data yet also allow employees to verify the accuracy of their own data. The rise of social media and scraping tools has turned the Internet into an enormous repository of data, where ***scraping and crawling tools*** include programs designed to scour and pull data from websites and other electronic sources in a systematic manner. In fact, a survey by SHRM in 2015 revealed that 84% of surveyed organizations recruited applicants using social media websites.[24]

Recognizability of an Individual's Data

The extent to which individual employee records can be recognized is largely dependent on how the data were collected in the first place. There are three terms to describe data in terms of recognizability: anonymous, confidential, and personally identifiable data. ***Anonymous data*** refers to those pieces of information that cannot be linked to any information that might link those responses to an individual, thereby disclosing the individual's identity. To be truly anonymous, data should be gathered without IP addresses, GPS coordinates, e-mail addresses, and demographic questions—all of which can be used to narrow down the respondent. ***Confidential data*** refers to data for which individuals' identities are known by the researchers due to the linking of a

Scraping and crawling tools Programs designed to scour and pull data from websites and other electronic sources in a systematic manner

Anonymous data Pieces of information that cannot be linked to any information that might identify an individual, thereby disclosing the individual's identity

Confidential data Information for which individuals' identities are known by the researchers due to the linking of a name or code but are not generally disclosed or reported

---

SPOTLIGHT ON LEGAL ISSUES

Scraping Data Can Lead to Big Legal Trouble

In 2010, a software engineer in Colorado named Pete Warden developed and deployed a program designed to "crawl" publicly available Facebook pages. In no time, he had gathered data from 500 million Facebook pages from 220 million Facebook users. The data gathered were identifiable, as they included names, locations, friends, and interests. In the interest of research, Mr. Warden created an anonymized version of the dataset and offered it to others to use.

However, this was not the end of his story. As Mr. Warden is quoted as saying, "Big data? Cheap. Lawyers? Not so much." Thus, in order to try to avoid

legal problems with Facebook, he deleted all copies of his dataset and never made it public. Data scraped or crawled (automatically extracted using computer software programs) from websites are subject to three major legal claims against their collection, including copyright infringement, the Computer Fraud and Abuse Act, and terms-of-use violations, among others. Subsequent data privacy issues emerged when Cambridge Analytica gathered data from Facebook users. These breaches of trust led Facebook to rethink which data are gathered and how much control users have over what is shared about them.[25]

Fitness Trackers and Data Privacy

Today, many organizations partner with vendors to address employee health and engagement. For example, with the goal of improving employee well-being for partnering organizations, Virgin Pulse provides employees with wearable devices and applications to track their sleep, stress, activity level, and other personal data. Companies like Virgin Pulse tout their commitment to data privacy, security, and compliance, thereby implying that employee data will not be shared in an unauthorized manner.

However, if an organization decided to provide employees with wearable devices instead of working through a third-party vendor like Virgin Pulse, this could pose an ethical dilemma under certain circumstances. Namely, without proper data privacy and compliance restrictions in place, the data could be used in ways that would compromise individuals' privacy and other personal rights. Although perhaps not illegal, HR professionals may run dangerously close to committing discrimination under the Americans with Disabilities Act (ADA) if they use

these data to make employment decisions. Poor or irregular sleep, for example, does not necessarily constitute a disability according to the ADA, but it could be an indicator of various physical diseases or psychiatric disorders, which are protected as disabilities under the ADA. Further, even if deemed legal, using employee health data in this manner could be construed as unethical, particularly if the data are used in a way that deviates from their intended use.[26]

Questions

1. How does the use of a third-party vendor like Virgin Pulse make it more ethical to have employees wear monitoring devices than it would be if the employer did so directly?

2. Do you think the use of monitoring devices should be optional for employees? How would you ensure that employees who opted out of using the device would not be penalized for nonparticipation?

---

name or code but are not generally disclosed or reported. This type of data is useful when dealing with sensitive issues such as salary, complaints, opinion survey responses, or exit interviews. In such cases, only those who need to know whose data they are have access to that information. *Personally identifiable data* refers to data that are readily linked to specific individuals.

The surprising thing with data recognizability is understanding how seemingly anonymous data, such as a query into a search engine, can give enough unique information to track that person down. For example, an IP address is a unique online identifier that may be tracked when a form is filled out or an online survey is taken. Although not 100% accurate, IP addresses can be used to identify a person or pinpoint their location, especially over a period of time as individuals travel to the same places (e.g., from their homes to work and back).

Social Security Numbers

One particularly sensitive issue is the safeguarding of Social Security numbers.[27] The Federal Trade Commission estimates that more than 9 million Americans have their identities stolen each year, and because Social Security numbers are such valuable targets to identity thieves, steps must be taken to ensure their safekeeping. Such steps include keeping all Social Security number information in secured locations (both virtually and physically) and allowing access from authorized-access computer stations. Only individuals with legitimate business reasons should have access. Any documents released should be destroyed by shredding, and all state and federal laws should be followed regarding the collection, storage, and destruction of Social Security numbers.

Data Security Concerns

Like data privacy, data security is a primary concern of both employees and managers. *Data security* refers to protective measures taken to prevent unauthorized access to employee data and to preserve the confidentiality and integrity of the data.[28] *Cybersecurity* can be thought

Personally identifiable data Data readily linked to specific individuals

Data security Protective measures taken to prevent unauthorized access to employee data and to preserve the confidentiality and integrity of the data

Cybersecurity Data security applied to information accessible through the Internet

of as data security applied to information accessible through the Internet. Data security can be threatened by a number of entities and for a variety of reasons. While data hacks, attacks, and viruses are real threats, human error is a huge risk when it comes to data security. An information system can have the most sophisticated password protection and security features, but an unintentional human error could still wreak havoc. Imagine a scenario in which you are logged into your company's HRIS while working on a company laptop in a coffee shop. You hear the barista announce your coffee order is ready and step away from your laptop for a moment, forgetting to log out. After picking up your order, you walk back to your table, and to your astonishment, your laptop is gone! An innocent human error and lapse of judgment on your part has put employees' personal data at risk. Unfortunately, human error is inevitable, but we can do our best to prevent these errors by training managers and employees on data security and providing rules and guidelines for protecting people data.

In 2010, Google purchased the large and historic Port Authority Terminal building in New York City for $1.9 billion. It is the fourth-largest building in the city. In addition to its size, another attractive feature of the building is that after it opened in 1932, it eventually sat atop one of the main fiber-optic arteries in NYC, making it strategically desirable for data transmission.[30]

As a relatively recent example, the U.S. Office of Personnel Management (OPM), a federal agency that manages many of the federal government's human resources, suffered an attack. In the summer of 2015, hackers stole more than 20 million current and former federal employees' work and personal data, including birthdates, Social Security numbers, and fingerprint records.[29] In the year that followed, it came to light that OPM was using outdated information systems in need of serious improvements, thereby putting OPM at risk for the data breach. Since the data breach took place, the American Federation of Government Employees has filed a class-action suit against OPM. Thus, beyond damages to its reputation and putting individuals' personal information at risk, the government stands to lose financially too. In addition, it is likely that federal employees lost trust in OPM's ability to secure their personal data, and if this is the case, OPM will need to regain the trust of its employees when it comes to data privacy and security.

Approaches for Maintaining Data Security

There are several common approaches for ensuring data security. Some are technological, including requiring strong passwords, training users, using two-step authentication, and applying blockchain technology. Other approaches have to do with proper training of the users of data.

Technological Security Measures Increasingly complex passwords are something that we are all familiar with as we are creating and maintaining online accounts. As we now realize that human error is a large factor in many data breaches, it is important to realize that one of the ways these problems manifest themselves is via lack of password security, such as passwords being written down near computers, remembered by computers, or shared with others. In addition, as computing power increases, it becomes easier for computer programs to be able to decode passwords. It might be surprising to know that Mark Zuckerberg, founder of Facebook, has had his Pinterest, LinkedIn, and Twitter accounts hacked.[31] Although many websites allow only a few attempts before locking out users, it is still advisable to select strong passwords, not to reuse the same password across multiple accounts, and to change your passwords to important sources of information frequently.

An extra layer of security can be had in the form of ***two-step authentication*** (also known as ***multifactor authentication***), an additional piece of information that only the user knows. For example, Apple computer, iPhone, or iPad users may be familiar with this authentication process when any new device is seeking to access Apple ID information. Of course, two-step authentication works well when you are in possession of your devices, but if a thief has access to both and they are not sufficiently password protected, that can be a bigger problem.

Two-step authentication (multifactor authentication) An extra layer of security that requires an additional piece of information that only the user would know

©iStock.com/designer491

MANAGER'S TOOLBOX
Tips for Creating Strong Passwords

Some of the tips for creating strong passwords are obvious, such as not writing down the password anywhere physically near your computer. However, other tips are not so obvious. The following are some key considerations when dealing with password management, including creating passwords:

- **Long.** The longer the better, with 8 or more characters currently recommended.

- **Contain numbers, letters, and symbols.** There are only 26 letters in the alphabet and 10 numbers. So mixing them up and using symbols helps to create more powerful passwords, which are exponentially more challenging to decode.

- **Include both upper- and lowercase letters.** Using both uppercase and lowercase letters creates more options for the user and makes it tougher for hackers to crack your password.

- **Unique.** Some of the most common passwords include 123456, qwerty, Password, starwars, and admin. It is estimated that 10% of people have used at least one of the worst (because they are commonly known) passwords on this list, with nearly 3% using 123456 alone.

- **Generated randomly.** There are random password generators available online. Although they make remembering passwords more challenging, they are more secure than using actual words. Using a password manager such as LastPass can help with that part, but such a treasure trove of information can be a highly attractive target for hackers, and even that company, LastPass, was hacked in 2015.

Blockchain A distributed incorruptible digital technology infrastructure that maintains a fully encoded database that serves as a ledger where all transactions are recorded and stored

©iStock.com/anyaberkut

Access requiring two-step authentication may require a verification code even if the user knows the username and password.

Technology has and will continue to shape the way HR is managed and implemented in a number of ways. *Forbes* declared 2018 to be the year that blockchain "establishes itself as the fastest-growing digital technology since the evolution of the Internet."[32] To that end, blockchain is poised to disrupt the current practice of HR. **Blockchain** is "a distributed incorruptible digital technology infrastructure which maintains a fully encoded database that serves as a ledger where all transactions are recorded and stored."[33] It has also been more simply described as an approach that "provides a decentralized and secure ledger that gives participating parties a way of validating the information related to a secure transaction."[34] Because it is more secure than other technology available today, it has the potential to be used in compensation, background checks, recruiting, and other HR functions in ways that we can only imagine at this point (and other ways that likely we cannot yet imagine). Although blockchain is relatively new and will continue to evolve rapidly in terms of its applications to business broadly and HR specifically, it is important to include it in our discussion of potential data security tools. Maintaining data security is especially consequential given that 1.4 billion data records were compromised in 2016, and experts predict that by 2020, 25% of the world's population will be affected by data breaches.[35]

SPOTLIGHT ON GLOBAL ISSUES

The General Data Protection Regulation (GDPR)

The General Data Protection Regulation (GDPR) is a regulation in European Union law regarding data protection and privacy that went into effect in 2018. Anyone working globally should be aware of GDPR and understand its rules and implications. Essentially, the law states that the European Union's (EU's) 500 million citizens have the "right to be forgotten." This means that companies that continue to collect and store data will face major fines and penalties of up to 4% of their annual worldwide revenue or 20 million euros (whichever one is the larger amount).[36] This is a major consideration for multinational companies, as this far-reaching law states that companies need to provide a "reasonable level" of protection for employees' personal data, but it does not explicitly define what reasonable protection is exactly.

Companies affected are those that have:

- a presence in an EU country, or no presence in the EU but process data of EU residents; and

- more than 250 employees or fewer than 250 employees but whose data processing impacts the rights and freedoms of data subjects more than occasionally or includes sensitive data.

A 2017 survey by PwC found that 92% of the companies surveyed viewed this law as one of their top data privacy and security priorities.[37]

User Training   One of the major entry points for data security breaches is human error, which is the number-one cause of data breaches, especially for small and medium-sized businesses.[38] Thus, it makes sense to consider training as an essential part of a data security program. Training might include awareness of key security issues, ethics and compliance when dealing with sensitive data, and security training for new employees or those moving to more information-sensitive positions within the company. There are several steps to consider when training employees, starting with a needs assessment aligned with the desired outcomes of the training. Many organizations have developed and offer such training programs for organizations not wishing to develop programs themselves. The key is to make sure the right employees are taking the training and engaging in safe data management behaviors.

Developing a Human Resource Information System

LO 3.4   Describe basic technical aspects of developing an HRIS.

As you have seen so far in this chapter, a complex and comprehensive HRIS can be a costly and time-consuming undertaking for an organization. Before deciding whether to do so and how, organizations are well advised to systematically work through a step-by-step process for evaluating the needs and feasibility of implementing an HRIS (see Figure 3.7).[39] After that, it is important to outline the features needed in such a system, to select a vendor, and to engage in activities designed to control costs.

Conducting a Needs Assessment

The process of conducting a needs assessment for an HRIS is much like what you will read about in Chapter 8 on training and development needs assessments. The ideas are parallel, in order to be sure that you design the right program by conducting an analysis of what exists, what should change, and what factors might hinder successful implementation. Thus, the best plan can be

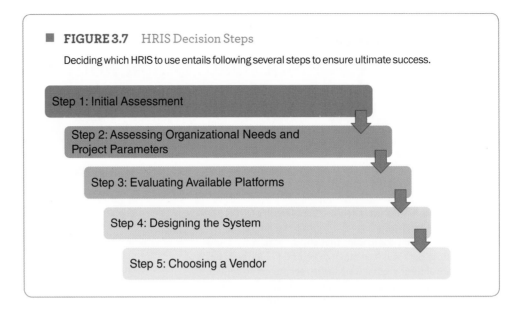

■ **FIGURE 3.7**   HRIS Decision Steps

Deciding which HRIS to use entails following several steps to ensure ultimate success.

Step 1: Initial Assessment

Step 2: Assessing Organizational Needs and Project Parameters

Step 3: Evaluating Available Platforms

Step 4: Designing the System

Step 5: Choosing a Vendor

developed to deal with potential setbacks and challenges during implementation, including identifying the key stakeholders who should be involved in the process.

Initial Assessment

In the initial assessment phase, a key question is whether the selection process is best led by internal HR individuals or whether engaging the services of an HRIS consultant to help with the process makes the most sense given time, experience, and cost factors. For example, if there seems to be a strong need for a new HRIS but the HR staff does not have a great deal of time or expertise in this area, it probably makes sense to bring in a consultant to help facilitate the process. During this phase, it is important to gain buy-in from management and key stakeholders by including them in the conversation; failure to do so may result in hurdles later on in the development and implementation process, as ultimately management and certain stakeholders may be gatekeepers to key resources.

Assess Organizational Needs

The next major activity is to assess organizational needs. The goal is to develop a system that meets all the current organizational needs as well as having room to expand in the future. Every organization will have a different set of needs, but all share some common goals with an HRIS, including the need to have a system that allows them to gather, organize, and securely maintain employee data. The system also has to allow for the generation of standardized compliance and strategic HR reports such as EEO, VETS-100, new hires, and turnover. Beyond that, the goal of this step is to determine the needed features of a potential system versus the wanted features of the system.

Many systems allow for optional HR-relevant modules to be added, such as compensation, benefits, onboarding, and performance management modules. However, the needs of the specific organization's HR functions and strategy will determine the specific configuration. One thing to keep in mind is the need for system integration. It is one thing to "have" the data, and as many organizations find out, it is a very different thing to access, retrieve, and merge such data.

Having standalone modules within HR that do not have the capability to link data with other organizational systems is not optimal. Thus, another key factor to consider in the needs assessment phase is various ways to handle the merging and joining of data from different databases. Finally, research consistently finds that understanding users' individual needs is a critical component of success when developing a new HRIS.[40]

SPOTLIGHT ON HR FOR SMALL AND MEDIUM-SIZED BUSINESSES

The Advantage of Starting From Scratch

As you saw in the opening case and throughout this chapter, changing, merging, and coordinating the computer systems of a multinational corporation is a major undertaking. Larger organizations are more likely to adopt HRIS systems.[41] However, in some respects, small and medium-sized businesses may actually have some advantages over their larger counterparts. Although they may have less working capital and leaner staffing, they may be better positioned to design their systems from scratch. That means that the system can start small and grow with the firm. Additionally, the latest technology translates into fewer headaches for small or medium-sized organizations, as larger organizations typically have to adapt dozens of legacy systems into newer ones. For small and medium-sized businesses, designing an HRIS is predicated on the assumption that the adopted platform can scale as the firm grows.

It might seem counterintuitive for small to medium-sized businesses to automate their HR systems when manually processing HR transactions is possible given the smaller numbers of employees. However, the efficiencies that come with an HRIS for smaller companies can be transformational. Namely, an HRIS can automate many transactional HR activities, which otherwise take up a lot of HR professionals' time, especially in small companies where there might only be one or a handful of HR professionals. Further, e-HRM, in general, allows smaller companies (and larger companies) to outsource HR functions in a way that can still electronically (potentially) integrate with their other HR functions that they do in-house. Finally, with advances in cloud computing, companies no longer need to house and manage their own servers and other costly hardware.

Designing the System

After identifying a list of minimum requirements and additional "wish list" items, assessing project parameters comes next, including budgetary, technological, and time constraints. Being as explicit and honest about these at this stage allows organizations to focus on features that are both feasible and desirable. These will lead directly into the design of the HRIS.

Two related but distinct factors are important to consider. These are logical design and physical design. On the one hand, *logical design* refers to the translation of business requirements into improved business processes.[42] For example, HR might identify all of the steps in the recruitment process, as well as the types of data that will be exchanged and stored. Often *data flow diagrams*, such as the one pictured in Figure 3.8, are used to depict the old and/or new business processes.

Logical design The translation of business requirements into improved business processes

Data flow diagrams Depict the logical design of how data move from one entity to the next and how data are processed within an information system

■ **FIGURE 3.8** Data Flow Diagram Excerpt

This excerpt from a data flow diagram depicts the logical design of a performance management system.

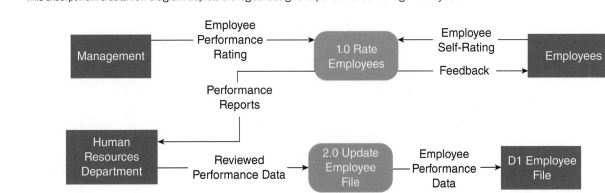

As the name implies, data flow diagrams show how data flow from one entity to the next, as well as how the data are processed.

On the other hand, *physical design* refers to determining the most effective way to translate business processes into the software and hardware solutions that make those processes a reality. For example, information technology experts might take the logical design of a recruitment system designed by HR and determine the software and hardware needed to bring the system to life and to integrate with other existing systems. As a general rule, the logical design (including process and data requirements) should precede the physical design (including both the associated hardware and software), as sometimes the logical design will reveal that the current physical design is actually fine and, thus, just the process needs to be changed.

Physical design The actual software and hardware solutions used to translate business processes into an actual information system

Selecting a Vendor

The first step in choosing a vendor is creating a list of what you want the HRIS to be able to accomplish. This list is included in a request for proposal (RFP), which is sent to several potential vendors. When writing an RFP, important considerations include the price and the configuration of the plan. For example, does the organization seek to purchase and install the hardware and software on internal machines staffed by internal staff? Or is the organization interested in software as a service so that a subscription to software makes sense and employees access the software via the Internet? There are, of course, pros and cons to either approach, so it is important to be clear regarding which of these options is desirable and viable when sending out the RFP. Small to medium-sized companies find the software-as-a-service option to be particularly attractive, as software can be accessed via web browsers without having to install it on local computers and other devices, such as tablets and smartphones. Easy access to HR systems and information paves the way for useful employee self-service functions such as benefits enrollment, tax information, and updating employee contact information, as well as more sophisticated functions such as access to onboarding materials, training and development programs, and performance management systems.

Identifying references is also important when considering different vendors. As the SHRM toolkit on designing and managing an HRIS notes, any reputable developer or reseller should provide references from current clients of similar size with comparable business processes.[43]

SHRM recommends that HR professionals ask vendors' references questions like these:

- How has the system improved HR functions?

- What modules are you using?

- Has the system met your expectations? If not, what is it missing?

- Are end users satisfied with the system?

- Has the system been expanded or upgraded since the original purchase? If so, how did the upgrade affect customizations and other features?

- How has the vendor responded to any problems?

- What do you like best about the system? What do you like least?

- Has the system provided the expected ROI? Why or why not?

- What was the implementation experience like? Did the vendor deliver on budget and on schedule?

After reviewing the different proposals that the organization receives and checking with vendor references, the selection committee should invite two to three vendors to give a demonstration of the HRIS platform to stakeholders within the organization. Finally, taking into consideration all of the available information, one vendor should be selected and a contract finalized. Among others, key points to consider in the contract are pricing, technical and maintenance support, and upgrades.

Implementing a Human Resource Information System

LO 3.5 Address key points of the process of HRIS implementation.

To this point, we have walked through the points to consider when considering, designing, and choosing a package. Next comes implementation. Although HRIS has the potential to transform organizations, and we covered several examples of HRIS successes, researchers note, "The available evidence suggests that in the vast majority of cases information technology (IT)–enabled HRIS have not helped produce a wholesale transformation of the HR function away from routine processing and compliance and towards the strategic business partner role that many were expecting."[44] Many of the challenges that get in the way of the potential benefits of HRIS are encountered during the implementation phase. Luckily, when it comes to implementing and maintaining an HRIS, there are some key points to consider in helping to ensure a successful project launch and ongoing implementation.

Managing Resistance to Change

Implementing a major HRIS or changing the way that data are gathered, stored, and retrieved can be a major change within an organization, and it can be challenging to handle effectively. It is not only about the software and hardware; it is also about the individuals whose work lives will be impacted by the change in procedures, job descriptions, and access to information. Thus, it is an organizational change process that must be managed, and such processes are, at their heart, people management challenges as well as opportunities. When it comes to changes to an HRIS, three specific groups are most likely impacted: those working in HR, who may have their work practices fundamentally altered; managers, who may have more access to information than ever before, which increases expectations of them; and employees, who may be asked to engage in more self-service HR activities than in the past. It is understandable that such behaviors might trigger concerns for organizational members.[45] In addition, we discuss other factors related to successful and unsuccessful change management attempts beyond understanding resistance to change.

"What if we don't change at all ... and something magical just happens?"

©iStock.com/andrewgenn

People react to change in a variety of ways, ranging from active resistance to enthusiastic support, as depicted in Figure 3.9. Given that a survey of 1,400 executives found that 82% see the pace of change in their organizations increasing and that a SHRM survey found that resistance to change is one of the top two reasons change efforts fail, it is not surprising that overcoming resistance to changes such as a new HRIS is an important part of the process.[46] Some individuals may also experience ambivalence to change, which is an opportunity to move them toward a positive attitude.[47] The closer to support that you can get individuals, the more likely the change implementation is to be successful. Whereas compliance is more helpful than passive or active resistance, the lack of enthusiasm can lead to short-lived gains, especially in the face of potential challenges or setbacks during implementation. Avon learned this the hard way when employees left in "meaningful numbers" following a challenging multiyear software overhaul project that was initially rolled out in Canada. Given the challenges during implementation, Avon opted to halt use of the new system and not to roll it out to the rest of the organization.[48] Thus, part of effective change management is knowing when to change course, as Avon did.

Effective managers learn to overcome resistance to change. That doesn't mean that changes always go exactly as planned or as the manager wants, but it does mean that they actively take steps to ensure a positive outcome. You might have a great idea, but people around you might not seem convinced, and/or they might express resistance. How do you make change happen?

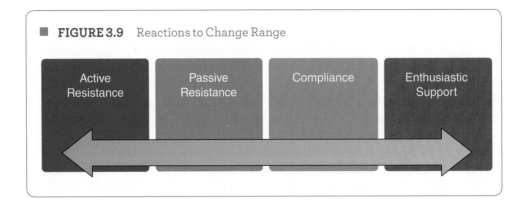

■ FIGURE 3.9   Reactions to Change Range

| Active Resistance | Passive Resistance | Compliance | Enthusiastic Support |

We recommend that you:

- recognize individuals may react negatively to change and plan accordingly,
- anticipate resistance and find ways to deal with it,
- listen to naysayers,
- show commitment and present a positive attitude toward the change,
- involve people in the process,
- ensure top management is visible and supportive,
- remind management and others that change is a process and successful change takes time,
- present data to your audience,
- appeal to your audience's ideals,
- reinforce change with incentives,
- communicate with employees and management,
- understand the reasons for resistance, and
- alter your approach if necessary.[49]

Organizational Culture and Realistic Timelines for Change

Part of understanding what is or is not a realistic timeline relates to understanding the organizational culture.[50] Is the culture one that embraces risk taking, or is the culture more conservative when it comes to change? Cultures vary in terms of how much they embrace collaboration, creating, controlling, or competing.[51] Because *clan cultures* are collaboration oriented and are characterized by valuing being cohesive, people oriented, team players, and empowering employees, when implementing change and setting timelines, consider doing so after involving all affected internal stakeholders in the decision-making process. For *adhocracy cultures,* which focus on creating and emphasize being entrepreneurial and flexible, taking risks, and being creative, aggressive timelines may be feasible and even encouraged. For *market cultures,* which are characterized by competition and value being aggressive, competitive, and customer-oriented, changes in the ways things are done can be challenging if they take more time. Although the long-term payoff may exist, the time urgency within market cultures can make time one of the most salient concerns of employees. *Hierarchy cultures* focus on controlling and value being efficient and timely, and consistent strategies that emphasize the efficiency of HRIS changes may offset concerns regarding the short-term challenges during the transition and training period.

Successful implementation of HRIS or any ERP depends on creating and utilizing realistic timelines regarding how long each step will take and when a complete switch-over can be undertaken. In 1999, three years after starting a transition to a new ERP, Hershey's was unable to fulfill $100 million worth of Kiss and Jolly Rancher candy orders due to a failed ERP transition. Part of the reason for this failure has been attributed to its attempt to set tight timelines without sufficiently changing them when things went wrong.[52]

Refreezing and Maintaining the New System

When approaching a major change such as a new HRIS, consider simple heuristics to help understand the key steps to follow during implementation. One such model was developed by Kurt Lewin in the 1940s. It is a simple model of change that many people continue to find useful even today. This involves three steps: ***unfreezing*** the current system and checking to see that individuals are ready for change, enacting the ***change***, and ***refreezing*** the new system in place so that it becomes the permanent replacement for the way things used to be done. Each phase is depicted in Figure 3.10 and features a unique set of opportunities and challenges. Much has been written about change management, and students interested in learning more about how to effectively enact and manage change are encouraged to read material covered in other courses such as "Organizational Behavior" or "Organizational Development."

Effective change managers are able to avoid the key reasons for systems failures by making sure sufficient and effective leadership is present, planning is well executed, change management best practices are followed, effective communication is present throughout the HRIS exploration and implementation process, and employees have sufficient training and support for the new systems.[53] Researchers have also identified five key areas for effective change champions to focus on during a change management process.[54] These include:

- creating the case for change,
- creating structural change,
- engaging others in the process and building commitment,
- implementing and sustaining change, and
- facilitating and developing capability.

Unfreezing Step 1 in the Lewin model of change, which refers to the process of unfreezing the current system and checking to see that individuals are ready for change

Change The second step in the Lewin model of change, this refers to enacting the change

Refreezing The third and final step in the Lewin change model, this step refers to refreezing the new system in place so that it becomes the permanent replacement for the way things used to be done

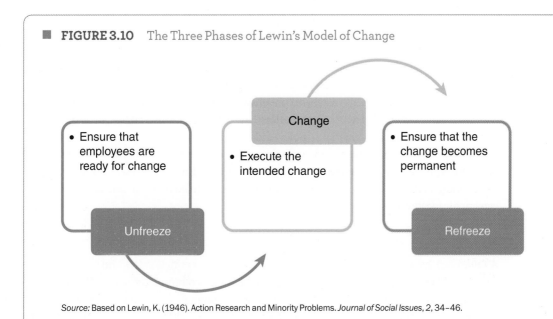

■ FIGURE 3.10   The Three Phases of Lewin's Model of Change

Source: Based on Lewin, K. (1946). Action Research and Minority Problems. *Journal of Social Issues, 2,* 34–46.

Following an effective unfreezing and subsequent change process, the next steps are to refreeze and maintain the change, which, in this case, means to solidify and stabilize the desired employee attitudes and behaviors in relation to the HRIS. During the refreeze and maintenance phases, organizations should consider several key questions: What will be needed to keep the new HRIS working effectively? How often will the effectiveness of the new HRIS be evaluated? When will updates be considered, and how will they be implemented? Who trains users on the new HRIS and associated changes, updates, and upgrades? Thinking through these questions initially as part of the process of HRIS feasibility helps avoid unpleasant surprises down the line. Research finds that employee attitudes and behaviors are affected by leadership before, during, and after an organizational change, which means that management involvement in the change process from start to finish is critical.[55]

Getting Technical: Core Information System Concepts

LO 3.6 Apply core information system concepts in HR management.

It is clear that data and how they are gathered, stored, and retrieved are critical to the ability of those within organizations to engage in effective analytics. Now that we have delved into the intricacies of designing and implementing an HRIS, we define some core concepts and terms that are integral for understanding what a generic information system is and how it operates. Specifically, in the following sections, we describe concepts associated with databases, users, and architectures.

Database Management

Database An organized collection of data that is both stored and accessed electronically

In simple terms, a ***database*** refers to a collection of organized data, its structure designed to facilitate the realization of business processes. A ***database management system (DBMS)*** refers to the software used to manage and maintain a database or multiple databases. For example, today's organizations commonly use applicant tracking systems—a type of DBMS—to collect, manage, analyze, and evaluate applicant data and the various processes associated with recruitment and selection efforts that might necessitate the flow of applicant data from one data store (or collection) to another and through different processes. Organizations commonly design their information systems around what is referred to as a relational database; however, it is becoming increasingly common for organizations to store data in an unstructured manner as well.

Database management system (DBMS) The software used to manage and maintain a database or multiple databases

A ***relational database*** is a specific type of database in which different subsets or collections of data are integrated through pieces of information residing within the data themselves. This avoids the need to include duplicate data in multiple locations within the database. Thus, data stored in different parts of the relational database can be linked through common identification number fields. For example, if a relational database contains a table filled with employee performance evaluation data and a table filled with compensation data, data from the two tables can be merged if a common field, such as one containing employee identification numbers, is present in both tables.

Relational database A specific type of database in which different subsets or collections of data are integrated through pieces of information residing within the data themselves

The software used to manage and maintain a relational database is referred to as a ***relational database management system (relational DBMS).*** Because different data sources can be linked in a relational DBMS, data are more readily shared by users from different functional areas and geographic locations.

Relational database management system (relational DBMS) The software used to manage and maintain a relational database

Table

Table A database object used to store data about cases and to add structure to the data

A ***table*** is a database object used to store data about cases (i.e., entities) and to add structure to the data. Often, a table takes the form of a matrix in which each column represents a different characteristic (or attribute) of cases and each row represents a unique case (or entity; see Table 3.2). In the absence of a table, data would be left unstructured, adding challenges regarding manipulating,

TABLE 3.2   An Example of a Table Containing Employee Data

	EmployeeID	EmployeeName	Gender
1	RDEA120	Waller, Anderson	Male
2	RDEA122	Clark, Jose	Male
3	RDEA123	Benton, Cora	Female
4	RDEA124	Rich, Belen	Female
5	RDEA125	Vega, Alejandra	Female
6	RDEA126	Hickman, Lukas	Male
7	RDEA127	Phillips, Aracely	Female
8	RDEA128	Bonilla, Cody	Male
9	RDEA129	Chaney, Orion	Male
10	RDEA121	Day, Linda	Female

managing, and analyzing the data. Each column in a table that represents a unique characteristic is referred to as a *field* or *variable*, and each case in a table is a *record*. For example, in a table containing employee personal data, one field might include the employees' names, and another field might include the employees' home phone numbers—both of which are characteristics of the employees. In this scenario, each row represents a unique employee record, such that by reading across a single row in a table, one can see the characteristics of the employee, as defined by the fields.

Field (variable) A column in a table that represents a unique characteristic

Record A case in a database

Key Variable

A relational database is composed of two or more tables, which are "connected" via a key variable. A *key variable*—sometimes referred to as a *linking variable*—provides the information necessary to construct the relationships between tables. For example, in many HRISs, a unique identifier is given to each employee (e.g., employee identification number). As shown in Table 3.3, the employee identification number serves as a key variable between the employee personal information table and the sales table. Note how a unique employee identification number is associated with each record (i.e., employee) in the employee personal information table but that employee identification numbers appear multiple times in the sales table. As described earlier in the chapter, relational databases reduce data redundancies by limiting the amount of repetition of identical data. Key variables are, consequently, used to connect tables so as to avoid data redundancies, which contribute to the process of database normalization.

Key variable Provides the information necessary to construct the relationships between tables and to join (or merge) data from different tables

Form

A *form* is a database object that provides a user interface with which to enter, edit, and/or display data contained within a database. A well-designed form can facilitate the manner in which users interact with the database. Figure 3.11 shows an example of a form used for data entry, which, in this case, is used to enter applicant data from a paper application. To reduce the occurrence of data-entry errors, the form closely resembles the actual paper application. Often, these forms are directly connected to the data housed within the database, enabling users to update database objects (e.g., tables, queries) directly.

Form A database object that provides a user interface with which to enter, edit, and/or display data in a database

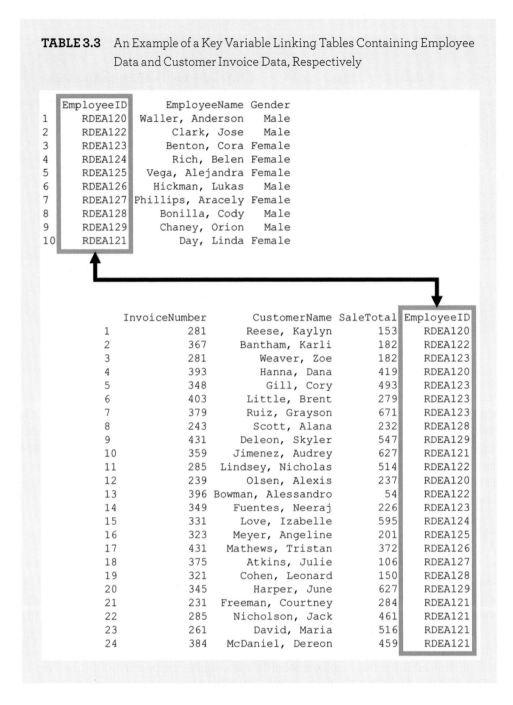

TABLE 3.3   An Example of a Key Variable Linking Tables Containing Employee Data and Customer Invoice Data, Respectively

	EmployeeID	EmployeeName	Gender
1	RDEA120	Waller, Anderson	Male
2	RDEA122	Clark, Jose	Male
3	RDEA123	Benton, Cora	Female
4	RDEA124	Rich, Belen	Female
5	RDEA125	Vega, Alejandra	Female
6	RDEA126	Hickman, Lukas	Male
7	RDEA127	Phillips, Aracely	Female
8	RDEA128	Bonilla, Cody	Male
9	RDEA129	Chaney, Orion	Male
10	RDEA121	Day, Linda	Female

	InvoiceNumber	CustomerName	SaleTotal	EmployeeID
1	281	Reese, Kaylyn	153	RDEA120
2	367	Bantham, Karli	182	RDEA122
3	281	Weaver, Zoe	182	RDEA123
4	393	Hanna, Dana	419	RDEA120
5	348	Gill, Cory	493	RDEA123
6	403	Little, Brent	279	RDEA123
7	379	Ruiz, Grayson	671	RDEA123
8	243	Scott, Alana	232	RDEA128
9	431	Deleon, Skyler	547	RDEA129
10	359	Jimenez, Audrey	627	RDEA121
11	285	Lindsey, Nicholas	514	RDEA122
12	239	Olsen, Alexis	237	RDEA120
13	396	Bowman, Alessandro	54	RDEA122
14	349	Fuentes, Neeraj	226	RDEA123
15	331	Love, Izabelle	595	RDEA124
16	323	Meyer, Angeline	201	RDEA125
17	431	Mathews, Tristan	372	RDEA126
18	375	Atkins, Julie	106	RDEA127
19	321	Cohen, Leonard	150	RDEA128
20	345	Harper, June	627	RDEA129
21	231	Freeman, Courtney	284	RDEA121
22	285	Nicholson, Jack	461	RDEA121
23	261	David, Maria	516	RDEA121
24	384	McDaniel, Dereon	459	RDEA121

Query

Query A question that is posed to a database

As the name implies, a *query* is a question that is posed to a database. Such questions can be used to perform a number of different actions. For example, a common use of queries is to retrieve certain segments or subsets of data from one or more tables within the database. A query can also be used to display and/or sort data, create new tables, manipulate data, or even perform a specified calculation. Queries come in handy when users find themselves posing the same question over and over again to the database. For example, if a manager wants to know how much sales revenue each member of her sales team generates each quarter, a query can be created that conducts the same actions, even when the data in the database are updated or changed. Commonly, structured query language (SQL) is used by

■ **FIGURE 3.11** Example of a Form

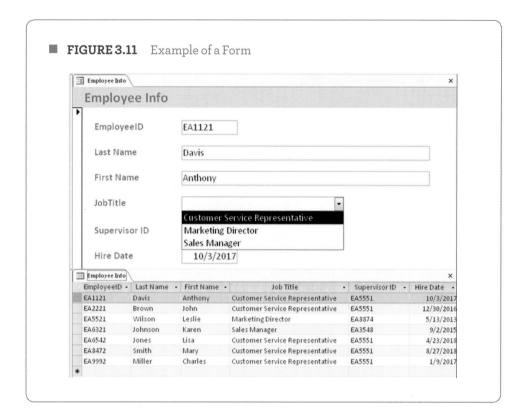

■ **FIGURE 3.12** An Example of a Simple Query to Compute Average of
Quantitative Data From a Column in a Table Using SQL

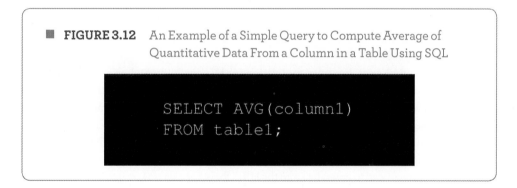

organizations to manage, maintain, and generate queries using their DBMS. Figure 3.12 provides an example of SQL script.

Report

A **report** is a database object that is used to organize, summarize, format, and present data residing in the database. The data used in a report can come from tables or queries. Like queries, reports are useful because they can be used to perform the same actions every time they are applied, even when the underlying data have been updated or changed. Recall the example used in the context of queries. The manager wants to go a step further than using the query to determine how much sales revenue each member of her sales team generated in the past quarter. Accordingly, the manager creates a report to summarize and format the total sales revenue data for each salesperson. Specifically, she creates a nicely formatted horizontal bar chart in which salespersons' names appear on the y-axis, and total sales revenue appears on the x-axis (see Figure 3.13).

Report A database object that
is used to organize, summarize,
format, and present data residing
in the database

■ **FIGURE 3.13**   Example of a Report Bar Graph

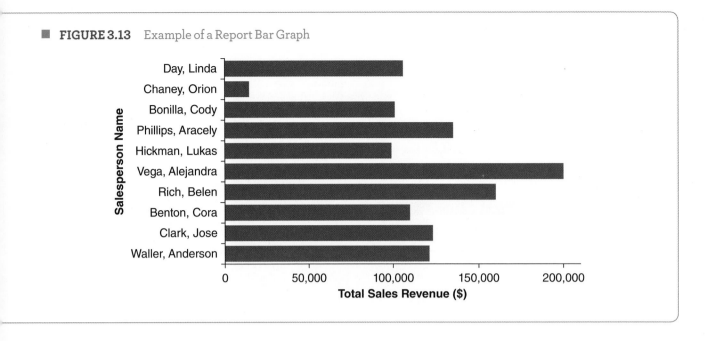

System Users

Different groups of individuals both within and outside of an organization may have reason to access and use an HRIS. As such, an HRIS should be designed with different system users in mind, as different system users often have different motivations or responsibilities when accessing an HRIS, and thus, user experience should be considered. Employees constitute a primary HRIS user group, as they need to access data within the system for entry, verification, analysis, and reporting purposes.

Even among employees, however, motivations or responsibilities when accessing the system may differ based on their roles. First, all employees need to interact with the HRIS for the purposes of viewing, changing, or verifying their own personal data. Many organizations allow employees to select their benefits during an open-enrollment period by accessing benefits self-service web portals. In this way, employees have direct control over their data in the HRIS instead of relying on a face-to-face meeting with a benefits administrator to select benefits. Second, some employees need to enter data into the HRIS for other users. Managers may be required to enter the performance appraisal ratings for each of their employees directly into the HRIS. Third, other employees play a more active role in updating the HRIS itself and/or analyzing and reporting data contained within the HRIS. For example, information technology employees are often responsible for implementing system design changes and fixing technology-related issues with the HRIS. In addition, HR analysts may analyze the existing HRIS data or collect new data for the purposes of finding answers to important HR-related questions. Finally, employees with managerial responsibilities may need to access actual employee data, but in many cases, they access data that are reported in aggregate about groups or units of employees. For example, CEOs may wish to know which organizational units have the highest turnover rates, and by accessing a dashboard with preconfigured yet customizable analytic findings, they can analyze turnover rates by organizational unit.

Other Users

In addition to an organization's employees, other users outside of the organization often need access to the HRIS. First, it is increasingly common for organizations to allow (potential) job applicants to enter their personal information, such as a résumé and applicant blank data, into

HR IN ACTION
Automatic Data Processing, Inc. (ADP)

Shutterstock.com

Christopher Goodney/Bloomberg via Getty Images

ADP chief executive officer Carlos Rodriguez

Since 1949, Automatic Data Processing, Inc. (ADP) has developed a global reputation for payroll processing products and services. For a number of years, the company had a AAA credit rating—the highest rating given—from both Moody's and Standard & Poor's. ADP has diversified in several ways since its inception. Notably, ADP now provides various products and services that connect the HRM function to company strategy by leveraging data analytics. In recent years, the company made headlines for developing a proprietary algorithm that predicts employees' risk of quitting based on several factors, such as employees' commuting distance and their income relative to neighbors' incomes.

Given the general decrease in the U.S. unemployment rate since 2009, there is a greater likelihood of increased turnover, as meta-analytic evidence indicates that individuals who are thinking about quitting will be more likely to do so when unemployment rates are lower. Consistent with that expectation, the United States has seen an uptick in turnover since 2012 as the unemployment rate has fallen. Because turnover—especially among high-performing employees—can be costly for organizations in terms of lost productivity and increased selection and training costs, adopting ADP's new algorithm as part of their HRM software packages may help organizations' bottom lines.

However, there may be some legal and ethical implications associated with using employee data of this kind. The kind of personal data used in the algorithm, such as commute length and neighborhood income, could be proxies for other factors, such as socioeconomic status, race, and ethnicity.[56]

the HRIS, often via an applicant tracking system. The system often allows applicants to log into the system at their convenience to check the status of their applications. Second, many organizations outsource some of their HR activities to third-party partners, and thus, some data need to be shared with these partners. For example, some organizations outsource their payroll functions to outside vendors; as a result, such vendors will need access to up-to-date compensation and benefits data for employees. Of course, sharing data with outside partners (or even internally with employee system users) may pose some data privacy and security risks.

System Architectures

System architectures for HRISs and other information systems have evolved since the advent of modern computing, and advancements in information technology are responsible for this evolution. For many decades, information systems were based on what are often called traditional tiered architectures, but in the past decade, there has been a rapid shift toward cloud-based architectures, especially as data transfer speeds and storage space have increased.

Traditional Tiered Architectures

In the mid-20th century, computers were the size of rooms and were so expensive that relatively few organizations had access to computers for information-system purposes. Nonetheless, some organizations devised systems so that a few users could directly interface with a computer mainframe, which meant that all databases and applications lived on the mainframe. These were called single-tier or one-tier architectures.

When personal computers were introduced, came down in price, and gained popularity during the 1970s and 1980s, client–server architectures (sometimes called two-tier architectures) were introduced. Specifically, many of the simpler functions with fewer processing demands were decentralized to personal computers that system users directly accessed via a user interface client, and the databases and applications lived on a server, thereby creating two tiers—one for the personal computers and one for the server. The next evolution in system architectures occurred when the server containing databases and applications was split into two separate servers so that more processing-intensive activities could be handled by a dedicated applications server.

Finally, with the advent of the Internet and expansion of its use, speed, and capabilities came what is referred to as N-tier architectures. (The "N" serves as a placeholder for any number that is four or greater.) By leveraging the Internet, N-tier architectures used the database and application servers of three-tier architectures but added web servers. Users no longer needed to download the user interface client onto personal computers because the user interface client was accessible via web servers. That is, through their personal computers, system users could log onto a web portal, which was hosted by web servers, to access and interface with the system. By introducing web servers, more and more devices, such as cell phones, could be used to access the system.

Cloud-Based Architectures

Today, we can access our music, movies, and software programs through the "cloud," or Internet-based databases and applications that are hosted remotely (from the perspective of the user). Cloud computing has revolutionized how we access information, as we can log on and interact with information through multiple devices and multiple locations, as long as there is a reliable Internet connection available. Cloud computing also has important implications for HRISs via cloud-based architectures, which allow organizational system users to access and interact with the HRIS in much the same way we access music and movies. In effect, cloud-based architectures move the database, application, and web servers of an N-tier architecture to the cloud. In this way, organizations do not need to house and manage their own servers; instead, their server needs are outsourced to a third-party entity that the organization partners with.

Software as a service (SaaS) Arrangements through which software and hardware associated with databases and applications are maintained and controlled by a third-party entity

A common application of cloud-based architectures is ***software as a service (SaaS)***, arrangements through which software and hardware associated with databases and applications are maintained and controlled by a third-party entity. An advantage of SaaS is that an organization can purchase access to databases and applications on a subscription basis, which means that the organization does not need to update DBMS software and hardware, as such responsibilities are taken care of by the SaaS provider. A potential disadvantage of SaaS and other cloud-computing architectures is that the organization relies on the cloud-computing provider to manage data security. Most providers take data security very seriously and put many safeguards and protections in place; however, using a provider along with other companies may increase the desirability for hackers to access the data.

CHAPTER SUMMARY

Managing data is important to HR because all organizations need to be able to make decisions about people, and data-informed decisions can be more effective. HR information systems, or HRIS, provide both opportunities and challenges. Opportunities include the ability to track employees through their employment life cycles, employee-centered HR functionality, data availability for metrics and analytics, and the ability to create effective data visualizations. Challenges to consider include cost, the HR skill set, data privacy concerns, and data security concerns. In developing an HRIS, an organization conducts a needs assessment, creates a design, and considers choosing a vendor. When an HRIS is implemented, the organization undergoes a process of change that culminates in refreezing; the HRIS must also be maintained over time. Core information system concepts include the management of databases and users, understanding of HRIS architecture, and relational database concepts.

KEY TERMS

human resource information system
    (HRIS)   69
people data   69
enterprise resource planning
    (ERP)   69
e-HRM   70
data lake   75
storytelling with data   75
data privacy   80
scraping and crawling tools   81
anonymous data   81
confidential data   81
personally identifiable data   82
data security   82

cybersecurity   82
two-step authentication   83
multifactor authentication   83
blockchain   84
logical design   87
data flow diagrams   87
physical design   88
unfreezing   91
change   91
refreezing   91
database   92
database management system
    (DBMS)   92
relational database   92

relational database management
    system (relational
    DBMS)   92
table   92
field (variable)   93
record   93
key variable   93
form   93
query   94
report   95
software as a service (SaaS)   98

Visit **edge.sagepub.com/bauer** to help you accomplish your coursework goals in an easy-to-use learning environment.

- Master the learning objectives using key study tools
- Watch, listen, and connect with online multimedia resources

- Access mobile-friendly quizzes and flashcards to check your understanding

HR REASONING AND DECISION-MAKING EXERCISES

MINI-CASE ANALYSIS EXERCISE: DETERMINING WHETHER TO CONTINUE HRIS CONSULTING

The Monday-morning meeting is just starting. The room is full of individuals from the HR team. As the newest member and most well trained on statistics and HR analytics, you are looked to by staff to help them frame questions, conduct research to answer the questions, and help walk them through the implications.

John Bettle, a senior HR manager within your division, walks in. He starts the meeting off with several scenarios that the team has been asked to address. As the new HR analytics guru in your group, you've been asked to address key questions.

The organization has been spending a lot of money bringing in HRIS consultants and experts to help with understanding the HRIS needs of the organization. The VP of HR, Raja Sutton, has asked John to let him know if he thinks the investment in time and money is worth it. John's gut tells him it is, but he's not sure how best to make the business case for this. Given that the request came from "up high," John is asking for your help in how to address it.

Now, decide what you would do. Share your approach to how the team might best respond to this request from the VP of HR.

1. What specifically would you tell John to say to justify the continued investment in understanding the organization's HRIS needs?

2. Be specific, and outline your recommendations for John, being sure to include key points from this chapter.

HR DECISION ANALYSIS EXERCISE: ISSUES WITH ADDRESSING A SKILLS GAP?

Your new CEO recently went to a technology conference. On returning, she shared her excitement about artificial intelligence (AI), big data, and analytics and their roles in the future of management. She mandated that the HR department create proposals for a new and improved HRIS to make sure the company stays current on these technology trends.

However, you are concerned that you may not have the right people with the right skills within the HR area, as most of them earned their college degrees many years ago. When you mentioned this to your manager, he said, "Well, maybe we need to retrain our current employees, or maybe we need to replace them with new talent that has the skills we need." How might you react to the suggestion to move forward in replacing current employees with those with better technology skills?

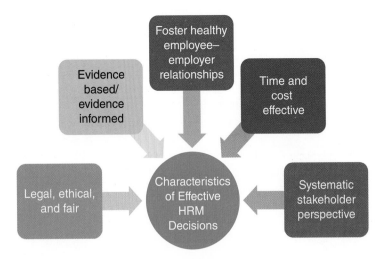

Please provide the rationale for your answer to each of the questions below.

Is this suggestion legal, ethical, and fair?

_____

_____

_____

_____

Is it evidence based/evidence informed?

_____

_____

_____

_____

Does it foster healthy employee–employer relationships?

_____

_____

_____

_____

Is it timely and cost effective?

_____

_____

_____

_____

Does it take a systematic stakeholder perspective?

_____

_____

_____

_____

Considering your analysis above, overall, do you think this would be an effective decision? Why or why not?

_____

_____

_____

_____

What, if anything, do you think should be done differently or considered to help make this decision more effective?

_____

_____

_____

_____

HR DECISION-MAKING EXERCISE: ORGANIZATIONAL ATTRACTIVENESS AUDIT

You work on a team of four other members of the customer service team at C-Zone, an auto-parts wholesaler. Your company has around 2,000 employees nationally. The company has low job acceptance rates of only 30%, which you suspect is too low, but since you do not work in HR, you have never mentioned anything about this. However, for a long time, you have believed that the high customer service turnover (75% each year) and low acceptance rates of jobs offered are related. Thus, it may be time for your team to think about what might be done about this. Your company recently implemented a new HRIS, which now makes it possible to get data on employees on request. You decide it is time for your five-person leadership team to start doing a little investigation.

1. Develop a plan to examine why employees are hesitant to join the organization and always seem to be leaving. How can you assess why employees turn down job offers? How might you assess why employees are leaving? After you choose your method of measurement (i.e., focus groups, survey, interviews), develop an instrument, including the questions to be included. How would you analyze the data to identify the top reasons for employee departures?

2. Let's assume that you found out the top three reasons for low job acceptance to your company are as follows:

   (a) Management is very authoritarian and not supportive of employees. When potential applicants read the comments on Glassdoor.com, it scares them off.
   (b) Compensation is below average compared with other similar organizations.
   (c) Employees feel they are working all the time with little downtime. This is especially true in the call center when calls can be stressful and plentiful at peak times.

3. What would be your proposed action plan to deal with these issues? Be specific, and make sure that your recommendations focus on recruitment, selection, training, compensation, and any other stages of the employment cycle.

DATA AND ANALYTICS EXERCISE: DATA CLEANING

One of the overarching goals of any HRIS is to provide users with accurate data. Further, the integrity of the data directly influences the integrity of the insights gleaned from the data, or in other words: garbage in, garbage out. Unfortunately, the data that reside within an HRIS are not always what we would hope or expect for. There are a number of reasons for this, but one of the most common reasons is human error.

Imagine that your HRIS is built around a relational database consisting of a number of different tables. In one of the tables, you store basic employee information, such as employee ID, employee name, job level, location, and department.

Here is an excerpt of the table:

EMPLOYEE ID	EMPLOYEE NAME	JOB LEVEL	LOCATION	DEPARTMENT
EA44312	Kim, Yeongjin	1	beaverton	Customer Service
EB58521	Dowsett, Jane	3	Hillsboro	
EA64533	Henderson, Lynn	4	Hillsboro	
EA89575	Mitchell, Terrance	1	Hillsboro	Customer Service
ET58748	Smith, John	1	Beaverton	Customer Service
ET96461	Martinez, David	4	Beavertn	Marketing
EB11248	Liu, Patricia	11	Beaverton	Customer Service

First, take a close look at the Location field. Do you notice anything? Note how the Beaverton location is spelled with a capital "B" for three of the cases and how it is spelled without the "o" for one case. Most likely, this difference in spelling was the result of an error during data entry. Errors like this might not seem like such a big deal, but down the road, they can lead to issues when it comes to merging and analyzing the data. Namely, many software programs such as Microsoft Access Excel will treat the two different versions of the word *Beaverton* (i.e., Beaverton, Beavertn) location as two distinct categories. That is, instead of treating the Location field as a categorical variable with two levels (i.e., Beaverton, Hillsboro), the Location field will be treated as a categorical variable with the following three levels: Beaverton, Beavertn, and Hillsboro. If you were to create a PivotTable in Excel to determine the frequency (i.e., counts) of employees who work at each location, you would end up with the following frequency table:

Row Labels	Count of Location
Beavertn	1
Beaverton	3
Hillsboro	3
Grand Total	**7**

Note how the frequency table correctly indicates that three employees work at the Hillsboro location but incorrectly indicates that three employees work at the Beaverton location and one employee works at the Beavertn location.

Second, take a close look at the rest of the table. Did you notice the missing data? Specifically, Jane Dowsett and Lynn Henderson are missing the names of the departments in which they work. More than likely these two employees work in a department that has a name. As such, it is important that these missing data are found and the table is updated.

Third, in this organization, there are only seven job levels, where a 1 corresponds to entry-level jobs and a 7 corresponds to executive jobs. Now take a look at the Job Level field. Note how Patricia Liu has a job level of 11, which is clearly beyond the 1–7 range. This might mean that someone accidentally entered 1 twice by mistake, resulting in 11. Again, a simple Excel PivotTable can be used to create a frequency table that displays how many employees fall into each job level. The frequency table here shows in the left column that one of the job levels is 11, which is not correct.

Row Labels	Count of Job Level
1	3
3	1
4	2
11	1
Grand Total	**7**

The best course of action is to prevent these errors in the first place. For instance, you can design tables with data validation rules that allow only predetermined values to be entered into cells (e.g., Beaverton, Hillsboro). Alternatively, in the context of a relational database, you can create a form that facilitates data entry by requiring data to be entered into certain fields and allowing only certain fields to be completed using drop-down menus with provided options.

If, however, you still find yourself with "dirty" data, you will need to clean the data prior to analysis. Fortunately, Excel and other programs offer several tools that can facilitate the data-cleaning process, such as the PivotTable tool that was highlighted in the example.

 EXCEL EXTENSION: NOW YOU TRY!

- On **edge.sagepub.com/bauer**, you will find an Excel exercise on data cleaning.

- First, you will learn how to use the filter feature to identify potential data integrity issues.

- Second, you will learn how to use the PivotTable tool to construct frequency tables that can be used to identify potential data integrity issues.

- Third, you will practice applying these tools and interpreting and communicating your findings.

CHAPTER 3 SUPPLEMENT: SAMPLE JOB DESCRIPTION FOR AN HRIS ANALYST

SAMPLE JOB DESCRIPTION FOR AN HRIS ANALYST

Source: SHRM. (2015). Designing and managing a Human Resource Information System. https://www.shrm.org/resourcesandtools/tools-and-samples/toolkits/pages/managingahumanresourceinformationsystem.aspx

Classification

[Indicate exempt or nonexempt.]

Salary Grade/Level/Family/Range

[Insert applicable information.]

Reports to

[Insert title of the position this job reports to, not name of current manager.]

Date

[Indicate date of Job Description creation or review.]

JOB DESCRIPTION

Summary/Objective

The HRIS analyst is an intermediate position within the HRIS structure. The primary focus of this position is to support the maintenance of the human resource management system (HRMS), in addition to other systems supported by the HRIS team. This position serves as a technical point of contact for assigned functional areas and assists subject matter experts with ensuring data integrity, testing of system changes, report writing, and analyzing data flows for process improvement opportunities. The HRIS analyst also supports HRMS upgrades, patches, testing, and other technical projects as assigned.

Essential Functions

Reasonable accommodations may be made to enable individuals with disabilities to perform the essential functions.

1. **System Maintenance** (5% of time): Assist in the review, testing, and implementation of HRMS upgrades or patches. Collaborate with functional and technical staff to coordinate application of upgrade or fix. Maintain HRMS tables. Document process and results.

2. **Production Support** (20% of time): Provide support for HRMS, including researching and resolving HRMS problems, unexpected results, or process flaws; performing scheduled activities; and recommending solutions or alternate methods to meet requirements.

3. **Projects/Process Improvement** (55% of time): Recommend process/customer service improvements, innovative solutions, policy changes, and/or major variations from established policy that must be approved by appropriate leadership prior to implementation. Serve as a key liaison with third parties and other stakeholders (e.g., payroll). Use project management skills in managing projects. May provide overall project management for a given HR initiative.

4. **Reports/Queries** (10% of time): Write, maintain, and support a variety of reports or queries using appropriate reporting tools. Assist in development of standard reports for ongoing customer needs. Help maintain data integrity in systems by running queries and analyzing data.

5. **Training** (5% of time): Develop user procedures, guidelines, and documentation. Train clients on new processes/functionality. Train new system users.

6. **Individual Development** (5% of time): Maintain awareness of current trends in HRMS with a focus on product and service development, delivery, and support and applying key technologies. Examine trends in information systems training, materials, and techniques. Through classes, reading, CBTs, or other mechanisms, continuously increase both HR knowledge and HRIS application/tools knowledge. Participate in user group meetings/conferences.

Competencies

1. Critical Evaluation
2. Consultation
3. Business Acumen
4. HR Expertise
5. Communication

Supervisory Responsibility

This position has no supervisory responsibilities.

Work Environment

This job operates in a professional office environment. This role routinely uses standard office equipment.

Physical Demands

The physical demands described here are representative of those that must be met by an employee to successfully perform the essential functions of this job.

While performing the duties of this job, the employee is regularly required to talk or hear. The employee frequently is required to stand; walk; use hands to finger, handle, or feel; and reach with hands and arms. Specific vision abilities required by this job include close vision, distance vision, color vision, peripheral vision, depth perception, and ability to adjust focus. This position requires the ability to occasionally lift office products and supplies, up to 20 pounds.

Position Type/Expected Hours of Work

This is a full-time position, and hours of work and days are Monday through Friday, 8:30 a.m. to 5 p.m.

Travel

Travel is primarily local during the business day, although some out-of-the-area and overnight travel may be expected.

Required Education and Experience

[Indicate education based on requirements that are job related and consistent with business necessity. See examples below.]

1. Bachelor's degree in computer science or related field or equivalent work experience.
2. Three to five years of HRIS or HR generalist or specialist experience.
3. One to two years of project management experience.
4. Systems implementation experience.

Preferred Education and Experience

[Indicate education based on requirements that are job related and consistent with business necessity. See examples below.]

1. SHRM Certified Professional (SHRM-CP) or Senior Certified Professional (SHRM-SCP).
2. Certified Associate in Project Management (CAPM).

Additional Eligibility Qualifications

None required for this position.

Work Authorization/Security Clearance (if applicable)

[This section lists visa requirements, H1-B sponsorship, special clearances, etc. If applicable, insert information if you have government contracts or special requirements.]

AAP/EEO Statement

[Insert AAP/EEO statement here if applicable.]

Other Duties

Please note this job description is not designed to cover or contain a comprehensive listing of activities, duties, or responsibilities that are required of the employee for this job. Duties, responsibilities, and activities may change at any time with or without notice.

Signatures

This job description has been approved by all levels of management:

Manager _____

HR _____

Employee signature below constitutes employee's understanding of the requirements, essential functions, and duties of the position.

Employee _____   Date _____

Diversity, Inclusion, and Equal Employment Laws

Opening Case

Diversity Challenges in the Tech Industry: The Case of Pinterest[1]

The San Francisco–based visual social media firm Pinterest is one of the first Silicon Valley companies that recognized the dismal state of diversity in the technology industry. In fact, a Pinterest engineer, Tracy Chou, is credited with starting the movement toward more data-driven diversity management. The 2013 blog post Ms. Chou wrote, titled "Where Are the Numbers?," motivated tech giants such as Facebook and Google to reveal the number of women and minorities in their workforce, particularly in technology and leadership positions. Pinterest's own numbers were revealed in this management-authorized blog post, with the assumption that by releasing the figures and making a public commitment, its team of more than 700 employees would become more diverse.

Unfortunately, the results at the end of the first year of this experiment showed that it was business as usual. Similar to other companies, Pinterest was half White and 43% Asian. It had 42% women, but this was because of the inclusion of all business units in these calculations. Men dominated technology (79%), engineering (81%), and leadership positions (84%).

One year into its commitment, the numbers had barely moved, even though the company had instituted several initiatives: mentored female programming students; recruited at African American, Hispanic, and female engineering events; and invested in unconscious bias training. What had gone wrong? Even though recruiters brought in a more diverse pool of candidates, hiring managers continued to use the same selection criteria, including prioritizing hiring from a small set of Ivy League schools (that happen to have a less diverse body of graduates). In retrospect, even though top management wanted to diversify hiring, they had not made a business case to everyone in the company. Thinking in terms of diversity had not become a part of a widespread mentality; it had remained an HR initiative.

As part of an overhaul, the company entered 2016 with explicit goals: It announced that in 2016, 30% of its new engineers would be female, and 8% would be underrepresented minorities. It was careful to clarify that these were to be used as guidelines and not quotas. It also started a partnership with the consulting firm Paradigm. This firm uses HR analytics to examine how recruitment and selection techniques affect

LEARNING OBJECTIVES

After reading and studying this chapter, you should be able to do the following:

4.1 Describe the challenges and benefits of diversity and inclusion in the workplace.

4.2 Identify major U.S. laws pertaining to equal employment opportunity and how they apply to various kinds of employment decisions.

4.3 Discuss the impact of Title VII of the Civil Rights Act.

4.4 Identify additional antidiscrimination acts and protections in the workplace.

4.5 Recommend ways in which organizations can maintain legal compliance and address key analytical, legal, ethical, and global issues associated with diversity and inclusion in HRM.

Tracy Chou is an engineer at Pinterest and a diversity advocate for the engineering profession.

the diversity of hires and presents suggestions to remove barriers to diversity. For example, Paradigm recommended that Pinterest help employees better prepare for an interview at a Silicon Valley company. Companies in the tech industry are known for their unusual hiring techniques, ranging from casual dress codes for applicants to intense team interviews. By sharing information about what to expect as part of the hiring process, it was able to prepare applicants better, give them more clarity, and limit the influence of nonessential factors on interview performance. Asking employees to refer potential hires from underrepresented groups also worked, increasing the number of female and Hispanic applicants for engineering jobs. In the same time period, the company hired its first head of diversity. Pinterest instituted programs such as apprenticeship and summer internship programs to increase diversity. Broadening their university outreach partners was also helpful. To avoid potential bias, in meetings and interviews, they started introducing applicants with their academic major and not the name of the university. Finally, the company instituted the National Football League's so-called Rooney Rule, requiring that for each leadership position, at least one female and one underrepresented minority would be interviewed.

Early results are promising: In 2017, women constituted 29% of all technical roles, up from 21% in 2015, whereas underrepresented ethnicities rose from 3% to 9%. Pinterest remains committed to sharing what it learned and continuing its data-driven approach to understanding and promoting diversity. The technology industry's diversity problem has many sources, ranging from a "leaky pipeline" (which means that women and minorities leave the industry due to discrimination and other factors) to organizational cultures that do not internalize diversity as a competitive advantage. Efforts such as those at Pinterest are noteworthy for their transparency and for their willingness to be part of the solution.

Case Discussion Questions

1. What is the difference between diversity goals and diversity quotas? Why do you think Pinterest was careful to distinguish between the two?

2. What are some of the challenges to diversity management in the technology industry? List and discuss what prevents companies from attracting and retaining diverse talent.

3. Consider the initiatives with which Pinterest is experimenting. Which ones hold greater promise? What else would you suggest it do?

4. What are your thoughts about the central roles of sex and racial diversity in the technology industry's diversification efforts?

 Click to learn more...

Read Tracy Chou's blog post at https://medium.com/@triketora/where-are-the-numbers-cb997a57252#.1305agqnk

As a collective characteristic, ***diversity*** refers to real or perceived differences among people with respect to sex, race, ethnicity, age, physical and mental ability, sexual orientation, religion, and attributes that may affect their interactions with others.[2] Having a diverse workforce and creating a culture of inclusion are good for business. By hiring, retaining, and supporting a diverse workforce, companies have the potential to achieve better business results and minimize the chances of costly lawsuits. This chapter discusses the basics of diversity management and the legal landscape relating to it.

Diversity Real or perceived differences among people with respect to sex, race, ethnicity, age, physical and mental ability, sexual orientation, religion, and attributes that may affect their interactions with others

Challenges and Benefits of Managing Diversity Effectively

LO 4.1 Describe the challenges and benefits of diversity and inclusion in the workplace.

As society becomes more diverse, organizations are following suit, as the following statistics indicate. In 2017, women constituted 47% of the workforce in the United States. White employees were 78%, Hispanics 17%, African Americans 12%, and Asian workers 6% of the labor force.[3] How organizations hire, manage, and retain a diverse workforce has implications for organizational effectiveness. There is a rich legal landscape that organizations need to be familiar with when managing their employees.

In this chapter, we first present the business case for diversity and explore why it still remains challenging to achieve a truly diverse workplace. Then we explore the legal landscape with regard to diversity in the United States, describing the most important laws and court decisions that HR managers need to be familiar with. Finally, we describe some best practices in managing diversity that organizations are advised to follow.

Is Diversity Beneficial for Work Groups and Organizations?

When employees work in a diverse group, do they experience benefits? Research on this question paints a complicated picture. Studies examining the relationship between the level of diversity in a group and outcomes show that diverse groups actually feel less cohesive, experience more conflict, misunderstand each other more, have higher rates of turnover, and have lower team performance. Similarly, individuals who work with others who are dissimilar to them feel less interpersonal attraction to their peers. In other words, simply diversifying a work group is no guarantee for immediate success. Instead, it may be a recipe for conflict and frustration.[4]

Inclusive environments Organizations or groups in which individuals, regardless of their background, are treated with dignity and respect, are included in decision making, and are valued for who they are and what they bring to the group or organization

At the same time, diversity's potential is unlocked when diversity is accompanied by inclusion. ***Inclusive environments*** are organizations or groups in which individuals, regardless of their background, are treated with dignity and respect, are included in decision making, and are valued for who they are and what they bring to the group or organization. Inclusiveness allows individuals to be themselves. Everyone is valued not only for their performance but also as human beings. Employees have input in decision making, and everyone's ideas are heard. Research shows that when accompanied by inclusion, diversity has positive effects on groups in the form of lower conflict, and the negative effects on unit performance disappear. At the company level, inclusive climate was associated with more positive relationships within the company and lower turnover rate. Further, perceptions of equal access to opportunities and fair treatment are associated with positive outcomes for individuals. These findings underline the importance of jointly considering diversity and inclusion in HR-related decision making.[5]

A key benefit of diversity is that diversity is critically important for innovation. When people with different life experiences and viewpoints come together and share information, disclose their viewpoints, and make an effort to integrate them, they arrive at more innovative decisions. As a result, diversity and innovation are related such that the more diversity that exists within a group, the more innovative it tends to be.[7] Consider product design. Today, many products target a diverse set of customers. Yet when a product design team is homogeneous, members typically consider only their own experiences with the product and neglect to consider unique challenges users dissimilar to them may experience. As a case in point, facial recognition software ranging from Hewlett-Packard's (HP) motion-tracking webcams to Google Photos had difficulty recognizing

The CEO of the financial firm TIAA, Roger Ferguson, leverages the power of diversity at work. He credits the firm's diversity at all levels for having pushed them to question the safety of investing in the subprime mortgage market and thereby avoiding the worst effects of the 2008 economic crash.[6]

Frank Polich/Bloomberg via Getty Images

©iStock.com/uatp2

Since the 1970s, automotive manufacturers used crash test dummies that represented the average American male, resulting in 47% higher injury rates for women wearing seatbelts. The situation was resolved with a federal law in 2011 requiring manufacturers to use a smaller female dummy in their tests.[8]

darker skin tones, causing frustration for end users. Analysts raised the possibility that lack of diversity in design teams could be contributing to these problems.

Diversity also has effects on firm reputation and performance. Diversity at the highest levels of a company signals that the firm understands and appreciates the value of diversity and gives power to a diverse group of individuals. Therefore, it has benefits for how the firm operates and how it is perceived in the external community. A study of Fortune 500 companies showed that the racial diversity of the board of directors was positively related to firm performance as measured by return on investment, because firms with diverse boards had a more positive reputation and greater investments in firm innovation as captured by investment in research and development (R&D).[9] However, in 2018, only 5% of Fortune 500 firms had female CEOs, and racial diversity was also lacking, with less than 1% of Fortune 500 being helmed by Black CEOs and 1% by Hispanic CEOs.[10]

Why Are Diversity and Inclusion Still Challenging to Achieve?

Even though diversity and inclusion are important for competitiveness, there are still barriers. Prejudices and biases continue to exist, and they may serve as barriers to hiring and retaining a diverse workforce. At the same time, the systemic absence of diversity in many industries and job categories is hard to explain solely through racism, sexism, ageism, or other forms of discrimination. Many of the challenges to achieving diversity and inclusion reflect simple human tendencies, which make it extremely difficult to eradicate them. In many cases, being aware of them is a useful first step, but instead of trying to change human nature, organizations are starting to design systems that recognize that these biases exist and seek to prevent them from affecting HR decisions in the first place.

Similarity-Attraction

Similarity-attraction hypothesis The theory that individuals prefer others who are similar to them

Perhaps the biggest challenge to having a diverse workforce and creating an inclusive work environment is the tendency of individuals to prefer others who are similar to them. Researchers name this tendency the *similarity-attraction hypothesis*. People tend to establish trust more quickly, show willingness to cooperate, and experience smoother communication with others who are similar to them. Similarity may not always refer to demographic characteristics such as sex, race, age, or nationality. It may also mean similarity in education level or functional background (e.g., marketing, finance, or HR major). This attraction could be a barrier to hiring employees who are different from the existing employee pool. For example, consciously or unconsciously, a hiring manager who is White may feel greater affinity for another White job applicant who is also of a similar age and went to the same college. Similarly, in a firm where Asian and male employees are the majority, non-Asian and female employees may experience greater difficulty getting hired. Often this tendency manifests itself as greater perceived chemistry, or a positive "gut feeling" signaling that one candidate is a better fit for the company or the team relative to the other candidates. Even in cases where employees who are different from the majority are hired, feeling different could result in a sense of alienation and isolation. Research has shown that individuals who are demographically different from others they work with are at a higher turnover risk, particularly early in their tenure in the company.[11]

Stereotypes and Unconscious Biases

Stereotypes Overly simplified and generalized assumptions about a particular group that may not reflect reality

Stereotypes may cause problems during and after hiring. *Stereotypes* are simplified and generalized assumptions about a particular group. These assumptions may be implicit or explicit. In other words, you may or may not be aware that you have these stereotypes, and often they live in your subconscious. For example, if you believe that younger people are more technology savvy, and you are aware that this is a perception you have, then this is an example of an explicit stereotype. However, if you don't consciously think that, and yet you are taken aback when you interact with an extremely tech-savvy older person, then you may have an implicit, or unconscious, bias about how age affects technical acumen. ***Unconscious (or implicit) bias*** refers to stereotypes individuals hold that reside beyond their conscious awareness. To explore your own potential implicit biases, try the implicit association test developed by Harvard University researchers (https://implicit.harvard.edu/implicit/takeatest.html).

Implicit or explicit, stereotypes and biases could serve as barriers to diversity and inclusion. In the hiring process, an older applicant interviewing for a job at a high-technology firm may simply seem "wrong" for the company culture because the employee does not look like the typical technology worker. After being hired, stereotypes may result in differential treatment. After having a baby, a female employee may be put on the "mommy track," with managers withholding challenging and developmental assignments with the assumption that the employee would no longer be interested in them. Using assumptions and generalizations when making decisions about specific individuals leads to unfair and potentially illegal decisions. And yet, particularly when they are a form of implicit bias, these tendencies are a challenge to eliminate. By definition, implicit biases are unconscious, and therefore a person may have difficulty identifying and eliminating them.

Confronting one's own biases and becoming more aware of how hidden biases affect organizational decision making is an essential first step in dealing with them. For example, Google developed a program training its employees on unconscious bias, giving employees a common understanding of implicit bias and a common language to collectively confront its effects and hold each other accountable. Organizations are designing structures and systems that start with the assumption that human decision makers are biased but prevent those biases from affecting decision making. One of the successful methods for dealing with lack of diversity in national orchestras has been to conduct auditions behind a screen, which has resulted in the admission of more female musicians to national orchestras even though they constituted only 5% of orchestra members in the 1970s. Comedian Samantha Bee, the first female to host a late-night comedy show, used a similar technique when hiring her diverse team of 50% female and 30% non-White writers. In addition to stripping all identifiers from applications, her selection process showed applicants how exactly to format submissions to eliminate inherent advantages of having industry experience, which resulted in the hiring of exceptional talent from unusual backgrounds, including a former Department of Motor Vehicles (DMV) employee.[12]

An Overview of Equal Employment Opportunity Laws

Effective management of diversity and inclusion goes beyond simply complying with the law, but legal compliance is an essential first step. An important reason for understanding the legal side of diversity and inclusion is to limit the organization's legal liability. Discrimination lawsuits are costly both in terms of legal fees and penalties and in terms of their costs to firm reputation. Although this chapter is not intended to give legal advice, it aims to create awareness of the basic federal laws and regulations that HR professionals need to be familiar with. When seeking specific legal advice, contact a lawyer.

There are two key factors that make diversity-related legal issues complicated. First, the legal landscape is dynamic and constantly changing. New federal and Supreme Court decisions set precedents that affect how the laws are interpreted in future cases. Therefore, HR professionals need to continually keep up with new developments in the legal field. Second, this book covers only federal laws relating to diversity. States and municipalities have their own laws, which offer additional protections to employees or place additional restrictions on businesses. Further, presidential ***executive orders***, which carry the force of law, may be applicable to HR issues. HR professionals and managers need to understand their legal obligations by becoming intimately familiar with the federal, state, and local laws affecting diversity management.

Unconscious (or implicit) bias Stereotypes individuals hold that reside beyond their conscious awareness

LO 4.2 Identify major U.S. laws pertaining to equal employment opportunity and how they apply to various kinds of employment decisions.

Executive orders Presidential orders that carry the force of law

Equal Employment Opportunity Commission (EEOC) An independent federal agency that ensures compliance with the law and provides outreach activities designed to prevent discrimination

Office of Federal Contract Compliance Programs (OFCCP) A division of the Department of Labor; monitors EEO compliance of federal contractors

EEOC is the primary federal agency responsible for handling workplace discrimination claims. In 2017, the agency received more than 84,000 individual filings.[14]

In the United States, federal law prohibits discrimination in employment decisions based on protected characteristics. These laws are referred to as Equal Employment Opportunity (EEO) laws. Most EEO laws pertaining to private, government, and state institutions are monitored and enforced by the ***Equal Employment Opportunity Commission (EEOC)***, an independent federal agency that ensures compliance with the law and provides outreach activities designed to prevent discrimination from occurring in the first place. In addition to EEOC, the ***Office of Federal Contract Compliance Programs (OFCCP)***, a division of the Department of Labor, monitors EEO compliance of federal contractors.[13]

Most EEO laws apply to organizations with 15 or more employees. EEO laws cover business, private employers, government agencies, employment agencies, and labor unions. These laws aim to prevent discrimination against employees, job applicants, and participants in training and apprenticeship programs. Note that independent contractors, because they are not employees, are not covered. Whether an individual is considered an independent contractor or an employee is complicated; the more control an employer exercises on an individual in how the job is done, the more likely it is for that person to be an employee for the purposes of these laws.[15] This section reviews the major EEO laws including the Equal Pay Act (1963), Title VII of the Civil Rights Act (1964 and 1991), Pregnancy Discrimination Act (1978), Age Discrimination in Employment Act (ADEA, 1967), Americans with Disabilities Act (ADA, 1990), and Genetic Information Nondiscrimination Act (GINA, 2008).

Excluding the Equal Pay Act, EEO laws require applicants or employees to file a complaint with EEOC as the first step. In other words, even though illegal discrimination may have occurred, individuals do not have the ability to file a lawsuit without filing a charge with EEOC first.[16] Before filing a charge, individuals need to make sure that they are actually protected by a specific EEO law. The laws also require employees or job applicants to file their complaint within a specific number of days following the discriminatory incident. Once a charge is filed,

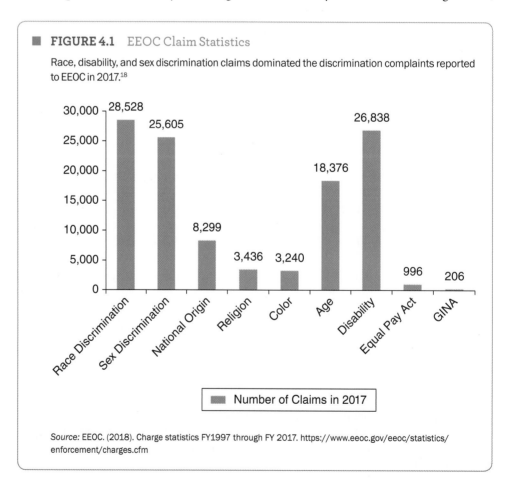

■ **FIGURE 4.1** EEOC Claim Statistics

Race, disability, and sex discrimination claims dominated the discrimination complaints reported to EEOC in 2017.[18]

Source: EEOC. (2018). Charge statistics FY1997 through FY 2017. https://www.eeoc.gov/eeoc/statistics/enforcement/charges.cfm

EEOC investigates claims of discrimination and seeks to help parties reach a settlement. Further, EEOC is authorized to file lawsuits in cases where there is evidence of bias. If EEOC finds evidence of discrimination but decides not to pursue a lawsuit, it issues a "right to sue" letter, allowing the individual to file a lawsuit on their own.[17] Figure 4.1 shows the number of EEOC claims for various types of discrimination in 1 year. Figure 4.2 provides an overview of the process from EEOC's perspective.

EEO laws apply to all aspects of the employment relationship. Specifically, employers are prohibited from engaging in discrimination in hiring, promotion, training, job assignments, compensation, discipline, termination, and any other aspects of the employment relationship. In order to avoid discrimination, organizations are advised to collect only information necessary for them to assess employees' fit for the job and base employment decisions on job-related criteria. EEO laws also deem it illegal to *retaliate* against an employee who complains about discrimination or files a discrimination claim. Similarly, it is illegal to retaliate against those otherwise involved in a discrimination claim, such as acting as a witness. Retaliation may result in reducing pay, termination, or transferring the employee to a less desirable position. It may also take the form of any action that would dissuade an employee from complaining in the first place. In one case, an employee who made a discrimination complaint to HR was assigned to work in a cubicle with no phone. The courts decided that attempts to isolate the employee and withholding equipment could be thought of as retaliation, even though no other changes were made to employment conditions.[19]

Retaliate Taking adverse action against an employee who complains about discrimination or files a discrimination claim

Equal Pay Act of 1963 (EPA)

Pay equity between men and women remains a concern, with women being paid an average of 83 cents for every dollar men made in 2014.[20] Reasons for this gap include segregation of sexes across different occupations with different pay averages, résumé gaps due to

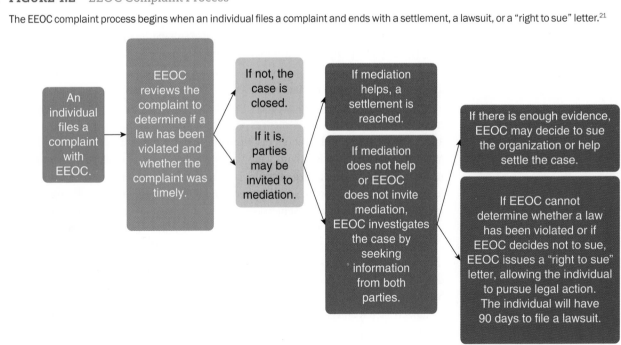

■ **FIGURE 4.2**   EEOC Complaint Process

The EEOC complaint process begins when an individual files a complaint and ends with a settlement, a lawsuit, or a "right to sue" letter.[21]

Source: EEOC. (2016). What you can expect after you file a charge. https://www.eeoc.gov/employees/process.cfm

child-rearing responsibilities, or sex discrimination. One piece of legislation aimed at closing the gap is the Equal Pay Act of 1963. This law applies to "employers engaged in commerce or production of goods," which means virtually all businesses. According to this law, in cases in which employees perform similar jobs requiring similar skills and under similar conditions, employees cannot be paid differently based on their sex. In order to make a claim, the employee would need to show that:

a. They and an employee of the other sex are working in the same place, doing equal work, *and*

b. They are paid differently for the same work.

As a defense, the employer would need to show that there is a reason other than sex for the pay difference, such as seniority, merit, or quality or quantity of production. Note that the individual does not need to prove that the organization acted intentionally when paying sexes differently; rather, simply showing that the difference exists is sufficient. The law covers all aspects of employee compensation and rewards, including salaries, benefits, commissions, stock options, and allowances. Even though job titles may be different, if the job is essentially the same, then the pay of men and women is expected to be the same. As a case in point, in 2016, a school district in Minnesota settled a case for $50,000. The school district was paying a female "custodial aide" lower wages compared to a male "custodian," even though the jobs were essentially the same. In other words, the nature of the jobs is more important than the job title in equal-pay claims.

When making pay decisions, HR professionals and managers will need to consider the existing pay distribution and ensure that there is internal and individual equity; that is, pay differences among individuals reflect differences in jobs or actual differences in performance. Further, if decision makers realize that there is unfairness in the pay structure, they would need to correct the situation. This correction can only occur by increasing the pay of the lower paid person. Reducing the pay of the highly paid individual would be another violation of the law.[22]

Title VII of the Civil Rights Act

LO 4.3 Discuss the impact of Title VII of the Civil Rights Act.

Title VII is the most comprehensive federal legislation relating to equal employment opportunities. The law, which applies to all employers with 15 or more employees, including state and government institutions, prohibits employment decisions based on sex, race, color, national origin, and religion. The law prohibits both intentional discrimination based on these protected characteristics and seemingly neutral decision criteria that have a discriminatory effect on different groups. The law includes harassment as part of discriminatory practices and prohibits retaliation against those who complain about discrimination, file a complaint, or are otherwise involved in facilitating a discrimination claim. Title VII applies to all groups equally. Discriminating against majority or historically privileged groups such as White or male employees is sometimes referred to as *reverse discrimination*. Note that there is no separate legislation prohibiting reverse discrimination: Discriminating against men as well as women, employees of all races, all religions, color, and national origin is against the law, regardless of who is the victim of discriminatory action.

Reverse discrimination
Discriminating against majority or historically privileged groups such as White or male employees

Equitable relief Payments made to a plaintiff to bring them back to the position they would have had if they were not discriminated against

Compensatory damages Providing financial relief to the complainant for damages incurred, such as mental and emotional stress suffered as a result of discrimination

Punitive damages Damages that are awarded if it is demonstrated that the company had engaged in reckless discrimination and failed to act in good faith

Title VII was originally passed in 1964 and then amended in 1991. The amendment allowed the plaintiff (the person or party bringing the case to court) to seek compensatory and punitive damages in addition to equitable relief. *Equitable relief* refers to payments made to a plaintiff to bring them back to the position they would have had if they were not discriminated against. This includes back pay and getting one's job back. *Compensatory damages* refer to providing financial relief to the complainant for damages incurred, such as mental and emotional stress suffered as a result of discrimination. *Punitive damages* are awarded if it is demonstrated that the company had engaged in reckless discrimination and failed to act in good faith. The 1991 amendment also introduced upper limits to compensatory and punitive damages. For example, if the employer has between 15 and 100 employees, the amount of damages a person may recover is limited to $50,000. At the same time, a group of individuals who have similar claims may sue as a group, creating a ***class action lawsuit***. In these cases, the limits apply to a single person, and a class action suit may include large numbers of individuals, leading to significant costs for businesses.[23]

What Is Discrimination Under Title VII?

Title VII prohibits two basic types of discrimination: ***Disparate treatment*** and ***disparate (or adverse) impact***. Disparate treatment refers to treating different groups of applicants or employees differently because of their race, color, religion, sex, or national origin. For example, if an organization requires a background check, it should be done for all employees regardless of employee race, sex, religion, or national origin. Using different tests, questions, and/or hiring and promotion procedures for different groups are examples of disparate treatment. Further, hiring or refusing to hire employees into a particular position based on these protected characteristics (such as giving preference to men for warehouse positions or giving preference to women for sales jobs in a store) is also illegal. Disparate impact involves using seemingly neutral criteria that has a discriminatory effect on a protected group. For example, a workplace policy prohibiting head coverings may seem neutral on the surface, but it is likely to have a disparate impact on Muslim, Sikh, and Orthodox Jewish employees.

Disparate Treatment

Despite the decades that have passed after the passage of Title VII in 1964, disparate treatment discrimination still occurs and continues to be costly to businesses. As a case in point, in 2010, Walmart agreed to pay more than $11 million in back pay and compensatory damages because it was ruled that for a period of 7 years, it had excluded women from warehouse positions and only hired men between the ages of 18 and 25 for these jobs, which is a violation of the law.[24] It is allowable for organizations to have physical ability requirements for particular positions, but they may not have policies segregating employees of different sexes or other protected characteristics into different positions.

Here is how a disparate treatment case is handled: Imagine that an applicant applies for a job at a retail store. She wears a hijab, a veil traditionally worn by Muslim women. She is qualified for the job. The interviewer asks several questions about her need to wear this particular clothing and her religion in general. After the interview, the applicant learns that she did not get the job. Instead, the company hires someone who has less experience in retail. The applicant would have ***prima facie evidence*** (at first glance, or preliminary evidence) that discrimination may have happened because:

a. The person applied for a job for which she was qualified;

b. She was rejected despite being qualified, and someone with similar or less qualifications was hired;

c. There is circumstantial evidence indicating that religion, a protected characteristic, may have been a factor.

After prima facie evidence has been established, the burden of proof shifts to the employer. Now the employer will need to demonstrate that there was a nondiscriminatory reason for the decision. For example, if the job candidate lacked critical skills or the person who was hired was chosen for a different and nondiscriminatory reason, such as a specific expertise, this would be the employer's defense. If there is strong evidence that religion was the reason for not hiring this applicant (e.g., e-mails come to light that display religious prejudice on the part of the hiring manager), then the employment decision would be deemed illegal.

If the employer can present a nondiscriminatory reason, the burden of proof once again shifts to the applicant. Now the applicant would need to show that the reason provided by the employer is a ***pretext***, or an excuse and not the real reason. This can be shown if the employer's reason is factually incorrect or there is some evidence that it was not the true reason.

Class action lawsuit When individuals who have similar claims sue as a group

Disparate treatment Treating different groups of applicants or employees differently because of their race, color, religion, sex, or national origin

Disparate (or adverse) impact When employers use seemingly neutral criteria that have a discriminatory effect on a protected group

Prima facie evidence At first glance, or preliminary evidence

Pretext An excuse given for a decision that is not the real reason

MANAGER'S TOOLBOX

Avoiding Illegal Interview Questions and Employment Practices

Consider the following interview questions and employment practices and why they may be potentially illegal.[25]

Are you married?	This question may violate state laws prohibiting marital status discrimination. If only asked to women, it may be an example of sex discrimination under Title VII. The organization may be trying to screen out female applicants who are likely to become pregnant, violating pregnancy discrimination. It is best to avoid asking this question during hiring.
How old are your children?	Again, if this is a question only asked to women, it would be an example of sex discrimination. Given its irrelevance to the hiring process and potential discriminatory effects, this question is best avoided.
You have an interesting accent. Where did you grow up?	This question could reveal the national origin of the applicant, which is a protected category.
Have you ever been arrested?	Statistically, Hispanic and Black men are more likely to have been arrested, and arrest record is not a reliable indicator of crime. Therefore, the use of this criterion could have disparate impact.
Using a thick accent as a reason not to hire	If the accent does not seriously interfere with one's performance at work, using someone's accent as a reason not to hire them may be discrimination based on national origin.
Using English-only rules	A policy forbidding the use of one language (e.g., no Spanish) would be illegal due to national origin discrimination. English-only rules may be legal as long as they are dictated by business necessity and job requirements. For this reason, implementing such rules during breaks will be suspect. If other languages are being used in a hostile way to harass others, English-only rules would be appropriate.
Using a language test as part of hiring	Even in cases in which communication in English is essential for the job, requiring language skills that go beyond what is needed during the regular performance of the job could be a violation of Title VII.
Do you have a disability that requires an accommodation? What impairments do you have?	Even with good intent, it is best to avoid this question. If the employee has a disability, the accommodation request should come from the employee. Learning about the applicant's disability in the prehire stage could result in liability. It is acceptable to ask whether the individual is able to perform the major functions of the job.

What Should Organizations Do to Proactively Defend Themselves Against Disparate Treatment Claims?

In Title VII disparate treatment cases, the employer may present two kinds of defense. First, they may show that there was a nondiscriminatory reason for the adverse action against the applicant or employee. To do that, employers would need to be aware of the law and must avoid using legally protected characteristics in their employment decisions. Additionally, they must keep careful records of all applicants following interviews and document all employment decisions to be able to defend them when necessary.

A second defense of the organization could be to show that the protected characteristic in this particular case is a ***bona fide occupational qualification (BFOQ)***, or an essential necessity of the

Bona fide occupational qualification (BFOQ)
A particular instance where a normally legally protected characteristic (such as age or gender) is an essential necessity of a job

job. BFOQ is a very narrow defense, and claims that a characteristic is important for the business in question because of customer preferences typically fail. Instead, successful uses of the BFOQ defense involve customers' privacy concerns. As a case in point, Beth Israel Medical Center was able to successfully defend itself in a lawsuit brought by a male OB/GYN. The doctor claimed the hospital was discriminating against him because it was accommodating female patients who expressed a preference for female doctors. In this case, the court found gender to be a BFOQ due to patients' privacy concerns. However, a similar argument was not effective when a spa owned by Marriott International, Inc., wanted to accommodate male customers who desired a female massage therapist. In this case, the BFOQ defense failed when the case reached the federal district court. Although there are circumstances that may make a protected characteristic a BFOQ, these cases are narrow, and customer preferences (other than privacy concerns) are unlikely to be considered a BFOQ.[26]

Disparate Impact

Discrimination that involves discriminatory intent, the use of different criteria, asking additional questions, or indicating a preference for one sex, race, religion, and national origin are types of disparate treatment. However, according to Title VII, discrimination does not necessarily involve discriminatory intent. Instead, employers may sometimes use seemingly neutral criteria that have a discriminatory effect on a protected group. This type of discrimination is termed *disparate impact* (or adverse impact). In fact, a charge of disparate impact does not imply intention on the part of an employer. For example, organizations often use tests that may lead to greater hiring of one group than others. The City of Chicago used a physical performance test to hire paramedics between 2000 and 2014. During this period, 98% of all men and 60% of all women who took the test passed. The court sided with the female paramedics who brought the lawsuit.[27] Even though it is a seemingly neutral criterion, the test had different effects on male and female candidates. Similarly, if an organization refuses to hire those who are shorter than 6 feet, they are less likely to hire women, Asians, and Hispanics. Certain personality and cognitive ability tests also affect different groups differentially. When a test has different effects on different groups, the company will need to demonstrate that there is a business necessity to use that specific test. If there is no compelling reason, then its use may be illegal under Title VII. Note that disparate impact claims are different from disparate treatment in that the plaintiff may not claim compensatory and punitive damages. The payments made to complainants are limited to equitable relief, in addition to an order to the organization to stop using the particular discriminatory practice.

Disparate impact claims do not necessitate showing evidence that discrimination was intentional. In a claim involving disparate impact, prima facie evidence can be demonstrated by showing that the selection criterion or employment policy has a differential effect on different groups. This requires a statistical analysis to assess the effects of the selection criterion. In 1978, EEOC, the Department of Labor, and the Department of Justice adopted the **Uniform Guidelines on Employee Selection Procedures**, which outline how selection systems can be designed to comply with EEO laws. According to the Uniform Guidelines, a simple way of establishing whether disparate impact occurred is to use the *4/5ths (or 80%) rule*. According to this rule, one group's selection ratio may not be less than 80% of the majority group's ratio. In the example of the City of Chicago's paramedics, the male paramedic selection ratio was 98%, whereas for women, it was 60%. The question is, Is this gap large enough to show that female applicants were negatively affected? To answer this question, multiply 98 by 80%, which is 78.4%. Given that female applicants had a selection ratio of 60%, which is less than 78.4%, there is prima facie evidence that the test was discriminatory. Alternatively, divide 60% by 98%, which is 61%. Because this is smaller than 80%, there is prima facie evidence that disparate impact exists. The 4/5ths rule is criticized because it is prone to giving false positives (shows discrimination when none exists). Instead, organizations may use more rigorous statistical tests such as a chi-square test, particularly if they have a large sample. An example of how to conduct the chi-square test to establish prima facie evidence for disparate impact appears in the *Data and Analytics Exercise* for this chapter.

Once prima facie evidence is established, the burden of proof shifts to the employer. Now they would need to demonstrate that the test in question is job related and is consistent with business

Uniform Guidelines on Employee Selection Procedures Guidelines adopted by EEOC, the Department of Labor, and the Department of Justice, which outline how selection systems can be designed to comply with EEO laws

4/5ths (or 80%) rule According to this rule, a protected group's selection ratio may not be less than 80% of the majority group's ratio

necessity. If the employer can prove that performance on this specific test is predictive of job performance and skills assessed on this test are essential to the safe and effective performance of the job, then the employer will be able to continue its use of this process. However, if the person challenging the selection procedure can demonstrate that there are other, nondiscriminatory alternatives to the test in question, then the employer may need to abandon their use of this criterion. The Uniform Guidelines (http://uniformguidelines.com/uniformguidelines.html#20) include information regarding how to validate selection tests and ensure that they comply with Title VII. In other words, an organization may continue to use a specific test if its validity can be established. However, often organizations have difficulty defending themselves because the requirements of selection tests may not reflect the reality of the jobs. For example, in manual jobs, the physical agility or ability requirements expected of job applicants may be harsher than what the job actually entails, leading to the conclusion that the test unnecessarily discriminates. Even though a test or other hiring method may *seem* valid, the organization needs to be able to defend its use through actual data.

What Should Organizations Do to Proactively Defend Themselves Against Disparate Impact Claims?

When it comes to disparate impact cases, the employer's defense is to establish that the test being used is job related and that there is a business necessity. To establish job relatedness, organizations need to be ready to defend the validity of their tests. The cutoffs used in selection tests should be reasonable and aligned with normal expectations in the day-to-day performance of the job. The Uniform

■ FIGURE 4.3   The Process of Showing Disparate Treatment and Disparate Impact

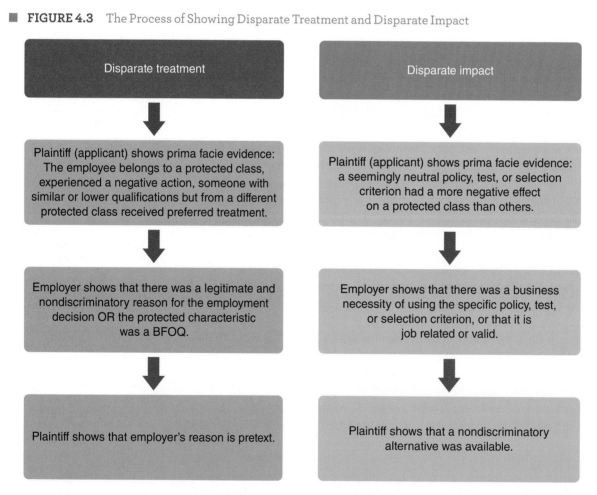

Source: Based on information from https://www.eeoc.gov/policy/docs/factemployment_procedures.html

Guidelines is an important source for HR professionals in charge of selecting tests and setting decision criteria used to screen out and make employment decisions about employees and applicants. Figure 4.3 summarizes the two processes for showing disparate treatment and disparate impact.

Title VII and Harassment

In addition to prohibiting discrimination based on disparate impact and disparate treatment, Title VII has prohibitions around harassment. *Harassment* involves unwelcome behaviors based on sex, race, religion, national origin, and other protected characteristics. Under Title VII, harassment that would be offensive to a reasonable person and that occurs on a frequent basis so that it creates a hostile work environment is illegal. Harassment may include name-calling; offensive jokes, pictures, or other explicit materials; and insults or mockery, among others. What is important to know about harassment is:

Harassment Unwelcome behaviors based on sex, race, religion, national origin, and other protected characteristics

a. Companies are liable for harassment perpetuated by supervisors, coworkers, nonemployees, and customers;

b. Harassment does not need to have financial consequences for the employee;

c. Even individuals who are not the direct victims of harassment may have a legal claim if being part of a hostile work environment has been negatively affecting them.[28]

Sexual harassment, which includes unwanted advances and other harassment that is sexual in nature, is also prohibited. Title VII does not contain specific clauses about sexual harassment, but courts have treated sexual harassment as a type of sex-based harassment, and therefore Title VII applies to cases of sexual harassment. The victim of sexual harassment may be male or female, and the victim and the perpetrator do not need to be of opposite sexes. EEOC defines two forms of sexual harassment. *Quid pro quo harassment* involves making employment decisions contingent on sexual favors. A manager hinting that a promotion or a raise depends on the employee providing a sexual favor or punishing an employee for refusing to fulfill a sexual request are examples of quid pro quo harassment. In other words, the use of sexual favors as a bargaining tool in employment decisions is prohibited. Alternatively, sexual harassment may be in the form of creating a *hostile work environment*, or conduct sexual in nature that contributes to an environment that a reasonable person would find offensive.

Christopher Polk/Getty Images for JumpLine

Sexual harassment took center stage in 2017 when women started speaking out against rampant sexual harassment by powerful men in entertainment, media, and politics. The #MeToo movement demonstrated the prevalence of harassment, with many celebrities sharing their stories.

What constitutes a hostile work environment? The following elements typically would need to be in place:

1. The plaintiff is a member of a protected class.

2. The plaintiff was subjected to harassment.

3. The plaintiff experienced harassment due to their protected class.

4. The conduct affected the employment of the plaintiff.

5. The employer knew about or should have known about the harassment and did nothing to protect the employee.

Sexual harassment Unwanted advances and other harassment that is sexual in nature

Quid pro quo harassment Involves making employment decisions contingent on sexual favors

Hostile work environment Behavior that contributes to an environment a reasonable person would find offensive

Because claims against organizations are more likely to be successful if the company had known and yet failed to act on the information, businesses should establish safeguards by training their managers and employees, ensuring that there are clear and safe mechanisms for employees to voice complaints, and any such complaints are taken seriously and resolved promptly. Recall that retaliating against complainants or resolving the issue in a way that punishes the victim (such as transferring the victim to a less desirable job) are problematic and increase the company's liability.

Title VII and Special Considerations Regarding Sex Discrimination

Title VII prohibits the use of one's sex in employment-related decisions. A simple way of thinking about this is that organizations may not classify jobs as "men's jobs" and "women's jobs" unless there is a strong reason to believe that sex is a BFOQ. Making assumptions about one's sex and using those stereotypes in employment decisions is also illegal. For example, an employer may not restrict jobs with physical demands to men with the assumption that men have greater physical endurance.

Title VII and the Equal Pay Act (EPA) both provide protections, even though EPA is solely concerned with pay differentials, whereas Title VII is more comprehensive and includes all types of employment decisions. A plaintiff concerned about pay discrimination can technically utilize either or both laws, but there are important differences. When filing a claim based on EPA, plaintiffs are not required to go through EEOC. This means they can initiate a lawsuit themselves. Further, EPA applies to businesses of all sizes, but Title VII only applies to businesses with 15 or more employees. EPA claims may be filed within a longer period of time, and the prima facie evidence is simpler to establish. In this case, the plaintiff simply needs to show that a man and a woman, doing essentially the same work, are paid differently. In the case of Title VII, the plaintiff would need to show that the difference was motivated by differences in sex. Companies are often asked to run statistics such as the chi-square test or t-tests to show that there is a statistically significant pay difference between men and women. One main advantage of Title VII for plaintiffs is that it allows them to recover more money at the end of the lawsuit.[29]

The maker of Sara Lee brands agreed to pay $4 million to settle a race discrimination suit in 2015. Jobs held exclusively by African American employees were subject to asbestos, mold, and other hazards, and employees noted that they experienced racial harassment and discrimination.[31]

Reasonable accommodation An accommodation provided to employees to help them perform their jobs that is reasonable given a firm's resources

Title VII, Race, and Color

Title VII prohibits discrimination in employment based on race or having policies and procedures that have a discriminatory impact on individuals of a particular race. Restricting certain positions to a particular race is a violation of the law. For example, in 2016, a temporary staffing agency settled a case for $435,000 because it had given preference to Hispanic employees in its placements and discriminated against African Americans and also retaliated against an employee who raised concerns about the situation. Treating employees of different races differently is also a violation. As a case in point, in 2016, a sheet metal union agreed to a $1.6 million settlement because EEOC's analysis showed that African American and Hispanic workers received fewer hours and lower wages. In other words, organizations are advised to examine their employment practices to ensure that there are job-related and defensible reasons for decisions that lead to differences in pay, hiring, promotion, and advancement of employees.[30] Finally, harassment based on one's race is illegal, and management is advised to take action immediately when informed of racial harassment.

Title VII and Religion

In addition to prohibiting discrimination in employment decisions based on religion, Title VII requires organizations to provide **reasonable accommodation.** Simple nondiscrimination is insufficient by itself, and in fact, uniform application of organizational rules with rigidity may be a cause for discrimination claims. Organizations are asked to make allowances for an employee for their religion unless doing so imposes an undue hardship on the employer. In other words, when the employer's dress code policy, work schedules, breaks, and time-off periods clash with employee religious needs, employers are expected to make a good-faith effort to accommodate them. This may involve making an exception for the employee with respect to the dress code or accommodating their schedule so they can take part in religious observances on a certain day of the week or time of year.

The law defines a religion as one's sincerely held beliefs, which include both mainstream religions and those practiced by a small minority. Title VII also protects individuals from being discriminated against because they have no religious beliefs. Finally, the expectation that the

SPOTLIGHT ON ETHICS

Applicants With Criminal History

Should an organization avoid hiring individuals with a criminal background? There is no federal law prohibiting discrimination against former inmates. Yet having blanket policies excluding those with criminal backgrounds has an ethical dimension. There are certainly legitimate reasons for not hiring someone with a criminal record, particularly when public health and safety are a concern. If the ex-convict commits a crime and harms a coworker or customer, the organization may be responsible for negligent hiring. At the same time, the rehabilitation of ex-convicts depends on finding employment. Depending on when the crime occurred and what it was, the risks to the business may be minimal. In some cases, individuals choose to plead guilty instead of fighting a conviction, which helps them avoid incarceration but results in a criminal record.

Businesses such as Seattle-based Mod Pizza and Oregon-based Dave's Killer Bread are committed to giving those with criminal backgrounds a second chance, and they benefit from a qualified and highly motivated workforce. There is also a movement ("ban the box") for states and jurisdictions to pass laws banning the question "Have you been convicted of a crime?" on employment applications. These laws typically do not prevent companies from using criminal history as part of the hiring process, but they require the employer to wait until a job offer is made before a criminal background check is conducted; the offer may then be revoked if needed. There are no easy answers, but whether and how criminal records should be used in employment decisions is an ethical dilemma.[32]

Questions

1. As a manager, suppose you need to decide whether to hire a candidate with excellent qualifications for the position but with a felony conviction in his/her background. What factors would you take into consideration to decide whether to hire this candidate?

2. Think of a case, or find one in the literature, of a company that encountered legal trouble as a result of hiring an employee with a criminal record. What could have been done differently? What did the company do right?

employee would need to be accommodated due to their religion may not be a reason to discriminate against an employee. In a 2015 Supreme Court case against the clothing retailer Abercrombie & Fitch, a job applicant was denied employment because she wore a hijab. The assumption was that the hijab would have clashed with the company's dress code prohibiting head caps. Even though the applicant had not mentioned her religion or asked for an accommodation, the use of assumptions about her religion as a reason not to hire her was ruled to be illegal.[33]

Training managers is a key first step of legal compliance. An important issue is to avoid asking questions about religion during job interviews. Instead, focus should be on job characteristics and whether employees are able to perform the job. If it becomes clear that the employee needs a religious accommodation, the organization must consider whether a reasonable accommodation is possible. This is a high bar: If the employer chooses not to accommodate, it must show that accommodation would have been unsafe or extremely costly or would significantly affect other employees. Mere inconvenience for the employer is not a justifiable reason not to accommodate. If an HR manager observes or hears that someone is being harassed because of their religion (or due to other reasons), immediate action should be taken. The organization should outline and inform employees about communication channels they should use if they experience harassment.

Title VII and National Origin

Title VII has protections against national origin discrimination. Taking adverse action against someone due to their nationality or due to the nationality of someone they are related to (e.g., married to) is prohibited under this law. Harassment of others based on nationality is also prohibited. Seeking to hire U.S. citizens, unless necessitated by a government contract or other special reason, is prohibited, given that U.S. citizenship is not necessary to be legally employed in the United States. Discriminating based on accent is prohibited under Title VII, and instituting English-only rules, unless there is a business necessity such as safety of others, is a practice that should be used cautiously. It is also important for businesses to disregard nationality-related information in employment decisions. For example, the consulting firm Accenture was faced with a class action lawsuit claiming that it paid software engineers from India (who were working in the United States) significantly less than what American engineers were being paid, forcing the company to settle the case for $500,000.[34]

LO 4.4   Identify additional antidiscrimination acts and protections in the workplace.

Additional Antidiscrimination Acts and Protections

Along with Title VII of the Civil Rights Act, additional acts and amendments have been put in place by states and municipalities to protect employees. These acts include, but are not limited to, the Pregnancy Discrimination Act of 1978, Age Discrimination in Employment Act of 1967, Americans with Disabilities Act of 1990, Genetic Information Nondiscrimination Act of 2008, and Lilly Ledbetter Fair Pay Act of 2009, along with additional protections for LGBTQ workers.

Pregnancy Discrimination Act (PDA) of 1978

This law is an amendment of Title VII and prohibits employers from discriminating against employees due to a pregnancy or related conditions. An individual's pregnancy or assumptions about pregnant individuals may not be used in hiring decisions as long as the person is capable of performing the major functions of the job. Further, all employment-related decisions including training, scheduling, benefits, and promotions are protected. In cases in which the employee seeks leave, the employer may not treat a pregnancy-related leave any differently than leave granted to employees due to other reasons. For example, the employer may not seek more evidence or information. Employers may not prevent an employee from returning to work following a pregnancy, and they may not assign them inferior work upon return.[35]

A common reason for pregnancy discrimination claims is the refusal on the part of employers to accommodate pregnant employees, and a 2015 Supreme Court decision reaffirms the importance of treating pregnancy-related requests similarly to other medical requests. In the legal case *Young v. UPS*, following her doctor's advice, a UPS driver sought to take on lighter duties with lower weight-lifting requirements during her pregnancy. UPS did not accommodate the employee's request, stating that its policy was to treat pregnancies similarly to an off-the-job injury, which meant that the employee was not entitled to special accommodations. The employee was instead put on unpaid leave, resulting in the loss of her medical insurance. However, employees injured on the job, employees with other disabilities, and those employees who had lost their Department of Transportation credentials were routinely accommodated through lighter duties, suggesting that temporarily accommodating employees was not an undue hardship for the business, and UPS was unable to present a nondiscriminatory and legitimate reason for why employees could not be accommodated for a pregnancy-related condition but other classes of employees could be accommodated for other temporary disabilities. The Supreme Court decision suggests that employers should treat a pregnancy as a form of temporary disability and react to it similarly.[36]

The PDA does not permit a paternalistic attitude in which businesses make assumptions about pregnant workers regarding their physical limitations or their ability to withstand particular work conditions. For example, in the Supreme Court case *UAW v. Johnson Controls* (1991), the company was challenged for its policy of excluding women who were of child-bearing age from certain jobs, with the rationale that they would become exposed to harmful levels of lead, harming their unborn children. This policy was found to violate PDA.[37] Instead, businesses need to make efforts to protect all employees and inform employees about any risks but leave decisions regarding working arrangements to employees. Restricting pregnant employees or those who might get pregnant to specific positions, even with the belief that such restrictions protect the employee, are prohibited.

The PDA is not the only legislation that pertains to pregnancy and related conditions. Pregnancy-related complications are protected under the Americans with Disabilities Act (ADA), which is discussed later in this chapter. The Family and Medical Leave Act (FMLA) covers leave employees are entitled to take, including for childbirth and adoptions. The Affordable Care Act (ACA) has provisions requiring some employers to accommodate the needs of new mothers by giving them sufficient break time to pump breast milk and a private space to do so. These legislative developments suggest that it would be helpful for employers to take a proactive approach toward pregnant employees to accommodate their needs and to ensure they do not experience discrimination.

©iStock.com/Yuri_Arcurs

The Pregnancy Discrimination Act protects employees during and after a pregnancy. Failing to give the employee the same or a similar job upon return to work may be a violation of PDA.

Age Discrimination in Employment Act of 1967 (ADEA)

Stereotypes about older workers persist, despite accumulated evidence that these assumptions and stereotypes are simply wrong in the face of empirical evidence.[38] The Age Discrimination in Employment Act (ADEA) applies to employers with 20 or more workers and prohibits employers from discriminating against an applicant or employee due to their age. The ADEA protects only individuals 40 years of age or older and only applies in cases where old age is used as a rationale to exclude an individual from opportunities. When an older worker is preferred over a younger one, even when age was a factor used in decision making, the decision is not necessarily illegal under ADEA. However, preferring a younger person to an older one is illegal, even when both are over the age of 40. In other words, if an organization favors a 50-year-old over a 60-year-old for a promotion and uses relative youth as a criterion, the decision would be illegal. Similar to other EEO laws, harassment due to one's age from managers, coworkers, or customers is also prohibited, and age-based comments and teasing that are frequent enough to create a hostile work environment would be illegal.[39] While the law provides protections, age discrimination is challenging to prove. The Supreme Court decision of *Gross v. FBL Financial Services* in 2009 suggests that plaintiffs have the burden of proof that age was the primary reason for the adverse employment decision (as opposed to the employer having to prove that it would have taken that action regardless of age).[40]

ADEA becomes particularly relevant when discussing retirement issues with older workers. Forcing employees to retire by insisting on it or by eliminating their position will introduce the possibility that the decision is biased. Firing or demoting an employee close to a time of retirement discussions also opens the company up for liability.

One important first step to defend a business against ADEA claims is to avoid asking questions about the employee's age, which surprisingly still happens. In a lawsuit involving an Indiana manufacturer, the job applicant was asked whether he was within the "ideal age range" for the position, which was 45 to 52. The applicant was denied employment when he admitted that he was older. The case resulted in a settlement of $100,000.[41] Similarly, the organization should avoid using age or age-related stereotypes in employment-related decisions. Having a legitimate and nondiscriminatory reason for all business decisions and application of all HR decisions consistently across age groups is particularly important.

Americans with Disabilities Act (ADA) of 1990

The ADA prohibits discrimination against individuals with disabilities who are able to perform the major functions of the job with or without accommodations. The act was amended in 2008 (Americans with Disabilities Act Amendment Act—ADAAA). The act applies to organizations with 15 or more employees and defines a disability as a physical or mental impairment that affects one's major life activities. ADAAA provides a list of major life activities in consideration of a disability and includes activities such as walking, reading, and communicating and major bodily functions such as functions of the immune system, respiratory, reproductive, and neurological functions. Having a history of a specific ailment and being perceived as disabled are two additional forms of protected disabilities. Impairments that are episodic are a disability if they limit major life activities when they are active. ADAAA provides a list of conditions that are always considered a disability (e.g., HIV infection, cancer, bipolar disorder). There is also a list of conditions that are *not* considered a disability: pedophilia, compulsive gambling, voyeurism, and exhibitionism, among others. Obesity may be a disability if it limits one's major life activities.

If an ailment does not affect major life activities, it is not considered a disability eligible for ADA protection. Consider employees terminated due to stuttering. The history of court cases suggests that when plaintiffs reported that they had mild stuttering that did not affect their performance or the rest of their lives, the courts found that stuttering did not constitute a disability for ADA purposes, and thus firing these employees was not a legally protected form of termination. However, in cases in which the plaintiff suffered from severe stuttering or stuttered in an episodic manner that constituted a major limit on their interactions with others, it was considered a qualifying disability. This means that it is the company's obligation to provide reasonable accommodations and not use the disability in employment-related decisions as long as the employee can perform the major functions of the job.[42]

Essential functions Job tasks or goals that every incumbent needs to perform

Marginal functions Job tasks or goals that can be assigned to others

Each job has ***essential functions*** that every incumbent needs to perform, as well as ***marginal functions*** that can be assigned to others. Essential functions are core tasks that are expected of all incumbents and are important for effective and safe performance of the job. If the person is not capable of performing the essential functions even with accommodations, the employer is not required to hire or retain the individual. However, if the disability is preventing the person from performing the marginal functions, these functions may be reassigned to others, and the disability may not be a factor in decision making. Finally, the law uses the term *reasonable accommodations* to indicate that as long as accommodating the person does not cause undue hardship on the business, the employer is expected to provide accommodations. What is reasonable depends on the size and resources available to the business, indicating that employers are expected to make a good-faith effort in providing accommodations.

In order to be able to accommodate the individual, the organization needs to know about the specific disability and the need for an accommodation. Unless a disability is obvious, the request needs to originate from the employee, and once a request is made, the employer and employee are expected to arrive at a mutual resolution. Employers are advised not to inquire whether the individual has a disability and to avoid asking medical questions as part of the hiring process. Among the accommodations available to employees may be unpaid leave, particularly if it is available to other employees. Employees with disabilities are expected to be treated similarly to other employees seeking leave, and if evidence is requested for the reason for leave, such evidence should be sought from all employees seeking leave. Organizations are allowed to set maximum limits on how much leave employees are entitled to take, but they may need to make exceptions in the case of disability-related leave, as long as doing so does not create an undue hardship for the business.[43] ADA compliance has few strict and specific rules other than making a genuine effort to consider the employee's request and provide accommodations within the organization's means.

ADA compliance requires careful planning. The organization would benefit from having updated job descriptions that clearly delineate essential job functions and marginal duties. Organizations should have job descriptions that reflect the actual job content as performed within the organization. Managers need to be trained in understanding what constitutes a disability. When a request for accommodation is received, it is essential for managers and HR to be open to ideas and work with the individual to arrive at solutions. Just because an accommodation is unusual is not a reason to dismiss it. The organization is not required to provide an extremely costly and burdensome accommodation, or even the first choice of the individual, but a good-faith effort is important. As with other EEO laws, organizations should ensure that employees are trained to be respectful to all colleagues, including those with disabilities.[44]

SPOTLIGHT ON GLOBAL ISSUES

EEO Laws in a Global Context

Each country approaches diversity and inclusion in its own way; some countries offer no protections, while others offer greater protections than are typically found in the United States. The EEO laws in this chapter apply to all businesses operating in the United States and its territories, regardless of where the business is headquartered. The EEO laws also cover U.S. citizens working in U.S.-based firms overseas. In the case of a multinational firm such as Microsoft or Facebook, all employees within in the United States and all U.S. citizens working for foreign subsidiaries are covered, but citizens of the other countries in which these businesses are located are not covered. Further, when operating overseas, U.S.-based firms are permitted to violate EEO laws if compliance would lead to violating the laws of the country in which they operate.[45]

One interesting divergence between the United States and other countries is that many other countries use quotas as a way to ensure diversity of operations. For example, Germany, Norway, France, Spain, Italy, and other European countries have laws dictating that a specific percentage of board of director members be female. In China, public and private employers are required to hire individuals with disabilities as 1.5% of their workforce, and those failing to meet the quota are fined. When doing business overseas, organizations need to be aware of the EEO laws of the locales in which they operate, if any.[46]

Genetic Information Nondiscrimination Act (GINA) of 2008

The Genetic Information Nondiscrimination Act (GINA) of 2008 is a federal law that prohibits organizations from discriminating against applicants or employees in employment decisions (and in health insurance) based on genetic information. Genetic information is defined as the results of genetic tests, as well as family health history. This means that employers covered by GINA are prohibited from using an employee's family history and other genetic information when making decisions about them. It is also illegal for employers to require employees to submit their genetic information. The law covers organizations with 15 and more employees. It does not cover federal employees or members of the military, but each institution is covered by separate laws against genetic discrimination. In some instances, employers may obtain genetic information, such as through voluntary participation in a company's wellness program, but the employer needs to keep this information separate from employment decisions and protect information privacy. According to EEOC rules, employees may not offer employees incentives to disclose genetic information, with the exception of wellness programs. Genetic disclosures as part of wellness programs are regulated as well, with upper limits to how much incentive employers may provide to encourage participation in wellness programs and requirements to avoid discrimination based on this information.[47]

GINA is a recent law, and therefore complaints based on GINA are still rare but growing. GINA complaints usually result from requiring applicants or employees to submit data on their family history. In the first case that went to trial (*Lowe v. Atlas Logistics Group*, 2015), the transportation company wanted to find out the culprits of an employee wrongdoing by conducting genetic tests. The company narrowed the suspects to a small number of employees based on their schedules and asked employees to submit to a DNA test. Two employees (who were not found to be matches) later filed GINA complaints to EEOC. The lawsuit ended with the plaintiffs being awarded $2.225 million (later reduced to $300,000 per person).[48]

Subsequent to this case, GINA violations have been based on requests for family medical information. For example, in 2016, EEOC sued a Pittsburgh manufacturer for requiring job applicants to note whether "they had a family history of [tuberculosis], cancer, diabetes, epilepsy, or heart disease" as part of the application form. GINA prohibits requesting this information from employees or applicants. Further, if an employee is asked to submit to a medical exam as a precondition for employment, the employer is responsible if the providers of these "fitness for duty" exams violate the law. In 2015, an EEOC lawsuit involved a newly hired employee being asked family medical history information as part of the fitness-for-duty exam conducted by an outside provider. The employee was fired because he refused to answer the questions and therefore did not complete the exam. The organization claimed that the provider was responsible for the violation, but the court upheld that the employer was responsible for actions taken on its behalf.[49]

Lilly Ledbetter Fair Pay Act of 2009

This law is an amendment to Title VII, ADEA, and ADA and specifically relates to pay discrimination cases. Prior to the passage of this law, a pay discrimination decision under these acts had to be filed within 180 days after discriminatory acts. This was highly impractical, because employees often do not become aware of discrimination until months or years after the fact. This was the situation for Lilly Ledbetter, who worked as a supervisor for Goodyear Tire until her retirement. Over time, her pay lagged behind that of her male peers, even those with less seniority. Ledbetter did not find out about the situation until she had worked there for 19 years, and therefore it was not possible for her to file a claim within 180 days. She filed a lawsuit, but the Supreme Court (*Ledbetter v. Goodyear Tire & Rubber Co.*, 2007) held that she should have filed the suit within 180 days. Under the Lilly Ledbetter Fair Pay Act (2009), the 180-day clock restarts with each paycheck, allowing employees to file a claim after they find out that discrimination occurred.[50]

Protections for LGBTQ Workers

Legal protections for gender identity and sexual orientation constitute an evolving field. Individuals may have gender identity or expression that differs from their biological sex, and they may be sexually or romantically attracted to the opposite sex, the same sex, both, or neither. In the United States, an estimated 9 million individuals identify as lesbian, gay, bisexual, transgender, questioning, or queer. Studies suggest that between 15% and 43% of homosexual individuals experienced discrimination, and 90% of transgender individuals experienced harassment and mistreatment at work. There is no specific federal law prohibiting employment discrimination based on sexual orientation or gender identity in private industry, although there are specific regulations for federal employers and contractors. As of 2016, 20 states, as well as the District of Columbia, Guam, and Puerto Rico, have laws prohibiting discrimination based on both sexual orientation and gender identity in private and public sectors. Additional states provide protections for sexual orientation but not gender identity, and some states provide protections in public but not private employment. In addition, some cities and localities provide protections even though the states in which they are located do not.[51]

EEOC regards gender identity and sexual orientation as part of Title VII's sex discrimination clause, taking the view that Title VII provides protections to LGBTQ workers. However, the U.S. Department of Justice does not endorse this view as of this writing.[52] In a growing number of court cases, EEOC interpretation was upheld, but in other cases, the EEOC interpretation was challenged.[53] The issue is controversial because Congress has repeatedly failed to pass specific legislation to prohibit discrimination based on sexual orientation. In fact, a bill called the Employment Non-Discrimination Act (ENDA) has been regularly introduced in Congress since 1994 but has not passed. Some courts took this to mean that Title VII sex discrimination was not intended as protection for LGBTQ workers.[54]

One area in which clear protections exist is the issue of same-sex sexual harassment. There is general consensus that Title VII prohibits sexual harassment regardless of the sex of perpetrator and victim, including same-sex harassment. Further, based on precedent, Title VII allows for a stronger case to be made for protections of transgender applicants and workers. Title VII's prohibitions against sex discrimination and gender stereotyping suggests that discriminating against an employee because they violate expectations of how a man or woman should act is considered discrimination. Therefore, courts have often interpreted claims by transgender individuals who did not conform to traditional gender notions as examples of sex discrimination. In a landmark Supreme Court case from 1989 (*Price Waterhouse v. Hopkins*), a female employee was denied partnership in the firm because she was considered to be "too macho"; she was told to go to "charm school" and learn how to "dress and walk like a woman." Although this case did not involve a transgender employee, it established the framework that discriminating against individuals because they do not conform to stereotypes about their biological sex is prohibited. Examples of successful cases involving transgender workers include occasions in which an employee was fired or was discriminated against after the employer found out about employee plans for transitioning, harassing a transgender employee by intentionally calling them by their former name, and disciplining them for failure to comply with the company dress code. Courts are split on whether employees are required to provide access to restrooms that match the employee's gender identity or whether failure to provide such access constitutes unlawful discrimination.[55]

In 2015, EEOC issued a ruling for the first time that it regards sexual orientation discrimination to be a form of sex discrimination and therefore covered under Title VII and filed lawsuits based on this rationale. The rationale is simple: Sexual orientation is intricately linked to sex. In the example provided by EEOC, if an employer takes adverse action against a female employee for displaying a picture of her female spouse but does not take similar action against a male employee displaying a picture of his female spouse, the female employee would have been discriminated against due to her sex. Whether this argument will be successful in cases against private employers remains to be seen. In cases in which the legal argument was based around a person not fitting the gender stereotype (e.g., looking and acting feminine or masculine), courts decided that Title VII protections applied.[56]

A 2016 Supreme Court case (*EEOC v. R.G. & G.R. Harris Funeral Homes*) may be considered a step back for LGBTQ worker protections. In the case of a funeral home employee fired for transitioning from male to female, the court upheld the employer's right to fire the employee due to the funeral home's argument that accommodating the employee would violate the employer's sincerely held religious beliefs. In the case of closely held businesses, employers' religious beliefs may shield employers from damages, at least according to the way the legal landscape stood as of 2016.[57]

Fear of disclosing one's gender identity and sexual orientation is associated with negative outcomes, whereas openness and the ability to be open and authentic about oneself have benefits for workplace outcomes including job attitudes, stress, and workplace adjustment.[58] Therefore, organizations are advised to be proactive with respect to adding protections for LGBTQ workers. Providing training for employees and managers, making allowances in the dress code for transitioning employees, using the correct names and gender pronouns, respecting confidentiality of employee plans to transition, and treating applicants and employees with dignity and respect regardless of their specific gender identity and sexual orientation are among the ways organizations may create an inclusive and respectful environment.[59]

Alan Joyce, CEO of the Australian Qantas airlines, was named the most powerful LGBT executive in the world in 2017. He credits the inclusive culture of Qantas for the turnaround of the company and recording the highest profits in its 95-year history.[60]

Brendon Thorne/Bloomberg via Getty Images

Diversity and Inclusion in the Age of HR Analytics

Up to this point, we have discussed the importance of diversity and inclusion and covered the legal terrain affecting diversity in the workplace. Now we address initiatives and methods companies are using in order to manage diversity effectively.

Should Companies Use Affirmative Action?

Affirmative Action Plans (AAPs) aim to increase hiring and labor participation of groups that suffered from past discrimination. Some companies are legally required to have AAPs. For example, under Executive Order 11246, businesses with at least 50 employees *and* government contracts

LO 4.5 Recommend ways in which organizations can maintain legal compliance and address key analytical, legal, ethical, and global issues associated with diversity and inclusion in HRM.

SPOTLIGHT ON LEGAL ISSUES
Gig Workers

EEO laws cover applicants and employees, but they do not apply to independent contractors. Who is an employee? This issue is becoming less straightforward with the rise of the gig economy. Today, many individuals hold temporary positions and perform specific tasks. Technology vendors bring together those willing to perform tasks for others and consumers seeking to fill a need. For example, Uber and Lyft match travelers and those who are willing to drive. TaskRabbit and Bellhops allow consumers to hire someone for specific errands. These companies rely on the assumption that individuals performing the services are contractors and not employees. But are they?

The distinction between who is an employee and who is an independent contractor is a fine line, and it has little to do with the title assigned to the individual. The more control a company exercises over workers, the more likely those individuals are regarded as employees from a legal perspective. Lawsuits brought against companies such as Uber and other technology providers allege that the independent contractor classification was a misnomer. In 2015, FedEx reached a settlement for $240 million with its drivers, who were misclassified as contractors. In 2016, Uber agreed to a settlement for up to $100 million in a lawsuit claiming that it misclassified workers (later rejected at federal court for being inadequate).

EEO laws apply to employees, but organizations need to understand the legal definition of *employee* to understand their legal obligations.[61]

exceeding $50,000 are legally required to develop AAPs for hiring women and minorities. Federal contractors with more than $10,000 worth of business are required to have AAPs for hiring of workers with disabilities. Those with contracts exceeding $100,000 and having at least 50 employees also need to establish written AAPs for hiring veterans. Finally, courts may order a company to temporarily institute an AAP in order to rectify past discrimination. Employers are permitted to institute AAPs to rectify significant imbalances, but these need to be narrow in scope and temporary.[62]

Two myths about affirmative action in employment are that (a) affirmative action requires using quotas and (b) affirmative action permits or even requires hiring a less-qualified individual. Both are *false*. Simply hiring someone because they are from an underrepresented minority due to their race, even though someone else is more qualified, is an example of illegal discrimination according to Title VII—regardless of whether the organization has an AAP in place. Further, race or sex quotas would violate Title VII. Organizations may not have different selection criteria or different cutoff scores to encourage hiring of different groups of individuals.

The Office of Federal Contract Compliance Programs (OFCCP) provides guidelines and sample AAPs. Part of affirmative action is to conduct a workforce analysis to identify barriers to hiring minorities, disabled workers, and women. When these roadblocks are identified, the organization is expected to take concrete steps. For example, a finding that African American and Hispanic employees have a high turnover rate may lead to the action plan that the organization will conduct exit interviews to assess reasons for their departure. The identification of disproportionately few female applicants for a position may result in an action plan in which the organization decides to contact vocational schools and women's community groups to recruit more female applicants for the position. A sample AAP is available from OFCCP's website (https://www.dol.gov/ofccp).

One challenge with AAPs is the potential for backlash on the part of nonrecipients of these programs and the potential for stigmatization of beneficiaries of AAP programs. Research suggests that AAP beneficiaries experience stigma regarding their competence and likeability, which affects their effectiveness at work. Broadly publicizing qualifications of AAP targets is a useful method to counteract some of these effects.[63] The backlash against AAP and the association of AAPs with quotas and lowering the bar (even though both are actually illegal) has led to the relative unpopularity of AAP programs. Today, many businesses shy away from the term *AAP* and instead focus

SPOTLIGHT ON HR FOR SMALL AND MEDIUM-SIZED BUSINESSES

EEOC Compliance

Complying with EEO laws is important for small and medium-sized enterprises. Many of the laws discussed in this chapter become effective once an organization reaches 15 employees, but all businesses regardless of size are covered by EPA. State laws and local ordinances may have lower size thresholds. There are many resources that are geared toward small businesses:

- EEOC has small-business liaisons in many states and cities that are available to answer questions to ensure compliance. https://www.eeoc.gov/employers/contacts.cfm

- EEOC has an online resource center that explains small-business legal responsibilities and provides posters, videos, and other materials to help with compliance. https://www.eeoc.gov/employers/smallbusiness/

- Small businesses with federal contracts need to comply with OFCCP, which makes resources available. https://www.dol.gov/ofccp/TAguides/sbguide.htm

Be sure to investigate your state and local laws to ensure compliance.

on diversity management and inclusion initiatives that aim to create more egalitarian workplaces. Further, AAP programs that are monitored by OFCCP are complex to create and monitor. Therefore, organizations today typically adopt AAPs only when they are required to do so.[64]

How to Comply With EEO Regulations

EEOC and OFCCP have specific expectations of businesses. At a minimum, there are precautions organizations need to adopt in order to remain on the right side of the law. These include:

- **Training decision makers** to understand their legal obligations are an essential first step in legal compliance.

- **Creating policies** around legally protected areas, such as family and disability-related leave, harassment, and nonretaliation.

- **Meeting documentation requirements set by EEOC** is important. For example, all private employers covered by Title VII that also have 100 or more employees and federal contractors with 50 or more employees are required to annually file an EEO-1 report with EEOC and OFCCP. This form requires the organization to count all full-time and part-time employees for each major job category and break them down by ethnicity, race, and sex.

Internal Complaint Mechanisms

Supreme Court decisions such as *Burlington Industries v. Ellerth* (1998) found that organizations are liable for unlawful harassment by supervisors. However, organizations may protect their employees and limit their legal liability by establishing internal complaint procedures and promptly investigating and taking action against discrimination and harassment.[65] As a result, establishing policies and procedures explaining what discrimination and harassment are and giving employees mechanisms through which they can file a complaint with HR may ensure that employees are protected in a timely fashion. This information should be included in the employee handbook and communicated to all employees clearly. Ignoring employee complaints and failing to take prompt action will increase the liability of the organization. Conversely, employees are expected to take advantage of these mechanisms when they believe that discrimination is occurring. Individuals who are victims of discrimination and harassment may have a stronger legal claim if they can demonstrate that they tried to take advantage of internal complaint procedures.

Diversity Initiatives

Many organizations have diversity initiatives aimed at increasing inclusion. Having a chief diversity officer, having support for employee resource groups, and having mentoring programs that ensure that employees are matched to a mentor are among the methods in use in many companies to facilitate an inclusive culture. However, simply having policies and practices is no guarantee that the organization actually has built an inclusive culture. In fact, according to studies, the presence of these programs may create the illusion that the organization is fair and inclusive in the eyes of White and male employees without actually achieving their intended outcomes.[66] Therefore, regarding diversity initiatives as a first step in the path toward building an inclusive culture rather than as an end in itself is important.

One of the popular initiatives in diversity and inclusion is unconscious bias training.[67] As human beings, we all have implicit biases, and being aware of them and consciously making efforts to minimize their effects may lead to more inclusive workplaces. Unconscious biases do not need to result in major discrimination. Instead, on a day-to-day basis, unconscious biases have implications for micro-inequities. If we feel closer to those of our own sex, we may be warmer, more helpful, or kinder toward them; perhaps smile at them more frequently; invite them out for lunch or coffee more often; or initiate conversations more often. If we have implicit biases that lead us to associate being a man with being a higher-potential employee, we may be more likely to give administrative and bureaucratic assignments to women while assigning more challenging ones to men. None of these actions are illegal or problematic if done once or twice, but when they constitute patterns of behavior, they affect how inclusive the workplace is. As mentioned earlier in the chapter, Google and Pinterest are examples of companies that have implemented programs to raise awareness of unconscious bias.

There is debate around whether diversity training initiatives actually work and add value. Unfortunately, hard data on this issue are hard to come by. Not surprisingly, if managers and employees view diversity training as motivated by minimizing the likelihood of lawsuits and do not personally feel accountable and engaged by diversity initiatives, these are less likely to be successful.[68] Therefore, goal setting, tracking diversity metrics, and sharing diversity data are regarded as more promising approaches. For example, in 2018, the UK-based Lloyds Banking Group set the goal that by 2020, 8% of its senior management would come from Black, Asian, and minority ethnic groups.[69]

In 2015, Intel announced double referral bonuses for women, minorities, and veterans and committed $300 million to combat their underrepresentation.[70]

Big Data as a Pathway to Increasing Diversity and Inclusion

Organizations may leverage analytics as a pathway to build more diverse and inclusive organizations. The opening case described how Pinterest partners with Paradigm, a firm that uses HR analytics to examine the effects on diversity of various selection and recruitment methods. Today's organizations can also reach a diverse base of customers through targeted advertisements, as software companies like Google and social media firms like Facebook analyze data on consumer demographics and tailor advertisements to the audience. When organizations are able to purchase ad space to reach a more diverse applicant base, they diversify their recruitment pool.[71]

Organizations can use HR analytics to prevent biases from entering into the decision-making process. Selection tools such as GapJumpers and Unitive allow organizations to blind themselves to applicant demographic characteristics, socioeconomic background, and other factors that could be sources of bias.[72] GapJumpers uses software that acts like a blind audition for businesses. Applicants solve skill-based challenges and their background information is hidden so that applicants are given a fair chance to demonstrate their skills.

Data analytics can also help with managing existing employees. A Chicago-based accounting firm used a proprietary analytics tool that gathers information from the HR information system and creates a dashboard. At a certain point, the tool revealed an increase in turnover of women in the fifth to sixth year of their employment in the company. This information allowed the firm to investigate the phenomenon and identify data-driven solutions. In sum, data analytics may be used in all stages of employment, starting from selection to promotions and training, to understand and identify the points at which some groups have an advantage, and the points at which employees of a particular gender, race, age, or background are more likely to be lost.[73]

Internal Audits

Organizations can ensure compliance with EEO laws by conducting internal audits to identify problems and correct them proactively instead of risking a costly lawsuit. In particular, pay audits that examine gender differences in pay are often valuable in enabling the organization to take corrective action. At the federal level, the Equal Pay Act and Title VII provide protections against sex discrimination in pay. California passed a statewide Equal Pay Act in 2015, prohibiting sex differences in "substantially similar" work, and similar legislation in other states motivates employers to adopt a proactive approach.

Even though it is straightforward to group jobs that are similar to each other and conduct a statistical difference test based on sex (or other protected characteristics), HR is strongly cautioned against conducting this analysis without top-management commitment. The results of a pay audit are "discoverable" in and of themselves as part of legal proceedings. For

SPOTLIGHT ON DATA AND ANALYTICS
Diversity Initiative at Kimberly-Clark

In 2009, Kimberly-Clark, maker of products such as Huggies, Kleenex, and Kotex, came to the realization that although its customer base was 83% female, its leadership consisted mostly of men. Making diversity and inclusion a key initiative became an important

business priority, and Kimberly-Clark tackled this question using data analytics. The analytics team analyzed data on which employees were promoted, derailed, and left the company and used the results to make specific changes.

One realization was that women were not applying for open internal positions unless they met most or all of the criteria, whereas men were more likely to apply if they met half the desired criteria. Some jobs required work experience that was unusual for women (e.g., mill experience), so the company moved to a comparable-experience approach rather than looking for narrow types of experience.

Despite the benefits of analytics, the company credits top management support as the key for the success of the initiative, which resulted in an 82% increase in women in high-level positions in 4 years, as well as helping create a more inclusive, creative, and innovative workplace.[74]

HR IN ACTION

Salesforce.com

©iStock.com/Bjorn Bakstad

Pay audits can be used to rectify past mistakes and achieve equity within the firm. In 2015, the cloud-based software company Salesforce.com spent $3 million to tackle gender imbalance in pay. In cases in which pay differences were not explainable by factors such as job function, location, or level, adjustments were made for both men and women and affected 6% of the workforce. A second global assessment in 2017 affected 11% of employees and again cost around $3 million.

CEO Marc Benioff sees addressing gender gaps in pay as only one piece of Salesforce.com's Women's Surge initiative. The company ensures that women are at least 30% of the attendees at every meeting, and their High Potential Leadership Program works to ensure fairness in advancement opportunities.[75]

example, if the pay audit reveals that there were unexplainable differences between men and women, and if these differences are not corrected, the results of the audit become evidence for potential discrimination and increases the company's liability. Therefore, if the audit finds such differences, it is essential to promptly correct them, which will require resources and top-management commitment to the issue. Working with legal counsel during this audit and ensuring that the audit findings are protected by attorney–client privilege is important. HR still plays a key role as part of diversity audits, ensuring that jobs are classified and grouped correctly, and reasons for pay differences across employees are well documented. HR should also ensure that initial pay offers and subsequent raises are based on justifiable criteria.[76] There may be many legitimate differences for observed pay differences, including number of years of experience, tenure within the organization, managerial responsibilities, cost-of-living differences, and having received merit pay based on clear criteria, among others. During the pay audit these differences would be statistically controlled for and any unexplained differences identified.

Big Data and Legal Compliance

One of the key uses of predictive analytics is in employee selection. Organizations may successfully eliminate human biases from their selection decisions by utilizing selection algorithms. As we discuss in Chapter 7, it is possible to statistically identify the profile of successful employees and hire employees that fit the profile of this "most likely to succeed" candidate. The idea to automate hiring using algorithms, or at least identifying criteria that are most likely to predict desired outcomes using big samples, is appealing due to potential cost savings and the desire to make more objective selection decisions. HR technology vendors such as Cornerstone OnDemand provide software that helps companies use predictive analytics using publicly available information, test scores, and biometric data. There is research indicating that Facebook "likes" may reveal a person's IQ (e.g., liking the movie *The Godfather*, the music of Mozart, and, inexplicably, curly fries), and linguistic software may identify personality traits of applicants by analyzing the words they use (e.g., neurotic personalities are more likely to use words such as *awful* and *horrible*).[77] Software that aggregates high volumes of publicly available information about applicants may be used in an employee selection algorithm.

What are the legal consequences of these approaches? Data scientists and industrial/organizational psychologists caution that big data may not always be better data.[78] Essentially, these algorithms codify what success looked like in the past. Depending on how they were formulated, these algorithms may codify and perpetuate past systematic discrimination or potentially result in disparate impact. Certain metrics picked up by algorithms as predictive of performance may in fact be proxies for age, sex, race, or other protected categories. For example, suppose the algorithm discovers that those with a short commute to work are more likely to stay longer and be more effective at work and therefore recommends not hiring those with a long commute. This may make the selection pool less diverse due to the exclusion of some geographic areas if such areas differ in their level of diversity, which they often do. In other words, equating big data with more objective and unbiased data can be a mistake, and overreliance on historical data may result in biased decision making while also creating the illusion that the selection system is based on data and therefore must be unbiased.

There are currently many unknowns regarding how organizations may benefit from predictive data analytics while also ensuring compliance with EEO laws. Selection decisions based on big data may be challenged based on the disparate impact theory, and future court decisions are important to follow to understand the best practices. Key issues include:[79]

- **Correlation does not equal causation**. What is included in the algorithm may be correlated with performance but may not be a cause of performance. For example, if performance evaluations are biased in favor of young men, factors identified as predictive of performance will be markers correlated with being young and male, but not because those factors lead to higher performance.

- **Publicly available information may be unevenly distributed**. When algorithms rely on scraping publicly available data, some groups may be underrepresented. For example, older workers may have a smaller digital footprint.

- **Algorithms are opaque**. A selection algorithm includes many metrics that change over time because of machine learning. There may be factors that result in disparate impact, but it is difficult for applicants to see how specific algorithms affect them, even if they know that they were screened out due to an algorithm. EEO laws apply to the use of software using predictive analytics, but it is unclear how compliance can be assured and how courts will treat them.

- **It is unclear how newer, complex algorithms should be validated**. The Uniform Guidelines require validating tests used to make selection decisions in order to ensure legal compliance. However, it is unclear how this may be done with more cutting-edge analytics developed in recent years. Since the early 20th century, selection systems have been validated by demonstrating that they predict performance using a simple statistical correlation or regression equation. Applying this logic, more complicated selection algorithms used today would be valid because they are statistically related to performance—and, in fact, this is why they are being used in selection. At the same time, some argue that this methodology is flawed for big data, given that relationships with performance may be spurious (i.e., two things may be correlated not because one causes the other, but because both are related to something else). Further, the concept of statistical significance becomes less meaningful when the number of individuals included in the sample grows large, as virtually every relationship will be statistically significant by traditional standards. We encourage you to stay up to date regarding the most recent developments.

CHAPTER SUMMARY

Diversity has advantages for businesses, ranging from increased innovation to higher firm performance, but the benefits of diversity necessitate having an inclusive work environment. Diversity management has its challenges, particularly because individuals are more likely to be interpersonally attracted to similar others and the existence of biases that may serve as barriers to employment and advancement. There are numerous federal and state laws, executive orders, and local ordinances that aim to prevent discrimination based on sex, race, color, religion, national origin, age, disability status, pregnancy, and genetic information. Although HR analytics may be a crucial tool, the legal implications of big data in employee selection and talent management are still uncharted territory, which means HR professionals should pay attention to this rapidly evolving field.

KEY TERMS

diversity   111
inclusive environment   111
similarity-attraction hypothesis   112
stereotypes   112
unconscious bias (implicit bias)   113
executive orders   113
Equal Employment Opportunity
    Commission (EEOC)   114
Office of Federal Contract Compliance
    Programs (OFCCP)   114
retaliate   115
reverse discrimination   116

equitable relief   116
compensatory damages   116
punitive damages   116
class action lawsuit   117
disparate treatment   117
disparate impact (adverse
    impact)   117
prima facie evidence   117
pretext   117
bona fide occupational qualification
    (BFOQ)   118

Uniform Guidelines on Employee
    Selection Procedures   119
4/5ths rule (80% rule)   119
harassment   121
sexual harassment   121
quid pro quo harassment   121
hostile work environment   121
reasonable accommodation   122
essential functions   126
marginal functions   126

Visit **edge.sagepub.com/bauer** to help you accomplish your coursework goals in an easy-to-use learning environment.

- Master the learning objectives using key study tools
- Watch, listen, and connect with online multimedia resources

- Access mobile-friendly quizzes and flashcards to check your understanding

HR REASONING AND DECISION-MAKING EXERCISES

MINI-CASE ANALYSIS EXERCISE: WORKPLACE DIVERSITY DILEMMAS

Imagine that you are working at a medium-sized business as an HR professional. You are faced with the following dilemmas. Decide how you would handle each issue in the short term and long term. What additional information would help you decide? What changes seem necessary to the company given these dilemmas, if any?

1. An African American job applicant has just been offered a position as a customer service representative in the company's call center. The job does not have any face-to-face customer contact and only involves phone interactions. The manager who conducted the interview just told the applicant that her hair, which is in dreadlocks, violates the company's dress code, which requires "professional" hairstyles. The manager asked the employee to cut her hair. The applicant refused. The manager is considering revoking the job offer to the employee. What would you do?

2. An applicant for your janitorial services is hearing impaired and is unable to speak. He was invited for a job interview. However, when contacted, the applicant informed management that he would need a sign language interpreter for the interview, and he can bring his sister as an interpreter. The hiring manager cancelled the job interview. What would you do?

3. An employee in your department sent you an e-mail stating that he examined the salaries of more than 100 employees working in the call center and found that male employees seemed to be paid more than female employees. What would you do?

HR DECISION ANALYSIS EXERCISE: FAIR ALGORITHM?

Your organization just started conversations with a consulting firm. The firm is offering its platform for use in employee selection. In your discussions with the firm, it disclosed that its research-based algorithm assigns higher scores to applicants who:

- Drive a car with a manual transmission
- Have no gaps in their résumés
- Have a history of staying at each job for at least 2 years

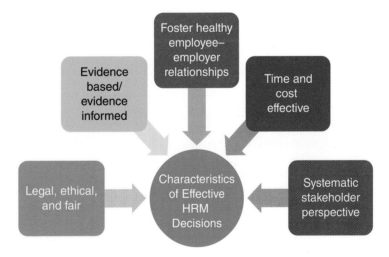

Should your organization use this selection system? Consider this decision using the following criteria.

Please provide the rationale for your answer to each of the questions below.

Is it legal, ethical, and fair?

_____

_____

_____

_____

Is it evidence based/evidence informed?

_____

_____

_____

_____

Does it foster healthy employee–employer relationships?

_____

_____

_____

_____

Is it time and cost effective?

_____

_____

_____

_____

Does it take a systematic stakeholder perspective?

_____

_____

_____

_____

Considering your analysis above, overall, do you think this was an effective decision? Why or why not?

_____

_____

_____

_____

What, if anything, do you think should be done differently or considered to help make this decision more effective?

_____

_____

_____

_____

HR DECISION-MAKING EXERCISE: ASSESSING DISPARATE IMPACT

Recently, your organization advertised openings for sales associates. The selection process includes gathering and evaluating information on a personality test and in-person interview.

Here is a breakdown of who applied and who was hired:

	APPLIED	HIRED
Men	150	15
Women	90	15
White	100	10
Asian American	50	10
African American	30	5
Hispanic	60	5

1. Using the 4/5ths rule, do you have prima facie evidence that disparate impact may have occurred? Explain your rationale.

2. If there is prima facie evidence for disparate impact, what information can you use as defense? What would be your action plan for the future?

DATA AND ANALYTICS EXERCISE: USING THE CHI-SQUARE TEST TO ASSESS DISPARATE IMPACT

Given the downsides of the 4/5ths rule, including its high rate of false positives and its sensitivity to sampling errors, companies may rely on more sophisticated analyses. The 4/5ths rule is simply a "rule of thumb" adopted by the courts and is not based on a formal statistical test. An alternative method is the chi-square test.[80]

Consider the following example. Assume that the use of a knowledge test resulted in the following distribution:

	PASS	FAIL	TOTAL
Men	70	90	160
Women	42	72	114
Total	112	162	274

These results indicate that if you disregard gender, 112 of 274 (40.9%) of all applicants passed the test, and 162 of 274 (59.1%) failed the test.

Now you need to calculate the distribution you would expect to see if gender plays no role. Without any systematic effects of gender, you would expect men and women to have the same pass and fail ratios. This is the **expected distribution**.

	PASS	FAIL	TOTAL
Men	65.4 (of 160 men, 40.9% should pass)	94.6 (of 160 men, 59.1% should fail)	160
Women	46.6 (of 114 women, 40.9% should pass)	67.4 (of 114 women, 59.1% should fail)	114
Total	112	162	274

Now you need to enter these data into Excel, as shown in the screenshot. Then insert the formula you see at the top into cell B12. The result is the "*p* value," which indicates whether the difference you observe between actual distribution and expected distribution is purely by chance, where a *p* value lower than .05 is considered statistically significant. The result presented below has a *p* value of .25, which is not statistically significant (which indicates that there is no evidence of a gender effect on selection).

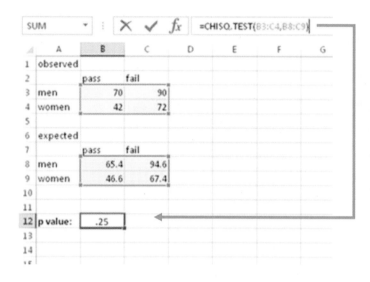

Use the formula listed at the top to calculate the *p* value for a chi-square difference test.

This test can easily be modified to have more than two groups (e.g., Whites, Hispanics, African Americans, and Asians).

 EXCEL EXTENSION: NOW YOU TRY!

- On **edge.sagepub.com/bauer**, use the Excel worksheet and consider the following observed distribution of selection method performance for White and African American job candidates.

  ○ Is there evidence of disparate impact according to your chi-square analysis?

  ○ If so, for which job candidates: African American candidates or White candidates?

	PASS	FAIL	TOTAL
African American	66	140	206
White	50	64	114

CHAPTER 4 SUPPLEMENT:
DEEPER DIVE INTO HRM—EEO-1 SAMPLE FORM

Joint Reporting Committee
- **Equal Employment Opportunity Commission**
- **Office of Federal Contract Compliance Programs (Labor)**

EQUAL EMPLOYMENT OPPORTUNITY

EMPLOYER INFORMATION REPORT EEO—1

Standard Form 100
REV. 01/2008

O.M.B.No. 3046-0007
FORM APPROVAL: www.reginfo.gov/public/do/PRAMain
100-214

Section A—TYPE OF REPORT
Refer to instructions for number and types of reports to be filed.

1. Indicate by marking in the appropriate box the type of reporting unit for which this copy of the form is submitted (MARK ONLY ONE BOX).

(1) ☐ Single-establishment Employer Report

Multi-establishment Employer:
(2) ☐ Consolidated Report (Required)
(3) ☐ Headquarters Unit Report (Required)
(4) ☐ Individual Establishment Report (submit one for each establishment with 50 or more employees)
(5) ☐ Special Report

2. Total number of reports being filed by this Company (Answer on Consolidated Report only)_____

Section B—COMPANY IDENTIFICATION (To be answered by all employers)

OFFICE USE ONLY

1. Parent Company

a. Name of parent company (owns or controls establishment in item 2) omit if same as label

Address (Number and street)			

City or town	State	ZIP code

2. Establishment for which this report is filed. (Omit if same as label)

a. Name of establishment

Address (Number and street)	City or Town	County	State	ZIP code

b. Employer Identification No. (IRS 9-DIGIT TAX NUMBER)

c. Was an EEO-1 report filed for this establishment last year? ☐ Yes ☐ No

Section C—EMPLOYERS WHO ARE REQUIRED TO FILE (To be answered by all employers)

☐ Yes ☐ No 1. Does the entire company have at least 100 employees in the payroll period for which you are reporting?

☐ Yes ☐ No 2. Is your company affiliated through common ownership and/or centralized management with other entities in an enterprise with a total employment of 100 or more?

☐ Yes ☐ No 3. Does the company or any of its establishments (a) have 50 or more employees AND (b) is not exempt as provided by 41 CFR 60-1.5, AND either (1) is a prime government contractor or first-tier subcontractor, and has a contract, subcontract, or purchase order amounting to $50,000 or more, or (2) serves as a depository of Government funds in any amount or is a financial institution which is an issuing and paying agent for U.S. Savings Bonds and Savings Notes?

If the response to question C-3 is yes, please enter your Dun and Bradstreet identification number (if you have one): ☐☐☐☐☐☐☐☐

NOTE: If the answer is yes to questions 1, 2, or 3, complete the entire form, otherwise skip to Section G.

Section D-EMPLOYMENT DATA

SF 100 – Page 2

Employment at this establishment – Report all permanent full- and part-time employees including apprentices and on-the-job trainees unless specifically excluded as set forth in the instructions. Enter the appropriate figures on all lines and in all columns. Blank spaces will be considered as zeros.

Job Categories	Number of Employees (Report employees in only one category)														
	Race/Ethnicity														
	Hispanic or Latino		Not-Hispanic or Latino												Total Col A - M
			Male						Female						
	Male	Female	White	Black or African American	Native Hawaiian or Other Pacific Islander	Asian	American Indian or Alaska Native	Two or more races	White	Black or African American	Native Hawaiian or Other Pacific Islander	Asian	American Indian or Alaska Native	Two or more races	
	A	B	C	D	E	F	G	H	I	J	K	L	M	N	O
Executive/Senior Level Officials and Managers 1.1															
First/Mid-Level Officials and Managers 1.2															
Professionals 2															
Technicians 3															
Sales Workers 4															
Administrative Support Workers 5															
Craft Workers 6															
Operatives 7															
Laborers and Helpers 8															
Service Workers 9															
TOTAL 10															
PREVIOUS YEAR TOTAL 11															

1. Date(s) of payroll period used: _____ (Omit on the Consolidated Report.)

Section E - ESTABLISHMENT INFORMATION (Omit on the Consolidated Report.)

1. What is the major activity of this establishment? (Be specific, i.e., manufacturing steel castings, retail grocer, wholesale plumbing supplies, title insurance, etc. Include the specific type of product or type of service provided, as well as the principal business or industrial activity.)

Section F - REMARKS

Use this item to give any identification data appearing on the last EEO-1 report which differs from that given above, explain major changes in composition of reporting units and other pertinent information.

Section G - CERTIFICATION

Check 1 ☐ All reports are accurate and were prepared in accordance with the instructions. (Check on Consolidated Report only.)
one 2 ☐ This report is accurate and was prepared in accordance with the instructions.

Name of Certifying Official	Title	Signature	Date
Name of person to contact regarding this report	Title	Address (Number and Street)	
City and State	Zip Code	Telephone No. (including Area Code and Extension)	Email Address

All reports and information obtained from individual reports will be kept confidential as required by Section 709(e) of Title VII.
WILLFULLY FALSE STATEMENTS ON THIS REPORT ARE PUNISHABLE BY LAW, U.S. CODE, TITLE 18, SECTION 1001

Source: https://www.eeoc.gov/employers/eeo1survey/upload/eeo1-2.pdf

The Analysis and Design of Work

Opening Case

The Development of SHRM's Competency Model for HR Practice

HR systems are designed to give employers a competitive advantage by focusing on how to attract and hire the best talent, as well as how to develop, train, and retain employees. This includes aligning jobs with organizational goals and strategies.

Thus, a key challenge for HR managers is to understand the tasks that need to be carried out by individual employees and how individual positions fit together to accomplish organizational goals. In addition, organizations must understand what knowledge, skills, abilities, and other characteristics (**KSAOs**) employees need to have in order to do their work most effectively. In short, a clear understanding of what employees do on their jobs and the skills employees need to do their jobs is the basis for building strong organizations.

This is true not only within organizations; it is true within specific professions as well. More and more, professions from health care to engineering[1] are defining what skills and abilities are needed to carry out their work. This provides credibility for the profession as a whole, and it also helps define what is needed for licensure and certification of individuals in order to protect the public. For example, how would you feel if an unlicensed physician took care of you or a family member?

It is for these reasons that the HR profession, through the Society for Human Resource Management (SHRM; see Chapter 1), systematically developed a competency model that defines the competencies required for success in the HR profession. SHRM developed its competency model to guide HR practitioners in achieving their professional goals and thus is developmental in nature. The model includes nine key competencies, which are listed and depicted in Figure 5.1.

- HR expertise (HR knowledge)
- Global and cultural effectiveness
- Relationship management
- Communication
- Consultation
- Critical evaluation

LEARNING OBJECTIVES

After reading and studying this chapter, you should be able to do the following:

5.1 Define job analysis and competency models and describe their purposes in organizations.

5.2 Demonstrate the use of different ways of collecting job analysis information.

5.3 Differentiate between job analysis and competency modeling and evaluate the advantages of each approach.

5.4 Explain how job design can be used to increase employee motivation, job attitudes, and performance.

5.5 Describe how flexible work environments affect employee well-being.

KSAOs Knowledge, skills, abilities, and other characteristics employees need to have in order to do their work most effectively

- Business acumen
- Ethical practice
- Leadership and navigation

Note that only one of the nine competencies is focused on technical knowledge of human resources. The other eight are less knowledge focused and reflect broader behaviors needed for success in organizations, including HR jobs. This is important since, according to the researchers who developed the SHRM competency model, successful HR practice entails more than just HR *knowledge*; it also requires the right *behaviors* for implementing this knowledge in an actual work organization.

A key aspect of SHRM's model is that it provides substantial detail in defining each competency, including the identification of subcompetencies. It also defines behaviors that reflect how each competency is manifested on the job. Finally, the model describes proficiency standards for each competency at four different career stages: early, mid, senior, and executive levels. As such, it serves as a helpful guide for HR professionals seeking to develop themselves in order to move on to the next stage of their careers. It is also helpful to organizational decision makers who want to know how best to develop and structure their HR functions.

■ **FIGURE 5.1**

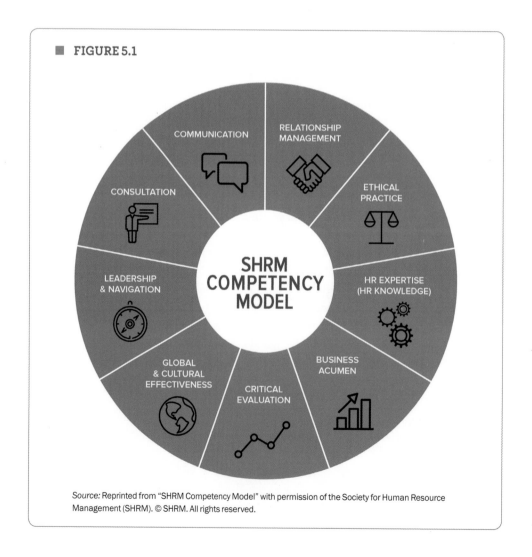

Source: Reprinted from "SHRM Competency Model" with permission of the Society for Human Resource Management (SHRM). © SHRM. All rights reserved.

To develop its HR competency model, SHRM used established best practices for analyzing jobs and building competency models.[2] Moreover, as described in Chapter 1, SHRM used a multistage process involving tens of thousands of participants, which included the following steps:

- An initial sample of more than 1,000 HR professionals in more than 100 focus groups in 29 cities worldwide, together with a survey of 640 HR leaders, was used to generate model content.
- Once the model was developed, SHRM surveyed tens of thousands of HR experts to confirm the importance of each competency.
- SHRM then studied more than 800 HR professionals and their supervisors with the goal of assessing the degree to which the competencies—both technical and behavioral—predict the job performance of HR professionals. This last step in the analysis shows "where the rubber meets the road" by demonstrating the robustness of the model through empirical validation.

The development of the SHRM competency model was an impressive feat that resulted in an enduring instrument that provides substantial guidance for the development of HR professionals. Going forward, a key goal for the model is to gain HR professionals a place at the table among organizational decision makers.[3]

Case Discussion Questions

1. Regardless of whether you plan to be an HR professional, how might you use this competency model for your professional development? Specifically, how would you go about gaining proficiency in each of these nine competencies? How might doing so help you succeed in your chosen occupation?

2. How might the robust empirical process used to develop the model be used to promote the model's credibility among business leaders? How would you argue in favor of the model to leaders in a government organization? In a multinational, private corporation?

3. What do you think about the relative value of each of the nine competencies at different career stages of HR practitioners? For example, how might an executive HR professional differ from an entry-level HR professional in their need for each of these competencies?

4. How do you think business schools and HR programs could use the model for curriculum development for both HR professionals and students in other fields of business administration?

5. How relevant do you think each of the nine competencies is for an employee's success in organizations, whether or not a person is associated with the HR function? Explain.

 Click to learn more . . .

To learn more about the SHRM competency model and its development, click on this report:
https://www.shrm.org/learningandcareer/competency-model/pages/default.aspx

Job analysis The analysis of work and the employee characteristics needed to perform the work successfully

To develop effective HR systems, organizations conduct *job analysis,* which is *the analysis of work and the employee characteristics needed to perform the work successfully.* Further, organizations must understand how individual jobs help achieve organizational goals and how the design of jobs can help support employees. In this chapter, we describe the science and best practices regarding how to analyze jobs and work processes to ensure organizational success. We also discuss how the job is experienced by employees and why the employee experience is important to organizations.

LO 5.1 Define job analysis and competency models and describe their purposes in organizations.

The Analysis of Work and Its Critical Role in HR Practice

In successful organizations, strategic goals at the highest levels must be translated down the organizational hierarchy into specific work processes. These processes must be further translated into the specific tasks and responsibilities of individual workers. In other words, employers must consider what work they do at the organizational level and then which specific employee responsibilities and job requirements are needed to carry this work out. They must understand their broader goals to know what workers in different roles actually do and what skills and abilities workers need in order to perform their work successfully.

This analysis of work and the employee characteristics needed to perform the work successfully is called *job analysis*. Job analysis is an essential HR function that forms the basis for all other HR functions, including recruitment, selection, promotion and succession planning, performance management, training and development, and pay and rewards.[4] For example, consider the job of firefighter. When developing legally defensible procedures to recruit and hire people who fit this job (see Chapters 4, 6, and 7), it would be advisable to have a deep understanding of what tasks firefighters perform and the skills and abilities they need to perform them. In fact, city governments frequently conduct job analyses for their public safety jobs, such as firefighters and police officers, to develop hiring criteria and selection procedures for them.

At the federal level, the U.S. Office of Personnel Management, which provides HR support for the millions of federal employees in civil service jobs, offers detailed technical guidelines about how to conduct job analyses for developing selection procedures for these workers.[5] And in the private sector, many corporations either conduct detailed job analyses or use the related process of competency modeling to better understand the different jobs in their companies and how they fit together to achieve organizational goals. For example, IBM has developed a competency model to document the core competencies of its professional employees worldwide.[6] In short, organizations recognize that an analysis of the work that individual employees do provides significant advantages in terms of managing their human capital. Although you may or may not ever actually conduct a job analysis yourself, you have probably benefited from a job analysis, which helps determine selection procedures, pay, and promotion considerations.

©iStock.com/rocketegg

It is commonplace for governments to maintain job analyses of their public safety jobs such as firefighter, a job that requires a number of specialized technical skills that are not familiar to members of the general public.

Tasks The elements of a job analysis that are typically used to describe the job itself

Technical Terms Used in Job Analysis and Competency Modeling

In this section we define some of the terminology used in job analysis and competency modeling. First, *tasks* are the elements of a job analysis that are typically used to describe the job itself. They usually contain an action verb followed by an object and are clarified in terms of how the work is performed (e.g., under what conditions, using what equipment, and for what purpose). In the case of a barista's job, a task might be "Makes (action verb) espresso drinks (object) using espresso maker and other coffee equipment to serve customer needs (clarification of conditions, equipment, and purpose)." As another example, think about the job of a teacher and write one task statement: "_____ (action verb) _____ (object) _____ (clarification of conditions, equipment, and purpose)."

Second, knowledge, skills, abilities, and other characteristics (KSAOs) are used to describe the attributes workers need to carry out their work effectively. *Knowledge* is generally something a person could learn from a book (e.g., knowledge of laws pertinent to the HR profession), a *skill* is something an employee can learn how to do (e.g., skill in the use of fire equipment), an *ability* is a relatively innate talent or aptitude (e.g., spatial relationships ability), and *other characteristics* refers to personality traits such as extraversion or integrity.

©iStock.com/joel-t

Third, the persons who provide information about the job are called ***subject matter experts (SMEs).*** In a job analysis, an SME is typically a job incumbent who performs the job as well as supervisors, as incumbents and supervisors each give unique information about what the job involves.[8]

Over the past few decades, organizations have increasingly begun to use the related processes of competency modeling in addition to job analysis. Generally speaking, the goals of ***competency modeling*** are to understand what types of attributes and behaviors are required for a group of jobs, perhaps over an entire organization. (We will discuss competency modeling in greater detail later in the chapter.) The primary elements of a competency model are the employee competencies that are needed to perform the job, such as "competency in working with team members." For simplicity's sake, in this chapter, the term *job analysis* refers to either job analysis or competency modeling. Also, because work in the 21st century can change quickly—and organizations may not necessarily have a series of finite, stable "jobs"—the term *work analysis* may sometimes be used in place of the older term *job analysis*. **Work analysis** implies that, over time, an employee may need to perform a variety of evolving jobs within an organization.[9]

In addition, it is important to distinguish between the concept of a ***job (or job classification)*** in an organization versus a ***position***. A job classification is a group of related duties within an organization, whereas a position is the duties that can be carried out by one person. For example, a city government may have the job classification of "police officer." There might be hundreds of individual police officers in that job classification, holding positions with titles such as "patrol officer" or "detective." Or a large, national drug store chain might employ individual pharmacists in thousands of positions across the country, but they would all be in the same job classification of "pharmacist."

It is also useful to distinguish between job analysis and the terms ***job descriptions*** and ***job specifications***. In general, a job analysis results in a very detailed document that allows a person who is relatively unfamiliar with the job to get a good idea of what the job involves in terms of tasks and required KSAOs. In fact, a detailed job analysis might list hundreds of tasks and dozens of KSAOs. In contrast, both job descriptions and job specifications are usually shorter documents than the full results of a job analysis, often a single page, although this can vary considerably across different organizations. It can be useful to have a relatively short document like this to show job applicants and current employees what the job involves. Table 5.1 is a brief example of a job description and a job specification for a hypothetical administrative assistant position.

Job descriptions provide the title and purpose of the job, as well as a general overview of the essential tasks, duties, and responsibilities (i.e., observable actions) associated with the job. The material in job descriptions can be used in recruitment materials for attracting new employees, job ads, and postings so that applicants know what the job involves and given to employees so that they understand their job.

IBM, with more than 400,000 employees worldwide, has developed a comprehensive competency model that defines the competencies required for all its professional workers. It created the model to better organize the vast amount of training and development material that had grown up across the many types of jobs within the organization into a single comprehensive framework.[7]

Subject matter experts (SMEs) People (e.g., employees, supervisors) who provide information about the job

Competency modeling A type of job analysis with the goal of understanding what types of attributes and behaviors are required for a group of jobs, perhaps over an entire organization

Work analysis A more recent term for job analysis, which is based on the idea that an employee may need to perform a variety of evolving jobs within an organization

Job classification A group of related duties within an organization

Position Duties that can be carried out by one person

Job descriptions Job descriptions provide the title and purpose of the job, as well as a general overview of the essential tasks, duties, and responsibilities (i.e., observable actions) associated with the job

Job specifications Job specifications focus on the characteristics of an employee who does the job

TABLE 5.1　Sample Brief Job Description and Job Specifications for an Administrative Assistant

Administrative Assistant Job Description
Overview and Purpose

The purpose of the administrative assistant position is to provide support to other workers (e.g., managers) in carrying out their job tasks.

Duties

The administrative assistant carries out a range of duties in support of organizational functions, including scheduling meetings and appointments and answering phone calls. Includes providing assistance in preparing reports and developing and implementing filing systems. May also include taking notes and minutes.

Major Tasks and Responsibilities

- Plan and organize meetings, including developing a meeting agenda and taking notes and minutes as needed.
- Coordinate with others within and outside of the organization, including other administrative assistants, as needed.
- Make appointments for other staff within the business unit.
- Answer phone calls in support of the work unit.
- Develop filing systems for work unit and implement.
- Order supplies as needed.
- Plan meetings and trips of office visitors, providing needed support.
- Develop office policies and procedures.
- Support simple bookkeeping functions within the unit such as reimbursements and paying of vendors.

Administrative Assistant Job Specifications
Job Requirements

- Organizational skills
- Interpersonal skills necessary for working with coworkers and outside clients
- Ability to prioritize work
- Knowledge of basic office practices and procedures
- Basic knowledge of office equipment including simple troubleshooting
- Oral and written communication skills
- Good attention to detail

Minimum Qualifications

- High school diploma (required); some college or college degree (desirable)
- Office experience, including at least 6 months working as an administrative assistant
- Demonstrated proficiency with typical office software

In contrast to job descriptions, job specifications focus on the characteristics of an employee who does the job. They describe what the general requirements are for an employee doing the job, including the KSAOs and any physical or emotional requirements. Job specifications also include the qualifications a person needs to fill the job in terms of experience and education and thus are essential to consider when recruiting for and filling a position. Maintaining and documenting job descriptions and job specifications, in a format that is consistent across jobs within the organization, are an essential role of HR departments.[10]

MANAGER'S TOOLBOX

Some Basics of Job Descriptions

Writing and updating job descriptions are some of the most basic functions of an HR department, because these descriptions are used for a range of useful functions. For example, job descriptions are:

- used to develop recruitment and job posting materials to attract job applicants and give them an idea about what the job involves;

- shared with job applicants during the selection process to provide a realistic preview of what a job actually entails; and

- provided to new and existing employees so that they know what is expected of them and what criteria can be used to evaluate them.

One of the challenges in organizations is keeping job descriptions up to date, and this is especially true in dynamic business environments in which jobs change quickly. There are some ways that HR practitioners can keep an eye on this issue:

- One practice, especially in quickly changing industries and organizations, is to update job descriptions annually.

- Reviewing an employee's job description might be most useful during annual performance appraisal meetings between supervisors and employees. During these meetings, employees can inform their supervisor if the job has changed to an extent that would warrant an updated job description.

What Are the Purposes of Job Analysis?

Job analysis is often considered the cornerstone of other HR functions, because it is essential to understand work processes and the human requirements for doing work to do other HR functions well. In short, good HR practice is based on a robust job analysis. Figure 5.2 shows the many HR functions that are dependent on a job analysis.

A job analysis is important for establishing the minimum qualifications the job requires, including education and experience. It is also used for recruitment, as it is necessary to understand the human requirements of a job prior to developing recruitment strategies and materials. For example, in hiring a software engineer, it is essential to understand the minimum qualifications of the job, such as the KSAOs and the amount of education and work experience needed (see Chapter 6). In addition, job analysis is necessary for developing selection procedures (see Chapter 7). This includes the basic requirements of the job (e.g., experience) and types of tests and assessments that should be used to determine a job applicant's fit with the job, including the KSAOs they should measure. Moreover, U.S. employment law requires that selection procedures be based on a job analysis in order to be legally defensible.

An analysis of jobs and how they relate to each other is necessary for good succession planning. Succession planning (or succession management; see Chapter 6) involves taking stock of which employees are qualified to fill positions that are likely to be vacated soon. If no candidates are currently prepared to move into those positions, the best candidates can be groomed to do so by giving them developmental experiences such as training and work assignments. For example, a medium-sized manufacturing company may realize that its plant manager will be retiring in 2 years. In preparation, the company can identify good candidates among current employees for taking on the plant manager's role. These candidates can then be trained or given appropriate work experiences so that they can take on the plant manager's job when the current plant manager retires. In this example, a job analysis would identify which KSAOs are required for the plant manager's job; other jobs in the company that are similar to the job of plant manager; which employees are in those other jobs and thus could be good candidates for plant manager; and what additional KSAOs they would still need to take on the plant manager's job.

■ **FIGURE 5.2**   Summary of the Relationship Between Job Analysis and Other HR Functions

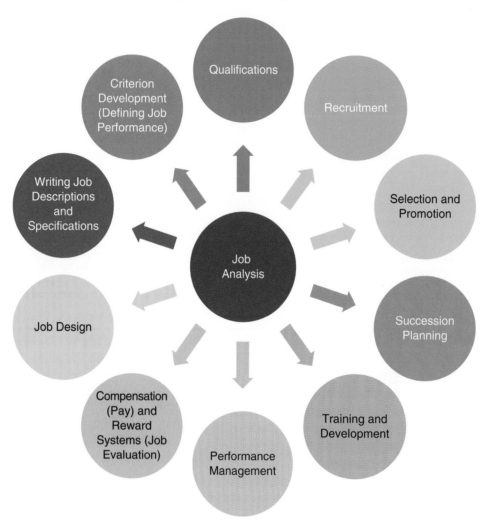

SPOTLIGHT ON LEGAL ISSUES

Job Analysis and Legal Defensibility of HR Systems

Because job analysis is often called a cornerstone of other HR functions, job analysis is key to their legal defensibility. This is perhaps best illustrated in the area of hiring.

For example, the U.S. federal government's Uniform Guidelines on Employee Selection Procedures (1978) state that with few exceptions, a job analysis is required to demonstrate the validity of selection procedures.[11] As we will see in Chapter 7, the validity of selection procedures is core to their legal defensibility. In other words, a valid selection procedure (i.e., one that predicts job performance well) needs to begin with a job analysis.

In addition, job analysis plays a critical role in implementation of the Americans with Disabilities Act (ADA, 1990). As noted in Chapter 4, a key aspect of complying with ADA is that employers identify essential functions of the job and include them in their job descriptions. An employer who makes a hiring decision based on requiring a nonessential function of the job or a marginal function that could be assigned to other workers could face legal challenges. The key is to carefully identify these essential job functions by means of a job analysis and to document them clearly in job descriptions following legally defensible procedures and guidelines.[12]

Job analysis is also necessary for developing the most effective training and development programs (see Chapter 8). Specifically, it is important to understand the KSAOs needed for a job when developing training and development programs, and it is a key part of conducting a training needs assessment. In addition, job analysis is needed in the development of performance standards to be used in performance management systems (see Chapter 9) that can most effectively assess employees' current skill and performance levels.

Regarding employee compensation and pay, a job analysis is needed to set pay scales that are both fair to employees and are competitive with the current employment market (see Chapter 11). This type of job analysis involved in setting pay in organizations is called job evaluation (see Chapter 11). Further, job analysis is important for designing jobs that will motivate employees in their work (discussed later in this chapter). Job analyses are essential for writing job descriptions and job specifications. Finally, job analyses play a critical role in developing criterion measures—that is, the specific measures and metrics. Organizations use these to evaluate the effectiveness of HR systems, such as whether they are successfully hiring the best people and training them appropriately.[13]

Clearly, the role of job analysis is critical in organizations: A well-produced job analysis can provide a strong basis for the success of an HR system, while a poor (or nonexistent) job analysis can decrease the effectiveness of an HR system.

Seeing the Big Picture: Work Flow Analysis

Most of this chapter is focused on the analysis of jobs and individual positions. However, before moving into a discussion of analyzing individual jobs, it is important to step back and consider how work is accomplished at the organizational level. This broad, organization-level focus on work within the organization and within organizational units is known as *work flow analysis*. It is often useful to think of this process in reverse order: Begin with the desired final output; then enumerate the tasks necessary to create this output; and go on to identify the organizational resources, equipment, and human capital necessary to carry out these tasks. In this way, managers can think critically about organizational processes and how they might be carried out more effectively using fewer resources. Such an analysis might also allow organizations to adjust to changes in the economic or technological environments. Work flow analysis can also provide guidance as to how to make jobs more motivating to workers, an issue we discuss later in this chapter.

> **Work flow analysis** A broad, organization-level focus on work within the organization and within organizational units and the input needed

As an example, a restaurant's managers might decide to analyze their operations. The restaurant's output is the production of food and drinks. They need to determine how they would measure this output, including measures of both the quantity and the quality of the output. From there they could decide what tasks need to be performed for producing this output, including tasks performed by the chef (e.g., preparing menus, cooking food) and those performed by others in the shop, such as the people operating the cash register (e.g., interacting effectively with customers, making change). From there they could determine the needed resources (e.g., chicken, lettuce, milk), equipment (e.g., oven, mixer, grill), and KSAOs (e.g., knowledge of recipes, skill at using equipment) that are needed to create the output. Note that work flow analysis is applied to a number of different types of work, from the manufacturing of high-tech equipment to research and development work to large retailers. It should also be applied not only to individual workers but also to teams and other organizational subunits, as well as the organization as a whole, to better understand their functioning and improve their efficiency.

Although many organizations may skip this systematic analysis of their work, the use of increasingly sophisticated analytics techniques in organizations might change this. Specifically, an analysis of an organization's operations can facilitate the use of work flow analysis to increase efficiency. This might include the use of more algorithms that assess how subtle changes in inputs can affect outputs, including the combined effects of inputs on work processes and outputs. In addition, online retailers such as Amazon and Walmart are constantly examining their work flow for ways to optimize them, as they must frequently adapt to ever-changing conditions, including supply, inventory, and delivery of goods.[14] A challenge for work flow analysis is the use of reliable measures

SPOTLIGHT ON DATA AND ANALYTICS

Analyzing and Advancing the Data Science Profession

A significant challenge appears in developing a job analysis or competency model when the job or profession is new or changing. The job of data scientist within the field of data analytics and big data presents just such a challenge. The EDISON Project

(http://edison-project.eu/), funded by the European Commission's Horizon 2020 research and innovation program, is an initiative that undertakes this challenge with the specific goal of accelerating the data science profession.

The EDISON Data Science Framework (EDSF) includes a number of freely available documents that define the data science profession in terms of the skills and competencies that make up the profession. These documents were developed to assist not only educators but also data scientists themselves and employing organizations. In addition, they give policy makers tools to more effectively determine how best to nurture the field of data science and to give individuals interested in pursuing a data science career tools for understanding the various paths available to them. Another goal of the project is to develop a curriculum for data scientists.[15]

of both the quantity and quality of outputs. Moreover, the application of sophisticated analytics to work flow analysis may be used to mitigate some of the negative outcomes (e.g., worker displacement) associated with the increased automation of work processes.[16]

LO 5.2 Demonstrate the use of different ways of collecting job analysis information.

Collecting Job Analysis Data

A number of methods may be used to collect job analysis data. First, *interviewing* SMEs (subject matter experts) is the most common method for collecting job analysis data; such interviews can be conducted individually or in small groups. The job analyst (typically an HR staff member) might discuss with SMEs (employees and supervisors) the job tasks they perform, the KSAOs needed to do the job, and critical job situations they might face. However, for more technical jobs, it may be necessary to *observe* people doing the work. For example, to understand the highly specialized equipment used by firefighters, it would probably be necessary for a job analyst to actually see how they use that equipment in their work. Similarly, it is common to do "ride-alongs" with law enforcement employees to gain a deeper understanding of the procedures they must follow. For practical reasons, when there are large numbers of job incumbents and supervisors, it is common to conduct *surveys* of SMEs instead of interviews. Surveys can facilitate obtaining a representative sample for large organizations where there may be variations in the way the work is done across the organization. For example, if a large hospital's HR managers were analyzing the job of emergency room nurse, they might want to be sure to gain input from nurses who work on different shifts, as the types of emergencies nurses deal with—and thus the tasks they do and the KSAOs they need—might vary considerably depending on the time of day. Note that software designed to help with the collection and processing of job analysis data is available from a number of vendors.

Often it is not necessary to carry out a job analysis from scratch. Rather, if there is an existing job analysis in place, it may be possible to begin with that one and simply update it. If not, existing job analysis materials are often available from professional organizations (e.g., a job analysis for engineers from an engineering professional association). In addition, a source of information about jobs is the O*NET, published by the U.S. Department of Labor and discussed later in this chapter. Note that existing job analysis sources such as these may not provide a complete job analysis in themselves, as they are not tailored to the specific job in the specific organization. However, these materials can provide a springboard to begin the job analysis process.[17]

Logistical Issues in Job Analysis

From an employee's perspective, a job analysis might be perceived as an organizational intervention: HR shows up asking about your job in order to make decisions about important issues like hiring, promotion, training, and pay. Thus, the selection of which SMEs will partici-

The American Association of Engineering Societies worked with the U.S. Department of Labor to develop a competency model for engineering jobs.[18]

pate in a job analysis is a major decision from an employee's perspective. SMEs should be chosen in such a way that they provide a representative sample of the employees in a particular job type. For example, if a chain of drugstores were developing the job analysis for a pharmacist, it might consider using a sample of pharmacist SMEs that represent the different geographical store locations, as the pharmacist job might be different in different locations, such as dealing with different types of health conditions and customer questions.

Additionally, SME samples should be demographically representative in terms of issues such as gender and ethnicity. Not only might these lead to different results, but just as important is that the job analysis process be seen as fair by employees. For example, if a city were doing a job analysis to develop a promotional procedure for fire captain but only asked SMEs from certain ethnic groups to participate, employees would likely—and rightly—see the job analysis process as unfair.

Preparing SMEs for Job Analysis

An issue that frequently comes up when collecting job analysis information is preparing SMEs for the process, in particular, letting them know why the job analysis is being conducted. From an employee's perspective, a person showing up from HR wanting to discuss their job could be seen as anything from a nuisance to a threat; in the worst case, a worker may worry that his or her job is being eliminated. Explaining to employees why the analysis is being done—for example, that information is being collected to develop better hiring procedures and could directly affect who will be hired to be their future team members and colleagues—not only allays employees' concerns but also increases their willingness to provide input into the process. Further, it can be very helpful to let SMEs know in advance what types of questions they will be asked in a job analysis interview, such as the types of tasks they perform and what KSAOs are needed to do their job. In this way, employees will not have to think on their feet but will have had a chance to consider what their job actually involves.

Specific Job Analysis Methods and Approaches

LO 5.3 Differentiate between job analysis and competency modeling and evaluate the advantages of each approach.

As described earlier, there are a number of ways to collect job analysis data. In addition, there are a number of specific job analysis methods and frameworks. Each produces a slightly different job analysis product and is thus best for different organizational goals. Further, some methods provide highly detailed information about jobs and the KSAOs needed to do them (e.g., task–KSAO analysis) or critical job situations often faced by employees (critical incidents technique). Others are focused on providing general information about jobs (e.g., Position Analysis Questionnaire), and still others provide a broad organizing framework within which to classify and compare jobs (e.g., O*NET content model). Then there are approaches that focus on the competencies needed to do jobs within a profession or a larger organization, allowing for comparisons in what is required across different job levels or at different career stages (competency models). Each of these is described in the following sections; note that the goal is not to provide a comprehensive list of job analysis methods, which can be found in other sources,[19] but rather to touch on some of the more commonly used examples.

Task–KSAO Analysis

Task–KSAO analysis is a job analysis approach focused on carefully defining the tasks that make up the job, as well as the KSAOs needed to do those tasks (see Figure 5.3). First, the job analyst determines the list of tasks that make up the job as well as the KSAOs that are needed to complete them. Second, the job analyst asks SMEs to document, often through a survey, that these tasks and KSAOs are critical to performing the job. Noncritical tasks and KSAOs are eliminated based on the analysis of these data. Third, the final list of KSAOs is reviewed by the SMEs to document that the KSAOs on the list really are needed to do the critical job tasks. Note that task/KSAO analysis is a detailed approach to job analysis, providing great detail about one or relatively few jobs. This detail involved in the analysis means that it is a more difficult method to use to analyze many jobs at one time if the goal is to compare an array of jobs. However, it is a good method to use for certain situations, when trying to understand job details such as when developing job-specific technical training or when developing content valid selection procedures (see Chapter 7). We also refer the reader to other sources that provide more information about how to carry out a task/KSAO analysis.[20]

Develop an Initial List of Tasks and KSAOs

The first step of task–KSAO analysis is to develop a list of tasks that describe the job and the KSAOs that a person needs to do them. This is typically done based on a number of sources described earlier. The job analyst may observe workers doing the job, interview a sample of SMEs, and review existing job analysis materials such as O*NET descriptions and previous job analyses. Existing job analyses may come from past analyses done by the organization, analyses done by professional organizations, or even from other organizations. In fact, it is common in the public sector for organizations to share their job analysis materials with each other. For example, a city that is conducting a job analysis for the job of police officer might request job analyses from other cities where policing is done in a similar way.

Based on this information, the job analyst would then develop a list of job tasks, which are usually stated in terms of an action verb, an object of the verb, and a purpose and clarification of conditions and equipment. For example, Figure 5.4 shows that one task for the job of administrative assistant might be *contacts* (action verb) *client* (object) *to coordinate meetings using e-mail*

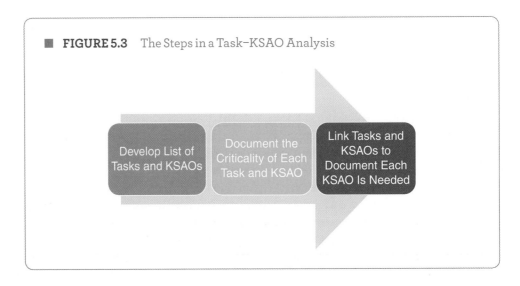

■ **FIGURE 5.3**   The Steps in a Task–KSAO Analysis

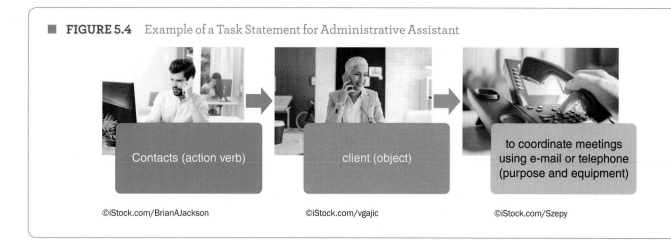

■ **FIGURE 5.4** Example of a Task Statement for Administrative Assistant

Contacts (action verb) → client (object) → to coordinate meetings using e-mail or telephone (purpose and equipment)

©iStock.com/BrianAJackson   ©iStock.com/vgajic   ©iStock.com/Szepy

or telephone (purpose and equipment). They would then develop a list of KSAOs based on their interviews and observations of SMEs and other research that would be needed to perform the task effectively. In the case of the administrative assistant task, some KSAOs might be "knowledge of how to use steamer/espresso maker" and "skill in assuring the proper consistency of frothed milk." Note that for most of the history of task analysis, the focus has been on observable tasks for physical jobs as those described. However, given the increased cognitive requirements of jobs, there has likewise been greater interest in ***cognitive task analysis***, which focuses on cognitive tasks that may not be observable by others but could be described by an SME. For example, in addition to the task of "Uses computer and internet to look up order status," a customer service representative's tasks might include "Determines best sources for looking up order status" or "Estimates time to delivery for a customer based on past experience."

Cognitive task analysis A type of job analysis that focuses on cognitive tasks that may not be observable by others but could be described by an SME

Document the Criticality of Tasks and KSAOs

Once a list of tasks and KSAOs has been developed, a key step is to document that they are indeed critical to the job. For example, if a city government were conducting job analysis to use as the basis for a test for police officer, they may have come up with a carefully developed list of 150 tasks that describe the job and 30 KSAOs needed to perform the job. It would be important to document that these tasks and KSAOs actually are critical to performance before basing a selection procedure on them. One approach would be to have a different group of SMEs review the tasks and KSAOs and ask them to eliminate or revise tasks and KSAOs that they believe are not critical—for example, that they are unimportant or performed relatively infrequently.

However, a more in-depth analysis of the criticality of tasks and KSAOs is through a ***criticality survey***, in which larger groups of SMEs rate each task and KSAO in terms of how critical or essential it is. Tables 5.2 and 5.3 show examples of task and KSAO criticality surveys for a hypothetical customer service job for a large retailer, in which SMEs would be asked to rate the importance of each task and KSAO.

Criticality survey A more in-depth analysis of the criticality of tasks and KSAOs, in which larger groups of SMEs rate each task and KSAO in terms of how critical or essential it is

Accordingly, Table 5.4 shows the results of the task criticality survey based on an administration of the surveys to 470 SMEs—specifically, 420 customer service specialists and 50 supervisors. As you can see, for most of the tasks and KSAOs, the mean importance ratings are fairly high (between 4 and 5). The standard deviation, which refers to the spread or dispersion of ratings (see Chapter 2), is fairly low (under 1). There are, however, some tasks and KSAOs for which this is not true. As you can see in Table 5.4, Task 31, "Cleans office kitchen area when it is their turn to do so," has a mean of only 1.4, indicating that most SMEs thought it was not critical and that it should probably be dropped. Additionally, Task 32, "Uses sit/stand desk correctly throughout the day to maintain own personal health," has a fairly high mean; but it has a high standard deviation as well, suggesting that there is a good

TABLE 5.2 Hypothetical Task Criticality Rating Form for a Customer Service Job

Please rate each task on the following scale:

How important is this task for a customer service specialist?

5 = Very important

4 = Important

3 = Moderately important

2 = Slightly important

1 = Not important

Customer Service Specialist Tasks	How important is this task for a customer service specialist? (circle one)
1. Speaks with customers who are interested in new products.	1 2 3 4 5
2. Works to solve customer complaints.	1 2 3 4 5
3. Coordinates with supervisor to resolve customer problems.	1 2 3 4 5
4. Stays abreast of current sales and specials provided by the company by speaking with supervisor and coworkers and checking company website.	1 2 3 4 5
5. Uses telephone system to answer customer calls promptly.	1 2 3 4 5
6. Uses computer to look up customer orders.	1 2 3 4 5
. . .	
31. Cleans office kitchen area when it is their turn to do so.	1 2 3 4 5
32. Uses sit/stand desk correctly throughout the day to maintain own personal health.	1 2 3 4 5
33. Provides customers with refunds, as appropriate, if there is any problem with the product.	1 2 3 4 5

TABLE 5.3 Hypothetical KSAO Rating Form for a Customer Service Job

KSAO	HOW IMPORTANT IS THIS KSAO FOR A CUSTOMER SERVICE SPECIALIST? (CIRCLE ONE)
A. Interpersonal skills	1 2 3 4 5
B. Product knowledge	1 2 3 4 5
C. Keyboarding skills	1 2 3 4 5
. . .	
J. Decision-making skills	1 2 3 4 5
K. Knowledge of online order tracking system	1 2 3 4 5

TABLE 5.4   Means and Standard Deviations for the Task Importance Ratings for Customer Service Specialist, Obtained From 420 Customer Service Specialists and 50 Supervisors

MEANS AND STANDARD DEVIATIONS FOR THE IMPORTANCE RATINGS OF EACH TASK

CUSTOMER SERVICE SPECIALIST TASKS	MEAN (1–5 SCALE)	STANDARD DEVIATION
1. Speaks with customers who are interested in new products.	4.4	0.8
2. Works to solve customer complaints.	4.8	0.2
3. Coordinates with supervisor to resolve customer problems.	4.1	0.8
4. Stays abreast of current sales and specials provided by the company by speaking with supervisor and coworkers and checking company website.	4.0	0.9
5. Uses telephone system to answer customer calls promptly.	4.8	0.2
6. Uses computer to look up customer orders.	4.9	0.1
. . .		
31. Cleans office kitchen area when it is their turn to do so.	(1.4)	.8
32. Uses sit/stand desk correctly throughout the day to maintain own personal health.	4.0	(1.9)
33. Provides customers with refunds, as appropriate, if there is any problem with the product.	4.4	.9

bit of disagreement among SMEs about the criticality of this task and that it should perhaps be dropped or at least reconsidered. Similar analyses can be done for the KSAOs as well.

Demonstrate That the KSAOs Are Linked to Critical Tasks

The final step of a task–KSAO analysis is to document that all of the KSAOs are actually linked to critical tasks. This is an important step, as the KSAOs will be used as the basis for a number of HR functions, such as the development of training programs. This can be done through simply asking a panel of SMEs to document that all KSAOs are linked to tasks. However, for larger groups of SMEs, it is also possible to document that KSAOs are actually needed for important tasks through a *linkage survey*. Table 5.5 shows an example of a linkage survey, in which a sample of SMEs would be asked to indicate how important each of the KSAOs is to each job task. KSAOs that are not linked to any critical job tasks would be eliminated from the job analysis.

As noted earlier, task–KSAO analysis provides rich, detailed information about jobs. However, as you might guess, it can be a time-consuming process, and it may feel onerous to the SMEs who must complete lengthy surveys answering multiple questions about their jobs. For these reasons, there are a number of "best practices" from the research on how to reduce the load on SMEs and to detect SMEs who are not taking the process seriously. These include

- providing incentives to SMEs who complete the surveys;
- breaking up task/KSAO surveys so that different groups of SMEs complete different parts of the survey; and
- introducing "carelessness" items on the survey—that is, items such as bogus tasks that can detect which SMEs are being careless while completing the survey so that their data can be eliminated.[21]

Linkage survey Where sample of SMEs would be asked to indicate how important each of the KSAOs is to each job task

TABLE 5.5   Task–KSAO Linkage Form for the Job of Customer Service Specialist

Using the following scale, please indicate how important each KSAO across the top is for performing each task in the left-hand column.

5—Essential

4—Very important

3—Important

2—Moderately important

1—Not important

Customer Service Specialist Tasks	A. Interpersonal Skills	B. Product Knowledge	C. Keyboarding Skills	. . .	J. Decision-Making Skills	K. Knowledge of Online Tracking System
1. Speaks with customers who are interested in new products.	1 2 3 4 5	1 2 3 4 5	1 2 3 4 5		1 2 3 4 5	1 2 3 4 5
2. Works to solve customer complaints.	1 2 3 4 5	1 2 3 4 5	1 2 3 4 5		1 2 3 4 5	1 2 3 4 5
3. Coordinates with supervisor to resolve customer problems.	1 2 3 4 5	1 2 3 4 5	1 2 3 4 5		1 2 3 4 5	1 2 3 4 5
4. Stays abreast of current sales and specials provided by the company by speaking with supervisor and coworkers and checking company website.	1 2 3 4 5	1 2 3 4 5	1 2 3 4 5		1 2 3 4 5	1 2 3 4 5
5. Uses telephone system to answer customer calls promptly.	1 2 3 4 5	1 2 3 4 5	1 2 3 4 5		1 2 3 4 5	1 2 3 4 5
6. Uses computer to look up customer orders.	1 2 3 4 5	1 2 3 4 5	1 2 3 4 5		1 2 3 4 5	1 2 3 4 5
. . .						
31. Cleans office kitchen area when it is their turn to do so.	1 2 3 4 5	1 2 3 4 5	1 2 3 4 5		1 2 3 4 5	1 2 3 4 5
32. Uses sit/stand desk correctly throughout the day to maintain own personal health.	1 2 3 4 5	1 2 3 4 5	1 2 3 4 5		1 2 3 4 5	1 2 3 4 5
33. Provides customers with refunds, as appropriate, if there is any problem with the product.	1 2 3 4 5	1 2 3 4 5	1 2 3 4 5		1 2 3 4 5	1 2 3 4 5

Critical Incidents Technique

Critical incidents technique
A technique that involves asking SMEs to describe critical job situations that they frequently encounter on the job

The **critical incidents technique** involves asking SMEs to describe critical situations that they frequently encounter on the job. SMEs are then asked to generate examples of good and poor responses to these critical incidents. This might include responses that they have seen other employees give or ways that they themselves responded to a critical job situation very well or very poorly.[22] As an example, a customer service representative could report that a common

HR IN ACTION
Job Analysis Guidelines for the U.S. Office of Personnel Management

Courtesy of United States Office of Personnel Management

The U.S. Office of Personnel Management (OPM) is the federal agency that manages many of the HR functions for U.S. government agencies such as recruitment, hiring, retention, and compensation. As such, OPM's HR practices affect millions of government employees. OPM notes that a robust job analysis provides important support for developing good selection procedures and plays a key role in their legal defensibility.

For these reasons, OPM provides detailed guidelines to federal agencies about how they should conduct job analyses, including how to develop lists of tasks describing the job and the competencies needed to do the job. OPM also specifies how frequently a job analysis needs to be done—for jobs that are dynamic and quickly changing such as those in information technology, this will be very frequent, perhaps even annually. OPM also provides assistance on how job analysis data can be used by federal agencies to develop selection procedures such as structured interviews (see Chapter 7).[23]

critical incident they must face is an angry customer. A positive response might be to figure out what the customer is angry about and come up with solutions that work well both for the customer and the organization, whereas a negative response might be to become angry with the customer, which would only make matters worse. In Figure 5.5, we show some examples of critical incidents for the job of barista.

■ FIGURE 5.5 Critical Incidents for the Job of Barista

A customer asks for a specialty drink (e.g., a caffe macchiato), which the barista mixes incorrectly. The customer complains to the barista that it's wrong.

- Positive: The barista apologizes and remixes the drink after checking for the correct recipe/procedure.
- Negative: The barista tells the customer that this is the way the drink is actually supposed to be and that they didn't do anything incorrectly.

A customer tells the barista that one of his/her coworkers was a big help to them when they lost their wallet in the coffee shop the previous week and asks them to give his/her coworker a gift card as an expression of thanks.

- Positive: The barista thanks the customer, tells them that this is unnecessary, but agrees to take the card and then passes it along to his/her coworker.
- Negative: The barista thanks the customer and then loses the gift card.

The critical incidents technique may be used on its own or in conjunction with other job analysis methods. The technique provides rich information about frequently occurring, important work situations, including both positive and negative performance on the part of employees and incidents that have actually happened on the job. This is invaluable information for such purposes as developing job-related interview questions for hiring employees (Chapter 7), developing training content (Chapter 8), and developing performance management systems (Chapter 9).

Position Analysis Questionnaire

Unlike task–KSAO analysis and the critical incidents technique, which each provide detailed information about jobs and are often built from scratch with direct input from SMEs, the Position Analysis Questionnaire (PAQ) takes a very different approach. The PAQ is an "off-the-shelf" job analysis survey consisting of 195 generic statements describing what characteristics a worker needs to possess.[24] For instance, in using the PAQ to conduct a job analysis, a job analyst might interview SMEs about their job, complete the PAQ survey based on the interviews, and then have the PAQ data scored online. Because the PAQ has been around since the 1960s, there is a substantial database, such that a detailed report can be generated about the job, giving recommendations for what types of selection procedures might be used for a job with this profile or what the pay should be relative to other jobs. The advantages of the PAQ are that it is far less labor intensive and thus less expensive than the task/KSAO analysis, and its generic items and rich database of jobs allow for comparisons across job types. On the other hand, it does not provide as rich of detail as other job analysis methods, and because its items are written at a fairly high reading level, it cannot simply be given to SMEs to complete, but rather it must be completed by a job analyst who has been trained in its use.[25]

HR IN ACTION

Analyzing What's Needed for Specific Professions

©iStock.com/ajr_images

This chapter focuses on how employers can conduct job analyses and develop competency models to better understand the work conducted in their organizations, as well as how individual jobs are related to each other. However, job analyses for specific jobs are also done by government agencies and professional organizations for developing licensure, credentialing, and certification exams that determine whether an individual is fit to work within a particular profession.[26]

As one example, the National Council of State Boards of Nursing, Inc. (NCSBN), conducted a detailed job analysis for the job of nurse aide. Through a series of SME panels and meetings, it developed a list of 113 activity statements (tasks) and 201 KSAO statements to reflect the work done by certified nurse aides at entry level.[27] Similarly, the National Council for Therapeutic Recreation Certification (NCTRC) developed a job analysis for Certified Therapeutic Recreation Specialists. Notably, its analysis included a survey of thousands of SMEs, identifying dozens of job tasks.[28]

Occupational Information Network (O*NET)

We have already mentioned the Occupational Information Network, or O*NET, published by the U.S. Department of Labor. O*NET is a handy source of job analysis data about a range of occupations, and it can provide a useful start to the job analysis process. However, it is important also to remember that O*NET provides a useful job analysis framework in itself. Figure 5.6 provides a summary of the O*NET framework, which includes elements used to describe what a worker needs to do a particular job (such as abilities, knowledge, skills, and work experience), as well as a job itself (such as tasks, general work activities, and labor market trends). The O*NET framework, because of its great depth, may even provide a framework for understanding the variety that can occur in jobs within an organization across different national contexts. The appendix to this chapter provides detailed information about O*NET including how the O*NET database is populated, and additional detail and documentation about O*NET can be found at the O*NET website (https://www.onetonline.org/). If you check out the O*NET website and enter a job title, you will see the significant amount of data that is provided by the website. For instance, just type in *data scientist*—or any job title that may be of interest to you—to get an idea of the typical tasks and KSAOs that are part of the job.[29]

Competency Modeling

Competency modeling began to emerge in the 1990s as an approach to analyzing jobs, and its use has increased steadily since then. The focus of competency modeling is similar to that of other job analysis methods in that it involves understanding what KSAOs are needed for doing a job and how these KSAOs—or competencies—are manifested on the job in terms of behaviors. However, competency modeling differs from traditional job analysis in several ways, and this is why competency models have grown in popularity. For example, as illustrated in our opening case, SHRM has taken a competency modeling approach to understanding HR jobs rather than using a traditional job analysis, as competency modeling offers a number of advantages.

■ **FIGURE 5.6**   The O*NET Job Analysis Framework

Elements That Are Used to Describe What a Worker Needs to Do the Job

- Worker Characteristics (such as abilities)
- Worker Requirements (such as knowledge and skills)
- Experience Requirements (such as work experience or certifications and licenses needed)

Elements Used to Describe the Work

- Occupational Requirements (such as work activities)
- Workforce Characteristics (such as current labor market trends)
- Occupation-Specific Information (such as tasks that are performed and tools that are used)

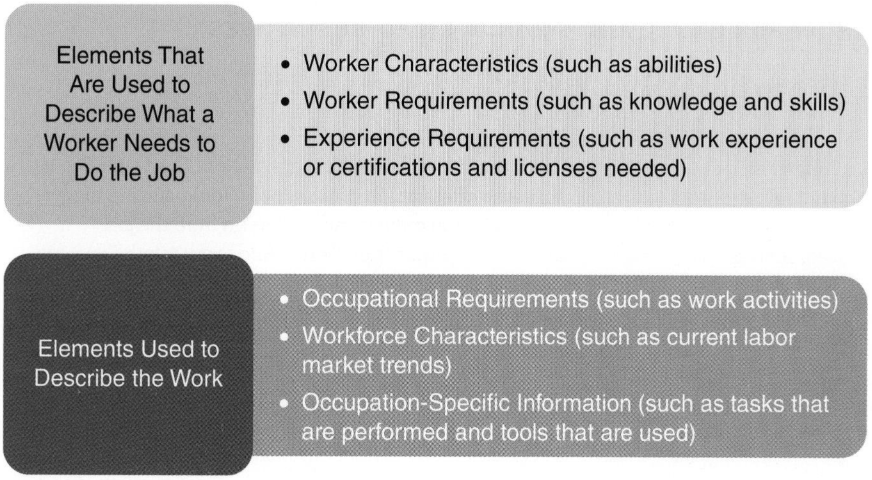

Source: Based on https://www.onetcenter.org/content.html

Alexander Alonso, PhD, SHRM-SCP, is the Society for Human Resource Management's (SHRM's) chief knowledge officer leading operations for SHRM's Certified Professional and Senior Certified Professional certifications, research functions, and the SHRM Knowledge Advisor service. He is responsible for all research activities, including the development of the SHRM Competency Model and SHRM credentials.

Perhaps the biggest difference between competency modeling and most job analysis methods is the comprehensive nature of competency models. Competency models are usually broad enough that they can describe a range of jobs within an organization and do so across multiple levels. In that sense, competency modeling is beneficial to organizations wanting to understand similarities and differences across jobs. For this reason, SHRM chose to use a competency modeling approach to capture a range of HR job types as well as the different levels of experience required for different types of HR jobs: The breadth of the competency modeling approach allowed for that. Similarly, IBM developed a competency model that allowed the company to organize the wide range of training needs of different jobs across a very large, global organization. Other large organizations such as Boeing and Microsoft have also taken a competency modeling approach.[30]

In addition, competency models typically allow organizations to capture their goals and values. For example, an organization that wanted to include a "Value for Diversity" across all of their jobs—and make sure that all employees realize the importance of this value for success in the organization—might include a "Value for Diversity" competency. As noted in the Spotlight on Ethics box, SHRM's competency model explicitly included the value of "Integrity" in HR work because of its desire to articulate the importance of integrity in HR work.

A review of the practice of competency modeling identified these and a number of other key differences between competency modeling and job analysis (see Table 5.6). For example, competency models are often directly related to organizational strategies: They identify differences in the ways that competencies are manifested across different job levels. Unlike traditional job analysis, which considers jobs as they are now, competency models often consider future job requirements—a critical factor in highly dynamic industries. In addition, the development of a competency model in an organization is often an organizational development intervention in itself, as it requires substantial input from its members, particularly from the top, in identifying the big picture of what an organization's members actually do and how that aligns with organizational goals across all organizational levels. Plus, competency modeling is far more likely to catch the attention of executives than a traditional job analysis would, for many of the reasons described in Table 5.6. This possibility of greater executive buy-in and support for competency

SPOTLIGHT ON HR FOR SMALL AND MEDIUM-SIZED BUSINESSES

Job Analysis in Smaller Organizations

Most of the job analysis and competency modeling techniques described in this chapter were developed in large public- and private-sector organizations. As a result, many of the processes used, such as large-scale surveys and review of materials with large numbers of SMEs, would be difficult or impossible to carry out in smaller organizations. However, that doesn't mean that job analyses and job descriptions aren't useful to smaller employers. The issue, rather, is to adapt these methods to a smaller scale. For example, this might mean speaking to current employees and their managers to identify and document the key job responsibilities and KSAOs; or it could simply mean developing a basic job

description for jobs in the organization. The O*NET database offers a rich starting point for analyzing many jobs, requiring only some adaptation from the job analyst with input from SMEs. And smaller public-sector organizations can often borrow job analysis information from other public agencies.

Even these simple job analysis activities can have a big payoff. They can facilitate other HR activities like recruiting the best candidates, developing great hiring interviews, measuring performance, setting pay and rewards, or onboarding and orienting new employees to their jobs.[31]

TABLE 5.6 Description of Competency Models and How They Differ From Job Analysis

1. Executives typically pay more attention to competency modeling than to job analysis.
2. Competency models often attempt to distinguish top performers from average performers.
3. Competency models frequently include descriptions of how the competencies change or progress with employee level.
4. Competency models are usually directly linked to business objectives and strategies.
5. Competency models are typically developed top down (start with executives) rather than bottom up (start with line employees).
6. Competency models may consider future job requirements either directly or indirectly.
7. Competency models may be presented in a manner that facilitates ease of use (e.g., organization-specific language, pictures, or schematics that facilitate memorableness).
8. Usually, a finite number of competencies are identified and applied across multiple functions or job families.
9. Competency models are frequently used actively to align the HR systems.
10. Competency models are often an organizational development intervention that seeks broad organizational change as opposed to a simple data collection effort.

Source: Reprinted from Campion, M. A., Fink, A. A., Ruggeberg, B. J., Carr, L., Phillips, G. M., & Odman, R. B. (2011). Doing competencies well: Best practices in competency modeling. *Personnel Psychology, 64,* 225–262.

modeling is an important consideration: It means that the process is more likely to be successful and that the results will be used in strategic decision making.

Because competency models—like job analyses—are used as the basis for other HR functions, it is important that they be carefully developed in order to be both accurate and legally defensible. For example, because competency models are used to capture a wide range of jobs across the company, it may be tempting to write competencies that are so broad as to be

SPOTLIGHT ON ETHICS

Designing Ethics and Integrity Into Work

Throughout this book, we illustrate the importance of ethics and integrity to the practice of HR through these Spotlight on Ethics boxes. Although ethical behavior is perhaps best modeled by company management, a key factor is to begin at the beginning of the HR process and to make ethical behavior an explicit part of the job analysis, competency model, and job description. In other words, the essential role of job analysis and competency modeling in other HR functions makes them critical to communicating the values of ethics and integrity to the organization's employees—and letting employees know that these are needed to get ahead in the organization. In this way, the value of ethical behavior will be echoed throughout the other HR functions, including recruitment, selection, training, and performance management.

There are a number of examples of how ethics can be incorporated into the job analysis process. For

example, the O*NET framework published by the U.S. Department of Labor includes integrity as one of its work styles. SHRM's competency model incorporated ethical practice as one of its core competencies; these also include integrity, courage, and professionalism. Such explicit inclusion of employee ethics in describing the job requirements should increase the odds of recruiting and hiring ethical workers, as well as rewarding ethical behavior.[32]

Questions

1. How would you define ethics and integrity? Do you see them as personal qualities, or can they also be characteristics of an organization?

2. Give some examples of events in the news involving ethics or integrity at the organizational level.

SPOTLIGHT ON GLOBAL ISSUES
Building Global Competencies

Given the increased globalization of work in the 21st century, it is not surprising that global issues are now becoming increasingly recognized in job analysis processes. Specifically, organizations that operate in multinational environments need to develop job analysis systems and competency models that are flexible enough to integrate multiple national contexts.

For example, the World Health Organization (WHO), an agency of the United Nations focused on public health worldwide, has developed a global competency model that includes competencies such as knowing and managing oneself, producing results, and respecting and promoting cultural differences, as well as management competencies and leadership competencies. SHRM's competency model places a value on global knowledge with its Global and Cultural Effectiveness competency.

In addition to emphasizing the need for managers and employees to navigate different global and cultural contexts, companies increasingly need to develop job analysis and competency modeling systems that can address the complexity of different jobs and the way they are structured in different parts of the world. Specifically, with the growth of multinational organizations working across multiple national contexts, there are challenges for balancing national and cultural differences while still maintaining an integrated organizational whole. For example, Deloitte Consulting cites this need to balance job architecture across multiple contexts for effective job classification and pay structures. Notably, as comprehensive job analysis frameworks such as the O*NET continue to develop, and as they become more flexible and easier to deploy because of improving technology and advanced analytics, developing job analysis systems that encompass a range of countries and cultures will become more feasible and commonplace.[33]

relatively useless. Other considerations in the development of robust competency models include ensuring their legal defensibility (e.g., if they will be used as the basis for personnel selection decisions), determining the level of detail required for the particular organization, and making sure that the list of competencies stays current over time as the organization, teams, and individual jobs evolve. HR practitioners and researchers have developed best practices in competency modeling, and these should be reviewed prior to undertaking the development of competency models. These include using rigorous job analysis methods to develop competencies, thinking of future organizational needs while creating the model, and linking the model to organizational goals and objectives.[34]

LO 5.4 Explain how job design can be used to increase employee motivation, job attitudes, and performance.

Designing Jobs to Enhance Motivation, Attitudes, Well-Being, and Performance

Throughout most of this chapter, our focus has been on how to analyze jobs to understand what a worker does on the job and the worker characteristics needed to do the job—and to define these as objectively as possible. Thus, the point of job analysis and competency modeling is to have a deep understanding of what the job involves to form the basis for developing HR functions such as selection, pay, or training, among others. However, it is also important to consider how jobs can be designed to better fit with human needs. Such an approach has been shown to have a number of benefits, such as reducing worker stress. In addition, employers need to consider ***job design*** in terms of how jobs are *experienced* by workers, regardless of the objective characteristics of the work. Designing or redesigning jobs based on how workers perceive and experience their work (e.g., stressful, boring, meaningful) is also important, as it can affect worker motivation, job attitudes, and job performance. In this section, we examine some of the approaches that have been taken to design jobs for workers and job characteristics that have been shown to be important in redesigning jobs. In addition, Chapter 15 will discuss how designing the physical aspects of jobs, such as from an ergonomic perspective, can help improve worker safety and health.

Job design The process of identifying how a job's characteristics are experienced from the employee's perspective in order to enhance well-being and performance

Before discussing approaches to designing jobs to address human needs, describing a few key concepts is in order. First, the concept of *job enlargement* involves the addition of more responsibilities to a job so that it is less boring and more motivating for workers. This might include adding some challenges that can make the job more interesting or allow workers to gain more skills. For example, having a worker take on a new project that is different from the ones she has taken on before could be a form of job enlargement. Second, *job enrichment* involves allowing workers to have greater decision-making power. For example, a team of workers in a high-tech manufacturing firm might be allowed to manage themselves rather than only being managed by the supervisor or team leader. Although job enlargement and job enrichment are both considered important for reducing boredom and improving employee motivation and performance, it is important to keep in mind that not all employees will do well with enriched or enlarged jobs: Some employees may prefer not to take on additional responsibilities, while others may not perform well with such responsibilities. Finally, *job rotation* includes rotating employees from one job to another, not only making their work less boring but also allowing them to learn new skills.[35]

Job Design Considerations

In the early 20th century, the scientific management approach (see Chapter 1) advocated for the simplification of jobs, such that a single worker would be required to do the same simple, repetitive task. Following this principle, jobs were often designed in ways that ignored issues such as worker boredom and social needs. The Hawthorne Studies (see Chapter 1) were the first major break from this approach, as their findings suggested the value of designing work in a way that was motivating and supportive to workers, taking into account the important roles that social processes, group norms, and work variety all play in work performance.

The Tavistock Mining Institute Studies, conducted in England in the mid-20th century, were an early illustration of actively redesigning jobs for actual people, who can become bored and need social interaction. These studies found that a highly "logical" redesign of coal mining jobs during World War II—with, for example, a decreased emphasis on the intact teams that had previously functioned to make this uncomfortable and dangerous work less stressful—had resulted in serious decreases in productivity. It was at that time that the importance of job design from the worker's perspective was first shown in stark relief.

Developed in the 1960s, Hackman and Oldham's *Job Characteristics Model (JCM)* was the first complete model of job design, explaining which characteristics are the most important to increasing worker motivation and productivity. Most of the subsequent job design models are largely based on it. Figure 5.7 shows the basics of the JCM and the process by which job characteristics were thought to affect worker outcomes. The model proposes that enhancing the characteristics of the job leads to improved psychological states, which leads to improved individual and organizational outcomes. Specifically, the characteristics of skill variety (applying a range of skills on the job), task identity (completing a complete piece of work on the jobs), and task significance (doing work that is important, for example, affects others) lead to experienced meaningfulness of work; autonomy (freedom in how the work gets done) leads to experienced responsibility; and feedback (the degree to which the job gives you feedback about performance) leads to knowledge of results. These three psychological states— meaningfulness, responsibility, and knowledge of results—all in turn lead to improved outcomes such as motivation and performance.

Later models of job design take a slightly different approach from the JCM, with a focus on understanding how workers' experiences might affect outcomes such as stress. The *Job Demands-Control Model (JDC)* emphasizes that employees experience stress when there are high job demands and little control over their job. In a more elaborated version of the JDC, the *Job Demands-Resources Model (JDR*; see Figure 5.8) emphasizes that job demands, such as workload and time pressure, can be counteracted by characteristics such as job control, participation, and supervisor support.[36] In fact, research suggests that providing factors like supervisor support can improve employee motivation and even health.

Job enlargement The addition of more responsibilities to a job so that it is less boring and more motivating for workers

Job enrichment Allowing workers to have greater decision-making power

Job rotation Rotating employees from one job to another, allowing them to learn new skills

Job Characteristics Model (JCM) The first complete model of job design, explaining which job characteristics are the most important to increasing worker motivation and productivity

Job Demands-Control Model (JDC) This model emphasizes that employees experience stress when there are high job demands and little control over their job

Job Demands-Resources Model (JDR) This model emphasizes that job demands, such as workload and time pressure, can be counteracted by characteristics such as job control, participation, and supervisor support

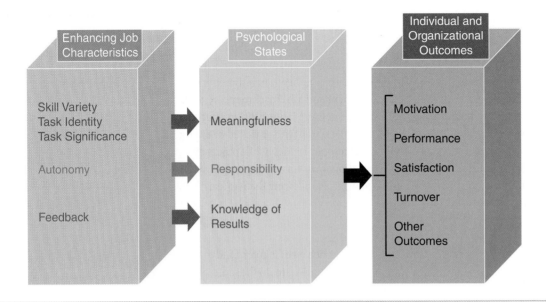

■ **FIGURE 5.7**   Hackman and Oldham's Job Characteristics Model

In the early 21st century, Morgeson and Humphrey developed a more comprehensive model of job design, which takes into account the dimensions from previous job design models (see Figure 5.9). The model includes 18 types of job characteristics falling into four broad categories: task characteristics, knowledge characteristics, social characteristics, and the work context (which includes more physical aspects of the job). In other words, according to this model, there are a number of job characteristics that may be seen as "levers" available to organizational decision makers who want to enhance workers' jobs to increase motivation, satisfaction, and performance.[37]

How Effective Are Job Design Considerations for Predicting Employee Outcomes?

Does improving the psychological characteristics of work actually pay off for organizations in terms of outcomes like job attitudes and performance? The research, as summarized in a large meta-analysis of 259 studies and more than 200,000 workers, suggests that it clearly does. For example, the experience of autonomy, task variety, and task significance among workers was positively related to increased job performance. Greater autonomy and task significance were

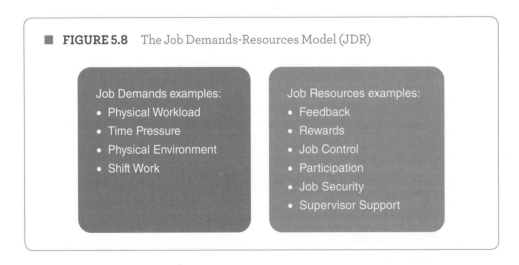

■ **FIGURE 5.8**   The Job Demands-Resources Model (JDR)

■ **FIGURE 5.9**   Morgeson and Humphrey's Comprehensive Job Design Model[38]

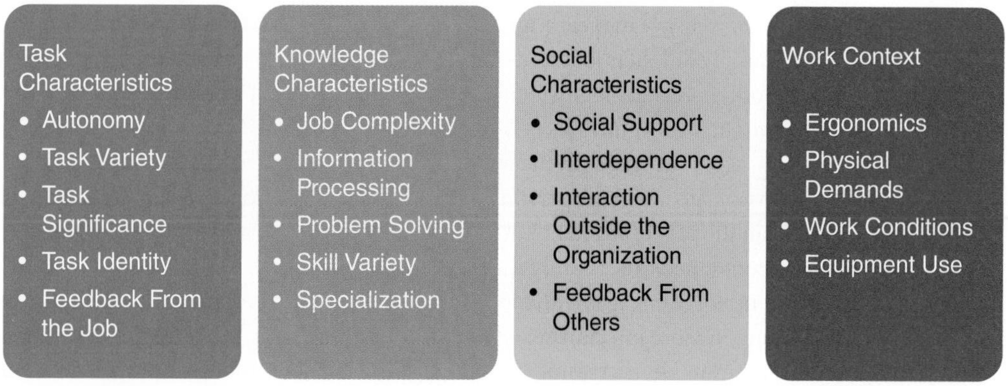

Task Characteristics	Knowledge Characteristics	Social Characteristics	Work Context
• Autonomy • Task Variety • Task Significance • Task Identity • Feedback From the Job	• Job Complexity • Information Processing • Problem Solving • Skill Variety • Specialization	• Social Support • Interdependence • Interaction Outside the Organization • Feedback From Others	• Ergonomics • Physical Demands • Work Conditions • Equipment Use

Source: Adapted from Morgeson, F. P., & Humphrey, S. E. (2006). The Work Design Questionnaire (WDQ): Developing and validating a comprehensive measure for assessing job design and the nature of work. *Journal of Applied Psychology, 91,* 1321–1399.

negatively related to employee burnout. Increased support from coworkers was negatively related to intention to quit the job. And higher levels of most of the job characteristics were positively associated with greater job satisfaction.[39]

Interestingly, however, despite increases in the technological sophistication of work today, there continue to be many boring, repetitive, unenriched, and unmotivating jobs even in most developed economies.[40] Given the negative effects of such jobs, employers need to understand employees' experiences of their work, which can be assessed through a range of methods, from sophisticated analytics to conversations and listening. Improving employees' experience of work through job redesign may provide a competitive edge for those organizations willing to make the investment.

Finally, it is important to know that some employees will value enriched jobs more than others; that is, enriching job characteristics may be beneficial to some employees but not to others. As one example, researchers have recently argued that the age of the employee may determine which job characteristics employees want and need in their work.[41] For instance, younger employees may especially need job characteristics like task variety that allow them to gain the experience they need to advance in their careers, whereas older employees may benefit from being allowed to apply the wide range of skills that they have already acquired throughout their careers. The empirical research does in fact suggest that older and younger workers may benefit from different job characteristics.[42] For example, one recent study showed that increasing autonomy led to increased job satisfaction and mental health of older construction workers compared to their younger counterparts.[43] However, many other factors, such as the particular type of job and industry, likely play a role as well.[44]

Job Crafting

Most of the discussion in this section has been about how employees experience their work and what organizations can do to enhance this experience. However, it has also been recognized that workers may be quite capable of ***job crafting***—redesigning their own jobs to fit their needs and personalities—provided they stay within the guidelines of the organization. Job crafting can lead to significant improvements in worker morale and performance.[45] For example, an employee may decide to take on additional challenges that could be helpful in gaining the work experiences that they need to advance in their career. You may have done some job crafting in your own work. Other employees may decide to craft their job as they gain expertise, or late-career employees may adapt their jobs to fit their changing needs.

In one early study of job crafting, researchers examined how cleaning crew workers in a hospital, a fairly low-skills job, experienced their work. In conducting interviews with these workers,

Job crafting Redesigning one's own job to fit one's needs (e.g., abilities, interests, personality)

the researchers found that some workers experienced their jobs to be rather boring and repetitive and without much meaning—just as you might expect. In contrast, other workers found their jobs to be quite meaningful. The difference was that these latter workers often performed tasks that were not in their original job descriptions, such as talking to patients. While the first group simply did their jobs as described, the latter group molded their jobs in ways that made their jobs more meaningful to them.[46] (You can see a short video describing this research here: https://youtu.be/C_igfnctYjA.)

Not surprisingly, the willingness and ability of workers to craft their jobs have often been associated with the personality characteristic of proactivity, as crafting requires an active role on the part of workers.[47] A recent meta-analysis of more than 120 studies and 35,000 workers confirmed this, finding that job crafting behaviors were related to proactive personality and employee engagement, meaning that more proactive and engaged employees reported engaging in more job crafting. Furthermore, job crafting seems to benefit the organization as well; for example, increasing challenging job demands among employees was found to be related to employee job performance.[48] With that said, the willingness and ability to craft are not just functions of the employee personality: Research suggests that job crafting is a skill that can be taught to employees.[49] For example, one recent study showed how training workers to craft their jobs around their personal strengths was especially useful to improving older workers' perceived fit with their jobs, although this effect was not found with younger workers.[50] In any case, for job crafting to be successful, organizations need to give employees sufficient latitude to enable them to craft their jobs.

Flexible Work Arrangements

LO 5.5 Describe how flexible work environments affect employee well-being.

Flextime A work arrangement in which workers can choose from a number of work schedules

Telecommuting A work arrangement in which an employee is not physically at an office or other location but instead works a substantial amount of time away from the office

There are other ways that organizations can design work to support employees. Many organizations offer flexible work arrangements to workers, with the goal of helping them to balance work and life needs. (We treat the issue of work–family issues in greater depth in Chapter 15.) One such work arrangement is *flextime*, in which workers can choose from a number of work schedules. For example, some workers in an organization may choose to work from 7:00 a.m. to 3:00 p.m., while others may choose to work from 9:00 a.m. to 5:00 p.m. Other examples include the possibility of working four 10-hour days each week. Some organizations allow workers to change their work schedules from day to day, while others require that workers choose a set time that they are at work. Of course, many of these flexible work schedules are not suitable for all kinds of work. For example, medical personnel would need to ensure that hospitals are always sufficiently staffed.

Many organizations have now taken this idea of flexible work schedules a step further, implementing flexible times and telecommuting. *Telecommuting*, or remote work, is a work arrangement in which an employee is not physically at an office or other location but instead works a substantial amount of time away from the office. For example, an employee might choose to work from home and only come in to work 2 days per week, or even 2 days per month. The idea is that such flexibility can allow workers to better manage their nonwork lives and save commuting time. In fact, there has been an increase in the popularity of telework at many organizations such as Dell, Xerox, and Aetna, which have adopted telecommuting with the goal of reducing energy consumption.[51]

But what does the research indicate about whether telecommuting actually benefits organizations and employees? The answer is generally favorable, but with some caveats. A meta-analysis of 46 employee samples comprising more than 12,000 employees showed that telecommuting was negatively related to work–family conflict, turnover intentions, and role stress for employees and also was positively associated with better job satisfaction and performance. However, heavy telecommuting (more than 2.5 days per week) led to more negative relationships with coworkers. In fact, one concern with telecommuting is that it can be hard to manage relationships at work, including the value of working face to face with collaborators for making real-time, data-based decisions. It is for these reasons that some companies like IBM, HP, and Bank of America decided in the early 2000s to pull the plug on telecommuting.[52] In short, although telecommuting has many advantages, it is not universally beneficial for all types of work. On the other hand, it can benefit certain worker groups. For example, one study in a health-care organization showed that allowing flexibility to older office workers in terms of location and time of work caused them to want to stay with the organization.[53]

Contingent Employees

Contingent employees are those who are hired for a limited, fixed term such as a short-term contract or a project consulting contract. The use of contingent employees has been expanded, with some sources citing that 40% of U.S. workers hold contingent types of jobs.[54] The organizational benefits cited for the use of contingent workers include the flexibility of hiring workers with specific skills only when they are needed, the ability to deal with fluctuations in production, the ability to reduce the need for training (i.e., hiring employees who are already trained up on certain skills), and to "try out" employees before making the commitment of hiring them permanently (temp-to-permanent).

In fact, the *gig economy* is a type of contingent work that uses highly skilled workers to link up with organizations using a digital platform. For instance, a company may need a team of highly qualified programmers for a short-term project; it would not have the need to hire them permanently. Thus, it might hire a team of programmers from around the country or around the world to work on the project.

Although there has been significant growth in contingent jobs, these work arrangements are not without their downsides to employees and to organizations. For example, gig-economy jobs have been criticized because they leave workers vulnerable to job insecurity and wage theft. Contingent workers are also more likely than permanent workers to have lower pay, higher poverty rates, and decreased access to health insurance.

Some organizations argue that the benefits of contingent workers are not completely clear and that hiring contingent workers does not necessarily lead to cost savings. For example, a simulation study on the cost effectiveness of various contingent workforce strategies in organizations suggests that the use of workers from temporary agencies may be associated with decreased performance and increased turnover. In comparison, the use of independent contractors was more cost effective, with the temp-to-permanent approach being the most cost effective. In summary, it is important for organizations not to simply assume that the use of contingent workers is always cost effective. Rather, they should carefully consider the particular circumstances and the advantages and disadvantages of using contingent workers, both for the workers themselves and for the organization.[55]

> **Contingent employees**
> Individuals who are hired for a limited, fixed term such as a short-term contract or a project consulting contract

CHAPTER SUMMARY

Job analysis is the basis for most HR functions, including recruitment, selection, training, performance management, and pay. It is also used to develop job descriptions and job specifications. Methods used to collect job analysis data include interviews, observations, surveys, government data (the O*NET), and existing job analyses. Various job analysis frameworks and approaches to analyzing work—such as task analysis, the critical incidents technique, and competency modeling—each have their own unique advantages and disadvantages. Understanding how work is experienced from the employee's perspective in terms of motivation is also key to approaching the analysis and design of work as ways of increasing worker engagement, satisfaction, and performance. Flexible work arrangements such as flextime, telecommuting, and contingent work are increasingly common, although organizational decision makers should analyze their implementation carefully for their advantages and disadvantages.

KEY TERMS

⑤SAGE edge™

Visit **edge.sagepub.com/bauer** to help you accomplish your coursework goals in an easy-to-use learning environment.

- Master the learning objectives using key study tools
- Watch, listen, and connect with online multimedia resources
- Access mobile-friendly quizzes and flashcards to check your understanding

HR REASONING AND DECISION-MAKING EXERCISES

MINI-CASE ANALYSIS EXERCISE: JOB ANALYSIS AND KSAO RATINGS

The city of Jasper has conducted a job analysis of its firefighters. Specifically, the job being analyzed is a fire apparatus operator/driver (FAOD). FAODs are workers who, in addition to conducting direct firefighting activities, also drive the fire equipment and apparatus to the fire incident, and who also have deep knowledge about operating the equipment.

Jasper has collected data from 35 FAODs and 10 of their supervisors, who served as subject matter experts (SMEs). The following table lists the means and standard deviations of the KSAO criticality ratings in terms of importance.

MEANS AND STANDARD DEVIATIONS FOR THE CRITICALITY (IMPORTANCE) RATINGS OF EACH KSAO		
FIRE APPARATUS OPERATOR/DRIVER (FAOD) KSAOS	MEAN (1–5 SCALE)	STANDARD DEVIATION
A. Ability to work within a team	4.9	0.2
B. Mechanical ability	4.8	0.3
C. Upper body strength	4.5	0.3
D. Ability to read maps (both paper and online) and to memorize all city streets	3.8	1.2
E. Knowledge of fire equipment functions and capacity	4.8	0.1
F. Ability to supervise crew	3.2	1.3
G. Knowledge of fire-suppression principles related to residential buildings	3.6	1.1
H. Knowledge of fire-suppression principles related to commercial/high-rise buildings	4.8	.3
I. Critical thinking/decision making	4.7	.2

1. Based on your initial review of the mean criticality ratings for each KSAO, which KSAOs would you consider dropping from the job analysis? Explain why.

2. You know that a key role of this job is driving fire equipment (e.g., fire trucks) to the fire scene. But KSAO D has a fairly low mean and a high standard deviation. Why might this be? Rather than tossing out this KSAO, do you see any issue with the way that the KSAO is currently written and how it might be edited?

3. You learn that the city of Jasper collected most of the data for this job analysis from SMEs who are located in urban areas of the city rather than in the more suburban areas. Knowing this, would it affect any of your decisions about which KSAOs to remove from the job analysis? How might the city approach future data collections like this differently?

HR DECISION ANALYSIS EXERCISE: STRATEGIC ISSUES IN CHOOSING A JOB ANALYSIS APPROACH

You are currently working in the HR department of Sintra, Inc., a mid-sized health services provider, with approximately 500 health personnel (e.g., physicians, nurses) and more than 100 administrative staff. Sintra's focus is on providing urgent care in your state, with approximately 30 offices spread across urban, suburban, and rural areas.

Sintra is considering a change in the work flow of the services it provides; for example, it is toying with the idea of creating intact teams of health professionals to provide health services. As part of this work flow analysis, Sintra has examined its existing job analyses. For its health providers, there are essentially just two job descriptions, one for physician and one for nurse. However, Sintra's leadership realizes the need to do more specific, detailed job analyses for the individual specialty areas of its physicians and nurses so as to better understand what specific types of physicians and nurses do and thus to assemble the most effective teams. It is estimated that in reality, there are at least three specialty areas among the nurses and four among the physicians, meaning that Sintra needs to plan to conduct at least seven job analyses to understand what its nurses and physicians actually do.

Not surprisingly, the nurses and physicians across Sintra are very interested in the results of these job analyses, as they will have a substantial effect on whom they work with and on the kind of care that they are able to deliver to patients. They are dedicated to their jobs, and they want to be able to express their views about what they do on the job and how they can most effectively serve patients.

The vice president of HR, Margot Russy, has charged you with taking on the task of conducting these job analyses for these nurse and physician jobs. Consistent with what is described above, her goal is to develop a comprehensive competency model that will reflect the range of nurse and physician jobs in the company. She also sees the value of doing these job analyses well so as to assemble the best teams of health providers. However, she tells you that Sintra is under considerable financial pressure from its investors to do these job analyses as inexpensively as possible. Thus, she asks if you might simply use Sintra's largest clinic, located in the downtown of the major city in the state, to confirm the different job descriptions already in place and the interrelationships among the jobs. She also reasons that this would allow the job analyses to happen quickly.

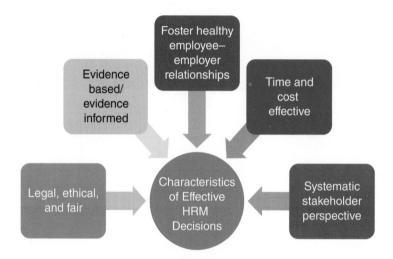

Please provide the rationale for your answer to each of the questions below.

Was the VP of human resources's approach legal, ethical, and fair?

_____

_____

_____

_____

Was her approach evidence based/evidence informed?

_____

_____

_____

_____

Would her decision foster healthy employee–employer relationships?

_____

_____

_____

_____

Would her recommendations for how to approach these job analyses be time and cost effective?

_____

_____

_____

_____

Did she take a systematic stakeholder perspective?

_____

_____

_____

_____

Considering your analysis above, overall, what would be an effective decision? Why?

_____

_____

_____

_____

What, if anything, do you think should be done differently or considered to help make this decision more effective?

_____

_____

_____

_____

HR DECISION-MAKING EXERCISE: USING O*NET

As discussed earlier in the chapter, O*NET was developed by the U.S. government to provide a general job analysis system to help employers to conduct their job and work analyses. Please go to the O*NET website at https://www.onetonline.org/ to answer the following questions.

1. Search for a job with which you are familiar. Were you able to find the job quickly, with the same job title you were using, or did O*NET use a slightly different job title? Or did it suggest multiple possible job titles? If so, why do you think this is?

2. Now look at the tasks, knowledge, skills, and abilities that O*NET notes as associated with that job. Do these match your impression of the job? Why might there be some differences between the job title you used and the job title in the O*NET database?

3. Sometimes no single O*NET job title captures the job for which you are searching. In your case, did it require piecing together the information from two or more jobs listed in the O*NET database to adequately describe the job you're looking for? If so, can you explain why this may have happened?

4. For most jobs you will search for, the O*NET job titles will not be a perfect fit for a particular job in a particular organization. More important, the content listed in the O*NET may not be a perfect match, either. Given these challenges, what do you see as the value to HR professionals using the O*NET when conducting job analyses?

DATA AND ANALYTICS EXERCISE: EVALUATING TASK–KSAO ANALYSIS DATA

When conducting a task–KSAO analysis, a list of tasks and KSAOs is generated for a particular job. To determine which tasks and KSAOs to retain, as well as which KSAOs are most important for performing each task, different questionnaires are administered to subject matter experts (SMEs), who rate the criticality (importance) of the tasks and KSAOs.

Two simple descriptive analytics—the *mean* and the *standard deviation (SD)*—can be used to determine which tasks and KSAOs are most critical, as well as the level of agreement of SMEs' ratings. First, a mean is a measure of central tendency. Assuming that ratings fall in a normal bell-shaped distribution, the mean represents the most central—or average—rating. In the context of a task–KSAO analysis, the mean rating for a particular task or KSAO represents its level of criticality. Thus, if a task or KSAO has a higher mean than another task or KSAO, it signifies that it is more critical in the eyes of the SMEs. Second, a standard deviation is a

■ FIGURE 5.10

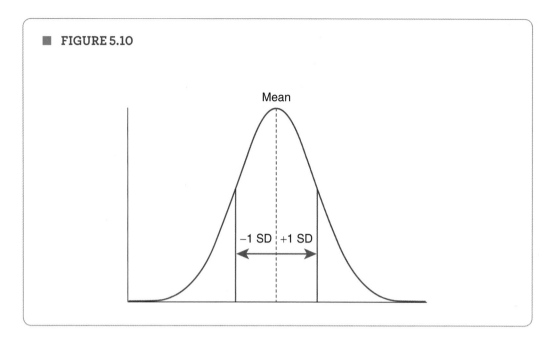

measure of dispersion or variation. Assuming that ratings fall in a normal distribution, the SD represents how dispersed or spread out the ratings are around the mean. Thus, in the context of a task–KSAO analysis, a smaller SD indicates that there is more agreement in SME ratings for a particular task or KSAO. Further, assuming a normal distribution of SME ratings, 68% of scores will fall between 1 SD below and above the mean rating, and 95% of scores fall within 2 SDs below and above the mean rating.

Excel software from Microsoft makes it easy to compute the mean and SD of a set of scores. To calculate the mean, use the =AVERAGE() function, and to calculate the SD, use the =STDEV.S() function. Within the parentheses of either function, simply enter the vector of scores for which you wish to calculate the mean or SD. For example, download the Excel spreadsheet containing subject matter expert (SME) data for task criticality ratings. Next, to calculate the mean and SD of the first task criticality ratings (i.e., 4, 3, 4, 4, 5, 2, 4, 5), you would enter the following in cells J2 and K2, respectively: =AVERAGE(B2:I2) and =STDEV.S(B2:I2). The mean is 3.88 and the SD is .99.

Tasks	SME 1	SME 2	SME 3	SME 4	SME 5	SME 6	SME 7	SME 8	Mean	SD
1. Speaks with customers who are interested in new products.	4	3	4	4	5	2	4	5	3.88	.99
2. Works to solve customer complaints.	5	5	5	5	5	5	5	5		
3. Coordinates with supervisor to resolve customer problems.	4	4	5	4	4	4	5	4		
4. Stays abreast of current sales and specials provided by the company by checking company website.	2	1	3	4	2	2	5	1		
5. Uses telephone system to answer customer calls promptly.	3	3	4	3	4	3	4	4		
6. Uses computer to look up customer orders.	4	4	5	4	4	4	4	4		
7. Uses telephone system to notify customers about products received.	1	1	2	1	2	2	1	1		
8. Uses email system to notify customers about products received.	5	5	4	3	3	3	4	5		
9. Cleans office kitchen area when it is their turn to do so.	2	2	4	2	2	3	2	2		
10. Uses sit/stand desk correctly throughout the day to maintain own personal health.	4	3	4	4	4	5	3	4		
11. Provides customers with refunds, as appropriate, if there is any problem with the product.	1	1	1	1	1	1	1	1		

✔ EXCEL EXTENSION: NOW YOU TRY!

- Now, on **edge.sagepub.com/bauer**, using the same Excel spreadsheet, calculate the means and SDs for the remaining task criticality ratings. Once you have done so, respond to the following questions:

  ○ Which task had the highest mean? Which task had the lowest mean?

  ○ Which task had the highest SD? Which task had the lowest SD? What do these SDs indicate?

- Based on the means and SDs, which three tasks would you definitely retain? Which three tasks would you definitely remove? Why?

CHAPTER 5 SUPPLEMENT: DEEPER DIVE INTO HRM: O*NET

Source: https://www.onetcenter.org/overview.html; https://www.onetcenter.org/dataCollection.html

The online O*NET job analysis system can provide significant support for organizations wishing to carry out a job analysis. As we discuss in the chapter, the O*NET database can provide a great starting point for an employer wishing to conduct a job analysis. However, the database can provide a good deal more, including a comprehensive framework within which most jobs can be organized. Specifically, the framework can organize jobs from the levels of

- major groups,
- minor groups,
- broad occupations, and
- detailed occupations.

In addition, it is necessary to populate the O*NET database with current information about various occupations and also to ensure that this information is updated on a regular basis. To accomplish these goals, the Department of Labor and the National Center for O*NET Development considered a number of strategies, focusing on what would provide the most accurate data as well as what would be the most cost-effective approach. In short, the goal was to obtain valid, reliable, current, and regularly updated data. Together they developed a two-stage process that includes

- randomly sampling businesses across the United States that are expected to employ large numbers of a particular occupation of interest, and
- surveying random samples of employees within these businesses to update the database.

In addition, the O*NET uses labor market data to make projections about the growth of certain jobs in the coming years and which jobs seem to be new or emerging. These are noted on the website as having a "bright outlook."

In short, then, the O*NET database provides employers with a rich, robust source of information about thousands of specific jobs.

Workforce Planning and Recruitment

Opening Case

Creating a College Recruitment Pipeline: The Case of PwC[1]

PricewaterhouseCoopers (PwC) is one of the Big 4 accounting firms that along with Deloitte, EY, and KPMG handle 80% of auditing for all U.S. public companies. PwC provides tax, assurance, and advisory services to clients around the world and employs more than 236,000 people across 158 countries in 736 locations. The work can be demanding. In order to keep the new employee pipeline open, PwC focuses a great deal on its college relationships and recruiting from new college graduate programs. PwC has invested and continues to invest time, effort, and money toward these programs. Several of its recruitment activities are covered in this chapter. For example, as of 2016, PwC had hired more than 11,000 students per year via college campus recruiting programs and relationships and offers new college graduates $1,200 per year to help them pay off student debt. Legally, firms are prohibited from asking about employees' personal debt, but nationally, 71% of college graduates have student loan debt of $35,000 on average. Thus, this benefit has the potential to be highly attractive to college students weighing their options for employment after graduation.

PwC also offers Career*Advisor,* a website designed to help students assess their strengths and interests, maximize their resources to identify opportunities, prepare for the job search, and identify ways to present

LEARNING OBJECTIVES

After reading and studying this chapter, you should be able to do the following:

6.1 Describe workforce planning and its role in HR.

6.2 Identify what recruiting is and its key components.

6.3 Describe the three stages of recruitment and what takes place in them.

6.4 Explain the various aspects of diversity in recruiting.

6.5 Explain key analytical, legal, ethical, and global issues associated with workforce planning and recruitment.

©iStock.com/NicolasMcComber

PwC has offices around the world including this location in London, UK.

themselves to make the best impression. Career*Advisor* offers articles, videos, assessments, and tools to help students succeed in their new careers regardless of where they choose to go. It also introduced video interviewing to help busy students work around their schedules and classes. But PwC is also hoping that by offering innovative recruitment tools, its employment brand and reputation will be enhanced, which can help attract and hire the best candidates. Rod Adams, PwC's U.S. recruiting leader, noted that the use of video interviews helps to free up time during a site visit after an offer is made, creating a more enjoyable experience. In his words, "It becomes a sell visit instead of an interview. The benefit is candidate experience because [candidates] come into the office, they're not nervous because they already have an offer, and they can really just absorb our environment and what we have to offer them versus worrying about their interview."

Finally, one major source of new employees is internships that turn into job offers. According to PwC, 90% of its interns receive full-time job offers (compared to the U.S. average of 72%). To help students prepare for internships, PwC offers information regarding what students can expect including coaching and real-time development during internships. Its continued investment in its internship program has helped PwC earn the 12th spot on the 20 Most Prestigious Internships list for 2018, according to *Forbes*.

Following are some job search tips from Alexa Merschel, a PwC recruiter, who has hired more than 500 people after reviewing 8,000 résumés and interviewing thousands of applicants:

- Keep your résumé short and up-to-date.
- Include volunteer experience.
- Include the name of the company to which you are applying in your résumé's "objective."
- Make sure your phone's voicemail greeting sounds professional.
- Create a profile on LinkedIn and make sure it is complete.
- Network widely.
- If interviewed, come prepared with stories illustrating your initiative and leadership skills, and be ready to answer specific questions about your accomplishments and leadership skills.

PwC is also working toward other strategic recruiting goals such as gamified training solutions, which allow trainees to engage in work scenario role playing online. Further, PwC maintains a robust alumni network, which lets it cultivate future employees and stay in touch with former employees as potential clients and returning employees.

Case Discussion Questions

1. Do you think PwC is offering the right mix of incentives to attract college graduates? Why or why not?

2. Are there other things PwC is not yet doing that you believe it should consider doing to attract college students and graduates?

3. Do you think the tips shared by Alexa Merschel, a PwC recruiter, would be helpful at other firms or in other industries? Why or why not?

4. PwC offers 90% of its interns full-time employment. What do you see as the pros and cons of this approach?

▶ Click to learn more...

Read more about PwC's college student programs for recruitment for college freshmen, sophomores, juniors, seniors, and fifth-year students at http://www.pwc.com/us/en/careers/campus/programs-events.html

This chapter discusses the basics of workforce planning and recruitment. By hiring, retaining, and supporting a workforce diverse in terms of KSAs, gender, race, religion, age, sexual orientation, physical abilities, and other characteristics, employers can achieve better business results and, if done correctly, minimize the chances of costly lawsuits. As we learned in Chapter 4, having diverse employees and creating a culture of inclusion are good for business. Studying this chapter will give you the knowledge and tools to engage in effective recruitment.

Understanding the Labor Landscape: Workforce Planning and Forecasting

LO 6.1 Describe workforce planning and its role in HR.

Chapter 2 discusses strategic HRM and planning as important parts of effective human resource management. Workforce planning and forecasting are not exceptions to this. In order to survive in both good and tough times, organizations that successfully plan for future needs can navigate challenging times and avoid some of the labor-related surprises that are likely to occur over time (Figure 6.1). Engaging in the process of workforce planning can help eliminate (or ameliorate)

■ **FIGURE 6.1** An Overview of Talent Flows and Staffing Processes

The recruitment process starts with building and planning and ends with a job offer being accepted. Understanding the potential labor pool is an important first step in the talent flow process.

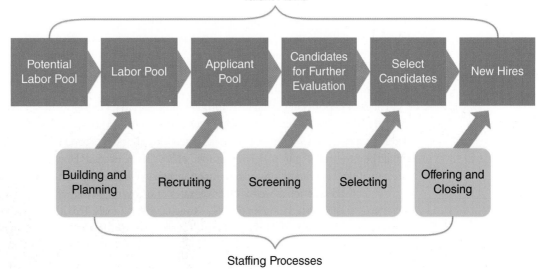

Source: Cascio, W. F., & Boudreau, J. W. (2011). Utility of selection systems: Supply-chain analysis applied to staffing decisions. In S. Zedeck (Ed.), *APA Handbooks in psychology. APA handbook of industrial and organizational psychology, Vol. 2. Selecting and developing members for the organization* (pp. 421–444). Washington, DC: American Psychological Association.

■ FIGURE 6.2   Workforce Planning and Recruitment Process Steps

Each step of the planning process is important for long-term recruitment success.

surprises, smooth out business cycles, identify problems early, prevent problems, and take advantage of opportunities.[2] Of course, no amount of planning can be 100% effective. However, as we will see in this chapter, planning and forecasting can help organizations avoid some obvious challenges out on the horizon. Plus, solving a talent problem that is years away from happening is much easier than trying to respond to one that is immediate. So what exactly is workforce planning and how is it done?

Workforce Planning

Workforce planning The process of determining what work needs to be done in both the short and long term and coming up with a strategy regarding how those positions will be filled

Workforce planning refers to the process of determining what work needs to be done in both the short and long term and coming up with a strategy regarding how those positions will be filled (Figure 6.2). Workforce planning is linked to strategic goals in many ways. For example, if the organization is considering entering a new industry sector, it will need to understand what skills are necessary to be successful in the new industry. For example, when Future Mobility Corp (a Chinese start-up backed by Tencent Holdings) decided to enter the electric vehicle market, it needed new expertise. It decided to acquire expertise in this area by hiring the entire electric vehicle development team from BMW.[3] Whether this decision was effective remains to be seen, but it is an illustration of a strategic acquisition decision.

Forecasting The act of determining estimates during workforce planning regarding what specific positions need to be filled and how to fill them

This chapter is especially focused on the role of recruitment in workforce planning, and a key step in this process is forecasting. *Forecasting* refers to the act of determining estimates regarding what specific positions need to be filled and how to fill them. This analysis includes understanding internal and external talent supply and demand, labor costs, company growth rates, and revenue. The forecast can be as detailed or general as makes sense for the organization depending on how volatile or stable the organization, industry, or economy is at a given point in time. However, even positions that have historically been easy to fill can become challenging to fill over time as the workforce ages, unemployment rates decrease, or positions change in terms of how attractive they are to potential applicants.

The next step after engaging in a thorough forecast is to set recruitment-specific goals that are aligned with the organization's strategic plans. The overarching goal is to identify and attract qualified applicants while avoiding problems associated with labor shortages or surpluses. Many questions should be answered (Figure 6.3). For example, what skills are needed? How many of those skills exist already within the organization and how many are new? What are the forecasted attrition rates during recruitment and selection as well as turnover rates, and how might they affect recruiting goals? The next step is to develop recruitment processes to achieve these goals. This is followed by implementation and, finally, evaluating the recruitment process for ways to improve it or alter it for the future.

Succession Planning and Leadership Development

Succession planning Taking stock of which employees are qualified to fill positions that are likely to be vacated soon

Leadership development The formal and informal opportunities for employees to expand their KSAOs

Succession planning refers to the active forecasting of leadership needs and the strategies for filling them over time. *Leadership development* refers to the formal and informal opportunities for employees to expand their KSAOs. It is important to recognize that both recruitment and

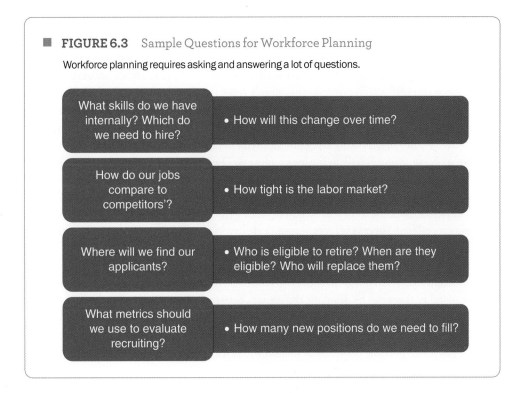

■ **FIGURE 6.3** Sample Questions for Workforce Planning

Workforce planning requires asking and answering a lot of questions.

| What skills do we have internally? Which do we need to hire? | • How will this change over time? |
| What skills do we have internally? Which do we need to hire? | • How tight is the labor market? |

What skills do we have internally? Which do we need to hire?

• How will this change over time?

How do our jobs compare to competitors'?

• How tight is the labor market?

Where will we find our applicants?

• Who is eligible to retire? When are they eligible? Who will replace them?

What metrics should we use to evaluate recruiting?

• How many new positions do we need to fill?

retention are tied to whether potential employees and existing employees perceive that there are developmental opportunities in the form of training and promotion. Thus, it is important to consider succession planning in terms of what KSAOs an employer will need, when they will need them, and how to develop employees so that transitions in leadership occur smoothly. Doing so is part of effective workplace planning. At a minimum, organizations need *replacement planning* to identify a minimal plan of individuals to take over top leadership roles over time. Succession planning involves both the identification and training of individuals who might serve as replacements of top leaders within the organization. Finally, *succession management* refers to identifying and developing successors at all levels of the organization.[4]

Labor Market Conditions

Labor market conditions refers to the number of jobs available compared to the number of individuals available with the required KSAOs to do those jobs. Earlier chapters referred to various Bureau of Labor Statistics (BLS) analyses, findings, and projections. The U.S. Department of Labor oversees the BLS, which is "the principal Federal agency responsible for measuring labor market activity, working conditions, and price changes in the economy. Its mission is to collect, analyze, and disseminate essential economic information to support public and private decision-making."[5] One of the important functions provided by this research arm of the Department of Labor is to help organizations understand labor market conditions, as this is a fundamental aspect of workforce planning and recruitment strategies.

Referring to the opening case, if a BLS report indicated that there are many qualified and interested applicants graduating from college every year without a lot of employment options, it would be less important for PwC to invest so heavily in its college relations and recruitment programs. However, if there is a lot of competition for a limited number of qualified graduates compared to the number PwC is seeking to employ, its college recruiting investment strategy makes sense.

Replacement planning The process of identifying a minimal plan of individuals to take over top leadership roles over time

Succession management The process of identifying and developing successors at all levels of the organization

Labor market conditions The number of jobs available compared to the number of individuals available with the required KSAOs to do those jobs

US Bureau of Labor Statistics

The BLS has provided economic information since 1884.

Workforce Labor Shortages

Workforce characteristics may influence recruitment in various ways, including through labor shortages and surpluses. A ***workforce labor shortage*** refers to labor market conditions in which there are more jobs available than workers to fill them. When there is a labor shortage, there is a "tight labor market," with recruiters consistently reporting that finding skilled job candidates is harder. For example, organizations seeking to hire women in the computer sciences face serious recruiting efforts, as women accounted for only 18% of college graduates with this degree, down from 37% in 1984.[6] A decreasing unemployment rate is one signal that labor market conditions may become more challenging for employers. The United States, Canada, Germany, and Japan have been experiencing falling unemployment rates, which can signal employment challenges.[7] In 2016, 69% of recruiters surveyed within the United States reported a lack of skilled candidates in the labor market as the largest obstacle to hiring. Labor shortages may change what applicants are offered. Surveys of recruiters indicate that job candidates are more willing to ask for higher salaries—especially in the technology and health-care sectors. In response, 68% of companies have increased the average salary offer made to job candidates in 2016 compared to 2015.[8] It is important to keep in mind that although the overall employment rate is one indication of labor availability, there can be dramatic differences between jobs, industries, and even locations depending on the requirements of the jobs. For example, when Amazon announced plans to add 100,000 new jobs over 18 months, it was good news for those looking for a job, but it was a situation that put added pressure on the labor market where the company was hiring.[9]

Workforce Labor Surpluses

Workforce labor surplus (***slack***) refers to labor market conditions in which there is more available labor than organizations can need. Such a situation can result in high unemployment rates and make finding a job tough for individuals. This can be nationwide, or it can happen within specific

---

HR IN ACTION
Labor Shortages for Basic Services

Job growth is brisk, with 7,000 new job openings expected by 2024. With that said, local and state governments around the United States are worried about whether they will be able to successfully fill water infrastructure positions, as a labor shortage is projected in this field. In fact, water treatment worker is one of the jobs most at risk in terms of not having enough qualified candidates, according to an employment report by the Conference Board. Websites seeking to attract applicants for the water treatment industry boast that such jobs require no college degree, offer good opportunities for advancement as well as great pay and benefits, are resistant to recessions, and provide the ability to benefit society.

You may not reflect on all the steps that the water you drink goes through before it comes out of your kitchen faucet. However, water treatment plant and system operators do. They monitor operating conditions, meters, and gauges among several other things at water treatment plants to make sure what you drink is safe. The job requires a high school diploma or equivalent and a license.

Other basic services jobs also have challenges. For example, the electric power industry is plagued by staggering estimates of 30% to 40% of its entire 400,000-person workforce being eligible to retire. The nursing profession has similar issues, with job openings continuing to grow due to the aging population in the U.S. but new nurses not entering the profession quickly enough to keep up with demand.[10]

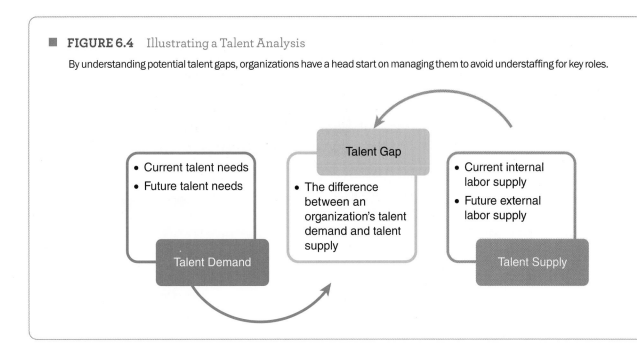

FIGURE 6.4 Illustrating a Talent Analysis

By understanding potential talent gaps, organizations have a head start on managing them to avoid understaffing for key roles.

regions or areas. For example, the logging industry was greatly curtailed in the Pacific Northwestern United States in the 1980s. Similarly, manufacturing jobs available have decreased in America's Midwestern states. Under such labor market conditions, the challenge becomes matching the skills needed to do the jobs with those in need of employment. Programs such as job retraining and educational reimbursements represent some ways that organizations, and at times the government, can seek to align skills in the local labor market more with local labor demands. Organizations facing a workforce labor surplus in their area or industry have an easier time finding employees to fill their positions. However, organizations must often compete for those with key skills.

Talent Analysis

A *talent analysis* refers to actively gathering data to determine potential talent gaps, or the difference between an organization's talent demand and its available talent supply (Figure 6.4). The talent supply, more often called a *talent pool*, is a group of individuals (employees or potential applicants) who possess the KSAOs to fill a particular role. As you can imagine, determining the needed KSAOs comes from job analysis information. Understanding the current and future talent needs is an important aspect of this analysis, as is understanding the current internal labor pool (those who already work for an organization) and future external labor pool (those who do not currently work for an organization but who might be hired in the future). For example, Boeing uses predictive workforce modeling techniques to predict and fill talent gaps before they develop. It considers several factors such as business trends, associated workforce skill needs, internal workforce demographics such as skill populations, job levels, age and retirement eligibility, economic trends, and expected employee life cycles.[11]

One way that the talent pool can be increased is via immigrants to the United States. Data show that more than 26 million individuals who were born outside of the United States were legally employed here in 2015.[12] Thus, immigrants serve as a major talent supply if they possess skills that are in demand.

Talent analysis The process of gathering data to determine potential talent gaps, or the difference between an organization's talent demand and the available talent supply

Talent pool A group of individuals (employees or potential applicants) who possess the KSAOs to fill a particular role

The Recruiting Process

Recruitment is the process of identifying and working to attract individuals interested in and capable of filling identified organizational roles. These individuals may be from either the external or internal labor markets. When it comes to recruitment, both quantity and quality matter.

LO 6.2 Identify what recruiting is and its key components.

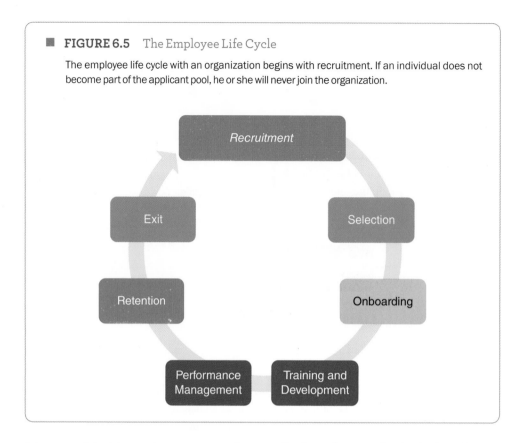

■ FIGURE 6.5   The Employee Life Cycle

The employee life cycle with an organization begins with recruitment. If an individual does not become part of the applicant pool, he or she will never join the organization.

Recruitment The process of identifying a group of individuals (employees or potential applicants) who possess the KSAOs to fill a particular role

It is a mutual decision-making process on the part of both employers and individuals, with organizational representatives considering such factors as needs, costs, and timing and individuals considering factors such as their reactions to the recruitment process, location of the job, and organizational reputation.

Why Recruitment Matters

Effective recruitment is a critical aspect of organizational success. Reasons for this include innovation, firm performance, and organizational culture.[13] In fact, recruitment has consistently been identified as one of the most impactful HR functions.[14] As you may recall, HRM is defined as *the constellation of decisions and actions associated with managing individuals throughout the employee life cycle to maximize employee and organizational effectiveness in attaining goals.* Thus, recruitment is the start of the employee life cycle and the source of human capital within an organization, as illustrated in Figure 6.5.

Recruitment Strategy

A recruitment strategy is the formalization of the recruitment process at a given organization. It includes recruitment objectives, strategy development, recruitment activities, recruitment results, and understanding the intervening job applicant variables, which may influence any of these factors.

Recruitment Objectives
Identifying recruitment objectives, or goals, at the start of the recruitment process sets the stage for the next steps. Objectives might include the number and qualifications and characteristics of applicants, time frame for recruitment, and how effective recruitment will be determined.

Strategy Development
There are many elements of a recruitment strategy, but overall, this is where needs are articulated including whom to recruit, where to find them, how to reach them, who will interact with them,

and what they will be offered to join the organization. ***Recruitment need*** refers to the results of the workforce planning process in terms of what KSAOs are needed within the organization as well as when they will be needed. ***Placement*** refers to two aspects of strategy development. First, where do we need the talent to be placed? Where in the organization are employees needed? Second, where will they be found? Will these be internal or external hires? Is the talent pool sufficient, or do steps need to be taken to develop the necessary talent?

Recruitment Activities

Recruitment activities include which methods will be used, what information about the job will be conveyed, and the details of the strategy developed in the previous step. One opportunity to make recruitment more effective is to closely align the recruitment process to selection and onboarding. Many organizations focus so much time and attention on recruiting that they forget how important it is to have everyone on the same page regarding what the job entails, what is expected of new employees, and what they can expect when they enter the organization. Research shows that the more highly these are aligned, the more effectively new employees adjust to their jobs.[15]

The Role of Recruiters in the Recruitment Process

Recruiters are an important part of the recruitment process. In addition, a ***hiring manager*** is defined as the person who asked for the role to be filled and/or whom the new hire will be reporting to as his or her manager. Thus, recruiters and hiring managers are the gatekeepers of the hiring process and, in the best case, are working as partners during the recruitment process. The goal of the selection process is to obtain large pools of qualified applicants. However, recruiters and hiring managers can become inundated with large numbers of applications, overburdening hiring personnel with more applications than they can process. This can result in nonstrategic, suboptimal decision making as, in general, decisions made under tight timelines are more likely to result in little thought on the part of decision makers, and research has shown that placing increased information-processing burdens on decision makers allows biases to enter the decision-making process.[16]

Further, recruitment decision makers need to feel confident that they can rely on the assessment solutions (e.g., employment tests, interviews) that they are using in the hiring process to help them find the best candidates possible. Thus, assessment solutions need to be valid predictors and legally defensible. In other words, recruiters need assessment systems that can provide large numbers of qualified applicants but that can effectively and efficiently determine who the best applicants are. Addressing these issues for recruiters will do much to increase the cost–benefit analysis of the hiring process.[17]

Considering the role of recruiters is important to understanding organizational effectiveness at attracting talent. Overall, the job of recruiter is seen as a desirable one. Corporate recruiter has been listed as one of the 50 best jobs in the United States based on salary, job openings, job score, and job satisfaction ratings.[18] But recruiters are human, which means that their effectiveness is subject to their strengths and weaknesses pertaining to their attitudes, decision making, and other behaviors. For example, have you ever wondered how the use of photos in social media affects the recruiting process? Photos can send positive or negative signals to recruiters, 41% of whom say that seeing a picture of a job candidate before they meet in person influences their first impression.[19] Even more potentially damaging are photos focused on alcohol and a perception by a majority of recruiters that "oversharing" on social media sites counts against an applicant. Impressions do not end there. Researchers in Belgium studied the influence of attractive profile photos on Facebook and found that candidates with more attractive photos obtained 38% more job interview invitations than those with less attractive photos.[20] Recent recruiter surveys indicate that typos, drug use, body odor, and dressing too casually for interviews negatively impact hiring decisions.[21] Factors that led to favorable impressions included applicant enthusiasm, command of job requirements and skills, culture fit, and strong conversation skills.[22]

Recruitment needs The results of the workforce planning process in terms of what KSAOs are needed within the organization as well as when they will be needed

Placement A part of strategy development, which involves determining where talent needs to be placed and where the talent can be found

Hiring manager The person who asked for the role to be filled and/or to whom the new hire will be reporting as their manager

LO 6.3 Describe the three stages of recruitment and what takes place in them.

Recruitment funnel A situation in which the number of applicants gets smaller as people move through the selection process.

Stages of Recruitment

The stages of recruitment move through a ***recruitment funnel*** (see Figure 6.6) in which the number of participants gets smaller the further down the funnel the applicant goes. It is important to understand how critical this recruitment funnel is. This is because only those individuals who become applicants can ultimately be hired, and thus, the initial applicant yield ratio (how many ultimately hired compared to those who applied) is important. Thus, the goal is to get a large number of qualified applicants from which the employer can choose. Further, any applicants who remove themselves from the process cannot be selected, so keeping applicants' interest so that they do not drop out is important. Thus, understanding this concept is helpful as we discuss the recruiting process.

At its most basic level, the idea behind the recruitment funnel is that the number of applicants needed at the start of the selection process is much larger than the ultimate number of hires made (see Figure 6.6). While every organization will identify its own ratios for success based on its workforce planning and actual number of hires per applicants, it is clear that as applicants move through the selection process and the best applicants are identified at each selection hurdle, fewer and fewer applicants are considered further. How wide or narrow the recruitment funnel is depends on the number of employees needed and the level of skills needed to perform the job. For example, when hiring a retail employee to help customers and ring up sales, there are often fewer requirements than when hiring a mechanic to fix cars. That is because retail employees can be more easily and quickly trained compared to mechanics, who take years to perfect their craft.

There are three fundamental stages of recruitment. The first is to identify and generate applicants, which is seen in Figure 6.6 in the first two parts of the recruitment funnel. The second stage focuses on maintaining applicant interest and participation as they continue through the assessment process. Thus, recruitment can really be thought of as a two-way process wherein the organization is trying both to assess and attract the best job applicants. Finally, the third stage is to influence job choice so that desired applicants are willing to accept offers made to them.

Generating Applicants

Generating applicants is an important first step to the recruitment process. It is one that has also garnered a great deal of well-deserved attention, as it represents a substantial

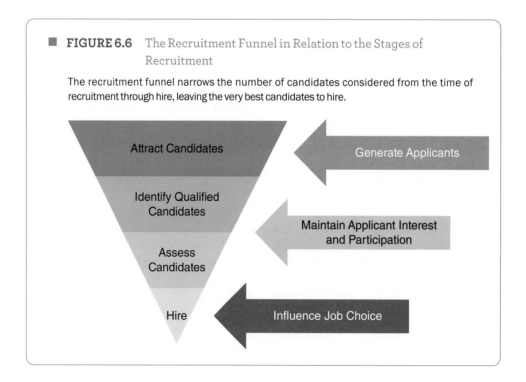

■ FIGURE 6.6   The Recruitment Funnel in Relation to the Stages of Recruitment

The recruitment funnel narrows the number of candidates considered from the time of recruitment through hire, leaving the very best candidates to hire.

Attract Candidates ← Generate Applicants

Identify Qualified Candidates ← Maintain Applicant Interest and Participation

Assess Candidates

Hire ← Influence Job Choice

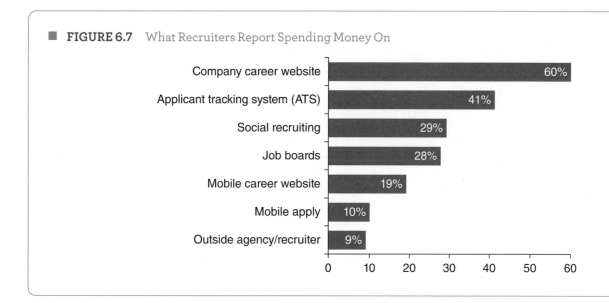

■ **FIGURE 6.7** What Recruiters Report Spending Money On

investment of both time and money on the part of the recruiting organization (see Figure 6.7). Generating applicants determines the talent pool that will be considered for positions within an organization. Following are some important considerations, starting with applicant quantity and quality.

Applicant Quantity and Quality

Although this chapter focuses on many aspects of recruitment, it is important to understand that there are two major goals within the first stage of the recruitment process.[23] The first goal is quantity: Generating a sufficient number of applicants during the first stage of the recruitment process is important for several reasons, including that the effectiveness of the selection process depends upon having a large enough talent pool that has the skills needed to do the job and meets other strategic needs such as diversity and succession planning. We know that lower selection ratios—and thus how "choosy" the employer can be—are achieved by attracting large numbers of applicants. It is not clear, however, whether the relationship is causal. It may be that well-run and profitable organizations are more attractive than other organizations. Nonetheless, this does highlight the importance of having sufficient numbers of applicants.

The second goal is quality. Quality relates to applicants having the requisite skills needed as well as representing a diverse pool of applicants. Research shows that low selection ratios are associated with positive organizations' financial performance.[24] As such, in addition to applicant quantity, applicant quality is important.

Realistic Job Previews

One important function of the recruitment process is to attract individuals to apply for jobs and be inclined to take a job if offered one. High turnover rates, however, can create recruitment challenges, as the organization needs to constantly recruit and hire new employees. Thus, an important consideration is to attract individuals to the job and organization while also being realistic enough that once they begin the job, they will not be disappointed and quit. One way in which organizations and researchers address these concerns is the ***realistic job preview (RJP),*** which offers potential applicants a realistic, and sometimes unappealing, view of the actual job.

For example, the Indiana Department of Child Services created a 35-minute video that frankly outlines the challenges and frustrations along with the rewards and joys of the job of child services caseworker. It starts with a warning that "Due to mature subject matter, viewer discretion is advised." It includes references to the job being "rewarding, complex, stressful,

Realistic job preview (RJP) Offers potential applicants a realistic view of the actual job, including both positive and negative information

©iStock.com/CatLane

In 2018, Amazon announced it would be implementing a $15-per-hour minimum wage for all full-time employees, contractors, and part-time workers. It remains to be seen whether this will influence Amazon's recruitment.

and sometimes a bit frightening."[25] On a lighter note, the Walt Disney Company shows job candidates a film depicting what it is like to work at Disney and outlines its employment policies and conditions. Some candidates self-select out of the recruitment process based on viewing this film, deciding it is not a good fit for them.[26] Research regarding RJPs has been mixed, with some studies finding support and others finding no appreciable differences between those who experience RJPs during recruitment and those who do not.[27]

One innovative example of an RJP is used by Zappos. It offers a financial incentive for new employees to quit after going through the training program, because it is only at that point that they can fully understand what the job would entail. Zappos effectively pays a new employee to quit if the employee doesn't feel he or she is a good fit. Specifically, Zappos pays for time invested in training, plus $4,000 if the person doesn't think it is the right position or company for him or her. About 2% to 3% of employees take the offer.[28]

Recruitment Sources

Perhaps no single aspect of recruitment has received more time and attention than recruitment sources. Deciding exactly how to reach potential applicants is both a strategic and a financial decision. Recruitment sources can be divided into two main categories, passive recruitment and active recruitment (see Figure 6.8).

Although research has been conducted around the globe in the hopes of identifying which recruitment sources are the most effective, what is effective for one organization may be less effective for another due to the differences in their recruitment strategies, brands, and industries. In addition, organizations may choose to focus on the recruitment of internal candidates, or they may look for talent outside of the organization. A recent SHRM survey found that 25%

■ FIGURE 6.8   Recruitment Sources May Be Passive or Active for Organizations and Applicants

Active	• Headhunters • Executive Search Firms • Employee Referrals • Social Media Search • University Relations	• Employee Referrals • Internal Hires • Internships • Alumni Relationships • Job Boards/Postings • Employment Agencies
Organization		
Passive		• Walk-in Applications • Unsolicited Résumé Submission • Networking
	Passive	**Applicant** *Active*

TABLE 6.1   General Recruitment Sources

Webpages
Unadvertised jobs
Job boards
Social networking sites
Internal sources
Internal transfers and promotions
Enlarge jobs for existing employees (e.g., longer hours, more responsibilities)
Alumni employees
External sources
Employee referrals
Search firms, agencies
University relations, internship programs
Freelance employees
Walk-ins
Competitors

of organizations filled positions with current internal employees and 75% with external hires.[29] Table 6.1 summarizes some of the main types of recruitment sources used by organizations.

Internal Recruiting Sources

Steve Kerr, senior advisor and former chief learning officer at Goldman Sachs, is quoted as saying, "It's very odd to me. The assets walk home at night. If people are your most important asset, you ought to develop them. It is Goldman's philosophy that not only do people have to be developed, it ends up being a huge competitive advantage." He further argues that development can help with "recruitment as well as retention."[31] As noted earlier, succession planning is an important piece of workforce planning. Another benefit of recruiting for positions internally is that advancement and development opportunities can be attractive to current employees and, thus, help with retention. If you are able to redeploy talent throughout the organization rather than losing it, the organization is able to retain valuable organizational knowledge.

External Recruitment Sources

External recruitment refers to an employer's actions that are intended to bring a job opening to the attention of potential job candidates outside of the organization and, in turn, influence their intention to pursue the opportunity. A key aspect to external recruitment is to identify the most effective external recruitment sources. Types of sources include external services such as search firms, employment agencies, on-demand recruiting services, alumni employees, and military transition services, as well as job postings such as those in newspapers, on social media, and on career sites. In addition, as the opening case of PwC's college recruitment programs demonstrates, some organizations find that cultivating an employee pipeline to keep up with anticipated talent demands is useful. Thus, many attend college job fairs, work with college placement offices, and utilize internship programs. Another option is to consider non-U.S. citizens for hard-to-fill positions. This might include off-shoring or visa sponsorship issues. Each of these sources has potential benefits and drawbacks that should be considered as part of an organization's recruitment strategy.

External recruitment An employer's actions that are intended to bring a job opening to the attention of potential job candidates outside of the organization and, in turn, influence their intention to pursue the opportunity

Webpages

For most organizations, the webpage is a vital part of recruitment because it sends signals regarding what the organization is like and because it contains employment information. Public

SPOTLIGHT ON DATA AND ANALYTICS
Internal Recruiting at Credit Suisse

©iStock.com/stockwerk

In the age of big data and analytics, it is not unheard of for an organization to identify who might be likely to quit. What is new is how accurate such estimates have become.

Credit Suisse, a multinational financial services holding company headquartered in Zurich, is using this information to identify employees who might benefit from internal recruitment efforts. In 2014, Credit Suisse began asking recruiters to contact such employees to alert them to internal job opportunities. They report that the program served to reduce turnover by 1% and prompted 300 employees to find new positions within the firm. They estimate that the program saved $75 million to $100 million in rehiring and training costs. This is a good example of pairing internal data, analytics, and an internal recruitment strategy to avoid unwanted attrition.[32]

webpages may serve as recruitment sources for both internal and external applicants. Internal webpages, which are accessible by only current employees, are another important source.

Unadvertised Jobs

Although the following sections outline both internal and external recruiting sources, another key recruitment source is word-of-mouth listings. About 50% of positions are actually filled via informal channels and may never have been formally advertised or listed.[30] As a best practice, we recommend making a recruitment pool as large as possible; however, there may be times when informal channels yield unique talent acquisition opportunities for an organization. Thus, it is important to consider the pros and cons of hidden job listings and informal hiring, although very little research has been conducted in that regard. However, hiring those one knows can lead to lower diversity in terms of approaches and ideas, can be perceived by others as unfair, and might run afoul of federal guidelines.

Internal Transfers and Promotions

Firms report filling positions with internal transfers and promotions a little more than 37% of the time.[33] A key aspect of managing internal transfers and promotions is the use of an internal *applicant tracking system (ATS)*, which offers a centralized way to house employee and applicant data in a single repository. This repository of data can then be linked with other HR information systems like that of retention and performance management to analyze the effectiveness of applicants from different recruitment sources, for example. It can also be used to track employee transfers and promotions over time. For a more detailed illustration of this, please see the Data and Analytics exercise at the end of this chapter.

Applicant tracking system (ATS) An internal system that offers a centralized way to house applicant and employee data and to enable electronic business processes related to recruitment

Internal Job Boards

Internal job boards allow organizations to post available positions internally before the rest of the potential talent pool sees them. When internal candidates are given early consideration for positions, it can be good for morale and for mobility within the organization. In fact, some organizations invest a considerable amount to help existing employees find new opportunities within the organization because this may serve to help boost retention rates and retain top talent.

Alumni Employees

More and more organizations are considering rehiring former employees. This includes PwC, and this practice of employing "boomerang employees" who return to the organization is common in accounting and consulting firms. In fact, Deloitte conducted a study of alumni rehires and found that rehires saved them $3.8 million in search fees alone.[34] For National Basketball Association (NBA) players, for example, research revealed that for players who left a team and later returned, success was related to leaving on good terms initially, being successful while they were away, and the terms of their reemployment.[35] In general, research shows that rehires are less likely to quit and have an easier time onboarding back into the organization.[36] Overall, nearly 7% of hires are former employees.[37] Organizations can cultivate effective alumni networks in several ways, including by creating a website with a directory of members, job boards, and information about networking events and professional development.[38] Microsoft traditionally has hired around 5% alumni employees each year. It launched the Microsoft Alumni Network in 1995, which currently has thousands of members.[39]

Employee Referrals

An employee referral is a specific recruitment method that taps existing employees for potential applicant suggestions. Some firms such as Google pay existing employees a bonus for a successful referral. The average bonus reported is between $1,000 to $2,499.[40] Other incentives might include a paid day off, gifts, or recognition at a staff meeting. Employers may give rewards immediately when referred employees are hired or after a set number of days of successful employment. They further work to ensure that current employees find the process pleasant by ensuring that referred individuals are contacted within 48 hours.[41] This can be an effective way to recruit, because existing employees understand the organizational culture and job demands and are in a good position to suggest potential candidates they feel would be successful. When surveyed, 78% of recruiters reported that employee referrals helped them find their best candidates. Referrals account for more than 22% of applicants.[42]

To help ensure that referral programs are legal and do not result in unfair hiring practices, SHRM recommends the following. SHRM also has an available online toolkit to help with designing referral programs.[43]

- *Reread legal recruitment guidelines.* This helps ensure that you are not unintentionally creating a system that is not consistent with existing laws.

- *Use a variety of recruiting methods when advertising job openings.* This will help keep the applicant pool more diverse.

- *Make employee referral programs open to the entire organization, not limiting them to specific employee groups, departments, or divisions.*

- *Evaluate all candidates—including employee-referred candidates—using the same qualification criteria.*

- *Conduct ongoing analyses of the workforce and the applicant pool to ensure that the employee referral program is effective and is yielding the intended results.* Included in the analyses should be diversity categories, the quality of hire, and resulting tenure from referrals. If the program is not meeting its intended goals and is negatively affecting workforce diversity, you may need to reevaluate it.

Search Firms

Search firms are paid to find candidates and to help organizations fill roles. Executive search firms focus on the upper levels of an organization. Some organizations use search firms to fill all their positions. Others use them rarely. For example, Time Warner, Inc., hired thousands of senior-level employees from 2005 and 2012 but used an executive-search firm only once.[44] Some industries, such as higher education, tend to use search firms to generate candidates for key positions like university president, provost, or dean. Search firms can also be used to fill open positions quickly in areas in which the organization does not have an established recruitment process or brand. For example, Apple hired a search firm to help it quickly staff its retail stores in China.[45] Regardless of who is responsible for the actual recruitment, it is imperative that positions are delineated so that job expectations and qualifications are clear and accurate. Not doing so can lead to higher levels of turnover and frustration for both those hired and organizations.

University Relationships

New college hires often originate from recruitment strategies aimed at leveraging university relationships such as targeting specific universities, attending university job fairs, and developing internship programs. Some schools even host "virtual" job fairs so that a wider number of hiring organizations and students can attend at a lower cost.[46] Research shows that job fairs have a significant impact on the perceptions students form of organizations.[47] Such relationships work for current students but can be effective for university alumni relations as well.

Located in the 30,000-person rural town of Bozeman, Montana, RightNow Technologies, Inc., struggled to find enough qualified software engineers and marketing professionals. To aid recruitment efforts, the company turned to Montana State University, figuring that former students would be aware of the livability of Bozeman and, thus, might be interested in returning if offered the right opportunity. This led RightNow to purchase a list of alumni from the school, which yielded such success that other firms in the area have adopted similar practices.[48]

Rosetta, a marketing and advertising company, created a Campus Ambassador Program in which past interns interested in staying involved with Rosetta were trained on the company's recruiting process and recruitment message. It provided them with giveaways to help promote Rosetta's brand and asked ambassadors to engage in specific programs such as conducting information sessions, participating in Rosetta's campus visits, and providing referrals. In 2015, 26% of its past interns participated, and applications were up 7% that year.[49]

Internship Programs

Internships can be an important tool for both organizations and students. For students, research shows that they almost double the chance of full-time job offers when they graduate. This makes sense, as many interns are eventually offered full-time employment. Further, those who have had internships earn more than those who do not, have lower turnover, and are more likely to report that their college degrees helped prepare them for their careers[50] (see Table 6.2).

Research shows that organizations that want to hire interns tend to be more open to their creativity, which helps to attract interns who are interested in full-time jobs after graduation.[51] For organizations, interns are seen as an important and effective source of recruitment. In a 2015 recruiter survey, 55% of respondents reported that intern-to-hire programs led to their best hires.[52] Thus, as we saw with PwC, some organizations invest heavily in their internship programs.

Internships are also very successful recruitment tools for small and medium-sized businesses. Resources for setting up internship programs can be found on the National Association of Colleges and Employers (NACE) website (http://www.naceweb.org/internships/15-best-practices.aspx). Best practices include

- providing interns with meaningful work assignments,
- holding orientations,
- providing a handbook or relevant website for addressing rules and frequently asked questions, and
- conducting exit interviews at the end of the internship experience to learn how it went and ways to improve future internship experiences.

TABLE 6.2 Which Organizations Are the Most Attractive to Students?

Vault.com surveyed 12,000 current and former interns, showed them a list of 50 large companies, and asked them to rate their prestige on a 1-to-10 scale. The research methodology used to compile this list included only large companies. Here are the results for 2018:

1. Google
2. Apple, Inc.
3. Facebook, Inc.
4. Microsoft Corporation
5. Goldman Sachs & Co.
6. Tesla Motors, Inc.
7. Amazon.com, Inc.
8. JPMorgan Chase
9. Morgan Stanley
10. The Walt Disney Company
11. Nike
12. PwC
13. IBM
14. Deloitte
15. The Boston Consulting Group, Inc.
16. Intel
17. ESPN
18. Mercedes-Benz
19. Berkshire Hathaway
20. The Coca-Cola Company

Source: Kauflin, J. (2017). The 20 most prestigious internships for 2018. *Forbes.* https://www.forbes.com/sites/jeffkauflin/2017/10/11/the-20-most-prestigious-internships-for-2018/#38d0cc823ab8

One thing to keep in mind is that the legality of unpaid internships can be questionable. Thus, it is important to be clear on the rules surrounding internships before launching a program.

External Job Boards

External job boards have made advertising jobs much easier than it has been in the past. They have largely replaced the idea of placing help-wanted ads in the newspaper. Online job boards allow organizations to post for current and potential jobs, direct applicants where to apply, and provide specific information to help applicants narrow down potential positions via a number of search parameters such as location, job requirements, or pay. Types of job boards range from those with jobs in all categories such as Monster.com (one of the oldest job boards), Glassdoor.com, and Indeed.com to more specific job boards such as AllRetailJobs.com or www.truckerswanted.ca, the latter of which is specific to the trucking industry in North America and free for both drivers and companies to use. ZipRecruiter.com allows organizations to post to more than 200 job boards at once. In the United States, nearly 10% of hires were found via job boards.[53] Globally, perhaps the largest job board is China's job51.com website, which reports having 81 million registered individuals, with 72 million résumés contained within its database.[54]

SPOTLIGHT ON ETHICS

Applicant Information Privacy

Job boards have become popular with organizations and job applicants. However, one major ethical concern has to do with information privacy. There are two considerations that seem especially important to consider.

First, who "owns" the data that applicants input into job board systems? Although online information privacy laws vary by country, with the European Union having stricter laws than the United States, the answer to this question is not clear. Imagine a scenario in which an online job board company tracks all your job application information and personal information and then sells this research about you. This is not as far-fetched as it sounds; there are documented accounts of job boards selling résumés and e-mail addresses.

A second concern is information security. Even if an organization does not plan to share your information with others, it is possible that cybercrime could lead to your information being stolen. For example, more than 1 million Monster.com subscribers had their information stolen. This is a serious concern, given how sensitive personal information such as Social Security numbers can be for identity theft. In response, Monster.com now allows users to make their résumés completely private so that employers cannot search for you but you can still search job listings and send out résumés and applications yourself.[55]

Questions

1. How would you discuss these ethical issues with the decision makers in your organization? Are there specific policies or practices you would recommend?

2. Beyond the issues described here, what other ethical questions might you ask about online job boards? Think of them from the perspective of the job applicant, the recruiting organization, the tech company that operates the board, and any other stakeholders.

Social Networking Sites

Each day, millions of people spend time on social media. These sites allow organizations to dramatically widen their reach when it comes to recruiting. Social networking sites such as Instagram, Twitter, Facebook, and Snapchat vary in the degree to which they have traditionally been considered recruitment sources. It is hard to ignore, however, the trend toward social networking sites being an important source for potential talent and networking. These sites are large and continue to add members. For example, LinkedIn reports having 530 million members.[56] On average, upward of 60,000 jobs are posted on Twitter daily.[57]

Using social media can help pinpoint specific skills and more narrow needs. For example, PepsiCo shares job openings and responds to candidate questions on Twitter.[58] Innovis Health runs specialty clinics in Minnesota and North Dakota. To help with physician recruitment, this company loads videos to YouTube to show potential recruits what the facilities look like and how they operate.[59] In China, Marriott launched a promotional campaign to help staff 20,000 positions in its new hotels. Marriott found that videos featured on its website as well as launching a social game online to allow users to virtually manage their own restaurants as a way of exposing them to Marriott's coveted customer service principles were helpful.[60]

Employment Agencies

Employment agencies vary a great deal in terms of the services they offer and roles they perform. For example, they might engage in roles such as information provider, matchmaker, or administrator. Employment agencies also provide employers with flexible workers. Flexible workers include contract, contingent, and part-time workers, who account for a little more than 16% of hires.[61] Further, within the United States, 81% of organizations report using flexible workers.[62] Staffing firms, also known as temporary employment agencies, can help organizations fulfill workforce needs and handle the administration of employees needed for only a short period of time. However, it is important to remember that those employers considering working with agencies should follow guidelines to ensure they work only with reputable firms, document any agreement with the agency with a written contract, and ensure that the staffing agency controls all aspects of the working relationships such as setting hours, paying their employees, and complying with employment laws.[63] Some organizations such as T-Mobile have turned to temporary workers to fill permanent positions such as engineers and technicians.[64] Regardless, organizations should continue to work to make sure all employment decisions comply with all antidiscrimination and similar laws even for temporary workers hired by staffing firms.

Freelance Employees

The gig economy is growing every year. As more and more individuals are choosing freelance work as their primary form of employment or as side employment, gig workers have become a viable source for organizations to find desired skills. Although previous chapters describe the pros and cons associated with hiring freelance employees, it is becoming easier and easier for employers to locate them using online marketplaces for work outsourcing. Sites such as Elance.com for business and engineering services, FlexJobs.com, Guru.com (which boasts 1 million jobs completed to date and 3 million freelancers), and GetAFreelancer.com help organizations locate the skills they need.[65]

Walk-Ins

Only a negligible 1% of new hires come from applicants applying in person at stores or facilities.[66] With that said, depending upon the type of job, walk-ins may be an important form of recruitment source. For example, in retail and hospitality sectors, walk-ins occur with greater frequency. Typically, individuals apply in person at local companies when seeking part-time work. The formula is simple: Organizations receptive to walk-ins should be prepared with job application forms. Depending on how strong the need is, some organizations give managers the freedom to interview prospective employees on the spot. One obvious and low-tech way to indicate that you are interested in walk-ins is to post a "help wanted" sign in the window of the business.

 SPOTLIGHT ON HR FOR SMALL AND MEDIUM-SIZED BUSINESSES

Recruitment Tips

Small businesses are big business in America. Businesses with five or fewer employees make up 62% of all businesses in the United States, and a third of the working population is employed at businesses with fewer than 100 employees. When it comes to recruitment, it is easy to think that large organizations have a major competitive advantage over smaller firms (60% of small-business owners do report recruitment to be a challenge). However, that may not always be the case.

There are, in fact, several potential advantages to working at a smaller organization, and these can be used to recruit potential employees at smaller firms. For example, small organizations tend to be less bureaucratic, with fewer formalized rules. They offer employees a chance to gain valuable work experience by allowing workers to engage in a wide breadth of activities rather than becoming more specialized, as is often the case at larger organizations. It is also easier to know everyone within your organization

if it is smaller, and the gap between managers and employees tends to be small. And smaller firms may be able to recruit more quickly due to fewer bureaucratic layers.[67]

But in order to compete, smaller organizations do need to be creative in recruiting. Some suggestions include

- Relying on team members to help with recruiting,
- Selling your company's high-growth potential,
- Cultivating learning opportunities for employees and emphasizing these to job applicants, and
- Finding potential top performers who share the organization's mission and vision and using them to help recruit new employees.

Hiring From Competitors

Another area of external sources of recruitment is other employers in the same industry and/or region. Competition among high-tech companies in the Silicon Valley has become so heated that pay and benefits have been driven up for new employees. This was a good situation for employees and job applicants but a costly one for companies. In 2017, the Walt Disney Company agreed to pay $100 million to end a "no-poaching" lawsuit, which claimed that the company colluded with other animation studios in California to not hire each other's employees. In response to the suit, DreamWorks Animation paid $50 million and Blue Sky Studios paid $19 million to settle the case. In 2015, Apple, Google, Intel, and Adobe Systems Inc. paid $415 million in response to similar claims.[68]

SPOTLIGHT ON GLOBAL ISSUES

International Hires

Global hires include employees who are able to secure company-sponsored H-1B visas. Organizations may employ non-U.S. employees by applying for and receiving H-1B visas. However, the number of such visas is determined by the government and varies from year to year. In 2016, H-1B visas were capped at 65,000 regular employees with an exemption for up to 20,000 foreign nationals holding a graduate degree from U.S. universities. It is important to understand the laws associated with hiring non-U.S. workers within the United States. Websites such as the United States Department of Labor contain useful information (https://www.dol.gov/general/topic/hiring/foreign).

Offshoring refers to obtaining goods or services from a foreign supplier rather than from within the United States. A company may choose to offshore services to reduce costs or to improve an organization's focus on its core competencies. To avoid problems, organizations should align their strategies with decisions around offshoring. For example, offshoring call centers to a country with cheaper labor may save money, but if customers leave due to poor customer service, the organization may actually lose money. In 2007, when other organizations were outsourcing their call centers, JetBlue Airways made a strategic decision not to outsource its call centers. In contrast, some firms such as Microsoft have effectively outsourced entire departments to other parts of the world.[69]

LO 6.4 Explain the various aspects of diversity in recruiting.

Recruiting for Diversity

Recruitment is covered by several laws designed to protect individuals from discrimination on the basis of their sex, race, age, or differential abilities. Laws such as Title VII of the Civil Rights Act, the Americans with Disabilities Act, and the Age Discrimination in Employment Act all serve to protect individuals. In addition to wanting to comply with legal requirements, organizations often also want to attract members of protected groups in order to leverage the positive aspects of having a more diverse workforce. In its survey of college employers, NACE found that 56% of respondents indicated that they have a formal diversity recruitment effort.[70] In reviewing specific issues and research findings associated with different groups, we also recognize that individuals vary a great deal in the degree to which they identify with each group as well as how their specific constellation of demographics and beliefs influences their reactions to recruitment and organizational attraction.

One thing that organizations can do to ensure stronger diversity within the organization is to treat their existing employees well and to invest in their career development once they are hired into the organization. If your organization does a reasonable job of attracting a diverse workforce but is not able to retain such individuals, it might be time to examine other factors such as the organization's culture and perceptions of how it is to work there from those on the frontlines.

It can also be illuminating to do an analysis of who is leaving to see if the numbers are equally distributed across different groups. For example, ride-sharing company Uber found out that ignoring such issues can lead to decreases in a diverse workforce as well as create a public relations problem, thereby affecting the bottom line.[71]

Gender Diversity

Some industries have a more challenging time recruiting and maintaining women than others. The high-tech industry has had an especially tough time with recruiting and retaining women for many reasons. Research shows that women are less likely to engage in persistent job-search behaviors. This is consistent with findings regarding promotions within organization such as for Google, wherein women were less likely to put themselves up for promotions and less likely to persist if passed over the first time they applied.[72] Nevertheless, organizations can enact key activities to attract and retain women at all ranks of the organization, including the creation of a united front in which the message and behavior are clear regarding how women are to be treated within the organization, the spreading of a wide recruitment net, the development of a female-friendly benefits program, the serious treatment of sexual harassment and gender discrimination, and the placement of women in positions of power.[73]

Recruitment is a process in which unconscious biases of both applicants and organizational decision makers may play a role, limiting diversity. This is particularly challenging because it is unconscious, meaning that employers may not be aware of how their recruitment efforts are not attracting a wide range of applicants. Therefore, conscious effort may be needed to reverse the effects. Research has shown that there are differences in how male- and female-dominated occupations advertise these positions, with traditionally male-dominated occupations using words such as *competitive* and *dominant* in position descriptions. Textio is a Seattle-based start-up that develops software to get around this problem by analyzing the text of job postings to make postings attractive to a diverse pool of applicants.[74]

The recruitment of greater numbers of individuals for jobs with labor shortages such as nursing has led to the ongoing need for the recruitment of men as well as women. At this point, men represent only 9% of the 3.5 million nurses in the United States.[75] Thus, when it comes to gender diversity, it is not solely a male or female issue. The key is to give everyone access to the same positions for which they are qualified. It is important that applicants are able to pass key selection criteria such as the ability to lift a certain amount of weight or to drag heavy hoses in the case of firefighters if those tasks are job-related. Diversity management is an ongoing process. These examples highlight the importance of considering diversity along a number of key dimensions.

Racial Diversity

Strategic ad placement can be an effective way to attract a more diverse applicant pool.[76] In addition to where ads are placed, the content of those ads may influence applicant attraction as well. Research found that African American applicants were more attracted to organizations indicating that they emphasize a commitment to equal opportunity, access to training, and to recruiting applicants of color.[77] In addition, studies show that recruitment materials matter a great deal for applicants. For example, recruitment materials depicting employees of color have been found to attract African Americans and Latinos without negatively affecting Caucasian applicants.[78] Further, when photos illustrated minorities in supervisory roles, positive effects were even stronger.[79] An important consideration is to firmly align the recruitment message with the organizational reality. It makes no sense to recruit individuals with false promises of an organization that does not exist, because this results in an *un*realistic job preview. Further, doing so creates a costly situation for both individuals and organizations and can serve to undermine diversity recruitment and retention in the long run.

ERIC PIERMONT/AFP/Getty Images

In 2009, Ursula Burns became the CEO of Xerox, making her the first African American woman CEO of a Fortune 500 company. She served in that role until 2017. She had been a lifelong Xerox employee who began as an intern in college and then was hired full time when she graduated. She credits much of her success to the mentoring and guidance of those she worked with over the years.[80]

Age Diversity

Chapter 1 states that by 2030, 20% or more of the U.S. population will be aged 65 or older. People are working longer due to longer life spans, and people of different ages will be working side by side as never before.[81] This has implications for recruitment as more and more individuals are choosing to continue working and may go for "encore" careers. Research shows that there are few differences between the performance of older and younger workers. In fact, older workers are more likely to engage in organizational citizenship behaviors and have fewer unexcused absences.[82] In a study examining common age stereotypes, researchers found that across all available data, few of the older worker stereotypes are true: There was no evidence that older workers were less motivated, more resistant to change, less trusting, less healthy, or more vulnerable to work–family imbalance, although they may be less interested in training and career-development activities.[83] Additionally, given their extensive experience, older workers can be seen as bringing important human capital to an organization.[84] Thus, attracting more seasoned employees is becoming more attractive to many companies. Organizations are beginning to take notice. For example, Walmart approached AARP (previously known as American Association of Retired Persons) in the hopes of recruiting older workers.[85] Organizations would benefit from considering how the recruitment methods they utilize affect the diversity of their applicant pool. For example, the exclusive use of college recruiting programs may exclude older applicants and violate the Age Discrimination in Employment Act (ADEA). Similarly, using wording such as *new college graduate* and *digital native* may repel older applicants and may run afoul of ADEA.[86] Further, recruiters play a key role, and they should be aware of their own biases against older applicants when making hiring decisions.

Veterans

There are approximately 22 million military veterans in the United States, making up 9% of the adult population. Once service members leave active duty and enter the civilian job market, they represent another potential source of recruitment. Matching the KSAOs of military positions to civilian positions, however, can pose a challenge within civilian organizations, because the job titles, duties, and requirements may differ greatly. In fact, in a SHRM survey, 60% of respondents indicated that they had experienced challenges related to the hiring of veterans for this very reason. Some companies see hiring veterans as an expression of goodwill.[87] Others see it as a win-win to close their talent gap.

For example, Raytheon Company hires thousands of engineers each year. As part of the U.S. Army's Partnership for Youth Success (PaYS) program, which connects new recruits with postservice jobs, Raytheon can hire qualified employees and get them security clearance, which is timely and can be expensive. Raytheon states, "Military professionals come to us with security clearances, and in many cases they've used our products, so they're familiar with the company and our processes. That's a big timesaver and cost-saver."[88]

Researchers suggest several strategies for success when considering veterans as a recruitment source, including[90]

- Understanding (and modifying as needed) beliefs about veterans,

- Hiring and training knowledgeable decision makers to work on recruitment,

The recruitment of veterans before and after they serve is an ongoing consideration for the military as well as civilian organizations. To recruit an additional 6,000 active-duty soldiers in 2017, the U.S. Army spent $300 million on bonuses and ads.[89]

- Increasing the organization's knowledge of military job-related tasks and KSAOs, and

- Socializing veterans in the role requirements and norms of civilian organizations.

It is also important to consider retention when it comes to employing veterans. Work done as part of the SERVe (Study for Employment Retention of Veterans) grant funded by the Department of Defense found that supervisors can play a large role in retaining veterans by including emotional and instrumental support and engaging in role modeling creative work–family solution management.[91]

Differently Abled Individuals

The Americans with Disabilities Act (ADA) (1990) prohibits discrimination against a qualified applicant or employee with a disability. Determining who is qualified to perform the major functions of the job with or without accommodations is based on a job analysis. The ADA applies to organizations with 15 or more employees and defines a disability as a physical or mental impairment that affects one's major life functions. The key point to understand is that the ADA includes both applicants and employees, so it is in full force during recruitment efforts and, if requested, reasonable accommodations must be made in terms of all aspects of recruitment and selection. For example, an organization would need to make sure that the recruitment methods it uses do not exclude applicants with disabilities. If recruitment activities are conducted on a college campus or at a job fair, the location needs to be accessible. If online sources are used, it is important to ensure that applicants with visual and hearing impairments can complete the application process.

SPOTLIGHT ON LEGAL ISSUES

General Guidelines for Recruitment

The information here should not be considered a substitute for legal advice. The application and impact of laws vary based on the specifics of the case, and laws may change over time. Thus, we encourage readers to seek out legal advice if unsure of the legality of specific programs or actions.

When it comes to recruitment, legal issues are an important consideration. As the EEOC's compliance manual says, "*Who* ultimately receives employment opportunities is highly dependent on how and where the employer looks for candidates." For instance, disparate racial impact occurs when a recruitment practice produces a significant difference in hiring for protected racial groups. It does not necessarily matter whether such differential impact is intentional—just that it occurred.[92]

Here are some questions to ask about your recruiting practices to help avert or curtail potential problems. Ideally, you will be able to answer yes to the following:

- Do you have standardized recruiting practices?

- Have you ruled out that your recruiting practices indicate possible disparate impact?

- Can you provide evidence that each of your recruiting practices is consistent with business necessity and is job related?

- Are you casting a wide net in your recruiting sources by using a variety of sources accessible to everyone?

- Are recruiters and agencies you work with familiar with discrimination laws and how to comply with them?

LO 6.5   Explain
key analytical, legal,
ethical, and global
issues associated with
workforce planning and
recruitment.

A Broader View of Workforce Planning and Recruitment

Up to this point, this chapter has focused on various aspects of recruitment. Let's now consider some broader issues, including how to evaluate the effectiveness of recruitment efforts, how to keep applicants interested and motivated throughout the process, and how to choose the right job for the right applicant.

Recruitment Results: Evaluating Effectiveness and Metrics

When it comes to measuring the quality of their college hires, the energy corporation Chevron says it looks at ethnic and gender diversity, schools attended, campus interview assessment scores, total internships the employee had, internships with Chevron, performance ratings, promotions, and turnover. As one of Chevron's recruiters says, "Being able to see what you're doing right and what needs attention is critical to the long-term health of your organization."[93] In their book *The Differentiated Workforce,* Brian Becker, Mark Huselid, and Richard Beatty suggest five principles when it comes to strategic workforce measures:

1. *Don't start with the measures.* While measures can be an important tool, they should not be the goal of strategic workforce planning and implementation.

2. *Don't rely on benchmarking.* By definition, benchmarking means matching what others do. Doing so will not generate competitive advantages to your organization.

3. *Don't expect measurement alone to fix problems.* While measurement can identify areas of strength and weakness in your recruitment processes, simply gathering the data is not enough to fix potential problems.

4. *Focus on the strategic impact of the workforce.* Not all individuals, teams, or divisions within an organization have the same impact on the organization's success on key goals. Focus on the places where it matters most.

5. *Measure both levels and relationships between workforce measures.* Some measures may go down when others go up. Understanding how they work together is important for getting a full picture of organizational functioning.

The key to implementing strategic recruitment is to think of these measures as a starting point rather than the goal. That is because such measures may serve to incentivize the wrong behaviors or mask important relationships with strategic implications. For example, time to hire and cost per hire are common metrics used in recruiting, and research shows a positive relationship between these metrics and firm performance. However, as Becker and colleagues note, it is important to pay attention to the outcome of measuring behavior. For example, potential efforts to later work to minimize measures might serve to encourage recruiters to engage in lowering how select they are when choosing recruitment channels or actual applicants. They argue that a better idea would be to focus on other metrics such as the quality of hires. And only 23% of organizations report that their organization measures quality of hire.[94] That could mask or create a problem. For example, if recruiters are given bonuses for hiring 20% of those who apply, they could increase their percentage by making offers to applicants with fewer alternatives. Although this could help them earn a bonus, it would hurt the organization overall because weaker employees are hired. All of these measures indicate the need for an effective tracking system to gather information, and adding new information such as new hire surveys is another way to tap into key metrics such as new hire satisfaction levels. Similarly, the only way to address hiring manager satisfaction is to ask managers how they feel.

Maintaining Applicant Interest and Participation

A major consideration when it comes to the recruitment process and associated activities is maintaining applicant interest and participation.[95] If an applicant withdraws from the process or

MANAGER'S TOOLBOX

Common Recruitment Key Performance Indicator (KPI) Metrics

A variety of potential workforce metrics may be used to assess recruitment effectiveness. We list several of these metrics below within their recruitment stage.

Generating Applicants

- *Application completion rate percentage* (number of applicants who complete the application process/number of applicants who start the application process)
- *Qualified candidates* (those moving past the phone screen stage)
- *Source of hire* (tracking, surveys)

Maintaining Applicant Participation

- *Applicants per hire* (number of applicants hired/number of applicants who start the application process)
- *Candidate experience* (survey)
- *Time to hire* (number of days between when a person applies and accepts an offer)
- *Yield ratio* (number of applicants who move from one recruitment hurdle to the next)

Job Acceptance

- *Acceptance rate* (number of accepted offers/ total number of offers)
- *Open vacancies versus positions filled*
- *Time to fill* (number of days a job is open)

After New Employee Organizational Entry

- *Cost per hire* ([internal costs + external costs]/ number of hires)
- *Diversity* (qualitative and quantitative approaches)
- *Hiring manager satisfaction* (survey)
- *New hire satisfaction* (survey)
- *Performance* (track performance ratings)
- *Turnover/retention rate percentage* ([number of employees employed after 1 year/number of employees hired 1 year ago] × 100)
- *Quality of fill* refers to a combination of metrics such as new employee satisfaction, performance, promotion, high potential ratings, and retention.

---

goes through the process without much enthusiasm for the organization and, ultimately, turns down a job offer, recruitment has not been effective. With this in mind, we cover some key factors related to the maintenance of applicant interest and participation.

Treatment During Recruitment

Research finds that recruiter behaviors such as how personable, competent, and informative they are matter. These behaviors are related to applicant perceptions of job attributes and how they feel about the organization and job, as well as the likelihood of accepting a job offer.[96] Timing and communication are fundamentally important factors when it comes to maintaining applicant interest and participation. Research shows that, overall, job applicants like to hear back quickly and have regular status updates. Not surprisingly, the *best* applicants have the most alternatives and are also the most likely to withdraw from the hiring process if they feel they are not being treated well.[97] Firms report greater success when they begin their recruiting process earlier. In order to help applicants understand where they stand in the recruitment process, Disney created a hiring dashboard through which applicants can track the status of their application.[98]

Interviews

There are two types of interviews to consider. The first is the ***informational interview***, which is defined as the exchange of information with the goal of learning more about the organization and its industry. If you have ever had an informal discussion with a recruiter at a job fair or

Informational interview The exchange of information between an individual and an organizational representative with the goal of learning more about the organization and its industry

interviewed an organizational insider about his or her job, you have already conducted an informational interview. The purpose of such interviews is to begin the process of getting to know more about the organization and industry and potential career opportunities in general. Even though such interviews are informal, they may still serve to influence the reactions that applicants have to that organization. Imagine you are a supply and logistics student looking to find out more about the packaging and distribution industry. You reach out to three organizations, requesting an informational interview, but only one replies. You have a great time at the interview and learn a lot. Although you are not looking for a job right now, imagine if you would be more or less likely to pursue a job with the two companies that never got back to you versus the one that did.

The other type of interview is the selection interview, which is what we traditionally think of as a job interview; this type of interview is covered in detail in Chapter 7. Even though the selection interview puts the applicant "on the spot," it is also important to approach it as a two-way process. While the employee is being evaluated, he or she is also gaining insights into what it would be like to work for the interviewing organization. And the organization is also still trying to attract the applicant to the job and the organization to increase the chances that the applicant accepts a potential offer. In these ways, selection interviews also serve a recruitment purpose.

Site Visits

Site visit When a job applicant physically agrees to go to the organization's location to meet with and to be interviewed by its representatives

One important part of the recruitment and selection process for both organizations and individuals is the site visit. On a *site visit*, the job applicant physically goes to the organization's location to meet with and to be interviewed by its representatives. Site visits serve many important functions, including presenting a chance for applicants to meet key organizational members, compare their expectations to the realities encountered during the visit, and allow for them to have a more substantial set of interactions. Research shows that applicants report several benefits related to site visits, including opportunities to meet current employees, high-level organizational members, and those with similar backgrounds. In terms of site visit logistics, they report being positively influenced by being treated professionally, having a likeable site visit host, quality hotels, and the site visit being well orchestrated.[99]

Influencing Job Choice

As seen in the previous section on maintaining applicant interest and participation, poor treatment at any stage of the recruitment process can lead job applicants to withdraw. In addition, there are organizational and individual considerations that influence job choice (see Figure 6.9).[100]

Organizational Image, Brand, and Reputation

NACE routinely surveys companies and finds that branding continues to be a key focus for university recruiting programs, and research supports the idea that organizational image affects applicants.[101] Slogans like "Work hard. Change the World," used at Amazon, help organizations signal important aspects of their culture. Being a well-regarded brand is a good problem to have, but it can make keeping up with the number of applications challenging. For example, Google receives millions of résumés each year. In 2014 alone, it received more than 3 million résumés.[102] Worried that it might alienate its brand if it relied on algorithms to decide who made the cut or not, Google modified its hiring process to ensure that human eyes look at every one of those millions of résumés.[103] And the importance of maintaining a company's brand is likely to continue. For example, the Conference Board surveyed CEOs and asked them to identify key challenges they anticipated in the coming years. At the top of the list was a need to use decision-making tools like data analytics to understand what is attractive about their brands and social media that reinforces a positive brand image.[104] Social media can also present opportunities and challenges

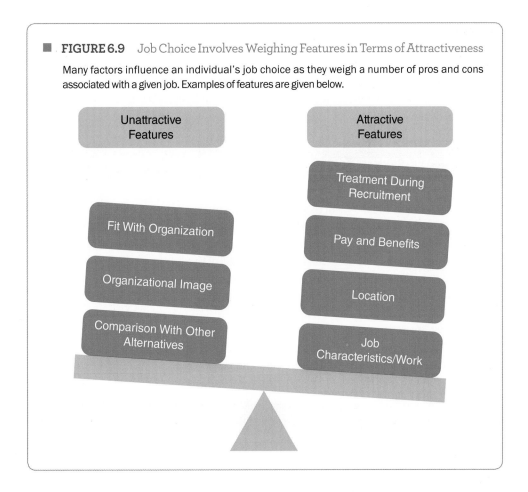

■ **FIGURE 6.9** Job Choice Involves Weighing Features in Terms of Attractiveness

Many factors influence an individual's job choice as they weigh a number of pros and cons associated with a given job. Examples of features are given below.

Unattractive Features

Attractive Features

Treatment During Recruitment

Fit With Organization

Pay and Benefits

Organizational Image

Location

Comparison With Other Alternatives

Job Characteristics/Work

for employment brands. The Twitter account of the Wendy's fast food chain got a great deal of attention based on online exchanges. In fact, the team who manages this account even has a publicist.[105] Research has shown that word-of-mouth opinions regarding the hiring process affect whether or not an applicant will choose a job.[106]

Organizational Fit

Research shows that applicants who highly identify with an organization are more likely to pursue jobs and to accept them if offered.[107] Organizational cultures vary a great deal, and they are not equally attractive to everyone. For example, someone attracted to a clan culture (e.g., Costco or Southwest Airlines) might be less attracted to a hierarchical culture (e.g., Walmart or Boeing). Research has found that specific values such as an organization's social and environmental responsibility are related to how attractive the company's is to job applicants.[108] Thus, organizational fit is another consideration that job candidates take into consideration when deciding whether to accept a job.[109]

Job Features

Pay and benefits are also important considerations for decision makers. For instance, 78% of Jobvite recruiter respondents say that medical/dental coverage is the most effective perk to attract new candidates, and 65% report that offering a 401(k) plan is also helpful, followed by 44% indicating that flexible schedules and a casual dress code are also attractive to potential employees. In addition to financial aspects of employment, the actual work that will be done and how it will be done (or job characteristics) also can serve to influence decision makers. In general, people tend to prefer work that affords them autonomy, is seen as meaningful, and allows them to receive feedback.

Alternative Offers

Finally, the process of individual decision making involves comparing potential alternatives. If a job candidate has multiple offers, they may simply decide that one offer is more attractive overall than another one. The best applicants tend to have the most job alternatives. Thus, organizations wanting to hire such individuals should consider putting their best offer forward as much as it can to attract them.

CHAPTER SUMMARY

Understanding the labor landscape makes it possible to follow the steps in the workplace planning and forecasting process, including succession planning, leadership development, assessing labor market conditions, and talent analysis. Effective recruitment begins with setting objectives in order to develop a strategy. Its advantages for organizations range from increased hiring success to higher firm performance to the ability to attract a diverse set of applicants. Recruitment stages include generating applicants, assessing the quantity and quality of applicants, and accessing sources of recruitment—both internal and external. Hiring for diversity means attending to multiple kinds of diversity, including gender, race, age, veteran status, and differently abled individuals. In the process of recruitment, organizations need to comply with various laws and policies. Organizations strive to maintain applicant interest and participation so that the best applicants accept job offers. Global considerations also come into play in attracting talent. Measuring effective recruitment using metrics and analytics is also an important part of recruitment.

KEY TERMS

workforce planning   182
forecasting   182
succession planning   182
leadership development   182
replacement planning   183
succession management   183
labor market conditions   183
workforce labor shortage   184

workforce labor
   surplus (slack)   184
talent analysis   185
talent pool   185
recruitment   185
recruitment need   187
placement   187
hiring manager   187

recruitment funnel   188
realistic job preview (RJP)   189
external recruitment   191
applicant tracking
   system (ATS)   192
informational interview   203
site visit   204

Visit **edge.sagepub.com/bauer** to help you accomplish your coursework goals in an easy-to-use learning environment.

- Master the learning objectives using key study tools
- Watch, listen, and connect with online multimedia resources

- Access mobile-friendly quizzes and flashcards to check your understanding

HR REASONING AND DECISION-MAKING EXERCISES

MINI-CASE ANALYSIS EXERCISE: EMPLOYEE TURNOVER RATE

You have been with your large high-tech organization for 3 years, having joined right after earning your college degree in business. You enjoy working in human resource management on the recruitment side of things. Lately, however, you have noticed that even though you are doing a good job at attracting applicants—you are able to keep them interested in the selection process and have established a strong acceptance rate among applicants—there is a problem. The turnover rate for employees within 18 months of being hired is at 34%. Although that isn't the highest rate in the industry, it certainly is higher than you'd like to see, and it is higher than it used to be.

You have done some initial analyses and determined that part of the issue seems to be that recruiters tell potential employees things to attract them to the organization, but the reality once they join is quite different. And especially for top performers, other options at other organizations quickly become attractive.

You have spoken with your boss, the VP of HR, and she has authorized you to create a task force to investigate the issue further and develop a strategy to solve the root causes of the problem. She suspects that the turnover rate is a symptom of bigger problems rather than the main problem.

1. Whom do you think you need to involve in this decision? Why?

2. How should you begin to tackle this problem in terms of your approach and sources of information?

3. What data should you gather?

4. Are there experiments you might do to test potential causes and to identify different solutions?

HR DECISION ANALYSIS EXERCISE:
FAIRNESS OF UNIVERSITY RELATIONS AND ALUMNI SUPPORT

Imagine that you are working as a college recruiter for your firm. As part of your job, you have a strong working relationship with the director of career services of one key university. The director's name is Les Sharp. You have developed an effective working relationship with him. Last week he suggested that if your company was willing to donate to his university's fundraising campaign, he would be sure to channel the best students to interview with your organization before any other firms. It is tempting to consider this, because the competition for top talent from this school is fierce, and your company has been pressuring you to increase both the quantity and quality of interns and hires from this school. In fact, your job may depend on it.

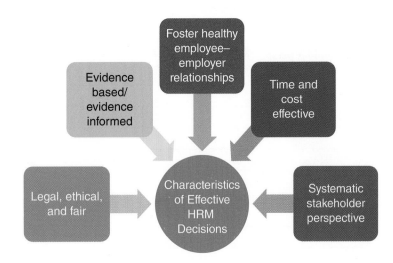

Should you make this deal? Consider this decision using the established criteria.

Please provide the rationale for your answer to each of the questions.

Is this deal legal, ethical, and fair?

_____

_____

_____

_____

_____

Is this deal evidence based/evidence informed?

_____

_____

_____

_____

_____

Does this deal foster healthy employee–employer relationships?

_____

_____

_____

_____

_____

Is this deal time and cost effective?

_____

_____

_____

_____

_____

Does this deal take a systematic stakeholder perspective?

_____

_____

_____

_____

_____

Considering your analysis above, overall, was your decision effective? Why or why not?

_____

_____

_____

_____

What, if anything, do you think should be done differently or considered to help make this decision more effective?

_____

_____

_____

_____

_____

HR DECISION-MAKING EXERCISE: RECRUITMENT AND BEYOND

Imagine that you and a small team of two to five colleagues are working with a medium-sized retail company that is expanding internationally. Although the headquarters will remain in Columbus, Ohio, the firm is opening a second office in Japan. They want to know what your team recommends in terms of recruiting for this new 30-person office. Your team's job is to decide how to handle recruiting in the short term and long term.

1. Should your company hire locally, hire expatriate employees, use a search firm, start developing a college recruiting program in Japan, or use a different recruiting approach? Explain the advantages and disadvantages of each of these approaches.

2. What additional information would help your team decide?

3. Where will your team begin its recruitment efforts?

DATA AND ANALYTICS EXERCISE: THE TRANSITION MATRIX AND EVALUATING MOVEMENT INTO, THROUGH, AND OUT OF AN ORGANIZATION

Understanding how employees move into, through, and out of different jobs in an organization is important for planning and staffing purposes. The transition matrix—also known as a Markov matrix—is a useful tool for examining such patterns of movement. As shown in what follows, a transition matrix communicates the number of employees or the proportion of employees who began in one job in one time period and who ended up in other jobs in the organization or even left the organization by another time period. First, take a look at the transition matrix with raw numbers, wherein the numbers represent employees. If read from left to right across a given row, the sum of the row values represents total number of employees who had a particular job title in the earlier time period. For example, a total of 15 (14 + 1) employees held the Research Scientist job title in 2014. Further, each row indicates where employees ended up in terms of their job titles at the later time period. For example, 14 out of the 15 Research Scientists from 2014 were still Research Scientists at 2017, and 1 out of 15 Research Scientists from 2014 exited the organization by 2017. Alternatively, if read from top to bottom by a given column, the sum of each overall column total represents how many employees held a given job title in 2017. For example, 20 (14 + 5 +1) employees held the job title of a Research Scientist in 2017. Further, 14 of those 20 individuals were also Research Scientists in 2014, 5 were Research Associates in 2014 but are now Research Scientists, and one was not in the organization in 2014 but is now a Research Scientist. Accordingly, a transition matrix comprised of raw numbers provides an indication of the number of employees who entered, moved within, and exited the organization, as well as which positions they held during their time in the organization.

TRANSITION MATRIX WITH RAW NUMBERS

		2017			
		RESEARCH SCIENTIST	RESEARCH ASSOCIATE	RESEARCH ASSISTANT	NOT IN ORGANIZATION
2014	Research Scientist	14			1
	Research Associate	5	26		4
	Research Assistant		11	43	2
	Not in Organization	1	2	12	

Second, take a look at the transition matrix with proportions, wherein the values represent the proportion of employees from the earlier time period who hold various jobs at the later time period. The transition matrix with proportions is constructed to be read from left to right across a given row, as the sum of each row's proportions totals to 1.0. Further, each row indicates the proportion of employees from an earlier time period who ended up in the same or different jobs (or even out of the organization) by a later time period. For example, .93 (or 93%) of individuals who held the job title of Research Scientist in 2014 continued to hold the title of Research Scientist in 2017, whereas .07 (7%) of individuals who held the job title of Research Scientist in 2014 left the organization by 2017.

TRANSITION MATRIX WITH PROPORTIONS

		2017			
		RESEARCH SCIENTIST	**RESEARCH ASSOCIATE**	**RESEARCH ASSISTANT**	**NOT IN ORGANIZATION**
2014	Research Scientist	.93			.07
	Research Associate	.14	.74		.10
	Research Assistant		.20	.77	.03
	Not in Organization	.06	.14	.80	

The transition matrix can be a useful descriptive analytics tool, as it can be used to describe the way in which employees have moved into, through, and out of the organization in the past. In addition, a transition matrix can serve as the basis for a predictive analytics tool called Markov chain analysis—an approach that can provide estimates for how employees will move into, through, and out of the organization in the future.

 EXCEL EXTENSION: NOW YOU TRY!

- On **edge.sagepub.com/bauer**, you will find an Excel spreadsheet containing the raw data for this exercise. You will complete this exercise using that Excel spreadsheet.

- Also on the textbook companion website, you will find a PDF tutorial document that explains step by step how to create a transition matrix with raw numbers and with proportions in Excel using the raw data.

CHAPTER 6 SUPPLEMENT: CAPABILITIES OFFERED BY ASSESSING ATTRACTION OUTCOMES

Reprinted from Carlson, K. D., Connerly, M. L., & Mecham, R. L. (2002). Recruitment evaluation: The case for assessing the quality of applicants attracted. *Personnel Psychology, 55*, 461–490.

CAPABILITIES OFFERED BY ASSESSING ATTRACTION OUTCOMES

Capability: Evaluation of alternative attraction practices.

How it adds value: Provides a means for organizations to compare the effectiveness of alternative recruitment activities. This approach also allows organizations to evaluate each phase of recruitment so strengths or weaknesses in attraction can be identified.

Capability: Comparisons of applicants across applicant pools.

How it adds value: Gives decision makers the opportunity to compare candidates from different applicant pools. Because scores are scaled to the applicant population rather than to specific applicant pools, scores for candidates from different applicant pools can be compared directly.

Capability: Evaluating alternative sources of candidates.

How it adds value: Provides organizations with a means of examining alternative sources of applicants. This can be particularly useful in college recruitment programs where organizations can objectively evaluate the potential of the applicant pools from different schools and be able to make determinations about which sources provide better applicants.

Capability: Evaluating the effectiveness of status maintenance and job acceptance activities.

How it adds value: Once attraction outcomes have been assessed, the assessment of status maintenance and job acceptance outcomes simply involves the recognition of the value lost when top candidates withdraw from the applicant pool prior to receiving a job offer or refuse to accept a job offer when one is offered.

Capability: Concurrent evaluation of attraction activities.

How it adds value: Because scores are developed for each applicant, attraction outcomes can be evaluated on an ongoing basis, even before organizations complete recruitment processes. This gives decision makers the opportunity to identify problems and adjust activities to reduce their negative effects while there is still time to do so.

Capability: Cost–benefit analyses of attraction activities.

How it adds value: Permits organizations to evaluate both the benefits and costs of alternative attraction, status maintenance, and job acceptance activities. Unambiguous interpretations of the relative effectiveness are possible.

Capability: Evaluating recruitment improvement opportunities.

How it adds value: Provides organizations the opportunity to compare how well they are performing recruitment activities against what could be possible with the applicant populations that exist and provides a means of estimating the value of those opportunities.

Selection Processes and Procedures

7

Opening Case

Finding the Best Fit: The Case of Selection at Google

Acquiring the best talent provides organizations with an important competitive advantage, particularly when selection systems are aligned with strategic objectives. Chapter 6 pointed out one key aspect of hiring the best talent: the recruitment and selection funnel. As noted there, having more candidates to choose from in the funnel gives an organization the highest probability of hiring the best. In other words, all things being equal, it's better to choose from 10 qualified job candidates than from just two.

Now consider the size of the recruitment and selection funnel at Google, which is one of the most admired employers in the world and has been ranked at the top of *Fortune*'s list of "best companies to work for" for many years. By some estimates, Google receives as many as 2 million job applications each year but only hires about 5,000 of those applicants. Thus, the chances of an applicant landing a job at Google are about 1 in 400; it is not impossible to get a job there, but it is not going to be easy. One thing is certain: The recruitment and selection funnel works in Google's favor.

In addition to having more qualified applicants from which to choose, companies also need valid, job-related selection procedures to be able to choose among job candidates. As this chapter discusses, managers who simply choose candidates "from the gut" tend not to choose the people who are the best fit for the job. Rather, systematic and rigorous selection procedures, such as a structured interview process in which all candidates are asked the same job-related questions, lead to hiring the best talent. Google is a leader in this area, applying the top research practices to optimize its interview process. For example, Google found through its research that conducting four interviews is the best way to optimize selection decisions. This is likely because having more than one interviewer compensates for the biases of any single interviewer, and it also takes into account that a candidate may simply have had a "bad day" when they participated in an interview. Google also found—again through robust analytics—that conducting many more interviews per candidate (e.g., 25) was not necessarily more effective and may in fact have made the selection process take too long. The point is that using research and analytics to understand the hiring process maximizes the chances of hiring success.

LEARNING OBJECTIVES

After reading and studying this chapter, you should be able to do the following:

7.1 Explain how job analysis and legal issues apply to recruitment and selection.

7.2 Describe the concepts of reliability, validity, and selection utility and how they are demonstrated.

7.3 Demonstrate the strategic choice and combination of various selection procedures.

7.4 Identify the different selection procedures available for making hiring decisions and their advantages and disadvantages.

7.5 Recognize and explain key analytical, legal, ethical, and global issues associated with personnel selection.

7.6 Describe the importance of applicant reactions to selection processes.

7.7 Explain how to deploy selection procedures within organizations to enhance job performance.

Other innovative approaches to recruitment and selection include Google's development of an international programming competition called Google Code Jam, which was established in 2003 to help the company identify top engineering talent. The competition culminates with the top 25 Code Jammers competing in the World Championship for $15,000 and bragging rights. Google sees this as a way to engage with the engineering community, celebrate those at the top of their game, and also to consider top talent recruited in a unique way. Google seems to have leveraged the best of proven selection science as well as creative applicant cultivation to its advantage.[1]

Case Discussion Questions

1. Although having more applicants to choose from is a good thing, can there be such a thing as too many applicants? For example, how might a company like Google process 2 million applicants per year, short of interviewing all candidates?

2. Although hiring "from the gut" is generally not the best approach to selection, do you think that this approach may have some advantages? If so, what are they? Do you think that this sort of approach enters into Google's hiring processes?

3. In addition to using interviews, how might Google select employees for certain jobs such as programmers? How would you decide which types of assessment(s) are most important for hiring programmers that best fit the job?

4. Teamwork and being able to admit mistakes are also factors that seem to fit well with success at Google. How could these sorts of factors be assessed in the selection process?

▶ Click to learn more...

Watch a video on getting a job at Google:

https://www.youtube.com/watch?v=k-baHBzWe4k

People are arguably an organization's most precious resources—they are one of the main factors that determine an organization's success. Luckily, there is a robust science on how to choose the employees that best fit the job and the organization and how to do so in a fair, legally defensible way that aligns with an organization's strategy. This chapter reviews the science of employee selection, including established data analytic techniques for enhancing the quality of hiring decisions. It also discusses the wide variety of selection procedures that are available to support hiring decisions and talent acquisition.

An underlying premise of this text is that the employees make the organization. This is in line with practice, as 75% of companies indicate that talent acquisition is critical to executing their business strategies.[2] That is, well-developed selection systems bring talented individuals into the organization, who in turn can help the organization realize strategic objectives. Chapter 6 discusses how to recruit so that an employer can choose among the best job applicants, and it emphasizes how important finding the right people for one's organization can be. In fact, Jeff Bezos, CEO of Amazon.com, is quoted as saying, "I'd rather interview 50 people and not hire anyone than hire the wrong person."[3] And the Mayo Clinic takes 3 years before it decides if a doctor has what it takes to remain there.[4] Let's say a company has 100 openings and is able to recruit 1,000 people to apply for that job. This would be a good problem to have. But then the next step is to address an important question: how to select the *best* 100 applicants and to do it in a way that is ethical and legal.

There are many choices when it comes to selection methods, including personality tests, background checks, and interviews—to name a few. But how useful are each of these methods, and which are the best? What are the ethical and legal issues surrounding the use of these methods, and what legal issues need to be addressed? How are data involved in making effective hiring decisions? To answer that question, we begin by reviewing some issues from previous chapters—strategy, job analysis, recruitment, legal issues, and diversity—to tie each of these topics to their relevance in areas of personnel selection.

Setting the Stage for Selection: Job Analysis, Recruitment, and Legal Issues

LO 7.1 Explain how job analysis and legal issues apply to recruitment and selection.

By carefully aligning employee selection with strategic objectives, an organization ensures that it will acquire the *right* talent to meet its unique needs and demands, which ultimately propels the organization in the right strategic direction. Accordingly, to achieve success, an organization requires selection systems that are aligned with organizational strategy. This is best considered in the use of effective recruitment strategies to attract the best talent (see Chapter 6) and identifying the needs of the job as it fits into the larger work unit and organization—all staying within legal and ethical guidelines.

Job Analysis

As noted in Chapter 5, job or work analysis and its cousin competency modeling involve the identification of the tasks that make up a job, and the KSAOs that are required for the job. Job analysis is important for choosing selection procedures, because different selection procedures capture certain KSAOs more effectively. For instance, an integrity test—specifically developed to assess applicant honesty—will generally be a better screener for honesty than will reviewing a résumé. To give a simple example, if you determined that a product-design job required engineering skills and teamwork, you would want to use hiring procedures that reflect these requirements. You might consider a personality test that reflects a person's abilities to work well as part of a team, and you might include relevant engineering and teamwork questions in the job interview. Although this example shows that basing selection procedures on a job analysis are in many ways common sense, it is important to keep in mind that some sort of job analysis is also legally required for selection procedures, and it is also recommended by professional guidelines.[5] PepsiCo and Starwood Hotels and Resorts are using analytics to understand the profile of their most successful current employees to inform their selection procedures for screening future candidates.[6]

Using Recruitment to Enhance Hiring Decisions

Chapter 6 discussed recruitment as a key way of increasing the odds of hiring the best employees. (As a reminder, see the recruitment funnel in Figure 7.1.) There are really two issues here. First, we want to increase the *size* of the applicant pool to increase the odds of selecting the best employees. For example, all things being equal, being able to choose from among 10 job candidates will increase a company's odds of hiring the best person, as opposed to being able to choose from only one candidate. But a second key goal of recruitment is to increase the number of *qualified* applicants. This is why it is so important during recruitment to focus on both getting a large number of people to apply *and* making sure that they are the best qualified applicants.[7]

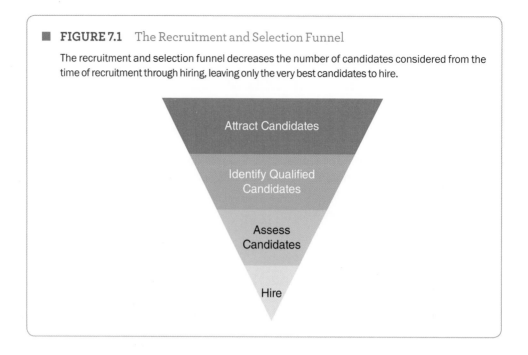

■ **FIGURE 7.1**   The Recruitment and Selection Funnel

The recruitment and selection funnel decreases the number of candidates considered from the time of recruitment through hiring, leaving only the very best candidates to hire.

Attract Candidates

Identify Qualified Candidates

Assess Candidates

Hire

Legal and Ethical Issues in Hiring

Chapter 4 discussed the centrality of legal issues to HR decision making. Perhaps the area in which legal issues are most evident—and which has the most developed history in terms of laws and court cases—is in selection. As a result of Title VII of the Civil Rights Act of 1964 and the subsequent court cases interpreting it (referred to as "case law"), a significant body of laws and legal guidelines has developed to guide employers in choosing, developing, and administering hiring procedures. To help employers make sense of this large, often complex set of laws and court cases, the EEOC, Department of Justice, and Department of Labor developed the Uniform Guidelines on Employee Selection Procedures (1978). Although the Uniform Guidelines are not technically laws in themselves, they do summarize the laws up until that time and are typically treated by the courts as if they were law. As described in Chapter 4, the Uniform Guidelines provide substantial legal guidance to employers on the implementation of recruitment programs and the determination of whether a test has adverse impact against protected groups, for example, by using the 4/5ths or 80% rule in terms of hiring ratios. We encourage you to review the material in Chapter 4 on adverse impact and how to calculate it, as it is a critical issue in understanding the implementation of selection procedures. In addition, the Uniform Guidelines set legal standards on a broad range of selection-related issues such as establishing the validity of selection procedures, setting cutoff scores, promoting diversity in organizations, and monitoring the diversity of an employer's applicant flow and workforce. Note that although the Uniform Guidelines summarize the legal issues up until 1978, they are now more than 40 years old, and there have been calls for them to be updated taking into account more recent developments regarding the science of selection. Further, note that in addition to these laws and government guidelines, there are also professional guidelines on the development and administration of selection procedures, published by the Society for Industrial and Organizational Psychology (SIOP's *Principles for the Validation and Use of Personnel Selection Procedures*, 2018; for more on these, please see Supplement 7.1).[8]

LO 7.2   Describe the concepts of reliability, validity, and selection utility and how they are demonstrated.

Data-Driven Criteria for Choosing Selection Procedures: Reliability, Validity, and Utility

Various sources of data can be used to determine whether the use of specific selection procedures influences key organizational outcomes such as performance and productivity.

SPOTLIGHT ON LEGAL ISSUES

Understanding Reasonable Accommodation as Outlined by the Americans with Disabilities Act (ADA) During Selection

Question. If an applicant has a disability and will need an accommodation for the job interview, does the Americans with Disabilities Act (ADA) require an employer to provide them with one?

Answer. Employers are required to provide "reasonable accommodation" (appropriate changes and adjustments) to enable applicants to be considered for a job opening. Reasonable accommodation may also be required to enable them to perform a job, gain access to the workplace, and enjoy the "benefits and privileges" of employment available to employees without disabilities. *An employer cannot refuse to consider an applicant because the person requires a reasonable accommodation to compete for or perform a job.*

Question. Can an employer refuse to provide an applicant with an accommodation because it is too difficult or too expensive?

Answer. An employer does not have to provide a specific accommodation if it would cause an "undue hardship" that would require significant difficulty or expense. However, an employer cannot refuse to provide an accommodation solely because it entails some costs, either financial or administrative. *If the requested accommodation causes an undue hardship, the employer still would be required to provide another accommodation that does not.*

Question. What are some examples of "reasonable accommodations" that may be needed during the hiring process?

Answer. Reasonable accommodation can take many forms. Accommodations that may be needed during the hiring process include (but are not limited to):

- providing written materials in accessible formats, such as large print, braille, or audiotape

- providing readers or sign language interpreters

- ensuring that recruitment, interviews, tests, and other components of the application process are held in accessible locations

- providing or modifying equipment or devices

- adjusting or modifying application policies and procedures.

Question. Because of a learning disability, an applicant believes they need extra time to complete a written test. Does the ADA require an employer to modify the way a test is given to the applicant?

Answer. An employer may have to provide testing materials in alternative formats or make other adjustments to tests as an accommodation for such an applicant. The format and manner in which a test is given may pose problems for persons with impaired sensory, speaking, or manual skills, as well as for those with certain learning disabilities. For example, an applicant who is blind will not be able to read a written test but can take the test if it is provided in braille, the questions are audio recorded, or an automated text reader is provided. A deaf person will not understand oral instructions, but these could be provided in a written format or through the use of a sign language interpreter. A 30-minute timed written test may pose a problem for a person whose learning disability requires additional time. Thus, *the ADA requires that employers give application tests in a format or manner that does not require use of an impaired skill unless the test is designed to measure that skill.*

Question. When does an applicant have to tell an employer that they need an accommodation for the hiring process?

Answer. It is best for applicants to *let an employer know as soon as they realize that they will need a reasonable accommodation* for some aspect of the hiring process. An employer needs advance notice to provide many accommodations, such as sign language interpreters, alternative formats for written documents, and adjusting the time allowed for taking a written test. An employer may also need advance notice to arrange an accessible location for a test or interview.

Question. How do applicants request a reasonable accommodation?

Answer. They must inform the employer that they need some sort of change or adjustment to the application/interviewing process because of their medical condition. They can make this request *orally or in writing,* or someone else might make a request for them (e.g., a family member, friend, health professional, or other representative, such as a job coach).

Source: Modified from material developed by the U.S. Equal Employment Opportunity Commission. (n.d.). Job applicants and the Americans with Disabilities Act. https://www.eeoc.gov/facts/jobapplicant.html

For example, selection procedures based on the "gut" impressions of hiring managers can be a legal liability for employers. Moreover, research shows that this approach generally results in poor outcomes—simply put, not a great approach.[9] In contrast, developing selection procedures based on systematic data collection and analysis can result not only in more legally compliant selection procedures but more predictive ones as well. Using such a data-driven approach, however, requires careful attention to the reliability, validity, and utility (dollar value) of selection procedures.

Ensuring the Quality of Selection Measures: Reliability and Validity

Psychometrics A science used to estimate the quality of psychological measures such as those used in personnel selection

Some selection procedures are of higher quality than others. There is a science—called *psychometrics*—used to estimate the quality of the measures used in personnel selection. Specifically, it is possible to examine how consistent or dependable various selection procedures are (called reliability), as well as how well or accurately they predict actual job performance (called validity; see Figure 7.2). Let's explore what reliability and validity mean and how they apply to HR selection.

Reliability

Reliability The consistency of measurement

Suppose that you are trying to hire highly conscientious applicants. You give an applicant a personality test that measures conscientiousness, and it says that they are highly conscientious. The applicant comes back in for an interview, and you give them the conscientiousness test again, and this time it says that they are not very conscientious. This is a problem: How can the test possibly be measuring a stable personality dimension like conscientiousness if it is not consistent? That is the heart of what is meant by *reliability*, or the consistency of measurement. It is a necessary condition for validity. A test has to first measure something consistently before we can decide whether it is actually measuring the underlying dimension. The reliability of a test or measure is expressed as a correlation coefficient, on a scale of 0 to 1, with 0 indicating low reliability and 1 high reliability.[10]

Validity

One of the key issues surrounding the use of selection procedures is the concept of validity, or the degree to which a predictor actually measures what it is supposed to measure, such as an important individual difference variable related to job performance. In other words, whereas

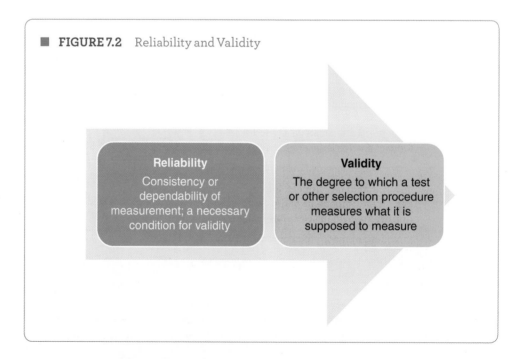

■ FIGURE 7.2   Reliability and Validity

Reliability
Consistency or dependability of measurement; a necessary condition for validity

Validity
The degree to which a test or other selection procedure measures what it is supposed to measure

reliability relates to how consistently we measure something, *validity* relates to how accurately we measure something. Note that although validity is a single concept, there are three common ways to show the validity of selection procedures: content validity, criterion-related validity, and construct validity. These are described in government guidelines such as the Uniform Guidelines on Employee Selection Procedures (see Chapter 4) as well as in professional guidelines (*SIOP Principles*).[11] Let's discuss each of these.

Content Validity

Content validity is actually an approach to test development focused on sampling the domain such as the job. This is typically done via a job analysis and SME input. If you wanted to demonstrate that a selection procedure had good content validity, you would develop the test based on a job analysis and review by subject matter experts (SMEs, generally job incumbents and supervisors). As an example, if a local or regional bank wanted to develop a content-valid selection procedure for a bank teller's job, it might conduct a job analysis of the job, shadow bank tellers to observe their work, and develop questions (perhaps for a written test and structured interview) accordingly. It might also have current bank tellers and their supervisors serve as SMEs and review the test questions to document that they reflect the job correctly. In showing content validity, there generally are no complex statistics involved; rather, the test's validity is demonstrated by documenting that the test is based on a job analysis and that SMEs have judged the test content to reflect the content domain of the job.[12] For instance, the Biddle Consulting Group used a content validation approach as part of its validation of the computer-based CritiCall test for hiring police and other emergency dispatchers. Specifically, it had 66 SMEs from the Florida Highway Patrol rate the test on dimensions such as whether test performance is essential to the job.[13]

Criterion-Related Validity

The gold standard in selection research is to show that there is an empirical relationship (usually a statistically significant correlation) between a test and measures of job performance—using either a sample of current employees (concurrent validity) or job applicants (predictive validity). Showing this empirical relationship is called *criterion-related validity*, and this correlation between the test score and job performance is referred to as the *validity coefficient*. As an example, a company might give a test of emotional stability to 75 employees who work closely together on teams, finding that the test is correlated .29 with a measure of employees' job performance, and that this correlation is statistically significant. In the personnel selection context, that correlation would be considered evidence for the validity of the emotional stability test in predicting job performance. In the case of the CritiCall test for dispatchers described earlier, it was found in a sample of 62 Florida Highway Patrol dispatchers and call-takers that CritiCall test scores were correlated .41 with job performance—a statistically significant correlation, and evidence of the test's criterion-related validity.[14]

When conducting research to demonstrate a test's criterion-related validity, there are two primary ways to approach it. *Predictive validity* involves administering the test to job applicants and then seeing how well the test scores correlate with their later job performance scores. For example, a clothing retailer might administer a test to its job applicants and then see whether those test scores are correlated to the actual sales numbers of hired applicants 1 year later. The second approach is through *concurrent validity*, which involves administering the test to current employees and showing that their test scores are correlated with their current job performance. In this case, the clothing retailer could ask current employees to take the test—assuring them that this is for research only and their test scores will not affect their jobs—and then correlate those test scores with job performance. If the correlation is statistically significant, it would suggest that the retailer is justified in using this test for making selection decisions. The CritiCall example is an example of a concurrent validation study. The concurrent approach is perhaps simpler and more straightforward, as it means that the employer does not have to wait to see whether the test is valid. On the other hand, the samples of current employees used in concurrent validity studies may not provide the most accurate estimates of a test's validity among applicants: For example,

Validity The accuracy of a measure, or the degree to which an assessment measures what it is supposed to measure

Content validity An approach to test development focused on sampling the domain such as the job, usually shown through job analysis or SME judgment

Criterion-related validity The demonstration of an empirical relationship between a predictor and measures of job performance

Validity coefficient The correlation between a selection procedure (e.g., a test) and job performance

Predictive validity Administering a selection procedure to job applicants and showing that their scores are correlated with their later job performance scores in order to demonstrate criterion-related validity

Concurrent validity Administering a selection procedure to current employees and showing that their scores are correlated with their current job performance in order to demonstrate criterion-related validity

current employees don't "act like" highly motivated job applicants in the actual testing situation. Still, predictive and concurrent validity approaches both provide evidence for whether the test is valid and should be used for making selection decisions.[15]

Construct Validity

Construct validity The demonstration that a test actually measures a particular construct of interest through an accumulation of evidence about the test, including its pattern of relationships with other measures

Construct validity involves the demonstration that a test actually measures a particular construct of interest, such as mechanical ability. This is typically shown through an accumulation of evidence about the test, including its pattern of relationships with other tests and measures that make sense from a theoretical or scientific point of view. For example, a test publisher might show that its test of conscientiousness has a pattern of correlations with other tests that makes logical sense: The test might show a high correlation with other tests of conscientiousness, a moderate correlation with tests of achievement orientation, and a relatively weak correlation with tests of verbal ability. On the other hand, if the conscientiousness test was found to correlate strongly with verbal ability, one might be concerned that it is not a clean measure of conscientiousness, since it also seems to be measuring verbal ability. In the hiring context, once a test's construct validity has been demonstrated, it might be used for hiring if that construct (in this case, conscientiousness) has been identified as important to the job through a job analysis.

Construct validity can be thought of as overarching the entire concept of validity—which is the idea of establishing that a test measures what it is supposed to measure. Given that construct validity is demonstrated by showing a pattern of accumulated evidence of a test's validity, we would also expect that the test would sample the content domain of conscientiousness (see content validity) and would correlate with supervisor ratings of an employee's willingness to help their coworkers. This reflects the original point: Validity is best conceptualized as a single, unitary concept, not as consisting of three "types."[16] For example, tests developed through a careful content validity approach should, theoretically, also show good criterion-related validity.[17] Rather, content, criterion-related, and construct validity are simply three convenient ways of demonstrating the validity of measures. Table 7.1 summarizes different validity strategies, along with examples of each in an organizational context.

Analytics: Showing the Importance of Validity in Hiring Decisions

The validity of personnel selection procedures is one of the most important key metrics used in HR decision making; ensuring validity provides a competitive advantage to organizations that understand it and manage it well. Specifically, if organizations choose selection procedures that are highly predictive of job performance, they are more likely to make good hires. Conversely, organizations that decide simply to "go with their gut" rather than systematically choosing the selection procedures with the best proven validity for choosing employees are losing out on a potential advantage over their competition (consider that gut decisions may also lead to unfair or illegal hiring decisions). In addition, it is necessary to demonstrate the validity of selection procedures to provide legal defensibility.

Figure 7.3 illustrates the importance of taking the time in organizations to research a test's validity. It shows a case of criterion-related validity—that is, the relationship between test score (on the x-axis) and job performance (on the y-axis) for jobs in a hypothetical company. We have marked where the passing score for the test is on the x-axis and where the break point is for employees who have acceptable performance and those with unacceptable performance on the y-axis. Based on a passing score on the test and the acceptable performance score, Figure 7.3 further breaks selection decisions down into accurate decisions (hits) and inaccurate decisions (misses). Hits include applicants who passed the test and turned out to be good employees (true positives), as well as applicants who failed the test and turned out to be unacceptable performers (true negatives). As you can see, the problem is the misses: These are the false positives—that is, employees who passed the test but turned out to be unacceptable performers, as well as false negatives, or employees who did not pass the test but who would have actually been good performers. Obviously, the goal in selection decision making is to increase the number of hits and avoid misses.

TABLE 7.1   Summary of Different Validation Strategies for Personnel Selection Procedures

STRATEGY FOR DEMONSTRATING VALIDITY	DEFINITION	EXAMPLE
Content Validity	Content validity involves developing a selection procedure such that it samples a particular domain. In the selection context, this is the job. Content validity thus involves developing the selection procedure based on a job analysis and with input from SMEs (e.g., incumbents) and documenting the process. It is often used when available sample sizes of employees and incumbents are too small to conduct empirical validation (criterion-related validity).	A city government needs to develop a knowledge test and simulation for selecting fire captains for promotion to a fire chief's position. It conducts a job analysis of the fire chief job and then develops the test and simulation with input from SMEs. SMEs also review the final test and simulation. The SMEs confirm that the two assessments sample the job and that the assessments measure knowledge and skills needed at the time the person is promoted. All processes are documented.
Criterion-Related Validity	Shown by demonstrating an empirical relationship—most commonly a statistically significant correlation—between a selection procedure (e.g., test score) and job performance.	
Predictive design	Uses job applicants as the sample. Test scores obtained during the application process are correlated with later job performance (e.g., 6 months later).	A company wants to validate a mechanical ability test for hiring factory workers. It administers the test to a group of job applicants. Then, 1 year later, it correlates the mechanical ability test scores with job performance scores among those applicants that were actually hired. The company finds a statistically significant relationship ($r = .38$) between the mechanical ability test scores and job performance, which is evidence of validity, and suggests that the test can be used for future selection decisions.
Concurrent design	Uses current employees (incumbents) as the sample. Test scores obtained from incumbents are correlated with their current job performance.	A company wants to validate a mechanical ability test for hiring factory workers. It administers the test to a group of volunteer employees and then correlates the mechanical ability test scores with current job performance scores. The company finds a statistically significant relationship ($r = .35$) between the mechanical ability test scores and job performance, which is evidence of validity, and suggests that the test can be used for future selection decisions.
Construct Validity	Accumulation of research evidence that the test or measure actually does measure the construct it purports to measure and does not measure unrelated constructs.	A test developer administers its new mechanical ability test to several groups, perhaps students as well as samples of employees obtained from its clients. It finds that the test has a high correlation with existing tests of mechanical ability, a moderate correlation with tests of spatial relationships, and a low correlation with tests of extraversion and verbal ability. These patterns suggest that the test is measuring mechanical ability and is not measuring unrelated constructs.

The importance of validity is seen in Figure 7.3. The first graph shows a case of moderate validity. Note the healthy number of hits but also some misses. The second graph shows what happens when validity drops down to zero: The number of hits and misses is nearly identical, meaning that the test was essentially useless. The third graph shows what happens when validity is nearly perfect—that is, when there is a very high correlation between the test and job performance. In this figure, you can see that the distribution of scores includes almost entirely hits and almost no misses.

■ FIGURE 7.3   The Importance of Predictor Validity to Accurate Selection Decisions

The validity of a selection procedure directly impacts the number of correct hiring decisions. When validity is moderate, there are a number of hits but also some misses as well. When validity falls to zero, there are as many misses as hits—essentially random selection. But as validity gets higher, the relative number of misses declines significantly.

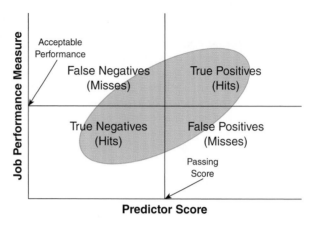

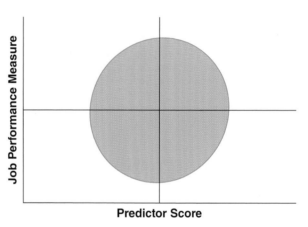

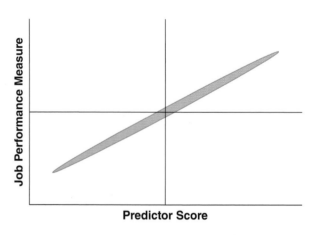

Although near-perfect validity is something that is rarely achieved in the real world, the point is that carefully researching the best selection procedures and using those to make hiring decisions can have an enormous impact on the quality of hiring decisions and, more important, may help hiring managers avoid costly mistakes. In short, it is well worth the time and effort for HR decision-makers to examine the validity of the selection procedures that they are considering, including conducting in-house studies of predictors (especially in larger organizations) and demanding that test vendors show validity evidence for their selection procedures, including complete descriptions of the research that test publishers have done in similar industries and jobs.

Do Organizations Have to Do Their Own Validity Research?

Employers that invest resources in examining the validity of selection procedures and choosing the best ones are at a definite advantage when hiring the best talent. However, one question is whether organizations have to do their own research on selection procedures or whether they can rely on existing studies done by test publishers. This is at the heart of the concept of *validity generalization*—that is, the assumption that selection procedures that have been validated for similar jobs in similar organizations can be assumed to be valid for new situations. As an example, let's say that the Vivace Company wants to use a selection procedure for hiring its online customer assistance agents. A test vendor approaches Vivace and points out that it has a situational judgment test (SJT) that it has used with other companies that employee online customer assistance agents and that the SJT has been found to have good predictive validity (i.e., it predicts the performance of customer assistance agents). Can Vivace confidently use this test for hiring its customer assistance agents? According to the theory of validity generalization, yes. This would especially be the case to the extent that the customer service jobs in these other companies are similar to Vivace's customer service jobs; this might be determined through a job analysis. Overall, the scientific evidence supports the use of a validity generalization approach; however, legal guidelines also suggest that showing that the two jobs in consideration are actually similar is important and that employers should do their own *local validation* study (i.e., showing the test's validity for a job in their own organization) at some point if possible.[18]

Validity generalization The assumption that selection procedures that have been validated for similar jobs in similar organizations can be assumed to be valid for new situations

Local validation Showing the test's validity for predicting job performance in a specific organization

Selection Utility

The first factor to consider when hiring is also the *utility* of selection decisions, or the degree to which selection procedures are worth the time and money to carry them out (see Figure 7.4). One of the most important ways to increase selection utility is to be sure that selection procedures are valid. To the extent that selection procedures are good predictors of job performance, they are more worthwhile to use. Conversely, if selection procedures are not valid, it is not worth taking the time and money to use them.

Utility The degree to which an HR function (e.g., a selection procedure) is worth the time or money it requires

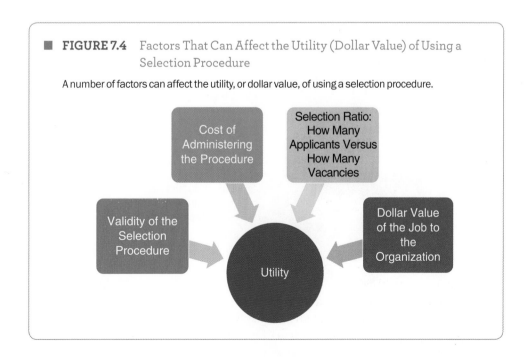

■ **FIGURE 7.4** Factors That Can Affect the Utility (Dollar Value) of Using a Selection Procedure

A number of factors can affect the utility, or dollar value, of using a selection procedure.

- Cost of Administering the Procedure
- Selection Ratio: How Many Applicants Versus How Many Vacancies
- Validity of the Selection Procedure
- Dollar Value of the Job to the Organization
- Utility

Second, the selection ratio, or the number of job vacancies relevant to the number of applicants, also affects the utility of selection procedures. Suppose you had two job vacancies and only two job applicants. It may not be worth the trouble to use any selection procedure other than to be sure that the applicants were minimally qualified and not a risk to the organization, because you know that you will need to hire both of these applicants in order to fill the two vacancies. Rather, when there are more applicants relative to the number of vacancies, it is worth it to take the time and money to give a test—the utility of using a good selection system goes up. This again illustrates the importance of effective recruitment procedures to successful selection procedures.

Third is the cost of the selection procedure. All things being equal, there is greater utility in using a cheaper selection procedure than one that is more expensive. Finally, if the job is of high-value to the organization, or if poor performance could seriously affect the organization (e.g., police officers for a municipality), the utility of using good selection procedures increases even further. For instance, a city government might decide that a valid test for emergency dispatchers has high utility because it fulfills a primary mission of the city and could even save lives. Recall the CritiCall test, which is used by public-sector organizations to hire emergency dispatchers, and that was found in a study of the Florida Highway Patrol to predict the performance of dispatchers.[19]

LO 7.3   Demonstrate the strategic choice and combination of various selection procedures.

Strategically Choosing and Combining Selection Procedures

Imagine that a company has done a lot of research to establish the selection procedures that are the most likely to be the best predictors for a customer service. Based on the job analysis and some background research, the company examines 10 tests to consider using it to make selection decisions. To do its research, the company administers the 10 tests—which include three possible

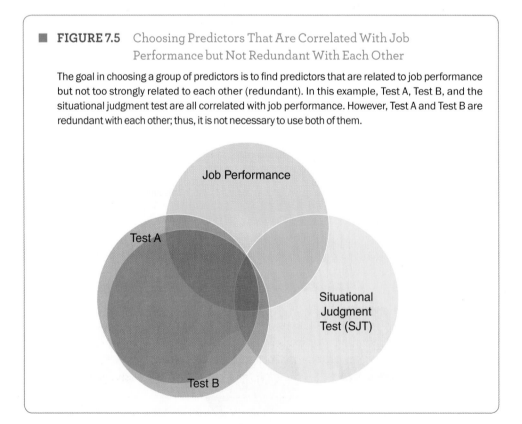

■ **FIGURE 7.5**   Choosing Predictors That Are Correlated With Job Performance but Not Redundant With Each Other

The goal in choosing a group of predictors is to find predictors that are related to job performance but not too strongly related to each other (redundant). In this example, Test A, Test B, and the situational judgment test are all correlated with job performance. However, Test A and Test B are redundant with each other; thus, it is not necessary to use both of them.

TABLE 7.2   Hypothetical Correlations Among Three Tests and Job Performance

	1	2	3	4
1. Conscientiousness A	-			
2. Conscientiousness B	.92	-		
3. Situational Judgment Test (SJT)	.19	.23	-	
4. Job Performance (Criterion)	.35	.37	.41	-

tests of conscientiousness—to 1,000 current employees (i.e., a concurrent validation study) and correlates the employees' test scores with employees' job performance, in this case, supervisor performance ratings. The company finds that all 10 tests have a significant correlation with the job performance measure. This means that all 10 tests are valid predictors of job performance—that is good news. But it also knows that administering 10 tests is impractical, as it would take too much time, be costly, and perhaps annoy the job applicants.

Some further analysis of the data from the 1,000 current employees can help. Conceptually, the goal is to have selection procedures that are correlated with job performance but are not overly correlated with each other (redundant). Related to this last idea, selection procedures should complement each other. In other words, each selection procedure should uniquely predict some aspect of job performance. Figure 7.5 illustrates this issue conceptually using a Venn diagram, and Table 7.2 shows a correlation matrix that illustrates the situation statistically. The figure and table each show three valid tests (Personality Test A, Personality Test B, and a situational judgment test or SJT) that are correlated with performance. In addition, the personality tests and the SJT complement each other in terms of prediction since the personality tests predict one aspect of job performance and the SJT predicts another aspect of performance. However, the two personality tests are highly correlated with each other (.92); they are redundant. In this case, it is best to use one of the personality tests but not both.

Selection Procedures

In the previous sections, we have discussed some of the technical aspects of different selection procedures. In practice, there is a broad array of selection procedures that are available to employers. Each of these selection procedures has advantages and disadvantages in terms of validity (how well it predicts job performance), utility (its cost), and its likelihood to cause adverse impact and thus affect the diversity of the organization. In this section, we describe the advantages and disadvantages of a wide range of selection procedures based on the research. We also will describe best practices for a number of these procedures so that organizations can get the best information from each. Keep in mind that there is no best selection procedure for choosing applicants. Rather than considering one selection procedure (e.g., a personality test) for choosing applicants, selection procedures are best thought of as complementing each other. Thus, some combination of selection procedures will usually provide the best prediction of job candidates. Websites such as Glassdoor.com allow individuals to share insights into the hiring process as well as specific interview questions. Of course, such anonymous information must be taken for what it is, but it can be worthwhile for candidates to research a company before interviewing with them. This discussion does not necessarily include an

LO 7.4 Identify the different selection procedures available for making hiring decisions and their advantages and disadvantages.

Deploying Selection Systems in Different Countries and Languages

One question in today's multinational companies is whether to make personnel selection procedures consistent across the organization, regardless of the country. Such consistency in selecting employees regardless of location could enhance the consistency of the organization's culture worldwide, but it can be difficult to implement a one-size-fits-all approach to selection across national boundaries given differences in employment laws. Moreover, different predictors may work well in one country but not in another. For instance, a test of agreeableness may be a good predictor in one country but not in another due to cultural differences.

Another issue is that of translating an assessment from one language to another. This is typically done via a method known as translation and back-translation.

As an example, an English test might be translated into Italian and then back-translated into English (see Figure 7.6). This back-translated English version would then be compared to the original English to help decide whether the Italian and English versions are basically equivalent.

Figure 7.6 is a specific example of the translation/back-translation process for an extraversion question, with the goal of creating an Italian item from the English. The final back-translated item is close enough to the original to suggest that the Italian item is an acceptable translation. Of course, the item would then need to be given to an Italian-speaking sample and the data analyzed (e.g., to assess its validity) in order to ensure that it actually is a good item.[20]

■ FIGURE 7.6

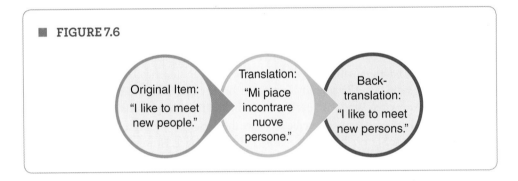

exhaustive list of all selection procedures that are available but instead focuses on the ones that are most commonly used. Throughout this section, you will want to refer to the summary of selection procedures in Table 7.3.

Interviews

The interview is the most commonly used selection procedure (see Figure 7.7). In fact, it is hard to imagine an employer not using some type of interview before hiring an employee. Due to the popularity of interviews and their long history, there is a large body of research examining the effectiveness of interviews in selection. Furthermore, there are a number of recommended best practices for enhancing the validity of *selection interviews*. We focus on the two main types of selection interviews, unstructured and structured interviews, their validity, and how to use them most effectively to make hiring decisions.

Unstructured Interviews

The most common type of selection interview, and perhaps the one that has been used for hiring employees through the ages, is the *unstructured interview,* in which the interviewer (e.g., a hiring manager or supervisor) has a conversation with the job applicant. There is no fixed

Selection interview
A conversation or discussion between a job applicant and an organizational representative used to screen job applicants

Unstructured interview When the interviewer has a conversation with a job applicant with no fixed protocol for each applicant

TABLE 7.3   A Summary of Selection Procedures, Their Validity, and Practical Considerations for Their Use

SELECTION PROCEDURE	VALIDITY (AVERAGE CORRELATION WITH JOB PERFORMANCE)	APPLICANT REACTIONS[21] MOST PREFERRED = *** PREFERRED = ** LEAST PREFERRED = *	PRACTICAL CONSIDERATIONS FOR USING THEM
Structured Interviews	Large (.44–.51)[22]	***	Behavioral interviews ("What have you done in the past?") may predict job performance slightly better than situational interviews ("What would you do in this situation?").[23]
Unstructured Interviews	Medium (.33–.38)[24]	***	The ability of unstructured interviews to predict job performance may vary because of inconsistency across applicants and interviewer biases.
Personality Tests	Small (.11–.25)[25]	**	Although personality tests have been criticized for having low validity, they are low-cost assessments with low adverse impact. Validity can be enhanced by telling the applicant to think about how they are "at work" when responding.
Integrity Tests	Medium (.26–.47)[26]	*	Solid predictors of counterproductive work behavior. Inexpensive, with fairly low adverse impact.
General Cognitive Ability	Large (.51)[27]	**	One of the most consistently valid predictors of job performance. Low cost. However, they can have adverse impact against certain ethnic groups.
Specific Cognitive Abilities (e.g., clerical ability, mechanical ability)	Varies	**	Validity varies by the specific type of cognitive ability assessed. Certain cognitive ability tests may have adverse impact (e.g., mechanical ability and women).
Work Samples	Large (.54)[28]	***	Work samples are highly correlated with job performance and preferred by applicants. Due to high administrative costs, work samples may be administered as a final hurdle to a smaller group of finalists rather than to all applicants.
Situational Judgment Tests (SJTs)	Small to Medium (.19–.43)[29]	***	Solid validity and appealing to applicants.
Assessment Centers	Medium (.45)[30]	***	Work samples are often used to assess manager candidates for promotion. Although they are expensive to administer, they may serve not only as a predictor of job performance but as a training and development tool as well.
Biographical Data	Medium to Large (.37–.52)[31]	**	Practical method for predicting job performance for large numbers of applicants. Primary costs are in the initial research and development for a particular company or industry.

Note: Correlations between .10 and .29 are considered small compared to correlations between .30 and .49, which are considered medium, and those between .50 and above, which are considered large.

■ **FIGURE 7.7**   Percentage of Organizations Using Different Selection Methods to Hire for Individual Contributor Positions

A 2016 SHRM survey found that structured interviews were the most frequently used selection technique for nonmanagement/individual contributor positions.

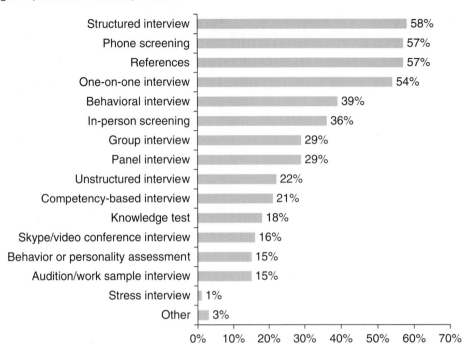

Selection Method	Percentage
Structured interview	58%
Phone screening	57%
References	57%
One-on-one interview	54%
Behavioral interview	39%
In-person screening	36%
Group interview	29%
Panel interview	29%
Unstructured interview	22%
Competency-based interview	21%
Knowledge test	18%
Skype/video conference interview	16%
Behavior or personality assessment	15%
Audition/work sample interview	15%
Stress interview	1%
Other	3%

Interviews are the most commonly used selection procedure, and there is a long history of research on how to make them most effective. Perhaps the most important finding of this research is that increasing the structure of the interview—such as asking all candidates the same job-related questions—can significantly increase the validity of the interview in predicting job performance.

protocol or set of questions for each applicant. In fact, different applicants are likely to be asked different questions, and the questions may not necessarily be particularly job related. Not surprisingly—and despite the confidence that some interviewers have in their own ability to choose the best job applicant based on their instincts or "gut reactions"—the unstructured interview has relatively low validity in terms of predicting job performance. This is especially true to the extent that the unstructured interview does not focus on job-related questions. Moreover, because different job applicants may be asked different questions, it is hard to compare the responses of different applicants, and there is a definite risk of applicants being treated unfairly or introducing interviewer biases, even if they are unintentional or unconscious. For these reasons, the unstructured interview has largely fallen out of favor regarding selection, at least in terms of being the primary basis for hiring decisions.

That said, unstructured interviews are likely to continue to be part of most hiring decisions, and this is not necessarily a bad thing as long as they are used wisely. It is hard to imagine a situation in which a hiring manager or supervisor would not want to have the opportunity to have a casual conversation with a job applicant prior to hiring them. For an example of how this might work, once the most qualified job applicants are identified through other selection methods, a supervisor may then decide to interview the top candidates via an unstructured interview. Furthermore,

TABLE 7.4 Structured Interview Questions With Rating Scales

You and a coworker are collaborating on a project that is due in 10 days. You are beginning to fall behind because your coworker is not working quickly enough. How would you handle this?

Rating scale:

1—Candidate either ignores the issue completely or handles it in way that makes things worse (e.g., confronts the worker in a negative way).

2

3—Candidate recognizes the problem, but they develop a suboptimal solution, such as telling their boss.

4

5—Candidate develops a constructive solution, such as speaking with the worker to find out what may be wrong, what he or she themselves may be doing to slow things down, or what they can do to help develop a solution.

Tell us about a time when you were dealing with a difficult customer. How did you handle the situation?

1—Candidate describes that they did something to make the situation worse, such as ignoring the customer or being rude back.

2

3—Candidate chooses a suboptimal solution such as passing the customer on to their supervisor.

4

5—Candidate worked with the customer to figure out what the problem is and to come up with a mutually acceptable solution.

unstructured interviews may be helpful to sell the applicant on the job, to give the applicant a realistic job preview (see Chapter 6), and to make an impression regarding the specific job and the organization.[32] Interviewers also give applicants an opportunity to ask questions about the organization, the job, and coworkers to help them decide if the job seems like a good fit. Although the research has shown that unstructured interviews have lower validity than structured interviews, unstructured interviews are not without their merits, including being a good way to assess interpersonal skills and some personality traits. In fact, it has been argued that unstructured interviews are simply measuring different characteristics than structured interviews, which are much more focused on job-related behaviors and skills.[33]

Structured Interviews

As mentioned earlier, the unstructured interview has been in use for many decades. However, research on unstructured interviews eventually caused selection researchers to conclude that the interview was generally not a valid selection procedure.[34] As a result, HR researchers and practitioners began to think of a different approach to selection interviewing in which all job applicants are asked the same, job-related questions. This approach, known as the ***structured interview,*** has been found to have good predictive validity in making hiring decisions (see Table 7.4). Figure 7.7 compares the frequency of use of various kinds of interviews and other assessment techniques.

There are two types of structured interviews: the situational interview and the behavioral interview. In the ***situational interview,*** job applicants are asked what they would do in a hypothetical work-related situation. For example, applicants for a supervisory role might be asked, "What would you do if you had an employee whose performance suddenly decreased? How would you handle the situation?"

In contrast, in the ***behavioral interview,*** applicants are asked how they handled a work-related situation in the past. As we noted in our opening case, Google is a leader in the selection space, and behavioral interviews are part of its selection procedures.[35] For the supervisor position, applicants might be asked, "What have you done when you had an employee whose performance suddenly decreased? How did you handle the situation?"

Structured interview An interview in which all job applicants are asked the same, job-related questions

Situational interview A type of structured interview in which job applicants are asked what they would do in a hypothetical work-related situation

Behavioral interview A type of structured selection interview that uses questions about how applicants handled a work-related situation in the past

In other words, the situational interview asks what an applicant would do, whereas the behavioral interview asks an applicant what they have actually done in the past. Both the situational and behavioral interview formats have good validity, and each approach could be appropriate depending on the particular circumstances. For instance, the situational interview might be more appropriate when job applicants have little work experience and thus could not be expected to answer behavioral interview questions. Moreover, research has suggested that these two types of structured interviews may each be assessing slightly different things: The situational interview appears to measure cognitive ability and job knowledge, whereas the behavioral interview measures personality variables and (not surprisingly) job experience.[36] In the Manager's Toolbox, we give some advice on how to use structured interviews to make good hiring decisions.

Finally, here are a few points about using interviews for selection. First, online interviews using video are becoming increasingly common. However, research has suggested that

---

MANAGER'S TOOLBOX

Best Practices: How to Add More Interview Structure

The basic premise of the structured interview is that adding greater structure helps increase the validity of the interview in making hiring decisions. "Structure" means asking the same questions of all interviewees. But what else is meant by "structure"? We describe a number of best practices identified in the research to make selection interviews more structured and thus more likely to lead to good hiring decisions.

1. *Develop job-related questions that are asked to all applicants.* This is one of the most important ways to increase interview validity. Consider what behaviors are performed on the job and what KSAOs are needed to perform them. These behaviors and skills can be derived from a job analysis or competency model. Further, an examination of critical incidents faced by employees on the job can help in the development of interview questions.

2. *Treat all interviewees consistently.* To the extent that all job candidates are interviewed under the same conditions—for example, in the same place and by the same interviewers—better information can be gained to compare job applicants.

3. *Train interviewers.* Train interviewers on how to interview applicants, and be sure that all interviewers use the same procedures when interviewing and evaluating job candidates. Note that interviews are susceptible to the same rating errors as performance appraisals such as the halo error and contrast error (discussed in Chapter 9), and thus rating errors are often included as part of their training. They can also be trained in the use of rating scales so that they are consistent in their ratings. Also, providing normative feedback to interviewers about how their ratings compare to those of other interviewers can reduce rating differences between interviewers and improve interview reliability.

4. *Have more than one interviewer interview each applicant.* Where possible, have two or more people interview each job candidate to check for consistency in interviewers. (Remember from our opening case that Google uses four interviews.) This also allows interviewers to discuss their ratings of candidates, a process that allows the observations of one interviewer to compensate for an issue that was missed by another interviewer.

5. *Have interviewers take notes.* This allows interviewers to check back as they compare different candidates, and it allows interviewers to compare their ratings with each other.

6. *Develop rating scales for each interview question.* Providing rating scales can be one of the most important ways to increase the validity of interviews. (Refer to Table 7.3, which shows rating scale examples for structured interview questions.) Robust rating scales also provide examples of poor, average, and excellent responses, such that interviewers have a consistent framework for rating job candidates and can compare their ratings with each other more effectively. Rating scales are typically developed with the assistance of SMEs. And if more than one interviewer is used (see item 4), the ratings from each interviewer can be averaged together, and any discrepancies among the interviewer ratings can be discussed.[37]

SPOTLIGHT ON HR FOR SMALL AND MEDIUM-SIZED BUSINESSES
Hiring in Smaller Organizations

We recommend that all organizations, regardless of their size, leverage the hiring procedure used by nearly all employers: the selection interview.

Any employer can take advantage of the benefits of incorporating a job-related, structured interview into its hiring process. As noted elsewhere, this includes:

- basing the interview questions on the job tasks and the KSAOs or competencies needed to carry out the tasks,

- asking all applicants the same job-related questions,

- using more than one interviewer where possible, and

- using the same criteria for rating applicants' responses.

In short, the structured interview is a well-established best practice for increasing the odds of making good hiring decisions and reducing interviewer bias.

interviewer ratings may be lower in technology-mediated interviews and that applicant reactions to the process may be lower for interviews that are not done in person.[38] Second, in recent years, the "group interview," in which multiple candidates are interviewed at one time, has seen increased use by organizations. Little empirical research on the validity of this approach has emerged in the literature, and we suggest caution in terms of having multiple interviewees compete within the same interview unless such competition is part of the job. At the same time, a recent study suggests that group interviews have acceptable applicant reactions except for applicants with certain personality traits (e.g., some introverts).[39] Finally, research suggests that first impressions in the interview matter to structured interview outcomes (i.e., interviewer ratings). The implications of this finding are only beginning to be understood.[40]

Personality Tests

Since the early 1990s, there has been a growing interest in personality tests for use in selection, with 62% of employers recently reporting that they use personality tests in hiring.[41] Here we discuss the reasons for this interest among employers in using personality to hire workers.

Five Factor Model (FFM) or the "Big Five"

The shift in interest in using personality tests in selection is partly due to a landmark meta-analysis conducted in 1991 by Murray Barrick and Michael Mount that examined the use of tests focused on the ***Five Factor Model (FFM)*** ("Big Five") personality typology, which found that personality is related to a number of work performance dimensions. The Big Five is a typology of normal adult personality.

The five dimensions are best remembered by the acronym *OCEAN*. They are: Openness to Experience, Conscientiousness, Extraversion, Agreeableness, and Neuroticism. Openness to experience has to do with a person's inquisitiveness and willingness to learn new things and was found to be related to employees' performance in training programs. Conscientiousness includes traits such as dependability and achievement orientation and was found to relate to job performance across most jobs. Extraversion, which includes traits such as sociability, was related to jobs such as sales and management. Agreeableness is the degree to which the person is kind, sensitive, and pays attention to others' feelings. Finally, Neuroticism (or its opposite, emotional stability) relates to anxiety and worry.[42] Table 7.5 shows sample items for each of the Big Five dimensions. There are numerous specific tests of the Big Five available.[43]

Interest in the use of personality inventories in selection has grown because most are relatively easy, quick, and inexpensive to administer, and they have generally been found to have

Five Factor Model (FFM)
A model of normal adult personality that includes the dimensions of Openness to Experience, Conscientiousness, Extraversion, Agreeableness, and Neuroticism

TABLE 7.5   Example of Big Five Items

(1–5 response scale, from "very inaccurate" to "very accurate"; the person would respond about how they perceive themselves to be)[44]

Openness to Experience	Conscientiousness	Extraversion
Have a rich vocabulary.	Am always prepared.	Am the life of the party.
Have a vivid imagination.	Pay attention to details.	Feel comfortable around people.
Have excellent ideas.	Get chores done right away.	Start conversations.
Am quick to understand things.	Like order.	Talk to a lot of different people at parties.
Use difficult words.	Follow a schedule.	Don't mind being the center of attention.
Spend time reflecting on things.	Am exacting in my work.	
Am full of ideas.		

Agreeableness	Neuroticism	
Am interested in people.	Get stressed out easily.	
Sympathize with others' feelings.	Worry about things.	
Have a soft heart.	Am easily disturbed.	
Take time out for others.	Get upset easily.	
Feel others' emotions.	Change my mood a lot.	
Make people feel at ease.	Have frequent mood swings.	
	Get irritated easily.	
	Often feel blue.	

Some personality variables can be useful for predicting job performance in certain specific jobs. For example, proactive personality has been shown to predict the job performance of real estate agents over and above conscientiousness and extraversion.

lower adverse impact than other selection tests such as cognitive ability tests (i.e., they are less likely to have a negative impact on an organization's diversity). However, their validity is not as high as some other selection procedures such as structured interviews.[45] Further, note that for legal reasons, personality tests developed to make clinical diagnoses—that is, those not focused on normal adult personality—should not be used for hiring except under very specific, limited circumstances.

In addition, some worry about the possibility of applicants faking on personality inventories—that is, applicants not providing honest answers about how they are but providing the responses that they believe an employer wants. However, some researchers suggest that personality tests are likely valid in spite of some faking activities on the part of applicants. Some researchers even suggest that faking behaviors can be positive: Applicants who infer what responses are expected of them may be demonstrating that they understand what would be required of them on the job. And other researchers say that the term *faking* is actually a misnomer, and it may simply reflect an applicant's relatively normal—and benign—tendency to want to show themselves in the best light so that they can get a job.[46]

Finally, it is important to know that the Big Five is only one approach to measuring job-related personality variables for use in selection. Other personality variables that have been found to be useful in selection include proactive personality; proactive people tend to recognize and act on opportunities at work. Research has shown, for instance, that proactive personality is a good predictor of performance of real estate agents, over and above conscientiousness and extraversion.[47]

Another personality variable that has gained research attention as a selection procedure is adaptability, which has to do with a person's ability to adjust to new situations. Dimensions of adaptability include cultural, interpersonal, and learning adaptability.[48] Although the use of adaptability in selection research is still early, the interest in this personality variable for selection is expected to grow given the dynamic nature of work today.

Integrity Tests

At one time, employers routinely used polygraph tests (lie detectors) to screen out job applicants who might steal or exhibit other types of counterproductive or antisocial behaviors while at work (e.g., using drugs at work; fighting with coworkers). However, because these polygraph tests were found to have a high rate of false positives (i.e., people who were a low risk to the company but failed the test), the use of polygraph tests in selection was generally outlawed in the 1980s except for very limited circumstances, such as for certain job applicants in security service firms and pharmaceutical manufacturers.[49] Thus, to help employers screen out applicants who are at the highest risk of exhibiting these negative behaviors on the job, the use of self-report *integrity tests* has grown significantly.

Integrity test A test specifically developed to assess applicants' tendency toward counterproductive and antisocial behavior

There are two primary types of integrity test formats: personality-based integrity tests and overt integrity tests. Table 7.6 presents examples of personality-based and overt integrity tests. Personality-based integrity tests are more subtle in their wording, and the wording is such that the "correct answer" may not be obvious to test takers. Most personality-based integrity tests are considered to be a function of conscientiousness, neuroticism, and agreeableness, plus an additional personality dimension referred to as "honesty-humility."[50] Overt integrity tests, in contrast, ask the test taker to give their opinions about negative behaviors at work (e.g., theft), whether such behaviors are acceptable, and whether they have engaged in these behaviors themselves.

Integrity tests might appear at first to be of little use to employers; for example, the overt items may seem overly simplistic at first glance and easily faked. However, there have been a number of meta-analyses on the topic of integrity tests, and the findings are that these tests correlate .47 with a number of negative work behaviors such as violence and theft.[51] Although there is still some difference of opinion among testing experts on just how valid these tests are for predicting performance, on balance, the research shows that integrity tests demonstrate sufficient validity, can pass legal muster, and provide value to employers trying to screen out job applicants who pose a risk to the organization and employees.[52] Moreover, integrity tests seem to exhibit relatively low adverse impact, and they seem to be valid in a number of cultural settings.[53] Integrity

TABLE 7.6   Examples of Overt and Personality-Based Integrity Test Items

SAMPLE INTEGRITY TEST ITEMS	
OVERT INTEGRITY TEST ITEMS	**PERSONALITY-BASED (COVERT) INTEGRITY TEST ITEMS**
I have used illegal drugs at work.	It's OK to make some mistakes when you work quickly.
It's OK to hit a coworker if they yell at you.	You need to take risks sometimes if you want to get the job done.
I have stolen money from my employer.	I am always seeking excitement and thrills in my life.
If a coworker is rude to me, I would do something to his car.	I don't get along with other people because I always stand up for my rights.

tests are perhaps best considered in combination with other selection procedures such as cognitive ability tests and interviews, providing a screen for job applicants who are most likely to be difficult employees at work.

Cognitive Ability Tests

Cognitive ability tests have a long history in personnel selection, going back into the early 20th century. Here we define a ***cognitive ability test*** as an assessment of the ability to "perceive, process, evaluate, compare, create, understand, manipulate, or generally think about information and ideas."[54] On the positive side, cognitive ability tests have been demonstrated to be one of the best predictors of job performance across a range of job types, with a correlation with job performance as high as .51.[55] This, combined with their relatively low cost, leads to their having high utility.

On the negative side, cognitive ability tests are prone to lead to adverse impact, with the mean score of certain groups (e.g., Blacks, Hispanics) being significantly lower than the mean score of other groups (e.g., Whites, Asians). (Note, of course, that there is still substantial overlap between the scores of these different subgroups, even if there are differences in the *mean* score for each group.) For reasons of adverse impact alone, many employers prefer to avoid the use of cognitive ability tests, both for reasons of diversity and for the possibility of legal challenges.[56] In fact, many HR researchers attribute increased interest in personality tests we discussed earlier as partly due to the fact that personality tests have relatively low adverse impact compared to cognitive ability tests.

There are a few different types of cognitive ability tests used by employers. First are tests of general cognitive ability, sometimes referred to as "*g*" by psychologists. One theory as to why tests of general cognitive ability are such good predictors of job performance (a correlation of .51 according to some meta-analyses) is that cognitive ability is related to knowledge acquisition skills. Thus, cognitive ability helps workers gain important job skills both during training and on the job. Further, this may explain why cognitive ability is thought to be such a good predictor for cognitively complex jobs.[57] One test of general cognitive ability that has a long history in personnel selection is the Wonderlic Personnel Test. The Wonderlic is a 50-item, 12-minute test that includes items such as math reasoning and verbal tasks. Available in many languages, the Wonderlic was first developed in the 1930s and has amassed a large database, including norms—that is, the scores associated with different occupations.[58] For example, Subway requires that prospective Subway franchisees take and get a certain score on the Wonderlic Personnel Test.[59]

In addition to tests of general cognitive ability, there are tests of specific cognitive abilities, such as tests of mechanical ability and clerical ability, which are designed for use with specific job types in which these abilities have been found to be important through a job analysis. The adverse impact issue with these tests of specific cognitive abilities varies by the type of test. For example, tests of mechanical ability have been found to have some adverse impact against women.[60]

Finally, tests of ***emotional intelligence (EI)*** have recently gained attention as predictors of job performance. Very broadly, EI is defined as one's ability to recognize and appraise emotions in oneself and others and behave accordingly.[61] Some researchers define EI primarily in terms of being a personality variable, although other researchers describe it as a cognitive ability that is focused on social skills. Accordingly, some tests of EI focus more on cognitive ability, whereas others focus more on personality traits. Given the interest in EI for making selection decisions, there have been numerous studies on EI, including meta-analyses, to better understand the role of EI in selection. Not surprisingly, research has found that EI tests are better predictors of job performance when jobs are high in emotional labor. Further, research suggests that certain types of EI tests do not predict job performance over and above traditional tests like personality and cognitive ability; in other words, this research suggests that the concept of EI is nothing new. Although more research is needed to understand definitively what different EI tests are actually

Cognitive ability test
A measure of the ability to perceive, process, evaluate, compare, create, understand, manipulate, or generally think about information and ideas

Emotional intelligence (EI) One's ability to recognize and appraise emotions in oneself and others and behave accordingly

SPOTLIGHT ON DATA AND ANALYTICS

Gamification of Personnel Selection Procedures

©iStock.com/Warchi

Gamification, or the transformation of an ordinary activity into a game-like activity to increase engagement, motivation, and competition, including scoring, has taken hold in a variety of fields from advertising to e-learning. Relevant to the present chapter, gamification of personnel selection procedures is now drawing increased interest from employers. For example, conventional hiring procedures might require job applicants to take

tests of cognitive ability or personality. In contrast, in gamified selection procedures, applicants might participate in a game activity to assess factors such as cognitive processing speed or risk tolerance. The idea is that such gamified assessments could attract job applicants who might not otherwise take conventional selection tests.

Some argue that gamified assessments offer other advantages such as longer—and thus more reliable—assessments. And because job applicants are engaged in the "flow" of a gamified assessment, they may be less likely to give dishonest or socially desirable responses. However, gamification of selection procedures is still fairly new, and more research is needed. For example, the validity of gamified assessments for predicting job performance relative to traditional selection tests is still relatively unknown. Further, research is needed with regard to how some groups of applicants (e.g., older applicants) might perceive gamified assessments. Certainly, employers considering the use of gamified assessments should conduct their own research to assess their value.[62]

measuring and their added value in selection decisions, some researchers point out that tests of EI may be a streamlined way for employers to predict job performance without using lengthy, time-consuming batteries of tests of personality and cognitive ability.[63]

Work Samples, Situational Judgment Tests (SJTs), and Assessment Centers

So far, we have discussed predictors that are "signs" of how a person would perform on the job—things like interviews and tests. However, another option is to consider sampling more directly a person's ability to do the job. In this section, we describe three different "families" of selection procedures that directly sample a person's potential job performance and hence their fit for the job. These three selection procedures are work samples, assessment centers, and situational judgment tests (SJTs).

Work Samples

A *work sample* is what the name implies: a sample or example of the work produced by an applicant. Suppose an organization needs to hire a computer programmer. The company has quite a few options for selection procedures, such as a cognitive test, interview, and of course a review of applicants' work history by means of applicants' résumés. In fact, the organization's competency model suggests that these methods can all be justified as measures of the competencies needed for this job. However, the hiring manager realizes that, although each of these methods provides a good idea of the likelihood of a person's success, none of them directly samples what the person

Work sample A sample or example of the work produced by a job applicant

Tests and an interview can tell you a lot about a job candidate's skills as a computer programmer. In addition, a work sample can indicate how well a person can actually perform many of the core job tasks. For instance, Google uses coding exercises as part of its selection procedures when hiring engineers.[65]

does on the job. To address this, the hiring manager decides to meet with each applicant and give them a short coding task to see how well they do. The hiring manager then has SMEs (current programmers) evaluate how well the applicants perform on the coding task.

As another example, JetBlue Airways used a job analysis to identify the key skills employees in its call center needed, and once it identified the desired KSAOs, it developed a call simulation test to use in the hiring process. With the use of this selection procedure, turnover decreased by 25%.[64]

This example of seeing how well an applicant performs the work tasks required on the job is the essence of a work sample. As you might guess, work samples have good validity. The research shows that they are correlated about .54 with work performance. In addition, they clearly have good content validity because they are an actual sample of the job. And applicants tend to like work samples, seeing them as very fair.[66] However, one drawback of work samples is that they are more expensive than other methods, usually requiring that one person at a time go through the assessment. Then applicants' performance on the work sample must usually be evaluated by trained SMEs. Given the cost of work samples—in terms of their individual administration and scoring—they are usually placed at the end of a series of cheaper selection hurdles. In a previous example, a company might decide to give cheaper tests and assessments to the original pool of qualified computer programmer applicants and then give interviews and work samples to the smaller group of top candidates.

Situational Judgment Tests (SJTs)

Situational judgment tests (SJTs) A test that captures some of the realism of work sample tests, but in a format (e.g., multiple-choice) that can be used more easily with large numbers of applicants

The value of work samples in terms of their validity and attractiveness to applicants led HR researchers to consider cheaper alternatives. This is where the concept of ***situational judgment tests***, or ***SJTs***, comes into play. SJTs are sometimes referred to as "low-fidelity simulations." Specifically, SJTs capture some of the realism of work sample tests, but in a format that can be used more easily with large numbers of applicants. An SJT might present the applicant with a scenario, in either paper or video format, and then ask the respondent to choose a series of alternatives. As an example of an SJT item, applicants for a retail job might be given a scenario in which they are working with one customer to help them choose the best product when another customer interrupts them. They would then be asked how they would handle the situation. Note that while many SJTs use a written, multiple-choice format, others ask candidates to choose which video response seems most appropriate, and others use an open-ended format that must be scored later.[67] Additional examples of SJT items are given in Table 7.7. Because of their relatively low administration costs, SJTs have gained popularity. In fact, you may have taken an SJT when you applied for a job. In addition, they have solid validity, with correlations with job performance of .19 to .43. For instance, one SJT focused on medical school applicants' predicted work performance years later.[68]

Assessment Centers

Assessment center A specific type of work sample, often used for manager selection

So far, we have described work-sample types of assessments that can be used for a large number of job types. In addition, a specific type of work sample known as the ***assessment center*** was developed to assess management skills. Assessment centers were first pioneered in U.S. businesses in the 1960s at AT&T, and their popularity has grown considerably over the years as a means of promoting people into management positions. Note that an assessment center is not an actual place maintained by the company. Rather, center assessments are typically carried out over a series of days at a remote site provided by the organization, such as a hotel.

TABLE 7.7   Situational Judgment Test (SJT) Items for a Retail Clothing Job

You are helping a customer choose a tie. Another customer approaches you and interrupts your conversation. What would be the best thing to do?

a. Ignore the customer who interrupted you.

b. Tell the customer who interrupted you that you are busy and that he should not interrupt a conversation.

c. Kindly tell the second person that you would be glad to help him in a few minutes.

d. Explain to the first customer that you have given him all the time you can and you need to help others.

You have a friend who admires the clothing in the store where you work. She tells you that, although she doesn't have much money, she would really like to have a blouse from the store. Which of the following would be the best thing for you to do?

a. Tell your friend when you see that there is a sale on the kind of blouse she likes.

b. Ask your boss if there are any extra blouses in the store so you can give one to your friend.

c. Take one of the blouses and give it to your friend.

A customer comes in to return a piece of clothing that is obviously defective. He is very angry about the failure of the item. Which of the following would be the best thing to do?

a. Tell the customer that this is not your fault personally, and so he should not be mean to you.

b. Tell the customer that you can replace the item and also give him a free gift card to make up for the inconvenience.

c. Try to calm down the customer by asking him to explain what happened and then work with him to find a solution.

A common type of assessment center exercise includes the role play, in which candidates might be asked to handle a situation with an actor or one of the assessors. For example, the candidate might be told that they will need to interact with an employee whose performance has declined in recent months, getting to the bottom of what the problem is and developing a solution. The actor would be trained to interact with the candidate in a way that reflects reality. Another common assessment center exercise is the in-basket or in-box, in which a candidate is told to provide responses to a series of e-mails that they have received that morning. They would be asked to explain how they handled each e-mail. Generally, assessment center exercises are evaluated by at least two raters, typically expert managers or trained psychologists.

Not surprisingly, assessment centers are good predictors, correlating .37 to .45 with job performance.[69] As with other work samples, they provide good content validity because they clearly sample the job domain. And not only can they be used to make promotion decisions, they are also good for training and development purposes, so that management candidates can see their strengths and weaknesses and determine where further development is needed. On the other hand, assessment centers are expensive, as they require the development of detailed, realistic materials and the use of teams of trained experts, often from outside of the organization, as assessors. For this reason, like work samples, assessment centers are typically not given to very large numbers of candidates but might be administered to smaller pools of finalists in the selection process.[70]

Biographical Data and Related Data Collection Methods

We have covered a lot of different selection methods and instruments up to this point. In addition, employers can also collect useful data for screening job applicants from questions about their backgrounds.

Doug Reynolds, PhD, is executive vice president at Development Dimensions International, where he directs the product development and technology functions. His department develops and implements software-based assessment centers, testing, and learning products for Fortune 500 companies. His consulting work focuses on the implementation of assessments in organizations, and he publishes on topics related to the intersection of I-O psychology and technology. He is a past president of the Society for Industrial and Organizational Psychology (2012–2013).[71]

Biographical data (biodata) Information about a job applicant based on their personal history that can be used to make selection decisions

Training and Experience Forms

One of the most common of these are training and experience (T&E) forms, which ask applicants about their work-related education, training, and experience. Applicants' training and experience are then tabulated and scored based on an existing rubric determined through a job analysis and input from SMEs. In this sense, T&E forms can be seen as another flavor of structured résumés (see what follows), at least from the viewpoint of applicants. T&E forms have a long history in personnel selection, especially for government jobs. There is considerable variability in their validity in predicting job performance, ranging from a correlation between T&E scores and performance as low as .11 up to .45.[72]

Biodata

Employers can also use **biographical data (biodata)** as a predictor of job performance, with the assumption that past behavior—whether at work or perhaps even outside of work—is the best predictor of future behavior. For instance, a retail employer might be concerned that the high turnover rate for certain jobs is causing serious financial losses for the company. If only they could get their employees to stay for at least 6 months, the costs invested in training them would be worthwhile. For this reason, they may ask applicants about how many jobs they have held in the last 3 years and then examine the relationship between the number of jobs a person has held and how long they remain on the job. Through this research, the company discovers that people who have held more than four jobs in the last 3 years are likely to quit in fewer than 6 months. In other words, employers find that this question allows them to determine which applicants are the best risk for staying with the organization.

In addition, biodata items could focus on nonwork experiences as predictors of work performance. As an early example of the use of biodata, in World War II, it was found that one item—whether an applicant for flight school played with model airplanes when growing up—was a good predictor of flight training performance. The idea was that an applicant who played with model airplanes was interested in flying and was thus a good bet for succeeding in flight school. Moving to recent times, a sports equipment retailer might find, through research, that people who participated in a range of different sports during their school years are the best at helping customers. This might be because these applicants are knowledgeable about a range of different sports and sports equipment, allowing them to help customers make good decisions in their purchases. Thus, employers can research a number of different types of background data that they suspect will predict job performance, choosing those that stand out as the best predictors in their research.[73] The key is for employers not to ask questions that might be unfair or have adverse impact, such as what part of town they live in. In addition, biodata items have solid validity, correlated about .35 with job performance.[74]

Résumés

Perhaps the most commonly used selection screening method is the résumé, in which job applicants describe their job-relevant education and work experience. The résumé is often used as a first-hurdle screening method, allowing a hiring manager, supervisor, or HR recruiter to narrow down the applicant pool to a more manageable size. Given the ubiquitous nature of the résumé, one might think that it is well researched and has good validity. However, this is not necessarily the case. One of the biggest problems with résumés is that there is not a single format to use, in terms of the types of education and experience reported, the way the education and experience are described, or even the font used. And some applicants are better at putting together a résumé than others. For this reason, résumés from various applicants are difficult to compare, limiting their value as a screening device. In addition, because of the sheer volume of résumés received by organizations, as well as their length and the time needed to read them, they may overwhelm the recruiter due to time and cognitive overload. This may result in less-than-satisfactory decisions due to cognitive biases (often an issue with decisions made under time pressure) as recruiters may need to quickly sort through hundreds of résumés in a short period of time.[75]

With these concerns, why do résumés remain popular? We see two reasons. First is that résumés are now an expected, customary part of many job application processes. Second, some applicants may like the résumé. Applicants may perceive résumés as giving them a bit of control and an opportunity to show what they know—even if it is difficult for applicants to guess what it is that may strike the fancy of the recruiter.[76] The good news is that there is an increasing interest in using structured résumés, in which applicants must complete a résumé using a structure determined by the employer and based on a job analysis. Structured résumés can be easier for recruiters to scan. Further, algorithms can now "read" these résumés to rank applicants based on job requirements—and avoid some cognitive biases of overwhelmed recruiters.

HR IN ACTION
Leveraging Résumés for Job Applications

One of the most common selection tools is the résumé. We have discussed employers' challenges of using résumés to screen job applicants and that applicants have a generally positive reaction to the use of résumés in hiring. On the other hand, many applicants experience some frustration with this selection procedure, sending out dozens or even hundreds of résumés with little success—and often with no response from employers.

What can applicants do to get better results from the submission of their résumés?

- First, be aware that résumés are often scanned electronically before a person even sees them. For this reason, it is important that the résumé include important keywords that match the job ad.

- Second, don't be shy about tailoring a résumé to a specific job application. Another way to think of this is to say that one résumé is probably not sufficient for the range of jobs a person might apply to.

- Third, consider the importance of a meaningful cover letter—one that is not too generic or that simply repeats what is already in the résumé.

Finally, try not to forget the personal touch—reaching out to an individual in the organization can often get you further than just sending in a résumé.[77]

References and Background Checks

Another screening device used by a number of employers is references from past employers, typically obtained through letters of reference. The idea behind references is that the best predictor of future behavior is past behavior, and knowing how a person behaved in previous employment situations can give some idea about their future behavior. Although the logic here is generally sound, obtaining robust data about an applicant in this way is not without its challenges. First, applicants will, logically, tend to provide only the names of people who they know will give a positive recommendation. Second, many employers have policies that only allow them to say whether a person worked for them and will not provide an assessment of the quality of that person's work. These two factors alone limit the amount of information that can typically be obtained through references. On the other hand, such references continue to be used by employers to screen out applicants who would be a high risk either to coworkers or to the company.[78]

Related to this, many employers, especially those hiring for high-security jobs (e.g., police officer, jobs working with children), may require some sort of background check (e.g., through legal databases) to ensure that the applicant is not a risk to others.[79] However, the use of criminal background checks is beginning to decline for many jobs and in certain U.S. states due to "ban the box" laws, described in Chapter 4. These laws continue to evolve and vary by state and municipality, but "ban the box" laws generally prohibit questions about past criminal convictions during the application process. In 2016, companies such as American Airlines, Starbucks, and Xerox were among many organizations pledging to voluntarily remove the box from their applications. Google banned the box in 2011, and Unilever claims to be one of the first companies to do so. Note that employers might still do background checks, including asking about convictions after a job has been offered. Rather, the goal is to avoid disqualifying an otherwise qualified applicant at the outset of the selection process.[80]

Physical Ability Tests

Physical ability tests are often used for physically demanding jobs such as police officer. There are generally two approaches to physical abilities testing. The first is like a standard work sample test, sampling the physical requirements. For example, a city might determine through a job analysis that a police officer's job requires them to run 50 yards in 8 seconds or to be able to climb a 6-foot fence. Thus, the physical ability test would include running 50 meters in 8 seconds or less and a portion that includes climbing a fence. The second approach to such physical abilities tests is to determine the various types of strength required for the job (e.g., hand strength, arm strength) and to develop tests that measure these physical abilities. For example, hand strength might be measured by the ability to squeeze a hand grip 10 times within 15 seconds. One concern with these physical abilities tests is that they can have adverse impact against women, and employers need to ensure that the abilities measures are job related (e.g., based on a job analysis, correlated with job performance) to ensure their legal defensibility. For example, recently the City of Chicago was successfully sued, and required to pay millions of dollars, for including a test of strength that was not considered to be job related and had adverse impact against women.[81] In addition, some organizations provide information or even practice sessions for job applicants to reduce adverse impact; of course, all applicants (i.e., not just women) would need to be provided with the opportunity to participate in these practice sessions. Note that the use of physical requirements such as height has generally been discontinued as these may have adverse impact against some ethnic groups and against women, while not tapping into whether applicants can actually do the job.[82]

©iStock.com/shaunl

Physical ability tests are often used as part of the selection procedure for physically demanding jobs such as police officer or firefighter. Which physical abilities do you think are especially important for most law enforcement jobs or firefighting? Are tests for these physical abilities likely to have adverse impact?

LO 7.5 Recognize and explain key analytical, legal, ethical, and global issues associated with personnel selection.

Emerging Issues in Selection

Social media are often used by employers in the recruitment process. In addition, there has been some interest in using applicant information obtained from social media to make hiring decisions as well. However, we recommend against employers using such information for making hiring decisions for a number of reasons. First, the information provided across different applicants is not consistent; that is, different applicants provide different types of information and different amounts of information, such that comparing different applicants to make a hiring decision would not be fair. In addition, research has shown that the information provided by social networking sites may not lead to good decisions. In one study, researchers found that recruiters' ratings of students' Facebook pages was not predictive of later work performance and that decisions made on the basis of this information favored White and female applicants, suggesting that such decisions would have systematic biases.[83] Of course, even though it is inadvisable for employers to use information from social networking sites, some may do so, and thus we suggest that job applicants remain cautious about what they post about themselves on these sites.

In addition, there has been some interest among employers in using credit history as an applicant screening method. The assumption among some employers is that a poor credit history

SPOTLIGHT ON ETHICS

Keeping Applicant and Employee Data Secure

As we discussed throughout this book, applicant information privacy is a major ethical issue faced by employers. We mentioned the issue of keeping applicant information secure—something that is more easily said than done due to the risks inherent in both human error and the ingenuity of cyber-criminals.

In 2014, McDonald's Canada's job website was hacked, which put the personal data of as many as 95,000 job applicants at risk of being stolen; the data included their home addresses, e-mail addresses, and phone numbers. As another example, a laptop theft at Coca-Cola involved the private data of more than 74,000 employees, contractors, and suppliers. These cases are likely to happen more and more frequently as employers such as PepsiCo seek to launch mobile-optimized application portals. Often, the cause of such data breaches is simple human error—errors that result from behaviors that many of us engage in on a regular basis.

How does an employer protect applicant data? It is recommended that HR work closely with IT staff, set up communication channels among employees to share insights for protecting data security, conduct a risk assessment of where things might go wrong, and train employees in the basics of keeping data secure.[84]

Questions

1. What practices and cautions are you familiar with that would help keep personal data secure, for yourself or for others such as job applicants at your workplace or university?

2. Look up the McDonald's or Coca-Cola data breach and read the details of what happened, how, and why. What could have been done differently? How did the employer respond once the breach happened?

---

may be a sign of other problems such as low conscientiousness.[85] However, there are a number of reasons to caution against using credit histories in selection, and their use appears to be on the decline among employers of late. First, given the recent economic downturn, many people may have a poor credit score due to factors that are no fault of their own, such as being laid off from their job. Second, the relationship between credit scores, personality, and performance is not at all clear. For example, one study showed that a poor credit score is not associated with workplace deviance and that a good score is actually associated with poor agreeableness. Third, there is also evidence that credit scores may show adverse impact. In short, credit scores cannot be assumed to predict job performance, and they may lead to adverse impact, such that they should not be used except when there is good reason to do so.

Applicant Reactions to Selection Methods and Procedures

LO 7.6 Describe the importance of applicant reactions to selection processes.

Through the years, most selection research and analysis have focused on the employer's perspective—that is, how to choose tests that are the most valid predictors of job performance. Although this continues to be the focus of most research in this area, there is a growing realization that the job applicants' perspective, or *applicant reactions*, matters as well. Research has shown that how applicants perceive the hiring process, including how fairly they believe that they were treated, can affect important outcomes such as their willingness to buy the company's products or even whether they accept a job offer.[86] In other words, organizations would do well to consider the *candidate experience* (the term for applicant reactions often used by employers) in developing their hiring procedures, and many now do so.

Many employers are concerned that a bad candidate experience could cause the best applicants to look for jobs elsewhere, and this may in fact be true. The British cable and mobile provider Virgin Media also realized that disgruntled candidates could be directly affecting their

Applicant reactions A job applicant's perspective regarding the selection procedures they encounter and the employer that uses them

Candidate experience A term for applicant reactions often used by employers

bottom line. Specifically, they found that a significant number of job candidates who had had a negative interview experience (e.g., a rude interviewer) switched providers as a result, costing the company the equivalent of $5.4 million per year. To attack this problem head-on, Virgin put together an intensive program to train interviewers—a gold standard on how to treat applicants with respect. Part of the program includes inviting candidates to share their experiences as feedback to the interview team. The program seems to have gained traction throughout the company, with managers now actively checking to see their unit's "scores" from applicants so they have feedback regarding how they are doing.[87]

An extensive body of research has examined what applicants want in a selection system. Applicants want to be treated fairly during hiring, and this perceived fairness in turn affects their attitudes and behaviors.[88] Applicants prefer selection methods that appear to be related to the job. As an example, applicants tend to prefer job interviews that ask clearly job-related questions rather than abstract questions with no obvious relationship to the job. In addition, applicants value feedback and communication from employers during the hiring process, and they also like methods that treat all applicants the same way. Finally, applicants want to be treated with respect: A cold or unfriendly person tells the applicant that cold relationships prevail in the organization. Interestingly, these characteristics of the selection situation that are valued by applicants seem to generalize across countries and cultures, having been found in North America, Europe, South America, and Asia.[89] A summary of some of the key factors that affect job applicants' perceptions are presented in Table 7.8.

This all leads to the question regarding which selection procedures applicants prefer (see Figure 7.8). Not surprisingly, they tend to prefer procedures that are obviously job related such as work samples, assessment centers, and job interviews; feel less positively toward more abstract selection procedures such as résumés, biodata, personality tests, cognitive tests, and references; and feel least positively toward graphology (handwriting analysis), which is still used for selection in France, the use of personal contacts, and integrity tests, which may seem the least job related.[90] Note that one challenge for employers is that some of the methods most preferred by applicants are not always the most cost effective to administer. For example, work samples are certainly valid predictors, but they can be quite expensive to administer and may be impractical for very large applicant pools. Research has also suggested that providing explanations to job applicants—for example, how a test that does not appear to be obviously job related actually has been carefully

TABLE 7.8   Characteristics of Selection Systems That Have Been Found to Affect Applicant Perceptions and Behaviors

SELECTION PROCEDURE CHARACTERISTICS	DEFINITION
Job-Relatedness	The selection procedure is either obviously related to the job (e.g., a work sample) or the applicant understands that it is important to the job (e.g., a test of agreeableness and extraversion for a customer service job).
Opportunity to Perform	The selection procedure gives the applicants a feeling that they can "show what they know" or "show what they can do" relative to what is required for the job.
Interpersonal Treatment	The applicant is treated with respect by people from the organization. This might include respect in communications with the applicant, both written and in person, and letting the applicant know the final outcome (e.g., the employer lets the applicant know if they got the job rather than simply saying nothing).
Feedback Timeliness	Applicants are given the results of the application process in a timely manner.
Consistency	Applicants are all treated in a consistent manner.

Sources: Based on information contained in Bauer, T. N., Truxillo, D. M., Sanchez, R. J., Craig, J., Ferrara, P., & Campion, M. A. (2001). Applicant reactions to selection: Development of the Selection Procedural Justice Scale (SPJS). *Personnel Psychology,* 54, 387–419; Gilliland, S. W. (1993). The perceived fairness of selection systems: An organizational justice perspective. *Academy of Management Review,* 18, 694–734; Hausknecht, J. P, Day, D. V., & Thomas, S. C. (2004). Applicant reactions to selection procedures: An updated model and meta-analysis. *Personnel Psychology,* 57, 639–683.

■ **FIGURE 7.8** Selection Procedures Preferred by Job Applicants

Most Preferred	Favorable Evaluation	Least Preferred
• Work Samples	• Résumés	• Honesty Tests
• Interviews	• Cognitive Tests	• Personal Contacts
	• References	• Graphology (handwriting analysis)
	• Biodata	
	• Personality Tests	

Sources: Anderson, N., Salgado, J. F., & Hülsheger, U. R. (2010). Applicant reactions in selection: Comprehensive meta-analysis into reaction generalization versus situational specificity. *International Journal of Selection and Assessment, 18,* 291–304; Hausknecht, J. P., Day, D. V., & Thomas, S. C. (2004). Applicant reactions to selection procedures: An updated model and meta-analysis. *Personnel Psychology, 57,* 639–683.

developed and researched to be quite valid—can help to alleviate applicant concerns.[91] The candidate experience is so important that the Talent Board, an organization that focuses on understanding the candidate experience, gives awards to organizations each year. In 2016, companies such as American Airlines, AT&T, Facebook, GE, Intel, LEGO Group, Marriott International, and Wells Fargo were among the 50 winners recognized by the Talent Board.[92] In short, in addition to considering the validity, utility, and legality of selection procedures, employers should consider applicants' perceptions of these procedures.

Deployment of Selection Procedures

LO 7.7 Explain how to deploy selection procedures within organizations to enhance job performance.

Suppose an employer has decided to use a personality test, an integrity test, and a structured interview to hire its programmers. There are approximately 10 vacancies, and the company expects to have 100 strong applicants due to a successful recruitment effort. One simple approach would be to administer all of the selection procedures at one time. So an applicant might come into the organization and take the personality and integrity tests and then move on to the interview. However, there are some problems with this approach, primarily with the use of resources involved: Given that there are 100 applicants, interviewing all 100 of them, especially when there are only 10 vacancies, would not be very cost effective in terms of using company resources and time. Instead, the company might decide to administer these selection procedures sequentially in what is called a ***multiple-hurdle approach*** (see Figure 7.9). Typically, the less expensive selection procedures—in this case the tests of personality and integrity—are put first. Those applicants who score sufficiently high on these two tests would then be put through the more costly structured interview.[93] You may have personal experience with this approach to selection, which is commonly used for hiring. Applicants might fill

■ **FIGURE 7.9** Example of the Multiple-Hurdle Selection Process

This is an example of a multiple-hurdle approach in which the least expensive selection procedures are put first with the full applicant pool, and the most expensive selection procedures are put last with fewer applicants to save on administration costs.

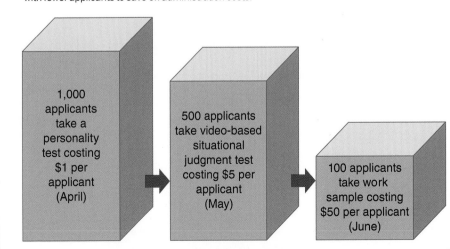

1,000 applicants take a personality test costing $1 per applicant (April)

500 applicants take video-based situational judgment test costing $5 per applicant (May)

100 applicants take work sample costing $50 per applicant (June)

Multiple-hurdle approach
When a series of selection procedures is administered sequentially and applicants must pass each hurdle to move to the next one

out an initial job application and take a test online, and the employer then follows up with an interview if these initial tests suggest that the applicant is a good enough fit.

It is important to note that the timeliness of decisions is important to applicants who would like to receive feedback quickly and who may also have other opportunities that they are considering. Thus, making applicants wait too long between selection hurdles can give applicants a negative impression of the company and may cause employers to lose the best talent to other employers who are willing to move more quickly. In other words, using selection hurdles rather than administering all selection procedures at once makes a lot of practical sense, as long as the delays between hurdles are not too lengthy.

CHAPTER SUMMARY

Obtaining the best talent provides an organization with a competitive advantage and is the main goal of selection. The technical issues involved in choosing among personnel selection procedures include assuring their validity and utility and complying with legal issues. Understanding reliability, validity, and selection utility enables organizations to choose the best predictors for a given hiring situation. A range of selection procedures are available to organizations, and these should be utilized according to their relative validity, practicality, and effects on workforce diversity. Practical issues such as the timing and sequencing of selection procedures to ensure cost effectiveness need to be considered along with the candidate experience.

KEY TERMS

psychometrics   218
reliability   218
validity   219
content validity   219
criterion-related validity   219
validity coefficient   219
predictive validity   219
concurrent validity   219
construct validity   220
validity generalization   223

local validation   223
utility   223
selection interview   226
unstructured interview   226
structured interview   229
situational interview   229
behavioral interview   229
Five Factor Model (FFM)   231
integrity test   233
cognitive ability test   234

emotional intelligence (EI)   234
work sample   235
situational judgment
    test (SJT)   236
assessment center   236
biographical data
    (biodata)   238
applicant reactions   241
candidate experience   241
multiple-hurdle approach   243

Visit **edge.sagepub.com/bauer** to help you accomplish your coursework goals in an easy-to-use learning environment.

- Master the learning objectives using key study tools
- Watch, listen, and connect with online multimedia resources

- Access mobile-friendly quizzes and flashcards to check your understanding

HR REASONING AND DECISION-MAKING EXERCISES

MINI-CASE ANALYSIS EXERCISE: SELECTION SYSTEMS FOR HIRING

You are working for a regional coffee chain, Al Bar. Currently the company has 900 employees, but it is expanding into several new urban areas, and moving forward, the CEO would like to be more systematic in the approach to hiring new baristas. Al Bar also needs a valid but practical and cost-effective approach given the large number of new hires expected in the coming years.

A glance at the O*Net database shows the following sorts of skills are typically required of baristas:

- Take orders from customers and give orders to coworkers for preparation.
- Prepare beverages such as espresso drinks, coffee, tea.
- Clean work area and equipment.
- Describe items on the menu to customers and suggest menu items that they might like.
- Take customer payments.

You have been asked to propose a new selection system for hiring baristas. Consider the following questions.

1. Which selection procedures would make the most sense for hiring baristas? Weigh each of your suggested selection procedures in terms of (a) validity, (b) enhancing workforce diversity, (c) utility, and (d) applicant reactions.

2. Once you have chosen your selection procedures, how would you deploy them? For example, in what order would you administer the selection procedures? Would you administer them in person or online (or some combination)? Explain why.

3. Assuming that you would use an interview at some point in the process, what would be some good interview questions? Would you use an unstructured interview, a behavioral interview, a situational interview, or some combination? Explain why.

4. Which selection procedures would you definitely not use for the barista job?

HR DECISION ANALYSIS EXERCISE:
A NEW APPROACH TO HIRING EMPLOYEES?

You are working in the human resources department at Moderne Electronics, a leader in the field of electronic health care products. Recently, the CEO of Moderne has been interested in gamified personnel selection tests, including tests of personality and cognitive ability. As a result, the CEO has interviewed three companies that sell gamified tests and decided to sign a contract with one of these companies, Avanguardia Testing. Your CEO wants to use these gamified tests because "this is what today's applicants expect." Moreover, the salespeople at Avanguardia have told your CEO that the tests are good predictors of job performance and that Avanguardia has used big data algorithms to prove it. However, Avanguardia has not yet provided documentation to this effect.

Your boss, the vice president of HR, has questioned the switch to the new gamified system, partly because implementation of the new gamified tests will require a significant overhaul of the HR system including thousands of hours of HR staff time. However, the VP of HR does admit that the tests provided by Avanguardia are attractive and fun.

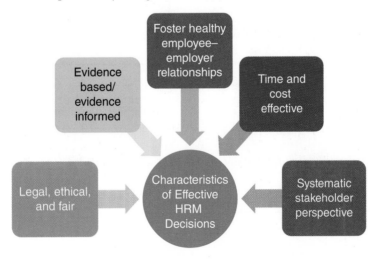

Please provide the rationale for your answer to each of the questions below.

Was the CEO's decision legal, ethical, and fair?

_____
_____
_____
_____

Was the CEO's decision evidence based/evidence informed?

_____
_____
_____
_____

Did the CEO's decision foster healthy employee–employer relationships?

_____
_____
_____
_____

Was the CEO's decision time and cost effective?

_____
_____
_____
_____

Did the CEO take a systematic stakeholder perspective?

_____
_____
_____
_____

Considering your analysis above, overall, do you think this was an effective decision? Why?

_____
_____
_____

What, if anything, do you think should be done differently or considered to help make this decision more effective?

_____
_____
_____

HR DECISION-MAKING EXERCISE: ASSESSING THE VALIDITY OF A NEW TEST FOR HIRING EMPLOYEES

A test vendor has approached the vice president of HR in your company with a new test of conscientiousness. The test vendor claims that the new conscientiousness test is at least as valid as the old test that your company is currently using—but the new test is half the price! As a result, the VP of HR has tasked you with determining whether the company should use this new test of conscientiousness or stick with the old test. This is important, because having a valid test affects hiring decisions regarding hundreds of new employees. Plus, as you know, the test's validity is also important to the legal defensibility of the test.

You have been able to give the new conscientiousness test to 200 current employees on two occasions, 1 week apart. In addition, you have given these employees the old conscientiousness test, as well as tests of "achievement striving" and "verbal skills." Finally, you also have supervisor performance ratings on file for each employee regarding their organizational citizenship. In other words, you have a lot of what you need to begin to assess the validity of the new test of conscientiousness in terms of predicting job performance!

The correlations among these different tests and measures follow. Note that statistically significant relationships are indicated by an asterisk (*).

TABLE 7.9   Correlations Among Tests and Measures

	1	2	3	4	5	6
1. New Conscientiousness Test Time 1	-					
2. New Conscientiousness Test Time 2	.97*	-				
3. Old Conscientiousness Test	.92*	.90*	-			
4. Achievement Striving Test	.62*	.65*	.58*	-		
5. Verbal Skills Test	.11	.12	.12		-	
6. Job Performance: Supervisor Ratings of Organizational Citizenship	.35*	.33*	.32*	.25*	.15*	-

Take a few minutes to orient yourself to this correlation matrix. Note that most of the information you need is in the first column, which shows the pattern of correlations between the new conscientiousness test with other measures. Then, answer the following questions.

1. What do you think about its **construct validity** (i.e., its pattern of correlations with other tests)? Why?

2. What is the evidence for the **criterion-related validity** of the new conscientiousness test?

3. What do you think about the **content validity** of the new conscientiousness test? (*Hint*: Is the information needed to answer this question available in the table?) Explain.

4. Would you recommend using the new test or the old test of conscientiousness for hiring workers? Why or why not?

DATA AND ANALYTICS EXERCISE: WEIGHTING PREDICTORS VIA REGRESSION

As we described earlier, criterion-related validity of selection procedures can be shown through a statistically significant correlation between a test and a job outcome like performance. Going one step further, regression can show a predicted score on the outcome based on a test.

For example, if you had a dataset that allowed you to develop a regression equation (through a statistical program), you would get an equation in this form:

$Y = bx + a$

Where Y is the predicted score on the outcome

X is the score a person obtained on the test

b is the weight of the test

And a is the constant or "y-intercept."

Let's say the specific equation you obtained from your dataset was as follows:

$Y = 3x + 1$

In this case, if a person obtained a 5 on the test, their predicted score on outcome would be 16. Note that this is not the score that all people with a 5 would get but is rather a *predicted* score or their most likely score.

Now let's go through an example where you have given three tests to a group of employees (concurrent design). The tests are proactivity, emotional intelligence, and situation judgment (SJT), all predicting customer service job performance.

You get the following results:

Correlations

		PROACTIVITY	EMOTIONAL INTELLIGENCE	SJT	CUSTOMER SERVICE
Proactivity	Pearson Correlation	1	.318**	.237**	.391**
	Sig. (2-tailed)		.000	.000	.000
	N	300	300	300	300
Emotional Intelligence	Pearson Correlation	.318**	1	.932**	.426**
	Sig. (2-tailed)	.000		.000	.000
	N	300	300	300	300
SJT	Pearson Correlation	.237**	.932**	1	.417**
	Sig. (2-tailed)	.000	.000		.000
	N	300	300	300	300
Customer Service	Pearson Correlation	.391**	.426**	.417**	1
	Sig. (2-tailed)	.000	.000	.000	
	N	300	300	300	300

** Correlation is significant at the 0.01 level (2-tailed).

All three tests have a significant correlation with customer service job performance. But the EI test and SJT are highly redundant, correlated .932. One of them should go.

Here is one way to settle this: You learn that the SJT costs $1 per person to administer, while the test of EI costs $10 per person. With thousands of applicants, you are concerned about the relative utility of the EI, and so you decide to drop it.

Now you have to decide how to weight the two remaining tests: proactivity and SJT. That would be found in the column listed as B.

	COEFFICIENTS	STD. ERROR	T STAT	P-VALUE
Intercept	5.527	.539	10.249	.000
Proactivity	.385	.064	6.031	.000
SJT	.567	.085	6.714	.000

In this case, the weight of SJT is .567, and the weight of proactivity is .385. The constant is 5.527. So the equation then becomes:

Y (predicted customer service score) $= 5.527 + .567$ (SJT score) $+ .385$ (proactivity score)

Thus, if a person obtained a 10 on the SJT, and a 10 on proactivity, their predicted customer service score would be

$Y = 5.527 + 5.670 + 3.850$

$Y = 15.047$

 EXCEL EXTENSION: NOW YOU TRY!

On **edge.sagepub.com/bauer**, in the Excel spreadsheet, run the requested regression models to get the regression weights.

CHAPTER 7 SUPPLEMENT: THE UNIFORM GUIDELINES AND THE SIOP *PRINCIPLES*[94]

As noted in this chapter, there are government and professional guidelines for the development, use, and validation of employee selection procedures. These guidelines were developed to help employers interpret the relevant laws; protect the rights of job applicants; and ensure that employers follow best practices for obtaining and developing the most valid selection procedures with the highest selection utility. Two of the main documents are the Uniform Guidelines on Employee Selection Procedures (commonly referred to among selection professionals just as "the Uniform Guidelines") and the *Principles for the Validation and Use of Employee Selection Procedures* published by the Society for Industrial and Organizational Psychology (SIOP). Both of these documents are quite extensive, such that reproducing them here is not possible, even as an appendix. However, links to each of these documents are provided for those students of HR who would like to review them.

UNIFORM GUIDELINES ON EMPLOYEE SELECTION PROCEDURES

The Uniform Guidelines were developed to provide guidance to employers, employment agencies, licensing and certification boards, labor unions, government contractors and subcontractors, and other entities. They provide technical guidelines for a range of selection topics such as guidelines for recruitment, validation, and affirmative action programs. Adopted by the Equal Employment Opportunity Commission (EEOC), Civil Service Department, Department of Labor, and Department of Justice, one purpose of the Uniform Guidelines was to summarize EEO "case law" (accumulated court cases that interpreted EEO legislation such as the Civil Rights Act of 1964) for employers. Technically not laws in themselves, the Uniform Guidelines are still given "great deference" by the courts. One criticism of the Uniform Guidelines is that they have not been updated since 1978 and do not take into account scientific developments that have occurred in selection science over the last 40 years. Generally, the Uniform Guidelines apply to employers with 15 or more employees. The Uniform Guidelines are available here:

https://www.gpo.gov/fdsys/pkg/CFR-2011-title29-vol4/xml/CFR-2011-title29-vol4-part1607.xml

PRINCIPLES FOR THE VALIDATION AND USE OF PERSONNEL SELECTION PROCEDURES

In contrast, SIOP's *Principles for the Validation and Use of Personnel Selection Procedures* (or "*Principles*") were most recently updated in 2018. As the leader in personnel selection science for most of the last century, SIOP's goal in producing the *Principles* is to describe both the scientific findings and best practices regarding the use of selection procedures. This includes a description of how to establish validity evidence, ensure the fairness of selection procedures, and conduct appropriate data analysis to maximize successful selection decisions. The most recent version of the SIOP *Principles* is available here:

http://www.siop.org/_principles/principles.pdf

Training, Development, and Careers

8 ←

LEARNING OBJECTIVES

After reading and studying this chapter, you should be able to do the following:

8.1 Describe the steps to a training needs assessment, including the purpose of each, and how they are used to develop training goals.

8.2 List the characteristics of the employee, the organizational context, and the training that can be leveraged to enhance training effectiveness.

8.3 Describe some of the most important training methods and media used by organizations and list their respective advantages and disadvantages.

8.4 Identify the major categories of criteria for assessing training effectiveness and demonstrate their use.

8.5 Analyze the factors associated with effective career development and management.

Opening Case

Using Training and Development to Drive Culture of Commitment: The Case of Igloo

Igloo, a Texas-based manufacturer of ice chests for more than 70 years, has undertaken a number of initiatives to train and develop its employees to promote its company culture of commitment. Igloo's operations in Texas employ 900 *associates*—the term Igloo uses for its employees. There are a number of key dimensions to Igloo's culture, such as trusting others, avoiding politics (decision making based on personal advantage), and promoting effective communication.

As keeper of the culture at Igloo, HR is central to promoting, supporting, and sustaining the culture. Thus, part of HR's job is to train associates on what Igloo's culture is, why it is important, and how to embrace it. This includes not only training on the culture for new hires during the onboarding process but also explaining the culture during annual goal-setting sessions, sales meetings, and strategic planning programs.

One key dimension of Igloo's culture of commitment is the "recipe for associate success." Training and development activities are a central part of this dimension, and thus Igloo has undertaken an ambitious training program for enhancing the skills of its associates. Part of the development of this training program included an assessment of training needs and tailoring the program to the needs of associates. The program's key features focus on training, but they also focus on the counseling and coaching of associates.

Further, Igloo developed a technical skills training program based on the latest neuroscience research on adult learning. This technical skills program includes these five steps:

- *Demonstration*: Knowledgeable associates show learners how to carry out the task at hand.

- *"By the numbers"*: Highly technical work is broken down into established, standardized steps so that it is more easily taught and is taught in a consistent manner to different employees.

- *Role reversal*: Learners act as instructors themselves. That is, they "teach" the skill to instructors to demonstrate to instructors what they can actually do. The idea is that a person must be highly proficient before they can teach a skill to another person.

Mike Powell via Getty Images

- *Practice with questions and answers*: Associates are given time to practice their new skills and ask questions about them so that they can build confidence.

- *Certification*: Final step in which Igloo determines whether associates are ready to go and "floor ready."

Igloo's culture of commitment demonstrates its emphasis on people—in short, safety and respect toward associates.[1]

Case Discussion Questions

1. Igloo has developed its culture around associates who primarily work in manufacturing. How effective would this approach to implementing culture be in other industries, for example, commercial construction? A high-tech start-up?

2. What are some of the drawbacks to Igloo's approach to managing its culture? Where might HR or top management face some challenges in the organization?

3. How would you decide what the appropriate culture is for an organization? How would you use the company's training and development function to help introduce and reinforce a new culture?

4. How might training be used to introduce a culture focused on respect for diversity? On employee safety?

5. What specific types of training content and exercises might you include if you were rolling out a training program for Igloo that was focused on its culture of commitment?

6. How would you assess the effectiveness of Igloo's efforts to introduce the culture of commitment? Consider (a) how you would know if the culture was actually adopted and (b) what metrics you might use to know whether the culture is actually supporting the success of the organization.

 Click to learn more…

To learn more about how to transform culture like Igloo did, click on this article: https://www.corpmagazine.com/human-resources/cultural-commitment-creating-a-workplace-where-people-feel-valued/

As we have stated in the preceding chapters, an organization's human capital is arguably its greatest asset. Developing employees through training may be one of the best investments an organization can make—if it is done well. Thus, it is important to implement best practices for training and developing employees in organizations throughout their careers.

■ **FIGURE 8.1** The Process for Developing, Implementing, and Evaluating an Organizational Training Program

Assess Training Needs

Address Characteristics of the Trainee, Organization, and Training to Enhance Learning

Choose Appropriate Training Method(s)

Assess Training Effects at the Individual and Organizational Levels

This chapter describes the process for developing and implementing a training program and demonstrating its value to the organization. As shown in Figure 8.1, this process involves conducting a training needs assessment, addressing characteristics of the worker and the organization, choosing the appropriate training methods, and evaluating the program's effectiveness. Whether you are in charge of the training program or are a manager making decisions about whether to invest in training, this chapter provides the expertise you need to develop a training program or critically assess its value.

The Importance of Training in Organizations

An organization's investment in its employees through training and development activities can be critical to its success. For this investment to pay off, it is important that the training address specific organizational needs, align with the organization's objectives, and fit the needs of employees. Additionally, the organizational decision makers should consider from the start how they will know whether the training worked.

These considerations are important given the sizable investment that organizations make in training. As shown in Figure 8.2, U.S. companies spend billions of dollars each year on training programs. Some sources estimate global expenditures on training at $362 billion.[2]

Most of you will be involved in organizational training and development activities at some point in your lives, certainly as a participant; but you will also likely be called upon to make decisions about whether to undertake a training program for your employees or even for an organization. The principles described in this chapter will help you to make more informed and effective decisions about training in your workplace. Given the large amounts of money that organizations invest in training programs each year, helping you, as an employee or as a manager, make better decisions about training is important. For example, much of the money organizations spend on training is paid to external vendors who specialize in various types of training. To promote their training programs, these vendors often cite examples of successes in other organizations. This is certainly a valid way for training vendors to illustrate that their training can be effective. However, managers should ask whether the training would actually be beneficial to their own organization, how training success was actually measured (e.g., was it simply trainee satisfaction, or can the vendor show that the training actually had an impact on knowledge and performance?), and

■ **FIGURE 8.2**   Corporate Training Expenditures in U.S. Organizations During 2017

Source: Size of training industry. (2017). https://www.trainingindustry.com/wiki/entries/size-of-training-industry.aspx

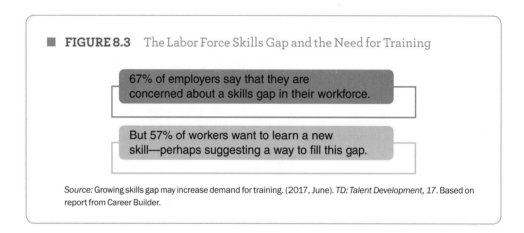

■ **FIGURE 8.3**   The Labor Force Skills Gap and the Need for Training

Source: Growing skills gap may increase demand for training. (2017, June). *TD: Talent Development, 17*. Based on report from Career Builder.

whether these previous clients can be contacted to get their experiences with the training program directly from them.

Despite these cautions, the potential payoff to organizations from training is substantial. Moreover, other research shows that workplace training can benefit not only the work organizations that provide it but also individual employees and even countries and societies. In fact, although managers may observe that there is a skills gap between the general workforce and the available jobs (see Figure 8.3), workers are eager to gain more training to advance their skills—a win-win-win for employers, workers, and the economy.

Training Needs Assessment

LO 8.1   Describe the steps to a training needs assessment, including the purpose of each, and how they are used to develop training goals.

Needs assessment
A systematic evaluation of the organization, the jobs, and the employees to determine where training is most needed and what type of training is needed

Training **needs assessment** is a systematic evaluation of the organization, the jobs, and the employees to determine where training is most needed and what type of training is needed. Training needs assessment is also a key part of developing clearly focused training goals that are aligned with organizational strategy and in understanding how to develop and implement the training program in ways that will have the greatest benefit to the organization.[3]

Today, HR functions face greater pressures for accountability. This is especially true of the training function because of the large amount of money that is spent on it. Still, although many organizations would be reluctant to invest in equipment without a good bit of analysis, many of these same organizations do not deeply analyze their training needs (see Figure 8.4) before

■ **FIGURE 8.4**   Misalignment Between Training Programs and Actual Training Needs Suggests the Importance of a Training Needs Assessment.

46% of employees who receive training say that the training they get isn't effective for helping them to do their job.

16% of employees say their training was ineffective because they were trained on the wrong skill.

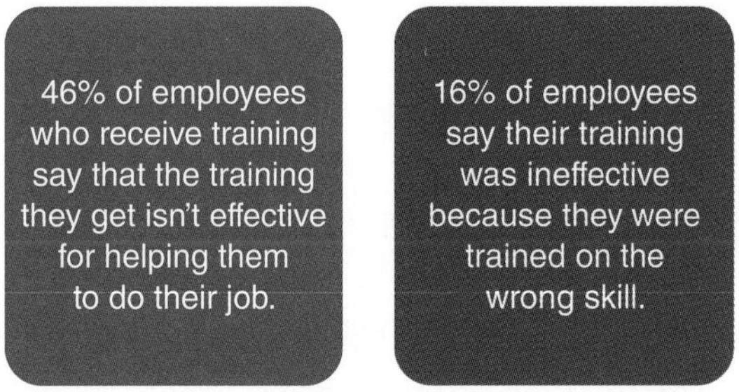

Source: Effectiveness of formal workplace training uncovered. (2017, March). *TD: Talent Development, 19*; The appalling state of employee training and how to improve it.https://axonify.com/news/axonify-announces-workplace-research-reveals-one-third-us-employees-receive-no-formal-job-training/

investing in training. First, companies often assume that problems are due to a lack of training, but this is not always the case; as a result, they can end up spending resources on unneeded training. For example, a restaurant chain may believe that its problem with decreasing sales is due to a skills gap among its servers and may decide to address the "problem" with training. In actuality, the problem may turn out not to be a training issue at all but something else (e.g., poor advertising). Second, even if top management in an organization correctly believes that there are training needs among its employees, their training efforts need to be correctly focused. Using the restaurant chain again as an example, even if the company is correct that its servers need additional training, the servers' specific skills gap needs to be identified. It would not be useful to train the servers on customer service skills, when in fact the problem is that the servers do not know or understand the items on the menu well enough to advise customers. It would hardly be a good use of company resources to train employees on topics on which they are already proficient.

In short, before spending the capital needed to train employees, it is wise to get a better grasp on what the organization's training needs actually are through some sort of a needs assessment process. In fact, conducting a training needs assessment may be the most important step in developing an effective training program. This process is typically conceptualized as having three components: organizational analysis, job analysis, and person analysis (see Figure 8.5).

■ **FIGURE 8.5**   The Three Phases of a Training Needs Assessment

Organizational Analysis
- Goals, strategies, objectives, culture
- Resources
- External environment

Job Analysis
- KSAOs and tasks of the focal job
- Competencies
- Critical incidents employees face on the job

Person Analysis
- Assess current KSAOs and competencies of employees
- Develop training goals
- Consider employee characteristics (e.g., demographics, motivation, education)

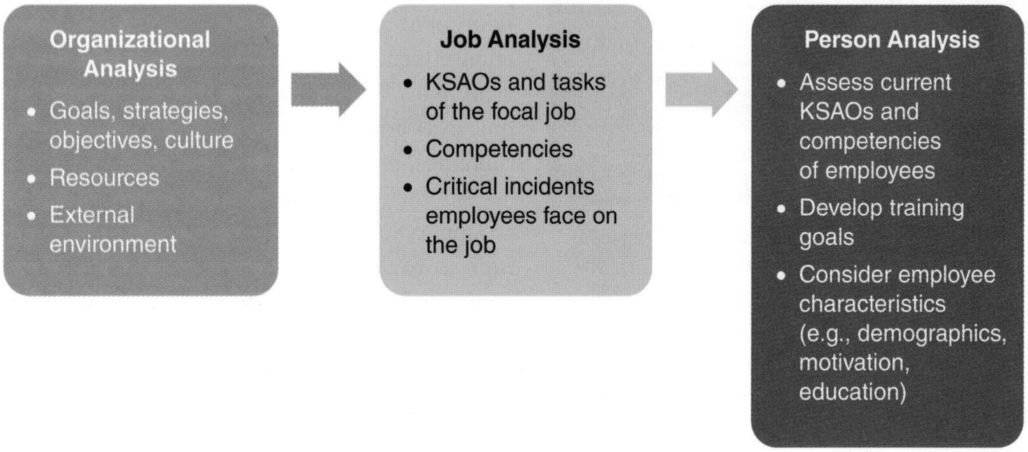

Organizational Analysis

Organizational analysis involves a number of steps for getting to know the organization at a broader level so a training program can be developed to fit the organization. This includes issues such as

- understanding the company's **goals and strategies** so that the goals of the training program are aligned with them,
- understanding the **organization's culture**, including the attitudes toward training among managers and employees,
- identifying the **resources** that the organization can devote to training, and
- analyzing the organization's **external environment**.

Organizational Goals and Strategies

Understanding organizational goals and strategies is important for all organizational activities—including training programs. Imagine that an organization's focus is to gain market share over the next 5 years. It may be worthwhile to consider training efforts focused on the sales force or on product development if these are seen as key to developing the market share. For example, as part of its social initiatives in 2015, Starbucks committed to a goal of hiring 10,000 youths (defined as between 16 and 24 years of age) who were neither employed nor in school. In pursuit of this goal, the company brought together more than 50 U.S.-based companies to form the "100,000 Opportunities Initiative" that trains, provides internships, and hires disadvantaged youth. The company opened several training stores to provide on-the-job training and met its goal 2 years earlier than expected.[4]

Organizational Culture

Similarly, understanding the company's culture—the shared beliefs that employees have about accepted behavioral norms—is key to implementing an effective training program. Although organizational decision makers may know that culture is important, the challenge becomes how to instill a strong, positive culture into the organization, starting with individual employees and teams. Research clearly demonstrates that supervisors and managers are key to communicating and supporting a positive culture. The research has also shown that organizational policies and practices play a significant role.

For example, if a company's culture valued nonconfrontational, subtle interpersonal relationships, developing a training program focused on promoting an assertive, confrontational interpersonal style could be damaging. As described in this chapter's opening case, Igloo gains great benefit from training that supports its "culture of commitment." Imagine how counterproductive it would be for such a company to have training that encouraged workers to work as quickly as possible, focusing on time–motion efficiency rather than thinking through the purpose and result.

Another issue that frequently comes up regarding culture is lack of support for training among managers and employees. If managers indicate relatively low support or value placed on training, or if the company has had failed training programs in the past, figuring out how to increase trainee motivation and support for training may be one of the most important challenges in designing the training program. In some cases, the culture may be so opposed to training that it is not a worthwhile investment at that moment. Consider cases in which supervisors may actually undermine training efforts, such

Some high-tech start-ups hire talent without planning to develop them further, focusing on getting the best people who don't need further development. However, that is not always the case, with some startups seeing the value in continually developing their people. As a case in point, Medallia stresses the importance of a learning culture, hiring employees who are interested in their own development—that is, those with a growth mindset—with Medallia supporting them in doing so.[5]

©iStock.com/monsitj

HR IN ACTION

Helping Subject Matter Experts Become Good Trainers

©iStock.com/PeopleImages

If you were being trained, you would like to be trained by an expert in the field, and this makes sense. However, one concern is that being a content expert does not necessarily mean that you are a good trainer or teacher. Consider the teachers and professors that you may have known over the years who were brilliant with regard to their field of expertise but were less than optimal teachers.

In organizations, it is often the subject matter experts (or SMEs) who are asked to step in and teach others about their content area. A classic example would be the information technology expert. But just because you are an expert on IT, that doesn't mean you are an expert on how to train others about IT. In fact, your expertise might even interfere with your ability to understand what novices do or do not know.

This is where the "train-the-trainer" concept comes in. Many professional trainers go through train-the-trainer instruction before going into the teaching environment. In addition, though, organizations have their own SMEs who act as internal trainers and go through a train-the-trainer course. This might include some basics like considering the needs of trainees and choosing the right methods to fit the learners and the topic. It might also include more sophisticated topics such as theories of adult learning and how to design training systems, as well as participating in simulations that have them design a training program, deliver it, and then go through a debrief as feedback from their peers and from instructors.[6]

that they tell employees not to perform the behaviors they learned in training. ("I know that's what you were taught in training, but that is not the way we actually do things here.") In this case, investment in training is unlikely to lead to transfer of skills to the job. One approach might be to get supervisors involved in the development of the training program as early as possible to get their input on how best to increase the usefulness of the training, as well as their support for the training program once it is implemented.

Organizational Resources

At the same time, it is important to understand what resources the organization is able and willing to invest in the training program. This includes the organization's mindset regarding whether to invest in training at all and also issues such as facilities and personnel. Some organizations may choose to focus on hiring the best talent ("buy" strategy). This strategy assumes that new hires will need little training. On the other hand, some employers may be willing to invest in training employees to align their skills with organizational needs ("develop" strategy). In addition, it is important to understand whether the company currently has employee subject matter experts (SMEs) who can act as trainers, or whether trainers will need to be brought in from the outside. Similarly, if the organization is considering the use of eLearning (discussed later in this chapter), do all employees have access to the computers or mobile devices that would be needed to train them? Or if the training is best delivered by means of classroom training, are those facilities available? How many employees can be trained at one time? The issue of resources must be understood early on so that the training can best be developed in a practical, scalable way, or the training may need to be limited to training for only certain employees on the most critical competencies.

Compliance training
Instruction focused on regulations, laws, and policies related to employees' daily work

External Environment

The organization's external environment should also be taken into account when developing the training program. This might involve various types of ***compliance training*** that is required for particular jobs, such as safety training. In addition, the organization's external competition is an issue that can inform the development of a training program. For example, a competitor may be providing certain key training to its employees that should also be considered. In addition, laws and regulations, such as equal employment opportunity laws, can be important to consider when putting together a training program, especially if access to or success in the training program can affect whether an employee is hired or allowed to remain in a job. In this sense, the training program could have the same effect as a selection procedure. If so, issues related to adverse impact (e.g., Do different groups perform at different levels in the program?) need to be considered, and the training program would need to be legally defensible as job related.

Job Analysis

Once organizational analysis has been conducted, providing a better understanding of the organization and which jobs should be the focus of the training program based on the organization's goals and resources, the next step in a training needs assessment is to conduct a job analysis. A job analysis helps determine which KSAOs, tasks, and competencies are associated with a job, as well as the critical incidents that employees face on the job, in order to develop an effective training program. We have discussed the range of options for job analysis and competency modeling as well as the basics of how to do them (e.g., interviews, surveys).

The task–KSAO approach is particularly well suited for the development of training, as it identifies the critical KSAOs, which will form the backbone of the training program.

SPOTLIGHT ON LEGAL ISSUES

Training Through the Legal Lens: Equal Access and Compliance

A number of legal issues are relevant to the training function in organizations. Broadly, these pertain to providing equal opportunity to employees via training programs and also to an employer's obligation to provide a number of types of job-related training to employees and supervisors.

First, consider the Uniform Guidelines on Employee Selection Procedures (discussed in Chapters 4 and 7). Although training may not be a selection procedure per se, to the extent that a training program affects which employees are retained or promoted, the training program is part of selection decisions. For example, if success in a training program for new supervisors is necessary for an employee to keep a supervisory job, the training program is being used as a selection procedure. Thus, the organization needs to ensure that passing rates in the training program for different subgroups are equivalent, or it should be prepared to show the validity/job relatedness of the training program in order to defend it. In addition,

employees should have fair access to training programs that can provide opportunities for them to advance in their careers.

Second, a number of types of training programs are required by employers to remain compliant with current government guidelines and to avoid legal liability. Such compliance training is focused on regulations, laws, and policies related to employees' daily work. These might include providing supervisors with the skills training they need to be effective; safety training, particularly for workers in safety-sensitive jobs; and diversity and sexual harassment training to protect all employees and provide a safe work environment. If employees are not sufficiently trained, and if then their actions result in injury to themselves or others, the company may be held liable for *negligent training*. In short, training programs should be examined with an eye to legal issues from their inception.[7]

In addition, understanding which tasks are linked to the KSAOs—that is, how the KSAOs are actually demonstrated on the job in terms of behavior—provides rich material for the development of training content. For example, it would be important to know that a job requires the KSAO of "interpersonal skills." However, it would be even more useful to know which interpersonal skills are demonstrated on the job. For example, an administrative assistant might, as part of their coordination activities, focus on interacting with members of the team as well as the leaders of other work groups. In contrast, customer service agents for an airline would use their interpersonal skills to interact with customers. This key difference would determine what type of training content would be included for each of these different types of jobs: For the executive assistant, there might be role plays focused on interacting with a difficult team member; for the airline customer service agent, the role play might focus on dealing with an unhappy passenger. Relatedly, it would be good to know what critical incidents employees face on their jobs—such as dealing with a difficult team leader from a different group in the case of the administrative assistant—to understand how to develop the most appropriate training scenarios.

Both administrative assistants and airline customer service agents have to deal with tricky interpersonal situations. These circumstances can be quite different in terms of whom the assistants and agents are dealing with, the levels of anger and anxiety involved in the interactions, and the mode of communication such as in person, by phone, or by e-mail. What kind of interpersonal skills training content would you recommend for each type of job?

Person Analysis

Once the critical competencies, KSAOs, and tasks of a job have been identified, it may seem that there is enough information to develop a training program. However, there are still a few issues that need to be determined in order to maximize training resources. Specifically, these can be broken down into two categories of information:

1. Which specific KSAOs or competencies need to be developed, and for which employees?

2. Which characteristics of the employees (referred to as demographics) need to be considered in order to develop the most effective training program?

Identifying KSAOs and Candidates for Development

One approach an organization might take is to train employees on every KSAO that is required for the job. But this would assume that employees are weak on all of the KSAOs, which is unlikely to be the case. The more likely scenario is that employees are fine in terms of some KSAOs and weaker on others. It is also likely that some employees need training more than others do. Let's tease apart these two issues.

First, to train employees on KSAOs at which they are already proficient would obviously be a waste of resources. For that reason, organizations tend to focus on the skills they believe most employees need to improve. For example, a company that sells large-scale computer equipment may find that most of its salespeople are good at finding new customers, reaching out to existing customers, and making sales. Due to rapid advances and innovations in computer equipment, however, salespeople don't know what the various types of equipment can do, which limits their ability to match customer needs with the appropriate equipment. In this case, the training program could be fairly straightforward, such that it brings salespeople up to speed about the current product knowledge.

Second, it may be that only some employees need training whereas others do not. Or it may be that some employees need training on some KSAOs, but other employees need training on different KSAOs. Using the sales example, the company may find that some salespeople need to be trained on the various computer products the company is currently selling, and others need to be trained on how to develop new client lists. The training program might therefore be tailored to address each of these different employee needs.

Note that a strategic decision regarding the training program is often whether all employees in a particular type of job should receive the same training or whether the training program should focus on individual employee needs. This decision is largely driven by balancing the difficulty of developing and delivering individualized employee training versus delivering a one-size-fits-all training program that sometimes trains employees on skills they already possess. There is no simple solution to this challenge. However, eLearning forms of training (discussed later in this chapter), which often allow employers (and employees) to choose from among thousands of possible training modules, to some extent facilitate the delivery of training customized to individual employee needs.

How are person analysis data obtained? A number of methods are available to decision makers, and there is no one "correct" method. The options include examining objective production or sales data, customer survey data, performance appraisals, and survey of employees regarding their training needs. Person analysis data can also be collected by having employees take tests (particularly if the focus is on knowledge) or go through job performance simulations. The most appropriate method depends largely on which KSAOs are being assessed as well as the practicality and cost.

Trainee Demographics

Later in this chapter, we discuss how different employee characteristics can affect the delivery of training. At this point, however, it is important simply to understand some basic employee demographics that might affect the type of training approach to be used. For example, employees' education level or age might affect the training methods the organization chooses to use. A group of employees with little exposure to computer technology may not be good candidates for an eLearning approach.

Developing Training Goals

Once the job analysis and person analysis data have been collected, an examination of the gap between the two can drive the development of training goals. In other words, the needs assessment will determine the gap between what the job requires and what KSAOs the trainees currently possess, and the goals of the training should be developed based upon this gap, as seen in Figure 8.6.

To the extent possible, training goals should be expressed in specific, behavioral terms. For example, a weak training goal might be: "By the end of training, the employee can assemble equipment." In contrast, a stronger, more useful training goal would be: "By the end of training, an employee can assemble two pieces of equipment per hour." The latter goal is more useful for the final users of the training goals: training developers and trainees. Training developers will use the goals as the basis for their training programs. Trainees need to be given their training goals to help in their learning the material. (We will discuss the importance of goal setting for learning later in this chapter.)

In summary, investing in a training needs assessment can provide significant value for organizations, determining not only whether there is a need for training but also what type of training and for whom. In addition, it is important to remember that it is not always necessary to perform a training needs assessment with the exact steps and stages described here. In fact, many organizations approach the needs assessment process a bit differently. The key is to keep the goals of each of the stages of needs assessment in mind and to stay focused on organization, job, and persons as much as possible prior to designing a training program.[8]

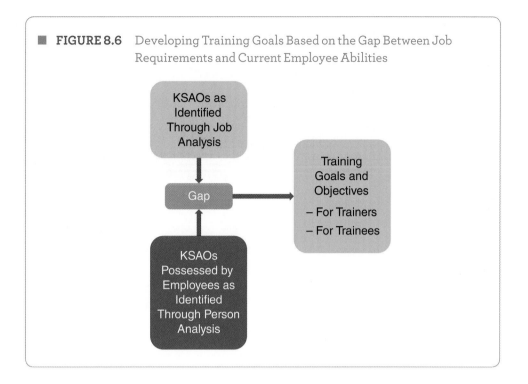

■ **FIGURE 8.6** Developing Training Goals Based on the Gap Between Job Requirements and Current Employee Abilities

Enhancing Learning

Once the training needs assessment is complete and the training goals are established, the next step is to consider ways to enhance learning. Learning can be defined as the acquisition of new knowledge, skills, and behaviors and can occur either within or outside of the training context.[9] Effective training programs take into account characteristics of the trainees, the organization, and the training to enhance learning (see Figure 8.7). Understanding who the trainees are as well as the organization they will be working in helps to implement a training system that will be most effective. In addition, this will allow for a consideration of how the training itself can be used to enhance training and transfer. The main idea here is that training is not a "one-size-fits-all" proposition, and consideration of the person and their context helps make the training more effective.[10]

Trainee Characteristics

A number of trainee characteristics may affect the success of a training program and should be taken into account to enhance the effectiveness of the training system. First, ***self-efficacy***, or a person's belief that they can accomplish a task, is one of the most important predictors of training effectiveness. If a person does not believe that they can master the material in a training course or that they can transfer their learned skills back to the job, they will not do as well in training. This is because people who don't feel they can master a particular skill will put less effort into accomplishing it. How can a training system address the possibility of low self-efficacy among some learners? One of the most effective approaches is to teach the material in small "bites" that allow people to feel a sense of mastery for specific aspects of a knowledge or skill.

Relatedly, ***trainee motivation*** is a significant predictor of training success. While you may be familiar with several theories of motivation, perhaps the most practical ones to consider for the training context are goal-setting theory and expectancy theory. ***Goal-setting theory*** states that setting specific, difficult yet achievable goals for people will lead to the highest performance. Performance can be further enhanced by adding rewards and providing feedback as to how well the person is achieving their goals. Goal setting should

LO 8.2 List the characteristics of the employee, the organizational context, and the training that can be leveraged to enhance training effectiveness.

Self-efficacy A person's belief that they can accomplish a task

Trainee motivation The sustained motivation of employees during the training process, which is a predictor of training success

Goal-setting theory The theory that setting specific, difficult, yet achievable goals for people will lead to the highest performance

- make the training goals specific but achievable,

- clearly communicate training goals to the learner, and

- provide feedback as to how well the goals are being achieved.

In sum, it should provide clear guidance for enhancing trainee motivation and training performance.

Further, goal accomplishment should be tied to rewards such as promotions, pay, or being able to do the job more effectively. Similarly, the ***expectancy theory*** of motivation suggests that if a person sees that their efforts will lead to greater performance, and if they believe that performance will lead to an outcome that they value, they will be more motivated. So in

Expectancy theory A theory that suggests that if a person sees that their efforts will lead to greater performance, and if they believe that performance will lead to an outcome that they value, they will be more motivated

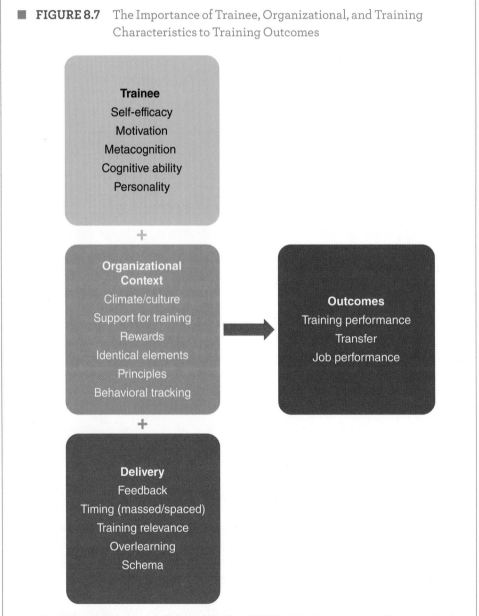

■ **FIGURE 8.7** The Importance of Trainee, Organizational, and Training Characteristics to Training Outcomes

Sources: Based on Colquitt, J. A., LePine, J. A., & Noe, R. A. (2000). Toward an integrative theory of training motivation: A meta-analytic path analysis of 20 years of research. *Journal of Applied Psychology, 85,* 678–707; Goldstein, I. L., & Ford, J. K. (2002). *Training in organizations: Needs assessment, development, and evaluation* (4th ed.). Belmont, CA: Wadsworth Cengage Learning.

the training context, this might include showing trainees that if they try to do well in training it will lead to training success, and this success can lead to an outcome they value such as better job performance.

A third factor related to training success is ***metacognitive skills***. You may not have heard of metacognitive skills before, but you probably use these skills on a regular basis in your coursework. Metacognition is the person's ability to step back and assess their own performance—are they doing well in training? Are there some topics that they find harder than others and that they need to brush up on? Some people are better at assessing their own performance than others, and this ability can have a serious effect on whether they learn. Consider two students, Carlos and Antonio, who both want As in a class. While Carlos is studying, he considers how well he is grasping the material, and he realizes that he is at best at the C level. As a result, Carlos digs into the material to study even harder so he can achieve an A. On the other hand, Antonio, whose knowledge level is also currently in the C range, doesn't really assess his own level of expertise and assumes that he is doing just fine by simply reading the chapters. Note the difference here: By being aware of his weaknesses, Carlos will address them with extra work and is more likely to earn an A in the class. In contrast, Antonio doesn't see his weaknesses and thus will be unlikely to do anything to address them. As a result, he is likely to get a C and be disappointed. In fact, the research suggests that poor performers are not only inaccurate in assessing their own skill levels but also tend to overestimate them.[11] How can the design of a training system address the fact that some people have poor metacognitive skills? As a solution, training can include giving learners frequent feedback about their actual performance levels and even remind them on occasion to step back and think about how well they are learning.

In addition, it is not surprising that both ***personality*** and cognitive ability can affect a person's learning. For example, proactive personality, conscientiousness, openness to experience, and extraversion have all been shown to be related to training performance. And of course, cognitive ability is related to a person's learning speed. One way to address these personality and cognitive differences among learners is to devise training systems that allow people to proceed at their own pace. For example, a training program could be made up of three modules. More proficient learners could move through the three modules quickly, while less proficient learners could go more slowly.

Organizational Context: Enhancing Transfer

Perhaps one of the most important issues in training is ***training transfer***, or whether the training results in changes in performance on the job. The idea of transfer is core to the purpose of training in organizations—a training program may create increased knowledge among employees, but if performance is not affected, the training is not creating value for the organization.

There are a number of factors that can affect whether training results in transfer. First, what is the ***training transfer climate*** as expressed by supervisors—that is, is there support for training in the organization? For example, a bank may implement a training program that causes increased knowledge about how to interact with customers. In fact, the trainees may show strong improvement in their interpersonal skills while in the training environment. But when they return to work, the bank managers tell them that the training is nonsense and that there is no time to interact with customers in this way. In other words, despite the strength of the training, training knowledge and skills are unlikely to transfer due to an unsupportive climate. In fact, until the climate can be changed—and this usually starts by top management communicating and rewarding the desired climate and modeling the associated behaviors themselves—it may not be worth implementing the training. Relatedly, employees need to be rewarded for carrying out their trained behaviors.

In addition, training is more likely to transfer to the extent that there are ***identical elements***, or that the training environment is like the work environment. Consider employee training focused on the use of a new software system. Company A gives its employees training on the

---

Metacognitive skills A person's ability to step back and assess their own skill, performance, or learning

Personality An individual's dispositional and relatively stable pattern of cognition, behavior, and emotion

Training transfer Whether the training results in changes in job performance

Training transfer climate Support for training transfer in the work environment from supervisors and coworkers

Identical elements The extent to which the training environment is the same as the actual work environment and thus enhances training transfer

Mobile technology can be used to enhance the transfer of training. Behavioral tracking programs administered through mobile devices such as smartphones can help trainees set goals for performing trained behaviors on the job and also send trainees daily reminders about performing trained behaviors back at work.[12]

Transfer through principles
Teaching learners the principles underlying a training concept in order to enhance transfer

Behavioral tracking A process in which trainees keep track of their on-the-job behaviors and whether they are performing the behaviors they learned in training

system using computer equipment that is the same system employees use on the job. Company B simply gives a lecture describing the new software and how to use it. In this case, Company B's training approach is not much like the work environment and is not likely to lead to good results.

Transfer through principles is when transfer is enhanced by training employees on the principles behind the content being taught. Consider a situation in which customer service workers are being trained on how to handle customer complaints. One company trains its employees on the issues involved—addressing customer complaints by balancing fairness and customer satisfaction, with the possibility of a small monetary concession from the company if the customer has a valid complaint or is a long-term customer. Company B, however, does not explain any such principles but only tells the trainees to apologize to customers if there is a complaint. Clearly, the employees in Company A will be better able to handle a range of customer service complaints and also to handle them in a way that results in customer satisfaction.

Finally, transfer can be enhanced through a process called *behavioral tracking*, a process in which trainees keep track of their on-the-job behaviors and whether they are performing the behaviors they learned in training. Specifically, trainees might set goals for performing behaviors on the job and keep track of how often they perform the behaviors. The use of the behavioral tracking approach is facilitated by the use of today's mobile technology. As an example, supervisors might go through a simple lecture about how to be supportive of their employees. Then they are asked to follow the behavioral tracking protocol for 3 weeks. Specifically, they are asked to set daily goals for performing supportive behaviors, and for 3 weeks they receive daily reminders on their smartphones asking them if they have shown support to their employees that day. As you can imagine, reminding trainees of their daily goals regarding applying training concepts on the job and asking them how well they have accomplished their goals can be a powerful tool in facilitating transfer.[13]

Training Delivery Characteristics

A number of characteristics of the training program can be used to enhance learning and transfer and some that may be useful in particular situations. First, as mentioned earlier, providing *feedback* to learners as to their training performance can greatly enhance the effectiveness of training. Consider a situation in which you are completing several online training modules as part of learning your new job. If you were never told how successful you were in completing the modules, not only would that be very unsatisfying, it would not provide you with information to adjust your performance in order to do better in the training. As such, providing feedback can help learners understand how well they are mastering the training material and adjust their performance if necessary. Second, *training relevance*, or the degree to which trainees see the training as important to their jobs, can have a significant impact on the amount of effort they invest in the training. Third, providing trainers with a learning *schema* at the beginning of the training process can also enhance learning. A schema is an outline or framework to help the learner organize the training material so that they will better retain the material. For example, a retail employer wanting to train employees to work in a store could explain to them the different skills they will learn over the week—how to interact with customers, how to handle money, how to handle customer returns—so that the learners know how to organize the material in their minds and thus retain the material more effectively. Often such a schema is given to learners in the form of a brief outline of the training material before training begins or in the form of a brief lecture. Clear training goals can also act as a schema to help employees organize the training content.

Feedback Information provided to an employee regarding his/her performance

Training relevance The degree to which trainees see the training as important to their jobs

Schema An outline or framework to help the learner organize the training material so that they will better retain the material

Two additional training delivery concepts can be considered for certain training situations. First, **overlearning** in training occurs when trainees repeatedly practice a particular behavior in the training situation so that they can perform the behavior automatically without much cognitive effort. Overlearning takes additional organizational resources—primarily the time of the trainer and trainees—and thus for practical reasons should not be used except under special circumstances. But overlearning can be very useful for training certain types of tasks, such as when the task is performed on the job infrequently or when it is performed under stressful conditions. For example, employees may rarely practice emergency safety procedures on the job, if at all, such that their knowledge of these procedures may decay. Moreover, emergency procedures are typically performed under stressful conditions—so much so that an employee might forget what to do when the emergency arises. By overlearning these emergency procedures during training through repeated drills, the employees will be more likely to handle the emergency situation if it arises.

Finally, the idea of **massed learning** versus **spaced learning** refers to whether the training occurs in one large chunk (massed) or through several sessions over time (spaced). Spaced learning is generally a more effective training method, as it allows learners to absorb the material, build self-efficacy incrementally, and even practice it on the job. However, many organizations opt for massed learning for practical reasons—it may be less expensive to deliver training in a large chunk rather than in small ones. For example, a New York company may hire a trainer to come in from Los Angeles and stay in New York overnight each time. The company could have the trainer come in once a week for 5 weeks (a spaced approach), or it could simply have one intensive session (a massed approach). Obviously, this massed approach would save money by reducing trainer travel expenses. Considering whether to use a massed or spaced approach to training has much to do with the type of training material and its suitability to massed training as well as cost.[14]

Overlearning When trainees repeatedly practice a particular behavior in the training situation so that they can perform the behavior automatically without much cognitive effort

Massed learning Training that occurs in one large chunk at one point in time

Spaced learning Training that occurs through several sessions over time

Training Methods

Training has been going on in industrialized organizations for more than 100 years. In that time, a number of common training methods have emerged, and there is some understanding of their levels of effectiveness. As with many HR practices, there is no one best way to train employees. Rather, one should take into account a number of issues such as the particular skill or ability that is being trained, how well the training method fits the characteristics of individual trainees and the organization (e.g., providing feedback, allowing people to work at their own pace), as well as practical issues such as cost. Further, it may be best to think about choosing the best combination of methods for training rather than one method. For example, rather than choosing between lectures and on-the-job training, an organization may choose to use a combination of both, interspersed together over weeks, to get the strongest effect at a reasonable cost.

In this section, we present an overview of some of the most common training methods, as well as their advantages and disadvantages. Keep in mind that the descriptions we provide here are broad and that there is quite a bit of variability within each category of training method. For example, "lecture" may include a one-way video of a person talking, or it may be given to a class of 30 trainees with a lot of interaction and questions and answers. "eLearning" may include giving an online slide presentation to trainees, a sophisticated set of learning modules, or a simulation of a work situation.

LO 8.3 Describe some of the most important training methods and media used by organizations and list their respective advantages and disadvantages.

On-the-Job Training

Perhaps the most commonly used training method is **on-the-job training (OJT)**, in which a more senior employee works with a new employee to teach him or her how to perform the job tasks. OJT is a key component of most **apprenticeship** programs, wherein a person enters and learns a trade or profession (e.g., electrician). In fact, you may have experienced some form of OJT. In theory, OJT could be the most effective type of training: The training and transfer

On-the-job training (OJT) When a new employee works on the job in order to learn it, usually under the supervision of a more senior employee

Apprenticeship A formal training program when a person enters and learns a trade or profession

situation are the same, assuring a high potential for transfer. However, in practice, the advantages of OJT are often not maximized. Often the employee doing the training is not given much support. That is, the "trainer" employee often has to continue doing their job, with the extra burden of training a new employee. Also, to do OJT well, the "trainer" employee should be given some training themselves on how best to do OJT, not just be told, "Go train this person." Still, mixed with other training methods such as lectures or online training, OJT can be a powerful training tool if done correctly.[15]

Lectures

Lectures are training events in which an expert speaks to a group of workers to explain and impart knowledge. Lectures have a bit of a bad reputation in terms of being boring and not very engaging. Although the lecture method does have its drawbacks, it also has its merits. Lectures can be great for getting information to a large number of people quickly. They can also be much more engaging and useful if they involve interaction between the lecturer and trainees, providing feedback for both the trainee (e.g., to see whether they understand the training content) and the trainer (e.g., to see whether trainees understand the material and in what ways the training may need to be adjusted). Lectures are also excellent supplements for other training methods. For example, a lecture, or a series of lectures interspersed with other training methods, allows learners to develop a schema for organizing the training content, and it allows learners to ask questions after trying to apply the trained skill. Further, despite lectures' negative reputation, meta-analytic research suggests that they can provide significant value in terms of training many types of tasks and skills.[16]

Simulators

We know that OJT is a potentially effective training method. But it can be very dangerous to conduct OJT with certain types of jobs such as commercial airline pilots, for which simulation use is the norm. As just one example, at its Aircrew Training Center in Atlanta, Delta Airlines has 37 flight simulators reflecting nine different types of aircraft.[17] Simulations attempt to balance the limitations of OJT by providing a safe environment to train employees. In addition, simulators can allow the trainer to expose the trainee to some important but rarely occurring conditions. In the case of airline pilots, this might include dangerous although rare weather conditions that a pilot would need to be able to act on safely. The simulator experience is often followed up by a debriefing to discuss what happened during the training session. The drawback of many types of simulators, including pilot simulators, is their cost, and thus they are often only used for very specific types of jobs in which safety is paramount.[18]

Programmed Instruction

Programmed instruction involves presenting the learner with a set of learning modules or steps. After each module, the learner takes a quiz to demonstrate that they have mastered the material. If they pass the quiz, they can go on to the next module. If not, they must repeat the module until they can demonstrate that they have mastered the material. Despite its name and the fact that it is often administered via computer or online, programmed instruction derives its name from the fact that it is a "program of instruction." In fact, programmed instruction has been around since at least the middle of the 20th century, with modules and quizzes presented in paper form. You likely are familiar with programmed instruction in some form.

Programmed instruction provides a number of advantages from a learning perspective. It provides learners with needed feedback on whether they are mastering the material. It allows learners to go at their own pace. It may also be helpful for those with poor metacognitive skills to gauge whether they understand the training material. And once the up-front development costs are invested, programmed instruction can be cost effective. In fact, programmed instruction is available from many vendors so that organizations do not necessarily have to develop their own materials. In fact, many eLearning platforms take a programmed instruction approach. Programmed instruction may sometimes, however, lead to disengaged trainees, especially if the modules are little more than a series of PowerPoint slides. In other words, the learning is only as good as the programmed instruction content, and some learners much prefer to work with a live trainer. With that said, programmed instruction can be a great way to teach certain types of skills and can be used in conjunction with other training methods, freeing up a trainer's time to focus on training more complex skills that are best handled through face-to-face training.[19]

eLearning

eLearning, or training that is delivered through an online platform via computers or mobile devices, is growing exponentially as an industry that provides training to organizations. Although online and computer-based training have been around for years, as seen in Figure 8.8, investment in learning technology has grown substantially just over 2 years. The flexibility and variety of eLearning means that companies have access to tens of thousands of eLearning modules, which can be tailored for specific skills within their particular industry. It also means that employees spread globally can have access to training that they may not have had in the past, and employers can even provide standardized training to their employees, regardless of location.

eLearning Training that is delivered through an online platform via computers or mobile devices

At the same time, eLearning should not be seen as a panacea for all types of training. Rather, it should be seen as a training method that fits into a larger training system that includes multiple training methods.[20] Also, some research evidence points to the potential ineffectiveness of entirely learner-centered training in which learners decide their own training approach, as many learners may not choose the most appropriate learning exercises and learning options. This strongly relates to our earlier discussion about metacognitive skills. Instead, online learning approaches that provide guidance to learners may prove most effective, and the development of more sophisticated eLearning platforms should help in this regard. As a positive point, a meta-analytic study showed that online training can be as effective as classroom training for teaching simple knowledge types of material, and it can be highly effective if it allows some learner control and provides feedback. In short, eLearning and other

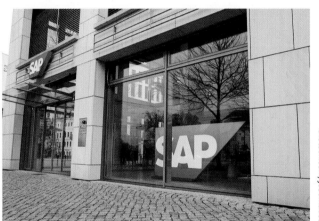

©iStock.com/josefkubes

eLearning platforms are sold by a number of online vendors, and the size of the course offerings is growing rapidly. One example is SAP's learning hub, which provides access to training 24 hours per day, 7 days per week.[21]

■ **FIGURE 8.8** Investment in Learning Technology

$6.5 billion was invested in learning technology companies in 2015

$17.3 billion was invested in learning technology companies in 2016

Sources: Global investment in learning technology firms surpasses previous year's record. (2017, April). *TD: Talent Development,* 19; Adkins, S.S. Metaari Advanced Learning Technology Research. (2017, January). The 2016 global learning technology investment patterns. http://www.metaari.com/assets/Metaari_s-Analysis-of-the-2016-Global-Learning-Technology-Investment-Pat25875.pdf

types of online systems hold promise for tailoring to individual workers' needs but are not the only solution for delivering training.[22]

Behavioral Modeling Training

Behavioral modeling training (BMT) usually involves a trainee observing a person (model) performing a behavior (either live or in a video), practicing it, and then receiving feedback about their own performance. Grounded in Bandura's social learning theory, BMT is based on the idea that people can learn from observing others and then can practice that skill themselves and receive feedback about their own performance. BMT is often used to train interpersonal types of skills and is thus a popular type of training for supervisors, who need to develop strong skills for dealing with subordinates and providing them with feedback. Meta-analytic results show that BMT is a powerful training tool and that its results last over time. Interestingly, BMT is more likely to result in good training transfer if learners are provided with both positive models (what to do) and negative models (what not to do).[23]

Diversity Training

Workplace diversity parallels increasing diversity within the U.S. population. It is also increasing due to growing numbers of work teams that comprise individuals from diverse cultural backgrounds working together remotely from around the world. One way that organizations seek to manage this diversity and even have it work in their favor is the introduction of diversity training. Although the question of how to conduct diversity training is far from settled, there are some conclusions to be drawn at this point. First, meta-analytic research suggests that diversity training does have an effect on affective (attitudes), cognitive (beliefs), and skill-based (behavioral) outcomes. Findings also showed that diversity training had stronger effects when spaced rather than massed (in this case, conducted face to face over time rather than in a single session). The researchers pointed out that more research is needed to understand how training can target unconscious processes (i.e., not only focusing on bias that participants are aware of), an approach that Google has taken in its gender diversity program. Others have noted that organizations will get better effects from diversity training if they frame it in positive terms to employees such as by making training voluntary, engaging employees, and increasing contact among workers from different backgrounds. And researchers have indicated the need for more in-depth research on how to better understand the process involved in diversity training and better increase its impact.[24]

Training to Increase Team Effectiveness

The workplace has become more oriented toward teamwork, and thus companies sometimes focus their training not only on individuals but on work teams as well. This could involve team members taking on each other's jobs or learning how to better communicate and coordinate among themselves. The research suggests that these approaches work. For example, a meta-analysis found that team training can positively impact team performance. Another study found that cross-training could help teams develop a shared "mental model"—or conceptualization—of their work, an important issue for team coordination.[25]

Cindy McCauley, PhD, is a senior fellow at the Center for Creative Leadership (CCL) in Greensboro, NC. During her 30 years at CCL, much of her work has focused on using leadership assessments and stretch assignments in the development of leaders. One of her projects helps groups improve their leadership processes by examining the critical outcomes of those processes: agreement on direction, aligned work, and mutual commitment to the group.[26]

Training for Managers and Leaders

Role-plays When trainees act in managerial situations such as counseling a difficult subordinate

Many of the training methods described thus far can also be used to train managers. There are also additional options for training managers. These include ***role-plays***, in which trainees act in managerial situations such as counseling a difficult subordinate; *case studies*, in which participants analyze a difficult business case; and *games and simulations*, in which teams challenge each other as if they were businesses in competition. In addition, assessment centers, which Chapter 7 discusses in terms of their use for selecting managers, can do double-duty as training and development exercises, providing managers with useful feedback about their strengths and weaknesses and giving advice for future development. In that same vein, *executive coaching* has grown in popularity as a way to provide individual advice and counseling to managers regarding their work and careers. In fact, it is also now possible to become certified as an executive coach. The research on the effectiveness of coaching is still scant, but researchers have pointed out that different types of coaches—such as trained psychologists versus those who have a management background—likely have different skill sets and can benefit managers in different ways. Managers' leadership skills and abilities can also be developed through the assignments that they are given. For example, a member of the sales team might be given a series of supervisory and managerial assignments in different geographical locations as preparation for a middle management role. Finally, given the complexities of managing a culturally diverse workforce, particularly with the rise of multinational companies, there is an increasing need for managers to develop their global leadership skills.[27]

Case studies A managerial training method wherein participants analyze and discuss a difficult business case

Games and simulations A type of managerial training in which teams challenge each other as if they were businesses in competition

Executive coaching Individual advice and counseling to managers regarding their work and careers

SPOTLIGHT ON GLOBAL ISSUES
Global Leadership Development

Being a leader can mean very different things around the world, and this determines the best ways to provide leadership training in different cultures. Consider the role of leaders in relation to their teams in different cultures. For example, individualistic cultures such as the United States tend to focus on individual goals, whereas more collectivist cultures might focus on how individuals' performance contributes to the performance of the group. Similarly, in hierarchical countries (e.g., India), it is assumed that a team has a leader with high decision-making authority. This is in contrast to countries where much more authority is afforded to individual team members. In other words, being a good leader in one culture can be quite different from effective leadership in another.

What is particularly challenging in today's global business environment is that leaders may need to be effective in their own cultural environment as well as in cultural environments different from their own. Increasingly, leaders manage people from multiple cultural backgrounds. A person may need to be able to understand different cultural styles of leadership and adjust their own behavior accordingly. Thus, the development of such global leaders is a complex process, and it may vary from person to person depending on their background. Global organizations may need to be willing to provide such individualized development as coaching and individual experiences in multiple cultural contexts. Global organizations may also include intensive sessions in which participants learn more about managing themselves and others in multiple cultural contexts and honing their own abilities in terms of cultural perception.[28]

Current Workplace Training Issues

A number of new types of training methods and approaches are emerging. The first of these is *mindfulness training*. Mindfulness is a state in which a person allows themselves to be in the present moment and also learns to notice things around them in a nonjudgmental way. Mindfulness is a topic of growing interest in organizations, especially its potential as a way of increasing employee well-being. Increased interest in mindfulness has led to the growing popularity of mindfulness training in organizations. Some results are promising in terms of affecting important outcomes, including reduced employee stress and better sleep.[29] According to some estimates, 22% of large employers offer mindfulness training to their employees, including Target, General Mills, and Google.[30]

Mindfulness training Teaches a person to be present in the moment and to notice things around them in a nonjudgmental way

Gamification Training that is made into a game or competition among employees in terms of scores on their training performance

A second type of training that is gaining recent attention in organizations is gamification. *Gamification* might include training that is made into a game or simply competition among employees in terms of scores on their training performance (e.g., earning badges, test scores after training). The assumption among proponents of gamified training is that it can increase trainee motivation and engagement. Although the number of vendors selling gamified training solutions is increasing quickly, the published research on gamified training is very limited, and the results do not lend themselves to simple recommendations for implementing gamified training in organizations. For example, gamified training may work for some employees but not for others: Those with a lot of gaming experience (e.g., video games) may prefer gamified training, while others with relatively little gaming experience may prefer traditional training delivery. The design of the competitive structure of the game can also lead to different results: Trainees who compete with others with skill levels lower than their own may benefit in terms of increased self-efficacy, but those with a more highly skilled competitor may be more engaged. In short, although gamification of training may hold promise, more research is needed about how and when to implement it and for whom it is most effective when compared to traditional training methods.[31]

Onboarding New Employees

Onboarding (organizational socialization) The process of helping new employees adjust to their new organizations by imparting to them the knowledge, skills, behaviors, culture, and attitudes required to successfully function within the organization

Onboarding (or *organizational socialization*) is the process of helping new employees adjust to their new organizations by imparting to them the knowledge, skills, behaviors, culture, and attitudes required to successfully function within the organization. When done right, onboarding can lead to positive outcomes for both organizations and individuals such as better new employee role clarity, feelings of connectedness with coworkers, confidence in their new role, higher performance, better job attitudes, and higher retention.[32] One study even found that better onboarding practices were related to higher financial performance for the firm. The goal of onboarding is to make sure that new employees have the information, orientation, training, and support they need to be successful.

Both organizations and new employees contribute to the success of onboarding. Organizations and organizational insiders engage in activities that may help or hinder new employees in adjusting to the organization. Similarly, new employees can engage in several specific activities and behaviors that can either help or hinder their own adjustment to their new organizations.

Effective Organizational Onboarding

Welcoming Activities that are intended to be friendly toward employees, such as giving them a personalized e-mail or call or having lunch with the new coworker

Informing Providing new employees with sources, materials, and training to help them learn what is expected of them

Orientation program A specific type of training designed to help welcome, inform, and guide new employees

Organizations can follow several onboarding best practices to set the stage for new employees' success. One way to think about how organizations can best direct their onboarding efforts is to focus on how to *welcome, inform,* and *guide* new employees.[33] *Welcoming* includes activities such as giving employees a welcome kit, giving them a personalized e-mail or call, having lunch with the new coworker, having the new employee meet their manager, providing the new employee with welcome gifts, or inviting them to a social activity or work meeting.

It is the *informing* portion of onboarding in which training comes into play. It is important for new employees to receive resources such as websites, internal discussion boards, materials, or orientations, on-the-job training, and additional training programs to help them learn what is expected of them and how to do their job well. The *orientation program*, a specific type of training designed to help welcome, inform, and guide new employees, is a great way to give new employees the information they need in a short amount of time. However, a key problem with orientation programs can be that they impart *too much* information all at once. Thus, it makes sense for organizations to think through what information is needed when. Zappos, for instance, spread the process of providing information to new employees out over 5 weeks as newcomers attended an onboarding training course that focused on understanding the culture and values that make the company unique. This brings up a key point: The onboarding process should be more than just the new employee orientation program. Organizations such as Microsoft, NASA, and PwC think of onboarding as lasting 1 year and beyond.[34]

Many different methods may be used during the informing phase of onboarding. For example, the Ritz-Carlton Hotel Company employs a systematic and innovative approach to employee

MANAGER'S TOOLBOX

What Can Managers Do to Maximize Onboarding Success?

- Make the first day on the job special.
- Implement formal orientation programs.
- Develop a written onboarding plan for every new employee.
- Consistently implement onboarding.
- Monitor and update onboarding programs over time.

- Use technology to help facilitate but not hinder the process.
- Engage organizational stakeholders in planning.
- Develop onboarding milestones and timelines.[35]

orientation and training to aid retention. In the 2-day classroom orientation, employees spend time with management and dine in the hotel's finest restaurant. To show what great customer service looks like, the new employees receive handwritten welcome notes and their favorite snacks during the break. During these 2 days, they are introduced to the company's intensive service standards, team orientation, and its own language. New employees also complete 100 hours of additional training, and they are tested on service standards and are certified if they pass.[36] As another example, Bank of America onboards its new executives through a number of HRM activities tied to its onboarding plan (see Figure 8.9).

Although large organizations may have the advantage of being able to invest more resources in developing onboarding programs, they face challenges as well due to their size. Specifically, larger organizations face two challenges: (1) determining how to scale their onboarding processes and (2) determining whether to create unique experiences in different business locations around the world. A key point is to survey new employees to understand how their onboarding process is going and to solicit ideas for how to improve upon it for future hires. In contrast, small and medium-sized organizations may actually have an advantage, as one-on-one onboarding can be very effective. The key for smaller organizations is to make sure that each new employee is able to get the information and support they need.

New employees who receive guidance from organizational insiders such as their coworkers, managers, and mentors are more successful than those who are left to find their own guidance. Thus, organizations may assign a "buddy" or peer to help a new employee with answers to questions, a tour of the facilities, and someone who checks in with the new employee on an ongoing basis. Other programs might be to assign mentors to newcomers. Yet another strategy organizations employ is to assign a single point of contact, starting with recruitment and hiring, and continuing until the new employee is fully adjusted. Research has consistently shown that organizational insiders are important for helping new employees adjust, so the extra effort to set up such relationships is worth it. For example, organizations such as CH2M Hill and Google create tools to help managers provide the right information and engage in the right behaviors at the right time for new employees.[37]

Effective Newcomer Onboarding Behaviors

Newcomers may feel overwhelmed during the adjustment process, but the good news is that much of their success is in their own hands. Engaging in proactive behaviors such as seeking feedback and information, socializing with coworkers, networking, seeking to build relationships with managers, and framing things positively to themselves all help newcomers adjust (see Table 8.1).[38] Research shows that newcomers who actively seek out information not only receive more of it but also get more ongoing attention from their managers.[39]

■ **FIGURE 8.9**   Onboarding Tools Used at Bank of America

ONBOARDING TOOL	WHY IS IT USED?	WHEN IS IT USED?
Orientation Program	Includes information on the business, history, culture, and values of Bank of America	Held on the first day on the job
Written Onboarding Plan	Helps new executives organize and prioritize the onboarding process	Provided in the first week after entry
Leadership Tools	Helps new executives understand the leadership frameworks at Bank of America	Provided in the first week after entry
Key Stakeholder Meetings	Allow for important flows of information and for expectation setting	Must be done in the first 2 months
New Leader–Team Integration	Helps accelerate the development of relationships between the new executive and his or her team members	Occurs between 2 and 3 months after entry
New Peer Integration	Helps accelerate the development of relationships between the new executive and the rest of the executive team	Occurs between 2 and 3 months after entry
Key Stakeholder Check-in Meetings	Help diagnose potential problems, receive developmental feedback, and create solutions	Occur between 3 and 4 months after entry
Executive Networking Forums	Help new executives connect and network with other executives	Held quarterly
360-Degree Feedback	Helps new executives gauge how they are performing on key metrics as measured by those around them	Occurs after 6 months after entry

Sources: Bauer, T. N. (2011). Onboarding new employees: Maximizing success. SHRM foundation's effective practice guidelines series. https://www.shrm.org/foundation/ourwork/initiatives/resources-from-past-initiatives/Documents/Onboarding%20New%20Employees.pdf; Bauer, T. N., & Elder, E. (2006). Onboarding newcomers into organizations. Presentation at the Society for Human Resource Management Annual Conference, Washington, DC; Conger, J., A., & Fishel, B. (2007). Accelerating leadership performance at the top: Lessons from the Bank of America's executive on-boarding process. *Human Resource Management Review, 17,* 442–454.

TABLE 8.1   What Can New Employees Do to Maximize Onboarding Success?

- Gather information
- Manage first impressions
- Invest in relationship development
- Seek feedback
- Show success early on

Source: Information summarized based on research by Talya Bauer.

LO 8.4   Identify the major categories of criteria for assessing training effectiveness and demonstrate their use.

Evaluating the Effectiveness of Training Programs

Accountability for different organizational functions is becoming an increasingly normal part of organizational life. Likewise, there is considerable pressure for HR departments to demonstrate the effectiveness of training programs. Perhaps even more important, evaluating a training program can be helpful to understanding where the program may be falling short and thus in which ways the training program can be adjusted or improved to better meet an organization's needs.

SPOTLIGHT ON ETHICS

The Training of Ethics in Organizations

We discussed the fact that ethics have been integrated into SHRM's competency model as a key competency. It's not surprising, then, that many organizations have integrated the training of ethics into their training curricula. This might include training in more general ethical issues such as diversity training. Or it might be more specific to certain types of jobs, such as how to handle monetary transactions, gifts from clients, or conflicts of interest. There have been recent discussions into the ethical issues that are faced by those working in the high-tech industry and how what they do can affect millions of lives. (Critics say that this sort of ethical training is not discussed enough within the industry, much less trained.) Still, other organizations do provide explicit training focused on ethics. For example, the National Institutes of Health (NIH) offers annual ethics training for its employees on understanding rules and issues such as those for gifts and financial conflicts of interest.[40]

Questions

1. Do you think people violate ethics because they lack training (i.e., they don't know what is ethical and unethical), or because they see some advantage to their unethical behavior? Give examples to support your opinion.
2. Find an example in the news or in the HR literature of an organization charged with ethics violations. What did the organization do right? What could the organization have done differently?

However, evaluation of training is not something that takes place in all organizations. This is for a number of reasons. First, in some organizations, there is still the belief that training evaluation is not necessary or to simply believe that if the trainees said that they liked it, the training must have been good enough. Second, even where there is an understanding that training evaluation is critical, some organizational decision makers may not want to undertake it for fear of finding that it did not work. Put differently, if you were the person who championed your company's new $100,000 eLearning platform, it could be a bit scary for you personally to find out that it didn't provide much demonstrable benefit to the organization. Relatedly, if the training is delivered by an external third party (e.g., a provider of an eLearning platform), they may have little motivation to look into the program's effectiveness or may simply rely on successes the program has had with previous clients as proof of the program's effectiveness.

Third, it is difficult to do a training evaluation well, and this in itself has its risks. As an example, let's say that an organization did not have great measures of performance—that they were a bit unreliable (see Chapter 7)—it would be very difficult to demonstrate a training program's effectiveness. Specifically, even if a program, in reality, increased employee knowledge and performance, the use of poor (unreliable) measures to evaluate the program will make it look like the program did not work. And related to this, many training professionals do not have sufficient training in how to do training evaluations effectively (see Figure 8.10).

Still, training evaluation is not an impossible undertaking, and organizations that do such evaluations and do them well not only can justify the use of organizational resources for training; they can also fine-tune how to improve their current program to make it even more effective. This section discusses the basics of how to evaluate an organizational training program. The primary goal is to describe how to conduct a robust training evaluation. The secondary goal is to provide information that helps managers who are not directly involved in the training function ask the right questions in order to better understand whether a training program is effective, and if not, whether it should be eliminated or adjusted to better support the achievement of organizational goals and objectives. Moreover, the increasing use of data analytics in organizations provides a number of advantages for quickly getting metrics regarding the success of a training program. First, we will discuss the different categories of training outcome measures that can be used to determine the effectiveness of a training program, along with their strengths and weaknesses.

■ **FIGURE 8.10** Training Staff May Need Further Evaluation Skills

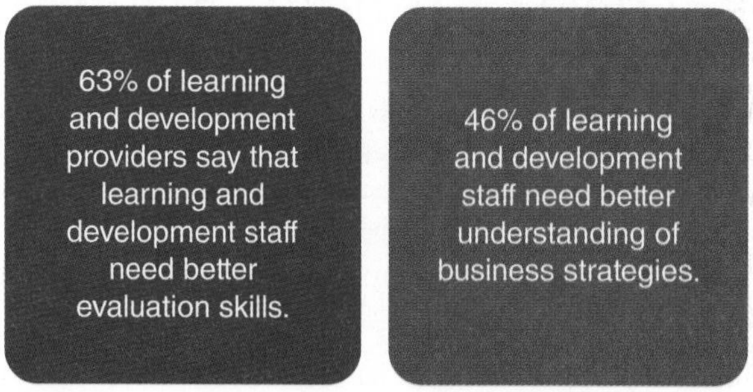

> 63% of learning and development providers say that learning and development staff need better evaluation skills.

> 46% of learning and development staff need better understanding of business strategies.

Source: From measurement/evaluation is the top skill needed by L&D pros. (2017, July). *TD: Talent Development,* 17. Based on a report from the Human Capital Institute.

Second, we will discuss some of the basics of how to analyze these training outcome measures to better understand how training is impacting employees and their performance.

Measures of Training Effectiveness

By far the dominant framework for classifying different measures of training effectiveness is the Kirkpatrick framework (see Figure 8.11). Kirkpatrick's model classifies training outcomes into four categories of training evaluation criteria: reactions, learning, behavior, and results. As Figure 8.11 suggests, the criteria can be conceptualized as existing on four levels, from the lowest and most basic (reactions) to the highest and most robust (results).

■ **FIGURE 8.11** Kirkpatrick's Four Levels of Training Outcomes

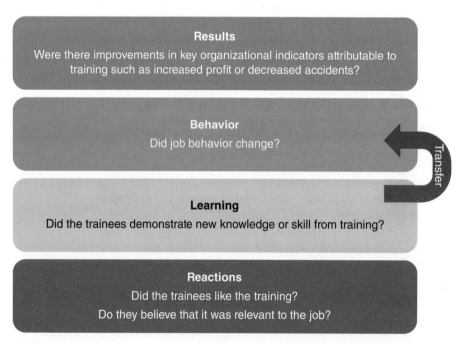

Results
Were there improvements in key organizational indicators attributable to training such as increased profit or decreased accidents?

Behavior
Did job behavior change?

Transfer

Learning
Did the trainees demonstrate new knowledge or skill from training?

Reactions
Did the trainees like the training?
Do they believe that it was relevant to the job?

Sources: Goldstein, I. L., & Ford, J. K. (2002). *Training in organizations: Needs assessment, development, and evaluation* (4th ed.). Belmont, CA: Wadsworth Cengage Learning; Kirkpatrick, D. L., & Kirkpatrick, J. D. (2006). *Evaluating training programs: The four levels.* San Francisco, CA: Berrett-Kohler Publishers.

Reactions criteria have to do with assessing how trainees react to the training, namely, whether they liked it. For example, an organization may send a survey to trainees after they have completed the training program asking them whether they enjoyed the training, thought the training was interesting, or liked the trainer. An example with which you are probably quite familiar is course evaluations within the university, which ask at the end of the course what your perceptions of the course, the instructor, or the materials might be. One important point, of course, is that while training reactions can be important to training effectiveness, they do not necessarily indicate whether the training actually increased employee knowledge or, even more important, whether the training actually transferred to the workplace in terms of increased performance. Note that some types of training reactions—*training utility reactions*, or trainees' belief that the training was actually relevant and useful to their jobs—have been shown to be useful metrics for suggesting transfer. In other words, some types of training reactions may be more useful than others in indicating the effectiveness of training.[41]

The next level in the framework is *learning criteria*, or whether the trainee actually gained some sort of knowledge or skill while in training. For example, a company may train its employees on the use of a new software system to track the delivery of its product to customers. To evaluate the training, the company might give the employees a test at the end of the training in which the employees demonstrate that they can use the software effectively. Note that this is a major step up from simply asking whether the trainees liked the training or thought it was effective.

Still, just because the trainees have gained knowledge or skill as the result of training does not in itself indicate the training is beneficial to the organization. For example, a company may provide training about safety practices on the job, and the employees may be able to pass a test about safe practices as a result of the training. But maybe the types of practices described in the training are not relevant to the employees' jobs. Or even if the safety rules are relevant, maybe the training will not transfer into actual safety behavior back at work, because supervisors and the culture are not supportive of it. This is where the next level in Kirkpatrick's model, behavior, comes in. *Behavior* refers to actual behavior on the job, perhaps as measured by the supervisor. In this example of safety training, perhaps after training, employees may rate each other higher than they did before training in terms of actually following safety practices. This suggests that the training actually transferred back to the job, resulting in improved safety performance.

The final and highest level of Kirkpatrick's training criteria is *results*, or whether the training actually translates into improvements in organizational outcomes such as profits and performance. Using the safety example presented here, the company may be able to demonstrate that, as a result of the training program, accidents actually decreased company-wide, and that there actually were decreases in employee injuries and medical claims as a result of injuries. These outcomes would thus reflect the ultimate goal of a safety program—reducing accidents, keeping employees from getting hurt, reducing costs. However, results criteria can often be the most difficult to tie back to training programs. For example, improvements in accidents, injuries, and medical claims could be attributed to many causes besides training.

It is important to make a few points about the Kirkpatrick framework. Its continued popularity for more than 50 years is largely attributable to its flexibility and intuitive appeal. These are important issues, but it is also important to note that the model may gloss over certain outcomes that are important to organizations, such as attitude change (one of the primary outcomes of diversity training). Moreover, the model's flexibility is demonstrated in that many of the metrics available—including some of the newest analytics—can be classified into the

©iStock.com/wdstock

To assess its training program, Bloomingdale's tracks its sales associates' knowledge acquisition, retention, and application. It can track this by employee and by store. Bloomingdale's can also analyze employee knowledge by individual knowledge categories and tie it back to employee behavior and results.[42]

Reactions criteria The assessment of how trainees react to training such as whether they thought it was valuable

Training utility reactions Trainees' belief that the training was actually relevant and useful to their jobs

Learning criteria Measures of whether the trainee actually gained some sort of knowledge or skill while in training

Behavior/behavior criteria Actual behavior on the job that is an outcome of training

Results criteria Whether the training actually translates into improved organizational outcomes

Harnessing Analytics to Enhance and Evaluate Training

Analytics has been associated with the training function for decades, at least in the most progressive organizations. After all, Kirkpatrick first introduced his four categories of training outcomes for measuring training success back in the 1950s, and these measures have been adopted by organizations in the intervening years.

However, as with other areas of HR, the development of more high-tech analytics in recent years has led to significant opportunities for organizations to more effectively manage and evaluate their training functions. First, the measurement of training outcomes in organizations has become not only more sophisticated but more easily accessible to organizational decision makers through useful summaries of the effectiveness of training on specific outcomes. As an example, Xerox evaluates its training efforts in terms of efficiency (e.g., number of trainees completing a training program; program cost), effectiveness (e.g., knowledge assessment scores), outcomes (e.g., whether the learner is engaging with

the training program, such as website visits), and alignment (e.g., the training function's net promoter scores within the organization). These types of outcomes can help organizational managers, both within and outside of training, make more informed decisions about what people are learning and how training can be improved. A key here is to make these outcome measures relatively easy and affordable for the organization to collect. Elegant but overly expensive measures of training effectiveness may not be practical.

Similarly, automation resulting from the use of artificial intelligence (AI) in organizations may also lead to enhanced training functions. In the months after the delivery of a training program, AI can be used to follow up with learners to reinforce certain key learning points, or it can be used to survey learners to assess their knowledge retention. In short, AI may become a significant tool for enhancing human learning in organizations.[43]

Kirkpatrick framework. The additional types of training outcomes available to organizations today may not suggest the need to replace Kirkpatrick's model but simply to augment it, as illustrated in the experience of Xerox highlighted in the Spotlight on Data and Analytics box.

Finally, one of the most challenging aspects of developing a training evaluation approach in an organization is demonstrating that the training outcomes are actually tied back to business objectives—that is, to results criteria. The use of analytics in organizations can be particularly helpful in this regard, allowing decision makers and managers to see whether training is impacting training outcomes and how these are impacting business outcomes. The key is to be able to measure these training outcomes accurately—not just quickly and cheaply—and in ways that can be meaningfully tied back to organizational outcomes. For example, an organization may implement a two-part training program, finding that although the training does increase employee skill levels and that this in turn leads to improved sales, it does not lead to increases in quality. Armed with this information, decision makers can determine how to tweak the program to provide better results. Thus, the linkage between training and organizational performance can be clearly illustrated in ways that can aid in organizational decision making—an approach used by Allstate Insurance and discussed in the HR in Action box.

Analyzing the Effects of Training on Training Criteria

Developing good measures of training effectiveness is the first step to training evaluation. The second step is tying these measures to the training program itself—in other words, gauging whether any change in the outcome can be attributed to the training program or to other factors. There is a robust science and deep literature on how to evaluate training data, but in this discussion, we provide only an overview of the key concepts. Let's explore a few different ways to conceptualize the effectiveness of a training program.[44]

HR IN ACTION

Tying Training Data to Performance to Drive Business Decision Making

©iStock.com/cnythzl

Research shows that organizational training enhances performance of individual employees and of organizations as well. Analytics provides an outstanding opportunity for companies to research the effectiveness of their training programs at improving organizational outcomes such as sales and productivity. These sorts of analytics can provide a substantial advantage to organizations that want to optimize their training functions to achieve the best organizational results.

The challenge, however, is finding practical ways to measure training effectiveness. We know that training outcomes can be broken down into reactions, learning, behavior, and results. But collecting these types of data in organizations isn't easy, and with the many types of training programs that may be used across a large organization, it can be challenging to consolidate the different training measures, much less consolidate them into a single coherent system of measures.

However, some organizations are learning how to address these challenges. Allstate Insurance developed a single system of standardized training performance measures. This standardization also allowed Allstate to produce analytics that tied these training performance measures—including reactions, learning, behavior, and results—to business performance. This includes assessing how learners are doing and tying this to the performance of their business units and facilitating the preparation of reports that can be used by decision makers.[45]

1. *Is it always necessary to determine whether a performance outcome is attributable to a training program?* We tend to think of training evaluation as measuring change in an outcome as a result of training. But in some limited circumstances this may not matter: The training will be delivered to employees no matter what, and all we really care about is whether performance is high enough after the training is done. An example here would be police training. It would be hard to think of a city that would decide not to train its new police recruits. And in evaluating the training, they would be more interested in whether the recruits' performance is high enough to put them on the streets interacting with the public, not the fine points of whether the training created changes in the recruits' knowledge. Thus, in some circumstances, the main focus may be not whether the training caused change but whether performance after training was high enough for employees to be effective in their jobs.

2. *Assuming that there seemed to be change in the training outcomes, can we actually attribute it to training?* Consider the example of an organization that measured test scores prior to training in January, and again after training in February. The results are shown in Figure 8.12. At first glance, it seems that the training worked—there was an increase in performance posttraining.

But now consider the information in Figure 8.13. Here it shows the same data plus a control group of employees who were not trained. As you can see in the figure, it looks like there was an improvement in the test scores regardless of whether the employees were trained. This may be due to a number of factors such as normal maturation of employees as they get more job experience (the training wasn't necessary); the fact that employees simply learned the test and got better at it (the training may have worked, but we can't tell from these data); or that the trained employees went back to their workplace and told their untrained colleagues about what they learned (the "control" group was actually trained by their trained coworkers). Note that this range of factors must be considered when attributing changes in measures to training.

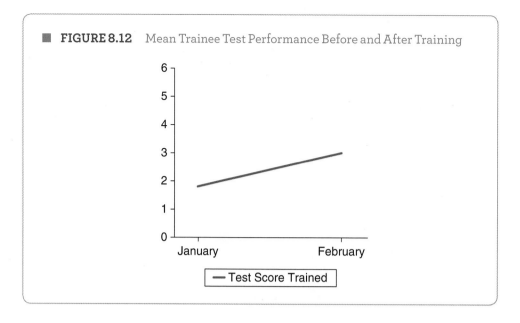

■ **FIGURE 8.12**   Mean Trainee Test Performance Before and After Training

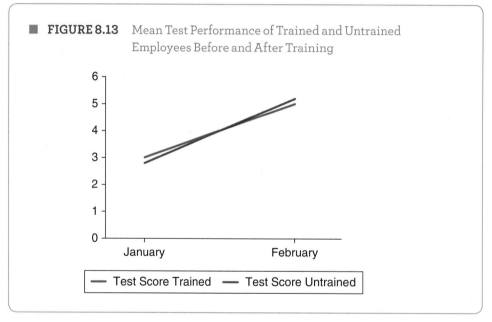

■ **FIGURE 8.13**   Mean Test Performance of Trained and Untrained Employees Before and After Training

3. *What is happening during the learning process, and how should we change or adjust the training to address any problems identified?* One of the biggest benefits of training evaluation is that it helps organizations to determine how to adjust or reinforce employee learning to maximize the training's effectiveness. Figure 8.14 shows the results for employee training on emergency procedures. The training occurred between January and February. The good news is that employee knowledge actually increased after the training. But then the levels of employee knowledge seemed to decline—a classic case of "decay." This may be because emergency procedures (we hope) rarely need to be used on the job; for this reason, employees begin to forget the procedures. The organization might address this issue in a few ways, perhaps by overtraining (mentioned earlier in this chapter) or by providing "booster" training to employees—short bits of training simply to remind employees of what they have already learned. This additional information can allow decision makers to address any shortcomings in the training program.

4. *Who are the end users of the training evaluation data? How can the results of the training evaluation be honed to fit their needs?* This last question can be illustrated with a simple example of whether to combine training measures into an average, or a composite, or to keep them separate (see Figure 8.15). In this case, the company is assessing training's effects on product knowledge,

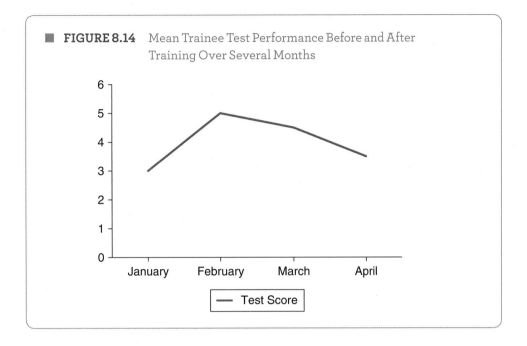

■ **FIGURE 8.14**   Mean Trainee Test Performance Before and After Training Over Several Months

team process skills, and knowledge of company procedures. It has also averaged the three training outcomes into a composite. The composite shows an improvement posttraining, but it masks the effect that the knowledge of company procedures didn't really improve posttraining. When deciding whether to combine training outcomes, the most important thing is to keep in mind who is the consumer of the data. Perhaps a top manager may only want to know the bottom-line results regarding whether the training worked, in which case the composite gives a bottom-line answer

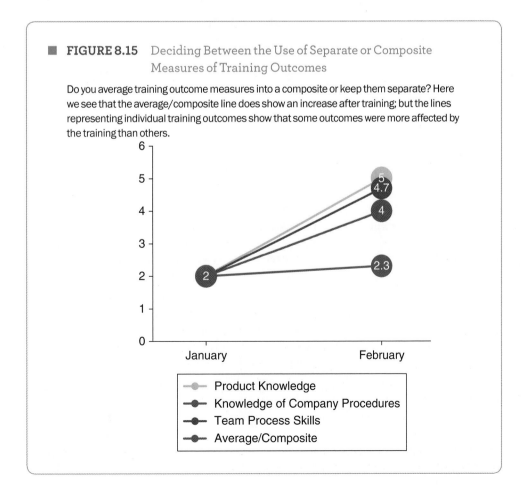

■ **FIGURE 8.15**   Deciding Between the Use of Separate or Composite Measures of Training Outcomes

Do you average training outcome measures into a composite or keep them separate? Here we see that the average/composite line does show an increase after training; but the lines representing individual training outcomes show that some outcomes were more affected by the training than others.

(yes, the training did work). But if the goal is to fine-tune the training and see where it could be improved, keeping the training outcomes separate is most important.[46]

In summary, a key part of training evaluation is being aware from the start of what the purpose of the evaluation is and deciding from there what the most valuable, practical measures of training effectiveness might be (see Table 8.2). To the extent that these can be tied to organizational goals, the better they will aid in making organizational decisions.

TABLE 8.2   A Checklist for Training Evaluation

STEP	ACTIONS	WHY
Clearly specify the purpose of the training evaluation (e.g., to see if specific key indicators are affected by the training; to adjust the training; to decide whether to continue to invest in training).	• Determine what you hope to accomplish by evaluating the training. • Link all subsequent decisions back to the purpose of the evaluation.	To ensure that time spent on evaluating the training was focused and worthwhile.
Evaluate the training at multiple levels if possible.	• Consider measuring reactions, learning, behavior, and results. • Use precise affective, cognitive, and/or behavioral indicators to measure the intended learning outcomes as uncovered during the needs assessment.	Allows well-grounded decisions about training, including any necessary modifications. Enables effective training to continue to be supported.

Source: Salas, E., Tannenbaum, S. I., Kraiger, K., & Smith-Jentsch, K. A. (2012). The science of training and development in organizations: What matters in practice. *Psychological Science in the Public Interest, 13,* 74–101.

SPOTLIGHT ON HR FOR SMALL AND MEDIUM-SIZED BUSINESSES

Training and Development in Smaller Organizations

Training and development in smaller organizations follow the same principles as in larger organizations, only on a different scale. Here are some ways to think about translating the principles in this chapter to smaller organizations:

- *Needs assessment*: Before undertaking a training initiative or hiring a trainer, ensure that the training fits an actual need or gap in the KSAOs of current employees and is consistent with the organization's goals.

- *Evidence for training effectiveness*: When hiring an outside trainer or purchasing a training program, be sure that evidence can be provided for the benefits of the program in other organizations.

- *Trainee characteristics*: When developing a training program, consider the characteristics of current employees, such as their interest in certain types of learning, and adapt the training program accordingly.

- *Evaluation*: Evaluate the effectiveness of a training program to see whether it should be continued or adapted to make it more effective. On a smaller scale, this might include speaking with trainees or asking them to rate the effectiveness of the program in terms of its usefulness to their work.

- *Career development*: Consider informal training and development activities, such as new work assignments, as a means for developing a "talent pipeline" for the future and show employees their value to the organization.

In addition, just as in larger organizations, smaller employers should keep in mind different types of required training such as safety training mandated by the Occupational Safety and Health Administration (OSHA; see Chapter 15). This includes developing a system to document required training for each employee.

Career Development and Management

Another important aspect of development relates to one's career. ***Career management*** is the continual process of setting career-related goals and planning a route to achieve those goals.[47] Understanding career management in the context of training and development is important because the needs of employees change over time.

Career Management Activities

Three categories of career management activities include work performed, personal relationships, and education. First, work performed includes ***job rotation***, which refers to employees who work on different assigned jobs within the same organization. Job rotation allows employees to develop a variety of skills and helps them to be more informed about various aspects of the business and to be exposed to different individuals, teams, and departments across the organization. At Raytheon, its multiyear job rotation program is a leadership development program that helps employees gain valuable leadership skills across a variety of settings within the organization.[48] In ***challenging assignments*** (or ***stretch assignments***), employees are given a task, project, or responsibility that is outside their current KSAOs. Challenging assignments can be a useful development activity for employees being groomed for management positions. The key is not to stretch employees so far that they fail.

Second, personal relationships at work are important. Relationships with managers can help make or break an employee's career. In addition, other organizational members or even someone outside of the organization may be helpful in mentoring employees to achieve positive career outcomes. Research consistently shows that having a mentor can be helpful in terms of career outcomes such as compensation, promotions, and career satisfaction.[49]

Third, employees may seek additional education to help them develop skills either at their own expense or via reimbursement from their organization. For example, in 2016, six of *Fortune* magazine's Best 100 Companies to Work For—Acuity, Boston Consulting Group, Burns & McDonnell, ARI, EY, and TDIndustries—gave unlimited tuition reimbursements to their employees.

Career Movements

Sometimes an employee's career path is defined, and redefined, by promotions, transfers, and even demotions. A promotion, when an employee is given a greater amount of responsibility within his or her job, is often accompanied by a pay increase to compensate for the additional level of work. At some companies, an employee must already be consistently performing at a level higher than they are currently placed before they will be considered for a promotion.[50] A transfer refers to an employee making a lateral move to part of the organization (domestic or international) without a major change in job duties, responsibilities, or compensation. Transfers can be helpful both for the organization (the better deployment of human capital) and to address employee needs.

Are Managers or Employees Responsible for Career Management?

Both organizations and individuals play an important role in career management. For example, strong career management pays off at Genentech, one of *Fortune's* "100 Best Companies to Work For." Genentech invested heavily in one-on-one career consulting, webinars, mentoring programs and support, career assessments, and short online video clips to help employees think about their careers in new ways. All of this led to an employee turnover rate of nearly 6% versus the industry average of 11%, and in 1 year alone it helped retain 76 high-potential employees.[51] For individuals, career management strategies include seeking mentoring relationships, understanding your own strengths and weaknesses, setting career goals, and taking on challenging assignments. Some best practices for both individuals and organizations are noted in Table 8.3.

LO 8.5 Analyze the factors associated with effective career development and management.

Career management The continual process of setting career-related goals and planning a route to achieve those goals

Job rotation Rotating employees from one job to another, allowing them to learn new skills

Challenging (stretch) assignments A task an employee is given that is outside their current KSAOs

TABLE 8.3   Career Development and Management Best Practices

BEST *INDIVIDUAL* PRACTICES FOR CAREER DEVELOPMENT AND MANAGEMENT	BEST *ORGANIZATIONAL* PRACTICES FOR CAREER DEVELOPMENT AND MANAGEMENT
• Build relationships.	• Invest in career development.
• Seek mentors including peer-to-peer mentors.	• Career development is aligned with employees' personal goals as well as corporate objectives.
• Develop self-awareness of your own strengths and weaknesses.	• Develop a culture that values, supports, and rewards learning.
• Set career goals and review them on a regular basis.	• Managers are given training on how to help employees with career development.
• Create a plan for developmental activities aligned with your career goals.	• Accountability for career development exists.
• Take on challenging assignments in areas related to your career goals.	• Employees are provided with the processes, information, tools, and resources they need to develop their careers.

Sources: Based on information contained in Berkeley Human Resources. Career planning: Career development action plan. http://hr.berkeley.edu/development/career-development/career-management/planning/action-plan; Lam, N., Dyke, L., & Duxbury, L. (2006). Career development in best-practice organizations: Critical success factors. *Optimum, The Journal of Public Sector Management, 29,* 22–30.

CHAPTER SUMMARY

Organizations invest significant resources in training and development, and this investment can pay significant dividends in terms of increased performance at the individual and organizational levels. The best practices described in this chapter include conducting a training needs assessment, considering trainee and organizational characteristics when developing a training program, choosing the appropriate training methods for the situation, and measuring training outcomes that are tied to organizational objectives. Guidelines for how to actually implement these best practices in organizations are summarized in Table 8.4. When done well, training forms part of overall career development, which benefits both the employee and the organization.

TABLE 8.4   Key Questions Human Resource Executives, Chief Learning Officers, and Business Leaders Should Ask About Training

For training in general throughout the organization or business unit:

• Have we *invested* sufficiently and wisely in training- and learning-related activities in our organization? How do we know?

• How have we determined and *prioritized* our most important training needs?

• How clear are we about the *competencies* we will need in order to compete successfully? How clear are we about where the gaps exist?

• What have we done to diagnose our organization's *learning environment*?

• What are we doing to make our organization more conducive to learning?

• What do you need me to do to send the *right signals* to our employees about the importance of training and learning in our organization?

• How will we know that our overall efforts in training and development have an impact? What *evidence* do we expect to see?

For a specific training program:

- What type of *training needs analysis* have we conducted to ensure we will be training the right things in the optimal way?

- What *training strategy* will be employed? How are we incorporating effective *instructional design* elements (e.g., information, demonstration, practice, and feedback)? How clear are the learning objectives?

- What are we doing to ensure we adequately *engage*, *motivate*, and *challenge* the trainees (and not simply ensure they are "happy")?

- What are we going to do *before and after* this training to ensure trainees can and will use what they have learned? What are we doing to prepare trainees, remove obstacles on the job, and reinforce and sustain learning?

- How is any training *technology* that we plan to use going to enhance learning and help trainees perform their jobs better and not just look cool?

- Should we be *evaluating* this training program? If so, for what purpose (e.g., to make adjustments or decide whether to continue it) and how?

Source: Reproduced from Salas, E., Tannenbaum, S. I., Kraiger, K., & Smith-Jentsch, K. A. (2012). The science of training and development in organizations: What matters in practice. *Psychological Science in the Public Interest, 13,* 74–101.

KEY TERMS

needs assessment   256

compliance training   260

self-efficacy   263

trainee motivation   263

goal-setting theory   263

expectancy theory   264

metacognitive skills   265

personality   265

training transfer   265

training transfer climate   265

identical elements   265

transfer through principles   266

behavioral tracking   266

feedback   266

training relevance   266

schema   266

overlearning   267

massed learning   267

spaced learning   267

on-the-job training   267

apprenticeship   267

eLearning   269

role-plays   270

case studies   271

games and simulations   271

executive coaching   271

mindfulness training   271

gamification   272

onboarding (organizational socialization)   272

welcoming   272

informing   273

orientation program   273

reactions criteria   277

training utility reactions   277

learning criteria   277

behavior/behavior criteria   277

results criteria   277

career management   283

job rotation   283

challenging (stretch) assignments   283

Visit **edge.sagepub.com/bauer** to help you accomplish your coursework goals in an easy-to-use learning environment.

- Master the learning objectives using key study tools

- Watch, listen, and connect with online multimedia resources

- Access mobile-friendly quizzes and flashcards to check your understanding

HR REASONING AND DECISION-MAKING EXERCISES

MINI-CASE ANALYSIS EXERCISE: EVALUATING TRAINING PROGRAMS

The Kehoe Company, which specializes in the sales of medical office software, has decided to invest in its sales force, specifically by providing training for its salespeople. The training includes live role plays and online training about the products themselves.

To evaluate the program, the company assessed sales performance and product knowledge in the year before and the year after the training. The company was not able to randomly assign employees to training and control groups but instead compared employees in two regions, Atlanta and Houston, which were considered to be equivalent in terms of their performance and demographics. All metrics are on a 10-point scale.

The table below shows the results of the training evaluation for the two offices. The metric used to evaluate the training is a composite of sales numbers and a measure of employees' product knowledge.

OFFICE	PRE-TRAINING COMPOSITE (AVERAGE) OF SALES PERFORMANCE AND PRODUCT KNOWLEDGE	POST-TRAINING COMPOSITE (AVERAGE) OF SALES PERFORMANCE AND PRODUCT KNOWLEDGE	SAMPLE SIZE
Atlanta (Trained)	8.4	9.2	449
Houston (Untrained/ Control)	8.5	8.7	398

1. Overall, based on these numbers, how effective would you say the training program is?

Next, the company decided to evaluate the effects of the training program on the two metrics separately. The first table shows a measure of average employee sales performance for the two offices pre- and posttraining. The second table shows a measure of product knowledge for the two offices pre- and posttraining.

OFFICE	PRE-TRAINING JOB PERFORMANCE (SALES)	POST-TRAINING JOB PERFORMANCE (SALES)	SAMPLE SIZE
Atlanta (Trained)	8.0	9.4	452
Houston (Untrained/Control)	8.5	8.6	398

OFFICE	PRE-TRAINING PRODUCT KNOWLEDGE TEST	POST-TRAINING PRODUCT KNOWLEDGE TEST	SAMPLE SIZE
Atlanta (Trained)	8.8	8.9	449
Houston (Untrained/Control)	8.5	8.8	403

2. Based on these numbers, what would you say is the effectiveness of the training program with regard to each of the training outcomes?

3. If the company wanted to adjust the training program, what would you recommend to it?

4. A colleague argues that sales numbers seem to be up as a result of the training program, so it doesn't matter whether employees showed an increase in product knowledge. What would be your response to that argument?

HR DECISION ANALYSIS EXERCISE: ARE TRAINING NEEDS ASSESSMENTS NECESSARY?

You are currently working at Meran, Inc., a 2,000-employee provider of hardware and parts to the telecommunications industry. Recently, Meran has become aware of the desire for training and development among many of its employees. This awareness has been as a result of requests from supervisors and employees both in product development and in manufacturing. In addition, top management has become acutely aware of the fact that Meran seems to provide fewer training opportunities than many of its industry competitors. In addition, the newest talent in the organization has voiced concern that they had been promised significant career development during the recruitment process, including mentoring from more experienced managers.

The HR director, Yuxin Zheng, has tasked you with finding a training program or programs that would be most suitable for Meran's needs. This includes the employees at multiple levels and divisions in the organization, along with multiple skill levels.

Although there are multiple indications that the company could use some additional types of training, your inclination is to perform some type of needs assessment to confirm what these needs really are. However, Zheng does not want to do a training needs assessment, suggesting that the organization already knows what is needed. In addition, he is proposing the use of an eLearning vendor, as it would allow the company to deliver a range of content. He argues that eLearning would allow for the delivery of training on mobile devices, something that he believes that the newer, younger employees would prefer over other types of training.

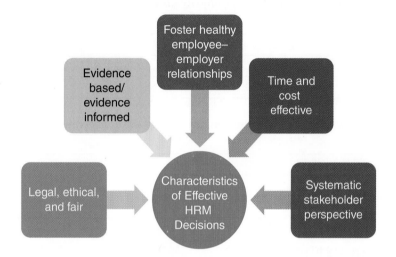

Please provide the rationale for your answer to each question.

Was Yuxin Zheng's approach legal, ethical, and fair?

_____

_____

_____

_____

Was his approach evidence based/evidence informed?

_____

_____

_____

_____

Does his decision foster healthy employee–employer relationships?

_____

_____

_____

_____

Are his recommendations for how to approach the choice of training programs time and cost effective?

_____

_____

_____
_____

Does he take a systematic stakeholder perspective?

_____
_____
_____
_____

Considering your analysis above, overall, what would be an effective decision? Why?

_____
_____
_____

What, if anything, do you think should be done differently or considered to help make this decision more effective?

_____
_____
_____
_____

HR DECISION-MAKING EXERCISE: INTERPRETING TRAINING AND SAFETY KNOWLEDGE ANALYTICS

The table below shows the average knowledge of safety practices related to chemical leak emergencies at a chemical plant, based on a sample of 221 chemical plant employees.

The employees were given a knowledge test at the time they were hired. They were then given the test again at multiple time points after their original hire date. They were trained on safety procedures at 3 months posthire.

TIME OF HIRE/BASELINE JOB KNOWLEDGE TEST SCORE (OUT OF 100)	1 MONTH POSTHIRE	2 MONTHS POSTHIRE	3 MONTHS POSTHIRE ONLINE SAFETY ↓ TRAINING	4 MONTHS POSTHIRE	6 MONTHS POSTHIRE	9 MONTHS POSTHIRE	12 MONTHS POSTHIRE
55	60	64		88	80	76	74

The data presented here can be considered a *time-series quasi-experimental design* that can be used in evaluating the safety training program.

Questions

1. These data indicate a slight increase in the employees' mean performance on the emergency safety procedures knowledge test at baseline and for the first 2 months after they are hired (prior to the online safety training). What are some possible reasons for this effect?

2. There is a "bump" in the employees' performance on the knowledge test immediately after they are trained. However, their knowledge then begins to decline over the next several months. What are some possible reasons for this effect?

3. Why would employees' knowledge in this particular domain decline, even though they are on the job? Put differently, wouldn't their working on the job continue to maintain their knowledge of emergency safety procedures? Why or why not?

4. Safety is a top priority in companies such as this one. If you were a manager, what could you do to remedy this decline in knowledge level among employees posttraining?

DATA AND ANALYTICS EXERCISE: EVALUATING A TRAINING PROGRAM

Evaluation of training is important yet sometimes forgotten or ignored. But without thoughtful evaluation, a company might continue with a training program in which employees fail to demonstrate sufficient levels of proficiency on key training outcomes. If you recall, we can classify training outcomes using Kirkpatrick's four levels: (1) reactions, (2) learning, (3) behavior, and (4) results.

Different inferential statistical analyses, such as *t*-tests or analyses of variance (ANOVA), can be used to evaluate training programs, and the most appropriate analysis will depend upon the type of design used (e.g., posttest-only design with a control group). Before running inferential statistical analyses, however, it is useful to compute descriptive analytics (e.g., mean, standard deviation) and create charts to generate a basic understanding of how individuals performed on training outcomes.

On the one hand, a *mean* is a measure of central tendency. It is the average score. In the training context, we often examine the mean of trained or untrained groups on some outcome measure. On the other hand, a *standard deviation (SD)* represents how dispersed or spread out the scores are around the mean. Thus, a larger SD indicates that there is more variation around the mean, whereas a smaller SD indicates that there is less variation.

In a normal distribution, 68% of scores fall between 1 SD below and above the mean, and 95% of scores fall within 2 SDs below and above the mean. If higher scores on a training outcome indicate better performance, organizations typically want to see a high mean coupled with a small SD, which would suggest that the average employee performed well and most employees performed at about the same level.

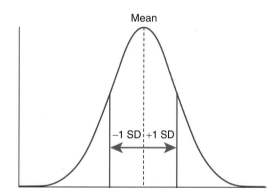

Fortunately, Excel makes it easy to compute the mean and SD of a set of scores. To calculate the mean, use the =AVERAGE() function, and to calculate the SD, use the =STDEV.S() function. Within the parentheses of either function, simply enter the vector of scores for which you wish to calculate the mean or SD. For example, to calculate the mean and SD for the set of training outcome scores (i.e., 7, 6, 4, 8, 6, 4) in the Excel sheet, you would enter the following in an empty cell: =AVERAGE(A2:A7) and =STDEV.S(A2:A7). Try this in Excel—you should get a mean of 5.83 and an SD of 1.60.

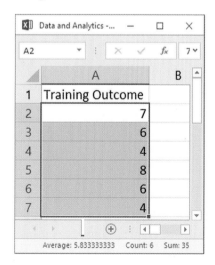

Now imagine that your company used a posttest-only with control group design to evaluate a safety training program. One group of trainees gets the new safety training program, and another group (control group) gets the old safety training program. The key training outcome is safety knowledge.

In this case, the big question is, *Did those in the new safety training program outperform those in the old safety training program*? Using an *independent-samples t-test*, we can assess whether two means are statistically different from one another. For example, if the p-value associated with the t-value we generate from the independent-samples t-test is less than the conventional cutoff .05, then we can conclude that the difference in means between the trainees in the new and old safety programs is significant.

 EXCEL EXTENSION: NOW YOU TRY!

- On **edge.sagepub.com/bauer**, you will find an Excel exercise on evaluating training programs.

- Using independent-samples t-tests, you will learn how to test different hypotheses and answer different questions based on training evaluation data.

CHAPTER 8 SUPPLEMENT: OSHA TRAINING REQUIREMENTS

As discussed in more detail in Chapter 15, many types of training are required by OSHA in particular industries and types of occupations. Tracking such training among employees is thus a critical issue for employers.

In addition, OSHA provides a number of publications to help employers understand what types of training their employees might be required to have. One of the key, detailed publications focuses on the types of training that employees require if they are working with particular types of equipment or materials, or if they are in certain types of jobs. The publication is available here:[52]

https://www.osha.gov/Publications/osha2254.pdf

Performance Management

Opening Case

Transforming Performance Management at Deloitte[1]

Among companies that have made major changes in their approach to performance management, the multinational consulting firm Deloitte provides an interesting example. In 2013, Deloitte conducted an internal study that revealed it was spending around 2 million hours on performance management–related activities. Performance management consisted of annual evaluations in which managers and employees set goals at the beginning of the year and then rated progress made at the end of the year. Despite the time spent on them, the system did not provide adequate or timely feedback to employees, nor did it provide organizational decision makers with sufficiently accurate performance data to be used in important decisions such as incentive pay. The company decided to give the system a makeover but also to change the company's view of what performance management is and how to approach it.

This transformation effort began with identifying what Deloitte needed the system to be able to accomplish. Erica Bank, performance management leader at Deloitte, describes the objectives as threefold: fuel performance, see performance, and recognize performance. To fuel performance, a key tool in the revamped system is frequent meetings in which the employee and the manager have future-oriented conversations, called "check-ins" or "one-on-ones." Managers and employees are encouraged to briefly meet weekly or biweekly to discuss ongoing work and employee career development. To get the employees and managers started, HR gave them ideas of what to talk about and sent weekly e-mails asking whether they had met (i.e., rather than force compliance, they simply nudged). The frequency and regularity of these meetings would ensure that the feedback received would be timely.

To see performance, managers are now asked to rate each employee they work with at the end of each project using a simple, four-question survey.

The questions are:

- Given what I know of this person's performance, I would always want him/her on my team. (*Responses reported on a five-point scale ranging from Strongly Disagree to Strongly Agree.*)

- This person is at risk for low performance (*Yes/No*).

- Given what I know of this person's performance, and if it were my own money, I would award this person the highest possible compensation increase. (*Responses reported on a five-point scale ranging from Strongly Disagree to Strongly Agree.*)

- This person is ready for promotion today (*Yes/No*).

LEARNING OBJECTIVES

After reading and studying this chapter, you should be able to do the following:

9.1 Differentiate between performance management and performance appraisals.

9.2 Compare the design features of different types of appraisals with respect to their benefits and downsides.

9.3 Identify best practices for making performance reviews fair and unbiased.

9.4 Explain how to implement performance management for maximum effectiveness.

9.5 Describe how teaching managers how to be good coaches helps improve performance management.

At a minimum, each employee is rated every quarter. Deloitte made the initial decision not to share each rating from individual managers with the employees, opting to share annual aggregated ratings with the rationale that this would allow managers to be more honest.

To recognize performance, Deloitte decided to use the performance ratings as a starting point. Chief Learning Officer Jeff Orlando notes that every "people decision" will be data informed but not data driven. HR and business leaders could use this information to decide whom to promote and whose performance needed intervention. The system is meant to help support (but not replace) decision makers in their efforts to recognize employee contributions.

Is the system working? Deloitte invested heavily in training managers on how the system would work, and encouraged adoption by allowing them to opt in. Deloitte will, no doubt, continue to change and shape the system in keeping with evolving demands. The initial reactions of its own employees have been positive. In 2016, ALM Intelligence named Deloitte a global leader in performance management consulting, indicating that the company is a thought leader in this arena and shares its performance management experience with its clients as well.

Case Discussion Questions

1. Which aspects of Deloitte's new performance management system do you find most radical?

2. If you were a manager at Deloitte, how would you have reacted to such a system? Would your answer change if you were an employee?

3. What are your thoughts regarding measuring performance with four simple questions? Do you think these are the right questions? How would you know if a particular question is effective?

4. How would you motivate managers to conduct frequent check-in meetings with employees? How would you counter the argument that these meetings take a lot of time?

5. How transparent is this system? Do you think Deloitte's decision not to share individual ratings with employees is warranted?

 Click to learn more . . .

Read the Deloitte University Press report titled *"Performance management is broken: Replace 'rank and yank' with coaching and development."*
https://dupress.deloitte.com/dup-us-en/focus/human-capital-trends/2014/hc-trends-2014-performance-management.html

Why is performance management important? The answer relates to a central concept of HR management: An organization's greatest asset is its people. Within organizations, employees need to know how well they are performing and how they can improve their performance so that the organization's objectives can be fulfilled. In addition, companies often use performance as a criterion when making pay and promotion decisions. They need ways of measuring, capturing, and comparing performance levels of different employees. For all these purposes, companies need accurate performance measures.

For the past several decades, the annual review in which managers completed long evaluation forms rating employee performance on numerous dimensions was standard practice and a ritual in most large corporations around the world. Now, many of the same companies are questioning the need for an annual review, with Adobe, GE, and Microsoft appearing in headlines as they abandon their traditional performance review systems.

In this chapter, we discuss performance appraisals, or performance measurement, focusing on different methods and what purposes performance appraisal serves. Then we shift our focus to performance feedback and discuss how performance management systems may incorporate effective feedback delivery systems.

What Is Performance Management?

Performance management is the process of measuring, communicating, and managing employee performance in the workplace so that performance is aligned with organizational strategy. If we unpack this definition, it will be easier to see the critical components of a performance management system. First, performance management involves obtaining some form of measurement of employee performance, or *performance appraisal*. Performance appraisals may take a number of different forms, ranging from subjective assessments in which managers evaluate employee performance to quantitative metrics resulting from employee actions such as sales performance, accounts opened, and the time in which a transaction is completed. There are many uses for this information, ranging from distributing rewards to identifying high-potential employees, determining training needs, and terminating employees to validating selection systems. Second, performance management systems involve giving feedback to employees regarding where they stand. This is important to motivate employees, ensure that their behaviors are aligned with the organization's goals, and address performance gaps. Third, the ultimate goal behind performance measurement systems is the management of performance. When successful, performance management systems help with employee engagement, retention, and the achievement of organizational objectives.

In practice, organizations have traditionally treated performance management and once-a-year performance appraisals synonymously. Even today, most performance management consists of managers completing an annual evaluation form, rating the employee on several dimensions, and then communicating their rating to the employee in a performance review meeting. The problem with these systems—as mentioned in the Deloitte opening case—is that feedback relegated to a once-a-year meeting has little hope of being useful to employees because it is too infrequent. Further, these ratings are often not regarded as fair or accurate, because managers approach these ratings with multiple motives, such as rating generously to reward their team and increase loyalty. To many managers, these performance management systems and the resulting conversations feel forced and are perceived as a waste of time. Therefore, it is not surprising that a SHRM study found that only 2% of the surveyed firms gave the performance management practices of their organization an A grade.[2] To solve these problems, companies have started experimenting with different formats, whereas some larger employers abandoned formal, end-of-year assessment altogether in favor of more frequent informal feedback sessions.

LO 9.1 Differentiate between performance management and performance appraisals.

Performance management The process of measuring, communicating, and managing employee performance in the workplace so that performance is aligned with organizational strategy

Performance appraisal An evaluation of employee performance

Objectives of Performance Appraisals

Performance appraisal is the process of measuring employees' performance using predetermined criteria and sharing this information with employees. Following are at least five critical reasons why organizations are interested in measuring employee performance in the workplace.

Giving Employees Feedback

One reason for conducting a formal performance assessment is to communicate to employees where they stand in the eyes of organizational decision makers. Individuals have their blind spots when it comes to their own performance. Knowing how they are perceived by managers, coworkers, or customers is useful for employees to develop their skills and find out through formal channels where they stand. The formal measurement of performance occurs annually, semiannually, or quarterly. Even if it happens several times a year, the formal performance review session has limitations as a medium for performance feedback. Because timeliness of feedback is so important, experts recommend supplementing these formal review sessions with regular **one-on-one meetings**, which are meetings managers have with their direct reports on a regular basis, usually weekly, to discuss performance goals, progress, and related issues. Still, regular formal performance reviews serve as tools to communicate to employees what they are doing well and what they can do better and to document their progress in an official capacity. In fact, companies such as education start-ups Quizlet and CareerFoundry found that once their company size reached 50 employees, workers started demanding a formal performance review system that gives them feedback about where they stand and documents their progress and performance.[3]

It is also important to note that simply providing feedback to employees is not a guarantee for performance improvements. In fact, a meta-analysis of the literature showed that about 33% of the time, feedback *reduced* performance instead of benefiting it.[4] This means that performance management programs should ensure that feedback recipients are provided with training to maximize the performance improvement potential.

Development and Problem Solving

Knowing where one stands with respect to performance criteria is a crucial step before taking corrective actions. An important objective of performance reviews is to identify employee strengths and deficiencies and develop ways to improve performance. This may take the form of employee training, providing additional coaching, taking corrective action in the form of putting the employee in a performance improvement plan, and supporting the employee in efforts to improve their performance. In other words, a key reason for conducting performance reviews is to take steps to improve future performance of the employee.

Decision Making

Organizations may want to make certain decisions using the performance metrics available to them. For example, reinforcement theory of motivation suggests that behaviors that are rewarded are more likely to be repeated.[5] When individual pay, incentives, and bonuses reflect employee contributions and performance, employees are likely to find the reward systems to be more equitable. In addition to providing data to be used in compensation-related decisions, the organization may use performance data to decide who is next in line for managerial positions as well as to identify employees who are not meeting the expectations of their jobs. Performance metrics provide input to numerous talent decisions organizations make.

Data Analytics

The ability of a firm to harness the power of data analytics depends on the availability of high-quality data on critical outcomes of interest. Performance is one such outcome that companies are interested in predicting and managing. For example, companies may use performance ratings to decide whether the employee selection methods in place are valid. As discussed in

One-on-one meetings
Meetings managers have with their direct reports on a regular basis, usually weekly, to discuss performance goals, progress, and related issues

Chapter 7, predictive and concurrent validity studies necessitate the availability of high-quality performance data.

For example, suppose a company is considering using a personality test as part of its selection system. It may administer the test to all applicants and hire without using the test scores. Then the company can examine the relationship between personality test scores and job performance metrics 6 months after hiring. A high correlation between the two would be good evidence for the predictive validity of the personality test in employee selection. Alternatively, the company may administer the test to existing employees and correlate test scores to job performance metrics. A high correlation would be evidence for the concurrent validity of the test. Demonstrating that selection procedures predict future performance is considered the gold standard of hire quality.[6]

But this pursuit will only be possible if the company has reliable performance data for its employees. Measuring and then mapping out the predictors of employee performance is an important area of opportunity for HR departments to add value using data analytics. Unfortunately, in many organizations, performance management systems do not cultivate high-quality, objective, and fair performance metrics that can be reliably used in data analytics efforts. The notable exception is when objective metrics such as call completion time, sales volume, or other productivity metrics are available. However, as this chapter later demonstrates, objective metrics have their own unique set of problems and may not necessarily be superior to more subjective evaluations. Performance management systems have the potential to produce data that can be predicted and managed using data analytic tools, but often the subjective and biased nature of these systems results in data that are not useful for analytics purposes—in other words, garbage in, garbage out.

SPOTLIGHT ON DATA AND ANALYTICS
Using Performance Metrics in Screening Job Applicants

Robert Alexander/Getty Images

In addition to their use in managing the performance of existing employees, predictive analytics can also be used in screening job applicants. Specifically, predictive analytics can identify factors that differentiate job applicants who will end up being high performers from those who are likely to fall behind. Algorithms can identify what aspects of a person's résumé, job experience, test scores, or interview answers do a

better job of yielding good employees. Performance metrics play an essential role in this process. In fact, predictive analytics will be only as good as the criterion variables, or outcomes we are trying to predict. What characteristics do applicants have that result in higher sales revenue, higher customer service performance, or accurately balancing their books?

For example, the commercial airline JetBlue developed predictive analytics for use in screening applicants for flight attendant and customer service agent positions. Using the services of a data analytics vendor, the Houston, Texas–based retail chain Mattress Firm administered an online assessment to its job applicants, measuring 39 traits. The profiles of applicants were compared to the profiles of the strongest performers among Mattress Firm's employees when making the selection. As can be seen, the ability of a firm to utilize these data-driven approaches relies on the availability of reliable, valid, and objective performance data about an organization's employees.[7]

©iStock.com/David Tran

Companies such as Adobe and J. P. Morgan made a move toward real-time feedback, eliminating annual reviews and ratings. These companies will need to take extra steps to document performance to manage their legal liability.

Legal Purposes

Performance metrics that are objective, accurate, and regularly collected are useful in defending organizations against costly lawsuits. Recall that Chapter 4 discusses numerous EEO laws that protect employee rights in organizations. Even though organizations have a lot of freedom in how they manage their workforces, there are several *non*permissible decisions they may make, such as using sex, age, disability status, religion, or any number of other protected characteristics to make decisions about employees.

Imagine an organization that fires an employee due to poor performance. However, the employee files a complaint against the organization suggesting that he firmly believes that his religion was the reason for the firing decision. The organization's main line of defense is to show that the motivation for the firing decision was the employee's poor performance. This necessitates providing records and documentation of the employee's performance over time, and regularly conducted, objective, and systematic performance reviews will be helpful in making the organization's case.

An example like this makes it clear how the new trend in some large employers to abandon formal performance reviews introduces legal challenges. For example, the EEOC noted that the absence of formal, regular, and consistent reviews in an organization may make it easier for the EEOC to defend a claim of bias. As a result, even organizations that decide to move toward more informal performance management will need to develop ways of documenting employee performance over time.[8]

Challenges of Conducting Fair and Objective Performance Appraisals

Performance appraisals provide important information to organizations that can be used to make critical HR decisions. At the same time, this chapter began by pointing out that performance appraisal systems are often disliked and regarded as unfair and that their accuracy and objectivity are often questioned. The challenge, then, is to design a system that is fair, relevant, and accurate.

Performance Appraisals as a Measurement Tool

The classical view of performance appraisals is that they are a measurement tool. This approach assumes that performance can be measured objectively, through the design of appropriate instruments. In fact, prior to the 1980s, most research into performance appraisals focused on examining the role of scale format in performance measurement in the hopes that it would make performance ratings more accurate. Once this approach proved unproductive, the focus shifted toward trying to understand how managers process the performance information they observe on a daily basis to form judgments about employees, with particular focus on the effects of prior expectations and memory on performance ratings. Scientists and practitioners experimented with different rating formats that would make it easier to eliminate unconscious biases from the review of performance. They also created systems and developed rater training programs that would increase managers' accuracy in observing, categorizing, and documenting performance information.[9]

Underlying all these efforts are the beliefs that performance appraisal is a measurement tool, raters have a desire to rate accurately, and if the right tools are designed, performance ratings will be objective and accurate. Decades of research in appraisals now show that this is a limited view of performance appraisals. It is true that some performance appraisal formats may increase the possibility of errors and bias. At the same time, it is naïve to regard performance appraisals as simply a tool of measurement. In fact, managers seem to have multiple motives (in addition to just giving accurate ratings) when evaluating the performance of their employees, suggesting that simply examining performance appraisals from an information processing perspective may be short-sighted. Further, researchers and practitioners began realizing that accuracy, although important, is not the only goal of performance measurement. Employee acceptance of the review is also a key goal, and acceptability of the feedback is essential for it to serve as a motivational tool.

Performance Ratings as Motivated Action

Today, there is greater recognition that performance rating accuracy and fairness are not achieved merely by presenting managers with the right tools to measure performance. Simply stated, managers are not always motivated to rate employee performance accurately. Instead, they have competing motives, such as a desire to preserve their relationship with the employee, to send a strong signal to their employees regarding "who's boss," to ensure that employees are indebted to the manager, to avoid a potentially unpleasant confrontation in the name of preserving harmony, or to make themselves look good to upper management, among others. In other words, performance appraisals can be as much a political tool as a measurement tool. This means that HR departments need to understand that the effectiveness of a performance appraisal system in generating performance data and serving as a motivational tool depends not only on system design features but also on user buy-in and rater motivation to be fair and accurate. In other words, effective performance management is not an activity solely owned by HR; and it is important to consider the context in which ratings take place and ensure that the organization has a strong culture of feedback.

Reacting to such considerations, companies such as Accenture and KPMG abandoned annual performance ratings altogether, moving toward systems that involve more frequent feedback and coaching. However, it is critical to recognize that such moves will only be effective if managers and employees take feedback seriously, managers are motivated and able to provide such feedback, and employees are motivated to accept such feedback. If annual performance reviews were failing because managers felt uncomfortable having frank conversations with their employees or did not see much value in such conversations, replacing annual reviews with frequent check-ins will not achieve much unless those underlying problems are resolved.

Characteristics of Effective Performance Appraisal Systems

Performance appraisal systems, or the way performance is measured in organizations, are expected to meet certain criteria for effectiveness. As shown in Figure 9.1, these include alignment with organizational strategy, perceived fairness, accuracy, and practicality.

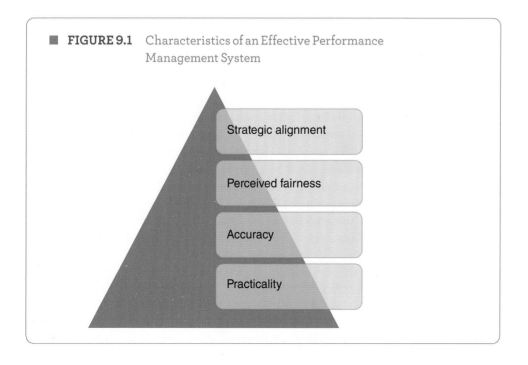

■ **FIGURE 9.1**   Characteristics of an Effective Performance Management System

Strategic alignment

Perceived fairness

Accuracy

Practicality

Strategic Alignment

The most effective performance appraisal systems are aligned with corporate strategy. They motivate employees to demonstrate behaviors and actions that are consistent with the strategic direction of the organization. For example, the online retailer Zappos had a performance appraisal system focusing on metrics such as meeting deadlines and being punctual. Realizing that the system lacked strategic alignment, it switched to a system in which the measurement criteria included how well employees demonstrate Zappos' 10 core values such as showing humility and demonstrating "wow" levels of customer service.[10]

Perceived Fairness

The usefulness of a performance appraisal system as a tool in performance management depends on the degree to which it is perceived as fair. If employees do not perceive their rating and the system producing their rating to be fair or feel that they do not receive feedback they consider to be fair, they are unlikely to be motivated to improve their performance. Therefore, fairness is a key criterion to determine the effectiveness of a performance appraisal system.[11]

Performance appraisals that give employees "due process" will protect employees' rights during the appraisal process and ensure that the resulting assessment is perceived as fair. Performance appraisal due process consists of three characteristics.[12] ***Adequate notice*** refers to the idea that employees should be evaluated using criteria and standards that were clearly communicated to the employee in advance. As a result, the measurement approach does not come as a surprise to the employee. ***Fair hearing*** involves a formal review meeting explaining to the employee why and how a particular rating was arrived at. Allowing employees voice in the evaluation process is also crucial to a fair hearing. When employees participate in the process and feel free to express their own opinions, fairness perceptions will be higher. ***Judgment based on evidence*** is the principle that performance standards are administered consistently across all employees, and the ratings are, to the degree possible, free from personal biases and prejudice. Research showed that performance appraisals that fit these criteria were associated with the most favorable user reactions to the system and evaluations of managers.

Accuracy

Accuracy is a challenging goal to strive toward in performance ratings because it is difficult to measure. Outside of laboratory settings, it is often impossible to know whether performance ratings of managers are accurate, given that "true scores" are not known. Nevertheless, accurate measurement is a good goal to strive toward. Measures perceived as inaccurate are likely to be perceived

Adequate notice The idea that employees should be evaluated using criteria and standards that were clearly communicated to them in advance

Fair hearing A formal review meeting explaining to the employee why and how a particular rating was given

Judgment based on evidence The principle that performance standards are administered consistently across all employees, and the ratings are, to the degree possible, free from personal biases and prejudice

as unfair.[13] Further, basing organizational decisions on inaccurate measures will be problematic. Accuracy has a lot to do with reliability and validity of ratings. As a reminder, reliability refers to the consistency of measurement. For example, given the same behaviors, different raters should evaluate the same person similarly (interrater reliability). Further, unless the individual's behavior has changed, the same rater who evaluates the individual on two different occasions should give very similar ratings (test–retest reliability). Validity involves using metrics that truly capture relevant dimensions of performance. For example, when defining and measuring the important dimensions of performance that matter for organizational effectiveness is difficult, some managers resort to "face time" or "chair time" when evaluating performance. Instead of focusing on criteria such as met deadlines, customer satisfaction, or goal achievement, raters may focus on how long the employee stays at the office, which is not an effective way of assessing employee performance. When the criteria used to assess performance are not perceived as valid, employees are frustrated, concerns regarding fairness abound, and efforts to maintain work–life balance suffer.[14]

Accuracy of measurement may be affected by unconscious biases (such as the case of a manager who rates an employee highly because the employee shares the manager's hobbies and they like each other), and intentional errors of raters (as in the case of a manager who rates an employee higher than warranted in order to avoid an unpleasant confrontation). Later, this chapter reviews factors contributing to rating errors and ways of minimizing their role in the performance evaluation process.

Practicality

An important aspect of an effective performance management system is its practicality. When the users of the system find it too time consuming and burdensome, they are more likely to regard it as paperwork pushed on them by HR departments, and their motivation to embrace the system will be low. As a result, perceived practicality will affect how motivated managers are to rate employees accurately and how engaged employees and managers are with the system.

Design Features of Performance Management Systems

Performance management system design is a responsibility usually spearheaded by HR departments. There are a number of critical decisions to be made in the design stage, including:

- Determining the purposes and desired outcomes of the performance appraisals,
- Defining performance,
- Determining specific performance criteria,
- Choosing the rating method,
- Choosing the source of performance information, and
- Deciding how closely performance ratings should be tied to compensation.

It is important to remember that system design features play a limited role in the eventual success of the performance management system. How the system is actually used by line managers and employees and the culture that supports performance and feedback remain more important to performance management system success. Therefore, any design effort must consider the user's perspective, and important decisions should be made with an eye toward securing user buy-in. For this purpose, securing top management commitment and gaining user buy-in through their involvement in the design stages are helpful steps to take. Top management sets the stage and helps to build a culture in which performance management is taken seriously and performance conversations occur regularly. As a result, top management is encouraged to display public support for performance management systems and model the expected behaviors. User involvement in system design is also useful because their perspective will help ensure that the system design is tailored to account for user reactions, with the eventual result being greater commitment to use the system.

LO 9.2 Compare the design features of different types of appraisals with respect to their benefits and downsides.

IBM has a history of involving employees in major initiatives. Its app-based performance review system, Checkpoint, was created with broad-based user involvement.[16]

Developmental purposes
A performance review conducted for the purpose of improving performance

Administrative purposes
A performance review conducted to make decisions in the organization

As one critic noted in *HR Magazine* regarding the increasing use of smartphone apps to facilitate frequent solicitation and delivery of feedback: "Ultimately it will be up to managers to make new variations of performance management work. No software can provide feedback that human beings aren't willing to give."[15]

Determining the Purposes and Desired Outcomes of Performance Appraisals

Organizations may have different reasons for why they conduct performance appraisals as part of performance management. Some may be utilizing performance reviews for *developmental purposes*, which means they are primarily interested in providing employees periodical, formal feedback on their performances. Other organizations may utilize performance appraisals for *administrative purposes*, which means that performance appraisals are used to make decisions in the organization, such as assigning merit pay and bonuses, or determining which employees will be sent to remedial training and which will be promoted. Typically, organizations use one performance appraisal for multiple purposes. However, it is important to remember that different purposes may be addressed via different types of appraisals. For example, it is important for a system in which the goal is to assign bonuses and promotions to meaningfully differentiate between employees. This means that the system will probably have to assign numerical ratings to employees. At the same time, it is important that the ratings assigned to each employee are different from each other so that the organization can see who the highest performers are. In contrast, in an organization in which the primary goal is to give feedback to employees, what is more critical is to have data from multiple perspectives and to provide a lot of qualitative information about the employees' behaviors in different contexts. In such a context, assigning a numerical rating to employee performance may not be an activity that adds a lot of value and in fact may detract from the main purpose of the appraisal, which is to give feedback. These organizations may benefit from a narrative review with open-ended questions, in which the most relevant feedback may be provided to each employee.

Therefore, organizations may benefit from giving serious consideration to the seemingly easy question of what they will do with the performance appraisal results. If it is clear to the organization that bonuses and merit pay will be assigned via a different method (such as sales numbers, seniority, or quarterly bonuses tied to specific goal accomplishment), then the organization may design the system with an eye toward maximizing feedback as opposed to differentiating among employees and quantifying performance. The opposite would be true if the system is expected to be used for the validation of selection systems or the evaluation of training programs. In these cases, it is useful to tell managers that their ratings will be used for research purposes only. In other words, organizations should consider which aspects of the appraisal system add value to organizational goals instead of designing a generic performance appraisal system that theoretically serves multiple purposes but in reality shortchanges each of them.

Defining Performance

What is performance? For example, when evaluating the effectiveness of a retail employee, what should be the focus? Should we measure product knowledge and dependability? Should we capture how often the employee goes out of their way to help a customer find what they need? Or should we measure how often employees were late in the past month and the value of the merchandise they actually sold?

HR IN ACTION
Accenture Transforms Performance Management

Slaven Vlasic/Getty Images for Advertising Week New York

With more than 400,000 employees worldwide, the global consulting and professional services company Accenture has a large number of employees receiving performance reviews every year. When Accenture realized that employees were not receiving the feedback they needed even though collectively 2 million hours were being spent on performance reviews, the company started a global effort to transform its performance management process.

Much of this work was shouldered by Ellyn Shook, the firm's chief leadership and human resources officer. The effort began by gathering input about what employees and managers needed. The response

was that employees expressed a need for real-time feedback, personalized career training, and more transparency from the company.

As a result of the input gathered, Accenture decided to engage in a culture transformation that abandoned the use of annual performance reviews, instead adopting a system to identify each employee's strengths and build on them. Shook noted that this effort was "probably the most significant talent transformation we've ever undergone in our history." Key pieces of the transformation include an in-house app that enables employees to share their priorities with their team and seek feedback. After testing the system on 20,000 employees, Accenture released it worldwide. As of 2017, the company also was in the process of training its managers in effective coaching of its employees. The resulting improvements will mean that managers and employees will spend more time managing performance, but they will find more value in the process.

It is important to note what Accenture *added* after it dropped the annual review. It is still early to tell if the transformation met its goals, but what is clear is that this was an effort at transforming the organization's performance culture rather than simply changing an appraisal system.[17]

These examples describe three different approaches to measurement of performance: traits, behaviors, or results. Each approach has important strengths but also limitations. It is important to note that irrespective of whether traits, behaviors, or results are to be used in conceptualizing performance, the specific dimensions should come from a strong job analysis and the resulting job description. Further, the criteria and metrics used to assess performance should be directly aligned with corporate strategy. For example, focusing on short-term sales volume may be inconsistent with an organizational strategy that emphasizes customer loyalty and customer service, because employees may become overly concerned with increasing their sales volume while neglecting to take care of customers once the sale is made.

Trait Appraisals

Trait appraisals focus on measuring employees' different attributes such as dependability, helpfulness, and product knowledge. These systems define performance as characteristics the employee has (rather than how they actually utilize or display these characteristics). The key advantage of traits is their simplicity of use. This approach does not necessitate identifying behaviors that constitute high performance, and therefore developing a trait-based appraisal is usually a simple and cost-effective process.

At the same time, trait appraisals have serious limitations that limit their usefulness. First, trait appraisals are associated with a greater number of rater errors and suffer more from lack of accuracy in ratings relative to behavioral appraisals. This is because they are quite vague—they require that the rater infer an employee trait rather than simply rating behaviors—and therefore open to interpretation by raters. In fact, research shows that when trait appraisals are used, agreement between different raters, such as self and managers, tends to be much lower, suggesting poor reliability.[18] This is likely to lead to negative reactions toward the feedback received and to contribute to a sense of unfairness. Second, trait appraisals describe the person and not the behavior. Therefore, they increase the likelihood that any negative feedback will be regarded as an attack on the employee's personality, which tends to be stable, rather than an observation regarding behaviors, which can be changed more easily.

Behavioral Appraisals

Behavioral appraisals assess the frequency with which employees demonstrate specific behaviors at work. For example, an organization that expects employees to approach customers about its extended warranty program may have a performance appraisal behavioral dimension related to how well the employee explains the warranty program to customers. A police officer performance evaluation may include behavioral dimensions such as whether the officer cleared the area of bystanders before confronting dangerous suspects. As you can see, these are specific, observable behaviors.

Behavioral appraisals are useful for feedback purposes, because delivering this assessment will make the employee aware of the types of behaviors employees are expected to demonstrate and point out gaps in performance. Behaviors are observable and are typically under the control of the employee. Therefore, they will give the employee the greatest amount of actionable feedback. At the same time, behavioral appraisals assume that there is a set, predetermined way in which performance can be accomplished. In reality, it may not be possible to create a list of behaviors that capture high performance in all jobs, and in fact, the use of behaviors for employees who have a lot of expertise may alienate the employees and reduce their perceived autonomy. Therefore, using behaviors for new employees rather than more experienced employees may be meaningful. The use of behavioral appraisals may also be more appropriate when employees are expected to always display a specific set of behaviors, such as greeting customers, making product recommendations, and offering to open a store credit card.

Results-Based Appraisals

Results-based appraisals define performance in terms of the outcomes of a job. Sales figures, number of mistakes, number of reservations taken, number of new clients, customer satisfaction ratings, and minutes taken to complete a phone call may all be important metrics that describe an employee's performance. Results-based assessments of performance have important advantages over traits and behaviors. Their key advantage resides in their objectivity. Unlike behaviors and traits, results are naturally occurring outcomes of performance at work, and their measurement usually does not necessitate one person rating another. Therefore, these metrics are less subjective than other appraisal methods.

This does not necessarily mean that results-based metrics are superior to assessments such as behavioral ratings, but results-based assessments are less likely to result in charges of favoritism and subjectivity. It is also easy to see how an individual's performance serves organizational goals: When employee sales performance is high, we can assume that the organization is benefiting from this.

At the same time, results-based assessments bring their own unique problems to performance measurement. To begin with, they are not always under the control of employees. For example, sales volume may depend on the territory assigned to the individual, quality of products, and availability of competition. If employees feel that the metrics used to assess them are not under their control, they will develop a sense of helplessness and will not be motivated to put forth effort. Second, some important aspects of an employee's performance may not have easily measured metrics. Sales volume, for instance, is easier to track compared to quality of customer interactions. As a result, employees may develop a single-mindedness with respect to the aspects of their performance captured by metrics and neglect other important aspects of their performance. Individual metrics may also have negative effects on cooperation if only employees' individual performance is being tracked and rewarded. Finally, metrics can be misleading. For example, the best doctors may have the highest patient mortality rates because the best physicians may attract patients who are in more critical condition. Similarly, the best salespeople may be assigned the more problematic customers because they are the only ones who can handle them. This means that simply looking at metrics may not provide an accurate picture of performance.

Goal Setting

An extension of results-based performance definitions is to engage in goal setting. Goal setting is one of the best methods available for increasing performance and therefore is a useful performance management tool.[19] Joint goal setting with one's manager at the beginning of a performance period, working toward a goal throughout the period, and assessing goal accomplishment at the end of the period are helpful methods for managing performance. Goal setting is a key part of *management by objectives (MBO)*, a management strategy in which organizational goals are translated into department goals, which in turn are converted into individual-level goals to ensure that individual and company goals and objectives are fully aligned. First, *key performance indicators (KPIs)* are defined at the company level. KPIs are measurable business metrics that are aligned with a company's strategy. These can be financial metrics such as profit or cost, customer related metrics such as customer satisfaction, people metrics such as turnover rate, or KPIs related to other strategic initiatives, such as organizational sustainability. Then these KPIs are translated into individual-level goals for employees, as discussed between the employee and the manager.

Goals that have the greatest motivational value are *SMART goals*:

- Specific,
- Measurable,
- Aggressive,
- Realistic, and
- Time-bound.

This means that the most effective goals are quantifiable, difficult enough to motivate the employee although remaining reachable, relevant to the performance of the employee's job and aligned with corporate strategy, and accomplished within a specific period of time. A goal such as "increase the fee income from service contracts by 10% by December of the calendar year" is an example of a SMART goal. As long as employees have abilities to reach the goal and are committed to the goal, having SMART goals is associated with higher levels of performance.

Goal setting can be an effective way of measuring and managing performance, but it comes with caveats. Perhaps the biggest concern with respect to goal setting is the possibility of ethics violations, such as cutting corners or using ethically questionable means to meet the goal. Further, goals narrow the focus of employees, leading to focusing on one or two dimensions of performance at the exclusion of others. Goals can also result in reduced motivation to learn new things and may lead to the creation of a culture of competition. All these downsides suggest that the use of SMART goals should be accompanied by careful monitoring and ensuring that *how* the goals are attained is not disregarded in the process.[20]

Management by objectives (MBO) A management strategy in which organizational goals are translated into department- and individual-level goals

Key performance indicators (KPIs) Measurable business metrics that are aligned with a company's strategy

SMART goals Goals that are specific, measurable, aggressive, realistic, and time-bound

SPOTLIGHT ON ETHICS
A Goal-Setting Scandal at Wells Fargo

Goal setting is one of the most effective and promising ways of motivating employees and aligning individual effort with department and organizational strategy. At the same time, goal setting can have a serious side effect that suggests the organizations using this strategy should take steps to avoid harmful consequences. In an aggressive culture that emphasizes ends and disregards means, goal setting may be a tool that corrupts employees and harms the company reputation.

Wells Fargo's experience with goal setting offers a cautionary tale. The company made headlines with the revelation that it had opened hundreds of thousands of unauthorized accounts for its customers, leading to charging of fees for accounts customers did not realize they had. The company agreed to pay $185 million in fines; its CEO at the time, John Stumpf (pictured here), resigned; and more than 5,000 employees were fired as a result.

The way goal setting was used at Wells Fargo illustrates some of the worst practices of goal setting and its consequences. Employees were required to reach impossible daily sales goals in order to keep their jobs. Managers did not seem to care *how* employees met the goals as long as they were met. In fact, in some cases managers encouraged employees to cheat, such as by opening up accounts for friends and family members or even opening accounts for customers without their knowledge, and apologizing afterward if the customer realized it. District managers pressured branches by discussing goal achievement four times a day. The company eventually replaced sales goals with a bonus structure emphasizing customer satisfaction.[21]

Questions

1. How would you advise your organization if top management proposed an aggressive goal-setting policy for employee performance? How might the organization reap the benefits of goal setting while avoiding negative consequences?

2. In your own work, how do you set goals for yourself and measure your progress in attaining them? What have you learned that might help you to gain more benefits from goal setting?

Choosing the Rating Method

Performance may be assessed using absolute ratings or relative rankings. Absolute ratings involve comparing employee behaviors or outcomes to performance criteria, whereas relative rankings involve comparing employees to each other. Both of these approaches involve quantifying performance in some way. In addition, some highly visible organizations have opted to abandon the tradition of assigning numbers to employee performance, switching to more qualitative approaches. Which approach to use should be motivated by the purpose of the performance assessment, but it is important to understand the strengths and limitations of each approach when making this decision. Figure 9.2 summarizes advantages and disadvantages inherent in each method.

Absolute Ratings

These systems involve a comparison of the employee's performance to predetermined criteria. These systems treat each performance score within a work group as independent from other

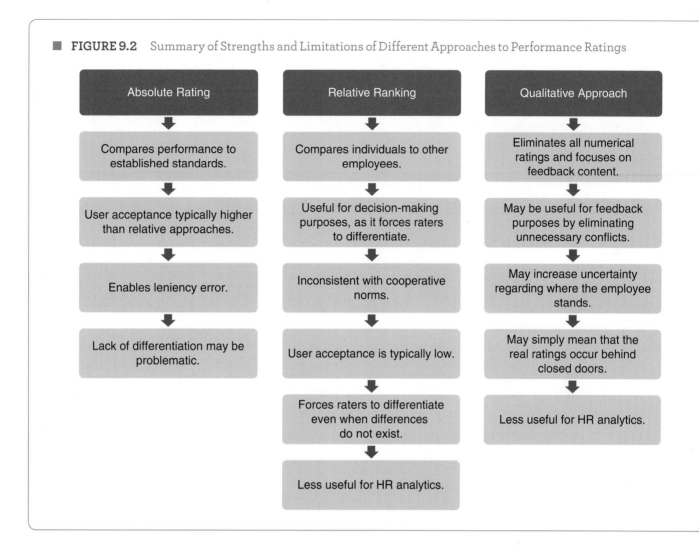

■ **FIGURE 9.2** Summary of Strengths and Limitations of Different Approaches to Performance Ratings

employees' scores. In these systems, all employees can technically be rated as "exceptional," or all employees may be rated as "needs improvement." One employee's rating is not expected to influence ratings given to other employees. The rater is expected to gather data about each employee's performance, compare performance to agreed-upon criteria, and then rate each employee. Systems that utilize absolute ratings may take the form of graphic rating scales, behaviorally anchored rating scales (BARS), and behavioral observation scales (BOS). The descriptions of these different rating methods can be found in Figure 9.3.

Relative Rankings

These systems involve comparison of each employee's performance to that of coworkers. Rankings may take the form of straight rankings, paired comparisons, and forced distribution. **Straight rankings** simply involve having the rater rank order all employees from best to worst. Depending on the number of employees to be ranked, this could be a cumbersome process. **Paired comparisons** involve creating rankings by comparing two employees at a time until every unique pair of employees has been compared and then compiling the results; this approach can be thought of as a round-robin tournament involving employee performance comparisons. The frequency of endorsement of one employee over others determines the

Straight rankings When a rater rank orders all employees from best to worst

Paired comparisons Creating rankings by comparing two employees at the same time until every unique pair of employees has been compared and then compiling the results

■ **FIGURE 9.3**　Descriptions of Different Absolute Rating Scale Formats

Graphic Rating Scale

Raters are presented with attributes and behavioral descriptions and are asked to rate the individual using an established scale.

Circle the number that describes the employee's

Quality of work

1	2	3	4	5
Unacceptable	Below Average	Average	Good	Exceptional

Quantity of work

1	2	3	4	5
Unacceptable	Below Average	Average	Good	Exceptional

Behaviorally Anchored Rating Scale (BARS)

Employee's behavior is measured on a scale that describes specific examples of behaviors that could occur for different levels of performance. These scales are developed following identification of critical incidents for high, moderate, and low performance levels. The purpose of the examples is to give all raters a common frame of reference and increase accuracy. These scales are useful as feedback tools, but could be challenging and costly to develop for all dimensions of performance.

Use the specific descriptions to rate the employee's customer service performance.

5 – Answers customer questions on the same day. Could be expected to investigate queries even when not directly within his/her line of responsibility.

3 – Answers customer questions respectfully and within a week.

1 – Treats customers with disrespect; customer inquiries are often ignored.

Behavioral Observation Scale

The rater assesses the frequency with which the employee displays the behaviors in question.

	Never 1	Rarely 2	Often 3	Usually 4	Always 5
Answers customer queries within the same day.					
	1	2	3	4	5
Greets customers within 60 seconds of them entering the store.	1	2	3	4	5

Forced distribution Also known as stack rankings; involves the rater placing a specific percentage of employees into categories such as exceptional, adequate, and poor

final ranking. Again, this could be mentally taxing for the rater if there is a large number of employees to be compared to each other. Finally, **forced distribution**, commonly known as "stack rankings," involves the rater placing a specific percentage of employees under the exceptional, adequate, and poor performer categories. The assumption behind ranking-based systems is that actual performance in organizations is normally distributed. Forced distribution was popularized by GE (but later abandoned by the firm in 2015, as well as by other early adopters such as Amazon and Microsoft), and is still in use in companies including Uber, Intel, and Cisco.[22]

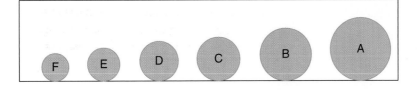

■ **FIGURE 9.4**   Example of a Forced Distribution System

When employees are ranked, the size of the differences in their performance will be disregarded. For example, the difference between B and C is much greater than the differences between C, D, E, and F.

Relative rankings have some limitations compared to absolute ratings. First, rankings are inconsistent with norms of cooperation, given that for some employees to be rated as exceptional, others will have to be rated as average or below average. In other words, performance is defined as if it were a zero-sum game in a work group. Second, recent evidence suggests that employee performance in organizations does not necessarily follow a normal distribution, violating a key assumption behind these systems. In fact, research shows that actual performance is distributed in such a way that a small percentage of employees show exceptional levels of success (superstars), whereas the remainder show performance that is below average.[23] As a result, trying to force employee performance into a bell-curve distribution seems problematic. Finally, managers and employees dislike these systems, given the necessity to differentiate between employees even when differences in performance are not large enough to be meaningful. For example, consider Figure 9.4, in which the size of the circles represents actual performance of each employee. When these employees are ranked, important information will be lost, such as the fact that the difference between A and B is actually smaller than that between B and C or that C, D, and E actually have very similar levels of performance or that both A and B are exceptional performers. The system will also force the rater to distinguish between C, D, and E even though their actual performances are so similar that the differences between them may be practically unimportant from the organization's perspective.

On a more positive note, though, these systems force the rater to differentiate among followers. Lack of differentiation in ratings even though there are real differences in performance can be a problem as serious as forced differentiation, and therefore using rankings may yield results that are more useful for decision-making purposes such as distributing bonuses, merit pay increases, and making decisions relating to promotions.

Qualitative Assessment

Some performance assessments do not utilize quantitative ratings. Instead, these systems rely on qualitative assessment, or describing the areas of strengths and limitations for feedback purposes, without assigning a numerical rating to each employee. An example of this approach is the ***critical incident method***, through which managers identify examples of exceptionally high and low incidents of performance and document them in narrative form.

In recent years, companies such as GE and Adobe have eliminated numerical ratings, replacing them with frequent check-ins and informal conversations. Such companies may choose not to quantify performance reviews because their primary purpose is developmental rather than administrative. In the absence of ratings, instead of getting overly focused on the rating they received or should have received, employees may more easily have a conversation around performance with their managers. For example, Cargill, the largest privately held corporation in the United States, found that the actual ratings were not sufficiently differentiated, and pay increases based on performance ratings were really small, leading to its decision to eliminate ratings.[24]

Critical incident method
A method through which managers identify examples of exceptionally high and low incidents of performance and document them in narrative form

The world's largest chip maker, Intel, conducted an internal experiment in which it gave employees feedback but no performance scores for 2 years. Eventually it went back to using ratings, believing that ratings increase healthy competition among employees.[25]

There is emerging evidence that eliminating ratings because employees do not like them and expecting that frequent feedback could replace them may be shortsighted. To begin with, the elimination of ratings may simply mean that the company continues to rate employees behind closed doors but stops sharing ratings with employees. Employee performance will need to be evaluated somehow, even when assessments are not revealed to employees. When ratings are abandoned in performance reviews, managers may still rate employees to determine pay raises and promotions, but the main change is that employees do not see or influence the ratings.[26] If ratings are replaced by these "shadow systems," it is likely that the lack of transparency will contribute to employee dissatisfaction in some companies, unless trust is already in place. This is one of the key reasons why Facebook decided to keep its formal ratings of employees.[27]

In a study by the consulting firm CEB on more than 10,000 employees, manager conversation quality, time spent on informal conversations, top performer satisfaction with their pay, and employee engagement were lower in firms that dropped ratings to move toward systems with informal conversations. In these firms, there was a tendency for managers to skip performance conversations altogether. Further, many managers gave feedback employees perceived as vague, and employees felt unsure where they stood with their managers. This is because the presence of a numerical rating communicates information that may be difficult to convey otherwise and serves a summative purpose. Similarly, an Aon Hewitt study of more than 2,000 employees showed that 64% of all survey respondents but 88% of high performers said that firms should have performance appraisals with numerical ratings.[28]

These results indicate that having clear ratings of performance may be particularly desirable to high performers who are more attracted to organizations that recognize their contributions. Scientific research on the effects of the presence, absence, or elimination of ratings is lacking. Organizations are advised to consider the benefits they derive from ratings (if any) and the costs of not providing performance ratings (if any) before making this decision.

Choosing the Source of Performance Information

Who should provide information about employee performance? There are many possibilities. Due to the nature of their jobs and responsibility for employee performance, managers are typically the primary raters in performance appraisals and serve the role of a major coach and source of feedback for employees. At the same time, information from managers may be supplemented with feedback from coworkers, subordinates, customers, and self. Utilizing *360-degree feedback*, or multiple-rater systems, presents employees with feedback from different stakeholders and has the potential to provide useful, rich information. At the same time, different sources have different limitations that need to be considered.

360-degree feedback
Multiple-rater systems, which present employees with feedback from different stakeholders and have the potential to provide useful, rich information

Managers

Because the role of a manager includes managing the performance of employees, managers are naturally involved in performance management. In industries such as manufacturing, the manager is the only rater during the annual or semiannual performance appraisal. Managers are often the most knowledgeable source in the assessment of employee performance, and they are in a position to collect more information if needed. They may provide higher-quality data to the performance assessment compared to other sources. For example, a meta-analytic study showed that the interrater reliability among different managers rating the same employee is typically higher than that among different coworkers rating the same employee.[29] Interestingly, this study showed that managers rated some dimensions of performance (productivity, quality) more reliably than other dimensions (interpersonal competence, communication competence), suggesting that supplementing manager ratings with those of coworkers for different dimensions of performance may add value.

Relying solely on a single manager as the rater could be problematic. In some contexts, managers may know little about the employee's performance. For example, this could occur if the employee is working in a field setting, when the manager is supervising a large number of employees and has limited interactions with each employee, or if the manager only recently started working with the employee. Although patrol officers are often supervised by a sergeant, they are often out on their own, and the sergeant has relatively little chance to observe their work behavior. Further, the nature of the relationship the manager has with the employee will affect the rating and the interactions during performance reviews, potentially resulting in skepticism among some employees that the appraisal process is biased. Adding multiple perspectives makes a lot of sense to ensure that ratings reflect diverse perspectives and capture the full picture of how the employee performs at work.

Coworkers

The involvement of coworkers in performance assessments introduces a rating source that potentially has more extended interactions with the focal employee. Because coworkers have the ability to rate certain aspects of performance (such as contributions to the team) more effectively, the introduction of coworkers as raters could increase perceived fairness of ratings. Given that work is increasingly performed in a team setting, coworkers are increasingly important stakeholders for employee performance, making their inclusion as a source of performance feedback natural. At the same time, coworker ratings have the potential to show bias toward the employee due to liking, similar to supervisor ratings.[30] As a result, companies often use these ratings for primarily developmental purposes rather than for reward or other administrative decisions. When coworker ratings are used, managers are typically also involved to ensure that the coworker raters remain anonymous and the feedback from the multiple sources is combined. For example, at Facebook, employees nominate three to five peers to evaluate them. This is followed by managers writing the review.[31]

In addition to their role in formal performance reviews, coworkers can be a good source of regular feedback. Companies such as the ride-hailing company Lyft are using software that scans employee calendars and invites coworkers to evaluate employee performance after meetings.[32]

Direct Reports

When the employee to be evaluated is a manager, the direct reports, or subordinates of the manager, are a relevant and important source of information. Feedback from the manager's direct reports could provide useful and actionable information and help the manager develop leadership skills. At the same time, anonymity of this feedback is essential to maintain the quality of subordinate feedback, as rating one's manager can be a threatening experience. In fact, research shows that when the source of subordinate feedback is known, raters (subordinates) have a tendency to inflate their assessments, resulting in distorted and unrealistic feedback.[33] This means that subordinates will be more useful as a source of feedback in large groups in which anonymity can plausibly be maintained. Further, similar to coworker ratings, feedback provided by subordinates also shows more evidence of a leniency bias as a result of liking, compared to assessments managers provide for their employees.

Customers

Internal and external customers provide a unique perspective to performance measurement. Internal customers are users of an employee's output within the same firm, whereas external customers are outside the organization. Feedback collected from customers is relevant and oftentimes is one of the more important indicators of performance. Seeking feedback from customers also signals to customers that their opinions matter, which may contribute to organizational reputation and customer relationships. A primary challenge will be to gather these data, as often customers are reluctant or uninterested in giving feedback unless they have complaints. Further, customers have little accountability and motivation to provide fair feedback, and they have little training to do so. As a result, their ratings may suffer from biases. In fact, research has shown that customer satisfaction ratings suffer from bias against women and minorities.[34]

Self-Assessment

Self-assessments have only moderate overlap with manager and coworker ratings. For example, a meta-analysis shows that self and manager ratings are correlated at only .22, which is a significant but still modest correlation. This is perhaps not surprising, given that self-assessment may capture the person's intentions in addition to actual behaviors and outcomes observable to others. You may assume that self-assessments that are part of a performance appraisal system will be inflated, but research actually shows that rating inflation is more likely to occur if the information will be used for decision-making purposes (as opposed to developmental purposes), and the leniency of these appraisals was reduced when individuals were told that their appraisals would be verified through other methods. Further, self and manager ratings were less likely to diverge when behavioral as opposed to trait criteria were used and when employees were asked to evaluate themselves relative to others. Self-ratings seem to be most useful for developmental purposes, as a way of getting employees to think about their strengths and weaknesses, and to have two-way dialogue during performance-related conversations, coaching sessions, and performance review meetings. Using self-assessments ensures that the employee is part of the conversation, has a chance to highlight their greatest contributions, and learns what their manager sees as their greatest strengths.[35]

Self-assessments are likely to be more useful if the criteria used for performance assessment are clear, objective, and unambiguous. For example, asking a student to evaluate their own "participation level" in class is likely to yield answers that may differ from the instructor's evaluation of the student, because students may define participation in class as attending the class, speaking up, coming to class prepared, discussing the class material with their peers in a small-group discussion, or any number of other ways. However, asking a student how often they spoke up in response to a question the instructor posed to the class is likely to yield answers more similar to what would be reported by the instructor or peers, because the question is more clearly defined and targeted. Similarly, asking employees to list their specific accomplishments within a period of time, tying ratings to a referent group (e.g., "compared to your coworkers"), may increase the usefulness of self-assessments and minimize disagreements between supervisor and employee ratings.

360-Degree Feedback

The 360-degree feedback approach is a method in which performance is evaluated from multiple perspectives all around the focal person, typically including manager, coworkers, and subordinates in the process. What we know about these different rating sources is that they each provide information that is not necessarily captured by the other. In other words, using multiple raters does not replicate information we already have; instead, different raters are better at evaluating different performance criteria. As a result, there is value in conducting 360-degree feedback in order to improve the quality of feedback available to the employee. At the same time, simply providing this feedback in raw form will not necessarily be useful for improving performance. For example, research shows that multisource feedback is perceived as more useful and actually resulted in behavioral changes when feedback was accompanied by a facilitator or coach who helped interpret the feedback and turn it into action. In contrast, simply receiving the feedback as a printout was like receiving no feedback.[36] Further, other research suggests that in 360-degree feedback systems, those who would benefit most from feedback—that is, the lowest performers—may not accept the feedback that they receive from the system.[37] A 360-degree feedback

The 360-degree feedback approach remains a popular developmental tool around the world, with some surprising uses. In 2016, Narendra Modi, the prime minister of India, instituted a system of 360-degree feedback in the promotion of key officers, hoping to make the government bureaucracy more performance oriented.[38]

Shutterstock.com

SPOTLIGHT ON GLOBAL ISSUES

Cultural Influences on Performance Management

Performance management has the potential to be strongly shaped by the cultural context. For example, in individualistic and low-uncertainty avoidant cultures such as the United States, performance management has a heavy feedback component, with employee voices strongly heard. More power-distant (hierarchical) and collectivistic cultures such as Singapore and Japan typically have more top-down feedback, with little employee involvement in the process. The effectiveness of 360-degree feedback is also culturally contingent, with these systems being a better fit for individualistic and low-power-distance (more egalitarian) cultures. In collectivist and highly power-distant cultures, giving feedback to peers

and supervisors is a serious challenge, resulting in appraisals that are quite lenient.

Companies are finding that their performance reviews work differently in their offices around the globe. In cases in which certain practices clash with local cultures, companies may choose to modify their global practices for particular local norms. For example, the French cosmetics company L'Oréal prides itself on its open culture in which employees feel free to confront each other. However, it quickly realized that open confrontation and criticism are frowned upon in its South American offices.[39] As another example, PepsiCo decided not to use 360-degree feedback in its offices in China.

system requires significant trust on the part of employees, as rating one's coworkers and managers can be a sensitive issue. In this sense, organizations may want to carefully develop and roll out a 360-degree feedback system should they choose to go this route and include features such as ways to protect the anonymity of raters.

Choosing the Ratee

So far, we have assumed that organizations are interested in measuring and managing individual performance. In reality, though, focusing on individual performance has a number of limitations. For example, with the increasing prevalence of teams in organizational settings, treating individual performance as if each individual performs independently may not exactly be realistic. Further, in many instances, individuals are expected to cooperate while performing their jobs. For example, a team of employees may make the sales, with input from each employee. Identifying which employee was responsible for making this sale may be challenging and may be inconsistent with the ultimate goal of cooperation.

Some organizations face the limitations of individual metrics by using *team appraisals* rather than individual-based measures. In these systems, goals and performance metrics may be at the team level. For example, banks often use "net promoter score" (a score that measures customers' likelihood to recommend the bank to others) to capture the performance of each branch. This is an important metric for banks, but it is unclear which employees have the most influence over a customer's likelihood to recommend the bank. Using team-based metrics may therefore focus employee attention on the unit's goals and encourage them to cooperate. In these organizations, individuals may receive team bonuses and team incentives depending either on team performance metrics or on whether their team meets specific targets. For example, Swiss banking software maker Avaloq utilizes a team-based review through which members evaluate the team's performance with respect to how well they worked together and whether the targets were reached.[40]

Team appraisals A team evaluation in which goals and performance are evaluated at the team level

A challenge of team-based appraisals is the possibility of employees not pulling their weight because they are not individually accountable. To tackle this problem, the organization may assess the degree to which the individual supports the team and complements coworker efforts.

Deciding How Closely to Link Performance Ratings to Compensation

Pay for performance, particularly in the form of bonuses, has established effects on future performance.[41] Research shows that employees who feel that they are treated fairly by the organization have stronger engagement and other positive job attitudes. Part of achieving fairness is ensuring that employees are rewarded and recognized in line with their contributions to the organization.[42] As Chapter 12 points out, companies utilize different methods of tying pay to individual, team, or organizational performance, in the hopes that employee pay reflects different contributions employees make to the organization.

When performance metrics are objective and reflect results that naturally follow employee performance (such as sales volume), tying pay to performance is more straightforward and less subject to bias. One concern with more subjective assessments is that the knowledge that performance ratings will be tied to performance may affect the rating managers give employees. Such knowledge may result in inflated performance ratings so that more employees receive raises or deflated ratings because the organization has a limited merit pay or bonus budget. Unfortunately, both of these approaches to performance reviews will result in a disconnect between the actual performance of the employee and the rating given.

Companies adopt different approaches to how they manage the link between pay and performance ratings. For example, Facebook uses a formula that minimizes manager influence over the compensation decision. A key benefit Facebook sees in this approach is that managers spend their time rating the employee, and once ratings are determined, compensation decisions are straightforward.[43] The difficulty of ensuring that performance appraisal ratings are error free is leading some organizations to sever the link between performance reviews and compensation, with the belief that linking pay to reviews takes away or diminishes their developmental value. However, motivation experts caution that this may lead to a situation in which the basis for bonuses is less transparent. Instead, some companies introduce several check-ins throughout the year but reserve one annual review for compensation-related decisions to ensure that employees know where they stand.[44]

When performance appraisals are used to distribute bonuses and merit pay, it makes sense to conduct **focal date reviews** in which performance review takes place on the same date for all employees. This way, the organization will find it easier to allocate its bonus or merit pay budget. One concern regarding focal date reviews is that all reviews within the company take place within the same short time period, resulting in a significant time investment for each manager supervising multiple employees. For instance, managers meeting individually with a large number of employees will incur a serious cognitive load as well as demands on their time.

An alternative to focal date reviews, particularly if evaluations will not be tied to compensation, is an **anniversary review** in which the employee is rated on the anniversary of their start date in the organization. This approach allows reviews to be spread out so that the performance review period does not become a significant burden on employees and managers.

Of course, with any yearly review system, one risk is that managers will not remember how employees were performing at the beginning of the review period but simply rely on their memory of the employee's performance over the last few weeks or months. Thus, conducting yearly reviews, regardless of when they take place, needs to be coupled with frequent check-ins and coaching meetings between employees and managers to make sure that performance is actually managed throughout the year.

Focal date reviews
Performance reviews that take place on the same date for all employees

Anniversary reviews
Performance reviews in which an employee is rated on the anniversary of their start date with the organization

Conducting Fair Performance Reviews

LO 9.3 Identify best practices for making performance reviews fair and unbiased.

The focus thus far has been on the design features of performance appraisals. Once the performance appraisal system is designed, implementation depends on the motivation and ability of raters to use the system in a fair and consistent manner. The rater is expected to work with the employees on a day-to-day basis, give regular feedback, and provide coaching and support throughout the evaluation period. When the time comes to give a performance review, the rater will have to look back on the employee's performance and provide an assessment. Although raters may have every intention of being fair and accurate, a number of errors can affect the rating process.

Factors Leading to Rating Errors

Performance assessment, particularly in jobs where quantitative metrics are not naturally available, requires raters to collect information about performance through observation and data gathering and then rate performance. Because this is a perceptual process, ratings oftentimes suffer from errors. Errors may include *leniency error* (the tendency of a rater to rate most employees highly), *severity error* (the tendency to rate most employees closer to the lower end of the scale), *central tendency error* (the tendency to rate almost all employees in the middle category), *halo error* (basing performance ratings on one or two performance dimensions, with one prominent dimension positively affecting how the employee is perceived on other dimensions), and *horns error* (the opposite of halo error; ratings on one dimension negatively influencing how the employee is perceived on other dimensions). Another issue in performance appraisals is the *recency error,* wherein a rater will focus on the most recent employee behaviors they have observed rather than focusing on the entire rating period. Manager awareness of factors that cause rating errors helps HR departments design training programs or other interventions for raters that will minimize the harmful effects of rater errors.

Leniency error The tendency of a rater to rate most employees highly

Severity error The tendency to rate almost all ratees low

Central tendency error The tendency to rate most employees in the middle category

Halo error Basing performance ratings on one or two performance dimensions, with one prominent dimension positively affecting how the employee is perceived on other dimensions

Horns error Ratings on one dimension negatively influencing how the employee is perceived on other dimensions

Recency error When a rater focuses on the most recent employee behaviors they have observed rather than focusing on the entire rating period

Impression Management

Employees are not passive recipients of performance ratings. In fact, they have the ability to influence the ratings managers give them through the careful use of impression management tactics. Impression management consists of behaviors individuals demonstrate to portray a specific image. Research shows that impression management tactics that are particularly effective in positively influencing performance ratings are supervisor-focused tactics, such as offering to do favors for the manager, complimenting the manager, and taking an interest in the manager's life. Impression management tactics that were more detrimental to performance ratings are self-focused, such as trying to show that one does a good job or working hard when performance is more visible to the manager. What differentiates these two types of impression management tactics is that supervisor-focused tactics positively shape the manager's belief that the employee is similar to the manager, whereas self-focused tactics negatively affect this perception. In other words, employees can influence the rating in ways that are different from working their hardest or increasing their performance.[45] It is easy to see that when managers fall prey to impression management tactics of employees who are perceived as poor performers by their coworkers, employees will likely question the validity of performance assessment and be concerned about favoritism.

Personal Characteristics of Raters and Ratees

There is some evidence that performance ratings are affected by ratees' personal characteristics. For example, rater–ratee race similarity is positively related to ratings, even though these effects are small. Attractiveness of the ratee seems to be an advantage for ratings of nonmanagerial women, to be a disadvantage for managerial women, and had no effects for men.[46] Other personal characteristics that can influence ratings include age,

SPOTLIGHT ON LEGAL ISSUES

Sex Discrimination Claims at Qualcomm

Performance appraisals can play a critically important role in employment discrimination lawsuits. Sometimes they provide key evidence supporting the organization's argument that a decision taken against an employee was due to poor performance as opposed to illegal discrimination. At other times, the absence of a legally defensible performance review serves to support claims of discrimination. One example of the latter is the case of Qualcomm, a San Diego–based chip designer with more than 30,000 employees worldwide.

In 2016, Qualcomm faced a sex discrimination lawsuit alleging discrimination against women engineers in pay and promotions. Instead of fighting the lawsuit in court, Qualcomm chose to settle it for $19.5 million and promised to make meaningful changes in its reward and promotion systems. Part of the discrimination claim was that the firm used performance ratings to allocate raises and

bonuses. In Qualcomm's system, managers rated employee performance with little guidance, and there was a lack of clear, quantifiable criteria to capture job performance. The rating rubric focused on qualitative criteria, and in this male-dominated environment, female employees routinely received lower performance evaluations relative to their male counterparts.

Performance reviews may have disparate impact on different groups of employees. As discussed in Chapter 4, disparate impact may not necessarily be illegal if the observed group differences are due to job-related differences. However, the use of subjective and vague criteria in performance reviews makes it harder to defend the legality argument. Although it is unclear how the Qualcomm lawsuit would have been resolved had it not been settled out of court, this case underlines the importance of reliable performance assessments for legal purposes.[47]

gender, pregnancy, religion, racial or ethnic background, and disability—all factors for which employment discrimination is illegal.

Rater personality also plays a role: Studies show that raters who are agreeable, emotionally stable, and extraverted rated their employees more highly, suggesting that raters' own personality could affect how lenient or harsh the rating is.[48] In other words, rater and ratee personality have the potential to lead to unconscious biases that may affect the fairness, accuracy, and eventual acceptance of performance reviews and feedback received based on these reviews.

Favoritism in performance ratings is an age-old problem. In the 3rd century, Chinese philosopher Sin Yu observed that "The Imperial Rater of Nine Grades seldom rates men according to his merits but always according to his likes and dislikes."[51]

Liking

One other possible source of rating distortion is liking, or favorable attitudes toward the ratee. Liking an employee may result in unintentional biases such as giving the employee the benefit of the doubt for low performance or giving more credit for high performance. Alternatively, managers may knowingly distort their ratings when they like an employee in an effort to preserve the relationship quality. Even though it seems plausible that liking an employee should be a major source of bias in performance ratings, research supporting this argument is limited. In fact, there is some evidence that liking may be a function of the performance level of the employee. If this is the case, then liking would not be a biasing factor in performance assessments and in fact could be a good indicator of how well the employee is performing.[49] Further, research indicates that the role of liking in the performance review process is contingent on system characteristics. For example, liking seems to lead to inflated ratings when raters are coworkers or subordinates. Further, trait appraisal formats, as opposed to more results-based metrics or behavioral appraisals, are more strongly affected by liking.[50]

©iStock.com/Lib Ferreira

Rater Motivation

Whether the rating actually reflects the employee's true performance level is also a function of how motivated the rater is to provide an accurate evaluation. Raters are thought to consider the advantages and downsides of rating the employee accurately versus inaccurately and how likely they are to get caught (or be called out for poor behavior). If the rater feels that giving the employee an inflated score is more advantageous and is likely to yield more positive outcomes for the rater, then the rating will be biased. This means that understanding why raters feel that inaccurate ratings are more beneficial will be helpful in counteracting this biasing factor. For example, rater discomfort with performance appraisals is known to yield overly positive ratings, presumably because raters are more highly motivated to avoid confrontation as opposed to providing high-quality feedback.[52] Retraining raters to alleviate discomfort helps increase rater motivation.

Improving the Effectiveness of Performance Management

LO 9.4   Explain how to implement performance management for maximum effectiveness.

There are a number of ways in which companies can improve the effectiveness of their performance management systems. Much like other HR systems, it is important to frequently explore improvement opportunities and ensure that the system in place continues to meet organizational needs over time.

Training Managers and Employees

Even though performance management is a key part of managers' roles, skills involved in effective performance management are often lacking. For example, a study by an HR consulting firm on 223 companies around the world revealed that only 45% of participants believed that managers had the skills to build actionable development plans, and 44% had the skills to provide high-quality feedback and coaching. These gaps point to important development opportunities for managers, given their critical role in the effectiveness of performance management systems.[53]

Interestingly, research indicates that teaching raters about the different types of rating errors such as halo effect, leniency, and strictness does not lead to more accurate ratings, and in fact it reduces rater accuracy. As a result, rating error awareness training does not have much support with respect to its usefulness. However, a specific type of training, *frame of reference (FOR) training*, has benefits. FOR training involves having raters observe specific instances of performance through videotapes or vignettes and then telling them the "true score" and why raters should rate in a particular way so that different raters are on the same page and pay attention to similar aspects of performance. The purpose of this training is to ensure that all raters evaluating similar types of employees share a common conceptualization of performance. FOR training has been shown to reduce rating errors and increase accuracy.[54] Other types of training that could be useful include training managers in confronting performance problems and delivering positive and negative feedback. Such training is likely to increase rater confidence and motivation to provide high-quality feedback and therefore can yield significant improvements in the quality of feedback employees receive.

Frame of reference (FOR) training Training that involves raters observing specific instances of performance through videotapes or vignettes and then telling them the "true score" and why raters should rate in a particular way

Increasing Rater Accountability

One assumption regarding performance appraisals is that keeping raters accountable for their ratings yields more accurate measurement. There is actually little research and empirical support for this argument. In fact, when raters are accountable to ratees (or when they know that they will have to explain their ratings to the employee they are rating), they are more lenient.[55] Raters may also be accountable to their own superiors, but research shows no effects of this type of accountability on performance ratings.

Despite the lack of research on this topic, companies expect that increasing rater accountability may motivate raters to take the performance appraisals seriously and may curb the effects of rater favoritism. Organizations utilize three primary means to increase rater accountability. First, managers' effectiveness in giving feedback and conducting appraisals

Shutterstock.com

What happens in calibration meetings reflects the core values of a company's culture. The law firm retained to conduct a culture audit at Uber recommended it drop the process of calibration of performance ratings. Calibration at Uber consisted of enforcing a strict curve, potentially making the ratings more subjective.[57]

Calibration meeting A meeting in which groups of managers come together and discuss the ratings they will give their employees before ratings are finalized

Diary keeping The practice of recording employee performance on a regular basis

may be a performance dimension in their own evaluations. This approach would communicate the expectation that effective managers take performance reviews seriously. Second, the manager's supervisor may have to sign off on the appraisals, introducing accountability to a higher-level manager. Third, organizations including Google and Intel utilize **calibration meetings**, a meeting in which groups of managers come together and discuss the ratings they will give their employees before ratings are finalized.[56] This approach makes managers accountable to each other by requiring them to justify their ratings and the distribution of their ratings to their peers. This method has its downsides, such as ratings being dependent on a manager's communication and negotiation abilities. Even though systematic information about the benefits of these methods is slow to emerge, it is important to know that these methods exist and are used with the hope that rater accountability improves ratee reactions to performance appraisals.

Having Raters Keep Records of Employee Performance

Rating performance periodically, even when it occurs regularly and frequently, such as on a quarterly basis, will require the rater to recall past performance for each employee reporting to them. As a result, raters would benefit from help in recalling performance information. **Diary keeping**, or keeping records of employee performance, is a method that has been shown to improve rating accuracy by enabling raters to recall specific information about their employees. Keeping a log of critical performance incidents could be helpful, even though managers may find it cumbersome. This method allows the manager to remember and recognize important milestones and provide feedback rich in detail.[58]

Auditing the System

One of the best practices of performance management is to periodically audit the system. An audit might reveal if raters are serious about evaluations, whether employees are satisfied with the quality of the feedback, and if they feel that their efforts are fairly rewarded and recognized. Performance reviews may not always work the way they were intended. For example, the system may have low user acceptance. Managers' lack of skills in confronting performance problems may lead to unproductive conversations. In some instances, the performance review criteria may become outdated as jobs change and evolve. Auditing the system periodically will help uncover and address these and other problems. As a case in point, Facebook has a team of analysts that go through reviews to identify potential evidence of bias. For example, they examine whether managers describe their male and female subordinates using similar language—the more frequent use of the word *abrasive* to describe female employees may capture unconscious biases, which may be worth further investigation to ensure that performance reviews and the resulting compensation are not biased.[59]

LO 9.5 Describe how teaching managers how to be good coaches helps improve performance management.

Teaching Managers How to Be Good Coaches and Build Trust

In companies that do the best job in performance management, managers serve as coaches to employees and give frequent feedback and support. Coaching is an important skill for a manager to have. Google's Project Oxygen, examining the behaviors that differentiated its more effective leaders from less effective ones, showed that coaching employees was among the eight differentiators. Coaches ask the right questions and model the right behaviors. They show employees how to complete difficult tasks, offer specific advice regarding how to tackle problems, and provide support.[60] As you can see, behaviors coaches perform are important for performance improvements.

Further, it is important to remember that the ongoing professional relationship between managers and employees and the trust that exists in this relationship provide the context in which feedback is delivered and performance is reviewed. As a result, thinking of performance reviews and feedback delivery in isolation from the relationship quality is a mistake. Unlike employee selection, in which job applicants are interacting with strangers and trying to make good first impressions, performance feedback is delivered to employees who have a history with the manager. Even though providing the right tools can help, in the absence of trust, feedback may not reach its potential and measurement may not be viewed as fair. For example, the same level of employee participation in the appraisal interview does not give employees the sense that they have voice in the process when trust in the manager is low.[61] This suggests that anything organizations can do to ensure that managers are trained in leading and that trust exists between management and employees should go a long way in improving the quality of performance management that takes place in the organization.

Developing a Feedback Culture

A ***feedback culture*** is one in which employees and managers feel comfortable giving and receiving feedback. The characteristics of an organization that has a supportive feedback environment can be seen in Figure 9.5. Top management support, role modeling for feedback, and training managers to realize the importance of feedback as a tool for performance improvement are among the steps companies may take to help create a feedback culture. Organizations are realizing that annual or semiannual reviews are woefully inadequate to provide useful feedback to employees. As a result, many organizations are instituting ways

Feedback culture A culture in which employees and managers feel comfortable giving and receiving feedback

---

MANAGER'S TOOLBOX
Feedback Delivery Best Practices

Feedback delivery is a skill that is useful to managers throughout their careers. Giving feedback allows a manager to recognize exemplary behaviors and confront performance that would benefit from improvement. Following are some best practices in feedback delivery that managers can apply in their organizations.[62]

Recognize contributions. Many managers assume that feedback is delivered only when something is wrong. This may mean that high performance and "extra mile" contributions go unrecognized. It is important to recognize positive behaviors using specific language. You may consider describing what you saw, explaining why this was a good behavior to demonstrate, and thanking the employee for doing it.

Conduct regular one-on-one meetings. These meetings are among the most helpful tools for ensuring that you will give the employee regular feedback and have opportunities to coach and develop the employee.

Be a role model for feedback. Your direct reports and coworkers will feel more comfortable receiving feedback from you if you are someone who takes feedback seriously, seeks it frequently, and displays an openness to learn about your own blind spots.

Focus on actual behaviors or results, not personality. When feedback targets an individual's personality, it may be perceived as unfair and taken personally. Instead, consider focusing on actual behaviors the employee may successfully change. For example, instead of "you seem low in energy," "you did not contribute any ideas in the past five meetings" is more behavioral and concrete and is less likely to put the employee on the defensive.

Use the "Start–Stop–Continue" model. One way of structuring your feedback is to specify what the employee should start doing, stop doing, and continue doing. This framework ensures that you will focus on both positive and negative behaviors.

■ **FIGURE 9.5**   Characteristics of a High-Quality Feedback Environment

Feedback provided by a credible source	Specific, useful, high-quality feedback	Feedback delivered in a considerate manner
Both positive and negative feedback provided	Feedback source is available to help and support the employee	The environment promotes feedback seeking

Source: Steelman, L. A., Levy, P. E., & Snell, A. F. (2004). The feedback environment scale: Construct definition, measurement, and validation. *Educational and Psychological Measurement, 64,* 165–184.

that employees can quickly and easily seek feedback at the conclusion of a project, a big meeting, or product launch. For example, Goldman Sachs and J. P. Morgan are among companies that rolled out tools accessible from smartphones to facilitate such feedback seeking any time during the year.[63] It is important to remember that such tools by themselves will not be useful unless there is a feedback culture in which employees feel comfortable and psychologically safe to seek and give feedback.

Establishing Performance Improvement Plans (PIP)

Performance improvement plan (PIP) Plan aimed at helping poor performers be accountable to meeting performance standards

The beginning of this chapter notes that performance reviews also serve as a tool to document poor performance. In cases of employees whose performances do not meet established performance standards, tying performance reviews to a ***performance improvement plan (PIP)*** could make these systems more developmental. Performance improvement plans keep poor performers accountable and also give them a chance to improve. The plan starts with documentation of poor performance using specific language. Then a collaborative process is used to establish an action plan. Using SMART goals as part of the action plan ensures that it is clear whether the struggling employee meets the expectations at the end of the agreed-upon period. Having a third party such as HR or the manager's own supervisor review the plan would be helpful to ensure that the plan is fair and free from tense emotions.

After a meeting between the manager and employee in which a plan is established, the manager and employee meet regularly to review improvements and roadblocks are removed along the way. The PIP concludes when the employee's performance improves and reaches the established goals. If performance does not improve, actions such as transfer or termination may be taken.[64]

©iStock.com/jetcityimage

Dow Chemical was able to defend itself when faced with a national origin discrimination lawsuit by showing that the complainant engineer was put on a performance improvement plan, and when performance did not improve under the plan, was then transferred to work with a different supervisor as a second chance to improve before termination.[65]

PIP is a tool to ensure that poor performers are given a fair chance to improve their performance. PIPs contribute to an overall sense of fairness in the organization and serve to protect the organization from costly lawsuits by showing that employees are treated fairly and given the benefit of the doubt. These plans emphasize the role management has to work with employees to improve performance rather than simply rating employees to make decisions about them.

CHAPTER SUMMARY

Performance management takes the form of measuring and documenting employee performance. It provides useful feedback, documentation, and a metric that can be tied to rewards. Companies need to assess the validity and reliability of data collected and analyzed if it is to lead to good performance management practices. The traditional annual performance appraisal is too infrequent to be useful for daily feedback. Therefore, performance appraisals need to be combined with other feedback, such as one-on-one meetings or tools that allow employees to seek and receive feedback in shorter intervals. Performance appraisals may measure traits, behaviors, or results, and performance information may be derived from multiple sources, including managers, coworkers, subordinates, and customers. Because performance appraisals often involve subjectivity, many errors may occur as part of the evaluation process, resulting in nonperformance factors affecting performance ratings. Ultimately, the effectiveness of a performance management system depends on user acceptance, and therefore involving users in designing the system, ensuring that managers and employees are trained in giving and receiving feedback, and helping develop a strong culture of feedback are among the steps organizations may take to strengthen performance management systems.

KEY TERMS

performance management   295
performance appraisal   295
one-on-one meetings   296
adequate notice   300
fair hearing   300
judgment based on evidence   300
developmental purposes   302
administrative purposes   302
management by objectives (MBO)   305
key performance indicators
(KPIs)   305

SMART goals   305
straight rankings   307
paired comparisons   307
forced distribution   308
critical incident method   309
360-degree feedback   310
team appraisals   313
focal date reviews   314
anniversary reviews   314
leniency error   315
severity error   315

central tendency error   315
halo error   315
horns error   315
recency error   315
frame of reference (FOR)
training   317
calibration meetings   318
diary keeping   318
feedback culture   319
performance improvement
plan (PIP)   320

Visit **edge.sagepub.com/bauer** to help you accomplish your coursework goals in an easy-to-use learning environment.

- Master the learning objectives using key study tools
- Watch, listen, and connect with online multimedia resources

- Access mobile-friendly quizzes and flashcards to check your understanding

HR REASONING AND DECISION-MAKING EXERCISES

MINI-CASE ANALYSIS EXERCISE: UNFAIR PERFORMANCE REVIEWS

You are the HR manager of a professional services firm with 300 employees. Your company utilizes annual performance reviews along with frequent check-in meetings throughout the year as part of performance management. Employees are evaluated on a number of questions assessing customer service quality and sales volume (results of a customer satisfaction survey and actual sales metrics, weighed at 60%) and demonstrating corporate values in day-to-day activities (mentoring others, driving change, and creativity, weighted at 40%).

The annual reviews have just been completed, and you heard from Orlando Nicholson, an employee who had been with the firm for 2 years. Orlando has a cordial but distant relationship with his manager. He asked for a meeting with you and revealed that he feels the most recent performance review he received is unfair. Orlando feels that his customer satisfaction scores are modest, but this is due to being assigned some of the most difficult clients the company has. In addition, the manager rated him as average in mentoring others, discounting the fact that he was heavily involved in the onboarding of two new employees 8 months ago. Orlando also feels that his relatively quiet and shy personality is being held against him. He feels that he heavily influences organizational change, but this happens informally and not in big meetings. In fact, there have been several times when he feels that other people took credit for his ideas.

How would you handle this situation?

Outline:

1. What would you advise Orlando to do in this meeting?

2. What would you tell his manager, if anything?

3. Are there any systemic changes you could think of that may help prevent instances like these from happening in the future?

HR DECISION ANALYSIS EXERCISE: SHOULD YOU ABANDON YEARLY REVIEWS?

You work for a large manufacturing organization with 8,000 employees. Your company has been struggling with having fair, accurate, and practical performance metrics. The performance review system consists of 360-degree feedback, semiannual reviews, and a combination of behaviors and results. You use end-of-year performance ratings to distribute performance bonuses. Managers are told to give employees feedback on a regular basis, but an employee opinion survey puts the average satisfaction with feedback quality at 3.2 on a 5-point scale.

Your company's CEO read in an airline magazine that many large companies are abandoning the use of annual appraisals. The article discussed real-time feedback tools that companies can acquire from various software vendors. These tools enable employees to seek and managers to give feedback regularly. The CEO also feels that the end-of-year review should be abandoned, and managers may simply rank their employees to determine performance bonuses at the end of the year. The CEO's opinion is that having to justify their ratings to employees makes managers more lenient, costing the company a lot of money in bonus payments.

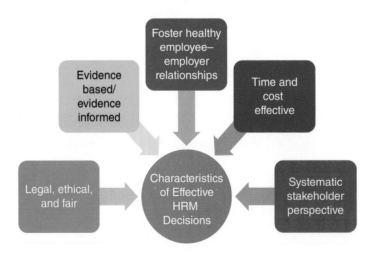

Should your organization switch to the system the CEO has read about? Consider this decision using the following criteria.

Please provide the rationale for your answer to each of the questions.

Is it legal, ethical, and fair?

_____
_____
_____
_____

Is it evidence based/evidence informed?

_____
_____
_____
_____

Does it foster healthy employee–employer relationships?

_____
_____
_____
_____

Is it time and cost effective?

_____
_____
_____
_____

Does it take a systematic stakeholder perspective?

_____
_____
_____
_____

Considering your analysis above, overall, do you think this would be an effective decision? Why or why not?

_____
_____
_____
_____

What, if anything, do you think should be done differently or considered to help make this decision more effective?

_____
_____
_____
_____

HR DECISION-MAKING EXERCISE:
DESIGNING A PERFORMANCE MANAGEMENT SYSTEM

You are in the process of developing a performance review system for Grimard Groceries, a regional retail chain with 80 stores. The job description of hourly employees includes:

- Preparing sandwiches
- Baking bread and cookies
- Making sure that shelves and displays are organized and attractive
- Working at the cash register
- Assisting customers with their questions about merchandise
- Providing efficient service
- Helping customers during checkout

Employees are expected to be helpful, friendly, and fun. The company emphasizes good-quality customer service to build customer loyalty.

If you were designing a performance management system for this company, what would it look like? Assuming that the company is interested in providing feedback to employees on a regular basis but also in tying pay to performance, propose a performance management system for the company. Please make sure that your answer includes specific details such as the forms to be used and the criteria with which performance will be measured.

DATA AND ANALYTICS EXERCISE: USING PREDICTIVE ANALYTICS TO UNDERSTAND PERFORMANCE

In order to improve performance, it helps to understand what factors contribute to it. Organizations may use predictive analytics to find the answers to this question. For example, let's assume that managers just completed measurement of performance using the company's performance appraisal form. We also have the following additional metrics on each employee:

Let's assume that you have information on four criteria that could affect performance.

- Product knowledge (results of a test the employees took part in).
- Personality (a measure of employee extraversion).
- Time management skills (evaluated by each associate's manager).
- Cooperativeness (evaluated by team members).

Which of these metrics are in fact good predictors of performance ratings? This is important information for the organization. For example, if we find that product knowledge is an important predictor, we can increase investment in training on product knowledge. If extraversion is an important predictor, then we could select employees based on extraversion.

EMPLOYEE	PRODUCT KNOWLEDGE	EXTRAVERSION	TIME MANAGEMENT	COOPERATIVENESS	PERFORMANCE RATING
1	3.75	2.33	2.67	4.67	4
2	3.4	3.8	4.4	2.5	2.5
3	3	2.33	4	4	4.33
4	4	4.67	4.33	4	4
5	4.8	3.75	3.33	3.4	3

EMPLOYEE	PRODUCT KNOWLEDGE	EXTRAVERSION	TIME MANAGEMENT	COOPERATIVENESS	PERFORMANCE RATING
6	3.5	2.67	4	4	4
7	4	2.6	3.5	4	4.6
8	5	5	5	2.67	2
9	4	4.6	5	2	2
10	3.4	2	2.3	4.3	4
11	4.5	2.5	4.4	3	4.5
12	3.5	2.3	4.5	3.6	4.3
13	3.8	2.1	2.8	5	5
14	3.7	5	3.2	3.5	4.3
15	3.4	4.5	4.3	5	3.4
16	4.3	4.8	3.75	3.33	3.4
17	4.8	3.5	3.67	4	4
18	3.5	3.67	4	4	4
19	3.5	5	4.4	4	3.4
20	5	2.3	4.5	4.3	5

This is the dataset we will analyze. In order to understand which of the four potential predictors are related to performance ratings, you could use simple bivariate correlations. However, you have four predictors and one outcome. If you use correlations, you will look at each relationship in isolation. In reality, our four predictors may be correlated with each other. This means that you may find that each of the four is correlated with performance ratings, but we would not know which ones are the best predictors once the others are accounted for.

For this reason, we will perform a regression analysis on these data. Note that this is actually a very small sample size to perform this analysis, but let's do it for illustration purposes.

We will use the "Data Analysis" function of Excel. (You can perform these analyses very easily in the statistics software SPSS or using a regression calculator that may be found online as well.) Once you click on Data Analysis, you will be able to perform a regression analysis, as follows:

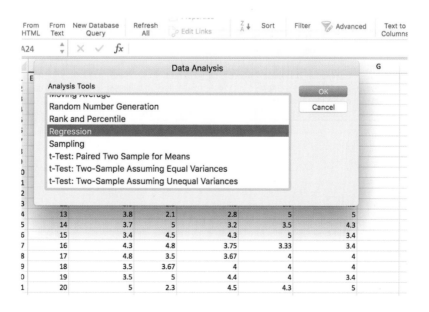

Now we will indicate the range of input. We marked the location of performance ratings under the Y range and the location of the other four variables under the X range. We included variable labels in the selection and then checked the "Labels" box to indicate that the selection includes variable names at the top.

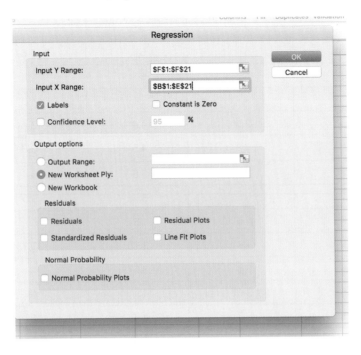

Once you hit OK, you will see a new sheet with the output:

	A	B	C	D	E	F	G	H	I	J
	SUMMARY OUTPUT									
	Regression Statistics									
	Multiple R	0.79765741								
	R Square	0.63625735								
	Adjusted R S	0.53925931								
	Standard Err	0.58922527								
	Observations	20								
	ANOVA									
		df	*SS*	*MS*	*F*	*Significance F*				
	Regression	4	9.1094587	2.27736467	6.55948661	0.00293277				
	Residual	15	5.2077963	0.34718642						
	Total	19	14.317255							
		Coefficients	*Standard Error*	*t Stat*	*P-value*	*Lower 95%*	*Upper 95%*	*Lower 95.0%*	*Upper 95.0%*	
	Intercept	2.23158768	1.81013451	1.23282975	0.23661228	-1.6266227	6.08979805	-1.6266227	6.08979805	
	Product Know	0.12193257	0.23449962	0.51996917	0.61067371	-0.3778915	0.62175669	-0.3778915	0.62175669	
	Extraversion	-0.3491473	0.13565507	-2.5737874	0.02117445	-0.6382893	-0.0600054	-0.6382893	-0.0600054	
	Time manag	0.02621841	0.22534763	0.11634651	0.90892133	-0.4540987	0.50653552	-0.4540987	0.50653552	
	Cooperativer	0.58024875	0.21603593	2.68589001	0.01693088	0.11977906	1.04071844	0.11977906	1.04071844	

Now let's take a look at the sections we marked in blue boxes. R-square tells us the percentage variation in performance ratings that is being explained by the four variables in our model. An R-square of 64% means that the four variables explain 64% of the differences in performance ratings.

P values tell us about the statistical significance of each predictor. This is an indicator of the probability that the relationship you observe between each predictor and the outcome is actually not different from zero. High *p* values mean that there is a very good chance that any relation you observe is really due to chance. Small *p* values indicate that the chance of the observed relationship being zero is really small. In this output, the *p* values are smaller than .05 for extraversion and cooperativeness. In other words, these are the predictors to pay attention to.

Finally, take a look at the "coefficients" column for extraversion and cooperativeness. Do you see anything interesting here? The sign of the extraversion coefficient is negative. This means that extraversion is actually *negatively* related to performance ratings. Using these data, you would conclude that in this company, introverted employees are actually higher performers. In contrast, there seems to be a positive relationship between cooperativeness and performance ratings. These results would help you make decisions such as where to invest your selection and training budget and where not to.

EXCEL EXTENSION: NOW YOU TRY!

On **edge.sagepub.com/bauer,** use the provided dataset and conduct a regression analysis to examine the relationship between four personality traits and job performance.

CHAPTER 9 SUPPLEMENT: COMPETENCY PERFORMANCE RATINGS

Sample competency performance rating form and behavior performance rating form. Special thanks to SHRM for their permission for us to reproduce these here.

COMPETENCY PERFORMANCE RATINGS

The table below presents the competency name, definition, and a set of example behaviors that describe performance associated with this competency. Please review this definition and each of these example behaviors before making your ratings.

HUMAN RESOURCE TECHNICAL EXPERTISE AND PRACTICE	
Definition: The ability to apply the principles and practices of human resource management to contribute to the success of the business	
1.	Maintains up-to-date knowledge of relevant laws, legal rulings, and regulations
2.	Effectively prioritizes own work duties
3.	Effectively prioritizes the work duties of others
4.	Maintains up-to-date knowledge of general HR practices, strategy, and technology
5.	Utilizes existing HR-related best practices
6.	Develops HR-related best practices
7.	Delivers customized HR solutions
8.	Engages in professional development

(Continued)

(Continued)

HUMAN RESOURCE TECHNICAL EXPERTISE AND PRACTICE	
9.	Maintains up-to-date knowledge of critical HR functions (e.g., strategic business management, compensation, and benefits)
10.	Identifies ways to improve work processes
11.	Effectively utilizes business and HR-specific technologies to address business needs
12.	Effectively applies knowledge of HR disciplines and functions to work

Consider each employee's job performance over the past year. Using the competency definition and illustrative behaviors listed above, please rate the job performance of each employee on this competency *relative to **all** other employees you have observed at the same career level* (not just compared to the other employees you are rating). If you have not had an adequate opportunity to observe the employee's performance, click on the button for "Not Observed/Cannot Rate."

	BELOW AVERAGE: BOTTOM 1/3 OF PEER GROUP		AVERAGE: MIDDLE OF THE PEER GROUP			ABOVE AVERAGE: TOP 1/3 OF PEER GROUP		NOT OBSERVED/ CANNOT RATE
	1	2	3	4	5	6	7	N/A
Employee 1	o	o	o	o	o	o	o	o
Employee 2	o	o	o	o	o	o	o	o
Employee 3	o	o	o	o	o	o	o	o

BEHAVIOR PERFORMANCE RATINGS

Following is a list of specific job-related behaviors associated with this competency. For this section of the survey, please rate each employee on the individual behaviors that follow. Consider each employee's job performance over the past year. Please rate the job performance of each employee on the behaviors that follow *relative to **all** other employees at the same career level* (not just compared to the other employees you are rating). If you have not had an adequate opportunity to observe the employee's performance, click on the button for "Not Observed/Cannot Rate."

Human Resource Technical Expertise and Practice **Definition:** The ability to apply the principles and practices of human resource management to contribute to the success of the business								
How well does this HR professional perform relative to other HR professionals at the same career level?	**Below Average:** Bottom 1/3 of peer group		**Average:** Middle of the peer group			**Above Average:** Top 1/3 of peer group		**Not Observed/ Cannot Rate**
	1	2	3	4	5	6	7	N/A
1 Maintains up-to-date knowledge of relevant laws, legal rulings, and regulations								
Employee 1	o	o	o	o	o	o	o	o
Employee 2	o	o	o	o	o	o	o	o
Employee 3	o	o	o	o	o	o	o	o
2 Effectively prioritizes own work duties								
Employee 1	o	o	o	o	o	o	o	o
Employee 2	o	o	o	o	o	o	o	o
Employee 3	o	o	o	o	o	o	o	o

3	Effectively prioritizes the work duties of others							
	Employee 1	o	o	o	o	o	o	o	o
	Employee 2	o	o	o	o	o	o	o	o
	Employee 3	o	o	o	o	o	o	o	o
4	Maintains up-to-date knowledge of general HR practices, strategy, and technology							
	Employee 1	o	o	o	o	o	o	o	o
	Employee 2	o	o	o	o	o	o	o	o
	Employee 3	o	o	o	o	o	o	o	o
5	Utilizes existing HR-related best practices							
	Employee 1	o	o	o	o	o	o	o	o
	Employee 2	o	o	o	o	o	o	o	o
	Employee 3	o	o	o	o	o	o	o	o

Managing Employee Separations and Retention

10

Opening Case

Keeping the Seats Occupied: Analytics as a Retention Management Tool in the Trucking Industry

Long-haul trucking often conjures images of open roads and beautiful scenery. Drivers are admired for the freedom and independence that are often associated with this lifestyle. The reality, however, bears little resemblance to this picture. Today, professional truck drivers typically drive predetermined and optimized routes, with their stops, rests, and speed strictly regulated and watched. They are continuously monitored via video cameras and dashboard "black boxes" or electronic logging devices. They are solo workers, spending long hours in isolation, and with a median salary around $40,000 nationwide, it is not a scheme to get rich quickly. As a result, it is no surprise that there is a nationwide shortage of truck drivers, with estimates that by 2024, the size of the shortage will reach 175,000 drivers.

Freight companies and private companies that rely on truck drivers as a critical part of their logistics network find it extremely difficult to fill open positions. This is an industry in which there is great pressure to hire anyone who is qualified and interested. Once hired, the problem is to hold on to new hires, because the annual turnover rate has been 100% for several years in a row. These data do not only capture voluntary leavers; some drivers leave due to retirements, and others are dismissed for problematic behavior. Still, holding on to good drivers is likely to give employers a key advantage in this highly competitive field.

Many carriers now rely on external vendor-generated solutions or build their own algorithms to benefit from predictive analytics for driver retention. A major use of analytics occurs in the hiring process. If characteristics that predict which truckers will leave quickly can be identified, the company can be more selective in the hiring process or utilize targeted interventions to retain particular groups of applicants. For example, a Tacoma, Washington–based carrier, Interstate Distributor Co., found that the turnover rate was lower among drivers who were referred by other employees. Iowa-based Decker Truck Line, Inc., identified retention problems among drivers who were hired directly from driving school, which led Decker to require at least 1 year of experience.

In addition to selecting employees for retention, analytics can be used to identify areas of improvement on the job or during the hiring process. For example, an external vendor called Stay Metrics partnered with

LEARNING OBJECTIVES

After reading and studying this chapter, you should be able to do the following:

10.1 Describe multiple aspects of managing employee retention and separations

10.2 Explain the costs of voluntary turnover to an organization

10.3 Identify the steps organizations should take to manage employee retention

10.4 Indicate the costs of dismissals to an organization

10.5 Estimate the cost of employee layoffs to an organization

©iStock.com/kali9

Professor Timothy Judge of Ohio State University to see which personal and job characteristics predicted turnover and to build a predictive model based on these factors. Their results showed that those who left within 90 days were more likely to be inexperienced, showed low satisfaction with their recruiter, were home less than they expected, and were dissatisfied with their dispatcher.

One of the improvements to the hiring process based on their findings is to have a consistent message during recruitment regarding how much time drivers may expect to spend at home. Using data routinely gathered during hiring and through employee attitude surveys and exit interviews, it is possible to identify factors contributing to driver turnover in the entire industry, as well as to turnover within the specific company. A Chicago-based vendor, Enlistics, has an app drivers may optionally log into via their Facebook account during hiring. If they choose to do this, information in their Facebook profiles becomes part of a model used to predict eventual turnover. For example, the company found in a different industry that applicants who use the expression "I am sick of…" in their social media profiles tend to have higher turnover rates.

Predictive analytics allow firms to make predictions about turnover risk of specific employees and intervene so that these high-risk employees are retained. For example, the trucking solutions vendor Omnitracs, LLC uses predictive analytics to assign drivers risk scores from 1 to 100 based on their likelihood to quit. Management periodically receives a list of high-risk employees. The next step is for a manager or HR representative to initiate a conversation with the driver to see what the problems might be. The system even sends prompts for a follow-up conversation with the driver. The users of these systems credit these solutions and the utilization of predictive analytics as a positive influence over their retention rates and an opportunity to make significant changes in their turnover rate.[1]

Case Discussion Questions

1. What types of data, in addition to those mentioned in the case, do you think can be used to develop predictive models regarding turnover? If you were developing such a model, what information would you want to collect so that you could predict turnover? Would you advise a company to use all information available to it in these predictive models?

2. Do you think the determinants of why employees quit and why they are dismissed would be different? What factors would you expect to be more closely related to voluntary turnover? What factors are more likely to predict whether the employee is dismissed?

3. What are the pros and cons of using social media profiles to predict turnover? What do you think about the ethics of this practice?

4. What are your thoughts about identifying the specific employees with high risk for turnover and intervening directly with them? What advantages and risks do you see in this approach? Do you think this approach is better than checking in with all employees regularly?

▶ Click to learn more …

Read Omnitracs' blog entry on truck driver retention:
http://www.omnitracs.com/blog/truck-driver-retention-direction---5-keys-happier-trucker

No employee will stay in an organization forever. Employees may decide to leave because they are unhappy with the job, have better alternatives, are retiring, are quitting the workforce to become a student or full-time caregiver, or are relocating. In other cases, organizations initiate the separation through either layoffs or dismissals. Understanding why employees leave is important for line managers and HR professionals. It is also important for them to know how to manage employee separations and retention in order to ensure that the organization has the right talent to get work done.

Understanding and Managing Employee Separations

Employee separations may take several different forms. **Voluntary turnover** is a departure initiated by an employee, and is typically because of the availability of better alternatives or unhappiness with current work. A specific type of voluntary turnover is **retirement**, which is the process of ending one's work life. Even though retirements are also voluntary, we discuss it separately because why people retire is distinct from other forms of voluntary separations. **Involuntary turnover** is a discharge initiated by the organization. This may take the form of a **dismissal**, or employment termination, because the worker failed to meet organizational expectations. Alternatively, involuntary turnover may be in the form of **layoffs**, which involve separation due to economic or strategic reasons. Such reasons can include technology-related productivity improvements necessitating fewer employees, downsizing, plant closing, outsourcing of work to a different organization, or offshoring of work to a different location, among others. In this chapter, we will consider each of these types of turnover separately.

Voluntary Turnover

Voluntary turnover occurs when employees quit their jobs. Quitting one's job may be regarded as the final stage of employee withdrawal at work. Employees, in fact, may withdraw from their jobs without actually quitting: Other forms of withdrawal include **tardiness**, or being late to work without giving advance notice, and **absenteeism**, or unscheduled absences from work. Even though tardiness and absenteeism may have many other causes, they may also be warning signs that the employee is psychologically and physically withdrawing from work, which may be followed by actual departure. Research has shown that absenteeism is a much stronger correlate of actual turnover relative to tardiness, which has a modest link to turnover.[2] This means frequent absenteeism may be treated as an early indicator of eventual turnover much more reliably than frequent lateness to work.

Turnover rate is an important metric to be familiar with in order to manage turnover. You may calculate an organization's turnover rate using the following formula.[3] This formula can be modified to calculate voluntary turnover (employee-initiated), involuntary turnover (employer-initiated), and overall turnover (employee + employer initiated). Simply adjust the numerator accordingly.

LO 10.1 Describe multiple aspects of managing employee retention and separations.

Voluntary turnover A departure initiated by an employee

Retirement The process of ending one's work life

Involuntary turnover An employee terminated by the organization against their own wishes

Dismissal Employment termination because the worker fails to meet organizational expectations

Layoffs Organizationally initiated termination of employment due to economic or strategic reasons

LO 10.2 Explain the costs of voluntary turnover to an organization.

Tardiness Being late to work without giving advance notice

Absenteeism Unscheduled absences from work

$$Turnover\ Rate = \frac{Number\ of\ departures\ during\ the\ year}{Average\ number\ of\ employees\ during\ the\ year} \times 100$$

For example, if a company had 10 departures every month during the year and had an average of 1,000 employees during the year, its annual turnover rate would be 12% (10 × 12/1,000) × 100. Is a turnover rate of 12% high? This is not an easy question to answer, but it is important to consider the turnover rate within the context of industry averages and the unemployment rate. If other firms in the same industry are averaging 30%, our example company is doing well relative to competitors. Further, unemployment rate will suppress turnover rates: When the unemployment rate is high, employees may feel lucky to have a job and are more likely to stay put. As the unemployment rate shrinks, employees who are unhappy will start departing at a faster rate.

Another helpful formula helps calculate the retention rate. This is somewhat different from the turnover rate. This is because an organization may have a few positions for which it is difficult to hold on to employees, inflating the turnover rate. For example, let's assume that a company has 10 employees. One leaves, and then the position is filled by four consecutive new hires who all quit during the year. Turnover rate for this company will be 5/10 × 100 = 50%. However, using the following formula,[4]

$$Retention\ Rate = \frac{Number\ of\ employees\ who\ stayed\ during\ the\ entire\ period}{Number\ of\ employees\ at\ the\ beginning\ of\ the\ period} \times 100$$

in the same company, retention rate will be 9/10 × 100 = 90%. This indicates that 90% of the people who were with the company at the beginning of the year are still there at the end of the year. The 50% turnover rate interpreted within the context of a 90% retention rate indicates that some positions are more prone to turnover than others. Both metrics are useful, complement each other, and are helpful in spotting trends and identifying patterns.

Costs of Voluntary Turnover

According to one estimate, replacing an employee who leaves may cost anywhere between 90% and 200% of the annual salary of the departing employee.[5] A meta-analysis has shown that voluntary turnover is negatively related to workforce productivity ($r = -.13$), with a particularly strong relationship in smaller businesses.[6] Of course correlation does not necessarily imply causation, so this correlation may mean that low productivity causes high turnover or that some problems the company experiences cause both high turnover and low productivity. Still, voluntary turnover is problematic for company performance for three key reasons. First, when employees leave, there are direct costs involved in replacing, onboarding, and training the replacements. Second, when employees leave, the organization loses human capital, or the collective KSAOs that employees bring to the organization. Employees build expertise and organization-specific knowledge over time, and when employees quit, the company loses access to this expertise. Third, turnover involves the loss of "social capital," or interpersonal connections employees have developed with coworkers, managers, and clients. For example, a key client who enjoys interacting with a particular employee may take their business elsewhere when that employee leaves, whereas coworkers may find that they no longer have someone to ask for information or advice on important matters.

Turnover is more harmful in some contexts than in others. For example, research has shown that in industries that require highly skilled professionals such as transportation and professional services, turnover has more negative effects on business outcomes relative to industries with more standardized business practices and fewer skill demands such as food services and retail. Similarly, business implications of managerial employees leaving are more negative relative to nonmanagerial employees leaving.[7] In general, when skilled and hard-to-replace employees leave, organizations will experience more negative consequences.

It is also important to recognize that not all turnover is harmful for organizations. You can imagine situations in which a particular employee's departure is a cause for relief and may be regarded as an opportunity to hire a better replacement. Researchers have proposed that every company has an optimum turnover rate at which the cost of turnover and costs associated with minimizing turnover are at their lowest. Still, even though the optimum level will vary by company, research shows that excessive turnover is problematic for company performance, and such negative effects on performance are stronger for long-term performance than short-term.[8] In other words, many of the harmful effects of turnover may be hidden and become easier to observe over time.

©iStock.com/PeopleImages

Causes of Voluntary Turnover

Why do employees quit their jobs? Much of the turnover literature views voluntary turnover as a function of ***desire to leave*** and ***ease of movement*** (see Figure 10.1). According to this view, employees desire to leave for the following reasons: dissatisfaction with different aspects of their job, lacking commitment to the organization, poor supervision or having an otherwise poor-quality relationship with their manager, and experiencing stress in the form of lack of role clarity, or the presence of role conflict (including work–life conflict).[10] A meta-analysis showed that average job satisfaction level within the organization (the degree to which employees report feeling satisfied with their jobs) and average job engagement level (involvement and enthusiasm for work) were both predictive of overall turnover rates, with satisfaction having a somewhat stronger correlation relative to engagement ($r = -.36$ vs. $-.30$, respectively). Even though this study included both voluntary and involuntary turnover, the results suggest that unhappiness and lack of engagement are among the key reasons for turnover.[11]

One of the industries with the highest turnover is retail. Poor pay, customer-related stress, and unpredictable hours push the turnover rate in this industry to 67% according to some estimates.[9]

Desire to leave When an employee would like to end their employment with an organization

Ease of movement The degree to which employees may leave an organization easily (due to factors such as a favorable job market that makes it easy to leave)

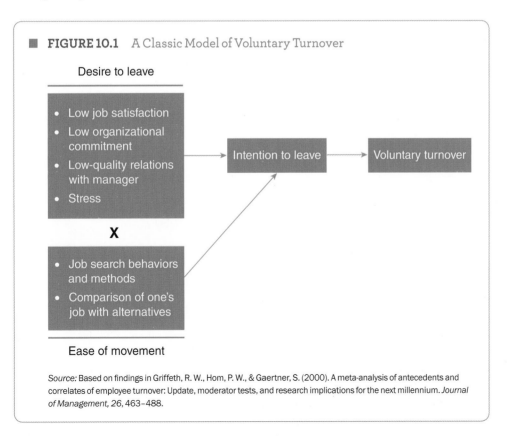

■ **FIGURE 10.1** A Classic Model of Voluntary Turnover

Source: Based on findings in Griffeth, R. W., Hom, P. W., & Gaertner, S. (2000). A meta-analysis of antecedents and correlates of employee turnover: Update, moderator tests, and research implications for the next millennium. *Journal of Management, 26,* 463–488.

On the ease-of-movement side, employees consider the job market, examine the availability of alternative jobs, and think about the likelihood of finding a job that is at least as good as their current job. Even if they have no other alternatives lined up, assessing how the job market is doing at the moment, how quickly coworkers with similar qualifications found jobs, and how high the demand is for the employee's skills will give employees ideas about the ease of movement. The outcome of this decision-making process is voluntary turnover. Finally, social media platforms like LinkedIn have made it easier for employees and employers to find each other, thereby providing employees with more information about the job market and the demand for certain skills.

Of course, this model does not summarize every possible quitting decision employees make. In fact, employees often leave even though they are happy at work. This could happen if the employee is relocating due to a spousal job change or quitting the workforce due to childcare or for health reasons. In other words, happiness at work is not a guarantee for employee retention, and turnover decisions do not require a prior steady decline in happiness. Researchers identified an ***unfolding model of turnover*** to describe exceptions to the classic model.[12] This model recognizes that employees often leave without lining up a new job. Sometimes they leave even though they have happily worked in that firm for years. The model explains the turnover decision as a result of "shocks" to the system. The employee experiences a critical incident or change, which shakes them out of their status quo and gets them to consider turnover as an option. The shock could be at work (e.g., the company was acquired by a larger firm with a poor reputation), in one's career (e.g., receiving an unsolicited invitation to interview elsewhere), or at home (e.g., the employee finds out that they are going to be a parent, motivating them to reassess career goals). Once a shock occurs, the employee may quit without lining up a new job, may start looking for a new job, or may decide that staying is better than leaving after all. The unfolding model suggests that shocks are more common predictors of turnover as opposed to simply feeling unhappy at work. The "shocks" that result in turnover may sometimes be psychological reflections rather than specific events. Research shows that job search activity increases around work anniversaries, milestone birthdays, and class reunions, which may all be times for reflecting on one's career.[13]

Turnover literature also examines why people stay.[14] In fact, even when employees are interested in and motivated to leave, often they choose to stay. The ***job embeddedness model***

Unfolding model of turnover A model that recognizes that employees often leave without lining up a new job and that turnover is often a result of "shocks" to the system

Job embeddedness model A model that explains that employees stay because of their links to others and fit with the context at work and in their communities and how much they would have to sacrifice by leaving their work and communities

TABLE 10.1   Job Embeddedness Model Explains Why Employees Stay

	WORK	COMMUNITY
Links	• Relations with manager • Relations with coworkers	• Membership in clubs and organizations • Spouse's work • Children's school and friends • Friends, neighbors
Fit	• Fit with organizational values • Fit with job	• Fit with community • Fit with city
Losses (what must be forfeited when leaving the job)	• Ability to negotiate parts of job • Nonportable benefits • Job stability and security • Social network • Pride of organizational membership	• Short commute • Familiarity with neighborhood

Source: Based on information contained in Mitchell, T. R., & Lee, T. W. (2001). The unfolding model of voluntary turnover and job embeddedness: Foundations for a comprehensive theory of attachment. *Research in Organizational Behavior, 23,* 189–246.

explains that employees stay because of their links to others and fit with the context at work and in their communities and how much they would have to sacrifice by leaving their work and communities, as illustrated in Table 10.1. According to this model, both on- and off-the-job embeddedness are negatively related to turnover. Note that the table lists only some examples of links, fits, and sacrifices. To illustrate, a high-level employee who worked for a highly reputable firm for a decade may find it challenging to leave due to high embeddedness. Changing jobs may mean relocation, which comes with forgoing one's current life, house, city, friendships, proximity to a beloved vacation spot, or any other number of off-the-job sacrifices along with leaving coworkers, managers, one's job, and social network at work. Leaving a highly reputable firm will also entail the sacrifice of how one is perceived due to organizational membership. For example, an employee who works for a well-known company such as Apple may receive respect and attention in their community as a result of being an Apple employee, which they would have to give up if they move to a firm that is less recognizable. As a result, even when unhappy at work, highly embedded employees may choose to stay. Interestingly, a meta-analysis showed that on-the-job embeddedness is more strongly and negatively related to turnover for employees in the public sector and, in female-dominated samples, suggesting that the role played by embeddedness is situational.[15]

Managing Employee Retention

LO 10.3   Identify the steps organizations should take to manage employee retention.

Given that excessive turnover is problematic and related to undesirable outcomes, what can organizations do to retain their employees? Many factors play key roles in an organization's retention of employees, including upper management's level of support for retention, the use of employee surveys and interviews, effective hiring and onboarding practices, investment in high-commitment HR practices, and attention to predictors of turnover. Moreover, since turnover is a fact of life in HR management, it is realistic to develop strategies for coping with turnover. In addition to retaining current employees, companies benefit from maintaining relationships with their former employees. Let's examine each of these factors.

Gain Upper-Management Support

An important aspect of increasing employee retention is to have upper management care about the turnover rate. In order to make a case to receive management support for reducing turnover, HR will need to calculate the rate of turnover, provide industry-level turnover rates for benchmarking purposes, and demonstrate the cost of turnover for the organization. For example, the Denmark-based manufacturing firm Hydratech Industries calculated the cost of turnover of a trade worker to be $53,000, including overtime costs for other employees covering the employee who leaves, recruiting, onboarding, training, and lost productivity until the newcomer gets up to speed. By calculating these numbers, it was easier to combat dismissive attitudes from upper management thinking that any departure is simply an isolated incident of an employee who did not work out.[16]

Leverage Engagement and Attitude Surveys

With the advent of predictive analytics, organizations have important tools at their disposal to predict with greater confidence which employees will stay and which ones will leave. One of the best predictors of voluntary turnover is reported intentions to leave. Asking questions about how much someone agrees with statements such as "I intend to leave my job in the next year" or "I intend to stay in this company for more than a year" is useful. Interestingly, though, turnover intentions only explain around 10 to 15% of variance in actual turnover. This is because turnover is a costly decision for employees, both financially and psychologically. Reporting turnover intentions is much easier than actually quitting, so many of those who report quit intentions may not take that step for some time. Employees who are less risk averse, who have more internal locus of control (i.e., who feel strong control over their own destiny), and who are low social monitors

Using Sentiment Analysis for Engagement

A data analytics tool that will likely increase in utilization is sentiment analysis. This is the analysis of text and natural language to extract the mood of the conversation. Employers have access to employee speech and conversations in the form of e-mail exchanges, texts, and written feedback to open-ended questions in employee surveys. These exchanges are treasure troves of data, but it is impossible for one or more experts to sift through and analyze them manually.

However, as technology that can conduct text analysis advances, organizations are increasingly capable of identifying the mood of their employees on an ongoing basis, note changes, and intervene early.

For example, when IBM utilized text analysis on employee survey feedback, it noted a pattern indicating that employees were frustrated about the available choices for computers in the workplace. This led it to offer more choices, including Apple computers. Such identification of emerging problems ensures that engagement throughout the company remains high. The company also analyzes comments employees leave in the internal social

networking platform (Connections) to identify patterns.

Similarly, Twitter contracted with a company named Kanjoya (later acquired by Ultimate Software) to conduct text analysis on internal surveys. To obtain richer data, Twitter started surveying employees more frequently and added more open-ended questions. The text analysis identifies patterns and presents them to the executive team.

This technology is not perfect. Among other shortcomings, it may give false alarms. For example, "I hate my boss" may be too similar to "I hated my boss" (referring to one's former job) for the software to distinguish. In addition, it is unclear how employees will react to having their text messages, e-mails, and online conversations monitored. Companies can and do monitor these conversations, but structuring and formalizing this monitoring may create feelings of mistrust. Ultimately, these technologies exist, and they may be helpful in understanding how employees feel at a given time, but their usefulness will depend on how and for what purposes businesses use them.[17]

(i.e., who are less sensitive to social cues in their actions) will have a stronger relation between reported turnover intentions and actual turnover.[18] This means that the predictive models of turnover may be improved through consideration of individual personalities.

Yearly attitude and engagement surveys can be used to identify factors that share the strongest relation with actual turnover. Using these data, organizations may implement targeted interventions. Boston Consulting Group, a management consulting firm operating in 48 countries, observed that its mid-career, high-potential female employees had higher turnover than male employees at the same career stage. An examination of its employee engagement survey showed that the female employees who ended up leaving sometime after responding to the survey responded with its lowest scores on items relating to mentoring and feedback received (as opposed to work–life balance or low career ambitions, which would have been the stereotypical explanations). Armed with this finding, the company instituted an Apprenticeship in Action program teaching managers how to build connections, give feedback, and provide high-quality coaching and mentoring. After the program implementation, attitudes toward feedback and mentoring improved across the board, and the gender differences in turnover rates in mid-career level disappeared.[19]

Pulse surveys Short, frequent surveys

Companies may also utilize **pulse surveys,** which are short, frequent surveys. These surveys do not necessarily replace the rich and detailed information that can be obtained via annual surveys but could be used to predict and manage turnover and to even detect "shocks" like those discussed earlier in the chapter. The media marketing company HubSpot, Inc. uses an outside vendor to send a single, anonymous question to employees every week. A sample question is "How happy are you working here on a scale of 1 to 10?" If an employee leaves written feedback, the manager of the employee can respond directly to feedback, ask additional questions, and retain anonymity, which helps identify problems and resolve conflicts.[20]

Utilize Exit Interviews

Companies may learn why a particular employee is leaving by conducting exit interviews with them relating to their departure. These interviews are opportunities to learn why employees are leaving and make changes in the organization to increase retention. For exit interviews to be useful, organizations need to conduct them regularly, analyze the data, and disseminate the data among decision makers who can enact changes. Many employees will be reluctant to share the reason for their departure, as they may worry that being honest will cost them a positive reference, or they simply may have little motivation to share their reasons. Companies may use exit interviews to understand which HR practices and departmental, managerial, and organizational factors contribute to departure and make systematic changes. Experts recommend the following:[22]

Listening to employee concerns is a successful way of building employee engagement and ultimately retention. Dunkin' Brands changed crew member uniforms in response to employee feedback and adjusted training curriculum to give managers coaching skills. The company sees employee engagement as one of the pillars of employee retention.[21]

©iStock.com/eyewave

- Exit interviews may be conducted by HR, but having a manager higher than the employee's own manager conduct the interviews has benefits, as they will have power to make actual changes. The employee's own manager should not be present or conduct exit interviews, as they often play some role in employee reasons for leaving.

- It is beneficial to make exit interviews mandatory for some positions.

- Conducting the interview halfway between employee giving notice and actual departure will have benefits because the employee will not have mentally "checked out" yet. Alternatively, conducting the interview sometime after the employee leaves could be useful, as it allows the employee to give a less emotional and more reflective answer.

- The interview may be face to face or via telephone. Either method provides rich information, although face-to-face interviews could be more helpful to build rapport.

- Information obtained in these interviews should be collated, analyzed, and shared among decision makers.

- When changes are made, it is useful to let other employees know that the changes came about from exit interview information so that employees see value in exit interviews—which could make them more forthcoming when they themselves leave.

- These interviews should be supplemented with *stay interviews* of employees who are not leaving. What is making them stay? Is the employee happy on the job and with their career? Having these conversations regularly with employees and making changes along the way may reduce the need for exit interviews in the first place.

Stay interviews
Interviews of employees who are not leaving to understand what keeps them on their jobs and identify problems that may eventually result in turnover

Hire for Fit

Employees often leave because they are not a good fit with what the organization needs and provides. Therefore, hiring for skills, values, preferences, and personalities that will maximize happiness and engagement at work in the specific company is an essential tool for retention. Organizations can identify the traits, background, and experience factors that are best predictors of retention and performance and select employees based on those characteristics. Further, as

Chapters 5 and 6 discuss, it is important to give employees a realistic job preview (RJP) in order to ensure that employees can assess their own level of fit. Providing employees with information about their tasks, responsibilities, level of autonomy, job demands, and expected degree of change and stability are among the issues that would benefit from a realistic preview.[23] There is much organizations can do during recruiting in order to affect retention. For example, Boys & Girls Clubs of America in Atlanta reduced focus on time-to-hire metrics as a way of assessing the effectiveness of their recruitment, instead increasing focus on retention metrics that highlighted finding hires who would stay. Further, the organization increased the use of more "high-touch" methods of recruiting, with multiple interviews with company insiders.[24]

Structure Onboarding Experiences

In a Korn Ferry survey of 1,817 executives, more than half of respondents noted that 10 to 25% of newly hired employees leave within their first 6 months. As you may recall from Chapter 8, successful onboarding can help increase the retention of new employees. As discussed earlier, employees are less likely to quit when they are embedded into their jobs and communities. Conversely, newcomers will have the least embeddedness because they have not yet established fit or relationships and, thus, they do not need to sacrifice much when leaving the company. Onboarding teaches newcomers about the company culture, welcomes them to the organization, connects them to others, and sets them off to a good start. The same Korn Ferry study suggests that only 29% of respondents collect data from new employees, which can be used to link early experiences to retention over time and to make changes and improvements in the onboarding practices.[25]

Invest in High-Commitment HR Practices

HR practices that indicate investment in long-term and high-quality management–employee relationships have been shown to reduce employee turnover.[26] Specifically, HR practices that indicate commitment to employees, such as providing internal mobility opportunities and advancement possibilities, employee participation initiatives, and engaging in selective hiring, are among the HR practices useful for retention. In contrast, HR and employment practices that signal strict short-term performance expectations and practices that reduce employee empowerment such as electronic monitoring of employees and routinization of work are associated with higher levels of turnover rates at the firm level. Finally, HR practices that increase embeddedness of employees are related to lower turnover. For example, the proportion of union representation is negatively related to turnover.

Interestingly, some HR practices that develop employee skills may create a high-quality relationship between the employee and the employer and could increase retention. However, they may also increase the ability of the employee to find an alternative job, potentially paving the way to voluntary turnover. Tuition reimbursement programs are a good example of this. Companies such as Chipotle, Starbucks, Walmart, and UPS pay for partial or full tuition for eligible employees.[27] While these programs contribute to retention during the employees' educational studies, their overall effects on retention are more complicated. One study in a high-tech firm showed that when employees completed graduate degrees, they were more likely to leave, whereas obtaining an undergraduate degree or course enrollment without obtaining a degree did not contribute to turnover. Further, the turnover rate among those who earned graduate degrees but were promoted afterward was 56% less than those who benefited from tuition reimbursement but were not promoted. These findings show that simply investing in human capital will not generate high engagement and loyalty to the company; the organization will need to provide a job that is commensurate with the employee's newly acquired qualifications as well.[28]

Satisfying employees' advancement needs is an essential part of high-commitment HR practices. Today, organizations and employees have a more transactional relationship in which employers rarely promise long-term employment. As a result, the focus has shifted toward *employability* of the employee: Employees expect their current work to keep them employable

Employability The degree to which an individual is able to gain initial employment and obtain new employment if required

HR IN ACTION

For the Love of Candy? Employee Retention at Mars, Inc.

©iStock.com/Ekaterina79

Mars, Incorporated is a private, global corporation, owning brands in pet care (Banfield Pet Hospital, Pedigree); supermarket food items (Uncle Ben's), chewing gum (Wrigley's); and, of course, chocolate candy (Dove, M&Ms, Mars, Milky Way, Snickers, and Twix). Mars is more than 100 years old, still a family-owned business, operates in 73 countries, and boasts a low turnover rate: around 5%. This is a company in which an employee's family may have been employed for several generations. What is the secret to such high loyalty and retention?

This third-largest privately owned company in the United States is in some ways very old-fashioned and does not look like a candidate for the Best Places to Work lists. For example, all employees, including the president, have to clock in and out every day; their pay will be docked if they are late. There is no free food or in-house chefs, although there are free candy-dispensing machines.

Instead, the company invests in its people. Mars provides high levels of opportunities for mobility and advancement. Employees (also called Martians) may find their true home after working in several different departments, and additional skills and education are rewarded and utilized with advancement and increased responsibilities. Formal rotation programs are used to help employees build new skills. In fact, many employees also get a mentor to help them chart their path. Employees are also given significant autonomy. Because the company is not publicly traded, its every move is not scrutinized by Wall Street, which translates into greater ability to take risks. The company shares financials with employees, and employees receive significant bonuses based on their team's performance. Managers are available and accessible, with a workplace climate emphasizing collaboration and camaraderie.

The company also takes care of its employees. Benefits include a pension plan, 401(k) plans with Mars matching up to 6% of the employee's salary, 16 hours of paid time off for volunteer work, 30 days of paternity leave (in addition to 60 days fully paid maternity leave), and generous health care coverage.

Mars focuses on doing good and helping employees follow their passions. The Mars Ambassador Program allows employees to work in one of the company's partner organizations (e.g., World Wildlife Foundation) for up to 6 weeks to share their expertise. It seems that when an organization invests in its people, treats them with dignity and respect, and shows consideration, employees are loyal and engaged.[29]

over time. This means employees expect to gain skills and abilities that will help them find a job and be successful in their careers and do not necessarily define career success as advancement within a specific firm. In other words, the expectation is to keep one's skills current so that one can find employment as needed. Changing jobs frequently and moving across organizations are increasingly common.

This strategy seems to pay off for some employees. For example, a study of a large cohort of German professionals revealed that those who stayed within one firm over a period of 5 years had seen annual pay raises averaging 11%, whereas those who had worked for three or more firms during the same period had pay raises of 15% annually. Further, the promotion rates of job changers and stayers were not different, suggesting that firms do not necessarily reward those who stay with frequent promotions. Given that "job hopping" and job search are more normalized and common, organizations need to invest in the futures of their employees and, paradoxically, keep employees' skills marketable in order to retain them.[30]

Focus on Turnover Predictors

We know from research that important predictors of turnover include job satisfaction, work engagement, organizational commitment, manager–employee relationship quality, and stress. This means that by focusing on these factors, organizations may make progress in reducing turnover. *Job satisfaction* refers to employees' contentment with different facets of their work, including the work itself, supervision, pay, and advancement opportunities. ***Work engagement*** refers to feelings of emotional connection to work and a state of being in which employees bring their personal selves to work. Satisfaction and engagement are closely related, with a strong positive correlation ($r = .53$),[31] and both are related to organization-level turnover.

What can organizations do in order to increase engagement, contribute to employee satisfaction, and build attachment to the workplace? Figure 10.2 outlines factors that are most strongly related to work engagement. Companies that are deliberate about designing jobs and working conditions that satisfy employee needs and desires will find it easier to attract and retain workers. For example, Facebook provides an environment in which employees take initiative, work on meaningful projects, and learn and grow on the job through feedback and coaching.[32] In contrast, performing work in an understaffed department for extended periods of time will contribute to turnover because stressful working conditions erode engagement, which could encourage employees to seek jobs elsewhere.

Stress is another reason employees quit their jobs. Difficulty balancing work with other obligations such as school and child- and eldercare responsibilities cost businesses in the form of turnover. Taking steps, such as introducing flexibility to schedules, allowing employees to work remotely as needed, and facilitating access to quality care facilities, are among the benefits organizations may provide that would reduce stress. Similarly, ensuring that each department is adequately staffed and employees are not working long hours is beneficial.

Finally, building a trust-based relationship with employees is a key driver of employee retention. By recognizing employee contributions, ensuring that employee jobs provide sufficient challenge and meaning to employees along with providing development opportunities, eliminating unnecessary stressors, and providing social support, effective managers make a big difference in whether employees are attached to the organization and interested in leaving and how long they stay. A strong bond with one's manager is hard to leave behind, whereas poor management often drives employees to quit.

Job satisfaction An employee's contentment with different facets of their work

Work engagement Feelings of emotional connection to work and a state of being in which employees bring their personal selves to work

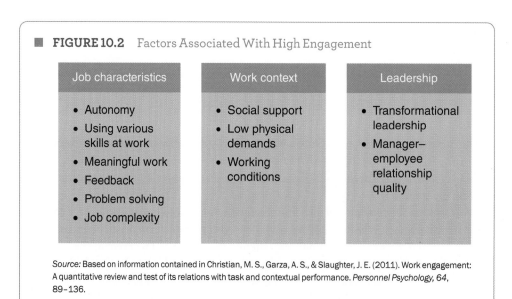

■ **FIGURE 10.2**   Factors Associated With High Engagement

Job characteristics	Work context	Leadership
• Autonomy • Using various skills at work • Meaningful work • Feedback • Problem solving • Job complexity	• Social support • Low physical demands • Working conditions	• Transformational leadership • Manager–employee relationship quality

Source: Based on information contained in Christian, M. S., Garza, A. S., & Slaughter, J. E. (2011). Work engagement: A quantitative review and test of its relations with task and contextual performance. *Personnel Psychology, 64,* 89–136.

Learn How to Cope With Turnover

In some businesses, the turnover rate is high, and it is likely to remain high. In industries in which turnover is chronically high, organizations will need to combine a turnover reduction strategy with a turnover management strategy. In other words, while taking the steps mentioned earlier to reduce turnover rate, businesses will also need to cope with the negative effects of expected turnover. For example, the U.S. military deliberately limits the deployment of military personnel to war zones to 6 months or a year. This means, in some departments, there will be 100% turnover in a given office. These constraints are important to limit separations from family, exposure to dangerous work conditions, and long hours with no downtime. The military copes with this high planned turnover in individual offices by ensuring that jobs are standardized and simplified, the organizational structure is consistent across branches, and employees use the simplest technology that the majority of personnel will be familiar with.[33] In high-turnover businesses, each departing employee will take away organizational knowledge, so it is particularly important for organizations to make special efforts to ensure that knowledge is not compartmentalized and is accessible to everyone.

Managing Relations With Former Employees

It may be natural for managers to feel disappointment when a high-performing employee leaves. However, former employees may provide key benefits to organizations even after their departure. Many organizations are realizing the importance of leveraging the power of their alumni network. Chapter 6 points out that a company's *alumni*, or former employees, may be a source of referrals for future employees, may provide useful business intelligence, serve as brand ambassadors, and even become customers of the organization.[34] Some companies deliberately invest in alumni relations and stay in touch with them.

Alumni Former employees of an organization

For example, McKinsey & Company provides a well-developed alumni network with a members-only website. It organizes events and gatherings for members and employs an alumni engagement person at each site. Being part of this exclusive alumni network is a selling point in McKinsey recruitment efforts for newcomers, and alumni bring significant business to McKinsey.

Boomerang employees Former employees who rejoin an organization

The amount of time and money invested in alumni networks will vary by industry and company strategy, but it is important to recognize that although turnover may conclude the employer and employee relationship, the two parties may still cross paths.

Sometimes former employees decide to come back to the organization, earning them the moniker *boomerang employees*. Even though some businesses refuse to hire former employees to encourage loyalty of current workers, those who choose to consider hiring them experience possible benefits. Hiring former employees requires less time investment, given the mutual experience. Onboarding takes less time for these employees. Finally, employees who choose to go back make the organization look good from a reputational perspective.[36]

©iStock.com/tomch

The electronic payment company PayPal was acquired by eBay, but its alumni went on to cofound some of the most successful technology companies, including Tesla, SpaceX, Palantir Technologies, LinkedIn, YouTube, Yammer, and Yelp, attesting to the potential power of corporate alumni networks.[35]

Research shows that departing employees are more likely to come back if they left for personal reasons (such as a relocation, family obligations), as opposed to leaving because they were unhappy with their work. Also, alumni are more likely to come back if they stayed away for a relatively short period of time, if they had chosen to stay in the same industry, or if they had a career break.[37] Finally, not all boomerang employees will have high performance when they return. A study conducted on National Basketball Association players is informative: Boomerang

MANAGER'S TOOLBOX
Retaining Top Talent

Every organization will have "star employees" whose voluntary turnover would constitute a major loss. How can an organization be proactive in retaining these employees? Top performers stay when they do meaningful work and have the opportunity to perform at their top level. To retain top talent, organizations may engage in the following targeted actions:[38]

Identify top performers. The first step in retaining top performers is to know who they are. Performance reviews, or simply asking managers to identify top performers, could serve this purpose.

Track retention data for top performers. Companies would benefit from calculating their top performer turnover rate. Although the company may have an incentive to tackle overall turnover, knowing how serious the issue of top talent retention is would be helpful to generate targeted interventions.

Be aware of their job attitudes. The organization may break down the results of their engagement or attitude surveys by performance level to see what factors are systematic problems for high performers. In addition, having one-on-one conversations with them to understand their frustrations would be helpful.

Identify risk factors. Organizations may use data analytics to identify factors most strongly related to voluntary departure of high-performing employees. Knowing the risk factors would allow the organization to identify who are at greater risk of leaving in the near future.

Rerecruit and reenergize. Having "stay interviews" with these employees to find out why they stay and to give them reasons to stay are helpful tools. These meetings can be helpful in redefining their job to keep employees motivated and challenged. Further, the organization should make sure that over time, the employment conditions remain competitive with the market. For example, Netflix adjusts the salaries of high performers to the market periodically to ensure that employees find their current pay rate attractive and have little reason to consider the market for a pay raise.

Counteroffer or let them go? No one, including high performers, will stay forever. Even though it is a great idea to be proactive in retaining them, there will be instances when the employee decides to leave. Should the organization present a counteroffer? Keeping an unhappy worker by paying them more may not make sense. If there is a way to reengage them and deal with problems that motivated them to leave, having that conversation could be helpful. Investing in the future of the employee sometimes may mean letting them go. Remember, they may want to come back some day or support the organization in other ways.

---

employees' performance after they return depended on their performance before departure and whether they stayed away long enough to acquire new skills, but not too long.[39] In other words, organizations may want to follow a selective strategy for boomerang employees, considering their prior performance and the conditions under which they left, and also consider reaching out to employees they would be interested in rehiring in a proactive manner rather than waiting for some to come back on their own.

Retirements

Retirements are normally a type of voluntary turnover (except in rare cases in which it is legally mandated), but it is worthwhile to consider them separately. Retirement is a type of work withdrawal where the employee chooses to finish working activities, replacing work with other life activities or perhaps to pursue a different career. When employees retire, the organization may experience some benefits in the form of the ability to hire lower-paid employees who may bring a fresh perspective to the job and organization. At the same time, retirement costs organizations in the form of lost expertise.[40] As a result, organizations have an incentive to manage retirements, potentially creating programs to utilize retired employees and preventing retirement that is due to withdrawal from work. Particularly with the mass retirement of baby boomers, organizations are faced with the possibility of losing critical expertise in a short period of time.

A review of the literature shows that retirement may be due to personal and work-related reasons. Among personal factors, the worker's age and health play key roles. Among work-related factors, performing jobs with high physical and psychological demands, dissatisfaction with work, and feeling "tired of work" are noteworthy. Further, those who have a strong attachment to their careers and those who see work as central to their identities are less likely to retire, whereas commitment to leisure activities contributes to the decision to retire. Finally, research examined the role of age-related stereotypes and negative treatment of older workers as potential factors contributing to retirement decisions.[41]

©iStock.com/spooh

Organizations may continue to benefit from the skills and knowhow of employees considering retirement by providing an "age-friendly workplace," allowing workers to switch to part-time roles, offering flexibility, ensuring that tasks still match employee capabilities, paying attention to workplace ergonomics, and building a workplace culture that supports age diversity. Many individuals find it difficult to leave the workforce altogether due to financial reasons and the desire to remain active and maintain social connections, so it may be possible to arrive at a solution that meets the needs of both parties. Many older workers are embracing **bridge employment** in the form of reducing one's hours or reducing job demands within the same or a different organization (and often reducing one's pay as well) instead of exiting the workforce. In the United States, bridge employment before full retirement is common, with around 60% choosing this option.[43]

Retirements may cause labor shortages, such as the one expected in the aviation industry, in which commercial airline pilots have a mandatory retirement age of 65. In June 2017, Horizon Air announced cancellation of 300 flights scheduled between August and September due to pilot shortages.[42]

Bridge employment
Reducing one's hours or reducing job demands within the same or a different organization in preparation for full retirement

Are there ways for organizations to encourage employees to retire? Because employees close to retirement are likely to be among the higher-paid workers due to their higher tenure, sometimes organizations see value in encouraging these workers to retire early. It is important to understand the legal implications of these moves. The organization may design an early retirement incentive plan (ERIP) for employees who meet particular criteria with respect to age, department, or position, offering them incentives such as continued health insurance coverage, severance pay (pay typically provided to dismissed employees), or access to pension benefits if they retire within a given window.

However, it is important to ensure that these programs remain voluntary, as forcing employees to retire is illegal under the Age Discrimination in Employment Act. Mandatory retirement due to age exists in only a small number of jobs such as law enforcement, commercial airline pilots, air traffic controllers, and judges in some states. Therefore, the organization needs to ensure that there is no coercion involved in these programs (such as hinting that the employee will lose their job anyway, so it is to their advantage to accept the program).[44] In fact, questioning an employee about their retirement plans, asking whether they are planning to retire soon, or implying that at their age they should consider retirement may become part of age-related discrimination cases.[45]

Organizations considering using early retirement programs are advised to seek legal counsel. Further, it is essential to conduct careful analyses before implementing such programs, because a larger number of employees than expected may take advantage of these programs, leaving the organization short staffed and with losses in critical expertise.

Involuntary Turnover: Dismissals

LO 10.4   Indicate the costs of employee dismissals to an organization.

The employment relationship typically starts optimistically. However, sometime after organizational entry, it may become clear that an employee was a poor fit for the job. An employee's

SPOTLIGHT ON HR FOR SMALL AND MEDIUM-SIZED BUSINESSES
Employee Retention

Research has shown that high turnover has stronger negative effects on workforce productivity in small businesses than in larger ones.[46] Owners and managers in small businesses may feel that it is hard to compete with larger businesses when it comes to employee retention. They may find that they have fewer benefits and perks to offer employees. However, research findings on predictors of turnover suggest that there are many tools small and medium-sized businesses may use to increase employee retention.

Factors such as relations with one's manager and coworkers fit with organizational values, and the ability of employees to craft the job in ways that are suitable for them are key elements in employee retention. All are within the means of small businesses. Further, tools such as exit interviews and stay interviews remain invaluable for small businesses given their value in identifying problem areas.

performance may fall short of expectations due to reasons such as poor person–job fit, poor work ethic, or behavioral problems. Therefore, the organization may decide to terminate the employment relationship.

Costs of Dismissals

Terminating a poorly performing or disruptive employee, while giving the organization a chance to hire a better replacement, comes with costs to the organization. Even in situations in which the problems are so egregious that it is obvious to everyone that the employee should be fired, there are risks to the organization. For example, the employee may say negative things about the company in person or online. The employee may sue the company for wrongful dismissal, which will cost time and energy to defend against even if the organization ultimately prevails. The terminated employee may engage in acts of sabotage or aggression. In some cases, the organization needs to continue to have a professional relationship with the dismissed employee; for example, a dismissed employee may be hired by a client organization and put in charge of the organization's account, essentially becoming a client to be pleased. All of these are not reasons to avoid dismissing an employee, but they indicate that a dismissal decision is not one that should be made in anger or impulsively. Developing fair procedures around how to dismiss employees, being systematic, treating employees consistently over time (and not being lenient to an offense that led to the termination of another employee), and making an effort to be respectful to the employee at every step of the process are helpful in minimizing these costs. In fact, research shows that when faced with a negative outcome, employees are most likely to retaliate when they are treated in a procedurally or interpersonally unfair manner.[47]

Although dismissals are costly, it is also important to remember that *not* dismissing some employees has its own costs, and in fact the organization may be considered guilty of negligence. For example, research shows that a "toxic worker" costs a team more than $12,000 by inducing their coworkers to leave.[48] Poor performers and disruptive workers may reduce morale and harm the ability of others to do their jobs. In fact, employees who harass, intimidate, or simply do not pull their weight may poison the group's atmosphere or cause other employees' performance to suffer.

When to Dismiss an Employee

When deciding whether to dismiss an employee for disruptive behavior or poor performance, there are a few questions to answer:

- *Did you investigate the root cause of performance deficiencies?* Is this a case of an employee mismatched with the current role but who could be valuable in a different role? Is this a previously good employee going through rough times? In some cases, the investigation may show that the solution is retraining or referring them to an Employee Assistance Program (EAP). It is important to understand the root causes, because if the problem is the context, replacing the employee will not solve the problem.

- *Did you give the employee feedback and opportunities to improve?* Ideally, before you reach the termination decision, the employee should be given feedback and ample opportunities to improve. Having the employee perform at unacceptable levels without confronting the problem and then dismissing the employee for poor performance is unfair, as the employee may have thought that the current level of performance was satisfactory. Chapter 9 reviewed the basics of performance management, including performance improvement plans (PIPs). When feedback does not solve the problem, the employee may be placed on a PIP, with clear goals outlined for acceptable levels of performance.

- *Did you follow organizational procedures?* In order to ensure that termination decisions are systematic and fair, many organizations embrace a ***progressive discipline*** system. As shown in Figure 10.3, these systems aim to ensure that employees have a chance to correct their behavior and are given multiple chances. There may be some offenses that are cause for immediate termination, whereas others would follow the full spectrum of stages.

Progressive discipline
The process of using increasingly severe steps to correct a performance problem

FIGURE 10.3 Stages of Progressive Discipline

Verbal warning → Written warning → Suspension → Termination

Organizations are not required to have progressive discipline procedures unless there is a collective bargaining agreement in place that requires them. However, a formal discipline process ensures consistent treatment of all employees and provides legal defense in case of a lawsuit by ensuring that problematic behaviors have been documented and dealt with systematically.[49]

- *Did you consider the timing of your decision?* Firing the employee at the wrong time may open the company up for a discrimination lawsuit or cause other difficulties. For example, terminating an employee shortly after the employee files a discrimination complaint will appear like retaliation, even when this is not the intent. (Note that firing an employee in retaliation for filing an EEOC complaint *is* illegal.)

The Legal Side of Dismissals

In the United States, with some exceptions, ***employment at will*** prevails, although it has been eroding in recent decades. This means that organizations have the right to terminate the employment of anyone at any time, and employees have the right to quit at any time. In fact, even though it is courteous, providing a 2-week notice before quitting is not a legal requirement given the at-will doctrine. Both the employee and the employer are free to initiate and terminate the relationship at any time.

At the same time, there are numerous exceptions to at-will employment, suggesting that from the organization's side, there are limits to when and why an employee may be dismissed.

Employment at will
When organizations have the right to terminate the employment of anyone at any time, and employees have the right to quit at any time

A dismissal that violates the law is termed ***wrongful dismissal***. For example, employees who are covered by a *collective bargaining agreement* are subject to the contract negotiated between the union and the employer regarding when and how to terminate employment. There may also be an *employment contract* between the employer and employee with respect to terms and duration of employment and conditions for termination (such as one that may exist for teachers). If a contract is in place, the organization needs to follow it rather than assume that employment is at will. Sometimes, there may be an *implied contract* between the employee and the organization. For example, if the organization verbally mentioned that employees in this organization are not fired without a reason, this may constitute a legally binding verbal contract, an exception to employment at will. *Public policy exception* suggests that the employee may not be fired in a way that violates public interest, such as firing an employee for performing jury duty or reporting illegal behavior of the organization. *Statutory exceptions* refer to myriad federal and state laws that prohibit discrimination based on specific actions or protected characteristics. Chapter 4 outlines many federal laws that protect employees, and these laws along with other federal and state laws are exceptions to at-will employment. Finally, some states endorse the principle of *covenant of good faith*. This means that in these states, it is illegal to dismiss the employee in a malicious way. An example of this is the dismissal of an employee to avoid paying them their earned sales commissions. All these exceptions suggest that in reality, employment is rarely "at will," and organizations benefit from being familiar with state and federal laws that limit their ability to dismiss employees.[50]

When an employee is dismissed, there is the potential for a costly lawsuit if the employee suspects that the dismissal is unlawful. For example, imagine a situation in which a recovering alcoholic has been dismissed shortly after revealing past alcoholism, with the stated reason being tardiness to work. The company may be sued because alcoholism is a protected disability under the Americans with Disabilities Act as long as it does not adversely affect job performance. In order to protect itself from the lawsuit, the organization will need to show that the real reason was tardiness. What is the organization's policy around tardiness? Was the employee given opportunities to improve? How were other employees with similar levels of tardiness treated? If the company has clear rules and procedures around tardiness and a progressive discipline policy, it will be easier to show that the real reason was tardiness.

The Dismissal Interview

Experts agree that there are right and wrong ways of conducting the termination interview. In the best-case scenario, the employee may still be unhappy with the outcome but will feel that they were treated with dignity and respect. Following are some recommendations to facilitate a less negative interview.

- *Be there.* Ultimately, it is the responsibility of the dismissed employee's manager to communicate the news. A representative from HR may be a part of the dismissal meeting. However, the manager likely has more information about events leading up to the dismissal decision. Also, the manager is usually the person who made the decision. Instead of expecting HR to do the talking, it is reasonable to expect that HR play a supportive role.

- *Be straightforward.* Although thanking the employee for their contributions is a good idea, discussing how difficult this decision was for the manager or mentioning the strengths of the employee may appear patronizing. In fact, a study showed that even though mentioning positives of the employee seems to add to feelings of being respected, this positive effect actually reverses if the employee is then escorted out of the building, indicating that inconsistent treatment where actions and words clash is regarded as disrespectful.[51]

- *Do not lie.* Telling the employee that their position is being eliminated to spare their feelings is sure to backfire when you are looking for a replacement. Such behavior erodes the company's credibility and is also likely to increase its legal exposure.[52]

- *"It is not me, it is you."* When communicating difficult news, a natural tendency is to apologize, mention the employee's good qualities, and place the blame on the situation. Experts warn that this strategy is undesirable, may cause the employee to blame the organization, and may increase legal liability. Therefore, it is important to clarify that even though what happened is unfortunate, the blame solely rests on the actions or inactions of the dismissed employee. A quick summary of the steps that happened before you got to this point is warranted.[53]

- *Clarify the timeline.* This meeting is also a good opportunity to discuss what happens next. When is the employee's last day? Is the employee eligible for severance pay? (See more details later in this chapter.) What happens to unused vacation time and insurance?

Explaining the Decision to the Team

When an employee is dismissed, it is important to communicate the decision to the remaining employees. This is because employees try to make sense of organizational changes, including when a colleague is dismissed. There will be speculation about what happened. Employees will also wonder whether something similar could happen to them. As a result, it is important to reassure coworkers that the dismissed employee was treated with dignity and was given opportunities to improve, or simply provide a brief explanation of what happened. It is important to protect the privacy of the employee being dismissed but also to reassure the team that the decision was just. Firing an employee in an unfair manner may lead to loss of trust on the part of the dismissed employee's coworkers, and therefore the organization will need to provide an explanation to counteract the situation and reassure employees.[54]

SPOTLIGHT ON LEGAL ISSUES
Wrongful Termination at United Airlines

In 2013, United Airlines fired two flight attendants who had served the company a combined total of 70 years and 30,000 flight hours. The employees had exemplary records and had never been disciplined or received complaints. In fact, they had received multiple awards for service and dedication over their careers. They were fired when a supervisor observed them watching an iPad for 15 minutes during a flight and noticed that they did not wear their aprons while serving customers. They were notified about the termination decision and were offered the option to retire instead.

The flight attendants filed a lawsuit in which they claimed that the real reason for the termination decision was age. The case was decided in favor of the plaintiffs, and they were awarded $800,000 for back pay and damages. The cost of the lawsuit to United is estimated to be around $1.5 million.

Organizations are advised to ensure that termination decisions are not made lightly. Firing long-serving employees for a first offense, or for reasons that might seem frivolous, lends support to the argument that the decision is actually for a different, potentially illegal reason. Organizations can take several steps to stay on the right side of the law, such as:

- Being sure that employees are not terminated for illegal reasons.

- Ensuring that the organization establishes and follows consistent procedures for termination decisions.

- Having strong documentation of past performance. It is not permissible to go back and create a paper trail for past offenses. Instead, managers need to document problem behavior along the way, communicate with the employee, and ensure compliance.[55]

LO 10.5   Estimate the
cost of employee layoffs
to an organization.

Involuntary Turnover: Layoffs

When organizations are faced with pressures to contain and reduce costs, reducing the number of employees is one method available to them. Layoffs refer to involuntary turnover of employees due to organizational restructuring, downsizing, or other strategic or economic reasons. Unlike dismissals, layoffs involve discharge of employees through no fault of their own. Some layoffs occur due to a desire to reduce payroll expenses in the short run. Others occur because the company may have strategically decided to switch focus, move out of a specific market or out of a particular line of work, or may have decided to offshore (i.e., move some aspects of production overseas to benefit from cost savings) or outsource production (i.e., instead of performing some operations inside the company, starting to purchase them from outside vendors). In each of these cases, the company decides that some positions, jobs, stores, or plants are no longer needed, resulting in layoff decisions.

Layoffs typically involve discharge of multiple employees, often reaching hundreds or even thousands. For example, in 1993, IBM laid off 60,000 employees in order to restructure the organization from one focused on mainframe computers to one focused on business solutions. More recently, in 2008, Citigroup cut 50,000 jobs during the credit crisis.[56] Layoffs are painful for employees being let go and their coworkers and managers, as well as families. As the numbers get larger, the effects may spread throughout the community in which the business is located, increasing the unemployment rate in the area and affecting housing and demand for the products of unrelated businesses.

Costs of Layoffs

The literature and the popular press treat layoffs as traumatizing events with good reason. In fact, the terminology used to describe these events often reflects this: Those directly affected by layoffs are sometimes termed "victims" of a layoff, whereas employees who escape the layoff are "survivors." Of course, this view is overly simplistic. In any layoff, there will be some employees who would prefer to be (and sometimes volunteer to be) among those who are being laid off; some employees may have been looking for an exit anyway, and the accompanying financial packages, such as a generous severance pay, may seem an attractive way of leaving an organization they were not committed to. Alternatively, among those who are laid off, there will be some who look at it as a blessing in disguise: an opportunity to pursue a career, job, or life change that they were hesitant to take while employed. At the same time, barring these exceptions, layoffs have numerous significant and negative effects and costs to employees, business outcomes, communities, customer relations, and the reputation of a business; thus, it is important to understand the direct and indirect implications of layoffs.

Layoffs negatively affect the psychological and physiological well-being of layoff victims, layoff survivors, and managers in charge of delivering the bad news.[57] When organizations engage in downsizing, it is often perceived as a violation of one's psychological contract with the organization. Employee justice perceptions, job involvement, loyalty, trust, creativity, and job performance suffer following downsizing.[58] In fact, research shows that these effects are not limited to feelings of injustice and anger toward the organization they are leaving. Layoff victims have lower trust in their next employer, express cynicism about the intentions of the new employer, and even worry that they will be mistreated by the new organization.[59] Further, an individual's layoff history has been linked to voluntary turnover in jobs following the layoff. This is partially because employees are more likely to be underemployed or hold poor-quality jobs following layoffs but also because the psychological contract violation and trust violation following a layoff becomes part of an individual's personal history, preventing them from forming strong attachments to their next employer.[60] In other words, layoffs are traumatic in the sense that they erode trust in employers in general and lead to a pervading sense that organizations are not trustworthy.

Interestingly, whether layoffs ultimately improve organizational performance is controversial. Organizational downsizing is not always the result of a well-thought-out plan to benefit the organization: Sometimes it occurs through organizational mimicry when other firms in the industry downsize. Research shows that downsizing may result in some reductions in labor costs, but it also disrupts organizational relations, erodes the skill base of the organization, and harms the business, with several studies suggesting a negative relationship between downsizing and organizational performance. In cases in which studies identified positive effects on organizational performance, these were realized several years after downsizing, suggesting that any positive effects typically happen in the long term.[61]

Layoffs also have some direct financial costs. ***Unemployment insurance*** is payment made to unemployed individuals (see Chapter 13). Unemployment insurance is a federal program providing income continuation to employees who lost their jobs through no fault of their own. The program is administered by individual states, and therefore the amount and conditions vary by the state. Unemployment benefits are funded by a payroll tax, and the amount of this tax varies by an organization's experience with layoffs. In other words, this tax rate goes up as the organization lays off more employees and those employees end up drawing funds from the unemployment insurance. Also note that employees who are dismissed (as opposed to laid off) may also be eligible for unemployment insurance, but state laws vary about this, and in most cases employees who were dismissed due to misconduct are not eligible. In contrast, employees who leave voluntarily are never eligible for unemployment benefits.[62] In order to manage these costs, organizations may consider alternatives to layoffs such as retraining employees to utilize them elsewhere and speed up the process of finding a new job for laid-off employees through referrals, providing leads, and other forms of assistance in finding a new job.

Unemployment insurance Payment made to unemployed individuals

---

SPOTLIGHT ON GLOBAL ISSUES
Cultural Influences on Employee Separations

Historically, countries differed greatly in the long-term employment protections they provided to workers. This situation is changing, with layoffs becoming more prevalent around the world. Still, employment laws in various countries may provide greater or lesser worker protections, making it more difficult to dismiss or lay off employees. For example, in summer 2017, information technology giants including WiPro Limited, Cognizant, and Infosys announced plans to lay off 56,000 employees collectively in India.[63] Some of these employees appealed to the nation's justice system with a lawsuit, which in December 2017 was decided in the workers' favor.[64] As another example, the law in Spain provides employment protection for employees with fixed-term contracts, which are typically held by older workers with more seniority. As a result, research shows that the problem of job insecurity is more common among younger workers in Spain,[65] who find it difficult to enter the labor market and secure fixed-term contracts.

In Japan, lifetime employment is becoming a thing of the past, but certain protections still make it difficult to lay off employees. To encourage employees to leave voluntarily, Sony sends employees it cannot lay off to "Career Design Rooms" or "boredom rooms," where they sit reading newspapers while collecting their paychecks. Each employee reports back to management at the end of the day and files a report on the day's activities. Other large companies in Japan such as Hitachi, Toshiba, and Seiko also reportedly follow this practice, or they may assign menial and meaningless tasks to employees with the hope that these employees will eventually choose to leave.[66]

When dismissing employees for cause, there are different procedures to be followed depending on the country or jurisdiction in which the dismissal takes place. Firing an employee in France requires notification of the employee via a registered letter, a waiting period, and considerable paperwork. In the United Kingdom, the organization needs to provide notice before dismissal of up to 12 weeks, based on the employee's tenure.[67]

Overall, the negative effects of layoffs and the resulting feelings of job insecurity are contingent on the institutional context within a particular society and the social safety net and legal rights unemployed individuals have. Whether laying off workers or dismissing for cause, organizations operating in multiple countries are strongly advised to ensure that their employee separation procedures follow the local law.

Lincoln Electric, a manufacturer of welding products founded in 1895, follows a no-layoffs policy for its workforce of more than 10,000.[69]

Benefits of Job Security

Job insecurity, or the feeling and worry that individuals may suddenly lose their jobs, is an important stressor, with consequences for employee well-being and job attitudes. Although feelings of job insecurity may originate from individual factors such as personality and qualifications, having gone through layoffs and other adverse organizational changes in the past play an important role in generating feelings of job insecurity.[68]

In order to avoid the negative consequences of layoffs and the resulting job insecurity, some organizations make a concerted effort to avoid layoffs. For example, Southwest Airlines and the San Diego, California–based Scripps Health have policies around avoiding layoffs and instead invest in retraining employees.[70] Companies that pursue zero-layoff policies aim to build long-term relations with their employees and seek alternative ways of managing their payroll expenses. Having such policies in place is likely to contribute to a sense of job security and help build attachment to the company, thereby improving employee engagement and retention.

HR can play a role in minimizing the need for layoffs through effective workforce planning. If an organization is in the habit of laying off employees regularly in response to seasonal fluctuations in demand and rehiring employees because key talent is lost after layoffs, these may be indications that this process is not being managed well. For example, in the United Kingdom, the Department for Work and Pensions was criticized when it announced plans to hire 3,000 employees on fixed-term contracts a few weeks after thousands of employees were laid off through a volunteer process. Instead, organizations may take a long-term view to layoffs by considering alternatives to layoffs and regarding layoffs as a last resort (see Table 10.2).

Deciding Layoff Criteria

Organizations will decide how to handle layoffs depending on their needs. Some layoffs will involve entire departments or plants being shut down, whereas others may utilize reducing headcount in every department by a certain percentage. As long as the layoff criteria are not illegal (i.e., choosing employees based on their age, disability status, sex, or race), organizations are allowed to set the criteria to fit their business purposes. The organization may decide which skills are essential to retain and hold on to employees who have critical skills and let go of employees who have documented performance problems. Layoffs may be **seniority-based** and **performance-based**. When layoffs are based on seniority, the organization retains the most senior workers and lets go of the newer workers. Even though this may lead to the loss of newly acquired key talent, this method has the advantage of ease of implementation. Employees are simply let go based on their hire date, and the implementation is likely to be systematic. When performance is used as the layoff criterion, the organization will be able to retain higher performers. In practice, however, as reviewed in Chapter 9, any biases and subjectivity inherent in performance measurement systems will affect layoff decisions, which may lead to feelings of unfairness.

Regardless of the criteria to be used, organizations are advised to keep good records of what criteria were used to implement layoffs and to ensure that the implementation is systematic.[71] Further, it is important to conduct an adverse-impact analysis to identify the effects on diversity. In many organizations, women and minorities may be clustered in staff functions and may have less tenure. Therefore, a seemingly neutral layoff criterion like seniority may wipe out one demographic group from the department. Understanding how different criteria will affect the level of

Seniority-based layoffs Using seniority as the layoff criterion such that the most senior employees are retained while newer employees are let go

Performance-based layoffs Using performance as the layoff criterion such that the employees with higher performance are retained while employees with lower performance are let go

TABLE 10.2   Alternatives to Layoffs[72]

METHOD	DESCRIPTION
Bonuses for productivity	Organizations may offer bonuses to employees who improve productivity or cut costs.
Reduced hours	The company may cut back on the hours of nonexempt employees or cut the number of work days along with the pay of exempt employees.
Furlough	Employees may be put on mandatory unpaid time off.
Unpaid time off	Employees may be offered unpaid time off for a period of time on a voluntary basis.
Seek ideas from employees	The organization may share information about the current financials of the company and seek ideas to save money.
Pay cut	The salaries or wages of some or all employees may be reduced.
Hiring freeze	The organization may cease hiring anyone for an extended period of time. Coupled with natural departures, this method results in a reduced headcount.
Job sharing	One full-time job may be divided between multiple part-time workers.
Offering early retirement	The organization may offer enticements to encourage employees to retire early.
Moving toward a contingent workforce	By utilizing temporary workers for jobs in which the demand for employees fluctuates, the organization may avoid seasonal layoffs.
Temporarily stopping production	The organization may stop production for a period of time and not pay employees for that period.
Retraining employees	Instead of laying off workers, the organization may invest in retraining and redeploying these employees.
Utilizing work-share programs	The organization may apply for state work-share programs to reduce work hours and pay of some employees, and employees receive unemployment insurance benefits while keeping their jobs.

diversity within the organization may motivate the organization to consider multiple criteria and to ensure that the criteria being used are fair and defensible.[73]

The Legal Side of Layoffs

When an organization is planning a layoff, an important federal law to be familiar with is the Worker Adjustment and Retraining Notification (WARN) Act. This act covers employers with at least 100 full-time employees or employers with at least 100 part-time and full-time employees who work a combined total of 4,000 hours per week. Federal, state, and local government employees are *not* covered by this law. Further, when calculating the size of a business, employees who had been employed for fewer than 6 months in the past 12 months are excluded. Covered organizations who intend to do one of the following are required to provide 60-day written advance notice to employees:

a. close a plant or facility and therefore lay off at least 50 employees within a single site for a period of 6 months or more, or

b. conduct a mass layoff in which the organization lays off 50 to 499 employees within a single site within a 30-day period, and that number is at least 33% of the organization's workforce, or

c. the organization will lay off 500 or more employees within a 30-day period.

Even when a single layoff may not reach one of these thresholds, the organization may still be covered by the WARN Act if the organization lays off two or more groups of employees through which the total reaches one of these thresholds within a 90-day period. Further, in addition to laying off employees, if the organization is planning to reduce the hours of employees by more than 50% for 6 months, the WARN Act's notification requirements are triggered. If the organization fails to provide advance notice, the organization is responsible for back pay and benefits up to 60 days.

Some organizations choose not to provide written advance notice, instead opting to provide 60 days' pay and benefits in lieu of notice and lay off employees immediately. This is technically a violation of the WARN Act, but this approach means that the organization has satisfied its WARN Act obligations by paying the penalty for violating the act.[74]

In addition to the federal WARN Act, state laws often extend the advance notice requirements for businesses engaged in layoffs. For example, states such as California, Illinois, New Hampshire, and New York have their own WARN Acts. In California, businesses with 75 or more employees (as opposed to the 100-employee threshold in the federal law) are covered. Further, the California law requires advanced notice for a layoff, plant closing, or relocation of 50 or more employees.[75]

One question to consider is where a gig worker is a contractor or employee. The distinction matters when deciding whether a layoff is covered by the WARN Act. When the San Francisco, California–based Homejoy, a cleaning services company, went bankrupt, it faced lawsuits from its workforce suggesting that they should have been classified as employees rather than contractors.[76]

The layoff decision needs to be compliant with the EEOC laws outlined in Chapter 4. When layoff criteria utilized by the organization intentionally or unintentionally discriminates against a protected group, the layoff decision may run afoul of the law. For this reason, as well as to maintain the fairness of the decisions, experts recommend that layoff decisions are based on objective criteria that can easily be verified, such as possessing multiple skills, seniority, and experience, as opposed to subjective criteria such as "attitude" or "initiative."[77]

Delivering the Message

Once the organization decides who the specific employees to be laid off are, it is important to deliver the news in a professional and compassionate manner. Layoffs often are emotionally charged and come as unexpected news to employees. Employees who learn about their impending layoff may feel anger and humiliation. Anything the organization may do to alleviate the negative consequences of layoffs (in the form of severance pay or outplacement assistance) and provide support to departing employees to help deal with the resulting uncertainty may result in better management of layoffs.

How the layoff victims are treated matters not only because fair treatment is the right thing to do but also because it affects the job attitudes, performance, and retention of layoff

SPOTLIGHT ON ETHICS
Compassionate Delivery of Layoff News

Even though not every layoff "victim" may feel like a victim, learning about one's impending layoff may be met with anger, humiliation, and a feeling that one is disposable. In some companies, the news is delivered in an unnecessarily careless and humiliating way. Ideally, layoff news should be delivered by showing compassion and respect to the employees. Here are some examples that miss the mark on this issue.

Escorted by security. It is common for organizations to have security presence during mass layoffs or when retaliation and aggression are expected, but should escorting employees to the exit be routine practice? Organizations need to strike a balance between ensuring safety and showing compassion. A senior executive who was a long-time employee shared his experience: "I had to go down, grab some things quickly, and there was some security guards waiting. And then I got marched out of the building. And I thought that was so demeaning.... And the thing that I did find humiliating, I had to ring up and ask permission to come back and collect all my stuff."[78]

Learning about it last. One employee reports that his company was conducting layoff meetings while outgoing voicemails of departing employees were being changed. An employee's wife found out about the layoff of her husband from a voicemail message stating that the employee no longer worked there.[79]

Mass announcements. Companies sometimes find it cumbersome to conduct one-on-one meetings with employees to be laid off and resort to mass announcements. Although this method is efficient and legally permissible, employees often find it disrespectful and unfair, especially when the announcement is not made in a face-to-face meeting. In one case, a Ford assembly plant in Chicago notified laid-off employees via an automated phone call on Halloween. Many employees thought it was a prank

and showed up to work the next day, only to find that their ID badges had been disabled.[80]

Can you come back and teach us what you do? An employee who performed a task vital to the company's operations was laid off. A few days later, she received a call from HR. Apparently, no one had realized how important her job was to the operations until after she was laid off. Would she consider coming back for a few days and teaching what she did to someone still employed in the company?[81]

Questions

1. What reasons can you think of to explain why employers chose to use what can be perceived as insensitive layoff announcements like those described here?

2. Find an example in the news or in the HR literature of a layoff that was handled with respect and compassion for the workers. Were there any problems nevertheless? What did the company do right, and what could have been done better?

---

survivors. Poor treatment of layoff victims may harm the company's reputation. Social media and websites such as Glassdoor.com, where current and former employees leave comments about their treatment by a company, make it easier for tales of unfair treatment to spread to potential job applicants and clients. In contrast, in a study on highly educated layoff victims, workers who were treated fairly during layoffs were more likely to recommend their former employer to others and report that they would return to work in that organization if given the chance.[82]

It is also important to remember that delivering layoff news is stressful for managers, who may experience feelings such as guilt, worry about employees' reactions, anger at the organization's decision, and doubt regarding their self-image as an effective manager. Therefore, it is essential to train managers in delivering layoff news. Figure 10.4 shows the elements of an effective layoff communication training, which includes the components of *bad news delivery* and *procedural fairness*. In other words, managers need to be trained in how to structure the layoff interview to ensure that the bad news is delivered in a professional way and to ensure that the process teaches managers to be fair. Researchers showed in a series of two laboratory studies that a training program that followed this structure was successful in ensuring that layoff news was communicated in a fairer manner, and the negative emotions reported by managers delivering the news were lower when trained. Unfortunately, such training is not common because layoffs are a relatively infrequent event, but managers need to learn how to deliver bad news in general, particularly when it comes to layoff news.[83]

Severance Pay

Severance pay refers to payments made to departing employees during organizationally initiated turnover. It is important to note that severance pay is usually not a federal legal requirement in the United States. However, many organizations choose to provide severance pay, and when severance pay is promised in an employee handbook or employment contract, it becomes a legally binding obligation. According to a study by the Institute of Management and Administration (IOMA), more than 70% of study participants working in organizations with at least 2,500 employees provided severance pay to all terminated employees, whereas only 15% of businesses

Severance pay Payments made to departing employees during organizationally initiated turnover

■ **FIGURE 10.4**   Elements of a Bad News Delivery Training in a Layoff Context

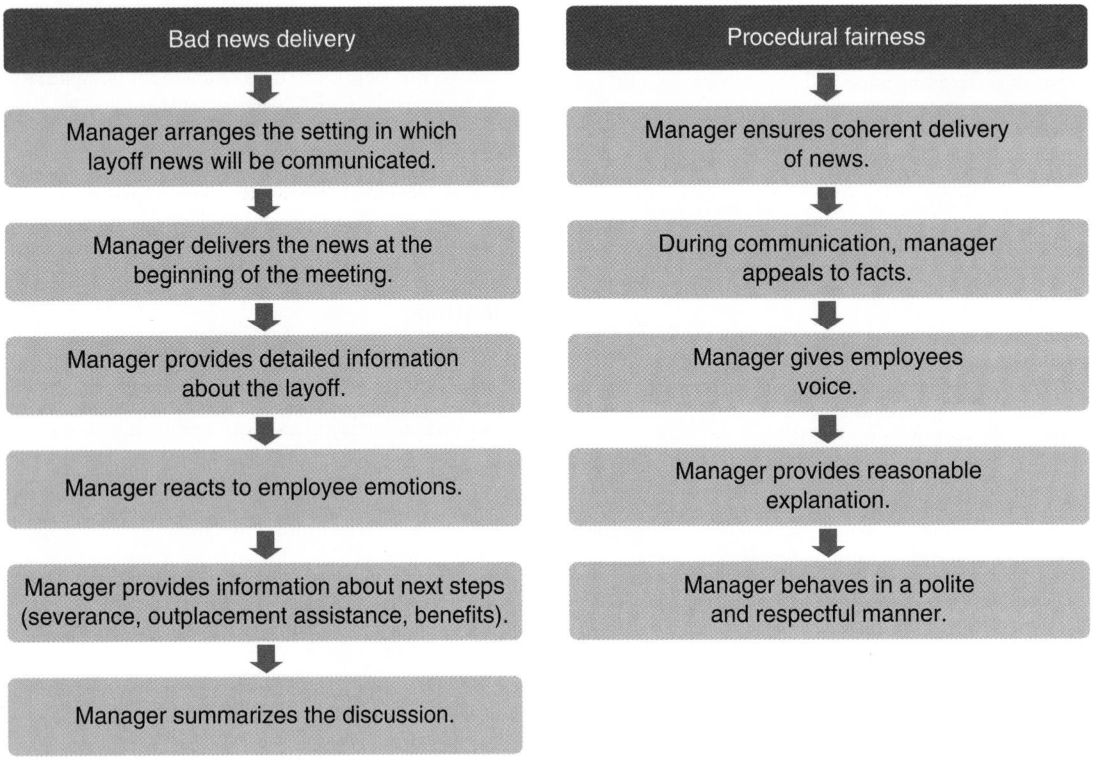

Source: Based on information contained in Richter, M., König, C. J., Koppermann, C., & Schilling, M. (2016). Displaying fairness while delivering bad news: Testing the effectiveness of organizational bad news training in the layoff context. *Journal of Applied Psychology, 101,* 779–792.

with fewer than 50 employees did so. Further, it was most common to provide severance based on the length of the employee's service.[84]

Severance packages often include 1 or 2 weeks of pay for each year the employee has been employed by the organization. Further, they may include additional benefits, such as an extension of employee health insurance for a period of time. Even though severance may be provided for both dismissals and layoffs, organizations may choose not to provide severance when an employee is terminated for cause (such as stealing money, violating company policy, or willfully behaving in a way damaging to the company), whereas organizations with severance policies typically provide them to all laid-off employees.

Employees may want to provide a generous severance pay during layoffs in order to soften the blow and help out displaced workers. Even in the best-case scenario, employees may find themselves unemployed for several months, and providing a generous severance package helps deal with the financial stress that arises from the layoff decision. In addition to helping out the involuntarily displaced employee, severance packages play a protective role for organizations: Organizations usually provide severance pay in exchange for a waiver of one's right to sue the company for reasons of discrimination. In practice, signing a severance agreement and receiving severance payment do not automatically prevent an employee from suing for discrimination; the court may still decide that the waiver is not valid. However, this waiver is usually valid if the departing employee signed it willingly and understood what it meant upon signing.[85] In other words, some companies are motivated to provide severance pay in order to potentially lower the likelihood of a lawsuit after the employee departs. This means that the severance agreement should be prepared in consultation with legal expertise. Further, if you ever find yourself in the role of the departing employee, it is important for you to understand the terms and conditions of receiving severance pay and the legal rights you may be waiving in the process.

Outplacement Assistance

In addition to providing laid-off employees with severance pay, some organizations also provide services that assist laid-off workers to find reemployment quicker. A study of more than 1,000 organizations showed that such programs benefit organizations by reducing unwanted turnover of employees and increasing survivor job satisfaction after layoffs. Helping employees find new employment is part of showing concern for them.[86]

Outplacement services are typically provided by outside companies contracted by the organization. Ideally, the program will be individualized and tailored to the person. For example, key elements of these programs include having a one-on-one meeting with a counselor who helps the person cope with the emotions arising from the layoff, a comprehensive assessment of the employee's skills and an analysis of how the person may fit with the job market, and providing training to help the employee brush up on their job search, interviewing, and negotiation skills.[87]

Managing Survivors

An important aspect of managing layoffs is to have a plan for how the layoffs will be communicated to layoff survivors (or those employees who are not being laid off) and how these remaining employees will be reengaged and motivated. When layoffs are occurring, survivors will experience anxiety not only on behalf of the employees being laid off but also about what will happen next, who will take over the workload of employees who are departing, what changes the reduced workforce will have to face, and whether layoffs are expected to occur in the future. As a result, considering and managing survivor reactions to layoffs is crucial.

Because layoffs generate anxiety on the part of employees that the economic future of the company is uncertain and that future layoffs are likely, the organization may end up losing critical talent it had no intention of laying off. When key talent unexpectedly leaves, the organization may find itself short-staffed and unable to meet its commitments. Even small-scale layoffs may increase voluntary turnover drastically. A study of 267 firms from multiple industries showed that layoffs targeting just 1% of the population were followed by an average of 31% increase in voluntary turnover.[88] As a case in point, when a software company was acquired by a larger firm, it announced plans to lay off 30 employees (out of 600). However, the company ended up losing 150 employees to voluntary turnover within a period of 3 months: The anxiety over the future of the company, a shaken sense of trust, and simply the change in how they see the company (i.e., from a company providing stable employment to a "downsizer") are among the reasons survivors may leave an organization shortly after downsizing.

A strong communication plan may mitigate some of the negative effects of layoffs on survivors. Communication by management and ethical treatment of layoff victims were found to mitigate some of the harmful effects of layoffs on survivor work satisfaction, fairness, and empowerment.[89] Organizations have an incentive to clearly communicate the reasons and consequences of layoffs for the remaining workforce, as well as to provide the necessary reassurances if they are able. For example, if the layoffs were to be a one-time event and no other layoffs are expected or planned in the near future, communicating this information is beneficial. However, management needs to be honest: If layoffs are going to occur in the near future, providing reassurances may comfort employees in the short run but is bound to break trust when promises are not kept.[90]

CHAPTER SUMMARY

Employee turnover may take the form of voluntary turnover such as quitting and retiring and involuntary turnover such as dismissals and layoffs. Because turnover is very costly to organizations in terms of time and effort as well as money, it is important for HR professionals to understand how to manage employee retention. Retention is influenced by many factors, including upper management's level of support for retention, the use of employee surveys and interviews, effective hiring and onboarding practices, investment in high-commitment HR practices, and attention to predictors of turnover. Although some forms of turnover may have benefits for organizations in the short and long term, organizations need to be deliberate in managing employee separations to ensure that they have access to the talent they need in order to reach organizational goals. Effective HR practices may aid in turnover management, but ultimately managers play a key role in motivating employees to quit their jobs or retire, as well as how employee dismissals and layoffs are handled in the organization. Therefore, managing employee separation requires a true partnership between HR departments and line managers.

KEY TERMS

voluntary turnover   333
retirement   333
involuntary turnover   333
dismissal   333
layoffs   333
tardiness   333
absenteeism   333
desire to leave   335
ease of movement   335

unfolding model of turnover   336
job embeddedness model   336
pulse surveys   338
stay interviews   339
employability   340
job satisfaction   342
work engagement   342
alumni   343
boomerang employees   343

bridge employment   345
progressive discipline   347
employment at will   347
wrongful dismissal   348
unemployment insurance   351
seniority-based layoffs   352
performance-based layoffs   352
severance pay   355

Visit **edge.sagepub.com/bauer** to help you accomplish your coursework goals in an easy-to-use learning environment.

- Master the learning objectives using key study tools
- Watch, listen, and connect with online multimedia resources
- Access mobile-friendly quizzes and flashcards to check your understanding

HR REASONING AND DECISION-MAKING EXERCISES

MINI-CASE ANALYSIS EXERCISE: DISMISSING AN EMPLOYEE

You work for the HR department of a manufacturing firm. The company has 500 employees, a significant portion of whom have long tenure in the company.

Eric Jenkins, a department manager who was hired 2 years ago, contacted you, saying that he is interested in dismissing Laura Harrison. Laura has been with the company for the past 25 years. He is concerned that Laura is not adapting well to the new technological changes that took place in the company over the past year. Plus she is always debating every point with Eric, trying to argue that "this is not how we do things around here." Eric feels that Laura's knowledge of the business is stale, and she is displaying strong resistance to change and innovation. He also feels that she is not respecting him because she is much older than he is. They have had performance conversations in the past, but Laura does not seem interested in improving. Eric gave Laura a 3 out of 5 (meets expectations) in her last performance review, which was about a year ago.

Your company is not unionized and does not have a formal discipline procedure.

Questions:

1. What would you advise Eric to do? Should Eric dismiss Laura? Explain your rationale. What would be the consequences of dismissing and not dismissing Laura?

2. What additional information would be helpful to you in making your recommendation about this case?

3. Let's say you decided not to dismiss Laura in the short run. What would be your recommended action plan to solve this problem?

4. What type of procedures would be helpful to have in this company? Provide your recommendations for structural changes so that cases such as these are more easily resolved.

HR DECISION ANALYSIS EXERCISE: FULL DISCLOSURE

Your company is in the process of laying off 100 of its 1,000 employees due to efforts to streamline its processes. As the owner, you know that you will most likely lay off another 50 employees in 3 months and 50 more 6 months after that. However, you are concerned about morale, and you intend to have a meeting with the remaining employees, reassuring them that the jobs of those who are left behind are secure. Should you reassure the layoff survivors by telling them that layoffs are not likely in the future and their jobs are safe, given that you anticipate future layoffs?

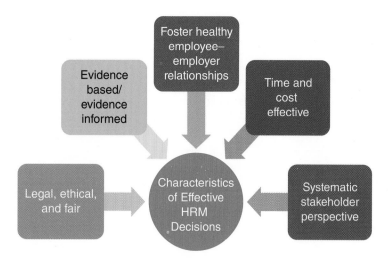

Please provide the rationale for your answer to each of the questions below.

Is your idea to reassure layoff survivors legal, ethical, and fair?

_____

_____

_____

_____

Is it evidence based/evidence informed?

_____

_____

_____

_____

Does it foster healthy employee–employer relationships?

_____

_____

_____

_____

Is it time and cost effective?

_____

_____

_____

_____

Does it take a systematic stakeholder perspective?

_____

_____

_____

_____

Considering your analysis above, overall, do you think this would be an effective decision? Why or why not?

_____

_____

_____

What, if anything, do you think should be done differently or considered to help make this decision more effective?

_____

_____

_____

HR DECISION-MAKING EXERCISE: CREATING A RETENTION MANAGEMENT SYSTEM

You are working at Shek, Inc., an organization providing private and group surfing and scuba diving lessons, adventure tours, and rental services to tourists in Hawaii. Your company has around 200 employees consisting of instructors, sales, marketing, and office personnel. The company has an annual turnover rate of 80%, which you suspect is too high.

1. How would you assess why employees are leaving? After you choose your method of measurement (survey, interviews), develop questions to include in your instrument. How would you analyze the data to identify the top reasons for employee departures?

2. Let's assume that you found out the top three reasons for turnover in this company are:

    a. Management is very authoritarian and not supportive of employees.
    b. Employee schedules vary a lot and often are announced with very short notice.
    c. Employees feel they are working all the time with little downtime.

What would be your proposed action plan to deal with these issues? Be specific, and make sure that your recommendations focus on recruitment, selection, training, compensation, and any other stages of the employment cycle.

DATA AND ANALYTICS EXERCISE: HOW HIGH IS YOUR TURNOVER?

Shaffer Technologies is an educational software firm in the San Francisco area. This firm had the following number of departures and number of employees during the past calendar year:

MONTH	NUMBER OF DEPARTURES	NUMBER OF EMPLOYEES
January	24	1070
February	88	1347
March	67	1213
April	29	1200
May	45	1422
June	77	1277
July	74	1286
August	18	1109
September	34	1272
October	14	1000
November	63	1263
December	72	1435

1. Calculate the annual overall turnover rate for this firm.

2. How would you decide whether this turnover rate is excessive for this firm? Explain the steps you would follow to make this decision.

3. Let's focus only on January. Assume that out of the 24 employees who are shown as departures, 2 left voluntarily, 9 of them are on FMLA leave, 5 of them were temporary agency workers who were let go, 2 retired, 4 were terminated for cause, and 2 were put on unpaid leave. What is the monthly turnover rate for January?

EXCEL EXTENSION: NOW YOU TRY!

- On **edge.sagepub.com/bauer,** you will find an Excel exercise on turnover involving a different organization.

- First, you will calculate the turnover rate for different units in an organization.

- Second, you will make recommendations based on your findings.

CHAPTER 10 SUPPLEMENT: SAMPLE POLICY FOR EMPLOYEE SEPARATIONS

Retrieved from https://www.shrm.org/resourcesandtools/tools-and-samples/policies/pages/cms_011005.aspx

Separation of Employment Policy: Procedures for Voluntary and Involuntary (Including Employee Death) Terminations

Jun. 19, 2017

PURPOSE

It is the policy of [Company Name] to ensure that employee terminations, including voluntary and involuntary terminations and terminations due to the death of an employee, are handled in a professional manner with minimal disruption to the workplace.

AT-WILL EMPLOYMENT

Employment with [Company Name] is voluntary and subject to termination by the employee or [Company Name] at will, with or without cause, and with or without notice, at any time. Nothing in these policies shall be interpreted to be in conflict with or to eliminate or modify in any way the employment-at-will status of [Company Name] employees.

VOLUNTARY TERMINATIONS

A voluntary termination of employment occurs when an employee submits a written or verbal notice of resignation to his or her supervisor or when an employee is absent from work for three consecutive workdays and fails to contact his or her supervisor (job abandonment).

PROCEDURES

1. Employees are requested to provide a minimum of two weeks' notice of their intention to separate from the company to allow a reasonable amount of time to transfer ongoing workloads. The employee should provide a written resignation notification to his or her manager.

2. Upon receipt of an employee's resignation, the manager will notify the human resource (HR) department by sending a copy of the resignation letter and any other pertinent information (e.g., employee's reason for leaving, last day of work).

3. The HR department will coordinate the employee's out-processing. This process will include the employee's returning all company property (e.g., keys, ID cards, parking passes); a review of the employee's post-termination benefits status; and the employee's completion of an exit interview.

4. The employee's manager will complete a Supervisory Termination Summary and deliver the completed form to HR.

5. Employees who possess a security clearance must meet with the security officer for a debriefing no later than their last day of employment.

INVOLUNTARY TERMINATIONS

An involuntary termination of employment, including layoffs of over 30 days, is a management-initiated dismissal with or without cause.

The inability of an employee to perform the essential functions of his or her job with or without a reasonable accommodation may also result in an involuntary termination. An employee may also be discharged for any legal reason, including but not limited to: misconduct, tardiness, absenteeism, unsatisfactory performance or inability to perform.

PROCEDURES

1. Before any action is taken to involuntarily discharge an employee, the employee's manager must request a review by the termination review board, which consists of the president, the vice president of HR and the employee's department head.

2. The termination review board will be responsible for reviewing the circumstances and determining if discharge is warranted. If the board recommends discharge, the employee's manager and an HR representative will notify the employee. The employee's manager should complete an Employee Change Form and notify HR and payroll of the last day worked by the employee.

DEATH OF AN EMPLOYEE

A termination due to the death of an employee will be made effective as of the date of death.

PROCEDURES

1. Upon receiving notification of the death of an employee, the employee's manager should immediately notify HR.

2. The benefits administrator will process all appropriate beneficiary payments from the various benefits plans.

3. The employee's manager should ensure that the payroll office receives the deceased employee's timecard.

FINAL PAY

An employee who resigns or is discharged will be paid through the last day of work, plus any unused paid time off (PTO), less outstanding loans, advances or other agreements the employee may have with the company, in compliance with state laws. In cases of an employee's death, the final pay due to that employee will be paid to the deceased employee's estate or as otherwise required under state law.

Developing a Pay Structure

Opening Case

Equal Pay for the U.S. Women's National Soccer Team

Avoiding pay discrimination is an important consideration when designing and implementing a compensation system, and it is a focal point of several U.S. employment and labor laws. Perhaps most well known is the Equal Pay Act, signed into law by President John F. Kennedy in 1963. Since then, additional legislation like the Civil Rights Act of 1964 and the Lilly Ledbetter Fair Pay Act of 2009 have been introduced to ensure equal pay for equal work.

In recent years, pay disparities between men's and women's professional sports have received increased scrutiny. The U.S. women's soccer team has featured prominently on the international stage by winning major competitions including Olympic gold medals in 1996, 2004, 2008, and 2012 and World Cup titles in 1991, 1999, and 2015. Some 30 million television viewers watched the U.S. women's team defeat Japan in the 2015 World Cup. Yet despite all of their success, the U.S. women have not received equal pay from the U.S. Soccer Federation as compared to the pay the men have received.

On the surface, the pay received by top U.S. men's and women's soccer players appears somewhat comparable. For instance, the U.S. men's star goalkeeper, Tim Howard, was paid a salary of $398,495 during 2014, and

LEARNING OBJECTIVES

After reading and studying this chapter, you should be able to do the following:

11.1 Explain the conceptual foundation of compensation and reward systems.

11.2 Describe how to develop internally, externally, and individually equitable and legally compliant pay structures.

11.3 Describe the development of a pay structure.

11.4 Identify basic principles underlying person-based pay structures.

11.5 Describe the philosophy and challenges of executive pay structures.

11.6 Evaluate issues of pay administration such as compression and pay transparency.

Vaughn Ridley - EMPICS/Contributor

The U.S. women's national soccer team celebrates after winning the 2015 World Cup championship in Vancouver, Canada.

the U.S. women's star goalkeeper, Hope Solo, was paid a salary of $366,000 in 2015. A closer look, however, reveals that Tim Howard played just 8 games, whereas Hope Solo played in 23 games. In other words, not only did Hope Solo make less overall, but Tim Howard's earnings came out to $49,812 per game, as compared to Hope Solo's earnings of $15,913 per game, which some have argued is compelling evidence of pay inequality. When looking farther down the list, even more striking pay differences appear. For example, the 50th-highest-paid U.S. men's player received $246,238 in cumulative pay between 2008 and 2016; in contrast, the 50th-highest-paid U.S. women's player received just $25,516 over that same period.

The differences in pay can be attributed to the pay structure and incentives: The U.S. Soccer Federation compensated men per game played, regardless of the outcome, whereas women were paid a base salary with relatively small financial incentives for winning games. Further, women received lower per diems to cover travel expenses and lower rates for sponsor appearances.

Some people contend that historically women's soccer has generated less revenue than men's soccer and thus argue that the ongoing pay discrepancy is justified. In contrast, those in favor of equal pay point to more recent data that show the U.S. women's team earned more revenue than the U.S. men's team in 2016. Some argue that the men and women do not perform equal work, pointing to the fact that, to qualify for the World Cup, the women's team must play five games over 2 weeks, whereas the men's team must play 16 games over a 2-year period. Because of this difference, some believe that the men's qualification schedule is more arduous than the women's, thereby warranting higher pay; but others argue that the women's schedule is more condensed and thus more intense.

The concern over equal pay came to a head in 2016 when five players from the U.S. women's team filed a formal complaint with the Equal Employment Opportunity Commission, a government body that investigates discrimination claims. In 2017, as part of a collective bargaining agreement, the U.S. women's team agreed to a new pay structure, which included a 30% increase in base pay as well as higher incentives for winning games. The new agreement did not yield pay equality between men and women, but it did take a large step toward closing the pay gap, moving the U.S. women's soccer team toward pay fairness.[1]

Case Discussion Questions

1. Why do you think pay fairness is important for employee job performance and retention?

2. If you were a leader at the U.S. Soccer Federation, how would you have responded to the U.S. women's team assertion that pay inequality existed?

3. How do you define *equal work* when it comes to the men's and women's soccer players?

4. Given what is described in this case, why do you think these pay discrepancies exist? Do you think that they are fair or unfair? Why?

5. In your opinion, when it comes to equal pay, what is the next step for the U.S. women's soccer team?

▶ Click to learn more…

Read a CBS News interview transcript with players from the U.S. women's national soccer team here: http://www.cbsnews.com/news/60-minutes-women-soccer-team-usa-gender-discrimination-equal-pay/

A *pay structure* refers to the way in which an organization applies pay rates to different jobs, skills, or competencies. An effective pay structure is an important part of an organization's broader compensation and reward systems, and it is important for attracting and retaining talented individuals, as well as for motivating existing workers to achieve higher levels of performance. Further, an effective pay structure distributes pay fairly, competes with the pay practices of other organizations, and abides by federal, state, and local employment and labor laws. Although pay represents just one aspect of rewarding workers, it is perhaps one of the most salient rewards for prospective job applicants and current employees. As such, the process of developing a pay structure requires a rigorous and systematic approach in order to establish effective pay policies that promote the organization's strategic goals and ensure fairness.

Pay structure The way in which an organization applies pay rates to different jobs, skills, or competencies

Pay as a Reward

Whether you are a manager or an employee, when thinking about rewarding employees, pay is likely the first thing that comes to mind—and for good reason. Pay, which includes wages and salaries, often accounts for nearly 70% of a total compensation package's overall value, where a total compensation package may also include benefits and other employment offerings such as health care and paid time off.[2] Managers and employees tend to view pay through different lenses. For managers, pay is often viewed as a major cost. For employees, pay often represents an entitlement offered in exchange for work. This chapter focuses on how to develop an effective pay structure that addresses the concerns of both managers and employees.

Despite its prominence as a reward, pay represents just one component of a total compensation package and, even more broadly, of a reward system. That is, employees seek and employers offer other returns for work beyond pay, which often include benefits, recognition, and status, to name a few. Moreover, although workers often emphasize the importance of pay for their decision to accept a job offer, pay is not the only reason workers gravitate to certain organizations. To that end, a 2017 survey by Korn Ferry revealed that only 4% of professionals ranked pay as the #1 reason for choosing one organization over another.[3] Accumulated research has revealed only a small correlation between employees' pay and their overall job satisfaction, meaning that employees who are paid more are only slightly more likely to be satisfied with their jobs.[4] Why might this be the case? Other factors, such as individuals' interactions and relationships with coworkers and supervisors, characteristics and conditions of work, HR practices, and even their own personalities, play important roles in employees' overall job satisfaction.[5]

LO 11.1 Explain the conceptual foundation of compensation and reward systems.

Reward Systems

Before focusing on pay as a form of compensation, it is important to understand how pay fits into a reward system. A *reward system* refers to the policies, procedures, and practices used by an organization to determine the amount and types of returns individuals, teams, and the organization receive in exchange for their membership and contributions. To provide a competitive advantage, reward systems must be integrated with other HR functions and aligned with organizational strategy. They must emphasize the attraction, motivation, and retention of individuals who directly or indirectly can contribute to the development, sale, or provision of the organization's products or services. First, as far as attraction is concerned, reward systems are less likely to attract talented individuals if recruitment information fails to reach them or if the selection procedures fail to identify the best candidates. Conversely, the most effective recruitment and selection processes can fail

Reward system The policies, procedures, and practices used by an organization to determine the amount and types of returns individuals, teams, and the organization receive in exchange for their membership and contributions

if the compensation package offered to top candidates is not competitive with offers made by other organizations. Second, without a competitive rewards package, an organization may struggle to motivate existing employees to use and apply their KSAOs. Third, an organization may struggle to retain workers when other organizations offer more attractive rewards packages or when workers are not rewarded fairly with respect to their contributions or position. Next, we distinguish between two overarching categories of rewards: relational returns and total compensation.[6]

Relational Returns

Relational returns include nonmonetary incentives and rewards, such as new learning and developmental opportunities, enriched and challenging work, job security, and recognition. As a classic example, the job of a tenured university professor offers the promise of lifetime employment as well as the intellectual freedom to pursue developmental opportunities and challenging work. As another example, Google offered a "20% time" policy in which employees were encouraged to spend 20% of their time working on personal projects of their own choosing that had the potential to benefit the company. This served not only as an enriching activity for employees but also as a source of potentially valuable new products and services, such as Gmail and Google News.[7]

Total Compensation

Total compensation subsumes compensation and benefits, which are often referred to as direct pay and indirect pay, respectively. **Compensation** includes base pay and variable pay, and **benefits** include health, life, and disability insurance; retirement programs; and work–life balance programs. A 2017 report by the Bureau of Labor Statistics found that, on average, compensation accounted for 68% of total compensation costs for employers, whereas benefits accounted for the other 32%.[8] This chapter describes how to develop a fair, attractive, and legally compliant pay structure, which is an important part of a compensation system.

Fairness of Rewards

An organization should strive for fair reward policies and practices. Specifically, an organization should design and implement rewards systems wherein employees perceive that (a) they are paid fairly relative to others inside and outside of their organization (i.e., internal and external equity, respectively) and (b) pay decisions are made and communicated in a fair manner. To understand reward system fairness, two psychological theories offer useful frameworks: equity theory and organizational justice theory.

Equity Theory

Equity theory provides a way of understanding how an individual's sense of fairness is influenced by others with whom they compare themselves. In the context of a reward system, it refers to an individual's perception of fairness as driven by the distributed rewards they receive (e.g., compensation) relative to how much they have contributed (e.g., effort, hours worked) and how that ratio of rewards to contributions compares to some other individual's ratio of rewards to contributions.[9] The other individual in this scenario is known as the *referent other* or simply the *referent*. Example referents include coworkers, colleagues, or others in the same field whom the employee knows. Equity theory includes the following propositions:

1. Individuals compare themselves to referents based on their perceived ratio of the following factors: rewards and contributions.

2. Individuals strive to maintain a state of perceived equity between themselves and referents. The greater the perceived inequity, the more tension individuals experience and the more motivated individuals become to adjust their rewards and contributions to improve the perceived equity of the situation.

Relational returns Nonmonetary incentives and rewards, such as new learning and developmental opportunities

Total compensation Package of compensation and benefits that employees receive

Compensation Employee reward that includes base pay and variable pay and is sometimes referred to as direct pay

Benefits Employee rewards that are sometimes referred to as indirect pay and include health, life, and disability insurance; retirement programs; and work–life balance programs

LO 11.2 Describe how to develop internally, externally, and individually equitable and legally compliant pay structures.

Equity theory Provides a way of understanding how an individual's sense of fairness is influenced by others with whom they compare themselves

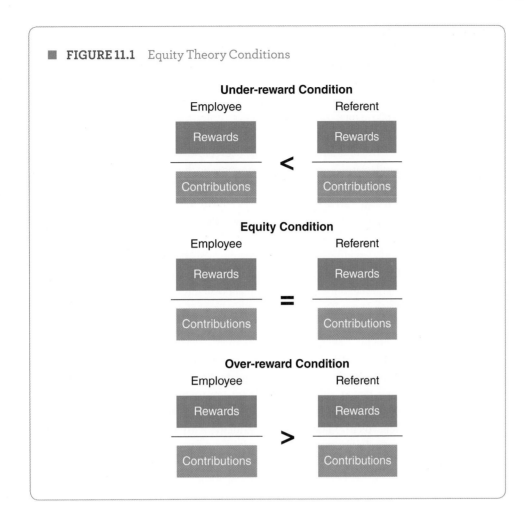

■ **FIGURE 11.1** Equity Theory Conditions

In the context of equity theory, equality and equity are not one and the same. Rather, equality means that two individuals receive the *same* rewards regardless of their contributions to their job and organization. In contrast, equity means that two individuals may have different levels of rewards and contributions so long as their *ratios* of rewards to contributions are the same. If an individual receives the same reward as another individual but contributed more, then the reward allocation could be considered equal but not equitable. Interestingly, individuals typically prefer equitable rewards when comparing themselves to others at work as part of a formal employment relationship, whereas they typically prefer equal rewards when comparing themselves to those with whom they share personal relationships, such as friends and family members.[10]

According to equity theory, individuals are sensitive to conditions of inequity, which can include under-reward and over-reward conditions, as shown in Figure 11.1. An individual who perceives they are being under-rewarded relative to another individual will be motivated to restore equity by increasing their rewards and/or reducing their contributions to adjust their ratio of rewards to contributions. Such an individual might be motivated to ask for a raise, reduce their effort at work, or both; or if the inequity cannot be addressed, they might choose to quit or even steal from the organization.[11] In support, research has shown that when faced with under-reward or a feeling of being underpaid, an individual might adjust their contributions by reducing their job performance or adjust their rewards by engaging in deviant behaviors like theft.[12] In contrast, an individual who perceives they are over-rewarded might be motivated to restore fairness by reducing their rewards and/or increasing their contributions. Or they may simply rationalize why they are over-rewarded compared to others. Not surprisingly, research has shown that individuals often do not, in fact, experience more tension when over-rewarded, and instead they tend to experience less tension in these situations.[13]

As an example of equity theory in action, consider the hypothetical case of Fatimah and Joanne, graduates of the same HR program who often confide in each other and share information about their jobs. Fatimah works as an external HR consultant for a for-profit consulting agency. Last year, Fatimah earned $95,000 in total compensation and worked on average 40 hours per week. Joanne also works as an external HR consultant but for a different for-profit consulting agency. Last year, Joanne also earned $95,000 in total compensation but, in contrast, worked on average 60 hours per week. Both Fatimah and Joanne began their current jobs at about the same time. All else being equal, do you think Joanne perceives under-reward inequity? Let's consider their rewards relative to contributions. Both Fatimah and Joanne earned the same amount and thus received the same reward, but when it comes to their respective contributions, Joanne works on average 20 hours more per week. Thus, Fatimah's ratio of rewards to contributions ($95,000 to 40 hours/week) is more favorable than Joanne's ratio ($95,000 to 60 hours/week), which increases the likelihood that Joanne will perceive under-reward inequity. To reduce this inequity, Joanne may feel motivated to ask for a raise or to work fewer hours and apply less effort. Alternatively, Joanne might decide to completely remove herself from this inequitable situation by leaving the organization and seeking out an organization that will provide higher pay or fewer hours. Finally, as another possibility, Joanne may change her perceptions or choose a different referent. That is, Joanne may realize that she overlooked a reward that she receives but that Fatimah does not, such as more challenging work or greater autonomy. Or perhaps Joanne learns that Fatimah's job—although ostensibly similar—is actually quite different in so many regards that Joanne switches her referent to another person who will serve as a better comparison.

Research shows that individuals vary with regard to their sensitivity to inequitable and equitable situations. The extent to which individuals are more or less sensitive to equity is referred to as their level of equity sensitivity. There are three equity sensitivity orientations: entitlement, equity sensitive, and benevolent.[14] Those with an entitlement orientation are more comfortable with over-reward inequity but less comfortable with under-reward inequity, and they tend to focus more on rewards than on their contributions. Those with an equity sensitive orientation prefer conditions of equity in which rewards are proportional to contributions. Those with a benevolent orientation are more comfortable with under-reward inequity but less comfortable with over-reward inequity, and they tend to focus more on their contributions than their rewards. Sauley and Bedian (2000) developed the equity sensitivity scale shown in Table 11.1, which you may complete as a self-assessment.[15]

Equity theory is not without its critics, as some have argued that people are not only concerned with the perceived fairness of their rewards relative to others but also to the reward system as a whole.[16] That is, it is entirely possible that an individual perceives a state of equity between

MANAGER'S TOOLBOX

Restoring Employees' Perceptions of Equity

Managers can play an important role when it comes to their employees' perceptions of equity. Remember, the concept of equity is perceptual in nature, and people do not always have all of the facts or entirely accurate information regarding their rewards and contributions relative to the rewards and contributions of others. Following are some steps that managers can take to restore an employee's perception of equity.

1. **Choose the right referent.** If the employee is comparing themselves to an inappropriate referent, encourage the employee to select a more appropriate referent.
2. **Get the facts.** Verify whether the rewards and contributions information used by the employee are accurate.
3. **Restore equity.** Discuss how the employee can increase rewards, such as by asking for a raise or promotion, or fix the rewards if an error has been made.[17]

TABLE 11.1   Self-Assessment: What Is Your Level of Equity Sensitivity?

Please read each of the following statements and indicate how much you agree with each of them using the following scale:
1 = strongly disagree, 2 = disagree, 3 = neither agree nor disagree, 4 = agree, 5 = strongly agree

1. I prefer to do as little as possible at work while getting as much as I can from my employer.
2. I am most satisfied at work when I have to do as little as possible.
3. When I am at my job, I think of ways to get out of work.
4. If I could get away with it, I would try to work just a little bit slower than the boss expects.
5. It is really satisfying to me when I can get something for nothing at work.
6. It is the smart employee who gets as much as they can while giving as little as possible in return.
7. Employees who are more concerned about what they can get from their employer rather than what they can give to their employer are the wise ones.
8. If I had to work hard all day at my job, I would probably quit.
9. When I have completed my task for the day, I help out other employees who have yet to complete their tasks.
10. Even if I received low wages and poor benefits from my employer, I would still try to do my best at my job.
11. I feel obligated to do more than I am paid to do at work.
12. At work, my greatest concern is whether or not I am doing the best job I can.
13. A job which requires me to be busy during the day is better than a job which allows me a lot of loafing.
14. At work, I feel uneasy when there is little work for me to do.
15. I would become very dissatisfied with my job if I had little or no work to do.
16. All other things being equal, it is better to have a job with a lot of duties and responsibilities than one with few duties and responsibilities.

Scoring:

Step 1: Sum your numeric responses to items 9–16.
Step 2: Reverse score your responses to items 1–8 by subtracting your numeric response from 6. For example, if you put down 2, subtract 2 from 6, which equals 4. Sum your reverse-scored responses for items 1–8.
Step 3: Add your numeric responses from Step 1 and Step 2. Your overall score can range from 16 to 80.
Step 4: If your overall score falls between 16–39, you likely have an entitlement orientation. If your overall score falls between 40–56, you likely have an equity sensitivity orientation. If your overall score falls between 57–80, you likely have a benevolence orientation.

Source: Items and scoring adapted from Sauley, K. S., & Bedeian, A. G. (2000). Equity sensitivity: Construction of a measure and examination of its psychometric properties. *Journal of Management, 26,* 885–910.

themselves and another person yet perceives the overarching reward system as inequitable or unfair. Nevertheless, equity theory offers a way to understand how perceived fairness is based, in part, on how individuals perceive their rewards and contributions relative to others. Moreover, because the theory is perceptual in nature, when an employee approaches a manager about perceived inequity relative to another employee, the manager should first consider whether the employee's perceptions are accurate, as one way to restore equity might be to simply correct the employee regarding the details of their own rewards and contributions or the rewards and contributions of the referent. Or perhaps the employee is comparing themselves to another individual who is not an appropriate referent, in which case the manager can intervene by suggesting a more appropriate referent.

Organizational Justice Theory

Organizational justice theory stems from equity theory and similarly focuses on perceptions of fairness in the workplace. Organizational justice theory extends equity theory by positing that individuals' emotions, thoughts, and behaviors are influenced by the extent to which they perceive distributive, procedural, and interactional justice at work (see Figure 11.2).[18] Considered in the context of reward systems, the theory provides a useful framework for understanding employee perceptions of existing reward systems as well as for designing and implementing new reward systems. Further, a general lack of organizational justice with regard to organizational

Organizational justice theory A theory that focuses on perceptions of fairness in the workplace

■ **FIGURE 11.2**   Three Types of Organizational Justice

DISTRIBUTIVE JUSTICE	Perceived fairness of the allocation of an outcome or resource, which can include rewards, punishments, or other organizational consequences. Originates from equity theory and is sometimes referred to as *outcome fairness*.
PROCEDURAL JUSTICE	Perceived fairness of the process used to determine how an outcome or resource is determined and doled out. Sometimes referred to as *process fairness*.
INTERACTIONAL JUSTICE	Perceived fairness of interpersonal treatment, such as with respect, consideration, dignity, and kindness, and of the manner and content of information provided, such as the explanation provided.

systems, policies, and practices can be consequential for the organization and its employees, as lower organizational justice has been linked to employee health problems, stress, and absenteeism.[19]

Distributive justice The perceived fairness or equity regarding the allocation of an outcome or resource, which can include rewards, punishments, or other organizational consequences

The first type of justice is called ***distributive justice,*** which is an outgrowth of equity theory and is sometimes referred to as *outcome fairness*. Distributive justice refers to the perceived fairness or equity regarding the allocation of an outcome or resource, which can include rewards, punishments, or other organizational consequences.[20] Although one might think that a lack of distributive justice is a part of daily life and thus fairly inconsequential, it turns out that low distributive justice is associated with lower job satisfaction, lower organizational commitment, lower trust, and a greater likelihood of quitting.[21] Thus, as much as is possible, care should be taken when distributing rewards to ensure employees perceive the outcome as fair.

Procedural justice The perceived fairness of the process used to determine *how* an outcome or resource is determined and distributed

The second type of justice is ***procedural justice***, which is also called *process fairness*. Procedural justice has to do with employees' perceptions of fairness regarding the process used to determine *how* an outcome or resource is determined and distributed.[22] In the context of reward systems, we can apply the principles of procedural justice to understand how employees perceive the policies, procedures, and practices used to determine who is rewarded and how much they are rewarded. To achieve high perceptions of procedural justice among employees, processes should be designed and applied with the following considerations in mind: consistency, bias suppression, accuracy, correctability, representativeness, and ethicality.[23] Accumulated research evidence has shown that employees who perceive lower levels of procedural justice tend to experience lower job satisfaction and organizational commitment along with lower trust and performance, as well as exhibit fewer helping behaviors and a greater desire to quit.[24]

Interactional justice The perceived fairness of an interpersonal or informational interaction—for example, being treated with respect and consideration or receiving adequate explanation about a process

The third type of justice is ***interactional justice***. Interactional justice entails individuals' perceptions that they are treated well interpersonally—such as with respect, consideration, dignity, and kindness—as well as provided with information in the form of an adequate explanation regarding the details of a particular process.[25] Research has shown that a lack of perceived interactional justice is associated with lower job satisfaction, organizational commitment, trust, and performance, as well as fewer helping behaviors and a greater desire to quit.[26]

Although organizations should strive to design and implement reward systems that are perceived as high in all three types of justice, sometimes it can be challenging to avoid low perceived distributive justice, as some outcomes may be particularly unlikeable. Fortunately, high procedural and interactional justice can buffer the negative effects of low distributive justice, and procedural justice becomes especially important in instances in which the distributed outcome is negative as opposed to positive.[27] Imagine that an employee is notified by his manager that he will not receive a year-end performance-based bonus, but the other members of the team will. Based on this information alone, the employee is likely to perceive low distributive justice. If, however, the manager delivered the bad news in a respectful manner and carefully explained the procedure used to determine who was eligible for the bonus, the employee may feel less upset

HR IN ACTION
Gravity Payments Raises Minimum Pay

Dan Price, CEO of Gravity Payments

In 2015, Dan Price—the CEO of a small company called Gravity Payments, which offers credit card processing—announced that all employees' annual pay would be raised to a minimum of $70,000 per year and that his $1 million in annual pay would be temporarily lowered to $70,000 to help cover the increased labor costs associated with the initiative. Price's inspiration for the change stemmed from a confrontation with an employee regarding pay and from a study by Kahneman and Deaton (2010). In that study, the researchers found that emotional well-being increased steadily along with increased pay until an annual income of about $75,000 was reached, at which point additional pay did not result in higher emotional well-being.

In the days that followed, Price's announcement was met with a mixture of praise, consternation, and criticism. On the one hand, Gravity Payments received an influx of résumés, interest from business scholars, and praise from some clients and even an elected official. On the other hand, the company faced criticism from clients who feared that the price of Gravity Payments' services would increase, from current employees who were concerned about the potential internal inequity of having positions of different worth being compensated at similar rates, and from members of the general public who thought the announcement was nothing but a publicity stunt.

Six months later, only two employees had left the company, alleviating potential concerns by some of a mass exodus due to perceived pay inequity. Around 18 months later, the company had seen a 67% increase in new clients and a 75% increase in revenues, and by about 2 years later, 10% of Gravity Payments' employees had purchased a home or planned to do so in the near future—a purchase that previously had seemed out of reach for many. In the end, what began as an initiative to improve the emotional well-being of those who earned less than $70,000 ended up helping the company's bottom line.[28]

about the outcome. In sum, when it comes to reward systems, careful attention should be paid to distributing equitable rewards, developing and implementing fair processes, treating employees with respect and consideration when allocating rewards, and explaining and communicating the process in a fair and transparent manner.

Developing a Pay Structure

LO 11.3 Describe the development of a pay structure.

As a component of a reward system, a pay structure refers to the way an organization applies pay rates to different jobs. When developing a pay structure, an overarching objective should be to ensure that its resulting policies adhere to the aforementioned principles of equity and fairness. Steps should be taken to ensure individual employees are paid equitably with respect to other employees in the organization and with respect to employees at other organizations performing similar work. Further, a pay structure and associated policies and practices should abide by the rules outlined in prevailing employment and labor laws so that ultimately pay is administered both fairly and legally. Thus, to develop and administer an effective pay structure and associated policies, an organization should strive for the following goals: (a) internal equity, (b) external equity, (c) individual equity, and (d) legal compliance (see Figure 11.3).

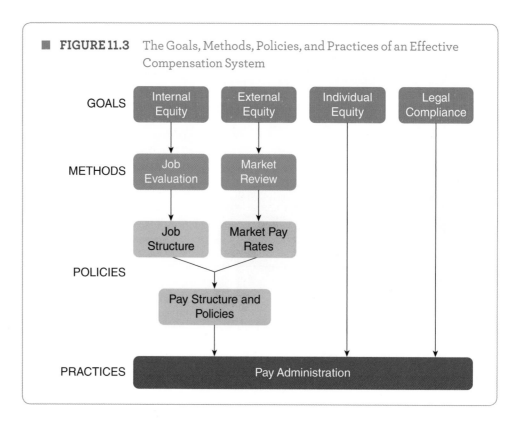

■ **FIGURE 11.3**   The Goals, Methods, Policies, and Practices of an Effective Compensation System

Ensuring Internal Equity

Internal equity The fairness of pay rates across jobs within an organization

When developing a pay structure, fairness should be a primary concern. ***Internal equity*** (sometimes called *internal alignment* or *internal consistency*) refers to the fairness of pay rates across jobs *within* an organization.[29] In other words, internal equity has to do with whether jobs of greater worth to an organization are compensated at a higher level.

Job Structure

Job structure The ranking of jobs within an organization based on their respective worth

Creating a fair job structure is an important step toward an internally equitable pay structure. A ***job structure***—sometimes called a *job hierarchy*—refers to the ranking of jobs based on their respective worth. Once a job structure is in place, a pay structure consisting of different pay levels or rates can be superimposed, such that differentials between pay levels reflect the relative worth or value of different jobs to the organization. Ultimately, both the job structure and pay structure should be aligned with organizational strategy, such that those who work in jobs that contribute more (directly) to the organization's attainment of strategic objectives are paid at a higher rate. Moreover, internally equitable job and pay structures can even be sources of motivation for employees, as they may inspire individuals to seek promotions to jobs that provide more pay.

Job Evaluation

Job evaluation A systematic process used to determine the relative worth of jobs within an organization

The creation of an equitable job structure requires a ***job evaluation***, which is a process used to determine the relative worth of jobs within an organization. Prior to doing so, however, a rigorous, up-to-date job analysis should be conducted for all jobs that will be evaluated in the job evaluation. The reason for this is that it is critical to identify the core tasks, KSAOs, and/or competencies associated with each job in order to systematically evaluate the relative worth of each job. In addition, a job analysis yields job descriptions and specifications that feed into the job evaluation and ultimately serve as the foundation of the job structure (as shown in Figure 11.4).

When conducting a job evaluation, an organization should take great care when determining who will be involved in the decision making and how decisions will be communicated to the rest of the organization. The job evaluation process requires many judgment calls, and thus employees have a tendency to perceive the process as overly subjective or entirely too political and

■ **FIGURE 11.4** Steps for Developing a Job Structure

Job Analysis
1. Define what tasks, duties, responsibilities, and KSAOs are actually required to perform benchmark jobs.

Job Descriptions
2. Using the data collected during the job analysis, create job descriptions for each of the benchmark jobs.

Job Evaluation
3. Based on the job descriptions, determine the relative worth of each job to the organization.

Job Structure
4. Create a hierarchy of jobs based on their relative worth to the organization.

therefore unfair. To alleviate such concerns, it is important to select subject matter experts (SMEs) whom employees trust and to clearly communicate how the job evaluation process will unfold. Common SMEs include job incumbents, supervisors of job incumbents, and internal or external compensation experts. Among the prominent approaches for conducting a job evaluation are the ranking method, classification method, and point-factor method.

The ***ranking method*** is perhaps the fastest and simplest way to perform a job evaluation, especially when there is a relatively small number of jobs.[30] Although it is less rigorous than the point-factor and factor-comparison methods, the ranking method captures the essence of what it means to order jobs by relative worth to create a job structure. In the ranking method, a team of SMEs evaluates the job descriptions and specifications for a selection of jobs and orders them in terms of their relative contribution to the organization's strategic objectives and mission. The results of the ranking process yield a job structure. However, the ranking method often lacks clear criteria for determining why and how jobs were ranked in a particular order, which can lead to (perceptions of) bias. Moreover, the ranking method provides an ordering of jobs based on their relative worth but does not indicate how much more one job is worth relative to another.

The ***classification method*** differs from the ranking method in that discrete classification levels—each comprising one or more jobs—are developed in advance to cover different job types or levels within the organization. A written classification description is developed for each classification level, and based on its job description, each job is matched by SMEs to a classification level in which the classification description is most similar. Job descriptions, job specifications, and input from SMEs are used to develop each classification level and its classification description.

Like a job description, classification descriptions are developed for each classification level to describe the work content covered. Typically, each classification description includes specific criteria that provide guidance for determining which job belongs to a particular classification level. Although some jobs can be easily assigned to a classification level by comparing their respective descriptions, other jobs are more challenging because they may appear to be similar to two or more classification levels. Like the ranking method, the classification method does not necessarily provide any indication of how much more valuable jobs in one classification level are to jobs in another classification level.[31]

The ***point-factor method*** is a common job evaluation approach in organizations given its rigor and relative objectivity.[32] Like the other approaches, the point-factor method requires a team of SMEs, preferably including at least one person who is an internal or external compensation expert or consultant.

The point-factor method requires SMEs to identify compensable factors and to develop and apply scales and weights to the compensable factors. ***Compensable factors*** are the common

Ranking method A job evaluation approach in which subject matter experts evaluate the job descriptions and specifications for a selection of jobs and order them in terms of their relative contribution to the organization's strategic objectives and mission

Classification method A job evaluation approach in which a written classification description is developed for each classification level, and based on its job description, each job is matched by subject matter experts to a classification level where the classification description is most similar

Point-factor method A job evaluation approach in which a team of subject matter experts systematically identifies compensable factors and develops and applies scales and weights for compensable factors, ultimately resulting in points being assigned to different jobs to describe their relative worth

Compensable factors The common dimensions by which jobs vary in terms of worth to the organization

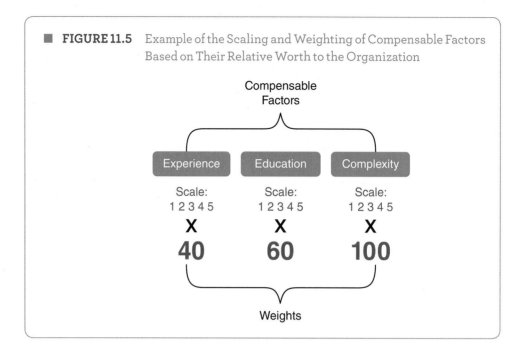

■ **FIGURE 11.5**   Example of the Scaling and Weighting of Compensable Factors Based on Their Relative Worth to the Organization

dimensions by which jobs vary in terms of worth to the organization. Examples of compensable factors might include the level of experience and education needed to do the job, the level of complexity inherent to the job, or even the danger and risk involved in performing the job. For instance, a job that requires an advanced degree and significant experience will pay more than an entry-level job requiring a high school degree, assuming education and experience are compensable factors. Further, compensable factors may vary in terms of their relative worth to the organization. For example, imagine the following three compensable factors: experience, education, and complexity. Based on its value to an organization, complexity might be weighted more heavily (100) than experience (40) and education (60), as is the case in the example provided in Figure 11.5.

The point-factor method earns its name by yielding a specific point value for each compensable factor for a given job based on the extent to which the job embodies each compensable factor. Further, this approach yields an overall point total for each job, such that the point total of one job can be compared to the point total of another job. As a result, this method results in a clear depiction of the relative worth of each job to the organization. Table 11.2 shows three benchmark jobs, where benchmark jobs are key jobs that are common across different organizations. Job #1 has the lowest overall point total and Job #3 has the highest. Look at the columns associated with the three compensable factors of experience, education, and complexity, and note that each job's relative worth is based on the level of each compensable factor required for performing the job. After scaling and applying weights to benchmark Jobs #1, #2, and #3, the same scales and weights can be applied to compute the points for nonbenchmark jobs. For a detailed explanation of the steps

TABLE 11.2   Example of Calculated Points for Benchmark Jobs Using the Point-Factor Method

BENCHMARK JOBS	COMPENSABLE FACTORS			
	EXPERIENCE	EDUCATION	COMPLEXITY	TOTAL
Job #1	200	60	200	**460**
Job #2	200	180	400	**780**
Job #3	200	300	500	**1000**

associated with a custom point-factor method, refer to Supplement 11.1.

Off-the-shelf point-factor method platforms exist for purchase, and one of the most famous is the Job Evaluation Manager by Hay Group (owned by Korn Ferry). The Job Evaluation Manager is often referred to as the Hay Plan or Hay System, and it scores each job based on three compensable factors: Know How, Accountability, and Problem Solving.[33]

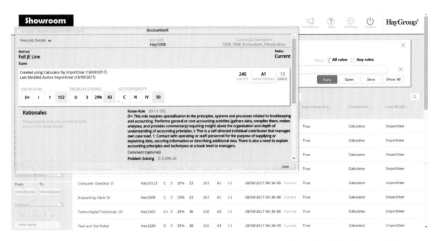

Example of Hay Group's Job Evaluation Manager point-factor method platform for the job of an accountant.

Ensuring External Equity

In addition to ensuring that jobs are internally aligned and internally equitable with respect to the job and pay structures, organizations should also establish a pay structure that is high in external equity. *External equity* (also known as *external competitiveness*) refers to the extent to which the pay for a particular job is competitive and fair relative to the pay of the same or similar jobs at other organizations.

In an ideal world, an organization would pay whatever it takes to attract, motivate, and retain top talent for each position; in actuality, such an approach would quickly exceed an organization's compensation budget. Nonetheless, in addition to considering what jobs are worth within the organization, an organization must also consider how competitors (i.e., the external labor market) are compensating similar jobs. As such, organizations must look to the external economic environment for guidance on how to pay people working in different jobs within the organization. This requires assessing the labor market and product market.

External equity The extent to which the pay for a particular job is competitive and fair relative to the pay of the same or similar jobs at other organizations

Labor market The availability of talent outside of an organization, which can be viewed through the lens of talent supply and demand

Labor Market

The *labor market* refers to the availability of talent outside of an organization, which can be viewed through the lens of talent supply and demand. Briefly, talent supply and demand are influenced by the unemployment rate, changes in technology, competition, shifts in populations, and various other factors. When talent supply exceeds talent demand, a talent surplus exists. Under talent surplus conditions, an organization will have more leeway when it comes to attracting and retaining talented individuals using pay, as employment opportunities for those in the labor pool are scarcer. Thus, employers may opt to pay employees less. Alternatively, when talent supply falls below talent demand, a talent shortage exists. Under talent shortage conditions, an organization may opt to pay more relative to competitors to ensure that they attract talented individuals from the more competitive market.

In September 2017, teachers on San Juan Island in Washington negotiated a new contract to receive more competitive pay relative to other teachers in other school systems. They argued that external equity was important for attraction and retention.[34]

Product market The final sale of products and services in the marketplace

Product Market

In addition to the labor market, an organization must consider the *product market*, which refers to the final sale of products and services in the marketplace. If an organization pays its workers more than competitors, it will likely have to charge more for the products or services it sells, and as a result, the organization may be less competitive in the marketplace. Selling fewer products or services may result in reduced revenue and profit, which can ultimately limit the budget for acquiring and retaining talent through pay. Accordingly, an organization must carefully consider how much it pays workers.

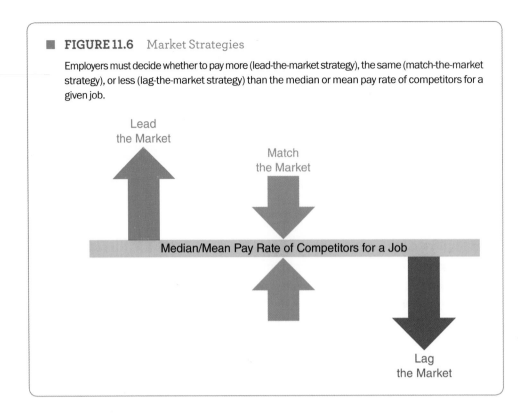

■ **FIGURE 11.6**   Market Strategies

Employers must decide whether to pay more (lead-the-market strategy), the same (match-the-market strategy), or less (lag-the-market strategy) than the median or mean pay rate of competitors for a given job.

Lead
the Market

Match
the Market

Median/Mean Pay Rate of Competitors for a Job

Lag
the Market

Market Strategies

By considering both the labor market and product market, an organization is poised to make a better decision when it comes to determining whether to lead, match, or lag the market for a given job (see Figure 11.6). A lead-the-market strategy occurs when an organization pays individuals with a given job more than competitors pay for those with the same or similar job. (*More* is typically defined as being above the mean or median market pay rate for that job.) A match-the-market strategy involves paying individuals about the same as the average competitor. A lag-the-market strategy means paying individuals less than the average competitor. Often, organizations enact a mixed-market position, which means that they choose to lead the market for some jobs and match or lag for others. So how do organizations determine whether they lead, match, or lag the market? The answer lies in market reviews.

Market Reviews

Market review The process of collecting pay data for benchmark jobs from other organizations

A *market review* is the process of collecting pay data for benchmark jobs from other organizations. As described previously, a benchmark job refers to a key job that is common across organizations and has more or less the same job description across organizations. Examples of benchmark jobs include: electrical engineer, psychiatrist, and customer service representative. Ultimately, the data collected by reviewing benchmark jobs can be combined with an organization's job structure data to create a pay structure that includes benchmark and nonbenchmark jobs alike.

Often, a market review is conducted with the help of a third-party survey company that collects pay data confidentially from employers or employees; sometimes these are referred to as *salary surveys* or *market surveys*. There are three primary sources of market review data:

- A *traditional survey* typically collects data from employers and is conducted by a government agency or professional organization. In some instances, access to survey data may be free. A traditional survey can provide important insights into the pay practices of other organizations, but sometimes it will lack the necessary level of specificity. For example, some traditional surveys report pay rates only at the national

TABLE 11.3 Example of Market Review Data for the Job of a Certified Nursing Assistant

DESCRIPTIVE STATISTICS (FOR SAMPLE OF ORGANIZATIONS)	BASE SALARY (MONTHLY)	BASE PAY (ANNUAL)	VARIABLE PAY (ANNUAL)	TOTAL CASH COMPENSATION (ANNUAL)	BENEFITS (ANNUAL)	TOTAL COMPENSATION (ANNUAL)	NUMBER OF ORGANIZATIONS	SAMPLE SIZE	MEAN WEEKLY HOURS
Mean	$2,833	$33,996	$0	$33,996	$5,456	$39,452	221	11,050	40
25th Percentile	$2,189	$26,268	$0	$26,268	$5,244	$31,512			
Median	$2,728	$32,736	$0	$32,736	$5,399	$38,135			
75th Percentile	$3,245	$38,940	$0	$38,940	$5,512	$44,452			

level, making it impossible to drill down to specific regions or organization types. In the United States, the Department of Labor provides wage and salary information through Bureau of Labor Statistics reports, which are publicly available. In addition, the Department of Labor sponsors the website CareerOneStop (careeronestop.com), which reports national- and state-level pay data for more than 900 benchmark jobs and links to O*NET (ONETonline.org). Other traditional surveys include those collected by WorldatWork, which charges a fee for accessing the results of such surveys.

- A *customized survey* collects pay data from employers in a more targeted manner to achieve higher accuracy and specificity. It is often administered by an external compensation consulting firm or an internal compensation or HR team and can be designed to focus on pay in a specific local job market where an organization is located (e.g., Silicon Valley). Further, depending on how dynamic the industry is, customized surveys may be conducted frequently to gather fresh data.

- A *web-based platform* typically collects data directly from employees via a website and offers up-to-date pay data, often for a fee.[35] Examples include Salary.com, PayScale .com, and SalaryExpert.com.

Regardless of the source, based on samples of participating employers or employees, most market reviews yield important pay information regarding the mean or median pay level for a particular benchmark job as well as the 25th and 75th percentiles, as shown for the job of a certified nursing assistant in Table 11.3. In addition, market review sources often collect and report information about the organizations to which the jobs belong. Information might include geographic location, industry, size, and type (e.g., for-profit, not-for-profit, private, public). This additional information allows market review users to drill down to pay information for benchmark jobs at a more granular level. For example, imagine a small critical outreach hospital with 25 beds located in a rural area in which the compensation analyst seeks pay information for the benchmark job of a registered nurse. If the compensation analyst were to identify the median pay rate for *all* registered nurses, regardless of hospital size and geographic location (e.g., rural, suburban, urban), then the median pay rate might not be an accurate representation of the market rate paid by small critical outreach hospitals in rural areas. Instead, the compensation analyst would be better off identifying the median pay level just for those hospitals located in rural areas with 10 to 50 beds.

Using the pay information generated from market reviews, an organization can reasonably compare its own pay practices for benchmark jobs with the pay practices for the same or similar benchmark jobs from other organizations to determine whether they are leading, meeting, or lagging the market. To ensure that market review survey data are accurate, it is important to match job descriptions, apply an aging factor, and apply survey weights.

Pay and Human Resource Information Systems

To design a competitive, externally equitable pay structure, an organization must obtain or access information about other organizations' pay practices. Traditionally, a consortium of organizations would subscribe to a third-party market survey and submit pay data confidentially, and in return, the organizations would receive a hard copy or an electronic copy of the survey results.

Today, some enterprise resource planning and HR information system vendors offer integrative solutions that reveal how well an organization is paying certain benchmark positions in relation to similar positions at other organizations. Both ADP and PayScale, for example, provide cloud-based software that facilitates the process by which organizations participate in market surveys, as well as off-the-shelf analytics and data visualizations for decision-making purposes.

Further, ADP leverages existing client pay information across different jobs to provide automated data analytics and visualizations, including information about pay equity related to race and sex. These advances place more pay information at the fingertips of key decision makers. Particularly in the case of pay equity data about protected groups (e.g., race, sex), however, organizations should think carefully about which employees are permitted to access pay equity data, and it is advisable that legal counsel be involved when analyzing any data that could reveal pay differences between protected groups.[36]

Match Job Descriptions

To conduct an effective market review, it is important to have up-to-date job descriptions available for benchmark jobs. Although market review sources often use similar job titles, sometimes the job descriptions vary across industries or between geographic areas. Alternatively, some jobs may have very different job titles but very similar job descriptions. As such, an accurate job description allows for the matching of an organization's benchmark job with the job description provided on a market review survey. Although this may sound like a straightforward process, the job descriptions included for market review surveys can vary from one sentence to a paragraph in length.

As a result, subject matter expertise in the jobs at hand and critical thinking skills are often required when comparing job descriptions to determine if the pay information from a market review source is an appropriate match. As an illustration of this issue, consider Table 11.4, which provides the job descriptions for a licensed practical nurse from CareerOneStop.com and Salary.com. First, note how CareerOneStop.com provides alternative job titles (*licensed practical nurse* and *licensed vocational nurse*), whereas Salary.com provides just the job title of *licensed practical nurse*. Second, note how the job descriptions provided by these two market review sources are very different in length and level of detail. Now imagine that your company completed a recent job analysis for the job of a licensed practical nurse, which yielded a job description that is specific to your organization. The challenge becomes determining whether the benchmark job as defined by a particular market review source matches your own job description.

Repeating the matching process for all benchmark jobs allows an organization to judge how competitive its pay is compared to competitors or other organizations in the industry. Table 11.5 shows a fictitious example of median monthly base pay rates pulled from three different market review surveys for benchmark jobs from the nursing job family.

Apply Aging Factor

After matching job descriptions and pulling market pay rates for benchmark jobs, it is often wise to "age" the pay data because (a) they were collected at some point in the past and (b) decisions based on the pay data will be implemented in the future. *Aging (of pay data)* refers to a process

Aging (of pay data) A process whereby previously collected market pay data are adjusted and updated based on market changes due to merit-based increases, cost-of-living adjustments, and other factors that affect pay

TABLE 11.4   Job Descriptions From Two Market Review Sources for the Job of a Licensed Practical Nurse[37]

MARKET REVIEW SOURCE	Careeronestop.com	Salary.com
JOB TITLE	Licensed practical and licensed vocational nurses	Licensed practical nurse
JOB DESCRIPTION	"Care for ill, injured, or convalescing patients or persons with disabilities in hospitals, nursing homes, clinics, private homes, group homes, and similar institutions. May work under the supervision of a registered nurse. Licensing required."	"Administers nursing care under the supervision of a registered nurse or other medical supervisor. Provides basic medical care, including changing bandages, administering medication, and collecting specimens. Ensures the health, comfort, and safety of patients by assisting with bathing, feeding, and dressing. Monitors and reports changes in patient's condition to supervisor. Requires graduation from approved LPN educational program. Requires a state license to practice. Years of experience may be unspecified. Certification and/or licensing in the position's specialty is the main requirement."

TABLE 11.5   Example of Market Review Data for the Nursing Job Family

	MEDIAN MONTHLY PAY RATE		
JOB TITLE	SURVEY 1	SURVEY 2	SURVEY 3
Certified Nursing Assistant (CNA)	$2,728	$2,216	$2,688
Licensed Practical Nurse (LPN)	$4,042	$3,674	$3,992
Registered Nurse (RN)	$6,078	$5,704	$5,947
Charge Nurse (CN)	$7,205	$6,845	$7,033
Nurse Practitioner (NP)	$8,928	$8,409	$8,771
Nursing Manager (NM)	$9,035	$8,722	$8,995
Nursing Director (ND)	$12,138	$10,038	$11,954

whereby the analyst identifies when the pay data were originally collected and then weights the data based on the expected change in the market pay rates resulting from merit-based increases, cost-of-living adjustments, and other factors that affect pay. For example, imagine that the pay data from Survey 1 in Table 11.5 were collected 10 months ago, and your team decides to age the data to 1 month in the future when the pay structure is expected to be implemented. Your team uses the following process to calculate and apply the aging factor:

1. Using a merit budget factor from a survey vendor like WorldatWork, you determine that the annual market movement rate is 2.5%.

2. Because the market movement rate represents an annual rate, you divide 2.5% by 12 to get a monthly rate of .002 (.025/12 = .002).

3. Because Survey 1 data were collected 10 months ago and you wish to forecast 1 month into the future, you will age the data by 11 months (10 + 1 = 11).

4. You multiply the monthly rate of .002 by 11 months to determine the aging factor for the 11-month period for which you are aging the data, and the resulting product is .022 or 2.2% ($.002 \times 11 = .022$).

5. Given that the market is forecasted to grow (and not decline), you add 1 to .022, which equals 1.022 ($1 + .022 = 1.022$), and this value reflects the aging factor.

6. Using the pay data for a licensed practical nurse from Survey 1 (Table 11.5), you apply the aging factor to the median monthly pay rate of $4,042. To do so, you multiply the aging factor by the median monthly pay rate, which yields $4,131 ($1.022 \times \$4,042 = \$4,131$).

7. Finally, you apply the aging factor to each of the median monthly pay rates for the remaining benchmark jobs found in Table 11.5 and then repeat this process for pay rates from Survey 2 and Survey 3.

Apply Survey Weights

Often, it is a best practice to use more than one market review survey to help account for sampling error in any one survey. That is, it is unlikely that any given survey obtained perfectly accurate pay data for the entire population of relevant jobs; rather, each survey collects pay data for a sample of jobs from the underlying population, which inevitably leads to sampling error, as a sample is unlikely to perfectly represent the population. In some cases, an organization may choose to apply different weights to each survey source based on how many organizations were included in the sample or based on the relative rigor used by each survey source. Using market review data from Table 11.5 as an example, you might decide to weight Survey 1 at 50% due to its higher rigor and larger sample and weight both Survey 2 and Survey 3 at 25%. For the sake of explanation, let us assume that the data presented in Table 11.5 have already been aged. Using this weighting scheme, you can compute the average median monthly pay rate for the job of a nurse practitioner in the following manner:

$$(\$8,928 \times .50) + (\$8,409 \times .25) + (\$8,771 \times .25) = \$8,759$$

As you can see, the median pay rate from Survey 1 carries more weight (50% or .50), which means it yields a larger contribution to the overall weighted average value of $8,759. Finally, in some instances, a sample-weighted average may be computed for each job from each market review source, assuming sample size is reported. This allows for the analyst to account for sampling error in a more direct manner. Finally, refer to Figure 11.7 for a summary of how to match job descriptions, apply the aging factor, and apply survey weights.

■ **FIGURE 11.7**   Process of Gathering and Preparing Market Review Data

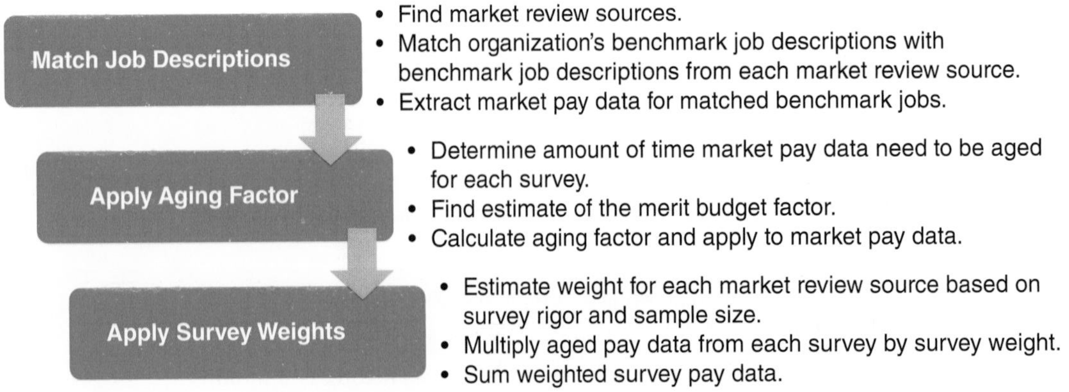

Match Job Descriptions
- Find market review sources.
- Match organization's benchmark job descriptions with benchmark job descriptions from each market review source.
- Extract market pay data for matched benchmark jobs.

Apply Aging Factor
- Determine amount of time market pay data need to be aged for each survey.
- Find estimate of the merit budget factor.
- Calculate aging factor and apply to market pay data.

Apply Survey Weights
- Estimate weight for each market review source based on survey rigor and sample size.
- Multiply aged pay data from each survey by survey weight.
- Sum weighted survey pay data.

Integrating Internal Equity and External Equity

So far, we have discussed internal equity and external equity separately; now we will explain how these two types of equity can be integrated to create a pay structure. Specifically, an organization can set the pay levels for all benchmark and nonbenchmark jobs by integrating the job structure data gathered during the job evaluation (internal equity) and the market pay data gathered from the market review (external equity). There are different ways to integrate job evaluation and market review data, and research has shown that compensation decision makers often place a greater emphasis on market review data as compared to job evaluation data; in other words, they tend to attribute more importance to external equity than to internal equity.[38] In fact, some organizations base their pay levels and pay structure directly on their competitors' pay levels and pay structures, a process that is referred to as ***market pricing***.[39]

For a balanced approach, an organization can use the point-factor method of job evaluation combined with market review data to determine how much a single point is worth in dollars. This information can be used to establish a market pay line and a pay policy line for both benchmark and nonbenchmark jobs. As a side note, more empirical research is needed to understand how to most effectively integrate internal and external factors when developing a pay structure and associated pay policies.[40]

Market pricing When an organization bases its pay levels and pay structure directly on its competitors' pay levels and pay structures

Market Pay Line

The ***market pay line*** reflects the relationship between the internal job structure of the organization for benchmark jobs—which is often represented in terms of job evaluation points—and the external pay practices of other organizations. To create a market pay line, we can use regression analysis. For example, using the data from Table 11.5, estimating the relationship between job evaluation points and *actual* market review pay rates results in the following regression equation:

Market pay line The relationship between the internal job structure of the organization for benchmark jobs and the external pay practices of other organizations

$$Monthly\ Base\ Pay\ (\$) = -8{,}988.99 + 19.71 \times Job\ Evaluation\ Points$$

In this equation, the Y-intercept (constant) is −8,988.99, and the slope (regression coefficient) is 19.71. The regression equation itself is a quantitative representation of the line-of-best-fit, and in this context, the line-of-best-fit represents the market pay line. Further, the R-squared value for the regression estimated equation is .98, which means that job evaluation points explain 98% of the variability in monthly base pay rates; in other words, the estimated market pay line closely fits the observed data. In Figure 11.8, the estimated market pay line is a solid black line; the jobs from

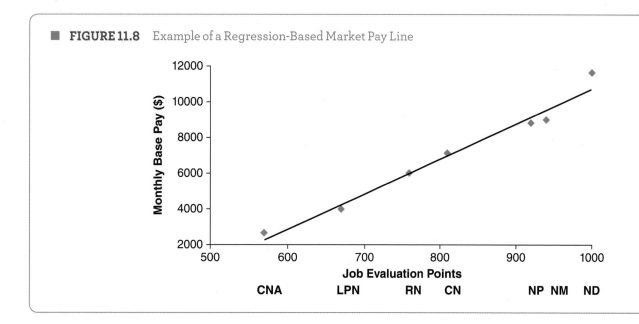

■ **FIGURE 11.8** Example of a Regression-Based Market Pay Line

the nursing job family and their respective job evaluation points are on the X-axis; the monthly base pay rates are on the Y-axis; and the blue diamonds represent the observed data on which the market pay line was derived. We can calculate the *predicted* market pay rates for each benchmark job in Table 11.5 by plugging their respective job evaluation points into the regression equation.

Assuming job evaluation points have been calculated for nonbenchmark jobs, the same regression equation can be used to calculate the market pay rates for nonbenchmark jobs. If a nonbenchmark job such as a nurse anesthetist received 920 job evaluation points, then that value can be entered into the regression equation to determine what a competitive monthly base pay would be. For the nurse anesthetist, this value is $9,144, which is calculated as follows:

$$\$9,144.21 = -8,988.99 + 19.71 \times 920$$

This process can be repeated for the remaining nonbenchmark jobs to calculate competitive market pay rates for all jobs in the job structure.

Pay Policy Line

Pay policy line Portrays an organization's operationalization of its market pay line, thereby representing how an organization translates information about its internal job structure and external pay rates of competitors into actionable pay practices

A **pay policy line** represents how an organization translates information about the internal job structure and external pay rates of competitors into actionable pay practices. One way to develop a pay policy line is to use the market pay line as a starting point. To do so, an organization specifies—depending upon its market strategy—whether it wants to pay above (lead), at (match), or below (lag) the market pay line. For instance, if the organization wants to pay 5% over the market pay line, the predicted market pay rates calculated from the market pay line regression equation are multiplied by 1.05 to realize the organization's strategy. For the nonbenchmark job of a nurse anesthetist, for which we determined that the predicted market pay rate is $9,144 per month, the 5% lead-the-market strategy results in a monthly pay rate of $9,601 ($9,144 × 1.05 = $9,601), which is called the pay policy rate. In Table 11.6, the pay policy rates are presented along with the predicted market pay rates and pay strategy factor from which they were derived.

Pay Grades

Pay grade A group of jobs with similar job evaluation point values that are then assigned common pay midpoint, minimum, and maximum values

A common practice is to establish pay grades based on the pay policy line. A **pay grade** represents a group of jobs with similar job evaluation point values that are then assigned common pay midpoint, minimum, and maximum values. Pay grades allow an organization to differentiate between employees holding the same job or similar jobs but who have different levels of performance, experience, or seniority. To create a pay grade, jobs with relatively similar job evaluation

TABLE 11.6 Job Evaluation Points, Actual Market Pay Rates, Predicted Market Pay Rates, and Pay Policy Line Pay Rates

JOB TITLE	JOB EVALUATION POINTS	ACTUAL MARKET PAY RATES	PREDICTED MARKET PAY RATES	PAY STRATEGY	PAY POLICY RATES (PREDICTED MARKET PAY RATES × PAY STRATEGY)
Certified Nursing Assistant (CNA)	570	$2,590	$2,246	+5%	$2,358
Licensed Practical Nurse (LPN)	670	$3,938	$4,217	+5%	$4,428
Registered Nurse (RN)	760	$5,952	$5,991	+5%	$6,290
Charge Nurse (CN)	810	$7,072	$6,976	+5%	$7,325
Nurse Practitioner (NP)	920	$8,759	$9,144	+5%	$9,601
Nursing Manager (NM)	940	$8,947	$9,538	+5%	$10,015
Nursing Director (ND)	1000	$11,567	$10,721	+5%	$11,257

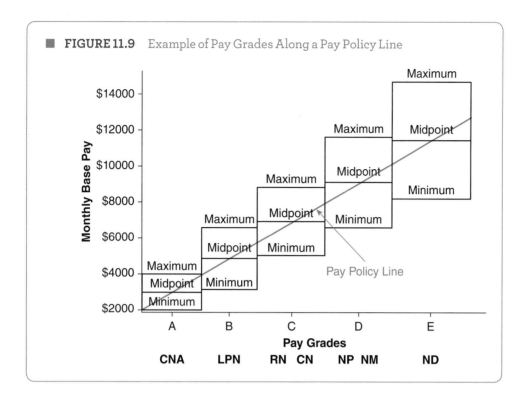

■ FIGURE 11.9 Example of Pay Grades Along a Pay Policy Line

points are grouped together. For example, the nurse practitioner and nursing manager jobs received 920 and 940 job evaluation points, respectively (as shown in Table 11.6), and thus they can be grouped together in a common pay grade. The pay policy rates for these two jobs are $9,601 and $10,015, respectively. To determine the pay grade midpoint, we might calculate the average of the two pay policy pay rates to arrive at $9,808:

$$\frac{\$9,601 + \$10,015}{2} = \$9,808$$

To establish the minimum and maximum values for the pay grade, market review data pertaining to the 25th and 75th percentiles for these two jobs can be used to set a floor and ceiling for the pay grade. Figure 11.9 shows five pay grades for the nursing job family, along with which jobs belong to which pay grade. Note how the pay policy line crosses the midpoint of each pay grade, as well as how different pay grades have different pay ranges, which reflects differences in their respective market-based minimum and maximum values.

Some organizations choose to use broadbanding instead of traditional pay grades. **Broadbanding** is the process of collapsing multiple pay grades into one large grade with a single minimum and maximum, resulting in fewer pay grades. Broadbanding may be used to complement **delayering**, the process by which the hierarchy in an organizational structure is reduced.[41] Broadbanding can be advantageous in certain industries and circumstances because it allows for more flexibility in terms of how managers make pay decisions, given the broad range of jobs within a band. In addition, broadbanding allows employees to move more easily across different functional areas while remaining in a single band. Like any pay policy, the decision to implement a pay structure using broadbanding should be based on the organization's strategy.

Broadbanding The process of collapsing multiple pay grades into one large grade with a single minimum and maximum, resulting in fewer pay grades

Delayering The process by which the hierarchy in an organizational structure is reduced

Ensuring Individual Equity

Once the pay structure and pay policies are in place, it is time to ensure that individual equity exists. **Individual equity** refers to the fairness of how pay is administered and distributed to individual employees working similar jobs within the same organization. For individual equity to exist, such

Individual equity The fairness of how pay is administered and distributed to individual employees working similar jobs within the same organization differences in pay rates should be attributable to differences in performance, seniority, and/or experience, as opposed to other factors that are not job related (e.g., race, sex). Using the minimum and maximum values of a pay grade or broadband as upper and lower limits, compensation analysts and/or managers can determine how much to compensate each individual employee. Individual equity will be higher when high-performing, more-senior, and more-experienced employees in a given pay grade are compensated at a higher rate than low-performing, less-senior, and less-experienced employees in the same pay grade.

Developing a Pay Structure in Small Organizations

Small businesses may lack employees or departments with dedicated expertise in reward and compensation system development, implementation, and administration. Further, when it comes to benchmark jobs, small businesses may find it unfeasible to compete with the pay rates of larger organizations. As such, they face unique challenges when it comes to determining what to pay employees. Fortunately, there are resources available through SHRM and websites like bls.gov, ONETonline.org, and CareerOneStop.org that provide guidance on how to develop internally equitable, externally equitable, individually equitable, and legal pay policies and practices.

Some small businesses may choose to outsource their pay administration function to an external vendor, or they might choose to hire external consultants who possess reward system expertise. In order to offer attractive and externally competitive compensation packages, some small businesses, such as start-ups, get creative by offering equity in the company or profit sharing.

Expatriates' and Host Country Nationals' Pay

Expatriates—also known as international assignees—are individuals who leave their home country to take an assignment in another country or the host country. In situations in which an expatriate takes an international assignment, they inevitably work side by side with host country nationals who are paid differently.

Understandably, concerns and conflicts can arise in situations in which two employees are performing ostensibly the same job but are earning markedly different incomes. Often, expatriates are paid using the *balance sheet approach*, in which the pay structure of expatriates is tied to that of their home countries, and additional pay in the form of allowances is provided to compensate for differences in living conditions and costs. The sometimes notably higher pay provided to expatriates can signal to host country nationals that the company values expatriates more, and this can lead to tension and perceptions of unfairness owing to an "us versus them" mindset, especially if the only identifiable difference between employees is their country of origin. Further, research has shown that, in general, the greater the difference in pay between expatriates and host country nationals, the greater the unfairness perceived by host country nationals.

As such, multinational companies should take steps to understand different host countries and to implement pay policies and practices that respond to host countries' cultural norms and values. Multinational companies can also set expectations for expatriates to contribute more in terms of professionalism, knowledge, and relationships with headquarters, thereby justifying their higher pay.[42]

Ensuring Legal Compliance

In addition to ensuring internal, external, and individual equity, a pay structure and the resulting pay policies, procedures, and practices should comply with federal, state, and local guidelines. In most cases, federal legislation is overseen and enforced by the Equal Employment Opportunity Commission (EEOC) or Office of Federal Contract Compliance Programs (OFCCP). Over the years, a number of pieces of congressional legislation and executive orders have shaped the pay landscape in the United States.

Fair Labor Standards Act

Enacted in 1938, the **_Fair Labor Standards Act (FLSA)_** introduced major provisions aimed at regulating overtime pay, minimum wage, hours worked, and recordkeeping. The FLSA covers nonexempt employees who work for organizations in which the annual gross volume of sales or business meets or exceeds $500,000 or those who are engaged in interstate commerce or in the production of goods for commerce. Hospitals, businesses providing nursing or medical services, schools, preschools, and government agencies are also covered by the law. Some exceptions to FLSA coverage include workers with disabilities, those who work in tipped employment, and full-time students.[43]

An important component of the FLSA is the distinction between exempt and nonexempt employees. The term **_exempt_** refers to those employees who do not fall under the purview of the minimum wage and overtime provisions, whereas the term **_nonexempt_** refers to those employees who are directly affected by the provisions. Although there has been a recent attempt to increase the salary requirements needed to be classified as exempt,[44] as it currently stands, to be classified as exempt, an employee must typically meet all three of the following tests:

- Earn $455 or more per week (which equals $23,660 per year);
- Receive a salary or charge a fee (and not an hourly wage);
- Perform exempt job duties.[45]

For more information on how to determine whether an employee should be classified as exempt, as well as what constitutes an exempt job duty, please refer to Supplement 11.2.

Overtime

The overtime provision of the FLSA mandates that organizations pay at least 1.5 times a nonexempt worker's regular pay for time worked beyond 40 hours in a week.[46] Those workers classified as exempt are not eligible for overtime. Some cities and states have passed legislation to augment the federal minimum. For instance, California includes a provision in which nonexempt workers who work more than 12 hours in a single day must be compensated with 2 times their regular pay. Consider enacting the following actions when administering overtime pay.[47]

- At the time of hire, clearly state the overtime policy.
- In the employee handbook, clearly describe the overtime policy.
- For all employees who are eligible for overtime, ensure that they are paid appropriately.
- Display an FLSA poster in the organization (e.g., in the break room) detailing the overtime provision and other provisions.
- At the very least, nonexempt employees are eligible for overtime at 1.5 times their regular pay should they work more than 40 hours in a week; however, be sure to check with your state and local legislation, as some states and cities offer more generous overtime provisions.

Fair Labor Standards Act (FLSA) Enacted in 1938, this act introduced major provisions aimed at regulating overtime pay, minimum wage, hours worked, and recordkeeping

Exempt A term that refers to those employees who do not fall under the purview of the minimum wage and overtime provisions

Nonexempt A term that refers to those employees who are directly affected by minimum wage and overtime provisions

Minimum Wage

The minimum wage provision of the FLSA establishes an income floor, thereby providing some protection to workers in terms of unfair pay practices and bringing workers closer to a livable wage. As of 2009, the federally mandated minimum wage was $7.25/hour,[48] which some have argued has not kept pace with inflation and the general cost of living. In response, some attempts have been made to increase the minimum wage for certain populations of workers. For example, in 2015, Executive Order 13658 introduced a $10.10/hour minimum wage for individuals working on federal contracts. Further, although cities and states are not permitted to establish a minimum wage that falls below the federal level, some cities and states have passed legislation to increase the minimum wage. For example, the minimum wage is $12.50/hour for the District of Columbia and $10.25/hour for Oregon.[49]

Hours Worked and Recordkeeping

In addition to minimum wage and overtime, the FLSA also defines what constitutes hours worked for nonexempt employees as well as what information is required for recordkeeping purposes. Regarding hours worked, the FLSA defines a number of key concepts relevant for determining how hours are counted and tracked, such as waiting time, on-call time, rest and meal periods, and travel time, to name a few.[50] As for recordkeeping, the FLSA requires that employers keep a record of nonexempt employees' names, addresses, birth dates (if younger than 19), sex, occupation, hours worked each day, regular hourly pay rate, overtime earnings, as

Employee Weekly Timesheet

Employee Name: Pay Period:
ID Number: Department:
Manager: Position Code:

Week 1

	Monday	Tuesday	Wednesday	Thursday	Friday	Saturday	Sunday
Time In							
Time Out							
Time In							
Time Out							
Reg. Hours							
Overtime							
Sick Time							
Vacation							
Total							

Week 2

	Monday	Tuesday	Wednesday	Thursday	Friday	Saturday	Sunday
Time In							
Time Out							
Time In							
Time Out							
Reg. Hours							
Overtime							
Sick Time							
Vacation							
Total							

Signature: _____   Date: _____

Shutterstock.com

The Fair Labor Standards Act mandates that employers track nonexempt employees' hours worked. Accurate recordkeeping ensures that nonexempt employees are paid correctly and receive overtime pay if more than 40 hours per week are accrued.

well as other information relevant to pay.[51] It should be noted that many modern HR information systems facilitate the tracking of these data and that employers must retain these data for at least 3 years.

Executive Order 11246

The issuing of **Executive Order 11246** by President Lyndon B. Johnson in 1965 expanded the protections for different forms of employment discrimination—such as employee pay—to include employers with federal contracts or subcontracts in excess of $10,000.[52] The executive order reflected the federal government's increased focus on discrimination-related issues, including pay discrimination. In an effort to prevent pay discrimination by increasing pay transparency, in 2015, the OFCCP revised Executive Order 11246 to clarify that individuals—job applicants or employees—who discuss pay may not be discriminated against or discharged by a federal contractor.[53]

Executive Order 11246 An executive order issued by President Lyndon B. Johnson that expanded the protections for different forms of employment discrimination—such as pay-based discrimination—to include employers with federal contracts or subcontracts in excess of $10,000

National Labor Relations Act

Enacted in 1935, the **National Labor Relations Act (NLRA)** includes a provision related to pay transparency. Specifically, Section 7 of the NLRA stipulates that employees protected under the act have a right to discuss pay as part of activities related to collective bargaining and protection, thereby providing an avenue through which employees may uncover pay discrimination.[54] In terms of coverage, most private-sector employees are protected under the NLRA; however, NLRA coverage specifically *excludes* public-sector employees, including individuals who work for federal, state, and local governments, as well as those employed as independent contractors or agricultural workers.

National Labor Relations Act (NLRA) Enacted in 1935, this act stipulates that employees protected under the act have a right to discuss pay as part of activities related to collective bargaining and protection

Internal Revenue Code

In addition to complying with antidiscrimination and fair-pay practices laws, employers and employees must also adhere to tax laws. The **Internal Revenue Code** of 1986 stipulates income and payroll tax regulations.[55] On the one hand, taxpayers, which include individual employees and business entities, must pay income taxes, which are based on the amount of income or profits earned. On the other hand, employers must pay payroll taxes, which are based on how much employers pay their employees. Additional income and payroll taxes may be imposed by local and state governments.

Internal Revenue Code Stipulates income and payroll tax regulations

---

SPOTLIGHT ON LEGAL ISSUES

Pay Discrimination at Checkers Restaurant

The Equal Pay Act of 1963 and Title VII of the Civil Rights Act of 1964 prohibit pay discrimination based on sex. Differences in pay between men and women are permitted only if they are based on seniority, merit, quantity or quality of production, or some factor other than sex. When an organization is suspected of paying men and women at different rates for performing equal work, the Equal Employment Opportunity Commission (EEOC) can step in to investigate the employment practices and sue the organization in question.

In 2013, the EEOC did just that when it sued Market Burgers, LLC—the company that operates Checkers fast-food restaurants—for pay discrimination. The EEOC alleged that male cashiers/sandwich makers and shift managers at a Checkers in West Philadelphia, Pennsylvania, were paid systematically more than their female counterparts who performed equal work. The EEOC suit also alleged that male workers were often scheduled more than 30 hours a week, whereas female workers were scheduled between 20 to 25 hours; thus, male workers in these positions had greater opportunities to work more hours to earn a larger paycheck.

In 2014, Market Burgers, LLC, settled the EEOC suit by agreeing to pay $100,000, matching female workers' wages to those of male workers performing equal work, and providing workers with training on pay discrimination and compliance with the Equal Pay Act and Title VII.[56]

LO 11.4   Identify basic principles underlying person-based pay structures.

Person-based pay structures   A pay structure that emphasizes individuals' unique competencies or skills when determining pay, such that a person who possesses a particular competency or skill receives additional pay

Person-Based Pay Structures

The chapter focus thus far has been on job-based pay structures, wherein pay rates are determined by the content of the job that a person occupies. In contrast, ***person-based pay structures*** emphasize individuals' unique competencies or skills when determining pay, such that a person who possesses a particular competency or skill receives additional pay.[57]

Person-based structures offer organizations greater agility when managing work flow, as those with certain competencies or skills are matched with appropriate tasks and paid accordingly. In doing so, organizations can avoid the rigidity of job-based structures in which employees are rewarded only for performing the tasks outlined in their job description, even if they possess competencies and skills that may contribute to task completion beyond their prescribed job. Further, job-based pay structures compensate employees who perform the same job relatively uniformly, even if some individuals lack proficiency in certain aspects of their job. Research has shown that person-based pay structures are linked to greater production quality and quantity, lower labor costs, greater individual skill change, and better attitudes.[58] However, compensating employees based on the skills or competencies they possess does not necessarily mean they are applying a particular skill or competency with regularity (or even at all). As such, it is important to make sure employees actually apply the skills or competencies for which they are being rewarded.

LO 11.5   Describe the philosophy and challenges of executive pay structures.

Executive Pay

During the financial crisis of 2008, executive pay became a popular topic of conversation, as greater attention was paid to the often-large pay discrepancies between company CEOs and the average worker. This discrepancy between CEO pay and average worker pay is called pay dispersion, or a pay gap, and has direct implications for perceptions of internal equity. In addition to costing companies a lot of money, large pay dispersions related to CEOs and other executive positions have been shown to have negative implications for short- and long-term company performance.[59] Yet over the years, the pay gap between CEOs and average workers has continued to rise in the United States, which led to the Dodd-Frank Wall Street Reform and Consumer Protection Act of 2010, which requires all publicly listed companies to report pay dispersion between the CEO and the average employee.[60]

Recent evidence has shown that U.S. CEOs earn 354 times more than the average unskilled worker.[61] In general, larger companies, companies with more board members, and companies with more independent board members tend to compensate their CEOs at higher rates.[62] Further, some companies weigh market review data heavily when creating their executive compensation packages, which ensure high levels of external equity but not necessarily internal equity.[63] The reasons for such large pay dispersions also have to do with the fact that CEO pay has outpaced average-worker pay over the past 4 decades. After adjusting for inflation, CEO pay grew by 937% from 1978 to 2013, whereas average-worker pay grew by just 10.2% over that same time period.[64] This imbalance can be attributed, in part, to record-breaking company profits, resulting in corresponding gains in the stock market for publicly traded companies. Because CEOs often receive a sizeable proportion of their total compensation from stock options and other ownership programs, they stand to benefit tremendously from profit gains.

Regardless of which factors drive executive pay, employee perceptions of fairness play an important role. If executives are paid exorbitant sums compared to the average employee, employees and other stakeholders may perceive the system as unjust and internally inequitable. Some local governments have taken steps to address organizations with large pay gaps between their CEOs and employees. For example, in 2017, the City Council of Portland, Oregon, voted to introduce a 10% surtax on organizations in which CEO pay is 100 times greater than the median pay of employees and a 25% surtax on organizations in which CEO pay is 250 times greater.[65]

Marc Lore, CEO, U.S. e-commerce for Walmart Stores Inc., was the most highly compensated CEO in the United States in 2016 and was awarded nearly $237 million in total compensation. His base salary was approximately $350,000, but the bulk of his total compensation came from his bonus and acquisition awards, which totaled $236.5 million.[66]

Pay Administration

Once a pay structure and policies have been designed, an organization must implement and administer them. When it comes to pay administration, there are a number of issues to consider. Here the chapter focuses on the following issues: pay compression and inversion, adherence to pay policies, and pay transparency and secrecy.

Pay Compression and Inversion

Pay compression and inversion can occur when a pay structure is strongly influenced by prevailing market pay practices, particularly when growth in the external market pay practices outpaces growth in an organization's internal pay practices. On the one hand, ***pay compression*** refers to one of two situations within a single organization: (a) a more recently hired employee with less experience earns nearly as much or the same as a more experienced, longer-tenured employee in the same job or (b) an employee in a lower-level job earns nearly as much or the same as another employee in a higher-level job, the latter of whom might even be the supervisor of the employee performing the lower-level job.[67] On the other hand, ***pay inversion*** constitutes a more severe form of compression and occurs when a newer, less-experienced employee in a given job earns (a) *more* than another, more-experienced employee in the same job or (b) *more* than another employee in a higher-level job. As an illustration of pay inversion, consider the following scenario: Julie was hired as a software engineer 3 years ago at an annual salary of $100,000/year, and since she was hired, Julie has received exceptional performance reviews. Over the past 3 years, an external labor shortage emerged for software engineers, which resulted in organizations offering increasingly higher salaries to attract talented individuals. As a result, the organization hired Carlos, who has the same qualifications as Julie except for fewer years of on-the-job experience, yet his starting salary was $120,000/year, which is an inversion of $20,000/year in favor of Carlos. Understandably, widespread compression and inversion may negatively impact employees' perceptions of pay-system fairness. Further, pay compression and inversion are indicative of low individual equity.

Pay compression Occurs when more recently hired employees with less experience earn nearly as much or the same as more experienced, longer-tenured employees in the same job or when employees in a lower-level job earn nearly as much or the same as employees in a higher-level job

Pay inversion A more severe form of pay compression that occurs when a newer, less-experienced employee in a given job earns more than another, more-experienced employee in the same job or more than another employee in a higher-level job

Adherence to Pay Policies

Evidence of pay compression and inversion may indicate that an organization is failing to adhere to the pay policies and pay structure that are in place. An HR metric called the compa-ratio can be a useful source of information when evaluating an organization's adherence to its pay policies. The ***compa-ratio*** reflects how much employees are actually paid for a given job or pay grade as compared to the espoused pay structure and policies and thus can be used to assess whether systematic compression or inversion is occurring.[68] The compa-ratio is a useful metric for identifying the extent to which an organization is adhering to the pay policies and pay structure. To calculate the compa-ratio, simply divide the average pay for employees in a given job or pay grade by the pay range or grade.

Compa-ratio A ratio that reflects how much employees are actually paid for a given job or pay grade as compared to the espoused pay structure and policies and thus can be used to assess whether systematic compression or inversion are occurring

$$Compa\text{-}Ratio\ for\ a\ Group\ of\ Employees = \frac{Average\ Actual\ Pay\ of\ Employees}{Midpoint\ of\ Pay\ Range\ or\ Grade}$$

A compa-ratio value of 1.00 indicates that employees are paid, on average, at the midpoint of their pay range or grade, which reflects that pay practices generally adhere to pay policies. A compa-ratio value that is greater than 1.00 indicates that, on average, employees are paid more than the midpoint of their pay range or grade, which may indicate, for example, that competitive market pay rates are growing faster than expected, and thus the pay policies and pay structure need to be updated accordingly. Conversely, a compa-ratio value that is less than 1.00 indicates that, on average, employees are paid less than the midpoint of their pay range or grade, which

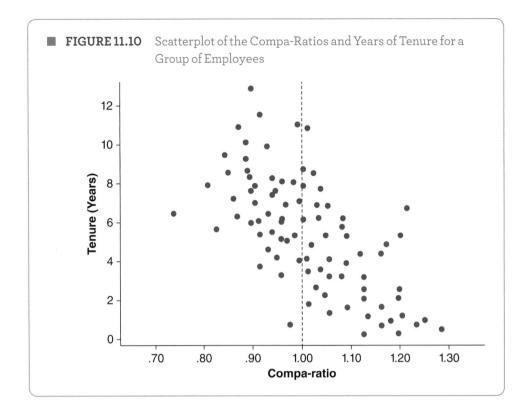

■ **FIGURE 11.10**   Scatterplot of the Compa-Ratios and Years of Tenure for a Group of Employees

indicates employees' pay may need to be upwardly adjusted to adhere to the pay policies, if the pay policy strategy of the organization is to match or lead the market.

A compa-ratio can also be calculated for individual employees by dividing the individual's pay by the midpoint of the pay range or grade to which they belong.

$$Compa\text{-}Ratio \; for \; One \; Employee = \frac{Actual \; Pay \; of \; Employee}{Midpoint \; of \; Pay \; Range \; or \; Grade}$$

Calculating the compa-ratios for individual employees can be a useful practice for detecting pay compression and inversion, especially when information about employee tenure is taken into consideration. For example, consider the scatterplot presented in Figure 11.10 in which individual employees' compa-ratios are plotted in relation to their tenure. Note that compa-ratio is on the X-axis, tenure is on the Y-axis, and each circle represents a single employee. If the organization's policy is to pay more-tenured employees at higher rates than less-tenured employees, then the scatterplot reveals that the organization's actual pay practices depart dramatically from that espoused policy. In this example, employees with the shortest tenure tend to have the highest compa-ratios, which indicate that more recent newcomers to the organization earn notably higher wages than the midpoint of their pay range. The opposite appears to be true for employees with longer tenures in the organization. For these reasons, this scatterplot is illustrative of pay compression and inversion.

Pay Transparency and Secrecy

Pay transparency and secrecy have emerged as important yet controversial topics. **Pay transparency** refers to the extent to which an organization communicates pay information and the extent to which employees are permitted to discuss pay with each other; the term is sometimes called *pay openness.*[69] In contrast, **pay secrecy** refers to the extent to which an organization has policies and practices aimed at suppressing the communication and exchange of pay information.

Pay transparency The extent to which an organization communicates pay information and the extent to which employees are permitted to discuss pay with each other

Pay secrecy The extent to which an organization has policies and practices aimed at suppressing the communication and exchange of pay information

On the one hand, proponents of pay transparency argue that making pay information publicly available is an important step in reducing the sex and race/ethnicity earnings gaps and in preventing discriminatory pay practices. Estimates from a 2018 Bureau of Labor Statistics report indicate that U.S. full-time women workers earned $0.81 for every $1.00 that full-time men workers earned; although this is an improvement over the 1979 $0.62-to-$1.00 ratio, a relatively wide gap still exists.[70] Regarding race/ethnicity, African-American/Black and Hispanic/Latino workers earned $0.75 and $0.74, respectively, for every $1.00 White workers earned, whereas White workers earned $0.84 for every $1.00 Asian workers earned.[71]

On the other hand, opponents of pay transparency argue that while publicly communicating pay information may reduce discriminatory pay practices, it may also put the organization at risk, as it may lead to dissatisfaction, lower productivity, and turnover. It is argued that public pay information may challenge workers' sense of worth and contribution to the organization; if they view themselves as top performers but learn they earn less than others, they may initiate thoughts of leaving the organization or decreasing performance. Further, open pay communication may encourage workers to engage in more frequent social comparisons with each other.[72]

In the United States, pay transparency is required for only certain groups of employees and employers, yet some organizations voluntarily and publicly communicate pay information.

SPOTLIGHT ON ETHICS
Pay Transparency at Google

Pay transparency remains a very controversial topic, and Google has been part of that controversy due to allegations of discriminatory pay practices. In July 2015, a former Google employee named Erica Baker posted a series of tweets about an unofficial pay transparency spreadsheet intended to elucidate potentially discriminatory pay practices at Google. In the publicly available spreadsheet, Baker allowed current and former Google employees to post pay and demographic information, and as of 2017, approximately 1,200 U.S.-based Google employees had submitted pay data. Using pivot tables and other spreadsheet tools, people analyzed the spreadsheet data, which revealed potential evidence of systematic gender differences in pay.

Baker described in her tweets how some managers were not pleased with her pay transparency initiative. Despite this resistance, employees continued to post their pay data to the spreadsheet, and some Google employees even used data from the spreadsheet to argue for pay raises, according to Baker. After this became a national news story, a Google spokesperson critiqued the data in the spreadsheet, stating that the spreadsheet contained only a small, nonrepresentative sample of employees; further, she defended the rigorous pay-related analyses conducted at Google, citing that women at Google are paid 99.7% of what men are paid.

After the news broke, the U.S. Department of Labor began investigating evidence regarding Google's pay practices. By July 2017, however, the Department of Labor learned it would not gain complete access to a large sample of Google employees' data, which the government agency had initially requested. A judge ruled that the Department of Labor's request for employees' personal data (e.g., names, addresses) could put the employees at risk of identity theft should the data be hacked.

The employee-driven spreadsheet at Google highlights the importance of pay fairness and legal compliance. Pay transparency represents one approach for reducing pay disparities. By making pay data freely available to employees (and even to the public), some argue that more pressure will be placed on organizations to make fair, ethical, and legal pay decisions. Still, others offer the counterargument that pay transparency can actually cause more harm than good, leading to conflict between employees and managers and higher turnover rates.[73]

Questions

1. On the whole, which do you think is better for an organization and its employees: pay transparency or pay secrecy? Give reasons and examples to support your answer.

2. Explain how this example relates to ethics and what your own reactions to the information contained in the case are.

Section 7 of the National Labor Relations Act ensures that most private-sector employees have a right to discuss pay information, and this right extends to work-related discussions on social media (e.g., Facebook, Twitter).[74] According to the Department of Labor, only about half of U.S. workers are allowed to discuss pay with coworkers in their respective organizations.

Although many organizations choose to keep pay information secret, some have taken steps to communicate earnings data across jobs and levels of the organization. For example, Whole Foods Market IP, LP, gained a reputation for pay transparency based on its 1986 initiative in which the company made wage information available to all employees.[75] As a recent example, the tech company Salesforce.com, Inc. spent $3 million in 2015 to work toward gender pay parity across its 17,000 employees. The impetus for the change came when two employees, Cindy Robbins and Leyla Seka, alleged that the men were paid more than women in the company. In response, the company analyzed pay across different positions, and in instances in which earnings differed to a statistically significant extent between men and women, Salesforce elevated women's salaries. Further, Salesforce audited recruiting, leadership, and parental leave policies and practices, which can serve as root causes of the earnings gaps.[76]

Research on the effects of pay transparency has yielded mixed findings. For example, communicating pay information may lead to envy of those who are paid more but may also lead to better performance.[77] In sum, pay transparency may help reduce pay gaps between protected groups, but it may also lead to some negative consequences in the short term.

CHAPTER SUMMARY

Pay, or compensation, represents one type of formal reward. A reward system encompasses relational returns (e.g., recognition, challenging work) and total compensation, where the latter includes compensation (e.g., base pay, variable pay) and benefits (e.g., health insurance, income protection). An effective pay structure requires fairness in the form of internal, external, and individual equity, as well as legal compliance. Regarding internal equity, a rigorous job evaluation ensures that jobs are internally aligned, such that jobs are structured hierarchically in terms of worth. As for external equity, using a thorough market review, an organization can look to the pay practices of other peer organizations to determine whether its pay practices are externally competitive. Integrating the principles of internal equity and external equity offers an opportunity to create an internally aligned and externally competitive pay structure. Once a pay structure and associated policies are in place, an organization should maintain individual equity, such that differences in pay for individual employees working similar jobs within an organization are attributable to differences in performance, seniority, and/or experience, as opposed to other job-unrelated factors. Executive pay represents another important equity consideration, as executive pay tends to be much higher than that of the average worker, which can be controversial. Above all, a pay structure and associated pay policies should adhere to prevailing employment and labor laws, and care should be taken to ensure that pay is administered properly and fairly.

KEY TERMS

pay structure   367
reward system   367
relational returns   368
total compensation   368
compensation   368
benefits   368
equity theory   368
organizational justice theory   371
distributive justice   372

procedural justice   372
interactional justice   372
internal equity   374
job structure   374
job evaluation   374
ranking method   375
classification method   375
point-factor method   375
compensable factors   375

external equity   377
labor market   377
product market   377
market review   378
aging (of pay data)   380
market pricing   383
market pay line   383
pay policy line   384
pay grade   384

Visit **edge.sagepub.com/bauer** to help you accomplish your coursework goals in an easy-to-use learning environment.

- Master the learning objectives using key study tools
- Watch, listen, and connect with online multimedia resources

- Access mobile-friendly quizzes and flashcards to check your understanding

HR REASONING AND DECISION-MAKING EXERCISES

MINI-CASE ANALYSIS EXERCISE: COMPENSATION INVESTIGATION

Karyn is the compensation analyst for a large manufacturing company with 20,000 employees. In her role, Karyn has administrative rights for both the compensation and employee personal information databases, which allow her to access employees' pay data as well as demographic information like their names, sex, race, and age. In fact, using employees' unique IDs, she has the ability to link employees' rewards data with their personal data.

Lately, Karyn has begun to wonder whether the employees of different sexes, races, and ages are paid similarly. Based on her data analytics training, she knows that t-test and correlation analyses would allow her to investigate whether systematic pay differences exist between protected groups in general and whether systematic pay differences exist for specific jobs and pay grades more specifically.

Karyn recently asked you if she can investigate if systematic pay differences exist. As Karyn's manager, you must decide whether you will grant Karyn permission to run the requested analyses. How would you handle this situation?

1. Do you have any concerns about allowing Karyn to run the requested analyses? Why or why not?
2. Is there any other person or entity you would like to involve in the decision-making process? If so, who?
3. What would you advise Karyn to do regarding the analyses?

HR DECISION ANALYSIS EXERCISE: IS MARKET PRICING THE WAY TO GO?

Your company's current pay structure was developed using the point-factor method in conjunction with market review data. Following the lead of other companies in the industry, however, your CEO proposes that she would like to overhaul the current pay structure by using market pricing exclusively. Recall from this chapter that market pricing refers to the process of basing a pay structure (almost) entirely off of competitors' pay practices. The CEO declares that the overhauled pay structure will do a better job at attracting and retaining top talent, as pay will match or exceed that of competitors.

You are the vice president of HR at the company, and the CEO values your opinion on HR-related topics and issues. The CEO has asked you to evaluate her proposal and provide her with feedback.

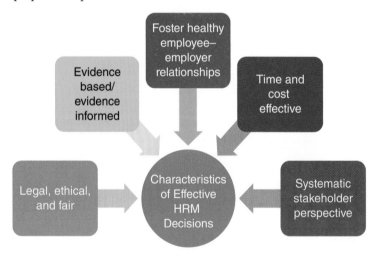

Should the organization overhaul the current pay structure using market pricing? Evaluate this decision using the following criteria.

Please provide the rationale for your answer to each of the questions below.

Is market pricing legal, ethical, and fair?

_____

_____

_____

Is it evidence based/evidence informed?

_____

_____

_____

Does it foster healthy employee–employer relationships?

_____

_____

_____

Is it time and cost effective?

_____

_____

_____

Does it take a systematic stakeholder perspective?

_____

_____

_____

Considering your analysis above, overall, do you think this would be an effective decision? Why or why not?

_____

_____

_____

What, if anything, do you think should be done differently or considered to help make this decision more effective?

_____

_____

_____

HR DECISION-MAKING EXERCISE: CONDUCTING A MARKET REVIEW

A video game company named Zenyah with 8,000 employees recently hired your consulting firm to develop a more externally equitable pay structure. Zenyah began as a start-up 10 years ago and has grown very rapidly ever since. Lately, the company has been having difficulty recruiting and selecting talented candidates for key software development, marketing, and sales jobs, which is likely due to the external labor shortage for individuals qualified for those jobs. As such, Zenyah has asked your consulting firm to conduct a market review for the following benchmark jobs:

- Computer programmer
- Systems software developer
- Applications software developer
- Market research analyst

- Marketing manager
- Advertising sales agent
- Advertising and promotions manager
- Sales representative

As part of the contract, Zenyah has requested that your consulting firm conduct new job analyses on the benchmark jobs, as it suspects that the job descriptions are out of date and inaccurate. As a starting point, you decide to use O*NET (ONETonline.org) to draft initial job description summaries that you can use to compare to the job description summaries that appear in the market review sources.

1. Using O*NET, write three- to five-sentence job description summaries for each benchmark job.

2. Using Salary.com and CareerOneStop.com as free market review sources, gather pay data for as many of the benchmark jobs as you can, and enter the data into a table. Be sure to match the job description summaries you created for Zenyah with the job description summaries in the market review sources to ensure you are making an appropriate comparison.

3. Imagine that the data in Salary.com and CareerOneStop.com were collected 1 month ago and need to be aged to 8 months from now. Use an annual aging factor of +3.5%.

4. Calculate the market-based pay midpoint for each of the benchmark jobs.

DATA AND ANALYTICS EXERCISE: EVALUATING PAY COMPRESSION

The compa-ratio can be a useful metric when investigating whether pay compression might be an issue for those employees who work the same job and thus belong to the same pay grade. For this exercise, you will calculate compa-ratios for individual employees using the following formula:

$$Compa\text{-}Ratio \ for \ One \ Employee = \frac{Actual \ Pay \ of \ Employee}{Midpoint \ of \ Pay \ Grade}$$

For example, if an employee earns $42,000/year and the midpoint of the employee's pay grade is $40,000, then the compa-ratio will be equal to 1.05 ($42,000/$40,000 = 1.05). Because this compa-ratio value is greater than 1.00, it indicates that the employee is paid more than the midpoint of the pay grade. If the compa-ratio had been less than 1.00, then it would have indicated that the employee was paid less than the midpoint of the pay grade. Now let's imagine that there are 100 total employees who work the same job, and we compute compa-ratios for each of them. In addition to each employee's compa-ratio, we also know the length of time (in years) that the employee has worked in that position (i.e., tenure). Using the compa-ratio and tenure variables, we can construct a scatterplot to understand how these employees are compensated relative to their length of tenure.

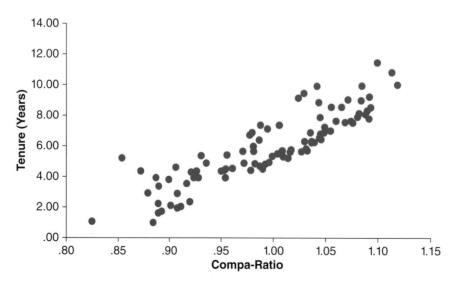

The scatterplot indicates that employees with higher compa-ratios tend to have worked in the job more years. In other words, there does not appear to be evidence of pay compression, as individuals who have worked fewer years in the job tend to earn less pay relative to the midpoint than those who have worked more years.

 EXCEL EXTENSION: NOW YOU TRY!

- On **edge.sagepub.com/bauer**, you will find an Excel exercise on evaluating pay compression.

- First, you will compute the compa-ratios for groups of employees who work the same job.

- Second, you will construct a scatterplot to visualize the relationship between the compa-ratio and tenure variables.

- Third, you will evaluate whether there is evidence of pay compression.

CHAPTER 11 SUPPLEMENT 11.1: STEPS FOR USING THE POINT-FACTOR METHOD[78]

Step 1: Perform job analyses for benchmark jobs

As the first step, conduct rigorous job analyses for all benchmark jobs, where benchmark jobs refer to key jobs in the organization, often ones that are common in the industry. If it is determined that relatively recent, rigorous job analyses have been conducted for benchmark jobs, then the resulting job analysis data—including tasks, duties, responsibilities, KSAOs, and/or competencies—can be fed into the following step.

Step 2: Identify the compensable factors

For the second step, a team of subject matter experts evaluates the content of the benchmark jobs and identifies common factors by which all jobs in the organization can be compared and evaluated, which are referred to as compensable factors. For example, as shown in Figure 11.S1, from the job analysis data, the subject matter experts may determine that all benchmark jobs vary along the continua of three compensable factors: experience, education, and complexity. Ideally, the compensable factors should address the skill, effort, responsibility, and work conditions required to complete each job, as these criteria are the basis for legally defensible differences in pay according to the Equal Pay Act of 1963.

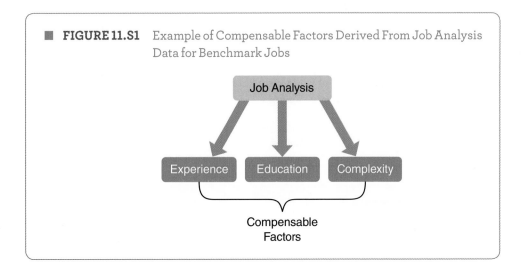

■ **FIGURE 11.S1**   Example of Compensable Factors Derived From Job Analysis Data for Benchmark Jobs

Step 3: Scale the compensable factors

The same or a different group of subject matter experts scale the compensable factors. This scaling process involves applying a numeric rating format to each of the compensable factors identified in Step 2. For example, as shown in Figure 11.S2, the compensable factors of experience, education, and complexity might be scaled with a 1–5 rating format, wherein 1 refers to low levels of the compensable factor are required for performing the job and 5 refers to high levels of the compensable factor are required for performing the job. Using the education factor as a more specific example, a rating of 1 on the scale might correspond to requiring a high school diploma, whereas a rating of 5 might correspond to requiring a doctoral degree of some kind. Note, however, that it is not necessary to use the same scale for each compensable factor, as some factors might warrant more or fewer degrees.

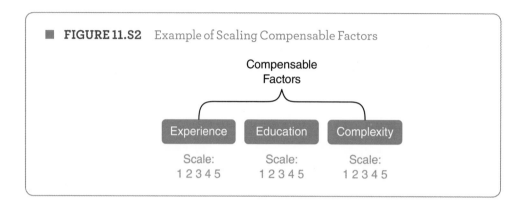

■ **FIGURE 11.S2**   Example of Scaling Compensable Factors

Step 4: Create weights for compensable factors based on importance

The fourth step involves deriving a weight for each of the compensable factors, where the weight of a given compensable factor reflects its relative worth to the organization compared to other compensable factors. There are two prevailing approaches for deriving weights: expert judgment and statistical analysis. The *expert judgment approach* typically involves a team of subject matter experts who distribute 100 percentage points across the compensable factors to determine the relative importance of each compensable factor, such that compensable factors with greater relative importance receive more percentage points. For example, as shown in Figure 11.S3, compensable factors of experience, education, and complexity might be allocated relative importance percentages of 20%, 30%, and 50% (respectively), which sum to 100%. Thus, according to these percentages, the complexity factor is the most important for the organization. After the relative importance percentages are assigned, it is time to allocate point values; we recommend using a total pool of 1,000 points given that the number 1,000 is relatively easy to multiply and divide by; as such, a job worth all 1,000 points would require maximum levels on all compensable factors. Continuing with the example, the relative importance percentages are multiplied by 1,000 to arrive at the total possible number of points for each compensable factor. For example, experience is assigned a total point value of 200 (1,000 × .20 = 200), whereas education and complexity would be assigned total point values of 300 and 500, respectively. Using these new point values, the weight of each compensable factor can be calculated by

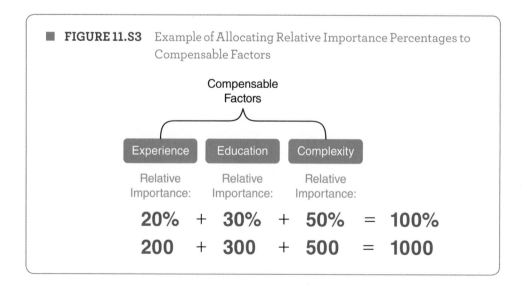

■ **FIGURE 11.S3**   Example of Allocating Relative Importance Percentages to Compensable Factors

dividing the total point value for the factor by the number of scale degrees. In other words, the weighting value represents the number of points that each scale degree is worth for a given compensable factor. For example, for the experience compensable factor, the weight is 40 (200 / 5 = 40), and for education and complexity, the values are 60 and 100, respectively (see Figure 11.S4). Now the benchmark jobs are ready to be scored using the point-factor system.

Another popular approach for weighting compensable factors involves *statistical analysis*, and sometimes this approach is referred to as policy capturing. Often the statistical analysis approach requires either internal or external pay data for benchmark jobs. First, subject matter experts must rate each compensable factor for each benchmark job using the rating scales. Second, using a multiple linear regression analysis, compensable factor weights are determined empirically by regressing pay levels onto each compensable factor's ratings. Using the ongoing example, the pay level for the benchmark jobs would be regressed onto the experience ratings, education ratings, and complexity ratings for the same benchmark jobs. The regression coefficients—or weights—estimated from the regression model represent the empirically derived compensable factor weights.

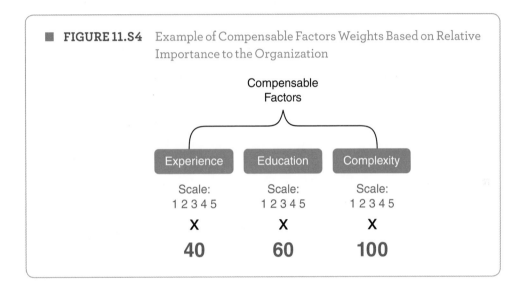

■ **FIGURE 11.S4** Example of Compensable Factors Weights Based on Relative Importance to the Organization

Step 5: Calculate the points for benchmark jobs

Once the compensable factors have been scaled and weighted, a group of subject matter experts scores each job by rating the compensable factors using the scale and multiplying by the weighting value. As shown in the example depicted in Figure 11.S5, for benchmark Job #1, the compensable factor called experience was rated as a 5 out of 5, indicating that this

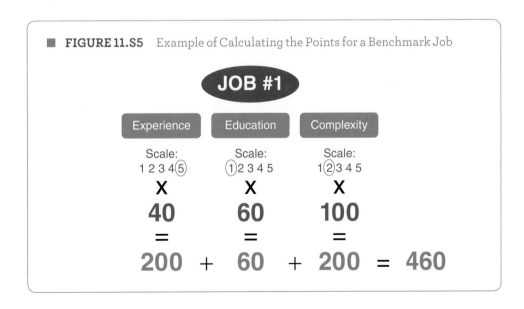

■ **FIGURE 11.S5** Example of Calculating the Points for a Benchmark Job

job requires the highest level of experience. When the rating of 5 is multiplied by the weight value of 40, it yields 200 points for experience—or in other words, the maximum points possible for this compensable factor. Following the same process for the education factor yields 60 points and for the complexity factor yields 200 points. By summing the compensable factor points, we arrive at the overall point value for this particular benchmark job, which is 460 points ($200 + 60 + 200 = 460$). Finally, this scoring process is then repeated for the other benchmark jobs (see Table 11.S1). Note how benchmark Job #1 is worth 460 points, whereas benchmark Jobs #2 and #3 are worth 780 and 1,000 points, respectively. As you can see, the point-factor method results in a rank order of the jobs based on points as well as showing how much more one job is worth compared to another based on their points.

TABLE 11.S1   Example of Calculated Points for Benchmark Jobs Using Point-Factor Method

BENCHMARK JOBS	COMPENSABLE FACTORS			
	EXPERIENCE	EDUCATION	COMPLEXITY	TOTAL
Job #1	200	60	200	**460**
Job #2	200	180	400	**780**
Job #3	200	300	500	**1000**

Step 6: Calculate the points for nonbenchmark jobs

After scoring benchmark jobs, users are trained how to score the nonbenchmark jobs. With thoughtful communication to employees and managers, the point-factor method can improve internal equity.

CHAPTER 11 SUPPLEMENT 11.2: DETERMINING WHETHER A JOB IS EXEMPT OR NONEXEMPT

Note to Employers: This questionnaire serves as a basic outline for an employer's initial analysis of positions being considered for exemption under the FLSA and is meant to serve as one of several tools in an employer's analysis. Job titles are insufficient to determine exempt status. SHRM strongly recommends that employers have legal counsel review their analysis efforts and exemption decisions.

Position: _____

Employee: _____

Date: _____

Completed by: _____

Completion of this questionnaire helps determine the exemption status of a position. Check the appropriate exemption (Executive, Administrative, Professional, Computer-Related, Outside Sales, and Highly Compensated). Then check all boxes under the selected exemption that are applicable. To qualify for an exemption, all boxes must be checked for that exemption. To access the Department of Labor (DOL) online resources for FairPay (CFR 29, Part 541), click here: http://webapps.dol.gov/elaws/elg/minwage.htm.

EXECUTIVE (examples: chief executive officer, controller, vice president, director)

❑	Regularly receives a predetermined amount constituting all or part of the employee's salary, which is not subject to reduction because of variations in the quality or quantity of work performed. To link to the DOL salary basis information, click here: https://www.dol.gov/whd/overtime/fs17g_salary.pdf.
❑	Is paid at least $455 weekly.
❑	Primary duty consists of managing the enterprise or a customarily recognized department or subdivision of the enterprise.
❑	Customarily and regularly directs the work of two or more full-time employees or their equivalents (for example, one full-time employee and two half-time employees).
❑	Has the authority to hire or fire other employees **OR** makes recommendations that carry particular weight as to the hiring, firing, advancement, promotion, or any other change in status of other employees.

To link to the DOL Executive Exemption information, click here: https://www.dol.gov/whd/overtime/fs17b_executive.pdf.

ADMINISTRATIVE (examples: manager, supervisor, administrator)

❑	Regularly receives a predetermined amount constituting all or part of the employee's salary, which is not subject to reduction because of variations in the quality or quantity of work performed. To link to the DOL salary basis information, click here: https://www.dol.gov/whd/overtime/fs17g_salary.pdf.
❑	Is paid at least $455 weekly.
❑	Primary duty consists of performing office or nonmanual work directly related to the management or general business operations of the employer or the employer's customers.
❑	Work includes the exercise of discretion and independent judgment with respect to matters of significance.

To link to the DOL Administrative Exemption information, click here: https://www.dol.gov/whd/overtime/fs17c_administrative.pdf.

PROFESSIONAL: LEARNED AND CREATIVE (examples: accountant, nurse, engineer, composer, singer, graphic designer)

❑	Regularly receives a predetermined amount constituting all or part of the employee's salary, which is not subject to reduction because of variations in the quality or quantity of work performed. To link to the DOL salary basis information, click here: https://www.dol.gov/whd/overtime/fs17g_salary.pdf.
❑	Is paid at least $455 weekly. Note: For teachers, licensed or certified practitioners of law and medicine, medical interns, and residents covered under this exemption, the salary basis and salary requirements do **NOT** apply.

Learned Professional

❑	Primary duty consists of the performance of work that requires advanced knowledge (beyond high school) and that is predominantly intellectual in character and consistently includes the exercise of discretion and independent judgment.
❑	The advanced knowledge is in a field of science or learning.
❑	The advanced knowledge was acquired by a prolonged course of specialized intellectual instruction (position possesses the appropriate academic degree or has substantially the same knowledge level and performs substantially the same work as degreed employees but possesses advanced knowledge only through a combination of work experience and intellectual instruction)

Creative Professional

❑	Primary duty consists of the performance of work requiring invention, imagination, originality, or talent in a recognized field of artistic or creative endeavor as opposed to routine mental, manual, mechanical, or physical work.

To link to the DOL Professional Exemption information, click here: https://www.dol.gov/whd/overtime/fs17d_professional.pdf.

COMPUTER-RELATED (examples: network or database analyst, developer, programmer, software engineer)

❑	Is paid at least $455 weekly **OR** $27.63 per hour. That is, this exemption does **NOT** have to meet the salary basis requirement to regularly receive a predetermined amount constituting all or part of the employee's salary, which is not subject to reduction because of variations in the quality or quantity of work performed **IF** paid at least $27.63 on an hourly basis.
❑	Primary duty consists of: ❑ The application of system-analyst techniques and procedures, including consulting with users to determine hardware, software, or systems functional specifications, OR ❑ The design, development, documentation, analysis, creation, testing, or modification of computer systems or programs, OR ❑ The design, documentation, testing, creation, or modification of computer programs related to machine-operating systems, OR ❑ A combination of these duties that requires the same level of skills.

To link to the DOL Computer-Related Exemption information, click here: https://www.dol.gov/whd/overtime/fs17e_computer.pdf.

OUTSIDE SALES (examples: salespersons, contract negotiators)

The salary basis and salary requirements do **NOT** apply for this exemption. That is, this exemption does **NOT** have the salary basis requirement to regularly receive a predetermined amount constituting all or part of the employee's salary, which is not subject to reduction because of variations in the quality or quantity of work performed, **AND** this exemption does **NOT** have to be paid a minimum salary.

❑	Primary duty consists of making sales or obtaining orders for contracts for services or for the use of facilities for which consideration will be paid by the client or customer.
❑	Customarily and regularly is engaged away from the employer's place or places of business.

To link to the DOL Outside Sales Exemption information, click here: https://www.dol.gov/whd/overtime/fs17f_outsidesales.pdf.

HIGHLY COMPENSATED EMPLOYEES PERFORMING EXECUTIVE, PROFESSIONAL, OR ADMINISTRATIVE DUTIES

❑	Is paid an annual total compensation of $100,000 or more, which includes at least $455 per week paid on a salary basis. The required total annual compensation of $100,000 or more may consist of commissions, nondiscretionary bonuses, and other nondiscretionary compensation earned during a 52-week period but does not include credit for board or lodging, payments for medical or life insurance, or contributions to retirement plans or other fringe benefits.
❑	Primary duty consists of performing office, nonmanual work. Note: No matter how highly paid, manual workers or other blue-collar workers, including nonmanagement construction workers, who perform work involving repetitive operations with their hands, physical skill, and energy are not eligible for this exemption.
❑	Customarily and regularly performs at least one of the exempt duties or responsibilities of the Executive, Professional, or Administrative Exemption.

Rewarding Performance

Opening Case

Improving Patient Care With
Financial Rewards: Geisinger Health System

Geisinger Health System is a physician-led, not-for-profit health care system headquartered in Danville, Pennsylvania, with more than 30,000 employees and plans for further expansion. Over a 7-year period beginning in 2002, Geisinger reconfigured and implemented new pay-for-performance programs to motivate physicians to deliver high-quality patient care while also keeping costs under control. The organization tied approximately 20% of physicians' compensation to pay-for-performance programs aimed at achieving strategic goals associated with patient care and productivity, with the remaining 80% of compensation tied to the traditional piecework incentives used in health care such as the number of patients seen and the number of procedures performed.

As an example of a specific pay-for-performance program, Geisinger rewarded physicians for signing patients up for the organization's online portal so as to better manage patient care data; this initiative contributed to fewer patient appointment no-shows and fewer phone calls, thereby improving physician productivity. Further, the organization challenged physicians to ensure they met all 120 best-practice treatment requirements when performing elective coronary artery bypass surgery. The physicians attained the strategic goal, which led to a 67% improvement in patients' relative mortality rate and to an 18% reduction of costs. In recognition of the physicians' performance, Geisinger provided financial rewards.

Interestingly, early on during the process of implementing the pay-for-performance programs, Geisinger lost a number of physicians to voluntary turnover, presumably because they took issue with the new reward system initiative. The organization weathered the attrition by retaining those physicians who were motivated to earn performance-based incentives. In the process, the organization shifted to a more results- and performance-oriented culture. Consequently, Geisinger not only changed how physicians are compensated but also changed the organization's values to focus more directly on patient care quality.[1]

Case Discussion Questions

1. In addition to patient care quality, what other physician-related outcomes could Geisinger improve by using pay-for-performance programs? What might result from focusing on these additional outcomes?

LEARNING OBJECTIVES

After reading and studying this chapter, you should be able to do the following:

12.1 Describe the motivating potential of pay and other rewards.

12.2 Identify the prevailing theories of motivation and goal setting.

12.3 Explain how pay can be used strategically to motivate desired behavior.

12.4 Describe common individual and group pay-for-performance programs.

12.5 Assess common challenges and opportunities of pay-for-performance programs.

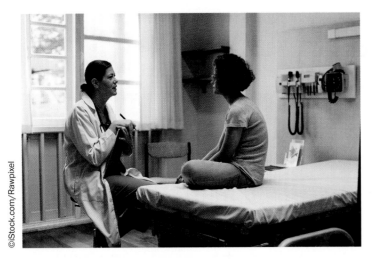

©iStock.com/Rawpixel

2. List some of the reasons why you think some physicians decided to leave Geisinger after the company implemented the new pay-for-performance programs.

3. Geisinger distributed approximately 20% of physicians' compensation as pay for performance. This was tied to achieving strategic goals associated with patient care and productivity. In the future, do you think Geisinger should increase or decrease this percentage? Why?

4. What unanticipated patient and physician outcomes might result from taking a pay-for-performance approach?

5. In your opinion, should all health care systems develop and implement pay-for-performance programs for physicians? What about for nurses and other direct-care providers?

▶ Click to learn more …

To learn about how Geisinger Health System leverages big data and analytics to inform patient care and change physician behavior, read the *Harvard Business Review* article by Erskine, Karunakaran, Slotkin, and Feinberg called "How Geisinger Health System Uses Big Data to Save Lives" (https://hbr.org/2016/12/how-geisinger-health-system-uses-big-data-to-save-lives).

Pay for performance Financial rewards offered in exchange for meeting certain levels of performance or achieving certain goals

Many employers reward performance in some manner, with pay-for-performance programs representing a common approach. ***Pay for performance***—sometimes called *performance-contingent pay*—refers to financial rewards offered in exchange for meeting certain levels of performance or achieving certain goals and can be an integral component of an organization's broader reward system. Well-designed pay-for-performance programs help attract, motivate, and retain high-potential and high-performing individuals. Such programs can also be used to reward individuals, teams and units, and the organization as a whole. However, pay for performance can have unintended consequences when poorly designed or poorly thought out. For example, pay-for-performance programs can motivate behaviors that are unethical and uncooperative in nature and can lead to budgeting problems with labor costs. Nevertheless, an effective pay-for-performance program can facilitate the realization of strategic objectives, especially when the program motivates behaviors that are strategically aligned.

This chapter focuses on changes in an individual's pay level and differences between individuals' pay levels based on their performances or the performance of their group. The chapter also addresses the motivating potential of distributing pay in recognition of performance and achievement of behavior-based and/or result-based objectives.

LO 12.1 Describe the motivating potential of pay and other rewards.

Pay as a Motivator

Pay is a common form of compensation and an integral part of a reward system, where a reward system comprises relational returns (e.g., recognition, job security), compensation (e.g., base pay, variable pay), and benefits (e.g., health insurance, work–life balance programs). The respective pay levels of individuals who hold the same job may vary in response to individual equity considerations such as individuals' respective levels of seniority, experience, and/or performance. To understand pay-for-performance programs, we begin by distinguishing pay-for-performance programs from traditional-pay programs.[2]

Traditional-pay programs reward employees based on the content of their job description, title, and/or level. They usually correspond to the relatively stable and fixed base-pay component of individual employees' compensation package. Think of traditional-pay programs as being a wage or salary guarantee; in exchange for organizational membership and holding a particular job, employees receive a base pay amount that is commensurate with the organizational worth of the job they were hired to perform. As long as employees hold onto their jobs, they receive their base pay, regardless of how well they perform. Of course, employees who fail to perform at minimally acceptable levels and fail to do so consistently over time—even after progressive disciplinary action by the organization—will likely lose the entirety of their base pay after being terminated.

In contrast, *pay-for-performance programs* reward employees for the behaviors they actually exhibit at work and for the results or goals they actually achieve. That is, pay is distributed as a reward for demonstrating a certain level of performance. The performance levels required for attaining rewards may be predetermined or decided upon after the fact. Compared to traditional-pay programs, pay-for-performance programs are more strongly linked to on-the-job motivation, as pay is thought to motivate employees to perform certain behaviors with greater efficiency or effectiveness. For instance, as described in the opening case on Geisinger Health System, pay-for-performance programs for physicians resulted in improved patient care and reduced costs—two very important outcomes in the health care industry. Research shows that pay-for-performance programs not only motivate individuals to perform at a higher level on the job but also serve as a vehicle to attract high-potential applicants and to retain high-performing incumbents.[3]

Defining Motivation

Employee motivation is a proximal outcome of pay-for-performance programs. The concept of motivation is broad and has been defined in many different ways. For our purposes, we conceptualize *motivation* as a psychological force that propels an individual (or a group of individuals) to enact certain behaviors or to strive for a goal or result. Moreover, motivation has to do with the direction, form, effort, and duration of an individual's (or a group's) behavior(s). First, *direction* refers to the behaviors, goals, or results on which an individual focuses attention. Second, *form* refers to the types of behaviors an individual enacts or the types of goals and results an individual pursues. Third, *effort* refers to the intensity with which an individual focuses on and/or enacts behaviors or pursues goals and results. Finally, *duration* refers to how long an individual persists in enacting certain behaviors or pursuing certain goals and results. Thus, when conceptualizing pay as a motivator, consider how pay signals the direction or form of desired behavior and encourages the effort and duration of behaviors and goal pursuit (see Figure 12.1).

When attempting to understand what motivates individuals, it is important to distinguish between two broad types of motivation: extrinsic and intrinsic (see Figure 12.2). Both are important for performance, but accumulated research indicates that they differ with respect to how they influence performance and what types of performance they influence.

Extrinsic Motivation

Motivation that originates outside of an individual and the work itself is known as *extrinsic motivation*; it serves as an external, environmental force that compels an individual to action.[4] An extrinsic motivator is simply a source of extrinsic motivation. The classic example of an extrinsic motivator is pay; other extrinsic motivators include nonmonetary awards and recognition such as praise or validation from a supervisor. With extrinsic motivators, individuals are not necessarily enacting certain behaviors or pursuing certain goals because they have the internal desire

Traditional-pay programs Compensation programs that reward employees based on the content of their job description, title, and/or level

Pay-for-performance programs Compensation programs that reward employees based on the behaviors they actually exhibit at work and the results or goals they actually achieve

Motivation A psychological force that propels an individual (or a group of individuals) to enact certain behaviors or to strive for a goal

Extrinsic motivation An external, environmental force that compels an individual to action

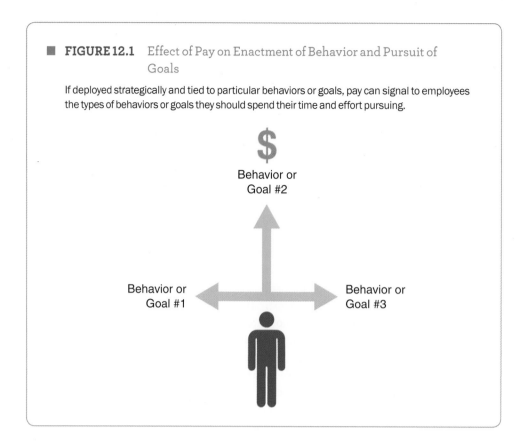

■ **FIGURE 12.1**   Effect of Pay on Enactment of Behavior and Pursuit of Goals

If deployed strategically and tied to particular behaviors or goals, pay can signal to employees the types of behaviors or goals they should spend their time and effort pursuing.

to do so, but rather, they enact these behaviors and pursue these goals because they receive some kind of compensation, reward, or award.

However, the extent to which a particular external, environmental force is motivating varies between individuals. For example, for some individuals, receiving pay may be perceived as very valuable and important and thus more extrinsically motivating. For others, pay may hold less value and importance and thus be less extrinsically motivating.

Intrinsic Motivation

Intrinsic motivation
A force that originates inside an individual and compels the individual to action because they perceive the action as innately rewarding

Unlike extrinsic motivation, **intrinsic motivation** originates inside an individual; it compels the individual to action because the individual perceives the action as innately rewarding, meaningful, challenging, and/or enjoyable.[5] For example, in the workplace, some people might feel intrinsically motivated to write code for a computer program because they simply enjoy the process of building something new and challenging. Others might be compelled to action based on their perceived sense of autonomy, competence, or interest in their work. For example, an individual who is promoted to a supervisory role may feel energized by the increased level of responsibility and control over how work is conducted and completed. Just as extrinsic motivation varies from one person to another, a given action or behavior may be more or less intrinsically motivating for different individuals.

Motivation and Performance

In general, higher motivation leads to higher performance. However, extrinsic and intrinsic motivations play different roles when it comes to performance. In a meta-analytic review of 183 studies on extrinsic and intrinsic motivation spanning 40 years, researchers found that extrinsic motivation was more strongly linked to the *quantity* of performance—or rather, *how much* an individual produces, completes, or provides in terms of products and services.[6] In contrast, intrinsic motivation was more strongly linked to the *quality* of performance—or rather, *how well* an individual produces, completes, or provides products and services. Interestingly, a positive association between intrinsic motivation and overall performance was found to be even stronger when extrinsic

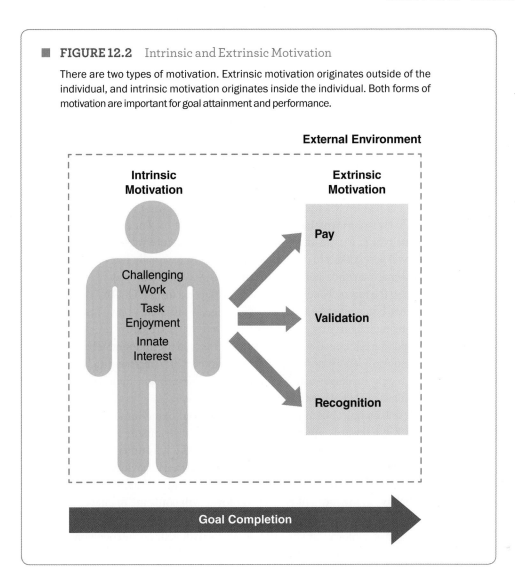

■ **FIGURE 12.2** Intrinsic and Extrinsic Motivation

There are two types of motivation. Extrinsic motivation originates outside of the individual, and intrinsic motivation originates inside the individual. Both forms of motivation are important for goal attainment and performance.

External Environment

Intrinsic Motivation

Extrinsic Motivation

Pay

Challenging Work

Task Enjoyment

Innate Interest

Validation

Recognition

Goal Completion

motivation was present. That is, the meta-analytic review indicates that extrinsic motivation may actually enhance performance by working in tandem with intrinsic motivation. Thus, if properly designed and implemented, pay-for-performance programs and other extrinsic motivators have the potential to enhance the quantity of employees' performance. Further, if applied in conjunction with intrinsic motivators, extrinsic motivators such as pay-for-performance programs can improve employees' overall performance, which includes both the quantity and quality of performance.

Theories of Motivation

Theories of motivation provide us with a framework for designing, explaining, and understanding the effects of pay-for-performance programs on behavior and goal attainment. Three prominent motivational theories are especially relevant to understanding how and why pay can motivate behavior: reinforcement theory, expectancy theory, and goal-setting theory.

Reinforcement Theory

Reinforcement theory provides a useful framework for understanding pay as an extrinsic motivator, particularly when pay is used for behavior modification, as in many pay-for-performance programs. Reinforcement theory is rooted in research on behaviorism and operant conditioning

LO 12.2 Identify the prevailing theories of motivation and goal setting.

Reinforcement theory
A motivational theory that provides a useful framework for understanding pay as an extrinsic motivator, particularly when pay is used for behavior modification

by Edward Thorndike, Ivan Pavlov, and B. F. Skinner, three influential social scientists from the early part of the 20th century.[7] The theory is predicated on the assumption that environmental consequences, which include extrinsic motivators such as providing or withholding rewards and punishments, influence behavior. According to the theory, such environmental consequences signal to individuals which behaviors they should continue or discontinue in the future.

The principles of reinforcement theory can be applied to encourage desired workplace behaviors and dissuade undesired workplace behaviors. If a reward is given when an individual enacts a desired behavior, then the individual will be more likely to perform that behavior again in the future. For example, if employees receive a bonus each time they make their end-of-quarter sales quota, they will be more likely to strive to meet their sales quota in future quarters. On the other hand, if a punishment is given when an individual enacts an undesired behavior, then the individual will be less likely to perform the behavior again in the future. For example, if employees receive a waste penalty (e.g., a pay deduction) each time they produce waste during the production process, they will be less likely to produce waste in the future. Finally, if a reward is withheld when an individual enacts an undesired behavior, then the individual will be less likely to perform the behavior again in the future. For example, Marissa Mayer, a former CEO of Yahoo Inc., did not receive her annual bonus after she and colleagues allegedly mishandled two security breaches that affected more than 1 billion users' personal information.[8] Yahoo's board of directors made the decision to withhold Mayer's annual bonus, presumably to avoid the undesirable behavior in the future. Mayer subsequently left her position at Yahoo in January 2017, receiving a $23 million severance package and equity holdings worth more than $200 million; thus, in the long term, failing to receive an annual bonus might not have been such a disincentive.[9]

In general, research has shown that to elicit a desired behavior, an environmental consequence—such as a reward or punishment—should be distributed soon after the behavior is exhibited. If too much time passes before the behavior's environmental consequence is presented, the likelihood of an individual performing the desired behavior again in the future begins to diminish. The more quickly rewards are distributed (or withheld) after an employee demonstrates a behavior, the more likely the employee will continue to enact (or cease to enact) that particular behavior again in the future.

It is worth noting that reinforcement theory does not focus directly on the cognition of individuals with respect to their motivation and behavior. Rather, the theory focuses on the actual manifestation of their behavioral responses to environmental consequences such as the distribution of pay. Thus, reinforcement theory does not directly help us understand *why* the provision of pay is motivating. Other theories, such as expectancy theory, help us answer those "why" questions.

Expectancy Theory

Expectancy theory A theory that suggests that if a person sees that their efforts will lead to greater performance, and if they believe that performance will lead to an outcome that they value, they will be more motivated

Expectancy theory offers a set of propositions that can be useful for understanding *why* pay-for-performance programs drive the direction, form, effort, and duration of behavior enactment and goal striving. Expectancy theory frames motivation in terms of the following psychological concepts: expectancy, instrumentality, and valence.[10] Some have argued that expectancy, instrumentality, and valence share a multiplicative relationship, such that if one falls to zero, then motivation falls to zero. For example, the theory proposes that an individual's motivation to attain a goal will drop if they perceive high valence and high expectancy but low instrumentality. The conceptual formula is as follows:

$$Motivation = Expectancy \times Instrumentality \times Valence$$

Expectancy The extent to which an individual perceives that applying effort will lead to higher performance

As depicted in Figure 12.3, *expectancy* refers to the perceived connection between individuals' effort and performance, such that individuals perceive greater expectancy when they *expect* that exerting more effort will lead to better performance. Imagine that your supervisor assigns you the following performance goal: *Sell 100 software licenses by the end of the month.* If you

■ **FIGURE 12.3** Expectancy Theory

Expectancy theory proposes that motivation consists of three components: expectancy, instrumentality, and valence. Expectancy refers to the perception that effort will lead to performance, instrumentality refers to the perception that performance will lead to a reward, and valence refers to the perception that a reward is valuable.

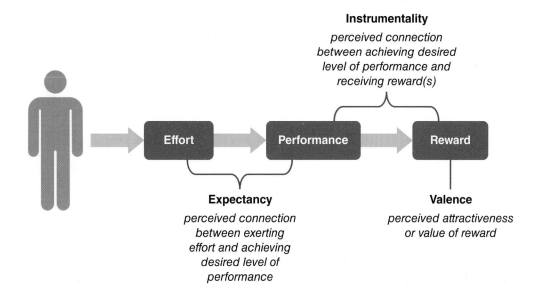

possess the knowledge of the software product and skills to sell it (as well as any other relevant KSAOs), then you will likely perceive that applying effort will help you accomplish the sales goal; you will experience a relatively high level of expectancy.

Instrumentality refers to the perceived connection between performance and rewards, such that individuals experience higher instrumentality when they perceive a direct link between demonstrating performance and, subsequently, receiving rewards. In other words, they perceive that performance is *instrumental* for receiving rewards. As an example, if your organization fails to communicate that selling 100 software licenses by the end of the month will lead to a bonus, then you will be less likely to perceive that selling 100 software licenses will be instrumental for receiving additional pay. Alternatively, if your organization communicates that selling 100 software licenses will result in a bonus, then you will perceive higher instrumentality, especially if, in the past, you saw the same or similar reward schemes work as communicated. Perceiving that a reward is directly contingent upon performance will heighten the degree to which you are motivated to earn that reward.

Valence is the extent to which individuals perceive a reward as being attractive or important. It refers to the value individuals attach to a reward, which differs across people. For example, you will likely perceive much higher valence if the month-end reward for selling 100 software licenses is $1,000 as opposed to $5; consequently, you will be more motivated to apply effort toward demonstrating the level of performance necessary for attaining the reward when the reward itself is more highly valued.

In sum, the perceived valence, instrumentality, and expectancy attached to a pay-for-performance program help us understand how, why, and under what conditions pay acts as a motivating force. In general, the amount of pay influences individuals' perceptions of valence, such that higher pay should be viewed as more attractive and ultimately more motivating. The degree to which performance is perceived to lead to pay closely aligns with instrumentality. In fact, instrumentality can reflect the quality of the respective performance management and reward systems, as well as the degree to which they are integrated effectively. If performance is not

Instrumentality The extent to which an individual perceives that achieving higher performance will lead to reward attainment

Valence The extent to which individuals perceive a reward as being attractive or important

MANAGER'S TOOLBOX

Evaluating Pay-for-Performance Programs Using Expectancy Theory

Without thoughtful communication and consideration of employee perceptions, a pay-for-performance program may fail to improve employee motivation and performance. Managers can apply expectancy theory to determine why the pay-for-performance program does not lead to higher motivation and performance.

1. **Expectancy.** If employees do not perceive a link between their effort and attaining a performance goal, then a manager should consider the following:

   - *Do employees have the requisite KSAOs necessary to meet the goal?* If not, the employees may need training.
   - *If a group pay-for-performance program is in place, do employees understand their role in the group and how they can contribute to the group's attainment of the goal?* If not, the manager should explain to employees how their efforts contribute to the group's success.

2. **Instrumentality.** If employees do not perceive a link between attaining a performance goal and receiving a reward, then the manager should consider the following:

   - *Do employees understand how the pay-for-performance program works?* If not, the

manager should explain the program and, in particular, how rewards are determined and why they are distributed.

   - *Is performance measured consistently, accurately, and fairly?* If not, the performance management system may need to be improved by enhancing the measurement tools, training users on how to use the measurement tools, or addressing office politics that influence the way performance is measured.
   - *Is the reward distributed in a timely manner after the goal is attained?* If not, the manager should work to ensure that the reward is distributed soon after the goal is met.

3. **Valence.** If employees do not perceive the reward to be attractive or of value, then the manager should consider the following:

   - *Is the size of the reward commensurate with the amount of effort and the level of performance it takes to earn the reward?* If not, the amount of the reward or the type of reward may need to be changed.
   - *Do employees want a monetary reward?* If not, the manager should ask employees what non-monetary rewards they might find valuable (e.g., praise, challenging work, flexible work schedule).

tracked and measured accurately, then employees may perceive the allocation of pay to be arbitrary, ultimately leading to diminished levels of perceived instrumentality and thus lower motivation. Alternatively, if pay is provided inconsistently as a reward (or not at all) for demonstrating high performance, then employees may also perceive lower levels of instrumentality and motivation.

Finally, when administering group incentives, employees' perceptions of expectancy should be considered. Specifically, in situations in which a group as a whole is rewarded for its performance, individual group members may have a difficult time understanding how their efforts lead to higher group performance, particularly when there is a large number of group members. Thus, they may perceive low expectancy when there is not a clear line of sight between their effort and the performance of the group.

Goal-Setting Theory

Tying performance-based pay to specific performance goals can increase the motivating potential of a pay-for-performance program, as rewards can signal the importance of goals and encourage greater effort to be applied to goal attainment. Indeed, the overarching objective of most pay-for-performance programs is to encourage employees to attain goals that are important

TABLE 12.1 Managers and employees can apply the SMART goal acronym to craft motivating goals.

Specific	Is your goal specific and well defined?
Measurable	Can you measure goal progress or completion?
Aggressive	Is your goal difficult and challenging?
Realistic	Do you have the right KSAOs to complete the goal?
Time-bound	Have you set a deadline for completing your goal?

to the organization. By integrating effective goal setting into a pay-for-performance program, an organization may be able to capitalize on increased extrinsic and intrinsic motivation, as pay can serve as an external, environmental motivator, and challenging goals can stimulate a sense of innate enjoyment and fulfillment. Compared to fixed forms of pay (e.g., hourly pay), some evidence has shown that pay-for-performance programs, such as individual incentives and bonuses, can increase employees' commitment to goals.[11]

Originally introduced by Gary Latham and Edwin Locke, ***goal-setting theory*** offers a framework for understanding how and why certain goals lead to higher motivation and performance. Goal-setting theory has existed for more than half a century, and the tenets of the theory have been applied to work, educational, and sports settings. Over time, several best practices have emerged regarding the development of motivating goals. In most circumstances, individuals who strive for specific yet difficult (but not impossible) goals reach higher levels of performance than those who strive for do-your-best, easy, or abstract goals.[12]

Goal-setting theory The theory that setting specific, difficult, yet achievable goals for people will lead to the highest performance

The SMART acronym encapsulates goal-setting best practices (see Table 12.1). SMART goals are specific, measurable, aggressive, realistic, and time-bound. The specific, measurable, and time-bound components of the SMART acronym reflect the aforementioned research that has shown that specific goals often lead to higher motivation and performance than goals that are general or ambiguous. When pursuing a specific, measurable, and time-bound goal, an individual will have a better idea of

- the direction in which they should focus their effort and what form their effort and behavior should take (specific);
- how successful goal completion is defined and measured (measurable); and
- how much time is available to complete the goal (time-bound).

Further, the aggressive and realistic components of the SMART acronym reflect research that has shown individuals are more motivated by difficult goals than by easy goals. Difficult (aggressive) goals push the individual to apply greater effort—sometimes for greater durations of time—thereby opening the door for potentially higher levels of performance when compared to easy goals. Difficult goals can also inspire intrinsic motivation, particularly for people who revel in new challenges. Finally, goals should be attainable (realistic) and not excessively difficult or impossible. A goal should reflect an individual's KSAOs and not exceed an individual's capabilities given the timeline for completion. Goals that are too difficult or unattainable may be met with frustration and withdrawal, which ultimately may diminish motivation and performance.

How does one determine if a goal is sufficiently specific and difficult and meets the definition of a SMART goal? Some of the best approaches include eliciting employees' feedback about their perceptions of the goals; breaking very difficult goals into smaller, manageable chunks; and including employees in the goal-setting process.[13] Recall that in some circumstances, a seemingly impossible goal may be due to a lack of requisite KSAOs on the employee's part, or it may be that successful goal attainment is beyond the control of the employee. Regarding the latter, it is important to ensure that there are not any roadblocks in the employee's path to success. For example, imagine that you are an employee striving to make a sales goal so that you can earn your year-end bonus. Although the sales goal might seem realistic at the outset, a number of different (external) forces may come into play that hinder the degree to which goal attainment remains realistic. Perhaps your ability to sell the product in question is largely contingent upon the estimated delivery date, and if a supplier runs behind schedule, customers may be unable to buy the product because the estimated delivery dates are too far in the future. In this situation, what seemed likely a reasonable yet difficult goal at first might morph into a virtually impossible target to hit. Accordingly, managers should work closely with employees, monitor their goal attainment, and request feedback to stay on top of such situations.

Although goals can be specific to individuals, they can also be group based. By attaching pay or other rewards to team goal attainment, an organization can signal that working together and interdependently is important. Research on goal-setting theory points to the importance of aligning team goals with the individual goals of specific team members.[14] Individual goals that lack alignment with team goals can lead to conflict and to individuals focusing more on their individual goals than the team goals. If designed properly, team goals can improve team performance. Team goals should be aligned with individual goals and thereby operate as part of an integrated system.

Strategy and Pay for Performance

LO 12.3 Explain how pay can be used strategically to motivate desired behavior.

A survey by PayScale found that in 78% of companies, the CEO plays a role in approving pay decisions, and in 33% of companies, an entire team is devoted to developing reward systems.[15] These statistics point to the strategic value of pay for an organization, as pay can be an instrumental force for motivating employees to attain strategic goals. In fact, a WorldatWork survey revealed that approximately two-thirds of large organizations have a formal, written compensation strategy in place, whereas the majority of the remaining large organizations have an unwritten compensation strategy.[16] Yet only 3% of organizations indicate that almost all employees understand their company's compensation strategy.[17] As such, developing a compensation strategy is a necessary but not sufficient step in the process of successfully implementing pay systems. Instead, once a strategy is developed, an organization should make a concerted effort to disseminate and explain the strategy to employees. Without careful communication, even the most thoughtfully developed strategy may go unnoticed or be misunderstood.

With regard to pay-for-performance programs, specifically, pay and other forms of reward can be contingent upon meeting strategic performance objectives. Attaching financial incentives to the enactment of certain behaviors and fulfillment of certain goals can direct employees' attention to and align their behaviors with the objectives considered most critical for companywide success.[18] After all, pay is a finite resource within organizations, and thus distributing performance-contingent pay can signal the importance of pursuing some goals over others.

Pay-for-Performance Programs

LO 12.4 Describe common individual and group pay-for-performance programs.

Recall that pay-for-performance programs reward employees for the types of behaviors they exhibit at work and the goals they attain. Pay-for-performance programs can be designed to reward individuals or groups. In terms of time orientation, they can be attached to short- or long-term goals. The following sections address some of the more common types of pay-for-performance programs.

Individual Pay-for-Performance Programs

In the United States, employees generally prefer individual pay-for-performance programs over group pay-for-performance programs.[19] Pay-for-performance programs aimed at rewarding individuals can be broadly organized using the categories of merit pay and variable pay. Variable-pay programs may include bonuses, spot awards, and individual incentives. These programs reward individuals for demonstrating key behaviors or achieving certain goals or results; however, they operate differently in terms of how rewards are distributed and their potential effects on motivation and performance.

©iStock.com/AndreyPopov

Merit-pay increases are often contingent upon the ratings an employee receives during a performance evaluation.

Merit pay Pay distributed to employees and integrated into their base pay as a reward for the ratings and/or feedback they receive on a performance evaluation measure

Merit Pay

Pay distributed to employees based on the ratings and/or feedback they receive on a performance evaluation measure is known as **merit pay**. By being integrated into an employee's base pay, merit pay results in the pay increase carrying forward to subsequent pay periods. Of those organizations with a formal performance management system and performance evaluation process, 87% tie merit-pay increases to performance ratings or rankings, according to a WorldatWork survey.[20] In many cases, higher performance ratings result in larger merit-pay increases. For example, imagine an organization that uses a four-point performance evaluation measure, where a rating of 4 indicates exceptional performance. Under a merit-pay program, an employee who receives a 4 rating would receive a larger pay increase than an employee who receives a 3 rating. In other cases, a fixed merit-pay increase is provided in exchange for surpassing a given performance threshold. For example, the organization might distribute the same merit-pay increase to anyone who receives a rating of 3 or 4.

Research shows that in general, employees who receive merit-pay increases tend to show higher performance than those who do not receive merit-pay increases.[21] However, employees often perceive a weak link between their level of performance and the amount of merit pay they receive,[22] which may be attributable to the fact that managers often feel uncomfortable differentiating between employees when it comes to performance evaluations.[23]

From the employer's perspective, merit-pay programs require thoughtful budgeting and management, because under these programs, pay increases are integrated into individuals' base pay. Based on a PayScale survey of 7,700 organizations, 31% of companies reportedly budgeted 3% of their total organizational salary budget for merit pay, whereas 10% of companies budgeted more than 5%.[24] With respect to performance management, an effective merit-pay program is predicated upon a well-designed performance evaluation measure and fair, unbiased performance ratings by supervisors. A merit-pay program depends upon close alignment between subjective performance evaluations and reward distribution.

Bonuses

More and more organizations have begun to adopt variable-pay programs, such as bonuses, spot awards, and individual incentives. As of 2016, approximately 88% of organizations reported having some type of variable-pay programs, a statistic which does not include sales commission programs.[25] Of those organizations with variable-pay programs, 81% use a bonus program. Unlike merit pay, **bonuses** are a form of variable pay, which means that they are not integrated into an individual's base pay. Instead, bonuses are distributed as a one-time payout in recognition of performance after the fact; they may be attached to a performance rating or to a completed goal. Bonuses can be distributed in recognition of individual performance, but they can also be distributed in recognition of team, unit, facility, or organizational performance. Because bonuses are not integrated into employees' base pay, they can be less expensive for the employer than distributing pay in the form of merit pay.[26]

Bonuses A form of variable pay distributed as a one-time payout in recognition of performance after the fact, which may be attached to a performance rating or to a completed goal

Spot awards A type of after-the-fact recognition that is often reserved for exceptional levels of performance on a project or for exceptionally high overall job performance

Spot Awards

Another type of after-the-fact recognition is **spot awards**, which are often reserved for exceptional levels of performance on a project or for exceptionally high overall job performance. More

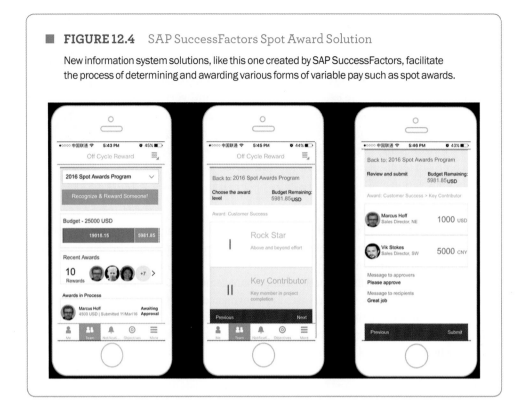

■ **FIGURE 12.4**   SAP SuccessFactors Spot Award Solution

New information system solutions, like this one created by SAP SuccessFactors, facilitate the process of determining and awarding various forms of variable pay such as spot awards.

than half of organizations recognize employees using spot awards and other similar programs.[27] Organizations vary with respect to the level of formality they apply to spot awards. Some organizations, such as the University of California, Berkeley, develop formal policies and procedures that describe the criteria for earning spot awards, eligibility guidelines, timing, and the amount of awards.[28] To support decision making around spot awards, companies like SAP SuccessFactors offer information system and technology solutions designed to facilitate the process of establishing guidelines and identifying potential spot-award candidates (see Figure 12.4).[29]

Individual Incentives

A survey by WorldatWork found that approximately one-third of organizations use some type of individual incentive program, which makes individual incentive programs one of the least commonly used individual pay-for-performance programs.[30] Nonetheless, research has shown that individual incentive programs generally have a positive effect on performance outcomes.[31] **Individual incentives** refer to the distribution of pay in response to the attainment of certain predetermined and objective levels of performance. In general, they are nondiscretionary, which means managers do not have much say when it comes to who receives individual incentives and the amount of the distributed rewards. Examples of individual incentives include piecework and standard-hour plans.

Piecework Plans

In a *piecework plan*, employees are compensated based on their respective production levels. We can distinguish between two types of piecework plans: straight piecework plans and differential piecework plans. In a ***straight piecework plan***, employee variable pay is based on the units they produce in a given time period, such that there is a direct correspondence between the amount of pay distributed and the number of units produced. For example, imagine that Cheryl works for a medical device company, and her main task is to assemble feeding tubes that will ultimately be used for patient care. A portion of her total compensation is variable and is distributed in accordance with a straight piecework plan. According to the plan, Cheryl earns $0.25 for every feeding tube she assembles within a pay period. Thus, if Cheryl assembles 2,000 feeding tubes in a pay period, she will receive $500 in variable pay (2,000 × $0.25 = $500).

Individual incentives The distribution of pay in response to the attainment of certain predetermined and objective levels of performance

Piecework plan An individual-incentive program in which employees are compensated based on their respective production levels

Straight piecework plan An individual-incentive program in which employee variable pay is based on the units they produce in a given time period, such that there is a direct correspondence between the amount of pay distributed and the number of units produced

In a ***differential piecework plan***, employees are paid one rate for units produced below a particular standard in a given time period, and they are paid a higher rate for units produced above that standard. In some instances, a differential piecework plan may include more than one standard and thus three or more pay rates for units produced. The goal underlying differential piecework plans is to incentivize employees to strive for the highest levels of production.

Differential piecework plan An individual-incentive program in which employees are paid one rate for units produced below a particular standard in a given time period and a higher rate for units produced above that standard

For example, imagine that Cheryl finds a new job at a different medical device company. Instead of a straight piecework plan, her new company distributes a portion of pay in accordance with a differential piecework plan. Under this plan, Cheryl earns $0.25 for each of the first 1,500 feeding tubes she assembles within a pay period and $0.30 for every additional feeding tube she assembles beyond 1,500. Thus, if Cheryl assembles 2,000 feeding tubes in a pay period at her new company, she will earn $525 in variable pay ($1,500 \times \$0.25 + 500 \times \$0.30 = \$525$).

Standard-Hour Plans

In a ***standard-hour plan***, employee pay is based on the completion of a particular task within a predetermined time period. These plans are often based on established hourly rates and expected completion times. Standard-hour plans are commonly used in service mechanic jobs. For instance, imagine that a bicycle shop determines that the services provided by bicycle mechanics are worth $25 per hour. Different tasks require different amounts of time, such that fixing a flat tire might take the average mechanic 10 minutes, whereas building a wheel might take the average mechanic 1.5 hours. Based on historical data, the bicycle shop concludes that the average mechanic should be able to complete a bicycle overhaul (i.e., disassembling, cleaning, adjusting, and lubricating components) in 2 hours. Given the bicycle mechanics' hourly worth of $25, each mechanic will earn $50 for completing a bicycle overhaul (25×2 hours = $50), regardless of whether the task takes the mechanic 1.5 hours or 2.5 hours. If the task is completed in 1.5 hours, the mechanic earns $50 in less time than expected, which frees up additional time to get started on other tasks and thus the potential to earn more money. Ambitious mechanics might find a standard hour plan to be highly motivating; however, for these plans to work, it is important that the estimated completion times for common tasks be fair and reasonable. After all, if mechanics consistently take longer than the estimated task completion times, then they may perceive lost income potential, especially when making comparisons with other bicycle shops that offer a set hourly wage and no standard hour plan.

Piecework plans are common in industries where production levels are easily quantified and tracked, such as in manufacturing.

Standard-hour plans are common for the job of a mechanic.

Sales Commissions

Those who have worked in sales are likely familiar with ***sales commissions,*** which reward the sale of a product or service as opposed to the production of a product or provision of a service. Workers who sell products and services such as cars, real estate, stocks, consumer packaged goods, medical devices, software, telecommunications, and insurance are commonly paid in commissions or a combination of base pay plus commissions. Typically, the amount of a sales commission is based on the percentage of the revenue or profit associated with each sale, overall sales volume, or customer satisfaction.

Standard-hour plan An individual-incentive program in which employee pay is based on the completion of a particular task within a predetermined time period

Sales commissions Pay-for-performance programs that reward the sale of a product or service as opposed to the production of a product or provision of a service

HR IN ACTION
Paying for Weight Loss

Poor employee health can be costly for organizations. In particular, employee obesity often leads to higher organizational costs due to higher rates of absenteeism and lower performance. As a result, four out of five U.S. organizations offer some kind of incentive to employees in order to meet weight-loss objectives, whether the incentive be a reduction in health insurance premiums or a monetary incentive added to employees' paychecks. The motivating potential of such incentives seems clear: Lose weight and receive a financial reward of some kind.

The research on the effectiveness of such incentive programs has produced mixed results. Some research has shown no change in employees' respective weights, on average, regardless of whether the incentive was to reduce health insurance premiums for meeting weight-loss goals or to provide lump-sum monetary incentives. Other research, however, has highlighted some promising approaches. For instance, in a study by Kullgren and colleagues, employees who participated in a team-based incentive program lost significantly more weight than employees who participated in an individual-based incentive program and a program with no incentive. The team-based incentive program was structured such that each five-person team was allocated $500 at the beginning of each month, and at the end of each month, the $500 was divided evenly among those employees who met or exceeded their target weight-loss goal. For example, if two out of five employees met or exceeded their goals, the two employees would receive $250 each, and if all five employees met or exceeded their goals, the five employees would receive $100 each. In contrast, the individual-based incentive in this study was structured such that an employee received $100 each month that they met or

exceeded their weight-loss goal. Overall, it was the team-based incentives that showed promise in this particular instance.

Research on other health behaviors, such as smoking cessation and exercise promotion, point to certain characteristics of weight-loss incentive programs that may enhance their effectiveness. First, monetary incentives tend to work (better) when they are clearly separated from employees' insurance premiums. A study by Volpp and colleagues showed that employees who received cash or checks that were separate from their paychecks tended to quit smoking at noticeably higher rates than those who did not receive such an incentive. Second, employees may be more sensitive to financial losses for failing to meet a health goal than to financial gains for meeting one. A study by Patel and colleagues showed that participants were more likely to meet their daily physical-activity goals when they received $42 at the beginning of each month and lost $1.40 every day that they failed to meet their goal, as compared to participants in a control group who did not receive an incentive. In contrast, participants who received $1.40 for every day that they met their goal did not outperform participants in the control group in terms of goal attainment. Interestingly, at the end of each month, participants in the loss incentive group and the gain incentive group would receive the same monetary amount if they met the same amount of daily goals, highlighting the greater sensitivity of individuals to monetary loss as compared to monetary gain.

Despite the potential promise of using financial incentives to promote health, there may be some downsides. Although financial incentives may encourage health behaviors (e.g., weight loss) in the short term, as shown in the meta-analysis by Ng and colleagues, such extrinsic motivators may in fact have deleterious effects on individuals' mental health and quality-of-life outcomes in the long term. Thus, financial incentives might encourage employees to lose weight in the near future, but the effects might not be lasting. For more lasting effects, employers can create an environment in which employees perceive that they have control over their weight-loss program, feel competent in their ability to lose weight, and perceive social support from peers, which ultimately may lead employees to experience higher intrinsic motivation and to achieve long-term weight-loss goals.[32]

SPOTLIGHT ON ETHICS

Merit Pay for Teachers

Implementing merit pay for teachers has been a contentious issue, particularly in the United States. Supporters contend that merit pay motivates teachers to do a better job, thus leading to better outcomes for students in terms of academic achievement and eventual employment success. Critics, on the other hand, contend that the ways in which teacher performance is evaluated can lack transparency and may be beyond teachers' direct control.

Selecting key performance indicators for teachers can be particularly challenging given that teachers can be evaluated based on their own behavior or on the behavior of their students and that student behavior can be influenced by many factors other than the teachers' classroom performance. That is, teachers may exert some degree of influence over students' behavior, including test scores, but students also arrive in a classroom with their own personal histories and unique circumstances that may affect how receptive and prepared to learn they are. Some critics argue that it can be unethical to base a substantial portion of teachers' take-home pay on their students' performance, particularly if performance is defined based on their students' success on standardized tests.

In the United States, the push for pay-for-performance programs in educational settings gained traction in the 1980s and early 1990s. At about that time, a statistician named William Sanders began advising Tennessee lawmakers on a method for evaluating teachers based on the extent to which they improved their students' standardized test scores, referred to as the *value-added approach*. The value-added approach takes into account the historical trends in students' test scores, such as whether they improved, stayed the same, or declined, and determines whether a teacher improved their students' test scores more than would be expected given that history.

Critics argue that the value-added approach is unfair, as there are a number of factors outside of teachers' direct control that can affect their value-added scores. Moreover, some teachers teach subjects that do not have an associated standardized test, which can make it difficult to evaluate them in the same manner as their peers. Analytical software companies like SAS Institute have developed algorithms to calculate the value-added scores of teachers. Some teachers and administrators have complained that these algorithms are difficult for nonstatisticians to understand, and due to the often proprietary nature of the algorithms, there can be a lack of transparency when it comes to communicating how the value-added scores are computed. Supporters of the value-added approach point to evidence that students of high value-added teachers are more likely to attend college and to go on to earn higher salaries than other students.

In terms of empirical research on the topics, research has shown that incentivizing teachers with merit pay does not always lead to higher teacher motivation or better student outcomes. In fact, the empirical findings are mixed. Some evidence indicates that merit pay leads to higher student scores in math, science, and reading, whereas other evidence suggests that merit pay may have some effect on students' math scores but not on reading scores and that teachers do not find merit-pay programs to be motivating. As a way forward, some education reform advocates contend that rewarding teacher performance should not necessarily be thrown out; rather, the structure and organization of the schools themselves should also be taken into consideration when recognizing teacher performance.[33]

Questions

1. Given the risk that low-performing teachers may do a poor job of preparing their students for eventual career success, do you think it is ethical to pay teachers without taking into account their performance? Why or why not?

2. Do you think it is ethical to base teacher pay on key performance indicators that may be, to some extent, beyond teacher control? Why or why not? Give some examples to support your opinion.

The way in which sales performance is operationalized in terms of target metrics can have important consequences for the behaviors that a program incentivizes. For example, basing sales commissions entirely on sales volume or on the percentage of revenue or profit generated may motivate aggressive selling behavior, such that salespersons focus their attention and effort predominantly on making more sales in the short term, perhaps at the expense of cultivating quality

Sales commission programs are common at car dealerships, where salespeople may earn a percentage of the revenue of each car they sell.

relationships with customers and helping out with other aspects of the sales process like processing customer returns. To motivate salespersons to build viable, long-term relationships with customers and to support other aspects of the sales process, an organization might also base sales commissions partly on customer satisfaction metrics. Establishing the right mix of metrics on which a sales commission program is based can help align the behavior of salespersons with the strategic goals of the organization.[34]

Perhaps unsurprisingly, evidence suggests that imposing upper limits on the total amount of commission salespersons can earn results in diminished motivation and sales performance when they reach that upper limit, whereas imposing no limit results in higher motivation and sales performance.[35] Further, it is important to note that the proportion of total compensation represented by a sales commission program should vary in accordance with organizational strategy. Specifically, organizations that employ a sales commissions program should consider carefully how much salespersons' pay will be contingent upon sales performance versus base pay or other forms of variable pay.

Group Pay-for-Performance Programs

Many organizations distribute rewards for group performance. In fact, some argue that deploying pay-for-performance programs only at the individual level may discourage collaboration and effective teamwork.[36] The strategic deployment of group pay-for-performance programs—generically called *success-sharing* plans—can improve group performance under certain circumstances, and group performance can be operationalized at the team, unit, facility, or organizational level.[37] Research has shown that group incentives tend to be more effective when the group in question is relatively small, such as a team, rather than the organization as a whole.[38] The following sections discuss some of the common types of group pay-for-performance programs.

Team Rewards

Because work today is increasingly team based and interdependent, team performance–contingent rewards have become more commonplace.[39] Just like individual programs, an organization can use financial rewards to motivate teams to achieve goals and reach specified performance levels. For instance, an organization might provide a year-end bonus for the manufacturing team that reduces waste the most during the manufacturing process. Meta-analytic evidence has shown that, indeed, team rewards can lead to higher performance, particularly when the team task is more complex in nature.[40] That is, more complex and complicated tasks may require greater collaboration and integration among team members, and thus team pay-for-performance programs provide additional motivation to work together in the service of their collective, shared goal. However, care must be taken to ensure that team rewards align with any individual rewards that might already be in place. Without thoughtful alignment, employees' attention might be pulled in competing—or even conflicting—directions.

Examples of team pay-for-performance programs exist across a wide variety of industries. In the professional sports industry, for example, organizations often reward teams for winning games, tournaments, series, or championships. In 2017, the National Hockey League (NHL) rewarded the Nashville Predators team $2.6 million for reaching the Stanley Cup Final in a best-of-seven series against the Pittsburgh Penguins, and the Pittsburgh Penguins received $4.325 million for winning that championship series. It was up to team management to determine how each team would distribute the financial rewards among individual team members, but ultimately it was each team's performance that determined how much pay *could* be distributed to the team.[41] Thus, beyond what individuals could receive in terms of their guaranteed base salary, NHL players also had opportunities to earn variable pay based on their team's performance. Interestingly, in other nonsports work contexts, some evidence has suggested that evenly distributing rewards to team members based on the team's overall performance may result in slower speeds but higher accuracy when it comes to the team's work, as compared to distributing rewards to team members based on their individual performance.[42]

As another example, in 2004, Google introduced its Founders' Awards, given to teams that made outstanding accomplishments on a project.[43] In the inaugural year, $12 million in stock was given to two project teams in recognition of their accomplishments. One of the award-winning teams created a process whereby Google users would be presented with advertisements that would be most relevant to them—an online experience that is ubiquitous today but was groundbreaking at the time. This team award served as a vehicle to motivate teams to continue pursuing excellence and maximize their contributions to the company. In addition to the financial reward, winning teams received accolades and recognition from their company and peers.

Gainsharing

One type of group pay-for-performance program that rewards a group of employees—often a unit or facility—for achieving certain milestones is called *gainsharing*. More than half of organizations use gainsharing as a way to reward groups of employees.[44] As the name implies, individual employees share in the success of the overall *gains* of their group, such as those related to productivity, quality, and customer service. Further, gainsharing programs can be implemented to improve individual employee involvement and participation in their group.[45] Research has shown that gainsharing can lead to higher productivity,[46] particularly when employees envision how their own actions contribute to the group's gains.

Gainsharing A type of group pay-for-performance program that rewards a group of employees for collectively achieving certain goals or objectives

Between 2006 and 2009, the Beth Israel Medical Center in New York City implemented a gainsharing program aimed at decreasing costs at the hospital level.[47] In total, 184 physicians participated in the gainsharing program, and through their involvement and participation, the 1,000-bed teaching hospital reduced costs by $25.1 million, while measures of patient care quality remained unchanged. Individual physicians shared in the hospital gains by receiving a portion of cost savings that was relative to their individual performance. In doing so, Beth Israel Medical Center managed to recognize individual contributions to hospital-level gains, thereby providing physicians with a clearer indication of how much they uniquely contributed to the hospital's success. This example of a gainsharing program illustrates how an organization can recognize individual performance in the context of a group pay-for-performance program.

Although gainsharing programs are generally beneficial for employee performance, the effects may not be as consistent or as large as those of individual pay-for-performance programs.[48] Namely, group dynamics come into play, such that individuals may have a difficult time understanding the extent to which they are contributing to the group's success. In addition, some individuals might engage in social loafing, yet if their group still achieves the goal, these individuals will still receive the same reward as those who worked harder and contributed more to the group's success.

When designing and implementing gainsharing programs, legal and ethical considerations should be front and center in the decision-making process, just as in any other HR program. In 2016, current and former employees of Whole Foods Market in the Washington, D.C., area filed a class-action lawsuit against the company, claiming that the management gamed the company's gainsharing program. The program provided monetary rewards when its departments achieved a surplus by operating under budget. According to the lawsuit, the management shifted labor costs from successful departments to other departments to avoid giving rewards to employees. Whole Foods corporate representatives argued that the issue only existed in a small number of stores and thus was not systemic; further, the company stated that it was investigating the matter. Nevertheless, this lawsuit illustrates the importance of ensuring that pay-for-performance programs are implemented fairly and in accordance with relevant policies and procedures, as well as the importance of communicating clearly the policies and procedures.[49]

Profit Sharing

Profit sharing A pay-for-performance program in which employees share in their organization's profits

As the name implies, ***profit sharing*** refers to pay-for-performance programs in which employees share in their organization's profits (e.g., return on assets). Profit-sharing rewards may be distributed as cash or placed in a retirement fund. According to the results of a WorldatWork survey, 20% of organizations use a profit-sharing program.[50] Under profit-sharing programs, the organization shares profits with its employees when targets are met or exceeded. In many cases, organizations use a formula for determining how much each individual employee receives as part of the profit sharing; however, in other cases, the amount received by each employee may be discretionary in nature.[51] In general, evidence suggests that organizations with profit-sharing programs tend to have higher productivity than comparable organizations that do not have such programs, and employees often have favorable attitudes toward these programs.[52] Further, a study of 912 employees from 45 organizations found that the positive effects of individual pay-for-performance programs on employees' perceptions of instrumentality were even stronger in organizations with an effective profit-sharing program.[53] (Recall from expectancy theory that instrumentality refers to perceptions that performance leads to rewards.) Because profit-sharing programs typically make rewards contingent upon the organization's success, employees may perceive less control over their ability to influence organizational profitability targets. Accordingly, employees may believe that profit-sharing programs carry more risk to their financial well-being than programs targeted at the individual, team, unit, or facility level.

©iStock.com/Flightlevel80

Delta Air Lines uses a profit-sharing program to motivate its employees. In 2017, the company distributed more than $1.1 billion in profit sharing to approximately 80,000 employees, with the payout constituting 10% of employees' gross income.[54]

 SPOTLIGHT ON GLOBAL ISSUES

Cultural Differences in Pay-for-Performance Programs

Pay-for-performance programs generally lead to beneficial employee and organizational outcomes. Nevertheless, regarding employee preferences for different programs, research has shown that some differences exist between collectivistic and individualistic cultures, as delineated in the cultural dimensions proposed by researcher Gert Hofstede. In individualistic cultures, individuals tend to emphasize their own unique identity and focus more on their own outcomes. In comparison, employees in collectivistic cultures tend to respond more favorably to team incentive programs and to perceive that they are procedurally fair. Further, those in collectivistic cultures are more likely to believe that their team can meet the team performance goals and, as a result, that their team will earn the reward. That is, individuals in collectivistic cultures often better understand how their individual contributions add to the team's

collective performance and thus may be more motivated by team incentives when compared to those living in individualistic cultures. As an additional difference, employees in individualistic cultures tend to prefer performance-based individual incentives, whereas employees in collectivistic cultures tend to prefer rewards that are distributed equally to all members.

As a result, multinational corporations must consider how their pay-for-performance programs are designed and implemented in relation to the prevailing cultures in the locations where they have employees. This is particularly important if cultural differences in collectivism and individualism exist. They need to ask themselves what types of pay-for-performance programs are most effective in the cultures they operate within.[55]

Stock Options

A type of group pay for performance that makes employees partial owners of the organization is the provision of ***stock options***, which allow employees to purchase a certain number of stock shares at a fixed price in a given time frame. Stock options are a long-term incentive because an employee may begin exercising these options only after a vesting period. Exercising stock options means that they may sell their stock options at a price that is higher than the fixed price when they purchased the stocks originally, resulting in a financial gain. Some research has shown that organizations tend to have higher returns on assets when they have more managers who are eligible for stock options.[56]

However, if the company stock shares fail to exceed the original fixed price at which they were purchased, then the employee gains nothing. Thus, employees may perceive stock option programs as risky, and organizations may find it difficult to attract and retain high-performing employees if stock prices follow a downward trend. As a point of caution, corporate scandals and other outside forces that devalue shares may undermine employees' faith in stock option programs, given that employees often have little influence over such matters. For example, in 2017, Adidas shares dropped immediately following the announcement of criminal charges wherein the director of global sports marketing allegedly helped bribe high school basketball players by providing them with products in exchange for signing an endorsement deal with the company should they later turn professional.[57]

Stock options A type of pay-for-performance program that makes employees partial owners of the organization by allowing employees to purchase a certain number of stock shares at a fixed price in a given time frame

Employee Stock Ownership Plans

Like stock options, ***employee stock ownership plans (ESOPs)*** reward employees when company stock shares increase in value and can only be used after a vesting period. ESOPs are also a type of defined-contribution retirement plan. Under these plans, the organization provides employees with stock shares and places these shares in an account. Employees never actually have possession of the shares while employed at the organization; rather, the organization disseminates the stock shares when an employee retires, dies, becomes disabled, or is fired by the organization. Some research has shown that ESOPs improve organizational performance, but the significant, positive effects of ESOPs tend to be relatively small.[58] Further, it is questionable how much ESOPs influence employees' motivation, as financial gains are often doled out years in the future. ESOPs position employees as owners of their company, which may lead employees to feel more invested in their company and more motivated to participate in organizational decisions, especially when they are dissatisfied with the state of their company.[59] That is, one might argue that the interests of the employees and company owners are more likely to align under ESOPs because employees begin to take on the added perspective of being company owners.

Employee stock ownership plan (ESOP) A type of pay-for-performance program and defined-contribution retirement plan that rewards employees when company stock shares increase in value and can only be used after a vesting period

Bob's Red Mill Natural Foods is a grain company based in Oregon. The company uses an employee stock ownership plan (ESOP), which makes its employees owners of the company.[60]

Challenges and Opportunities in Rewarding Performance

LO 12.5 Assess common challenges and opportunities of pay-for-performance programs.

Like any HR system, pay-for-performance programs face challenges and also present opportunities. In particular, challenges and opportunities related to performance measurement, sorting effects, labor costs, and unintended behavioral consequences are important to consider.

Performance Measurement

Effective pay-for-performance programs are predicated upon sound performance measurement. Yet this is easier said than done, as performance on a particular job is often multifaceted and nuanced, making it challenging to measure accurately. Performance can be assessed using a variety of measures, including both subjective performance evaluations and objective performance

SPOTLIGHT ON DATA AND ANALYTICS

Using Data to Evaluate Pay-for-Performance Programs

Some companies assume that pay-for-performance programs work unconditionally. That is, if you offer employees a monetary incentive, employees will improve their performance. In actuality, pay-for-performance programs are susceptible to bias and decision-making errors when it comes to determining performance levels of employees. Performance indicators, metrics, and measures are subject to unreliability and inaccuracy such that employees' true levels of performance may not be adequately captured. This can become problematic in merit-based pay-for-performance programs in which pay increases are contingent upon performance evaluations. The presence of bias (e.g., favoritism) and decision errors (e.g., omission of key performance episodes when completing rating) during performance evaluations can result in strong performers who fail to receive a reward and weak performers who receive a reward.

Fortunately, companies can use data analytics to gain insights into the quality of their pay-for-performance programs. First and foremost, a correlation can be calculated between performance evaluation scores and the amount of pay received. If pay is supposed to be based entirely on performance, then one would expect a strong correlation between performance and pay. And if a small or negligible-sized correlation is found, then it likely indicates that pay decisions are being made based on factors other than performance. Should this be the case, companies can analyze whether protected group characteristics such as age, race, and gender, as well as other factors like tenure, leave history, or education, are associated with differences in performance and pay. Significant associations between these other characteristics and pay or performance might point to problems in the measurement of performance or in the distribution of pay.

Companies with pay-for-performance programs often have (or should have) data at their disposal to diagnose the extent to which the program actually bases pay on performance, as well as potential sources of bias and decision errors.

indicators (e.g., sales volume). The quality of these measures, in terms of their reliability and validity, should not be treated as a foregone conclusion. Regardless of whether a performance measure is subjective or objective in nature, care should be taken to ensure that the measures used in a pay-for-performance program are well designed, relatively free of bias and judgment errors, and transparent and easy to understand. Ultimately, employee perceptions of fairness should be a primary focus when developing and implementing a performance measure, particularly when tied to administrative outcomes like pay increases.

Meta-analytic evidence has shown that subjective performance measures, such as those found in supervisor-rated performance evaluations, often suffer from lower-than-desired interrater reliability—a lack of consistency between raters in evaluating the same group of employees.[61] In some instances, inconsistency between raters may be attributed to measure contamination or deficiency. Imagine a performance evaluation measure designed for the job of an office manager in which supervisors are instructed to rate job incumbents using a five-point scale along three behavioral dimensions: fiscal affairs management, staff management, and event management. If the behavioral dimension of event management is not relevant to the job but is still assessed, then the performance evaluation measure will suffer from contamination. If, on the other hand, a behavioral dimension called "office promotion" is relevant to the job but is not assessed, then the performance evaluation measure will suffer from deficiency. Given concerns regarding contamination and deficiency, subjective performance evaluation measures should be designed or selected based on an up-to-date, rigorous job analysis, and supervisors should be trained on how to rate employees using the measures. Moreover, when designing or selecting objective measures of performance, efforts should be made to use only those measures that are relevant to how performance is conceptualized for the job in question so as to avoid contamination and deficiency.

SPOTLIGHT ON LEGAL ISSUES

Accusations of Discrimination at the U.S. Secret Service Agency

The U.S. Secret Service is a federal law enforcement agency tasked with protecting the president, the vice president, and their family members. It also investigates financial, cyber, terrorism, and child-exploitation crimes. In 2000, a small group of African American Secret Service agents filed a lawsuit against the agency, alleging racial discrimination in various employment practices, including performance evaluations and bonus pay. In 2008, a senior Secret Service inspector acknowledged that documents related to the lawsuit had been destroyed. Later, a federal judge ruled that the agency "made a mockery" of the law by refusing to provide documents requested by the African American plaintiffs during the

discovery process and defying court orders, among other things. The number of plaintiffs eventually increased to include more than 100 African American agents, and the case became a class action.

In 2017, the U.S. Secret Service agreed to settle the lawsuit by paying $24 million to the group of African American agents, which could include lump-sum payments of $300,000 for each agent. Upon the announcement of the settlement agreement and resolution, Secretary of Homeland Security Jeh C. Johnson issued an official statement, which concluded, "This settlement is also, simply, the right thing to do."[62]

Bias, office politics, and other sources of error can also affect the integrity of performance measures on which pay-for-performance programs are based. Yahoo Inc. found this out first-hand when a former employee sued the company for allegedly distorting and manipulating the performance evaluation rating system.[63] The lawsuit contended that Yahoo managers were required to sort employees into one of five different performance levels such that only a certain percentage of employees were allowed to be categorized into each level, resulting in some employees who were sorted into different performance levels even though they demonstrated the same or similar performance. The lawsuit alleges that Yahoo's system lacked transparency and relied on higher-level managers, who often had little contact with the employees in question, to provide input into the performance rankings. The allegations in this lawsuit highlight the importance of using performance measures that employees perceive as fair and are able to understand, particularly when such performance measures are used for administrative purposes like determining pay, promotions, or termination.

Incentive and Sorting Effects

Thus far the chapter has focused primarily on the *incentive effects* of pay-for-performance programs. Incentive effects refer to the extent to which pay-for-performance programs motivate employees' on-the-job behavior and pursuit of goals. However, pay-for-performance programs may also have other effects on employee and nonemployee behavior. Empirical evidence has shown that individuals tend to gravitate to jobs with reward systems that fit their disposition, goals, and performance capabilities, and the associated processes of attraction, selection, and attrition are referred to collectively as *sorting effects*.[64] That is, individuals who view themselves as high performers or who are (or have been) high performers often prefer pay-for-performance programs, as they stand to gain when participating in such programs. In addition, to some extent, individuals who have a dispositional aversion to risk taking often avoid pay-for-performance programs and are less motivated by pay-for-performance incentives, whereas those who have a higher need for achievement and self-efficacy find pay-for-performance programs to be more attractive.[65]

Sorting can be understood by applying the attraction–selection–attrition model, which proposes that organizational employees become more homogenous over time through the

Incentive effects The extent to which pay-for-performance programs motivate employees' on-the-job behavior and pursuit of goals

Sorting effects The associated processes of attraction, selection, and attrition that occur when employees gravitate toward jobs with reward systems that fit their disposition, goals, and performance capabilities

■ **FIGURE 12.5** The Attraction–Selection–Attrition Model

The attraction–selection–attrition model can be used to understand sorting effects. For example, people who prefer pay-for-performance programs and who are likely to reap the benefits of such programs prefer organizations with pay-for-performance programs. Consequently, they are more likely to be attracted to an organization with a pay-for-performance program, more likely to be selected by an organization with a pay-for-performance program, and more likely to leave an organization that lacks a pay-for-performance program.

processes of attraction, selection, and attrition, resulting in a more uniform organizational culture (see Figure 12.5).[66] The process of attraction occurs when, through recruiting materials, image advertising, and word of mouth, potential employees learn the characteristics of an organization (e.g., values, required KSAOs) and ultimately base their attraction to the organization on their own perceived fit to the organization. Meta-analytic evidence has shown that individuals who perceive a stronger fit between themselves and an organization form a stronger sense of attraction to the organization, making it more likely that they will apply for a vacant position.[67] As such, individuals who believe that they possess the required KSAOs and who value pay-for-performance programs (and believe that they stand to benefit from them) will be more attracted to organizations with such programs.

The process of selection occurs when an organization chooses those applicants with the KSAOs and values that are most similar to the KSAOs and values already possessed by current employees. An organization with a pay-for-performance program will be more likely to select applicants who have the required KSAOs and who value pay-for-performance programs.

The process of attrition occurs when, after some length of time, those employees who do not fit well into the organization ultimately leave the organization, resulting in a more homogenous group of employees within the organization. With respect to pay-for-performance programs, individuals who possess KSAOs that enable high performance in an organization and whose values align with pay-for-performance programs will be more likely to stay in organizations with such programs.

Labor Costs

Labor costs, such as those associated with pay-for-performance programs, can account for 70% of an organization's total costs, which means that they should be invested wisely, monitored closely, and forecasted accurately.[68] Despite potential positive effects on employee motivation and performance, pay-for-performance programs can make it challenging to predict future labor costs, particularly when the number of employees earning performance-contingent rewards varies over time (see Figure 12.6). Because employees' performance levels fluctuate across time and can be influenced by forces in the external environment (e.g., ups and downs in the economy), the number of employees reaping rewards from pay-for-performance programs inevitably varies as well.

To plan for the anticipated labor costs associated with pay-for-performance programs, statistical modeling and expert judgment can be used. First, the application of statistical modeling allows an organization to use prior evidence (e.g., performance, pay, and other factors potentially

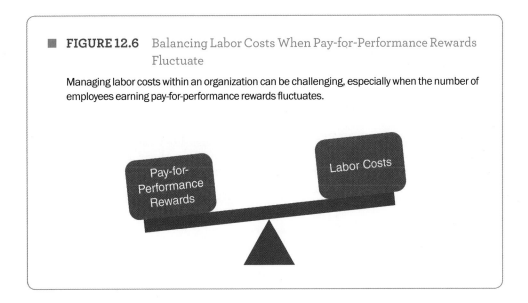

■ **FIGURE 12.6** Balancing Labor Costs When Pay-for-Performance Rewards Fluctuate

Managing labor costs within an organization can be challenging, especially when the number of employees earning pay-for-performance rewards fluctuates.

influencing performance and pay) to project how much money should be set aside to cover future labor costs. One limitation of such an approach is that statistical modeling assumes that whatever happened in the past will continue to happen in a similar manner in the future. As such, in situations in which a historically rare or unexpected occurrence happens, statistical models may not provide accurate labor cost estimates. As another limitation, it is important to remember that models of any kind, whether statistical, mathematical, or conceptual, are parsimonious approximations of reality. It is unlikely that a statistical model will include all relevant factors, and thus it is also unlikely that a statistical model will perfectly predict a future event. Statistical modeling is often a luxury available only to companies that have a sufficiently large workforce to generate a sufficiently powerful sample size; smaller companies may not have enough employees to reliably and accurately estimate model parameters.

Second, the application of expert judgment allows an organization to draw upon the subject-matter expertise of individuals who understand the industry, the employees, and the economic environment within which the organization operates. Expert judgment can augment the information gleaned from statistical models and other sources of information, particularly in instances in which unexpected or unusual events occur that may have an impact on labor costs. For instance, imagine that an unexpected economic recession occurs. For an organization that chooses to respond by laying off employees, what effect may such an event have on remaining employees' performance? Individuals can offer expert judgment based on their knowledge of pay-for-performance programs and human behavior to anticipate the extent to which a layoff will affect employee performance and ultimately the potential labor costs. Yet expert judgment has its limitations, as it is subject to any number of cognitive biases and judgment and decision-making errors. As such, expert judgment is by no means a panacea when it comes to projecting future labor costs associated with a pay-for-performance program. Nonetheless, when used in tandem, statistical modeling and expert judgment can make a formidable team by leading to more accurate forecasts.

Unintended Behavioral Consequences

Pay-for-performance programs can lead to unintended behavioral consequences, particularly when management fails to monitor employee behavior. The purpose of pay-for-performance programs is to motivate employees to enact behaviors to help realize the organization's strategic objectives. When unmonitored by management or poorly thought out, pay-for-performance programs may lead to such problems as employees demonstrating fewer organizational citizenship behaviors, more unethical behaviors, and, in the context of group pay-for-performance programs, less effort and cooperation.

The Role of Pay-for-Performance Programs

Empirical evidence points to the importance of pay-for-performance programs in small businesses. Based on data collected from 444 organizations, each with fewer than 500 employees, Wang, Thornhill, and Zhao investigated the extent to which pay-for-performance programs affected employee and organizational outcomes in small organizations. Results indicated that employees in organizations with a broader variety of pay-for-performance programs participated more frequently in various organizational activities and programs, such as job rotation and cross-training, organization-improvement meetings, and quality-assurance and workflow troubleshooting. In turn, organizations with greater employee participation in the aforementioned programs tended to show higher profit margins, growth rates, and value added per employee. These findings suggest that employees who work in small organizations with a variety of pay-for-performance programs (e.g., merit pay, individual incentives, profit sharing) tend to be more motivated to involve themselves in organizational activities and programs; this greater level of employee involvement is associated, in turn, with better organizational outcomes.

Interestingly, in this study, employees showed the highest frequency of participation in organizational activities and programs when they worked in small organizations where pay-for-performance programs constituted a moderate proportion of overall direct compensation (including base pay), as opposed to a low or high proportion. Similarly, profit margins, growth margins, and value added per employee were highest in small organizations in which pay-for-performance programs constituted a moderate proportion of overall direct compensation. Accordingly, if the proportion of performance-contingent pay relative to overall pay is too low, then employees feel less motivated to participate in organizational activities and programs because so much of their pay is fixed, thereby providing less of an incentive to become involved and seek rewards. Conversely, if the proportion of performance-contingent pay is too high, then employees feel less motivated to participate due to feelings of stress and fatigue, as so much of their pay is contingent upon their performance and thus, to some degree, uncertain. Finally, the extent to which employees participate in organizational activities and programs is consequential for organizational outcomes, as more involved and participative employees lead to better outcomes.

Overall, the findings from this study highlight the importance of pay-for-performance programs in small businesses. Namely, small organizations should consider offering a breadth of pay-for-performance programs, yet at the same time, they should be careful not to distribute too much of employees' pay in the form of variable pay. In this study, the researchers found that, on average, organizations distributed 13% of employees' total pay in the form of pay for performance, with a standard deviation of 23%, which was consistent with prior studies. The proportion of pay-for-performance compensation relative to overall direct compensation that is best for any particular organization will depend on a number of factors, including industry, organizational culture, and employee preferences.[69]

Organizational Citizenship Behaviors

Research has shown that pay-for-performance programs may motivate employees to enact core task behaviors and demotivate them to enact organizational citizenship behaviors, the latter of which include discretionary helping behaviors.[70] That is, pay-for-performance programs may, at times, do such an effective job of focusing employees' attention on task behaviors that employees ignore or forget to engage in nontask, helping behaviors. When employees' values are aligned with the values of the organization, the demotivating effect of pay-for-performance programs on organizational citizenship behaviors seems to disappear.[71] Thus, it is important to select and retain individuals who fit the organization's culture and values, particularly when pay-for-performance programs are used. Further, to encourage organizational citizenship behaviors, additional rewards can be made contingent upon enactment of organizational citizenship behaviors, and management can take an active role in encouraging employees to remember to help one another and the organization.

Unethical Behaviors

Another potential unintended consequence of pay-for-performance programs is unethical behavior. When a reward is contingent upon enactment of a particular behavior, individuals are more likely to enact that behavior in order to receive the reward, even if that behavior is unethical. Not surprisingly, research has shown that rewarding individuals for engaging in unethical behavior leads to even more unethical behavior.[72] Interestingly, pay-for-performance programs can also encourage unethical behavior even when unethical behavior was not directly or intentionally incentivized. For example, Wells Fargo made major news headlines in 2016 after it was revealed that employees opened and closed unauthorized bank accounts for customers, which is not only unethical and discourteous but also illegal.[73] Employees engaged in this unethical behavior because they received financial incentives based on meeting their sales goals, which were contingent upon how many customer accounts they opened. Thus, from a reinforcement theory perspective, the organization provided rewards in the form of additional pay when employees opened new accounts, thereby reinforcing the act of opening accounts. Perceiving the instrumentality of opening accounts and receiving rewards, some employees took advantage of the pay-for-performance program by opening accounts in order to increase their pay, and without the knowledge or consent of customers. Wells Fargo leadership was somewhat sluggish in its attempts to investigate the unethical behavior and allowed it to remain unchecked for some time.[74] In the aftermath, Wells Fargo was fined $185 million and terminated thousands of employees who engaged in these unethical and illegal behaviors.

As another example, in 2014, the U.S. Secretary of Veterans Affairs (VA) resigned amid a scandal in which employees hid the long wait times of veterans who sought medical care. Some have suspected that a pay-for-performance program used in at least one VA hospital may have inadvertently incentivized employees to engage in the unethical behavior. Specifically, in one hospital, physicians received financial rewards for minimizing the number of patient follow-up visits. The case of Wells Fargo and the case of the VA illustrate the importance of anticipating unintended consequences of pay-for-performance programs by carefully considering theories of motivation when designing such programs and by encouraging management to take an active role in monitoring the implementation of the program.

Effort and Cooperation

Rewards targeted at team or group performance may not necessarily lead to more effort and cooperative behaviors.[75] Group pay-for-performance programs are often introduced to encourage collectives of employees to work more effectively and efficiently; the underlying logic is that individuals working together experience certain synergies that allow them to tackle large and complicated tasks. As this chapter describes, research has shown that group pay-for-performance programs (e.g., gain sharing, profit sharing) can lead to higher group performance; however, the degree to which the pay-for-performance program inspires group performance will depend upon the group's history, how the program is structured, and the degree to which the program is monitored.[76] Further, just because a reward is linked to group performance, groups will not necessarily cooperate well with other groups; rather, group rewards may inadvertently lead to competition between different groups, which may result in diminished information sharing between groups.[77]

When groups become too large or are left unmonitored, some members may engage in social loafing and free riding, wherein they apply less effort and thus fail to contribute their fair share.[78] In addition, in larger groups, individuals often find it challenging to understand how their own efforts contribute to the group's overall performance.[79] To help mitigate some of these unintended consequences, individual rewards can be used in tandem with group rewards—as long as they are aligned—to encourage the engagement of *all* group members. Further, to avoid inter-group competition, organizations might consider adding a unit-, facility-, or organization-level pay-for-performance program (e.g., gainsharing, profit sharing) if one does not already exist. The addition of such a program may provide incentive for groups to work together (or at least avoid competing with one another) for the greater good of the organization.

CHAPTER SUMMARY

Unlike traditional-pay programs, pay-for-performance programs reward performance directly. That is, in pay-for-performance programs, if an employee meets performance standards or goals, the employee receives a reward. Pay is a classic example of an extrinsic motivator, as it represents an external environmental force that can affect an employee's effort. We can apply different theories, such as reinforcement theory, expectancy theory, and goal-setting theory, to understand and explain when and why different pay and pay-for-performance programs enhance motivation and performance. A variety of pay-for-performance programs exist; some reward individual performance, whereas others reward group performance. Individual pay-for-performance programs include merit pay, bonuses, spot awards, individual incentives, and sales commissions. Group pay-for-performance programs include team incentives, gainsharing, profit sharing, stock options, and employee stock ownership plans. Organizations face several challenges and opportunities when designing and implementing pay-for-performance programs. For instance, by deploying well-designed performance measures, organizations can maximize the effectiveness of their pay-for-performance programs, as well as ensure fairness and mitigate bias. Further, calculating labor costs for pay-for-performance programs can be challenging because many complex factors influence those costs. Finally, pay-for-performance programs can motivate employees to exhibit negative behaviors, and organizations need to be vigilant against these types of unintended consequences.

KEY TERMS

pay for performance (performance-contingent pay)   408
traditional-pay programs   409
pay-for-performance programs   409
motivation   409
extrinsic motivation   409
intrinsic motivation   410
reinforcement theory   411
expectancy theory   412
expectancy   412

instrumentality   413
valence   413
goal-setting theory   415
merit pay   417
bonuses   417
spot awards   417
individual incentives   418
piecework plans   418
straight piecework plan   418
differential piecework plan   419

standard-hour plans   419
sales commissions   419
gainsharing   423
profit sharing   424
stock options   425
employee stock ownership plans (ESOPs)   425
incentive effects   427
sorting effects   427

$SAGE edge™

Visit **edge.sagepub.com/bauer** to help you accomplish your coursework goals in an easy-to-use learning environment.

- Master the learning objectives using key study tools
- Watch, listen, and connect with online multimedia resources
- Access mobile-friendly quizzes and flashcards to check your understanding

HR REASONING AND DECISION-MAKING EXERCISES

MINI-CASE ANALYSIS EXERCISE: PAY FOR PERFORMANCE AND GOAL SETTING

Several years ago, Xeon Manufacturing introduced a new pay-for-performance program. The program was designed to provide manufacturing workers with financial rewards for meeting individual goals related to waste reduction and units produced. Today, upper management is concerned that the pay-for-performance program has failed to motivate its manufacturing workers, as they have not observed discernible improvements in waste reduction and units produced. Interestingly, the manufacturing workers have communicated that the amount of financial rewards attached to goal completion is appropriate. Thus, the question remains, why aren't the manufacturing goals motivating?

Upper management has asked you to investigate why the pay-for-performance program is not, in fact, improving motivation and performance. You decide to use goal-setting theory (and the SMART goal acronym) to inform your investigation.

Questions:

1. Based on goal-setting theory, what types of goals tend to lead to greater motivation and greater performance? Why?

2. Using goal-setting theory as a framework, if you were to interview current manufacturing employees about the motivating potential (or lack thereof) of the goals pertaining to waste reduction and units produced, what questions might you ask?

HR DECISION ANALYSIS EXERCISE: ALIGNING INDIVIDUAL AND TEAM REWARDS

For the past decade, your company has encouraged sales teams to work together in a cooperative and cohesive manner. This initiative is closely aligned with one of the company's core values: *"Together, we achieve more."* To motivate sales associates to cooperate with one another in their respective teams, at the end of each fiscal year, team managers evaluate their respective teams by rating them on a number of behavioral dimensions related to cooperation and cohesion. Teams that receive high marks on their evaluations receive year-end bonuses, and this bonus program accounts for 10% of compensation for those working as salespeople; the remaining 90% of compensation is distributed in the form of a base salary. Thus far, the company has found this pay-for-performance system to be quite effective, as team cooperation and cohesion have improved demonstrably.

Lately, your company has lost some of its top sales associates to competitors, and exit interviews revealed that some sales associates believed that they were not recognized and rewarded for their unique, individual contributions to the organization—namely, their sales productivity. To address this issue, the company has decided to implement a new pay-for-performance program designed to reward individual sales associates for their sales productivity; specifically, the company plans to implement a sales commission program. This new variable-pay program constitutes 40% of their compensation, and the remaining 60% will be distributed in the form of a base salary (50%) and a team bonus based on manager ratings of team cooperation and cohesion (10%). Ultimately, the organization wants to incentivize team cooperation and cohesion as well as individual sales productivity in an effort to encourage collaboration and individual contributions.

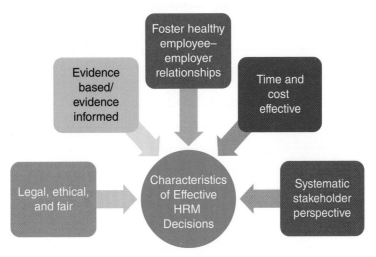

Consider the entire compensation package from a systems perspective. Do you have any concerns regarding the implementation of the new sales commission program? Do you think there will be any unintended consequences? Consider this decision using the following criteria.

Please provide the rationale for your answer to each of the questions below.

Is the compensation package legal, ethical, and fair?

_____
_____
_____
_____

Is it evidence based/evidence informed?

_____
_____
_____
_____

Does it foster healthy employee–employer relationships?

_____
_____
_____
_____

Is it time and cost effective?

_____
_____
_____
_____

Does it take a systematic stakeholder perspective?

_____
_____
_____
_____

Considering your analysis, overall, do you think this would be an effective decision? Why or why not?

_____
_____
_____
_____

What, if anything, do you think should be done differently or considered to help make this decision more effective?

_____
_____
_____

HR DECISION-MAKING EXERCISE: APPLYING EXPECTANCY THEORY TO UNDERSTAND PAY FOR PERFORMANCE

Three years ago, a large clothing retailer called La Ropa de Moda developed and implemented a new pay-for-performance program targeted at sales associates. The relatively new program is a sales performance incentive fund (SPIF) that provides a bonus for selling certain items of clothing. La Ropa de Moda learned that one of its competitors used SPIFs to sell old inventory to great effect. Because La Ropa de Moda has been having issues selling clothes from prior seasons, the company decided to implement a similar program. Unfortunately, La Ropa de Moda has found that even when a SPIF is attached to certain items of clothing, much of the old inventory sits on sales floors across the company's many locations. Thus, to date, the SPIF program has been largely ineffective when it comes to motivating employees to sell old inventory.

Sales associates' base hourly wage ranges from $14 to $19, and differences in hourly wage are attributable to years of experience in retail, seniority, and merit-based pay increases. SPIFs are attached to specific clothing items from prior seasons and range in value from $1 to $5. In addition to the SPIF program, sales associates receive a 7% commission on each article of clothing they sell. For example, if a sales associate sells a $100 pair of jeans, then the associate will earn a commission of $7. The average cost of an article of clothing in the store is $50, and on a typical 8-hour day, the average salesperson will sell $600 worth of clothing. The average salesperson works 33 hours per week.

On the one hand, the base wage and commissions earned by sales associates each pay period are distributed in a biweekly paycheck. On the other hand, the annual SPIFs earned by a single sales associate are paid out in one year-end lump-sum bonus, and thus SPIFs are not included in the paycheck corresponding to the pay period in which they were earned.

Apply the principles of expectancy theory to understand why the pay-for-performance program at La Ropa de Moda is failing to motivate sales associates to sell old inventory.

1. Identify and discuss the core components and propositions of expectancy theory.

2. Based on the information provided, do you think that low perceived *expectancy* among sales associates explains the lack of motivation to sell old items with SPIFs attached? Why?

3. Discuss whether sales associates' perceptions of *instrumentality* explain the lack of motivation to sell items with SPIFs.

4. Discuss whether sales associates' perceptions of *valence* explain the lack of motivation to sell items with SPIFs.

DATA AND ANALYTICS EXERCISE: EVALUATING COMPENSATION

A reward system typically represents a major cost for an organization. As such, it is important to evaluate the system and its constituent components. One important metric is the *total compensation expense factor*. The metric is calculated to describe how much an organization spends on total compensation (i.e., compensation, benefits) for all employees relative to total operating expenses.

$$Total\ Compensation\ Expense\ Factor = \frac{Compensation\ Expenses + Benefits\ Expenses}{Total\ Operating\ Expenses}$$

For example, if the sum of compensation and benefits expenses across all employees for the year is $10.3 million and the total annual operating expenses for the company are $12.9 million, then the total compensation expense factor is .798 ($10.3 million / $12.9 million = .798). An organization can use this metric to benchmark (i.e., compare) its total compensation expenses with those of other organizations. Further, an organization can track this metric over time to identify trends or to budget for total compensation expenses in the future. Moreover, an organization may drill down to pay-for-performance program expenses (or other specific reward expenses) relative to total operating expenses by calculating the *pay-for-performance expense factor*.

$$Pay\text{-}for\text{-}Performance\ Expense\ Factor = \frac{Pay\text{-}for\text{-}Performance\ Expenses}{Total\ Operating\ Expenses}$$

For example, if the annual expenses associated with pay-for-performance program expenses are $1.2 million, and the total annual operating expenses for the company are $12.9 million, then the pay-for-performance expense factor is .093 ($1.2 million / $12.9 million = .093).

Another important metric is the *total compensation revenue factor*, which can be used to describe how much an organization spends on total compensation for all employees relative to the amount of revenue generated.

$$Total\ Compensation\ Revenue\ Factor = \frac{Compensation\ Expenses + Benefits\ Expenses}{Total\ Revenue}$$

For example, if the sum of compensation and benefits expenses across all employees for the year is $10.3 million and the total annual revenue for the company is $13.9 million, then the total compensation revenue factor is .741 ($10.3 million / $13.9 million = .741). Like the total compensation expense factor, the total compensation revenue factor can be benchmarked against those of other organizations and can be tracked over time for the purposes of trend identification and financial planning and budgeting. Further, an organization can drill down to pay-for-performance expenses (or other specific reward expenses) relative to total revenue by calculating the *pay-for-performance revenue factor*.

$$Pay\text{-}for\text{-}Performance\ Revenue\ Factor = \frac{Pay\text{-}for\text{-}Performance\ Expenses}{Total\ Revenue}$$

For example, if the annual expenses associated with pay-for-performance programs are $1.2 million, and the total annual revenue for the company is $13.9 million, then the pay-for-performance revenue factor is .086 ($1.2 million / $13.9 million = .086). In this context, the metric is useful for evaluating the extent to which increases in pay-for-performance program expenses are associated with corresponding increases in total revenue generated. For instance, if the pay-for-performance program expenses grew to $1.4 million the following year and total revenue stayed the same, then the metric would increase to .101 ($1.4 million / $13.9 million = .101). The shift from .086 to .101 from one year to the next might signal that the pay-for-performance programs need to be critically evaluated, as employees reaped greater rewards but did not generate more revenue.

✓ EXCEL EXTENSION: NOW YOU TRY!

- On **edge.sagepub.com/bauer**, you will find an Excel exercise on evaluating a reward system.

- First, compute the total compensation expense factors and total compensation revenue factors across 3 years.

- Second, compute the pay-for-performance expense factors and pay-for-performance revenue factors across the same 3 years.

- Third, identify and interpret any notable trends.

CHAPTER 12 SUPPLEMENT: CERTIFIED COMPENSATION AND BENEFITS PROFESSIONALS

Today, HR professionals who design and manage their organization's reward systems, including compensation and benefits programs, often pursue some type of certification. WorldatWork offers some of the most popular certification programs that are specific to compensation and benefits. Through WorldatWork, HR professionals can earn the following certifications: Certified Compensation Professional (CCP), Advanced Certified Compensation Professional (ACCP), Master Certified Compensation Professional (MCCP), Certified Executive Compensation Professional (CECP), Certified Sales Compensation Professional (CSCP), Certified Benefits Professional (CBP), and Work Life Certified Professional (WLCP). These certifications signal expertise and proficiency in the administration of various types of reward systems, and they are earned by passing required exams. For example, to become a Certified Compensation Professional (CCP), one must pass the following exams:

- Total Rewards Management

- Accounting and Finance for the Human Resources Professional

- Strategic Communication in Total Rewards

- Job Analysis, Documentation and Evaluation

- Market Pricing—Conducting a Competitive Pay Analysis
- Variable Pay—Improving Performance With Variable Pay
- Quantitative Principles in Compensation Management
- Regulatory Environments for Compensation Programs
- Base Pay Administration and Pay for Performance
- Business Acumen for Compensation Professionals

More information on WorldatWork certifications can be found on its website: https://www.worldatwork.org/certification

Managing Benefits

13

Opening Case

Providing Benefits to Gig Workers at Care.com

A gig refers to a single project or task that an individual completes for pay, and individuals who complete gigs are often referred to as gig workers. Examples of gigs range from driving for Uber and Lyft to performing assignments for TaskRabbit and Postmates. Estimates suggest that more than 23 million Americans work in the gig economy, and a 2017 MetLife survey indicated that 51% of workers expressed interest in gig work instead of a full-time, salaried position at a single organization. Because many gig workers earn most of their income through part-time employment or independent contracts, they typically do not have access to the employer-sponsored benefits that full-time employees have. As such, a common complaint among gig workers is the lack of certain voluntary benefits—something that an organization called Care.com has sought to change.

Founded in 2007, Care.com is the world's largest online marketplace aimed at connecting families with caregivers, babysitters, and nannies. The company's overarching objective is "to improve the lives of families and caregivers by helping them connect in a reliable and easy way." Care.com's online marketplace connects millions of families with gig workers who provide care services. Amid calls for added protections and benefits for gig workers, in 2016, Care.com unveiled an initiative to contribute up to $500 per year to each care provider for health care, educational, and transportation expenses—a benefit that is relatively unheard of among gig workers.

Care.com funds this employee benefit with a portion of the transaction fee charged to families who use the company's services. In addition to having up to $500 to spend each year on qualified expenses, the benefit allows workers to roll unspent money forward to the following year. With health care costs increasing, $500 per year is likely not enough to pay for all health care, educational, and transportation expenses. However, the Patient Protection and Affordable Care Act provides workers who are not covered under employee health insurance with an opportunity to purchase relatively affordable health care policies. As such, when the $500-per-year sum is applied toward health care plan premiums, deductibles, and other expenses, care providers at Care.com can significantly reduce their annual out-of-pocket expenditures.

Care.com's initiative was among the first of its kind and is at the forefront of a larger movement toward providing more benefits to gig workers. Some groups, such as the Independent Drivers' Guild in New York City,

LEARNING OBJECTIVES

After reading and studying this chapter, you should be able to do the following:

13.1 Understand how benefits act as rewards and support organizational strategy.

13.2 Identify the different types of legally required benefits.

13.3 Describe the different types of voluntary benefits.

13.4 Assess the common challenges and opportunities associated with administering benefits programs.

13.5 Assess the common challenges and opportunities associated with communicating benefits programs.

©iStock.com/yacobchuk

have advocated for legislation that would require a fee to be added to gig-economy transactions—similar to the one implemented by Care.com—to provide portable benefits that workers could use even after switching to new gigs. In Seattle, the city council voted unanimously to allow taxi and ride-sharing drivers for companies such as Lyft and Uber to unionize, which provides independent contractors and gig workers with greater influence when it comes to introducing and changing benefits. As more workers take on gigs, other companies and governments may initiate new benefits, policies, and practices out of consideration for gig workers.[1]

Case Discussion Questions

1. What type of benefit did Care.com introduce for its gig workers? Why?

2. In addition to offsetting health care, educational, and transportation expenses, what other benefits could Care.com provide to its gig workers? What types of benefits would be most valuable to gig workers?

3. What effect might gig workers' ability to unionize have on their access to benefits?

4. In your opinion, in the future, will gig workers receive greater access to benefits, or will societal expectations of benefits change such that gig workers no longer expect access to employer-sponsored benefits? Why?

▶ Click to learn more...

To learn more about the challenges many gig workers face and how portable benefits might help, watch this video published by the *Wall Street Journal*:

https://www.wsj.com/video/series/financial-inclusion-in-america/america-changing-workforce-independent-and-gig-workers/A8D181BC-7494-4D6D-BE8A-250EBDFD841F

Benefits Employee rewards, which are a type of indirect pay, that include health, life, and disability insurance; retirement programs; and work–life balance programs

Benefits are an important component of an organization's broader reward system and constitute an important part of an employee's total compensation package. We often think of compensation as direct pay—base and variable salary or wages—but benefits are a form of indirect pay, which means they are not typically distributed as part of base or variable pay. Rather, benefits include programs, services, and perquisites related to health care, retirement, work–life balance, and income protection. Some benefits are required by law, and thus all organizations must offer these benefits. Other benefits are voluntary, meaning organizations can weigh the costs of providing such benefits in relation to the potential gains when it comes to attracting, motivating, and retaining employees. Ideally, voluntary benefits will be selected and implemented strategically and in the service of the organization's values, mission, and objectives. In many companies, HR plays a big role in administering and, sometimes, even selecting which benefits will be offered. In addition, HR professionals often play key roles in communicating what the benefit plan offering(s) entail(s), particularly if the organization will be contributing to employees' plans in some way.

Benefits as Rewards

LO 13.1 Understand how benefits act as rewards and support organizational strategy.

In 2018, the U.S. Bureau of Labor Statistics (BLS) reported that 72% of civilian workers had access to medical benefits, which are one of the most common forms of voluntary benefits; access to such benefits was notably higher (88%) among workers who had a full-time position within their company.[2] The BLS also reported that benefits, on average, accounted for 32% of organizations' total compensation costs.[3] Further, a Society for Human Resource Management (SHRM) report indicated that for 29% of surveyed employees, benefits offerings were a reason to seek jobs outside their current organization, signaling the importance of benefits from an employee-retention standpoint.[4] Moreover, from the employee's perspective, there are often tax benefits when receiving rewards in the form of benefits versus cash compensation.

Many U.S. workers have access to voluntary benefits, and although benefits represent a major cost for organizations, they also represent an opportunity for attracting, motivating, and retaining workers. Because organizations differ in terms of which voluntary benefits they provide, employees may be more attracted to some organizations than others based on the differences in benefits packages offered. Likewise, employees may be more likely to remain in their current organization if the benefits offerings meet their needs. Regarding motivation, some retirement programs, such as profit-sharing and employee stock ownership programs, offer benefits that are contingent upon the company's performance, thereby incentivizing employees to focus on company goals and objectives. Some organizations even offer paid time off and flexible work arrangements as incentives for meeting performance goals.[5]

Benefits have the potential to support organizational strategy and play an important role in achieving a competitive advantage, particularly when properly aligned with strategic objectives. In fact, SHRM reported in 2018 that over the prior year, 34% of surveyed employers reported expanding their voluntary benefits offerings over the previous year, signaling their strategic value. Perhaps not surprisingly, in a SHRM report from 2017, employers that leveraged benefits strategically to boost recruitment and retention efforts reported higher organizational performance and higher-than-average recruitment and retention effectiveness.[6]

As with a compensation strategy, developing a benefits strategy is a necessary but not sufficient step in the process of successfully implementing benefits offerings. That is, once a strategy is developed, a concerted effort must be made to disseminate and explain the benefits strategy to employees. Without careful communication, even the most promising strategy may go unnoticed or misunderstood. After all, benefits typically account for one-third of total compensation costs, and sometimes this nonnegligible value is ineffectively communicated to employees, leaving employees unaware of the value of their benefits.

Later in the chapter, we will discuss how to communicate the value of benefits to employees. But first, we review the two broad classifications of employee benefits in greater detail: legally required benefits and voluntary benefits (see Figure 13.1). Both types of benefits evolve continuously, as they are shaped by new regulations and legislation, as well as the changing preferences and needs of employers and their employees.

Legally Required Benefits

LO 13.2 Identify the different types of legally required benefits.

In the United States, certain benefits are required by law. Some legally required benefits are referred to as social insurance programs, as they address societal problems that many or all

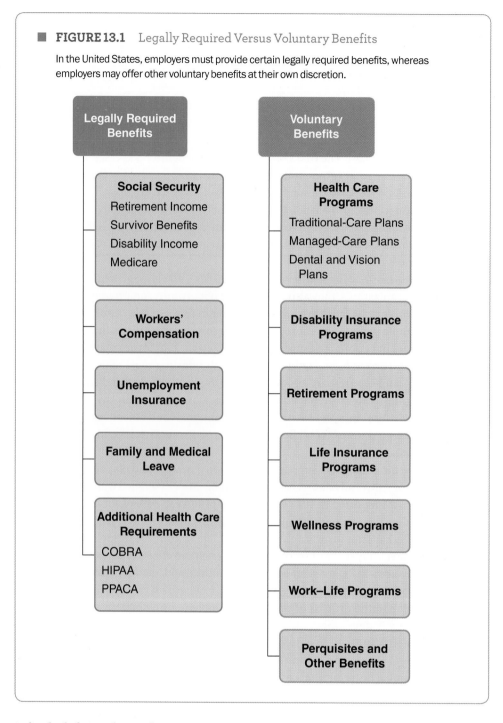

■ **FIGURE 13.1** Legally Required Versus Voluntary Benefits

In the United States, employers must provide certain legally required benefits, whereas employers may offer other voluntary benefits at their own discretion.

Legally Required Benefits

Social Security
Retirement Income
Survivor Benefits
Disability Income
Medicare

Workers' Compensation

Unemployment Insurance

Family and Medical Leave

Additional Health Care Requirements
COBRA
HIPAA
PPACA

Voluntary Benefits

Health Care Programs
Traditional-Care Plans
Managed-Care Plans
Dental and Vision Plans

Disability Insurance Programs

Retirement Programs

Life Insurance Programs

Wellness Programs

Work–Life Programs

Perquisites and Other Benefits

individuals face and provide a minimum income floor. Among civilian workers in the United States, legally required benefits account for, on average, 23% of employers' total benefits costs, and payroll tax contributions to such programs are a significant expense for most employees (as well as their employer).[7] The following sections describe the legally required benefits of Social Security, workers' compensation, unemployment insurance, and family and medical leave, as well as legally required health care programs.

Social Security

In 1935, the U.S. Congress passed the ***Social Security Act*** as part of the New Deal aimed at helping the United States recover from the Great Depression, which had left many Americans

Social Security Act Passed by the U.S. Congress in 1935 as part of the New Deal to help the United States recover from the Great Depression by providing economic security for old-age individuals and, later, additional programs for mothers and children in need, individuals with disabilities, the unemployed, and those whose family members have died

out of work and with few resources at their disposal. The act originally focused on the provision of economic security for old-age individuals, but through subsequent amendments, additional programs have been introduced for mothers and children in need and for individuals with disabilities, those who are unemployed, and those whose family members have died. Together, these programs make up the bulk of what is called the old-age, survivors, disability, and health insurance (OASDHI) program, whereas Medicare accounts for the remainder of the program. Approximately 20% of Americans receive some type of Social Security benefit, which ensures that they are provided with a minimum floor of income and supplements other sources of income.[8]

Bettmann/Contributor

The U.S. Congress passed the Social Security Act of 1935, and President Franklin D. Roosevelt signed it into law.

Social Security benefits are funded through a tax based on the amount of a worker's income (with a few exceptions). This tax is called the ***Federal Insurance Contributions Act (FICA)*** and is deducted from payroll, and both the employee and the employer contribute a set percentage of the employee's earnings to FICA; self-employed individuals are responsible for paying both the employee and the employer tax.[9] FICA tax contributions fund current Social Security beneficiaries, with any remainder placed in trust funds, which will be drawn from at a later date. To determine whether an individual is eligible to draw upon certain Social Security benefits, a work credits system is used, wherein each person must earn a particular number of work credits to become eligible to receive certain benefits at different points in their life. These work credits accrue throughout a person's life, such that a person can earn up to four work credits per year, assuming they generate enough income. For example, in 2018, an individual earned one work credit for every additional $1,320 in annual income until four work credits were reached. Finally, the amount of benefit an individual receives is dependent, in part, upon the average income they earned during their life.

Federal Insurance Contributions Act (FICA) A federal payroll tax paid by both employees and employers that funds current Social Security beneficiaries

Retirement Income

Retirement income is one of the primary benefits provided through Social Security. To be eligible for Social Security retirement income, an individual must have earned 40 work credits during their life and apply for the benefit. At the earliest, an eligible individual can begin receiving benefits at 62 years but will receive a permanently reduced benefit, as 62 years is not considered full retirement age in the United States. The current full retirement age ranges from 66 to 67 years, and the exact age depends on an individual's year of birth, as the age requirement has been increasing over time. An individual may maximize the benefit amount by delaying receipt of benefits after reaching full retirement age.[10]

Survivor Benefits

If an individual who is eligible for Social Security benefits dies, some family members may be eligible to receive survivor benefits. For example, a surviving spouse can receive a one-time $255 payment and potentially recurring monthly benefits, and under certain conditions, surviving children, parents, or even a divorced spouse may be eligible for monthly benefits as well.[11] Any monthly benefit received by a surviving family member will be contingent upon the deceased person's average lifetime earnings as well as the age of the surviving family member(s) and their relationship to the deceased person.

Disability Income

Like other Social Security benefits, disability income is intended to be a societal safety net. Specifically, disability income was created to support those who develop or face a disability that inhibits their ability to participate in the workforce. Eligibility for Social Security disability income depends on an individual's current age, the age at which they first experienced the disability, and their accrued work credits, such that younger workers may qualify with fewer work credits accrued over a shorter time frame. The disability benefit may also extend to a worker's spouse under certain circumstances or to a worker's adult child if the child developed the disability before reaching 22 years of age. An individual will continue to receive disability income for the duration of their disability, and if they reach full retirement age, then they will shift over to receiving retirement benefits. The disability income benefit also provides incentives and assistance aimed at helping individuals transition back to the workforce.[12]

Medicare

As a Social Security benefit, Medicare is a government-funded health insurance program designed for those who are 65 years or older and for those individuals who are under the age of 65 and have qualifying conditions, such as disabilities, permanent kidney failure, or amyotrophic lateral sclerosis (i.e., Lou Gehrig's disease). Medicare is designed to cover some but not all health care costs.[13] Thus, Medicare offers health insurance to those who no longer work and, as a result, who are no longer the potential recipients of employer-sponsored health insurance or do not have sufficient income to pay for other health insurance.

Workers' Compensation

Workers' compensation
Program funded entirely by the employer in the form of payroll taxes that provides medical coverage and income replacement for an individual who is injured or becomes ill on the job due to an accident or hazard

One program funded entirely by the employer in the form of payroll taxes is called *workers' compensation*. It typically provides medical coverage, including rehabilitation services and income replacement, for an individual who was injured or fell ill due to accidents or hazards at work.[14] In addition, workers' compensation programs often provide benefits to an individual's family members in the event the individual dies due to an injury or illness sustained from work. It is important to point out that such programs are not the same as Social Security disability insurance programs. Nearly all states mandate that employers offer workers' compensation programs to employees. Many private employers purchase workers' compensation coverage through insurance companies, whereas public employers provide coverage through government programs. The amount of payroll taxes an employer must contribute to workers' compensation programs varies by industry, such that industries with higher rates of injuries and illnesses contribute more.

Unemployment Insurance

As another example of legally required social insurance, the U.S. federal–state unemployment insurance program provides income replacement and job-search services to individuals who become unemployed through no fault of their own yet are still able to work and available for work, assuming they meet certain eligibility requirements. For example, during the economic recession that began around 2008, many workers found themselves out of a job, and unemployment insurance benefits helped many of these workers meet their basic needs while searching for new employment opportunities. The unemployment insurance program is funded through payroll taxes contributed by employers and is overseen and administered by the U.S. Department of Labor.[15] The Social Security Act incentivizes states to pass unemployment insurance laws by allowing employers to credit up to 90% of their state unemployment tax contributions to a federal unemployment tax.[16] The weekly benefit distributed to eligible individuals through unemployment insurance is a function of past income, with the amount of benefits received limited by certain minimums and maximums. During 2017, nearly 6 million individuals were beneficiaries of the U.S. federal-state unemployment insurance program.[17]

Family and Medical Leave

Family and Medical Leave Act (FMLA) Introduced in 1993 to protect employees' job security when they need to take unpaid leave due to family or medical issues

Attending to a family or medical issue is often stressful in its own right, and having to take time off from work to attend to such matters exacerbates already heightened stress levels. Fortunately, the U.S. *Family and Medical Leave Act (FMLA)* was introduced in 1993 to protect employees' job security in instances in which they need to take unpaid leave due to family or medical issues.

Eligible employees may use up to 12 weeks of unpaid leave in a year, during which their job and health care benefits remain protected, and a spouse or family member of a service member may use up to 26 weeks of FMLA in a year to care for the injured or ill service member. Importantly, employees can take FMLA all at once or intermittently, but in general, employees must provide supporting documentation to their employer at least 30 days prior to taking leave, and the employer must grant the leave request. FMLA covers virtually all public and private employers with 50 or more employees. To be eligible to take leave under FMLA, an employee must have worked at least 1,250 hours for their employer for at least 12 months, must have worked at an employer's location (e.g., campus, facility) that has at least 50 employees working within a 75-mile radius, and must face at least one of the following challenges:

- Being unable to work due to a serious health issue;

- Giving birth or caring for their own infant, including receiving treatment for pregnancy complications;

- Adopting a child or placing a child in their own foster care;

- Providing care for an immediate family member who is experiencing a serious health issue.[18]

Additional Health Care Requirements

In addition to the health care benefits required through the Social Security Act and workers' compensation laws, many U.S. employers must abide by other important health care laws—namely, the Employee Retirement Income Security Act and its amendments and the Patient

SPOTLIGHT ON GLOBAL ISSUES

Paid Paternity Leave in the European Union

The United States does not require paid parental leave at the federal level, but some states such as California, New Jersey, and Rhode Island offer some form of paid parental leave. In many developed nations, however, including members of the European Union (EU), paid parental leave has become commonplace. Yet there are significant differences in policies for paid maternal leave (leave for mothers) compared with those for paid paternal leave (leave for fathers). Employers in all EU countries must provide at least 14 weeks of maternity leave, with each country determining when maternity leave can be taken and for how much pay. In contrast, paternity leave remains unregulated by the EU; nevertheless, two-thirds of EU countries do offer some form of paid paternity leave, although the amount compensated varies by country.

Finland offers one of the most generous paternity leave policies of any EU country. Specifically, Finland provides 9 weeks of dedicated leave for new fathers, and fathers may use these 9 weeks at any time from the day the child is born until the child reaches 2 years of age; with that said, fathers can only take a maximum of 18 days of paternity leave concurrently with the child's mother. In terms of payment, Kela, Finland's Social Insurance Institution, typically provides each father with a monetary allowance that is approximately 70% of the father's income. Despite this benefit, the proportion of Finnish fathers who take advantage of paternity leave remains very low.

Other EU countries offer shorter paid paternity leave times but compensate fathers at 100% of their typical salary. Not surprisingly, some evidence indicates that fathers are more likely to take advantage of paternity leave in countries where they are compensated at a higher percentage of their overall income. Portugal is notable for making paternity leave mandatory: The government requires that all fathers must take 2 weeks of paid paternity leave. It also requires employers to allow an additional 2 weeks of paid leave after the mandatory leave period, and all 4 weeks must be compensated at 100% of the father's income.[19]

Protection and Affordable Care Act. The *Employee Retirement Income Security Act (ERISA)* of 1974 and subsequent amendments established minimum standards for many private employers' health care plans and did so as a means of protecting employees.[20] (We discuss ERISA as it relates to retirement plans later in the chapter.) Two amendments to ERISA have implications for many employers and their health care coverage: the Consolidated Omnibus Budget Reconciliation Act (COBRA) and the Health Insurance Portability and Accountability Act (HIPAA).

The *Consolidated Omnibus Budget Reconciliation Act (COBRA)* of 1985 protects employees' (and their beneficiaries') health care coverage for a designated amount of time in the event of voluntary or involuntary job loss, work-hour reductions, or another major occurrence (e.g., death, divorce).[21] For example, imagine that a worker gets laid off, and amid the stress of hunting for a new job, they have to seek out new health insurance. COBRA can alleviate some anxiety in this situation, as the worker has an opportunity to continue the existing health insurance coverage while seeking a new place to work. An eligible employee may have to pay for the entire cost of the plan and a 2% administrative fee. COBRA protections apply to employers with 20 or more employees that offer group health insurance plans, and COBRA allows individuals to continue their health care coverage even after the aforementioned major job and life events. COBRA protection can last for a maximum of 36 months, and the specific length of coverage is dependent upon the type of qualifying job or life event that the individual experienced.

The *Health Insurance Portability and Accountability Act (HIPAA)* of 1996 adds protections to the portability of employees' health care coverage as well as protections to ensure the privacy and security of employees' health care data.[22] More specifically, HIPAA put into place certain protections for preexisting health conditions, where previously a health insurer might exclude individuals with certain conditions (e.g., genetic predispositions) or a prior claim history. In addition, HIPAA protects individuals against discrimination in which they are targeted for their general health condition and/or specific illnesses or injuries.

Beyond ERISA and its amendments, the *Patient Protection and Affordable Care Act* of 2010, commonly known as the Affordable Care Act or the *ACA*, offers rights and protections associated with access to health care coverage. (Some refer to the ACA as "Obamacare," as it was signed into law by President Barack Obama.) The ACA requires insurance providers to eliminate exclusions on the basis of preexisting conditions as well as other discriminatory practices and requires all marketplace plans and many other plans to cover preventive medical services. To improve the affordability of health care for those with or without access to employer-sponsored health care plans, the ACA offers tax credits to individuals and their families, which they can use to purchase coverage through a government-operated marketplace. Further, the ACA has added other protections, such as those that allow children and other dependents to remain on their parents' insurance plan until they reach 26 years of age and eliminate lifetime and certain annual benefits limits. As of 2018, individuals who can afford and have access to health care but choose not to purchase coverage may have to pay a tax penalty, and employers must offer affordable health care plans to full-time employees or potentially pay a fee.[23] However, in December 2017, a new law was enacted that repealed the individual mandate; the change was set to take effect in the 2019 tax year.[24]

LO 13.3 Describe the different types of voluntary benefits.

Voluntary Benefits

In addition to legally required benefits, many organizations voluntarily provide benefits to employees. Voluntary benefits can add value by helping to attract, motivate, and retain talent; yet at the same time, many of these benefits have substantial financial costs for both the organization and its employees, leaving the organization to weigh the potential short- and long-term advantages of offering such benefits relative to the short- and long-term disadvantages of doing so. Some of the most common employer-sponsored voluntary benefits include health care, retirement, life insurance, and work–life programs. Table 13.1 describes the characteristics of three common funding structures for voluntary benefits.

TABLE 13.1   Funding Structures for Voluntary Benefits[25]

Group Insurance	• The employer issues an insurance policy, and the employees are insured under that policy as a voluntary benefit.
	• The employer is allowed to pay anywhere from none to all of the coverage costs associated with the voluntary benefit, often with the employees paying any remainder.
	• A less risky and burdensome funding structure for the employer in terms of financial risk because the insurer is responsible for administering most components of the policy and for bearing the risk that the amount of benefits paid to those covered by the policy exceed original expectations.
	• It is commonly used for medical, dental, vision, life, and retirement insurance.
Self-Funding	• The employer is responsible for administering, bearing the risk, and covering all costs associated with the voluntary benefit.
	• It is commonly used for paid time off, work–life programs, and wellness programs, as well as some perquisites.
Individual Insurance	• A voluntary benefit offered by the employer in which the employee bears all of the coverage costs associated with the benefit if the employee decides to participate in the benefit.
	• Examples include some executive benefits as well as some supplemental life insurance plans.

Health Care Programs

As voluntary benefits, health care programs provide employees with access to health care providers and services. Employees participate in health care programs to prevent and treat medical, dental, and vision conditions.

Medical Plans

Medical plans provide health care and treatment opportunities for those who are plan members. According to a Kaiser Family Foundation report, premiums have been rising for employer-sponsored medical plans. Individuals, on average, contribute 18% of the premium for single coverage plans and 31% of the premium for family coverage plans as part of the cost-sharing mechanism.[26] To keep the cost of premiums steady, some organizations, such as the online vintage-inspired clothing retailer called ModCloth, have raised deductibles substantially.[27] Although lower premiums provide immediate financial relief for employees, higher deductibles can pose challenges for employees who are not financially prepared for the out-of-pocket expenses associated with major procedures or surgeries. It is not uncommon for employers to offer employees more than one medical plan from which to choose, each with different associated costs. In the following sections, we review some common types of medical plans as well as health savings options.

Traditional-Care Plans   Also called *conventional-indemnity plans*, **traditional-care plans** allow participants to select any provider of their choosing without affecting how they are reimbursed, and participants' expenses are reimbursed as they are incurred. Over the past century, true traditional-care plans have become increasingly rare, as more organizations opt for managed-care plans.

Managed-Care Plans   Designed to provide wide-ranging health care services to plan participants, **managed-care plans** are preferable to traditional plans when it comes to meeting cost-containment goals and managing the quality and use of services. A common theme among managed-care plans is that participants incur lower cost sharing when they use in-network providers and services. In-network refers to providers and services that are members of the managed-care plan, and out-of-network refers to providers that are not members.

Traditional-care plans Also called conventional-indemnity plans, a medical plan that allows participants to select any provider of their choosing without affecting how they are reimbursed, and participants' expenses are reimbursed as they are incurred

Managed-care plans A medical plan designed to provide wide-ranging health care services to plan participants while managing the cost, quality, and use of services, where participants incur lower cost sharing when they use in-network (as opposed to out-of-network) providers and services

TABLE 13.2 Common Managed-Care Plans and Health Savings Options

MANAGED-CARE PLANS	CHARACTERISTICS
Health Maintenance Organization (HMO)	*Definition:* a plan in which out-of-network, nonemergency services are not covered, and plan participants select an in-network primary care physician who acts as a gatekeeper for in-network specialists. • Provides a comprehensive array of health care providers and services, ranging from generalists to specialists, as well as physical therapists and mental health providers. • Most require lower out-of-pocket costs for plan participants and sometimes even lack a deductible. • May not cover physician and specialist visits that are deemed out of network.
Preferred-Provider Organization (PPO)	*Definition:* a plan in which participants incur lower cost sharing for in-network service providers, and seeing a primary care physician is not required prior to seeing a specialist.[28] • Unlike an HMO, PPO participants may see providers outside of their network; however, going out of network will result in higher cost sharing by participants. • Unlike an HMO, PPO participants are not typically required to select a primary care physician. • According to a Kaiser Family Foundation report, nearly half of workers with employer-sponsored coverage enroll in PPOs, making it one of the most common and popular plans.
Exclusive-Provider Organization (EPO)	*Definition:* a specific type of PPO in which participants are only covered when they seek services from in-network providers, except in the event of an emergency.
Point-of-Service (POS)	*Definition:* a plan that is essentially a hybrid between an HMO and a PPO.[29] • Like an HMO, participants must select an in-network primary care physician who typically serves as the gatekeeper for referrals to specialists. • Like a PPO, participants may go out of network to find service providers at higher cost sharing. • In some plans, visiting a primary care physician and receiving preventive services do not contribute to the deductible, which reduces the out-of-pocket costs for routine care and treatment. • In 2017, 1 in 10 employees covered under employer medical plans enrolled in POS plans, which is similar to the enrollment rate found for HMOs.
High-Deductible Health Plan (HDHP)	*Definition:* a plan with a high deductible (and often higher out-of-pocket maximums than other plans). • According to the Internal Revenue Service, as of 2018, a plan becomes an HDHP when the annual deductible meets or exceeds $1,350 for an individual or $2,700 for a family. • Technically, an HDHP may be a special type of HMO, PPO, or POS that includes a high deductible. • Typically, an HDHP offers more affordable plan premiums than other plans and incentivizes participants to think carefully about which service providers they visit and which treatments they pursue.
Consumer-Driven Health Plan (CDHP)	*Definition:* an HDHP that is combined with a health reimbursement arrangement (HRA) or health savings account (HSA), resulting in certain tax advantages.[30]

Managed-care plans use a variety of provisions aimed at managing costs, quality, and use. For instance, some plans may have preadmission provisions, wherein plan participants must receive authorization or complete certain tests prior to being admitted to a hospital for nonemergency situations. As another example, some plans may require participants to receive a second opinion after a provider recommends them for elective or nonemergency surgery, a policy designed to be a cost-saving mechanism. Table 13.2 describes some of the most common managed-care plans.

Health Savings Options   In the United States, there are various health savings options, and we review three that are recognized by the Internal Revenue Service: health flexible spending arrangement, health reimbursement arrangement, and health savings account (see Table 13.3). These programs offer tax advantages aimed at reducing overall out-of-pocket health care expenses for individuals. Each option differs with respect to eligibility requirements and specific savings stipulations.[31]

©iStock.com/hedgehog94

Dental and Vision Plans   Insurance plans for dental care and eye care may be offered as a supplement to medical plans or as standalone plans. A 2018 SHRM survey indicated that 97% of surveyed employers offered dental insurance and 90% offered vision insurance.[32] Dental and vision plans typically operate much like a medical plan in that there is a designated network of approved service providers, premiums, deductibles, coinsurance, and copayments. With regard to dental plans specifically, many plans provide coverage for routine preventive and maintenance services like X-rays, cleanings, and fillings. Dental plans often differ with respect

Many employers offer some type of dental plan, yet many plan participants do not know what their dental plan covers and how much they will be expected to pay out of pocket. As such, employers should communicate plan details and costs to help employees recognize the value of their benefit.

TABLE 13.3   Common Health Savings Options

HEALTH SAVINGS OPTIONS	CHARACTERISTICS
Health Flexible Spending Arrangement (Health FSA)	*Definition:* an option that offers tax advantages for individuals who are enrolled in some employer-sponsored health care plans.[33] • Permits employees (and optionally employers) to set aside funds into an untaxed account, which means employees do not pay taxes on the money within a health FSA. • Imposes certain limitations regarding how the funds can be used. For example, funds cannot be used to pay premiums but can be used to pay deductibles, copayments, prescription medication, and medical equipment, as well as other qualified medical and dental expenses. • With some exceptions, participants cannot roll the entirety of account funds forward to the subsequent year in the event they do not use all of the funds.
Health Reimbursement Arrangement (HRA)	*Definition:* an option that allows an employer (and not the employee) to contribute unlimited funds to an account, such that the account reimburses the employee on a tax-free basis for qualified medical costs.[34] • For each coverage period, there is an upper limit on how much tax-free reimbursement a participant can apply toward qualified medical costs. • At the end of the year, any remaining funds can be rolled forward to the subsequent year. • Because the employer owns the HRA, the employer retains control of the funds should the employee leave the organization, and thus some view the HRA as an employee retention inducement.
Health Savings Account (HSA)	*Definition:* an option that permits participants to contribute a portion of pretax income to an account that can be used to pay for services. • Contributed funds are not taxed. • Funds can accumulate tax-deferred interest. • At the end of the year, any remaining funds can be rolled forward to the subsequent year.

Health Care Terminology and Concepts

Employees often ask their managers for help understanding their benefits. Health care programs, in particular, involve several terms and concepts that a manager may need to define and explain.

- **Participant:** an individual who is enrolled in a plan during a coverage period, allowing them to have access to the plan benefits.

- **Cost sharing:** a reimbursement model in which a participant is reimbursed for qualified services and procedures at a specified rate, subject to certain exceptions and limitations.

- **Premium:** a fee for a plan coverage period, which may be paid by any or all of the following entities: employer, employee, or union.

- **Deductible:** a set amount that a participant must pay during a coverage period for services rendered before the insurance provider begins contributing payments for expenses.

- **Coinsurance:** a cost sharing between the insurance provider and the participant, wherein the participant pays a percentage of expenses and the insurance reimburses the rest; typically comes into effect when a participant reaches the deductible for the coverage period (or if there was no deductible in the first place).

- **Copayment (or copay):** a fee charged when a participant receives a particular service or visits a particular provider; may be as little as $5 for preventive care such as an annual physical.

- **Maximum out-of-pocket expense:** an upper limit for how much the participant will pay for a coverage period after reaching the deductible (if applicable); once reached, the insurance provider typically covers subsequent expenses.

- **Maximum plan limit:** an upper limit of how much an insurance provider will pay to cover a participant's expenses for a coverage period or during the participant's lifetime; the Patient Protection and Affordable Care Act prohibits annual and lifetime limits, except when applied to certain services that are not considered essential.

- **Primary care physician:** a physician who provides most routine and preventive services (known in the past as a general practitioner or family doctor) and who serves as the main contact for the participant; may also be a gatekeeper who must authorize referrals to specialists and non-emergency hospital visits; some medical plans require participants to select a primary care physician.

- **Specialist:** a health care provider who provides less-routine or highly specialized services, such as the services provided by a dermatologist, obstetrician-gynecologist, neurologist, oncologist, or cardiologist.

to what and how much a plan will cover when it comes to more costly procedures such as root canals or orthodontics.

Interestingly, a 2017 survey of 1,000 adults by Lincoln Financial Group found that 54% of respondents rated employer-sponsored dental insurance as being a "must have," yet only 25% of those with dental insurance reported that they had visited the dentist during the prior year. The reason given for the low rate of dental visits was the perceived cost of such care.[35] Given that many employees pay relatively little out of pocket for routine cleanings and preventive services under most plans, a low rate of utilization may be due to general misunderstandings about the nature of their respective dental plans; this points to the importance of effective communication when administering any benefits plan.

Disability Insurance Programs

In addition to legally required workers' compensation and Social Security disability insurance, employers may also offer voluntary benefits in the form of short- and/or long-term disability insurance plans through private providers. Unlike workers' compensation, employees

SPOTLIGHT ON ETHICS

Making Changes to Health Insurance Plans

It is not unusual for employers to change health insurance plans. For example, an employer may switch to a plan with lower monthly premiums and a higher deductible or may switch from offering a preferred-provider organization (PPO) to a health maintenance organization (HMO). Employers may make such changes to achieve cost savings over the previous plan, or they may do so in an attempt to improve employee coverage or benefits utilization. Many health insurance plans are inherently complex and nuanced, such that employers and employees alike may experience unintended positive or negative consequences when changes are made. Given this uncertainty, it is incumbent upon organizational decision makers, particularly benefits experts, to do their due diligence when determining what changes to make to a plan, which might include a benefits utilization analysis, survey, or cost-benefit analysis.

Consider an organization that originally used a three-tiered employer cost-sharing system, wherein employees who earned the least income were placed in the first income tier and employees who earned the most were placed in the third income tier. Employers in the lowest tier received the highest employer cost-sharing contributions to monthly insurance premiums, whereas those in the highest tier received the lowest. In an attempt to refine the cost-sharing tier system, decision makers subsequently designed and implemented a five-tier system based on the same cost-sharing principle.

The decision makers in this scenario hoped that this refinement would make benefits administration fairer, as the additional tiers made the differentiations between employees of different incomes more nuanced. Unfortunately, there was an unintended consequence that adversely affected some of the most vulnerable employees. Specifically, some employees who were originally in the first tier subsequently moved to the second tier based on this change. This resulted in higher monthly premiums for those individuals, leaving them with lower take-home pay after the benefits were deducted from their paychecks. Some of these individuals ended up leaving the organization.

If the organization had applied data analytics to model the potential effects prior to making the decision to implement the new five-tiered system, they would likely have anticipated the negative impact on certain employees. This example illustrates why it is an organization's ethical responsibility to identify potential unintended consequences of changes to benefits. By leveraging the available data, an organization can avoid an unfortunate outcome.[36]

Questions

1. In your opinion, to what extent are employers ethically obligated to provide employer-sponsored health insurance for their workers? Give examples to support your answer.

2. In the scenario described, how might the company's HR administrators have intervened after the new five-tiered system was implemented to prevent employees from leaving due to reduced take-home pay?

---

may be eligible to draw upon disability insurance benefits even if their disability originated outside of work. Both short- and long-term disability insurance plans provide income protection to plan participants, and with the exception of some states, employers may voluntarily contribute fully or partially to employees' disability insurance. A 2018 SHRM survey indicated that 64% of employers provided short-term disability insurance and 72% provided long-term disability insurance.[37]

Short-term disability insurance is a form of income protection for employees who temporarily become unable to work as a result of an illness or injury, whether sustained at work or during their personal time. In California, Hawaii, New Jersey, New York, Rhode Island, and the District of Columbia, employers (with some exceptions) are required to offer short-term disability insurance to employees working in those jurisdictions.[38] In most organizations, employees first draw upon accrued paid time off prior to accessing any short-term disability benefits covered through their plan. For the majority of short-term disability insurance plans, employees may receive their income protection benefit for 90 to 180 days, and the income protection benefit

Short-term disability insurance A form of income protection for employees who temporarily become unable to work as a result of illness or injury usually covers 60% to 75% of their base pay.[39] As long as the combined benefit received does not exceed 100% of base pay, employees may coordinate short-term disability insurance benefits with other programs, such as workers' compensation, if applicable.

Long-term disability insurance A form of income protection for employees that is similar to short-term disability insurance, except it offers longer-term benefits activated once short-term disability insurance benefits expire

Long-term disability insurance is similar to short-term disability insurance, except that it offers longer-term benefits that activate once short-term disability insurance benefits expire. In addition, although long-term disability insurance also provides income protection benefits, the percentage of overall base pay is sometimes lower than the percentage afforded by short-term disability insurance benefits. Some plans stipulate a maximum time period for receiving income protection benefits, whereas other plans allow individuals to continue receiving the benefits through retirement. Like short-term disability insurance, those who draw income protection benefits from long-term disability insurance can coordinate their income protection benefits from other programs, as long as the combined benefit does not exceed 100% of their base pay.[40]

Retirement Programs

An employer may offer employees a variety of different retirement plans, which might include defined-benefit and defined-contribution plans, as well as plans designed to contribute to employees' individual retirement plans. In fact, a 2018 SHRM report indicated that 95% of employers offered at least one type of retirement plan to their employees.[41]

For many retirement plans, the U.S. federal government oversees voluntary retirement plans and provides protections for employees. The Employee Retirement Income Security Act (ERISA), mentioned earlier in this chapter, established minimum standards for many private-sector retirement plans (as well as health care plans) in order to put into place various protections for employees.[42]

Notably, ERISA does not cover plans maintained by government entities or religious institutions. Further, ERISA does not mandate that employers provide retirement plans for their employees; rather, ERISA states that private-sector employers with retirement plans must implement certain minimum plan standards. Under ERISA, employees participating in voluntary retirement plans have a right to:

- access critical information regarding the retirement plan, such as how it is funded and what the specific characteristics of the plan entail;

- fair and time-efficient processes pertaining to benefit claims under such plans, such as those related to appeals and grievances;

- sue for issues related to benefits provision or fiduciary duty breaches.

Pension Benefit Guaranty Corporation (PBGC) A U.S. government agency that insures private-sector retirement plans

If a retirement plan is terminated or fails, ERISA also protects employees' rights to certain benefits, which is accomplished using the ***Pension Benefit Guaranty Corporation (PBGC)***.[43] A U.S. government agency set up by Congress, the PBGC insures private-sector retirement plans, such that when a voluntary retirement plan is terminated or fails, PBGC steps in as trustee to ensure employees receive the benefits owed to them.[44] Consistent with ERISA, PBGC does not cover government- or religious-institution–maintained plans. Further, PBGC does not cover 401(k), profit-sharing, employee stock ownership, money-purchase, or health care plans. In sum, the U.S. government has put certain safeguards into effect to protect the retirement plans of private-sector workers.

In the following sections, we distinguish between two types of retirement plans that are commonly offered: defined-benefit and defined-contribution retirement plans (see Figure 13.2).

Defined-Benefit Plans

Defined-benefit plan Also known as a traditional pension plan, a type of retirement plan in which the employer provides plan participants with a pre-established benefit to be paid out over a fixed time period

Also known as a *traditional pension plan,* a ***defined-benefit plan*** is a type of retirement program in which the employer provides plan participants with a pre-established benefit to be paid out over a fixed time period. Sometimes a defined-benefit plan may stipulate an exact amount to

---

■ **FIGURE 13.2** Two Types of Voluntary Retirement Programs

Defined-benefit plans and defined-contribution plans are the two types of voluntary retirement programs.

Defined-Benefit Plans		**Defined-Contribution Plans**
Retirement program in which the employer provides participating individuals with an established benefit to be paid out over a fixed time period	vs.	Retirement program that does *not* yield an established benefit for the employee and is instead based on employee and/or employer contributions

---

be distributed, such as $2,000 per month at retirement. The funding for these plans sometimes differs between the public and private sectors. Often, both the employee and the employer are required to contribute to defined-benefit plans in public organizations, whereas in many cases, only the employer contributes to such plans in private organizations.[45] Compared to other retirement programs, defined-benefit plans allow employers to contribute more. Plus, by definition, defined-benefit plans offer predictable benefit amounts that can be accrued relatively quickly, which may be appealing to many employees, particularly those who have a discomfort for taking or incurring risk.

Depending on the employer, defined-benefit plans may be paid out to employees on a fixed periodic basis or in a single lump sum. The amount of the pre-established, determinable benefit for each employee is typically calculated using an actuarial formula based on employee earnings, years of service, and age. For instance, some plans use an employee's age and/or their pay over the three most recent years to determine the amount of the benefit. Although they are still offered by many companies, defined-benefit plans are becoming less common as more companies opt for defined-contribution plans. Part of this trend may be attributable to the more costly and administratively complex nature of establishing and maintaining defined-benefit plans compared to defined-contribution plans.[46]

A **cash balance plan**, sometimes referred to as a *guaranteed account plan,* is a type of defined-benefit plan. Under these plans, participants are provided with an account that is credited annually with a compensation credit and an interest credit. The compensation credit will often take the form of a percentage of the compensation an employee earns from the employer, and the interest credit refers to a guaranteed interest rate (either fixed or variable). Unlike other defined-benefit plans, under cash-balance plans, the amount of the deposits to participants' accounts is not based on their age.[47]

Cash balance plan Also known as a guaranteed account plan, a type of defined-benefit plan in which participants are provided with an account that is credited annually with a compensation credit and an interest credit

Defined-Contribution Plans

Differing from a defined-benefit plan is the **defined-contribution plan**, which does not yield a pre-established, fixed benefit for the employee. Instead, a defined-contribution plan is predicated on employee and/or employer contributions to an investment fund and the investment gains and/or losses of that fund.[48] Typically, such plans permit certain contribution levels from the employee or employer and enforce a maximum contribution level for the year. Employee contributions are typically **tax deferred**, which means that the taxable income an employee contributes to a plan will not be taxed until a later date, often when the earnings are distributed. Plan contributions are invested, resulting in the employee absorbing investment risk. That is, despite the employee and/or employer making consistent contributions over time, investment gains and/or losses can have a significant effect on the amount of earnings distributed upon retirement (or termination).[49] Consequently, defined-contribution plans are riskier than defined-benefit plans given their reliance on investment performance. Common types of defined-contribution plans include 401(k), 403(b), profit-sharing, employee stock ownership, and money-purchase pension plans.

Defined-contribution plan A type of retirement plan in which the employee and/or employer contributes to an investment fund

Tax deferred Taxable income that is not taxed until a later date, often when earnings are distributed

401(k) and 403(b) Plans   Both 401(k) and 403(b) plans are types of defined-contribution plans, and according to PayScale survey results published in 2018, 67% of surveyed employers offered a 401(k) or 403(b) plan.[50] Both types of plans typically allow employees to direct their own investments. Under both plans, employees are often allowed to transport their plan balance to another employer's plan should they switch jobs.

An employee enrolled in a ***401(k) plan*** makes contributions to an individual account in the form of deferred income, and depending upon the parameters of a particular plan, the employer may also be able to contribute to the employee's plan. In fact, some plans, such as safe harbor and SIMPLE 401(k) plans, *require* the employer to make plan contributions. As long as employer contributions fall under section 404 of the IRS code, employers may deduct the contributions on their federal tax returns.[51] Some plans allow employees to make contributions on a before-tax basis, whereas other plans require employees to make contributions on an after-tax basis.[52] Further, some plans allow employees to withdraw benefits prior to retirement, such as in the event of personal hardship or loans.

Regarding vesting of 401(k) plans, employee and employer contributions operate differently. For employees, from the moment they defer income from their paycheck to their plan, they are considered 100% vested, which means that they have control over the entirety of the funds they contributed; however, they may be subject to additional taxes if they withdraw prior to a specified age. Employer contributions, on the other hand, often vest on a graduated schedule, which means that employees may not be able to access the employer portion of their benefit until they have worked for that employer for a specified amount of time.[53]

Interestingly, when employers offer to match employee contributions, employees do not always take full advantage of such programs; however, a research study conducted by Google and academic researchers found that employees who received an extra "nudge" (i.e., additional information about the matching benefit) were more likely to increase their 401(k) contributions, resulting in greater retirement savings.[54]

A ***403(b) plan*** is sometimes referred to as a tax-sheltered annuity plan. A 403(b) plan is very similar to a 401(k) plan, but a notable difference between the two is that 403(b) plans are reserved for public schools and universities, religious organizations, and certain tax-exempt organizations such as charities.[55] Similar to a 401(k), the employee (and sometimes the employer) contributes to an individual account using deferred income. A 403(b) plan typically allows employee income to be deferred on a before-tax basis.[56]

Profit-Sharing Program   A ***profit-sharing program*** is one type of pay-for-performance program that can double as a retirement plan. Employees earn rewards by sharing in their organization's profits (e.g., return on assets), and rewards may be distributed as cash or placed in a retirement plan. Employers typically use a formula for determining how much each individual employee receives as part of the profit sharing. When designed for retirement, a profit-sharing program can be considered a type of defined-contribution plan and may even include a 401(k) option.[57] Under a profit-sharing program, employers are under no legal obligation to make certain levels of contributions or to contribute every year. Further, unlike a 401(k), true profit-sharing programs are based solely on employer contributions, and the moment that a profit-sharing program incorporates deferred income from employees, it becomes a 401(k) plan.[58] In terms of withdrawal, employee personal loans are permitted under a profit-sharing program. With that said, any withdrawal made when the employee is under age 59.5 years may be subject to an additional tax. Finally, stock bonus plans are similar to a profit-sharing program; however, under stock bonus plans, employers contribute stock as opposed to cash.

Employee Stock Ownership Plan (ESOP)   Like profit-sharing programs, an employee stock ownership plan can double as a pay-for-performance program and a retirement program. Specifically, an ***employee stock ownership plan (ESOP)*** rewards employees

---

401(k) plan A type of defined-contribution plan in which an employee (and in some cases the employer) makes contributions to an individual account in the form of deferred income

403(b) plan Also known as a tax-sheltered annuity plan, a type of defined-contribution plan in which an employee (and in some cases the employer) makes contributions to an individual account in the form of deferred income; reserved for public schools and universities, religious organizations, and certain tax-exempt organizations such as charities

Profit-sharing program A type of pay-for-performance program in which the employee earns rewards by sharing their organization's profits, and earned rewards can be placed in what can be considered a type of defined-contribution plan

Employee stock ownership plan (ESOP) A type of pay-for-performance program and defined-contribution plan in which the bulk of contributions are invested in an employer's stock, thereby rewarding employees when company stock shares increase in value and the vesting period has passed

when company stock shares increase in value and can only be used after a vesting period. Some research has shown that organizations with ESOPs tend to show slightly better organizational performance than organizations without ESOPs.[59] As an employee benefit, ESOPs are defined by the U.S. Internal Revenue Service as a defined-contribution plan, wherein the bulk of contributions are invested in an employer's stock.[60] ESOPs are different from stock options and stock purchase plans in that ESOPs typically allow employees to collectively own a substantially larger portion of the organization (and sometimes even own the organization outright). Further, only employees are eligible to participate in ESOPs, and thus, when employees separate from their organization, they are required to cash out of their ESOPs.[61] Those who participate in ESOPs stand to benefit should their organization perform well throughout their tenure, thereby leaving a healthy sum for retirement and motivating employees to contribute to their organization's strategic objectives.

Money-Purchase Plan   In the defined-contribution plan known as a ***money-purchase plan***, employers simply contribute a specified amount to each plan participant's account. Compared to some of the other plans, these plans are relatively straightforward and simple for employees to understand. The amount specified for each employee can be a percentage of annual compensation, and up to 25% of the amount of a participant's annual compensation can be contributed to their plan. Like other defined-contribution plans, contributions to money-purchase plans are invested into a fund, which means that the amount of participants' funds at retirement will be a function of all employer contributions to the fund as well as the investment gains or losses of the fund over time.[62] For example, imagine that Jorge's company contributes 8% of each employee's pay to a money-purchase plan. Because Jorge earns $65,000 a year, his company will contribute $5,200 ($65,000 × 0.08 = $5,200) to his money-purchase plan at the end of the year, and over time, investment gains or losses will affect the fund value at the time of his retirement.

Money-purchase plan A relatively straightforward defined-contribution plan in which employers contribute a specified amount to each plan participant's investment fund

Individual Retirement Plans

Plans that allow individuals to make tax-deferred investments for retirement are called ***individual retirement plans*** or ***individual retirement arrangements*** (IRAs). Although individual retirement plans can be employer sponsored, they need not be. Any individual who earns income or is compensated, whether as an employee or through self-employment, may be eligible

Individual retirement plan (individual retirement arrangement) A plan that allows an individual to make tax-deferred contributions to an investment fund and that does not need to be employer sponsored

TABLE 13.4   Traditional vs. Roth IRA

TRADITIONAL IRA	ROTH IRA
Does not allow individuals older than 70½ years old to contribute.	Does not allow individuals to contribute if their modified adjusted gross income is larger than specified amounts.
Individuals can deduct their contributions, but the tax deduction may be limited if they also participate in an employer retirement plan and earn an income above specified amounts.	Individuals cannot deduct their contributions.
Individuals must begin withdrawing or distributing minimum amounts the year after they turn 70½ years old.	Individuals are not required to take minimum distributions or withdrawals at any point as long as they are the original owner of the plan.
Withdrawals and distributions are taxable.	Withdrawals and distributions are not taxable, with some exceptions.

Source: U.S. Internal Revenue Service. (n.d.). Traditional and ROTH IRAs. https://www.irs.gov/retirement-plans/traditional-and-roth-iras

SPOTLIGHT ON HR FOR SMALL AND MEDIUM-SIZED BUSINESSES

Simplified Employee Pension Plans and Savings Incentive Match Plans for Employee IRAs

Simplified Employee Pension (SEP) plans and Savings Incentive Match Plans for Employees (SIMPLE) IRAs make it easier for smaller businesses to make contributions to employee retirement plans. Namely, both SEP plans and SIMPLE IRAs allow employers to contribute to traditional IRAs, and both tend to be more affordable for employers—particularly small employers—than more traditional, employer-sponsored retirement plans, as they require fewer operating and administrative costs.

When an employer makes a contribution to a traditional IRA under an SEP plan, the resulting plan is called an SEP-IRA. Such a plan permits employers to make contributions to employees' traditional IRAs and to their own retirement account. Further, SEP-IRAs adhere to the same investment and distribution rules as traditional IRAs, but SEP-IRAs permit notably larger annual contributions. Because employers are not required to make the same contributions each year, SEP plans are relatively flexible and thus may be attractive to small employers.

SIMPLE IRAs are similar to SEP plans but are *only* available to small employers that do not have any other retirement plan. They require fixed annual contributions and allow employer matching of up to 3% of employees' compensation for employees who choose to contribute. Alternatively, for employees who choose not to contribute to their plans, employers must make a nonelective contribution equal to 2% of employees' compensation up to an annual limit.[63]

to contribute to an individual retirement plan—subject to some restrictions.[64] Thus, individual retirement plans may be especially beneficial for those who are self-employed or lack access to employer-sponsored retirement plans.

Examples of individual retirement plans include traditional individual retirement accounts or annuities (traditional IRAs) and Roth IRAs, both of which offer tax advantages and impose restrictions on the overall amount of contributions made each year. Traditional IRAs and Roth IRAs do, however, differ in key ways, as shown in Table 13.4.

Life Insurance Programs

Life insurance program
Provides financial compensation for designated beneficiaries when the insured individual dies

Life insurance programs are frequently offered by employers as a voluntary employee benefit. Specifically, *life insurance programs* provide financial compensation for designated beneficiaries when the insured individual dies, and the compensation can be distributed in the form of a lump-sum payment.[65] According to a 2018 report by the U.S. Bureau of Labor Statistics, 60% of employees work in organizations with life insurance programs, and of those employees, 98% enrolled in a program, signifying that life insurance plans are popular benefits when offered.[66] More than half of full-time employees are enrolled in plans in which the benefit is paid out as a fixed multiple of employees' respective annual earnings, whereas the remainder are enrolled mostly in plans in which the benefit is paid out as a flat dollar amount.[67] Regardless of how the benefit is paid out, an employee should meet with those who are knowledgeable about the different benefits offered through the employer-sponsored life insurance program in order to ensure the employee selects the benefit that will be most appropriate for their family's financial needs in the event of the employee's death.

Wellness Programs

Wellness programs include those employer-sponsored or -provided initiatives aimed at promoting healthy behaviors among participating employees. More than half of surveyed organizations in a Kaiser Family Foundation report indicated that they provide wellness programs, such as smoking cessation, weight management, and behavioral and lifestyle coaching programs.[68] Some employers provide employees with incentives for participating in wellness programs, such as reductions in health care premium contributions.

Accumulated evidence indicates that, in general, wellness programs work (and employers believe that they work), as they are associated with positive employee health and work outcomes, as well as organizational financial outcomes.[69] Many organizations seem poised to maintain or expand their investments in employee wellness programs, as evidenced by the results of a SHRM report issued in 2018. The report indicated that of those surveyed organizations that increased benefit offerings over the prior year, 44% increased their wellness-program offerings.[70]

To promote healthy behaviors, 40% of the more than 3,000 SHRM member organizations surveyed in 2018 offered smoking cessation as a wellness program.[71]

Work–Life Programs

Organizations do not exist in a vacuum. Work demands have the potential to influence employees' personal lives, and demands from employees' personal lives have the potential to influence their work. As such, programs that help employees navigate the competing demands of their work and nonwork lives can be especially attractive and useful. For instance, employees benefit from programs that enable them to receive pay while taking time away from work due to sickness, travel, holidays, or other reasons. They also benefit from assistance with legal issues, caring for a family member, or pursuing educational opportunities. Research has shown that when employees' perceive work–life programs as useful, they tend to engage in more helping behaviors at work as well as perceive that their organizations supports them.[72]

Payment for Time Not Worked

Employees require time away from work for a variety of legitimate reasons. At the federal level, the Fair Labor Standards Act of 1938 does not require employers to pay employees for time away from work due to sickness, vacations, holidays, or other circumstances.[73] However, some state and local laws do require payment for time not worked under certain circumstances. Further, many employers voluntarily provide payment for time not worked. In the following paragraphs, we describe different types of payment for time not worked.

Paid Time Off (PTO)   When an employer compensates employees for time away from work, it is most often under a ***paid time off (PTO)*** program. Approved reasons for using PTO often include vacation, holidays, non–work-related illness or injury, and personal days. In addition, some employers offer PTO for jury duty, military duty, or other unforeseen circumstances or absences. It is becoming more common for employers to treat PTO as an inclusive program in which there is little or no distinction regarding the reason an employee takes time away from work. In many organizations, employees accrue PTO based on the number of hours worked and years of service, and the PTO accumulates into a pool until the employee decides to use some or all of it. Some employers place restrictions on how PTO can be used, such as limiting how many PTO days can be used for vacation versus sickness, whereas other employers allow employees to use PTO as needed without a specific reason.[74]

Interestingly, a 2018 survey by PayScale showed that 54% of organizations offered accrued PTO, 12% offered PTO as a reward for high performance, and 6% offered unlimited PTO.[75] Although still relatively rare, employers that offer unlimited PTO allow employees to take as much time away from work as they need as long as they meet performance expectations and, in many companies, if their supervisor approves the time off. The video-streaming company Netflix

Paid time off (PTO) A program that provides employees with compensation when they take time away from work, subject to employer approval

©iStock.com/Sezeryadigar

gained attention when it announced an unlimited PTO program in 2004—a benefit that Netflix continues to offer to this day.[76] Even still, introducing an unlimited PTO program may lead to some administrative challenges. For example, the Family and Medical Leave Act (FMLA) protects qualified employees' jobs while they are on leave, whereas extended leave under PTO does not necessarily do so. Thus, ideally, employers and employees should distinguish FMLA leave from traditional PTO to ensure that an employee's job remains protected.[77]

Sick time (sick leave)
A program that permits employees to take time off from work due to a personal or immediate family member's health issue

Sick Time   When an employee takes time off from work due to a foreseen or unforeseen personal health issue or an immediate family member's health issue, it is referred to as *sick time* or *sick leave*. As an example, if an employee takes time away from work due to the flu, this could be considered sick time. Alternatively, if an employee takes a day off to care for a child who is having outpatient surgery, this could also be considered sick time. In many cases, sick time is accrued each year based on the cumulative time worked.

Holiday pay A program that provides employees with compensation when taking time away from work for a recognized federal, state, or local holiday

Holiday Pay   When employees take time off from work on a recognized federal, state, or local holiday, employers use *holiday pay* to compensate workers. Examples of recognized U.S. federal holidays include Martin Luther King Jr. Day, Independence Day, and Thanksgiving Day.

Vacation pay A program that provides employees with compensation for taking time away from work for a planned reason

Vacation Pay   A great many employers provide *vacation pay*, which is compensation for taking time away from work for planned reasons, such as for relaxation or travel. Typically, an employee must schedule vacation time in advance and receive approval from a supervisor. In many organizations, paid vacation time is accrued based on cumulative time worked per year. Because many employer vacation pay policies allow employees to roll unused vacation time forward to subsequent years, it is not uncommon for employees to have unused vacation time when they leave an employer, and states vary with respect to whether an employer is required to "pay out" any unused vacation time.[78]

Personal leave A benefit employers use to supplement vacation and sick-time offerings by allowing employees to take paid or unpaid time away from work

Personal Leave   Often used as a catch-all for any foreseen or unforeseen time away from work, *personal leave* is a benefit employers use to supplement their vacation and sick time offerings. Employers may offer personal leave as paid or unpaid. Personal leave is distinguishable from leaves of absence covered under the Family Medical and Leave Act (FMLA) or the Uniformed Services Employment and Reemployment Rights Act.

Compensatory Time Off

Compensatory time off (comp time) A program that allows nonexempt employees to receive paid time off (instead of earning time-and-a-half pay) in exchange for working overtime hours

When a nonexempt employee works overtime hours and receives paid time off rather than earning time-and-a-half pay for the extra hours worked, it is known as *compensatory time off* or, more commonly, *comp time*. In the United States, comp time is currently only permitted for employees who work in the public sector, although some HR professionals have encouraged the U.S. Congress to introduce legislation that would require private employers to offer comp time.[79] To illustrate how comp time works, consider the following scenario: A nonexempt public-sector employee works 48 hours in a week, and the employee applies the extra 8 hours (beyond 40 hours) to comp time, which enables the employee to take 8 hours of paid time off at a later time.

Child and Elder Care

Today, a historically large proportion of the U.S. workforce consists of women, women with children, and dual-earner couples, which means that many working parents require child care when they are at work.[80] In addition, a sizeable number of U.S. workers provide unpaid elder care, which can impose time and financial challenges on families.[81] In fact, many workers find themselves caring and providing for children and parents simultaneously, a phenomenon referred to as the "sandwich generation," as adults are sandwiched between younger and older individuals in need of care. From a financial perspective, accessing or providing such care can be costly. For example, the Care Index estimates that the U.S. national average for at-home child care is $28,354 per year, and for in-center child care, the national average is $9,589 per year.[82]

Employer-sponsored or -subsidized child and elder care can help workers cope with the challenges of balancing work and caring for loved ones. Some employers provide child care services on site. As an example, The Home Depot offers the Little Apron Academy at a location in Atlanta. This center provides affordable on-site child care and educational services for employees' children aged 6 weeks to 5 years.[83] In addition to providing low-cost services, the Little Apron Academy offers The Home Depot employees convenience, as they do not need to drop their child off at a separate location or rush across town if their child becomes ill. Even though child care services represent an immediate cost to the employer, they can achieve a net reduction in costs for the organization and improve employee outcomes. Among other advantages, access to child care is associated with fewer employee absences, lower turnover, and improved employee recruitment.[84]

Flextime and Telecommuting

Many U.S. workers have partners who also work, and many of these dual-earner couples also have children. Allocating time for family responsibilities can be difficult with a rigid work schedule. In addition, many workers spend a substantial amount of time commuting to work; the U.S. Census Bureau estimates that the average worker spends 25 minutes commuting from home to work.[85] To cope with such demands, many employees seek flexible work schedules and arrangements. Flextime and telecommuting have emerged as two prominent forms of flexible work arrangements. Flextime occurs when an employer permits employees to adjust their work schedule to meet family and nonwork demands while also meeting their overall work-hours requirement, whereas telecommuting occurs when an employee works from home or another remote location, such as from a library or a coffee shop.

College Savings Plans

To help employees save for future college expenses, employers can contribute to or offer college savings plans. One plan, called the 529 College Savings Plan (529 Plan), even offers certain tax advantages.[86] Namely, many states allow for tax credit or deduction after payments have been made to a 529 Plan. Further, the funds in a 529 Plan can be invested, and federal taxes are not applied to investment gains. Finally, the funds from a 529 Plan can be withdrawn for qualified higher-educational expenses without being subject to state or federal income taxes. Although individuals can open their own 529 Plans, some employers administer 529 Plans as a voluntary benefit, which enables employees to apply after-tax income directly to their plan.[87] Some lawmakers have proposed legislation that would make it easier for employers to contribute to employees' 529 Plans.

Educational-Assistance Programs

In addition to administering and/or contributing to college savings plans, employers can also offer direct financial assistance for educational expenses. An ***educational-assistance program*** refers to an employee benefit program wherein the employer provides financial assistance for employee educational expenses, which may come in the form of tuition assistance, payment toward qualified educational expenses, or employer-sponsored scholarship programs. Under certain circumstances, an employer can apply these financial contributions as a tax deduction, and under the American Taxpayer Relief Act of 2012, employees do not have to pay income tax on their employer's contributions if the contributions are $5,250 or less per year.[88] A growing number of employers are partnering with universities as part of their educational-assistance programs. For instance, Starbucks partnered with Arizona State University to offer full-tuition support toward a bachelor's degree for full- and part-time U.S. employees.[89]

Educational-assistance program A program whereby the employer provides financial assistance for employee educational expenses

Legal-Services and Identity-Theft Benefits

Legal services and identity theft can impose heavy demands on employees' time and finances, which not only disrupt their family and nonwork lives but also have the potential to disrupt their work lives. Common reasons for legal services include divorce, bankruptcy, lawsuits, wills or trusts, and traffic violations. Some employers sponsor legal services to help employees through legal difficulties and to support their physical presence and psychological focus at work. Like other voluntary benefits, legal services can be deducted from participants' paychecks. Alternatively, employers

Companies in the high-tech industry have been leaders in employee perks. Some offer on-site massage treatments gratis or at a discounted rate.

©iStock.com/Wavebreakmedia

Perquisites (perks) Nonmonetary services or benefits provided by an employer

may also opt to provide a referral service—possibly through an employee-assistance program—wherein employees are referred to outside legal resources.[90] Finally, with identity theft on the rise, more individuals are facing the inconvenience and difficulties that come when identities are stolen.[91] As such, employers may offer identity-theft benefits to help employees protect their personal information.

Perquisites and Other Benefits

Nonmonetary services or benefits that an employer provides to its employees are referred to as *perquisites*, or *perks*. Essentially, the term *perks* is a catch-all for any voluntary benefit that does not fit neatly into one of the classic programs previously covered in this chapter. Typical examples of company perks include a designated parking space or an office with a view. Over the past several decades, many companies have expanded their perks by introducing new types of benefits that set them apart from their competitors. For example, companies like SAS and Google were leading pioneers in the perks arena. SAS—which was on several occasions ranked number one on *Forbes* magazine's list of the 100 Best Companies to Work For—offers live music in the subsidized cafeteria, oil changes, tire rotation, indoor swimming pools, and no dress code.[92] Famously, Google provides employees with free food via small displays, kitchen areas, and cafeterias; in fact, to encourage healthy eating choices, Google places the healthiest free-food options closer to eye level and less-healthy options in places that are harder to see and reach.[93] Google also offers on-site hair salons, dry cleaning, and bike repair as conveniences, although employees must pay for those.[94] Perks represent one more way that employers can differentiate themselves from their competitors.

LO 13.4 Assess the common challenges and opportunities associated with administering benefits programs.

Administering Benefits Programs

If benefits are selected and deployed in house, internal HR professionals must possess the knowledge and skills necessary to administer legally required and voluntary benefits programs. In fact, larger organizations often have a team of individuals who work as dedicated benefits specialists. Regardless of who administers benefits, HR information systems often play a critical role in gathering, storing, analyzing, and reporting the data. In the following sections, we describe the common challenges and opportunities associated with benefits administration.

Flexible Benefits Plans

Flexible benefits plans Offer employees some degree of choice for the employer-sponsored voluntary benefits they select and the benefits they are able to receive on a pretax basis

Some employers choose to administer flexible benefits plans. As the name implies, employer-sponsored *flexible benefits plans* offer employees some degree of choice when it comes to the voluntary benefits they select and the benefits they are able to receive on a pretax basis. Employees typically make contributions to flexible benefits plans as paycheck deductions, and the employer also pays a portion of the costs. The plan might provide employees with credits, which they can use to purchase the benefits that best suit their needs. For example, using their allotted credits, employees might choose from various medical, life insurance, and retirement plans, and they may be entitled to cash out a portion of their unused credits.

Research has shown that employees perceive higher procedural justice (i.e., process fairness) for flexible benefits plans than traditional benefits plans, which can be explained by the fact that flexible benefits plans provide employees with greater control over benefits selection while still offering consistent benefits choices across employees.[95] Further, adopting a flexible benefits plan may improve employees' satisfaction with their benefits.[96] As such, employers may find more favorable outcomes should they opt for a flexible benefits plan.

Flexible benefits plans go by other names, such as flex plans or cafeteria plans—the latter name communicates how these plans work: Employees may choose from a variety of benefit offerings as though they were walking through a cafeteria line and choosing from a variety of food options. In addition, these plans are also referred to as Section 125 plans—a label that references the applicable section of the U.S. Internal Revenue Code.[97] Section 125 permits flexible benefits plan participants to select two or more benefits, where at least one benefit is taxable and at least one benefit is qualified. Under Section 125, taxable benefits include cash payments that are taxed upon receipt. Qualified benefits include the following approved benefits that are received on a pretax basis (with certain limitations):

- employer-sponsored accident and health plans,
- group life insurance plans,
- child, elder, and other dependent care plans,
- adoption assistance programs, and
- health savings accounts (HSAs).

Different variations on flexible benefits plans exist, which include modular plans, core-plus options plans, full-choice plans, and flexible spending accounts.

Taxes and Accounting

By this point, you have probably noticed that there are different laws and taxes that must be considered when administering benefits. Moreover, different benefits often have different sets of rules, regulations, reporting standards, and taxes. Accordingly, successful benefits administration entails partnering with individuals, departments, or consulting firms with expertise in taxes and accounting. A comprehensive review of all pertinent tax and accounting forms and statements (e.g., Statement of Financial Accounting Standards 106) is beyond the scope of this textbook. However, we encourage interested readers to review documentation provided by government and professional organizations, such as the Internal Revenue Service (www.irs.gov) and the Financial Accounting Standards Board (www.fasb.org).

Discrimination

As with other core HR functions, benefits should not be administered in a manner that intentionally or unintentionally discriminates against different legally protected groups. As such, the following pieces of U.S. legislation covered in Chapter 4 can be extended to employee benefits administration: Title VII of the Civil Rights Act of 1964, Age Discrimination in Employment Act

---

SPOTLIGHT ON LEGAL ISSUES

Same-Sex Marriage and Spousal Benefits

In June 2015, the U.S. Supreme Court ruled that the Constitution guarantees the right to same-sex marriage. In the years leading up to the Court's decision, 37 states and the District of Columbia had already ruled in favor of same-sex marriage. Nonetheless, this landmark case guaranteed the right to same-sex marriage and spousal benefits at the federal level and across all states, in the process becoming the law of the land. Two years prior, the Supreme Court voted to strike down a federal law that denied spousal benefits to married same-sex couples; however, the Social Security Administration continued to deny same-sex spousal benefits for some individuals in states where same-sex marriage was not yet recognized. As such, the subsequent 2015 ruling provided blanket protections across the 50 states and the District of Columbia, and in the case of the Social Security Administration, spousal Social Security benefits for married same-sex couples became guaranteed.[98]

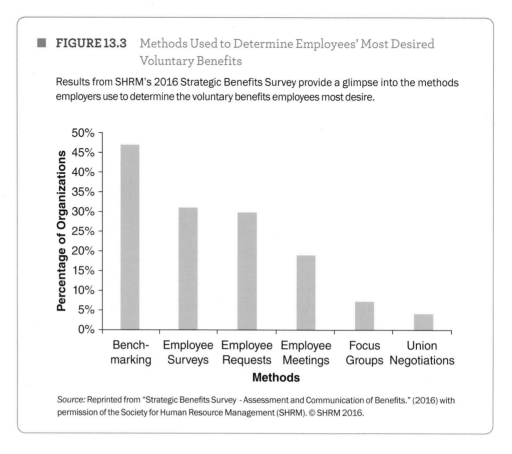

■ **FIGURE 13.3**   Methods Used to Determine Employees' Most Desired Voluntary Benefits

Results from SHRM's 2016 Strategic Benefits Survey provide a glimpse into the methods employers use to determine the voluntary benefits employees most desire.

Source: Reprinted from "Strategic Benefits Survey - Assessment and Communication of Benefits." (2016) with permission of the Society for Human Resource Management (SHRM). © SHRM 2016.

of 1967, Pregnancy Discrimination Act of 1978, Americans with Disabilities Act of 1990, and Genetic Information Nondiscrimination Act of 2008. That is, collectively, these pieces of legislation prohibit discrimination on the basis of race, color, religion, sex, national origin, age, pregnancy and associated medical conditions, disability, and genetic information.

To be classified as a qualified benefit, voluntary benefits programs must meet certain guidelines—one of which relates to discrimination in favor of highly compensated employees. In the United States, qualified benefits plans offer several potential tax advantages for the employer and employee: (a) employer tax deduction, (b) employee pretax payroll contribution, and (c) tax-free investment returns. As such, to earn the "qualified" distinction, an employer must demonstrate that all employees, regardless of their compensation levels, have access to the benefit and are helped by the benefit in similar ways.

Selecting Benefits

To strategically deploy voluntary benefits to attract, motivate, and retain talented workers, organizational decision makers must think carefully about which benefits programs to offer. Regarding initial voluntary benefit selection, a variety of data-gathering methods can be implemented (see Figure 13.3). Regardless of the method used, the overarching objectives should be to (a) determine the benefits employees want and (b) the benefits competitors offer. Regarding the first objective, employee surveys represent a relatively efficient data-gathering method to determine which benefits employees want because a large number of surveys can be sent out quickly (or even instantaneously). High survey response rates from all departments or units can help ensure that employees' responses are representative of all employees in the organization. Although potentially less efficient than surveys, employee focus groups offer an opportunity to gather rich, in-depth information regarding the most sought-after benefits. With respect to the second objective, competitor benchmarking based on market reviews remains one of the best approaches for determining what benefits other organizations offer.

SPOTLIGHT ON DATA AND ANALYTICS

Evaluating Benefits Offerings

Offering voluntary benefits to employees has the potential to add value for both employees and the organization. Analytics can be used as a decision-making tool (a) to determine which voluntary benefits to offer and (b) to evaluate the extent to which employees utilize different voluntary benefits. In fact, data analysis may reveal differences between the benefits employees say they want and the benefits they actually use.

To determine if any new voluntary benefits should be offered, HR professionals should collect systematic data on employee needs and wants. One of the most efficient ways to collect data from a large number of employees across the organization is to use an employee survey, and the survey should include items (i.e., questions or prompts) aimed at measuring employees' attitudes and behaviors toward existing benefits and potential benefits offerings. For example, to gauge employees' overall level of satisfaction with current benefits offerings, you might ask employees to rate the extent to which they agree with the following survey item, using a 1-to-5 scale (1 = *strongly disagree*, 5 = *strongly agree*): "Overall, I am satisfied with the company's current employee benefits offerings."

To avoid disappointing employees, make sure that any potential benefits offerings mentioned in the survey are actually ones that the organization has the means to implement. Otherwise, if the employees overwhelmingly respond in favor of a particular benefit but the organization is unable to offer the benefit, the employees may feel disappointed and dissatisfied. In other words, be sure to manage employees' expectations.

After designing the survey, efforts should be made to collect survey responses from a representative sample of employees. Consider that, collectively, all employees in the organization constitute the

employee population. To gather a representative sample of employees, steps must be taken to encourage responses from as many employees as possible and to ensure that employees from all functional areas and units respond to the survey. Once survey data collection has been completed, the demographic characteristics (e.g., age, gender, race, ethnicity, functional area) of the sample can be compared to the demographic characteristics of the entire employee population in the organization. Ideally, the demographic characteristics of the sample should be similar to the population. In doing so, HR professionals can ensure that any decisions made regarding benefits offerings are based on data that are representative of the entire organization. Finally, as a best practice, any time an organization collects data via employee surveys, the organization should report the aggregate findings back to the employees so that they know that their voices have been heard.

In addition to collecting data related to offering new voluntary benefits, the organization will need to determine which existing benefits offerings to change or eliminate. Data analytics can be used as a decision-support tool for benefits utilization. Using data that are perhaps already captured in the HR information system, an organization can analyze the number of employees enrolled in each benefit and the frequency with which employees access or use each benefit. In doing so, the organization can assess which benefits presumably reflect employees' needs and wants. Further, low utilization of a particular benefit may signal that the organization needs to better communicate the details of the benefit and/or its value. Finally, using data analytic tools like regression, analysts can investigate whether the enrollment in or use of certain benefits is associated with important employee and organizational outcomes such as turnover and performance.[99]

Communicating Benefits Programs

LO 13.5 Assess the common challenges and opportunities associated with communicating benefits programs.

The importance of effectively communicating benefits programs to (prospective) employees cannot be overstated, which includes communicating program details and communicating the value of benefits. In the early 1990s, researchers found that employees' awareness of their benefits offerings could be enhanced by providing them with informational materials about available benefits and by meeting with employees to discuss the available benefits.[100] More recently, SHRM conducted a 2017 survey in which HR professionals were asked which benefits communication methods they perceived as being most effective.[101] The results indicated that HR professionals generally preferred face-to-face communication methods, with 51% perceiving one-on-one communications as being very effective and 40% perceiving onboarding or orientations as being

HR IN ACTION

Using Data Visualizations to Communicate Value of Benefits

■ **FIGURE 13.4**   Communicating the Value of Benefits Using Data Visualizations

Data visualizations such as the pie chart can be used to communicate the relative value of different benefits.

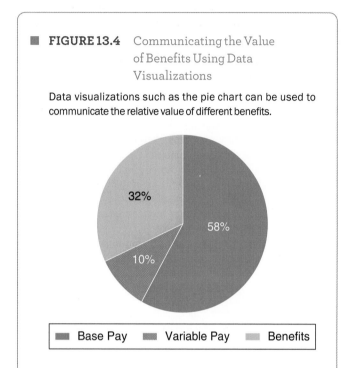

■ Base Pay   ■ Variable Pay   ■ Benefits

Although a pay stub presents employee and employer contributions to most benefits programs, the information is not typically presented in a compelling way that informs and engages the employee. Data visualizations are tools that can be used to enhance employees' understanding of the value of their benefits. For example, a simple pie chart with percentage value labels (such as the one shown in Figure 13.4) communicates visually the relative value of benefits relative to the total compensation package. Some vendors have created user-friendly dashboards that allow employees to interact with specific details of their benefits programs, such as how much paid time off they have remaining, and data visualizations like the pie chart often feature prominently in dashboards, as they present information in an at-a-glance and intuitive format.

very effective. Regarding virtual communication methods, approximately one-third of HR professionals found online benefits portals to be very effective. Thus, not surprisingly, face-to-face methods seem to work well for communication, as they offer synchronous information flow and access to immediate answers to questions. With that said, virtual communication methods may be more efficient and cost effective, particularly if well designed and implemented.

In addition to communicating information about benefits programs, HR professionals should make a concerted effort to communicate the value of benefits programs. Employee benefits represent a major cost for organizations, and evidence indicates that employees tend to underestimate the amount their employer contributes to their benefits.[102] In fact, many individuals may be unaware of how much benefits are worth. Regarding prospective employees, communicating the value of benefits can be the difference between the job candidate accepting an organization's offer or going with a competitor's offer, so it is advisable to provide job candidates with an accurate preview of what benefits will be available to them should they accept, as well as how much those benefits are worth. As for current employees, although pay stubs include information about employee and employer contributions to legally required and voluntary benefits programs, the information is often presented in tabular form such that the relative cost sharing between the employer and employee may not "jump off the page" for employees; as described in *HR in Action*, data visualizations like the pie chart can be effective tools for communicating the value of benefits. Finally, HR managers may lack the time or expertise to conduct formal communication about benefits and thus may benefit from partnering with public relations managers or firms to determine how and when to deliver benefits communications.[103]

CHAPTER SUMMARY

Benefits are part of the organization's broader rewards system, and thus, like other rewards, strategic deployment and administration of benefits can have important implications for attracting, motivating, and retaining workers. In the United States, legally required benefits include Social Security benefits, workers' compensation, federal and state unemployment insurance, and certain health care benefits. Voluntary benefits are discretionary in nature, and thus employers must think carefully and strategically to decide which benefits they will offer. They must also monitor the extent to which employees are using already available benefits. Examples of voluntary benefits include various forms of medical, dental, vision, life, and retirement insurance, as well as wellness programs. Finally, employers may face certain challenges and opportunities when it comes to administering and communicating benefits programs.

KEY TERMS

benefits   440
Social Security Act   442
Federal Insurance Contributions Act
   (FICA)   443
workers' compensation   444
Family and Medical Leave Act
   (FMLA)   444
Employee Retirement Income Security
   Act (ERISA)   446
Consolidated Omnibus Budget
   Reconciliation Act (COBRA)   446
Health Insurance Portability and
   Accountability Act (HIPAA)   446
Patient Protection and Affordable Care
   Act (ACA)   446
traditional-care plans   447
managed-care plans   447

short-term disability insurance   451
long-term disability insurance   452
Pension Benefit Guaranty Corporation
   (PBGC)   452
defined-benefit plan   452
cash balance plan   453
defined-contribution plan   453
tax deferred   453
401(k) plan   454
403(b) plan   454
profit-sharing program   454
employee stock ownership plans
   (ESOPs)   454
money-purchase plan   455
individual retirement plans (individual
   retirement arrangements)   455
life insurance programs   456

paid time off (PTO)   457
sick time (sick leave)   458
holiday pay   458
vacation pay   458
personal leave   458
compensatory time off (comp
   time)   458
educational-assistance
   program   459
perquisites (perks)   460
flexible benefits plans   460

Visit **edge.sagepub.com/bauer** to help you accomplish your coursework goals in an easy-to-use learning environment.

- Master the learning objectives using key study tools
- Watch, listen, and connect with online multimedia resources
- Access mobile-friendly quizzes and flashcards to check your understanding

HR REASONING AND DECISION-MAKING EXERCISES

MINI-CASE ANALYSIS EXERCISE: COMMUNICATING THE VALUE OF BENEFITS

Trident Health System has been experiencing difficulties attracting and retaining registered nurses (RNs) at its central hospital. Based on data from follow-up surveys with former applicants and from exit interviews conducted with former employees who voluntarily left the organization, HR leaders have concluded that a large number of individuals have been lured to a local competitor called Advantage Health. In particular, a number of former applicants and employees have reported that their primary reason for leaving was because Advantage Health paid RNs higher hourly wages as well as higher night and weekend pay differentials.

The HR leadership at Trident Health System acknowledges that they pay RNs lower wages than Advantage Health. However, based on market review data, they have reason to believe that Trident Health System offers one of the most generous benefits packages of any similar-sized health care organization in the region. Specifically, they offer generous employer cost-sharing contributions to employee medical, dental, and vision plans, as well as on-site subsidized child care services and a free employee cafeteria. Despite their generous benefits package, HR leaders are concerned that perhaps they are not doing a good enough job communicating information about their benefits to job candidates and current employees. At this time, job candidates and current employees can access information about benefits via the company's benefits webpage, and current employees can also look at their benefits deductions presented in their biweekly pay stub.

Questions:

1. What can Trident Health System do to improve how it communicates benefits to job candidates? What about current employees?

2. What methods would you recommend that Trident Health System use to communicate the value of its benefits offerings? Why?

3. What data-collection method(s) can the HR leaders use to determine which benefits employees (a) say they want and (b) actually utilize?

HR DECISION ANALYSIS EXERCISE: UNINTENDED CONSEQUENCES?

For the past 12 years, your company has offered an employer-sponsored health-maintenance organization (HMO) medical plan to employees and their dependents. After employer contributions are taken into account, employees contribute $38 per biweekly paycheck, on average, to pay for their plan premiums. The HMO does not have a deductible, and the annual out-of-pocket maximum is $1,250 for an individual and $2,500 for a family. The HMO does not cover out-of-network providers, procedures, or services.

Over the past few years, an increasing number of employees have come to your company's benefits specialists with complaints about the lack of out-of-network coverage. For instance, one employee conveyed a tragic story about how her husband, who was covered under her plan, chose not to see a nearby world-renowned oncologist for his cancer treatment because the oncologist was out of network; ultimately, he died from complications due to cancer. Based on your recommendation as the director of benefits, the company replaced the HMO with a preferred-provider organization (PPO), with the goal of providing some financial relief for those receiving care from out-of-network providers. It is estimated that the average biweekly premium paid by employees is now $51, which is higher than the average premium for the old HMO. In addition, the annual out-of-pocket maximums are $1,500 for an individual and $3,000 for a family, both of which are higher than the out-of-pocket maximums for the HMO. Finally, the copays and coinsurance for the PPO are roughly the same as the HMO.

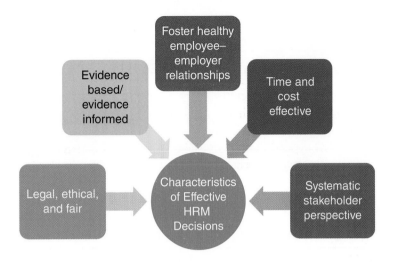

Do you have any concerns about switching to the PPO from the HMO? Do you think there will be any unintended consequences of switching to the PPO? Consider this decision using the following criteria.

Please provide the rationale for your answer to each of the questions below.

Is this decision legal, ethical, and fair?

_____
_____
_____
_____

Is it evidence based/evidence informed?

_____
_____
_____
_____

Does it foster healthy employee–employer relationships?

_____
_____
_____
_____

Is it time and cost effective?

_____
_____
_____
_____

Does it take a systematic stakeholder perspective?

_____
_____
_____
_____

Considering your analysis above, overall, do you think this would be an effective decision? Why or why not?

_____

_____

_____

What, if anything, do you think should be done differently or considered to help make this decision more effective?

_____

_____

_____

HR DECISION-MAKING EXERCISE: PAID PARENTAL LEAVE AT JEMBE BANKS

Jembe Banks is a regional bank that is headquartered in Detroit, Michigan, and has branches throughout Michigan, Indiana, Wisconsin, and Illinois. The bank currently employs nearly 350 employees at its headquarters and more than 2,300 employees at its various branches.

Each year, the HR team at Jembe Banks conducts a benefits survey designed to measure employees' preferences and attitudes regarding different benefits, as well as which benefits they plan to enroll in during the next fiscal year. At the end of each year's survey, the HR team provides the following open-ended question: "Is there a benefit that you would like for Jembe to offer in the future? Explain why." After reviewing responses from last year's survey, the HR team discovered that 121 employees out of the 899 who completed the survey stated that they wanted Jembe to offer paid parental leave. Respond to and discuss the following questions:

1. Legally, does the company have to provide paid parental leave? Explain.

2. If the company decides to provide paid parental leave, how many weeks of paid leave should the company provide? Why?

3. Should the company provide the same amount of paid parental leave to mothers and fathers alike? Why or why not?

4. Should a mother and father who are both employed by Jembe be allowed to take their paid leave concurrently? Why or why not?

DATA AND ANALYTICS EXERCISE: EVALUATING EMPLOYEES' SATISFACTION WITH BENEFITS

Offering the right mix of benefits can be quite challenging. Employers want to manage costs while also providing benefits that attract, motivate, and retain potential and current employees, and employees want benefits that meet their needs. Even the best assortment of benefits offerings can face problems if program details are not properly communicated and explained to employees. Employee surveys can be a powerful data collection tool when used to understand employees' attitudes toward benefits and how to improve benefits offerings.

Imagine an employee survey with items (e.g., questions) pertaining to the following attitudinal and behavioral concepts: overall benefits satisfaction, turnover intentions, and attendance at a benefits information session. Overall benefits satisfaction and turnover intentions are assessed with five-item measures, where employees rated each item using a 1 = "strongly disagree" and 5 = "strongly agree" response scale. An example item for overall benefits satisfaction is: "I am satisfied with the company's current medical plan offerings." A sample item for turnover intentions is: "I am considering leaving the organization in the next 6 months." A single item is used to assess attendance at a benefits information session, such that employees respond either "yes, I attended" or "no, I did not attend."

In what follows, we include a sample of employee response data for illustration purposes, where each row contains a unique employee's data and each column contains employees' scores on each of the three attitudinal and behavioral concepts. To simplify things, the average of employees' responses (i.e., scores) on the five-item measures for overall benefits satisfaction and turnover intentions have already been computed.

OVERALL BENEFITS SATISFACTION	TURNOVER INTENTIONS	ATTENDED A BENEFITS INFORMATION SESSION
3.78	2.87	Yes
4.60	1.91	Yes
3.19	2.14	Yes
4.12	1.90	Yes
3.88	2.90	Yes
3.84	1.64	Yes
4.68	1.63	Yes
3.46	3.29	Yes
3.26	2.45	Yes
4.52	2.07	Yes
2.06	2.98	No
2.84	2.97	No
3.63	3.01	No
3.36	3.17	No
3.64	3.45	No
2.84	4.09	No
2.71	3.40	No
2.84	3.14	No
2.86	2.83	No
2.93	2.66	No

Given these data, we will attempt to answer the following questions:

- Is there a negative correlation between overall benefits satisfaction and turnover intentions, such that employees with higher overall satisfaction with benefits offerings have fewer intentions to leave the company?
- Do employees who attended a benefits information session have higher overall satisfaction with their benefits than employees who did not?

To answer the first question, we can use simple linear regression, where overall benefits satisfaction is specified as the predictor variable and turnover intentions is specified as the outcome variable. Using Excel, we find the following:

	COEFFICIENTS	STANDARD ERROR	T STAT	P-VALUE	LOWER 95%	UPPER 95%
Intercept	4.81	.61	7.89	.00	3.53	6.09
Overall Benefits Satisfaction	−.60	.17	−3.49	.00	−.97	−.24

The results indicate that the regression coefficient for overall benefits satisfaction in relation to turnover intentions is −.60, which means that the association between the two variables is negative. Such an association means that for every one-point increase in overall benefits satisfaction, we tend to see turnover intentions drop by .60 points. The corresponding p-value is less than the conventional two-tailed cutoff (alpha) value of .05, which means we can treat the regression coefficient of −.60 as being statistically significant. Together, these two pieces of information provide evidence that, indeed, employees with higher overall satisfaction with benefits offerings have fewer intentions to leave the company.

Regarding the second question, we can run an independent-samples *t*-test using Excel to determine whether the average overall benefits satisfaction score for those who attend a benefits information session is significantly higher than the average overall benefits satisfaction score for those who did not attend a session.

	YES	NO
Mean	3.93	2.97
Variance	.29	.22
Observations	10	10
Pooled Variance	.26	
Hypothesized Mean Difference	0	
df	18	
t-Statistic	4.22	
P(T≤t) one-tail	.00	
t Critical one-tail	1.73	
P(T≤t) two-tail	.00	
t Critical two-tail	2.10	

The results indicate the *t*-statistic that corresponds to the difference between the two means (averages) is 4.22, and the associated two-tailed *p*-value is less than the conventional cutoff of .05. Based on this information, we have evidence that in fact there is a statistically significant difference between the average overall benefits satisfaction score for those who attended a benefits information session and the average overall benefits satisfaction score for those who did not attend a session. To determine whether those who attended the information session had a higher average, we can look at the mean scores. The mean for the group of employees who indicated "yes, I attended" was 3.93, whereas the mean for those who indicated "no, I did not attend" was 2.97. Thus, we found support that indeed those who attended an information session tended to have higher satisfaction with the company's current benefits offerings.

 EXCEL EXTENSION: NOW YOU TRY!

- On **edge.sagepub.com/bauer**, you will find an Excel exercise that provides additional practice evaluating employees' satisfaction with benefits offerings.

- Using regression and independent-samples *t*-tests, you will test different hypotheses and answer different questions based on employee survey data.

CHAPTER 13 SUPPLEMENT: QUESTIONS TO CONSIDER WHEN DESIGNING AND IMPLEMENTING A PAID TIME OFF (PTO) PROGRAM

The Society for Human Resource Management (SHRM) recommends that employers consider the following questions when deciding how to design and implement a paid time off (PTO) program:[104]

1. What will be done with unused PTO at the end of the year? Will employees be able to roll forward all of their PTO to the next year, or will there be limits to how much PTO can be rolled forward?

2. Will employees be permitted to "cash out" any unused PTO at the end of the year? Can they contribute the cash-out value of unused PTO to another benefit, such as a retirement plan or a health savings account?

3. Is the current HR information system and/or payroll system equipped to handle potentially complicated PTO transactional and administrative activities?

4. Is there a plan for how to communicate to employees how PTO accrual, year-end rollover, and other plan features operate?

5. Are managers trained and/or prepared for the implications of a PTO program as it relates to their responsibilities? Do managers know how to schedule employee time off using the new program and understand how to approve requested PTO?

Employee and Labor Relations

Opening Case

The First B Corp Certified U.S. Grocery Store: The Case of New Seasons Market

New Seasons Market is an Oregon-based grocery store chain founded in 2000 by three families who set the goal of "rethinking what a grocery store could be." The store is known for offering local and organic products. As of 2018, the company had 21 stores and more than 4,000 employees.

From the start, New Seasons Market was dedicated to both socially and environmentally responsible initiatives, including advocating for raising the minimum wage and the need for affordable housing. The stores divert more than 90% of all their waste from landfills via programs focused on composting, donations, and recycling. Fulfilling the company's mission statement "to be the ultimate neighborhood store," New Seasons Market offers events and classes, provides opportunities for its employees to do community volunteer work, and gives back 10% of after-tax profits to nonprofit organizations.

In 2013, New Seasons Market became the first grocery store in the United States to achieve B Corp certification. B Corps are for-profit companies that are certified by the nonprofit B Lab if they meet rigorous standards of social and environmental performance, accountability, and transparency and strive to use the power of markets to help solve social and environmental problems. B Corp certification is voluntary and can be changed at any time. B Lab is not a legal designation, but it is seen by some as important. For example, Rose Marcario, CEO of Patagonia, argues, "The B Corp movement is one of the most important of our lifetime, built on the simple fact that business impacts and serves more than just stakeholders—it has an equal responsibility to the community and to the planet." While New Seasons Market is not a publicly traded company, one key aspect of B Corps in general is that they don't have to focus solely on maximizing shareholder value. More than 2,000 Certified B Corps exist in 50 countries across 130 industries. Many of these companies are small to medium-sized, which is where much of the growth in this type of company has emerged. This certification is an independent, third-party certification that consists of an application of 170 questions covering such aspects of the business as energy efficiency and employee programs and practices. As a result of a company's answers to these questions, a total of 200 points is possible, but the certification does not expect that any company will ever be able to achieve a perfect score. In fact, a score of 80 points is enough to become certified. In its initial application, New Seasons Market earned 121 points, which is higher than the average of 97 points and higher than some

LEARNING OBJECTIVES

After reading and studying this chapter, you should be able to do the following:

14.1 Define *employee and labor relations* and identify key factors that influence them.

14.2 Compare different types of organizational policies and procedures.

14.3 Recognize the role that the labor movement plays globally.

14.4 Outline the collective bargaining process.

14.5 Evaluate the possible courses of action when negotiating parties fail to reach an agreement.

©iStock.com/Steve Debenport

companies known for their environmental and social responsibility missions, such as Patagonia. Other notable companies with B Corp certification include Ben & Jerry's (the first wholly owned subsidiary to get certified), Etsy, and Kickstarter. Natura, a Brazilian cosmetics company, became the first publicly traded Certified B Corp in 2014. Beyond those companies that formally apply for certification, more than 40,000 organizations use the free self-assessment tool available at www.bimpactassessment.net to help them benchmark and improve their social and environmental impact.

One major challenge for New Seasons Market is to manage relations with its workforce as the company continues to grow and expand into new parts of the country. Its expansion in 2016 to Mercer Island, Washington, was met with resistance by the United Food and Commercial Workers union's UFCW21 over the lack of a unionized workforce and concerns over the number of hours worked required for employees to receive benefits. Also, some workers in Portland, Oregon, began a union drive in 2017 as benefits were changing as part of the growth of the company. In response, in 2018, New Seasons decided to reassess its plans to expand into California as a result of the changes necessary to align across different states. Effectively managing employee relations will continue to be a major part of New Seasons Market's strategy for success.[1]

Case Discussion Questions

1. If you were a manager at New Seasons Market, how would you have reacted to B Lab certification? Would your answer change if you were an employee?

2. What are your thoughts regarding the pros and cons of measuring social and environmental impact of organizations? How would you know if a particular question on the certification is effective?

3. Prior to reading this case, had you heard about B Corp certification? What new things did you learn about this concept from the case?

4. Do you agree or disagree with Patagonia CEO Rose Marcario that "The B Corp movement is one of the most important of our lifetime"? Please explain your answer.

5. Do you think that New Season Market's B Corp certification has positive or negative implications for employee relations? Please explain your answer.

▶ Click to learn more...

To hear more about New Seasons Market becoming a B Corporation, view this YouTube video: https://youtu.be/Z9p88J9ZGeE

Employee relations The collective relationships between different employees as well as between employees and management in an organization

Employee relations refers to the collective relationships between different employees as well as between employees and management in an organization. Much of employee relations is tied to an organization's HR policies and procedures. In addition, organizations must adhere to formal labor laws such as terms of employment and particularly labor laws relating to unions and collective bargaining, referred to as ***labor relations***. Employee relations and labor relations are related to a wide range of HRM topics you have already learned about in this book such as rewards, benefits, training, and job security.

This chapter explores the key components of both employee relations and labor relations from both historical and modern organizational perspectives. We begin by delving into the definition of employee relations and factors related to this concept. Then we shift the focus to organizational policies and procedures, employee rights and responsibilities, and grievance procedures, which are also aspects of employee and labor relations. We discuss the labor movement and issues associated with union formation, functioning, and dispute management. We then outline the collective bargaining process and the alternative methods of resolving negotiations when an agreement cannot be reached.

Labor relations Managing in response to labor laws relating to unions and collective bargaining

Factors Influencing Employee Relations

Many factors influence employee relations. If you have taken an organizational behavior or principles of management course, you are probably familiar with such factors, as entire chapters are devoted to many of them; this textbook has touched on several of these issues as well. Here the focus is on these five important factors that might influence employee relations: culture, fair treatment, working conditions, employment laws, and unions (see Figure 14.1).

LO 14.1 Define *employee and labor relations* and identify key factors that influence them.

Culture

Culture is defined as the shared assumptions that members of an organization have, which affect how they act, think, and perceive their environment. Therefore, the culture that evolves within an organization can exhibit a major positive or negative effect on employee relations. It is also important to keep in mind that subcultures may also develop within organizations such that different groups may have different perceptions or experiences that influence their employee relations. One major factor that affects culture and employee relations is how individuals are treated in terms of both procedures and outcomes. In fact, employment law attorney Aaron Zandy says the key to avoiding employment lawsuits is to do three things: *be fair*, *be consistent*, and *do not surprise employees*.[2] Thus, the next point we will cover is how fair (or unfair) treatment may affect employee relations.

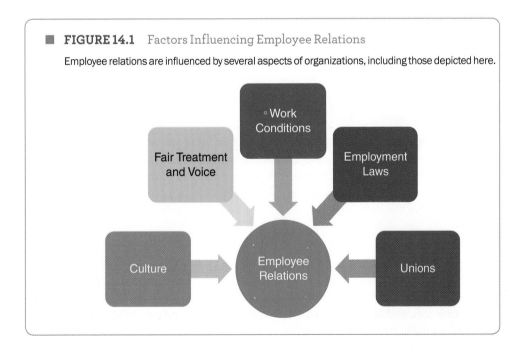

■ **FIGURE 14.1** Factors Influencing Employee Relations

Employee relations are influenced by several aspects of organizations, including those depicted here.

Not complying with employment labor laws can be costly. For example, in 2002, Starbucks paid $18 million in a dispute regarding overtime pay, and in 2008, it paid $105 million in a dispute over tips to settle lawsuits in California.

Fair Treatment and Voice

Fair treatment is so important for employee relations that SHRM's Code of Ethics (see Chapter 1) includes Fairness and Justice. Specifically, it reads, "As human resource professionals, we are ethically responsible for promoting and fostering fairness and justice for all employees and their organizations." This includes cultivating an environment of inclusiveness, developing and administering policies that are fair and consistent, and respecting individuals. When individuals feel that they are not being treated fairly, they tend to have lower job attitudes, poorer performance and greater withdrawal behaviors, and are more likely to join a union.[3] Thus, organizations wishing to develop and maintain positive employee–employer relations should keep fairness in mind when interacting with employees and applicants, to gather feedback from employees regularly to see what issues and improvements might be addressed, and to keep fairness and justice in mind when making decisions that impact employees. Even better, research finds that when employees have more voice in how organizations function due to programs like profit sharing, worker ownership, or worker participation in decision making, higher productivity is found as well.[4]

Working Conditions

When we refer to working conditions, there are many possible aspects of work that relate to employee relations. For example, rewards and benefits are aspects of work that are often reasons for employees to passively withdraw or actively look for employment elsewhere. Similarly, working in unsafe conditions can be a major concern and has been related to strained employee relations. In other instances, the actual workplace might be physically safe but create stress due to shift work, overtime, or a lack of flexibility in how or when work gets done. As the opening case on New Seasons indicates, changes to benefits led to strained employment relations and union activity. Some companies such as Costco are known as leaders in their industry in terms of wages and benefits even in the low-margin world of groceries and retail. The company is known for promoting from within, like Craig Jelinek, a 3-year veteran who took over as CEO in 2012. In fact, 98% of store managers have been promoted from within stores. Costco also pays well, with an average of $22/hour versus the average of $13.38/hour at Walmart, a store offering similar items, or the national average of around $11/hour for retail employees. Employees also receive full health benefits, a 401(k) retirement plan with stock options after 1 year, and generous vacation and family leave policies.[5]

Employment Laws

In the United States, employment laws are a major factor in the practice of HR. Understanding how they influence and regulate employee relations is important. Employment laws matter for the practice of HRM and for what employees expect in terms of employment relations with organizational members and the organization as a whole.

Unions

Finally, as we saw in the opening case and you will read in the pages that follow, the mere possibility of an organization's workforce joining a labor union (referred to as "unionization") may influence employee relations. However, once a union is in place, employee relations become formalized in specific and prescribed ways. Much of this chapter focuses on understanding the history of labor unions, trends in unionization, how they are formed, and how they function. Also covered are organizational policies and procedures, which exist regardless of whether a union is in place. Keep in mind, however, that unions are tasked to bargain over policies as well, so at times, they are deeply involved in forming, informing, and monitoring organizational policies and procedures.

Organizational Policies and Procedures

LO 14.2 Compare different types of organizational policies and procedures.

Designing, implementing, and enforcing organizational policies and procedures are often managed by HR departments. When unions are in place, these policies are negotiated, as we will see in greater detail in the sections that follow. However, it is important to understand how organizational policies and procedures are communicated and what they typically entail regardless of how they came to be.

Employee Handbooks

Organizational policies and procedures outline the rules and expectations for both employees and employers. Although there are laws that require employers to inform their employees about their specific workplace rights, it is not a legal mandate to have an actual employee handbook. However, many organizations do create handbooks including such information because they are useful for employees and managers to understand what is expected of them. Some handbooks are long and read like legal documents. Others are short and written simply. However, it is critical that employees of all levels understand that handbooks are part of the HR compliance process, so what is written in the handbook provides an answer if disputes occur between managers and employees. Thus, it is important that what is included is accurate, consistently enforced,

SPOTLIGHT ON HR FOR SMALL AND MEDIUM-SIZED BUSINESSES

Getting Started on an Employee Handbook

Whether you are working for a small established company or starting one of your own, creating a new employee handbook from scratch can be a daunting task. It helps to understand what information is required to be included by federal, state, and local laws. Examples include information regarding family medical leave policies, equal employment and nondiscrimination policies, and workers' compensation policies should an injury occur. It is important to keep in mind that employee handbooks are not contracts; a handbook overrides all other policies and procedures and should note that policies are subject to change within the handbook materials.[6] Another point to consider is that an employee handbook may be perceived as an implied contract, creating an exception to employment at will. To avoid this, include an at-will disclaimer in your employee handbook and avoid any promises of job security.[7] SHRM recommends that handbooks be reviewed by legal counsel at least annually. You should also ask all employees to sign a document acknowledging that they have received, read, and understand the handbook materials.

Resources exist to help create handbooks. Many free and low-cost templates are available. For example, SHRM offers free sample handbooks for members as well as a more advanced Handbook Builder that walks users through a set of questions.[8]

Following is a list of additional items to consider including in an employee handbook:

- Company history
- Time-off policy
- Employee behavior, standards of conduct
- Wages and salary
- Benefits
- Promotions
- Reasonable accommodations
- Employee communications
- Social media policies

Valve Gets Creative With Employee Handbook

Some organizations seek to signal their organizational culture through their use of unique employee handbooks. For example, Valve Corporation, the online gaming platform company that owns Steam, makes it clear that its culture is not like other organizations by beginning its handbook with a section entitled *How to Use This Book*: "This book isn't about fringe benefits or how to set up your workstation or where to find source code. Valve works in ways that might seem counterintuitive at first. This handbook is about the choices you're going to be making and how to think about them. Mainly, it's about how not to freak out now that you're here." The handbook also includes headings such as *Welcome to Valve, Settling In, How Am I Doing*?, and *Valve Is Growing*. After an employee posted a copy of it online, the handbook went viral, but not all employees agree that the handbook is an accurate depiction of the company's culture as they experienced it.[10] The company shares the handbook in nine languages on its recruitment web page.

See the full handbook here: http://media.steampowered.com/apps/valve/Valve_Handbook_LowRes.pdf

and understood by everyone within the organization. Not doing so can put organizations at risk should an employee complaint be filed.

Normally, new employees receive their handbooks as part of the onboarding process of orientation and compliance. Handbooks can make for pretty dry reading, and it might be tempting to skip reading it while trying to adjust to one's new job. Some companies such as The Motley Fool, which has appeared on Glassdoor.com's Best Places to Work list, have created fully interactive onboarding experiences, which include a video introduction from the CEO, as well as specific company policies and procedures, and a list of key terms for employees. Zappos.com's employee handbook is written in a comic book style and features a story of a grandmother explaining Zappos' culture, policies, and procedures.[9] Regardless of how entertaining the information is, all new employees should take the time to read and understand the handbook given what an important document it is as the basis for the employment relationship.

Examples of Types of Organizational Policies

Organizations vary in how many policies they include in their employee handbook depending on a number of factors, including the organization's industry, size, age, and culture, as well as state and local requirements. Rather than review all the potential policies that might be included, the focus is on five different types of policies that might be included: legally required information, code of conduct, leaves, appearance, and social media policies.

Legally Required Information

Although employee handbooks are not legally required, they are often included in them, as policies that must be addressed by law are important to outline and share with employees. These include worker's compensation policies, family medical leave policies, and EEOC nondiscrimination policies as required by the U.S. Department of Labor. Requirements change over time, so the suggestion to review the content shared with new employees is an ongoing task.

Code of Conduct

The code of conduct might include information about expectations for workplace behaviors such as respect, confidentiality, EEO compliance, and unacceptable behaviors such as discrimination or sexual harassment. It is important that organizations communicate their expectations regarding what constitutes a *conflict of interest* that might unduly influence decisions or have the appearance of doing so. Such policies should include definitions of conflicts of interest and what to do if such conflicts exist. Some organizations include code-of-conduct training that all employees must complete. Often employees will be asked to sign that they have read, understand, and agree to the code of conduct.

Leave Policy

Beyond the Family Medical Leave Act considerations, some organizations prescribe and strictly enforce how sick days, personal days, and/or vacation days are to be taken. Other organizations such as GrubHub, LinkedIn, Kronos, and Netflix have no limit on the amount of leave that can be taken.[11] Instead, they trust employees to behave responsibly and only take as much time as they need while keeping up with their responsibilities. Regardless of where a company is on this continuum, it is important to be clear about what the policy is and how employees should schedule days off to avoid confusion or resentment.

Appearance

There are many aspects of employee appearance that may or may not be outlined in an employee handbook. For example, dress codes, personal hygiene, facial hair, and body art and piercings may be addressed. Dress codes range from business formal, such as wearing a specific uniform, to casual. The type of dress code often depends on a number of factors such as the type of industry the organization is in, the type of work an employee does, whether special dress or equipment is needed for safety such as when working in construction sites, geography, or the organizational culture. Personal hygiene issues range from a safety requirement at work such as a restaurant employee washing their hands before returning to work to an uncomfortable topic to discuss at work regarding body odor. Managers and employees need guidance in how to handle such matters with sensitivity, and SHRM reminds us that odors may be caused by many factors outside of an employee's control such as a medical condition or a specific diet. Thus, such issues must be addressed appropriately to avoid violating the Americans with Disabilities Act or triggering other claims of discrimination.[12] Including guidelines on what

---

SPOTLIGHT ON LEGAL ISSUES

Tattoos in the Workplace

In the United States, more than 20% of adults and nearly 40% of millennials aged 18 to 29 have at least one tattoo, according to a study by Pew Research.[13] In general, employers have the right to choose not to hire someone, or to fire them, for tattoos. An exception to this is when tattoos are due to religious reasons. In one case, Red Robin restaurant fired a server for having tattoos that were part of his religious practice. Red Robin lost its case for termination in court and paid the server $150,000.[14] However, this is relatively rare in terms of outcomes for such court cases—especially those simply dealing with personal-expression or freedom-of-speech arguments. Another way employers can get into trouble, however, is if they discriminate against some types of tattoos but not others. The key for organizations is to be consistent

and fair in applying their dress code and grooming standards across all employees.

The First Amendment of the United States Constitution protects the rights of individuals to free speech, and this includes the display of tattoos. But that does not mean that employers in the private sector have to allow them. A survey found that 60% of HR professionals felt that visible tattoos would negatively impact an applicant's chances of securing employment, and 74% felt that way about facial piercings. It is not clear how these negative reactions may evolve over time given the growing number of individuals with tattoos in the United States. The key for organizations is to be consistent and fair in applying the dress code and grooming standards across all employees.

is expected and whether perfumes and colognes are allowed in the workplace can be helpful for employees and those who work around them to deal with the issues professionally and discreetly. Overall, the thing to keep in mind is that organizations have the legal right to adopt whatever dress codes and grooming requirements they desire to fit their culture and/or promote a particular brand or look as long as they do not discriminate on the basis of a protected class. However, the policies they choose to enact will most likely have an influence on employee relations.

Social Media

Nordstrom is famous for having a handbook that fits on a 5 × 8 card. It includes the following:

> *Our number one goal is to provide outstanding customer service. Set both your personal and professional goals high. We have great confidence in your ability to achieve them, so our employee handbook is very simple. We have only one rule. . . . Our one rule: Use best judgment in all situations. There will be no additional rules.*

That, however, is not the end of Nordstrom's workplace policies. For example, Nordstrom's social media guidelines point to 10 guidelines as an offshoot of its original rule stating, "If you use social media accounts to connect and share about Nordstrom, we ask that you use good judgment and follow these additional guidelines."[15] Keep in mind that policies should follow employment laws like those related to the right of employees to discuss working conditions, as this is behavior protected by the National Labor Relations Board (NLRB) laws. For example, an ambulance company, American Medical Response of Connecticut, fired an employee for criticizing her supervisor on Facebook, and the NLRB filed a complaint that this violated worker rights.[16] Organizations should clearly delineate their policies regarding social media both during and outside of work hours, as this has become an increasingly controversial issue.

LO 14.3 Recognize the role that the labor movement plays globally.

The Labor Movement

The history of the labor movement and the growth of labor unions can be traced back to fundamental changes in the workplace. In the early 1900s, factories began to set up procedures to address concerns regarding employee wages and additional labor concerns. However, following the Great Depression in the 1930s and then World War II, a surge in union membership took place through the 1950s. Union membership has been on a steady decline in the United States in recent decades. Whereas the decision to organize or join a union is a personal one for each employee, there are some common reasons why employees pursue unionization in their workplaces. There are also a number of different types of unions.[17] We next turn our attention to some potential reasons why employees seek to unionize.

Reasons Employees Unionize

Employees unionize for a variety of reasons including job dissatisfaction, working conditions, and employee disengagement. We start with job dissatisfaction.

Job Dissatisfaction

Dissatisfaction with one's job is a major reason employees organize and join unions. This makes sense, because when an individual is unhappy about a situation at work, they may engage in a number of behaviors in response. Different reactions to job dissatisfaction are illustrated using the exit–voice–loyalty–neglect framework, which argues that employee behavioral reactions range in terms of how active workers are as well as how constructive they are. Behaviors directed toward withdrawing from the organization include employee lateness, absenteeism, and turnover and are termed *exit*. Active and constructive responses

Pictured here is a worker wearing a sign on his hat that says "Bread or Revolution" at an Industrial Workers of the World labor rally in New York City in 1914.

■ **FIGURE 14.2** Four Possible Reactions to Job Dissatisfaction

Employees may respond to dissatisfaction through exit, voice, neglect, or loyalty.

Active

Exit	Voice

Destructive ←→ Constructive

Neglect	Loyalty

Passive

to dissatisfying working conditions include *voice*, through which employees attempt to improve conditions. *Neglect* and *loyalty* are passive and refer to allowing the conditions to worsen or hoping they will get better. Figure 14.2 illustrates these four possible reactions in terms of these factors. Attempts to organize and unionize represent one potential form of voice behavior.

Working Conditions

So what specific things might employees be dissatisfied about? There are a number of reasons related to working conditions that may affect whether employees are motivated to organize or join a union. These include concerns regarding working conditions such as pay, benefits, safety, job security, hours, the working environment, and treatment. In other words, employees interested in voting for a union believe that the union will help them get more of the financial and nonfinancial working conditions they value.[18]

The 40-hour work week did not come into existence in the United States until 1937 with the passage of the Fair Labor Standards Act at the urging of unions, leading to the union slogan "Labor Unions: The folks who brought you the weekend."[19]

One study found that membership in a labor union was related to better coping and lower stress for individuals working in a chemical plant.[20] Although union membership has been declining, the inequality in hourly wages has been increasing, indicating that unions do influence wages.[21] In support of the argument that union workers enjoy greater levels of compensation, on average, union members earn more and enjoy better benefits (e.g., health insurance and retirement accounts) than their nonunionized counterparts across the United States within the same occupations.[22] For example, across all industries, union workers earn a median weekly pay rate of $1,004 versus $802 for nonunion workers in 2016.[23] Bus drivers for Facebook received $9-per-hour raises after their union negotiated for higher wages, better benefits, additional pay for shift work, and the establishment of grievance procedures. Google and Apple increased the hourly pay and benefits for their own shuttle drivers shortly after Facebook's agreement with its employees represented by Teamsters Local 853.[24]

■ **FIGURE 14.3**   Results of an Employee Engagement Pulse Survey

Qualtrics, a survey platform company, advocates for the benefits of pulse surveys, which are shorter and administered more frequently than annual opinion surveys. Such surveys allow organizations to track changes in responses month to month and quarter to quarter such as the results shown here.

Source: Courtesy of Qualtrics. https://www.qualtrics.com/human-resources/employee-pulse-surveys/

Employee Disengagement

How engaged employees are at work is also related to whether employees are interested in unionizing. Employees who report not being engaged with their work also reported being more likely to vote yes to a union and to become union members.[25]

Employees who are disengaged or dissatisfied or feel unfairly treated can work with organizations toward improvement. But organizations need tools to do so. One such tool is the administration of an annual employee opinion survey to gauge employee attitudes and to identify problems and potential problems within the organization. Such surveys are big undertakings in terms of employee time to respond as well as the effort to create, administer, and analyze the results. Although large organizations such as Disney, Walmart, and Ford Motor Company already administer such surveys, more and more organizations are also beginning to administer smaller surveys more frequently (see Figure 14.3).

Why Do Some Organizations Resist Unionization?

Not all organizations resist unionization, but it is common for organizations to work to avoid it for a number of reasons including profit concerns and decreased autonomy. We discuss each of these in the section that follows.

Profit Concerns

It makes sense that organizations might be concerned that if they pay workers more in terms of wages or increase worker benefits and programs, they will become less profitable. However, that is only true if there are no financial benefits to workers being satisfied, such as stronger productivity or innovation. There is a great deal of debate regarding whether belonging to a union makes employees more or less satisfied overall.[26] Similarly, it is not clear if organizations with unions are more or less profitable than their nonunionized counterparts, as it depends on a variety of factors.[27] For example, a meta-analysis of 73 global studies examining the relationship between productivity and unions found that, in the United Kingdom, there was a negative association. For the United States, however, there was a positive association in general, as well as for within U.S. manufacturing.[28] Even though the reality for a given organization within a given country or industry is unclear in terms of profit, it is clear that unions do decrease an organization's autonomy to make decisions that impact employees.

Decreased Autonomy

As you will see in the pages that follow, when an organization's workforce is unionized or has a union in place, it serves to decrease how much discretion the organization has to alter wages and benefits and to set policies that affect employees. Rather than having full autonomy to make changes as long as they are legal, organizations with union members must consider the contract in place. This can make them less able to respond quickly to changes in the market or to changing conditions. This can be a concern for organizations. In fact, research shows that the worse the market conditions are, the more likely executives of a firm are to choose union-avoidance strategies rather than union–labor cooperation strategies.[29] Business and labor do not have to have an adversarial relationship. In countries such as Denmark, unions and employers work together closely, and Denmark is considered one of the easiest countries in the world in which to conduct business. It is ranked behind New Zealand and Singapore according to the World Bank (the United States was ranked sixth).[30]

Unions and Laws

To really understand the context of labor movements, it is important to trace the series of laws associated with their growth and regulation from the 1930s through today. First and foremost, unions exist in a legal context. Now that we have covered some of the reasons modern employees join unions as well as types of unions, we will move to a discussion of the different laws that set the legal context for work and workers. While many laws relate to employees and unions, we will highlight some of the most important acts related to HR practices, starting with the Norris-LaGuardia Act.

Norris-LaGuardia Act (1932)

This act was a critical step toward changing national labor relations. It outlawed the ability of federal courts to stop union activities such as pickets or strikes. It also outlawed agreements from employees to employers that they would not form or join a union. The passage of this act signaled a new era of support for unions and their activities. Although not a comprehensive act in itself, it is regarded as being important in laying the foundation of changing attitudes toward supporting labor movements in the United States.

National Labor Relations (or Wagner) Act (1935)

Building upon the legislative momentum of the Norris-LaGuardia Act, the **National Labor Relations** (or Wagner) **Act** regulated national labor relations by granting unions fundamental rights and powers. These included important provisions such as the right to collective bargaining, the definition of **unfair labor practices**, and importantly, it established penalties for companies that violated these rights. The act describes five key unfair labor practices that include the right to

> *self-organization, to form, join, or assist labor unions, to bargain collectively through representatives of their own choosing, and to engage in other concerted activities for the purpose of collective bargaining or other mutual aid or protection, and shall also have the right to refrain from any or all such activities. . . .*

These rights, however, do not extend to the railway or airline industries. Finally, the act established the **National Labor Relations Board (NLRB)**. As an independent United States governmental agency, the NLRB is tasked with supervising union elections and is empowered to investigate suspected unfair labor practices. The NLRB consists of a five-person board, and general counsel is appointed by the president of the United States with Senate consent. In 2017, the NLRB handled nearly 19,000 unfair practice charges (see Figure 14.4). For example, the NLRB argued that the following provisions within T-Mobile's employee handbook violated the Wagner Act: maintaining

National Labor Relations Act Stipulates that employees protected under the act have a right to discuss pay as part of activities related to collective bargaining and protection, thereby providing an avenue through which employees may uncover pay discrimination

Unfair labor practices Defined in the U.S. as actions taken by either unions or employers which violate the National Labor Relations Act or other legislation. Such acts are investigated by the National Labor Relations Board.

National Labor Relations Board (NLRB) An independent United States governmental agency, the NLRB is tasked with supervising union elections and is empowered to investigate suspected unfair labor practices

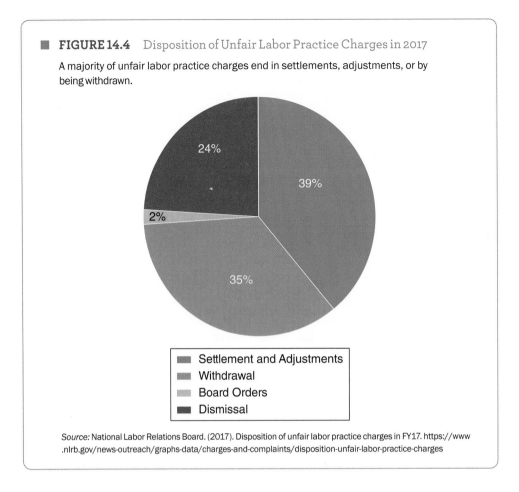

FIGURE 14.4　Disposition of Unfair Labor Practice Charges in 2017

A majority of unfair labor practice charges end in settlements, adjustments, or by being withdrawn.

- 39%
- 35%
- 2%
- 24%

■ Settlement and Adjustments
■ Withdrawal
■ Board Orders
■ Dismissal

Source: National Labor Relations Board. (2017). Disposition of unfair labor practice charges in FY17. https://www.nlrb.gov/news-outreach/graphs-data/charges-and-complaints/disposition-unfair-labor-practice-charges

a positive work environment, not arguing or fighting, failing to be respectful or to demonstrate appropriate teamwork, outlawing all photography and audio or video recording in the workplace, and barring access to electronic information by individuals not approved. The court ruled that these handbook items did not violate the act and that "a reasonable employee would be fully capable of engaging in debate over union activity or working conditions, even vigorous or heated debate, without inappropriately arguing or fighting, or failing to treat others with respect."[31]

Labor Management Relations Act (1947)

Labor Management Relations Act (1947) Also known as the Taft-Hartley Act; amended the National Labor Act and restricts the activities and power of labor unions

This act, also known as the Taft-Hartley Act, amended and limited the National Labor Relations Act in key ways. For example, it added additional unfair labor practices employees might engage in rather than limiting such unfair acts to companies. In essence, the act was designed to limit the power of unions and to limit the ability of labor to strike. Specifically, it prohibited jurisdictional strikes so that only unions directly related to the work of a targeted business could participate; prohibited unions and corporations from making independent expenditures for federal candidates; outlawed closed shops that required employers to only hire union members; allowed states to pass right-to-work laws; required unions and employers to give 80 days advance notice before striking; gave the president of the United States the power to stop strikes if they might create a national emergency; allowed employers to terminate supervisors for supporting union activity; and gave employers the right to oppose unions. Finally, the act gave federal court jurisdiction to enforce collective bargaining agreements. We will cover the details of such agreements later on in this chapter.

Labor–Management Reporting and Disclosure Act (LMRDA) (1959)

Labor–Management Reporting and Disclosure Act (LMRDA) (1959) Requires labor organizations to report financial transactions and administrative practices of unions, employers, and labor consultants

This act, also known as the Landrum-Griffin Act, deals with the relationship between a union and its members by prescribing how unions are internally regulated. The act protects union funds and was established to promote union democracy and fair elections. It requires labor

■ **FIGURE 14.5** Right-to-Work States

States shown in blue are right-to-work states where employees decide whether to join or financially support a union. States shown in green are non-right-to-work states and may require all employees within unionized organizations to pay union dues, whether or not they are union members.

Disclaimer: State laws, include employment laws, are in a constant state of flux. Always check the most recent edition of your state's laws to ensure compliance with the latest provisions.

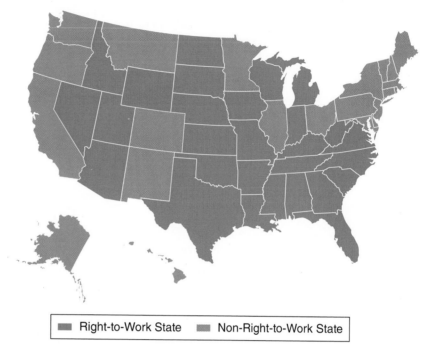

■ Right-to-Work State   ■ Non-Right-to-Work State

Source: Based on information from National Right to Work Foundation, http://www.nrtw.org/right-to-work-states/

organizations to file annual financial reports and reports on labor relations practices and established standards for the election of union officers as well as a Bill of Rights for union members. The act is administered by the Office of Labor–Management Standards.[32]

Right-to-Work Laws

A highly political topic involves who is covered and required to financially participate in unionized settings. There has been a shift in terms of this that has taken the form of state ***right-to-work laws*** (Figure 14.5). Such laws, if enacted, mean that no one within that state may be compelled to join a union to obtain or keep their job. In states without this law, employees who benefit from union activities such as collective bargaining, even if they choose not to join it, may be compelled to pay their "fair share" of union dues. The Labor Relations Act (also known as the Taft-Hartley Act), section 14(b), grants the right of states to enact such laws. The first two states to enact this were Arkansas and Florida in 1944. Since that time, as of 2017, 26 additional states had joined them. In 2018, the Supreme Court ruled that nonunion workers cannot be forced to pay fees to public-sector unions, which overruled a 40-year-old ruling that led to fair-share fees.

Right-to-work laws Vary from state to state but generally prohibit requiring employees to join a union or pay regular or fair-share union dues in order to obtain or keep a job

Trends in Union Membership

The Great Depression began in 1929 in the United States, and although unemployment was at record high levels, union membership grew by 300%. Unions had fewer than 3 million members in 1933 and more than 10 million by 1941.[33] That trend has reversed itself in the last 35 years,

■ **FIGURE 14.6**   Union Membership, 1983–2017

This chart illustrates how union membership (as a percentage of employed workers in the United States) continued to decrease. We have seen a high of 20.1% in 1983 to a low of 10.7% in 2017.

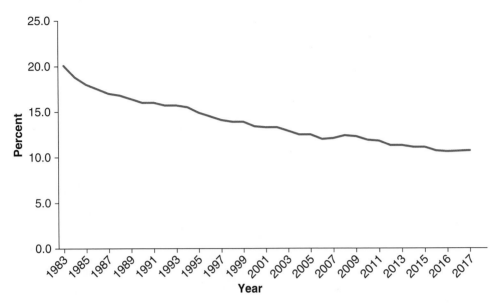

Sources: Bureau of Labor Statistics. (2015). https://www.bls.gov/opub/ted/2015/union-membership-rate-in-private-industry-and-public-sector-in-2014.htm and Union Membership (Annual) News Release. https://www.bls.gov/news.release/union2.htm; Union Member Summary. (2017). https://www.bls.gov/news.release/union2.nr0.htm

and union membership has been on the decline in the United States, with 14.6 million workers belonging to a union in 2016, down from a high of 17.7 million workers in 1983.

Union Membership in the United States

Union membership has decreased by nearly half since the 1980s, with 20% of all workers belonging to a union in 1983 and only 10.7% belonging to unions in 2017, according to the Bureau of Labor Statistics (see Figure 14.6). Some of this is due to the changing nature of work. Unions tend to be highly concentrated within certain industries such as transportation and utilities, construction, manufacturing, education and health services, wholesale and retail trade, and public-service employees.[34] However, even in many of those industries, membership has been declining. It is interesting that unions are actually winning more workplace elections (i.e., elections that would allow them to form a union in their workplaces), with 72% of the elections conducted by the National Labor Relations Board in 2016. Additionally, 61% of adults generally support labor unions during this period of decline, but fewer elections are being held.[35]

Global Unionization

The global landscape stands in sharp contrast with the trend in the United States. For example, 92% of workers in Iceland belong to a union. Figure 14.7 indicates that the United States has a relatively low percentage of unionized workers compared to much of the world. For multinational corporations, which must deal with different labor laws and norms in different countries, it is important to understand the concept of *works councils*. These comprise elected employee representatives who work alongside management to help make decisions regarding working conditions. Work councils are mandated by law for organizations operating in EU countries if they exceed certain sizes.[36] In Norway, the Working Environment Act regulates key provisions for employment relationships: Employees work 37.5 hours per week; flexible hours are encouraged; employees get 5 weeks of holidays per year, with employees more than 60 years old getting an additional week of vacation; 43 weeks of paid parental leave are available for employees working for at least 6 months;

SPOTLIGHT ON GLOBAL ISSUES
Labor Union Membership Rates Vary Around the World

FIGURE 14.7   The State of the Union's Labor Union Memberships

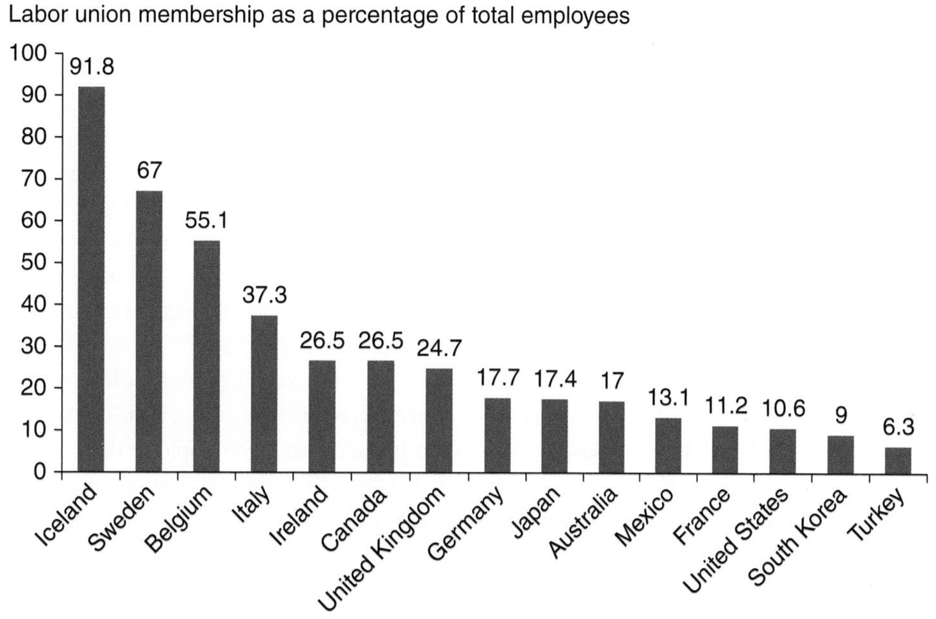

Labor union membership as a percentage of total employees

Country	Percentage
Iceland	91.8
Sweden	67
Belgium	55.1
Italy	37.3
Ireland	26.5
Canada	26.5
United Kingdom	24.7
Germany	17.7
Japan	17.4
Australia	17
Mexico	13.1
France	11.2
United States	10.6
South Korea	9
Turkey	6.3

Source: OECD. (2017). https://www.forbes.com/sites/niallmccarthy/2017/06/20/which-countries-have-the-highest-levels-of-labor-union-membership-infographic/#2c6e601f33c0

A number of factors influence the percentage of employees who are represented by a union such as history, politics, laws, and employment conditions. As you can see here, global union membership as a percentage of total employees in several countries varies a great deal. For example, only 6.3% of employees belong to unions in Turkey versus nearly 92% in Iceland. The U.S. has relatively fewer union members as a percentage of total workers than countries such as Iceland, Sweden, Belgium, or Italy. However, it is also important to note that the 10.6% in the U.S. still represents a large number of individuals, as it has nearly 327 million citizens versus the number of individuals in a smaller country such as Iceland, which has fewer than 350,000 citizens.

and employers have obligations to provide systematic training on health and safety issues.[37] It can be challenging for companies to navigate the different union rules and cultures, as they vary from country to country. For example, Amazon faced strong opposition in Germany from warehouse workers who wanted to organize toward a union. Whereas resistance to such activities might be common within the United States, in Germany "that's virtually unheard-of."[38]

Union Formation and Dissolution

Even though union membership is in decline in the United States, it is still important to understand how unions are formed and dissolved, as 14.6 million workers is still a sizable number of

Shutterstock.com

Concerns regarding wages are a common reason for unionization. Demonstrators, including labor unions and allied groups, rally at the Philadelphia International Airport during contract negotiations with American Airlines subcontractors in 2017.

individuals, and the potential for unionizing exists in most industries even if it is not traditionally a union industry. For example, digital news media has seen a surge of unionization, with 220 Huffington Post staffers joining the Writers Guild of America and East becoming the largest digital news company to become unionized.[39] Further, social media technology such as Unionbase by Larry Williams Jr. is making it easier than ever for labor to connect with unions.[40]

Steps to Forming a Union

The first step to the formation of a union is to conduct an organizing campaign. Formation is dependent on the union organizers getting at least 30% of the employees in the bargaining unit to sign an authorization card to prompt a union election. In order to secure those signatures, organizers normally need to have identified key issues that might motivate employees to want a union. This is because employees who are satisfied and feel they are treated fairly are less likely to join a union.

If the union organizers are successful in gathering 30% to 50% of the required signatures, they can file an election petition and conduct a union election online or via paper ballots.[41] It is important for employers to understand what is possible to do as well as what is not possible to do during an organizing campaign (see Table 14.1).

Achieving more than 50% of signed authorization cards may lead to the union organizers requesting that the company voluntarily recognize the union. If the employer does, the National Labor Relations Board is asked to certify the union. If the employer does not recognize the union, things can become more complicated. If the union wins the election, officers are elected, and they or a designated team begin negotiations with the employer on their membership's behalf. Figure 14.8 summarizes the steps to forming a union.

MANAGER'S TOOLBOX
Employer Obligations

TABLE 14.1

DURING A UNION ORGANIZING CAMPAIGN, EMPLOYERS AND MANAGERS MAY NOT:
• Threaten employees with loss of jobs or benefits if they join or vote for a union
• Threaten to close the place of work if employees select a union to represent them
• Question employees about their thoughts about unions or union activities
• Promise benefits to employees to discourage their union support
• Transfer, lay off, terminate, or assign employees more difficult work tasks, or punish employees for engaging in union activities or for filing an unfair labor practice charge

Source: National Labor Relations Board. (2018). Employer/union rights and obligations. https://www.nlrb.gov/rights-we-protect/employerunion-rights-and-obligations

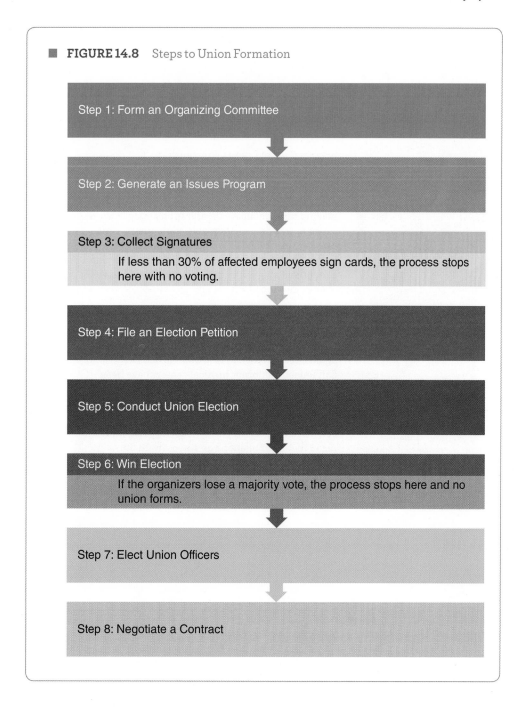

■ **FIGURE 14.8** Steps to Union Formation

Step 1: Form an Organizing Committee

Step 2: Generate an Issues Program

Step 3: Collect Signatures
If less than 30% of affected employees sign cards, the process stops here with no voting.

Step 4: File an Election Petition

Step 5: Conduct Union Election

Step 6: Win Election
If the organizers lose a majority vote, the process stops here and no union forms.

Step 7: Elect Union Officers

Step 8: Negotiate a Contract

Decertifying Unions

The Labor Management Relations Act (Taft-Hartley Act), discussed earlier in this chapter, laid out employees' rights to elect union leaders of their own choosing. In much the same way in which unions are formed, they can also be disbanded, or decertified. This may happen for a number of reasons, such as if employees do not think the union is doing a good job of representing them or if they prefer a different union. The process is parallel to union formation, with at least 30% of the workers in the bargaining unit needing to sign the petition to vote to decertify the union. However, the timing of union decertification is important. A decertification election may not take place when a contract is in place or within 1 year following a union's certification by the National Labor Relations Board.[42] In the 4 years between 2012 and 2016, unions lost 596 of 970 decertification elections.[43]

HR IN ACTION

The Coalition of Kaiser Permanente Unions

©iStock.com/shapecharge

The Coalition of Kaiser Permanente Unions, AFL-CIO, is a federation of 32 local unions associated with health care in California. This coalition includes 11 international unions and represents 120,000 health care workers. The Kaiser-Permanente/coalition agreement represents the largest, longest-lasting labor–management partnership in the United States.[44]

This partnership has a history going back to the early 1990s. At that time, in response to increasingly strained labor relations, the coalition was formalized in 1996. It sought to adopt new policies including a new constitution and bylaws. It also proposed a "new" idea to work with Kaiser Permanente to develop a partnership that included participation in decision-making throughout the organization and to "have a say in how to deliver affordable, high-quality care." The key was that coalition members were involved in the development of ideas rather than just talking about them after the organization had proposals already developed.

This partnership has been lauded as an effective example of how working together can be more powerful in long-term win-win solutions than against one another. In fact, both its San Diego and San Rafael, California, medical centers have been featured in case studies at Cornell University titled "How Labor–Management Partnerships Improve Patient Care, Cost Control, and Labor Relations."[45] Of course, having such a partnership does not always mean that labor relations go smoothly. In 2017, Kaiser Permanente reached a collective bargaining agreement with 1,200 registered nurses at the Los Angeles Medical Center after 17 months of heated contract negotiations and two short-term strikes.[46]

LO 14.4 Outline the collective bargaining process.

Collective bargaining The process of negotiating in good faith toward agreed terms on wages, hours, and working conditions

The Collective Bargaining Process

If a union is in place, it is responsible for negotiating with the employer on behalf of its members. This is one of the major functions of a union. The final agreement addresses details outlining wages, hours, and working conditions for employees. The process of negotiating in good faith toward agreed terms on wages, hours, and working conditions is called *collective bargaining*. In other words, the union and employer engage in negotiations on behalf of the employees/union members. Engaging in effective negotiations includes having a conflict management approach, which we discuss in the following section.

Conflict Management Approaches

Although negotiations are not necessarily conflicts, they can sometimes be perceived that way or become that way. This is especially true in high-stakes negotiations between unions and management. Thus, it is helpful to recognize and understand that individuals and groups differ in their approach to conflict management. This includes the level of cooperation (focusing on both parties keeping conflict limited) as well as the level of competition (focusing on getting what they want) they engage in and their preferences for each approach. These approaches are summarized in Figure 14.9 and include avoidance, accommodation, compromise, competition, and collaboration. *Avoidance* refers to low cooperation and

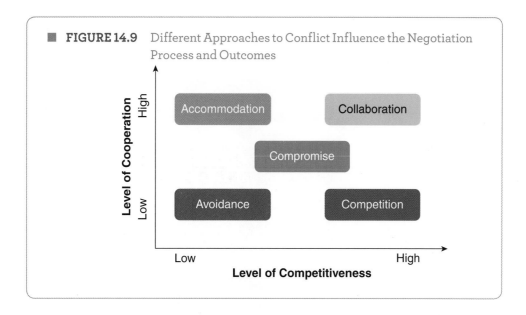

■ **FIGURE 14.9**   Different Approaches to Conflict Influence the Negotiation Process and Outcomes

competitiveness. *Accommodation* refers to low competitiveness but high levels of cooperation. *Compromise* refers to an approach predominantly in the middle range of cooperative and competitive approaches. *Competition* refers to an approach that is low on cooperation but high on competition. And finally, *collaboration* refers to approaches that seek to find win-win solutions by being high on both cooperation and competition. Research shows that conflict and negotiation preferences may vary by national culture.[47] But generally, labor relations should be better when win-win collaboration strategies are sought because both parties will see their needs met at least partially. In a study of unionized manufacturing facilities, areas with more collaborative labor relations had lower costs, less scrap, higher productivity, and a higher return on direct labor hours than those characterized as more adversarial.[48] In another study of 305 branches of a large unionized bank in Australia, cooperative labor relations were related to better information sharing and pursuing win-win solutions as well as higher productivity and customer service.[49]

Negotiation Phase and Collective Bargaining Content

Negotiation is defined as the give-and-take process between two or more parties aimed toward reaching an agreement. Because collective bargaining is a form of formal negotiation, it helps to understand the five phases of the negotiation process. These phases are the investigation, BATNA determination, presentation, bargaining, and closure phases. These phases are summarized in Figure 14.10.

Negotiation Give-and-take process between two or more parties aimed toward reaching an agreement

Phase 1: Investigation
In this first stage of the negotiation process, both sides gather information and investigate what the key issues are, identify the key goals that the team wishes to accomplish, what data they have to support their positions, and what might have been done related to these issues in the past. Although this is a critical first step, not all negotiators spend enough time engaging in investigation at this phase, which can lead to suboptimal outcomes in the process. Research shows that the specific goals and interests being negotiated have an impact on how the negotiations are approached as well as the final negotiated outcome.[50]

Phase 2: BATNA Determination
BATNA stands for best alternative to a negotiated agreement.[51] While this second phase is important for any negotiator, it is especially important in a union negotiation process, because the alternatives can be quite costly to the organization, union, and employees, as well as to those

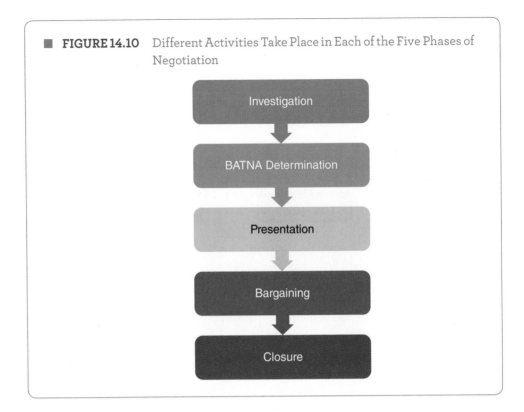

■ **FIGURE 14.10**   Different Activities Take Place in Each of the Five Phases of Negotiation

who depend on the organization's work to be done in the case of a strike. Best practices for determining your BATNA include:

- Brainstorming a list of alternatives that you are willing to accept as a worst-case scenario;

- Considering the modification of proposals to make them more attractive to both sides if necessary;

- Going into the negotiation with back-up alternatives in case what you have planned to present does not work as well as you had planned;

- Revising your BATNA over time as the negotiations progress; and

- Keeping your BATNA private within your team.

After the investigation and BATNA phases are complete, it is time to formally prepare for the negotiation presentation.

Phase 3: Presentation

In the third phase of the negotiation process, all the information is summarized and presented in a manner that supports the negotiator's case. Both parties present their initial offers to one another.

Phase 4: Bargaining and Content of a Labor Agreement

In the bargaining phase, each party discusses their initial presentation of their offer. As part of this process, concessions are normally made. In other words, parties do not normally walk into collective bargaining negotiations expecting to get every single one of their demands met, as that is not realistic. Thus, having some idea of how to offer and accept concessions is helpful during bargaining.

SPOTLIGHT ON ETHICS

The 2007–2008 Writers Guild of America Strike

Charley Gallay/Getty Images

In November 2007, 12,000 screenwriters for film, TV, and radio represented by the Writers Guild of America went on strike over what they perceived as an unfair portion of profits made by studios on the shows compared to writers of those shows. The fundamental issues revolved around DVD residuals (a type of pay), new media such as Internet download and streaming videos (another issue of pay), and whether reality and animation shows should be covered by the Writers Guild. These writers worked for 397 entertainment companies including CBS, NBCUniversal, News Corp./Fox, Walt Disney Company, and Warner Bros., among others. They

were joined by members of the Screen Actors Guild including actor Katherine Heigl, pictured here, of the TV show *Grey's Anatomy* at the time. The strike went on for 100 days. It is estimated that the strike cost $2.1 to $3 billion and shut down more than 60 TV shows. The final agreement was ratified, with nearly 94% of members voting in favor.

The Guild has engaged in three major strikes, including one in 1959 that lasted nearly 6 months and one in 1988 that lasted 155 days. On May 1, 2017, members voted to strike, but an agreement was reached in the early-morning hours of May 2, 2017, narrowly averting a repeat of this 8- to 10-year cycle. Balancing the ethical implications of studio owners paying writers fairly versus the fiscal implications of strikes continues to be a challenging dilemma.[52]

Questions

1. What do you see as the ethical aspects of going on strike? Examine this question from the workers' point of view and from the employer's point of view.

2. Some categories of workers in the United States are legally prohibited from striking. What ethical grounds do you see for such laws?

Wages, hours worked, and benefits are three types of mandatory bargaining items established by the National Labor Relations Act. These items directly affect employees and may be bargained until an impasse takes place. It is also legal for employees to strike and for employers to lock out employees in the hopes of obtaining a mandatory item of bargaining. Permissive (or voluntary) bargaining items are not directly related to work. Examples include ground rules for negotiations and how unfair labor charges will be settled. Thus, both parties may agree to bargain over these; however, they are not required to, and they are not legally allowed to strike over permissive items. Finally, illegal bargaining items include closed-shop provisions or discrimination. Such items may not legally be entered into a collective bargaining agreement.

Phase 5: Closure

The final phase of the negotiation process is closure, in which both parties come to an agreement on the negotiated offers or if one party determines that the final offer is unacceptable. If an agreement is reached and signed by both parties, it becomes a written, legally enforceable contract for the specific period of time as negotiated (often 1 year). It includes details of the conditions of employment including working conditions, terms of employment, and procedures for dispute resolution. This may be known as a labor agreement, labor contract, or union agreement. What happens if the parties fail to reach an agreement? The failure to reach an agreement may result in an impasse. An *impasse* may be resolved via mediation or arbitration, or it may result in a strike.

impasse Failure to reach an agreement

LO 14.5   Evaluate the possible courses of action when negotiating parties fail to reach an agreement.

Failure to Reach an Agreement

Unfortunately, research shows that negotiators who fail to reach an agreement may become less willing to work together in the future, share information, or behave cooperatively. Thus, having negotiators with experience and confidence in their negotiating abilities can be effective in helping to buffer these negative effects of impasse.[53] In addition, helping negotiators reach an agreement can be important for labor relations.

Alternative Dispute Resolution

Alternative dispute resolution Methods of resolving disputes that do not involve litigation

When two parties fail to reach an agreement, alternative dispute resolution may be entered into either voluntarily or involuntarily. *Alternative dispute resolution* is defined as any method of resolving disputes that does not involve litigation. There are several different types of alternatives including mediation, fact finders, and arbitration, which we discuss next.

Mediation

In mediation, the two parties are still in control of reaching a mutually acceptable agreement. The mediator is an impartial, third-party individual who helps the parties communicate more effectively and may be helpful in cases in which the ongoing relationship is important to preserve, such as in the case of collective bargaining. However, if one or both of the parties are unwilling to cooperate, mediation may not result in a resolution of the disputed contract terms.

JOHN VIZCAINO/AFP/Getty Images

Fact Finders

With fact finding, an impartial third party listens to the evidence and makes specific nonbinding recommendations to both parties. Fact finders gather and assess the information presented to them and also gather new information via investigation and consultation with experts. Their goal is to evaluate the facts of the case objectively to propose resolutions.

Arbitration

An arbitrator is an impartial third party who hears the facts of the case and then decides the outcome of the disputed contract terms. Arbitration may be *binding*, meaning that both parties agree to abide by the arbitrator's decision and not seek other options to resolve the dispute. A *nonbinding* resolution means parties may pursue a trial if they do not accept the recommended outcome.

Failure to reach an agreement often results in a strike. Strikes can be disruptive, as Avianca discovered. The Colombian airline was founded in 1919 and is tied with KLM as the oldest continuously operating airline in the world. It faced major disruption in service and the suspension of ticket sales when more than half of its 1,300 pilots went on strike (pictured here) in 2017 over failure to reach an agreement on wages and benefits. The Colombian government convened an arbitration court to help resolve the situation.[54]

Strikes and Work Stoppages

The history of HR was powerfully impacted when workers organized and began to demand better treatment. In fact, it was following a bitter strike in 1901 that the first human resource department was established by the National Cash Register Company. Thus, it is clear that the failure to reach an agreement can end in a strike or work stoppage (see Figure 14.11). A *strike* is defined as a type of work stoppage as the result of a concerted refusal of employees to work. The number of strikes in the United States has been decreasing since the 1940s. At the same time, in China, strikes are becoming increasingly common, with 2,726 strikes in 2015 compared to only 185 in 2011.[55] In 2016 in the United States, there was a total of 15 work stoppages involving nearly 100,000 employees.[56] Another type of work stoppage is a *lockout*, defined by the Bureau of Labor Statistics as "a temporary withholding or denial of employment during a labor dispute in order to enforce terms of employment upon a group of employees."[57] Lockouts are initiated by the management of an organization.

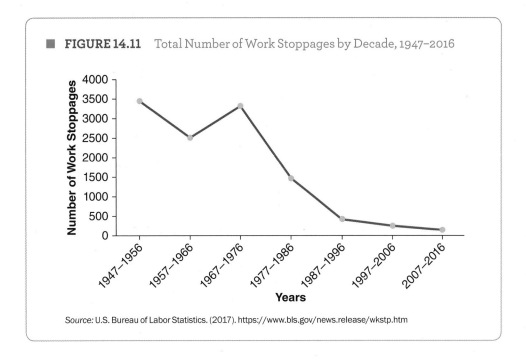

■ **FIGURE 14.11** Total Number of Work Stoppages by Decade, 1947–2016

Source: U.S. Bureau of Labor Statistics. (2017). https://www.bls.gov/news.release/wkstp.htm

Disputes and Grievances

As you might imagine, even with an accepted labor agreement or following a successfully completed strike, labor relations may remain strained, which may result in employees feeling unfairly treated. Thus, unions are responsible for ensuring that the terms of the contract are followed. If a member feels that the agreement is being violated, they may file a grievance, or a formal complaint. For example, if a unionized construction employee feels they have been required to perform practices that are unsafe and not in their job description, they may file a grievance against the company. How grievances are handled is normally specified in the labor agreement. Typically, the *grievance procedure* consists of four steps.[58]

Step 1: Inform
The first step in a grievance procedure is normally to inform one's supervisor formally or informally. Often a grievance form must be completed.

Step 2: Evaluate
After the first step, three things may happen. First, it may be determined by the supervisor and the union representative that the grievance is not valid. If this occurs, the process ends. Second, the grievance may be resolved to the satisfaction of the employee. If so, the process stops at this step. Finally, if the grievance is not resolved to the employee's satisfaction, it moves to the next step.

Step 3: Escalation
In step 3, the grievance is escalated to the next level in the organizational hierarchy. If the grievance is resolved at this level, the grievance process stops here. If this grievance is not resolved, the next step typically involves moving outside of the organization.

Step 4: External Resolution
In step 4, an outside arbitrator may be called upon to help reach a resolution. And ultimately, if the grievance remains an ongoing concern, either the employee or the union may end up pursuing litigation. One reason that organizations have grievance procedures in place is to avoid such public resolutions of disputes within their organization.

SPOTLIGHT ON DATA AND ANALYTICS
Tracking Grievance-Related Metrics

Organizations without unions often have grievance procedures in place to give employees a process to share concerns. Although not necessarily a common HR practice, it is recommended that organizations track metrics related to employee grievances. This becomes more and more important the larger the organization becomes because it is more challenging to know what employees are thinking as the number of employees grows. As data are gathered, summarized, and monitored, individuals within the organization can use these data to gain a better understanding of what is working in terms of employee relations and where there is room for improvement before small problems become large ones. Understanding the causes for grievances may require a combination of analytics in terms of numbers such as the following as well as qualitatively examining themes that emerge.

To get started, recommended metrics include:

- The number of grievances per month, quarter, and year by number of employees;

- A calculation of the cost of grievances including the time spent by managers, HR, lawyers, and other organizational members to handle the complaints;

- A determination of the root cause of grievances so that corrections may be made;

- Average time to close or complete the grievance and make a decision; and

- Return on investment can be calculated as revenue or profit per employee before and after changes to employee grievance procedures.

As Missildine-Martin, formerly of Dovetail Software, says, "Data leads to insights; insights lead to action."[59]

CHAPTER SUMMARY

Employee relations can be influenced by many different factors such as culture, fair treatment, working conditions, employment laws, and unions. Employee relations are managed through organizational policies and procedures. The types of policies an employer has will set the tone for the employee experience in that organization. Businesses use employee handbooks to ensure that workers know what is expected of them, including code of conduct, rules or guidelines for appearance, and the use of social media. The labor movement can be a major issue in the workplace. Reasons employees may seek to organize or unionize include job dissatisfaction, working conditions, and employee disengagement. Conversely, employers may resist unions based on concerns about profit and loss of autonomy for the business. HR professionals need to know about types of unions, laws pertaining to labor relations, and procedures to form and dissolve a union. The collective bargaining process includes conflict management approaches, negotiation phases, and what alternatives are available if an agreement cannot be reached. Proactively managing employee relations in a way that helps keep employees satisfied is a key component to promoting and ensuring more positive employee–employer relations.

KEY TERMS

employee relations   474
labor relations   475
National Labor Relations
    Act (1935)   483
Unfair labor
    practices   483

National Labor Relations Board
    (NLRB)   483
Labor–Management Reporting
    and Disclosure Act (LMRDA)
    (1959)   484
right-to-work laws   485

Labor Management Relations Act
    (1947)   484
collective bargaining   490
negotiation   491
impasse   493
alternative dispute resolution   494

⑤SAGE edge™

Visit **edge.sagepub.com/bauer** to help you accomplish your coursework goals in an easy-to-use learning environment.

- Master the learning objectives using key study tools
- Watch, listen, and connect with online multimedia resources

- Access mobile-friendly quizzes and flashcards to check your understanding

HR REASONING AND DECISION-MAKING EXERCISES

MINI-CASE ANALYSIS EXERCISE: GROWING PAINS

You are a manager at a small firm with 85 employees. Not long ago, your firm had just 15 employees, and it felt like a big family more than a workplace. But as you've grown, the "family feeling" has dissipated. You just heard from your good friend Robert that employees are starting to complain about management not listening to them or caring about them. He has even heard some talk about interest in considering a union to make sure that they are heard.

Given the highly competitive market your firm competes in and how slim the profit margins are, you are worried that the potential move to a union would be devastating and result in people actually losing their jobs if the firm couldn't afford to give everyone raises and instead had to lay people off. When you talk to your boss, Kelvin, he says that you are 100% right. There is no way that the firm would survive becoming a union shop, and you must do everything you can to stop the employees from unionizing. You keep thinking back to your HRM course from 7 years ago and have a lingering concern that this may not be legal, but you aren't sure. You want to do what is best for the firm and the employees, but you aren't sure what that is.

How would you handle this situation?

1. What kind of actions are you legally able to take in this situation?

2. What would you tell your boss, Kelvin, if anything?

3. How common or unique do you think this situation is? In other words, how likely is it that dealing with this type of situation might happen to someone taking an HRM course at some point in their career? Please discuss your rationale.

4. Are there any systemic changes you could think of that might help prevent more concerns like these from happening in the future?

HR DECISION ANALYSIS EXERCISE: ONLINE SURVEILLANCE?

You work for a large retail organization with more than 16,000 employees nationwide. Because so much of your business occurs during the months leading up to the winter holidays, historically you have hired a large number of seasonal workers who come on for 3 months and then are let go. In the 14 years you have been with the company, this has never been a big issue. However, you have noticed that the shrinkage (the unexplained loss of inventory) rates go up each holiday season and then back down again afterward. In other words, you see a big spike in theft during the same time that the seasonal workers are working in the stores.

After bringing this up at the next meeting at your company headquarters, the consensus is to begin monitoring all employees with cameras throughout the office, including in the restrooms. Kris, another team member at the meeting, voices concerns that this may be an invasion of privacy, but the consensus in the room is that it is an important enough issue that doing whatever it takes to catch those stealing from the company is worth it in the long run. Although the investment in a new video monitoring system is large, you have been tasked with implementing and running the program for the entire organization nationally.

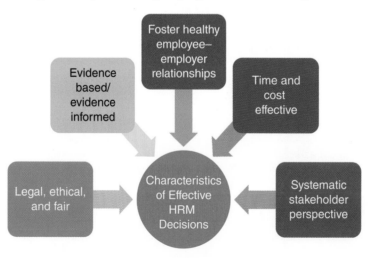

Should your organization switch to a system like this? Consider this decision using the following criteria.

Please provide the rationale for your answer to each of the questions below.

Is it legal, ethical, and fair?

_____
_____
_____
_____

Is it evidence based/evidence informed?

_____
_____
_____
_____

Does it foster healthy employee–employer relationships?

_____
_____
_____
_____

Is it time and cost effective?

_____
_____
_____
_____

Does it take a systematic stakeholder perspective?

_____
_____
_____
_____

Considering your analysis above, overall, do you think this would be an effective decision? Why or why not?

_____
_____
_____
_____

What, if anything, do you think should be done differently or considered to help make this decision more effective?

_____
_____
_____
_____

HR DECISION-MAKING EXERCISE: A TALE OF TWO TRAINING PROGRAMS

You are in the business of developing training and development materials and programs for work organizations. Your company is currently in the process of developing new training products. As someone who oversees a large 30-person team that develops, sells, and administers different workplace training programs, you have always made money each year, and how much profit you have to reinvest in developing new programs is directly tied to the number of trainings held each year. Your team recently came up with a new training program that is in big demand. Each of the sessions is selling out quickly, and you need to add more and more training days to meet demand. On the other hand, one of your other training products that helped build up the company and has been taught for the last 20 years is seeing decreasing demand. The two programs are very different. There are five individuals who are solely dedicated to the older program but only three to the new one. Unfortunately, the five employees working on the more established but less attractive training program can't teach the new ones, as they do not have the right expertise. Your company is small, and the trends are clear that demand is growing for the new program and dwindling for the older one. If the trend continues, pretty soon the company will be paying five employees to conduct fewer than one training per week, whereas the other three are giving three and four trainings per week. If you cancel the older program, you will have to let these five employees go. You don't see any way around these issues, but you want to let the group make recommendations.

Please answer the following questions. Be sure that your answer includes specific details such as what you think needs to be done and the goals you are trying to achieve.

- Given the current trends you have observed, what do you think your training team should recommend to address this growing problem?
- What do you think they will recommend?
- How might you guide them?

DATA AND ANALYTICS EXERCISE: USING OPINION SURVEY DATA TO GAUGE EMPLOYEE SATISFACTION

Gathering and analyzing opinion survey data from existing employees is a common practice for medium and large businesses. However, small businesses can also benefit from this activity. It doesn't have to be a long, time-intensive survey to help small businesses track how satisfied their employees are over time. Such data can also be helpful in understanding reactions to organizational changes because you have the data both before and after.

1. All of your employees have been filling out an anonymous survey every year they have been with your small but growing organization. In 2010, there were eight employees. Since 2010, you've been averaging hiring around three new employees each year but sometimes only one in a given year.

2. You want to analyze the data to see what trends are occurring in terms of their overall job satisfaction scores for each year, which range from 1 (*completely dissatisfied*) to 7 (*completely satisfied*). The data from those annual surveys follow:

	2010	2011	2012	2013	2014	2015	2016	2017	2018
1									5.1
2							6.2	5.9	5.0
3				4.5					
4	7.0	6.8	5.1	2.0					
5	5.9	5.8	5.8	5.6	5.7	5.9	5.6	5.8	5.9
6	6.3	6.2	6.5	5.9	6.1	6.6	6.3	6.3	5.8

	2010	2011	2012	2013	2014	2015	2016	2017	2018
7	6.4	6.6	6.7	4.1	5.1	5.5	6.2	5.8	5.1
8	4.0	4.0	4.0	4.0	4.0	4.0	4.0	4.0	4.0
9						6.2	5.9	5.0	5.0
10					5.0	5.0	5.0	5.0	5.0
11				7.0	6.8	6.6	6.0	5.3	5.0
12				5.0	5.0	5.0	5.0	5.0	5.0
13		6.0	6.0	3.8	5.0	5.2	5.1	5.6	5.4
14									7.0
15									6.8
16								7.0	7.0
17				4.0	5.2	5.2	5.4	5.5	5.5
18						4.0	3.8	3.6	3.0
19			7.0	6.2	6.8	6.0	6.1	6.4	6.0
20						6.6	6.0	5.3	5.0
21		6.0	6.0	5.0	6.0	6.0	6.0	6.0	6.0
22								6.3	6.4
23						5.4	5.3	5.5	5.7
24						5.4	5.3	5.5	5.7
25					1.0	1.0	1.0	1.0	1.0
26	7.0	7.0	7.0	7.0	7.0	7.0	7.0	7.0	7.0
27				5.5	4.9	5.1	5.4	5.5	5.5
28				4.0	5.2	5.1	5.5		
29			2.0	2.0	2.0	2.0	2.0	2.0	2.0
30							5.0	5.0	5.0
31				5.9	5.4	5.2	5.5	5.5	6.1
32				5.4	5.9	5.1	5.5	5.6	5.7
33			5.1	5.4	5.9	5.1	5.5	5.6	5.7
34				6.4	6.1	5.3	5.1	4.8	4.2
35	7.0	7.0	7.0	7.0	7.0	7.0	7.0	7.0	7.0
36									
37	5.3	5.6	5.3	5.4	5.9	5.1	5.5	5.6	5.7
38								5.3	5.7

QUESTIONS TO ADDRESS

1. Do you have any concerns about these data? Why or why not?

2. Is it truly anonymous? Explain your rationale.

3. What questions would you ask about these data?

4. What action would you take based on these data?

 EXCEL EXTENSION: NOW YOU TRY!

- On **edge.sagepub.com/bauer**, you will find an Excel exercise on evaluating employee survey data.

- First, you will learn how to create a heat map.

- Second, you will practice interpreting and communicating the results.

CHAPTER 14 SUPPLEMENT: MANAGEMENT–UNION COMMUNICATION GUIDELINES

Retrieved from https://www.shrm.org/resourcesandtools/hr-topics/labor-relations/pages/tips-foe.aspx

During a union-organizing campaign, business leaders will naturally come to HR for guidance. They need a firm understanding of the basic communication expectations.

Before a campaign launches in your workplace, train managers about what they can and cannot say to employees, and use role-playing techniques, which will help them get through what may be difficult interactions.

Employer Union Communication Guidance

CANNOT ENGAGE IN (TIPS):

 Threats
It is illegal to threaten employees because of their support for a union.

 Interrogation
It is illegal to question employees about their alignment with union messages or the alignment of their peers.

 Promises
It is illegal to promise or grant special favors of benefits in exchange for a vote for the company instead of a vote for the union.

Surveillance
It is illegal to engage in any surveillance or to spy on lawful union activity.

CAN SHARE (FOE):

 Facts
It is legal to share publicly available facts from the National Labor Relations Act, the website unionfacts.com, and other reputable sources.

 Opinions
It is legal to share why you feel a union is not needed for employees at your worksite. Use your company's position statement and the aforementioned TIPS as your guide.

 Examples
It is legal to share real examples and stories of others to highlight why a union might not be the right choice.

In the moment, leaders are going to want to respond to questions from their employees and must be prepared to educate employees with the relevant facts to include the company's position relative to unions. Leaders should be empowered to answer all questions but also need to know the types of things they can and cannot say.

Employee Safety, Well-Being, and Wellness

15

Opening Case

Putting the Brakes on Train Derailments: Promoting Safety on Public Railways

Supporting the safety of employees and customers is a stated goal for most organizations. Besides its importance for individual employees and for society more broadly, safety is linked to organizational success. For example, safety is directly linked to decreased liability, health, workers' compensation, and medical costs. It is also associated with greater employee satisfaction and retention. And visible cases of lapses in safety can severely damage an organization's reputation.

The question, then, is why some organizations continue to struggle with supporting workplace safety despite the demonstrated value of doing so. Part of the problem is that employee and customer safety is the result of multiple, complicated factors, including organizational culture, climate, rules, and policies; leadership; employee training; and even employee health. It is also a function of the physical work environment and the safeguards that are put into place by the organization.

The passenger rail industry provides a vivid illustration of the multiple factors that can affect safety and the challenges organizations face in trying to improve safety. In recent years, there have been a number of high-profile cases of the failure of train safety systems, and some similar patterns emerge from these cases.

LEARNING OBJECTIVES

After reading and studying this chapter, you should be able to do the following:

15.1 Give reasons why workplace well-being is important for employers and regulatory agencies.

15.2 Describe the main workplace safety outcomes measured by organizations and what organizations can do to promote safety.

15.3 Summarize issues around workplace stress and well-being.

15.4 Identify the characteristics of the variety of workplace wellness programs that are offered by employers.

15.5 Identify examples of focused workplace well-being interventions.

15.6 Explain what is meant by an integrated Total Worker Health™ approach.

Amtrak train derailment south of Seattle, Washington.

Stephen Brashear/Getty Images

On September 29, 2016, a New Jersey Transit passenger train crashed in the Hoboken, New Jersey, station. Although it had been traveling at only 10 mph as it first entered the station, and even though the engineer had earlier sounded the horn to signal the train's approach, it suddenly accelerated to 21 mph within the station. The train was moving so quickly that it plowed through a train bumper and onto the platform, killing one person with falling debris and injuring 100 others. The engineer said he had no memory of the accident and woke up after the train had stopped. It was later found that he was severely overweight and was diagnosed with severe sleep apnea, a sleep disorder often associated with obesity and one that can cause people to fall asleep during the day. In addition, despite continued calls to include an automatic braking system, or to use a "positive train control" system, which notifies the engineer that the train is traveling too fast and can, if needed, even stop the train, the train did not have this type of technology. Note that this technology has been around for many years, and Congress has mandated that such systems be installed. However, the deadline for the system's installation has been pushed back several times due to the high costs cited by the railroad industry.

Similarly, on January 4, 2017, a Long Island Railroad train crashed into the Brooklyn station, destroying a bumper, ramming into a room just beyond the end of the track, and injuring more than 100 people. Again, the engineer said he remembered approaching the station but had no memory of the crash. The National Transportation Safety Board found that he too was overweight and had sleep apnea. (After the crash, Long Island Railroad immediately started testing its engineers for sleep apnea; at one point, 8 of the 34 engineers that had been tested—nearly 25%—had sleep apnea.) Also, like the New Jersey Transit case, it had been recommended that positive train control be installed, but it was not in place on the Long Island line at the time of the crash.

On December 18, 2017, an Amtrak train traveling from Seattle, Washington, to Portland, Oregon (see photo), derailed just south of Seattle, killing four people and injuring dozens. At the time of the accident, the train was traveling into a curve at more than double the posted speed limit of 30 mph. Although at this writing the cause of the derailment is still under investigation, it appears that the engineers were not using their personal electronic devices; in other words, they were not distracted by them. A positive train control system had been installed on this line, but it was not yet in use. If it had been, it would have prevented the train from traveling too fast. The lack of a warning system has been cited as a factor that might have prevented the accident. Some analysts have also noted that although most railroads in the United States are behind in meeting their goals to install these types of automated safety systems due to costs, the railroads do continue to invest in other infrastructure such as new train stations.[1]

Case Discussion Questions

1. Given the examples of these three organizations, why do you think that these types of accidents continue to occur? Consider multiple issues and stakeholders that might be affecting railroads' decisions about preventing accidents, including short-term versus long-term goals.

2. Based on these cases, do you think that these three organizations have a safety culture in which workers perceive that management views safety as a priority? Which factors in the cases make you say that? Could it be that the culture is positive in some ways but not in others? How might these cultures be improved?

3. Consider the multiple variables, including employee characteristics and behaviors, and factors in the physical environment that would help prevent transportation accidents such as these. Then develop a plan for a passenger railroad system that would help to prevent accidents.

4. What would be your argument to organizational leaders about the relative value of each of your suggestions? What data and metrics would you want to have available to you to make your arguments?

5. In two of the cases described here, the health of the engineers might have played a role in the accident. What is the employer's responsibility for monitoring and maintaining the health of their employees when it can have a direct impact on public safety?

▶ Click to learn more…

Watch this video with the president of the National Safety Council on positive train control technology: https://youtu.be/PJqOfc93mtU

In this chapter, we will discuss the strategic role that HRM plays in maintaining the safety, health, and well-being of employees. This includes how HRM can promote effective workplace safety programs along with promoting cybersecurity in organizations. In addition, we will discuss the outcomes of workplace stress and ways to manage it and the increasing role of workplace wellness programs, including the range of possible programs and their benefits. We conclude by describing an integrated organizational strategy, Total Worker Health™, that takes into account the safety, well-being, and wellness and that is gaining increased attention among today's employers. For each of these topics, we will discuss some of the key metrics that can help employers deploy programs that best fit their needs and evaluate program effectiveness.

The Role of HRM in Worker Safety and Health

HRM plays a key role in attracting, hiring, developing, and rewarding employees to serve the strategic goals of the organization. Given this enormous investment in talent, organizations also have an interest in the safety, health, and well-being of their employees. This includes developing a culture of safety; providing a healthy, safe, and secure work environment; and actively supporting the health of employees through wellness programs—all with the goal of retaining the best talent, reducing health care costs, improving performance, and reducing legal liability. We begin by reviewing the importance of well-being and government regulatory agencies and resources.

LO 15.1 Give reasons why workplace well-being is important for employers and regulatory agencies.

The Case for Employee Well-Being

Organizations work to attract the best candidates, select those that are the best fit, and then work to develop and reward them as employees to help achieve organizations' goals. In addition, a great deal is invested in rewarding and training employees as well. Many organizations feel it is an ethical obligation to keep their workers safe, healthy, and happy. Taken together, these concepts of the safety, health, satisfaction, and engagement of employees are often referred to as worker *well-being*.[2] But organizations also have a stake in worker well-being because it affects organizational productivity and effectiveness. For example, an unhealthy workforce can lead to high medical costs. High employee stress can lead to turnover and to distractions that cause accidents and injuries. Nonsecure systems that are open to cyberattacks can lead to the loss of both employee and customer privacy and pose serious risks to a company's reputation and can be highly disruptive to its work processes as well. Workplace safety is an important goal in itself, and violating safety regulations can lead to fines and to legal liability.

Well-being A worker's well-being is composed of their safety, health, satisfaction, and engagement

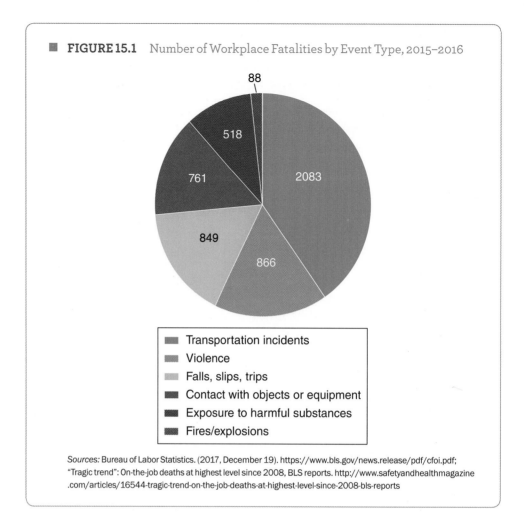

■ FIGURE 15.1   Number of Workplace Fatalities by Event Type, 2015–2016

Legend:
- Transportation incidents
- Violence
- Falls, slips, trips
- Contact with objects or equipment
- Exposure to harmful substances
- Fires/explosions

Sources: Bureau of Labor Statistics. (2017, December 19). https://www.bls.gov/news.release/pdf/cfoi.pdf; "Tragic trend": On-the-job deaths at highest level since 2008, BLS reports. http://www.safetyandhealthmagazine .com/articles/16544-tragic-trend-on-the-job-deaths-at-highest-level-since-2008-bls-reports

On the positive side, an organization's reputation as a healthy and safe place to work is an excellent recruitment tool. Decreasing employee stress can lead to improved performance. And providing a safe, healthy environment can increase employee retention. It is not surprising, then, that many of the most successful organizations treat workplace safety and health as a key organizational goal and invest heavily in metrics to assess a range of safety and health indicators.

Yet maintaining workplace safety and health is an ongoing challenge. For example, there was an uptick in deaths due to on-the-job injuries in 2016, with more than 5,100 worker deaths (see Figure 15.1). This is an increase of 7% from 2015 and the highest number of worker fatalities since 2008. Further, more than a third of employees in a recent survey by the American Psychological Association said that they have chronic work stress.[3]

Considering the opening case, it is clear that developing a safe and healthy workforce is very complicated, with multiple causal variables. Accidents and injuries can be caused by the physical work environment, a factor that is not easy or inexpensive to address. Employee stress can be caused by a plethora of factors such as a difficult supervisor or coworkers, poorly designed work, or work–life imbalance. Poor health can be caused by many factors outside of the workplace and seemingly outside of the employer's control, yet poor health can increase employer costs (e.g., medical costs, sick time) and even lead to accidents and injuries, as illustrated in the opening case.

Employers have a number of effective tools available to them to support the safety and health of their workers. For example, wellness programs can help workers manage their existing illnesses and decrease medical costs. Employers can train managers to be more supportive of employees not only to increase work–life balance but also to improve their sleep. Organizations can focus on ways to communicate with employees about safety not only to demonstrate its importance but also to gain input from workers about safety hazards and how to prevent them. These are all methods that have been tested as effective in improving a range of metrics that reflect the health of workers.

The Legal Backdrop: Government Agencies and Resources

In the United States, there are a number of government agencies tasked with regulating the area of workplace well-being and also with providing a number of important resources to employers. The *Occupational Safety and Health Administration (OSHA)* was established through the Occupational Safety and Health Act of 1970. Under the U.S. Department of Labor, OSHA's purpose is to ensure safe and healthy working conditions for employees by setting and enforcing safety and health standards. It also provides training and outreach, education, and assistance to both employers and employees. For example, OSHA provides a range of materials to help employers monitor safety conditions in their organizations. In addition to OSHA, 26 states, Puerto Rico, and the Virgin Islands have their own equivalent to OSHA, which provides additional workplace safety oversight.[4] Further, the *National Institute for Occupational Safety and Health (NIOSH)* is the federal agency that supports research on workplace safety and health and makes recommendations to employers. As part of its mission, NIOSH also can provide recommendations to employers regarding interventions and other initiatives that can help improve worker well-being.[5]

> **Occupational Safety and Health Administration (OSHA)** Under the U.S. Department of Labor, OSHA's purpose is to ensure safe and healthy working conditions for employees by setting and enforcing safety and health standards
>
> **National Institute for Occupational Safety and Health (NIOSH)** The federal agency that supports research on workplace safety and health and makes recommendations to employers

---

SPOTLIGHT ON HR FOR SMALL AND MEDIUM-SIZED BUSINESSES

Safety Efforts in Smaller Organizations

Small and medium-sized businesses need to protect their workers just as large corporations do. But by definition, smaller organizations will have fewer resources available to devote to safety and health.

For that reason, OSHA publishes a number of documents specifically for small and medium-sized organizations to ensure compliance with safety standards. For instance, OSHA publishes a number of "small entity" guides for smaller organizations. These guides include topics ranging from how to safely use construction equipment and how to work safely in confined spaces to how to handle dangerous substances.

In addition, OSHA has a full handbook dedicated to the issues of smaller businesses and how to scale down OSHA rules to make them manageable for smaller businesses. Much of this handbook involves a series of simplified safety checklists and worksheets that can be more easily applied in smaller organizations. OSHA also stresses the same key steps for maintaining safety

that would be used in larger companies: (a) Ensure manager and employee commitment to and involvement in safety; (b) continuously be on the lookout for safety hazards; (c) establish mechanisms to control and manage hazards; and (d) train managers, supervisors, and employees about how to prevent, spot, and deal with hazards.

OSHA notes that the key to these safety efforts in smaller organizations is to clearly designate someone in the company as being in charge of safety. This can be challenging for this individual, as he or she may end up being a "safety committee of one." Professionals recommend that the person in this unique—and sometimes isolating—position stay visible in the organization, which includes holding regular safety meetings for employees; staying close to workers and their safety issues, even working with them side by side to better understand their jobs; and working to get both employees and managers focused on safety.[6]

Workplace accidents Accidents sustained while on duty in the workplace

Workplace injuries Injuries sustained while on duty in the workplace

Workplace fatalities Fatalities that occur while on duty in the workplace

Near misses Situations in which an accident almost occurred but did not

Safety behavior The type of work behaviors that employees exhibit with regard to safety

Safety compliance behavior The extent to which workers follow the safety rules and regulations

Workplace Safety

Workplace illness, injury, and mortality are important due to their human toll on workers and families. In addition, medical costs associated with work-related injury and disease are estimated at $67 billion, with indirect costs of $183 billion based on one estimate.[7] Not surprisingly, reducing work-related accidents and injuries is a major focus of most organizations, with HR taking a central role in implementing such safety-related programs. For example, semiconductor manufacturer Texas Instruments has a strong safety program it is proud of, with a lost-time injury rate that is a fraction of the industry average. Part of its approach includes the collection and analysis of data that can help managers understand the causes of injuries in order to prevent them.[8] This section is concerned with the many antecedents of workplace accidents and injuries and how to address them, plus the regulatory environment for worker safety in the United States. Also highlighted is cybersecurity, a developing workplace safety issue.

Workplace Safety Outcomes and Their Antecedents

When tracking the issue of workplace safety, there are multiple types of safety and health outcomes that can be measured and analyzed by organizations. These include **workplace accidents**, such as spilling a hazardous chemical. More dramatic would be **workplace injuries**, with the most extreme and rare being **workplace fatalities**; these might include workers being injured or killed by a chemical exposure.

On March 25, 1911, in New York City, 145 garment workers died in the Triangle Shirtwaist Factory fire. The factory was located on floors 8 through 10 of the building. Because the exit doors had been locked, the workers were trapped and died of smoke inhalation, the fire itself, or jumping or falling to their deaths. One of the deadliest industrial disasters in U.S. history, the fire served as an impetus for the development of early workplace safety regulations.[12]

Keystone/Getty Images

However, in addition to these more dramatic safety outcomes, it is important for organizations to keep an eye on the much more frequent issues that are antecedents of outright accidents and injuries. One safety measure frequently discussed in organizations is that of **near misses**, or when an accident could have occurred but did not. As an example of a near miss, an electrician working on wiring an office in a new building forgot to turn off the electrical current before proceeding to install a section of the heating system, but a coworker noticed the problem and turned off the power just in time. In this example, there was no accident or injury because the coworker acted in time, and in fact the workers and the employer might think that there was nothing to report or to discuss. If the coworker had not intervened, the electrician could have been seriously injured or killed. The point here is that analyzing near misses is important to understanding potential causes of accidents, and they should be given careful consideration and analysis in safety discussions. Near misses are typically measured by worker self-reports, or they are uncovered in discussions within the team, but they can provide an essential part of understanding situations in which accidents and injuries may occur and how to prevent them.[9]

One challenge for organizations trying to prevent serious and fatal injuries is knowing which data to collect in order to understand their causes. It is estimated that only a relatively small percentage of the standard "recordable events" required by OSHA reporting lead to fatalities. One way to uncover this important data is to speak with workers out in the field to better understand specific circumstances in which no one was injured but that might have led to a serious accident. For example, if an employee working on a tall building were to slip on a wet surface, it might not lead to an injury if they righted themselves in time. But understanding what led to that slip—that may otherwise have led to a fatal accident—is key to injury prevention.[10]

Another factor that is important to understanding the causes of safety outcomes is employees' **safety behavior**.[11] Safety behavior is the type of work behaviors that employees exhibit with regard to safety. The research has generally identified two different types of safety behavior. First, **safety compliance behavior** is the extent to which workers follow the safety rules and regulations,

■ **FIGURE 15.2** Heinrich's Triangle

A summary of Heinrich's triangle, which suggests that fatalities and catastrophes, though relatively rare, are a function of much more frequent problems like unsafe behaviors.

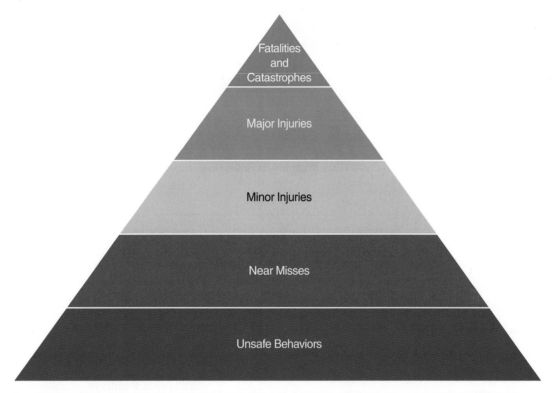

Fatalities and Catastrophes

Major Injuries

Minor Injuries

Near Misses

Unsafe Behaviors

Sources: Based on information contained in Heinrich, H. W. (1931). *Industrial accident prevention: A scientific approach.* New York, NY: McGraw-Hill; Marshall, P., Hirmas, A., & Singer, M. (2018). Heinrich's pyramid and occupational safety: A statistical validation methodology. *Safety Science, 101,* 180–189; Martin, D. K., & Black, A. A. (2015, September). Preventing serious injuries and fatalities. *Professional Safety,* 35–43.

such as wearing personal protective equipment (PPE) to protect them from the specific hazards that they are exposed to in their jobs. In the electrician's example, safety compliance behavior might include always following the rules about checking that a power source is turned off before performing electrical installations. Second, *safety participation behavior* refers to employees' willingness to support safety among their coworkers. This might include explaining the safety rules to new workers or mentioning a safety problem that they have seen (e.g., broken safety equipment) to a supervisor so it can be taken care of. In the electrician example, the fact that a second employee was aware of her surroundings and took notice that her teammate had not turned off the power source and did it herself before any injury could happen is an example of safety participation behavior. In this sense, safety behaviors include both a worker's willingness to follow safety rules themselves and their willingness to support safety among colleagues and teammates.

Safety participation behavior Employees' willingness to support safety among their coworkers

Safety compliance and safety participation are often measured by self-ratings or supervisor and coworker observations and ratings. One of the challenges with measuring and thus preventing the most costly and catastrophic safety problems is what is referred to as the low-base-rate problem. That is, serious accidents and injuries are relatively rare—although when they do happen, they can take an enormous human and economic toll. One way to consider this problem is through a diagram referred to as Heinrich's triangle, shown in Figure 15.2, which illustrates that thousands of unsafe behaviors and near misses usually occur before a serious accident or injury. Although there has been some debate over the exact nature of the triangle, such as the precise number of behaviors that occur before an accident, the triangle shows the value of examining the behaviors that lead up to accidents and injury before they occur. A key goal of HRM, particularly

■ **FIGURE 15.3**   Safety Climate and Individual Characteristics

Both the safety climate and characteristics of the individual worker play critical roles in safety performance and workplace accidents.

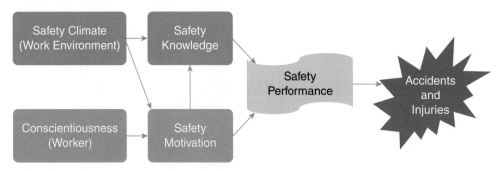

Source: Christian, M. S., Bradley, J. C., Wallace, J. C., & Burke, M. J. (2009). Workplace safety: A meta-analysis of the roles of person and situation factors. *Journal of Applied Psychology, 94,* 1103–1127.

Safety knowledge Workers' understanding of how to protect themselves and others on the job

Safety motivation Workers' perceived value for safety and desire to perform safely on the job

Hotel workers face the workplace hazard of sexual harassment and assault from hotel guests. This issue came to light most dramatically in the high-profile case of Dominique Strauss-Kahn, the head of the International Monetary Fund, who was accused of sexual assault by a hotel housekeeper in 2012 in New York City. As a result of this issue, some cities are now requiring that hotels provide "panic buttons" and similar devices for their workers to alert security when they are concerned for their safety.[14]

for those individuals who are focused on safety, is to uncover the factors that may lead to serious accidents, such as poor safety behaviors and near misses, so as to identify and prevent safety problems. In fact, larger employers might use data analytics to identify high-risk areas of the organization, such as those with large numbers of safety violations, near misses, or unsafe behaviors that can lead to injuries, health risks, and legal liability. And the use of sensors and wearable technology can be used to monitor hazardous conditions (e.g., combustible dust and gases, hazardous sound levels) and the safe use of equipment (e.g., ladders, motorized equipment) in real time.[13]

In addition, the idea of a number of factors leading to accidents and injuries is illustrated in Figure 15.3, which shows a model that has been developed and confirmed through a meta-analysis of the safety literature. The model illustrates a point that we have already made, namely, that accidents and injuries are a result of safety behaviors or performance on the part of workers. But there are additional antecedents as well, most of which can be addressed by the organization. First, *safety knowledge*, or workers' understanding of how to protect themselves and others on the job, is a key antecedent of accidents and injuries. In other words, organizations need to train workers regarding safety in general and about specific hazards that may be inherent in their jobs, such as how to handle dangerous equipment or specific chemicals and substances. It is for this reason that OSHA requires employers to conduct safety training and even requires specific types of training for certain types of jobs and in certain industries.

Second, *safety motivation*, or the worker's value for safety and desire to perform safely on the job, is another key factor that has been shown repeatedly to be important for safe behaviors. The organization needs to be sure to reward safe behaviors (such as following safe procedures) and not reward unsafe behaviors (such as ignoring safe procedures due to pressure to work too quickly). The employer may also choose to hire workers that are a lower safety risk, especially for particularly hazardous jobs, such as by considering the worker's conscientiousness (see Chapter 7).

Third, the model also identifies the critical role of *safety climate*, or the shared understanding that workers have about the importance of safety, which is a key part of the workplace environment. Research has consistently shown that a strong safety climate, both within the team and in the organization overall, is one of the most important predictors of safe behavior at work. Thus, safety climate has become a central focus of most workplace safety programs.[15] Research has shown that management plays a central role in promoting and supporting the safety climate through showing that they take safety seriously. This can take the form of modeling and rewarding safe behaviors, encouraging workers to identify any safety concerns that they observe, and training managers and workers on the importance of safety. For instance, one study of a heavy manufacturing company showed that improved supervisor–employee communications improved safety climate as well as safety behavior and safety audit scores.[16] And as a more specific example, at Valvoline, a worldwide distributor of auto and industrial lubricants, the safety approach includes a strong safety culture/climate.[17]

Safety climate The shared understanding that workers have about the importance of safety

Another employee safety and well-being concern is workplace aggression, including verbal abuse, harassment, intimidation, and physical assaults.[18] This is especially true for certain types of jobs. For example, there are nearly as many violent attacks among health care workers as in all other industries combined—even though health care workers make up only 9% of the workforce. And the rate of attacks against nurses has more than doubled in the last decade. OSHA recognizes the violence faced by health care workers and recommends that employers work with employees to identify hazards; carefully examine incidents to learn why a specific violent attack occurred; and train supervisors and managers to spot dangerous situations so that workers are not placed into them.[19] Workplace aggression is a serious hindrance to effective workplace functioning, as research shows that aggression from supervisors, coworkers, and outsiders can affect job attitudes (e.g., job satisfaction), behavior (e.g., work performance), and health (e.g., depression).[20]

Other Antecedents of Workplace Safety

Although workers and supervisors play a role in maintaining safety, the ***physical environment*** obviously plays a role as well. Recall from the opening case that one of the factors in the train accidents was a device to warn the engineers about speeding was either not in place or not used. This illustrates the importance of physical factors organizations can use do improve safety. One approach to this issue is shown in Figure 15.4, which illustrates the ***hierarchy of controls*** that an organization can use to reduce safety hazards. The hierarchy illustrates that although elimination of the safety hazard is most effective, there are other, less effective approaches that the organization can take.

Physical environment The natural and human-made components of one's surroundings

Hierarchy of controls Methods that an organization can use to reduce safety hazards, organized into a hierarchy based on their degree of effectiveness

As an example, a manufacturing company may be working to eliminate the noise hazards for workers that result from the use of noisy equipment. The most effective way for them to protect workers would be to completely eliminate the source of the hazardous noise. As a "second-best" alternative, they could find equipment that is quieter and substitute it for the noisy equipment. Or if the equipment cannot be changed, the company could "engineer out" some of the noise by putting up noise barriers between the workers and the equipment. Less effective might be to take what is called an administrative approach that will reduce employees' exposure to the noise, such as by scheduling workers in such a way as to reduce their exposure, say, by only letting workers use the noisy equipment for a brief, set amount of time each day. If these options are not possible, the company might provide some sort of personal protective equipment (e.g., headphones) to employees to reduce their noise exposure. Although this last option would be the least effective in solving the noise problem, it is certainly better than nothing.[21]

Another factor that can affect workplace safety is worker health. As described in the opening case, the fact that engineers had a health issue (sleep apnea) was seen as a possible cause of the accidents. Similar concerns about the role of sleep apnea in safety have been noted among long-haul truck drivers. For example, a study by the University of Pennsylvania found 28% of commercial truck drivers have mild to severe sleep apnea.[22] And work ***stressors***, such as work–life balance issues, can lead to distractions and to errors and accidents as well.[23]

Stressors Demands in the environment to which a person must respond

Safety officer An individual who is assigned to support safety and health issues in the workplace such as the promotion of safe practices and compliance with safety policies and rules

Safety committee Provides employees with a voice and an opportunity to participate in safety-related decisions in the organization

Given the range of factors that can affect safety, such as employee behaviors and near misses, the climate developed by managers and employees, the physical environment, health, and stress, measuring and analyzing the many factors that can affect safety outcomes is an important function in organizations. Typically, there is a ***safety officer*** assigned to examine these and other workplace safety and health issues in the workplace such as the promotion of safe practices and compliance with safety policies and rules. Or there may be a ***safety committee*** that provides employees with a voice and an opportunity to participate in safety-related decisions

FIGURE 15.4   The Hierarchy of Controls

An organization can control workplace hazards in several ways, from most effective (elimination) to least effective (PPE: personal protective equipment).

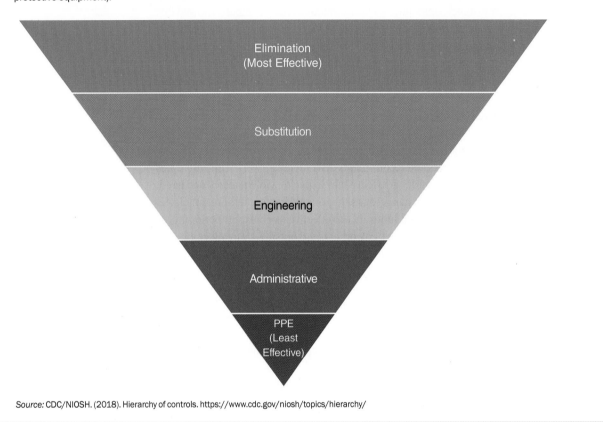

Source: CDC/NIOSH. (2018). Hierarchy of controls. https://www.cdc.gov/niosh/topics/hierarchy/

in the organization. In any case, HR plays a central role in analyzing the causes of potential safety and health issues and developing an effective safety program to address them (including for remote workers; see Table 15.1), a process that can be enhanced by the measurement of safety-related variables, and where possible, the use of analytics to better understand how to

TABLE 15.1   What Are the OSHA Requirements for Your Organization?

With the frequency of people working from home these days, it may not occur to some employers that there are some safety and security issues for workers working remotely. Here are a few tips for managing a remote workforce safely.
1. Be sure to have an at-home work policy, and be sure that employees are aware of it.
2. Require that the employee has a dedicated work area at home that is up to the employer's specifications.
3. Be sure that the employee has the correct insurance to cover any damage or liability.
4. Be sure that the employer's insurance covers issues like at-home workers and business travel.
5. Ensure computer security, including for workers who use their own equipment.
6. Be sure to have frequent contact with employees.

Source: Reprinted from "How to Manage Workplace Safety Issues for Remote Employees" (2017) with permission of the Society for Human Resource Management (SHRM). © SHRM. All rights reserved.

prevent accidents and protect employee health. This includes ensuring management commitment; facilitating communication about the program; encouraging worker involvement; conducting worksite analysis to uncover current and potential safety issues; working on hazard prevention and control; and training at all levels—employees, supervisors, and managers.[24] What is key is to view safety as a systemic issue with multiple antecedents. Further, workplace safety should be incorporated into an organization's business strategy with support at all levels including investment in workplace safety.

OSHA Regulations and Compliance

As noted earlier, OSHA was established to protect the safety and health of workers, and compliance with OSHA regulations is a serious matter for employers. Employers with more than 10 employees must maintain safety records about OSHA "recordable events" such as work-related fatalities, injuries, and illnesses (including days away from work). Note that OSHA provides significant support to employers in terms of answering questions about workplace safety and health and how to comply with OSHA regulations for organizations of all sizes. (See Table 15.2 about determining which OSHA regulations are relevant to your organization.) In addition, OSHA provides guidelines and advice for organizations on how to develop emergency preparedness and response plans, such as to natural disasters, chemical spills, or even security threats (e.g., dangerous intruders).[25] Further, employers must provide training to employees so that they can do their work safely. Note that OSHA may conduct workplace inspections (see Supplement for an OSHA publication on inspections), typically without advance notice to employers and when there is a specific reason. Figure 15.5 provides a sampling of the safety and health issues that are covered by OSHA regulations.[26]

In addition, OSHA spells out the rights of workers, providing them with guidance and assistance if they are facing a workplace hazard. For example, OSHA will take complaints from workers who believe that they are facing an unsafe or unhealthy workplace and will conduct an inspection if a worker believes there is a serious hazard or OSHA violation. They also provide protection for workers in situations in which an employer has retaliated against a worker. OSHA also can provide a worker with an inspection history of their employer if a worker is concerned that the employer has a history of violations.

■ **FIGURE 15.5** Workplace Issues Covered by OSHA

Drinking water, restroom use, and sanitation	Hazardous chemicals	Indoor air quality, temperature, and weather-related issues	Personal protective equipment (PPE)
Industry-specific rules and regulations	Wages, hours worked, and workers' compensation	Working alone	Workplace violence
Training	Employer responsibilities and assistance	Employee rights	Monitoring and reporting of accidents and injuries

Source: OSHA frequently asked questions. (n.d.). https://www.osha.gov/OSHA_FAQs.html#!employerassist

SPOTLIGHT ON LEGAL ISSUES

Safety, Health, and OSHA Compliance

As discussed in this chapter, the Occupational Safety and Health Administration (OSHA) is charged with protecting the safety and health of workers in the United States. This includes setting and enforcing standards, as well as providing training, outreach, and assistance to employers and workers. Thus, OSHA provides a range of resources for organizations of all sizes and across industries with the goal of providing healthy and safe working conditions to employees. At a broad level, OSHA requirements ensure the following:

- Workers should feel free to report unsafe or hazardous working conditions to their employers without fear of retaliation. Retaliation on the part of employers is, in fact, illegal. For instance, OSHA recently fined an employer $105,000 for terminating an employee who had reported a workplace mold issue.

- Workers should receive training about job hazards, including training about hazardous substances on their jobs. This training should be provided to workers in language and at a level that they can understand.

- Workers can confidentially report any employer violations to OSHA.

- Employers must post the OSHA poster "Job Safety and Health: It's the Law" in a prominent place. (See Supplement for a copy of this poster.)

What are the most typical types of OSHA violations? In 2017, some of the most common violations had to do with failure to protect workers from falls, unsafe scaffolding, unsafe ladders, inadequate lockout-tagout procedures (e.g., being sure that equipment that is being serviced cannot accidentally be turned back on again), inadequate respiratory protection, having inadequate guards to protect workers from dangerous equipment, electrical hazards, the use of industrial trucks, and inadequate hazard communication.[27]

TABLE 15.2   What Are the OSHA Requirements for Your Organization?

One important step in developing an effective workplace safety program is determining which safety regulations and requirements apply to your particular organization. For example, some industries are considered at least partially exempt (e.g., finance, real estate, retail), whereas other industries have industry-specific OSHA regulations and guidelines. Here are some suggestions for determining what the safety requirements are for a particular organization.

1. **Determine the industry code for the organization.** OSHA organizes its data by specific industries to better analyze and report its statistics. Knowing this code also tells the organization which industry standards it must comply with.

2. **Comply with the General Duty Clause**, which requires that employers provide a safe and healthy workplace.

3. **Adhere to poster requirements from the U.S. government as well as local state government (if there is one).** For example, employers need to provide a poster explaining workers' rights in terms of workplace safety. (One of the most important of these posters is provided in the Supplement to this chapter.)

4. **Determine the requirements for recording and reporting workers' injuries.** Note that organizations with 10 or more employees must maintain certain OSHA forms.

5. **Take care of electronic reporting requirements.** Note that organizations with 250 employees or more, or in certain high-risk industries, must also turn in electronic reports.

6. **Determine and follow OSHA training requirements.** These may vary by the particular industry.

Source: Society for Human Resource Management. (2017, December 1). How to determine regulatory requirements for safety. https://www.shrm.org/resourcesandtools/tools-and-samples/how-to-guides/pages/determiningregulatoryrequirements.aspx

Ergonomics and Office Design

In Chapter 5, we discussed job design in terms of designing the psychological characteristics of work—issues like making work less boring and giving workers more autonomy. In addition, an important workplace well-being issue is fitting the physical aspects of the job, often referred to as *ergonomic design*. The goal for most ergonomic approaches is to reduce musculoskeletal disorders such as muscle strain, back injury, or carpal tunnel syndrome. OSHA provides general guidance for specific industries such as nursing homes and food-processing work. In addition, OSHA recommends worker involvement to identify problems, provide training to workers and supervisors to avoid ergonomic problems, and develop and evaluate solutions.[28] For example, L.L.Bean, Maine's iconic outdoor equipment company, recently initiated a redesign of its warehouse, which included the use of machines rather than people for heavy lifting. Originally designed to protect the safety and health of its aging workforce, the redesign resulted in improved ergonomic conditions for workers of all ages.[29]

Sit-stand desks allow the user to alternate between sitting and standing while doing desk work, which allows for increased blood circulation. As an ergonomic solution, the use of sit-stand desks may reduce back pain and also the chances of obesity and cardiovascular disease.[30]

In addition, there has been much attention paid to issues around office design as well and its effects on health. For example, one issue is the effects of office *natural lighting* on worker health. One recent study found that workers working in windowless offices reported poorer sleep (i.e., shorter sleep duration, poorer sleep quality) and less physical activity than workers exposed to natural light.[31] Another recent trend in office design is the idea of *open offices*, where employees work in open spaces, without cubicles, with the idea that such work arrangements would lead to greater creativity and sharing of ideas. Thus far, however, the research on open offices has been less than encouraging, suggesting that these arrangements may lead to decreased satisfaction and greater stress due to less privacy and more chaotic work environments.[32]

Ergonomic design Fitting the physical aspects of the job to the human body

Natural lighting Lighting provided by sunlight

Open offices An office arrangement in which employees work in open spaces

Cybersecurity

Within the topic of workplace safety, it is important to examine the issue of cybersecurity. Cybersecurity is an evolving issue but one that involves HRM for several reasons. Much of the private information used in organizations is stored, analyzed, and reported by HR personnel, including everything from Social Security numbers to health issues and even some day-to-day work activities. Thus, HR professionals are responsible for maintaining the security of other employees' data as well as that of clients—and employees can do considerable damage either by mistake or on purpose. For example, in a recent UK court case, a disgruntled employee of Morrisons Supermarket published the personal information of about 100,000 employees on the Internet. Morrisons was successfully sued by those affected, even though it had done all it could to protect against breaches.[33] Although at this writing that case is still pending, it suggests that data security is a serious issue. Besides technological solutions to data breaches, human error is considered one of the greatest organizational vulnerabilities, where, for example, an employee might fall for a phishing scam and thus threaten the security of the entire system. Employee training is seen as one of the most useful solutions to this vulnerability.

Another emerging issue is employee monitoring, especially in the context of ensuring employees are not mishandling personal or sensitive data, either intentionally or unintentionally. New software solutions continue to develop to facilitate monitoring. However, organizations should consider such monitoring carefully before undertaking it for several reasons. First, employee monitoring can erode employee trust. Second, such monitoring involves a range of legal issues, such as laws around employee monitoring and data breaches. In addition, there may be state laws to consider (as employee monitoring laws may vary by state) and ensuring employees' legal consent to be monitored. Recommendations include clearly articulating the business case for monitoring employee data, encrypting data to restrict data access, and involving employees in such monitoring solutions to gain employee buy-in.[34] Finally, it is important to realize that employee privacy issues differ around the world, with European rules much more focused on protecting the workers' rights.

SPOTLIGHT ON ETHICS
Privacy, Technology, and Human Error

The vast amount of highly personal data available to employers provides huge opportunities to better understand employee behavior. Such safety and health data can help uncover ways to support employees' well-being. However, it also presents an array of ethical issues regarding employees' rights to privacy. In addition, large datasets of personal information present challenges to employers with maintaining the security of data that, if released, could be damaging to employees, job applicants, or customers. One recent example was the data breach at Uber, in which the private accounts of 57 million drivers and customers were stolen, and the company paid the hackers $100,000 to delete the data. (Uber also covered up the breach for several months, leading to the firing of its chief security officer and harming its reputation.)

Some security vulnerabilities can be addressed by technological solutions; that is, an organization could work to ensure that the data are protected from hacking by third parties. But other security vulnerabilities are the result of human error. It might take only a single employee to mistakenly give out their login credentials in a phishing attack to make the entire database of all employees and customers available. For example, a recent survey suggests that a majority of U.S. health care providers rank e-mail as a leading source of their security problems. Similarly, despite the highly sensitive nature of the data they maintain, a recent survey of corporate attorneys found that fewer than 45% of them provided employee training on how to avoid cybersecurity threats. Such

training generally includes the advice to change administrative passwords frequently, limit who has access to sensitive data, and include multilevel authentication for access to data.

The ethical issue of maintaining the security of private data is one that will continue to evolve with technological advances—advances on the side of those seeking data and on the side of organizations working to protect such data. What is clear, however, is that an organization is ethically responsible for maintaining the safety and security of its employees' and clients' personal information.[35]

Questions

1. Individuals working in HR have access to a great deal of private information about employees. If you had access to such data and someone approached you with an offer of money or other rewards in exchange for disclosing confidential employee information, what specific steps would you take to respond to the situation? What kind of training content should an employer provide for its employees so that they would know how to respond to such a scenario?

2. Describe some everyday situations in which an employee in HR or another area could accidentally compromise employees' private data. How can workers prevent or contain the damage of such a lapse?

SPOTLIGHT ON GLOBAL ISSUES
Safety and Health Standards and Norms Worldwide

This chapter discusses issues associated with worker safety, health, and privacy primarily from a U.S. perspective. However, it is important to keep in mind that laws and norms around these issues can vary from country to country and in different cultures.

With regard to safety and health, U.S. employers mainly focus on compliance with worker safety regulations established by OSHA or the specific

U.S. state. However, individual countries where the company operates may have different rules and standards for safety. As one example, many European countries require that office workers have natural light in their offices, typically via a window, because of the positive effects of natural light on worker health—something that is often disregarded in the design of offices in the United States. In addition, the International Labor Organizations (ILO), an agency of the United Nations, can provide significant guidance to employers regarding labor standards, safety and health, and worker protection. The ILO also provides a number of publications to help guide employers. Although some of these are broad health and safety guidelines, others focus on specific industries such as construction, agriculture, and mining, or on specific hazards such as asbestos and chemical exposures.

There are also differences in privacy standards afforded to workers in the United States compared to workers in other countries. For example, European privacy standards are more stringent. As one illustration, in 2017, a European Union (EU) advisory panel advised against employers issuing Fitbits or other health tracking devices to employees, even if employees are told how their data will be used and who will have access to it and can opt out of the health tracking program. This is because the power differences between employers and employees may be implicitly coercive. In fact, EU privacy rules that went into effect in 2018 stipulate that employers should carry out impact assessments before the implementation of any technology that might affect workers' privacy rights. One implication is that, at the very least, EU employers may need to have third parties process their employees' health data for them, providing it to the employer only in aggregate form.[36]

Workplace Stress

LO 15.3 Summarize issues around workplace stress and well-being.

Work stress is something we hear about on a regular basis. It is very common to hear a friend, family member, or coworker describe how stressful their work is. The estimate of how stressed workers are varies, but a recent survey by the American Psychological Association found that 37% of working Americans experience work stress, whereas another poll by CareerCast found that almost three in four workers were experiencing stress.[37] And although workers perceive many aspects of their work lives to be improving, apparently stress is not one of them: A Gallup poll found that stress was workers' number one complaint about their jobs.[38] Although the human cost of work stress is substantial, there are additional reasons why work stress is an important issue for organizations. For example, high stress may lead workers to be distracted and thus lead to workplace accidents.[39]

Stress also can affect the health of an organization's workforce, even to the point of being deadly. The results of a study on the mortality of more than 2,363 workers in their 60s in high-demand (stressful) jobs are striking, particularly taking into account the degree to which they had control over their work. The researchers found that workers who had low levels of control of their work had a 15% higher risk of death; on the other hand, those with high control had a 34% lower death risk. Among those workers in the study who didn't die, low control combined with high demands was associated with a higher body mass index (BMI). The researchers note that one solution is for organizations to provide employees with greater input into their work.[40]

In addition, stress can have negative effects on productivity and retention, with one poll showing that 42% of employees say that they have switched jobs because of stress. Top stressors may include relationship with the boss or coworkers, work overload, and poor work–life balance.[41] In short, worker stress can have serious implications for organizational competitiveness. At the same time, HRM can play a significant strategic role in reducing stress at work.

In discussing stress issues, it is important to differentiate the terms *stressors* and *strain,* which are both integral to stress. Stressors are demands in the environment to which a person must respond. Workplace stressors might include dangerous work conditions, a difficult boss, ambiguity in a person's work role, or a heavy workload. **Strain** refers to a person's reaction to stressors, such as heart disease, burnout, or depression, or behavioral outcomes such as low performance and turnover. Workplace stress has also been shown to lead to expressions of anger, aggression, and violence by employees, as well as to excessive alcohol consumption.[42] These strains in turn can lead to lower organization productivity, increased employee onboarding and training costs, and increased health care costs. Thus, it is increasingly common for many organizations to monitor workplace stressors, strains, and strain outcomes among their employees. Table 15.3 shows some common work stressors as identified by employees.

Strain A person's reaction to stressors, such as heart disease, burnout, or depression; or behavioral outcomes such as low performance and turnover

TABLE 15.3   Results of a Survey of the Leading Stressors at Work

A survey of more than 1,000 respondents identified the following issues as the leading causes of worker stress.

ISSUE	PERCENTAGE OF RESPONDENTS
1. Deadlines	30%
2. Life of another at risk	17%
3. Competitiveness	10%
4. Physical demands	8%
5. Working in the public eye	8%
6. Lack of growth	7%
7. Life at risk	7%
8. Hazards	5%
9. Meeting the public	4%
10. Travel	3%

Source: CareerCast. (2017). 2017 stressful jobs reader survey. http://www.careercast.com/career-news/2017-stressful-jobs-reader-survey; Wilkie, D. (2017, March 2). No. 1 stressor at work: Deadlines. https://www.shrm.org/resourcesandtools/hr-topics/employee-relations/pages/workplace-stress.aspx

In Chapter 5, we introduced the Job Demands-Resources (JDR) model as a way to consider the design of work. In addition, the JDR model provides a comprehensive view of sources of stress. As a recap, the JDR model describes a number of work demands that can negatively impact work engagement and performance. These demands include categories like the physical workload, time pressure, physical environment, and shift work. Variables that are typically seen as job demands that can act as negative stressors include role conflict (having conflicting roles at work); role ambiguity (a lack of clarity about what your role and responsibilities are in the organization and how your job fits in with other jobs); interpersonal conflicts with a boss or coworkers; risks, hazards, and poor work conditions; work–life conflict; emotionally demanding work; job insecurity (worry that you may lose your job); and performance demands. On the other hand, the JDR model also discusses resources that can support workers and thus mitigate stress such as supervisor support, control over your work, job security, participation, and feedback (see Figure 15.6).

From an organizational perspective, the more that employers can do to mitigate the stressful factors with improved resources, the better. For example, if employees are unsure about what their roles are, the organization can provide greater clarity through developing and updating job descriptions. Supervisors might also be trained to give workers support in dealing with emotionally demanding jobs. Or if employees are experiencing high work–life conflict due to lack of schedule control, the organization can provide greater control over work schedules to the extent possible.[43] Not surprisingly, the best approach is for organizations to carefully analyze the particular sources of stress, including those that may be associated with certain types of work, so that they can most effectively address the situation.

As one example, poor patient care is a serious outcome of physician stress. Physicians also have double the suicide rates of other professions. The causes of physician stress are complex, but they include a number of stressors such as increasing patient loads, increasing time pressures associated with documentation of electronic health records, and the fact that physicians need to deal with conflict and patients' emotional difficulties with relatively little training.[44]

Physicians have their own stress issues, with high burnout rates and high levels of emotional exhaustion and feelings of depersonalization (feeling disengaged from one's surroundings).

■ **FIGURE 15.6**   Some Common Sources of Workplace Stress and Factors
That Mitigate Them

Potential Sources of Stress in Organizations

- Role conflict
- Role ambiguity
- Interpersonal conflicts
- Risks, hazards, and poor work conditions
- Work–life conflict
- Emotionally demanding work

Factors Organizations Can Use to Reduce Stress

- Supervisor support
- Flexibility and control over work
- Job security
- Participation
- Constructive feedback

Sources: Based on Demerouti, E., Bakker, A. B., Nachreiner, F., & Schaufeli, W. B. (2001). The Job Demands-Resources model of burnout. *Journal of Applied Psychology, 86,* 499–512; Schaufeli, W. B., & Taris, T. W. (2014). A critical review of the Job Demands-Resources model: Implications for improving work and health. In *Bridging occupational, organizational and public health* (pp. 43–68). Springer Netherlands.

Challenge and Hindrance Stressors

It would be a mistake, however, to assume that all stressors are bad. In fact, some work stress is good: Even the earliest models of stress emphasized that there is also what is called "eustress" (good stress), or that some level of stress is good to increase activation, motivation, and performance. More recently, this idea has been carried further with the concepts of challenge and hindrance stressors. *Hindrance stressors* include negative stressors, things like workplace hassles, organizational politics, poor resources, role overload, and constraints. These hindrance stressors are linked to lower engagement and lower performance among employees. In contrast, *challenge stressors* are factors like role demands and time urgency, and they are thought to be positively linked to factors like work engagement. They are also thought to be associated with the experience of growth and achievement for employees. A meta-analysis on challenge and hindrance stressors showed that although both types of stressors can have negative effects on workers, challenge stressors are more likely to improve worker outcomes (e.g., job satisfaction), and hindrance stressors are more likely to hurt worker outcomes. The point here is that some degree of stress, especially certain types of stress, may actually be positive for some employees.[45]

Hindrance stressors Negative stressors, such as workplace hassles, organizational politics, poor resources, role overload, and constraints

Challenge stressors Job factors like role demands and time urgency that are thought to be positively related to work engagement

Work–Life Balance

For many workers these days, the quantity and pace of work are challenging. A recent Gallup poll found that the standard "40-hour workweek" is not a reality for many U.S. workers, who work on average 47 hours per week, which is almost a full workday beyond the "standard" 40 hours. Many employees—especially salaried workers—put in upward of 60-hour weeks, which means that they are either working 12-hour days, working on weekends, or both.[46] However, such expectations can be a source of stress for workers in terms of burnout and work–life balance problems—even for those who may seem to accept the "always on" situation. For example, before sending an e-mail, managers and coworkers may want to consider whether after-hours e-mails are appropriate and how they might affect both the employee and their family. And of course, the nature of the e-mails, such as how long they take to respond to and the tone of the e-mail, are important as well.[47]

This translates into less time for nonwork activities such as caring for children or aging parents, personal life, or outside interests. Further, always being connected by e-mail after work and on weekends is another challenge facing workers trying to balance their work and nonwork

Work-to-family conflict When work interferes with nonwork responsibilities

Family-to-work conflict When nonwork responsibilities interfere with work responsibilities

lives, with some countries even passing legislation to control e-mail. For example, in 2017, a "right to disconnect" law went into effect in France, requiring that organizations with more than 50 employees establish hours when it is unacceptable to send or respond to work e-mails.[48] The issue of balancing work and nonwork time is usually thought of as *work-to-family conflict*, which is when work interferes with nonwork responsibilities, and *family-to-work conflict*, which is when nonwork responsibilities interfere with work responsibilities.[49]

Given the potential consequences associated with work–family conflict for both organizations and individuals—such as decreased job satisfaction and performance, increased turnover, and depression—it is not surprising that there is considerable interest in what organizations can do to support workers dealing with this imbalance between their work and nonwork lives. These include employer policies focused on providing increased flexibility and support for employees balancing work and nonwork demands. Examples of workplace policies include flexible work hours and compressed workweeks (e.g., fewer than 5 days per week as well as flexible work locations). Other examples include flexible location and teleworking to provide caregiving control over work time and breaks, and sabbaticals and other types of employee leave. HRM plays a central role in implementing these types of workplace policies and programs, such as ensuring that the work gets done and defining the roles of both managers and employees in carrying out such policies.[50] In any case, providing this type of work–life support can have a big payoff in organizations. For example, SAS, a North Carolina–based business analytics software company, has had a reputation since it was founded in 1976 of supporting employees' work and nonwork spheres, including a subsidized cafeteria and on-site medical care. This even includes a 35-hour workweek for many employees. Not surprisingly, SAS has one of the lowest turnover rates in the industry and a frequent spot on "best places to work" lists.[51] In addition, this type of visible and tangible support for employees can provide a definite advantage in terms of recruitment.

Ways for Organizations to Reduce Stress

In addition to working to help employees with work–life balance, there are some other ways for organizations to help reduce some of the more toxic types of stress faced by employees.

Determine the Sources of Employee Stress

As we have emphasized throughout this book, there is rarely a one-size-fits-all solution to organizational challenges. Of course, organizations should evaluate the levels of outcomes such as sick leave use, turnover, and performance issues. But the most successful organizations will also dig deeper to find the sources of these negative outcomes. This might include surveys and interviews with individual employees and managers. For example, Hackensack University Medical Center regularly surveys its staff and benchmarks their results against a national database.[52] In any case, because many employers do not really understand their employees' level of stress or do not understand what is causing it, they may approach the problem in the wrong way. Also, keep in mind that different employees, in different types of jobs and at different levels, will often have different sources of stress.[53]

Eliminate the Root Causes of Employee Stress Before Looking for Fixes

Stress management programs intended for individual employees can be effective, but organizations should first see whether the primary sources of stress can be addressed.[54] For example, *workplace bullying*, either by supervisors or by coworkers, as well as an employee culture or climate that supports bullying, is a serious source of employee stress and dissatisfaction with work.[55] If employees perceive that there is a problem with difficult supervisors, removing or training those supervisors would be in order rather than training employees how to deal with it. Or if there is a technical aspect of the job that is disruptive to employees, address that first. For example, when a Starbucks employee work-scheduling algorithm was found to be disrupting employees' personal lives with constant last-minute changes, the company revamped it.[56]

Workplace bullying Consistent mistreatment by others in the workplace

Training Programs

A range of training programs can be used to support employees, such as training supervisors or employees on how to reduce stress.

Encourage and Allow for
Employee Recovery Experiences

Detaching from work can be essential for employees trying to recover from stress. In fact, studies have shown that good detachment experiences can lead to higher energy levels at work. Not only can workers be trained about how to detach and have the most successful recovery experiences, but organizations can also provide greater experiences for employee recovery.[57] Depending on the nature of the work or the types of employee stress, this might mean setting up e-mail policies that protect employees' nonwork time or allowing for short "sabbaticals" in which employees can recover. For example, accounting firm PwC provides a 4-week sabbatical to employees who have been with the organization for 5 to 7 years.[58] In addition, employers can encourage workers to take vacation days, as many employees, especially in the United States, might let their vacation days—and thus an opportunity for recovery—go to waste. Some organizations may encourage employees to take short naps at work, as naps can increase performance, and the value of naps during the workday is recognized by companies such as Uber, Google, and Zappos.[60] Providing personal days, either paid or unpaid, can allow employees to take care of personal needs off the job and to manage their work–life balance.

With the aging of the industrialized workforce, organizations have become interested in ways to support their older workers and keep them productive. BMW pioneered a model work redesign program among aging factory line workers.[59]

Consider How to Redesign Work and Work Areas to Fit Employee Needs

This includes quiet areas where employees might be able to take a break. Or it could be more extensive, such as BMW's overhaul of some of its manufacturing facilities to address its aging workforce, introducing features like wood floors (that are easier on joints), seated assembly work, and easier grips. BMW found a 7% increase in productivity with the introduction of these changes.[61]

Support the "Corporate Athlete"

Remaining in the stressful corporate world requires that employees take care of themselves in the same way that athletes would in terms of healthy behaviors, such as exercise and recovery. Organizations can play a role in supporting their "corporate athletes" to build and sustain their physical, emotional, mental, and spiritual capacities.[62]

In short, there are a number of ways that HRM professionals can work with organizational leaders to get a handle on employee stress and its negative impact on the employees and on the bottom line. In the next section, we discuss the role of wellness programs to support the safety, health, and well-being of workers.

Employee Wellness Programs

As you can see, there are considerable benefits to organizations that consider the stress, health, and well-being of their employees—benefits to both the employees and the organization. One challenge, then, is what organizations can do to actively promote employee health and well-being to provide a competitive edge. **Employee wellness programs** are organizational initiatives that promote the health, fitness, and well-being of workers.[63] These programs have been increasing in popularity, with an estimate of $6 billion spent on them each year.[64] In addition, more than half of employers typically offer wellness programs, and the percentage is even higher for large employers.[65] Because of their potential benefits both to organizations and to workers, wellness programs have taken center stage in HRM of late, and HRM practitioners are centrally involved in the most effective, strategic implementation of wellness programs.

LO 15.4 Identify the characteristics of the variety of workplace wellness programs that are offered by employers.

Employee wellness programs Organizational initiatives that promote the health, fitness, and well-being of workers

As we will see, wellness programs can take many forms, given the needs and resources of organizations, employees, and the particular industry. They include everything from helping employees manage illnesses (e.g., diabetes), increase exercise, or quit smoking to providing onsite medical screenings and care or improving their financial knowledge. For example, Cisco Systems, a multinational technology company, offers a wide range of options in its wellness program, including disease-management programs, onsite health care, fitness, child care facilities, mindfulness training, and generous parental leave policies.[66] The key is to offer the program that is the best fit for the employee and their situation.

Benefits of Wellness Programs

The increased interest in employer wellness programs is a sign that organizational decision makers think that these programs matter. A recent survey by *The Economist* Intelligence Unit surveyed 255 U.S. senior executives and 630 workers employed at organizations that have wellness programs.[67] Although only 31% of executives said they had used rigorous methods to assess the value of the programs, 70% said that they still considered the programs to be cost effective because of other intangible benefits—that a good wellness program is part of a progressive HR strategy that benefits the employer in other ways, such as attracting the best talent. Employees indicated that among the factors that would get them to participate in these programs would be to allocate some hours during the workday to wellness activities and provide on-site wellness facilities. One of the challenges of getting a good payoff from a wellness program is getting employees to participate in it. Both the executives and employees identified two leading factors that could reduce employee participation: Employees do not have the time to participate, and employees worry that their information may not remain confidential. These findings are consistent with other studies that show that most employers use wellness programs to improve well-being and to attract and retain the best talent, and only a minority of employers use wellness as a way to reduce tangible costs such as medical costs.[68]

Mark Bertolini is the CEO of Aetna, a Fortune 500 health benefits company. Bertolini emphasizes the need to go beyond assessing return on investment (ROI) when determining the value of a wellness program and to focus instead on how the program affects the organization's people and their well-being.[69]

That said, there are data that suggest the dollar value of wellness programs, at least for certain types of programs, and taking into account short-term versus long-term return on investment (ROI). A Rand study showed that disease-management programs that focus on helping workers with certain specific illnesses do seem to have the greatest short-term benefit in terms of saving money on health care costs, generating as much as $136 in savings per person and a 30% reduction in hospital admissions.[70] For example, a program that supports workers with heart disease could lead to a reduction in heart attacks; a program that supports workers with diabetes might lead to fewer amputations. On the other hand, "lifestyle management" programs that focus on issues like exercise and better eating habits might lead to long-term benefits like reduced rates of cancer or hypertension. Other reviews of the payoff from wellness programs cite lower medical costs and decreased absenteeism and presenteeism (working while having health problems).[71] Still, many would argue that given the value of worker well-being to increased engagement, performance, morale, and retention, an overly strong focus on ROI alone misses the point.[72]

Types of Wellness Programs

Wellness programs can include a range of elements (see Figure 15.7). We discuss only some of the more common examples in what follows. Note that most organizations would not

HR IN ACTION

A Premier Employee Wellness Program at Johnson & Johnson

Johnson & Johnson, the U.S.-based multinational focused on pharmaceuticals and medical devices, is a recognized leader in the area of employee wellness.

Johnson & Johnson takes an evidence-based view of wellness and health, using the following approach:

1. Assess factors that might influence a person's health behavior (e.g., smoking, exercise). This happens through an annual employee survey.

2. Apply evidence-based science on behavior change to improve that health behavior.

3. Measure the impact of programs.

4. Use data analytics to measure program effectiveness and to gain insights about potential improvements to the process.

Another key component is that Johnson & Johnson promotes a culture of health for all workers, from the manufacturing floor to the boardroom. The program is multifaceted, including a range of factors such as making healthy foods available on site, encouraging workers to get up from their desks, and making exercise available to workers.

Does Johnson & Johnson's wellness program work? As reported by the company, the general answer is yes. Smoking has decreased among Johnson & Johnson's employees. Heart disease and hypertension among its employees are lower than national U.S. standards. Health care costs have gone down per employee per year. But Johnson & Johnson does not focus just on medical cost savings. Rather, the company sees wellness as a factor supporting employee and company performance. In short, Johnson & Johnson reports that its wellness program has resulted in a good return on investment and seems to be linked to company market performance as well.[73]

---

include all of these elements but would instead select the types of wellness products that best fit their employees.[74] Some broad categories include the following:

- **Fitness club memberships and centers.** These can involve actually providing an on-site gym or special rates, discounts, or reimbursements at local fitness centers.

- **Nutrition education and healthy eating.** These types of programs provide instructions for employees on eating well. Some include making healthful food and snacks available on site or even an on-site farmers market.

- **Disease management.** Disease-management programs, which have existed since the early 2000s, are better researched than some other types of wellness programs, and they appear to be good at reducing medical costs and employee mortality. These include providing help, support, and guidance for employees who know that they have chronic conditions, such as heart disease or diabetes, so that they can better manage their diseases.

- **Emotional well-being.** With a focus on things like yoga instruction, mindfulness, and other ways to control employee stress, these programs have become more popular since the days of early wellness programs, which had a greater focus on physical health. As an example, Vancouver-based Mobify offers twice-weekly yoga classes to its employees.

■ **FIGURE 15.7**   Workplace Wellness Programs

Such programs have expanded in their popularity and breadth, and they can take many different forms. Here are examples of just some of the many possible elements of a workplace wellness program.

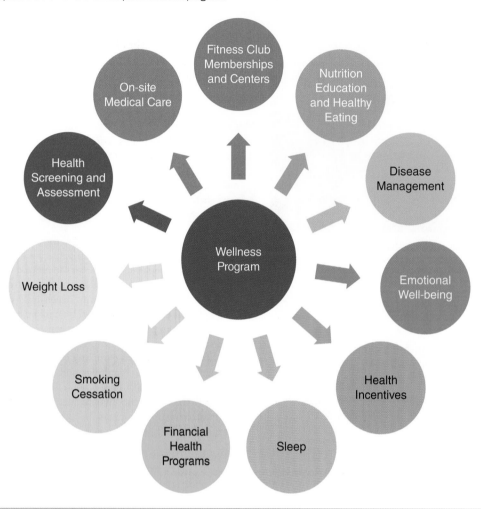

- **Health incentives.** An organization may choose to reward any number of health behaviors such as smoking cessation, weight loss, or steps. Implementing health incentives should take into account the type of employee. The key is for workers to feel engaged, not coerced.

- **Sleep.** These programs may focus on anything from sleep hygiene education (explaining the value of sleep and how to develop good sleep habits) to workplace naps. For example, Asana offers its employees "nap rooms" where they can take a quick nap during work hours. And at LinkedIn, a recent focus of its wellness program was sleep health, including a "sleep fair."[75]

- **Financial health programs.** A number of surveys have shown that employees are not financially healthy (in terms of their personal finances), and the stress from this could affect their workplace behavior. Employer-sponsored financial programs can take any number of forms, ranging from financial education and advice to paying student loans. Nearly half of all companies offer such financial advice, according to a SHRM survey.

- **Smoking cessation.** Smoking cessation programs support people trying to quit. These are used at many organizations such as Microsoft.

- **Weight loss.** Weight-loss programs are often included as part of healthy eating and exercise programs and may also include Weight Watchers meetings and weight-loss competitions.

- **Health screening and assessment.** Sometimes employees are unaware that they have health risks. Simply offering employees the chance to get some basic health screening might uncover if they have particular medical needs (the privacy of which would also need to be protected).

- **On-site medical care.** This is not something that all companies can offer. In fact, only about 8% of companies have such a program, according to a SHRM survey. But given that employees are sometimes pressed for time and do not get around to taking care of their personal health needs, some companies such as Cisco are offering these on-site medical services to employees.

Employee Assistance Programs (EAPs)

Employee assistance programs (or EAPs) are in some ways the predecessors of wellness programs, but with a decidedly different approach. Rather than taking an active role in promoting employee health and well-being and preventing illness, EAPs are focused on identifying employees' personal problems that may be affecting their work and helping them with these existing problems. The problems that they often address include a range of issues such as alcohol and substance abuse, emotional challenges, and financial problems. The services offered by EAPs can take different forms depending on the type of problems, like providing basic legal assistance, counseling, advice on child or eldercare services, and/or nursing advice by telephone. Typically paid for by the employer, EAP services generally support not only the employee but their family as well.[76] One classic example is the EAP offered by Accenture, which includes confidential support for issues such as anxiety, depression, and substance abuse, as well as support for financial issues.[77]

What began in the 1940s and 1950s with a primary focus on alcohol abuse has expanded through the years to become a program that is standard in most organizations, with many outside entities providing services (e.g., counseling) paid for by the employer. It is important to note that, like wellness programs, EAPs vary considerably from one organization to the next in what types of specific services they offer. Most medium- and large-sized organizations provide some type of EAP services to their employees. Many EAPs also require:

- the development of consistent EAP rules and guidelines with input from employees and, in unionized organizations, from unions;

- legal guidance on the appropriateness of EAP rules and procedures;

- procedures for maintaining employee confidentiality;

- training for supervisors on appropriate methods for identifying employee performance problems that might be appropriate for referral to EAP;

- consultation services for supervisors dealing with a possible employee EAP issue; and

- a system for monitoring and follow-up.[78]

What is the role of HRM in EAPs? One issue is to ensure employee privacy and security of employee information, including which EAP services are used by individual employees.

In addition, most employers, except for very large organizations, outsource EAP services given the highly specialized nature of the work in such matters, such as counseling and substance abuse treatment. In fact, one SHRM report notes that EAP services may be the most commonly outsourced HR function, with 62% of employers outsourcing the function. Thus, HR personnel are heavily involved in selecting EAP vendors, developing EAP policies, and explaining to employees which EAP services are available.[79] This last issue may be particularly important, as it has been argued that employees tend to underuse EAP services either due to issues such as privacy concerns or not really being aware of which EAP services are offered. By one estimate, despite the fact that 97% of large companies have EAPs, only about 40% of employees know whether their employer offers these services.[80]

Best Practices for Implementing Wellness Programs and the Role of HRM

Given the costs of wellness programs, their careful implementation is essential to providing value to the organization. It is here that HRM plays a central role by ensuring that the program fits employees' needs as well as those of the organization.[81]

SPOTLIGHT ON DATA AND ANALYTICS

Wearable Technology in the Workplace

One of the biggest sources of data workplace safety and health analytics is wearable technology ("wearables") worn by employees. This can take a number of forms, such as fitness trackers or employee badges that monitor employee movements and their proximity to each other.

Perhaps one of the most commonly cited uses of such wearables is for wellness programs. For example, a wearable allows employees to see not only their own steps in a day but how much their coworkers are walking as well. Wearables may allow employees to become aware of dysfunctional behaviors that they are not aware of or to see where they might make simple changes to improve their health. Similarly, wearables can allow employers to set up incentives for employees to increase their activity or allow them to tailor health programs to fit the needs of an individual employee.

Wearables can be used in the realm of employee safety as well. For example, some wearable solutions alert employees operating heavy equipment when they are too close to other employees. And wearable technology has even been cited as a way for organizations to track worker well-being in terms of their happiness at work, with the hopes of improving worker happiness.

Workplace wearables are not without their challenges, however. First, you can imagine the vast amount of data that an employer might be able to collect via wearables—far more data than most organizations are equipped to analyze or to interpret. Relatedly, collecting such data about employees raises the issue of who will have access to them and how the employer will protect the data from third parties. In addition, monitoring employees in such personal ways—say, the amount they exercise or their health—can backfire and may actually increase worker stress because workers feel that they are always "on." In fact, it has been argued that an employer that wants to improve employee health and well-being may do better to reduce hours and let employees detach from work rather than introducing competitions or monitoring health behavior. Further, monitoring by their employers may not be to the liking of many workers. For example, the collection of such personal data by employers has been challenged within the European Union, which has far more stringent privacy laws than the United States. A recent news story indicated that wearables can lead to serious security issues, such as when the wearables used by U.S. soldiers gave away their locations—which were not supposed to be revealed.

In short, workplace wearables can provide a tremendous opportunity to both employers and workers. Although they are not a panacea for all health and safety problems, they can provide considerable benefits if implemented with awareness of the pitfalls and with considerable planning.[82]

Tips for Implementing an Effective Wellness Program

Fitness programs come in a wide range of shapes and sizes, with varying costs and payoffs. These can vary by organization and by individual employees. Plus, starting a wellness program that isn't a good fit—for example, one that makes employees feel like they are being coerced into participating—may make matters worse. Here are some ideas to keep in mind when implementing a wellness program.

1. **Find out what employees actually want and need.** Whereas some employees may want assistance with financial planning, others may want gym memberships. The point is that an assessment of employee needs and interests—in other words, a program that employees will actually use—should guide the adoption of a new program.

2. **To the extent possible, make the program flexible to address individual employees' needs.** Focus not only on what most employees want but also on what different groups of employees want. A program that allows some flexibility to address the different needs of different workers should be well received.

3. **Think about how to encourage participation.** Some employees may be motivated to join a wellness program after some feedback about their current health. Others may be motivated by some sort of health competition among employees—although this could be a definite turnoff for other workers. Keep in mind what would work best for different employees in your organization.

4. **Consider the marketing angle.** This might be as simple as providing sufficient knowledge of the program. It might also mean carefully choosing the names for the program elements that won't "turn off" employees.

5. **Make participation convenient for employees.** An unused program is an unwise investment, so make it easy for employees to use. For example, if the focus is on greater exercise, consider whether employees might be more likely to participate in a gym program that is located on site or near the worksite. When it is easier for employees to use a program, it is easier for them to adopt it.

6. **Leverage technology.** Technology can help with wellness programs in numerous ways, such as apps that help employees with meeting their health goals, attending webinars, or scheduling medical appointments.[83]

- **Needs assessment.** As with all other HR functions, the wellness program should be designed to fit what employees want and to address organizational concerns. For example, if a key goal of the organization is to be seen as a healthy place to work, the wellness program might focus on nutrition and exercise. Or if medical claims are seen as a particular financial drain, the focus might be on disease management. Further, a program that does not fit a need felt on the part of employees is of little value. In other words, the program should also be tailored to the needs of the employees.

- **Engagement of leadership.** Research has shown that like so many other organizational initiatives, buy-in at all levels is necessary to ensure support and the success of the program.

- **Communication.** Another central role for HR is to ensure that employees know about the wellness services available to them. This means clear, consistent, and frequent messaging.

- **Ensure that the program is easy for employees to use.** Examples might include the decision to provide on-site child care or on-site health care services so that employees are more likely to use these services.

- **Evaluation.** We have noted that the payoff on wellness programs may not be as tangible as return on investment (ROI)—although sometimes it is. In any case, whether it is reduced health costs, absenteeism, employee satisfaction and morale, or better retention, some evaluation of the program should be included to illustrate its value. For example, measurement and evaluation are a standard part of Johnson & Johnson's wellness program. The use of metrics, such as physical activity and biometric screening (e.g., blood pressure, BMI), is becoming part of the natural landscape in evaluating wellness programs.

- **Ensure integrity of private employee data.** Part of having rich data to evaluate wellness programs is the ethical responsibility to protect these data. Ensuring the safety and security of employee data as well as regulatory compliance can best assure employee buy-in.

- **Consider the use of incentives.** A wellness program that is never used by employees is a waste of money. In fact, the measurement of employee adoption of various wellness offerings may be one of the most important metrics of the program's value. But there are many ways to encourage adoption. One method is to provide financial incentives for employee participation in wellness programs. Such incentives generally seem to work, at least for certain types of wellness programs, although they may work better for certain types of health behaviors (e.g., eating more fruits and vegetables) than others (e.g., stopping smoking). Other ways to incent employees into participating in wellness programs is to introduce employee competitions for those who wish to participate in this way. Incentives should be seen as fair by employees and not coercive. The *Manager's Toolbox* presents a number of suggestions for ensuring the success of a wellness program in organizations.

LO 15.5 Identify examples of focused workplace well-being interventions.

Workplace intervention
A solution implemented within an organization that focuses on a very specific workplace well-being issue

Workplace Interventions: Solutions to Address Specific Well-Being Issues

This chapter describes the role of HRM in employee safety and well-being, including a number of programs that employers can implement to support workplace safety and well-being. Sometimes, rather than implementing an entire program, employers uncover the need to focus on a very specific outcome (e.g., employee stress) or problematic issue (e.g., poor safety climate), or they may want to focus on the needs of their employee population (e.g., truckers). In these cases, they may choose to apply a more narrowly focused *workplace intervention* as a solution to address their needs. In this section, we describe a few examples of workplace interventions that have been rigorously evaluated for their effectiveness.

Improving Work–Life Balance

As described earlier, work–life balance issues are a growing challenge for many organizations, with factors such as intrusion of e-mail outside of work playing a role. One intervention called STAR (Support, Transform, Achieve, Results), developed by Leslie Hammer and colleagues to support work–life balance, included training supervisors to support work–life balance among employees and helping supervisors apply these skills on the job through software and workshops. When applied to 30 health care facilities, the researchers found that in groups that went through the STAR intervention, there were improvements in safety behavior and organizational citizenship behavior compared with groups that did not get the intervention. In other studies, STAR was also found to reduce smoking and improve workers' sleep.[84]

Enhancing Safety Through Improved Leadership and Communication

Through a series of studies, Dov Zohar and colleagues examined ways to enhance the communication between leaders and employees to improve safety. These interventions focused on the effects of giving supervisors feedback about the quality of the safety-focused conversations with their team members and whether leaders discussed safety with team members on a daily basis. The effects on safety outcomes were compelling. Although teams in which the leader did not receive the intervention showed improvement, teams where the leader did receive the intervention showed significant improvements in safety behavior, safety climate, and safety audit scores.[85]

Addressing the Needs of Specific Occupations

Some interventions are developed to address the health and safety challenges of specific professions. For example, long-haul truck driving is a sedentary job that often requires extended periods away from home and involves a number of health and safety risks. In addition to the risk of accidents, long-haul truckers have rates of obesity, diabetes, and smoking that are double the rates of other workers. Many also report limited physical activity and poor sleep.[86] Therefore, some safety and health interventions are specifically focused on long-haul truckers, taking into consideration the specific nature of their work. One such intervention is the Safety and Health Involvement for Truckers (SHIFT) intervention developed by Ryan Olson and colleagues, which was designed to address the sedentary nature of long-haul trucking. The SHIFT intervention included computer training, employees monitoring their own behaviors, and a weight-loss competition. An evaluation of SHIFT with a sample of 452 drivers across five trucking companies demonstrated that drivers who received the intervention showed lower BMI and increased fruit and vegetable consumption compared to those who did not receive the intervention.[87]

Total Worker Health™: An Integrated Approach to Worker Well-Being

LO 15.6 Explain what is meant by an integrated Total Worker Health™ approach.

Throughout this chapter, we have discussed the issues of workplace safety, worker stress and well-being, and wellness programs as separate issues. In reality, however, these are all linked, because an employer concerned with worker safety will also be concerned with worker well-being and will develop wellness programs to address these issues. Further, these issues are also all intertwined. Consider our opening case regarding railway accidents: The causes of these accidents included worker health issues (e.g., sleep apnea) that could have been addressed by means of a well-being program. Specifically, such a program could have identified the underlying medical problem and perhaps even reduced it through treatment, weight loss, and exercise; the accidents, however, were also the result of a physical work environment that did not include safeguards (e.g., speed monitoring systems) to prevent accidents and perhaps a weak safety climate. The result was that workers with health problems were involved in accidents that caused injury to themselves and to the public.

Thus, there is a growing recognition of the value of integrating wellness programs with traditional workplace safety and health programs because such integration can bring about systemic change within the organization. The National Institute for Occupational Safety and Health (NIOSH) refers to these integrated safety, well-being, and wellness programs as *Total Worker Health™ (TWH™)* programs (see Figure 15.8).[88] As one example, Dow Chemical, which has 54,000 employees in 49 countries, adopted a TWH™ approach that integrates three distinct elements: healthy people, healthy workplace, and healthy culture. These are all part of Dow's integrated strategy to address the complex issues around protecting the safety, health, and well-being

Total Worker Health™ (TWH™) An integrated approach to safety, well-being, and wellness

■ **FIGURE 15.8**   The Broad Range of Systemic Factors Associated With TWH™ Approaches to Managing Safety, Health, and Well-Being

Control Hazards and Exposures (e.g., chemicals)	Organization of Work (e.g., stress prevention, safe staffing)	Built Environment (e.g., access to healthy food, accommodation of worker diversity)
Leadership (e.g., commitment to safety and well-being; worker recognition)	Compensation and Benefits (e.g., work–life programs, disease management)	Changing Workforce Demographics (e.g., multigenerational and diverse workforce)
Policy Issues (e.g., worker privacy, reducing bullying)	Community Design (e.g., easy access to health care in the community)	New Employment Patterns (e.g., contingent workforce)

Source: Based on recommendations from NIOSH. (2015). Total worker health frequently asked questions. https://www.cdc.gov/niosh/twh/pdfs/faq-for-total-worker-health_2015-03-01-trademark-amended-for-download.pdf

of its workers, and TWH™ is an explicit part of its 2025 Sustainability Goals.[89] Although the research on these integrated programs is still in the early stages, an initial review of 17 TWH™ interventions found that they may have more long-term impact on worker safety and health than narrower, piecemeal approaches.[90] Further, seeing worker safety, health, and well-being through this integrated lens can help organizations identify underlying causes of safety and health issues. For example, through the use of data analytics, a company may be able to identify the relationship between costly outcomes (e.g., employee medical costs; accidents) that are associated with an underlying cause (e.g., safety climate) that could be addressed by specific management practices (e.g., top management support, supervisor training).

CHAPTER SUMMARY

HRM plays a central role in workplace safety, well-being, and wellness. HR professionals need to know the government agencies and resources devoted to safety and the safety regulations with which employers must comply. Proactive HRM will work to uncover workers' safety and health issues and their causes. HRM will also take steps to identify and implement appropriate solutions, including employee wellness programs and more specific interventions and integrated Total Worker Health™ approaches. Organizations with a culture of safety communicate the importance of safety and health to both managers and employees. Looking at the big picture of safety and health across the organization is a key strategy in supporting employee health and well-being and organizational success.

KEY TERMS

well-being   507
Occupational Safety and Health
    Administration (OSHA)   509
National Institute for Occupational
    Safety and Health (NIOSH)   509
workplace accidents   510
workplace injuries   510
workplace fatalities   510
near misses   510

Visit **edge.sagepub.com/bauer** to help you accomplish your coursework goals in an easy-to-use learning environment.

- Master the learning objectives using key study tools
- Watch, listen, and connect with online multimedia resources

- Access mobile-friendly quizzes and flashcards to check your understanding

HR REASONING AND DECISION-MAKING EXERCISES

MINI-CASE ANALYSIS EXERCISE: SAFETY FOR ALL

You are working for a small construction company specializing in interior and exterior painting of newly built homes. You are the sole safety officer in this small company of 50 employees. The company is fairly young—5 years old—but it is growing rapidly with the high rate of construction in your metropolitan area. And so far, things are going well from a safety perspective, with no severe accidents or injuries yet reported.

The company handles a number of safety issues well. It posts the required OSHA publications regarding employee rights and employer responsibilities. In addition, you have been able to use the checklists that OSHA publishes to improve safety standards and to demonstrate the need to provide safety training to employees on the hazards that are characteristic of this type of work.

However, you notice that the owner and the three lead supervisors in the company see safety as an issue that is addressed primarily through your role, not theirs. For example, the owner of the company rarely follows the company's own rules regarding safety, especially with regard to the handling of chemicals (e.g., solvents) that are used in painting work. Similarly, he and the three supervisors are very much focused on company growth and encourage workers to work quickly; in your view, this is sometimes at the expense of safety. In addition, you have noticed that when employees do voice a concern or suggestion regarding a safety problem, the suggestion is not welcomed by your supervisors— at least not in terms of their body language. You are trying to decide on your next steps in managing the safety function in the company.

1. What concerns do you have with the safety climate of this company? In what ways might these issues have a negative impact on worker safety?

2. What steps could you take in your role as safety officer to better illustrate to management the safety issues that you are observing in this company?

3. What arguments could you make to these top managers about the importance of safety climate and the role they play in it? What suggestions would you make to them as to how they might foster a positive safety climate?

HR DECISION ANALYSIS EXERCISE: THE WELLNESS COMPETITION

Tabular Communications runs a group of four call centers across the United States, with locations in Vermont, Iowa, Arizona, and California. Several retailers use Tabular's services. Specifically, Tabular's call center employees assist customers of these retailers with making purchases, also providing customers with product information.

These customer service jobs are highly sedentary. In addition, because these call centers are not located near restaurants, in the past employees could not easily purchase healthy food for lunch and for breaks, relying either on food they bring from home or on vending machines. In recognition of this issue, the HR team has persuaded Tabular's management to include some healthy options in the vending machines and even to provide on-site employee cafés with a range of food options. These innovations appear to be quite popular with employees.

To go a step further, the HR director has recently proposed that management initiate an employee wellness program that incorporates competition among employees. Specifically, the director would like to provide health-tracking devices to employees. These would allow employees not only to track their own steps but also to compete with other employees, with the company awarding prizes to those with the most steps. The program would also include a competition between the different call center locations. The director points out that getting up and moving around more would be especially beneficial to employees in these types of sedentary jobs. Furthermore, data collected from the health tracking devices might help the company figure out ways to cut its health care costs.

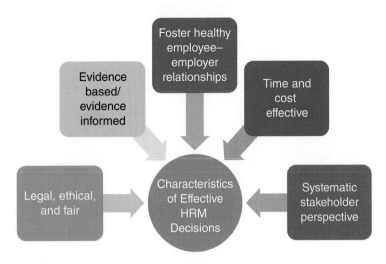

Please provide the rationale for your answer to each of the questions below.

Does this wellness program seem legal, ethical, and fair?

_____
_____
_____
_____

Is it evidence based/evidence informed?

_____
_____
_____
_____

Does it foster healthy employee–employer relationships?

_____
_____
_____
_____

Is it time and cost effective?

_____
_____
_____
_____

Does it take a systematic stakeholder perspective?

_____
_____
_____
_____

Considering your analysis above, overall, do you think that undertaking this aspect of the wellness program would be an effective decision? Why or why not?

_____

_____

_____

_____

What, if anything, do you think should be done differently or considered to help make this decision more effective?

_____

_____

_____

_____

HR DECISION-MAKING EXERCISE:
ASSESSING THE VALUE OF A WELLNESS PROGRAM

A manufacturing company is preparing to implement a company wellness program within its East Coast, Southeastern, and West Coast locations, which employ approximately 1,800 workers in total.

The proposed wellness program would involve five possible components:

- on-site exercise equipment;

- smoking cessation program;

- mindfulness training;

- free mental health counseling; and

- financial education.

The company's CEO is very supportive of a wellness program, having seen the benefits where she worked previously. But she is also concerned about justifying the program in terms of its costs and benefits. Thus, she would like to know which of these proposed components of the program—or which combination of components—the company should consider undertaking.

1. How would you investigate the potential value of each of these components prior to implementation? Aside from company data, what specific sources would you use to the possible value of each component?

2. What types of company data would you use to determine if each of these components is needed? Be specific in describing both (a) the type of data you would want to review and (b) what data patterns would suggest a need for the specific component.

3. Should you roll out the entire program at once, or should each component be rolled out separately? What would be the advantages and disadvantages of each approach? In crafting your response, consider whether the three company locations might be used differently for the rollout.

4. In the event that the program was implemented by the company, describe what types of data—from objective data to employee attitudes—the company should collect to evaluate whether each component is effective.

5. Are there any "intangible" outcomes that might be considered in assessing the value of the wellness program?

DATA AND ANALYTICS EXERCISE: INVESTIGATING EMPLOYEE STRESS

Recall that employee stress can lead to workplace accidents, as well as to lower productivity and higher turnover. Stress can be conceptualized as a process involving stressors and strain, where stressors are demands in the environment to which a person must respond and strain refers to a person's reaction to stressors. Employees' perceptions of stressors and strain can be measured using surveys, and the data from such surveys can be used to understand which organizational units perceive the highest levels of stressors and strain and whether stressors and strain are associated with important outcomes, such as employee attitudes (e.g., job satisfaction, turnover intentions) and performance. Regression analysis can be used to understand whether the relationship between a stressor or strain variable and an outcome variable is statistically significant and, if so, the direction of the association (positive vs. negative). For example, consider the following dataset. It contains employees' perceptions of a common workplace stressor called interpersonal conflict and their turnover intentions. Each row represents a unique employee's set of responses to the different survey questions, and the numeric scores associated with each variable represent the employee's average response to items/questions associated with that particular variable.

SURVEY NUMBER	INTERPERSONAL CONFLICT	TURNOVER INTENTIONS
1	4.6	4.1
2	4.7	3.4
3	3.7	4.0
4	3.9	3.1
5	3.6	3.7
6	2.0	3.9
7	3.3	2.9
8	2.9	3.4
9	3.2	3.7
10	2.9	4.0
11	2.9	3.4
12	3.1	3.4
13	3.3	3.8
14	2.0	2.9
15	2.5	3.4
16	2.3	2.5
17	2.5	2.7
18	3.5	2.3
19	2.6	2.1
20	1.4	1.5

If you were to plug these variables into a linear regression analysis, wherein interpersonal conflict is entered as a predictor variable and turnover intentions is entered as an outcome variable, you would find that the association between the two variables is statistically significant because the *p*-value equals .03, which is less than the conventional cutoff of .05. Further, the unstandardized regression coefficient for interpersonal conflict is .58, which means that the association is positive and that for every 1.0-point increase in interpersonal conflict scores, turnover intentions scores tend to increase by .58 points. An excerpt from the regression analysis output is provided.

	COEFFICIENTS	STANDARD ERROR	*T* STAT	*P*-VALUE	LOWER 95%	UPPER 95%
Intercept	1.20	.80	1.50	.15	−.48	2.88
Interpersonal Conflict	.58	.24	2.37	.03	.06	1.09

If the regression coefficient for interpersonal conflict were nonsignificant (i.e., the *p*-value were equal to or greater than .05), then we would conclude that there is no association between the two variables.

EXCEL EXTENSION: NOW YOU TRY!

- On **edge.sagepub.com/bauer**, you will find an Excel exercise on investigating employee stress.

- First, you will learn how to run a regression analysis in Excel.

- Second, you will run several regression analyses in which you investigate the associations between different stressor and strain variables and different outcome variables.

- Third, you will practice interpreting and communicating the results of the analyses.

CHAPTER 15 SUPPLEMENT:
OSHA POSTER AND INFORMATION SHEET

Required OSHA Poster (available at https://www.osha.gov/Publications/poster.html)

OSHA Inspections Information Sheet (available at https://www.osha.gov/OshDoc/data_General_Facts/factsheet-inspections.pdf)

■ **FIGURE 15.9**   Job Safety and Health—It's the Law

All workers have the right to:

- A safe workplace.
- Raise a safety or health concern with your employer or OSHA, or report a work-related injury or illness, without being retaliated against.
- Receive information and training on job hazards, including all hazardous substances in your workplace.
- Request an OSHA inspection of your workplace if you believe there are unsafe or unhealthy conditions. OSHA will keep your name confidential. You have the right to have a representative contact OSHA on your behalf.
- Participate (or have your representative participate) in an OSHA inspection and speak in private to the inspector.
- File a complaint with OSHA within 30 days (by phone, online or by mail) if you have been retaliated against for using your rights.
- See any OSHA citations issued to your employer.
- Request copies of your medical records, tests that measure hazards in the workplace, and the workplace injury and illness log.

This poster is available free from OSHA.

Contact OSHA. We can help.

Employers must:

- Provide employees a workplace free from recognized hazards. It is illegal to retaliate against an employee for using any of their rights under the law, including raising a health and safety concern with you or with OSHA, or reporting a work-related injury or illness.
- Comply with all applicable OSHA standards.
- Report to OSHA all work-related fatalities within 8 hours, and all inpatient hospitalizations, amputations and losses of an eye within 24 hours.
- Provide required training to all workers in a language and vocabulary they can understand.
- Prominently display this poster in the workplace.
- Post OSHA citations at or near the place of the alleged violations.

FREE ASSISTANCE to identify and correct hazards is available to small and medium-sized employers, without citation or penalty, through OSHA-supported consultation programs in every state.

1-800-321-OSHA (6742) • TTY 1-877-889-5627 • **www.osha.gov**

Source: Occupational Safety and Health Administration. "Job Safety and Health. It's the Law!" https://www.osha.gov/Publications/osha3165.pdf

■ **FIGURE 15.10**   OSHA Fact Sheet

OSHA®FactSheet

OSHA Inspections

The Occupational Safety and Health Administration is committed to strong, fair and effective enforcement of safety and health requirements in the workplace. OSHA inspectors, called compliance safety and health officers, are experienced, well-trained industrial hygienists and safety professionals whose goal is to assure compliance with OSHA requirements and help employers and workers reduce on-the-job hazards and prevent injuries, illnesses and deaths in the workplace.

Normally, OSHA conducts inspections without advance notice. Employers have the right to require compliance officers to obtain an inspection warrant before entering the worksite.

Inspection Priorities

OSHA cannot inspect all 7 million workplaces it covers each year. The agency seeks to focus its inspection resources on the most hazardous workplaces in the following order of priority:

1. Imminent danger situations—hazards that could cause death or serious physical harm receive top priority. Compliance officers will ask employers to correct these hazards immediately or remove endangered employees.

2. Severe injuries and illnesses—employers must report:

- All work-related fatalities within 8 hours.
- All work-related inpatient hospitalizations, amputations, or losses of an eye within 24 hours.

3. Worker Complaints—allegations of hazards or violations also receive a high priority. Employees may request anonymity when they file complaints.

4. Referrals of hazards from other federal, state or local agencies, individuals, organizations or the media receive consideration for inspection.

5. Targeted inspections—inspections aimed at specific high-hazard industries or individual work-places that have experienced high rates of injuries and illnesses also receive priority.

6. Follow-up inspections—checks for abatement of violations cited during previous inspections are also conducted by the agency in certain circumstances.

Phone/Fax Investigations

OSHA carefully prioritizes all complaints it receives based on their severity. For lower-priority hazards, with permission of a complainant, OSHA may telephone the employer to describe safety and health concerns, following up with a fax providing details on alleged safety and health hazards. The employer must respond in writing within five working days, identifying any problems found and noting corrective actions taken or planned. If the response is adequate and the complainant is satisfied with the response, OSHA generally will not conduct an on-site inspection.

On-site Inspections

Preparation—Before conducting an inspection, OSHA compliance officers research the inspection history of a worksite using various data sources, review the operations and processes in use and the standards most likely to apply. They gather appropriate personal protective equipment and testing instruments to measure potential hazards.

Presentation of credentials—The on-site inspection begins with the presentation of the compliance officer's credentials, which include both a photograph and a serial number.

Opening Conference—The compliance officer will explain why OSHA selected the workplace for inspection and describe the scope of the inspection, walkaround procedures, employee representation and employee interviews. The employer then selects a representative to accompany the compliance officer during the inspection. An authorized representative of the employees, if any, also has the right to go along. In any case, the compliance officer will consult privately with a reasonable number of employees during the inspection.

Walkaround—Following the opening conference, the compliance officer and the representatives will walk through the portions of the workplace covered by the inspection, inspecting for hazards that could lead to employee injury or illness. The compliance officer will also review worksite injury and illness records and the posting of the official OSHA poster.

During the walkaround, compliance officers may point out some apparent violations that can be corrected immediately. While the law requires that these hazards must still be cited, prompt correction is a sign of good faith on the part of the employer. Compliance officers try to minimize work interruptions during the inspection and will keep confidential any trade secrets they observe.

Closing Conference—After the walkaround, the compliance officer holds a closing conference with the employer and the employee representatives to discuss the findings. The compliance officer discusses possible courses of action an employer may take following an inspection, which could include an informal conference with OSHA or contesting citations and proposed penalties. The compliance officer also discusses consultation services and employee rights.

Results

When an inspector finds violations of OSHA standards or serious hazards, OSHA may issue citations and fines. OSHA must issue a citation and proposed penalty within six months of the violation's occurrence. Citations describe OSHA requirements allegedly violated, list any proposed penalties and give a deadline for correcting the alleged hazards. Violations are categorized as willful, serious, other-than-serious, *de minimis*, failure to abate, and repeated. In settling a penalty, OSHA has a policy of reducing penalties for small employers and those acting in good faith. For serious violations, OSHA may also reduce the proposed penalty based on the gravity of the alleged violation. No good faith adjustment will be made for alleged willful violations. For information on penalty ranges, see www.osha.gov/penalties.

Appeals

When OSHA issues a citation to an employer, it also offers the employer an opportunity for an informal conference with the OSHA Area Director to discuss citations, penalties, abatement dates or any other information pertinent to the inspection. The agency and the employer may work out a settlement agreement to resolve the matter and to eliminate the hazard. OSHA's primary goal is correcting hazards and maintaining compliance rather than issuing citations or collecting penalties.

Alternatively, employers have 15 working days after receipt of citations and proposed penalties to formally contest the alleged violations and/or penalties by sending a written notice to the Area Director. OSHA forwards the contest to the Occupational Safety and Health Review Commission for independent review. Alternatively, citations, penalties and abatement dates that are not challenged by the employer or settled become a final order of the Occupational Safety and Health Review Commission.

This is one in a series of informational fact sheets highlighting OSHA programs, policies or standards. It does not impose any new compliance requirements. For a comprehensive list of compliance requirements of OSHA standards or regulations, refer to Title 29 of the Code of Federal Regulations. This information will be made available to sensory-impaired individuals upon request. The voice phone is (202) 693-1999; teletypewriter (TTY) number: (877) 889-5627.

For assistance, contact us. We can help. It's confidential.

U.S. Department of Labor

www.osha.gov (800) 321-OSHA (6742)

DEP FS-3783 08/2016

Source: Occupational Safety and Health Administration. "OSHA Fact Sheet." https://www.osha.gov/OshDoc/data_General_Facts/factsheet-inspections.pdf

Opportunities and Challenges in International HRM

16

LEARNING OBJECTIVES

After reading and studying this chapter, you should be able to do the following:

16.1 Describe the advantages and disadvantages to standardizing HR practices in different locations of a business and barriers to standardization.

16.2 Examine the considerations an organization should make when expanding its business practices across borders such as cultural differences, unionization rates, and legal context.

16.3 Identify HRM practices that would benefit from local adjustments and those that would benefit from standardization across borders.

16.4 Summarize the forces affecting adjustment of expatriates to their overseas assignments and identify ways in which organizations can prepare expatriates for successful assignments.

16.5 Identify alternatives to long-term relocation assignments.

Opening Case

Talent Management in the Danger Zone: The Case of Mercy Corps

Consider the following job attributes: good pay and benefits; meaningful work where you are able to make a difference in people's lives, save them from danger, help them to get jobs, and bring aid to places where it is needed most. You have opportunities to learn something new every day, and a lot of travel is involved. If this sounds like your dream job, note that the job is actually in a war or disaster zone with poor living conditions, scarce medical support, and physical danger. Many organizations encounter risks as they do business, but for an international nongovernmental organization (INGO) such as Mercy Corps, danger *is* the business.

Nongovernmental organizations (NGOs) are humanitarian nonprofit organizations that aim to effect change in environmental, social, human rights, or other issues, and as an INGO, Mercy Corps performs this mission on a global scale. Whether it is bringing relief to refugees in Syria, helping farmers in Ethiopia prepare for drought conditions, or providing educational and employment opportunities to marginalized populations in Nigeria, working in international tough spots is everyday work for Mercy Corps employees. The Portland, Oregon–based organization operates in 40 countries and employs around 4,000 employees, fewer than 200 of whom are based in the United States. The agency deploys talent to where it is needed, which may mean sending African employees to work in the Middle East or Indonesian employees to South Sudan.

To a degree, all companies struggle with hiring, onboarding, managing, and retaining talent. However, Mercy Corps' HR challenges put it in a category of its own. For example, even though there is a large pool of individuals who are interested in volunteering and making a difference through their work, Mercy Corps is often looking for a specific set of skills as well as experience living and working under dangerous and volatile conditions, leading the organization to compete with other NGOs for a very small pool of talent for hiring. In addition to skills, it seeks characteristics that will make someone resilient and adaptable: Sensitivity, flexibility, curiosity, and emotional stability under pressure are traits it looks for. CEO Neal Keny-Guyer views "cultural intelligence" as a critical competency in hiring.

In addition to finding the right talent, keeping them is another challenge. Once hired, onboarding matters a great deal to ensure that new hires

A Mercy Corps translator at the Melissa Center for migrant women, which offers various classes to refugee women in Athens.

can hit the ground running and be effective quickly. They need to ensure that employees can be transported to safety if problems arise, prevent burnout of employees through regular rest and recovery, and provide extensive training that will enable employees to function effectively in a given geography. For example, field workers are trained on topics such as curfews, travel restrictions, how to interact with locals, and communication procedures during emergencies (often by trainers with a military background). Finally, Mercy Corps cannot solely rely on its meaningful mission to attract and retain workers, given the intense competition for talent among INGOs seeking personnel with similar skill sets. Thus, developing an employer brand that supports and engages employees is among the responsibilities of its HR team.

Given how critical employees are to Mercy Corps' mission, it is no surprise that HR is a strategic partner within the company. To be effective, HR leaders of Mercy Corps need a deep understanding of the company's operations, which may explain the appointment of Nigel Pont, a former regional director for Middle Eastern Operations, to the role of chief people and strategy officer. Part of how Mercy Corps enables business success is to ensure that the local teams are supported by local HR teams and that local HR teams have a voice within the country-level operations.

A key initiative for Mercy Corps is to build in-house expertise in data analytics and ensure that data are harnessed to increase the efficiency of all of its operations. For example, data analytics can be used to forecast how many people will arrive at a specific aid distribution center, ensuring that sufficient staff and resources are available to meet the needs of new arrivals. With the help of a partnership with Cisco, the company aims to make faster, more accurate, and more effective decisions that will help it meet the humanitarian challenges it faces every day.[1]

Case Discussion Questions

1. What do you think the unique and similar challenges are for NGOs versus for-profit companies in terms of HR and HR strategy?

2. What advantages do you think Mercy Corps has in recruiting, hiring, training, and managing employees relative to a domestic business? What are the challenges?

3. Cultural intelligence is the ability to work effectively across cultures. How do you think Mercy Corps can hire based on this skill? How can this skill be developed?

4. How do you think improved expertise in data analytics would affect the HR functions of Mercy Corps?

5. Organizations have a choice in centralizing or decentralizing their operations, including those of HR. To what degree do you think that centralized HR operations would be beneficial for Mercy Corps? Which operations would benefit from centralization? Which ones are better left to the discretion of local teams?

 Click to learn more...

Watch the "culture and values" video of Mercy Corps.
https://www.youtube.com/watch?v=qcBKc3WIMFs

For businesses, national boundaries have been losing their relevance. Many iconic "all-American" brands established in the United States such as Budweiser, 7-Eleven, and IBM now have non-U.S.-based owners. Companies including Intel, Nike, GE, and McDonald's receive more than half their revenue from their overseas sales and operations. HR professionals are increasingly operating in a world in which they need to go outside of the local talent pool for recruitment, learn how to train and manage a global workforce, and ensure that they create HR systems that explicitly consider the context in which they are operating. This chapter discusses international influences on the theory and practice of HRM.

Global markets often represent an important growth opportunity for businesses, providing the chance to reach previously untapped markets. Having access to a global talent pool may make companies more competitive and innovative. Moving production to a different country where labor, land, or raw materials are cheaper may provide advantages from a cost perspective. Regardless of its reasons, doing business globally is fast becoming the norm rather than the exception. Most multinationals have been headquartered in developed countries such as the United States, Europe, and Japan. However, this situation is changing, as exemplified by China-based Sinopec and PetroChina joining the list of largest multinational corporations in the world in terms of revenue.[2]

Global Transfer of HR Practices

Organizations vary in their degree of internationalization. For example, *international companies* export and import, but their investments are within one home country. Most large firms these days are international given that they source at least some materials from overseas. *Multinational companies* operate in multiple countries but with clearly designated headquarters in their home country. The headquarters typically set the standards for how host-country or subsidiary operations will function. Examples include Ikea (based in Sweden) and Amazon (based in the United States). *Transnational companies* have operations in multiple countries. However, they act like a borderless company and do not consider any one country as the center of operations. These businesses are more decentralized and adapt their operations following the best practices that may emerge from different operations. Transnationals are a type of multinational organization. Examples include Nestlé and Unilever. Internationalization is not only occurring in private-sector and for-profit organizations. In fact, even universities are becoming multinational: Georgia Institute of Technology has a campus in Lorraine, France, and Carnegie Mellon University has a campus in Rwanda, Africa.[3]

An important trend resulting in internationalization of businesses is *offshoring*. Companies often find that producing physical goods or performing some of their operations overseas has cost advantages. As a result, they may move some of their operations to an overseas location. Offshoring may help companies to deal with talent shortages in local markets as well, such as the shortage in engineering and sciences graduates in the United States. Offshoring is more likely to occur when decision makers believe that the infrastructure will be supportive and that they will have access to high-quality and affordable human resources.[4] Note that offshoring is different from and may not involve *outsourcing*. Outsourcing refers to moving some operations of the company to a different company. For example, a company may decide to stop handling its own payroll operations and instead contract another company to provide this service. Outsourcing does not necessarily involve an international operation: A firm may outsource to another company in the same country or region. Offshoring

LO 16.1 Describe the advantages and disadvantages to standardizing HR practices in different locations of a business and barriers to standardization.

International companies
Companies that export or import, but their investments are within one home country

Multinational companies
Companies operating in multiple countries but with clearly designated headquarters in their home country

Transnational companies
Companies that have operations in multiple countries and do not view themselves as belonging to any one country

Offshoring When companies produce physical goods or perform some of their operations overseas

Outsourcing Moving some operations of the organization to a different organization

■ **FIGURE 16.1**   Methods of Achieving Global Integration in a Multinational Organization

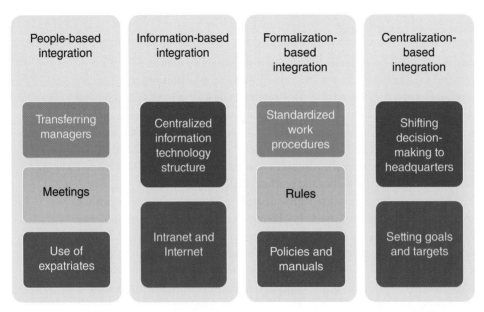

Source: Based on information contained in Kim, K., Park, J. H., & Prescott, J. E. (2003). The global integration of business functions: A study of multinational businesses in integrated global industries. *Journal of International Business Studies, 34,* 327–344.

Global integration When a company standardizes its HR practices around the world

Local differentiation When organizations vary their HR practices in consideration of the local environment

may be combined with outsourcing, such as Apple's use of Taiwanese manufacturer Foxconn to produce its iPhones and iPads.

In a global organization, a key decision that needs to be made with respect to HR practices is striking a balance between ***global integration*** and ***local differentiation***: Should the organization standardize its HR practices around the world? Or should it vary its practices in consideration of the local environment? There are clear advantages to having all units use the same selection, training, performance management, and reward systems so that operations are more consistent and coherent. Having standardized HR practices around the world will prevent efforts to "reinvent the wheel." Global integration ensures that the company establishes a common corporate culture and common ways of doing business, which could be helpful in achieving fairness across different operations. In fact, the desire to transmit headquarter practices to subsidiaries will be strong, because HR practices that are in use at the country of origin will often be perceived as the "right way" of doing business.

Figure 16.1 summarizes different types of methods companies use to transfer HR practices from headquarters to subsidiaries. Companies may transfer their practices across units through the use of people, information technology, standardized procedures and rules, and centralizing particular decisions in one location. For example, an organization interested in globally integrating its diversity-management practices might utilize people-, information-, formalization-, or centralization-based practices. People-based integration could involve ensuring that diversity managers around the globe have regular meetings and coordinate their activities. Information-based integration might entail including similar types of information in the corporate website in different localities. Formalization-based integration could take the form of using diversity-related metrics in performance evaluations around the globe. Finally, centralization-based integration might include drawing up a corporate-level diversity strategy in the headquarters.[5]

At the same time, there are good reasons not to transfer all or even some HR practices and instead follow a local differentiation strategy. For example, headquarter HR practices might not fit with the regulatory or cultural context of subsidiaries. If transported, these practices could make it more difficult to attract or retain employees. In fact, subsidiaries may sometimes develop their own HR practices that the company could be interested in disseminating to other overseas operations or to headquarters. Trying to centralize HR operations might prevent these opportunities from taking place.

There are occasions when headquarters will not try to transfer its policies to other locations. For example, a company that uses unlimited vacation days and telecommuting for headquarters employees may decide not to transfer these practices to overseas operations with the belief (correct or not) that such policies may be too expensive, not fit with the business context, and may be abused given lack of precedence in a particular location. Further, there are instances in which overseas employees may prefer that the company uses headquarters' policies. As a case in point, in countries where informal business practices based on personal relationships dominate the business landscape, multinational firms may be attractive to employers because they will have policies and practices ensuring systematic and procedurally fair decisions in hiring, promotions, and pay. In other words, subsidiary employees may prefer that the firm transfer HR practices from headquarters rather than allow each locality to develop its own. As can be seen, the decision to transfer some or all HR practices to overseas operations is not a simple one.[6]

When considering the question of global integration versus local differentiation, it is important to remember that this is not an "all or nothing" proposition; it is a matter of degree. Companies may choose to standardize some HR practices, whereas other practices may be subject to localization. Further, it is important to distinguish between HR philosophy and HR practices. The company may have HR practices that are adapted to each locality but may also have a centralized HR philosophy guiding HR-related decisions. As long as there is shared understanding about the company's fundamental values with respect to workforce management, the company may differentiate its HR practices yet manage to coordinate effectively across business units.

Important Considerations When Transferring HR Practices Across Borders

When a multinational organization is interested in transferring particular HR practices across borders, it may run into difficulties. Cultural differences, unionization rates, and legal context are three of the many reasons businesses may find that their best practices in one country may not be possible or desirable in other countries.

Legal Context

Even though the discussions of HR-related laws may have led you to believe to the contrary, businesses in the United States actually have a lot of freedom regarding talent management. For example, Chapter 10 discusses the principle of employment at will as the norm in most organizations, although its influence has been eroding over time due to several exceptions that have emerged. As a reminder, employment at will is the assumption that employees have the freedom to join and leave organizations any time they like, and businesses have the freedom to hire and terminate employees as they see fit. In contrast, in Europe, the commonly held assumption is that businesses need to be monitored, controlled, and constrained so that they do not harm employees. There are simply more protections for employees that constrain the autonomy of European businesses. For example, terminating an employee in Europe for any reason requires following specific procedures, giving employees advance notice, and providing generous severance pay. Most other countries around the world mandate paid time off for employees and new parents. The employee–organization relationship in the United States is often based on terms set by the company in negotiation with the employee, which is an assumption that is not necessarily the case in many other countries.

Differences in the legal environment may be as fundamental as whether a specific worker is an employee. Whether someone is an employee or not is an important distinction, as employee status

LO 16.2 Examine the considerations an organization should make when expanding its business practices across borders such as cultural differences, unionization rates, and legal context.

usually confers specific rights. Someone who is considered a contractor or a freelancer in one context may have to be recognized as an employee in a different national context, requiring the organization to modify its HR practices. For example, the ride-hailing company Uber is battling a lawsuit in the United Kingdom, where in 2017, the employment tribunal found that drivers should be recognized as "workers," because of the amount of control Uber exerts over drivers. "Worker" is a legal status in between self-employment and employee and comes with rules around working hours, minimum wage, mandatory break periods, and paid holidays.[7] France is a country with strong protections for workers. The workweek is limited to 35 hours, and employees have the "right to disconnect," or have the right to hours during which they are not required to check or answer e-mail.[8]

Unionization Rates

Chapter 14 discusses the decline of union membership in the United States, with labor union membership among the lowest in the world as a percentage of the workforce. Unlike the 10% seen in the United States, this rate was over 90% in Iceland, 55% in Belgium, 26% in Canada, and 13% in Mexico as of 2017.[9] Further, European Union law requires most companies to establish employee representation committees. This means that having an adversarial relationship with the union will make it very difficult to conduct business. Instead, when operating in countries with a strong tradition of unions, businesses need to involve union representatives in their decision-making process and follow more participatory approaches to management.

Cultural Differences

HR practices that work well in one context may also be difficult to transfer to other contexts due to differences in culture. A Dutch researcher, Geert Hofstede, conceptualized national culture as consisting of four dimensions (later versions added more dimensions), as shown in Table 16.1.

TABLE 16.1   Dimensions of Culture Based on Hofstede's Framework

DIMENSION	DEFINITION	EXAMPLE OF COUNTRIES HIGH AND LOW ON THIS DIMENSION
Individualism versus collectivism	The degree to which individuals define themselves as individuals as opposed to through their relationships. Collectivists emphasize loyalty to the group, face saving, and cooperation within the in-group.	Highly individualistic: Australia, US, UK Highly collectivistic: Ecuador, Guatemala, West Africa
Power distance	The degree to which the society accepts power in the society is distributed unequally and hierarchy is naturally accepted.	High power distance: Guatemala, Panama, Philippines, Romania, Slovakia Low power distance: Austria, Denmark, Israel
Uncertainty avoidance	The degree to which the society feels uncomfortable with uncertainty and risk and emphasizes procedures or traditions to deal with it.	High uncertainty avoidance: Australia, Greece, Guatemala, Portugal, Uruguay Low uncertainty avoidance: Denmark, Jamaica, Singapore
Masculinity versus femininity	Masculine cultures are those that embrace values such as achievement and materialism. Feminine cultures emphasize modesty, caring for the weak, and quality of life.	Highly masculine cultures: Japan, Slovakia Highly feminine cultures: Costa Rica, Netherlands, Norway, Sweden

Sources: https://www.hofstede-insights.com/models/national-culture/; https://harzing.com/download/hgindices.xls

Note that countries are not homogeneous with respect to cultural values: Some cities, regions, or different segments of the population will show variability. Still, the differences across countries with respect to average cultural values are important to consider.

When transferring HR practices that are regarded as highly successful in one location to cultures that are different from the country of origin, cultural differences may serve as a barrier. For example, overall, the United States is a highly individualistic, relatively highly masculine culture, with moderately low values in power distance and uncertainty avoidance. (Definitions of these values are in Table 16.1.) Let's say that a U.S.-based multinational is doing business in Colombia. Colombian culture is collectivistic and has higher power distance and uncertainty avoidance relative to the United States. The two countries are about the same in terms of masculinity, which suggests that both cultures are similarly materialistic. As a result, motivating individual employees through material awards is not very different between the two countries. However, the high level of collectivism in Colombia makes it more of a challenge to transfer reward systems that pit individuals against each other such as in individual sales competitions.

Some countries have specific traditions and norms around particular HR practices, necessitating that multinational companies adopt local practices. For example, in many countries in Asia, structured annual recruitment of new college graduates is widely practiced. Major companies hire a cohort of new graduates and subject them to specific and preplanned developmental experiences, preparing them for future managerial roles. Job applicants will expect major firms to follow this practice, and failing to adopt this practice may serve as a disadvantage in hiring. As a result, companies headquartered in a specific country may adopt certain selection practices regardless of their country of origin when they operate within a particular geography.[10]

Management practices may also be interpreted differently in different cultural contexts. For example, a flat organizational structure, absence of managerial supervision, and having a lot of autonomy over one's work may be regarded as empowering in cultures that emphasize low power distance. However, in cultures that emphasize high power distance such as India, the same practices may be disappointing to workers because they afford fewer opportunities for promotions and career growth. Japanese employees may react negatively to telecommuting and work-from-home arrangements because in their culture, work is expected to happen at the office, and Japanese homes are traditionally small, leaving little room for a home office to be set up. Organizations interested in transferring HR practices may benefit from considering the suggestions in Figure 16.2.

■ **FIGURE 16.2** Suggestions for Facilitating the Transfer of HR Practices Into Different Cultural Contexts

Explain the intent behind practices.

Consider having a cultural liaison to interpret the practice and provide support.

Provide space for experimentation and learning from failures.

Do not blame employees for failing to embrace a practice that may be a misfit for their cultural context.

Source: Based on information contained in Hinds, P. (2016, June 27). Research: Why best practices don't translate across cultures. *Harvard Business Review.* https://hbr.org/2016/06/research-why-best-practices-dont-translate-across-cultures

HR IN ACTION
Leveraging Culture for Success at L'Oréal

Shutterstock.com

Based in France and operating in 140 countries, L'Oréal is a global corporate giant. It employs more than 89,000 workers, and counts the brands Maybelline, Redken, Ralph Lauren (United States), Lancôme and Yves Saint Laurent (France), and Shu Uemura (Japan) among its offerings. Whereas the demand for cosmetics is global, what makes a product appealing in a particular geography varies greatly, requiring any company operating in multiple geographies to master cultural differences. In this arena, L'Oréal has important lessons to offer.

At first glance, L'Oréal does not seem a likely candidate for a textbook case on multiculturalism. The company, in its century-long history, has had only five CEOs, only one of whom was not French. Senior executives typically are promoted from within and count few non-French among them. What makes the difference in the international success of L'Oréal is the deliberate efforts to infuse multiculturalism into its product-development teams. The company brings experienced employees from subsidiaries, recruits from competitors, and new hires from top international business

schools to its product development operations. Candidates for these positions receive a year-long training in Rio de Janeiro, Singapore, Paris, or New York, then take part in a management-development program before being placed in their teams in the Paris headquarters. After working in these teams for a few years, these employees are placed back in its home-country operations as director-level employees. Using this methodology, the company ensures that it develops a pool of talented and multicultural managers who first are involved in product development and then take charge in subsidiary operations. This approach allows the company to develop future leaders who can create products that fit the local environment while also embracing the company's core values.

At L'Oréal, HR is a distributed function, where different operations around the world have their own HR leads. This approach allows the company to be closer to employees, connect with them more easily, and be more responsive to employee needs in each locality.

Despite all efforts to embrace multiculturalism, employees are the first to admit that it is not always easy, and L'Oréal does not always adopt local norms. For example, the headquarters culture embraces the values of confrontation and disagreement, which is not a good fit with its subsidiaries in Indonesia or Mexico, where harmony is valued. The company offers a program called "Managing Confrontation" to train employees. Even when it goes against employee instincts, the program underlines what the company values are and teaches employees the importance of effectively handling disagreements.[11]

Even though culture matters, it is important not to overestimate the effects of national culture as a reason particular HR practices may not work in a given context. Experts caution that differences in legal context, unemployment rates, and economic conditions may be more important than culture as the reasons why particular practices fail. For example, the reason employees may react negatively to pay-for-performance programs such as bonuses in some contexts may not be a fundamental difference in cultural values but rather the uncertainty

SPOTLIGHT ON ETHICS

Managing Ethics Globally in Multinationals

What do Rolls-Royce, Walmart, Royal Dutch Shell, and SAP have in common? These companies and others have faced investigations of corruption and bribing government officials to facilitate winning government contracts, getting permits, or obtaining licenses. A challenge all multinationals face is to uphold global ethical standards in diverse regions, including locations where anticorruption laws are loosely enforced or nonexistent and bribing government officials is considered a normal way of doing business. How can global businesses ensure that they uphold global principles of ethics in their operations around the world while conducting business effectively?

Global organizations will benefit from enforcing a culture of ethics and integrity throughout their operations. This seems like common sense, given that allowing bribery and corruption in some parts of their operations threatens the culture and reputation of the entire operation. It is also important to remember that even though local businesses may in fact be using bribes to speed the process of approvals or facilitate their operations, multinationals are often held to a different and higher standard in other countries, making their ethics violations all the more damaging. A few steps multinationals can take and HR can facilitate are as follows:

Commitment to a culture of integrity. Multinationals should have top management who value and embrace ethics in global operations. This means a strong commitment for doing the right thing, dealing with unethical actions quickly, and holding people accountable.

Eliminate undue performance pressures. Often, unethical actions are a symptom of pressures for short-term results. When headquarters evaluate

performance of subsidiaries using short-term results such as how quickly a store was opened, pressure increases on local employees to get things done at all costs. It also signals to third parties that the company is in a hurry, giving them leverage to pressure the company.

Providing training and policies. It is important to provide training not only about defining acceptable and unacceptable behaviors but also teaching employees what to do when confronted with questionable requests. Monitoring compliance via committees and audits can also help.

Eliminate a culture of silence. It is important to encourage people to speak up about questionable ethical behaviors. Giving employees anonymous ways of reporting unethical behaviors and ensuring that reports are followed by action will help create a culture of ethics.[12]

Questions

1. As an HR professional, suppose you are assigned to arrange for your company's international employees to receive ethics training to define acceptable and unacceptable behaviors and to know what to do when confronted with questionable requests. How would you develop a set of training objectives? Would you hire an outside training vendor, and if so, how would you select the vendor?

2. Find an example in the news or in the HR literature of a global company that was accused of corruption. How was the case resolved? What did the individuals involved do right, and what could they have done better?

---

introduced by economic factors, leading employees to believe that their effort will not lead to higher performance.[13]

Causes and Forms of Internationalization

The reason a company chooses to internationalize is a key consideration in whether the organization chooses global integration in favor of local adaptations.[14] In some organizations, subsidiaries require close coordination with the parent company. Examples of this are Ford or General Motors, which offshore manufacturing in order to take advantage of lower labor costs overseas. Because the cars are manufactured for the global market, ensuring that subsidiaries around the world are closely coordinated with headquarters is important. In other cases, the reason subsidiaries exist is to reach overseas markets, as in the case of global food and beverage companies like Kellogg's and Kraft. Because local responsiveness in product design and marketing is important, the companies may give greater autonomy to subsidiaries and make greater efforts to ensure that HR practices fit the needs of each locality.

When deciding how to approach its HR functions, the amount of autonomy the company has will also depend on the structure of its internationalization efforts. A company may have ***wholly owned subsidiaries*** overseas, giving the parent company full control over its overseas operations. Alternatively, the company may have less control over its overseas operations if it has a ***joint venture*** or a ***strategic alliance***. A joint venture involves two companies coming together and investing to create a new company, whereas a strategic alliance is a partnership with other companies. Joint ventures and strategic alliances have the advantage of allowing the company to access local resources and expertise but will also prevent the organization from exercising complete control over overseas operations.[15]

Wholly owned subsidiaries When an organization has subsidiaries overseas and gives the parent company full control over their overseas operations

Joint venture A joint venture involves two companies coming together and investing to create a new company

Strategic alliance A partnership with other companies

LO 16.3 Identify HRM practices that would benefit from local adjustments and those that would benefit from standardization across borders.

Managing HR Globally

Organizations need to design their HR practices to leverage the advantages of operating in multiple geographies, such as access to a wider talent pool and the ability to transfer expertise across locations. They must also face challenges such as understanding the fundamental cultural, legal, and economic differences and adapting practices accordingly. It is important to note that there are also some best practices that companies could benefit from replicating. For example, researchers contend that giving newcomers an orientation, arriving at pay decisions using systematic analyses, and utilizing salary surveys are among the best practices that may be standardized across operations.[16] In this section, we discuss individual HR practices and important adaptations that often take place when operating globally.

Recruitment and Selection

Operating overseas necessitates hiring employees in diverse national contexts, which could be a major challenge. A key decision that needs to be made is to determine the proper mix of parent

SPOTLIGHT ON GLOBAL ISSUES

Cultural Influences on High-Performance Work Systems

HR practices designed to improve organizational performance are referred to as *high-performance work systems* (HPWS). These systems include selectivity in hiring decisions, investing in training, linking pay with performance, and involving employees in decision making. To what extent should these practices be adapted to the cultural context?

A meta-analysis conducted in 29 countries examined whether these practices had to fit with national culture in order to influence organizational performance. Researchers have shown that there was an overall positive correlation between HPWS and organizational performance. Further, researchers found no support for

the argument that when these practices were a good fit with national culture, their effects were more positive. In fact, the results showed that in highly collectivistic and highly power-distant cultures, presumably contexts in which these practices should not be a very good fit, the effects of HPWS were even more positive.

These findings suggest that there are actually best practices in HRM. The practices covered thus far as "best practices" seem to work regardless of the cultural context in which they are implemented. It appears that investing in people is good practice regardless of context or country.[17]

country nationals, host-country nationals, and third-country nationals to be employed in a specific overseas operation. The degree to which the local labor market meets the multinational's needs will vary by industry and geography, and there are costs and benefits associated with different mixes.

Multinational firms often find that they have to compete with other multinational and local firms for the best talent. A well-known multinational company with positive brand recognition overseas may have a built-in advantage in recruiting local employees, but it also needs to provide a work environment and inducements that are competitive in order to attract talent. As IBM's loss of talent to local firms such as Infosys in India shows, companies should not assume that being well known globally will be sufficient for recruiting the best talent. Alternatively, a firm well known in its country of origin may have little name recognition in the subsidiary location, which may limit the ability to attract talent. Sometimes, the country of origin may serve as a barrier to recruitment. For example, some Indian multinationals operating in industrialized country contexts report experiencing difficulties attracting managerial employees and having to rely on sending expatriates instead of localizing their management team due to negative perceptions of Indian firms as employers with respect to their global image and concerns regarding some corporate policies being a poor fit to the local environments.[18] Organizations will need to invest in developing their brand as an employer and building a good reputation in the markets in which they operate.

Finding the necessary talent is also made difficult in markets in which demand for skilled talent exceeds local availability. Organizations may need to provide in-house training to employees to make them employment ready in localities where educational institutions fall short of meeting the training needs of organizations. At the same time, providing training introduces the problem of poaching by other organizations.[19]

Understanding how local employees expect to find job openings and their expectations for fair compensation will increase the competitiveness of the firm. For example, when educational technology company Blackboard tried to hire employees in the Netherlands, it was surprised by the low response rate its job posting generated, only to realize that in that market and for that job category, hiring was done through staffing agencies—a recruiting approach it hadn't used.[20]

In Europe, Asia, the Middle East, and South America, a company car is often a critical recruitment and retention tool and is intended to meet business and status needs. Determining who is eligible, whether to provide the car or a car allowance, and what make and model to allocate to different job levels requires careful consideration of each local market.[21]

Motivating, Rewarding, and Managing Employees

Multinational companies often differentiate their reward systems and benefits around the world in order to fit the national context. To begin with, businesses need to be aware of differences in legal requirements that affect compensation practices. In many parts of the world, companies are mandated to provide 13th- or 14th-month bonuses (e.g., Brazil, Costa Rica, and Ecuador). In other countries, providing these bonuses is customary (e.g., Austria and Japan). Typically, these amount to 1/12 of the employee's pay. Different countries will have different requirements relating to who is eligible for 13th- or 14th-month bonuses, and payment schedules vary.[22]

Having extrinsic rewards that fit a given context is essential for attracting and retaining talent. In addition to cultural differences, workforce demographics may necessitate regional adaptation. For example, some countries have aging populations: Japan and Germany have populations with a median age of 47, whereas India, Ecuador, and South Africa have a median age of 27.[23] Such differences will inevitably affect benefits packages and workplace conditions employees find desirable.

At the same time, some benefits that are popular in the United States are finding positive reception in other contexts as well. As a case in point, historically, global firms relied on Social Security provided by local governments and avoided providing retirement benefits, but this is changing. According to Willis Towers Watson 2016 International Pension Plan Survey, 13% of the 668 firms surveyed reported that they cover local employees in their retirement plans.[24] Multinational firms are finding that by establishing defined-contribution plans similar to 401(k) plans (see Chapter 13), multinational firms may experience recruitment and retention advantages. In contexts such as Russia, companies experience tax advantages when they set up defined-contribution retirement programs. Companies may need to make adaptations to the local context, such as investing the funds overseas if permissible and determining if the local financial system is unstable.[25]

Employee Separations

Organizations that operate in multiple countries need to be aware of differences in how separations are handled, given the differences in labor law. For example, in Europe, employment is regarded as a fundamental right, and taking away that right may not be done in an arbitrary fashion. Given the high levels of unionization and prevalence of works councils (similar to unions) in Europe, organizations need to work with labor representatives in setting up procedures for

---

SPOTLIGHT ON LEGAL ISSUES

The Legal Side of Working Internationally

When managing an international workforce, legal compliance is complicated due to the need to reconcile multiple legal frameworks. Here are a few important considerations:[26]

- When moving an employee overseas either as an expatriate or in short-term operations, the employee will likely need to acquire a work permit or visa.

- When an employee is staying in a different country for 6 months or more, the stay may trigger tax implications for the employer. This means that monitoring short-term assignments is important. U.S. citizens generally pay taxes to the United States regardless of where they work, so this may introduce a double taxation case. Further, many domestic insurance policies cover health care overseas for 6 months, and a different health care policy may be needed for longer assignments.

- EEOC laws discussed in Chapter 4 cover all employees of a U.S. employer working in the United States. For example, a Chinese citizen working in a U.S. firm is covered by EEOC laws. Some non-U.S. employers operating in the United States may be exempt. Foreign organizations operating in the United States

based on a mutual treaty may be permitted to show preference to their own nationals for some positions. Host-country employees of U.S. firms are not subject to EEOC laws (e.g., Japanese employees of a U.S.-based multinational in Japan are not covered), but a U.S. citizen expatriate sent to work in the Japanese operations of a U.S.-based multinational is covered.

- When two laws clash, companies are required to follow the laws of the countries they operate in, even if this means violating the U.S. law.

- Educating employees on local laws is important to protect employees. Toyota found this out the hard way: An American executive moving to Japan was arrested and imprisoned for 20 days on suspicion of illegally importing a prescription painkiller.

- Organizations have a "duty of care," or a moral and legal obligation, to act in ways that will avoid preventable and foreseeable injuries and risks to their employees. Although the legal framework around duty of care varies around the world, taking care of employees proactively will help establish trust and prevent costly legal battles.

terminating employees. Approaching the termination process systematically and respectfully, creating strong employment contracts, specifying how performance and absenteeism are to be handled, and ensuring that notice periods and severance pay follow the national legal requirements in each locality are essential for success.[27]

Handling of Personal Data

Recall from Chapter 3 that European Union countries have implemented General Data Protection Regulation (GDPR), which overhauls how businesses store, safeguard, and use personal data. This law gives more power to individuals and has clear implications for human resource functions that routinely retain, access, and use data about current and former employees as well as job applicants. For example, according to the law, companies need to have consent to store unsuccessful job candidates' details. If they fail to secure consent, companies must remove the data from their records. Employees have the right to access their own personal data with a required maximum turnaround time of 1 month. Companies may be required to designate a data-protection officer depending on the scope of data they handle. Faced with steep penalties for failures in compliance, companies need to make structural changes in collecting, storing, and using employee data.[28]

Management of Expatriates

When doing business internationally, a critically important HR issue relates to the management of expatriates. An *expatriate* (or expat) is a person who is living and working in a different country than their country of origin. Expatriate assignments typically describe a move overseas that is longer than 6 months. In multinational enterprises, expatriates are *organizationally assigned*, or sent by the organization for a predetermined time to work in an overseas operation. Alternatively, a *self-initiated expatriate* is a skilled professional who moves to a different country for a specific period of time with the intention of gaining overseas work experience. Although much can be learned from self-initiated expatriates, note that this chapter focuses on organizationally assigned expatriates, given the importance of HR functions in systematically facilitating the process of effective expatriation.

Benefits and Downsides of Using Expatriates

Expatriate assignments provide a variety of benefits to organizations and individuals. By moving talented employees overseas, companies aim to meet specific business needs and close skill gaps. Moving employees overseas ensures that they gain skills in global management. Completing an overseas assignment successfully may be a boon to the career of the expatriate, helping them develop unique skills and achieve visibility. Expatriate assignments play an important role in knowledge diffusion, such as transferring innovations across units. Expatriates can facilitate direct knowledge sharing across units and indirect knowledge sharing by linking home- and host-country operations and acting as "boundary spanners" that tie units to each other. Research has shown that expatriate assignments in which headquarters employees are assigned to overseas locations facilitate knowledge transfer from the headquarters to host-country operations, whereas host-country employees working in headquarter locations (sometimes referred to as *inpatriates*) facilitate knowledge transfer from local operations to headquarters.[30] Tonya Hallett, the HR director of Cadillac, sees global exposure of employees as

Expatriate A person who is living and working in a different country than their country of origin

Organizationally assigned expatriate When an expat is sent by the organization for a predetermined time to work in an overseas operation

Self-initiated expatriate A skilled professional who moves to a different country for a specific period of time with the intention of gaining overseas work experience

Inpatriates Host-country employees working in headquarter locations

LO 16.4 Summarize the forces affecting adjustment of expatriates to their overseas assignments and identify ways in which organizations can prepare expatriates for successful assignments.

©iStock.com/Pere_Rubi

Employees in sales and marketing at Adidas may apply for the company's Talent Carousel program, allowing them to work in a different country for 2 years, which may be followed by another round of overseas assignment or returning home. The company is planning to open this talent development program to other departments.[29]

key to the company's competitiveness. In a car show in Switzerland, a European driver's remark to a Cadillac employee that the car was not designed for narrow European streets is an example she gives for the value of a global mindset.[31]

At the same time, there are potential downsides to the use of expatriates, and it is important to consider these when deciding whether to deploy expatriates. First, from the organization's perspective, overreliance on expatriates or using expatriates for the wrong types of positions may backfire. For example, research has shown that using expatriates for transfer of knowledge that does not require cultural adaptations (e.g., technical knowledge) facilitates subsidiary performance, whereas using them for types of assignments in which location-specific knowledge is needed (such as marketing knowledge) actually impedes the ability of the subsidiary to benefit from parent company expertise.[32] As discussed earlier, the use of expatriates is a way of transferring home-country practices overseas, and using expatriates may make it difficult to utilize regional knowledge. In other words, the organization should carefully consider whether a local employee is not in fact a better candidate for a given position. Second, expatriate assignments run the risk of failure and necessitate careful planning. Moving to a different country and taking on a new role is stressful, and poor adjustment results in low job satisfaction, low effectiveness, and premature return from the assignment.[33] Finally, expatriate assignments are costly: It is estimated that each international posting may cost as much as twice the salary of the employee, and even higher in the case of failed assignments.[34] Given high costs and risk, understanding factors that facilitate quick adjustment is important to design expatriate assignments effectively.

Expatriate Adjustment

Expatriate adjustment refers to the degree of comfort and lack of stress associated with being an expatriate. Research shows that three forms of adjustment matter for expatriates. ***Cultural adjustment*** refers to adjusting to the new culture one is now living in, including factors such as transportation, entertainment, health system, education, and general living conditions. ***Work adjustment*** involves feeling comfortable at work and with one's new tasks. ***Interactional adjustment*** is the comfort felt with interacting with local individuals inside or outside work. In other words, being successful as an expatriate relies not only on feeling comfortable at work but also on achieving comfort with interpersonal interactions and with general living conditions. Which of these do you think is most important to an expatriate's success? Although work adjustment has the strongest effect on expatriate job satisfaction, the desire to quit the expatriate assignment is most strongly affected by cultural adjustment; simply mastering one's job will not be sufficient for a successful expatriate assignment. Self-initiated and organizationally assigned expatriates have important differences, with the former having greater desire for adventure and confidence living abroad, whereas the latter are more motivated by seeking a career challenge and interest in skill development.[35] Other key factors that affect the pace of adjustment and the degree of adjustment success, including characteristics of expatriates, organizational factors, and nonwork factors, are shown in Figure 16.3.[36]

Spouse Adjustment

Research shows that the biggest influence over an expatriate's cultural adjustment is the adjustment of the spouse. When spouses have difficulty adjusting to the culture, the risk of a premature return increases, suggesting that preparing spouses for the assignment and ensuring that they are ready and willing will have benefits for the success of the experience. In fact, one's family situation and relationships are key reasons mentioned for refusing to accept an expatriate assignment in the first place.[37] Experts suggest that before a move as a family, it is important to be on the same page and discuss how the spouse will spend time, identify sources of social support, inquire into work and social activities for the spouse, and realistically examine the impact of the move for the whole family. If the expatriate is moving alone, then the

Cultural adjustment Adjusting to the new culture one is now living in, including factors such as transportation, entertainment, health system, education, and general living conditions

Work adjustment Feeling comfortable at work and with one's new tasks

Interactional adjustment The comfort felt with interacting with local individuals inside or outside work

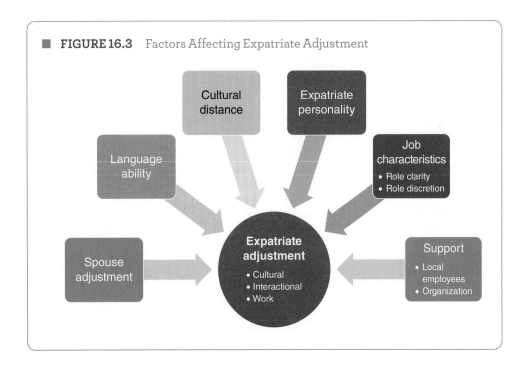

■ **FIGURE 16.3** Factors Affecting Expatriate Adjustment

risk is one of social isolation and loneliness, which necessitates identifying sources of social support prior to and early in the move.[38] Realizing the importance of spouses for expatriate adjustment, many companies have programs that facilitate spouses' adjustment. For example, some companies provide support to spouses in getting a job in the local market as part of their relocation packages. This policy is valuable due to the rise in the number of dual-career couples. In cases in which the spouse is working in the same company, offering jobs for both may be another strategy in providing a type of support that will make a big difference in the adjustment of the expatriate.[39]

Language Ability

Interestingly, research shows a stronger effect for language ability on interactional and cultural adjustment and no effects on work adjustment. In fact, language ability seems to matter for work adjustment primarily when non-English speakers were sent to an English-speaking country, as opposed to vice versa.[40] It is likely that English emerges as the business language in workplaces around the world, so when an English speaker is sent to a non-English-speaking country, their work adjustment is not in serious jeopardy.

At the same time, for all expatriates, not speaking the local language affects one's ability to adjust to the culture and social interactions. Language not only facilitates interpersonal communication, it also affects power and status relationships. For example, research has shown that when multinational companies embrace a language as the official language of the company, those employees who speak that language fluently gain power and status over others who do not speak it well.[41] Further, host-country employees often try to make sense of expatriates' behavior, attempting to understand how well-intentioned they are toward the local employees and how much respect they have toward their culture. One qualitative study in China found that when expatriates showed a willingness to learn the local language, local employees expressed more acceptance toward them. Such effort on the expatriates' part was interpreted as a sign of goodwill. Local employees also respected expatriates who allowed them to speak their native language in meetings, asking for a summary of the discussion at the end, instead of forcing everyone to speak English. Unfortunately, simply good intentions were not sufficient to build relationships over time. Trying but failing to speak the local language resulted in overreliance on a few people to interpret

MANAGER'S TOOLBOX
Being Effective in Global Teams

In global organizations, there is often a need to work across borders. For example, a software development team may include employees from France, Russia, India, and the United States. Here are some tips on how to be more effective in these teams:[42]

1. **Do not confuse language fluency with job effectiveness.** It is likely that the team will include members with varying fluency in the language in which the team communicates. It is important for the team leader to understand that those who are the most articulate are not necessarily the best performers, and valuing their contributions more may affect team morale and sense of fairness.

2. **Be inclusive.** The team leader may create an inclusive climate by deliberately asking questions to the more silent members, giving members time to articulate their thoughts, and asking open-ended questions. The team leader may also frame a question as being within the expertise of some of the silent members of the group, putting them in positions of expertise, which may also encourage the participation of silent members.

3. **Providing cultural training.** Providing training on how culture affects assumptions

and attributions may facilitate more effective communication with those from different cultural backgrounds.

4. **Learn how to "code switch."** Understanding that different cultures have different norms is one thing. Learning how to adapt your behavior to fit the demands of the situation (such as giving more indirect feedback or being more authoritarian than you are used to) without feeling inauthentic is a learned skill. Remind yourself of the importance of understanding and practicing the norms of new contexts you enter. At the same time, be careful to calibrate the switch; it is easy to overswitch, which will introduce problems of its own. For example, knowing that directness is valued in one culture may encourage someone to be overly aggressive and confrontational, potentially damaging relationships.

5. **Invest in relationship development.** When working with those from a different cultural upbringing, mistakes and misunderstandings are bound to happen. Forgiveness is easier to achieve if you have an existing relationship. Relating to your team members and bonding with them is not a waste of time: It is an investment that will pay off throughout the life of the project and beyond.

the work environment and difficulties getting work done and building relationships. Not showing any interest resulted in social isolation and being segregated from the host-country nationals.[43]

Cultural Distance

The cultural distance between one's own country of origin and the destination seems to have a negative effect on adjusting to a new culture.[44] This is perhaps not surprising, as a culture that emphasizes values that directly contradict one's own will pose more challenges. At the same time, it is important to note that cultural similarity may be a double-edged sword. A U.S. expatriate moving to South Korea will certainly encounter unfamiliar situations. At the same time, some potential expatriates will opt out of this move due to expectations of such difficulties, which means that those interested in moving will be the ones who are motivated to invest time and effort in preparing for the move. In contrast, a U.S. expatriate moving to Australia may assume that given the similarity in language, the move will be free of cultural challenges. However, despite speaking the same language, there are clear and important cultural differences between the two countries, and different leadership styles and ways of doing business, which may lead to misunderstandings and frustrations.

Expatriate Personality

The expatriate's social and relational skills affect all three forms of adjustment. Regardless of what their specific job description is, expatriates will need to be able to work with people who are different from themselves and influence them in ways that will facilitate their own adjustment, get accepted, and get things done. This is no small feat and requires exceptional relational skills. Further, the expat's self-confidence matters a great deal for successful adjustment.[46] Researchers also noted that learning-oriented expatriates who view their assignment as a challenge to master and expatriates who are sociable are more likely to seek support from locals, which should help them build a network of supportive relationships.[47]

Job Characteristics

Research shows that the two job-related factors that matter the most to expatriate adjustment are role clarity and role discretion. In other words, there needs to be crystal-clear communication between management and the expatriate with respect to expectations, and expatriates should be given autonomy to perform their jobs effectively.[48]

Support

For successful adjustment of expatriates to their work, two sources of organizational support seem critical: support of the host country employees and support from the organization itself. Support of local coworkers matters a great deal. Local employees are in a position to interact with the expatriate every day, share information, and give tips about how to get things done, facilitating all three forms of adjustment. One of the reasons local employees may choose not to cooperate with expatriates is that expatriates are likely to be classified as "out-group" members by local employees due to their dissimilarity to locals.[49] For example, it has been proposed that Japanese employees are typically very polite to expatriates on the surface but classify expatriates as out-group members, often resulting in expatriates feeling that achieving social integration will not be possible regardless of how hard they try.[50] In order to prevent the new expatriate from being classified as an out-group member, organizations sometimes resort to sending an expatriate with ties to the local context (such as sending an employee who identifies as ethnic Chinese to their operations in China). However, this practice is not always successful and actually may sometimes create even more hostility, envy, or resentment among local employees.[51] Expatriates themselves also play a role in how much support they receive from local employees. Researchers proposed that expatriates who are motivated to seek support from the "right" coworkers who are capable and motivated to help them are likely to establish support networks, facilitating their own adjustment process.[52]

Organizational support is also critical to expatriate adjustment. Expatriates who feel that the organization cares about them, values them, and is invested in them report higher levels of adjustment in their assignments.[53] Organizations can also support expatriates by providing logistical support. This involves taking care of mundane but important details of the move, such as identifying appropriate housing, schools for children moving with the expatriate, opening bank accounts, and other daily details that are bound to create stress for the expatriates.

Preparing Expatriates for Their Assignments

Organizations may do a great deal to facilitate expatriates' adjustment into their new locale in the predeparture stage. Preparation may pay big dividends by facilitating quicker adjustment and preventing premature departures. Organizations will need to ensure that they (a) select the right person, (b) prepare them for the role, and (c) provide ongoing support.

Selecting Expatriates

Historically, companies chose expatriates based on their specific job knowledge and job-related skills. This approach was quickly revealed as misguided, as success in an expatriate assignment takes much more than being good at one's job. Just because someone is good at marketing products in

©iStock.com/typhoonski

A survey of 13,000 people in 188 countries in 2017 ranked Bahrain as the best destination for expatriates. The country is known for being open and friendly to expatriates, and the expatriate population actually outnumbers the local population, creating a diverse and welcoming culture.[45]

Global mindset Refers to being open to learning about different cultures, having a sense of adventure, being comfortable dealing with ambiguity, and having a nonjudgmental attitude toward those from other cultures

In 2017, 11% of Fortune 500 companies had foreign-born CEOs, including Sundar Pichai, CEO of Google, pictured here. Research shows that people with international experience are more effective and creative problem solvers and are promoted faster, pointing to the benefits of expatriate experience for companies and individuals.[56]

Culture shock The feeling of disorientation individuals experience when they enter a new culture

the United States is no guarantee that they will be equally good at doing so in Thailand. Therefore, experts recommend that the selection process also consider personality and social skills. Relational skills, or the ability to build effective relationships with key stakeholders, will be important. A *global mindset* is also important: Individuals who are open to learning about different cultures, have a sense of adventure, are comfortable dealing with ambiguity, and have a nonjudgmental attitude toward those from other cultures are more likely to be successful, and therefore assessing these skills as part of the selection process could be helpful.[54]

Identifying candidates who are excited about serving as expatriates also matters. When few candidates exist for an expatriate position, offering financial incentives may be an option, but companies often feel that pointing to developmental benefits of an expatriate assignment works better. For example, the Mexican multinational CEMEX faced resistance to expatriate assignments in the past, with headquarter employees not wanting to work outside of Mexico. Over time, by communicating the benefits of an expatriate assignment for employees' careers, the company was able to create a pool of interested candidates. Similarly, German multinational Siemens does not pay a financial incentive to accept an overseas assignment to avoid attracting applicants motivated solely by money. Instead, the company requires overseas experience to be promoted above a certain level, resulting in clear career benefits to expatriate assignments.[55]

Cultural Training

An important barrier to effectiveness in a new location is lack of understanding of cultural differences. Expatriates may be frustrated because their normal ways of behaving at work may no longer be appropriate and in fact may generate very different reactions. The feeling of disorientation individuals experience when they enter a new culture is termed *culture shock*. For example, an expatriate who is used to relating to people and building quick relationships with others may realize that the idea of small talk is foreign in cultures such as Germany or Japan. In these cultures, relationships develop over a long period of time through mutually lived experiences and trust. Discussions of weather or traffic, or other lighthearted conversation that does not communicate anything real about the person, will not be useful in building relationships.[57] Understanding these and other cultural differences may facilitate the adjustment process by helping expatriates be attuned to instances in which they need to vary either their own behavior or interpretations of others' actions.

Companies vary in the amount of cultural training they provide, and there are examples of companies that do a thorough job with expatriate training. For example, Nike assigns expatriates and their families a cultural trainer who will stay in touch with them throughout the assignment and help them adjust to and decode the new culture.[58]

Relocation Assistance

The amount of assistance and the form of assistance provided will vary by the level of resources the company can afford, the specific location one is moving into, and the organizational level of the expatriate. For example, moving from one Western country to another will require different resources relative to moving to a big city in China such as Hong Kong, Shanghai, or Beijing. Conversely, different resources are necessary when moving from a large city to a less developed inland city in China such as Chengdu or Wuhan. Moving to a remote location may mean that the expatriate will need to deal with lack of adequate medical care, difficulty identifying international schools for kids, and lack of housing that matches what the expatriate is used to. The more declines expatriates are expected to experience in their quality of life relative to their home country, the more generous the expatriate relocation assistance and pay packages will need to be. Contracting the services of a global relocation services provider may make this process easier and more professional, as HR professionals are rarely experts in employee mobility.

SPOTLIGHT ON HR FOR SMALL AND MEDIUM-SIZED BUSINESSES
Getting Help Going International

Large firms have a lot of built-in resources when they decide to go international. What about a small or medium-sized business going international for the first time? Following are a few resources that could be helpful in this endeavor.[59]

- The U.S. Small Business Administration operates the Office of International Trade, which provides small businesses with support in international trade and offers a variety of resources for this purpose.

- In the country of operations, locate a chamber of commerce for help with local resources.

- Connect with local universities. They may have alumni networks in place that might help with the hiring efforts.

- Consider contracting a relocation assistance firm for any employees who will relocate overseas. Large firms may have in-house staff to handle these operations, which may become a challenge for the smaller enterprises.

Organizations often cap the amount they will pay as relocation assistance. For example, only 42% of companies participating in a survey reported that they pay the entire cost of relocation. This means that relocation services firms had to reduce the types of services they offer to contain costs (e.g., moving hard-to-transport items). Further, companies are more likely to pay a lump-sum amount when expatriates are low-level employees, as opposed to covering the costs on an ongoing basis.[60] Working with a relocation company may help expatriates avoid numerous hassles they would not even expect to encounter during their initial move.

Compensation

Staffing overseas positions with expatriates is expensive. When determining pay packages, it is important to ensure that the expatriate does not suffer a serious financial penalty as a result of accepting the assignment. Key components of the pay package are summarized in Table 16.2. Additionally, benefits such as travel insurance; home, auto, and property insurance; and health insurance must be provided. Expatriate compensation packages have become subject to increased scrutiny over the years, and many organizations have reduced the types of benefits and allowances they provide. For example, in the past, Ford used to allow expatriates to sell their homes to the company at an assessed value. Ford abandoned this policy following the 2008 recession. Although it still covers the full housing costs for expatriates, it does not provide support for the homes that are left behind.[61]

As summarized in Table 16.2, companies make a choice regarding whether to make the home country pay or the host country pay the basis for expatriate pay. The approach chosen will depend on where the assignment is located. For example, assignments taking place in Hong Kong and Singapore are often on a "local-plus" package, given the high salaries, high quality of life, and high cost of living of these locations. The salary is localized, with a few expatriate benefits added to it such as housing and education allowances.[62]

When determining the pay and benefits packages, one size may not fit all, and it is important to consider the issues that are relevant for the expatriate and the family. For one family, educational opportunities for children may be the most important, whereas for another, finding employment for the spouse may be critical. Providing a compensation package that is consistent and fair while also considering the unique needs of each expatriate may increase the success of the assignment. For this purpose, one option is to use a ***coreflex plan***, which provides some services (such as paying for movers and travel expenses) to all expatriates, with the remainder of benefits personalized to the unique situation of the expatriate (such as trips to look for a new house or assistance in identifying private schools). According to one estimate, 9% of companies currently have such plans in place, but these plans are expected to become more popular as companies become more cost conscious.[63]

Coreflex plan A plan that provides some services (such as paying for movers and travel expenses) to all expatriates, with the remainder of benefits personalized to the unique situation of the expatriate

TABLE 16.2   Components of an Expatriate's Compensation Package

COMPONENT	EXPLANATION
Base pay	Most companies use a *home-country-based approach* to determining expatriates' base pay. The expatriate's regular pay in the home country is divided into taxes, housing, savings, and spending components, and the organization makes adjustments so that the employee does not lose money on the move. This approach protects the expatriate from cost differences in the new location. According to SHRM, 76% of all assignments use this approach. In a *host-country-based approach*, the expatriate is treated as a local employee for their salary. This approach is used in 14% of long-term assignments. The *headquarters-based approach* assumes that all expatriates are paid headquarters salaries regardless of location.
Performance-based pay	The expatriate may also be offered financial incentives in recognition of reaching performance targets or stock-based rewards.
Housing allowance	In some locations, the company may offer company-owned housing or pay for the differences between housing in home- and host-country locations. If the employee is moving with their family, this may be a larger allowance.
Cost-of-living adjustment	The employee's pay is adjusted for cost-of-living differences between home and host locations.
Hardship/hazard pay	When employees are assigned to a hazardous location, the pay package also includes hazard pay to compensate for the differences in living conditions and quality of life. This may be 10 to 50% of base pay.
Educational assistance	When local educational options are inadequate, the company may pay for the costs of dependents' educational expenses in a private school or offer a stipend to partly cover the costs.
Home leave	Companies usually cover travel expenses of the expatriate and their family to their home country once a year or more, and in long assignments, they may offer a period of leave to be spent in the home country. This policy will be more generous for expatriates in stressful locations.

Source: Based on information contained in Anonymous. (2017, April 3). Designing global compensation systems. https://www.shrm.org/ResourcesAndTools/tools-and-samples/toolkits/Pages/designingglobalcompensation.aspx

Risk Management

Organizations need to ensure the safety and security of their employees when sending them overseas. The world is increasingly unpredictable, and political turmoil, health risks (remote location, unsanitary conditions), individual high crime rates (murder, theft, break-ins), organized crime (terrorism, gang activities, kidnappings), and natural risks (earthquakes, extreme weather) pose serious threats and uncertainty to companies operating in some regions. Certain areas may pose a threat to expatriates in particular, such as the increasing frequency of kidnappings of expatriates in oil-producing Nigeria.[64] In Latin America and Eastern Europe, someone who is dressed nicely may be subject to an "express kidnapping" in which they are forced to walk to an ATM and withdraw cash.[65] There are also more familiar catastrophes that could occur while the employee is traveling: What happens if the expatriate has a heart attack on the plane? Or the expatriate has a car accident or a family member becomes ill?

Organizations are responsible for ensuring the safety of all employees, and securing the services of professional security consultants may be done in some locations. It may be impossible for a company doing overseas business to eliminate all risks, as many of these are inherent in doing business everywhere and are often unpredictable, but these risks must be managed. Companies should decide whether expatriates need to be sent to a particular location or whether employing local employees is possible. Regardless of whether expatriates or locals are employed, the company will need to take steps to keep employees safe. In some locations, this may involve having work performed in a barricaded compound or hiring bodyguards or providing bulletproof cars. A decision must be made regarding whether families are allowed to accompany the expatriate. Emergency evacuation procedures and protocols should be established. Finally, it is important to explain all the risks involved to prospective employees before they are sent, and proper training should be provided if they choose to accept the assignment.[66]

Special Considerations Relating to Women and LGBTQ Employees as Expatriates

Women constitute 20% of the expatriate population. These numbers depend on location (higher in Asia, lower in Europe and Africa) and industry (higher in consumer goods, lower in energy), but women as a group experience particular challenges as expatriates.[67] Stereotypes about women's unwillingness to serve as expatriates and potential inability to operate in other cultures have been debunked. At the same time, organizational decision makers' worries about sending women as expatriates have been identified as a reason for the lower representation of women among expatriates.[68] Still, in cultures where sexism has been institutionalized, female expatriates report greater problems such as being excluded from social activities, being insulted, and experiencing physical violence.[69]

Research shows that organizational support and absence of family problems serve as buffers for female expatriates dealing with local employees' prejudices.[70] Despite challenges in some locations, organizations are advised against excluding female employees from expatriate opportunities. Instead, organizations may offer training to potential expatriates as well as work to introduce zero-tolerance policies in their subsidiaries regarding discrimination and harassment. By sending the signal that everyone is considered equally for expatriate positions and supported throughout the process, organizations benefit from the talent and skills of all their employees.

Similar concerns exist for LGBTQ employees. Research suggests that many LGBTQ employees are highly motivated to accept expatriate positions and have ways of facilitating their own adjustment such as via connections to the local LGBTQ community.[71] At the same time, serious concerns exist. More than 70 countries criminalize homosexuality, and 13 view it as punishable by death.[72] Thus, LGBTQ employees may also experience hurdles not experienced by other expatriates, such as difficulty obtaining visas for their spouses, lack of legal protection and presence of institutionalized harassment, and possibilities for social exclusion. Obtaining current information regarding legal and social climate in the target location is important. The organization should educate prospective expatriates regarding what to expect, provide resources that are inclusive in language and content (such as spousal-support policies inclusive of same-sex couples and their children), and provide information and support throughout the assignment.[73]

Repatriation

In many cases, the conclusion of the expatriate assignment means repatriation, or relocating the expatriate to their country of origin. The repatriation process presents challenges. Expatriates are valuable to their companies given the investments the company made in their career development. However, many companies have difficulty retaining expatriates. According to one estimate, 38% of expatriates leave their company within 1 year of their return.[74]

Sometimes, repatriation is a challenge because expatriates may not be interested in going back. This may be due to financial reasons: An employee who is relocated from India to the United Kingdom will likely have had their salary adjusted to the higher-cost location, which means that they will experience a significant pay cut when they return to India. Further, expatriates may not have a desirable job waiting for them when they return home. In most cases, the company will have to find a new job for them, as their old job would have already been filled by someone else, and they may have outgrown their former job. Research has shown that perceptions of underemployment in the job they return to was a precursor to turnover intentions among expatriates.[75] Upon return, expatriates may also experience a ***reverse culture shock***. Expatriates may find that they have changed during the assignment and that their home country and company have also changed during their absence, resulting in the feeling that their country of origin does not feel like home anymore.

Unfortunately, despite the cost of an expatriate assignment to a company, organizations do not always approach repatriation of expatriates in a systematic way and often do not know what to do with expatriates once they return. For example, a study by Ernst & Young suggested that 47% of responding companies reported doing little to help expatriates reintegrate into the company.[76] Given that employees increasingly regard their careers as boundaryless (as opposed to specific to

Reverse culture shock
A situation in which expatriates return to their country of origin and find that their country of origin does not feel like home anymore

one organization), it is not surprising that when organizations are unable to absorb the additional experience and skills employees develop during an international assignment, they are likely to leave.

LO 16.5 Identify alternatives to long-term relocation assignments.

Alternatives to Long-Term Relocation Assignments

Instead of sending expatriates on long-term assignments, organizations are increasingly designing short-term assignments to contain costs and reduce the disruptive effects of long-term stays on employees and their families. Instead of sending an employee as an expatriate for 3 years, the company may choose to send them for 3 months, extending the stay as needed or sending the employee multiple times. Extended business travel may be a useful way to meet short-term staffing needs. For example, tax season in Germany is in September, whereas it is in April in the United States, so KPMG brings in tax professionals from Germany to the United States to meet the high seasonal demand. eBay sends U.S.-based employees to Europe to cover for employees on maternity leave. Walmart has Action Learning Groups in which teams are sent to a region to solve specific business problems. It also has short-term internship programs of 12 weeks in different countries to ensure that best practices are shared.[78]

"Global nomads," or employees who move from country to country across different assignments, are on the rise, introducing challenges with respect to ensuring continuous medical coverage and retirement benefits for these employees, who may not have a home base.[77]

Short-term assignments usually do not have much of the organizational support involved for expatriates: Typically there is no adjustment in pay or relocation allowances, and the company's investment may be limited to travel expenses for the expatriate to and from the location. Short-term assignments are also less burdensome for employees. In particular, employees with families may benefit from such assignments given the difficulty of moving an entire family overseas for several years. In short-term assignments, the employee's permanent job will usually not be given away, so repatriation will not be as challenging. The employee will typically retain their regular reporting relationships but most likely will also report to a local manager as well. As long as such arrangements meet business needs, there may be advantages for businesses (low cost) and employees (low risk while also carrying developmental benefits).[79]

SPOTLIGHT ON DATA AND ANALYTICS

Tracking Expatriates Around the World

A volcano is erupting in Bali. Do you know where your employees are? This question may not have an easy answer for global firms that operate in multiple countries and those that have expatriates, frequent business travelers, and "global nomads" who do not even have a permanent place of assignment.

In addition to knowing where everyone is physically, companies need to ensure that their expatriate experience is managed smoothly. This means making sure that every paycheck is correct, preassignment experiences and requirements are checked off, visas are valid, and medical benefits are up to date.

Each expatriate assignment generates valuable data that companies can utilize to continuously improve

the experience and manage the repatriation process. Expatriate satisfaction surveys, turnover data, and performance data may be analyzed to gain clues as to which systematic problems exist in each country of operations.

Tracking such data may be handled via Excel or other in-house products. For companies that employ hundreds of expatriates, investing in tracking technology is another option. Regardless of the method used, integrating data generated from expatriates with the remainder of HRIS systems will provide benefits by making sense of how the company is managing the expatriate experience and what keeps expatriates committed to the company.[80]

Cross-border commuters represent another alternative to expatriate assignments. Employees may work in a different country during the week, returning home on weekends. These arrangements are popular in Europe. For example, it is not unusual for an employee to live in Italy and work in Switzerland. Such arrangements are often outside of formal mobility programs, but they still must be monitored. The company needs to comply with tax-withholding requirements in multiple countries, ensure that the employee has the appropriate work permit, and fulfill data privacy and legal requirements.[81] Companies often find that these programs are expensive, given the need to pay for a hotel or a serviced apartment and to pay for travel during peak travel periods.[82]

In conclusion, increasing globalization of businesses introduces novel challenges for management of human resources. Managing a workforce that transcends local borders and managing employees who are mobile across borders are only two common challenges and ways in which HR can add value to businesses.

CHAPTER SUMMARY

HR faces many challenges when business goes global. One challenge is to determine the proper balance of global integration and local differentiation. There are advantages to standardizing HR practices, but local laws, differences in attitudes toward unions, national culture, and the reason the company chose to internationalize will influence how much standardization is appropriate. When operating in different countries, recruitment and selection, separations, compensation, and treatment of employees must consider local norms. An important HR challenge is to manage mobility of employees, either through short-term or longer-term expatriate assignments. There are both benefits and disadvantages to hiring expatriates. HR can add value by recognizing various kinds of adjustments expatriates and their families must make and by providing preparation and cultural training. Finally, organizations can be creative in devising alternatives to long-term relocation assignments.

KEY TERMS

international companies 545
multinational companies 545
transnational companies 545
offshoring 545
outsourcing 545
global integration 546
local differentiation 546

wholly owned subsidiaries 552
joint venture 552
strategic alliance 552
expatriate 555
organizationally assigned expatriate 555
self-initiated expatriate 555
inpatriates 555

cultural adjustment 556
work adjustment 556
interactional adjustment 556
global mindset 560
culture shock 560
coreflex plan 561
reverse culture shock 563

Visit **edge.sagepub.com/bauer** to help you accomplish your coursework goals in an easy-to-use learning environment.

- Master the learning objectives using key study tools
- Watch, listen, and connect with online multimedia resources
- Access mobile-friendly quizzes and flashcards to check your understanding

HR REASONING AND DECISION-MAKING EXERCISES

MINI-CASE ANALYSIS EXERCISE: DEVELOPING A GLOBAL MINDSET

Your company recently started marketing its products in different overseas markets, including China and France. Realizing that international expansion will drive the future of business, your CEO wants to make sure that managers over a certain organizational level all have "a global mindset." One idea the CEO has is to require all managers above a certain level to have at least 6 months of overseas experience to qualify for a promotion.

You are not really sure whether this is the right strategy. You worry that this will lead some high-potential individuals to quit or to feel resentment and a sense of unfairness. You agree that a global mindset is important to the future of business, but is requiring international experience for all managers the right way to go about ensuring it?

What would you advise your CEO that the company do? Develop a concrete proposal about how to develop a global mindset in the company and provide justification for your plan. Be sure to include a discussion of the resource requirements of your plan.

HR DECISION ANALYSIS EXERCISE: EXCEPTIONS TO THE RULE?

Your company is managing 100 expatriates located in 10 different countries. In an effort to approach the treatment and compensation of expatriates systematically, your company has strict rules around what the company will and will not pay for regardless of country. For example, the company specifically pays for housing of the immediate family and educational expenses of children. In addition, the company limits the number of trips back to the United States it will pay for. These rules are relatively specific and inflexible in order to achieve fairness among employees.

Requests for three exceptions to these rules have come across your desk for three expatriates based in Zurich. One employee would like to bring his mother from Egypt, as he is an only child and sole caretaker for his mother. This would mean moving the family to bigger housing and paying for the extra travel expenses. Another employee would like her child to attend nursing school during the relocation. A third expatriate wants to secure an extra trip to the United States to attend her grandmother's 100th birthday. However, the company directive is clear not to make exceptions. Analyze these company policies for expatriates in light of these requests.

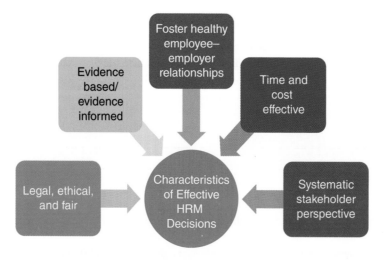

Please provide the rationale for your answer to each of the questions below.

Are the policies legal, ethical, and fair?

Are they evidence based/evidence informed?

_____

_____

_____

_____

Do they foster healthy employee–employer relationships?

_____

_____

_____

_____

Are they time and cost effective?

_____

_____

_____

_____

Do they take a systematic stakeholder perspective?

_____

_____

_____

_____

Considering your analysis above, overall, do you think refusing to make exceptions would be an effective decision? Why or why not?

_____

_____

_____

_____

What, if anything, do you think should be done differently or considered to help make this decision more effective?

_____

_____

_____

_____

HR DECISION-MAKING EXERCISE: ASSESSING THE EFFECTIVENESS OF EXPAT MANAGEMENT

You are the HR director of Moore Markets, a grocery retailer that is in the process of overseas expansion. The company is U.S. based and just opened up several stores and branch offices in Mexico, Canada, China, and Germany. You currently have more than 50 expatriates working in these countries. These employees have been deployed as needed, working on assignments that will last anywhere between 1 and 3 years. Anecdotally, you know that a few expatriates who repatriated from these assignments will quit within 6 months. You also know that several expatriates cut their assignments short and asked to return early. Expatriates also voiced concerns that local employees often compare their pay and benefits with what they perceive as generous expatriate packages, expressing resentment. You realize that you are not really tracking the return on investment of expatriates. You do not really know whether your company is doing a good job managing expatriates and whether the company is having systematic problems with them.

Questions

1. How would you go about measuring the effectiveness of your expatriate program? What type of information would you collect, and how? Develop a plan to collect the information you need.

2. Would you assess whether you are sending the right employees for these assignments? Describe what steps you would follow.

3. Effectiveness of expatriates relies on their ability to cooperate with local employees, and perceived unfairness and resentment on the part of locals could hamper expatriate effectiveness. What can you do to prevent such resentment?

DATA AND ANALYTICS EXERCISE: MANAGING EXPATRIATES USING DATA

Ettinger Manufacturing currently has 30 expatriates working in three countries. They perform similar jobs, and they started their expatriate assignments at about the same time. A sample of the data collected from them is shown here. What would you do with such data to understand how best to manage expatriates at Ettinger Manufacturing?

EXPATRIATE ID	ASSIGNMENT SATISFACTION	FAMILY SATISFACTION	PAY SATISFACTION	COWORKER SATISFACTION	RECEIVED PREDEPARTURE TRAINING (1 = YES)	LOCATION
1	4.57	3.55	2.70	2.85	1	Turkey
2	5.00	3.00	3.30	2.55	1	Turkey
3	4.14	3.19	3.00	3.19	1	Turkey
4	4.71	3.56	3.38	2.88	1	Turkey
5	4.57	4.13	3.13	3.25	1	Turkey
6	4.57	4.31	3.06	1.81	1	Turkey
7	4.14	3.00	2.58	1.50	0	Turkey
8	3.00	2.69	3.38	1.63	1	Turkey
9	1.57	1.38	1.50	1.13	0	Turkey
10	2.71	3.42	3.08	1.08	0	Turkey
11	3.14	2.50	3.31	1.31	1	Canada
12	3.86	2.88	3.00	1.88	1	Canada
13	3.86	2.83	2.67	1.17	0	Canada
14	2.71	1.95	2.05	1.40	0	Canada
15	3.86	3.25	2.25	1.80	1	Canada
16	3.57	2.82	2.57	1.57	1	Canada
17	4.71	4.00	2.42	1.17	0	Canada
18	4.86	3.50	1.69	1.13	0	Canada
19	4.00	3.15	2.05	1.55	1	Canada

EXPATRIATE ID	ASSIGNMENT SATISFACTION	FAMILY SATISFACTION	PAY SATISFACTION	COWORKER SATISFACTION	RECEIVED PREDEPARTURE TRAINING (1 = YES)	LOCATION
20	2.71	2.63	2.13	1.63	0	Canada
21	4.00	2.78	2.84	1.84	0	Spain
22	3.00	1.38	2.13	1.50	0	Spain
23	3.50	1.90	2.70	1.20	1	Spain
24	3.57	2.50	1.38	1.00	1	Spain
25	3.29	2.75	2.63	2.38	1	Spain
26	3.00	2.75	2.63	1.63	1	Spain
27	4.86	4.06	2.75	2.19	1	Spain
28	4.43	3.19	3.00	1.94	1	Spain
29	4.57	3.69	3.44	2.38	0	Spain
30	4.00	3.50	2.94	2.44	0	Spain

 EXCEL EXTENSION: NOW YOU TRY!

- On **edge.sagepub.com/bauer**, you will find these same data in an Excel sheet. Analyze these data and consider what your recommendations would be to management. Consider using regression, *t*-test, and one-way analysis of variance in your analyses. Questions you could consider by analyzing the data include:

  ○ Does expatriate satisfaction depend on which country they are assigned to?

  ○ What factors are significantly related to expatriate satisfaction?

  ○ Do you find that training expatriates before departure is useful?

CHAPTER 16 SUPPLEMENT: DESIGNING GLOBAL COMPENSATION SYSTEMS

Retrieved from https://www.shrm.org/resourcesandtools/tools-and-samples/toolkits/pages/designingglobalcompensation.aspx

TOOLKITS

DESIGNING GLOBAL COMPENSATION SYSTEMS

Scope—This article highlights some of the considerations related to designing compensation plans for globally mobile employees. It discusses the primary design elements for compensating employees on international assignments. It does not discuss other numerous elements of managing expatriates, such as hiring, training, motivating, communicating and repatriating.

Overview

An international assignment compensation system has to finely balance adequately rewarding and motivating expatriates while keeping costs under control for corporate headquarters. The cost of a three-year international assignment can easily exceed $3 million.

Because of the enormous investment, developing a comprehensive global compensation system for expatriates is one of the most critical challenges facing global human resource management.

Developing a Compensation Philosophy and Strategy

Companies with multinational operations need to develop compensation plans for employees that are in line with their global business strategy. Companies that articulate a clear global pay philosophy and develop corresponding compensation programs are best positioned to effectively execute their strategy. An effective global compensation strategy creates consistency in pay management and facilitates global employee mobility.

Establishing guidelines and practices with consistent communication of key messages is vital to the success of the compensation program.

Although multinational employers are striving to globalize their compensation practices, local and regional approaches to international pay are still most common.

Approaches to Global Compensation

International assignment compensation has many moving parts and is difficult to standardize. Many factors affect the compensation of a particular expatriate, including assignment type and length, location, family needs (if any), and benefits. The main compensation items for expatriates involve base pay, cost-of-living adjustments, housing allowances, home leave, education assistance for dependents and premium pay.

The U.S. Department of State indexes the living costs abroad, quarters allowances, hardship differentials and hazard pay allowances. The information, published quarterly, is used by many organizations to assist in establishing private compensation systems.

Compensation Plan Elements

A global compensation plan includes elements typical of any rewards strategy along with a few extra incentives and allowances, depending on the host country.

Base pay

When an employee accepts an international assignment, it is up to the employer to determine the base rate of pay (referred to as the base salary). The base salary is normally related to pay ranges in the home country, which then may be adjusted based on local variances (i.e., fluctuations in the economy). Companies take one of the following approaches to establish base salaries for expatriates:

- **The home-country-based approach.** The objective of a home-based compensation program is to equalize the employee to a standard of living enjoyed in his or her home country. The 2016 Cartus Global Mobility Policy & Practices Survey found that 76 percent of long-term assignments and 75 percent of short-term assignments use a home country pay structure.[1] Under this system, the employee's base salary is broken down into four general categories: taxes, housing, goods and services, and discretionary income.

- **The host-country-based approach.** With this approach, the expatriate employee's compensation is based on local national rates. Many companies continue to cover the employee in its defined contribution or defined benefit pension schemes and provide housing allowances. Only 14 percent of long-term assignments and 5 percent of short-term assignments base pay on local rates, according to the Cartus survey.[2]

- **The headquarters-based approach.** This approach assumes that all assignees, regardless of location, are in one country (i.e., a U.S. company pays all assignees a U.S.-based salary, regardless of geography). Cartus found that a small percentage of companies use headquarters-based approaches for long-term assignments (4 percent) and short-term assignments (5 percent).[3]

- **Balance sheet approach.** In this scenario, the compensation is calculated using the home-country-based approach with all allowances, deductions and reimbursements. After the net salary has been determined, it is then converted to the host country's currency. Since one of the primary goals of an international compensation management program is to maintain the expatriate's current standard of living, developing an equitable and functional compensation plan that combines balance and flexibility is extremely challenging for multinational companies. To this end, many companies adopt a balance sheet approach. This approach guarantees that employees in international assignments maintain the same standard of living they enjoyed in their home country. A worksheet lists the costs of major expenses in the home and host countries, and any differences are used to increase or decrease the compensation to keep it in balance.

Some companies also allow expatriates to split payment of their salaries between the host country's and the home country's currencies. The expatriate receives money in the host country's currency for expenses but keeps a percentage of it in the home country currency to safeguard against wild currency fluctuations in either country.

Variable/incentive compensation

The globalization of business has increased the use of variable and incentive pay around the world. But some cultures do not readily accept the practice of linking pay to individual or group performance. Other roadblocks to pay for performance include financial (not enough funding of the pool), target setting (defining performance parameters) and pay equity. Yet when it is done right, pay for performance effectively allocates limited rewards and retains top performers. As such, variable pay has become an increasingly important compensation element in many countries.

Variable pay plans generally fall into one of two categories:

- Short-term incentive plans are usually annual plans that link awards based on meeting individual or group performance criteria and objectives. Unlike long-term plans, these incentive pay plans provide for the payout to be awarded yearly.

- Long-term incentive plans, on the other hand, can vary in length from three to five years. These plans typically include equity-based incentives, such as stock options, restricted share grants and other types of equity-based plans like phantom stocks or stock appreciation rights. Awards are closely linked to the achievement of company goals and objectives over the three- to five-year period.

Participation and eligibility for each type of plan, as well as the level of incentives and average payouts, vary greatly among different companies, industries and countries around the world.

Premiums and allowances

Premiums and allowances are added to the base salary so expatriate employees can maintain their standard of living. Those add-ons are removed when the employee repatriates. Some types of premiums and allowances are as follows:

- **Hardship and hazard/danger pay.** Employers sometimes need to send employees on assignments to host countries where conditions are difficult or hazardous (i.e., remote locations or countries with high rates of violence). As a result, a hardship allowance may be granted as an additional incentive to compensate employees for accepting assignments in less-than-desirable countries. Premiums typically range from 10 percent to 50 percent of base pay, depending on the severity of the hardship. For assignments in developing countries that have a history of violence or are experiencing political unrest, expatriates often receive some form of hazard pay, such as an additional 25 percent of their base salary.

- **Cost-of-living adjustments.** A cost-of-living adjustment is an increase or decrease of an expatriate employee's pay in response to fluctuations in the economy, such as inflation or deflation. To prevent attrition of the global employee's purchasing power, companies often raise the employee's base salary to keep up with inflation. When price levels drop, companies may also decrease the base salary accordingly.

- **Educational assistance.** Educational assistance for dependents of expatriate employees varies based on conditions in the host country. Assistance is usually not provided if local educational institutions are deemed adequate. When the educational system of the host country is substandard, employers may use a variety of benefits, such as employers operating a school in the foreign country; paying for dependents' educational expenses, including room and board, to attend schools in the United States; or providing an allowance for attendance at private schools in either the United States or the host country. Other employers may simply choose to pay employees a specified amount (stipend) considered necessary for schooling at the nearest adequate school, and the employees make up any difference to send their dependents to an institution of their choice.

- **Housing assistance.** Assistance for housing is usually provided either in the form of free company-owned housing or via a housing allowance that is typically equal to the difference in housing costs between the home and host countries or based on a specified percentage of an employee's base salary. Housing allowance rates are usually calculated based on either a single person or a two-person household. For employees with larger families living with them, employers may provide an additional supplement, typically ranging from 10 percent to 30 percent of the two-person allowance.

- **Home leave.** The objective of home leave policies is to give the assignee and his or her family the opportunity to maintain personal and business relationships and remain abreast of any economic, political, social or cultural changes in the home country. Although home leave policies vary among multinational corporations, most policies grant leave based on the employee's level within the organizational structure. Executives, managers and more senior-level professionals are most often granted home leave once a year, or once every other year for a duration of up to four weeks, and lower-level employees may be allowed only a single visit during the course of their assignment. Companies that provide home leave allowances generally purchase or reimburse the employee for any travel-related expenses, such as airline tickets for the employee, spouse or partner and any dependent children younger than college age.

Benefits

Global benefits for expatriates can be complicated for HR professionals to navigate, given the myriad national health care and pension systems and the laws governing foreign residents.

Health care plans

Health care coverage can pose significant challenges for expatriate employees because not all U.S. health care plans provide coverage for employees residing abroad. For this reason, the practice of providing health care benefits varies greatly among multinational companies. Multinational companies can provide coverage to employees in one of the following ways:

- Include the assignee in an international health care plan.
- Continue coverage under the U.S. health care plan.
- Provide coverage for the employee through a host country health care plan.

Retirement plans

Regardless of the compensation approach a multinational company chooses to adopt, most companies commonly provide assignees with the same level of Social Security and pension plan benefit coverage, without any interruption in service, as enjoyed by other employees in the home country location.

Some countries require expatriate employees to participate in their social security or other government welfare benefit schemes. In this case, many companies provide for reimbursement of any payments made to the host country's government scheme.

Spousal/partner assistance

Since approximately half of all U.S. marriages are dual-earner partnerships, dealing with international assignments can pose significant challenges for the trailing spouse or partner, the expatriate employee and the sponsoring organization.

Trailing spouses face many challenges to finding suitable employment in the host country, including language and legal barriers as well as differences in educational, professional or licensing requirements.

Assistance with job searches, visas or work permits, career and educational counseling, and resume writing are just a few examples of the types of assistance a multinational employer can provide spouses or partners of transferring employees. A less common approach is to offer a financial sum to spouses of expatriate employees for any loss of income resulting from the relocation.

Training

Other add-ons that are less commonly offered but can significantly ease expatriate package negotiations include cultural competence training, language training and repatriation assistance.

Cross-cultural training

The purpose of these programs is to enhance the knowledge and awareness about the employee's new location and the cultural differences affecting communication, behaviors and viewpoints. Training programs typically last a few days; however, for assignments to more remote or difficult locations, programs may also include security training that lasts for a longer period of time. The length and type of training should be directly related to the perceived level of assignment difficulty or differences in the assignment country.

Employers may conduct training either as an individual program for a single transferring employee and his or her family or as a group program when a number of employees are transferring to the same location within the same general time frame. However, it is advisable when conducting group training to also provide individuals with one-on-one time with the trainer to discuss any specific issues related to the employee's job responsibilities or to address any other more personal concerns or issues.

Language training

The inability to communicate can create a sense of vulnerability and loss of control. A basic knowledge of the language empowers expatriate employees to build critical relationships with host country nationals. Some jurisdictions require that employee communications be in the local language.

Most companies provide some form of language training for expatriate employees assigned to countries where they are nonnative speakers. Training program options include the following:

- Intensive total immersion courses.
- Cross-cultural training with integrated language instruction.
- Private tutoring or coaching.
- Group language classes.
- Use of language software or audiovisual applications.

Repatriation/reassignment

Expatriate pay considerations do not end when the assignment ends. Pay can be a significant factor in making it difficult for a person to repatriate. Often employees returning home realize they made considerably more money with a lower cost of living in the host country; returning to the home country means a cut in pay and standard of living. If the foreign compensation package is disproportionate, an expatriate can suffer financial issues upon repatriation or reassignment to the home or other foreign country. Expatriate families and employees benefit from repatriation training to help readjust to living in the home country and returning to the original work environment. The length of the training often depends on the length of the assignment and the ages of the employees' children.

Similarly, if the leading motivator of the expatriate employee is the long-term career aspect, the company needs to provide a challenging assignment upon return to the home office or shortly thereafter. If this is not feasible, communication about future plans for such an assignment and the timing should come from a mentor or a member of the senior management team. Otherwise, the company may risk losing its entire investment to turnover of returning expatriate employees.

Compensating Third-Country Nationals

Third-country nationals (TCNs) are employees who are not from the home country or the host country. TCNs have traditionally been technical or professional employees hired for short-term employment and are often considered international freelance employees.

In the case of TCNs, multinational companies have one of three options regarding compensation:

- Pay the TCNs as if they were local nationals.

- Treat them as any other U.S. citizen would be treated.

- Establish an arrangement based primarily on the third country's existing pay ranges.

The option a company chooses depends primarily on how these employees were hired into the organization or how they obtained the international assignment. The most common practices include the following:

- If the company is hiring locally in the host country, a TCN who applies for a job (including a professional or managerial position) may be assumed to be applying under the terms being offered. In this case, unless the TCN was specifically targeted and individually recruited for the position, he or she would most likely be offered the same compensation package provided to other local nationals.

- If a TCN who is already employed by the company transferred or reassigned from another country, the compensation arrangement usually depends on the individual's particular career pattern. TCNs who occupy positions that involve regular transfers or reassignments are most likely to be compensated on the same basis as any one of their U.S. counterparts who are also subject to frequent transfers. This approach, however, may require that these employees be paid based on U.S. salary ranges that are adjusted to support differences in locations each time a transfer occurs.

Tax Compliance

United States citizens and resident aliens are taxed on their worldwide income, whether the person lives inside or outside the United States. Multinational companies take one of four approaches to ensure tax compliance:

- Employees are responsible for their own taxes.
- The employer determines tax reimbursement on a case-by-case basis.
- The employer pays the difference between taxes paid in the United States and the host country.
- The employer withholds U.S. taxes and pays foreign taxes.

Qualifying U.S. citizens and resident aliens who live and work abroad may be able to exclude from their income all or part of their foreign salary or wages, or amounts received as compensation for their personal services. In addition, they may also qualify to exclude or deduct certain foreign housing costs.

The foreign earned income exclusion allows up to $92,900 of annual employment earnings to be exempt from U.S. gross income. The foreign housing exclusion provides for the amount of housing expenses in excess of U.S. norms to be excluded from taxable income. A foreign tax credit of the amount of foreign tax imposed on overseas earnings can be used to offset the amount of U.S. tax otherwise due by the U.S. citizen or resident.

A common misconception that contributes to the international tax gap is that this potentially excludable foreign earned income is exempt income not reportable on a U.S. tax return. In fact, only a qualifying individual with qualifying income may elect to exclude foreign-earned income, and this exclusion applies only if a tax return is filed and the income is reported.

U.S. income tax is calculated on foreign-source income and translated to U.S. dollars at the time of receipt. Blocked currency, which is foreign income that is not readily convertible into U.S. dollars, does not constitute taxable income and may generally be deferred until the currency is convertible into U.S. dollars or is used for nondeductible personal expenses. Withholding of U.S. income tax is not required if the employer is required to withhold the host country's income tax.

The U.S. Social Security tax is mandatory if services are performed by a U.S. citizen or resident, and if the employment is for a U.S. employer or for an affiliate of a U.S. company with a 3121(l) agreement. An entity is an affiliate if the U.S. company owns at least a 10 percent interest in the voting stock or profits of the entity. However, employees performing services for an international organization are exempt from FICA, FUTA and federal income tax withholding because services rendered for international organizations do not constitute employment, and remuneration for services rendered to international organizations does not constitute taxable income. Organizations that qualify as international organizations are those that have been designated as such by the president of the United States. The exemption applies to citizens and residents of the United States as well as to nonresident aliens.

Although foreign tax rules vary significantly by location, local taxing authorities also reserve the right to impose taxes on any income earned by the expatriate employee in the host country.

Equalization, reduction and totalization agreements

To prevent an expatriate employee from suffering excess taxation of income by both the U.S. and host countries, many multinational companies implement either a tax equalization or a tax reduction policy for employees on international assignments.

A tax equalization policy is an agreement between the employer and the employee to reduce the employee's wages, for which the employer agrees to assume the obligation for the worldwide tax liabilities of the employee. Equalization is accomplished by the use of a hypothetical tax. The hypothetical tax is calculated as if the employee had never left the United States, and it represents the employee's normal or expected tax liability for U.S. income.

Tax equalization is implemented by the use of advances to the employee; proceeds of the advance go to the tax authorities on the employee's behalf. These advances are settled at year end. The result is deferred compensation to the employee, which the host country does not tax.

Under a tax reduction policy, expatriates gain from the differences in income taxes in the United States and the foreign country to which they are assigned, or the compensation of expatriates is adjusted so they experience no loss in income as a result of the net effect of income taxes, both foreign and U.S.

Additionally, the United States government has Totalization Agreements in effect with several countries. These agreements eliminate dual coverage of employees by both the home and host countries. U.S. International Social Security Agreements coordinate with comparable programs in other countries. These agreements assign coverage according to objective rules, provide for no individual coverage elections and require that the employee remains covered by the home country and is exempt in the host country. The expatriate assignment must be for a period of five years or less, and the employee must remain an active employee of the sending employer.

All agreements exempt expatriates from the host country's version of the U.S. Old Age, Survivors, Disability and Health Insurance (OASDHI) program. Some agreements also exempt them from other foreign benefits, such as health insurance, unemployment insurance, workers' compensation, family allowances, cash sickness benefits and maternity benefits.

Tax treaties

The United States has income tax treaties with a number of foreign countries. Under these treaties, residents (not necessarily citizens) of foreign countries are taxed at a reduced rate or are exempt from U.S. income taxes on certain items of income they receive from sources within the United States. These reduced rates and exemptions vary among countries and specific items of income. Treaty provisions generally are reciprocal in that they apply to both treaty countries. Therefore, a U.S. citizen or resident who receives income from a treaty country and who is subject to taxes imposed by foreign countries may be entitled to certain credits, deductions, exemptions and reductions in the rate of taxes of those foreign countries. Treaty benefits generally are available to residents of the United States. They generally are not available to U.S. citizens who reside outside the United States. However, certain treaty benefits and safeguards, such as nondiscrimination provisions, are available to U.S. citizens residing in the treaty countries.

State taxes

Many states impose taxes on the foreign income of expatriate employees who maintain a home in that state. In addition, states also may impose unemployment insurance taxes on employers that have employees with homes in that state. The reasoning is that, like other resident citizens, the employee derives certain benefits from the state, and the state where the employee resides is the most plausible place for an unemployed worker to seek unemployment compensation.

Templates and Tools

Agencies and organizations

U.S. Department of State

Sample policies

International Assignment Management: Expatriate Policy and Procedure

International Assignment Management: Rest and Recuperation Policy

Supplement Endnotes

[1]Cartus. (2016). *2016 trends in global relocation: Global mobility policy & practices.* https://www.cartus.com/files/2214/8796/3083/Cartus-2016-Global-Mobility-Policy-and-Practices-Survey_Full_Survey_inclusive_of_all_charts.pdf

[2]Ibid.

[3]Ibid.

Appendix

2016 SHRM Body of Competency and Knowledge

Chapter 1: Introduction to Human Resource Management

HR Expertise (HR Knowledge Areas)

Required Content: Undergraduate Curriculum

Chapter 2: Strategic HRM, Data-Driven Decision Making, and HR Analytics

HR Expertise (HR Knowledge Areas)

Required Content: Undergraduate Curriculum

Chapter 3: Data Management and Human Resource Information Systems

Chapter 4: Diversity, Inclusion, and Equal Employment Laws

HR Expertise (HR Knowledge Areas)

Required Content: Undergraduate Curriculum

Chapter 5: The Analysis and Design of Work

HR Expertise (HR Knowledge Areas)

Required Content: Undergraduate Curriculum

Employee Engagement & Retention

Total Rewards

Learning & Development

Talent Acquisition

Chapter 6: Workforce Planning and Recruitment

HR Expertise (HR Knowledge Areas)

Required Content: Undergraduate Curriculum

Employee Engagement & Retention

Total Rewards

Learning & Development

Chapter 7: Selection Processes and Procedures

HR Expertise (HR Knowledge Areas)

Required Content: Undergraduate Curriculum

Employee Engagement & Retention

Chapter 8: Training, Development, and Careers

HR Expertise (HR Knowledge Areas)

Required Content: Undergraduate Curriculum

Employee Engagement & Retention

Learning & Development

Talent Acquisition

Structure of the HR Function

HR Strategic Planning

Diversity & Inclusion

Chapter 9: Performance Management

Chapter 10: Managing Employee Separations and Retention

HR Expertise (HR Knowledge Areas)

Required Content: Undergraduate Curriculum

Chapter 11: Developing a Pay Structure

Chapter 12: Rewarding Performance

HR Expertise (HR Knowledge Areas)

Required Content: Undergraduate Curriculum

Employee Engagement & Retention

Chapter 13: Managing Benefits

HR Expertise (HR Knowledge Areas)

Required Content: Undergraduate Curriculum

Employee Engagement & Retention

Chapter 14: Employee and Labor Relations

HR Expertise (HR Knowledge Areas)

Required Content: Undergraduate Curriculum

Workforce Management

Risk Management

Chapter 15: Employee Safety, Well-Being, and Wellness

HR Expertise (HR Knowledge Areas)

Required Content: Undergraduate Curriculum

Employee Engagement & Retention

Total Rewards

Learning & Development

Talent Acquisition

Structure of the HR Function

HR Strategic Planning

Diversity & Inclusion

HR in the Global Context

Technology Management

Organizational Effectiveness & Development

Chapter 16: Opportunities and Challenges in International HRM

Glossary

Ability-motivation-opportunity model: A model that proposes a system of HR practices that influences employee outcomes and, ultimately, operational and functional outcomes to the extent that the practices target three different elements: ability to perform, motivation to perform, and opportunity to perform

Absenteeism: Unscheduled absences from work

Adequate notice: The idea that employees should be evaluated using criteria and standards that were clearly communicated to them in advance

Adhocracy culture: Organizations with adhocracy cultures are creation focused and emphasize entrepreneurship, flexibility, risk taking, and creativity

Administrative purposes: An appraisal given for administrative purposes is used to make decisions in the organization

Aging (of pay data): A process whereby previously collected market pay data are adjusted and updated based on market changes due to merit-based increases, cost-of-living adjustments, and other factors that affect pay

Alternative dispute resolution: Methods of resolving disputes that do not involve litigation

Alumni: Former employees of an organization

Anchoring bias: The tendency when making a judgment to rely on the first piece of information that one receives

Anniversary reviews: Performance reviews in which an employee is rated on the anniversary of their start date with the organization

Anonymous data: Pieces of information that cannot be linked to any information that might identify an individual, thereby disclosing the individual's identity

Applicant reactions: A job applicant's perspective regarding the selection procedures they encounter and the employer that uses them

Applicant tracking system (ATS): An internal system that offers a centralized way to house applicant and employee data and to enable electronic business processes related to recruitment

Apprenticeship: A formal training program when a person enters and learns a trade or profession

A-S-A framework: The process of attraction, selection, and attrition that defines an organization's culture

Assessment center: A specific type of work sample, often used for manager selection

Availability bias: The tendency to rely more on information that is more readily available than alternative information

Balanced scorecard: The evaluation of organizational performance based on the extent to which the organization satisfies different stakeholder needs, such as the needs of customers, investors, shareholders, employees, and the broader community

Behavior: Actions on the job

Behavior/behavior criteria: Actual behavior on the job that is an outcome of training

Behavioral interview: A type of structured selection interview that uses questions about how applicants handled a work-related situation in the past

Behavioral tracking: A process in which trainees keep track of their on-the-job behaviors and whether they are performing the behaviors they learned in training

Benchmarking: The measurement of the quality of an organization's practices in comparison with those of a peer organization

Benefits: Employee rewards, which are a type of indirect pay, that include health, life, and disability insurance; retirement programs; and work–life balance programs

Biases: A tendency, feeling, or opinion, especially one that is preconceived, unreasoned, and unsupported by evidence

Big data: Large amounts of unstructured, messy, and sometimes quickly streaming data, which can be described in terms of volume, variety, velocity, and veracity

Biographical data (biodata): Information about a job applicant based on their personal history that can be used to make selection decisions

Blockchain: A distributed incorruptible digital technology infrastructure that maintains a fully encoded database that serves as a ledger where all transactions are recorded and stored

Bona fide occupational qualification (BFOQ): A particular instance where a normally legally protected characteristic (such as age or gender) is an essential necessity of a job

Bonuses: A form of variable pay distributed as a one-time payout in recognition of performance after the fact, which may be attached to a performance rating or to a completed goal

Boomerang employees: Former employees who rejoin an organization

Bridge employment: Reducing one's hours or reducing job demands within the same or a different organization in preparation for full retirement

Broadbanding: The process of collapsing multiple pay grades into one large grade with a single minimum and maximum

Business ethics: A system of principles that govern how businesses operate, how decisions are made, and how people are treated

Calibration meetings: When groups of managers come together and discuss the ratings they will give their employees before ratings are finalized

Candidate experience: A term for applicant reactions often used by employers

Career management: The continual process of setting career-related goals and planning a route to achieve those goals

Case studies: A managerial training method wherein participants analyze and discuss a difficult business case

Cash balance plan: Also known as a guaranteed account plan, a type of defined-benefit plan in which participants are provided with an account that is credited annually with a compensation credit and an interest credit

Categorical variable: A variable that consists of multiple levels, without any particular order or inherent numeric values

Central tendency error: The tendency to rate most employees in the middle category

Challenge stressors: Job factors like role demands and time urgency that are thought to be positively related to work engagement

Challenging (stretch) assignments: A task an employee is given that is outside their current KSAOs

Change: The second step in the Lewin model of change, this refers to enacting the change

Clan culture: Organizations with clan cultures are collaboration and people oriented and value cohesion,

employee empowerment, and team players

Class action lawsuit: When individuals who have similar claims sue as a group

Classification method: Where written classification descriptions are developed for each classification level, and based on its job description, each job is matched by subject matter experts to a classification level where the classification description is most similar

Cognitive ability test: A measure of the ability to perceive, process, evaluate, compare, create, understand, manipulate, or generally think about information and ideas

Cognitive task analysis: A type of job analysis that focuses on cognitive tasks that may not be observable by others but could be described by an SME

Collective bargaining: The process of negotiating in good faith toward agreed terms on wages, hours, and working conditions

Compa-ratio: A ratio that reflects how much employees are actually paid for a given job or pay grade as compared to the espoused pay structure and policies and thus can be used to assess whether systematic compression or inversion are occurring

Compensable factors: The common dimensions by which jobs vary in terms of worth

Compensation: Includes base pay and variable pay and is sometimes referred to as direct pay

Compensatory damages: Providing financial relief to the complainant for damages incurred, such as mental and emotional stress suffered as a result of discrimination

Compensatory time off (comp time): A program that allows nonexempt employees to receive paid time off (instead of earning time-and-a-half pay) in exchange for working overtime hours

Competency: A cluster of knowledge, skills, abilities, and other

characteristics (KSAOs) necessary to be effective at one's job

Competency modeling: A type of job analysis with the goal of understanding what types of attributes and behaviors are required for a group of jobs, perhaps over an entire organization

Compliance training: Instruction focused on regulations, laws, and policies related to employees' daily work

Concept: A theoretical phenomenon or construct

Concurrent validity: Administering a selection procedure to current employees and showing that their scores are correlated with their current job performance in order to demonstrate criterion-related validity

Confidential data: Information for which individuals' identities are known by the researchers due to the linking of a name or code but are not generally disclosed or reported

Consolidated Omnibus Budget Reconciliation Act (COBRA): Protects employees' and their beneficiaries' health care coverage for a designated amount of time in the event of job loss, work-hour reductions, or another major occurrence

Construct validity: The demonstration that a test actually measures a particular construct of interest through an accumulation of evidence about the test, including its pattern of relationships with other measures

Content validity: An approach to test development focused on sampling the domain such as the job, usually shown through job analysis or SME judgment

Contingent employees: Individuals who are hired for a limited, fixed term such as a short-term contract or a project consulting contract

Continuous variable: A variable that consists of a continuum of numerically ordered values

Coreflex plan: A plan that provides some services (such as paying for movers and travel expenses) to all expatriates, with the remainder of benefits personalized to the unique situation of the expatriate

Criterion-related validity: The demonstration of an empirical relationship between a predictor and measures of job performance

Critical incident method: A method through which managers identify examples of exceptionally high and low incidents of performance and document them in narrative form

Critical incidents technique: A technique that involves asking SMEs to describe critical job situations that they frequently encounter on the job

Criticality survey: A more in-depth analysis of the criticality of tasks and KSAOs, in which larger groups of SMEs rate each task and KSAO in terms of how critical or essential it is

Cultural adjustment: Adjusting to the new culture one is now living in, including factors such as transportation, entertainment, health system, education, and general living conditions

Culture shock: The feeling of disorientation individuals experience when they enter a new culture

Cybersecurity: Data security applied to information accessible through the Internet

Database: An organized collection of data that is both stored and accessed electronically

Database management system (DBMS): The software used to manage and maintain a database or multiple databases

Data-driven decisions: Decisions that are made based on the analysis and interpretation of relevant, accurate, and timely data

Data flow diagrams: Depict the logical design of how data move from one entity to the next and how data are processed within an information system

Data lake: Stores a vast amount of raw data in its native (and often unstructured) format

Data privacy: Individuals' control over the collection, storage, access, and reporting of their personal data

Data security: Protective measures taken to prevent unauthorized access to employee data and to preserve the confidentiality and integrity of the data

Data visualization: Pictorial and graphic representations of quantitative or qualitative data

Defined-benefit plan: Also known as a traditional pension plan, a type of retirement plan in which the employer provides plan participants with an established benefit to be paid out over a fixed time period

Defined-contribution plan: A type of retirement plan in which the employee and/or employer contributes to an investment fund

Delayering: The process by which the hierarchy in an organizational structure is reduced

Descriptive analytics: Focuses on understanding what has already happened, which implies a focus on the past

Desire to leave: When an employee would like to end their employment with an organization

Developmental purposes: A performance review conducted for the purpose of improving performance

Diary keeping: The practice of recording employee performance on a regular basis

Differential piecework plan: An individual-incentive program in which employees are paid one rate for units produced below a particular standard in a given time period and a higher rate for units produced above that standard

Dismissal: Employment termination

Disparate (or adverse) impact: When employers use seemingly neutral criteria that have a discriminatory effect on a protected group

Disparate treatment: Treating different groups of applicants or employees differently because of their race, color, religion, sex, or national origin

Distributive justice: The perceived fairness or equity regarding the allocation of an outcome or resource, which can include rewards, punishments, or other organizational consequences

Diversity: Real or perceived differences among people with respect to sex, race, ethnicity, age, physical and mental ability, sexual orientation, religion, and attributes that may affect their interactions with others

Ease of movement: The degree to which employees may leave an organization easily (due to factors such as a favorable job market that makes it easy to leave)

Educational-assistance program: A program whereby the employer provides financial assistance for employee educational expenses

e-HRM: Internet-based information systems and technology that span across organizational levels

eLearning: Training that is delivered through an online platform via computers or mobile devices

Emotional intelligence (EI): One's ability to recognize and appraise emotions in oneself and others and behave accordingly

Employability: The degree to which an individual is able to gain initial employment and obtain new employment if required

Employee relations: The collective relationships between different employees as well as between employees and management in an organization

Employee Retirement Income Security Act (ERISA): Introduced in 1974 to establish minimum standards for many private employers' health care plans in order to protect employees

Employee stock ownership plans (ESOPs): A type of pay-for-performance program and defined-contribution plan in which the bulk of contributions are invested in an employer's stock, thereby rewarding employees when company stock shares increase in value and the vesting period has passed

Employee wellness programs: Organizational initiatives that promote the health, fitness, and well-being of workers

Employment at will: When organizations have the right to terminate the employment of anyone at any time, and employees have the right to quit at any time

Enterprise resource planning (ERP): Integrated business-management software intended to coordinate and integrate processes and data across different functional areas of a company, such as accounting, sales, human resource management, and finance

Equal Employment Opportunity Commission (EEOC): An independent federal agency that ensures compliance with the law and provides outreach activities designed to prevent discrimination

Equitable relief: Payments made to a plaintiff to bring them back to the position they would have had if they were not discriminated against

Equity theory: Provides a way of understanding how an individual's sense of fairness is influenced by others with whom they compare themselves

Ergonomic design: Fitting the physical aspects of the job to the human body

Essential functions: Job tasks or goals that every incumbent needs to perform

Executive coaching: Individual advice and counseling to managers regarding their work and careers

Executive orders: Presidential orders that carry the force of law

Executive Order 11246: An executive order issued by President Lyndon B. Johnson that expanded the protections for different forms of employment discrimination—such as pay-based discrimination—to include employers with federal contracts or subcontracts in excess of $10,000

Exempt: A term that refers to those employees who do not fall under the purview of the minimum wage and overtime provisions

Expatriate: A person who is living and working in a different country than their country of origin

Expectancy: The extent to which an individual perceives that applying effort will lead to higher performance

Expectancy theory: A theory that suggests that if a person sees that their efforts will lead to greater performance, and if they believe that performance will lead to an outcome that they value, they will be more motivated

External equity: The extent to which the pay for a particular job is competitive and fair relative to the pay of the same or similar jobs at other organizations

External recruitment: An employer's actions that are intended to bring a job opening to the attention of potential job candidates outside of the organization and, in turn, influence their intention to pursue the opportunity

Extrinsic motivation: An external, environmental force that compels an individual to action

Fair hearing: A formal review meeting explaining to the employee why and how a particular rating was given

Fair Labor Standards Act (FLSA): Enacted in 1938, this act introduced major provisions aimed at regulating overtime pay, minimum wage, hours worked, and record keeping

Family and Medical Leave Act (FMLA): Introduced in 1993 to protect employees' job security when they need to take unpaid leave due to family or medical issues

Family-to-work conflict: When nonwork responsibilities interfere with work responsibilities

Federal Insurance Contributions Act (FICA): A federal payroll tax paid by both employees and employers that funds current Social Security beneficiaries

Feedback: Information provided to an employee regarding his/her performance

Feedback culture: A culture in which employees and managers feel comfortable giving and receiving feedback

Field: A column in a table that represents a unique characteristic

Five Factor Model (FFM): A model of normal adult personality that includes the dimensions of Openness to Experience, Conscientiousness, Extraversion, Agreeableness, and Neuroticism

Flexible benefits plans: Offer employees some degree of choice for the employer-sponsored voluntary benefits they select and the benefits they are able to receive on a pretax basis

Flextime: A work arrangement in which workers can choose from a number of work schedules

Focal date reviews: Performance reviews that take place on the same date for all employees

Forced distribution: Also known as stack rankings; involves the rater placing a specific percentage of employees into categories such as exceptional, adequate, and poor

Forecasting: The act of determining estimates during workforce planning regarding what specific positions need to be filled and how to fill them

Form: A database object that provides a user interface with which to enter, edit, and/or display data in a database

401(k) plan: A type of defined-contribution plan in which an employee (and in some cases the employer) makes contributions to an individual account in the form of deferred income

403(b) plan: Also known as a tax-sheltered annuity plan, a type of defined-contribution plan in which an employee (and in some cases the employer) makes contributions to an individual account in the form of deferred income; reserved for public schools and universities, religious organizations, and certain tax-exempt organizations such as charities

4/5ths (or 80%) rule: According to this rule, a protected group's selection ratio may not be less than 80% of the majority group's ratio

Frame of reference (FOR) training: Training that involves raters observing specific instances of performance through videotapes or vignettes and then telling them the "true score" and why raters should rate in a particular way

Gainsharing: A type of group pay-for-performance program that rewards a group of employees for collectively achieving certain goals or objectives

Games and simulations: A type of managerial training in which teams challenge each other as if they were businesses in competition

Gamification: Training that is made into a game or competition among employees in terms of scores on their training performance

Gig: A single project or task that a worker is hired to do on demand

Gig economy: The prevalence of temporary employment positions, where individuals are employed as independent workers instead of actual employees of an organization

Global integration: When a company standardizes its HR practices around the world

Global mindset: Individuals who are open to learning about different cultures, have a sense of adventure, are comfortable dealing with ambiguity, and have a nonjudgmental attitude toward those from other cultures

Goal-setting theory: The theory that setting specific, difficult, yet achievable goals for people will lead to the highest performance

Halo error: Basing performance ratings on one or two performance dimensions, with one prominent dimension positively affecting how

the employee is perceived on other dimensions

Harassment: Unwelcome behaviors based on sex, race, religion, national origin, and other protected characteristics

Hawthorne effect: The alteration of one's behavior to fit what you think is wanted of you, as a result of the knowledge of being studied or observed

Health Insurance Portability and Accountability Act (HIPAA): Introduced in 1996 to add protections to the portability of employees' health care coverage and ensure the privacy and security of employees' health care data

Hierarchy culture: Organizations with hierarchy cultures focus on control and value being efficient, timely, and consistent

Hierarchy of controls: Methods that an organization can use to reduce safety hazards, organized into a hierarchy based on their degree of effectiveness

High-performance work practices: Bundles of HR universal best practices, such as promoting within the organization and offering training

Hindrance stressors: Negative stressors, such as workplace hassles, organizational politics, poor resources, role overload, and constraints

Hiring manager: The person who asked for the role to be filled and/or to whom the new hire will be reporting as their manager

Holiday pay: A program that provides employees with compensation when taking time away from work for a recognized federal, state, or local holiday

Horns error: Ratings on one dimension negatively influencing how the employee is perceived on other dimensions

Hostile work environment: Behavior that contributes to an environment a reasonable person would find offensive

HR business partner: Someone who serves as a consultant to management on HR-related issues

HR generalist: A person who fulfills an HR generalist function attends to multiple HR functions

HR specialist: A person who fulfills an HR specialist function attends to all aspects of one specific HRM function

Human capital: The knowledge, skills, and abilities that people embody across an organization

Human resource (HR) analytics: The process of collecting, analyzing, interpreting, and reporting people-related data for the purpose of improving decision making, achieving strategic objectives, and sustaining a competitive advantage

Human Resource Information Systems (HRIS): Systems used to collect, store, manage, analyze, retrieve, and report HR data and allow for the automation of some HR management functions

Human resource management (HRM): The decisions and actions associated with managing individuals throughout the employee life cycle to maximize employee and organization effectiveness

Identical elements: The extent to which the training environment is the same as the actual work environment and thus enhances training transfer

Incentive effects: The extent to which pay-for-performance programs motivate employees' on-the-job behavior and pursuit of goals

Inclusive environments: Organizations or groups in which individuals, regardless of their background, are treated with dignity and respect, are included in decision-making, and are valued for who they are and what they bring to the group or organization

Individual equity: The fairness of how pay is administered and distributed to individual employees working similar jobs within the same organization

Individual incentives: The distribution of pay in response to the attainment of certain predetermined and objective levels of performance

Individual retirement plans (individual retirement arrangements): A plan that allows an individual to make tax-deferred contributions to an investment fund and that does not need to be employer sponsored

Informational interview: The exchange of information between an individual and an organizational representative with the goal of learning more about the organization and its industry

Informing: Providing new employees with sources, materials, and training to help them learn what is expected of them

Inpatriates: Host-country employees working in headquarter locations

Instrumentality: The extent to which an individual perceives that achieving higher performance will lead to reward attainment

Integrity test: A test specifically developed to assess applicants' tendency toward counterproductive and antisocial behavior

Interactional adjustment: The comfort felt with interacting with local individuals inside or outside work

Interactional justice: The perceived fairness of an interpersonal or informational interaction—for example, being treated with respect and consideration or receiving adequate explanation about a process

Internal equity: The fairness of pay rates across jobs within an organization

Internal Revenue Code: Stipulates income and payroll tax regulations

International companies: Companies that export or import, but their investments are within one home country

Intrinsic motivation: A force that originates inside an individual and

compels the individual to action because they perceive the action as innately rewarding

Involuntary turnover: An employee terminated by the organization against their own wishes

Job analysis: The analysis of work and the employee characteristics needed to perform the work successfully

Job Characteristics Model (JCM): The first complete model of job design, explaining which job characteristics are the most important to increasing worker motivation and productivity

Job classification: A group of related duties within an organization

Job crafting: Redesigning one's own job to fit one's needs (e.g., abilities, interests, personality)

Job Demands-Control Model (JDC): This model emphasizes that employees experience stress when there are high job demands and little control over their job

Job Demands-Resources Model (JDR): This model emphasizes that job demands, such as workload and time pressure, can be counteracted by characteristics such as job control, participation, and supervisor support

Job descriptions: Job descriptions provide the title and purpose of the job, as well as a general overview of the essential tasks, duties, and responsibilities (i.e., observable actions) associated with the job

Job design: The process of identifying how a job's characteristics are experienced from the employee's perspective in order to enhance well-being and performance

Job embeddedness model: A model that explains that employees stay because of their links to others and fit with the context at work and in their communities and how much they would have to sacrifice by leaving their work and communities

Job enlargement: The addition of more responsibilities to a job so that it is less boring and more motivating for workers

Job enrichment: Allowing workers to have greater decision-making power

Job evaluation: A systematic process used to determine the relative worth of jobs within an organization

Job rotation: Rotating employees from one job to another, allowing them to learn new skills

Job satisfaction: An employee's contentment with different facets of their work

Job specifications: Job specifications focus on the characteristics of an employee who does the job

Job structure: The ranking of jobs within an organization based on their respective worth

Joint venture: A joint venture involves two companies coming together and investing to create a new company

Judgment based on evidence: The principle that performance standards are administered consistently across all employees, and the ratings are, to the degree possible, free from personal biases and prejudice

Key performance indicators (KPIs): Measurable business metrics that are aligned with a company's strategy

Key variable: Provides the information necessary to construct the relationships between tables and to join (or merge) data from different tables

KSAOs: Knowledge, skills, abilities, and other characteristics employees need to have in order to do their work most effectively

Labor Management Relations Act (1947): Also known as the Taft-Hartley Act; amended the National Labor Act and restricts the activities and power of labor unions

Labor market: The availability of talent outside of an organization, which can be viewed through the lens of talent supply and demand

Labor market conditions: The number of jobs available compared to the number of individuals available with the required KSAOs to do those jobs

Labor relations: Managing in response to labor laws relating to unions and collective bargaining

Labor–Management Reporting and Disclosure Act (LMRDA) (1959): Requires labor organizations to report financial transactions and administrative practices of unions, employers, and labor consultants

Layoffs: Organizationally initiated termination of employment due to economic or strategic reasons

Leadership development: The formal and informal opportunities for employees to expand their KSAOs

Learning criteria: Measures of whether the trainee actually gained some sort of knowledge or skill while in training

Leniency error: The tendency of a rater to rate most employees highly

Life insurance programs: Provides financial compensation for designated beneficiaries when the insured individual dies, often distributed in the form of a lump-sum payment

Linkage survey: Where sample of SMEs would be asked to indicate how important each of the KSAOs is to each job task

Little data: Structured data that are gathered in small volumes, usually for a previously planned purpose

Local differentiation: When organizations vary their HR practices in consideration of the local environment

Local validation: Showing the test's validity for predicting job performance in a specific organization

Logical design: The translation of business requirements into improved business processes

Long-term disability insurance: A form of income protection for employees that is similar to short-term disability insurance, except it offers longer-term benefits activated once short-term disability insurance benefits expire

Magnitude: The size of a relationship

Managed-care plans: A medical plan designed to provide wide-ranging health care services to plan participants while managing the cost, quality, and use of services, where participants incur lower cost sharing when they use in-network (as opposed to out-of-network) providers and services

Management by objectives (MBO): A management strategy in which organizational goals are translated into department- and individual-level goals

Marginal functions: Job tasks or goals that can be assigned to others

Market culture: Organizations with market cultures are characterized by competition and as being aggressive, competitive, and customer oriented

Market pay line: The relationship between the internal job structure of the organization for benchmark jobs and the external pay practices of other organizations

Market pricing: When an organization bases its pay levels and pay structure directly on its competitors' pay levels and pay structures

Market review: The process of collecting pay data for benchmark jobs from other organizations

Massed learning: Training that occurs in one large chunk at one point in time

Mean: The average of a group of numeric values

Measure: A tool used to assess the level(s) of a theoretical concept, such as a survey used to assess employee engagement

Merit pay: Pay distributed to employees and integrated into their base pay as a reward for the ratings and/or feedback they receive on a performance evaluation measure

Metacognitive skills: A person's ability to step back and assess their own skill, performance, or learning

Mindfulness training: Teaches a person to be present in the moment and to notice things around them in a nonjudgmental way

Mission: A core need that an organization strives to fulfill and thus represents the organization's overarching purpose

Money-purchase plan: A relatively straightforward defined-contribution plan in which employers contribute a specified amount to each plan participant's investment fund

Motivation: A psychological force that propels an individual (or a group of individuals) to enact certain behaviors or to strive for a goal

Multifactor authentication: An extra layer of security that requires an additional piece of information that only the user would know

Multinational companies: Companies operating in multiple countries but with clearly designated headquarters in their home country

Multiple-hurdle approach: When a series of selection procedures is administered sequentially and applicants must pass each hurdle to move to the next one

National Institute for Occupational Safety and Health (NIOSH): The federal agency that supports research on workplace safety and health and makes recommendations to employers

National Labor Relations Act: Stipulates that employees protected under the act have a right to discuss pay as part of activities related to collective bargaining and protection, thereby providing an avenue through which employees may uncover pay discrimination

National Labor Relations Board (NLRB): An independent United States governmental agency, the NLRB is tasked with supervising union elections and is empowered to investigate suspected unfair labor practices

Natural lighting: Lighting provided by sunlight

Near misses: Situations in which an accident almost occurred but did not

Needs assessment: A systematic evaluation of the organization, the jobs, and the employees to determine where training is most needed and what type of training is needed

Negotiation: Give-and-take process between two or more parties aimed toward reaching an agreement

Nonexempt: A term that refers to those employees who are directly affected by minimum wage and overtime provisions

Occupational Safety and Health Administration (OSHA): Under the U.S. Department of Labor, OSHA's purpose is to ensure safe and healthy working conditions for employees by setting and enforcing safety and health standards

Office of Federal Contract Compliance Programs (OFCCP): A division of the Department of Labor; monitors EEO compliance of federal contractors

Offshoring: When companies produce physical goods or perform some of their operations overseas

Onboarding: The process of helping new employees adjust to their new organizations by imparting to them the knowledge, skills, behaviors, culture, and attitudes required to successfully function within the organization

One-on-one meetings: Time managers spend with their direct reports on a regular basis, usually weekly, to discuss performance goals, progress, and related issues

On-the-job training (OJT): When a new employee works on the job in order to learn it, usually under the supervision of a more senior employee

Open offices: An office arrangement in which employees work in open spaces

Organizational culture: Assumptions shared by organization members, which affect their actions, thoughts, and perceptions

Organizational justice theory: A theory that focuses on perceptions of fairness in the workplace

Organizational performance: The extent to which employee

learning and growth, internal business process efficiency, customer attitudes and behavior, and financial performance contribute to the organization's mission and strategy

Organizationally assigned expatriate: When an expat is sent by the organization for a predetermined time to work in an overseas operation

Orientation program: A specific type of training designed to help welcome, inform, and guide new employees

Outsourcing: Moving some operations of the organization to a different organization

Overconfidence bias: The tendency for an individual to be more confident in their own beliefs than reality would suggest

Overlearning: When trainees repeatedly practice a particular behavior in the training situation so that they can perform the behavior automatically without much cognitive effort

Paid time off (PTO): A program that provides employees with compensation when they take time away from work, subject to employer approval

Paired comparisons: Creating rankings by comparing two employees at the same time until every unique pair of employees has been compared and then compiling the results

Patient Protection and Affordable Care Act (ACA): Introduced in 2010 to provide rights and protections associated with access to health care coverage

Pay compression: Occurs when recently hired employees with less experience earn nearly as much or the same as more experienced, longer-tenured employees in the same job or when employees in a lower-level job earn nearly as much or the same as employees in a higher-level job

Pay grade: A group of jobs with similar job evaluation point values

that are then assigned common pay midpoint, minimum, and maximum values

Pay inversion: A more severe form of pay compression that occurs when a newer, less-experienced employee in a given job earns (a) more than another, more-experienced employee in the same job or (b) more than another employee in a higher-level job

Pay for performance: Financial rewards offered in exchange for meeting certain levels of performance or achieving certain goals

Pay-for-performance programs: Compensation programs that reward employees based on the behaviors they actually exhibit at work and the results or goals they actually achieve

Pay policy line: Portrays an organization's operationalization of its market pay line, thereby representing how an organization translates information about its internal job structure and external pay rates of competitors into actionable pay practices

Pay secrecy: The extent to which an organization has policies and practices aimed at suppressing pay information

Pay structure: The way in which an organization applies pay rates to different jobs, skills, or competencies

Pay transparency: The extent to which an organization communicates pay information and the extent to which employees are permitted to discuss pay with each other

Pension Benefit Guaranty Corporation (PBGC): A U.S. government agency that insures private-sector retirement plans

People data: Data associated with various groups of humans that are associated with an organization, such as employees and other stakeholders

Performance appraisal: An evaluation of employee performance

Performance improvement plan (PIP): Plan aimed at helping poor performers be accountable to meeting performance standards

Performance management: The process of measuring, communicating, and managing employee performance in the workplace so that performance is aligned with organizational strategy

Perquisites (perks): Nonmonetary services or benefits provided by an employer

Personal leave: A benefit employers use to supplement vacation and sick-time offerings by allowing employees to take paid or unpaid time away from work

Personality: An individual's dispositional and relatively stable pattern of cognition, behavior, and emotion

Personally identifiable data: Data readily linked to specific individuals

Person-based pay structures: A pay structure that emphasizes individuals' unique competencies or skills when determining pay, such that a person who possesses a particular competency or skill receives additional pay

Physical design: The actual software and hardware solutions used to translate business processes into an actual information system

Physical environment: The natural and human-made components of one's surroundings

Piecework plans: An individual-incentive program in which employees are compensated based on their respective production levels

Placement: A part of strategy development, which involves determining where talent needs to be placed and where the talent can be found

Point-factor method: A common job evaluation approach in which a team of subject matter experts systematically identifies, scales, and develops weights for compensable factors, ultimately resulting in points being assigned to different jobs to describe their relative worth

Position: Duties that can be carried out by one person

Predictive analytics: Focuses on what is likely to happen in the future based on available data

Predictive validity: Administering a selection procedure to job applicants and showing that their scores are correlated with their later job performance scores in order to demonstrate criterion-related validity

Prescriptive analytics: Focuses on what actions should be taken based on what is likely to happen in the future

Pretext: An excuse given for a decision that is not the real reason

Prima facie evidence: At first glance, or preliminary evidence

Procedural justice: The perceived fairness of the process used to determine *how* an outcome or resource is determined and distributed

Product market: The final sale of products and services in the marketplace

Profit sharing: A pay-for-performance program in which employees share in their organization's profits

Profit-sharing program: A type of pay-for-performance program in which the employee earns rewards by sharing their organization's profits, and earned rewards can be placed in what can be considered a type of defined-contribution plan

Progressive discipline: The process of using increasingly severe steps to correct a performance problem

Psychometrics: A science used to estimate the quality of psychological measures such as those used in personnel selection

Pulse surveys: Short, frequent surveys

Punitive damages: Damages that are awarded if it is demonstrated that the company had engaged in reckless discrimination and failed to act in good faith

Qualitative data: Nonnumeric information that includes text or narrative data, such as interview transcripts

Quantitative data: Numeric data that can be counted or measured in some way

Query: A question that is posed to a database

Quid pro quo harassment: Involves making employment decisions contingent on sexual favors

Ranking method: A job evaluation approach in which subject matter experts evaluate the job descriptions and specifications for a selection of jobs and order them in terms of their relative contribution to the organization's strategic objectives and mission

Reactions criteria: The assessment of how trainees react to training such as whether they thought it was valuable

Realistic job preview (RJP): Offers potential applicants a realistic view of the actual job, including both positive and negative information

Reasonable accommodation: An accommodation provided to employees to help them perform their jobs that is reasonable given a firm's resources

Recency error: When a rater focuses on the most recent employee behaviors they have observed rather than focusing on the entire rating period

Record: A case in a database

Recruitment: The process of identifying a group of individuals (employees or potential applicants) who possess the KSAOs to fill a particular role

Recruitment funnel: A situation in which the number of applicants gets smaller as people move through the selection process

Recruitment needs: The results of the workforce planning process in terms of what KSAOs are needed within the organization as well as when they will be needed

Refreezing: The third and final step in the Lewin change model, this step refers to refreezing the new system in place so that it becomes the permanent replacement for the way things used to be done

Reinforcement theory: A motivational theory that provides a useful framework for understanding pay as an extrinsic motivator, particularly when pay is used for behavior modification

Relational database: A specific type of database in which different subsets or collections of data are integrated through pieces of information residing within the data themselves

Relational database management system (relational DBMS): The software used to manage and maintain a relational database

Relational returns: Nonmonetary incentives and rewards, such as new learning and developmental opportunities

Reliability: The consistency of measurement

Replacement planning: The process of identifying a minimal plan of individuals to take over top leadership roles over time

Report: A database object that is used to organize, summarize, format, and present data residing in the database

Resource-based view: Proposes that a resource holds value to the extent that it is rare and inimitable, where example resources include physical, financial, organizational, and human resources

Results criteria: Whether the training actually translates into improved organizational outcomes

Retaliate: Taking adverse action against an employee who complains about discrimination or files a discrimination claim

Retirement: The cessation of work at the end of one's work life

Reverse culture shock: A situation in which expatriates return to their country of origin and find that their country of origin does not feel like home anymore

Reverse discrimination: Discriminating against majority or historically privileged groups such as White or male employees

Reward system: The policies, procedures, and practices used by an organization to determine the amount and types of returns individuals, teams, and the organization receive in exchange for their membership and contributions

Right-to-work laws: Vary from state to state but generally prohibit requiring employees to join a union or pay regular or fair-share union dues in order to obtain or keep a job

Role-plays: When trainees act in managerial situations such as counseling a difficult subordinate

Safety behavior: The type of work behaviors that employees exhibit with regard to safety

Safety climate: The shared understanding that workers have about the importance of safety

Safety committee: Provides employees with a voice and an opportunity to participate in safety-related decisions in the organization

Safety compliance behavior: The extent to which workers follow the safety rules and regulations

Safety knowledge: Workers' understanding of how to protect themselves and others on the job

Safety motivation: Workers' perceived value for safety and desire to perform safely on the job

Safety officer: An individual who is assigned to support safety and health issues in the workplace such as the promotion of safe practices and compliance with safety policies and rules

Safety participation behavior: Employees' willingness to support safety among their coworkers

Sales commissions: Pay-for-performance programs that reward the sale of a product or service as opposed to the production of a product or provision of a service

Schema: An outline or framework to help the learner organize the training material so that they will better retain the material

Scientific process: A method used for systematic and rigorous problem solving that is predicated on the assumption that knowledge requires evidence

Scraping and crawling tools: Programs designed to scour and pull data from websites and other electronic sources in a systematic manner

Selection interview: A conversation or discussion between a job applicant and an organizational representative used to screen job applicants

Self-efficacy: A person's belief that they can accomplish a task

Self-initiated expatriate: A skilled professional who moves to a different country for a specific period of time with the intention of gaining overseas work experience

Seniority-based layoffs: Using seniority as the layoff criterion such that the most senior employees are retained while newer employees are let go

Severance pay: Payments made to departing employees during organizationally initiated turnover

Severity error: The tendency to rate almost all ratees low

Sexual harassment: Unwanted advances and other harassment that is sexual in nature

Short-term disability insurance: A form of income protection for employees who temporarily become unable to work as a result of illness or injury

Sick time (sick leave): A program that permits employees to take time off from work due to a personal or immediate family member's health issue

Sign: The positive or negative direction of a relationship between variables

Similarity-attraction hypothesis: The theory that individuals prefer others who are similar to them

Site visit: When a job applicant physically agrees to go to the organization's location to meet with and be interviewed by its representatives

Situational interview: A type of structured interview in which job applicants are asked what they would do in a hypothetical work-related situation

Situational judgment tests (SJTs): A test that captures some of the realism of work sample tests but in a format (e.g., multiple-choice) that can be used more easily with large numbers of applicants

SMART goals: Goals that are specific, measurable, aggressive, realistic, and time-bound

Social Security Act: Passed by the U.S. Congress in 1935 as part of the New Deal to help the United States recover from the Great Depression by providing economic security for old-age individuals and, later, additional programs for mothers and children in need, individuals with disabilities, the unemployed, and those whose family members have died

Software as a service (SaaS): Arrangements through which software and hardware associated with databases and applications are maintained and controlled by a third-party entity

Sorting effects: The associated processes of attraction, selection, and attrition that occur when employees gravitate toward jobs with reward systems that fit their disposition, goals, and performance capabilities

Spaced learning: Training that occurs through several sessions over time

Spot awards: A type of after-the-fact recognition that is often reserved for exceptional levels of performance on a project or for exceptionally high overall job performance

Spurious correlation: A correlation observed between two variables that are not actually related

Stakeholders: A number of different groups that an organization must appeal to, including customers and investors

Standard deviation: The amount of variation of a group of numeric values around their mean

Standard-hour plan: An individual-incentive program in which employee

pay is based on the completion of a particular task within a predetermined time period

Stay interviews: Interviews of employees who are not leaving to understand what keeps them on their jobs and identify problems that may eventually result in turnover

Stereotypes: Overly simplified and generalized assumptions about a particular group that may not reflect reality

Stock options: A type of pay-for-performance program that makes employees partial owners of the organization by allowing them to purchase a certain number of stock shares at a fixed price in a given time frame

Storytelling with data: Communicating data in a manner that brings them to life for the audience, with a focus on simplicity and ease of interpretation and comprehension

Straight piecework plan: An individual-incentive program in which employee variable pay is based on the units they produce in a given time period, such that there is a direct correspondence between the amount of pay distributed and the number of units produced

Straight rankings: When a rater rank orders all employees from best to worst

Strain: A person's reaction to stressors, such as heart disease, burnout, or depression; or behavioral outcomes such as low performance and turnover

Strategic alliance: A partnership with other companies

Strategic human resource management: The process of aligning HR policies and practices with the objectives of the organization, including employee, operational, stakeholder, and financial outcomes

Strategy: A well-devised and thoughtful plan for achieving an objective

Strategy formulation: The process of planning what to do to achieve organizational objectives

Strategy implementation: The enactment of a strategic plan

Strategy type: A general approach for how an organization will bring its mission, vision, and values to life

Stressors: Demands in the environment to which a person must respond

Structured interview: An interview in which all job applicants are asked the same, job-related questions

Subject matter experts (SMEs): People (e.g., employees, supervisors) who provide information about the job

Succession management: The process of identifying and developing successors at all levels of the organization

Succession planning: Taking stock of which employees are qualified to fill positions that are likely to be vacated soon

SWOT analysis: An analysis of the internal strengths and weaknesses of an organization and the external opportunities and threats to that organization

Systems perspective: The view of how all pieces of a system and its sub-systems fit together

Table: A database object used to store data about cases and to add structure to the data

Talent analysis: The process of gathering data to determine potential talent gaps, or the difference between an organization's talent demand and the available talent supply

Talent pool: A group of individuals (employees or potential applicants) who possess the KSAOs to fill a particular role

Tardiness: Being late to work without giving advance notice

Tasks: The elements of a job analysis that are typically used to describe the job itself

Tax deferred: Taxable income that is not taxed until a later date, often when earnings are distributed

Team appraisals: A team evaluation in which systems, goals, and performance are evaluated at the team level

Telecommuting: A work arrangement in which an employee is not physically at an office or other location but instead works a substantial amount of time away from the office

360-degree feedback: Multiple-rater systems, which present employees with feedback from different stakeholders and have the potential to provide useful, rich information

Total compensation: Package of compensation and benefits that employees receive

Total Worker Health™ (TWH™): An integrated approach to safety, well-being, and wellness

Traditional-care plans: Also called conventional-indemnity plans, a medical plan that allows participants to select any provider of their choosing without affecting how they are reimbursed, and participants' expenses are reimbursed as they are incurred

Traditional-pay programs: Compensation programs that reward employees based on the content of their job description, title, and/or level

Trainee motivation: The sustained motivation of employees during the training process, which is a predictor of training success

Training relevance: The degree to which trainees see the training as important to their jobs

Training transfer: Whether the training results in changes in job performance

Training transfer climate: Support for training transfer in the work environment from supervisors and coworkers

Training utility reactions: Trainees' belief that the training was actually relevant and useful to their jobs

Transfer through principles: Teaching learners the principles underlying a training concept in order to enhance transfer

Transnational companies: Companies that have operations in multiple countries and do not view themselves as belonging to any one country

Two-step authentication: An extra layer of security that requires an additional piece of information that only the user would know

Unconscious bias: Stereotypes individuals hold that reside beyond their conscious awareness

Unemployment insurance: Payment made to unemployed individuals

Unfair labor practices: Defined in the U.S. as actions taken by either unions or employers that violate the National Labor Relations Act or other legislation. Such acts are investigated by the National Labor Relations Board.

Unfolding model of turnover: A model that recognizes that employees often leave without lining up a new job. Sometimes they leave even though they have happily worked in that firm for years.

Unfreezing: Step 1 in the Lewin model of change, which refers to the process of unfreezing the current system and checking to see that individuals are ready for change

Uniform Guidelines on Employee Selection Procedures: Guidelines adopted by EEOC, the Department of Labor, and the Department of Justice, which outline how selection systems can be designed to comply with EEO laws

Unstructured interview: When the interviewer has a conversation with a job applicant with no fixed protocol for each applicant

Utility: The degree to which an HR function (e.g., a selection procedure) is worth the time or money it requires

Vacation pay: A program that provides employees with compensation for taking time away from work for a planned reason

Valence: The extent to which individuals perceive a reward as being attractive or important

Validity: The accuracy of a measure, or the degree to which an assessment measures what it is supposed to measure

Validity coefficient: The correlation between a selection procedure (e.g., a test) and job performance

Validity generalization: The assumption that selection procedures that have been validated for similar jobs in similar organizations can be assumed to be valid for new situations

Values: Parameters and guidelines for decision making that help an organization realize its vision

Variable: A column in a table that represents a unique characteristic

Vision: An extension of an organization's mission that describes what the organization will look like or be at some point in the future

Voluntary turnover: A departure initiated by an employee

Welcoming: Activities that are intended to be friendly toward employees, such as giving them a personalized e-mail or call or having lunch with the new coworker

Well-being: A worker's well-being is composed of their safety, health, satisfaction, and engagement

Wholly owned subsidiaries: When an organization has subsidiaries overseas and gives the parent company full control over its overseas operations

Work adjustment: Feeling comfortable at work and with one's new tasks

Work analysis: A more recent term for job analysis, which is based on the idea that an employee may need to perform a variety of evolving jobs within an organization

Work engagement: Feelings of emotional connection to work and a state of being in which employees bring their personal selves to work

Work flow analysis: A broad, organization-level focus on work within the organization and within organizational units and the input needed

Work sample: A sample or example of the work produced by a job applicant

Workers' compensation: Program funded entirely by the employer in the form of payroll taxes that provides medical coverage and income replacement for an individual who is injured or becomes ill on the job due to accident or hazard

Workforce labor shortages: Labor market conditions in which there are more jobs available than workers to fill them

Workforce labor surplus (or slack): Labor market conditions in which there is more available labor than organizations can need

Workforce planning: The process of determining what work needs to be done in both the short and long term and coming up with a strategy regarding how those positions will be filled

Workplace accidents: Accidents sustained while on duty in the workplace

Workplace bullying: Consistent mistreatment by others in the workplace

Workplace fatalities: Fatalities that occur while on duty in the workplace

Workplace injuries: Injuries sustained while on duty in the workplace

Workplace intervention: A solution implemented within an organization that focuses on a very specific workplace well-being issue

Work-to-family conflict: When work interferes with nonwork responsibilities

Wrongful dismissal: A dismissal that violates the law

Notes

Chapter 1

1. Case partially based on information in Eat This, Not That! (2018). 16 things you don't know about Chobani. https://www.eatthis.com/chobani/; Durisin, M. (2013). Chobani CEO: Our success has nothing to do with yogurt. *Business Insider*. http://www.businessinsider.com/the-success-story-of-chobani-yogurt-2013-5; Hager, H. (2012). HR shared services: It's not all Greek to Chobani. http://www.humanresourcesiq.com/hr-shared-services/articles/hr-shared-services-it-s-not-all-greek-to-chobani; *Industry News*. (2013). Chobani founder named world entrepreneur 2013. https://www.qsrmagazine.com/news/chobani-founder-named-world-entrepreneur-2013; McGregor, J. (2016). Chobani's CEO is giving up to 10 percent of his company to employees. *Washington Post*. https://www.washingtonpost.com/news/on-leadership/wp/2016/04/27/chobanis-ceo-is-giving-up-to-10-percent-of-his-company-to-employees/; Strom, S. (2016). At Chobani, now it's not just the yogurt that's rich. *New York Times*. http://www.nytimes.com/2016/04/27/business/a-windfall-for-chobani-employees-stakes-in-the-company.html?_r=0; Weisul, K. (2012). 6 hiring secrets from Chobani HR. *Inc.com*. http://www.inc.com/kimberly-weisul/hiring-secrets-chobani-hamdi-ulukaya-craig-gomez.html; Chobani. (2018). About Chobani. https://www.chobani.com/about

2. Nutt, P. C. (2002). *Why decisions fail*. Oakland, CA: Berrett-Koehler Publishers.

3. Coff, R. W. (2002). Human capital, shared expertise, and the likelihood of impasse on corporate acquisitions. *Journal of Management, 28*, 107–128.

4. Employee relations best practices: Costco's approach to HR. http://i-sight.com/resources/employee-relations-best-practices-costco/; Chu, J., & Rockwood, K. (2008). CEO interview: Costco's Jim Sinegal. https://www.fastcompany.com/1042487/ceo-interview-costcos-jim-sinegal; La Monica, P. R. (2015). The best CEOs of the year are . . . *CNN Money*. http://money.cnn.com/gallery/investing/2015/12/23/best-ceos-2015/; 11 reasons to love Costco that have nothing to do with shopping. *Huffington Post*. http://www.huffingtonpost.com/2013/11/19/reasons-love-costco_n_4275774.html; https://www.marketwatch.com/investing/stock/cost

5. Virgin Air website. (2015, January 26). Why is looking after your employees so important? https://www.virgin.com/entrepreneur/why-is-looking-after-your-employees-so-important

6. Gallup Press. (2013). Gallup: State of the American workplace. http://www.gallup.com/poll/188144/employee-engagement-stagnant-2015.aspx

7. Seppala, E., & Cameron, K. (2015). Proof that positive work cultures are more productive. *Harvard Business Review*. https://hbr.org/2015/12/proof-that-positive-work-cultures-are-more-productive

8. Huselid, M. A. (1995). The impact of human resource management practices on turnover, productivity, and corporate financial performance. *Academy of Management Journal, 38*, 635–672; Pfeffer, J. (1998). *The human equation: Building profits by putting people first*. Boston, MA: Harvard Business School Press; Pfeffer, J., & Veiga, J. F. (1999). Putting people first for organizational success. *Academy of Management Executive, 13*, 37–48; Welbourne, T., & Andrews, A. (1996). Predicting performance of Initial Public Offering firms: Should HRM be in the equation? *Academy of Management Journal, 39*, 910–911.

9. Schein, E. (1996). Culture: The missing concept in organization studies. *Administrative Science Quarterly, 41*, 229–240.

10. Cameron, K. S., & Quinn, R. E. (1999). Diagnosing and changing organizational culture: Based on the competing values framework. Reading, MA: Addison-Wesley.

11. Figure partially based on information contained in Cameron, K. S., & Quinn, R. E. (2011). *Diagnosing and changing organizational culture*. Jossey-Bass; Tong, Y. K., & Arvey, R. D. (2015). Managing complexity via the Competing Values Framework. *Journal of Managerial Development, 34*, 653–673.

12. Zielinski, D. (2015, November). The gamification of recruitment. *HR Magazine*, 59–60.

13. U.S. Department of Commerce, U.S. Census Bureau. (2014). The baby boom cohort in the United States: 2012-2060. https://www.census.gov/prod/2014pubs/p25-1141.pdf

14. U.S. Bureau of Labor Statistics. http://www.bls.gov/opub/

reports/womens-earnings/ archive/highlights-of-womens-earnings-in-2014.pdf

15. Pew Research Center. (2015). Projected U.S. population by race and Hispanic origin, 2015–2065, with and without immigrants entering 2015–2065. http://www .pewhispanic.org/2015/09/28/ modern-immigration-wave-brings-59-million-to-u-s-driving-population-growth-and-change-through-2065/ ph_2015-09-28_immigration-through-2065-a2-06/

16. Dougherty, C. (2008, August 14). Whites to lose majority status in US by 2042. *Wall Street Journal*, A3.

17. U.S. Bureau of Labor Statistics. (2016). Employment situation summary Table A. Household data, seasonally adjusted. http://www.bls .gov/news.release/empsit.a.htm

18. Edelman, D. J. (2015). Freelancing in America: 2015. http://www .slideshare.net/upwork/2015-us-freelancer-survey-53166722/1

19. Torpey, E., & Hogan, A. (2016). Working in a gig economy. U.S. Department of Labor, Bureau of Labor Statistics. http://www.bls.gov/ careeroutlook/2016/article/what-is-the-gig-economy.htm

20. France-Presse, A. (2017). Sweden rejects quotas for women on boards of listed companies. *The Guardian*. https://www.theguardian.com/ world/2017/jan/12/sweden-rejects-quotas-women-boardroom-listed-companies; Frenkel, S. (2018). Tech giants brace for Europe's new data privacy rules. *New York Times*. https://www.nytimes .com/2018/01/28/technology/europe-data-privacy-rules.html; Petroff, A., & Cornevin, O. (2017, January 2). France gives workers "right to disconnect" from office email. *CNN Money*. http://money.cnn. com/2017/01/02/technology/france-office-email-workers-law/index.html

21. Krantz, M. (2015, July 15). 10 U.S. companies take the most foreign money. *USA Today*. http://americasmarkets.usatoday .com/2015/07/15/10-u-s-companies-take-the-most-foreign-money/

22. Intel. (2015). Celebrating 50 years of Moore's Law. http://download.intel .com/newsroom/kits/ml50/pdfs/ moores-law-50-years-infographic-entire.pdf

23. Deloitte University Press. (2015). Global human capital trends 2015: Leading in the new world of work. http://www2 .deloitte.com/content/dam/Deloitte/ at/Documents/human-capital/ hc-trends-2015.pdf

24. SHRM Foundation. (2015). What's next?: Use of workforce analytics for competitive advantage. https:// www.shrm.org/about/foundation/ ShapingtheFuture/Documents/ EIU%20Theme%203%20 Analytics%20Report-FINAL.pdf

25. Liberatore, S. (2016). What happens in an Internet second. *Daily Mail*. http:// www.dailymail.co.uk/ sciencetech/article-3662925/ What-happens-Internet-second-54-907-Google-searches-7-252-tweets-125-406-YouTube-video-views-2-501-018-emails-sent.html; Pappas, S. (2016). How big is the Internet, really? LiveScience. http://www.livescience.com/ 54094-how-big-is-the-Internet .html; http://www .Internetlivestats.com/one-second/

26. Wetherill, D. (2016). Broken links: Why analytics investments have yet to pay off. *The Economist*. http://www .zsassociates.com/-/media/files/ publications/public/broken-links-why-analytics-investments-have-yet-to-pay-off.pdf?la=en

27. Business ethics and compliance timeline. (2018). https://www .ethics.org/eci/research/free-toolkit/ ethics-timeline

28. Ethical education in business schools. (2004). http://www.aacsb .edu/~/media/AACSB/Publications/ research-reports/ethics-education. ashx

29. Groth, A., & Bhasin, K. (2011). 18 amazing facts about small businesses in America. *BusinessInsider*. http://www .businessinsider.com/facts-about-small-businesses-in-america-2011-8;

Nazar, J. (2013). 16 surprising statistics about small businesses. *Forbes*. https://www.forbes.com/ sites/jasonnazar/2013/09/09/ 16-surprising-statistics-about-small-businesses/#37afdfd5ec88; U.S. Census Bureau. (2014). SUSB annual data tables by establishment industry https://www.census.gov/ data/tables/2014/econ/susb/2014-susb-annual.html; Non-employer establishments growth rate, 2005–2015. Istrate, E., & Harris, J. (2017). NACo analysis of U.S. Census Bureau data. http://www .naco.org/featured-resources/ future-work-rise-gig-economy

30. Hunter, S. T., Bedell, K. E., & Mumford, M. D. (2007). Climate for creativity: A quantitative review. *Creativity Research Journal*, *19*, 69–90; Zohar, D., & Luria, G. (2005). A multilevel model of safety climate: Cross-level relationships between organization and group-level climates. *Journal of Applied Psychology, 90*, 616–628; Mayer, D. M., Kuenzi, M., & Greenbaum, R. L. (2010). Examining the link between ethical leadership and employee misconduct: The mediating role of ethical climate. *Journal of Business Ethics, 95*, 7–16.

31. Osterhaus, E. (2014). Study:What employers are looking forin HR positions. http://new-talent-times.softwareadvice.com/what-employers-look-for-hr-jobs-0514/

32. Society for Human Resource Management at https:// www.shrm.org

33. Bureau of Labor Statistics, U.S. Department of Labor, Occupational Outlook Handbook, 2016–17 Edition, Human Resources Managers. (2018). http://www.bls .gov/ooh/management/human-resources-managers.htm

34. Glassdoor.com. (2018). 25 best jobs in America. https://www.glassdoor .com/List/Best-Jobs-in-America-LST_KQ0,20.htm

35. Bureau of Labor Statistics, U.S. Department of Labor. (2018). Occupational Outlook Handbook, 2016-17 Edition, Human Resources Managers. http://www.bls.gov/ooh/

management/human-resources-managers.htm and Human Resources Specialists. http://www.bls.gov/ooh/business-and-financial/human-resources-specialists.htm

36. Ibid. http://new-talent-times.softwareadvice.com/what-employers-look-for-hr-jobs-0514/

37. Lengnick-Hall, M. L., & Aguinis, H. (2012). What is the value of human resource certification? A multi-level framework for research. *Human Resource Management Review, 22,* 246–257.

38. Campion, M. A., Fink, A. A., Ruggeberg, B. J., Carr, L., Phillips, G. M., & Odman, R. B. (2011). Doing competencies well: Best practices in competency modeling. *Personnel Psychology, 64,* 225–262; Shippman, J. S., Ash, R. A., Battista, M., Carr, L., Eyde, L. D., Hesketh, B., Kehoe, J., Pearlman, K., Prien, E. P., & Sanchez, J. I. (2000). The practice of competency modeling. *Personnel Psychology, 53,* 703–740; SHRM. (2016). The SHRM Competency Model. https://www.shrm.org/LearningAndCareer/competency-model/PublishingImages/pages/default/SHRM%20Competency%20Model_Detailed%20Report_Final_SECURED.pdf

39. U.S. Bureau of Labor Statistics. (2017). Industrial-Organizational Psychologists. https://www.bls.gov/oes/current/oes193032.htm

40. Academy of Management. (2018). https://aom.org/; Society for Industrial-Organizational Psychology. (2018). What is I-O? www.siop.org

41. EEOC. (2018). Charge statistics FY 1997 through FY 2017. https://www.eeoc.gov/eeoc/statistics/enforcement/charges.cfm

42. Bauer, T., Erdogan, B., Short, J., & Carpenter, M. (2015). *Principles of management*. Washington, DC: Flat World Knowledge.

43. Lindzon, J. (2015). Welcome to the new era of human resources. *Fast Company*. http://www.fastcompany.com/3045829/the-new-rules-of-work/welcome-to-the-new-era-of-human-resources

Chapter 2

1. Collins, L., Fineman, D. R., & Tsuchida, A. (2017, February 28). People analytics: Recalculating the route. https://www2.deloitte.com/insights/us/en/focus/human-capital-trends/2017/people-analytics-in-hr.html#endnote-sup-16; Lewis, G. (2017, March 30). 3 ways data shapes the talent strategy at Tesla, Chevron, and LinkedIn. https://business.linkedin.com/talent-solutions/blog/talent-analytics/2017/3-ways-data-shapes-the-talent-strategy-at-tesla-chevron-and-linkedin; McKeon, A. (2017). How some companies reap rewards of people analytics tools. http://searchhrsoftware.techtarget.com/feature/How-some-companies-reap-rewards-of-people-analytics-tools; Thibodeau, P. (2018, February 14). HR is failing to use people analytics tools, new report says. http://searchhrsoftware.techtarget.com/news/252435104/HR-is-failing-to-use-people-analytics-tools-new-report-says

2. SAS Institute Inc. (n.d.). Jim Goodnight, co-founder & CEO. http://www.sas.com/en_us/company-information/leadership/jim-goodnight.html

3. Strategy. In *Merriam-Webster's online dictionary*. http://www.merriam-webster.com/dictionary/strategy

4. Hambrick, D. C., & Fredrickson, J. W. (2001). Are you sure you have a strategy? *Academy of Management Executive, 15,* 48–59.

5. About Tesla. https://www.tesla.com/about. Musk, E. (2006, August 2). The secret Tesla Motors Master Plan (just between you and me). https://www.tesla.com/blog/secret-tesla-motors-master-plan-just-between-you-and-me; Musk, E. (2016, July 20). Master Plan, part deux. https://www.tesla.com/blog/master-plan-part-deux

6. Hamilton, A. (2008, October 29). Best inventions of 2008: Invention of the year. http://content.time.com/time/specials/packages/article/0,28804,1852747_1854195,00.html

7. Boudette, N. E. (2017, July 3). Tesla's first mass-market car, the Model 3, hits production this week. *New York Times*. https://www.nytimes.com/2017/07/03/business/tesla-model-3-elon-musk.html; Boudreau, J. (2012, June 22). Tesla Motors begins delivering Model S electric cars in Silicon Valley milestone. http://www.mercurynews.com/2012/06/22/tesla-motors-begins-delivering-model-s-electric-cars-in-a-silicon-valley-milestone-2/

8. Hull, D. (2016, November 1). Tesla sees SolarCity boost in 3 years as Musk hits critics. http://www.bloomberg.com/news/articles/2016-11-01/tesla-motors-says-solarcity-will-add-to-tesla-s-balance-sheet

9. Gans, J. (2016, July 25). Why Elon Musk's new strategy makes sense. *Harvard Business Review*. https://hbr.org/2016/07/why-elon-musks-new-strategy-makes-sense

10. Cole, J. (2016, May 18). Tesla, Musk plan $2 billion stock sale to build Model 3, 373,000 people reserved. InsideEVs. http://insideevs.com/tesla-to-raise-2-billion-373000-people-have-reserved-a-model-3

11. Agencies. (2006, March 17). L'Oréal buys Body Shop for £652m. https://www.theguardian.com/business/2006/mar/17/retail.money; http://www.thebodyshop-usa.com/about-us/aboutus_anita-roddick.aspx; Values Report. http://www.thebodyshop.ca/en/pdfs/valuescampaigns/Values_report_lowres_v2.pdf

12. Learned, E. P., Christensen, C. R., Andrews, K. R., & Guth, W. D. (1969). *Business policy: Text and cases*. Homewood, IL: R. D. Irwin.

13. Porter, M. E. (1980). *Competitive strategy: Techniques for analyzing industries and competitors*. New York, NY: Free Press.

14. Barney, J. (1991). Special theory forum the resource-based model of

the firm: Origins, implications, and prospects. *Journal of Management, 17*, 97–98; Burrows, D. (2011, October 6). Apple's stock dips afterdeath of Steve Jobs. http://www.cbsnews.com/news/apples-stock-dips-after-death-of-steve-jobs/; Colt, S. (2015, January 31). Here's how good Tim Cook has been for Apple in one chart. *Business Insider.* http://www.businessinsider.com/apples-stock-price-has-doubled-since-tim-cook-became-ceo-2015-1; How does Tim Cook's management style differ from Steve Jobs? (2015, October 28). http://www.investopedia.com/articles/professionals/081715/how-does-tim-cooks-management-style-differ-steve-jobs.asp; Isaacson, W. (2015). *Steve Jobs.* New York, NY: Simon & Schuster Paperbacks; O'Marah, K. (2015, March 25). Is Tim Cook a better CEO than Steve Jobs? *Forbes.* http://www.forbes.com/sites/kevinomarah/2015/03/25/is-tim-cook-a-better-ceo-than-steve-jobs/#26561cf7776f; Taube, A. (2014, May 23). Steve Jobs thought the "think different" ad that went viral after his death was "horrible." *Business Insider.* http://www.businessinsider.com/steve-jobs-hated-apple-think-different-ad-2014-5

15. Oyedele, A. (2016, October 21). McDonald's is still killing it because of all-day breakfast. *Business Insider.* http://www.businessinsider.com/mcdonalds-reports-third-quarter-earnings-and-beats-on-comp-sales-2016-10

16. Guth, W. D., & MacMillan, I. C. (1986). Strategy implementation versus middle management self-interest. *Strategic Management Journal, 7*, 313–327; When CEOs talk strategy, is anyone listening? (2013, June). https://hbr.org/2013/06/when-ceos-talk-strategy-is-anyone-listening; Eisenhardt, K. M. (1989). Agency theory: An assessment and review. *Academy of Management Review, 14*, 57–74; Wright, P. M., Smart, D. L., & McMahan, G. C. (1995). Matches between human resources and strategy among NCAA basketball

teams. *Academy of Management Journal, 38*, 1052–1074.

17. Schuler, R. S., & Jackson, S. E. (1987). Linking competitive strategies with human resource management practices. *The Academy of Management Executive (1987–1989)*, 207–219.

18. Legge, K. (1995). What is human resource management? In *Human resource management: Management, work and organisations.* London, UK: Palgrave.

19. Abelson, J. (2005, July 13). Gillette and P&G shareholders approve takeover. *New York Times.* http://www.nytimes.com/2005/07/13/business/worldbusiness/gillette-and-pg-shareholders-approve-takeover.html?_r=0; Kanter, R. M. (2009, October). Mergers that stick. https://hbr.org/2009/10/mergers-that-stick. Sierra-Cedar 2016–2017 HR Systems Survey White Paper, 19th Annual Edition. (n.d.). http://www.sierra-cedar.com/white-papers/; Sorkin, A. R., & Lohr, S. (2005, January 28). Procter said to reach a deal to buy Gillette in $55 billion accord. *New York Times.* http://www.nytimes.com/2005/01/28/business/procter-said-to-reach-a-deal-to-buy-gillette-in-55-billion-accord.html

20. Ferris, G. R., Barnum, D. T., Rosen, S. D., Holleran, L. P., & Dulebohn, J. H. (1995). Toward business–university partnerships in human resource management: Integration of science and practices. In G. R. Ferris, S. D. Rosen, & D. T. Barnum (Eds.), *Handbook of human resource management* (pp. 1–16). Cambridge, MA: Blackwell Publishers.

21. Clark, M., & Schramm, J. (2012). *Future insights: The top trends according to SHRM's HR subject matter experts.* Alexandria, VA: Society for Human Resource Management.

22. Huselid, M. A., Becker, B. E., & Beatty, R. W. (2005). *The workforce scorecard: Managing human capital to execute strategy.* Cambridge, MA: Harvard Business Review Press; Kaplan, R. S., & Norton, D. P. (1996). Using the balanced

scorecard as a strategic management system. *Harvard Business Review*, 75–85.

23. Marler, J. H. (2012). Strategic human resource management in context: A historical and global perspective. *Academy of Management Perspectives, 26*, 6–11.

24. Ibid.

25. Huselid, M. A. (1995). The impact of human resource management practices on turnover, productivity, and corporate financial performance. *Academy of Management Journal, 38*, 635–672; Pfeffer, J. (1998). Seven practices of successful organizations. *California Management Review, 40*, 96–124.

26. Pfeffer, J. (1998). Seven practices of successful organizations. *California Management Review, 40*, 96–124.

27. Huselid, M. A. (1995). The impact of human resource management practices on turnover, productivity, and corporate financial performance. *Academy of Management Journal, 38*, 635–672.

28. Tzabbar, D., Tzafrir, S., & Baruch, Y. (2016). A bridge over troubled water: Replication, integration and extension of the relationship between HRM practices and organizational performance using moderating meta-analysis. *Human Resource Management Review, 27*, 134–148.

29. Boxall, P., & Macky, K. (2009). Research and theory on high-performance work systems: Progressing the high-involvement stream. *Human Resource Management Journal, 19*, 3–23.

30. Huselid, M. A. (1995). The impact of human resource management practices on turnover, productivity, and corporate financial performance. *Academy of Management Journal, 38*, 635–672.

31. Milliman, J., Von Glinow, M. A., & Nathan, M. (1991). Organizational life cycles and strategic international human resource management in multinational companies: Implications for congruence theory. *Academy of Management Review, 16*, 318–339; Schuler, R. S.,

Dowling, P. J., & De Cieri, H. (1993). An integrative framework of strategic international human resource management. *Journal of Management, 19,* 419–459; Taylor, S., Beechler, S., & Napier, N. (1996). Toward an integrative model of strategic international human resource management. *Academy of Management Review, 21,* 959–985.

32. Jackson, S. E., Schuler, R. S., & Jiang, K. (2014). An aspirational framework for strategic human resource management. *Academy of Management Annals, 8,* 1–56.

33. Lepak, D. P., Liao, H., Chung, Y., & Harden, E. E. (2006). A conceptual review of human resource management systems in strategic human resource management research. *Research in Personnel and Human Resources Management, 25,* 217–271.

34. Dineva, B. (2015, May 11). Data: Referrals strongly impact retention and depend on employee performance. https://business .linkedin.com/talent-solutions/ blog/2015/05/data-referrals- strongly-impact-retention-and- depend-on-employee-performance; Lewis, G. (2017, March 30). 3 ways data shapes the talent strategy at Tesla, Chevron, and LinkedIn. https://business.link edin.com/talent-solutions/blog/ talent-analytics/2017/3-ways- data-shapes-the-talent-strategy- at-tesla-chevron-and-linkedin; Kazmierczak, K. (2015, March 9). Tesla Motors—growing rapidly and strategically. http://www.hci.org/ blog/tesla-motors-growing-rapidly- and-strategically

35. The Economist Intelligence Unit report for PwC. (2014). *Guts & gigabytes.* PwC.

36. Rasmussen, T., & Ulrich, D. (2015). Learning from practice: How HR analytics avoids being a management fad. *Organizational Dynamics, 44,* 236–242.

37. Angrave, D., Charlwood, A., Kirkpatrick, I., Lawrence, M., & Stuart, M. (2016). HR and analytics: Why HR is set to fail the big data challenge. *Human Resource Management Journal, 26,* 1–11; Lohr, S. (2013, April 20). Big data, trying to build better workers. *New York Times.* http://www.nytimes .com/2013/04/21/technology/big- data-trying-to-build-better-workers .html; Ransbotham, S., Kiron, D., & Prentice, P. K. (2016, March 8). Hard work behind analytics success: Why competitive advantage from analytics is declining and what to do about it. *MIT Sloan Management Review*; Silverman, R. E., & Waller, N. (2015, March 13). The algorithm that tells the boss who might quit. *Wall Street Journal.* http://www .wsj.com/articles/the-algorithm- that-tells-the-boss-who-might- quit-1426287935; Streitfield, D. (2015, August 17). Data-crunching is coming to help your boss manage your time. http://www.nytimes .com/2015/08/18/technology/data- crunching-is-coming-to-help-your- boss-manage-your-time.html

38. Lewis, G. (2017, March 30). 3 ways data shapes the talent strategy at Tesla, Chevron, and LinkedIn. https://business .linkedin.com/talent-solutions/blog/ talent-analytics/2017/3-ways-data- shapes-the-talent-strategy-at-tesla- chevron-and-linkedin

39. SHRM Foundation. (2016, May). *Use of workforce analytics for competitive advantage.* https:// www.shrm.org/about/foundation/ shapingthefuture/documents/ eiu%20theme%203%20analytics%20 report-final.pdf

40. Deloitte University Press. (2015). *Global human capital trends 2015.*

41. Davenport, T. (n.d.). In praise of "light quants" and "analytical translators." https://www2.deloitte .com/us/en/pages/deloitte-analytics/ articles/in-praise-of-light-quants- and-analytical-translators.html

42. SHRM Foundation. (2016, May). Use of workforce analytics for competitive advantage. https:// www.shrm.org/about/foundation/ shapingthefuture/documents/ eiu%20theme%203%20analytics%20 report-final.pdf

43. Cascio, W. (1991). *Costing human resources: The financial impact of behavior in organizations* (3rd ed.). Boston, MA: PWS-Kent; Mobley, W. H. (1982). *Employee turnover: Causes, consequences, and control.* Menlo Park, CA: Addison-Wesley.

44. Fitz-Enz, J. (1997). It's costly to lose good employees. *Workforce, 76*(8), 50–52; Hale, J. (1998). Strategic rewards: Keeping your best talent from walking out the door. *Compensation and Benefits Management, 14,* 39–50.

45. Griffeth, R. W., Hom, P. W., & Gaertner, S. (2000). A meta- analysis of antecedents and correlates of employee turnover: Update, moderator tests, and research implications for the next millennium. *Journal of Management, 26,* 463–488; Kristof-Brown, A. L., Zimmerman, R. D., & Johnson, E. C. (2005). Consequences of individuals' fit at work: A meta-analysis of person–job, person–organization, person–group, and person– supervisor fit. *Personnel Psychology, 58,* 281–342.

46. Bauer, T. N. (2010). Onboarding new employees: Maximizing success. https://www.shrm.org/ about/foundation/products/ documents/onboarding%20 epg-%20final.pdf

47. *The National Law Review.* (2016, October 14). EEOC convenes meeting to discuss "Big Data" analytics. http://www.natlawreview .com/article/eeoc-convenes-meeting- to-discuss-big-data-analytics

48. IBM Big Data & Analytics Hub. (n.d.). The four V's of big data. http://www.ibmbigdatahub.com/ infographic/four-vs-big-data

49. Wilhelmy, A., Kleinmann, M., König, C. J., Melchers, K. G., & Truxillo, D. M. (2016). How and why do interviewers try to make impressions on applicants? A qualitative study. *Journal of Applied Psychology, 101,* 313–332.

50. The White House. (2016, May 4). Big risks, big opportunities: The intersection of big data and civil rights. https://obamawhitehouse

.archives.gov/blog/2016/05/04/big-risks-big-opportunities-intersection-big-data-and-civil-rights

51. O'Neill, C. (2016). *Weapons of math destruction: How Big Data increases inequality and threats democracy.* New York, NY: Crown.

52. Knaflic, C. N. (2015). *Storytelling with data: A data visualization guide for business professionals.* Hoboken, NJ: Wiley.

53. Potts, R., & LaMarsh, J. (2004). *Managing change for success: Effecting change for optimum growth and maximum efficiency.* Duncan Baird.

54. Cohen, P. (2015, April 13). One company's new minimum wage: $70,000 a year. *New York Times.* http://www.nytimes.com/2015/04/14/business/owner-of-gravity-payments-a-credit-card-processor-is-setting-a-new-minimum-wage-70000-a-year.html; Cohen, P. (2015, July 31). A company copes with backlash against the raise that roared. *New York Times.* http://www.nytimes.com/2015/08/02/business/a-company-copes-with-backlash-against-the-raise-that-roared.html?smid=fb-nytimes&smtyp=cur&_r=1

55. Kavanagh, M. J., Thite, M., & Johnson, R. D. (2015). *Human resource information systems: Basics, applications, and future directions* (3rd ed.). Thousand Oaks, CA: Sage.

Chapter 3

1. Byrne, N. (2010). Nissan North American transforms HR services. https://www.hrexchangenetwork.com/hr-shared-services/articles/nissan-north-america-transforms-hr-services; Campbell, P. (2017). Renault-Nissan alliance becomes world's largest carmaker. *Financial Times.* https://www.ft.com/content/fe682336-7365-11e7-aca6-c6bd07df1a3c; Carey, S. (2017). Renault follows in Nissan's tracks with global Workday rollout for HR. ComputerWorldUK. https://www.computerworlduk.com/cloud-computing/what-expect-from-aws-reinvent-2016-3648942/; Ghosn, C. (2002). Saving the business without losing the company. *Harvard Business Review.* https://hbr.org/2002/01/saving-the-business-without-losing-the-company; Ghosn, C., & Riés, P. (2004). *Shift: Inside Nissan's historic revival.* Crown Business; McLain, S., & Stoll, J. (2017). Carlos Ghosn steps down as Nissan CEO. *Wall Street Journal.* https://www.wsj.com/articles/carlos-ghosn-resigns-as-nissan-ceo-1487807319; Statista (2017). Number of Nissan employees from FY 2009 to FY 2016. https://www.statista.com/statistics/370511/number-of-nissan-employees/; Statista (2017). Number of Renault Group employees between 2012 and 2016. https://www.statista.com/statistics/387166/number-of-renault-group-employees/

2. Tannenbaum, S. I. (1990). Human resource information systems: User group implications. *Journal of Systems Management, 41,* 27–32.

3. Ruël, H., Bondarouk, T., & Looise, J. K. (2004). E-HRM: Innovation or irritation. An explorative empirical study in five large companies on web-based HRM. *Management Review,* 364–380.

4. EmployeeConnect (2016). DHL case study: Best online solution with EmployeeConnect. https://www.employeeconnect.com/blog/portfolio_page/dhl-case-study/

5. Miracle, K. (2004). Case study: The City of Virginia Beach's innovative tool for workforce planning. *Public Personnel Management, 33,* 449–458.

6. Beulen, E. (2008). The contribution of a global service provider's human resources information system (HRIS) to staff retention in emerging markets—comparing issues and implications in six developing countries. Paper presented at the Information Systems Workshop on Global Sourcing: Services, Knowledge, and Innovation.

7. Kavanaugh, M. J., Thite, M., & Johnson, R. D. (2015). *Human resource information systems: Basics, applications, and future directions.* Thousand Oaks, CA: Sage, p. 6, emphasis in original.

8. Carlson, K. D., & Kavanaugh, M. J. (2015). HRIS in Action from HR metrics and workforce analytics chapter. Reprinted with permission from M. J. Kavanaugh, M. Thite, & R. D. Johnson (2015). *Human resource information systems: Basics, applications, and future directions.* Thousand Oaks, CA: Sage.

9. Maier, C., Laumer, S., Eckhardt, A., & Weitzel, T. (2013). Analyzing the impact of HRIS implementations on HR personnel's job satisfaction and turnover intention. *Journal of Strategic Information Systems, 22,* 193–207.

10. Maier, C., Laumer, S., Eckhardt, A., & Weitzel, T. (2012). Analyzing the impact of HRIS implemention on HR personnel's job satisfaction and turnover intention. *Journal of Strategic Information Systems, 22,* 193–207.

11. Marler, J. H., & Floyd, B. D. (2015). Database concepts and applications in HRIS. In M. J. Kavanagh, M. Thite, & R. D. Johnson (Eds.). *Human resource information systems: Basics, applications, and future directions* (3rd ed.). Thousand Oaks, CA: Sage.

12. SHRM (2015). Designing and managing a Human Resource Information System. https://www.shrm.org/resourcesandtools/tools-and-samples/toolkits/pages/managingahumanresourceinformationsystem.aspx

13. Carlson, K. D., & Kavanaugh, M. J. (2015). HRIS in Action from HR metrics and workforce analytics chapter. Reprinted with permission from M. J. Kavanaugh, M. Thite, & R. D. Johnson (2015). *Human resource information systems: Basics, applications, and future directions.* Thousand Oaks, CA: Sage.

14. Cleveland, W. S., Diaconis, P., & McGill, R. (1982). Variables on scatterplots look more highly correlated when the scales are increased. *Science, 216,* 1138–1141.

15. Knaflic, C. N. (2015). *Storytelling with data: A data visualization guide for business professionals.* Hoboken, NJ: Wiley.

16. Ibid.

17. Hussain, Z., Wallace, J., & Cornelius, N.E. (2007). The use and impact of human resource information systems on human resource management professionals. *Information & Management, 44,* 74–89; Lawler, E. E., Levenson, A., & Boudreau, J. W. (2004). HR metrics and analytics: Use and impact. *Human Resource Planning, 26,* 15–29; Ngai, E. W. T., & Wat, F. K. T. (2006). Human resource information systems: A review and empirical analysis. *Personnel Review, 35,* 297–314.

18. Vorhauser-Smith, S. (2014). The little word behind Big Data in HR. *Forbes.* https://www.forbes.com/sites/sylviavorhausersmith/2014/11/10/the-little-word-behind-big-data-in-hr-who/2/#590371fd4bd0

19. Beadles, N., Lowery, C., & Johns, K. (2005). The impact of human resource information systems: An exploratory study in the public sector. *Communications of the IIMA, 5,* 39–46; Bussler, L., & Davis, E. (2002). Information systems: The quiet revolution in human resource management. *Journal of Computer Information Systems, 42,* 17–20; Hussain, Z., Wallace, J., & Cornelius, N. E. (2007). The use and impact of human resource information systems on human resource management professionals. *Information & Management, 44,* 74–89.

20. Teo, T. S. H., Lim, G. S., & Fedric, S. A. (2007). The adoption and diffusion of human resources information systems in Singapore. *Asia Pacific Journal of Human Resources, 45,* 44–62.

21. Stone, E. F., & Stone, D. L. (1990). Privacy in organizations: Theoretical issues, research findings, and protection mechanisms. *Research in Personnel and Human Resources Management, 8,* 349–411.

22. Lukaszewski, K. M., Stone, D. L., & Stone-Romero, E. F. (2008). The effects of the ability to choose the type of human resources system on perceptions of invasion of privacy and system satisfaction. *Journal of Business & Psychology, 23,* 73–86.

23. Eddy, E. R., Stone, D. L., & Stone-Romero, E. E. (1999). The effects of information management policies on reactions to human resource information systems: An integration of privacy and procedural justice perspectives. *Personnel Psychology, 52,* 335–358.

24. SHRM. (2016). *SHRM survey findings: Using social media for talent acquisition: Recruitment and screening.* Alexandria, VA: Society for Human Resource Management. https://www.shrm.org/hr-today/trends-and-forecasting/research-and-surveys/Documents/SHRM-Social-Media-Recruiting-Screening-2015.pdf

25. Rao, P. S., Frenkel, S., & Schreuer, M. (2018). Mark Zuckerberg to meet European Parliament members over Facebook's data use. *New York Times.* https://www.nytimes.com/2018/05/16/technology/zuckerberg-europe-data-cambridge-analytica.html; Snell, J., & Care, D. (2013). Use of online data in the Big Data Era: Legal issues raised by the use of web crawling and scraping tools for analytics purposes. *Bloomberg Law.* https://www.bna.com/legal-issues-raised-by-the-use-of-web-crawling-and-scraping-tools-for-analytics-purposes/

26. Virgin Pulse: Personalized wellbeing. https://www.virginpulse.com/our-products/; EEOC Enforcement Guidance on the Americans with Disabilities Act and Psychiatric. Disabilities. https://www.eeoc.gov/policy/docs/psych.html

27. SHRM. (2014). Record-keeping policy: Safeguarding Social Security numbers. https://www.shrm.org/ResourcesAndTools/tools-and-samples/policies/Pages/cms_015266.aspx

28. Stallings, W., & Brown, L. (2015). *Computer security: Principles and practice* (3rd ed.). Boston, MA: Pearson.

29. Naylor, B. (2016). One year after OPM data breach, what has the government learned? *NPR.* http://www.npr.org/sections/alltechconsidered/2016/06/06/480968999/one-year-after-opm-data-breach-what-has-the-government-learned; Sanders, S. (2015). Massive data breach puts 4 million federal employees' records at risk. *NPR.* http://www.npr.org/sections/thetwo-way/2015/06/04/412086068/massive-data-breach-puts-4-million-federal-employees-records-at-risk

30. Gustin, S. (2010). Google buys giant New York building for $1.9 billion. *Wired.* https://www.wired.com/2010/12/google-nyc/

31. Lomas, N. (2016). Zuckerberg's Twitter, Pinterest, LinkedIn accounts hacked. *Tech Crunch.* https://techcrunch.com/2016/06/06/zuckerbergs-twitter-pinterest-linkedin-accounts-hacked/

32. Anthes, M. (2018). Three ways blockchain will disrupt traditional business and impact marketing in 2018. *Forbes.* https://www.forbes.com/sites/forbesagencycouncil/2018/01/29/three-ways-blockchain-will-disrupt-traditional-business-and-impact-marketing-in-2018/#4b2d39915e26

33. Ibid.

34. Brown, G., & Smit, N. (2017). Will blockchain disrupt the HR technology landscape? Deloitte. https://www2.deloitte.com/nl/nl/pages/human-capital/articles/will-blockchain-disrupt-the-hr-technology-landscape.html

35. EMI Blogger. (2017). Data breach stats show almost 1.4B records were compromised in 2016. https://cybersec.buzz/data-breach-stats-show-almost-1-4b-data-records-compromised-2016/; Leech, M. (2017). Data breach statistics 2017: First half results are in. https://blog.gemalto.com/security/2017/09/21/new-breach-level-index-findings-for-first-half-of-2017/

36. Fontana, J. (2016). Tough new privacy laws in EU could signal global changes. *ZDNet.* http://www.zdnet.com/article/tough-new-privacy-laws-in-eu-could-signal-global-changes/

37. PwC. (2017). Pulse survey: US companies ramping up General Data Protection Regulation (GDPR) budgets. https://www.pwc.com/us/en/increasing-it-effectiveness/publications/assets/pwc-gdpr-series-pulse-survey.pdf

38. Rayome, A. D. (2017). Negligent employees are no. 1 cause of cybersecurity breaches at SMBs. *TechRepublic.* https://www.techrepublic.com/article/report-negligent-employees-are-no-1-cause-of-cybersecurity-breaches-at-smbs/; 2017 state of cybersecurity in small & medium sized businesses. https://keepersecurity.com/2017-State-Cybersecurity-Small-Medium-Businesses-SMB.html

39. How to select an HRIS (2015). SHRM. https://www.shrm.org/resourcesandtools/tools-and-samples/how-to-guides/pages/howtoselectanhrissystem.aspx

40. Wilson-Evered, E., & Hartel, C. E. J. (2009). Measuring attitudes to HRIS implementation: A field study to inform implementation methodology. *Asia Pacific Journal of Human Resources, 47,* 374–384.

41. Teo, T. S. H., Lim, G. S., & Fedric, S. A. (2007). The adoption and diffusion of human resources information systems in Singapore. *Asia Pacific Journal of Human Resources, 45,* 44–62.

42. Kavanaugh, M. J., & Johnson, R. D. (2018). *Human resource information systems* (4th ed.). Thousand Oaks, CA: Sage.

43. SHRM. (2015). Designing and managing a Human Resource Information System. https://www.shrm.org/resourcesandtools/tools-and-samples/toolkits/pages/managingahumanresourceinformationsystem.aspx

44. Dery, K., Hall, R., Wailes, N., & Wiblen, S. (2013). Lost in translation? An actor-network approach to HRIS implementation. *Journal of Strategic Information Systems, 22,* 225–237.

45. Sung, W., Woehler, M. L., Fagan, J. M., Grosser, T. J., Floyd, T. M., &

Labiance, G. (2017). Employees' responses to an organizational merger: Intraindividual change in organizational identification, attachment, and turnover. *Journal of Applied Psychology, 102,* 910–934.

46. Change management: The HR strategic imperative as a business partner. (2007, December). *HR Magazine, 52*; SHRM. (2017). Managing organizational change. https://www.shrm.org/resourcesandtools/tools-and-samples/toolkits/pages/managingorganizationalchange.aspx

47. Oreg, S., & Sverdlik, N. (2011). Ambivalence toward imposed change: The conflict between dispositional resistance to change and the orientation toward the change agent. *Journal of Applied Psychology, 96,* 337–349.

48. Kepes, B. (2013). Avon's failed SAP implementation a perfect example of the enterprise IT revolution. *Forbes.* https://www.forbes.com/sites/benkepes/2013/12/17/avons-failed-sap-implementation-a-perfect-example-of-enterprise-it-revolution/#6cb5dc4e31a6

49. Bartlett, J. E., & Bartlett, M. E. (2013). Introduction to Human Resource Information Systems-SHRM. https://www.shrm.org/.../Bartlett%20HRIS%20PPTto%20Post%20Online.pptx; McGoon, C. (1995, March). Secrets of building influence. *Communication World, 12*(3), 16; Michelman, P. (2007, July). Overcoming resistance to change. *Harvard Management Update, 12*(7), 3–4; Stanley, T. L. (2002, January). Change: A common-sense approach. *Supervision, 63*(1), 7–10.

50. Davis, F. D., Bagozzi, R. P., & Warsaw, P. R. (1989). User acceptance of computer technology: A comparison of two theoretical models. *Management Science, 35,* 982–1003; Goodhue, D. L. (1995). Understanding user evaluations of information systems. *Management Science, 41,* 1827–1844.

51. Cameron, K. S., & Quinn, R. E. (1999). *Diagnosing and changing*

organizational culture: Based on the competing values framework. Reading, MA: Addison-Wesley.

52. Gargeya, V. B., & Brady, C. (2006). Success and failure factors of adopting SAP in ERP system implementation. *Business Process Management Journal, 11,* 501–516.

53. Kavanaugh, M. J., & Johnson, R. D. (2018). *Human resource information systems* (4th ed.). Thousand Oaks, CA: Sage.

54. Higgs, M., & Rowland, D. (2011). What does it take to implement change successfully? A study of the behaviors of successful change leaders. *Journal of Applied Behavioral Science, 47,* 309–335.

55. Zhao, H. H., Seibert, S. E., Taylor, S. M., Lee, C., & Lam, W. (2016). Not even the past: The joint influence of former leader and new leader during leader succession in the midst of organizational change. *Journal of Applied Psychology, 101,* 1730–1738.

56. Rooney, B. (2010, February 5). Buffett's Berkshire loses top S&P credit rating. *CNN Money.* http://money.cnn.com/2010/02/05/news/companies/Berkshire_Hathaway_credit_rating/index.htm, https://www.adp.com/solutions/large-business/services/benefits-administration/analytics-and-decision-support.aspx; Nash, K. S. (2016, May 31). ADP's CIO says algorithms measure employee flight risk. *Wall Street Journal.* http://blogs.wsj.com/cio/2016/05/31/adp-algorithms-tackle-employee-flight-risk/; U.S. Bureau of Labor Statistics, Labor Force Statistics from the Current Population Survey. http://data.bls.gov/timeseries/LNS14000000; Carsten, J. M., & Spector, P. E. (1987). Unemployment, job satisfaction, and employee turnover: A meta-analytic test of the Muchinsky model. *Journal of Applied Psychology, 72,* 374–381; U.S. Bureau of Labor Statistics, Job Openings and Labor Turnover Survey. http://data.bls.gov/timeseries/JTS00000000TSR

Chapter 4

1. Bellstrong, K. (2015, August 4). Why Pinterest's new diversity goals actually matter. Fortune.com. http://fortune.com/2015/08/03/pinterest-diversity-goals/; Cohen, D. (2017, December 20). Pinterest updated its progress on its 2017 diversity efforts. http://www.adweek.com/digital/pinterest-diversity-2017/; Guynn, J. (2015, July 31). Pinterest launches diversity project to see what sticks. *USA Today*; Kokalitcheva, K. (2016, January 21). Pinterest hires its first head of diversity. *Fortune*. https://www.forbes.com/sites/kathleenchaykowski/2016/01/06/pinterest-hires-its-first-head-of-diversity/#6dfe0a1a787f; Lorenzetti, L. (2015, August 4). What Pinterest is learning from Pittsburgh Steelers about diversity. *Fortune*. http://fortune.com/2015/07/30/pinterest-diversity-initiative; Rao, L. (2016, March 15). Tech's diversity fixer. *Fortune*. http://fortune.com/2016/03/15/tech-diversity-problem; Vara, V. (2015, November). Pinterest's great expectations. *Fast Company*, 33–36.

2. Bell, M. P. (2012). *Diversity in organizations*. Mason, OH: Cengage.

3. U.S. Bureau of Labor Statistics. (2016). Labor force statistics from the current population survey. https://www.bls.gov/cps/cpsaat11.htm

4. Bell, S. T., Villado, A. J., Lukasik, M. A., Belau, L., & Briggs, A. L. (2010). Getting specific about demographic diversity variable and team performance relationship: A meta-analysis. *Journal of Management, 37,* 709–743; Roberge, M. E., & van Dick, R. (2010). Recognizing the benefits of diversity: When and how does diversity increase group performance? *Human Resource Management Review, 20,* 295–308.

5. Boehm, S. A., Kunze, F., & Bruch, H. (2014). Spotlight on age-diversity climate: The impact of age-inclusive HR practices on firm-level outcomes. *Personnel Psychology, 67,* 667–704; Chrobot-Mason, D., & Aramovich, N. P. (2013). The psychological benefits of creating an affirming climate for workplace diversity. *Group & Organization Management, 38,* 659–689; Nishii, L. H. (2013). The benefits of climate for inclusion for gender-diverse groups. *Academy of Management Journal, 56,* 1754–1774.

6. Diel, S. (2010). TIAA-CREF chief Roger W. Ferguson Jr. tells Birmingham audience that diverse companies outperform others. *The Birmingham News* (2010, November 4). http://blog.al.com/businessnews/2010/11/tiaa-cref_chief_roger_w_fergus.html; Reuters (2008, April 4). Chief is selected at TIAA-CREF. *New York Times.* https://www.nytimes.com/2008/04/04/business/04pension.html; Carter, D. A., Simkins, B. J., & Simpson, W. G. (2003). Corporate governance, board diversity, and firm value. *The Financial Review, 38,* 33–53.

7. van Dijk, H., van Engen, M. L., & van Knippenberg, D. (2012). Defying conventional wisdom: A meta-analytical examination of the differences between demographic and job-related diversity relationships with performance. *Organizational Behavior and Human Decision Processes, 119,* 38–53.

8. Ferro, S. (2016, March 1). Here's why facial recognition tech can't figure out black people. *Huffington Post*; McKay, P. F., Avery, D. R., Liao, H., & Morris, M. A. (2011). Does diversity climate lead to customer satisfaction? It depends on the service climate and business unit demography. *Organization Science, 22,* 788–803; Shaver, K. (2012, March 25). Female dummy makes her mark on male-dominated crash tests. *Washington Post.* https://www.washingtonpost.com/local/trafficandcommuting/female-dummy-makes-her-mark-on-male-dominated-crash-tests/2012/03/07/gIQANBLjaS_story.html?utm_term=.12ce7957f5ea

9. Miller, T., & Triana, M. D. C. (2009). Demographic diversity in the boardroom: Mediators of the board diversity-firm performance relationship. *Journal of Management Studies, 46,* 755–786.

10. Anonymous. (2017, June 7). These are the women CEOs leading Fortune 500 companies. *Fortune*. http://fortune.com/2017/06/07/fortune-500-women-ceos/; Mariño, K. J. (2016). Top 10 Latino CEOs at Fortune 500 companies you should know about. *Latin Post.* http://www.latinpost.com/articles/107285/20160108/top-10-latino-ceos-at-fortune-500-companies-you-should-know-about.htm

11. Sacco, J. M., & Schmitt, N. (2005). A dynamic multilevel model of demographic diversity and misfit effects. *Journal of Applied Psychology, 90,* 203–231.

12. Guynn, J. (2015, May 13). Google's bias busting talks tackle prejudices. *USA Today.* https://www.usatoday.com/story/tech/2015/05/12/google-unconscious-bias-diversity/27055485; Nededog, J. (2016, June 30). "Full frontal" producer talks the hiring process for one of TV's most diverse writing staffs. *Business Insider.* https://www.businessinsider.com/how-samantha-bee-found-her-diverse-writing-team-2016-6; Rice, C. (2013, October). How blind auditions help orchestras to eliminate gender bias. *The Guardian.* https://www.theguardian.com/women-in-leadership/2013/oct/14/blind-auditions-orchestras-gender-bias

13. U.S. Department of Labor. (2016). Equal employment opportunity. https://www.dol.gov/general/topic/discrimination

14. EEOC. (2018). Charge statistics FY 1997 through FY 2017. https://www.eeoc.gov/eeoc/statistics/enforcement/charges.cfm

15. EEOC. (2016). Coverage. https://www.eeoc.gov/employers/coverage.cfm

16. EEOC. (2018). Filing a lawsuit. https://www.eeoc.gov/employees/lawsuit.cfm

17. EEOC. (2016). Employees and job applicants. https://www.eeoc.gov/employees/index.cfm

18. EEOC. (2018). Charge statistics FY1997 through FY 2017. https://www.eeoc.gov/eeoc/statistics/enforcement/charges.cfm

19. Banished to a cubicle: Does isolation = retaliation? (2016, May). *HR Specialist: Employment Law, 46.5*, 3.

20. U.S. Bureau of Labor Statistics. (2016, January 15). Women's earnings 83 percent of men's, but vary by occupation. http://www.bls.gov/opub/ted/2016/womens-earnings-83-percent-of-mens-but-vary-by-occupation.htm

21. EEOC. (2016). What you can expect after you file a charge. https://www.eeoc.gov/employees/process.cfm

22. EEOC. (2016). Facts about equal pay and compensation discrimination. https://www.eeoc.gov/eeoc/publications/fs-epa.cfm; *HR and Employment Law News* (2016, September 27). Job titles irrelevant in equal pay claims, settlement shows. http://hr.blr.com/HR-news/Discrimination/Equal-Pay-Comparable-Worth/Job-Titles-Irrelevant-Equal-Pay-Claims-Settlement/#

23. EEOC. (2016). Remedies for employment discrimination. https://www.eeoc.gov/employees/remedies.cfm

24. EEOC. (2010). Walmart to pay more than $11.7 million to settle EEOC sex discrimination suit. https://www.eeoc.gov/eeoc/newsroom/release/3-1-10.cfm

25. Fitzke, S., Gorajski, S., & Parker, B. (2015, March). Weigh EEOC guidance when considering criminal histories. *HR Specialist: Minnesota Law, 8.3*, 6; National origin discrimination: What managers need to know. (2015, May). *HR Specialist: Minnesota Employment Law, 4.* Zachary, M. K. (2015). Language requirements and the law. *Labor Law for Supervisors,* 19–23.

26. EEOC. (2002). Title VII: BFOQ. https://www.eeoc.gov/eeoc/foia/letters/2002/titlevii_bfoq.html; Shorter, T. N., McLaughlin, C. L., & O'Day, T. (2007). Can we use gender in our hiring decisions? The discrimination Bona Fide Occupational Qualification (BFOQ) applied to health care. http://www.gklaw.com/news.cfm?action=pub_detail&publication_id=544;

27. Progress Illinois. (2016, September 20). Appeals court sides with Chicago female paramedics in sex discrimination suit. http://progressillinois.com/news/content/2016/09/20/appeals-court-sides-chicago-female-paramedics-sex-discrimination-suit

28. EEOC. (2016). Harassment. https://www.eeoc.gov/laws/types/harassment.cfm

29. Equal Pay and Discrimination against women. http://employment.findlaw.com/employment-discrimination/equal-pay-and-discrimination-against-women.html

30. Robinson-Jacobs, K. (2015, December 21). EEOC to announce $4 million settlement in Sara Lee race discrimination case. http://www.dallasnews.com/business/business/2015/12/21/eeoc-to-announce-largest-settlement-against-sara-lee-parent-in-race-discrimination-case

31. Ahearn, T. (2016, September 1). Temporary staffing agency to pay $430,000 to settle EEOC race discrimination suit. http://www.esrcheck.com/wordpress/2016/09/01/temporary-staffing-agency-to-pay-435000-to-settle-eeoc-race-discrimination-suit; Gurrieri, V. (2016). Sheet metal union to pony up $1.6M in EEOC race bias case. http://www.law360.com/articles/784572/sheet-metal-union-to-pony-up-1-6m-in-eeoc-race-bias-case

32. Jensen, C. (2016, October 5). Entrepreneurship puts returning citizens back in the game. http://streetsense.org/article/entrepreneurship-returning-citizens-jobs-reentry/#.WBE3YuErL-Y; National employment law project. (2016, December 1). Ban the box: US cities, counties, and states adopt fair hiring policies. http://www.nelp.org/publication/ban-the-box-fair-chance-hiring-state-and-local-guide/; Second chance employment. http://www.daveskillerbread.com/media/second-chance-employment/; Schmitt, J., & Warner, K. (2010, November). Ex-offenders and the labor market. http://cepr.net/documents/publications/ex-offenders-2010-11.pdf; Smialek, J. (2014, February 7). Putting released prisoners back to work. *Bloomberg*.com; Vega, T. (2015, October 30). Out of prison and out of work: Jobs out of reach for former inmates. http://money.cnn.com/2015/10/30/news/economy/former-inmates-unemployed/

33. Diamond, T. E. (2016, May). 6 issues to consider when updating your employee handbook. *HR Specialist: Pennsylvania Employment Law, 11.5*, 6.

34. Wickham, A. (2016). Accenture reaches $500k settlement in bias class action. http://www.law360.com/articles/851153/accenture-reaches-500k-settlement-in-bias-class-action

35. EEOC. (2016). Pregnancy discrimination. https://www.eeoc.gov/eeoc/publications/fs-preg.cfm

36. Rhodan, M. (2015, March 26). Supreme Court rules in favor of protecting pregnant women in the workplace. *Time*.com; Supreme Court creates new pregnancy discrimination framework. (2015, May). *HR Specialist: California Employment Law, 9.5*, 7.

37. Dunlap, N. B. (2015, November). Supreme Court "delivers" new life to pregnancy discrimination claims in *Young v. United Parcel Service, Inc. Florida Bar Journal,* 59–63.

38. Ng, T. W. H., & Feldman, D. C. (2012). Evaluating six common stereotypes about older workers with meta-analytic data. *Personnel Psychology, 65,* 821–858.

39. EEOC. (2016). Age discrimination. https://www.eeoc.gov/laws/types/age.cfm

40. *Gross v. FBL Financial Services.* http://caselaw.findlaw.com/us-supreme-court/557/167.html

41. Gould, T. (2016, January 8). EEOC wins big in age bias, wage discrimination cases. http://www.hrmorning.com/eeoc-wins-big-in-age-bias-wage-discrimination-cases/

42. SHRM. (2014, October 14). Disability accommodations: Conditions: Does the Americans with Disabilities Act (ADA) provide a list of conditions that are covered under the act? https://www.shrm.org/resourcesandtools/tools-and-samples/hr-qa/pages/cms_011495.aspx; Weiner, C., & Tetnowski, J. A. (2016, July). Stuttering discrimination under the law. *The ASHA Leader*, 52–57.

43. EEOC issues new guidance on leave and the ADA. *Payroll Manager's Letter*, 6–7.

44. Mook, J. R. (2010, September 9). Five steps to protect your company from claims under new ADA. http://www.hrhero.com/hl/articles/2010/09/09/five-steps-to-protect-your-company-from-claims-under-new-ada/

45. EEOC. (2016). The equal employment opportunity responsibilities of multinational employers. https://www.eeoc.gov/facts/multi-employers.html

46. Berkowitz, P. M. (2015). Gender, diversity, European quotas, and U.S. law. https://www.littler.com/publication-press/press/gender-diversity-european-quotas-and-us-law; International Labor Organization. (2016). Facts on people with disabilities in China. http://www.ilo.org/wcmsp5/groups/public/---asia/---ro-bangkok/---ilo-beijing/documents/publication/wcms_142315.pdf

47. EEOC proposed rule clarifies wellness rules under GINA. (2016, January). *HR Specialist: California Employment Law, 10*.1, 7; GINA Genetic Information Nondiscrimination Act. http://ginahelp.org/#

48. Miller, S. (2015). United States District Court for the Northern District of Georgia finds employer liable for violation of Genetic Information Nondisclosure Act (GINA) in the case of the "devious defecator." *American Journal of Law & Medicine, 41*, 684–687.

49. Employer—not vendor—is liable for fitness-for-duty exam GINA violations. (2015, December). *HR Specialist: Minnesota Employment Law, 8*.12, 3. Family medical history is none of your business. (2016, March). *HR Specialist: Employment Law, 46*.3, 3.

50. EEOC. (2016). Equal Pay Act of 1963 and Lilly Ledbetter Fair Pay Act of 2009. https://www.eeoc.gov/eeoc/publications/brochure-equal_pay_and_ledbetter_act.cfm

51. Human Rights Campaign. (2016). http://www.hrc.org/state_maps; Sangha, K. K. (2015). LGBT protection in the workplace: A survey of state and local laws. *Employment Relations Today, 42*, 57–68.

52. Frankel, A. (2017, September 11). How Trump DOJ's about-face on LGBT workplace bias could backfire at Scotus. https://www.reuters.com/article/us-otc-lgbt/how-trump-dojs-about-face-on-lgbt-workplace-bias-could-backfire-at-scotus-idUSKCN1BM2DD

53. EEOC. (2016). What you should know about EEOC and the enforcement protections for LGBT workers. https://www.eeoc.gov/eeoc/newsroom/wysk/enforcement_protections_lgbt_workers.cfm

54. Munoz, S. T., & Kalteux, D. M. (2016, March). LGBT, the EEOC, and the meaning of "sex." *The Florida Bar Journal*, 43–48.

55. Joiner, E., & Lyons, A. (2016, Summer). Creating an inclusive workplace for LGBT employees. *Corporate Counsel Litigation, 30*, 3.

56. Cheri Gay, V. (2015). 50 years later . . . still interpreting the meaning of "because of sex" within Title VII and whether it prohibits sexual orientation discrimination. *The Air Force Law Review, 73*, 61–109; More reason for sexual orientation policy: EEOC files first Title VII gay-bias suit. (2016, April). *The HR Specialist, 14*.4, 3; Munoz, S. T., & Kalteux, D. M. (2016, March). LGBT, the EEOC, and the meaning of "sex." *The Florida Bar Journal*, 43–48.

57. Grant, A. (2017, October 26). World's 100 most successful LGBT executives and business leaders, 2017. http://ceoworld.biz/2017/10/26/worlds-100-most-successful-lgbt-executives-and-business-leaders-2017/; Hewett, J. (2016, March 4). Alan Joyce says management diversity was key to getting Qantas through turbulent times. https://www.theaustralian.com.au/business/in-depth/perpetual/alan-joyce-says-management-diversity-was-key-to-getting-qantas-through-turbulent-times/news-story/5afe123042f7d2e20b8d3a5f001477b8

58. http://www.workplaceclassaction.com/2016/08/eeoc-loses-landmark-transgender-discrimination-case/

59. King, E. B., & Cortina, J. M. (2010). The social and economic imperative of lesbian, gay, bisexual, and transgendered supportive organizational policies. *Industrial and Organizational Psychology, 3*, 69–78.

60. Joiner, E., & Lyons, A. (2016, Summer). Creating an inclusive workplace for LGBT employees. *Corporate Counsel Litigation, 30*, 3.

61. Benn, K. (2016, April 21) Uber settles two class actions with drivers for up to $100M. https://www.law360.com/articles/787770/uber-settles-2-class-actions-with-drivers-for-up-to-100m; Wood, R. (2015, June 16). W. FedEx settles independent contractor mislabeling case for $228 million. *Forbes*. http://www.forbes.com/sites/robertwood/2015/06/16/fedex-settles-driver-mislabeling-case-for-228-million/#199f59165f5a

62. SHRM. (2015). Affirmative action: General: When would my company need to have an affirmative action program? https://www.shrm.org/resourcesandtools/tools-and-samples/hr-qa/pages/whenisanaapneeded.aspx

63. Leslie, L. M., Mayer, D. M., & Kravitz, D. A. (2014). The stigma of affirmative action: A stereotyping-based theory and meta-analytic test of the consequences for

performance. *Academy of Management Journal, 57,* 964–989.

64. SHRM. (2015, November 9). Affirmative action: General: When would my company need to have an affirmative action program? https://www.shrm.org/resourcesandtools/tools-and-samples/hr-qa/pages/whenisanaapneeded.aspx

65. EEOC. (2018). Enforcement guidance on vicarious employer liability for unlawful harassment by supervisors. https://www.eeoc.gov/policy/docs/harassment.html

66. Phillis, M. (2016, June). You have a chief diversity officer, but is your workplace inclusive? *Workforce,* 20–21.

67. Huet, E. (2015, July 17). Women who code: We have to start making commitments on diversity. *Forbes.com*; Goodman, N. (2016, September/October). Diversity is reality; inclusion is a choice. *Training,* 56–57.

68. Dobbin, F., & Kalev, A. (2016, July/August). Why diversity programs fail. *Harvard Business Review.* https://hbr.org/2016/07/why-diversity-programs-fail

69. Cox, J., & Musaddique, S. (2018, February 12). Lloyds banking group sets ethnic diversity target. http://www.independent.co.uk/news/business/news/lloyds-bank-ethnic-diversity-target-bame-increase-numbers-ftse-100-a8207046.html

70. Zakrzewski, C. (2015, August 5). Corporate news: Intel seeks to boost diversity in hiring. *Wall Street Journal,* B9.

71. Morgan, W. B., Dunleavy, E., & DeVries, P. D. (2016). Using big data to create diversity and inclusion in organizations. In S. Tonidandel, E. King, & J. Cortina (Eds.), *Big data at work: The data science revolution and organizational psychology* (pp. 310–335). New York: Routledge.

72. Morse, G. (2016, July/August). Designing a bias-free organization. *Harvard Business Review, 94*(7/8).

73. Waxer, C. (2015, April). Combating the diversity dearth with analytics. *Computerworld,* 11–18.

74. Murray, S. (2014, April 1). How one company put women in charge. http://blogs.wsj.com/atwork/2014/04/01/how-one-company-put-women-in-charge/; Petrilla, M. (2014, December 11). How analytics helped Kimberly-Clark solve its diversity problem. *Fortune.com.* http://fortune.com/2014/12/10/kimberly-clark-dodsworth-diversity/

75. Smith, A. (2016, July/August). Analyzing pay. *HR Magazine,* 69–72.

76. Peck, E. (2015, April 23). Salesforce CEO takes radical step to pay men and women equally. *Huffington Post.* http://www.huffingtonpost.com/2015/04/23/salesforce-pay-gap_n_7126892.html; Robbins, C. (2017, April 4). 2017 salesforceequal pay assessment update. https://www.salesforce.com/blog/2017/04/salesforce-equal-pay-assessment-update.html; Zarya, V. (2016, July 12). Salesforce spent $3 million on equal pay—Here's how many employees got raises as a result. *Fortune.* http://fortune.com/2016/03/08/salesforce-equal-pay/

77. Winsborough, D., & Chamorro-Premuzic, T. (2016, Spring). Talent identification in the digital world: New talent signals and the future of HR assessment. *People & Strategy, 39*(2), 28–31.

78. Bridgeford, L. C. (2015, September). Experts discuss big data's effect on hiring, bias claims. *HR Focus,* 4–6; Macheel, T. (2016, September 8). Women in banking: Is big data a weapon of mass discrimination? *American Banker.* https://www.americanbanker.com/opinion/women-in-banking-is-big-data-a-weapon-of-mass-discrimination

79. McGowan, K. (2016, July 29). When is big data bad data? When it causes bias. http://www.bna.com/big-data-bad-n73014445584

80. SHRM. (2015, September 14). Avoiding adverse impact in employment practices. https://www.shrm.org/resourcesandtools/tools-and-samples/toolkits/pages/avoidingadverseimpact.aspx

Chapter 5

1. National Council of State Boards of Nursing, Inc. (NCSBN®). (2015). Report of Findings from the 2014 Nurse Aide Job Analysis and Knowledge, Skill and Ability Study. https://www.ncsbn.org/15_2014NNAAP_Job_Analysis_vol65.pdf; American Association of Engineering Societies and U.S. Department of Labor. (2015). Engineering competency model. www.aaes.org/sites/default/files/Engineering%20Competency%20Model_Final_May2015.pdf

2. Campion, M. A., Fink, A. A., Ruggeberg, B. J., Carr, L., Phillips, G. M., & Odman, R. B. (2011). Doing competencies well: Best practices in competency modeling. *Personnel Psychology, 64,* 225–262; Shippmann, J. S., Ash, R. A., Battista, M., Carr, L., Eyde, L. D., Hesketh, B., Kehoe, J., Pearlman, K., Prien, E. P., & Sanchez, J. I. (2000). The practice of competency modeling. *Personnel Psychology, 53,* 703–740.

3. Alonso, A., Kurtessis, J. N., Schmidt, A. A., Strobel, K., & Dickson, B. (2015). A competency-based approach to advancing HR. *People + Strategy, 28,* 38–44; Alonso, A. (2017, March 27). Certify this! The role of competency-based certification in HR. https://blog.shrm.org/blog/certify-this-the-role-of-competency-based-certification-in-hr; Society for Human Resource Management. (2012). SHRM Competency Model. https://www.shrm.org/LearningAndCareer/competency-model/Documents/Full%20Competency%20Model%2011%202_10%201%202014.pdf

4. Morgeson, F. P., & Dierdorff, E. C. (2011). Work analysis: From technique to theory. In S. Zedeck (Ed.), *APA handbook of industrial and organizational psychology* (vol. 2, pp. 3–41), Washington, DC: APA.

5. U.S. Office of Personnel Management. (2007). Delegated

examining operations handbook: A guide for federal agency examining offices. https://www.opm.gov/policy-data-oversight/hiring-information/competitive-hiring/deo_handbook.pdf

6. PDRI. (2014). Validating the global competency model. https://www.pdri.com/images/uploads/PDRI_EP_CM_IBM_FW.pdf

7. Ibid.

8. Brannick, M. T., Levine, E. L., & Morgeson, F. P. (2007). *Job and work analysis: Methods, research, and applications for human resource management.* Thousand Oaks, CA: Sage; Cascio, W. F., & Aguinis, H. (2011). *Applied psychology in human resource management* (7th ed.). Upper Saddle River, NJ: Prentice Hall; Morgeson, F. P., & Dierdorff, E. C. (2011). Work analysis: From technique to theory. In S. Zedeck (Ed.), *APA handbook of industrial and organizational psychology* (vol. 2, pp. 3–41). Washington, DC: APA.

9. Sanchez, J. I., & Levine, E. L. (2012). The rise and fall of job analysis and the rise of work analysis. *Annual Review of Psychology, 63*, 397–425.

10. Brannick, M. T., Levine, E. L., & Morgeson, F. P. (2007). *Job and work analysis: Methods, research, and applications for human resource management.* Thousand Oaks, CA: Sage; Cascio, W. F., & Aguinis, H. (2011). *Applied psychology in human resource management* (7th ed.). Upper Saddle River, NJ: Prentice Hall.

11. Uniform Guidelines on Employee Selection Procedures. (1978). *Federal Register, 43*, 38290–38315.

12. Mook, J. R. (2010, September 9). Five steps to protect your company from claims under new ADA. http://www.hrhero.com/hl/articles/2010/09/09/five-steps-to-protect-your-company-from-claims-under-new-ada/

13. Morgeson, F. P., & Dierdorff, E. C. (2011). Work analysis: From technique to theory. In S. Zedeck (Ed.), *APA handbook of industrial and organizational psychology* (vol. 2, pp. 3–41). Washington, DC: APA.

14. Burroughs, A. (2017, January 3). The digitalization of retail means broad continuous change. *Smart Business.* http://www.sbnonline.com/article/digital-transformation-retail-broad-continuous-change/

15. The EDISON project, http://edison-project.eu/; The EDISON data science framework (EDSF), http://edison-project.eu/sites/edison-project.eu/files/attached_files/node-488/edison-general-introduction-edsf.pdf

16. Lee, K. F. (2017, June 24). The real threat of artificial intelligence. *New York Times.* https://www.nytimes.com/2017/06/24/opinion/sunday/artificial-intelligence-economic-inequality.html; Kerstetter, J. (2017, June 26). Daily report: Technology's effects on developing economies. *New York Times.* https://www.nytimes.com/2017/06/26/technology/daily-report-automations-effect-on-developing-tech-economies.html

17. Brannick, M. T., Levine, E. L., & Morgeson, F. P. (2007). *Job and work analysis: Methods, research, and applications for human resource management.* Thousand Oaks, CA: Sage; Gatewood, R., Feild, H., & Barrick, M. (2011). *Human resource selection.* Mason, OH: Cengage Learning.

18. American Association of Engineering Societies and U.S. Department of Labor. (2015). Engineering competency model. http://www.aaes.org/sites/default/files/Engineering%20Competency%20Model_Final_May2015.pdf

19. Brannick, M. T., Levine, E. L., & Morgeson, F. P. (2007). *Job and work analysis: Methods, research, and applications for human resource management.* Thousand Oaks, CA: Sage.

20. Ibid.; Gatewood, R., Feild, H., & Barrick, M. (2011). *Human resource selection.* Mason, OH: Cengage Learning.

21. Brannick, M. T., Levine, E. L., & Morgeson, F. P. (2007). *Job and work analysis: Methods, research, and applications for human resource management.* Thousand Oaks, CA: Sage; Gatewood, R., Feild, H., & Barrick, M. (2011). *Human resource selection.* Mason, OH: Cengage Learning; Green, S. B., & Stutzman, T. (1986). An evaluation of methods to select respondents to structured job-analysis questionnaires. *Personnel Psychology, 39*, 543–564.

22. Flanagan, J. C. (1954). The critical incident technique. *Psychological Bulletin, 51*, 327–358.

23. U.S. Office of Personnel Management. (2007). Delegated examining operations handbook: A guide for federal agency examining offices. https://www.opm.gov/policy-data-oversight/hiring-information/competitive-hiring/deo_handbook.pdf

24. McCormick, E. J., Jeanneret, P. R., & Mecham, R. C. (1972). A study of job characteristics and job dimensions as based on the position analysis questionnaire (PAQ). *Journal of Applied Psychology, 56*, 347–368.

25. Brannick, M. T., Levine, E. L., & Morgeson, F. P. (2007). *Job and work analysis: Methods, research, and applications for human resource management.* Thousand Oaks, CA: Sage; Gatewood, R., Feild, H., & Barrick, M. (2011). *Human resource selection.* Mason, OH: Cengage Learning.

26. Raymond, M. R. (2001). Job analysis and the specification of content for licensure and certification examinations. *Applied Measurement in Education, 14*(4), 369–415.

27. National Council of State Boards of Nursing, Inc. (NCSBN®). (2015). Report of findings from the 2014 Nurse Aide Job Analysis and Knowledge, Skill and Ability Study. https://www.ncsbn.org/15_2014NNAAP_Job_Analysis_vol65.pdf

28. National Council for Therapeutic Recreation Certification. (2015). 2014 CTRS job analysis report. https://nctrc.org/wp-content/uploads/2015/02/5JobAnalysis.pdf

29. Peterson, N. G., Mumford, M. D., Borman, W. C., Jeanneret,

P. R., Fleishman, E. A., Levin, K. Y., Campion, M., Mayfield, M. S., Morgeson, F. P., Pearlman, K., Gowing, M. K., Lancaster, A. R., Silver, M. B., & Dye, D. M. (2001). Understanding work using the Occupational Information Network (O* NET): Implications for practice and research. *Personnel Psychology, 54,* 451–492.

30. Campion, M. A., Fink, A. A., Ruggeberg, B. J., Carr, L., Phillips, G. M., & Odman, R. B. (2011). Doing competencies well: Best practices in competency modeling. *Personnel Psychology, 64,* 225–262; Shippmann, J. S., Ash, R. A., Battista, M., Carr, L., Eyde, L. D., Hesketh, B., Kehoe, J., Pearlman, K., Prien, E. P., & Sanchez, J. I. (2000). The practice of competency modeling. *Personnel Psychology, 53,* 703–740.

31. Dobbins, C., & Ehmke, C. (2005). Developing effective job descriptions for small businesses and farms. Purdue University, Purdue Extension. https://www.extension.purdue.edu/extmedia/ec/ec-728.pdf; Doucette, C. (2018). What happens if an organization doesn't conduct a job analysis? *Chron.* http://smallbusiness.chron.com/happens-organization-doesnt-conduct-job-analysis-15562.html; White, D., & White, P. (2015). 6 benefits of writing job descriptions for your business. *Entrepreneur.* https://www.entrepreneur.com/article/247829.

32. Society for Human Resource Management. (2012). SHRM competency model. https://www.shrm.org/LearningAndCareer/competency-model/Documents/Full%20Competency%20Model%2011%202_10%201%202014.pdf; Department of Labor, O*NET Database. https://www.onetcenter.org/dictionary/21.3/excel/work_styles.html

33. Deloitte Consulting, LLP. (2015). Job architecture. Laying the building blocks of effective Human Capital Management. https://www2.deloitte.com/content/dam/Deloitte/us/

Documents/human-capital/us-cons-job-architecture-041315.pdf; World Health Organization. WHO Global Competency Model. http://www.who.int/employment/competencies/WHO_competencies_EN.pdf

34. Campion, M. A., Fink, A. A., Ruggeberg, B. J., Carr, L., Phillips, G. M., & Odman, R. B. (2011). Doing competencies well: Best practices in competency modeling. *Personnel Psychology, 64,* 225–262; Sanchez, J. I., Levine, E. L. (2009). What is (or should be) the difference between competency modeling and traditional job analysis? *Human Resource Management Review, 19,* 53–63; Shippmann, J. S., Ash, R. A., Battista, M., Carr, L., Eyde, L. D., Hesketh, B., Kehoe, J., Pearlman, K., Prien, E. P., & Sanchez, J. I. (2000). The practice of competency modeling. *Personnel Psychology, 53,* 703–740.

35. Parker, S. K. (2014). Beyond motivation: Job and work design for development, health, ambidexterity, and more. *Annual Review of Psychology, 65,* 661–691; Parker, S. K., Morgeson, F. P., & Johns, G. (2017). One hundred years of work design research: Looking back and looking forward. *Journal of Applied Psychology, 102,* 403–420.

36. Demerouti, E., Bakker, A. B., Nachreiner, F., & Schaufeli, W. B. (2001). The job demands–resources model of burnout. *Journal of Applied Psychology, 86,* 499–512; Hackman, J. R., & Oldham, G. R. (1975). Development of the job diagnostic survey. *Journal of Applied Psychology, 60,* 159–180; Karasek, R. A. (1979). Job demands, job decision latitude, and mental strain: Implications for job redesign. *Administrative Science Quarterly, 24,* 285–308.

37. Morgeson, F. P., & Humphrey, S. E. (2006). The Work Design Questionnaire (WDQ): Developing and validating a comprehensive measure for assessing job design and the nature of work. *Journal of Applied Psychology, 91,* 1321–1399.

38. Morgeson, F. P., & Humphrey, S. E. (2006). The Work Design

Questionnaire (WDQ): Developing and validating a comprehensive measure for assessing job design and the nature of work. *Journal of Applied Psychology, 91,* 1321–1399.

39. Humphrey, S. E., Nahrgang, J. D., & Morgeson, F. P. (2007). Integrating motivational, social, and contextual work design features: A meta-analytic summary and theoretical extension of the work design literature. *Journal of Applied Psychology, 92,* 1332–1356.

40. Parker, S. K. (2014). Beyond motivation: Job and work design for development, health, ambidexterity, and more. *Annual Review of Psychology, 65,* 661–691.

41. Truxillo, D. M., Cadiz, D. A., Rineer, J. R., Zaniboni, S., & Fraccaroli, F. (2012). A lifespan perspective on job design: Fitting the job and the worker to promote job satisfaction, engagement, and performance. *Organizational Psychology Review, 2,* 340–360.

42. Zaniboni, S., Truxillo, D. M., & Fraccaroli, F. (2013). Differential effects of task variety and skill variety on burnout and turnover intentions for older and younger workers. *European Journal of Work and Organizational Psychology, 22,* 306–317; Zaniboni, S., Truxillo, D. M., Fraccaroli, F., McCune, E. A., & Bertolino, M. (2014). Who benefits from more tasks? Older versus younger workers. *Journal of Managerial Psychology, 29,* 508–523.

43. Zaniboni, S., Truxillo, D. M., Rineer, J. R., Bodner, T. E., Hammer, L. B., & Krainer, M. (2016). Relating age, decision authority, job satisfaction, and mental health: A study of construction workers. *Work, Aging and Retirement, 2,* 428–435.

44. Bouville, G., Dello Russo, S., & Truxillo, D. (2018). The moderating role of age in the job characteristics–absenteeism relationship: A matter of occupational context? *Journal of Occupational and Organizational Psychology, 91,* 57–83.

45. Parker, S. K. (2014). Beyond motivation: Job and work design for development, health, ambidexterity,

and more. *Annual Review of Psychology, 65,* 661–691; Tims, M., Bakker, A. B., & Derks, D. (2012). Development and validation of the job crafting scale. *Journal of Vocational Behavior, 80,* 173–186.

46. Lebowitz, S. (2015). A Yale professor explains how to turn a boring job into a meaningful career. *Business Insider.* http://www .businessinsider.com/turn-a-boring-job-into-a-meaningful-career-job-crafting-2015-12; Wrzesniewski, A., & Dutton, J. E. (2001). Crafting a job: Revisioning employees as active crafters of their work. *Academy of Management Review, 26,* 179–201.

47. Parker, S. K. (2014). Beyond motivation: Job and work design for development, health, ambidexterity, and more. *Annual Review of Psychology, 65,* 661–691.

48. Rudolph, C. W., Katz, I. M., Lavigne, K. N., & Zacher, H. (2017). Job crafting: A meta-analysis of relationships with individual differences, job characteristics, and work outcomes. *Journal of Vocational Behavior, 102,* 112–138.

49. Heuvel, M., Demerouti, E., & Peeters, M. C. (2015). The job crafting intervention: Effects on job resources, self-efficacy, and affective well-being. *Journal of Occupational and Organizational Psychology, 88,* 511–532; Kooij, D. T., van Woerkom, M., Wilkenloh, J., Dorenbosch, L., & Denissen, J. J. (2017). Job crafting towards strengths and interests: The effects of a job crafting intervention on person–job fit and the role of age. *Journal of Applied Psychology, 102,* 971–981.

50. Kooij, D. T., van Woerkom, M., Wilkenloh, J., Dorenbosch, L., & Denissen, J. J. (2017). Job crafting towards strengths and interests: The effects of a job crafting intervention on person–job fit and the role of age. *Journal of Applied Psychology, 102,* 971–981.

51. Fell, S. S. (2015). How telecommuting reduced carbon footprints at Dell, Aetna and Xerox. *Entrepreneur.* https://www .entrepreneur.com/article/245296

52. Gajendran, R. S., & Harrison, D. A. (2007). The good, the bad, and the unknown about telecommuting: Meta-analysis of psychological mediators and individual consequences. *Journal of Applied Psychology, 92,* 1524–1541; Tobak, S. (2017). IBM signals end of telecommuting craze. *Entrepreneur.* https://www.entrepreneur.com/ article/294656

53. Cahill, K. E., James, J. B., & Pitt-Catsouphes, M. (2015). The impact of a randomly assigned time and place management initiative on work and retirement expectations. *Work, Aging and Retirement, 1,* 350–368.

54. Pofeldt, E. (2015). Shocker: 40% of workers now have "contingent" jobs, says U.S. government. *Forbes.* https://www.forbes.com/ sites/elainepofeldt/2015/05/25/ shocker-40-of-workers-now-have-contingent-jobs-says-u-s-government/#4ad6ceec14be

55. Fisher, S. L., & Connelly, C. E. (2017). Lower cost or just lower value? Modeling the organizational costs and benefits of contingent work. *Academy of Management Discoveries, 3,* 165–186; Pofeldt, E. (2015). Shocker: 40% of workers now have "contingent" jobs, says U.S. government. *Forbes.* Tran, M., & Sokas, R. K. (2017). The gig economy and contingent work: An occupational health assessment. *Journal of Occupational and Environmental Medicine, 59,* e63–e66.

Chapter 6

1. Adams, S. (2014). Job search secrets from a campus recruiter. *Forbes.* http://www.forbes.com/ sites/susanadams/2014/03/26/ job-search-secrets-from-a-campus-recruiter/#eace97a236bf; PwC. (2017). Recruiting process. http:// www.pwc.com/us/en/careers/ campus/recruiting.html; PwC. (2017). Practice areas. http://www .pwc.com/us/en/careers/campus/ why-pwc/what-we-do.html; NACE.

(2016). Video interviewing helps PwC boost candidate experience. http://www.naceweb.org/ s02102016/video-interviewing-helps-boost-candidate-experience .aspx; Malcolm, H. (2015). PwC to start giving employees $1,200 a year in student loan debt assistance. *USA Today.* http:// www.usatoday.com/story/money/ personalfinance/2015/09/22/pwc-offering-student-loan-assistance-to-employees/72565522/; Walker, J. (2010). PwC pays for priority: New recruiting tool for college students gives accounting firm top billing. *Wall Street Journal.* https://www .wsj.com/articles/SB1000142405 27487040293045755266412946 99972; Statista. (2018). Number of PwC employees worldwide from 2013–2017, by region. https://www .statista.com/statistics/189763/ number-of-employees-of-pwc-by-region-2010/

2. Sullivan, J. (2002). Why you need workforce planning. *Workforce.* http://www.workforce .com/2002/10/24/why-you-need-workforce-planning/

3. Boston, W. (2016). BMW loses core development team of its i3 and i8 electric vehicle line. *Wall Street Journal.* https://www .wsj.com/articles/bmw-loses-core-development-team-of-its-i3-and-i8-electric-vehicle-line-1461086049

4. Day, D. (2007). Developing leadership talent. SHRM Foundation. https://www.shrm.org/ foundation/ourwork/initiatives/ resources-from-past-initiatives/ Documents/Developing%20 Leadership%20Talent.pdf

5. U.S. Bureau of Labor Statistics. (2017). About BLS. https://www.bls .gov/bls/infohome.htm

6. NACE. (2016). Trends: Fewer women in computer sciences. http://www.naceweb.org/talent-acquisition/trends-and-predictions/ trends-fewer-women-in-computer-sciences/; Sherman, E. (2015, March 26). Report: Disturbing drop in women in computing field. *Fortune.* http://fortune.com/2015/03/26/

report-the-number-of-women-entering-computing-took-a-nosedive/

7. The Conference Board. (2014). International comparisons of annual labor force statistics. https://www.conference-board.org/ilcprogram/index.cfm?id=25444

8. Jobvite. (2016). Jobvite recruiter national report: The annual social recruiting survey. http://web.jobvite.com/Q316_Website_2016RecruiterNation_LP.html

9. Schwartz, N. D., & Wingfield, N. (2017). Amazon to add 100,000 jobs as bricks-and-mortar retail crumbles. *New York Times*. https://www.nytimes.com/2017/01/12/business/economy/amazon-jobs-retail.html?_r=0; Swartz, J. (2017). Amazon is creating 100,000 U.S. jobs, but at what cost? *USA Today*. https://www.usatoday.com/story/tech/columnist/2017/01/13/amazons-jobs-creation-plan-comes-amid-labor-pains/96488166/

10. U.S. Bureau of Labor Statistics. (2017). Occupational outlook handbook: Water and wastewater treatment plant and system operators. https://www.bls.gov/ooh/production/water-and-wastewater-treatment-plant-and-system-operators.htm; The Conference Board. (2014). International comparisons of annual labor force statistics. https://www.conference-board.org/ilcprogram/index.cfm?id=25444; Top 10 reasons to get a career in the water treatment industry. http://watergrades.com/1960/top-10-reasons-to-get-a-career-in-the-water-treatment-industry/; Roberts, B. (2010). Can they keep our lights on? SHRM. https://blog.shrm.org/workforce/can-they-keep-our-lights-on; Nursing shortage. http://www.nursingworld.org/nursingshortage

11. Berman-Gorvine, M. (2013). Boeing soars over potential talent gaps with its workforce planning strategies. *Bloomberg*. https://www.bna.com/boeing-soars-potential-n17179872416/

12. U.S. Bureau of Labor Statistics. (2016). Foreign-born workers: Labor force statistics. https://www.bls.gov/news.release/pdf/forbrn.pdf

13. Barber, A. E. (1998). *Recruiting employees: Individual and organizational perspectives*. Thousand Oaks, CA: Sage; Kim, Y., & Ployhart, R. E. (2014). The effects of staffing and training on firm productivity and profit growth before, during, and after the great recession. *Journal of Applied Psychology, 99*, 361–389.

14. Sullivan, J. (2012). Recruiting has the highest business impact of any HR function. www.ere.net; Boston Consulting Group. http://www.bcg.com/expertise/capabilities/people-organization/human-resources.aspx

15. Bauer, T. N., & Green, S. G. (1994). Effect of newcomer involvement in work-related activities: A longitudinal study of socialization. *Journal of Applied Psychology, 79*, 211–223; Major, D. A., Kozlowski, S. W., Chao, G. T., & Gardner, P. D. (1995). A longitudinal investigation of newcomer expectations, early socialization outcomes, and the moderating effects of role development factors. *Journal of Applied Psychology, 80*, 418–431; Saks, A. M. (1994). A psychological process investigation for the effects of recruitment source and organization information on job survival. *Journal of Organizational Behavior, 15*, 225–244; Wanous, J. P., Poland, T. D., Premack, S. L., & Davis, K. S. (1992). The effects of met expectations on newcomer attitudes and behaviors: A review and meta-analysis. *Journal of Applied Psychology, 77*, 288–297.

16. Truxillo, D. M., Cadiz, D. M., & Rineer, J. R. (2014). The aging workforce: Implications for human resource management research and practice (S. Jackson, Ed.). *Oxford Handbooks Online: Business & Management*. https://www.researchgate.net/publication/282348874_The_Aging_Workforce_Implications_for_Human_Resource_Management_Research_and_Practice

17. Truxillo, D. M., & Bauer, T. N. (2015). Maximizing candidate and recruiter experiences and organizational outcomes. Findly White Paper. Available upon request from the first author.

18. Glassdoor.com. (2017). 50 best jobs in America. https://www.glassdoor.com/List/Best-Jobs-in-America-LST_KQ0,20.htm

19. Jobvite. (2016). Jobvite recruiter national report: The annual social recruiting survey. http://web.jobvite.com/Q316_Website_2016RecruiterNation_LP.html

20. Baert, S. (2017). Facebook profile picture appearance affects recruiters' first hiring decisions. *New Media & Society, 20*, 1220–1239.

21. Jobvite. (2016). Jobvite recruiter national report: The annual social recruiting survey. http://web.jobvite.com/Q316_Website_2016RecruiterNation_LP.html

22. Ibid.

23. Carlson, K. D., Connerley, M. L., & Mecham, R. L. (2002). Recruitment evaluation: The case for assessing the quality of applicants attracted. *Personnel Psychology, 55*, 461–490; Collins, C. J., & Han, J. (2004). Exploring applicant pool quantity and quality: The effects of early recruitment practice strategies, corporate advertising, and firm reputation. *Personnel Psychology, 57*, 685–717.

24. Huselid, M. A. (1995). The impact of human resource management practices on turnover, productivity, and corporate financial performance. *Academy of Management Journal, 38,* 635–872.

25. Indiana Department of Child Services. (2011). Family case manager. http://www.in.gov/dcs/3209.htm http://www.in.gov/dcs/3209.htm

26. Jones, B. I. People management lessons from Disney. https://cdns3.trainingindustry.com/media/3532077/disneypeoplemanagementlessons.pdf

27. Breaugh, J. A., Macan, T. H., & Grambow, D. M. (2008). Employee recruitment: Current knowledge and directions for future research. In G. P. Hodgkinson & J. K. Ford (Eds.), *International review of industrial and organizational psychology* (vol. 23, pp. 45–82). New York: John Wiley & Sons; Breaugh, J. A. (2008). Employee recruitment: Current knowledge and important areas for future research. *Human Resource Management Review, 18,* 103–118; Earnest, D. R., Allen, D. G., & Landis, R. S. (2011). Mechanisms linking realistic job previews with turnover: A meta-analytic path analysis. *Personnel Psychology, 64,* 865–897.

28. Burkus, D. (2016). Why Amazon bought into Zappos' "pay to quit" policy. *Inc.* http://www.inc.com/david-burkus/why-amazon-bought-into-zappos-pay-to-quit-policy.html; Snyder, B. (2015). 14% of Zappos' staff left after being offered exit pay. *Fortune.* http://fortune.com/2015/05/08/zappos-quit-employees/

29. SHRM. (2016). Talent acquisition: Selection. *HRToday.* https://www.shrm.org/hr-today/trends-and-forecasting/research-and-surveys/Documents/Talent-Acquisition-Selection.pdf

30. Weber, L., & Kwoh, L. (2013). Beware the phantom job listing. *Wall Street Journal.* https://www.wsj.com/articles/SB10001424127887323706704578229661268628432

31. Day, D. (2007). Developing leadership talent. SHRM Foundation. https://www.shrm.org/foundation/ourwork/initiatives/resources-from-past-initiatives/Documents/Developing%20Leadership%20Talent.pdf

32. Garland, P. (2016, September). Why people quit their jobs. *Harvard Business Review.* https://hbr.org/2016/09/why-people-quit-their-jobs

33. CareerXroads. (2015). Source of hire report. http://www.slideshare.net/gerrycrispin/2015-careerxroads-source-of-hire-report-56847680

34. Zimmerman, E. (2006). The boom in boomerangs. Workforce Management Online. http://www.workforce.com/section/06/feature/24/25/79/%20index.html

35. Rediff. (2014, July 15). Hiring former employees is beneficial. http://www.rediff.com/money/report/hiring-former-employees-is-beneficial/20140715.htm

36. Shipp, A. J., Furst-Holloway, S., Harris, T. B., & Rosen, B. (2014). Gone today but here tomorrow: Extending the unfolding model of turnover to consider boomerang employees. *Personnel Psychology, 67,* 421–462; Tugend, A. (2014). Employees who leave increasingly return to the fold. *New York Times.* https://www.nytimes.com/2014/07/26/your-money/employees-who-leave-are-increasingly-returning-to-the-fold.html; Zottoli, M. A., & Wanous, J. P. (2000). Recruitment source research: Current status and future directions. *Human Resource Management Review, 10,* 353–383.

37. Zimmerman, E. (2006). The boom in boomerangs. Workforce Management Online. http://www.workforce.com/section/06/feature/24/25/79/%20index.html

38. *Nitsch v. DreamWorks Animation SKG Inc.,* 14-cv-04062, U.S. District Court, Northern District of California (San Jose); Rosenblatt, J. (2017). Disney agrees to pay $100 million to end no-poaching lawsuit. *Bloomberg.* https://www.bloomberg.com/news/articles/2017-02-01/disney-agrees-to-pay-100-million-to-end-no-poaching-lawsuit

39. Zimmerman, E. (2006). The boom in boomerangs. *Workforce.* http://www.workforce.com/2006/01/25/the-boom-in-boomerangs/

40. WorldatWork. (2014, June). *Bonus programs and practices.* https://www.worldatwork.org/adimLink?id=75444

41. Bock, L. (2015). *Work rules! Insights from inside Google that will transform how you live and lead.* New York: Twelve.

42. Jobvite. (2015). The Jobvite recruiter nation survey. https://www.jobvite.com/wp-content/uploads/2015/09/jobvite_recruiter_nation_2015.pdf

43. SHRM. (2016). Designing and managing successful employee referral programs. https://www.shrm.org/resourcesandtools/tools-and-samples/toolkits/pages/tk-designingandmanagingsuccessfulemployeereferralprograms.aspx

44. Lublin, J. S. (2012). More executive recruiting shifts in-house. *Wall Street Journal.* https://www.wsj.com/articles/SB10000872396390443294904578046421729938416

45. Bersin, J. (2013). Corporate recruiting explodes: A new breed of service providers. *Forbes.* https://www.forbes.com/sites/joshbersin/2013/05/23/corporate-recruitment-transformed-new-breed-of-service-providers/#3648c3c840a9

46. Agnvall, E. (2007). Job fairs go virtual. *HR Magazine.* https://www.shrm.org/hr-today/news/hr-magazine/Pages/0707agenda_empstaff.aspx

47. Roheling, M. V., & Cavanaugh, M. A. (2000). Student expectations of employers at job fairs. *Journal of Career Planning & Employment, 60,* 48–53.

48. Spors, K. K. (2007, June 4). For company in remote location, ex-residents offer promising pool. *Wall Street Journal.* https://www.wsj.com/articles/SB118081823563622771

49. NACE. (2016). Campus ambassadors help Rosetta extend its reach. http://www.naceweb.org/talent-acquisition/branding-and-marketing/campus-ambassadors-help-rosetta-extend-its-reach/

50. NACE. (2012). The skills and qualities employers want in their class of 2013 recruits. http://www.naceweb.org/s10242012/skills-abilities-qualities-new-hires/; Stone, C., van Horn, C., & Zukin, C. (2012, May). *Chasing the American dream: Recent college graduates and the Great Recession.* Report from

the John J. Heldrich Center for Workforce Development at Rutgers University; Taylor, M. S. (1988). Effects of college internships on individual participants. *Journal of Applied Psychology, 73*, 393–401.

51. Zhao, H., & Liden, R. C. (2011). Internship: A recruitment and selection perspective. *Journal of Applied Psychology, 96*, 221–229.

52. Jobvite. (2015). 2015 Recruiter nation survey. http://web.jobvite.com/Q315_Website_2015RecruiterNation_LP.html

53. Jobvite. (2016). Jobvite recruiter national report: The annual social recruiting survey. http://web.jobvite.com/Q316_Website_2016RecruiterNation_LP.html

54. Jobboard Finder. (2018). https://www.jobboardfinder.net/jobboard-51job-china

55. Doyle, A. (2016, July 5). How to avoid identity theft when you are job searching. https://www.thebalance.com/how-to-avoid-identity-theft-when-you-are-job-searching-2062151; Feldman, D. C., & Klaas, B. S. (2002). Internet job hunting: A field study of applicant experiences with on-line recruiting. *Human Resource Management, 41*, 175–192; Gohring, N. (2009, January 23). Monster.com reports theft of user data. *PCWorld.* http://www.pcworld.com/article/158270/monster_reports_theft.html; Gueutal &, H., & Stone, D. L. (2005). *The brave new world of eHR: Human resources in the digital age.* New York: John Wiley & Sons.

56. Statista. (2018). Number of LinkedIn members from 1st quarter 2009 to 3rd quarter 2016 (in millions). https://www.statista.com/statistics/274050/quarterly-numbers-of-linkedin-members/

57. Budzienski, J. (2015). 3 ways to be constantly recruiting star talent through social media. *Entrepreneur.* https://www.entrepreneur.com/article/245295

58. Sharma, P. (2016). How Disney and 5 other top employers use Twitter to recruit. http://theundercoverrecruiter.com/how-disney-and-5-other-top-employers-use-twitter-to-recruit/

59. Arnold, J. T. (2009). Twittering and Facebooking while they work. *HR Magazine, 54*, 12, 53–55.

60. Osawa, J., & Mozur, P. (2012). In China, recruiting gets social. *Wall Street Journal.* https://www.wsj.com/articles/SB10000872396390444226904577561643928840040

61. Crispin, G., & Hoyt, C. (2015). Source of hire 2015. *CareerXroads.* http://www.slideshare.net/gerrycrispin/2015-careerxroads-source-of-hire-report-56847680

62. Bonet, R., Cappelli, P., & Hamori M. (2013). Labor market intermediaries and the new paradigm for human resources. *The Academy of Management Annals, 7*, 341–392.

63. Donham, C. (2013). Five things to know about working with staffing firms. *Workforce Magazine.* http://www.workforce.com/2013/10/16/five-things-to-know-about-working-with-staffing-firms/

64. Zappe, J. (2005, June). Temp-to-hire is becoming a full-time practice at firms. *Workforce Magazine*, 82–85.

65. Collamer, N. (2014). 10 great sites to find gigs and part-time work. *Forbes.* https://www.forbes.com/sites/nextavenue/2014/04/04/10-great-sites-to-find-gigs-and-part-time-work/#50b0009f5502; Flandez, R. (2008). Help wanted—and found. *Wall Street Journal.* https://www.wsj.com/articles/SB122347721312915407

66. Jobvite. (2016). Jobvite recruiter national report: The annual social recruiting survey. http://web.jobvite.com/Q316_Website_2016RecruiterNation_LP.html

67. U.S. Small Business Administration. Firm size data. https://www.sba.gov/advocacy/firm-size-data; How to attract talent to a small company. *Wall Street Journal.* http://guides.wsj.com/small-business/hiring-and-managing-employees/how-to-attract-talent-to-a-small-company/; Puri, R. (2014). Four ways small businesses can recruit top talent. *Forbes.* https://www.forbes.com/sites/sage/2014/02/18/four-ways-small-businesses-can-recruit-top-talent/#18100945d6a1

68. *Nitsch v. DreamWorks Animation SKG Inc.*, 14-cv-04062, U.S. District Court, Northern District of California (San Jose); Rosenblatt, J. (2017). Disney agrees to pay $100 million to end no-poaching lawsuit. *Bloomberg.* https://www.bloomberg.com/news/articles/2017-02-01/disney-agrees-to-pay-100-million-to-end-no-poaching-lawsuit

69. U.S. Bureau of Labor Statistics. (2016). Labor force characteristics of foreign-born workers summary. https://www.bls.gov/news.release/forbrn.nr0.htm; SHRM. (2007). Call centers come home. https://www.shrm.org/hr-today/news/hr-magazine/pages/0107fraseblunt.aspx

70. NACE. (2017). Benchmarks: Diversity recruiting efforts, target groups. http://www.naceweb.org/talent-acquisition/trends-and-predictions/benchmarks-diversity-recruiting-efforts-target-groups/

71. Kelleher, K. (2017). Uber is facing a leadership crisis that could cause lasting damage. *Time.* http://time.com/4687491/uber-travis-kalanick-crisis-pr-brand-ipo-image-sexism-privacy/

72. Bock, L. (2015). *Work rules! Insights from inside Google that will transform how you live and lead.* New York: Twelve; Lang, J., & Zapf, D. (2015). Quotas for women can improve recruitment procedures: Gender as a predictor of the frequency of use of passive job search behavior and the mediating roles of management aspirations, proactivity, and career level. *Journal of Personnel Psychology, 14*, 131–141.

73. ERE. (2017). 5 keys to recruiting women for your workforce. www.eremedia.com

74. Gaucher, D., Friesen, J., & Kay, A. C. (2011). Evidence that gendered wording in job advertisements exists and sustains gender inequality.

Journal of Personality and Social Psychology, 101, 109–128; Wild, J. (2017, March 7). Wanted—a way with words in recruitment ads. *Financial Times.* https://www .ft.com/content/9974b0ce-e7bb- 11e6-967b-c88452263daf

75. fastaff. (2016). Male nursing statistics. http://www.fastaff.com/ blog/male-nursing-statistics

76. Avery, D. R., & McKay, P. F. (2006). Target practice: An organizational impression management approach to attracting minority and female job applicants. *Personnel Psychology, 59*, 157–187.

77. Highhouse, S., Stierwalt, S. L., Bachiochi, P., Elder, A. E., & Slaughter, J. E. (1999). Effects of advertised human resource management practices on attraction of African American applicants. *Personnel Psychology, 52*, 425–442; Slaughter, J. E., Sinar, E., & Bachiochi, P. D. (2002). Black applicants' reactions to affirmative action plans: Effects of plan content and previous experience with discrimination. *Journal of Applied Psychology, 87*, 333–344.

78. Avery, D. R., Hernandez, M., & Hebl, M. (2004). Who's watching the race? Racial salience in recruitment advertising. *Journal of Applied Social Psychology, 34*, 146–161; Walker, H. J., Feild, H. S., Bernerth, J. B., & Becton, J. B. (2012). Diversity cues on recruitment websites: Investigating the effects on job seekers' information processing. *Journal of Applied Psychology, 97*, 214–224.

79. Avery, D. R. (2003). Reactions to diversity in recruitment advertising—are differences black and white? *Journal of Applied Psychology, 88*, 672–679.

80. Whitney, L. (2010, March 30). Anne Mulcahy to retire as Xerox chairman. *CNET News.* http://news .cnet.com/8301-1001_3-20001412- 92.html; Bryant, A. (2010, February 20). Xerox's new chief tries to redefine its culture. *New York Times.* http://www.nytimes .com/2010/02/21/business/21xerox

.html?pagewanted=1&8dpc; Xerox at a glance. http://www.xerox.com/ about-xerox/company-facts/ enus.html

81. Truxillo, D. M., Cadiz, D. M., & Hammer, L. B. (2015). Supporting the aging workforce: A review and recommendations for workplace intervention research. *Annual Review of Organizational Psychology and Organizational Behavior, 2*, 351–381.

82. Ng, T. W. H., & Feldman, D. C. (2008). The relationship of age to tend dimensions of job performance. *Journal of Applied Psychology, 93*, 392–423.

83. Ng, T. W. H., & Feldman, D. C. (2012). Examining six common stereotypes about older workers with meta-analytical data. *Personnel Psychology, 65*, 821–858.

84. Truxillo, D. M., Cadiz, D. M., & Rineer, J. R. (2014). The aging workforce: Implications for human resource management research and practice (S. Jackson, Ed.). *Oxford Handbooks Online: Business & Management.* https://www.researchgate.net/ publication/282348874_The_Aging_ Workforce_Implications_for_ Human_Resource_Management_ Research_and_Practice

85. Freudenheim, M. (2005, March 23). More help wanted: Older workers please apply. *New York Times,* p. A1.

86. Evans, M. (2017, February 24). The stubborn problem of ageism in hiring. https://www.citylab.com/ work/2017/02/ageism-in-hiring-is- rife-and-not-easy-to-fix/517323/; McGuireWoods (2017, March 6). Are college recruiting programs age discrimination? http://www .lexology.com/library/detail .aspx?g=c08e77fc-9c83-4630-9344- b4d9e80136d4

87. SHRM. (2016). Employing military personnel and recruiting veterans: What HR can do. https://www.shrm .org/ResourcesAndTools/hr-topics/ benefits/Documents/10-0531%20 Military%20Program%20Report_ FNL.pdf

88. Meinert, D. (2016). Why hiring veterans makes good business sense. *HR Magazine.* https:// www.shrm.org/hr-today/news/ hr-magazine/1116/pages/why- hiring-veterans-makes-good- business-sense.aspx

89. Vanden Brook, T. (2017). Army to spend $300 million on bonuses and ads to get 6,000 more recruits. *USA Today.* https://www.usatoday.com/ story/news/politics/2017/02/12/ army-spend-300-million- bonuses-and-ads-get-6000-more- recruits/97757094/

90. Stone, C., & Stone, D. L. (2015). Factors affecting hiring decisions about veterans. *Human Resource Management Review, 25*, 68–79.

91. SERVe. (2018). https://servestudy .org/about

92. EEOC Compliance Manual. (2006). https://www.eeoc.gov/policy/docs/ race-color.html; EEOC Prohibited Employment Policies/Practices. https://www.eeoc.gov/laws/ practices/; Harris, M. M. (2006). EEOC is watching you: Recruitment discrimination comes to the forefront. https://www.eremedia .com/ere/eeoc-is-watching-you- recruitment-discrimination-comes- to-the-forefront/

93. NACE. (2015). Measuring your organization's quality of hire. http:// www.naceweb.org/s10212015/ measuring-quality-of-hire.aspx

94. SHRM. (2016). Talent acquisition: Selection. *HR Today.* https://www .shrm.org/hr-today/trends-and- forecasting/research-and-surveys/ Documents/Talent-Acquisition- Selection.pdf

95. Hausknecht, J. P. (2010). Candidate persistence and personality test practice effects: Implications for staffing system management. *Personnel Psychology, 63*, 299–324; Walker, H. J., Helmuth, C., Feild, H. S., & Bauer, T. N. (2015). Watch what you say: Job applicants' justice perceptions from initial organizational correspondence. *Human Resource Management, 54*, 999–1011; Walker, J., Bauer, T. N., Cole, M. S., Bernerth, J. B.,

Feild, H. S., & Short, J. C. (2013). Is this how I will be treated? Reducing uncertainty through recruitment interactions. *Academy of Management Journal, 56,* 1325–1347.

96. Harris, M. M., & Fink, L. S. (1987). A field study of applicant reactions to employment opportunities: Does the recruiter make a difference? *Personnel Psychology, 40,* 765–784.

97. Boswell et al. (2003). Individual job-choice decisions and the impact of job attributes and recruitment practices: A longitudinal field study. *Human Resource Management, 42,* 23–37; Chapman, D. S., Uggerslev, K. L., Carroll, S. A., Piasentin, K. A., & Jones, D. A. (2005). Applicant attraction to organizations and job choice: A meta-analytic review of the correlates of recruiting outcomes. *Journal of Applied Psychology, 90,* 928–944; Rynes et al. (1991). The importance of recruitment in job choice: A different way of looking. *Personnel Psychology, 50,* 309–339.

98. Disney. https://www.youtube.com/watch?v=Lv7o-Q4IbjY

99. Boswell, W. R., Roehling, M. V., LePine, M. A., & Moynihan, L. M. (2003). Individual job-choice decisions and the impact of job attributes and recruitment practices: A longitudinal field study. *Human Resource Management, 42,* 23–37; Rynes, S. L., Bretz, R. D., & Gerhart, B. (1991). The importance of recruitment in job choice: A different way of looking. *Personnel Psychology, 50,* 309–339; Turban, D. B., Campion, J. E., & Eyring, A. R. (1995). Factors related to job acceptance decisions of college recruiters. *Journal of Vocational Behavior, 47,* 193–213.

100. Boswell, W. R., Roehling, M. V., LePine, M. A., & Moynihan, L. M. (2003). Individual job-choice decisions and the impact of job attributes and recruitment practices: A longitudinal field study. *Human Resource Management, 42,* 23–37; Lievens, F., & Highhouse, S. (2003). The relation of instrumental and symbolic attributes to a company's attractiveness as an employer. *Personnel Psychology, 56,* 75–102; Uggerslev, K. L., Fassina, N. E., & Kraichy, D. (2012). Recruiting through the stages: A meta-analytic test of predictors of applicant attraction at different stages of the recruiting process. *Personnel Psychology, 65,* 597–660.

101. Cable, D. M., & Yu, K. Y. T. (2006). Managing job seekers' organizational image beliefs: The role of media richness and media credibility. *Journal of Applied Psychology, 91,* 828–840.

102. Dishman, L. (2015). A former Google recruiter reveals the biggest résumé mistakes. *Fast Company.* https://www.fastcompany .com/3052371/hit-the-ground-running/a-former-google-recruiter-reveals-the-biggest-resume-mistakes

103. Google. (2017). How we review applications (and what happens next). https://careers.google.com/how-we-hire/apply/

104. The Conference Board. (2017). CEO challenge 2017: Meeting the customer relationships/corporate brand and reputation challenge. https://www.conference-board.org/publications/publicationdetail .cfm?publicationid=7400&centerId=9

105. Murphy, B. (2018). Wendy's can't stop trolling McDonald's on Twitter. *Inc.* https://www.inc.com/bill-murphy-jr/wendys-cant-stop-trolling-mcdonalds-on-twitter-heres-latest-burn.html; Whitten, S. (2017). A Wendy's tweet just went viral for all the wrong reasons. *CNBC.* http://www.cnbc .com/2017/01/04/wendys-saucy-tweets-are-hit-and-miss-on-social-media.html

106. van Hoye, G., & Lievens, F. (2009). Tapping the grapevine: A closer look at word-of-mouth as a recruitment source. *Journal of Applied Psychology, 94,* 341–352.

107. Griepentrog, B. K., Harold, R. M., Holtz, B. C., Klimoski, R. J., & Marsh, S. M. (2012). Integrating social identity and the theory of planned behavior: Predicting withdrawal from an organizational recruitment process. *Personnel Psychology, 65,* 723–753.

108. Bauer, T. N., & Aiman-Smith, L. (1996). Green career choices: The influence of ecological stance on recruiting. *Journal of Business and Psychology, 10,* 445–458; Gully, S. M., Phillips, J. M., Castellano, W. G., Han, K., & Kim, A. (2013). A mediated moderation model of recruiting socially and environmentally responsible job applicants. *Personnel Psychology, 66,* 935–973.

109. Dineen, B. R., Ash, S. R., & Noe, R. A. (2002). A web of applicant attraction: Person–organization fit in the context of web-based recruitment. *Journal of Applied Psychology, 87,* 723–734; Swider, B. W., Zimmerman, R. D., & Barrick, M. R. (2015). Searching for the right fit: Development of applicant person–organization fit during the recruitment process. *Journal of Applied Psychology, 100,* 880–893.

Chapter 7

1. https://code.google.com/codejam/; Fallows, J., & Coates, T. N. (2016, April 10). The science of smart hiring. *The Atlantic Monthly.* https://www.theatlantic.com/business/archive/2016/04/the-science-of-smart-hiring/477561/; Lamont, T. (2015, April 6). How to get a job at Google: Meet the man who hires and fires. *The Guardian.* https://www.theguardian.com/technology/2015/apr/04/how-to-get-job-at-google-meet-man-hires-fires; The 100 Best Companies to Work For 2017. *Fortune.* http://beta .fortune.com/best-companies/

2. Aberdeen Group. (2016). Talent acquisition trends 2016: Candidates take command. http://www.aberdeen.com/research/12582/12582-rr-talent-acquisition-trends/content.aspx

3. Deutschman, A. (2004). Inside the mind of Jeff Bezos. *Fast Company.*

https://www.fastcompany.com/50541/inside-mind-jeff-bezos

4. Nisen, M. (2013). It takes Mayo Clinic 3 whole years to decide if a doctor's good enough for them. *Business Insider.* http://www.businessinsider.com/mayo-clinics-hiring-process-is-incredibly-rigorous-2013-2

5. Society for Industrial and Organizational Psychology (SIOP). (2003). *Principles for the validation and use of personnel selection procedures* (4th ed.). Bowling Green, OH: Author; Uniform Guidelines on Employee Selection Procedures. (1978). *Federal Register, 43,* 38290–38315.

6. Chamorro-Premuzic, T. (2015). 3 emerging alternatives to traditional hiring methods. *Harvard Business Review.* https://hbr.org/2015/06/3-emerging-alternatives-to-traditional-hiring-methods

7. Gatewood, R., Feild, H., & Barrick, M. (2011). *Human resource selection.* Mason, OH: Cengage Learning.

8. Society for Industrial and Organizational Psychology (SIOP). (2003). *Principles for the validation and use of personnel selection procedures* (4th ed.). Bowling Green, OH: Author; Uniform Guidelines on Employee Selection Procedures. (1978). *Federal Register, 43,* 38290–38315.

9. Kuncel, N. R., Klieger, D. M., Connelly, B. S., & Ones, D. S. (2013). Mechanical versus clinical data combination in selection and admissions decisions: A meta-analysis. *Journal of Applied Psychology, 98,* 1060–1072.

10. Gatewood, R., Feild, H., & Barrick, M. (2011). *Human resource selection.* Mason, OH: Cengage Learning.

11. Society for Industrial and Organizational Psychology (SIOP). (2018). *Principles for the validation and use of personnel selection procedures* (5th ed.). Cambridge, MA: Cambridge University Press; Uniform Guidelines on Employee Selection Procedures. (1978). *Federal Register, 43,* 38290–38315.

12. Lawshe, C. H. (1975). A quantitative approach to content validity. *Personnel Psychology, 28,* 563–575.

13. Biddle Consulting Group. (2013). Content-related and criterion-related validation study of CritiCall. http://ww1.prweb.com/prfiles/2013/09/19/11143327/Florida%20Highway%20Patrol%20CritiCall%20Content%20and%20Criterion%20Validation%20Report%209-3-13.pdf

14. Ibid.

15. Sackett, P. R., Putka, D. J., & McCloy, R. A. (2012). The concept of validity and the process of validation. In N. Schmitt (Ed.), *The Oxford handbook of personnel assessment and selection* (pp. 91–118). New York, NY: Oxford University Press; Schmitt, N., Gooding, R. Z., Noe, R. A., & Kirsch, M. (1984). Meta analyses of validity studies published between 1964 and 1982 and the investigation of study characteristics. *Personnel Psychology, 37,* 407–422.

16. Landy, F. J. (1986). Stamp collecting versus science: Validation as hypothesis testing. *American Psychologist, 41,* 1183–1192.

17. Sackett, P. R., Walmsley, P. T., Koch, A. J., Beatty, A. S., & Kuncel, N. R. (2016). Predictor content matters for knowledge testing: Evidence supporting content validation. *Human Performance, 29,* 54–71; Spitzmuller, M., Sin, H. P., Howe, M., & Fatimah, S. (2015). Investigating the uniqueness and usefulness of proactive personality in organizational research: A meta-analytic review. *Human Performance, 28,* 351–379.

18. Gatewood, R., Feild, H., & Barrick, M. (2011). *Human resource selection.* Mason, OH: Cengage Learning; Society for Industrial and Organizational Psychology (SIOP). (2018). *Principles for the validation and use of personnel selection procedures* (5th ed.). Cambridge, MA: Cambridge University Press; Uniform Guidelines on Employee Selection Procedures. (1978). *Federal Register, 43,* 38290–38315.

19. Biddle Consulting Group. (2013). Content-related and criterion-related validation study of CritiCall.

20. Brislin, R. W. (1970). Back-translation for cross-cultural research. *Journal of Cross-Cultural Psychology, 1,* 185–216; Steiner, D. D. (2012). Personnel selection across the globe. In N. Schmitt (Ed.), *The Oxford handbook of personnel selection and assessment* (pp. 740–767). New York, NY: Oxford University Press; Tippins, N. T. (2010). Making global assessments work. *The Industrial-Organizational Psychologist, 48,* 59–64.

21. Anderson, N., Salgado, J. F., & Hülsheger, U. R. (2010). Applicant reactions in selection: Comprehensive meta-analysis into reaction generalization versus situational specificity. *International Journal of Selection and Assessment, 18,* 291–304; Hausknecht, J. P., Day, D. V., & Thomas, S. C. (2004). Applicant reactions to selection procedures: An updated model and meta-analysis. *Personnel Psychology, 57,* 639–683.

22. McDaniel, M. A., Whetzel, D. L., Schmidt, F. L., & Maurer, S. D. (1994). The validity of employment interviews: A comprehensive review and meta-analysis. *Journal of Applied Psychology, 79,* 599–616; Schmidt, F. L., & Hunter, J. E. (1998). The validity and utility of selection methods in personnel psychology: Practical and theoretical implications of 85 years of research findings. *Psychological Bulletin, 124,* 262–274.

23. Levashina, J., Hartwell, C. J., Morgeson, F. P., & Campion, M. A. (2014). The structured employment interview: Narrative and quantitative review of the research literature. *Personnel Psychology, 67,* 241–293.

24. McDaniel, M. A., Whetzel, D. L., Schmidt, F. L., & Maurer, S. D. (1994). The validity of employment interviews: A comprehensive review and meta-analysis. *Journal of Applied Psychology, 79,* 599–616; Schmidt, F. L., & Hunter, J. E. (1998). The validity and utility of

selection methods in personnel psychology: Practical and theoretical implications of 85 years of research findings. *Psychological Bulletin, 124*, 262–274.

25. Shaffer, J. A., & Postlethwaite, B. E. (2012). A matter of context: A meta-analytic investigation of the relative validity of contextualized and noncontextualized personality measures. *Personnel Psychology, 65*, 445–493.

26. Ones, D. S., Viswesvaran, C., & Schmidt, F. L. (1993). Comprehensive meta-analysis of integrity test validities: Findings and implications for personnel selection and theories of job performance. *Journal of Applied Psychology, 78*, 679–703; Van Iddekinge, C. H., Roth, P. L., Raymark, P. H., & Odle-Dusseau, H. N. (2012). The criterion-related validity of integrity tests: An updated meta-analysis. *Journal of Applied Psychology, 97*, 499–530.

27. Schmidt, F. L., & Hunter, J. E. (1998). The validity and utility of selection methods in personnel psychology: Practical and theoretical implications of 85 years of research findings. *Psychological Bulletin, 124*, 262–274.

28. Hunter, J. E., & Hunter, R. F. (1984). Validity and utility of alternative predictors of job performance. *Psychological Bulletin, 96*, 72–98; Schmidt, F. L., & Hunter, J. E. (1998). The validity and utility of selection methods in personnel psychology: Practical and theoretical implications of 85 years of research findings. *Psychological Bulletin, 124*, 262–274.

29. Christian, M. S., Edwards, B. D., & Bradley, J. C. (2010). Situational judgment tests: Constructs assessed and a meta-analysis of their criterion-related validities. *Personnel Psychology, 63*, 83–117.

30. Arthur, W., Day, E. A., McNelly, T. L., & Edens, P. S. (2003). A meta-analysis of the criterion-related validity of assessment center dimensions. *Personnel Psychology, 56*, 125–153.

31. Hunter, J. E., & Hunter, R. F. (1984). Validity and utility of alternative predictors of job performance. *Psychological Bulletin, 96*, 72–98; Vinchur, A. J., Schippmann, J. S., Switzer, F. S., III, & Roth, P. L. (1998). A meta-analytic review of predictors of job performance for salespeople. *Journal of Applied Psychology, 83*, 586–597.

32. Wilhelmy, A., Kleinmann, M., König, C., Melchers, K., & Truxillo, D. M. (2016). How and why do interviewers try to make impressions on applicants? A qualitative study. *Journal of Applied Psychology, 101*, 313–332.

33. Blackman, M. C. (2002). Personality judgment and the utility of the unstructured employment interview. *Basic and Applied Social Psychology, 24*, 241–250; Dipboye, R. L., Macan, T., & Shahani-Denning, C. (2012). The selection interview from the interviewer and applicant perspectives: Can't have one without the other. In N. Schmitt (Ed.), *The Oxford handbook of personnel assessment and selection* (pp. 323–352). New York, NY: Oxford University Press; Wilhelmy, A., Kleinmann, M., König, C., Melchers, K., & Truxillo, D. M. (2016). How and why do interviewers try to make impressions on applicants? A qualitative study. *Journal of Applied Psychology, 101*, 313–332.

34. Arvey, R. D., & Campion, J. E. (1982). The employment interview: A summary and review of recent research. *Personnel Psychology, 35*, 281–322.

35. Friedman, T. L. (2014). How to get a job at Google. *New York Times.* https://www.nytimes.com/2014/02/23/opinion/sunday/friedman-how-to-get-a-job-at-google.html?_r=0

36. Arvey, R. D., & Campion, J. E. (1982). The employment interview: A summary and review of recent research. *Personnel Psychology, 35*, 281–322; Janz, T. (1982). Initial comparisons of patterned behavior description interviews versus unstructured interviews. *Journal of*

Applied Psychology, 67, 577–580; Latham, G. P., Saari, L. M., Pursell, E. D., & Campion, M. A. (1980). The situational interview. *Journal of Applied Psychology, 65,* 422–427; Levashina, J., Hartwell, C. J., Morgeson, F. P., & Campion, M. A. (2014). The structured employment interview: Narrative and quantitative review of the research literature. *Personnel Psychology, 67*, 241–293.

37. Campion, M. A., Palmer, D. K., & Campion, J. E. (1997). A review of structure in the selection interview. *Personnel Psychology, 50*, 655–702; Chapman, D. S., & Zweig, D. I. (2005). Developing a nomological network for interview structure: Antecedents and consequences of the structured selection interview. *Personnel Psychology, 58*, 673–702; Hartwell, C. J., & Campion, M. A. (2016). Getting on the same page: The effect of normative feedback interventions on structured interview ratings. *Journal of Applied Psychology, 101,* 757–778.

38. Blacksmith, N., Willford, J. C., & Behrend, T. S. (2016). Technology in the employment interview: A meta-analysis and future research agenda. *Personnel Assessment and Decisions, 2*, 12–20.

39. Bye, H. H., & Sandal, G. M. (2016). Applicant personality and procedural justice perceptions of group selection interviews. *Journal of Business and Psychology, 31*, 569–582.

40. Swider, B. W., Barrick, M. R., & Harris, T. B. (2016). Initial impressions: What they are, what they are not, and how they influence structured interview outcomes. *Journal of Applied Psychology, 101*, 625–638.

41. Kantrowitz, T. M. *Global Assessment Trends 2014.* CEB-SHL Talent Management. https://www.cebglobal.com/content/dam/cebglobal/us/EN/regions/uk/tm/pdfs/Report/gatr-2014.pdf

42. Barrick, M. R., & Mount, M. K. (1991). The Big Five personality dimensions and job performance: A meta-analysis. *Personnel Psychology, 44*, 1–26.

43. International Personality Item Pool: A Scientific Collaboratory for the Development of Advanced Measures of Personality Traits and Other Individual Differences. http://ipip.ori.org/

44. Goldberg, L. R. (1999). A broad-bandwidth, public domain, personality inventory measuring the lower-level facets of several five-factor models. *Personality Psychology in Europe, 7*, 7–28; International Personality Item Pool: A Scientific Collaboratory for the Development of Advanced Measures of Personality Traits and Other Individual Differences. http://ipip.ori.org/

45. Morgeson, F. P., Campion, M. A., Dipboye, R. L., Hollenbeck, J. R., Murphy, K., & Schmitt, N. (2007). Reconsidering the use of personality tests in personnel selection contexts. *Personnel Psychology, 60*, 683–729.

46. Hogan, J., Barrett, P., & Hogan, R. (2007). Personality measurement, faking, and employment selection. *Journal of Applied Psychology, 92*, 1270–1285; Kleinmann, M., Ingold, P. V., Lievens, F., Jansen, A., Melchers, K. G., & König, C. J. (2011). A different look at why selection procedures work: The role of candidates' ability to identify criteria. *Organizational Psychology Review, 1*, 128–146. Marcus, B. (2009). Faking from the applicant's perspective: A theory of self-presentation in personnel selection settings. *International Journal of Selection and Assessment, 17*, 417–430; Van Hooft, E. A., & Born, M. P. (2012). Intentional response distortion on personality tests: Using eye-tracking to understand response processes when faking. *Journal of Applied Psychology, 97*, 301–316.

47. Crant, J. M. (1995). The Proactive Personality Scale and objective job performance among real estate agents. *Journal of Applied Psychology, 80*, 532–537; Spitzmuller, M., Sin, H. P., Howe, M., & Fatimah, S. (2015). Investigating the uniqueness and usefulness of proactive personality in organizational research: A meta-analytic review. *Human Performance, 28*, 351–379.

48. Cullen, K. L., Edwards, B. D., Casper, W. C., & Gue, K. R. (2014). Employees' adaptability and perceptions of change-related uncertainty: Implications for perceived organizational support, job satisfaction, and performance. *Journal of Business and Psychology, 29*, 269–280.

49. U.S. Department of Labor. (2009). Other workplace standards: Lie detector tests. https://www.dol.gov/compliance/guide/eppa.htm

50. Marcus, B., Lee, K., & Ashton, M. C. (2007). Personality dimensions explaining relationships between integrity tests and counterproductive behavior: Big Five, or one in addition? *Personnel Psychology, 60*, 1–34; Sackett, P. R., & Wanek, J. E. (1996). New developments in the use of measures of honesty, integrity, conscientiousness, dependability, trustworthiness, and reliability for personnel selection. *Personnel Psychology, 49*, 787–829.

51. Ones, D. S., Viswesvaran, C., & Schmidt, F. L. (1993). Comprehensive meta-analysis of integrity test validities: Findings and implications for personnel selection and theories of job performance. *Journal of Applied Psychology, 78*, 679–703.

52. Ones, D. S., Viswesvaran, C., & Schmidt, F. L. (2012). Integrity tests predict counterproductive work behaviors and job performance well: Comment on Van Iddekinge, Roth, Raymark, and Odle-Dusseau. *Journal of Applied Psychology, 97*, 537–542; Sackett, P. R., & Schmitt, N. (2012). On reconciling conflicting meta-analytic findings regarding integrity test validity. *Journal of Applied Psychology, 97*, 550–556; Van Iddekinge, C. H., Roth, P. L., Raymark, P. H., & Odle-Dusseau, H. N. (2012). The criterion-related validity of integrity tests: An updated meta-analysis. *Journal of Applied Psychology, 97*, 499–530.

53. Berry, C. M., Sackett, P. R., & Wiemann, S. (2007). A review of recent developments in integrity test research. *Personnel Psychology, 60*, 271–301; Marcus, B., Lee, K., & Ashton, M. C. (2007). Personality dimensions explaining relationships between integrity tests and counterproductive behavior: Big five, or one in addition? *Personnel Psychology, 60*, 1–34.

54. Guion, R. M. (1998). *Assessment, measurement, and prediction for personnel decisions*. Mahwah, NJ: Lawrence Erlbaum Associates.

55. Schmidt, F. L., & Hunter, J. E. (1998). The validity and utility of selection methods in personnel psychology: Practical and theoretical implications of 85 years of research findings. *Psychological Bulletin, 124*, 262–274.

56. Ones, D. S., Dilchert, S., & Viswesvaran, C. (2012). Cognitive abilities. In N. Schmitt (Ed.), *The Oxford handbook of personnel assessment and selection* (pp. 179–224). New York: Oxford University Press; Roth, P. L., Bevier, C. A., Bobko, P., Switzer, F. S., & Tyler, P. (2001). Ethnic group differences in cognitive ability in employment and educational settings: A meta-analysis. *Personnel Psychology, 54*, 297–330; Ryan, A. M., & Powers, C. (2012). Workplace diversity. In N. Schmitt (Ed.), *The Oxford handbook of personnel assessment and selection* (pp. 814–831). New York: Oxford University Press.

57. Ones, D. S., Dilchert, S., & Viswesvaran, C. (2012). Cognitive abilities. In N. Schmitt (Ed.), *The Oxford handbook of personnel assessment and selection* (pp. 179–224). New York: Oxford University Press; Schmidt, F. L., & Hunter, J. (2004). General mental ability in the world of work: occupational attainment and job performance. *Journal of Personality and Social Psychology, 86*, 162–173.

58. Guion, R. M. (1965). *Personnel testing*. New York: McGraw-Hill.

59. Subway, Inc. Study guide for taking the Wonderlic Basic Skills Test. http://subconinc.net/subconinc/resources/1/study_guide.pdf

60. Gatewood, R., Feild, H., & Barrick, M. (2011). *Human resource selection.* Mason, OH: Cengage Learning.

61. Salovey, P., & Mayer, J. D. (1990). Emotional intelligence. *Imagination, Cognition and Personality, 9,* 185–211.

62. A video game that slays hiring bias and airdrops you into the right job. (2016, October 12). *Fast Company.* https://www.fastcompany.com/3063881/a-video-game-that-slays-hiring-bias-and-airdrops-you-into-the-right-job; Gamification in recruitment: Psychometric selection for diverse talent. (2016, August 1). *Personnel Today.* http://www.personneltoday.com/hr/gamification-recruitment-psychometric-selection-diverse-talent/; Riley, P. Should we play? Gamification in assessment and selection. *Assessment and Development Matters, 7,* 13–16. http://ptc.bps.org.uk/sites/ptc.bps.org.uk/files/Documents/Assessment%20%26%20Development%20Matters/Should%20we%20Play%20-%20Philippa%20Riley.pdf

63. Joseph, D. L., Jin, J., Newman, D. A., & O'Boyle, E. H. (2015). Why does self-reported emotional intelligence predict job performance? A meta-analytic investigation of mixed EI. *Journal of Applied Psychology, 100,* 298–342; Joseph, D. L., & Newman, D. A. (2010). Emotional intelligence: An integrative meta-analysis and cascading model. *Journal of Applied Psychology, 95,* 54–78.

64. JetBlue: hiring crewmembers with the skills to thrive. https://rework.withgoogle.com/case-studies/JetBlue-hiring-crewmembers-with-skills-to-thrive/

65. Block, K. (2016). I hire engineers at Google. Here's what I look for (and why). *Fast Company.* https://www.fastcompany.com/3062713/i-hire-engineers-at-google-heres-what-i-look-for-and-why

66. Hausknecht, J. P., Day, D. V., & Thomas, S. C. (2004). Applicant reactions to selection procedures: An updated model and meta-analysis. *Personnel Psychology, 57,* 639–683; Schmidt, F. L., & Hunter, J. E. (1998). The validity and utility of selection methods in personnel psychology: Practical and theoretical implications of 85 years of research findings. *Psychological Bulletin, 124,* 262–274.

67. Bauer, T. N., Truxillo, D. M., Mack, K., & Costa, A. B. (2011). Applicant reactions to technology-based selection: What we know so far. In N. T. Tippins & S. Adler (Eds.), *Technology-enhanced assessment* (pp. 190–223). San Francisco: Jossey-Bass.

68. Christian, M. S., Edwards, B. D., & Bradley, J. C. (2010). Situational judgment tests: Constructs assessed and a meta-analysis of their criterion-related validities. *Personnel Psychology, 63,* 83–117; Lievens, F., & Sackett, P. R. (2012). The validity of interpersonal skills assessment via situational judgment tests for predicting academic success and job performance. *Journal of Applied Psychology, 97,* 460–468.

69. Arthur, W., Day, E. A., McNelly, T. L., & Edens, P. S. (2003). A meta-analysis of the criterion-related validity of assessment center dimensions. *Personnel Psychology, 56,* 125–153; Schmidt, F. L., & Hunter, J. E. (1998). The validity and utility of selection methods in personnel psychology: Practical and theoretical implications of 85 years of research findings. *Psychological Bulletin, 124,* 262–274.

70. Lievens, F., & De Soete, B. (2012). Simulations. In N. Schmitt (Ed.), *The Oxford handbook of personnel assessment and selection* (pp. 383–410). New York: Oxford University Press.

71. http://www.siop.org/lec/2009/reynolds_bio.aspx; http://www.ddiworld.com/company/our-management-team/douglas-reynolds

72. Schmidt, F. L., & Hunter, J. E. (1998). The validity and utility of selection methods in personnel psychology: Practical and

theoretical implications of 85 years of research findings. *Psychological Bulletin, 124,* 262–274.

73. Cucina, J. M., Caputo, P. M., Thibodeaux, H. F., & Maclane, C. N. (2012). Unlocking the key to biodata scoring: A comparison of empirical, rational, and hybrid approaches at different sample sizes. *Personnel Psychology, 65,* 385–428; Gatewood, R., Feild, H., & Barrick, M. (2011). *Human resource selection.* Mason, OH: Cengage Learning.

74. Schmidt, F. L., & Hunter, J. E. (1998). The validity and utility of selection methods in personnel psychology: Practical and theoretical implications of 85 years of research findings. *Psychological Bulletin, 124,* 262–274.

75. Ibid.

76. Hausknecht, J. P, Day, D. V., & Thomas, S. C. (2004). Applicant reactions to selection procedures: An updated model and meta-analysis. *Personnel Psychology, 57,* 639–683.

77. Getting past the first cut with a résumé that grabs digital eyes. (2016, July 8). *New York Times.* https://www.nytimes.com/2016/07/10/jobs/getting-past-the-first-cut-with-a-resume-that-grabs-digital-eyes.html; How to write a cover letter people will actually read. (2016, October 21). *New York Times.* https://www.nytimes.com/2016/10/22/business/how-to-write-a-cover-letter-that-stands-out.html; Job hunting in the digital age. (2016, April 8). *New York Times.* https://www.nytimes.com/2016/04/10/education/edlife/job-hunting-in-the-digital-age.html

78. Gatewood, R., Feild, H., & Barrick, M. (2011). *Human resource selection.* Mason, OH: Cengage Learning.

79. Ibid.; Society for Human Resource Management. (2010, January 22). Background checking: Conducting reference background checks: SHRM poll. *Survey Findings.* http://www.shrm.org/Research/SurveyFindings/Articles/Pages/ConductingReferenceBackgroundChecks.aspx

80. The White House. (2016). White House launches the fair

chance business pledge. https://obamawhitehouse.archives.gov/the-press-office/2016/04/11/fact-sheet-white-house-launches-fair-chance-business-pledge; https://www.laboremploymentlawblog.com/2017/07/articles/background-investigations/criminal-background-checks/; https://www.shrm.org/resourcesandtools/legal-and-compliance/state-and-local-updates/xperthr/pages/ban-the-box-laws-by-state-and-municipality-.aspx

81. Chicago to pay $3.8 million as part of Fire Department gender bias case. (2016, December 9). *Chicago Tribune*. http://www.chicagotribune.com/news/local/politics/ct-chicago-fire-department-lawsuit-gender-bias-met-20161209-story.html

82. Baker, T. A., & Gebhardt, D. L. (2012). The assessment of physical capabilities in the workplace. In N. Schmitt (Ed.), *The Oxford handbook of personnel assessment and selection* (pp. 274–296). New York: Oxford University Press; Courtright, S. H., McCormick, B. W., Postlethwaite, B. E., Reeves, C. J., & Mount, M. K. (2013). A meta-analysis of sex differences in physical ability: Revised estimates and strategies for reducing differences in selection contexts. *Journal of Applied Psychology, 98*, 623–641.

83. Van Iddekinge, C. H., Lanivich, S. E., Roth, P. L., & Junco, E. (2016). Social media for selection? Validity and adverse impact potential of a Facebook-based assessment. *Journal of Management, 42*, 1811–1835.

84. Based on information contained in 74,000 data records breached on stolen Coca-Cola laptops. (2014, January 27). *Infosecurity Magazine*. http://www.infosecurity-magazine.com/view/36627/74000-data-records-breached-on-stolen-cocacola-laptops-/; Are you doing enough to protect your sensitive HR data? (2016, October 19). *People HR*, https://www.peoplehr.com/blog/index.php/2016/10/19/are-you-doing-enough-to-protect-your-sensitive-hr-data/

85. Bernerth, J. B., Taylor, S. G., Walker, H. J., & Whitman, D. S. (2012). An empirical investigation of dispositional antecedents and performance-related outcomes of credit scores. *Journal of Applied Psychology, 97*, 469–478.

86. Harold, C. M., Holtz, B. C., Griepentrog, B. K., Brewer, L. M., & Marsh, S. M. (2016). Investigating the effects of applicant justice perceptions on job offer acceptance. *Personnel Psychology, 69*, 199–22; McCarthy, J. M., Bauer, T. N., Truxillo, D. M., Anderson, N. R., Costa, A. C., & Ahmed, S. M. (2017). Applicant perspectives during selection: A review addressing "so what?," "what's new?," and "where to next?" *Journal of Management, 43*, 1693–1725.

87. Steiner, K. (2017). Bad candidate experience cost Virgin Media $5M annually—and how they turned it around. https://business.linkedin.com/talent-solutions/blog/candidate-experience/2017/bad-candidate-experience-cost-virgin-media-5m-annually-and-how-they-turned-that-around

88. Bauer, T. N., Truxillo, D. M., Sanchez, R. J., Craig, J., Ferrara, P., & Campion, M. A. (2001). Applicant reactions to selection: Development of the Selection Procedural Justice Scale (SPJS). *Personnel Psychology, 54*, 387–419; Gilliland, S. W. (1993). The perceived fairness of selection systems: An organizational justice perspective. *Academy of Management Review, 18*, 694–734; Hausknecht, J. P, Day, D. V., & Thomas, S. C. (2004). Applicant reactions to selection procedures: An updated model and meta-analysis. *Personnel Psychology, 57*, 639–683; McCarthy, J. M., Bauer, T. N., Truxillo, D. M., Anderson, N. R., Costa, A. C., & Ahmed, S. M. (2017). Applicant perspectives during selection: A review addressing "so what?," "what's new?," and "where to next?" *Journal of Management, 43*, 1693–1725.

89. Anderson, N., Salgado, J. F., & Hülsheger, U. R. (2010). Applicant reactions in selection: Comprehensive meta-analysis into reaction generalization versus situational specificity. *International Journal of Selection and Assessment, 18*, 291–304; Hoang, T. G., Truxillo, D. M., Erdogan, B., & Bauer, T. N. (2012). Cross-cultural examination of applicant reactions to selection methods: United States and Vietnam. *International Journal of Selection and Assessment, 20*, 209–219; Steiner, D. D., & Gilliland, S. W. (1996). Fairness reactions to personnel selection techniques in France and the United States. *Journal of Applied Psychology, 81*, 134–141.

90. Gilliland, S. W. (1993). The perceived fairness of selection systems: An organizational justice perspective. *Academy of Management Review, 18*, 694–734; Hausknecht, J. P, Day, D. V., & Thomas, S. C. (2004). Applicant reactions to selection procedures: An updated model and meta-analysis. *Personnel Psychology, 57*, 639–683.

91. Truxillo, D. M., Bauer, T. N., Campion, M. A., & Paronto, M. E. (2002). Selection fairness information and applicant reactions: A longitudinal field study. *Journal of Applied Psychology, 87*, 1020–1031; Truxillo, D. M., Bodner, T. E., Bertolino, M., Bauer, T. N., & Yonce, C. A. (2009). Effects of explanations on applicant reactions: A meta-analytic review. *International Journal of Selection and Assessment, 17*, 346–361.

92. CandE Awards. (2016). CandE winners. http://www.thetalentboard.org/cande-awards/cande-winners/

93. Guion, R. M. (2011). *Assessment, measurement, and prediction for personnel decisions*. New York: Routledge.

94. Society for Industrial and Organizational Psychology (SIOP). (2018). *Principles for the validation and use of personnel selection procedures* (5th ed.). Cambridge, MA: Cambridge University Press; Uniform Guidelines on Employee Selection Procedures. (1978). *Federal Register*, 43, 38290–38315.

Chapter 8

1. Winters, J. (2017, April). A principles-driven culture pushes Igloo to success. *TD: Training and Development*, 36–40.

2. Size of training industry. (2017). https://www.trainingindustry.com/wiki/entries/size-of-training-industry.aspx

3. Goldstein, I. L., & Ford, J. K. (2002). *Training in organizations: Needs assessment, development, and evaluation* (4th ed.). Belmont, CA: Wadsworth Cengage Learning.

4. QSR. (2017, February 1). Starbucks' hiring plans reach veterans, youth, and refugees. https://www.qsrmagazine.com/news/starbucks-hiring-plans-reach-veterans-youth-and-refugees; The Financial. (2017, July 20). Starbucks to open first store in Bed-Stuy, Brooklyn. https://www.finchannel.com/business/66705-starbucks-to-open-first-store-in-bed-stuy-brooklyn

5. Bingham, T., & Galagan, P. (2016, December). Lessons from the Silicon Valley fast lane. *TD: Talent Development*, 30–35; Dweck, C. (2016). *Mindset: The new psychology of success*. New York: Penguin Random House LLC.

6. Lechner, H. G., Zavaleta, K. W., & Shinde, A. S. (2017, June). Preparing subject experts to teach. *TD: Training and Development*, 68–69; Van Daele, C. (2017, April). Beyond tech pro to tech trainer. *TD: Training and Development*, 104–105.

7. Rients, S. (2017, February 1). Compliance training doesn't have to be boring. *Association for Talent Development*. https://www.td.org/Publications/Magazines/TD/TD-Archive/2017/02/Compliance-Training-Doesnt-Have-to-Be-Boring; Uniform Guidelines on Employee Selection Procedures. (1978). *Federal Register, 43*, 38290–38315.

8. Goldstein, I. L., & Ford, J. K. (2002). *Training in organizations: Needs assessment, development, and evaluation* (4th ed.). Belmont, CA: Wadsworth Cengage Learning.

9. Kraiger, K., Ford, J. K., & Salas, E. (1993). Application of cognitive, skill-based, and affective theories of learning outcomes to new methods of training evaluation. *Journal of Applied Psychology, 78*, 311–328; Salas, E., Tannenbaum, S. I., Kraiger, K., & Smith-Jentsch, K. A. (2012). The science of training and development in organizations: What matters in practice. *Psychological Science in the Public Interest, 13*, 74–101.

10. Colquitt, J. A., LePine, J. A., & Noe, R. A. (2000). Toward an integrative theory of training motivation: A meta-analytic path analysis of 20 years of research. *Journal of Applied Psychology, 85*, 678–707; Goldstein, I. L., & Ford, J. K. (2002). *Training in organizations: Needs assessment, development, and evaluation* (4th ed.). Belmont, CA: Wadsworth Cengage Learning.

11. Kruger, J., & Dunning, D. (1999). Unskilled and unaware of it: How difficulties in recognizing one's own incompetence lead to inflated self-assessments. *Journal of Personality and Social Psychology, 77*, 1121–1132.

12. Hammer, L. B., Truxillo, D. M., Bodner, T., Rineer, J., Pytlovany, A. C., & Richman, A. (2015). Effects of a workplace intervention targeting psychosocial risk factors on safety and health outcomes. *BioMed Research International, 2015*; Olson, R., & Winchester, J. (2008). Behavioral self-monitoring of safety and productivity in the workplace: A methodological primer and quantitative literature review. *Journal of Organizational Behavior Management, 28*, 9–75.

13. Hammer, L. B., Truxillo, D. M., Bodner, T., Rineer, J., Pytlovany, A. C., & Richman, A. (2015). Effects of a workplace intervention targeting psychosocial risk factors on safety and health outcomes. *BioMed Research International, 2015*; Olson, R., & Winchester, J. (2008). Behavioral self-monitoring of safety and productivity in the workplace: A methodological primer and quantitative literature review. *Journal of Organizational Behavior Management, 28*, 9–75.

14. Colquitt, J. A., LePine, J. A., & Noe, R. A. (2000). Toward an integrative theory of training motivation: A meta-analytic path analysis of 20 years of research. *Journal of Applied Psychology, 85*, 678–707; Goldstein, I. L., & Ford, J. K. (2002). *Training in organizations: Needs assessment, development, and evaluation* (4th ed.). Belmont, CA: Wadsworth Cengage Learning.

15. Goldstein, I. L., & Ford, J. K. (2002). *Training in organizations: Needs assessment, development, and evaluation* (4th ed.). Belmont, CA: Wadsworth Cengage Learning.

16. Arthur, W., Jr., Bennett, W., Jr., Edens, P. S., & Bell, S. T. (2003). Effectiveness of training in organizations: A meta-analysis of design and evaluation features. *Journal of Applied Psychology, 88*, 234–245; Goldstein, I. L., & Ford, J. K. (2002). *Training in organizations: Needs assessment, development, and evaluation* (4th ed.). Belmont, CA: Wadsworth Cengage Learning.

17. Simulators and training devices. https://www.delta.com/content/www/en_US/about-delta/business-programs/training-and-consulting-services/pilot-training/simulators-and-training-devices.html

18. Goldstein, I. L., & Ford, J. K. (2002); Villado, A. J., & Arthur W., Jr. (2013). The comparative effect of subjective and objective after-action reviews on team performance on a complex task. *Journal of Applied Psychology, 98*, 514–528.

19. Goldstein, I. L., & Ford, J. K. (2002).

20. Slade, T. (2017, March). Five lessons for new eLearning designers. *TD: Training and Development*, 60–64.

21. SAP Learning Hub. https://training.sap.com/shop/learninghub

22. Bell, B. S., & Kozlowski, S. W. (2002). Adaptive guidance: Enhancing self-regulation, knowledge, and performance in technology-based training. *Personnel Psychology, 55*, 267–306. Bell, B. S., & Kozlowski, S. W. (2008). Active learning: Effects of core training design elements on self-regulatory processes, learning, and adaptability. *Journal of Applied Psychology, 93*, 296–316; Sitzmann, T., Kraiger, K., Stewart, D., & Wisher, R. (2006). The comparative effectiveness of web-based and classroom instruction: A meta-analysis. *Personnel Psychology, 59*, 623–664.

23. Baldwin, T. T. (1992). Effects of alternative modeling strategies on outcomes of interpersonal-skills training. *Journal of Applied Psychology, 77*, 147–154; Bandura, A. (1977). *Social learning theory.* Englewood Cliffs, NJ: Prentice Hall; Taylor, P. J., Russ-Eft, D. F., & Chan, D. W. (2005); A meta-analytic review of behavior modeling training. *Journal of Applied Psychology, 90*, 692–709.

24. Alhejji, H., Garavan, T., Carbery, R., O'Brien, F., & McGuire, D. (2016). Diversity training programme outcomes: A systematic review. *Human Resource Development Quarterly, 27*, 95–149; Dobbin, F., & Kalev, A. (July–August, 2016). Why diversity programs fail and what works better. *Harvard Business Review,* 52–60; Kalinoski, Z. T., Steele-Johnson, D., Peyton, E. J., Leas, K. A., Steinke, J., & Bowling, N. A. (2013). A meta-analytic evaluation of diversity training outcomes. *Journal of Organizational Behavior, 34*, 1076–1104; Lindsey, A., King, E., Hebl, M., & Levine, N. (2015). The impact of method, motivation, and empathy on diversity training effectiveness. *Journal of Business and Psychology, 30*, 605–617; Manjoo, F. (2014). Exposing hidden bias at Google. *New York Times.* http://www.nytimes.com/2014/09/25/technology/exposing-hidden-biases-at-google-to-improve-diversity.html

25. Marks, M. A., Sabella, M. J., Burke, C. S., & Zaccaro, S. J. (2002). The impact of cross-training on team effectiveness. *Journal of Applied Psychology, 87*, 3–13; Salas, E., DiazGranados, D., Klein, C., Burke, C. S., Stagl, K. C., Goodwin, G. F., & Halpin, S. M. (2008). Does team training improve team performance? A meta-analysis. *Human Factors, 50*, 903–933.

26. Center for Creative Leadership. (n.d.). https://www.ccl.org/people/cindy-mccauley-2/; The long view: Cindy McCauley. (2017, February). *TD: Training and Development,* 62–63.

27. Bono, J. E., Purvanova, R. K., Towler, A. J., & Peterson, D. B. (2009). A survey of executive coaching practices. *Personnel Psychology, 62*, 361–404; Goldstein, I. L., & Ford, J. K. (2002). *Training in organizations: Needs assessment, development, and evaluation* (4th ed.). Belmont, CA: Wadsworth Cengage Learning.

28. Byebierggaard, P., & Yoder, B. (2017, May). The sense-making loop. *TD: Training and Development,* 38–43.

29. Hülsheger, U. R., Feinholdt, A., & Nübold, A. (2015). A low-dose mindfulness intervention and recovery from work: Effects on psychological detachment, sleep quality, and sleep duration. *Journal of Occupational and Organizational Psychology, 88*, 464–489; Roeser, R. W., Schonert-Reichl, K. A., Jha, A., Cullen, M., Wallace, L., Wilensky, R., . . . Harrison, J. (2013). Mindfulness training and reductions in teacher stress and burnout: Results from two randomized, waitlist-control field trials. *Journal of Educational Psychology, 105*, 787–804.

30. Schaufenbruel, K. (2015, December 29). *Harvard Business Review.* https://hbr.org/2015/12/why-google-target-and-general-mills-are-investing-in-mindfulness; Wieczner, J. (2016, March 12). Meditation has become a billion dollar business. *Fortune.* http://fortune.com/2016/03/12/meditation-mindfulness-apps/

31. Landers, R. N., & Armstrong, M. B. (2017). Enhancing instructional outcomes with gamification: An empirical test of the Technology-Enhanced Training Effectiveness Model. *Computers in Human Behavior, 71*, 499–507; Santhanam, R., Liu, D., & Shen, W. C. M. (2016). Research Note—Gamification of technology-mediated training: Not all competitions are the same. *Information Systems Research, 27*, 453–465.

32. Bauer, T. N., Bodner, T., Erdogan, B., Truxillo, D. M., & Tucker, J. S. (2007). Newcomer adjustment during organizational socialization: A meta-analytic review of antecedents, outcomes, and methods. *Journal of Applied Psychology, 92*, 707–721; Saks, A. M., Uggerslev, K. L., & Fassina, N. E. (2007). Socialization tactics and newcomer adjustment: A meta-analytic review and test of a model. *Journal of Vocational Behavior, 70*, 413–446.

33. Klein, H. J., & Polin, B. (2012). Are organizations on board with best practices onboarding? In C. Wanberg (Ed.), *The Oxford handbook of organizational socialization* (pp. 267–287). New York: Oxford University Press.

34. Personal communication with Talya N. Bauer.

35. Information summarized based on research by Talya Bauer.

36. Bauer, T. N., & Erdogan, B. (2016). *Organizational behavior.* Boston: Flat World Knowledge; Durett, J. (2006, March 1). Technology opens the door to success at Ritz-Carlton. http://www.managesmarter.com/msg/search/article_display.jsp?vnu_content_id=1002157749; Elswick, J. (2000, February). Puttin' on the Ritz: Hotel chain touts training to benefit its recruiting and retention. *Employee Benefit News, 14*, 9; The Ritz-Carlton Company: How it became a "legend" in service. (2001,

Jan.–Feb.). *Corporate University Review, 9,* 16.

37. Bauer, T. N. (2015). Onboarding: The critical role of hiring managers. SuccessFactors. https://www.researchgate.net/publication/286447336_The_critical_role_of_the_hiring_manager_in_new_employee_onboarding

38. Ashford, S. J., & Black, J. S. (1996). Proactivity during organizational entry: The role of desire for control. *Journal of Applied Psychology, 81,* 199–214.

39. Ellis, A. M., Nifadkar, S. S., Bauer, T. N., & Erdogan, B. (2017). Your new hires won't succeed unless you onboard them properly. *Harvard Business Review.* https://hbr.org/2017/06/your-new-hires-wont-succeed-unless-you-onboard-them-properly

40. National Institutes of Health NIH Ethics Program. (2018). https://ethics.od.nih.gov/training.htm; Raicu, I. (2017, May 26). Rethinking ethics training in Silicon Valley. *The Atlantic.* https://www.theatlantic.com/technology/archive/2017/05/rethinking-ethics-training-in-silicon-valley/525456/

41. Alliger, G. M., Tannenbaum, S. I., Bennett, W., Jr., Traver, H., & Shotland, A. (1997). A meta-analysis of the relations among training criteria. *Personnel Psychology, 50,* 341–358.

42. McIntosh, C. (2017, June). Swapping training delivery for knowledge building. *TD: Talent Development,* 60–61.

43. Bushée, D. (2017, March). Analyze this. *TD: Training and Development,* 28–29; Ketter, P. (2017, April). Artificial intelligence creeps into talent development. *TD: Talent Development,* 22–25.

44. Goldstein, I. L., & Ford, J. K. (2002). *Training in organizations: Needs assessment, development, and evaluation* (4th ed.). Belmont, CA: Wadsworth Cengage Learning.

45. Russell, G. (2017, March). Program measurements get streamlined. *TD: Training and Development,* 24–27.

46. Goldstein, I. L., & Ford, J. K. (2002). *Training in organizations: Needs assessment, development, and evaluation* (4th ed.). Belmont, CA: Wadsworth Cengage Learning.

47. Association Adviser. (2015). Professional development vs. career management. http://www.associationadviser.com/index.php/professional-development-career-management/

48. Are you ready to take on a brand new challenge? https://jobs.raytheon.com/college-jobs

49. Allen, T. D., Eby, L. T., Poteet, M. L., Lentz, E., & Lima, L. (2004). Career benefits associated with mentoring for protégés: A meta-analysis. *Journal of Applied Psychology, 89,* 127–136.

50. Myers, F. R., Gerber, S., McDowell, G. L., Levinson, J. C., Perry, D. E., Molidor, J. B., & Parus, B. (2014). *Find the career you want.* New York: Wiley.

51. *Fortune.* (2017). 100 Best companies to work for, Genentech. http://fortune.com/best-companies/2015/genentech-9/; Training. (2015). 2015 best practice and outstanding training initiative award winners. https://trainingmag.com/trgmag-article/2015-best-practice-and-outstanding-training-initiative-award-winners

52. Occupational Safety and Health Administration. (2015). *Training requirements in OSHA standards.* https://www.osha.gov/Publications/osha2254.pdf

Chapter 9

1. Banks, E. (2016, January 13). Reinventing performance management at Deloitte. https://www.td.org/Publications/Blogs/Learning-Executive-Blog/2016/01/Reinventing-Performance-Management-at-Deloitte; Buckingham, M., & Goodall, A. (2015, April). Reinventing performance management. *Harvard Business Review,* 40–50; Deloitte (2016, August 1). Deloitte named a global leader in performance management consulting by ALM intelligence. https://www2.deloitte.com/global/en/pages/about-deloitte/articles/deloitte-performance-management-consulting-alm-intelligence.html; Lee, J. (2016). Traditional performance reviews get a makeover. *Benefits Canada, 40*(3), 42–43; Orlando, J. (2016, Summer). It all adds up to change at Deloitte. *People + Strategy,* 11; Orlando, J., & Bank, E. (2016, April). Case study: A new approach to performance management at Deloitte. *People + Strategy,* 42–44.

2. SHRM. (2014, October 20). HR professionals' perceptions about performance management effectiveness. https://www.shrm.org/hr-today/trends-and-forecasting/research-and-surveys/Pages/2014-performance-management.aspx#sthash.DoYdBNJT.dpuf

3. Mohan, P. (2017). Ready to scrap your annual performance reviews? Try these alternatives. *Fast Company.* https://www.fastcompany.com/40405106/ready-to-scrap-your-annual-performance-reviews-try-these-alternatives

4. Kluger, A. N., & DeNisi, A. (1996). The effects of feedback interventions on performance: A historical review, a meta-analysis, and a preliminary feedback intervention theory. *Psychological Bulletin, 119,* 254–284.

5. Skinner, B. F. (1969). *Contingencies of reinforcement: A theoretical analysis.* Century Psychology Series. Englewood Cliffs, NJ: Prentice Hall.

6. Murphy, J. P. (2016, Summer). Quality of hire: Data makes the difference. *Employment Relations Today,* 5–15.

7. Fleck, C. (2016, June). An algorithm for success. *HR Magazine,* 130–135; Roberts, G. (July, 2016). Predictive analytics is essential to your candidate pre-screening process—Here's why! *Workforce Solutions Review,* 36–37.

8. Anonymous. (2016, March). Tossing formal, annual reviews may affect workplace litigation. *HR Focus,* 4.

9. Bretz, R. D., Milkovich, G. T., & Read, W. (1992). The current state of performance appraisal research and practice: Concerns, directions, and implications. *Journal of Management, 18,* 321–352; DeNisi, A. S., & Murphy, K. R. (2017). Performance appraisal and performance management: 100 years of progress? *Journal of Applied Psychology, 102,* 421–433; Landy, F. J., & Farr, J. L. (1980). Performance rating. *Psychological Bulletin, 87,* 72–107.

10. Pyrillis, R. (2011, May 5). Is your performance review underperforming? http://www.workforce.com/2011/05/05/is-your-performance-review-underperforming/

11. Folger, R., Konovsky, M. A., & Cropanzano, R. (1992). A due process metaphor for performance appraisal. *Research in Organizational Behavior, 14,* 129–177.

12. Taylor, M. S., Tracy, K. B., Renard, M. K., Harrison, J. K., & Carroll, S. J. (1995). Due process in performance appraisal: A quasi-experiment in procedural justice. *Administrative Science Quarterly, 40,* 495–523.

13. DeNisi, A., & Smith, C. E. (2014). Performance appraisal, performance management, and firm-level performance: A review, a proposed model, and new directions for future research. *Academy of Management Annals, 8,* 127–179.

14. Behson, S. (2016, April 6). Work–life balance is easier when your manager knows how to assess performance. *Harvard Business Review,* 2–4.

15. Wilke, D. (2016, February). Beyond the annual performance review, *HR Magazine,* 7.

16. Hassell, B. (2016, April). IBM's new checkpoint reflects employee preferences. *Workforce.com,* 12.

17. Cunningham, L. (2015, July 21). In big move, Accenture will get rid of annual performance reviews and rankings. *Washington Post.* https://www.washingtonpost.com/news/on-leadership/wp/2015/07/21/in-big-move-accenture-will-get-rid-of-annual-performance-reviews-and-rankings/; Rafter,

M. V. (2017, January/February). Upon further review. http://www.workforce.com/2017/01/10/upon-further-review/

18. Heidemeier, H., & Moser, K. (2009). Self-other agreement in job performance ratings: A meta-analytic test of a process model. *Journal of Applied Psychology, 94,* 353–370.

19. Locke, E., & Latham, G. P. (1990). *A theory of goal setting & task performance.* Englewood Cliffs, NJ: Prentice Hall.

20. Ordóñez, L. D., Schweitzer, M. E., Galinsky, A. D., & Bazerman, M. H. (2009, February). Goals gone wild: The systematic side effects of overprescribing goal setting. *Academy of Management Perspectives,* 6–14.

21. Egan, M. (2016, September 9). Workers tell Wells Fargo horror stories. http://money.cnn.com/2016/09/09/investing/wells-fargo-phony-accounts-culture/index.html?iid=EL; Egan, M. (2017, January 6). Wells Fargo's notorious sales goals to get a makeover. http://money.cnn.com/2017/01/06/investing/wells-fargo-replace-sales-goals-fake-accounts/index.html

22. Griswold, A. (2017, February 27). Uber is designed so that for one employee to get ahead, another must fail. https://qz.com/918582/uber-is-designed-so-that-for-one-employee-to-succeed-another-must-fail/

23. O'Boyle, E., & Aguinis, H. (2012). The best and the rest: Revisiting the norm of normality of individual performance. *Personnel Psychology, 65,* 79–119.

24. Pulakos, E. D., Hanson, R. M., Arad, S., & Moye, N. (2015). Performance management can be fixed: An on-the-job experiential learning approach for complex behavior change. *Industrial and Organizational Psychology, 8,* 51–76.

25. Cappelli, P., & Tavis, A. (2016, October). The performance management revolution: The focus is shifting from accountability to learning. *Harvard Business Review,* 58–61.

26. Mohan, P. (2017). Ready to scrap your annual performance reviews? Try these alternatives. *Fast Company.* https://www.fastcompany.com/40405106/ready-to-scrap-your-annual-performance-reviews-try-these-alternatives

27. Goler, L., Gale, J., & Grant, A. (2016, November). Let's not kill performance evaluations yet. *Harvard Business Review,* 91–94.

28. AON Hewitt. (2016). Workforce mindset study. https://www.bookeseminars.com/sites/default/files/AB_Consumer_Workforce_Mindset_Report_2016.pdf; CEB Blogs. (2016, May 12). The real impact of removing performance ratings on employee performance. https://www.cebglobal.com/blogs/corporate-hr-removing-performance-ratings-is-unlikely-to-improve-performance/

29. Viswesvaran, C., Ones, D. S., & Schmidt, F. L. (1996). Comparative analysis of the reliability of job performance ratings. *Journal of Applied Psychology, 81,* 557–574.

30. Levy, P. E., & Williams, J. R. (2004). The social context of performance appraisal: A review and framework for the future. *Journal of Management, 30,* 881–905.

31. Mohan, P. (2017). Ready to scrap your annual performance reviews? Try these alternatives. *Fast Company.*

32. Feintzeig, R. (2017, May). The never-ending performance review; Companies are transitioning to more frequent evaluations. *Wall Street Journal.* https://www.wsj.com/articles/the-never-ending-performance-review-1494322200

33. Antonioni, D. (1994). The effects of feedback accountability on upward appraisal ratings. *Personnel Psychology, 47,* 349–356.

34. Hekman, D. R., Aquino, K., Owens, B. P., Mitchell, T. R., Schilpzand, P., & Leavitt, K. (2010). An examination of whether and how racial and gender biases influence customer satisfaction. *Academy of Management Journal, 53,* 238–264.

35. Farh, J. L., & Werbel, J. D. (1986). Effects of purpose of the appraisal and expectation of validation on

self-appraisal leniency. *Journal of Applied Psychology, 71,* 527–529; Heidemeier, H., & Moser, K. (2009). Self–other agreement in job performance ratings: A meta-analytic test of a process model. *Journal of Applied Psychology, 94,* 353–370.

36. Seifert, C. F., Yukl, G., & McDonald, R. A. (2003). Effects of multisource feedback and a feedback facilitator on the influence behavior of managers toward subordinates. *Journal of Applied Psychology, 88,* 561–569.

37. Brett, J. F., & Atwater, L. E. (2001). 360° feedback: Accuracy, reactions, and perceptions of usefulness. *Journal of Applied Psychology, 86,* 930–942.

38. Mishra, R. (2017, May 24). Modi's new acid test for bureaucrats. http://www.thehindubusinessline.com/specials/modis-new-acid-test-for-bureaucrats/article9711806.ece

39. Cho, I., & Payne, S. C. (2016). Other important questions: When, how, and why do cultural values influence performance management? *Industrial and Organizational Psychology: Perspectives on Science and Practice, 9,* 343–350; Meyer, E. (2015, October). When culture doesn't translate. *Harvard Business Review.* https://hbr.org/2015/10/when-culture-doesnt-translate

40. Papp, F. (2017, March 14). Avaloq: Employees evaluate team performance. http://www.finews.com/news/english-news/26590-avaloq-where-employees-get-to-decide-about-bonuses

41. Nyberg, A. J., Pieper, J. R., & Trevor, C. O. (2016). Pay-for-performance's effect on future employee performance: Integrating psychological and economic principles toward a contingency perspective. *Journal of Management, 42,* 1753–1783.

42. Cohen-Charash, Y., & Spector, P. E. (2001). The role of justice in organizations: A meta-analysis. *Organizational Behavior and Human Decision Processes, 86,* 278–321.

43. Goler, L., Gale, J., & Grant, A. (2016, November). Let's not kill performance evaluations yet. *Harvard Business Review,* 91–94.

44. Caprino, K. (2016, December 13). Separating performance management from compensation: New trend for thriving organizations. *Forbes.* https://www.forbes.com/sites/kathycaprino/2016/12/13/separating-performance-management-from-compensation-new-trend-for-thriving-organizations/; Papp, F. (2017, March 14). Avaloq: Employees evaluate team performance. http://www.finews.com/news/english-news/26590-avaloq-where-employees-get-to-decide-about-bonuses

45. Wayne, S. J., & Liden, R. C. (1995). Effects of impression management on performance ratings: A longitudinal study. *Academy of Management Journal, 38,* 232–260.

46. Bretz, R. D., Milkovich, G. T., & Read, W. (1992). The current state of performance appraisal research and practice: Concerns, directions, and implications. *Journal of Management, 18,* 321–352.

47. Freeman, M. (2016, July 26). Qualcomm enters $19.5 million gender bias settlement. *San Diego Union Tribune.* http://www.sandiegouniontribune.com/business/technology/sdut-qualcomm-lawsuit-gender-bias-women-stem-2016jul26-story.html; Freeman, M. (2016, July 27). Qualcomm settles gender-discrimination lawsuit. *Los Angeles Times.* http://www.latimes.com/business/la-fi-qualcomm-women-20160727-snap-story.html; Sanford Heisler Sharp LLP. Qualcomm gender discrimination class action - $19.5 million settlement. https://sanfordheisler.com/wp-content/uploads/2016/07/Endorsed-Complaint.pdf

48. Harari, M. B., Rudolph, C. W., & Laginess, A. J. (2015). Does rater personality matter? A meta-analysis of rater Big Five–performance rating relationships. *Journal of Occupational and Organizational Psychology, 88,* 387–414.

49. Robbins, R. L., & DeNisi, A. S. (1994). A closer look at interpersonal affect as a distinct influence on cognitive processing in performance appraisal. *Journal of Applied Psychology, 79,* 341–353.

50. Levy, P. E., & Williams, J. R. (2004). The social context of performance appraisal: A review and framework for the future. *Journal of Management, 30,* 881–905.

51. Murphy, K. R., & Cleveland, J. (1965). *Understanding performance appraisal: Social, organizational, and goal based perspectives.* Thousand Oaks, CA: Sage.

52. Villanova, P., Bernardin, H. J., Dahmus, S. A., & Sims, R. L. (1993). Rater leniency and performance appraisal discomfort. *Educational & Psychological Measurement, 53,* 789–799.

53. Fludd, V. (2016, March). Performance management for managers. *TD,* 12.

54. Arvey, R. D., & Murphy, K. R. (1998). Performance evaluation in work settings. *Annual Review of Psychology, 49,* 141–168; Athey, T. R., & McIntyre, R. M. (1987). Effects of rater training on rater accuracy: Levels-of-processing theory and social facilitation theory perspectives. *Journal of Applied Psychology, 72,* 567–572.

55. Harari, M. B., & Rudolph, C. W. (2017). The effect of rater accountability on performance ratings: A meta-analytic review. *Human Resource Management Review, 27,* 121–133.

56. Lebowitz, S. (2015, June 15). Here's how performance reviews work at Google. *Business Insider.* http://www.businessinsider.com/how-google-performance-reviews-work-2015-6

57. Sitrin, C. (2017, June 13). Here's what Eric Holder's law firm thinks Uber should do to fix its toxic culture. https://www.vox.com/technology/2017/6/13/15793712/uber-holder-report-sexual-harassment-travis-kalanick

58. DeNisi, A. S., & Peters, L. H. (1996). Organization of information in memory and the performance appraisal process: Evidence from the field. *Journal of Applied Psychology, 81,* 717–737.

59. Goler, L., Gale, J., & Grant, A. (2016, November). Let's not kill performance evaluations yet. *Harvard Business Review*, 91–94.

60. Pulakos, E. D., Hanson, R. M., Arad, S., & Moye, N. (2015). Performance management can be fixed: An on-the-job experiential learning approach for complex behavior change. *Industrial and Organizational Psychology, 8*, 51–76.

61. Meinecke, A. L., Klonek, F. E., & Kauffeld, S. (2017). Appraisal participation and perceived voice in annual appraisal interviews: Uncovering contextual factors. *Journal of Leadership & Organizational Studies, 24*, 230–245.

62. Porath, C. (2016). Give your team more effective positive feedback. *Harvard Business Review.* https://hbr.org/2016/10/give-your-team-more-effective-positive-feedback

63. Hoffman, L. (2017, April 21). Goldman goes beyond annual review with real-time employee feedback; changes are part of bigger shift in the way companies track and grade workers' performance. *Wall Street Journal.* https://www.wsj.com/articles/goldman-goes-beyond-annual-review-with-real-time-employee-ratings-1492786653

64. SHRM. (2017, March 6). How to establish a performance improvement plan. https://www.shrm.org/resourcesandtools/tools-and-samples/how-to-guides/pages/performanceimprovementplan.aspx

65. Anonymous. (2017, April). Performance falling short? Offer second chance with new boss before terminating. *HR Specialist: Texas Employment Law, 12*(4), 2.

Chapter 10

1. U.S. Bureau of Labor Statistics. (2016). Heavy and tractor-trailer truck drivers. https://www.bls.gov/ooh/transportation-and-material-moving/heavy-and-tractor-trailer-truck-drivers.htm; Huff, A. (2015, November 24). Data analysis proves beneficial in driver recruiting, retention. http://www.ccjdigital.com/data-analysis-proves-beneficial-in-driver-recruiting-retention/; Huff, A. (2016, December 16). Stay metrics research shows root causes of early driver turnover. http://www.ccjdigital.com/stay-metrics-research-shows-the-root-causes-of-early-driver-turnover/; Huff, A. (2017, February 22). Predicting driver turnover: The model sends a message. http://www.ccjdigital.com/predicting-driver-turnover-the-model-sends-a-message/; Jaillet, J. (2017). Advanced tools help carriers keep, reward drivers before they quit. http://www.ccjdigital.com/tech-toolbox-retaining-drivers/; Kilcarr, S. (2014, September). New solutions being aimed at driver shortage. *Fleet Owner, 109*(9).

2. Griffeth, R. W., Hom, P. W., & Gaertner, S. (2000). A meta-analysis of antecedents and correlates of employee turnover: Update, moderator tests, and research implications for the next millennium. *Journal of Management, 26*, 463–488.

3. Glebbeek, A. C., & Bax, E. H. (2004). Is high employee turnover really harmful? An empirical test using company records. *Academy of Management Journal, 47*, 277–286.

4. Maurer, R. (2017, March 21). Data will show you why your employees leave or stay. https://www.shrm.org/resourcesandtools/hr-topics/talent-acquisition/pages/data-retention-turnover-hr.aspx

5. Allen, D. G., Bryant, P. C., & Vardaman, J. M. (2010). Retaining talent: Replacing misconceptions with evidence-based strategies. *Academy of Management Perspectives, 24*, 48–64.

6. Park, T. Y., & Shaw, J. D. (2013). Turnover rates and organizational performance: A meta-analysis. *Journal of Applied Psychology, 98*, 268–309.

7. Hancock, J. I., Allen, D. G., Bosco, F. A., McDaniel, K. R., & Pierce, C. A. (2013). Meta-analytic review of employee turnover as a predictor of firm performance. *Journal of Management, 39*, 573–603.

8. Based on Glebbeek, A. C., & Bax, E. H. (2004). Is high employee turnover really harmful? An empirical test using company records. *Academy of Management Journal, 47*, 277–286.

9. Becker, S. (2017, May 11). Bad jobs? 7 jobs with the highest turnover rates. https://www.cheatsheet.com/money-career/bad-jobs-7-jobs-with-the-highest-turnover-rates.html/?a=viewall

10. Griffeth, R. W., Hom, P. W., & Gaertner, S. (2000). A meta-analysis of antecedents and correlates of employee turnover: Update, moderator tests, and research implications for the next millennium. *Journal of Management, 26*, 463–488.

11. Harter, J. K., Schmidt, F. L., & Hayes, T. L. (2002). Business-unit-level relationship between employee satisfaction, employee engagement, and business outcomes: A meta-analysis. *Journal of Applied Psychology, 87*, 268–279.

12. Mitchell, T. R., & Lee, T. W. (2001). The unfolding model of voluntary turnover and job embeddedness: Foundations for a comprehensive theory of attachment. *Research in Organizational Behavior, 23*, 189–246.

13. Anonymous. (2015, October). Talent quitting time. *Harvard Business Review*, 34; Anonymous. (September 2016). Talent: Why people quit their jobs. *Harvard Business Review*, 20–21.

14. Hom, P. W., Lee, T. W., Shaw, J. D., & Hausknecht, J. P. (2017). One hundred years of employee turnover theory and research. *Journal of Applied Psychology, 102*, 530–545.

15. Jiang, K., Liu, D., McKay, P. F., Lee, T. W., & Mitchell, T. R. (2012). When and how is job embeddedness predictive of turnover? A meta-analytic investigation. *Journal of Applied Psychology, 97*, 1077–1096.

16. Krell, E. (2012, April). 5 ways to manage high turnover. *HR Magazine*, 63–64.

17. Staley, O. (2017, February 14). Employers are creepily analyzing your emails and

Slack chats to see if you're happy. https://qz.com/910394/employers-are-using-sentiment-analysis-and-analyzing-your-emails-and-slack-chats-to-see-if-youre-happy-at-work; Waddell, K. (2017, September 29). The algorithms that tell bosses how employees are feeling. https://www.theatlantic.com/technology/archive/2016/09/the-algorithms-that-tell-bosses-how-employees-feel/502064/; Zielinski, D. (2017, May 15). Artificial intelligence and employee feedback. https://www.shrm.org/resourcesandtools/hr-topics/technology/pages/-artificial-intelligence-and-employee-feedback.aspx

18. Allen, D. G., Weeks, K. P., & Moffitt, K. R. (2005). Turnover intentions and voluntary turnover: The moderating roles of self-monitoring, locus of control, proactive personality, and risk aversion. *Journal of Applied Psychology, 90,* 980–990.

19. Stohlmeyer Russell, M., & Lepler, L. M. (2017, May 19). How we closed the gap between men's and women's retention rates. *Harvard Business Review.* https://hbr.org/2017/05/how-we-closed-the-gap-between-mens-and-womens-retention-rates

20. Anonymous. (2014, November). One engagement question a week helps company maintain culture, manage turnover. *HR Focus,* Issue 91–11, 1–2; Fox, A. (2012, July). Drive turnover down. *HR Magazine,* 23–27.

21. Krell, E. (2012, April 1). 5 ways to manage high turnover. https://www.shrm.org/hr-today/news/hr-magazine/pages/0412krell.aspx

22. Anonymous. (2008, July). How to learn more from exit interviews. *HR Focus,* 3–6; Spain, E., & Groysberg, B. (2016, April). Making exit interviews count. *Harvard Business Review,* 88–95.

23. Maurer, R. (2017, March 31). New hires skip out when the role doesn't meet expectations. https://www.shrm.org/resourcesandtools/hr-topics/talent-acquisition/pages/new-hires-retention-turnover.aspx

24. Fox, A. (2012, July). Drive turnover down. *HR Magazine,* 23–27.

25. Maurer, R. (2017, March 31). New hires skip out when the role doesn't meet expectations. https://www.shrm.org/resourcesandtools/hr-topics/talent-acquisition/pages/new-hires-retention-turnover.aspx

26. Heavey, A. L., Holwerda, J. A., & Hausknecht, J. P. (2013). Causes and consequences of collective turnover: A meta-analytic review. *Journal of Applied Psychology, 98,* 412–453.

27. Burry, M. (2017, April 23). Top 15 companies that offer tuition reimbursement programs. https://www.thebalance.com/companies-offer-tuition-reimbursement-4126637

28. Benson, G. S., Finegold, D., & Mohrman, S. A. (2004). You paid for the skills, now keep them: Tuition reimbursement and voluntary turnover. *Academy of Management Journal, 47,* 315–331.

29. Kaplan, D. A. (2013, January 17). Mars incorporated: A pretty sweet place to work. *Fortune.* http://fortune.com/2013/01/17/mars-incorporated-a-pretty-sweet-place-to-work/; Moss, D. (2016, September 20). Profiles in HR: Tracey Wood, Mars Chocolate North America. https://www.shrm.org/hr-today/news/hr-magazine/1016/pages/profiles-in-hr-tracey-wood-mars-chocolate-north-america.aspx; Zimmerman, K. (2016, August 8). Are rotational programs the key to retaining millennial employees? *Forbes.* https://www.forbes.com/sites/kaytiezimmerman/2016/08/08/can-a-millennial-quarter-life-crisis-be-cured-by-their-employer/

30. Hamori, M., Koyuncu, B., Cao, J., & Graf, T. (2015, Fall). What high-potential young managers want? *MIT Sloan Management Review,* 61–68.

31. Christian, M. S., Garza, A. S., & Slaughter, J. E. (2011). Work engagement: A quantitative review and test of its relations with task and contextual performance. *Personnel Psychology, 64,* 89–136.

32. Goler, L. (2015, December 16). What Facebook knows about engaging millennial employees. *Harvard Business Review.* https://hbr.org/2015/12/what-facebook-knows-about-engaging-millennial-employees

33. Murnieks, C. Y., Allen, S. T., & Ferrante, C. J. (2011). Combating the effects of turnover: Military lessons learned from project teams rebuilding Iraq. *Business Horizons, 54,* 481–491.

34. Hoffman, R. (2014, September 1). Four reasons to invest in a corporate alumni network. https://business.linkedin.com/talent-solutions/blog/2014/09/four-reasons-to-invest-in-a-corporate-alumni-network

35. Khan, I. (2017, March 1). 7 unicorns founded by PayPal alumni. https://dare2disrupt.com/2017/03/01/7-unicorns-founded-by-paypal-alumni/

36. Apy, F. A., & Ryckman, J. (2014). Boomerang hiring: Would you rehire a past employee? *Employment Relations Today,* 13–19.

37. Shipp, A., Furst-Holloway, S., Harris, T. B., & Rosen, B. (2014). Gone today but here tomorrow: Extending the unfolding model of turnover to consider boomerang employees. *Personnel Psychology, 67,* 421–462.

38. Fox, A. (2014, April). Keep your top talent: The return of retention. *HR Magazine,* 31–40; Hamori, M., Koyuncu, B., Cao, J., & Graf, T. (2015, Fall). What high-potential young managers want? *MIT Sloan Management Review,* 61–68; Knight, R. (2015, September 29). When the competition is trying to poach your top employee. *Harvard Business Review.* https://hbr.org/2015/09/when-the-competition-is-trying-to-poach-your-top-employee

39. Swider, B. W., Liu, J. T., Harris, T. B., & Gardner, R. G. (2017). Employees on the rebound: Extending the careers literature to include boomerang employees. *Journal of Applied Psychology, 102,* 890–909.

40. Leonard, D., Swap, W., & Barton, G. (2014, December 2). What's lost when experts retire. *Harvard Business Review*, 2–4.

41. Wang, M., & Shultz, K. S. (2010). Employee retirement: A review and recommendations for future investigation. *Journal of Management, 36*, 172–206.

42. Ostrower, J. (2017, July 31). The U.S. will face a staggering shortage of pilots. http://money.cnn.com/2017/07/27/news/companies/pilot-shortage-figures/index.html

43. Fisher, G. G., Chaffee, D. S., & Sonnega, A. (2016). Retirement timing: A review and recommendations for future research. *Work, Aging and Retirement, 2*, 230–261.

44. EEOC. (2000). EEOC compliance manual. https://www.eeoc.gov/policy/docs/benefits.html#VI.%20Early%20Retirement%20Incentives

45. Waltemath, J. (2013, May 2). Memo to management: Please don't ask them when they are going to retire. http://www.employmentlawdaily.com/index.php/2013/05/02/memo-to-management-please-dont-ask-them-when-they-are-going-to-retire/

46. Park, T. Y., & Shaw, J. D. (2013). Turnover rates and organizational performance: A meta-analysis. *Journal of Applied Psychology, 98*, 268–309.

47. Skarlicki, D. P., & Folger, R. (1997). Retaliation in the workplace: The roles of distributive, procedural, and interactional justice. *Journal of Applied Psychology, 82*, 434–443.

48. Berman-Gorvine, M. (2016, February). Having a toxic worker costs employers minimum of $12,500. *HR Focus, 2*, 10.

49. Plump, C. M. (2010). Dealing with problem employees: A legal guide for employers. *Business Horizons, 53*, 607–618.

50. Doyle, A. (2016, October 17). Exceptions to employment at will. https://www.thebalance.com/exceptions-to-employment-at-will-2060484; Holzschu, M. (2017). Just cause vs. employment-at-will.

https://www.businessknowhow.com/manage/justcausevsfreewill.htm; National Conference of State Legislatures. (2017). The at-will presumption and exceptions to the rule. http://www.ncsl.org/research/labor-and-employment/at-will-employment-overview.aspx

51. Wood, M. S., & Karau, S. J. (2009). Preserving employee dignity during the termination interview: An empirical examination. *Journal of Business Ethics, 86*, 519–534.

52. DePree, C., & Jude, R. K. (2007, August). Ten practical suggestions for terminating an employee. *The CPA Journal, 77*(8), 62–63.

53. Knight, R. (2016, February 5). The right way to fire someone. *Harvard Business Review*. https://hbr.org/2016/02/the-right-way-to-fire-someone

54. Wadors, P. (2015, October 2). Letting good people go when it's time. *Harvard Business Review*. https://hbr.org/2015/10/letting-good-people-go-when-its-time

55. Matousek, M. (2018, March 21). 2 veteran United flight attendants won $800,000 in a lawsuit after a supervisor made an absurd claim about iPads. *Business Insider*. http://www.businessinsider.com/united-flight-attendants-lawsuit-against-airline-2018-3; Nicholson, K. (2018, March 7). Two former United airlines employees awarded $800,000 in age discrimination lawsuit. https://www.denverpost.com/2018/03/06/united-airlines-age-discrimination-lawsuit/

56. Zillman, C. (2015, September 20). The 10 biggest corporate layoffs of the past two decades. *Fortune*. http://fortune.com/2015/09/20/biggest-corporate-layoffs/

57. Grunberg, L., Moore, S. Y., & Greenberg, E. (2001). Differences in psychological and physical health among layoff survivors: The effects of layoff contact. *Journal of Occupational Health Psychology, 6*, 15–25; Grunberg, L., Moore, S. Y., & Greenberg, E. S. (2006). Managers' reactions to implementing layoffs: Relationship to health problems

and withdrawal behaviors. *Human Resource Management, 45*, 159–178; McKee-Ryan, F., Song, Z., Wanberg, C. R., & Kinicki, A. J. (2005). Psychological and physical well-being during unemployment: A meta-analytic study. *Journal of Applied Psychology, 90*, 53–76.

58. Datta, D. K., Guthrie, J. P., Basuil, D., & Pandey, A. (2010). Causes and effects of employee downsizing: A review and synthesis. *Journal of Management, 36*, 281–348.

59. Pugh, S. D., Skarlicki, D. P., & Passell, B. S. (2003). After the fall: Layoff victims' trust and cynicism in re-employment. *Journal of Occupational and Organizational Psychology, 76*, 201–212.

60. Davis, P. R., Trevor, C. O., & Feng, J. (2015). Creating a more quit-friendly national workforce? Individual layoff history and voluntary turnover. *Journal of Applied Psychology, 100*, 1434–1455.

61. Datta, D. K., Guthrie, J. P., Basuil, D., & Pandey, A. (2010). Causes and effects of employee downsizing: A review and synthesis. *Journal of Management, 36*, 281–348.

62. Doyle, A. (2017, July 3). Can I collect unemployment if I am fired? https://www.thebalance.com/can-i-collect-unemployment-if-i-am-fired-2064150; Grossman, R. J. (2012, February). Hidden costs of layoffs. *HR Magazine*, 24–30.

63. Sood, V. (2017, May 12). Top 7 IT firms including Infosys, Wipro to lay off at least 56,000 employees this year. http://www.livemint.com/Industry/4CXsLIIZXf8uVQLs6uFQvK/Top-7-IT-firms-including-Infosys-Wipro-to-lay-off-at-least.html

64. Ghanate, N. (2017, December 29). Hyderabad: Mass layoffs shake IT industry in 2017. *Deccan Chronicle*. https://www.deccanchronicle.com/nation/current-affairs/291217/hyderabad-mass-layoffs-shake-it-industry-in-2017.html

65. Keim, A. C., Landis, R. S., Pierce, C. A., & Earnest, D. R. (2014). Why do employees worry about their jobs? A meta-analytic review of

predictors of job insecurity. *Journal of Occupational Health Psychology, 19*, 269–290.

66. Tabuchi, H. (2013, August 16). Layoffs taboo, Japan workers are sent to the boredom room. *New York Times.* http://www.nytimes .com/2013/08/17/business/global/ layoffs-illegal-japan-workers-are-sent-to-the-boredom-room.html; Torres, I. (2013, May 30). Japanese companies using "banishment rooms" to push employees to resign. http://japandailypress .com/japanese-companies-using-banishment-rooms-to-push-employees-to-resign-3029793/

67. Dowling, D. C. (2013, June 5). What to expect when dismissing employees outside the U.S. https:// www.shrm.org/resourcesandtools/ hr-topics/global-hr/pages/ dismissing-employees-overseas.aspx

68. Keim, A. C., Landis, R. S., Pierce, C. A., & Earnest, D. R. (2014). Why do employees worry about their jobs? A meta-analytic review of predictors of job insecurity. *Journal of Occupational Health Psychology, 19*, 269–290; Sverke, M., & Hellgren, J. (2002). The nature of job insecurity: Understanding employment uncertainty on the brink of a new millennium. *Applied Psychology: An International Review, 51*, 23–42.

69. Koller, F. (2010). *Spark: How old-fashioned values drive a twenty-first century corporation.* New York: PublicAffairs.

70. Becker, S. (2017, January 8). Job search? These 5 companies have policies that prevent layoffs. https://www.cheatsheet.com/ money-career/job-search-these-companies-have-policies-that-prevent-layoffs.html/?a=viewall; Van Gorder, C. (2015, January 26). A no-layoffs policy can work, even in an unpredictable economy. *Harvard Business Review.* https:// hbr.org/2015/01/a-no-layoffs-policy-can-work-even-in-an-unpredictable-economy

71. Maingault, A. (2009, July). Layoff criteria, severance pay, student interns. *HR Magazine,* 16.

72. Partially based on information contained in Anonymous. (2009, April). Maximize productivity, minimize layoffs. *HR Focus,* 10–15; Mirza, B. (2008, December 29). Look at alternatives to layoffs. https://www.shrm.org/ resourcesandtools/hr-topics/ behavioral-competencies/ leadership-and-navigation/pages/ alternativestolayoffs.aspx

73. Kalev, A. (2016, July 26). How "neutral" layoffs disproportionately affect women and minorities. *Harvard Business Review.* https:// hbr.org/2016/07/how-neutral-layoffs-disproportionately-affect-women-and-minorities

74. Anonymous. (2009, February). Know your layoff rules and procedures. *HR Focus.* U.S. Department of Labor. Warn advisor. https://webapps.dol.gov/elaws/eta/ warn/faqs.asp

75. Anonymous. (2009, February). Know your layoff rules and procedures. *HR Focus, 86*, 2; SHRM (2012, December 27). What is the California WARN act and how does it differ from federal WARN? https://www .shrm.org/resourcesandtools/ tools-and-samples/hr-qa/pages/ californiawarnact.aspx

76. Ho, C. (2017, August 24). When a gig economy company folds, workers can be left holding the bag. *San Francisco Chronicle.* http://www .sfchronicle.com/business/article/ When-a-gig-economy-company-folds-workers-can-be-11954057.php

77. Anonymous. (2009, February). Know your layoff rules and procedures. *HR Focus, 86*, 2.

78. Vickers, M. H., & Parris, M. A. (2009). Layoffs: Australian executives speak of being disposed of. *Organizational Dynamics, 39*, 57–63.

79. Vickers, M. H., & Parris, M. A. (2009). Layoffs: Australian executives speak of being disposed of. *Organizational Dynamics, 39*, 57–63.

80. Pete, J. S. (2014, November 3). Robocall to 100 Ford workers: "You are fired." http://www.nwitimes .com/business/local/robocall-to-ford-workers-you-re-fired/ article_3b821381-0a50-5631-847d-6647a51f8d6c.html

81. Nobel, C. (2015, January 7). The quest for better layoffs. http://hbswk.hbs.edu/item/ the-quest-for-better-layoffs

82. Blau, G., Petrucci, T., & McClendon, J. (2012). Effects of layoff victims' justice reactions and emotional responses on attitudes toward their previous employer. *Career Development International, 17*, 500–517.

83. Richter, M., König, C. J., Koppermann, C., & Schilling, M. (2016). Displaying fairness while delivering bad news: Testing the effectiveness of organizational bad news training in the layoff context. *Journal of Applied Psychology, 101*, 779–792.

84. Anonymous. (2009, November). Exclusive survey results: How employers are handling severance. *HR Focus, 86*, 7–13.

85. EEOC. (2009). Understanding waivers of discrimination claims in employee severance agreements. https://www.eeoc.gov/policy/docs/ qanda_severance-agreements .html#II

86. Anonymous. (2014, February). Cutting staff? Offering outplacement services benefits everyone, survey finds. *HR Focus,* 16.

87. Martin, H. J., & Lekan, D. F. (2007). Reforming executive outplacement. *Organizational Dynamics, 37*, 35–46.

88. Trevor, C. O., & Nyberg, A. J. (2008). Keeping your headcount when all about you are losing theirs: Downsizing, voluntary turnover rates, and the moderating role of HR practices. *Academy of Management Journal, 51*, 259–276.

89. Maertz, C. P., Wiley, J. W., LeRouge, C., & Campion, M. A. (2010). Downsizing effects on survivors: Layoffs, offshoring, and outsourcing. *Industrial Relations, 49*, 275–285.

90. Wadors, P. (2015, October 2). Letting good people go when it's time. *Harvard Business Review.* https://hbr.org/2015/10/letting-good-people-go-when-its-time

Chapter 11

1. Cauterucci, C. (2017, April 5). The U.S. women's soccer team finally has a better contract, but not equal pay. http://www.slate.com/blogs/xx_factor/2017/04/05/the_u_s_women_s_soccer_team_finally_has_a_better_contract_but_not_equal.html; Das, A. (2016, April 21). Pay disparity in U.S. soccer? It's complicated. *New York Times.* https://www.nytimes.com/2016/04/22/sports/soccer/usmnt-uswnt-soccer-equal-pay.html; Das, A. (2016, March 31). Top female players accuse U.S. soccer of wage discrimination. *New York Times.* https://www.nytimes.com/2016/04/01/sports/soccer/uswnt-us-women-carli-lloyd-alex-morgan-hope-solo-complain.html; Das, A. (2017, April 5). Long days, Google docs and anonymous surveys: How the U.S. soccer team forged a deal. https://www.nytimes.com/2017/04/05/sports/soccer/uswnt-us-soccer-labor-deal-contract.html; History: U.S. Soccer Team Honors. (n.d.). https://www.ussoccer.com/about/history/awards; O'Donnell, N. (2016, November 10). Team USA members on historic fight for equal pay in women's soccer. http://www.cbsnews.com/news/60-minutes-women-soccer-team-usa-gender-discrimination-equal-pay/

2. U.S. Bureau of Labor Statistics. (2018). Employer costs for employee compensation—March 2018 (USDL-18-0944). https://www.bls.gov/news.release/pdf/ecec.pdf

3. Quest for Kudos: Korn Ferry Survey Finds Highly Skilled Professionals Are Motivated More by Recognition and Meaningful Work than by Pay. (2017, July 27). https://www.kornferry.com/press/quest-for-kudos-korn-ferry-survey-finds-highly-skilled-professionals-are-motivated-more-by-recognition-and-meaningful-work-than-by-pay/

4. Judge, T. A., Piccolo, R. F., Podsakoff, N. P., Shaw, J. C., & Rich, B. L. (2010). The relationship between pay and job satisfaction: A meta-analysis of the literature. *Journal of Vocational Behavior, 77,* 157–167.

5. Humphrey, S. E., Nahrgang, J. D., & Morgeson, F. P. (2007). Integrating motivational, social, and contextual work design features: A meta-analytic summary and theoretical extension of the work design literature. *Journal of Applied Psychology, 92,* 1332–1356; Judge, T. A., Heller, D., & Mount, M. K. (2002). Five-factor model of personality and job satisfaction: A meta-analysis. *Journal of Applied Psychology, 87,* 530–541; Kaplan, S., Bradley, J. C., Luchman, J. N., & Haynes, D. (2009). On the role of positive and negative affectivity in job performance: A meta-analytic investigation. *Journal of Applied Psychology, 94,* 162; Kinicki, A. J., McKee-Ryan, F. M., Schriesheim, C. A., & Carson, K. P. (2002). Assessing the construct validity of the job descriptive index: A review and meta-analysis. *Journal of Applied Psychology, 87,* 14–32; Kooij, D. T., Jansen, P. G., Dikkers, J. S., & De Lange, A. H. (2010). The influence of age on the associations between HR practices and both affective commitment and job satisfaction: A meta-analysis. *Journal of Organizational Behavior, 31,* 1111–1136.

6. Newman, J. M., Gerhart, B., & Milkovich, G. T. (2017). *Compensation* (12th ed.). Boston, MA: McGraw Hill.

7. D'Onfro, J. (2015, April 17). The truth about Google's famous "20% time" policy. *Business Insider.* http://www.businessinsider.com/google-20-percent-time-policy-2015-4

8. U.S. Bureau of Labor Statistics. (2018). Employer costs for employee compensation—March 2018 (USDL-18-0944). https://www.bls.gov/news.release/pdf/ecec.pdf

9. Adams, J. S. (1963). Towards an understanding of inequity. *The Journal of Abnormal and Social Psychology, 67,* 422.

10. Greenberg, J., & Cohen, R. L. (1982). The justice concept in social psychology. In J. Greenberg & R. L. Cohen (Eds.), *Equity and justice in social behavior* (pp. 1–47). Cambridge, MA: Academic Press.

11. Greenberg, J. (1990). Employee theft as a reaction to underpayment inequity: The hidden cost of pay cuts. *Journal of Applied Psychology, 75,* 561–568.

12. Carrell, M. R., & Dittrich, J. E. (1978). Equity theory: The recent literature, methodological considerations, and new directions. *Academy of Management Review, 3,* 202–210; Goodman, P. S., & Friedman, A. (1971). An examination of Adams' theory of inequity. *Administrative Science Quarterly,* 271–288; Greenberg, J. (1993). Stealing in the name of justice: Informational and interpersonal moderators of theft reactions to underpayment inequity. *Organizational Behavior and Human Decision Processes, 54,* 81–103.

13. Austin, W., & Walster, E. (1974). Reactions to confirmations and disconfirmations of expectancies of equity and inequity. *Journal of Personality and Social Psychology, 30,* 208–216; Evan, W. M., & Simmons, R. G. (1969). Organizational effects of inequitable rewards: Two experiments in status inconsistency. *Administrative Science Quarterly,* 224–237.

14. Huseman, R. C., Hatfield, J. D., & Miles, E. W. (1987). A new perspective on equity theory: The equity sensitivity construct. *Academy of Management Review, 12,* 222–234; King, W. C., Miles, E. W., & Day, D. D. (1993). A test and refinement of the equity sensitivity construct. *Journal of Organizational Behavior, 14,* 301–317.

15. Sauley, K. S., & Bedeian, A. G. (2000). Equity sensitivity: Construction of a measure and examination of its psychometric properties. *Journal of Management, 26,* 885–910.

16. Carrell, M. R., & Dittrich, J. E. (1978). Equity theory: The

recent literature, methodological considerations, and new directions. *Academy of Management Review, 3,* 202–210.

17. Schmitt, D. R., & Marwell, G. (1972). Withdrawal and reward reallocation as responses to inequity. *Journal of Experimental Social Psychology, 8,* 207–221.

18. Greenberg, J. (1987). A taxonomy of organizational justice theories. *Academy of Management Review, 12,* 9–22.

19. Robbins, J. M., Ford, M. T., & Tetrick, L. E. (2012). Perceived unfairness and employee health: A meta-analytic integration. *Journal of Applied Psychology, 97,* 235–272.

20. Homans, G. C. (1961). *Social behavior: Its elementary forms.* New York: Harcourt Brace Jovanovich.

21. Colquitt, J. A., Conlon, D. E., Wesson, M. J., Porter, C. O., & Ng, K. Y. (2001). Justice at the millennium: A meta-analytic review of 25 years of organizational justice research. *Journal of Applied Psychology, 86,* 425–445; Colquitt, J. A., Scott, B. A., Rodell, J. B., Long, D. M., Zapata, C. P., Conlon, D. E., & Wesson, M. J. (2013). Justice at the millennium, a decade later: A meta-analytic test of social exchange and affect-based perspectives. *Journal of Applied Psychology, 98,* 199–236.

22. Leventhal, G. S. (1980). What should be done with equity theory? In K. J. Gergen, M. S. Greenberg, & R. H. Wills (Eds.), *Social exchange: Advances in theory and research* (pp. 27–55). New York: Springer US.; Thibaut, J. W., & Walker, L. (1975). *Procedural justice: A psychological analysis.* Hillsdale, NJ: Lawrence Erlbaum Associates.

23. Leventhal, G. S. (1980). What should be done with equity theory? In K. J. Gergen, M. S. Greenberg, & R. H. Wills (Eds.), *Social exchange: Advances in theory and research* (pp. 27–55). New York: Springer US. Leventhal, G. S., Karuza, J., & Fry, W. R. (1980). Beyond fairness: A theory of allocation preferences. *Justice and Social Interaction, 3,* 167–218.

24. Colquitt, J. A., Conlon, D. E., Wesson, M. J., Porter, C. O., & Ng, K. Y. (2001). Justice at the millennium: A meta-analytic review of 25 years of organizational justice research. *Journal of Applied Psychology, 86,* 425–445.

25. Bies, R. J., & Moag, J. F. (1986). Interactional justice: Communication criteria for fairness. In R. J. Lewicki, B. H. Sheppard, & M. H. Bazerman (Eds.), *Research on negotiations in organizations* (vol. 1, pp. 43–55). Greenwich, CT: JAI Press.

26. Colquitt, J. A., Conlon, D. E., Wesson, M. J., Porter, C. O., & Ng, K. Y. (2001). Justice at the millennium: A meta-analytic re view of 25 years of organizational justice research. *Journal of Applied Psychology, 86,* 425–445.

27. Brockner, J., & Wiesenfeld, B. M. (1996). An integrative framework for explaining reactions to decisions: Interactive effects of outcomes and procedures. *Psychological Bulletin, 120,* 189–208; Folger, R. (1977). Distributive and procedural justice: Combined impact of voice and improvement on experienced inequity. *Journal of Personality and Social Psychology, 35,* 108–119.

28. Cohen, P. (2015, July 31). A company copes with backlash against the raise that roared. *New York Times.* https://www.nytimes.com/2015/08/02/business/a-company-copes-with-backlash-against-the-raise-that-roared.html?smid=fb-nytimes&smtyp=cur&_r=1; Cohen, P. (2015, April 13). One company's new minimum wage: $70,000 a year. *New York Times.* https://www.nytimes.com/2015/04/14/business/owner-of-gravity-payments-a-credit-card-processor-is-setting-a-new-minimum-wage-70000-a-year.html; Drew, K. (2017, June 21). Seattle company paying $70K salaries to employees expands, workers see housing boom. http://komonews.com/news/local/seattle-company-with-70k-salaries-for-employees-doubles-office-space; Kahneman, D., & Deaton, A. (2010). High income improves evaluation of life but not emotional well-being.

Proceedings of the National Academy of Sciences, 107, 16489–16493; Keegen, P. (n.d.). Here's what really happened at that company that set a $70,000 minimum wage. https://www.inc.com/magazine/201511/paul-keegan/does-more-pay-mean-more-growth.html

29. Newman, J. M., Gerhart, B., & Milkovich, G. T. (2017). *Compensation* (12th ed.). Boston, MA: McGraw Hill.

30. Heneman, R. L. (2003). Job and work evaluation: A literature review. *Public Personnel Management, 32,* 47–71.

31. Ibid.

32. Kilgour, J. G. (2008). Job evaluation revisited: The point factor method: The point factor method of job evaluation consists of a large number of discretionary decisions that result in something that appears to be entirely objective and, even, scientific. *Compensation & Benefits Review, 40,* 37–46; Performing Job Evaluations. (2016, October 27). https://www.shrm.org/resourcesandtools/tools-and-samples/toolkits/pages/performingjobevaluations.aspx

33. Job Evaluation Manager. (n.d.). http://www.haygroup.com/en/our-services/evaluate/job-evaluation-manager/#tpfCID0

34. Javier, L. (2017, September 4). San Juan Island teachers ratify contract, end 4-day strike. http://www.king5.com/news/education/san-juan-island-teachers-ratify-contract-end-4-day-strike/470850074

35. How to Perform Compensation Benchmarking & Set Salary Ranges. (n.d.). http://www.payscale.com/content/whitepaper/Perform-Compensation-Benchmarking.pdf

36. ADP. (n.d.). https://www.adp.com. Benchmark. (n.d.). http://www.payscale.com/hr/product-benchmark. Smith, A. (2016, July 1). HR's role in pay analyses. https://www.shrm.org/hr-today/news/hr-magazine/0716/pages/hrs-role-in-pay-analyses.aspx

37. Based on information contained in Licensed Practical Nurse. (n.d.). http://swz.salary.com/salarywizard/

Licensed-Practical-Nurse-Job-Description.aspx; Salary Finder: Wages for Licensed Practical and Licensed Vocational Nurses in Oregon. https://www.careeronestop.org/toolkit/wages/find-salary.aspx?keyword=Licensed%20 Practical%20and%20Licensed%20 Vocational%20Nurses&s occode=292061 &location=OREGON

38. Weber, C. L., & Rynes, S. L. (1991). Effects of compensation strategy on job pay decisions. *Academy of Management Journal, 34*, 86–109.

39. Barcellos, D. (2005). The reality and promise of market-based pay. *Employment Relations Today, 32*, 1–10.

40. Dulebohn, J. H., & Werling, S. E. (2007). Compensation research past, present, and future. *Human Resource Management Review, 17*, 191–207.

41. Abosch, K. S. (1995). The promise of broadbanding. *Compensation & Benefits Review, 27*, 54–58.

42. Bonache, J., Sanchez, J. I., & Zárraga-Oberty, C. (2009). The interaction of expatriate pay differential and expatriate inputs on host country nationals' pay unfairness. *The International Journal of Human Resource Management, 20*, 2135–2149; Mahajan, A. (2011). Host country national's reactions to expatriate pay policies: Making a case for a cultural alignment pay model. *The International Journal of Human Resource Management, 22*, 121–137; Shelton, T. (2008). Global compensation strategies: Managing and administering split pay for an expatriate workforce: Multinational companies need an effective and efficient solution to manage, track and calculate complex split-pay compensation arrangements. *Compensation & Benefits Review, 40*, 56–60; Toh, S. M., & Denisi, A. S. (2003). Host country national reactions to expatriate pay policies: A model and implications. *Academy of Management Review, 28*, 606–621.

43. U.S. Department of Labor. (n.d.). Wage and hour division: Compliance assistance–wages and the Fair Labor Standards Act (FLSA). https://www.dol.gov/whd/flsa/

44. Held, A. (2017, June 27). Labor Department rethinking Obama-era overtime pay rule. *NPR.* http://www.npr.org/sections/thetwo-way/2017/06/27/534597018/labor-department-rethinking-obama-era-overtime-pay-rule; U. S. Department of Labor. (n.d.). Wage and hour division: Final rule: Overtime. https://www.dol.gov/whd/overtime/final2016/

45. U.S. Department of Labor. (2018). Wage and hour division: Fact Sheet #17A: Exemption for executive, administrative, professional, computer & outside sales employees under the Fair Labor Standards Act (FLSA). https://www.dol.gov/whd/overtime/fs17a_overview.pdf

46. U.S. Department of Labor. (n.d.). Wage and hour division: Overtime pay. https://www.dol.gov/whd/overtime_pay.htm

47. Schwartz, S. C. (n.d.). Employment rules & regulations in the Trump administration. https://www.lexisnexis.com/communities/corporatecounselnewsletter/b/newsletter/archive/2017/05/18/employment-rules-amp-regulations-in-the-trump-administration.aspx

48. U.S. Department of Labor. (n.d.). Wage and hour division: Minimum wage. https://www.dol.gov/whd/minimumwage.htm

49. U.S. Department of Labor. (n.d.). Wage and hour division: Consolidated minimum wage table. https://www.dol.gov/whd/minwage/mw-consolidated.htm

50. U.S. Department of Labor. (2008). Wage and hour division: Fact Sheet #22: Hours worked under the Fair Labor Standards Act (FLSA). https://www.dol.gov/whd/regs/compliance/whdfs22.pdf

51. U.S. Department of Labor. (2008). Wage and hour division: Fact Sheet #21: Recordkeeping requirements under the Fair Labor Standards Act (FLSA). https://www.dol.gov/whd/regs/compliance/whdfs21.pdf

52. U.S. Department of Labor. (n.d.). Office of Federal Contract Compliance Programs (OFCCP): Executive Order 1124–Equal Employment Opportunity. https://www.dol.gov/ofccp/regs/compliance/ca_11246.htm; U.S. Equal Employment Opportunity Commission. (1965, September 28). Executive Order No. 11246. https://www.eeoc.gov/eeoc/history/35th/thelaw/eo-11246.html

53. U.S. Department of Labor. (n.d.). Office of Federal Contract Compliance Programs (OFCCP): Executive Order 11246: Pay transparency regulations. https://www.dol.gov/ofccp/PayTransparency.html

54. U.S. National Labor Relations Board. (n.d.). Employee rights. https://www.nlrb.gov/rights-we-protect/employee-rights; U.S. National Labor Relations Board. (n.d.). National Labor Relations Act. https://www.nlrb.gov/resources/national-labor-relations-act

55. U.S. Government Publishing Office. (1954, August 16). Title 26–Internal Revenue Code. https://www.gpo.gov/fdsys/pkg/USCODE-2011-title26/pdf/USCODE-2011-title26.pdf

56. U.S. Equal Employment Opportunity Commission. (2014, April 2). Checkers franchise will pay $100,000 to settle EEOC pay discrimination lawsuit. https://www.eeoc.gov/eeoc/newsroom/release/4-2-14.cfm; U.S. Equal Employment Opportunity Commission. (2013, August 12). EEOC sues Checkers for pay discrimination. https://www.eeoc.gov/eeoc/newsroom/release/8-12-13.cfm; Moran, G. (2016, April 12). Here's what it takes to sue for gender pay discrimination—and win. *Fortune.* http://fortune.com/2016/04/12/how-to-sue-for-gender-pay-discrimination/

57. Gupta, N., & Shaw, J. D. (2001). Successful skill-based pay plans. In C. H. Fay, M. A. Thompson, & D. Knight (Eds.), *The executive handbook of compensation.* New York: Free Press; Lawler,

E. E. (1994). From job-based to competency-based organizations. *Journal of Organizational Behavior, 15*, 3–15.

58. Dierdorff, E. C., & Surface, E. A. (2008). If you pay for skills, will they learn? Skill change and maintenance under a skill-based pay system. *Journal of Management, 34*, 721–743; Mitra, A., Gupta, N., & Shaw, J. D. (2011). A comparative examination of traditional and skill-based pay plans. *Journal of Managerial Psychology, 26*, 278–296; Murray, B., & Gerhart, B. (1998). An empirical analysis of a skill-based pay program and plant performance outcomes. *Academy of Management Journal, 41*, 68–78.

59. Connelly, B. L., Haynes, K. T., Tihanyi, L., Gamache, D. L., & Devers, C. E. (2016). Minding the gap: Antecedents and consequences of top management-to-worker pay dispersion. *Journal of Management, 42*, 862–885; Jaskiewicz, P., Block, J. H., Miller, D., & Combs, J. G. (2017). Founder versus family owners' impact on pay dispersion among non-CEO top managers: Implications for firm performance. *Journal of Management, 43*, 1524–1552.

60. Mishel, L., & Sabadish, N. (2012). CEO pay and the top 1%: How executive compensation and financial-sector pay have fueled income inequality. *Economic Policy Institute, 331*, 1–7.

61. Kiatpongsan, S., & Norton, M. I. (2014). How much (more) should CEOs make? A universal desire for more equal pay. *Perspectives on Psychological Science, 9*, 587–593.

62. Tosi, H. L., Werner, S., Katz, J. P., & Gomez-Mejia, L. R. (2000). How much does performance matter? A meta-analysis of CEO pay studies. *Journal of Management, 26*, 301–339; Van Essen, M., Otten, J., & Carberry, E. J. (2015). Assessing managerial power theory: A meta-analytic approach to understanding the determinants of CEO compensation. *Journal of Management, 41*, 164–202.

63. Clifford, S. (2017, June 14). How companies actually decide what to pay CEOs. https://www.theatlantic.com/business/archive/2017/06/how-companies-decide-ceo-pay/530127/

64. Davis, A., & Mishel, L. (2014). CEO pay continues to rise as typical workers are paid less. *Economic Policy Institute, 380*, 1–12.

65. Morgenson, G. (2016, December 7). Portland adopts surcharge on C.E.O. pay in move vs. income inequality. *New York Times.* https://www.nytimes.com/2016/12/07/business/economy/portland-oregon-tax-executive-pay.html

66. Melin, A. (2017, May 10). Dealmaker Weinberg cracks ranks of best paid executives for 2016. https://www.bloomberg.com/graphics/2017-highest-paid-ceos/

67. Newman, J. M., Gerhart, B., & Milkovich, G. T. (2017). *Compensation* (12th ed.). Boston, MA: McGraw-Hill.

68. Ibid.

69. Marasi, S., & Bennett, R. J. (2016). Pay communication: Where do we go from here? *Human Resource Management Review, 26*, 50–58.

70. U.S. Bureau of Labor Statistics. (2017, August). Highlights of women's earnings in 2016 (Report 1069). https://www.bls.gov/opub/reports/womens-earnings/2016/home.htm; U.S. Bureau of Labor Statistics. (2018, July 18). Usual weekly earnings of wage and salary workers: Second quarter 2018 (Report USDL-18-1180). https://www.bls.gov/news.release/pdf/wkyeng.pdf

71. U.S. Bureau of Labor Statistics. (2018, July 18). Usual weekly earnings of wage and salary workers: Second quarter 2018 (Report USDL-18-1180). https://www.bls.gov/news.release/pdf/wkyeng.pdf

72. Card, D., Mas, A., Moretti, E., & Saez, E. (2012). Inequality at work: The effect of peer salaries on job satisfaction. *American Economic Review, 102*, 2981–3003; Obloj, T., & Zenger, T. (2015). Incentives, social comparison costs, and the proximity of envy's object. HEC Paris Research Paper No. SPE-2015-1085; Zenger, T.

(2016, September 30). The case against pay transparency. *Harvard Business Review.* https://hbr.org/2016/09/the-case-against-pay-transparency

73. Burns, J. (2017, April 8). Women at Google face "extreme, systemic" wage gap, according to Labor Dept. suit. *Forbes.* https://www.forbes.com/sites/janetwburns/2017/04/08/u-s-labor-dept-women-at-google-face-extreme-systemic-wage-gap/#73526033b5c5; Buxton, M. (2017, September 8). A Google employee spreadsheet shows pay disparities between men and women. https://finance.yahoo.com/news/google-employee-spreadsheet-shows-pay-223500784.html; Fung, B. (2017, July 16). The probe into Google's alleged gender pay gap just hit a snag. *Washington Post.* https://www.washingtonpost.com/news/the-switch/wp/2017/07/16/the-labor-department-just-lost-a-battle-with-google-over-its-alleged-gender-pay-gap/?tid=a_inl&utm_term=.f96e4d5c67f5; McHugh, M. (2015, July 20). What happens when you talk about salaries at Google. https://www.wired.com/2015/07/happens-talk-salaries-google/; Zenger, T. (2016, September 30). The case against pay transparency. *Harvard Business Review.* https://hbr.org/2016/09/the-case-against-pay-transparency

74. U.S. National Labor Relations Board. (n.d.). Employee rights. https://www.nlrb.gov/rights-we-protect/employee-rights; U.S. National Labor Relations Board. (n.d.). The NLRB and social media. https://www.nlrb.gov/news-outreach/fact-sheets/nlrb-and-social-media

75. Griswold, A. (2014, March 3). Here's why Whole Foods lets employees look up each other's salaries. *Business Insider.* http://www.businessinsider.com/whole-foods-employees-have-open-salaries-2014-3

76. Lam, B. (2015, November 10). One tech company just erased its gender pay gap; https://www.theatlantic

.com/business/archive/2015/11/salesforce-equal-pay-gender-gap/415050/; Robbins, C. (2016, March 8). Equality at Salesforce: The equal pay assessment update. https://www.salesforce.com/blog/2016/03/equality-at-salesforce-equal-pay.html

77. Bamberger, P., & Belogolovsky, E. (2010). The impact of pay secrecy on individual task performance. *Personnel Psychology, 63*, 965–996; Belogolovsky, E., & Bamberger, P. A. (2014). Signaling in secret: Pay for performance and the incentive and sorting effects of pay secrecy. *Academy of Management Journal, 57*, 1706–1733; Futrell, C. M., & Jenkins, O. C. (1978). Pay secrecy versus pay disclosure for salesmen: A longitudinal study. *Journal of Marketing Research*, 214–219.

78. Kilgour, J. G. (2008). Job evaluation revisited: The point factor method of job evaluation consists of a large number of discretionary decisions that result in something that appears to be entirely objective and, even, scientific. *Compensation & Benefits Review, 40*, 37–46; Newman, J. M., Gerhart, B., & Milkovich, G. T. (2017). *Compensation* (12th ed.). Boston, MA: McGraw-Hill.

Chapter 12

1. Krize, N. (2017, March 1). Geisinger Health System hiring 2,000 people. http://wnep.com/2017/03/01/geisinger-health-system-hiring-2000-people/; Lee, T. H., & Cosgrove, T. (2014). Engaging doctors in the health care revolution. *Harvard Business Review*. https://hbr.org/2014/06/engaging-doctors-in-the-health-care-revolution; McCarthy, D., Mueller, K., & Wrenn, J. (2009). Geisinger Health System: Achieving the potential of system integration through innovation, leadership, measurement, and incentives. *The Commonwealth Fund, 9*, 1–16. http://www.commonwealthfund.org/~/media/Files/Publications/Case%20Study/2009/Jun/McCarthy_Geisinger_case_

study_624_update.pdf; Steele, G. D. (2015). A proven new model for reimbursing physicians. *Harvard Business Review*. https://hbr.org/2015/09/a-proven-new-model-for-reimbursing-physicians

2. Aguinis, H. (2012). *Performance management* (3rd ed.). Upper Saddle River, NJ: Pearson.

3. Carrell, M. R., & Dittrich, J. E. (1976). Employee perceptions of fair treatment. *Personnel Journal, 55*, 523–524.

4. Amabile, T. M. (1993). Motivational synergy: Toward new conceptualizations of intrinsic and extrinsic motivation in the workplace. *Human Resource Management Review, 3*, 185–201; Herzberg, F. (1966). *Work and the nature of man.* Cleveland, OH: World.

5. Amabile, T. M. (1993). Motivational synergy: Toward new conceptualizations of intrinsic and extrinsic motivation in the workplace. *Human Resource Management Review, 3*, 185–201; Deci, E. L., & Ryan, R. M. (2000). The "what" and "why" of goal pursuits: Human needs and the self-determination behavior. *Psychological Inquiry, 11*, 227–268.

6. Cerasoli, C. P., Nicklin, J. M., & Ford, M. T. (2014). Intrinsic motivation and extrinsic incentives jointly predict performance: A 40-year meta-analysis. *Psychological Bulletin, 140*, 980–1008.

7. Skinner, B. F. (1953). *Science and human behavior.* New York, NY: Macmillan; Steers, R. M., Mowday, R. T., & Shapiro, D. L. (2004). Introduction to special topic forum: The future of work motivation theory. *Academy of Management Review, 29*, 379–387; Thorndike, E. L. (1911). *Animal intelligence.* New York: Macmillan.

8. Liedtke, M. (2017). Yahoo withholds CEO Marissa Mayer's bonus as punishment for security breach response. *Chicago Tribune*. http://www.chicagotribune.com/bluesky/technology/ct-yahoo-marissa-mayer-bonus-20170301-story.html

9. La Monica, P. R. (2017). Marissa Mayer leaves Yahoo with nearly

$260 million. *CNN Money*. http://money.cnn.com/2017/06/13/investing/yahoo-marissa-mayer-severance-stock-verizon/index.html

10. Porter, L. W., & Lawler, E. E. (1968). *Managerial attitudes and performance.* Homewood, IL: Irwin; Vroom, V. H. (1964). *Work and motivation.* New York: Wiley.

11. Wright, P. M. (1989). Test of the mediating role of goals in the incentive–performance relationship. *Journal of Applied Psychology, 74*, 699–705; Wright, P. M. (1992). An examination of the relationships among monetary incentives, goal level, goal commitment, and performance. *Journal of Management, 18*, 677–693.

12. Locke, E. A., & Latham, G. P. (1984). *Goal setting: A motivational technique that works!* Upper Saddle River, NJ: Prentice Hall.

13. Locke, E. A., Latham, G. P. (2006). New directions in goal-setting theory. *Current Directions in Psychological Science, 15*, 265–268.

14. Seijts, G. H., Latham, G. P., & Whyte, G. (2000). Effect of self- and group efficacy on group performance in a mixed-motive situation. *Human Performance, 13*, 279–298.

15. PayScale. (2017). Comp is culture: 2017 compensation best practices report. https://www.payscale.com/compensation-today/2017/02/payscales-2017-compensation-best-practices-report

16. WorldatWork. (2016). Compensation programs and practices survey. https://www.worldatwork.org/adimLink?id=80656

17. Ibid.

18. March, J. G., & Simon, H. A. (1958). *Organizations.* Oxford, UK: Wiley.

19. Cable, D. M., & Judge, T. A. (1994). Pay preferences and job search decisions: A person–organization fit perspective. *Personnel Psychology, 47*, 317–348; Le Blanc, P. V., & Mulvey, P. W. (1998). Research study: How American workers see the rewards of work. *Compensation & Benefits Review, 30*, 24–28.

20. WorldatWork. (2016). Compensation programs and practices survey. https://www.worldatwork.org/adimLink?id=80656

21. Heneman R. L. (1992). *Merit pay: Linking pay increases to performance ratings.* New York: Addison-Wesley.

22. Hay Group. (1994). *The Hay Report: Compensation and benefit strategies for 1995 and beyond.* Philadelphia, PA: Hay Group.

23. Longenecker, C. O., Sims, H. P., Jr., & Gioia, D. A. (1987). Behind the mask: The politics of employee appraisal. *The Academy of Management Executive.* 183–193.

24. PayScale. (2017). Comp is culture: 2017 compensation best practices report. https://www.payscale.com/compensation-today/2017/02/payscales-2017-compensation-best-practices-report

25. WorldatWork. (2016). Compensation programs and practices survey. https://www.worldatwork.org/adimLink?id=80656

26. Newman, J. M., Gerhart, B., & Milkovich, G. T. (2017). *Compensation* (12th ed.). New York: McGraw-Hill.

27. WorldatWork. (2016). Compensation programs and practices survey. https://www.worldatwork.org/adimLink?id=80656

28. Berkeley Human Resources. (n.d.). Spot awards. https://hr.berkeley.edu/compensation-benefits/compensation/recognition/spot-awards

29. Saunders, N. (2016). Motivate and retain top talent with spot awards. https://blogs.sap.com/2016/05/23/motivate-and-retain-top-talent-with-spot-awards/

30. WorldatWork. (2016). Compensation programs and practices survey. https://www.worldatwork.org/adimLink?id=80656

31. Rynes, S. L., Gerhart, B., & Parks, L. (2005). Personnel psychology: Performance evaluation and pay for performance. *Annual Review of Psychology, 56,* 571–600.

32. Finkelstein, E. A., DiBonaventura, M. D., Burgess, S. M., & Hale, B. C. (2010). The costs of obesity in the workplace. *Journal of Occupational and Environmental Medicine, 52,* 971–976; Kullgren, J. T., Troxel, A. B., Loewenstein, G., Asch, D. A., Norton, L. A., Wesby, L., . . . & Volpp, K. G. (2013). Individual-versus group-based financial incentives for weight loss: A randomized, controlled trial. *Annals of Internal Medicine, 158,* 505–514; Ng, J. Y., Ntoumanis, N., Thøgersen-Ntoumani, C., Deci, E. L., Ryan, R. M., Duda, J. L., & Williams, G. C. (2012). Self-determination theory applied to health contexts: A meta-analysis. *Perspectives on Psychological Science, 7,* 325–340; Patel, M. S., Asch, D. A., Rosin, R., Small, D. S., Bellamy, S. L., Heuer, J., . . . & Wesby, L. (2016). Framing financial incentives to increase physical activity among overweight and obese adults: A randomized, controlled trial. *Annals of Internal Medicine, 164,* 385–394; Patel, M. S., Asch, D. A., Troxel, A. B., Fletcher, M., Osman-Koss, R., Brady, J., . . . & Volpp, K. G. (2016). Premium-based financial incentives did not promote workplace weight loss in a 2013–15 study. *Health Affairs, 35,* 71–79; Patel, M. S., Asch, D. A., & Volpp, K. G. (2016). Paying employees to lose weight. *New York Times.* https://www.nytimes.com/2016/03/06/opinion/sunday/paying-employees-to-lose-weight.html?mcubz=0&_r=1; Volpp, K. G., Troxel, A. B., Pauly, M. V., Glick, H. A., Puig, A., Asch, D. A., . . . & Corbett, E. (2009). A randomized, controlled trial of financial incentives for smoking cessation. *New England Journal of Medicine, 360,* 699–709.

33. Carey, K. (2017). The little-known statistician who taught us to measure teachers. *New York Times.* https://www.nytimes.com/2017/05/19/upshot/the-little-known-statistician-who-transformed-education.html?_r=0; Chetty, R., Friedman, J. N., & Rockoff, J. E. (2014). Measuring the impacts of teachers II: Teacher value-added and student outcomes in adulthood. *The American Economic Review, 104,* 2633–2679; Dee, T. S., & Keys, B. J. (2004). Does merit pay reward good teachers? Evidence from a randomized experiment. *Journal of Policy Analysis and Management, 23,* 471–488; Hanushek, E. A. (2011). The economic value of higher teacher quality. *Economics of Education Review, 30,* 466–479; Johnson, S. M. (2012). Having it both ways: Building the capacity of individual teachers and their schools. *Harvard Educational Review, 82,* 107–122; Murnane, R., & Cohen, D. (1986). Merit pay and the evaluation problem: Why most merit pay plans fail and a few survive. *Harvard Educational Review, 56,* 1–18; Woessmann, L. (2011). Cross-country evidence on teacher performance pay. *Economics of Education Review, 30,* 404–418; Yuan, K., Le, V. N., McCaffrey, D. F., Marsh, J. A., Hamilton, L. S., Stecher, B. M., & Springer, M. G. (2013). Incentive pay programs do not affect teacher motivation or reported practices: Results from three randomized studies. *Educational Evaluation and Policy Analysis, 35,* 3–22.

34. O'Connell, B. (1996). Dead solid perfect: Achieving sales compensation alignment. *Compensation & Benefits Review, 28*(2), 41–48.

35. Misra, S., & Nair, H. S. (2011). A structural model of sales-force compensation dynamics: Estimation and field implementation. *Quantitative Marketing and Economics, 9,* 211–257.

36. Deming, W. E. (1986). *Out of the crisis.* Cambridge, MA: MIT Center for Advanced Engineering Study; Pfeffer J. (1998). *The human equation.* Boston, MA: Harvard Business School Press.

37. Rynes, S. L., Gerhart, B., & Parks, L. (2005). Personnel psychology: Performance evaluation and pay

for performance. *Annual Review of Psychology, 56,* 571–600.

38. Kaufman, R. T. (1992). The effects of Improshare on productivity. *Industrial Labor Relations Review, 45,* 311–322.

39. Devine, D. J., Clayton, L. D., Philips, J. L., Dunford, B. B., & Melner, S. B. (1999). Teams in organizations: Prevalence, characteristics, and effectiveness. *Small Group Research, 30,* 678–711; Ilgen, D. R., Hollenbeck, J. R., Johnson, M., & Jundt, D. (2005). Teams in organizations: From input-process-output models to IMOI models. *Annual Review of Psychology, 56,* 517–543; Johnson, S. T. (1993). Work teams: What's ahead in work design and rewards management. *Compensation and Benefits Review, 25,* 35–41; Martin, A., & Bal, V. (2006). *The state of teams.* Greensboro, NC: Center for Creative Leadership.

40. Garbers, Y., & Konradt, U. (2014). The effect of financial incentives on performance: A quantitative review of individual and team-based financial incentives. *Journal of Occupational and Organizational Psychology, 87,* 102–137.

41. Vingan, A. (2017). How much did Predators players make during playoffs? http://www.tennessean.com/story/sports/nhl/predators/2017/07/17/predators-players-salaries-during-stanley-cup-nhl-playoffs/478023001/

42. Beersma, B., Hollenbeck, J. R., Humphrey, S. E., Moon, H., Conlon, D. E., & Ilgen, D. R. (2003). Cooperation, competition, and team performance: Toward a contingency approach. *Academy of Management Journal, 46,* 572–590; Johnson, M. D., Hollenbeck, J. R., Humphrey, S. E., Ilgen, D. R., Jundt, D., & Meyer, C. J. (2006). Cutthroat cooperation: Asymmetrical adaptation to changes in team reward structures. *Academy of Management Journal, 49,* 103–119.

43. Hafner, K. (2005, February 1). New incentives for Google employees: Awards worth millions. *New York Times.* http://www.nytimes.com/2005/02/01/technology/new-incentive-for-google-employees-awards-worth-millions.html

44. WorldatWork. (2016). Compensation programs and practices survey. https://www.worldatwork.org/adimLink?id=80656

45. Gardner, A. C. (2011). Goal setting and gainsharing: The evidence on effectiveness. *Compensation & Benefits Review, 43,* 236–244.

46. Welbourne, T. M., & Gomez-Mejia, L. (1995). Gainsharing: A critical review and a future research agenda. *Journal of Management, 21,* 559–609.

47. Leitman, I. M., Levin, R., Lipp, M. J., Sivaprasad, L., Karalakulasingam, C. J., Bernard, D. S., . . . & Shulkin, D. J. (2010). Quality and financial outcomes from gainsharing for inpatient admissions: A three-year experience. *Journal of Hospital Medicine, 5,* 501–507.

48. Rynes, S. L., Gerhart, B., & Parks, L. (2005). Personnel psychology: Performance evaluation and pay for performance. *Annual Review of Psychology, 56,* 571–600.

49. Moyer, J. W. (2016). Whole Foods accused of cheating workers out of bonuses in class-action lawsuit. *Washington Post.* https://www.washingtonpost.com/local/public-safety/whole-foods-accused-of-cheating-workers-out-of-bonuses-in-class-action-lawsuit/2016/12/21/104dfd7c-c705-11e6-bf4b-2c064d32a4bf_story.html?utm_term=.b6938691b6de

50. WorldatWork. (2016). Compensation programs and practices survey. https://www.worldatwork.org/adimLink?id=80656

51. Designing and managing incentive compensation programs. (2018, January 12). https://www.shrm.org/resourcesandtools/tools-and-samples/toolkits/pages/designingincentivecompensation.aspx

52. Doucouliagos, C. (1995). Worker participation and productivity in labor-managed and participatory capitalist firms: A meta-analysis. *Industrial Labor Relations Review, 49,* 58–77; Weitzman, M. L., & Kruse, D. L. (1990). Profit sharing and productivity. In A. S. Blinder (Ed.), *Paying for productivity* (pp. 95–140). Washington, DC: Brookings Institute.

53. Han, J. H., Bartol, K. M., & Kim, S. (2015). Tightening up the performance–pay linkage: Roles of contingent reward leadership and profit-sharing in the cross-level influence of individual pay-for-performance. *Journal of Applied Psychology, 100,* 417–430.

54. Farber, M. (2017). Delta Air Lines employees just got $1.1 billion in profit sharing. *Fortune.* http://fortune.com/2017/02/16/delta-airlines-profit-sharing-billion/

55. Fong, S., & Shaffer, M. (2003). The dimensionality and determinants of pay satisfaction: A cross-cultural investigation of a group incentive plan. *International Journal of Human Resource Management, 14,* 559–580; Hofstede, G. (1991). *Culture and organisations: Software of the mind.* London: McGraw-Hill; Ramamoorthy, N., & Carroll, S. J. (1998). Individualism/collectivism orientations and reactions toward alternative human resource management practices. *Human Relations, 51,* 571–588.

56. Gerhart, B., & Milkovich, G. T. (1990). Organizational differences in managerial compensation and financial performance. *Academy of Management Journal, 33,* 663–691.

57. Ozanian, M. (2017). Shares of Adidas hammered by college bribery scandal. *Forbes.* https://www.forbes.com/sites/mikeozanian/2017/09/26/shares-of-adidas-hammered-by-college-bribery-scandal/#1f55b24a3ecb

58. Blasi, J., Conte, M., & Kruse, D. (1996). Employee stock ownership and corporate performance among public companies. *ILR Review, 50,* 60–79.

59. French, J. L. (1987). Employee perspectives on stock ownership:

Financial investment or mechanism of control. *Academy of Management Review, 12,* 427–435.

60. Bob's Red Mill. (n.d.). Proudly employee-owned. https://www.bobsredmill.com/bobs-way-meet#ESOP

61. Viswesvaran, C., Ones, D. S., & Schmidt, F. L. (1996). Comparative analysis of the reliability of job performance ratings. *Journal of Applied Psychology, 81,* 557–574.

62. Domonoske, C. (2017). Secret Service, agents settle over racial discrimination allegations. *NPR.* https://www.npr.org/sections/thetwo-way/2017/01/18/510396659/secret-service-agents-settle-over-racial-discrimination-allegations; Hassan, A. (2017). A Secret Service agent's path from recruitment to bias lawsuit. *New York Times.* https://www.nytimes.com/2017/02/25/us/secret-service-bias-lawsuit-ray-moore.html?_r=0; Secret Service penalized in discrimination case. (2008). *NBC News.* http://www.nbcnews.com/id/28303789/ns/us_news-crime_and_courts/t/secret-service-penalized-discrimination-case/#.WgspAFtSzIV; U.S. Department of Homeland Security. (2017, January 17). Statement by Secretary of Homeland Security Jeh C. Johnson on U.S. Secret Service resolution. https://www.dhs.gov/news/2017/01/17/statement-secretary-homeland-security-jeh-c-johnson-us-secret-service-resolution; U.S. Secret Service inspector destroyed documents. (2008, February 21). https://www.rcfp.org/browse-media-law-resources/news/us-secret-service-inspector-destroyed-documents

63. Longenecker, C. O., Sims, H. P., Jr., & Gioia, D. A. (1987). Behind the mask: The politics of employee appraisal. *The Academy of Management Executive,* 183–193; Masunaga, S., & Lien, T. (2016). Yahoo ex-employee sues, alleging manipulation of performance reviews and gender bias. *Los Angeles*

Times. http://www.latimes.com/business/technology/la-fi-tn-yahoo-lawsuit-20160202-story.html

64. Gerhart, B., & Rynes, S. L. (2003). *Compensation: Theory, evidence, and strategic implications.* Thousand Oaks, CA: Sage; Lazear, E. P. (1986). Salaries and piece rates. *Journal of Business, 59,* 405–431.

65. Bretz, R. D., Ash, R. A., & Dreher, G. F. (1989). Do people make the place? An examination of the attraction-selection-attrition hypothesis. *Personnel Psychology, 42,* 561–581; Cable, D. M., & Judge, T. A. (1994). Pay preferences and job search decisions: A person–organization fit perspective. *Personnel Psychology, 47,* 317–348; Cadsby, C. B., Song, F., & Tapon, F. (2007). Sorting and incentive effects of pay for performance: An experimental investigation. *Academy of Management Journal, 50,* 387–405.

66. Schneider, B. (1987). The people make the place. *Personnel Psychology, 40,* 437–453.

67. Uggerslev, K. L., Fassina, N. E., & Kraichy, D. (2012). Recruiting through the stages: A meta-analytic test of predictors of applicant attraction at different stages of the recruiting process. *Personnel Psychology, 65,* 597–660.

68. Blinder, A. (1990). *Paying for productivity.* Washington, DC: Brookings Institution.

69. Wang, T., Thornhill, S., & Zhao, B. (2016). Pay-for-performance, employee participation, and SME performance. *Journal of Small Business Management, 56,* 412–434.

70. George, J. M., & Jones, G. R. (1997). Organizational spontaneity in context. *Human Performance, 10,* 153–170; Wright, P. M., George, J. M., Farnsworth, S. R., & McMahan, G. C. (1993). Productivity and extra-role behavior: The effects of goals and incentives on spontaneous helping. *Journal of Applied Psychology, 78,* 374–381.

71. Deckop, J. R., Mangel, R., & Cirka, C. C. (1999). Getting more than you pay for: Organizational citizenship

behavior and pay-for-performance plans. *Academy of Management Journal, 42,* 420–428.

72. Hegarty, W. H., & Sims, H. P. (1978). Some determinants of unethical decision behavior: An experiment. *Journal of Applied Psychology, 63,* 451.

73. Barro, J. (2016). Wells Fargo's scandal is a cautionary tale about incentive pay. *Business Insider.* http://www.businessinsider.com/wells-fargos-scandal-is-a-cautionary-tale-about-incentive-pay-2016-9

74. Bomey, N., & McCoy, K. (2017). Wells Fargo clawing back $75.3 million more from former execs in fake accounts scandal. *USA Today.* https://www.usatoday.com/story/money/2017/04/10/wells-fargo-compensation-clawback/100276472/

75. DeMatteo, J. S., Eby, L. T., & Sundstrom, E. (1998). Team-based rewards: Current empirical evidence. *Research in Organizational Behavior, 20,* 141–183.

76. Nalbantian, H. R., & Schotter, A. (1997). Productivity under group incentives: An experimental study. *The American Economic Review,* 314–341.

77. Lawler, E. E., & Cohen, S. G. (1992). Designing pay systems for teams. *ACA Journal, 1,* 6–19; Mohrman, A. M., Mohrman, S. A., & Lawler, E. E. (1992). The performance management of teams. In W. J. Bruns Jr. (Ed.), *Performance measurement, evaluation, and incentives* (pp. 217–241). Boston, MA: Harvard Business School Press; Wageman, R. (1996). Interdependence and group effectiveness. *Administrative Science Quarterly, 40,* 145–180; Wageman, R., & Baker, G. (1997). Incentives and cooperation: The joint effects of task and reward interdependence on group performance. *Journal of Organizational Behavior, 18,* 139–158.

78. Latané, B., Williams, K., & Harkins, S. (1979). Many hands make light the work: The causes and consequences of social loafing.

Journal of Personality and Social Psychology, 37, 822–832.

79. Milkovich, G. T., & Wigdor, A. K. (1991). *Pay for performance: Evaluating performance appraisal and merit pay.* Washington, DC: National Academies Press.

Chapter 13

1. Care.com introduces groundbreaking peer-to-peer benefits platform for caregivers. (2018). https://www.care.com/press-release-carecom-introduces-caregiver-benefits-platform-p1186-q81381650.html; Company overview. (2018). https://www.care.com/company-overview; Katz, L. F., & Krueger, A. B. (2016). The rise and nature of alternative work arrangements in the United States, 1995–2015. Working paper. https://benefittrends.metlife.com/us-perspectives/work-redefined-a-new-age-of-benefits/; Scheiber, N. (2016, September 14).Care.com creates a $500 limited for benefit gig-economy workers. *New York Times.* https://nyti.ms/2cM6luB; Semuels, A. (2017, November 6). Could a tax fix the gig economy? *The Atlantic.* https://www.theatlantic.com/business/archive/2017/11/gig-economy/544895/; Stonier, M. (2017, October 13). This state wants to offer universal benefits for gig workers. *Fortune.* http://fortune.com/2017/10/13/gig-economy-workers-benefits/; Torpey, E., & Hogan, A. (2016, May). Career outlook: Working in a gig economy. U.S. Bureau of Labor Statistics. https://www.bls.gov/careeroutlook/2016/article/what-is-the-gig-economy.htm

2. U.S. Bureau of Labor Statistics. (2018, March). Table 1. Medical care benefits: Access, participation, and take-up rates. https://www.bls.gov/news.release/ebs2.t01.htm https://www.bls.gov/news.release/ebs2.t02.htm; U.S. Bureau of Labor Statistics. (2018, July 20). News release: Employee benefits in the United States—March 2018. USDL-18-1182. https://www.bls.gov/news.release/archives/ebs2_07202018.pdf

3. U.S. Bureau of Labor Statistics. (2018, June 8). News release: Employer costs for employee compensation—March 2018. USDL-18-0944. https://www.bls.gov/news.release/pdf/ecec.pdf

4. Society for Human Resource Management. (2018). 2018 employee benefits: The evolution of benefits. SHRM. https://www.shrm.org/hr-today/trends-and-forecasting/research-and-surveys/Documents/2018%20Employee%20Benefits%20Report.pdf

5. PayScale. (2018). 2018 compensation best practices report: The great divide: How a lack of trust is driving HR & managers apart. PayScale. https://www.payscale.com/content/report/2018-compensation-best-practices-report.pdf

6. Society for Human Resource Management. (2017). 2017 strategic benefits survey: Strategize with benefits. SHRM. https://www.shrm.org/hr-today/trends-and-forecasting/research-and-surveys/pages/strategize-with-benefits.aspx; Society for Human Resource Management. (2018). 2018 employee benefits: The evolution of benefits. SHRM. https://www.shrm.org/hr-today/trends-and-forecasting/research-and-surveys/Documents/2018%20Employee%20Benefits%20Report.pdf

7. U.S. Bureau of Labor Statistics. (2018, June 8). News release: Employer costs for employee compensation—March 2018. USDL-18-0944. https://www.bls.gov/news.release/pdf/ecec.pdf; Beam, B. T., & McFadden, J. J. (2007). *Employee benefits* (8th ed.). Chicago, IL: Dearborn Financial Publishing.

8. U.S. Social Security Administration. (2018). https://www.ssa.gov/

9. U.S. Social Security Administration. Updated 2018. (2018). https://www.ssa.gov/pubs/EN-05-10003.pdf

10. U.S. Social Security Administration. (2018). Retirement benefits. https://www.ssa.gov/benefits/retirement/

11. U.S. Social Security Administration. (2018). Survivors benefits. https://www.ssa.gov/benefits/survivors/

12. U.S. Social Security Administration. (2018). Disability benefits. https://www.ssa.gov/benefits/disability/; U.S. Social Security Administration. (2018). Types of beneficiaries. https://www.ssa.gov/oact/ProgData/types.html

13. U.S. Social Security Administration. (2018). Medicare benefits. https://www.ssa.gov/benefits/medicare/

14. Posthuma, R. A. (2009). Workers' compensation. SHRM. https://www.shrm.org/academicinitiatives/universities/teachingresources/Documents/Workers%27%20Comp%20IM%20Final.pdf

15. U.S. Department of Labor. (2018). Unemployment insurance. https://www.dol.gov/general/topic/unemployment-insurance

16. U.S. Social Security Administration. (2012). Unemployment insurance program description and legislative history. https://www.ssa.gov/policy/docs/statcomps/supplement/2012/unemployment.html

17. U.S. Department of Labor. (2018). Unemployment insurance data. https://oui.doleta.gov/unemploy/DataDashboard.asp

18. U.S. Department of Labor. (2018). Wage and Hour Division (WHD): Family and Medical Leave Act. https://www.dol.gov/whd/fmla/

19. Belle, J. V. (2016). RAND Europe: Paternity and parental leave policies across the European Union. RAND Corporation. https://www.rand.org/pubs/research_reports/RR1666.html; Dishman, L. (2016, February 16). How U.S. employee benefits compare to Europe's. *Fast Company.* https://www.fastcompany.com/3056830/how-the-us-employee-benefits-compare-to-europe; Lorenzo, G. (2015, October 7). How does life for working parents in Finland compare to those in the U.S.? *Fast Company.* https://www.fastcompany

.com/3051689/how-does-life-for-working-parents-in-finland-really-compare-to-the-us; Kela. (2015). Home and family: Benefits for families with children and housing benefits. https://www.kela.fi/documents/10180/1978560/2015_Home_family.pdf; Helsinki: Ministry of Social Affairs and Health. (2013). Child and family policy in Finland. http://julkaisut.valtioneuvosto.fi/bitstream/handle/10024/69916/URN_ISBN_978-952-00-3378-1.pdf

20. U.S. Department of Labor. (2018). Health plans & benefits: ERISA. https://www.dol.gov/general/topic/health-plans/erisa

21. U.S. Department of Labor. (2018). Health plans & benefits: Continuation of health coverage—COBRA. https://www.dol.gov/general/topic/health-plans/cobra; U.S. Department of Labor. (2018). History of EBSA and ERISA. https://www.dol.gov/agencies/ebsa/about-ebsa/about-us/history-of-ebsa-and-erisa

22. U.S. Department of Labor. (2018). Health plans & benefits: Portability of health coverage. https://www.dol.gov/general/topic/health-plans/portability; U.S. Department of Labor. (2018). History of EBSA and ERISA. https://www.dol.gov/agencies/ebsa/about-ebsa/about-us/history-of-ebsa-and-erisa

23. HealthCare.gov. (2018). Health coverage rights and protections. https://www.healthcare.gov/health-care-law-protections/; U.S. Internal Revenue Service. (2018). Employer shared responsibility provisions. https://www.irs.gov/affordable-care-act/employers/employer-shared-responsibility-provisions; U.S. Government Publishing Office. (2010, March 23). Public Law 111-148—Mar. 23, 2010. https://www.gpo.gov/fdsys/pkg/PLAW-111publ148/pdf/PLAW-111publ148.pdf

24. Mukherjee, S. (2017, December 20). The GOP tax bill repeals Obamacare's individual mandate. Here's what that means for you.

Fortune. http://fortune.com/2017/12/20/tax-bill-individual-mandate-obamacare/

25. Beam, B. T., & McFadden, J. J. (2007). *Employee benefits* (8th ed.). Chicago, IL: Dearborn Financial Publishing.

26. The Kaiser Family Foundation and Health Research & Educational Trust. (2017). *Employer health benefits.* Menlo Park, CA: Henry J. Kaiser Family Foundation.

27. Scheiber, N., & Corkery, M. (2017, November 27). As Walmart buys online retailers, their health benefits suffer. *New York Times.* https://www.nytimes.com/2017/11/27/business/economy/walmart-online-health.html?_r=1

28. The Kaiser Family Foundation and Health Research & Educational Trust. (2017). *Employer health benefits.* Menlo Park, CA: Henry J. Kaiser Family Foundation.

29. Ibid.

30. Song, G. Y. (2010, October 25). Consumer-driven health care: What is it, and what does it mean for employees and employers. U.S. Bureau of Labor Statistics. https://www.bls.gov/opub/mlr/cwc/consumer-driven-health-care-what-is-it-and-what-does-it-mean-for-employees-and-employers.pdf

31. U.S. Internal Revenue Service. (2017). Publication 969 (2017), Health savings accounts and other tax-favored health plans. https://www.irs.gov/publications/p969

32. Society for Human Resource Management. (2018). 2018 employee benefits: The evolution of benefits. SHRM. https://www.shrm.org/hr-today/trends-and-forecasting/research-and-surveys/Documents/2018%20Employee%20Benefits%20Report.pdf

33. U.S. Internal Revenue Service. (2013, September 30). Internal Revenue Bulletin: 2013-40. https://www.irs.gov/irb/2013-40_IRB

34. U.S. Internal Revenue Service. (2013, September 30). Internal Revenue Bulletin: 2013-40. https://www.irs.gov/irb/2013-40_IRB; U.S. Internal Revenue Service.

(2018). Health reimbursement arrangements (HRAs). https://taxmap.irs.gov/taxmap/pubs/p969-003.htm

35. Lincoln Financial Group. (2017). 2017 Dental Research Series: Part 1—Consumer insights. http://newsroom.lfg.com/sites/lfg.newshq.businesswire.com/files/doc_library/file/2017_LFG_Dental_Series_Consumer_Data_6.27.17.pdf; Lincoln Financial Group. (2017, June 27). Lincoln Financial Group dental study informs both dentists and employers of consumers' needs and wants. http://newsroom.lfg.com/press-release/dental-coverage/lincoln-financial-group-dental-study-informs-both-dentists-and-employe

36. Richardson, C. M. (1998). Ethics and employee benefits. *Benefits Quarterly, 14,* 9–16.

37. Society for Human Resource Management. (2018). 2018 employee benefits: The evolution of benefits. SHRM. https://www.shrm.org/hr-today/trends-and-forecasting/research-and-surveys/Documents/2018%20Employee%20Benefits%20Report.pdf

38. Morley, T. (2018). Temporary disability insurance requirements by state. https://www.shrm.org/resourcesandtools/legal-and-compliance/state-and-local-updates/xperthr/pages/temporary-disability-insurance-requirements-by-state.aspx

39. Society for Human Resource Management. (2014, December 11). Disability benefits: What are short-term disability and long-term disability? https://www.shrm.org/resourcesandtools/tools-and-samples/hr-qa/pages/stdandltd.aspx

40. Society for Human Resource Management. (2014, December 11). Disability benefits: What are short-term disability and long-term disability? https://www.shrm.org/resourcesandtools/tools-and-samples/hr-qa/pages/stdandltd.aspx

41. Society for Human Resource Management. (2018). 2018 employee benefits: The evolution of

benefits. SHRM. https://www .shrm.org/hr-today/trends-and-forecasting/research-and-surveys/Documents/2018%20Employee%20Benefits%20Report.pdf

42. U.S. Department of Labor. (2018). Health plans & benefits: ERISA. https://www.dol.gov/general/topic/health-plans/erisa

43. U.S. Department of Labor. (2018). Participant rights. https://www .dol.gov/general/topic/retirement/participantrights; U.S. Department of Labor. (2018). Retirement plans and ERISA FAQs. https://www .dol.gov/agencies/ebsa/about-ebsa/our-activities/resource-center/faqs/retirement-plans-and-erisa-consumer

44. Pension Benefit Guaranty Corporation. (2018). PBGC pension insurance: We've got you covered. https://www.pbgc.gov/wr/find-an-insured-pension-plan/pbgc-protects-pensions; https://www .pbgc.gov/workers-retirees

45. Beam, B. T., & McFadden, J. J. (2007). *Employee benefits* (8th ed.). Chicago, IL: Dearborn Financial Publishing; Society for Human Resource Management. (2015, April 24). Pension plan: Defined benefit: General: What is a defined benefit plan? https:// www.shrm.org/resourcesandtools/tools-and-samples/hr-qa/pages/whataredefinedbenefitplans.aspx

46. U.S. Internal Revenue Service. (2018). Choosing a retirement plan: Defined benefit plan. https://www .irs.gov/retirement-plans/choosing-a-retirement-plan-defined-benefit-plan

47. Beam, B. T., & McFadden, J. J. (2007). *Employee benefits* (8th ed.). Chicago, IL: Dearborn Financial Publishing.

48. Beam, B. T., & McFadden, J. J. (2007). *Employee benefits* (8th ed.). Chicago, IL: Dearborn Financial Publishing; U.S. Department of Labor. (2018). Types of retirement plans. https://www.dol.gov/general/topic/retirement/typesofplans

49. U.S. Internal Revenue Service. (2018). Definitions. https:// www.irs.gov/retirement-plans/plan-participant-employee/definitions

50. PayScale. (2018). 2018 compensation best practices report: The great divide: How a lack of trust is driving HR & managers apart. PayScale. https://www.payscale .com/content/report/2018-compensation-best-practices-report.pdf

51. U.S. Internal Revenue Service. (2018). 401(k) plan overview. https://www.irs.gov/retirement-plans/plan-sponsor/401k-plan-overview

52. U.S. Internal Revenue Service. (2018). 401(k) plans. https://www .irs.gov/retirement-plans/401k-plans

53. U.S. Internal Revenue Service. (2018). Choosing a retirement plan: 401(k) plans. https://www.irs .gov/retirement-plans/choosing-a-retirement-plan-401k-plan

54. Chang, A., & Kurkoski, J. (2017, August 22). Nudge employees to save more for retirement. https:// rework.withgoogle.com/blog/nudge-to-save-for-retirement/; Choi, J. J., Haisley, E., Kurkoski, J., & Massey, C. (2017). Small cues change savings choices. *Journal of Economic Behavior & Organization, 142*, 378–395.

55. U.S. Internal Revenue Service. (2018). Tax-sheltered annuity plans. https://www .irs.gov/retirement-plans/irc-403b-tax-sheltered-annuity-plans

56. U.S. Internal Revenue Service. (2018). Choosing a retirement plan: 403(b) tax-sheltered annuity plan. https://www.irs.gov/retirement-plans/choosing-a-retirement-plan-403b-tax-sheltered-annuity-plan

57. U.S. Internal Revenue Service. (2018). Definitions. https:// www.irs.gov/retirement-plans/plan-participant-employee/definitions

58. U.S. Internal Revenue Service. (2018). Choosing a retirement plan: Profit-sharing plan. https://www.irs .gov/retirement-plans/choosing-a-retirement-plan-profit-sharing-plan

59. Blasi, J., Conte, M., & Kruse, D. (1996). Employee stock ownership and corporate performance among public companies. *ILR Review, 50,* 60–79.

60. U.S. Internal Revenue Service. (2018). Employee stock ownership plans (ESOPs). https://www.irs .gov/retirement-plans/employee-stock-ownership-plans-esops; U.S. Internal Revenue Service. (2018). Definitions. https:// www.irs.gov/retirement-plans/plan-participant-employee/definitions

61. Sammer, J. (2016, February 4). ESOPs turn workers into owners. https://www.shrm.org/resourcesandtools/hr-topics/benefits/pages/esops-workers-owners.aspx

62. Beam, B. T., & McFadden, J. J. (2007). *Employee benefits* (8th ed.). Chicago, IL: Dearborn Financial Publishing; U.S. Department of Labor. (2018). Types of retirement plans. https://www.dol.gov/general/topic/retirement/typesofplans; U.S. Internal Revenue Service. (2018). Choosing a retirement plan: Money-purchase plan. https://www.irs .gov/retirement-plans/choosing-a-retirement-plan-money-purchase-plan

63. Beam, B. T., & McFadden, J. J. (2007). *Employee benefits* (8th ed.). Chicago, IL: Dearborn Financial Publishing; U.S. Internal Revenue Service. (2018). Choosing a retirement plan: SEP. https://www .irs.gov/retirement-plans/choosing-a-retirement-plan-sep; U.S. Department of Labor. (2018). Types of plans. https://www.dol .gov/general/topic/retirement/typesofplans

64. Beam, B. T., & McFadden, J. J. (2007). *Employee benefits* (8th ed.). Chicago, IL: Dearborn Financial Publishing.

65. Foster, A. C. (1997). Employee benefits: Life insurance. U.S. Bureau of Labor Statistics. https://www.bls .gov/opub/mlr/cwc/life-insurance .pdf

66. U.S. Bureau of Labor Statistics. (2018, March). News release: Employee benefits in the United

States—March 2018. USDL-18-1182. https://www.bls.gov/news .release/archives/ebs2_07202018.pdf

67. Blanco, R. M. (2012). Life insurance benefits: Variations based on workers' earnings and work schedules. U.S. Bureau of Labor Statistics. https://www.bls.gov/opub/ mlr/cwc/life-insurance-benefits-variations-based-on-workers-earnings-and-work-schedules.pdf

68. The Kaiser Family Foundation and Health Research & Educational Trust. (2017). *Employer health benefits.* Menlo Park, CA: Henry J. Kaiser Family Foundation.

69. Goetzel, R. Z., Henke, R. M., Tabrizi, M., Pelletier, K. R., Loeppke, R., Ballard, D. W., . . . & Serxner, S. (2014). Do workplace health promotion (wellness) programs work? *Journal of Occupational and Environmental Medicine, 56,* 927–934; Mattke, S., Liu, H., Caloyeras, J., Huang, C. Y., Van Busum, K. R., Khodyakov, D., & Shier, V. (2013). Workplace wellness programs study. *Rand Health Quarterly, 3*(2), 7; Gebhardt, D. L., & Crump, C. E. (1990). Employee fitness and wellness programs in the workplace. *American Psychologist, 45,* 262–272; Parks, K. M., & Steelman, L. A. (2008). Organizational wellness programs: A meta-analysis. *Journal of Occupational Health Psychology, 13,* 58–68.

70. Society for Human Resource Management. (2018). 2018 employee benefits: The evolution of benefits. SHRM. https://www .shrm.org/hr-today/trends-and-forecasting/research-and-surveys/ Documents/2018%20Employee%20 Benefits%20Report.pdf

71. Ibid.

72. Lambert, S. J. (2000). Added benefits: The link between work–life benefits and organizational citizenship behavior. *Academy of Management Journal, 43,* 801–815.

73. U.S. Department of Labor. (2018). Holiday pay. https://www.dol.gov/ general/topic/wages/holiday

74. Sammer, J. (2017, January 9). Employers are banking on paid

time off. https://www.shrm.org/ resourcesandtools/hr-topics/ benefits/pages/banking-on-paid-time-off.aspx

75. PayScale. (2018). 2018 compensation best practices report: The great divide: How a lack of trust is driving HR & managers apart. PayScale. https://www.payscale .com/content/report/2018-compensation-best-practices-report .pdf

76. Umoh, R. (2018, April 28). 5 companies with employee perks that rival Google's. https://www.cnbc .com/2018/04/27/facebook-netflix-amazon-and-others-offer-perks-that-rival-google.html

77. Sammer, J. (2014, December 15). Unlimited paid time off: A good or bad idea? https://www.shrm .org/resourcesandtools/hr-topics/ benefits/pages/unlimited-pto.aspx

78. Deschenaux, J. (2015, June 16). Put vacation policies in writing. https:// www.shrm.org/resourcesandtools/ legal-and-compliance/state-and-local-updates/pages/put-vacation-policies-in-writing-.aspx

79. Smith, A. (2017, April 6). SHRM to Congress: Make comp time available to businesses. https:// www.shrm.org/resourcesandtools/ legal-and-compliance/employment-law/pages/shrm-congress-comp-time-businesses.aspx; Society for Human Resource Management. (2016, August 31). Legal & regulatory: Compensatory time: Is compensatory time allowed in the private sector? https://www.shrm .org/resourcesandtools/tools-and-samples/hr-qa/pages/ iscompensatorytimeallowed intheprivatesector.aspx

80. U.S. Bureau of Labor Statistics. (2016). Employment characteristics of families (USDL-16-0795). https:// www.bls.gov/news.release/famee .nr0.htm; U.S. Bureau of Labor Statistics. (2013). Women in the labor force: A databook. http://stats .bls.gov/cps/wlf-databook-2012 .pdf; U.S. Bureau of Labor Statistics. (2015a). Employment characteristics of families (USDL-15-0689). https://

www.bls.gov/news.release/archives/ famee_04232015.pdf

81. U.S. Bureau of Labor Statistics. (2015b). Unpaid eldercare in the United States: Data from the American Time Use Survey (USDL-15-1851). https://www.bls.gov/news .release/pdf/elcare.pdf

82. The state of child care in the U.S. (2018). https://www.care.com/ care-index

83. Dalton, M. (2017, December 21). Companies realize benefits of pitching in for child care. https:// www.wabe.org/companies-realize-benefits-pitching-child-care/

84. Shellenback, K. (2004). *Child care & parent productivity: Making the business case.* Ithaca, NY: Cornell Cooperative Extension. http:// government.cce.cornell.edu/doc/ pdf/ChildCareParentProductivity .pdf; Childcare Partnership Project. Engaging business partners. http://www.nccic.acf.hhs.gov/ ccpartnerships/facts.fs11.htm

85. McKenzie, B., & Rapino, M. (2011, September). Commuting in the United States: 2009. U.S. Department of Commerce. https:// www.infrastructureusa.org/ wp-content/uploads/2011/09/ census-commuting.pdf

86. Hopkins, J. (2016, September 15). Understanding the tax benefits of 529 plans. *Forbes.* https:// www.forbes.com/sites/ jamiehopkins/2016/09/15/ understanding-the-tax-benefits-of-529-plans/#3a7cf53a19aa

87. Kenney, J., & Mason, L. (2012, February 17). Strengthen employee loyalty with corporate 529 plans. SHRM. https://www.shrm.org/ resourcesandtools/hr-topics/ benefits/pages/529plans.aspx; LearnVest. (2017, April 1). College savings plans: The nextbig employee benefit? *Forbes.* https://www.forbes .com/sites/learnvest/2017/04/01/ college-savings-plans-the-next-big-employee-benefit/#46fcae6272ce; Ward, L. (2016, March 27). The latest corporate benefit: The 529 plan. *Wall Street Journal.* https://www.wsj.com/articles/

the-latest-corporate-benefit-the-529-plan-1459130786

88. Society for Human Resource Management. (2015, November 14). Designing and managing educational assistance programs. https://www.shrm.org/resourcesandtools/tools-and-samples/toolkits/pages/educationalassistanceprograms.aspx; U.S. Congress. (2013, January 2). H.R.8—American Taxpayer Relief Act of 2012. https://www.congress.gov/bill/112th-congress/house-bill/8/text?overview=closed

89. Starbucks college achievement plan. (2018). https://www.starbucks.com/careers/college-plan

90. Sammer, J. (2014, July 10). The case for legal services and ID theft benefits. SHRM. https://www.shrm.org/resourcesandtools/hr-topics/benefits/pages/legal-services.aspx

91. Federal Trade Commission. (2014, February). Consumer Sentinel Network: Data book. SHRM. https://www.shrm.org/ResourcesAndTools/hr-topics/benefits/Documents/sentinel-cy2013.pdf

92. Brenoff, A. (2017, December 6). 8 reasons why employees never want to leave this amazing company. *Huffington Post.* https://www.huffingtonpost.com/2013/11/18/best-places-to-work_n_4240370.html; Crowley, M. C. (2013, January 22). How SAS became the world's best place to work. *Fast Company.* https://www.fastcompany.com/3004953/how-sas-became-worlds-best-place-work; Leung, R. (2003, April 18). Working the good life: SAS provides employees with generous work incentives. *CBS News.* https://www.cbsnews.com/news/working-the-good-life/

93. Stewart, J. B. (2013, March 15). Looking for a lesson in Google's perks. *New York Times.* http://www.nytimes.com/2013/03/16/business/at-google-a-place-to-work-and-play.html

94. D'Onfro, J. (2015, April 7). Here are all of Google's employees, and how much they cost the company. *BusinessInsider.* http://

www.businessinsider.com/cost-benefit-of-google-perks-2015-4

95. Cole, N. D., & Flint, D. H. (2004). Perceptions of distributive and procedural justice in employee benefits: Flexible versus traditional benefit plans. *Journal of Managerial Psychology, 19*, 19–40.

96. Barber, A. E., Dunham, R. B., & Formisano, R. A. (1992). The impact of flexible benefits on employee satisfaction: A field study. *Personnel Psychology, 45*, 55–75.

97. U.S. Internal Revenue Service. (2018). Section 125: Cafeteria plans: Modification of application of rule prohibiting deferred compensation under a cafeteria plan. https://www.irs.gov/pub/irs-drop/n-05-42.pdf; U.S. Internal Revenue Service. Publication 15-B. (2017). Employer's tax guide to fringe benefits. https://www.irs.gov/publications/p15b#en_US_2017_publink1000193624

98. Liptak, A. (2015, June 26). Supreme Court ruling makes same-sex marriage a right nationwide. *New York Times.* https://www.nytimes.com/2015/06/27/us/supreme-court-same-sex-marriage.html; *United States vs. Windsor.* (2013). https://www.law.cornell.edu/supremecourt/text/12-307; Bernard, T. S. (2015, August 20). Gay couple are eligible for Social Security benefits, U.S. decides. *New York Times.* https://www.nytimes.com/2015/08/21/business/gay-couples-are-eligible-for-benefits-us-decides.html; Scheiber, N. (2016, December 2). Walmart settles discrimination suit over benefits for same-sex spouses. *New York Times.* https://www.nytimes.com/2016/12/02/business/walmart-same-sex-discrimination-lawsuit.html?_r=0; U.S. Equal Employment Opportunity Commission. What you should know about EEOC and the enforcement protections for LGBT workers. https://www.eeoc.gov/eeoc/newsroom/wysk/enforcement_protections_lgbt_workers.cfm; Freur, A. (2017, July 27). Justice

Department says rights law doesn't protect gays. *New York Times.* https://www.nytimes.com/2017/07/27/nyregion/justice-department-gays-workplace.html

99. Kass, E. M. (2017, July 19). Moving the meter on benefits utilization. https://www.benefitnews.com/news/moving-the-meter-on-benefits-utilization; Work redefined: A new age of benefits. https://benefittrends.metlife.com/us-perspectives/work-redefined-a-new-age-of-benefits/

100. Hennessey, H. W., Perrewe, P. L., & Hochwarter, W. A. (1992). Impact of benefit awareness on employee and organizational outcomes: A longitudinal field examination. *Benefits Quarterly, 8*, 90–96.

101. Society for Human Resource Management. (2017). 2017 strategic benefits survey: Strategize with benefits. SHRM. https://www.shrm.org/hr-today/trends-and-forecasting/research-and-surveys/pages/strategize-with-benefits.aspx

102. Wilson, M., Northcraft, G. B., & Neale, M. A. (1985). The perceived value of fringe benefits. *Personnel Psychology*, 38(2), 309–320.

103. Freitag, A. R., & Picherit-Duthler, G. (2004). Employee benefits communication: Proposing a PR-HR cooperative approach. *Public Relations Review, 30*, 475–482.

104. Sammer, J. (2014, January 9). Employers are banking on paid time off. SHRM. https://www.shrm.org/resourcesandtools/hr-topics/benefits/pages/banking-on-paid-time-off.aspx

Chapter 14

1. McIntosh, D. (2017). Union drive launches at New Seasons. nwLaborPress.org https://nwlaborpress.org/2017/11/union-drive-launches-at-new-seasons/; Tu, J. I. (2016). Controversy, competition greet New Seasons Market as it opens on Mercer Island. *Seattle Times.* https://www.seattletimes.com/business/retail/controversy-competition-greet-

new-season-market-as-it-opens-on-mercer-island/; Goodman, M. (2013). Make it good officially. *Entrepreneur.* http://www.bcorporation.net/sites/default/files/Entrepreneur_Mag_Feature.pdf; Freeland, C. (2013). Capitalism, but with a little heart. *New York Times.* http://www.nytimes.com/2013/07/19/us/19iht-letter19.html?_r=0; Why B Corps matter. http://www.bcorporation.net/what-are-b-corps/why-b-corps-matter; Taylor, N. (2017). New Seasons Market earns B Corp recertification. *Grocery Business.* http://www.winsightgrocerybusiness.com/new-seasons-market-earns-b-corp-recertification; New Seasons Market. Our story. https://www.newseasonsmarket.com/our-story/; B Corps. Our history. http://www.bcorporation.net/what-are-b-corps/the-non-profit-behind-b-corps/our-history; Honeyman, R. (2014). *The B Corp handbook: How to use business as a force for good.* Oakland, CA: Berrett-Koehler Publishers.

2. Meinert, D. (2014). Be fair, be consistent, avoid lawsuits. *HR Magazine.* https://www.shrm.org/hr-today/news/hr-news/pages/be-fair-be-consistent-avoid-lawsuits.aspx

3. Buttigieg, D. M., Deery, S. J., & Iverson, R. D. (2007). An event history analysis of union joining and leaving. *Journal of Applied Psychology, 92,* 829–839; Cohen-Charash, & Spector, P. E. (2001). The role of justice in organizations: A meta-analysis. *Organizational Behavior and Human Decision Processes, 86,* 278–321; Colquitt, J. A., Scott, B. A., Rodell, J. B., Long, D. M., Zapata, C. P., Conlon, D. E., & Wesson, M. J. (2013). Justice at the millennium, a decade later: A meta-analytic test of social exchange and affect-based perspectives. *Journal of Applied Psychology, 98,* 199–236.

4. Doucouliagos, C. (1995). Worker participation and productivity in labor-managed and participatory capitalist firms: A meta-analysis. *Industrial and Labor Relations Review, 49,* 58–77.

5. Gabler, N. (2016). The magic in the warehouse. *Fortune.* http://fortune.com/costco-wholesale-shopping/; Taube, A. (2014). Why Costco pays its retail employees $20 an hour. *Business Insider.* http://www.businessinsider.com/costco-pays-retail-employees-20-an-hour-2014-10

6. Inc. What to include in an employee handbook. (2010). *Inc.* https://www.inc.com/guides/2010/06/what-to-include-in-employee-handbook.html

7. Guerin, L. (2018). Does your employee handbook compromise at-will employment? https://www.lawyers.com/legal-info/labor-employment-law/human-resources-law/employee-handbooks-and-at-will-employment.html

8. SHRM. (2018). Employee handbooks. https://www.shrm.org/resourcesandtools/tools-and-samples/pages/employee-handbooks.aspx

9. Robinson, J. (2015). 6 inspiring employee handbook examples. *Nasdaq.* http://www.nasdaq.com/article/6-inspiring-employee-handbook-examples-cm459464

10. Warr, P. (2013). Former Valve employee: "It felt a lot like high school." *Wired.* https://www.wired.com/2013/07/wireduk-valve-jeri-ellsworth/

11. Strauss, K. (2017). 10 companies that offer unlimited vacation time. *Forbes.* https://www.forbes.com/sites/karstenstrauss/2017/07/19/10-companies-offering-unlimited-vacation-time/#6fa1a10c2082

12. SHRM. (2011). Dress & appearance: Body odor, what should HR do when an employee's body odor is affecting the workplace? https://www.shrm.org/resourcesandtools/tools-and-samples/hr-qa/pages/bodyodoraffectingworkplace.aspx

13. Pew Research. (2010). Millennials: Confident. Connected. Open to change. http://www.pewsocialtrends.org/2010/02/24/millennials-confident-connected-open-to-change/

14. Oliver, C. (2015). Tattoos in the workplace: Laws for covering art. *NBC News.* http://www.nbc-2.com/story/28241652/tattoos-in-the-workplace-laws-of-covering-art

15. Lucas, S. (20114). Nordstrom's awesome employee handbook is a myth. *CBS News MoneyWatch.* https://www.cbsnews.com/news/nordstroms-awesome-employee-handbook-is-a-myth/; Lutz, A. (2014). Nordstrom's employee handbook has only one rule. *Business Insider.* http://www.businessinsider.com/nordstroms-employee-handbook-2014-10

16. Greenhouse, S. (2010). Company accused of firing over Facebook post. *New York Times.* http://www.nytimes.com/2010/11/09/business/09facebook.html.

17. **Types of Unions: Industrial and craft unions.** Unions vary depending on the type of work their members do. The two types of unions are industrial unions and craft unions. *Industrial unions* cover all workers who are employed within a given industry. For example, the National Education Association represents teachers from a variety of fields and types of educational institutions, and the Order of Railway Conductors of America represents railroad workers. Conversely, *craft unions* represent individuals with a specific trade across different employers and locations. Examples include unions of plumbers, electricians, and ironworkers. Craft unions emerged from the guild system of the Middle Ages, with the first craft union within the United States being shoemakers in Philadelphia during colonial times. United States History. (2017). Craft unions. http://www.u-s-history.com/pages/h1746.html

National and international unions. Internationally, the largest union is the All-China Federation of Trade Unions, a state-controlled union comprising more than 280 million members. In 2006, Walmart has unionized employees working in its Chinese stores represented by this union. In the United States, the largest unions are much smaller, with the National Education Association having more than 2 million members and Service Employees International Union having close to 2 million members. Within the United States, many national unions are affiliated with the American Federation of Labor and Congress of Industrial Organizations (AFL-CIO). It is not a union but rather an association designed to help advocate for union worker rights nationally. UNITE HERE was established in 2004 via mergers with other unions and represents workers in industries such as airports, food service, hotels, textiles, transportation, and gaming. It is the fastest-growing union in the private-sector within the United States with more than 270,000 members. It is affiliated with the AFL-CIO along with 55 other unions representing 12.5 million working people. Groll, E. (2013). The world's most powerful labor unions. *Foreign Policy.* http://foreignpolicy.com/2013/09/02/the-worlds-most-powerful-labor-unions/; China's growing labour movement offers hope for workers globally. (2015). The Conversation. http://theconversation.com/chinas-growing-labour-movement-offers-hope-for-workers-globally-39921; Mernit, J. L. (2017). How millennials are trying to revive the labor movement. *Fast Company.* https://www.fastcompany.com/40497318/how-millennials-are-trying-to-revive-the-labor-movement; UNITEHERE. http://unitehere.org/who-we-are/; AFL-CIO. (2017). Our affiliated unions. https://aflcio.org/about/our-unions-and-allies

Local Unions. Although national and international unions have a great deal of collective power due to their size and many local unions belong to national unions, for most union members, their local union has a greater impact on their day-to-day working lives. For example, union members elect local union officials such as the president, vice president, and secretary of the union. These individuals often form the team that negotiates with the organization during collective bargaining. It is possible for a bargaining team to be appointed to engage in bargaining on behalf of the local union members.

18. Youngblood, S. A., DeNisi, A. S., Molleston, J. L., & Mobley, W. H. (1984). The impact of work environment, instrumentality beliefs, perceived union image, and subjective norms on union voting intentions. *Academy of Management Journal, 27,* 576–590.

19. Baker, D. (2015). Labor unions: The folks who gave you the weekend. *Huffington Post.* https://www.huffingtonpost.com/dean-baker/labor-unions-the-folks-wh_b_8101242.html

20. Baugher, J. E., & Roberts, J. T. (2004). Workplace hazards, unions, and coping styles. *Labor Studies Journal, 29,* 1–24.

21. Western, B., & Rosenfeld, J. (2011). Unions, norms, and the rise in U.S. wage inequality. *American Sociological Review, 76,* 513–537.

22. Long, G. I. (2013). Differences between union and nonunion compensation, 2001–2011. *Monthly Labor Review.* https://www.bls.gov/opub/mlr/2013/04/art2full.pdf; Luhby, T. (2015). Want a raise? Join a union. *CNN Money.* http://money.cnn.com/2015/02/24/news/economy/union-wages/index.html

23. U.S. Bureau of Labor Statistics. (2016). Union Members—2016. https://www.bls.gov/news.release/pdf/union2.pdf

24. Wallace, G. (2015). Facebook's bus drivers set for raises after union vote. *CNN Money.* http://money.cnn.com/2015/02/22/technology/facebook-bus-drivers-union/index.html?iid=EL; Wong, Q. (2015). Facebook approves union contract for shuttle bus drivers. *siliconbeat.* http://www.siliconbeat.com/2015/03/12/facebook-approves-union-contract-for-shuttle-drivers/

25. Modern Survey. (2015). Employee engagement and unions. http://www.modernsurvey.com/resources/whitepapers; Tyler, J. (2009). Employee engagement and labor relations. *Gallup News Business Journal.* http://news.gallup.com/businessjournal/122849/employee-engagement-labor-relations.aspx

26. Laroche, P. (2016). A meta-analysis of the union–job satisfaction relationship. *British Journal of Industrial Relations, 54,* 709–741.

27. Becker, B. E., & Olson, C. A. (1992). Unions and firm profits. *Industrial Relations, 31,* 395–415.

28. Doucouliagos, C., & Laroche, P. (2003). What do unions do to productivity? A meta-analysis. *Industrial Relations, 42,* 650–691.

29. Cooke, W. N., & Meyer, D. G. (1990). Structural and market predictors of corporate labor relations strategies. *Industrial and Labor Relations Review, 43,* 280–293.

30. Martin, C. J. (2016). Business and labor don't have to be enemies. *Washington Post.* https://www.washingtonpost.com/news/in-theory/wp/2016/08/04/business-and-labor-dont-have-to-be-enemies/?tid=a_inl&utm_term=.51822ef21a8a; The World Bank. (2017). Ease of Doing Business Index. https://data.worldbank.org/indicator/IC.BUS.EASE.XQ?year_high_desc=false

31. Durham, C. (2017). Court upholds T-Mobile's positive workplace environment rules. SHRM. https://www.shrm.org/resourcesandtools/legal-and-compliance/employment-law/pages/court-report-positive-workplace-rules.aspx

32. U.S. Department of Labor. (2018). https://www.dol.gov/general/aboutdol/majorlaws; https://www.dol.gov/olms/regs/compliance/LMRDAQandA.htm#quest1

33. SHRM. (2016). https://www.shrm.org/resourcesandtools/legal-and-compliance/employment-law/pages/norris-laguardia-act.aspx

34. Dunn, M., & Walker, J. U.S. Bureau of Labor Statistics. (2016). Union membership in the United States.

https://www.bls.gov/spotlight/2016/union-membership-in-the-united-states/pdf/union-membership-in-the-united-states.pdf

35. Marsh, J. M., Bloom, H. M., & Rosen, P. B. (2017). Unions winning more elections, but organizing fewer new workers. https://www.laborandcollectivebargaining.com/2017/03/articles/collective-bargaining/unions-winning-elections-organizing-fewer-new-workers/#page=1; Swift, A. (2017). Labor union approval best since 2003, at 61%. Gallup News. http://news.gallup.com/poll/217331/labor-union-approval-best-2003.aspx

36. Employee involvement—European Works Councils. (n.d.). http://ec.europa.eu/social/main.jsp?catId=707&langId=en&intPageId=211

37. NHO. (2013). Basic labour law. https://www.nho.no/en/Business-in-Norway/Basic-Labour-Law/

38. Wingfield, N., & Eddy, M. (2013). In Germany, union culture clashes with Amazon's labor practices. *New York Times.* http://www.nytimes.com/2013/08/05/business/workers-of-amazon-divergent.html

39. Calderone, M. (2017). The *Huffington Post* ratifies union contract. *Huffington Post.* https://www.huffingtonpost.com/entry/huffington-post-union-contract_us_588f7523e4b0c90efefed41a

40. https://unionbase.org/; Wartzman, R. (2017). Meet the millennial who's trying to save the labor movement with a Facebook for unions. *Fast Company.* https://www.fastcompany.com/40461691/meet-the-millennial-whos-trying-to-save-the-labor-movement-with-a-facebook-for-unions

41. National Labor Relations Board. (2002). Your government conducts an election, For you—on the job. Information for voters in NLRB elections. https://www.nlrb.gov/sites/default/files/attachments/basic-page/node-3024/election.pdf

42. National Labor Relations Board. (2000). https://www.nlrb.gov/rights-we-protect/whats-law/employees/i-am-represented-union/decertification-election

43. Marsh, J. M., Bloom, H. M., & Rosen, P. B. (2017). Unions winning more elections, but organizing fewer new workers. https://www.laborandcollectivebargaining.com/2017/03/articles/collective-bargaining/unions-winning-elections-organizing-fewer-new-workers/#page=1

44. History of the coalition of Kaiser Permanente unions. (n.d.). https://www.unioncoalition.org/who-we-are/

45. Lazes, P. M., Figueroa, M., & Katz, L. (2012). How labor–management partnerships improve patient care, cost control, and labor relations. http://digitalcommons.ilr.cornell.edu/reports/59/

46. Agrawal, N. (2017). Kaiser nurses reach tentative labor agreement with Los Angeles Medical Center. *Los Angeles Times.* http://www.latimes.com/business/la-fi-kaiser-nurses-agreement-20170217-story.html

47. Tinsley, C. H. (2001). How negotiators get to yes: Predicting the constellation of strategies used across cultures to negotiate conflict. *Journal of Applied Psychology, 86,* 583–593.

48. Cutcher-Gershenfeld, J. (1991). The impact on economic performance of a transformation in workplace relations. *Industrial Labor Relations Review, 44,* 241–260.

49. Deery, S. J., & Iverson, R. D. (2005). Labor–management cooperation: Antecedents and impact on organizational performance. *Industrial and Labor Relations Review, 58,* 588–609.

50. Harinck, F., De Dreu, C. K. W., & Van Vianen, A. E. M. (2000). The impact of conflict issues on fixed-pie perceptions, problem solving, and integrative outcomes in negotiation. *Organizational Behavior and Human Decision Processes, 81,* 329–358.

51. Fisher, R., Ury, W. L., & Patton, B. (2011). *Getting to yes: Negotiating agreement without giving in.* New York: Penguin Books.

52. History.com. (2008). Writers' strike ends after 100 days. http://www.history.com/this-day-in-history/writers-strike-ends-after-100-days; Klowden, K., Chatterjee, A., & DeVol, R. (2008). The writers' strike of 2007–2008: The economic impact of digital distribution. *Milken Institute Review.* http://www.milkeninstitute.org/publications/view/347; Macaray, D. (2013). The 2007–2008 writers strike. *Huffington Post.* https://www.huffingtonpost.com/david-macaray/the-200708-writers-strike_b_3840681.html; Ng, D., James, M., & Faughnder, R. (2017). They avoided a strike, but negotiations between writers and studios were a true Hollywood thrilled. *Los Angeles Times.* http://www.latimes.com/business/hollywood/la-fi-ct-writers-guild-no-strike-20170501-story.html

53. O'Connor, K. M., & Arnold, J. A. (2001). Distributive spirals: Negotiation impasses and the moderating role of self-efficacy. *Organizational Behavior and Human Decision Processes, 84,* 148–176.

54. Reuters Staff. (2017). Colombia convenes arbitration court to resolve Avianca pilots strike. https://www.reuters.com/article/colombia-avianca/colombia-convenes-arbitration-court-to-resolve-avianca-pilots-strike-idUSL2N1MA0GN

55. Griffiths, J. (2016). China on strike. *CNN.* http://www.cnn.com/2016/03/28/asia/china-strike-worker-protest-trade-union/index.html

56. U.S. Bureau of Labor Statistics. (2017). Major work stoppages. https://www.bls.gov/news.release/wkstp.htm

57. U.S. Bureau of Labor Statistics. Frequently asked questions (FAQs). (n.d.). Work stoppages. https://www.bls.gov/wsp/wspfaq.htm

58. SHRM. (2012). Grievance procedures: What are the steps typically found in a grievance

procedure? https://www.shrm
.org/resourcesandtools/tools-
and-samples/hr-qa/pages/
aresolutionformanagementand
employees.aspx

59. Hastings, R. R. (2012). Measure
grievances to minimize costs.
SHRM. https://www.shrm.org/
resourcesandtools/hr-topics/
employee-relations/pages/
measuregrievancestominimize
costs.aspx

Chapter 15

1. Associated Press. (2017). Video:
Train crew not using electronic
devices before crash. https://www
.nytimes.com/aponline/2017/12/22/
us/ap-us-train-derailment-
washington-state.html; Barone, B.
(2017). NJ: Engineers in LIRR and
NJ Transit derailments had sleep
apnea, NTSB says. *AM New York.*
https://www.amny.com/transit/
engineers-in-lirr-and-nj-transit-
derailments-had-sleep-apnea-
ntsb-1.14241007; Fitzsimmons,
E. G. (2016). Train was traveling at
twice the speed limit just
before Hoboken crash. *New York
Times.* https://www.nytimes
.com/2016/10/07/nyregion/train-
was-traveling-at-twice-the-speed-
limit-just-before-hoboken-crash
.html; McGeehan, P., Mazzei, P., &
Johnson, K. (2017). Law requires
life-saving braking device. Most
trains don't have it. *New York
Times.* https://www.nytimes.com/
2017/12/20/us/amtrak-train-safety
.html; Shepardson, D. (2017).
U.S. Safety Board says train-crash
engineers had undiagnosed sleep
disorders. *Scientific American.*
https://www.scientificamerican
.com/article/u-s-safety-board-
says-train-crash-engineers-had-
undiagnosed-sleep-disorders/

2. Workplace well-being.
(2018). International Labor
Organization. http://www.ilo
.org/safework/areasofwork/
workplace-health-promotion-and-
well-being/WCMS_118396/lang—
en/index.htm

3. American Psychological
Association. (2017). 2017 work
and well-being survey. http://
www.apaexcellence.org/assets/
general/2017-work-and-well-being-
survey-results.pdf; Bureau of Labor
Statistics. (2017, December 19).
https://www.bls.gov/news.release/
pdf/cfoi.pdf; "Tragic Trent": On-the-
job deaths at highest level since
2008, BLS reports. http://www
.safetyandhealthmagazine.com/
articles/16544-tragic-trend-on-the-
job-deaths-at-highest-level-since-
2008-bls-reports

4. About OSHA. (n.d.) https://www
.osha.gov/about.html; State Plans.
https://www.osha.gov/dcsp/osp/
index.html

5. About NIOSH. (2018). http://
www.cdc.gov/niosh/about/
default.html

6. Musick, T. (2016). The one-person
safety team. *Safety + Health
Magazine.* http://www
.safetyandhealthmagazine.com/
articles/print/13592-the-one-
person-safety-team; Occupational
Safety and Health Administration.
(2005). *Small Business Handbook.*
https://www.osha.gov/
Publications/smallbusiness/small-
business.pdf

7. Leigh, J. P. (2011). Economic
burden of occupational injury and
illness in the United States. *Milbank
Quarterly, 89,* 728–772.

8. America's safest companies awards:
2017 America's Safest Companies.
(2017). EHS Today. http://www
.ehstoday.com/americas-safest-
companies-awards/2017-america-s-
safest-companies

9. Musik, T. (2017, August 27).
Preventing serious injuries
and fatalities. *Safety + Health
Magazine.* http://www
.safetyandhealthmagazine.com/
articles/16087-preventing-serious-
injuries-and-fatalities

10. Musik, T. (2017). Preventing serious
injuries and fatalities. *Safety +
Health Magazine.* http://www
.safetyandhealthmagazine.com/
articles/16087-preventing-serious-
injuries-and-fatalities

11. Neal, A., & Griffin, M. A. (2006).
A study of the lagged relationships
among safety climate, safety
motivation, safety behavior, and
accidents at the individual and
group levels. *Journal of Applied
Psychology, 91,* 946–953.

12. Triangle Shirtwaist Factory Fire.
(2009). http://www.history.com/
topics/triangle-shirtwaist-fire

13. IEEE. (2014). *Workplace safety
monitoring using RFIT sensors.*
https://ieeexplore.ieee.org/
document/7034494/; National
Institute for Occupational Safety
and Health. (2018). *Direct reading
and sensor technology.* https://www
.cdc.gov/niosh/topics/drst/
default.html

14. Edelson, J. (2017). Hotels add panic
buttons to protect housekeepers
from guests. *Bloomberg.* https://
www.bloomberg.com/news/
articles/2017-12-13/hotels-
add-panic-buttons-to-protect-
housekeepers-from-guests

15. Clarke, S. (2006). The relationship
between safety climate and safety
performance: A meta-analytic
review. *Journal of Occupational
Health Psychology, 11,* 315–327;
Zohar, D., & Luria, G. (2005).
A multilevel model of safety
climate: Cross-level relationships
between organization and group-
level climates. *Journal of Applied
Psychology, 90,* 616–628.

16. Zohar, D., & Polachek, T. (2014).
Discourse-based intervention
for modifying supervisory
communication as leverage for
safety climate and performance
improvement: A randomized field
study. *Journal of Applied Psychology,
99,* 113–124.

17. America's safest companies
awards: 2017 America's Safest
Companies. (2017). EHS
Today. http://www
.ehstoday.com/americas-safest-
companies-awards/2017-america-s-
safest-companies

18. Occupational Safety and Health
Administration. Workplace
violence. (n.d.) https://www.osha
.gov/SLTC/workplaceviolence/

19. Campbell, A. F. (2016). Why violence against nurses has spiked in the last decade. *The Atlantic.* https://www.theatlantic.com/business/archive/2016/12/violence-against-nurses/509309/; OSHA. (2016). Guidelines for preventing workplace violence for healthcare and social service workers. https://www.osha.gov/Publications/osha3148.pdf

20. Hershcovis, M. S. (2011). "Incivility, social undermining, bullying . . . oh my!": A call to reconcile constructs within workplace aggression research. *Journal of Organizational Behavior, 32,* 499–519.

21. CDC/NIOSH. (2018). Noise and hearing loss prevention. https://www.cdc.gov/niosh/topics/noise/reducenoiseexposure/noisecontrols.html

22. Federal Motor Carrier Safety Administration. (2018). Driving when you have sleep apnea. https://www.fmcsa.dot.gov/driver-safety/sleep-apnea/driving-when-you-have-sleep-apnea

23. Wallace, J. C., & Chen, G. (2005). Development and validation of a work-specific measure of cognitive failure: Implications for occupational safety. *Journal of Occupational and Organizational Psychology, 78,* 615–632.

24. Developing Effective Safety Management Programs. (2016). Society for Human Resource Management. https://www.shrm.org/resourcesandtools/tools-and-samples/toolkits/pages/developingsafetymanagementprograms.aspx

25. OSHA, Emergency Preparedness and Response. (2018). https://www.osha.gov/SLTC/emergencypreparedness/index.html; OSHA, Evacuation and Shelter in Place. (2018). https://www.osha.gov/SLTC/emergencypreparedness/gettingstarted_evacuation.html

26. OSHA frequently asked questions. (2018). https://www.osha.gov/OSHA_FAQs.html#!employerassist; OSHA Inspections. (2016). https://www.osha.gov/OshDoc/data_General_Facts/factsheet-inspections.pdf

27. Druley, K. (2017). OSHA's top-10 most cited violations for fiscal year 2017. *Safety + Health Magazine.* http://www.safetyandhealthmagazine.com/articles/16362-oshas-top-10-most-cited-violations-for-2017; OSHA (2015). Job Safety and Health: It's the Law. https://www.osha.gov/Publications/poster.html; OSHA fines employer $105,000 for retaliating against employee who complained about mold exposure. *National Law Review.* (2016). https://www.natlawreview.com/article/osha-fines-employer-105000-retaliating-against-employee-who-complained-about-mold

28. OSHA. (2018). https://www.osha.gov/SLTC/ergonomics/

29. Total Worker Health in Action! (2016). https://www.cdc.gov/niosh/twh/newsletter/twhnewsv5n3.html

30. Stromberg, J. (2014). Five health benefits of standing desks. *Smithsonian.* https://www.smithsonianmag.com/science-nature/five-health-benefits-standing-desks-180950259/

31. Boubekri, M., Cheung, I. N., Reid, K. J., Wang, C. H., & Zee, P. C. (2014). Impact of windows and daylight exposure on overall health and sleep quality of office workers: A case-control pilot study. *Journal of Clinical Sleep Medicine, 10,* 603–611.

32. Evans, G. W., & Johnson, D. (2000). Stress and open-office noise. *Journal of Applied Psychology, 85,* 779–783; Konnikova, M. (2014, January 7). The open-office trap. *The New Yorker.* http://www.newyorker.com/business/currency/the-open-office-trap

33. Whitaker, P. (2017, December 12). UK high court: Employers may be vicariously liable for employee data breaches. *The National Law Review.* https://www.natlawreview.com/article/uk-high-court-employers-may-be-vicariously-liable-employee-data-breaches

34. Marvin, R. (2017). The best employee monitoring software of 2018. *PC Magazine.* https://www.pcmag.com/roundup/357211/the-best-employee-monitoring-software;

Shartonn, B. R., & Neuman, K. L. (2017). The legal risks of monitoring employees online. *HarvardBusiness Review.* from https://hbr.org/2017/12/the-legal-risks-of-monitoring-employees-online

35. Isaac, M., Benner, K., & Frenkel, S. (2017). Uber hid 2016 breach, paying hackers to delete stolen data. *New York Times.* https://www.nytimes.com/2017/11/21/technology/uber-hack.html; *HIPAA Journal.* (2017, December 12). Email top attack vector in healthcare cyberattacks. https://www.hipaajournal.com/email-top-attack-vector-healthcare-cyberattacks/; Smith, A. (2016, January 8). Employee training to reduce cybersecurity breaches underused. SHRM. https://www.shrm.org/resourcesandtools/legal-and-compliance/state-and-local-updates/pages/training-reduces-cybersecurity-breaches.aspx

36. International Labour Organization. (n.d.). http://www.ilo.org/global/lang—en/index.htm; Kahn, J. (2017 September, 11). Fitness tracking startups are sweating due to EU privacy regulators. (2017). https://www.bloomberg.com/news/articles/2017-09-11/fitness-tracking-startups-are-sweating-due-to-eu-privacy-regulators; ECHY. (2018). Natural light and Europe lighting regulations. http://www.echy.fr/natural-light-and-europe-lighting-regulations/?lang=en

37. American Psychological Association. (2017). 2017 work and well-being survey. http://www.apaexcellence.org/assets/general/2017-work-and-well-being-survey-results.pdf; Careercast. (2017). 2017 stressful jobs reader survey. http://www.careercast.com/career-news/2017-stressful-jobs-reader-survey

38. Newport, F., & Harter, J. (2016). U.S. workers' satisfaction with job dimensions increases. http://news.gallup.com/poll/195143/workers-satisfied-job-dimensions.aspx

39. Wallace, J. C., & Chen, G. (2005). Development and validation of a work-specific measure of

cognitive failure: Implications for occupational safety. *Journal of Occupational and Organizational Psychology, 78*, 615–632.

40. Gonzalez-Mulé, E., & Cockburn, B. (2017). Worked to death: The relationships of job demands and job control with mortality. *Personnel Psychology, 70*, 73–112; Workers in stressful, low-control jobs have higher risk of early death: Study. (2016). *Safety + Health Magazine.* http://www .safetyandhealthmagazine.com/ articles/14913-workers-in-stressful- low-control-jobs-have-higher-risk- of-early-death-study

41. Dill, K. (2014). Survey: 42% of employees have changed jobs due to stress. *Forbes.* https://www.forbes .com/sites/kathryndill/2014/04/18/ survey-42-of-employees- have-changed-jobs-due-to- stress/#607fbecc3380

42. Liu, S., Wang, M., Zhan, Y., & Shi, J. (2009). Daily work stress and alcohol use: Testing the cross-level moderation effects of neuroticism and job involvement. *Personnel Psychology, 62*, 575–597.

43. Demerouti, E., Bakker, A. B., Nachreiner, F., & Schaufeli, W. B. (2001). The job demands-resources model of burnout. *Journal of Applied Psychology, 86*, 499–512; Schaufeli, W. B., & Taris, T. W. (2014). A critical review of the Job Demands- Resources Model: Implications for improving work and health. In *Bridging Occupational, Organizational and Public Health* (pp. 43–68). The Netherlands: Springer.

44. Klass, P. (2017). Taking care of the physician. *New York Times.* https:// www.nytimes.com/2017/11/13/well/ family/taking-care-of-the-physician .html

45. Crawford, E. R., LePine, J. A., & Rich, B. L. (2010). Linking job demands and resources to employee engagement and burnout: A theoretical extension and meta- analytic test. *Journal of Applied Psychology, 95*, 834–848; LePine, J. A., LePine, M. A., & Jackson, C. L. (2004). Challenge and

hindrance stress: Relationships with exhaustion, motivation to learn, and learning performance. *Journal of Applied Psychology, 89*, 883–891.

46. Saad, L. (2014). The "40-hour" work week is actually longer—by seven hours. http://news.gallup .com/poll/175286/hour-workweek- actually-longer-seven-hours.aspx

47. "Always on" email culture contributes to worker stress: Researchers. (2016, August 8). *Safety + Health Magazine.* http:// www.safetyandhealthmagazine .com/articles/14481-always-on- email-culture-contributes-to- worker-stress-research; Boswell, W. R., Olson-Buchanan, J. B., Butts, M. M., & Becker, W. J. (2016). Managing "after-hours" electronic work communication. *Organizational Dynamics, 45*, 291–297; Butts, M., Becker, W. J., & Boswell, W. R. (2015). Hot buttons and time sinks: The effects of electronic communication during nonwork time on emotions and work–nonwork conflict. *Academy of Management Journal, 58*, 763–788.

48. Morris, D. Z. (2017). New French law bars work emails after hours. *Fortune.* http:// fortune.com/2017/01/01/ french-right-to-disconnect-law/

49. Allen, T. D., Johnson, R. C., Saboe, K. N., Cho, E., Dumani, S., & Evans, S. (2012). Dispositional variables and work–family conflict: A meta- analysis. *Journal of Vocational Behavior, 80*, 17–26.

50. Kossek, E. E., Hammer, L. B., Thompson, R. J., & Buxbaum, L. B. (2014). Leveraging workplace flexibility for engagement and productivity. *SHRM Foundation's Effective Practice Guidelines Series.*

51. Brenoff, A. (2013). 8 reasons why employees never want to leave this amazing company. https://www .huffingtonpost.com/2013/11/18/ best-places-to-work_n_4240370 .html; Meaningful work, life balance makes SAS one of the world's best workplaces. (n.d.). https://www.sas.com/en_us/news/ press-releases/2017/october/gptw- multinational.html

52. Masterson, L. (2017). Nurses are burnt out. Here's how hospitals can help. https://www.healthcaredive .com/news/nurses-are-burnt- out-heres-how-hospitals-can- help/442640/

53. Pyrillis, R. (2017). Employers missing the point of rising employee stress. http://www.workforce .com/2017/03/14/employers- missing-point-rising-employee- stress/

54. Wellness Council of America. (WELCOA). (2018). The benefits of stress management for employees. https://www.welcoa.org/blog/ benefits-stress-management- employees/

55. Tepper, B. J., Simon, L., & Park, H. M. (2017). Abusive supervision. *Annual Review of Organizational Psychology and Organizational Behavior, 4*, 123–152; Yang, L. Q., Caughlin, D. E., Gazica, M. W., Truxillo, D. M., & Spector, P. E. (2014). Workplace mistreatment climate and potential employee and organizational outcomes: A meta- analytic review from the target's perspective. *Journal of Occupational Health Psychology, 19*, 315–335.

56. Kantor, J. (2014). Working anything but 9 to 5. *New York Times.* (2014, August 13). http://www.nytimes .com/interactive/2014/08/13/us/ starbucks-workers-scheduling- hours.html

57. Mäkikangas, A., Kinnunen, S., Rantanen, J., Mauno, S., Tolvanen, A., & Bakker, A. B. (2014). Association between vigor and exhaustion during the workweek: A person-centered approach to daily assessments. *Anxiety, Stress, & Coping, 27*, 555–575; Sonnentag, S., & Fritz, C. (2007). The Recovery Experience Questionnaire: Development and validation of a measure for assessing recuperation and unwinding from work. *Journal of Occupational Health Psychology, 12*, 204–221.

58. Shen, L. (2016). These 19 great employers offer paid sabbaticals. *Forbes.* http://fortune .com/2016/03/07/best-companies- to-work-for-sabbaticals/

59. Druley, K. Keeping aging workers safe. (2016). *Safety + Health Magazine*. http://www.safetyandhealthmagazine.com/articles/15023-aging-workers; Loch, C. H., Sting, F. J., Bauer, N., & Mauermann, H. (2010). How BMW is defusing the demographic time bomb. *Harvard Business Review, 88*, 99–102.

60. Herrera, T. (2017). Take naps at work. Apologize to no one. *New York Times*. https://www.nytimes.com/2017/06/23/smarter-living/take-naps-at-work-apologize-to-no-one.html; Six companies (including Uber) where it's OK to nap. (2015). *Inc.* https://www.inc.com/zoe-henry/google-uber-and-other-companies-where-you-can-nap-at-the-office.html

61. Druley, K. Keeping aging workers safe. (2016). *Safety + Health Magazine*. http://www.safetyandhealthmagazine.com/articles/15023-aging-workers; Loch, C. H., Sting, F. J., Bauer, N., & Mauermann, H. (2010). How BMW is defusing the demographic time bomb. *Harvard Business Review, 88*, 99–102.

62. Loehr, J., & Schwartz, T. (2001). The making of a corporate athlete. *Harvard Business Review*. https://hbr.org/2001/01/the-making-of-a-corporate-athlete

63. What is a wellness program? (2015). SHRM. https://www.shrm.org/resourcesandtools/tools-and-samples/hr-qa/pages/whatarewellnessbenefits.aspx

64. Do wellness programs save employers money? (2014). Rand Corporation. https://www.rand.org/content/dam/rand/pubs/research_briefs/RB9700/RB9744/RAND_RB9744.pdf

65. Mattke, S., Liu, H., Caloyeras, J. P., Huang, C. Y., Van Busum, K. R., Khodyakov, D., & Shier, V. (2013). *Workplace wellness programs study*. Rand Corporation. https://www.rand.org/pubs/research_reports/RR254.html

66. Milligan, S. (2017). Employers take wellness to a higher level. *HR Magazine*. https://www.shrm.org/hr-today/news/hr-magazine/0917/pages/employers-take-wellness-to-a-higher-level.aspx

67. Measuring wellness: From data to insights. (2014). The Economist Intelligence Unit. SHRM. https://www.shrm.org/ResourcesAndTools/hr-topics/benefits/Documents/EIU_HUMANA_WEB_FINAL_0.pdf

68. Milligan, S. (2017). Employers take wellness to a higher level. SHRM. https://www.shrm.org/hr-today/news/hr-magazine/0917/pages/employers-take-wellness-to-a-higher-level.aspx

69. Forget ROI: Aetna's CEO's perspective on wellness & functionality. (2017). *Corporate Wellness Magazine*. http://www.corporatewellnessmagazine.com/cwminterviews/aetna-ceo-perspective-on-wellness-functionality

70. Do wellness programs save employers money? (2014). Rand Corporation. https://www.rand.org/content/dam/rand/pubs/research_briefs/RB9700/RB9744/RAND_RB9744.pdf

71. Ibid.; Harris, M. M. (2016). The business case for employee health and wellness programs. Society for Industrial and Organizational Psychology. http://www.siop.org/WhitePapers/casehealth.pdf

72. Purcell, J. (2016). Meet the wellness programs that save companies money. *Harvard Business Review*. https://hbr.org/2016/04/meet-the-wellness-programs-that-save-companies-money

73. Milligan, S. (2017, September). Employee wellness blows up. *HR Magazine*, 60–67; Johnson & Johnson. Health and wellness at work. https://www.jnj.com/caring/patient-stories/health-and-wellness-at-work; Johnson & Johnson. (2016). The healthiest workforce. https://www.jnj.com/about-jnj/company-statements/healthiest-workforce; Johnson & Johnson. (2018). Our approach to health and wellness. https://www.jnj.com/jjhws; Moran, G. (2017). This is the future of corporate wellness programs. *Fast Company*. https://www.fastcompany.com/40418593/this-is-the-future-of-corporate-wellness-programs; Quinton, S. (2013). The Johnson & Johnson workout program: Improving productivity with diet and exercise. *The Atlantic*. https://www.theatlantic.com/business/archive/2013/06/the-johnson-amp-johnson-workout-program-improving-productivity-with-diet-and-exercise/425994/; Thompson, M. (2017). How to launch a corporate wellness program that works. *Forbes*. https://www.forbes.com/sites/melissathompson/2017/03/03/how-to-launch-a-corporate-wellness-program-that-works/#51d4f8e51a56

74. Designing and managing wellness programs. (2016). SHRM. https://www.shrm.org/resourcesandtools/tools-and-samples/toolkits/pages/designingandmanagingwellnessprograms.aspx; Martis, L. (2018). 7 companies with epic wellness programs. https://www.monster.com/career-advice/article/companies-good-wellness-programs; Milligan, S. (2017). Employers take wellness to a higher level. *HR Magazine*. https://www.shrm.org/hr-today/news/hr-magazine/0917/pages/employers-take-wellness-to-a-higher-level.aspx; Mattke, S., Liu, H., Caloyeras, J. P., Huang, C. Y., Van Busum, K. R., Khodyakov, D., & Shier, V. (2013). *Workplace wellness programs study*. Rand Corporation. https://www.rand.org/pubs/research_reports/RR254.html; 10 great examples of workplace wellness programs. (2018). https://risepeople.com/blog/workplace-wellness-programs/

75. Milligan, S. (2017). Employers take wellness to a higher level. *HR Magazine*. https://www.shrm.org/hr-today/news/hr-magazine/0917/pages/employers-take-wellness-to-a-higher-level.aspx

76. Employee assistance program (EAP): General. (2014, August 12). What is an employee assistance program? SHRM. https://www

.shrm.org/resourcesandtools/ tools-and-samples/hr-qa/pages/ whatisaneap.aspx

77. 10 great examples of workplace wellness programs. (2017). https://risepeople.com/blog/ workplace-wellness-programs/

78. Definitions of an employee assistance program (EAP) and EAP core technology. (October 2011). International Employee Assistance Association. http://www .eapassn.org/about/about-employee-assistance/eap-definitions-and-core-technology; Managing Employee Assistance Programs. (2015). SHRM. https://www .shrm.org/resourcesandtools/ tools-and-samples/toolkits/pages/ managingemployeeassistance programs.aspx

79. Managing Employee Assistance Programs. (2015). SHRM. https:// www.shrm.org/resourcesandtools/ tools-and-samples/toolkits/pages/ managingemployeeassistance programs.aspx

80. American Psychiatric Association. (2016). https://www.psychiatry .org/news-room/apa-blogs/ apa-blog/2016/07/employee-assistance-programs-an-often-overlooked-resource; Dunning, M. (2014). Employee assistance programs underutilized by employees. http://www .businessinsurance .com/article/20140105/ NEWS03/301059979

81. Designing and managing wellness programs. (2016). SHRM. https:// www.shrm.org/resourcesandtools/ tools-and-samples/toolkits/pages/ designingandmanagingwellness programs.aspx; Harris, M. M. (2016). The business case for employee health and wellness programs. Society for Industrial and Organizational Psychology. http://www.siop.org/WhitePapers/ casehealth.pdf; Mattke, S., Liu, H., Caloyeras, J. P., Huang, C. Y., Van Busum, K. R., Khodyakov, D., & Shier, V. (2013). *Workplace wellness programs study*. Rand Corporation. https://www.rand .org/pubs/research_reports/RR254

.html; Milligan, S. (2017, August 21). Employers take wellness to a higher level. *HR Magazine*. https:// www.shrm.org/hr-today/news/ hr-magazine/0917/pages/employers-take-wellness-to-a-higher-level.aspx

82. Beckman, K. (2017, June 28). Wearables technology gains traction in workplace safety. http://www .businessinsurance .com/article/00010101/ NEWS08/912314133/Wearables-technology-gains-traction-in-workplace-safety-; Harvard Business School Cold Call Podcast. (2018, January 4). How to monetize happiness. https:// hbswk.hbs.edu/item/how-to-monetize-happiness?cid=wk-rs; Kahn, J. (2017). Fitness tracking startups are sweating due to EU privacy regulators. *Bloomberg*. https://www.bloomberg.com/ news/articles/2017-09-11/fitness-tracking-startups-are-sweating-due-to-eu-privacy-regulators; Moran, G. (2017). This is the future of corporate wellness programs. *Fast Company*. https://www.fastcompany .com/40418593/this-is-the-future-of-corporate-wellness-programs; Sly, L. (2018). US soldiers are revealing sensitive and dangerous information by jogging. *Washington Post*. https:// www.washingtonpost.com/world/a-map-showing-the-users-of-fitness-devices-lets-the-world-see-where-us-soldiers-are-and-what-they-are-doing/2018/01/28/86915662-0441-11e8-aa61-f3391373867e_story .html?utm_term=.11e2967e71a4; Vanderkam, L. (2015). The darkside of corporate wellness programs. *Fast Company*. https://www.fastcompany .com/3047115/the-dark-side-of-corporate-wellness-programs

83. Milligan, S. (2017, August 21). Employers take wellness to a higher level. *HR Magazine*. https:// www.shrm.org/hr-today/news/ hr-magazine/0917/pages/employers-take-wellness-to-a-higher-level.aspx

84. Hammer, L. B., et al. (2016). Intervention effects on the safety compliance and citizenship behaviors: Evidence from the work, family, and health study. *Journal of

Applied Psychology, 101, 190–208; Hurtado, D. A., et al. (2016). Effects on cigarette consumption of a work–family supportive organizational intervention: 6-month results from the work, family and health network. *Journal of Epidemiology and Community Health. 70*, 1155–1161; Olson, R., et al. (2015). A workplace intervention improves sleep: Results from the randomized controlled Work, Family, and Health study. *Sleep Health, 1*, 55–65.

85. Zohar, D., & Luria, G. (2005). A multilevel model of safety climate: Cross-level relationships between organization and group-level climates. *Journal of Applied Psychology, 90*, 616–628; Zohar, D., & Polachek, T. (2014). Discourse-based intervention for modifying supervisory communication as leverage for safety climate and performance improvement: A randomized field study. *Journal of Applied Psychology, 99*, 113–124.

86. CDC Vital Signs. (March 2015). Trucker safety: Using a seatbelt matters. https://www.cdc.gov/ vitalsigns/truck-safety/index. html; Sieber, K. (2015). Long-haul truck driver health survey results. https://blogs.cdc.gov/niosh-science-blog/2015/03/03/truck-driver-health/; Sieber, W. K., et al. (2014). Obesity and other risk factors: The national survey of U.S., long-haul truck driver health and injury. *American Journal of Industrial Medicine, 57*, 615–626.

87. Olson, R., Wipfli, B., Thompson, S. V., Elliot, D. L., Anger, W. K., Bodner, T., Hammer, L. B., & Perrin, N. (2016). Weight control intervention for truck drivers: The SHIFT randomized controlled trial, United States. *American Journal of Public Health, 106*, 1698–1706.

88. Total worker health. (2015). https:// www.cdc.gov/niosh/twh/totalhealth .html

89. Total worker health in action! (2017, December). https://www.cdc.gov/ niosh/twh/newsletter/twhnewsv6n4 .html#Promising

90. Anger, W. K., Elliot, D. L., Bodner, T., Olson, R., Rohlman, D. S.,

Truxillo, D. M., . . . & Montgomery, D. (2015). Effectiveness of total worker health interventions. *Journal of Occupational Health Psychology, 20*, 226–247.

Chapter 16

1. Baker, L. (2016, March 28). A world on fire. *Oregon Business Magazine.* https://www.oregonbusiness.com/article/politics/item/16592-world-on-fire; Proulx, C. (2016, October 5). Five trends transforming the employee experience at INGOs .https://www.insidengo.org/blog/five-trends-transforming-employee-experience-ingos; Westcott, S. (2008, January 24). Recruiting in dangerous times. *Chronicle of Philanthropy.* https://www.philanthropy.com/article/Recruiting-in-Dangerous-Times/167475; Yoo, T., & Donald, A. (2017, September 7). Tech breakthroughs must reach the world's most vulnerable. https://medium.com/world-economic-forum/tech-breakthroughs-must-reach-the-worlds-most-vulnerable-61661c14f4cc; Yu, R. (2010, August 24). Fending off danger abroad. *USA Today,* Money, 1.

2. Investopedia. (2018). Multinational corporation: MNC. https://www.investopedia.com/terms/m/multinationalcorporation.asp

3. Lane, J., & Kinser, K. (2015, June 5). Is today's university the new multinational corporation? https://theconversation.com/is-todays-university-the-new-multinational-corporation-40681

4. Kedia, B. L., & Mukherjee, D. (2009). Understanding offshoring: A research framework based on disintegration, location, and externalization advantages. *Journal of World Business, 44*, 250–261.

5. Sippola, A., & Smale, A. (2007). The global integration of diversity management: A longitudinal case study. *International Journal of Human Resource Management, 18*, 1895–1916.

6. Almond, P. (2011). Re-visiting country of origin effects on HRM in multinational corporations. *Human Resource Management Journal, 21*, 258–271.

7. Saxena, S. (2017, December 15). Uber is at the centre of a challenge to the gig economy. https://www.bloombergquint.com/law-and-policy/2017/12/15/uber-is-at-the-centre-of-uks-challenge-to-gig-economy

8. Petroff, A., & Cornevin, O. (2017, January 2). France gives workers "right to disconnect" from office email. http://money.cnn.com/2017/01/02/technology/france-office-email-workers-law/index.html

9. McCarthy, N. (2017, June 20). Which countries have the highest level of union membership? *Forbes.* https://www.forbes.com/sites/niallmccarthy/2017/06/20/which-countries-have-the-highest-levels-of-labor-union-membership-infographic/#262682c233c0

10. Farndale, E., & Paauwe, J. (2007). Uncovering competitive and institutional drivers of HRM practices in multinational corporations. *Human Resource Management Journal, 17*, 355–375.

11. Churchard, C. (2013, August 23). Totally worth it. *People Management*, 36–38; Hong, H. J., & Doz, Y. (2013, June). L'Oréal masters multiculturalism. *Harvard Business Review.* https://hbr.org/2013/06/loreal-masters-multiculturalism; L'Oréal. (2016). Key figures. http://www.loreal.com/group/our-activities/key-figures; Meyer, E. (2015, October). When culture doesn't translate. *Harvard Business Review.* https://hbr.org/2015/10/when-culture-doesnt-translate

12. Albanese, C., DiPasquale, S., & Gilblom, K. (2017, December 20). Eni, Shell to face trial in Italy in $1 billion bribery case. *Bloomberg.* https://www.bloomberg.com/news/articles/2017-12-20/eni-shell-to-face-trial-in-italy-over-1-billion-bribery-case; Anonymous. (2017, January 18). Rolls-Royce apologises after £671m bribery settlement.

BBC. http://www.bbc.com/news/business-38644114; Auchard, E., & Brock, J. (2017, October 26). SAP faces U.S. probe into South Africa kickback allegations. https://www.reuters.com/article/us-sap-se-corruption-safrica/sap-faces-u-s-probe-into-south-africa-kickback-allegations-idUSKBN1CV0ZW; Currell, D., Davis Bradley, T. (2012, September). Greased palms, giant headaches. *Harvard Business Review.* https://hbr.org/2012/09/greased-palms-giant-headaches; Heineman, B. W. (2014, May 15). Who's responsible for the Walmart Mexico scandal? *Harvard Business Review.* https://hbr.org/2014/05/whos-responsible-for-the-walmart-mexico-scandal; Paine, L. S. (2010, June). The China rules. *Harvard Business Review,* 103–108.

13. Vaiman, V., & Brewster, C. (2015). How far do cultural differences explain the differences between nations? Implications for HRM. *International Journal of Human Resource Management, 26*, 151–164.

14. Brewster, C., Sparrow, P., & Harris, H. (2005). Towards a new model of globalizing HR. *International Journal of Human Resource Management, 16*, 949–970.

15. Colakoglu, S., Lepak, D. P., & Hong, Y. (2006). Measuring HRM effectiveness: Considering multiple stakeholders in a global context. *Human Resource Management Review, 16*, 209–218.

16. Morris, S. S., Wright, P. M., Trevor, J., Stiles, P., Stahl, G., et al. (2009). Global challenges to replicating HR: The role of people, processes, and systems. *Human Resource Management, 48*, 973–995.

17. Rabl, T., Jayasinghe, M., Gerhart, B., & Kühlmann, T. M. (2014). A meta-analysis of country differences in the high performance work system–business performance relationship: The roles of national culture and managerial discretion. *Journal of Applied Psychology, 99*, 1011–1041.

18. Thite, M., Wilkinson, A., & Shah, D. (2012). Internationalization and

HRM strategies across subsidiaries in multinational corporations from emerging economies: A conceptual framework. *Journal of World Business, 47*, 251–258.

19. Budhwar, P. S., Varma, A., & Patel, C. (2016). Convergence-divergence of HRM in the Asia-Pacific: Context-specific analysis and future research agenda. *Human Resource Management Review, 26*, 311–326.

20. Overman, S. (2016, February). Tapping talent around the globe. *HR Magazine*, 47–51.

21. WillisTowersWatson. (2017, September 18). A global approach to company car benefits policy. https://www.willistowerswatson.com/en-LB/insights/2017/09/A-global-approach-to-company-car-benefits-policy

22. Aon. (2017, September). Revisiting 13th and 14th month bonus rules in Latin America, Europe, Africa and Asia. https://radford.aon.com/insights/articles/2017/13th-and-14th-Month-Bonus-Rules-in-Latin-America-Europe-Africa-and-Asia

23. Central Intelligence Agency. (2017). *The world factbook.* https://www.cia.gov/library/publications/the-world-factbook/fields/2177.html

24. WillisTowersWatson. (2017, February 23). International pension survey 2016. https://www.willistowerswatson.com/en/insights/2017/02/International-pension-plan-survey-2016

25. Tobenkin, D. (2011, June). Attention to pensions. *HR Magazine*. 93–98.

26. Claus, L. (2010, February). International assignees at risk. *HR Magazine*, 73–75; EEOC. (2003). Employee rights when working for multinational employers. https://www.eeoc.gov/facts/multi-employees.html; Maurer, R. (2014, November). The rise of the accidental expat. *HR Magazine*, 12; Simms, J. (2017, February 21). The tricky logistics of global mobility—and HR's crucial role in getting it right. *People Management*, 46–48.

27. Onley, D. S. (2014, January). Terminating overseas employees. *HR Magazine*, 33–36.

28. Burgess, M. (2018, January 2). What is GDPR? WIRED explains what you need to know. http://www.wired.co.uk/article/what-is-gdpr-uk-eu-legislation-compliance-summary-fines-2018; Wright, A. D. (2017, July 31). HR urged to prepare for new data protection law in Europe. https://www.shrm.org/resourcesandtools/hr-topics/global-hr/pages/hr-urged-to-prepare-for-new-data-protection-law-in-europe.aspx

29. Doke, D. D. (2016, January 4). Adidas: Where talent rules. http://www.recruiter.co.uk/news/2015/12/adidas-where-talent-rules

30. Harzing, A. W., Pudelko, M., & Reiche, S. (2016). The bridging role of expatriates and inpatriates in knowledge transfer in multinational corporations. *Human Resource Management, 55*, 679–695.

31. Anonymous. (2015, November). Cadillac retooling HR as it aims for global approach. *HR Focus*, 4–6.

32. Fang, Y., Jiang, G. L. F., Makino, S., & Beamish, P. W. (2010). Multinational firm knowledge, use of expatriates, and foreign subsidiary performance. *Journal of Management Studies, 47*, 27–54.

33. Harzing, A. W. (1995). The persistent myth of high expatriate failure rates. *International Journal of Human Resource Management, 6*, 457–475; Naumann, E. (1993). Organizational predictors of expatriate job satisfaction. *Journal of International Business Studies, 24*, 61–79.

34. Anonymous. (2009). Best expatriate assignments require much thought, even more planning. *HR Trendbook*, 74–75.

35. Doherty, N., Dickmann, M., & Mills, T. (2011). Exploring the motives of company-based and self-initiated expatriates. *International Journal of Human Resource Management, 22*, 595–611.

36. Bhaskar-Shrinivas, P., Harrison, D. A., Shaffer, M. A., & Luk, D. M. (2005). Input-based and time-based models of international adjustment: Meta-analytic evidence and theoretical extensions. *Academy of Management Journal, 48*, 257–281.

37. Everson, K. (2014, July). Relocation sector keeps moving right along. *Workforce, 93*.

38. Clouse, M. A., & Watkins, M. D. (2009, October). Three keys to getting an overseas assignment right. *Harvard Business Review,* 115–119.

39. Clemetson, L. (2010, December 15). The globe-trotters. *Workforce Management, 89*. http://www.workforce.com/2010/12/15/special-report-on-globalization-the-globe-trotters/

40. Bhaskar-Shrinivas, P., Harrison, D. A., Shaffer, M. A., & Luk, D. M. (2005). Input-based and time-based models of international adjustment: Meta-analytic evidence and theoretical extensions. *Academy of Management Journal, 48*, 257–281.

41. Marschan-Piekkari, R., Welch, D., & Welch, L. (1999). In the shadow: The impact of language on structure: Power and communication in the multinational. *International Business Review,* 421–440.

42. Molinsky, A. L. (2012, January/February). Code switching between cultures. *Harvard Business Review,* 140–141; Molinsky, A. (2014, January 30). Encourage foreign-born employees to participate more in meetings. *Harvard Business Review.* https://hbr.org/2014/01/encourage-foreign-born-employees-to-participate-more-in-meetings; Molinsky, A. L. (2014, July 15). Adapt to a new culture - but don't go too far. *Harvard Business Review.* https://hbr.org/2014/07/adapt-to-a-new-culture-but-dont-go-too-far; Neeley, T., & Kaplan, R. S. (2014, September). What's your language strategy? *Harvard Business Review,* 70–76.

43. Zhang, L. E., & Harzing, A. W. (2016). From dilemmatic struggle to legitimized indifference: Expatriates' host country language learning and its impact on the expatriate–HCE relationship. *Journal of World Business, 51*, 774–786.

44. Peltokorpi, V. (2008). Cross-cultural adjustment of expatriates

in Japan. *International Journal of Human Resource Management, 19,* 1588–1606.

45. Anonymous. (2017, May 8). What is it like to live and work in Bahrain? https://www.expatfocus .com/c/aid=4190/articles/bahrain/ what-is-it-like-to-live-and-work-in-bahrain/; Steverman, B. (2017, September 6). The best and worst countries to live and work in, according to expats. https:// www.bloomberg.com/news/ articles/2017-09-06/the-u-s-and-u-k-are-getting-worse-and-worse-expats-say

46. Bhaskar-Shrinivas, P., Harrison, D. A., Shaffer, M. A., & Luk, D. M. (2005). Input-based and time-based models of international adjustment: Meta-analytic evidence and theoretical extensions. *Academy of Management Journal, 48,* 257–281.

47. Farh, C. I. C., Bartol, K. M., Shapiro, D. L., & Shin, J. (2010). Networking abroad: A process model of how expatriates form support ties to facilitate adjustment. *Academy of Management Review, 35,* 434–454.

48. Bhaskar-Shrinivas, P., Harrison, D. A., Shaffer, M. A., & Luk, D. M. (2005). Input-based and time-based models of international adjustment: Meta-analytic evidence and theoretical extensions. *Academy of Management Journal, 48,* 257–281.

49. Toh, S. M., & DeNisi, A. S. (2005). A local perspective to expatriate success. *Academy of Management Executive, 19,* 132–146.

50. Peltokorpi, V., & Froese, F. J. (2009). Organizational expatriates and self-initiated expatriates: Who adjusts better to work and life in Japan? *International Journal of Human Resource Management, 20,* 1096–1112.

51. Fan, S. X., Cregan, C., Harzing, A. W., & Köhler, T. (2018). The benefits of being understood: The role of ethnic identity confirmation in knowledge acquisition by expatriates. *Human Resource Management, 57,* 327–339.

52. Farh, C. I. C., Bartol, K. M., Shapiro, D. L., & Shin, J. (2010). Networking abroad: A process model of how expatriates form support ties to facilitate adjustment. *Academy of Management Review, 35,* 434–454.

53. Kraimer, M. L., Wayne, S. J., & Jaworski, R. A. (2001). Sources of support and expatriate performance: The mediating role of expatriate adjustment. *Personnel Psychology, 54,* 71–99.

54. Anonymous. (2009). Best expatriate assignments require much thought, even more planning. *HR Trendbook,* 74–75.

55. Anonymous. (2011, March). Developing your global know-how. *Harvard Business Review,* 71–75.

56. Gillenwater, S. (2017, June 16). Today's immigrant CEOs: Bringing a global sensibility to American business. https:// www.salesforce.com/blog/ 2017/06/immigrant-ceos-global-sensibility-business.html; Maddux, W. W., Galinsky, A. D., & Tadmor, C. T. (2010, September). Be a better manager: Live abroad. *Harvard Business Review,* 24.

57. Molinsky, A., & Hahn, M. (2015, April 8). Building relationships in cultures that don't do small talk. *Harvard Business Review.* https://hbr.org/2015/04/building-relationships-in-cultures-that-dont-do-small-talk

58. Frase, M. (2007, February). The road to (inland) China. *HR Magazine,* 71–78.

59. Overman, S. (2016, February). Tapping talent around the globe. *HR Magazine,* 47–51.

60. Everson, K. (2014, July). Relocation sector keeps moving right along. *Workforce, 93.*

61. Clemetson, L. (2010, December 15). The globe-trotters. *Workforce Management, 89.* http://www .workforce.com/2010/12/15/special-report-on-globalization-the-globe-trotters

62. Anonymous. (2010). Pay variations in Asia. *HR Magazine,* 6.

63. Gale, S. F. (2017, November/ December). Finding agility in employee mobility. *Workforce,* 58–59.

64. Refworld. (2014, July 31). Nigeria: Kidnapping for ransom, including frequency, profile of victims and kidnappers; response by authorities (2013–2014). http://www.refworld .org/docid/546dc1724.html

65. Bureau of National Affairs. (2011, January). Kidnappings remain a concern for firms doing business abroad. *HR Focus,* 6–8.

66. Wright, A. D. (2011, December). Open for business? *HR Magazine,* 105–107.

67. Bruning, N. S., & Cadigan, F. (2014). Diversity and global talent management: Are there cracks in the glass ceiling and glass border? *People & Strategy, 37*(3), 18–21.

68. Varma, A., & Russell, L. (2016). Women and expatriate assignments: Exploring the role of perceived organizational support. *Employee Relations, 38,* 200–223.

69. Bader, B. (2018, February 6). Do female expats experience a greater level of discrimination? *People Management.* https://www .peoplemanagement.co.uk/voices/ comment/female-expats-greater-discrimination

70. Shen, J., & Jiang, F. (2015). Factors influencing Chinese female expatriates' performance in international assignments. *International Journal of Human Resource Management, 26,* 299–315.

71. McPhail, R., McNulty, Y., & Hutchings, K. (2016). Lesbian and gay expatriation: Opportunities, barriers, and challenges for global mobility. *International Journal of Human Resource Management, 27,* 382–406.

72. Fenton, S. (2016, May 17). LGBT relationships are illegal in 74 countries, research finds. https://www .independent.co.uk/news/world/ gay-lesbian-bisexual-relationships-illegal-in-74-countries-a7033666 .html

73. Florian, J. (2018, April 2). Sending LGBTQ employees abroad poses challenges, requires planning. https://

www.bna.com/sending-lgbtq-employees-b57982090600/

74. Bolino, M. C., Klotz, A. C., & Turnley, W. H. (2017, April 18). Will refusing an international assignment derail your career? *Harvard Business Review*. https://hbr.org/2017/04/will-refusing-an-international-assignment-derail-your-career

75. Kraimer, M. L., Shaffer, M. A., & Bolino, M. C. (2009). The influence of expatriate and repatriate experiences on career advancement and repatriate intentions. *Human Resource Management, 48,* 27–47.

76. Clemetson, L. (2010, December 15). The globe-trotters. *Workforce Management, 89.* http://www.workforce.com/2010/12/15/special-report-on-globalization-the-globe-trotters

77. Anonymous. (2012, September). Rise in "global nomads" long-term expatriates presents challenge. *HR Focus,* 9–10.

78. Anonymous. (2011, March). Developing your global know-how. *Harvard Business Review,* 71–75.

79. Krell, E. (2011, December). Taking care of business abroad. *HR Magazine,* 44–48.

80. Hannibal, E., Traber, Y., & Jelinek, P. (2015, April). Tracking your expatriate software. *HR Magazine,* 63–65.

81. Maurer, R. (2014, November). The rise of the accidental expat. *HR Magazine,* 12.

82. Simms, J. (2017, February 21). The tricky logistics of global mobility—and HR's crucial role in getting it right. *People Management,* 46–48.

Index

Figures and tables are indicated by f and t, respectively, following the page number.